W9-ATP-651

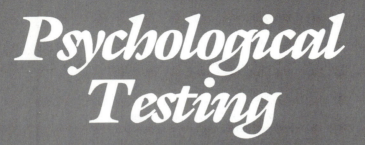

Psychological Testing

PRINCIPLES, APPLICATIONS, AND ISSUES

Third Edition

Robert M. Kaplan
University of California, San Diego

Dennis P. Saccuzzo
San Diego State University

Brooks/Cole Publishing Company
Pacific Grove, California

To Cathie and Lorraine

I(T)P™
The trademark ITP is used under license.

Consulting Editor: *Lawrence S. Wrightsman*

Brooks/Cole Publishing Company, a Division of Wadsworth, Inc.

© 1993, 1989, 1982 by Wadsworth, Inc., Belmont, California 94002. All rights reserved. No part of this book may be reproduced, stored in a retrieval system, or transcribed, in any form or by any means—electronic, mechanical, photocopying, recording, or otherwise—without the prior written permission of the publisher, Brooks/Cole Publishing Company, Pacific Grove, California 93950, a division of Wadsworth, Inc.

Printed in the United States of America
10 9 8 7 6 5 4

Library of Congress Cataloging-in-Publication Data
Kaplan, Robert M.
    Psychological testing : principles, applications, and issues /
Robert M. Kaplan, Dennis P. Saccuzzo. — 3rd ed.
      p. cm.
    Includes bibliographical references and indexes.
    ISBN 0-534-16230-4
    1. Psychological tests.   I. Saccuzzo, Dennis P., [date].
II. Title.
BF176.K36   1993
150′.28′7—dc20
                              92-23151
                                 CIP

Sponsoring Editor: *Marianne Taflinger*
Editorial Associates: *Heather Graeve* and *Virge Pirelli-Minetti*
Production Coordinator: *Fiorella Ljunggren*
Production: *Greg Hubit Bookworks*
Manuscript Editor: *Carol Reitz*
Permissions: *Helen Van Why*
Interior Design: *Christy Butterfield*
Cover Design: *Roy R. Neuhaus*
Art and Photo Coordinator: *Greg Hubit*
Interior Illustration: *Accurate Art, Inc.*, and *Susan Rogin*
Typesetting: *Bi-Comp, Inc.*
Cover Printing: *Lehigh Press Lithographers/Autoscreen*
Printing and Binding: *R. R. Donnelley & Sons Company, Crawfordsville*

Disclaimer for Figures 13-4, 13-7, 13-8, 13-9: Permission to reprint the referenced SAT questions does not constitute review or endorsement by Educational Testing Service or the College Board of this publication as a whole or of any other testing information it may contain.

Preface

Psychology is a broad, exciting field. Psychologists today work in a variety of settings, including everything from schools and clinics to biochemistry laboratories and industrial settings. Despite this diversity, two common themes link all psychologists: all study behavior, and all depend to some extent on its measurement. This book concerns a particular type of measurement, psychological tests, which measure characteristics pertaining to all aspects of behavior in human beings.

Psychological Testing is the result of a deep interest its authors share. As active participants in the development and use of psychological tests, we became disheartened because far too many undergraduate college students view psychological testing courses as boring and unrelated to their goals or career interests. In contrast, we view psychological testing as an exciting field. It has a solid place in the history of psychology, yet it is constantly in flux because of challenges, new developments, and controversies. A book on testing should encourage, not dampen, a student's interest. Thus we provide an overview of the many facets of psychological tests and measurement principles in a style that will appeal to the contemporary college student.

To understand all the applications and issues in psychological testing, the student must learn some basic principles. Because this requires some knowledge of introductory statistics, some reviewing and a careful reading of Part I will pave the way for an understanding of the applications of tests discussed in Part II. Part III examines the issues now shaping the future of testing. Such issues include test anxiety, test bias, and the interface between testing and the law. The very future of applied psychology may depend on the ability of psychologists to face these challenging issues.

Throughout the book there is a series of focused discussions and focused examples. These sections are designed to illustrate the material in the book through examples or to provide a more detailed discussion of a particular issue. There are also some technical boxes that are used to demonstrate technical material such as statistical calculations.

Students today often prefer informal discussions and personally relevant examples. Consequently we decided to use models from a variety of fields and to write in an informal style to maximize interest. However, testing is a serious and complicated field in which there are major disagreements among scholars and experts of the highest level. Therefore, we have treated these aspects of testing with more formal discussion and detailed referencing.

It has been more than ten years since the publication of the first edition of *Psychological Testing: Principles, Applications, and Issues*. On completion of the first edition, we believed that future revisions would be easy because psychological testing is a field that changes slowly. However, there have been many major developments since 1982, and we have attempted to reflect these developments in the second and third editions.

Since the initial publication of *Psychological Testing,* many of the major tests—including the Stanford-Binet Intelligent Scales, the Wechsler Intelligence Scale for Children, and the Strong-Campbell Interest Inventory—have been revised. We have done our best to provide updates on all of them as well as descriptions of new psychological tests. Further, we have attempted to grow with the field. For example, ten years ago psychological testing was relatively rare in medical settings. Today, psychological testing in hospitals and clinical medical settings is very common. To reflect these changes, we have added updated chapters on testing in health care settings and we have expanded our coverage of new developments such as clinical neuropsychology. Also, many social and political developments have affected testing. For example, the Civil Rights Bill of 1991 may have a significant impact on the way tests are administered. There is now talk of national testing programs and recommended new standards for the use of psychological tests. All of these developments are captured in this edition of the book.

We are highly indebted to the many reviewers and professors who offered feedback on this and the previous editions. Special thanks go to Jeff Bryson of San Diego State University, who neatly edited the second edition of the book. His contribution was invaluable. Raul Betterncourt of California State University, Fresno, and Mary Allen of California State University, Bakersfield, also provided many useful suggestions. We are also indebted to Darrell Anderson of the University of New Mexico, Robert Grissom of San Francisco State University, Leonard Jacobson of the University of Miami, Calvin Janssen of Tennessee Temple University, and Frank Rosekrans of Eastern Washington University for their thoughtful analyses.

The reviewers for the third edition were James R. Barclay; Nancy S. Breland of Trenton State College; Richard D. Draper of Montclair State College; Lisa Friedenberg of the University of North Carolina at Asheville; Tim Hartshorne of Central Michigan University; Elaine M. Heiby of the University of Hawaii; Richard A. Hudiburg of the University of North Alabama; Ron Jewett of North Central Bible College; Terry Newell of California State University, Fresno; Allen L. Shoemaker of Calvin College; and Mark T. Smircina of Blackburn College. We thank them all for their constructive criticisms and useful suggestions.

The three editions of this book have been developed under four different editors at Brooks/Cole. The earlier ones benefited from the patient and inspired supervision of Todd Lueders, C. Deborah Laughton, and Phil Curson. The current edition was completed under the watchful eye of Marianne Taflinger. Thank you to all of them. We are most indebted to Greg Hubit for the high-quality production of the book and to Carol Reitz for her excellent editing of the manuscript. And we are also indebted to the expert production team at Brooks/Cole, especially Fiorella Ljunggren, who supervised the production process, and Roy Neuhaus, who created the cover for the book.

Finally, we are very grateful to Robin Nordmeyer, Rachel Ingrum, Beverly Jones, Arlysse Kienle, Susan McLaughlin, Lorraine Saccuzzo, and Virginia Anderson, who contributed most of the important labor required to complete the third edition.

Robert M. Kaplan
Dennis P. Saccuzzo

Brief Contents

PART I   *Principles*   1

Chapter 1   Introduction   3
Chapter 2   Norms and Basic Statistics for Testing   28
Chapter 3   Correlation and Regression   63
Chapter 4   Reliability   98
Chapter 5   Validity   132
Chapter 6   Building a Test   155
Chapter 7   Selection and Decision Analysis   177
Chapter 8   Test Administration   197

PART II   *Applications*   213

Chapter 9   Interview Techniques   223
Chapter 10   Tests of Mental Ability: The Binet Scale   256
Chapter 11   The Wechsler Intelligence Scales   283
Chapter 12   Other Individual Tests of Ability   315
Chapter 13   Group Ability Tests: Intelligence, Achievement, and Aptitude   351
Chapter 14   Tests for Choosing Careers   385
Chapter 15   Structured Personality Tests   416
Chapter 16   Projective Personality Tests   455
Chapter 17   Alternatives to Traditional Psychological Tests   482
Chapter 18   Measures of Anxiety and Stress   508
Chapter 19   Testing in Health Care Setting   528

PART III   *Issues*   553

Chapter 20   Test Bias   555
Chapter 21   Testing and the Law   585
Chapter 22   The Future of Psychological Testing   623

Contents

PART I   *Principles*   **1**

Chapter 1   Introduction   **3**

I. Basic Concepts   6
   A. What a test is   6
   B. Types of tests   7
   C. Psychological testing and individual differences   10

II. Plan for the Book   10
   A. Principles of psychological testing   10
   B. Applications of psychological testing   11
   C. Issues of psychological testing   11

III. Historical Perspective   12
   A. Early antecedents   12
   B. Charles Darwin and individual differences   13
   C. Experimental psychology and psychophysical measurement   14
   D. The evolution of intelligence and standardized achievement tests   16
   E. Personality tests: 1920–1940   18
   F. The emergence of new approaches to personality testing   22
   G. The period of rapid changes in the status of testing   23
   H. The current environment   25

Summary   26

Chapter 2   Norms and Basic Statistics for Testing   **28**

I. Why We Need Statistics   29

II. Scales of Measurement   30
   A. Properties of scales   30
   B. Types of scales   32

III. Frequency Distributions 34

IV. Percentile Ranks 36

V. Percentiles 40

VI. Describing Distributions 41

    A. Mean 41

    B. Standard deviation 42

    C. Z score 45

    D. Standard normal distribution 48

    E. McCall's T 53

    F. Quartiles and deciles 54

VII. Norms 56

    A. Age-related norms 57

    B. Tracking 57

    C. Criterion-referenced tests 61

Summary 62

Chapter 3 Correlation and Regression **63**

I. The Scatter Diagram 64

II. Correlation 66

III. Regression 67

    A. The regression line 67

    B. The best-fitting line 69

    C. Testing the statistical significance of a correlation coefficient 78

    D. How to interpret a regression plot 80

IV. Other Correlation Coefficients 84

V. Terms and Issues in the Use of Correlation 86

VI. Multivariate Analysis (Optional) 90

    A. General approach 90

    B. An example using multiple regression 91

    C. Discriminate analysis 92

    D. Factor analysis 93

Summary 96

Chapter 4 Reliability   **98**

 I. History and Theory of Reliability 99

   A. Conceptualization of error 99
   B. Spearman's early studies 100
   C. Basics of test score theory 100

 II. Models of Reliability 103

   A. Sources of error 104
   B. Time sampling: Test–retest method 104
   C. Error associated with the use of particular items 106
   D. The domain sampling model 107
   E. Reliability of a difference score 116
   F. Reliability of criterion-referenced tests 120

 III. Reliability in Behavioral Observation Studies 120

 IV. Connecting Sources of Error with Reliability Assessment Method 121

 V. Using Reliability Information 124

   A. Standard errors of measurement and the rubber yardstick 124
   B. How reliable is reliable? 126
   C. What to do about low reliability 126

 Summary 130

Chapter 5 Validity   **132**

 I. Learning to Ask About the Validity Evidence 133

   A. The definition of validity 133
   B. Nature of evidence 134

 II. Types of Validity 134

   A. Face Validity 135
   B. Content-related validity 135
   C. Criterion-related validity 137

D. Construct-related validity   147

E. Relationship between reliability and validity   152

Summary   153

Chapter 6   Building a Test   **155**

I. Item Writing   156

A. Item formats   156

B. Other possibilities   163

II. Item Analysis   164

A. Item difficulty   164

B. Discriminability   165

C. Pictures of item characteristics   168

D. Items for criterion-referenced tests   173

E. Limitations of item analysis   175

Summary 175

Chapter 7   Selection and Decision Analysis   **177**

I. The Test Manual   178

II. Base Rates and Hit Rates   180

A. Taylor-Russell tables   184

B. Utility theory and decision analysis   189

C. Incremental validity   190

III. Locating Information about Published Tests   192

A. Tests in Print III   193

B. The Mental Measurements Yearbook   194

C. Test: A Comprehensive Reference for Assessment in Psychology, Education, and Business   194

D. Test Critiques   194

E. Measures of Personality and Social Psychological Attitudes   195

F. Unpublished Experimental Mental Measures   195

G. Handbook of Psychiatric Rating Scales   196

Summary   196

Chapter 8   Test Administration   **197**

   I. The Examiner and the Subject   198
      A. The race of the tester   198
      B. The examiner–test taker relationship   199
      C. Expectancy effects   200
      D. Effects of reinforcing responses   202
      E. Computer-assisted test administration   204
      F. Subject variables   206

   II. Behavioral Assessment Methodology   207
      A. Reactivity   207
      B. Drift   208
      C. Expectancies   208
      D. Problems in rating accuracy   209
      E. Statistical control of rating errors   210
   Summary   211

PART II   *Applications*   **213**

   Introduction to Part II: Applications   **215**

   I. The Issue of Test Use   216

   II. Concepts and Distinctions   218
      A. A test battery   218
      B. Testing versus assessment   219

   III. Criteria for Selection of Tests   219
      A. Ability tests   220
      B. Approach to personality tests   221
   Summary   221

Chapter 9   Interview Techniques   **223**

   I. The Interview as a Test   226

   II. Reciprocal Nature of Inverviewing   228

   III. Principles of Effective Interviewing   228

A. The proper attitudes 229

B. Responses to avoid 229

C. Effective responses 231

D. Responses to keep the interaction flowing 232

E. Measuring understanding 236

IV. Types of Interviews 239

A. Evaluation or assessment interview 239

B. Structured clinical interviews 240

C. Case history interview 244

D. Mental status examination 246

E. Employment interview 247

V. Developing Interviewing Skills 249

VI. Sources of Error in the Interview 249

A. Interview validity 250

B. Interview reliability 252

VII. Research Approaches to the Study of Interviewing 253

A. Nonverbal communication 253

B. Quantitative aspects of interview behavior 254

Summary 254

Chapter 10 Tests of Mental Ability: The Binet Scale **256**

I. Binet's Principles of Test Construction 259

A. Principle 1: Age differentiation 260

B. Principle 2: The concept of general mental ability 260

II. The Early Binet Scales 262

A. Nature of the 1905 Binet-Simon Scale 262

B. The 1908 scale 263

III. Terman's Stanford-Binet Intelligence Scale 266

A. The 1916 Stanford-Binet Intelligence Scale 266

B. The intelligence quotient (IQ) concept 266

C. The 1937 scale 268

D. Psychometric properties of the 1937 scale   268

E. The 1960 Stanford-Binet revision   270

IV. The Modern Binet Scale   272

    A. Model of the modern (1986) Binet Scale   274

    B. Characteristics of the 1986 revision   274

    C. Psychometric properties of the modern Binet   277

    D. Research on the modern Binet   280

    E. Evaluation of the modern Binet   281

Summary   282

Chapter 11   The Wechsler Intelligence Scales   **283**

I. The Wechsler Intelligence Scales   284

    A. Advances in intelligence testing: Point and performance scale concepts   285

    B. From the Wechsler-Bellevue Intelligence Scale to the WAIS-R   288

II. Scales and Subtests of the WAIS-R   288

    A. The verbal subtests   289

    B. Raw scores, scaled scores, and the verbal IQ   293

    C. The performance subtests   295

    D. Performance IQs   297

    E. Full-scale IQs   297

III. Interpretive Features of the WAIS-R   298

    A. Verbal-performance IQ comparisons   299

    B. Pattern analysis   299

    C. Hypothetical case studies   300

IV. Psychometric Properties of the WAIS-R   302

    A. Reliability   303

    B. Validity   304

V. Evaluation of the WAIS-R   305

VI. Downward Extensions of the WAIS-R: The WISC-III and WPPSI-R   306

    A. The WISC-III   306

B. Evaluation of the WISC-III   311

C. The Wechsler Preschool and Primary Scale of Intelligence (WPPSI-R)   312

Summary   313

Chapter 12 Other Individual Tests of Ability   **315**

I. General Features of Alternative Individual Ability Tests   316

A. Alternative individual ability tests compared with the Binet and Wechsler Scales   316

B. Alternatives compared with each other   318

II. Specific Alternative Individual Ability Tests   319

A. Infant scales   320

B. Major tests for young children   328

C. General individual ability tests for handicapped and special populations   336

D. Broad-range individual ability tests: Child through adult   341

III. Individual Tests of Ability for Specific Purposes   342

A. Learning disabilities   342

B. Visiographic tests   345

C. Creativity: Torrance Tests of Creative Thinking (TTCT)   348

D. Individual achievement tests: Wide Range Achievement Test, Revised (WRAT-R)   348

Summary   350

Chapter 13 Group Ability Tests: Intelligence, Achievement, and Aptitude   **351**

I. Comparison of Group and Individual Ability Tests   353

A. Advantages of individual tests   354

B. Advantages of group tests   355

II. General Features of Group Tests   356

    A. Characteristics of group tests   356

    B. Selecting group tests   356

    C. Using group tests   357

III. Group Tests in the Schools: Kindergarten Through 12th Grade   358

    A. Achievement tests versus aptitude tests   358

    B. Group achievement tests   359

    C. Group tests of mental abilities (intelligence)   362

    D. Summary of group tests in the schools   365

IV. College Entrance Tests   366

    A. College Board Scholastic Aptitude Test (SAT)   366

    B. Cooperative School and College Ability Tests (SCAT)   369

    C. The American College Test (ACT)   370

V. Graduate School Entrance Tests   371

    A. Graduate Record Examination Aptitude Test (GRE)   371

    B. Miller Analogies Test (MAT)   376

VI. Nonverbal Group Ability Tests   377

    A. Raven Progressive Matrices (RPM)   377

    B. Goodenough-Harris Drawing Test (G-HDT)   379

    C. IPAT Culture Fair Intelligence Test   380

VII. Group Tests for Specific Purposes   381

    A. Tests for use in industry: Wonderlic Personnel Test (WPT)   381

    B. Tests for assessing occupational aptitude   382

    C. Armed Services Vocational Aptitude Battery (ASVAB)   382

Summary   383

Chapter 14 Tests for Choosing Careers   **385**

I. Measuring Interests   386

A. The Strong Vocational Interest Blank   387

B. The Strong-Campbell Interest Inventory   388

C. The 1985 SCII revision   394

D. The Kuder Occupational Interest Survey   395

E. The Minnesota Vocational Interest Inventory   398

F. The Career Assessment Inventory   398

G. The Self-Directed Search   399

H. Eliminating sex bias in interest measurement   400

I. Aptitudes and interests   400

II. Measuring Personal Characteristics for Job Placement   401

A. Trait factor approach: Osipow's vocational dimensions   401

B. The Career Maturity Inventory: Super's development theory   402

C. The California Occupational Preference Survey: Roe's career-choice theory   483

D. Are there stable personality traits?   404

III. Measuring Characteristics of the Work Setting   405

A. The social-ecology approach   405

B. Classifying environments   407

C. Job analysis   410

IV. Measuring the Person-Situation Interaction   411

Summary   414

Chapter 15 Structured Personality Tests   **416**

I. Strategies of Structured Personality Test Construction   418

A. Overview of the strategies   418

B. Deductive strategies   419

C. Empirical strategies   420

II. Criteria Used in Selecting Tests for Discussion   422

III. The Logical-Content Strategy   422

A. Woodworth Personal Data Sheet   423

B. Early multidimensional logical-content scales   423

C. Mooney Problem Checklist   424

D. Criticisms of the logical-content approach   424

IV. The Criterion-Group Strategy   425

A. Minnesota Multiphasic Personality Inventory   425

B. California Psychological Inventory   436

V. The Factor Analytic Strategy   437

A. Guilford's pioneer efforts   438

B. Cattell's contribution   439

C. Problems with the factor analytic strategy   441

VI. The Theoretical Strategy   442

A. Edwards Personal Preference Schedule   442

B. Personality Research Form and Jackson Personality Inventory   445

C. Temperament: The Myers-Briggs Type Indicator   448

D. Self-concept   449

VII. Combination Strategies   449

A. The Millon Clinical Multiaxial Inventory   450

B. The NEO Personality Inventory   450

Summary   453

Chapter 16   Projective Personality Tests   **455**

I. The Projective Hypothesis   456

II. The Rorschach Inkblot Test   458

A. Historical antecedents   458

B. Stimuli, administration, and interpretation   459

C. Psychometric properties   468

III. An Alternative Inkblot Test: The Holtzman   470

IV. The Thematic Apperception Test   471

    A. Stimuli, administration, and interpretation   472

    B. Psychometric properties   476

V. Alternative Apperception Procedures   477

VI. Nonpictorial Projective Procedures   477

    A. Word association test   478

    B. Sentence completion tests   479

    C. Figure drawing tests   480

Summary 480

Chapter 17   Alternatives to Traditional Psychological Tests   **482**

I. The Status of Traditional Psychological Tests and an Overview of the Alternatives   484

II. Behavioral Assessment Procedures   485

    A. Procedures based on operant conditioning   487

    B. Self-report techniques   489

    C. Kanfer and Saslow's functional approach   494

    D. Cognitive-behavioral assessment procedures   495

    E. Psychophysiological assessment procedures   499

III. Computers and Psychological Testing   501

    A. Psychophysical and signal detection procedures   501

    B. The computerization of traditional tests   505

    C. Computerization of behavioral assessment   505

Summary   506

Chapter 18   Measures of Anxiety and Stress   **508**

I. Stress and Anxiety   509

II. General Measures of Anxiety   510

    A. The State-Trait Anxiety Inventory   510

    B. The Taylor Manifest Anxiety Scale   512

III. Measures of Test Anxiety 513

    A. The Test Anxiety Questionnaire 514

    B. The Test Anxiety Scale 515

    C. Other measures of test anxiety 517

IV. Treatments for Test Anxiety 518

V. Measures of Life Stress 519

    A. Life experiences survey 522

    B. Measures of coping 523

    C. Measures of social support 524

Summary 526

Chapter 19 Testing in Health Care Settings   **528**

I. Neuropsychological Assessment 529

    A. Clinical neuropsychology 529

    B. Developmental neuropsychology 530

    C. Adult neuropsychology 532

    D. California Verbal Learning Test (CVLT) 537

II. Quality of Life Assessment 540

    A. What is health-related quality of life? 540

    B. Common methods for the measurement of quality of life 542

Summary 551

PART III   *Issues*   **553**

Chapter 20 Test Bias   **555**

I. Why Is the Issue Controversial? 556

II. Test Fairness and the Law 556

III. The Traditional Defense of Testing 558

    A. Content validity 558

    B. Criterion validity 562

IV. Other Approaches to Testing Minority-Group Members 567

    A. Ignorance versus stupidity 567

    B. The Chitling Test 568

    C. The Black Intelligence Test of Cultural Homogeneity 569

    D. The System of Multicultural Pluralistic Assessment 571

V. Suggestions for Solutions 574

    A. Ethical concerns and the definition of test bias 574

    B. Improving the use of selection devices 578

    C. Developing different criteria 579

    D. Changing the social environment 581

Summary 583

Chapter 21 Testing and the Law   **585**

I. Laws Governing the Use of Tests 587

    A. Federal authorities 587

    B. Specific laws 595

II. Some Major Lawsuits 598

    A. Early desegregation cases 598

    B. *Stell* v. *Savannah-Chatham County Board of Education* 599

    C. *Hobson* v. *Hansen* 600

    D. *Diana* v. *State Board of Education* 601

    E. *Larry P.* v. *Wilson Riles* 602

    F. *Parents in Action on Special Education* v. *Hannon* 604

    G. *Crawford et al.* v. *Honig et al.* 605

    H. *Marshall* v. *Georgia* 609

    I. *Debra P.* v. *Turlington* 610

    J. *Regents of the University of California* v. *Bakke* 612

    K. *Golden Rule Insurance Company et al.* v. *Washburn et al.* 613

    L. Personnel cases 615

M. A critical look at lawsuits 621

Summary 621

Chapter 22 The Future of Psychological Testing   **623**

    I. Pressures Shaping the Field of Testing 623

        A. Professional issues 624

        B. Moral issues 629

        C. Ethical issues 631

        D. Social issues 633

    II. Current Trends 636

        A. Proliferation of new tests 636

        B. Higher standards, improved technology, and increasing objectivity 637

        C. Greater public awareness and influence 638

        D. The computerization of tests 639

    III. Future Trends 640

        A. Prediction 1: Future prospects for testing are promising 640

        B. Prediction 2: The proliferation of new and improved tests will continue unabated 641

        C. Revolutionary changes: "Perestroika" in school testing 642

        D. Prediction 3: Controversy, disagreement, and change will continue 644

    Summary 644

Appendix 1 Areas of a Standard Normal Distribution 645

Appendix 2 Publishers of Major Tests 648

Appendix 3 Critical Values of *r* for $\alpha = .05$ and $\alpha = .01$ (Two-Tailed Test) 651

Appendix 4 Critical Values of *t* 652

Appendix 5 Code of Fair Testing Practices in Education 654

Glossary 659

References 665

Author Index 703

Subject Index 711

List of Sample Test Profiles

Figure 10-8	Cover page of the Stanford-Binet Intelligence Scale	273
Figure 11-2	WAIS-R Expanded Record Form	287
Figure 11-5	A WAIS-R pattern	293
Figure 11-8	WISC-III-like items	307
Figure 13-3	Example of a score report for the Stanford Achievement Test	360
Figure 13-4	Sample items from the verbal and mathematical sections of the Scholastic Aptitude Test	367
Figure 13-7	GRE verbal ability sample items	372
Figure 13-8	GRE quantitative ability sample items	373
Figure 13-9	GRE analytical ability sample items	374
Figure 13-11	MAT sample items	376
Focused Example 14-1	SCII Profile for Jean A.	391–393
Figure 15-2	An MMPI profile	426
Figure 15-3	An MMPI-2 profile	433
Table 15-4	The primary source traits covered by the 16PF test	440
Figure 15-4	Jackson Personality Inventory profile sheets	446–447
Figure 15-5	NEO Personality Inventory profile	451
Table 16-1	Summary of Rorschach Scoring	465
Focused Example 16-2	The danger of basing Rorschach interpretations on insufficient evidence	466–467
	Sentence completion tests	479
Table 17-4	Examples of a behavioral self-report	491
Table 17-5	Sample questions from a behavioral assertiveness questionnaire	493
Table 18-2	Some of the questions used in the Test Anxiety Questionnaire	515
Table 19-3	Sickness Impact Profile categories and selected items	543
Figure 20-6	Sample SOMPA profile	573
Table 21-2	Examples of items from a minimum competence test	611
Table 22-1	Performance testing	643

PART I

Principles

CHAPTER 1
Introduction

CHAPTER 2
Norms and Basic Statistics for Testing

CHAPTER 3
Correlation and Regression

CHAPTER 4
Reliability

CHAPTER 5
Validity

CHAPTER 6
Building a Test

CHAPTER 7
Selection and Decision Analysis

CHAPTER 8
Test Administration

Chapter 1

Introduction

Learning Objectives

When you have completed this chapter, you should be able to:

- Define the basic terms pertaining to psychological and educational tests.
- Distinguish between an individual test and a group test.
- Define the terms *achievement, aptitude,* and *intelligence* and identify a concept that can encompass all of these terms.
- Distinguish between ability tests and personality tests.
- Define the phrase *structured personality test.*
- Explain how structured personality tests differ from projective personality tests.
- Explain what a normative or standardization sample is and why such a sample is important.
- Identify the major developments in the history of psychological testing.
- Explain the relevance of psychological tests in contemporary society.

Thirteen-year-old children in 12 industrialized nations were given problems such as the following from the International Assessment of Education Progress (IAEP):

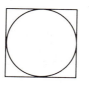

The length of a side of this square is 6. What is the radius of the circle?

A. 2   B. 3   C. 4   D. 6   E. 8   F. 9   G. Don't know

Figure 1-1
Percentage of
13-year-old
students at or
above level 600 on
the IAEP
mathematics scale.

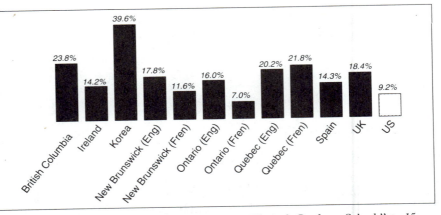

(*From "Performance at the Top: From Elementary Through Graduate School," p. 15.
Copyright © 1991 by Educational Testing Service. Reprinted by permission of
Educational Testing Service, the copyright holder.*)

Only one of the 12 countries ranked below the United States in the percentage
of 13-year-olds who had mastered such concepts (see Figure 1-1).

The results were similar for an IAEP science knowledge test (see Figure
1-2), which had questions such as the following:

Group A	Water vapor	**Group C**	Alcohol
	Oxygen		Water
	Air		Gasoline
Group B	Ice		
	Aluminum		
	Iron		

The substances above, each at room temperature, have been classified into groups.
On what property is the classification based?

A. Chemical composition   **C.** State of matter
B. Specific heat   **D.** Abundance within the earth's crust

Of what usefulness are tests such as these? Do these tests measure anything
meaningful? How accurate are they? To answer such questions, which are of
concern not only to every American but also to all members of the highly
competitive international community, it is necessary to understand the principles of psychological testing that you are about to learn.

Whether you like it or not, tests have a profound effect on you and your
family, and they will continue to do so. Tests can play a decisive role in which
college you attend, whether you get into an advanced degree program, and

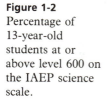

Figure 1-2
Percentage of 13-year-old students at or above level 600 on the IAEP science scale.

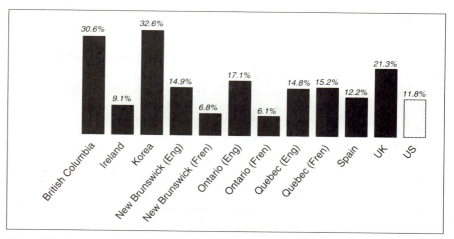

(From "Performance at the Top: From Elementary Through Graduate School," p. 15. Copyright © 1991 by Educational Testing Service. Reprinted by permission of Educational Testing Service, the copyright holder.)

even whether you will be accepted for employment after graduation. They may be used to determine whether you or someone in your family suffers from an emotional illness or to gauge the extent of emotional damages in litigation cases.

On April 18, 1991, President Bush released a proposal for reforming education in America to help bridge the alarming gap between the educational achievement of American children and that of their counterparts in other industrialized nations. *AMERICA 2000: An Educational Strategy* included a proposal for standardized national testing of all American school children. The idea was to set national standards and permit a direct comparison of children in every city and town. Is national testing of school children a bold solution to a pressing national problem, or is it another step toward the Big-Brother state portrayed in George Orwell's book, *1984?*

On July 8, 1991, at the national convention of the National Education Association (NEA) in Miami Beach, the teacher group vigorously criticized the idea of standardized national testing. According to a resolution passed by the NEA by a resounding voice vote, a national testing program would homogenize students and be "contrary to the diverse interests and needs of children." In spite of these objections, standardized national tests are now being developed and tested and may soon become a reality. Should you be alarmed or relieved?

To answer questions about tests you must understand the concepts presented in this book, such as reliability, validity, item analysis, and test constructions. Although a mastery of these concepts will require careful study and a knowledge of basic statistics, your efforts will be richly rewarded.

I. *Basic Concepts*

You are probably already familiar with some of the more elementary concepts of psychological testing. For the sake of clarity, however, it is important to begin with definitions of even the most basic terms so that you will know how they are used in this textbook.

A. *What a Test Is*

Every school child has had experience with tests. A **test** is a measurement device that quantifies behavior. A spelling test, for example, measures how well someone spells or the extent to which someone has mastered or learned to spell a specific list of words. At some time during the next few weeks it is likely that your instructor will want to measure the extent to which you have mastered the material of this book. To accomplish this, your instructor may give you a test.

As you well know, the test your instructor gives may not measure your full understanding of the material. This is because a test measures only a sample of behavior. There is always error associated with a sampling process. Test scores are not perfect measures of a behavior or characteristic, but as you will see, they do add significantly to the prediction process.

An **item** is a specific stimulus to which a person's overt behavioral response can be scored or evaluated (for example, classified, graded on a scale, or counted). Because psychological and educational tests are made up of items, the data they produce are explicit and hence subject to scientific inquiry.

In simple terms, items are the specific questions or problems that make up a test. The two problems presented at the beginning of this chapter are examples of test items. The overt response would be to fill in or blacken one of the spaces:

|| || || || || || ||
A B C D E F G

A **psychological test** or educational test is a set of items designed to measure characteristics of human beings that pertain to behavior. There are many types of behavior. Overt behavior is an observable activity by an individual. Some psychological tests attempt to measure the extent to which a human being might engage in or "emit" a particular overt behavior or whether the individual is even able to do so. Other tests measure the extent to which a person has previously engaged in some overt behavior. Behavior can also be covert. This behavior takes place within an individual and cannot be directly observed. For example, your feelings and thoughts are types of covert behavior. Some tests attempt to measure such behavior. Thus, psychological and educational tests measure past and present behavior. They also attempt to predict future behavior, such as success in college or the probability that you can complete an advanced degree program in law or medicine.

What does it mean when someone gets a score of 75 items correct on a 100-item test? One thing it means, of course, is that 75% of the items were answered correctly. In many situations, however, knowing the percentage of correct items a person obtained can be misleading. Consider two extreme examples. In one case, out of 100 students who took the exam, 99 obtained scores of 90% correct or higher and one got 75% correct. In another case, 99 of the 100 students obtained scores of 25% or lower, while one had 75% correct. The meaning of the scores can change dramatically depending on how a well-defined sample of individuals score on a test. To deal with such problems of interpretation, psychologists make use of scales, which relate raw scores on test items to some defined theoretical or empirical distribution. Later in the book you will learn about such distributions.

Scores on tests may be related to traits, which are enduring characteristics or tendencies to respond in a certain manner. Determination, sometimes seen as stubbornness, is an example of a trait; shyness is another. In contrast to traits, tests scores may be related to states, or the specific condition or status of an individual. A determined individual after many setbacks may, for instance, be in a weakened state and therefore less inclined than usual to manifest determination. Tests measure many types of behavior.

B. *Types of Tests*

Just as there are many types of behavior, so there are many types of tests. Tests that can be given to only one person at a time are known as **individual tests** (see Figure 1-3). The situation involved in an individual test is similar to that in individual psychotherapy. The examiner or **test administrator** (that is, the person giving the test) gives the test to only one person at a time, just as in individual psychotherapy; only one person is seen at a time. A **group test,** by contrast, can be administered to more than one person at a time by a single examiner, such as when your instructor gives everyone in the class a test at the same time.

Tests can also be categorized according to the type of behavior they measure. **Ability tests** contain items that can be scored in terms of speed, accuracy, or both. On an ability test, the faster or the more accurate one's responses, the better one scores on a particular characteristic. The more algebra problems you can correctly solve in a given amount of time, the greater is your ability in solving such problems.

Historically, experts have distinguished among achievement, aptitude,

Figure 1-3
Photo of an
individual
administration.
(*Ann Chwatsky/
Jeroboam*)

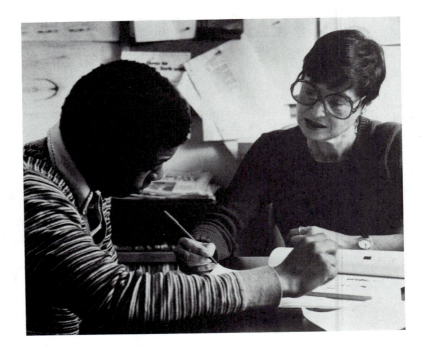

and intelligence as different types of ability. **Achievement** refers to previous learning. A test that measures or evaluates how many words you can spell correctly is called a spelling achievement test. **Aptitude,** by contrast, refers to the potential for learning or acquiring a specific skill. A spelling aptitude test measures how many words you might be able to spell given a certain amount of training, education, and experience. Your music aptitude refers in part to how well you might be able to learn to play a musical instrument given a certain number of lessons. Intelligence, in turn, has traditionally been distinguished from achievement and aptitude. **Intelligence** commonly refers to a person's general potential to solve problems, adapt to changing circumstances, think abstractly, and profit from experience, independent of prior learning. When you say a person is "smart," you are probably referring to intelligence. When a father scolds his daughter because she has not done as well in school as she is capable of doing, presumably he is saying that she has not used her intelligence (potential) to achieve (that is, acquire new knowledge).

The distinctions among achievement, aptitude, and intelligence, however, are not always so cut and dry, since all three are highly interrelated (Coleman & Cureton, 1954; Kelley, 1927, pp. 193–209). Attempts to separate prior learning from potential for learning, for example, have not been successful. There is a considerable overlap among achievement, aptitude, and intelligence tests. In view of this overlap, all three concepts are encompassed in the term **human ability** (see Carroll & Horn, 1981).

Figure 1-4
Self-report test
items.

	True	False
1. I like heavy metal music.	☐	☐
2. I believe that honesty is the best policy.	☐	☐
3. I am in good health.	☐	☐
4. I am easily fatigued.	☐	☐
5. I sleep well at night.	☐	☐

There is a clear-cut distinction between ability tests and personality tests. Whereas ability tests are related to capacity or potential, **personality tests** are related to the overt and covert dispositions of the individual—for example, the tendency that a person will show a particular behavior or response in any given situation. Remaining isolated from others, for instance, does not require any special skill or ability, but some people prefer or are disposed to remain thus isolated. This is their typical behavior. Personality tests measure typical behavior.

There are several types of personality tests. In Chapter 15 you will learn about structured (that is, objective) personality tests. **Structured personality tests** provide a statement, usually of the "self-report" variety, and require the subject to choose between two or more alternative responses such as "True" or "False" (see Figure 1-4).

In contrast to structured personality tests, projective personality tests are unstructured. A **projective personality test** is one in which the stimulus (test materials) and the required response or both are ambiguous. For example, in a projective test known as the Rorschach inkblot test, the stimulus is an inkblot. Furthermore, rather than being asked to choose among alternative responses as in structured personality tests, the individual is asked to provide a spontaneous response. The inkblot is presented to the subject, who is asked "What might this be?" The general idea behind projective tests is that a person's interpretation of an ambiguous stimulus will reflect his or her unique characteristics (see Chapter 16).

See Table 1-1 for a summary of ability and personality tests.

Table 1-1
Types of Tests

I. Ability tests: Measure skills in terms of speed, accuracy, or both.
  A. Achievement test: Measures previous learning.
  B. Aptitude test: Measures potential for acquiring a specific skill.
  C. Intelligence test: Measures potential to solve problems, adapt to changing circumstances, and profit from experiences.
II. Personality tests: Measure typical behavior—traits, temperaments, and dispositions.
  A. Structured (objective): Provides a self-report statement to which the person responds "True" or "False", "Yes" or "No".
  B. Projective: Provides an ambiguous test stimulus; response requirements are unclear.

C. *Psychological Testing and Individual Differences*

Psychological testing refers to the use of psychological and educational tests. It refers to all the possible uses, applications, and underlying concepts of tests. The main use of psychological and educational tests, though, is to evaluate *individual differences*, or variations among individuals. Such tests measure individual differences in ability and personality. It is assumed that the differences among individuals on the test are attributable to actual differences among individuals in their various capabilities or typical behaviors. For instance, individuals who score high on an IQ test are assumed to have a higher degree of intelligence than those who obtain low scores.

II. *Plan for the Book*

This book is divided into three parts: *principles, applications,* and *issues.* Together, these parts provide an extensive coverage of psychological testing from the most basic ideas to some of the most complex. Basic ideas and events are introduced early and stressed throughout so that newly acquired knowledge is reinforced through practice. In covering principles, applications, and issues, our intent is to provide not only the *who's* of psychological testing but also the *how's* and *why's* of major developments in the field. We also address an important concern of many students—relevance—by examining the diverse uses of tests and the resulting data.

A. *Principles of Psychological Testing*

By *principles of psychological testing* we mean the basic concepts and fundamental ideas that underlie all psychological and educational tests. These are covered in Part I. There are some basic statistical concepts, for example, that provide the foundation for understanding tests. These concepts are presented in Chapters 2 and 3. Chapters 4 and 5 cover two of the most fundamental concepts in testing: reliability and validity. **Reliability** refers to the accuracy, dependability, consistency, or repeatability of test results. In more technical terms, reliability refers to the degree to which test scores are free of measurement errors. As you will learn, there are many ways a test can be reliable. For example, test results may be reliable over time, which means that when the same test is given twice within any given time interval, the results tend to be the same or highly similar. In Chapter 4, you will learn about the different types of reliability. **Validity** is a term that refers to the meaning and usefulness of test results. More specifically, validity refers to the degree to which a certain inference or interpretation based on a test is appropriate. When we ask the question "What does this psychological test measure?" we are essentially asking "For what inferences is this test valid?"

Another principle or fundamental idea of psychological testing concerns how a test is created or constructed. The principles of test construction are covered in Chapter 6. Chapter 7 covers the selection of psychological tests and presents the basic knowledge one needs to select tests for specific purposes. The act of giving a test is known as **test administration.** Some tests are easy to administer, but others must be administered in a highly specific way. Chapter 8, the final chapter of Part I, covers the basic fundamentals of administering a psychological test.

B. *Applications of Psychological Testing*

Whereas the focus of Part I is on the principles of testing, the focus of Part II is on applications. Here we provide a detailed analysis of many of the most popular tests and how they are used or applied. Part 2 begins with an overview of the essential terms and concepts that relate to the application of tests. After this overview, Chapter 9 discusses interview techniques. An **interview** is a method of gathering information by conversations or direct questions. Not only has the interview traditionally been among the major techniques of gathering information in psychology in general, but interview data also provide an important complement to test results.

Chapters 10, 11, and 12 cover individual tests of human ability. As you will learn, there is a wide variety of fine tests of human ability. In Chapter 13, group tests of human ability are discussed. Chapters 14–17 cover the basic personality tests. Chapter 14 covers interests tests, which measure behavior relevant to such factors as occupational preferences. Chapter 15 covers structured personality tests, and Chapter 16 covers projective personality tests. In Chapter 17, we discuss many of the relatively new alternatives to the more traditional tests. We also consider the important influence of cognitive psychology on testing (Loftus, 1991; Neisser, 1991).

Taken together, Chapters 14–17 provide an in-depth coverage of the most widely used and newly developed personality and interest tests. These chapters not only provide descriptive information but also delve into the ideas underlying the various tests.

C. *Issues of Psychological Testing*

Beyond principles and applications, there are many social and theoretical issues related to testing, such as the controversial topic of racial differences in ability (Jensen, 1986; Zuckerman, 1990). Part 3, the last section of the book, covers many of these issues. To compromise between breadth and depth of coverage, we decided to focus on a comprehensive discussion of those issues that have particular importance in the current professional, social, and political environment.

Chapter 18 reviews the research on measures of stress and anxiety. Then in Chapter 19, the relatively new area of medical testing—tests for brain damage and health status—is covered. The next two chapters cover particularly sensitive controversies. Chapter 20 examines the issue of test bias, one of the most controversial issues in the field today (National Commission on Testing and Public Policy, 1990). Psychological tests have been accused of being discriminatory or biased against certain groups. Chapter 20 takes a careful look at both sides of this delicate controversy. Because of charges of bias and other problems, psychological testing is increasingly coming under the scrutiny of the law (Bersoff, 1981; Pinizzotto & Finkel, 1990). Thus, test bias is related to legal issues, and this relationship is examined in Chapter 21. In Chapter 22, a general overview is provided of other major issues that are presently shaping the future of psychological testing in America. From our review of the issues, we speculate on what the future holds for psychological testing.

III. *Historical Perspective*

Having given you an overview of the plan of the book, we will now briefly provide the historical context to give you a perspective. Consistent with our plan to proceed from the more basic concepts to the more complex ones and to reintroduce critical concepts to enhance learning, our historical discussion will touch on some of the material presented earlier in this chapter.

A. *Early Antecedents*

It is common to think of testing as both a recent and an American development. Indeed, most of the major developments in testing have occurred in this century, and a good number of them have taken place in the United States. The origins of testing, however, are neither recent nor American. Historians have obtained evidence that the ancient Chinese had a relatively sophisticated civil service testing program more than 4000 years ago (DuBois, 1966, 1970). Oral examinations were given every third year in China, and their results were used for work evaluations and promotion decisions.

By the time of the Han Dynasty (206 B.C. to A.D. 220), the use of test batteries (two or more tests used in conjunction) was quite common. These early tests related to such diverse topics as civil law, military affairs, agriculture, revenue, and geography. Tests had become quite well developed by the time of the Ming Dynasty (A.D. 1368–1644). During this period, there was a national multistage testing program that involved local and regional testing centers equipped with special testing booths. Those who had done well on the tests at the local level went on to provincial capitals for more extensive essay examinations. After this second testing, those with the highest test scores (best results) went on to the nation's capital for a final round of examinations. Only those who passed this third set of tests were eligible for public office.

The Western world most likely learned about testing programs through exposure to the Chinese. Reports by British missionaries and diplomats encouraged the English East India Company to copy the Chinese system in 1832 as a method for selecting employees for overseas duty. Testing programs worked well for the company, and so the British government adopted a similar system of testing for its civil service in 1855. After the British endorsement of a civil service testing system, the French and German governments followed suit. In 1883 the American government established the American Civil Service Commission, which developed and administered competitive examinations for certain government jobs. The impetus of the testing movement in the Western world grew rapidly around this time (Parkinson, 1957; Wiggins, 1973).

B. *Charles Darwin and Individual Differences*

Perhaps the most basic concept underlying psychological and educational testing pertains to individual differences. No two snowflakes are identical, and no two fingerprints are the same. Similarly, no two people are exactly alike in ability and typical behavior. Tests, as we have noted, are specifically designed to measure these individual differences in ability and personality among people.

Although human beings realized long ago that individuals differ, developing tools for measuring such differences, as you will see, was no easy matter. To develop a measuring device, we must understand what we want to measure. An important step toward understanding individual differences came with the publication of Charles Darwin's highly influential book, *The Origin of Species*, in 1859. According to Darwin's theory, higher forms of life evolved on this planet partially because of differences among individual forms of life within a species. Given that individual members of a species differ, some possess characteristics that are more adaptive or successful in a given environment. Darwin also believed that those with the best or most adaptive characteristics survive at the expense of those who are less fit, and that the survivors then pass their characteristics on to the next generation. Through this process, he argued, life has evolved to its presently complex and incredibly intelligent levels.

A relative of Darwin, Sir Francis Galton (see Figure 1-5), soon began applying Darwin's theories to the study of human individual differences. Given the concepts of survival of the fittest and individual differences, Galton set out to show that some humans possessed characteristics that made them more fit than other humans, a theory he articulated in his book, *Hereditary Genius*, published in 1869. Galton (1883) subsequently began a series of experimental

Figure 1-5
Sir Francis
Galton. (*From the
National Library
of Medicine.*)

studies to document the validity of his position. He concentrated on demonstrating that individual differences existed in human sensory and motor functioning, such as reaction time, visual acuity, and physical strength. In so doing, Galton initiated a search for knowledge concerning human individual differences, which is now one of the most important domains of scientific psychology.

Galton's work was extended by American psychologist James McKeen Cattell, who coined the term *mental test* (Cattell, 1890). Cattell's doctoral dissertation was based on Galton's work on individual differences in reaction time. In continuing Galton's exploration of human individual differences and introducing the term *mental test,* Cattell perpetrated and stimulated the forces that ultimately led to the development of modern tests. Galton's influence on Cattell is clearly revealed in the latter's statement that Galton is "the greatest man whom I have ever known" (Cattell, 1930, p. 116).

C. *Experimental Psychology and Psychophysical Measurement*

A second major foundation of testing can be found in experimental psychology and early attempts to unlock the mysteries of human consciousness through the scientific method. Prior to the development of psychology as a science, there were mathematical models, in particular those of J. F. Herbart who eventually used these models as the basis for educational theories that strongly influenced 19th-century educational practices. E. H. Weber followed Herbart and attempted to demonstrate the existence of a psychological threshold, the minimum amount of stimulus energy necessary to activate a sensory system. Weber originated the famous law expressing the relationship between the strength of a stimulus and the increase necessary to produce a noticeable difference:

$$\frac{\Delta I}{I} = C$$

where ΔI = the increment in stimulus intensity—the just noticeable difference

$\quad\quad I$ = the intensity of the original stimulus (that is, a standard stimulus)

$\quad\quad C$ = a constant within but not between the various senses

Following Weber's tradition was G. T. Fechner, who devised the law that the strength of a sensation grows as the logarithm of the stimulus intensity:

$$S = k \log I$$

where S = subjective, or perceived, magnitude

$\quad\quad I$ = stimulus intensity

$\quad\quad k$ = a constant

Wilhelm Wundt set up a laboratory at the University of Leipzig in 1879 and is credited with founding the science of psychology, following in the tradition of Weber and Fechner (Hearst, 1979). Wundt was succeeded by E. B. Titchner, whose student, G. Whipple, recruited L. L. Thurstone at the Carnegie Institute of Technology. Whipple provided the basis for immense changes in the field of testing by conducting a seminar at the Carnegie Institute in 1919 attended by Thurstone, E. Strong, and other prominent early American psychologists. From this seminar came the Carnegie Interest Inventory and later the Strong Vocational Interest Blank. Further on in this book, we will discuss in greater detail the contributions of these early pioneers to the testing field as well as the tests they helped develop.

Thus, psychological testing derives from two branches: one based on the work of Darwin, Galton, and Cattell on the measurement of individual differences and the other (more theoretically relevant and probably stronger) based on the work of German psychophysicists Herbart, Weber, Fechner, and Wundt. Experimental psychology developed from the latter branch. From this branch people in the field of psychological testing gained an understanding that testing is like an experiment and requires rigorous experimental control. Such control, as you will see, comes from administering tests under highly standardized conditions.

The efforts of these researchers, however necessary, did not alone result in the creation of modern psychological tests. Modern tests were born in response to important needs. One such need was to classify and identify the mentally and emotionally handicapped. One of the earliest tests resembling present-day procedures, the Seguin Form Board (Seguin, 1866), was developed in an effort to educate and evaluate the mentally retarded. Similarly, Kraepelin (1912) devised a series of examinations or tests for evaluating emotionally impaired persons.

An important breakthrough in the creation of modern tests came at the turn of the 20th century. The French minister of public instruction appointed a commission to study ways of identifying intellectually subnormal individuals in order to provide them with appropriate educational experiences. One member of that commission was Alfred Binet. Working in conjunction with French physician T. Simon, Binet developed the first major general intelligence test, which contained 30 items of increasing difficulty. Binet's early effort launched the first systematic attempt to evaluate individual differences in human intelligence (see Chapter 10).

D. *The Evolution of Intelligence and Standardized Achievement Tests*

The history and evolution of Binet's intelligence test are instructive. The first version of the test, known as the Binet-Simon scale, was published in 1905. As stated, this instrument contained 30 items of increasing difficulty and was designed to identify intellectually subnormal individuals. Like all well-constructed tests, the Binet-Simon scale of 1905 was augmented by a comparison or standardization sample. Binet's standardization sample consisted of 50 children who had been given the test under *standard conditions*—that is, with precisely the same instructions and format. In obtaining this standardization sample, the authors of the Binet test had norms with which they could compare the results from any new subject. Without such norms, the meaning of scores would have been difficult, if not impossible, to evaluate. However, by knowing such things as the average number of correct responses found in the standardization sample, it was at least possible to state whether a new subject was below or above it.

It is easy to understand the importance of a standardization sample. However, the importance of obtaining a standardization sample that represents the population from which new people come has sometimes been ignored or overlooked by test users. For example, if the standardization sample consisted of 50 white males from wealthy families, then the meaning of the score of a black female child from a poverty-stricken family could not be easily or fairly evaluated. Nevertheless, comparisons of this kind are not all that uncommon. Clearly, it is not appropriate to compare a person to a group if that individual does not belong or is not represented in that group.

Binet was aware of the importance of a standardization sample. Indeed, one facet in the evolution of the Binet test has been an attempt to increase the size and representativeness of the standardization or comparison sample. A **representative sample** is one that comprises individuals similar to those for whom the test is to be used. When the test is used for the general population, a representative sample must reflect all segments of the population in proportion to their actual numbers.

By 1908 the Binet-Simon scale had been substantially improved. It was revised to include nearly twice as many items (59) as the 1905 scale. Of even more significance, the size of the standardization sample was increased to more than 200. The 1908 Binet-Simon scale also introduced the historically significant concept of mental age. A child's mental age was determined by the test. In simplified terms, you might think of **mental age** as a measurement of a child's performance on the test relative to other children of that particular age group. If a child's test performance equaled that of the average 8-year-old, for example, then his or her mental age would be 8. That is, in terms of the abilities measured by the test, this child could be viewed as having a similar level of ability as the average 8-year-old. The actual, or chronological, age of the child might be 4 or 12, but in terms of test performance, the child functioned at the same level as the average 8-year-old. The mental age concept was one of the most important contributions of the revised 1908 Binet-Simon scale.

The Binet-Simon scale was revised again in 1911, but that revision contained only minor improvements. By this time, however, the idea of intelligence testing had swept across the world and was especially entrenched in the United States. By 1916, L. M. Terman of Stanford University revised the Binet test for use in America. (There had been earlier American versions, which will be discussed in Chapter 10.) Terman's revision, known as the Stanford-Binet Intelligence Scale (Terman, 1916), was the only American version of the Binet test that flourished and was characteristic of one of the most important trends in testing—the drive toward better and better tests.

Terman's 1916 revision of the Binet-Simon scale contained numerous improvements. The standardization sample was increased to include 1000 persons, original items were revised, and many new items were added. Terman's 1916 Stanford-Binet Intelligence Scale added respectability and momentum to the newly developing testing movement, which began in the United States around World War I in response to the demand for a quick, efficient way of evaluating the emotional and intellectual functioning of thousands of military recruits.

The Binet test was an individual test. World War I, however, created a demand for large-scale group testing because there was a shortage of trained personnel who could evaluate the huge influx of military recruits in terms of ability and emotional functioning. Therefore, shortly after the United States became actively involved in World War I, the Army requested the assistance of Robert Yerkes, who was the president in 1917 of the American Psychological Association (see Yerkes, 1921). Yerkes headed a committee of distinguished psychologists who soon developed group tests of human abilities: the Army Alpha and the Army Beta. The Army Alpha was a structured ability test that required reading ability. The Army Beta, by contrast, was designed to measure the intelligence of illiterate adults.

World War I saw the widespread development of group tests, in which many people could be tested simultaneously. Also about this time the scope of testing was broadened to include tests of achievement, aptitude, interest, and personality. As previously indicated, however, achievement, aptitude, and intelligence tests overlapped considerably; the distinctions proved to be more illusory than real. (Measures of personality have a separate history and will be discussed in a subsequent section.) It is noteworthy, however, that the 1916 Stanford-Binet Intelligence Scale appeared at a time of strong demand for and high optimism and faith in the potential of measuring human behavior through tests. World War I and the creation of group tests then added momentum to the testing movement. Shortly after the appearance of the 1916 Stanford-Binet Intelligence Scale and the Army Alpha test, schools, colleges, and industry began using tests. It appeared to many that this new phenomenon, the psychological test, held the key to the solution of the problems emerging from the rapid expansion of technology and population growth characteristic of modern-day societies.

Among the most important developments following World War I was the development of standardized achievement tests. In contrast to essay tests, standardized achievement tests provide multiple-choice questions that are standardized on a large sample of children in order to produce norms against which the results of new examinees can be compared.

The use of standardized achievement tests caught on quickly because of the relative ease of administration and scoring and the lack of subjectivity or favoritism that can occur in essay or other written tests. Through the use of standardized achievement tests it was possible to subject a large number of children to identical testing conditions and scoring standards. Such tests also allowed a broader coverage of content and were less expensive and more efficient than essays. In 1923 the work in the development of standardized achievement tests culminated with the publication of the Stanford Achievement Test by T. L. Kelley, G. M. Ruch, and L. M. Terman.

By the 1930s it was widely held that these new standardized tests were clearly superior to essay tests in their objectivity and reliability, and their use proliferated widely. Interestingly, as we will see later in the book, teachers of today appear to have come full circle. In its July 1991 meeting, the NEA advocated the use of written tests and work samples (portfolios) over standardized achievement tests as the best way to evaluate children.

For every movement there is a countermovement, and the testing movement in the United States in the 1930s was no exception. Critics soon became vocal enough to dampen enthusiasm and to put even the most optimistic advocates of tests on the defensive. Little by little, the limitations, weaknesses, and problems with existing tests were noted by researchers, who demanded nothing short of the highest possible standards. One of the most systematic, persistent, and organized attacks on tests by psychologists was directed at the so-called structured personality tests. However, no test was safe from criticism, not even the Stanford-Binet, which had been a landmark in the testing field. Thus, although tests were used between the two world wars and many new tests were developed, the accuracy and utility of tests remained under heavy fire.

Just prior to the outbreak of World War II in Europe in 1939, however, tests began to enjoy a renewed level of respectability. The knowledge and experience of the previous two decades were manifested in new, improved tests. By 1937 the Stanford-Binet was revised again. Among the many improvements was the inclusion of a standardization sample of more than 3000 individuals. No other individual intelligence test before or since has had a larger standardization sample. Only the group tests, such as the Scholastic Aptitude Test (SAT), which can be administered on a mass scale, have larger samples.

Only two years after the 1937 revision of the Stanford-Binet test, David Wechsler published the first version of the Wechsler intelligence scales (see Chapter 11), the Wechsler-Bellevue Intelligence Scale (W-B) (Wechsler, 1939). The Wechsler-Bellevue scale contained several interesting innovations in intelligence testing. Unlike the Stanford-Binet test, which produced only a single score (the so-called IQ, or intelligence quotient), Wechsler's test yielded several scores, permitting an analysis of an individual's pattern or combination of abilities. Among the various scores produced by the Wechsler test was the performance IQ. As you will see, performance tests do not require a verbal response.

Intelligence can be evaluated in a context that is as free as possible from verbal or language skills. The Stanford-Binet test had long been criticized because of its emphasis on language and verbal skills. With its verbal emphasis, the Binet test was inappropriate for many individuals (especially those who are nonverbal or illiterate). In addition, there are few people, if any, who believe that language or verbal skills play an exclusive role in human intelligence. Wechsler's inclusion of a nonverbal (performance) scale thus helped overcome some of the weaknesses of the Binet test that stemmed from its heavy verbal emphasis. The Binet test was drastically revised in 1986 to include performance subtests. (Performance scales and other important concepts in intelligence testing will be formally defined in Chapter 11, which covers the various forms of the Wechsler intelligence scales.)

E. *Personality Tests: 1920–1940*

During the period immediately preceding and following World War II, personality tests began to blossom. Whereas intelligence tests attempted to measure ability or potential, personality tests attempted to measure presumably stable characteristics or traits that theoretically underlie behavior. **Traits** can be defined as relatively enduring dispositions (tendencies to act, think, or feel in a certain manner in any given circumstance) that distinguish one individual from another. For example, it can be argued that some people are optimistic and some pessimistic. Optimistic people remain optimistic regardless of

Figure 1-6

The Woodworth
Personal Data
Sheet represented
an attempt to
standardize the
psychiatric
interview. It
contains questions
such as those
shown here.

	True	False
1. I wet the bed.	☐	☐
2. I drink a quart of whiskey each day.	☐	☐
3. I am afraid of closed spaces.	☐	☐
4. I believe I am being followed.	☐	☐
5. People are out to get me.	☐	☐
6. Sometimes I see or hear things that other people do not hear or see.	☐	☐

whether or not things are going well. A pessimist, by contrast, is always looking at the negative side of things. Optimism and pessimism can thus be viewed as traits. They are relatively enduring characteristics of an individual that manifest themselves across a wide variety of situations. They are characteristics of the individual that are brought to a situation. One of the basic goals of traditional personality tests is to measure traits. As you will learn, however, the notion of traits has important limitations.

The earliest personality tests were structured paper-and-pencil group tests. These tests provided multiple-choice and true/false questions that could be mass (group) administered. Because they provide a high degree of structure (that is, a definite stimulus and specific alternative responses that can be unequivocally scored), these paper-and-pencil group personality tests are often referred to as objective or structured personality tests. The first structured personality test, the Woodworth Personal Data Sheet, was developed during World War I and was published in final form just after the war (see Figure 1-6).

As indicated earlier, the motivation underlying the development of the first personality test was the need to screen military recruits. The history of testing indicates that tests such as the Binet or Woodworth were created by necessity to meet unique challenges. Like the early ability tests, however, the first structured personality test was simple by today's standards. Interpretation of results from the Woodworth test depended on the now-discredited assumption that the content of an item could be accepted at face value. If the person marked "False" to the statement "I wet the bed," then it was assumed that he or she did not wet the bed. As logical as this assumption seems, experience has shown that it is often false. In addition to problems with honesty, the person responding to the question may not interpret the meaning of "wet the bed" in the same way as the test administrator. (There are other problems with tests like the Woodworth, and these are discussed in Chapter 15.)

The introduction of the Woodworth test was enthusiastically followed by the creation of a variety of structured personality tests, all of which assumed the accuracy of a test response. However, just as ability tests such as the Binet had been scrutinized, analyzed, and criticized by researchers, so were the early structured personality tests. Indeed, the criticism of structured personality

Figure 1-7
Card 1 of the Rorschach inkblot test, a projective personality test. Such tests provide an ambiguous stimulus to which a subject is asked to make some response.

tests that relied on face value alone became so intense that they were nearly driven out of existence. What followed was the development of new tests based on more modern concepts that revitalized the use of structured personality tests (see Chapter 15). Thus, after an initial surge of interest and optimism during most of the 1920s, structured personality tests declined in use by the late 1930s and into the early 1940s. Following World War II, however, personality tests based on fewer or different assumptions were introduced, thereby rescuing the structured personality test concept.

During the brief but dramatic rise and fall of structured personality tests based on the assumed accuracy of a test response, interest in projective tests began to grow. In contrast to structured personality tests that, in general, provide a relatively unambiguous test stimulus and specific alternative responses, projective personality tests provide an ambiguous stimulus. Furthermore, in a projective test the response requirements are unclear. The scoring of projective tests is often subjective.

Unlike the early structured personality tests, interest in the projective Rorschach inkblot test grew slowly (see Figure 1-7). The rationale for the Rorschach test was first published by Herman Rorschach of Switzerland in 1921. However, several years passed before the Rorschach was introduced in the United States by David Levy. The first Rorschach doctoral dissertation written in a U.S. university was not completed until 1932, when Sam Beck, Levy's student, decided to scientifically investigate the properties of the Rorschach test. Although initial interest in the Rorschach test was lukewarm at best, its attractiveness progressed rapidly following Beck's work, despite suspicion, doubt, and criticism from the scientific community.

Adding to the momentum for the acceptance and use of projective tests was the development of the Thematic Apperception Test (TAT) by Henry Murray and Christina Morgan in 1935. Whereas the Rorschach test contained completely ambiguous inkblot stimuli, the TAT was more structured. Its stimuli consisted of ambiguous pictures depicting a variety of scenes and situations, such as a boy sitting in front of a table with a violin on it. Unlike the Rorschach test, which asked the subject to explain what the inkblot might be, the TAT required the subject to make up a story about the ambiguous scene. The TAT purported to measure human needs and thus to ascertain individual differences in motivation. (In Chapter 16 you will learn more about projective tests in general and about the Rorschach and the TAT in particular.)

F. *The Emergence of New Approaches to Personality Testing*

The popularity of the two most important projective personality tests, the Rorschach and TAT, grew rapidly by the late 1930s and early 1940s, perhaps because of disillusionment with structured personality tests (Dahlstrom, 1969a). However, many psychologists seem to have a deeply ingrained suspicion of projective tests, especially the Rorschach, so projective tests were far from universally accepted.

In 1943 the development of the Minnesota Multiphasic Personality Inventory (MMPI) began a new era for structured personality tests. The idea behind the MMPI, though not new, helped revolutionize structured personality tests. The problem with early structured personality tests, like the Woodworth, was that they made far too many assumptions that subsequent scientific investigations failed to substantiate. The authors of the MMPI, by contrast, argued that the meaning of a test response must be determined by empirical research. The MMPI, along with its updated companion the MMPI-2 (Butcher, 1989, 1990), is currently the most widely used and referenced personality test in existence. Its emphasis on the need for empirical data in determining the meaning of test results has stimulated the development of a wide body of knowledge (see Ben-Porath & Butcher, 1991).

Like other major tests that have appeared in the 20th century, the MMPI was met with initial enthusiasm followed by disillusionment as weaknesses were revealed and became glaringly apparent. However, because of the large number of research studies that provide insight to the meaning of its scores, the MMPI has enjoyed substantial popularity and support from the scientific as well as the professional community. Recently the MMPI has been revitalized by exceptionally rigorous methods (Butcher, 1989). In 1957 the California Psychological Inventory (CPI) was developed within the context of the same commitment to empirical research. As you will see in Chapter 15, both the original MMPI and the original CPI contain significant problems. However, with the restandardization of the MMPI that took place in 1986 and the revision of the CPI in 1987, many of the problems have been corrected.

Table 1-2
Summary of
Personality Tests

Woodworth Personal Data Sheet: An early structured personality test that assumed that a test response can be taken at face value.

The Rorschach Inkblot Test: A projective test that provided an ambiguous stimulus (an inkblot) and asked the subject what it might be.

The Thematic Apperception Test (TAT): A projective test that provided ambiguous pictures and asked subjects to make up a story.

The Minnesota Multiphasic Personality Inventory (MMPI): A structured personality test that made no assumptions about the meaning of a test response. Such meaning was to be determined by empirical research.

The California Psychological Inventory (CPI): A structured personality test developed according to the same principles as the MMPI.

The Sixteen Personality Factor Questionnaire (16PF): A structured personality test based on the statistical procedure of factor analysis.

Just about the time the MMPI appeared, personality tests based on the statistical procedure called *factor analysis* began to emerge. **Factor analysis** is a method for finding the minimum number of dimensions (characteristics, attributes) called factors to account for a large number of variables. We may say a person is outgoing, is gregarious, seeks company, is talkative, and enjoys relating to others. However, these descriptive adjectives contain a certain amount of redundancy, or overlap. A factor analysis can identify the extent of this overlap. For example, a factor analysis of the above characteristics might reveal that they all can be accounted for by or subsumed under a single dimension (or factor): extroversion.

The first serious attempt to use factor analytic techniques in the development of a structured personality test was made by J. P. Guilford in the early 1940s. By the end of that decade, R. B. Cattell introduced the Sixteen Personality Factor Questionnaire (16PF), which remains to this day one of the most well-constructed structured personality tests and an important example of a test developed with the aid of factor analysis. (Factor analytic structured tests will also be discussed in Chapter 15.) See Table 1-2 for a summary of personality tests.

G. *The Period of Rapid Changes in the Status of Testing*

The 1940s saw not only the emergence of a whole new technology in psychological testing but also the growth of applied aspects of psychology. The role and significance of tests used in World War I were reaffirmed in World War II. By this time the U.S. government had become interested in encouraging the continued development of applied psychological technology. As a result, considerable federal funding was funneled through the Veterans Administration to provide paid, supervised training experiences for clinically oriented psychologists. By 1949 formal university training standards were developed and accepted, and clinical psychology was born. Other applied branches of psychology—such as industrial psychology, counseling psychology, educational psychology, and school psychology—soon began to blossom.

One of the major functions of the applied psychologist was psychological testing. The Shakow et al. (1947) report (whose recommendations provided the foundation for the formal training standards in clinical psychology) specified that psychological testing was a unique function of the clinical psychologist and recommended that testing methods be taught to only doctoral psychology students. A position paper of the American Psychological Association published about seven years later (APA, 1954) reinforced that testing belongs to the clinical psychologist by its formal declaration that the psychologist would conduct psychotherapy only in "true" collaboration with physicians. Thus testing, but not psychotherapy, could be conducted independently by a psychologist. Indeed, as long as psychologists assumed the role of testers, they played a complementary, but often secondary or subservient, role vis-à-vis medical practitioners. The medical profession could have made clinical psychology's emergence difficult, but it did not because as tester the psychologist could be an aid to the physician. Therefore, the late 1940s and early 1950s saw the use of tests as the major function of the clinical psychologist (Shaffer, 1953).

For better or worse, depending on your perspective, the government's efforts to stimulate the development of applied aspects of psychology, especially clinical psychology, were extremely successful. Hundreds of highly talented and creative young people were attracted to clinical and other applied areas of psychology. These individuals, who were to utilize tests and other psychological techniques to solve practical human problems, were uniquely trained as scientific practitioners of the principles, empirical foundations, and applications of the science of psychology.

Soon the highly talented group of post–World War II psychologists began to reject the secondary role relative to the medical profession that was inherent in the testing situation as practiced in the 1940s and 1950s (Lewandowski & Saccuzzo, 1976). Many of these early clinical practitioners, armed with rather powerful knowledge from scientific psychology, must have felt like second-rate citizens when compared with physicians (see Saccuzzo & Kaplan, 1984). Unable to engage in the independent practice of psychotherapy, some psychologists perhaps sensed they were being treated like technicians whose purpose was to serve the medical profession. Psychologists began to reject playing a secondary role to the medical profession.

Many psychologists, furthermore, apparently associated tests with a secondary relationship to the medical profession and thus rejected tests (Lewandowski & Saccuzzo, 1976). At the same time, the potentially intrusive nature of tests and fears of misuse of tests began to create public suspicion, distrust, and contempt for tests. Attacks on testing came from within the profession of psychology and also from sources external to the profession. These attacks intensified and multiplied so fast that many psychologists jettisoned all ties to the traditional tests developed during the first half of this century, and testing again underwent a sharp decline in status in the late 1950s that persisted into the 1970s (see Holt, 1967).

H. *The Current Environment*

Most things seem to go through cycles, and psychological testing is no exception. Although the attacks and efforts to impose restrictions on tests continue unabated, interest in psychological testing remains strong. Traditional tests continue to be used, and new procedures are developed each year. As in the past, psychological testing remains one of the most important yet controversial topics in psychology. For you as a student, a thorough, up-to-date knowledge of the material in this text will be one of the most important aspects of your education. No matter what your major, you will find the basic principles discussed in the early chapters of this book invaluable.

If you are among those interested in using psychological techniques in an applied setting, then the information contained in the chapters ahead will be of great significance. Deep in the historical roots of psychology and through to the present, psychological tests have been among the most important instruments of the psychologist in general and of those who apply psychology in particular.

Testing is indeed one of the essential elements of psychology. Not all psychologists use tests and some psychologists are opposed to tests, yet all areas of psychology depend on measurement. In fact, all areas of psychology depend on knowledge gained in research studies in which measurements are taken. The meaning and dependability of these measurements are unmistakably among the most important foundations of research in psychology. An understanding of the basic principles of measurement is necessary for the effective study of any area of human behavior (see Matarazzo, 1990, 1991).

The use of specific psychological tests is one of the basic skills of the applied psychologist. In clinical settings, for example, testing is the unique function of the psychologist. Psychotherapy is often performed by psychiatrists, social workers, nurses, and even untrained volunteers. It is the psychologists, however, who administer and evaluate the results of psychological tests. Thus, training in psychological testing is one of the psychologist's most distinguishing marks. In industrial and educational psychology, knowledge of psychological testing is one of the most important distinguishing skills the psychologist brings to the job.

In today's complex society, the relevance of the principles, applications, and issues of psychological testing extends far beyond the field of psychology. Even if you do not plan to become a psychologist, you are very likely to encounter psychological tests at some time in the future. Attorneys, physicians, social workers, business managers, educators, and many other professionals are frequently confronted with reports based on psychological tests. To make adequate use of information based on psychological tests, you need the kind of knowledge presented in this book.

Even if you enter a profession or occupation with little relevance to psychological testing, the principles, applications, and issues of psychological testing will be of interest to you. The lives of you and your family are likely to be touched by psychological tests. The more you know about psychological tests, the better able you will be to ensure that your encounters with them are positive. Given the attacks on tests and threats to prohibit or greatly limit their use, you have a responsibility to yourself and to society to know as much as you can about psychological tests. The future of testing may very well depend on you and people like you. A thorough knowledge of testing will allow you to base your decisions on facts and to ensure that tests are used for the most beneficial and constructive purposes.

Tests have probably never been as important as they are in our contemporary society. To illustrate our point, let us consider just one type of testing—academic aptitude. Each year more than 2.5 million individuals take tests designed to give schools some evidence of their academic suitability, and the testing process begins early in students' lives. Prestigious presecondary schools require a test that is taken by more than 16,000 children each year. When these students become adolescents and want to get into college preparatory schools, about 20,000 take a screening examination. Very few students who want to go to a four-year college can avoid taking a college entrance test. The Scholastic Aptitude Test alone is given to more than 1.8 million high school students each year. Another 100,000 high school seniors take other tests in order to gain advanced placement in college.

These figures do not include the 75,000 persons who take a special test for admission to business school or the 120,000 persons who take a law school admission test. We have not even mentioned tests for graduate school, medical school, dental school, the military, and others. Millions of tests are given each year. As sources of information about human characteristics, the results of these tests are used to make critical life decisions.

Summary

The history of testing in America has been brief but intense. Although tests have always been available, psychological testing is very much a product of modern society with its unprecedented technology, population growth, and unique problems. By helping to solve the challenges posed by developments in modern times, tests have played a role in modern U.S. history. You should realize, however, that despite all the recent advances in the theory and technique of psychological testing, there are still many unsolved technical problems and hotly debated social, political, and economic issues. Nevertheless, the prevalence of tests in our society, despite strong opposition, indicates that although they are far from perfect, psychological tests must be fulfilling some important need in the decision-making process that permeates all facets of society. Because decisions must be made, with or without the aid of psychological tests, tests will flourish until a better or more objective way of making decisions emerges.

The modern history of psychological tests shows that they have evolved in a complicated environment in which hostile and facilitative forces have interacted to produce a balance characterized by innovation and a continual quest for better methods. One interesting thing about tests is that people seem to find it hard to remain neutral about them. If you are not in favor of tests, then you probably have some strong reservations about them. We ask that you maintain a flexible, open mind before forming an opinion. No matter what your attitude toward them, however, the study of psychological tests can be a most rewarding educational experience. If you know enough to form your own independent judgment of psychological testing after reading this text, then this book has accomplished its goal.

Chapter 2

Norms and Basic Statistics for Testing

Learning Objectives

When you have completed this chapter, you should be able to:

- Discuss three properties of scales of measurement.
- Determine why properties of scales are important in the field of measurement.
- Tell why methods are available for displaying distributions of scores.
- Describe the mean and the standard deviation.
- Define a Z score and explain how it is used.
- Relate the concepts of mean, standard deviation, and Z score to the concept of a standard normal distribution.
- Define quartiles, deciles, and stanines and explain how they are used.
- Tell how norms are created.
- Relate the notion of tracking to the establishment of norms.

We use numbers as a basic way of communicating: our money system requires us to understand and manipulate numbers, we estimate how long it will take to do things, we count, we express evaluations on scales, and so on. Think about how many times you use numbers in an average day. There is no way of avoiding them.

One advantage of number systems is that they allow us to manipulate numbers without changing the qualities they represent. Through sets of well-defined rules, we can use numbers to learn more about the world. Tests are devices used to translate observations of behavior into numbers. The outcome of a test is almost always represented as a score, and much of this book is about what scores mean. This chapter reviews some basic rules that are used to evaluate number systems. These rules and number systems will be our partners in learning about human behavior.

If you have had a course in psychological statistics, this chapter will reinforce the basic concepts. If additional review is needed, you should reread your introductory statistics book. Most introductory statistics books cover the information in this chapter. If you have not had a course in statistics, this chapter will provide some of the information needed for understanding other chapters in this book.

I. *Why We Need Statistics*

Modern psychology has advanced beyond centuries of speculation about human nature through its commitment to the scientific method. Scientific study requires systematic observations and an estimation of the extent to which our observations could have been influenced by chance alone. Statistical methods serve two important purposes in our quest for scientific understanding.

First, statistics help us describe. Numbers provide convenient summaries and allow us to evaluate some observations relative to others. For example, if you get a score of 54 on a psychology examination, you probably want to know what the 54 means. Is it lower than the average score, or is it about the same? Knowing the answer can make the feedback you get from your examination more meaningful. If you discover that the 54 puts you in the top 5% of the class, you might assume you have a good chance for an "A." If it puts you in the bottom 5%, you will feel differently.

Second, we can use statistics to make **inferences,** which are logical deductions about events that cannot be observed directly. For example, we do not know how many people watched a particular television movie unless we ask everyone. However, in using scientific sample surveys, we can make an inference about the percentage of people who saw the film. Data gathering and analysis might be considered analogous to criminal investigation and prosecution (Tukey, 1977). The first step is the detective work of gathering and displaying clues. This is what Princeton statistician John Tukey calls exploratory data analysis. Then there is a period of confirmatory data analysis, when the clues are evaluated against rigid statistical rules. This latter phase is like the work done by judges and juries.

Some students have an aversion to numbers and anything mathematical. If you are one of these people, you are not alone. Feeling uneasy about statistics is common not only among students but even among some professional psychologists. However, it is widely believed that statistics and the basic principles of measurement are at the center of the modern science of psychology. Scientific statements are usually based on careful study, and such systematic study requires some numerical analysis.

This chapter will review both descriptive and inferential statistics. **Descriptive statistics** are methods used to provide a concise description of a collection of quantitative information. **Inferential statistics** are methods used to make inferences from observations of a small group of people known as a sample to a larger group of individuals known as a population. Typically the psychologist wants to make statements about the larger group, but it is not possible to make all the necessary observations. Instead, observations are made on a relatively small group of subjects (sample), and inferential statistics are used to estimate the characteristics of the larger group.

Among the topics covered in this chapter are scales of measurement, the frequency distribution, the percentile distribution, the mean, the standard deviation, and norms.

II. *Scales of Measurement*

Measurement may be defined as the application of rules for assigning numbers to objects. The rules are the specific procedures used to transform qualities of attributes into numbers (Nunnally, 1978). For example, to rate the quality of wines, a wine taster must be given a specific set of rules. The wine might be rated on a 10-point rating scale, in which 1 means extremely bad and 10 means extremely good. For a taster to assign the numbers, the system of rules must be clearly defined. The basic feature of such systems is the scale of measurement. For example, to measure the height of your classmates, you might use the scale of inches; to measure their weight, you might use the scale of pounds.

In psychology we do not have clearly acknowledged and widely accepted scales of measurement. Nevertheless, we do have numerous systems by which we assign numbers. Indeed, the study of measurement systems is what this book is about. Before we consider any specific scale of measurement, it is important to consider general properties of measurement scales.

A. *Properties of Scales*

There are three important properties that make scales of measurement different from one another: magnitude, equal intervals, and an absolute 0.

Magnitude. Magnitude is the property of "moreness." A scale has the property of magnitude if we can say that one instance of the attribute represents more, less, or equal amounts of the quantity of interest than another instance of the attribute (McCall, 1980). On a scale of height, for example, if we can say that John is taller than Fred, then the scale has the property of magnitude. An example of a scale that does not have the property of magnitude is when a gym coach assigns numbers to teams in a league for identification (team 1, team 2, and so forth). Here the numbers are used only to label the teams, so the property of magnitude is not achieved. If the coach were to rank order the teams by the number of games they won, then the new numbering system (games won) would have the property of magnitude.

Figure 2-1
Hypothetical relationship between ratings of artwork and manual dexterity. In some ranges of the scale, the relationship is more direct than it is in others.

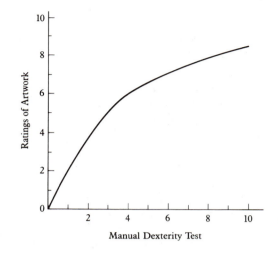

Equal intervals. The concept of equal intervals is a little more complex. A scale has the property of equal intervals if the difference between two points at any place on the scale has the same meaning as the difference between two other points that differ by the same number of scale units. For example, the difference between inch 2 and inch 4 on a ruler means the same as the difference between inch 10 and inch 12. The difference is exactly 2 inches in each case.

As simple as this concept seems, rarely is there good evidence that a psychological test has the property of equal intervals. For example, the difference between IQs of 45 and 50 does not mean the same thing as the difference between IQs of 105 and 110. Although each of these differences is 5 points $(50 - 45 = 5$ and $110 - 105 = 5)$, the 5 points at one level do not mean the same thing as 5 points at a higher level. When a scale has the property of equal intervals, the relationship between the measured units and some outcome can be described by a straight line or a linear equation in the form $Y = a + bX$. This equation tells us that as we increase in equal units on our scale, there are equal increases in the meaningful correlates of our units. For example, Figure 2-1 shows the hypothetical relationship between scores on a test of manual dexterity and ratings of artwork. Notice that the relationship is not a straight line. By examining the points of the figure, you can see that at some points the relationship is approximately linear: increases in manual dexterity are associated with increases in ratings of artwork. Then the relationship becomes nonlinear. The figure shows that after a manual dexterity score of about 5, greater increases in dexterity are needed to produce smaller increases in ratings of the quality of the artwork.

Absolute 0. An absolute 0 is obtained when there is nothing at all of the property being measured. For example, if you are measuring heart rate and observe that your patient has a rate of 0 and has died, you would conclude that

Table 2-1
Scales of
Measurement and
Their Properties

Type of Scale	Property		
	Magnitude	Equal Intervals	Absolute 0
Nominal	No	No	No
Ordinal	Yes	No	No
Interval	Yes	Yes	No
Ratio	Yes	Yes	Yes

there is no heart rate at all. For many psychological qualities it is extremely difficult, if not impossible, to define an absolute 0 point. For example, if we are measuring shyness on a rating scale with points 0 through 10, it is hard to say that 0 means the person is not shy at all (McCall, 1980).

Table 2-1 defines four scales of measurement based on the properties we have just discussed.

B. *Types of Scales*

Table 2-1 shows that a nominal scale does not have the property of magnitude, equal intervals, or an absolute 0. **Nominal scales** are really not scales at all; their only purpose is to name objects. For example, the numbers on the backs of football players' uniforms are nominal. In social science research, it has been common to label groups in sample surveys with numbers (such as 1 = white, 2 = black, and 3 = Mexican-American). However, when these numbers have been attached to categories, some statistical procedures applied to numbers themselves are not advisable. On the scale above for ethnic groups, a mean of 1.87 would have no meaning.[1]

A scale that has the property of magnitude but not the property of equal intervals or the property of an absolute 0 is known as an **ordinal scale.** An ordinal scale allows us to rank individuals or objects but not to say anything about the meaning of the differences between the ranks. If you were to rank order the members of your class in terms of their height, you would have an ordinal scale. Note that you would do this without concern for the differences among the ranks. For example, if Fred was the tallest, Susan the second tallest, and George the third tallest, you would assign them the ranks 1, 2, and 3, respectively. You would not give any consideration to the fact that Fred is 8 inches taller than Susan, but Susan is only 2 inches taller than George.

For most problems in psychology, we do not have the precision to measure

---

[1] This is not to say that sophisticated statistical analysis is not possible when the data are nominal. Indeed, several new and exciting developments in data analysis allow extensive and detailed inquiry with nominal data (see Daniel, 1990; Siegel & Castellan, 1988).

the exact differences between intervals. So most often we use ordinal scales of measurement. For example, IQ tests (see Chapter 10) do not have the property of equal intervals or an absolute 0, but they do have the property of magnitude. If they had the property of equal intervals, the difference between an IQ of 70 and one of 90 should have the same meaning as the difference between an IQ of 125 and one of 145. Because it does not, the scale can only be considered ordinal. Furthermore, there is no point on the scale at which there is no intelligence at all. Thus, the scale does not have the property of an absolute 0.

When a scale has the property of magnitude and equal intervals but not the property of an absolute 0, we refer to it as an **interval scale.** The most common example of an interval scale is the measurement of temperature in degrees Fahrenheit. This temperature scale clearly has the property of magnitude, since 35°F is warmer than 32°F, 65°F is warmer than 64°F, and so on. Also, the difference between 90°F and 80°F is equal to a similar difference of 10 degrees at any point on the scale. However, on the Fahrenheit scale temperature does not have the property of an absolute 0. If it did, the 0 point would be more meaningful. As it is, 0 on the Fahrenheit scale does not have a particular meaning. Freezing of water occurs at 32°F, and boiling of water occurs at 212°F. Because the scale does not have an absolute 0, it is not possible to make statements in terms of ratios. A temperature of 22°F is not twice as hot as 11°F, and a temperature of 70°F is not twice as hot as one of 35°F.

The Celsius scale of temperature is also an interval rather than a ratio scale. Although 0 represents freezing on the Celsius scale, it is not an absolute 0. Remember that an absolute 0 is a point at which nothing of the property being measured exists. Even on the Celsius scale of temperature, there is still plenty of room on the thermometer below 0. When the temperature goes below freezing, some aspect of heat is still being measured.

A scale that has all three properties (magnitude, equal intervals, and an absolute 0) is called a **ratio scale.** To continue our example with the scales of temperature, a ratio scale is one that has the properties of the Fahrenheit scale and the Celsius scale but also includes a meaningful 0 point. Physicists and chemists tell us that there is a point at which all molecular activity ceases. This is the point of absolute 0. The Kelvin scale of temperature is an example of a scale that is based on the absolute 0 point and is thus an example of a ratio scale. There are some examples of ratio scales in the numbers we see on a regular basis. For example, consider the number of yards gained by running backs on football teams. Zero yards actually means that the player has gained no yards at all. If one player has gained 1000 yards and another has gained only 500, then we can say that the first athlete has gained twice as many yards as the second.

Another example is the speed of travel. For instance, 0 mph (miles per hour) is the point at which there is no speed at all. If you are driving onto a highway at 30 mph and you increase your speed to 60 when you get in the lane, it is appropriate to say you have doubled your speed.

III. *Frequency Distributions*

A single test score means more if we relate it to other test scores. A distribution of scores summarizes the scores for a group of individuals. In testing, there are many ways of recording a distribution of scores.

The **frequency distribution** is a simple way of displaying data from tests. It is a technique for systematically displaying scores on a variable or a measure to reflect how frequently each value was obtained. With a frequency distribution, we define all the possible scores and determine how many people obtained

Table 2-2
Inches of Rainfall
in San Diego,
1967–1991

Year	Inches
1967	11.04
1968	8.04
1969	11.68
1970	6.48
1971	8.20
1972	6.24
1973	11.16
1974	6.68
1975	10.80
1976	9.24
1977	9.32
1978	17.56
1979	15.52
1980	15.72
1981	7.48
1982	12.04
1983	18.76
1984	5.44
1985	9.76
1986	15.20
1987	9.44
1988	12.64
1989	5.96
1990	7.76
1991	12.12
Sum	264.28
Mean	10.57
Variance	13.83
Standard deviation	3.72
$N = 25$	

Figure 2-2
Frequency
distribution
approximating
a normal
distribution
of 1000
observations.

each of these scores. Usually, when we make a frequency distribution, scores are arranged on the horizontal axis from the lowest to the highest value. The vertical axis is used to record how many times each of the values on the horizontal axis was observed. For most distributions of test scores, the frequency distribution is approximately bell shaped. A bell-shaped distribution has the greatest frequency of scores toward the center of the distribution, and the frequency of the values decreases as the values become greater or less than the value in the center of the distribution.

Figure 2-2 shows a frequency distribution of 1000 observations that takes on values between 61 and 90. Notice that the most frequent observations are the ones toward the center of the distribution around 75 and 76. As we look toward the extremes of the distribution, we find a systematic decline in the frequency with which the scores occur. For example, the score of 71 is observed less frequently than the score of 72, which is observed less frequently than the score of 73, and so on. Similarly, the score of 78 is observed more frequently than the score of 79, which is noted more often than the score of 80, and so forth.

This neat symmetric relationship is not characteristic of all sets of scores, but it occurs frequently enough in practice for us to devote special attention to it. In the section on the normal distribution, we will explain this concept in a little more detail.

Table 2-2 lists the rainfall amounts in San Diego, California, between the years 1967 and 1991. Figure 2-3 is a frequency distribution from the observations. Looking at the figure, we find a distribution that is slightly skewed. A skewed distribution is asymmetrical. Figure 2-3 has a positive skew because the tail goes off toward the higher or positive side of the x axis.

Another way of looking at this same set of rainfall data is to present them as a frequency polygon (see Figure 2-4). Here, the amount of rainfall is placed on the graph to represent the frequencies with which each interval occurs. Then lines are used to connect the frequencies.

Figure 2-3
Rainfall in San
Diego,
1967–1991.

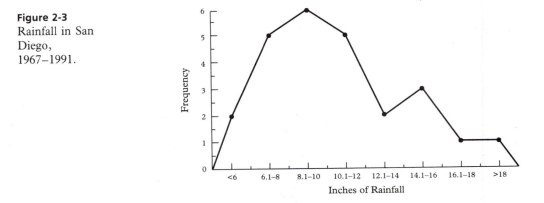

Whenever you draw a frequency distribution or a frequency polygon, you must decide on the width of the class interval. The **class interval** is the unit for the horizontal axis. For example, in Figures 2-3 and 2-4, the class interval is 3 inches. The demarcations along the x axis increase in 3-inch intervals as we move along it. The 3-inch class interval is used because it provides a convenient summary of rainfall, although the choice of 3 inches is arbitrary.

Figure 2-4
Frequency
polygon for the
data in Figure
2-3.

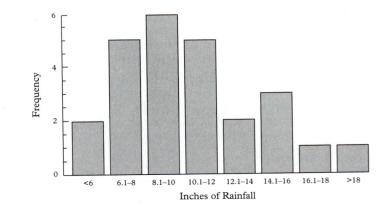

IV. *Percentile Ranks*

Percentile ranks replace simple ranks when we want to adjust for the number of scores in a group. A **percentile rank** answers the question "What percent of the scores fall below a particular score (X_i)?" To calculate a percentile rank, you need only follow these simple steps:

1. Determine how many cases are below the score of interest.
2. Determine how many cases are in the group.
3. Divide the number of cases below the score of interest (Step 1) by the total number of cases in the group (Step 2).
4. Multiply the result of Step 3 by 100.

The formula is

$$P_r = \frac{B}{N} \times 100 = \text{percentile rank of } X_i$$

where P_r = percentile rank
X_i = the score of interest
B = the number of scores below X_i
N = the total number of scores

This means that you form a ratio of the number of cases below the score of interest and the total number of scores. Because there will always be either the same or fewer cases in the numerator (top half) of the equation than there are in the denominator, this ratio will always be less than or equal to 1. To get rid of the decimal points, we multiply by 100.

As an example, let us consider the runner who finishes 62nd out of 63 racers in a gym class. To obtain the percentile rank, we divide 1 (the number of people who finish behind the person of interest) by 63 (the number of scores in the group). This gives us $\frac{1}{63}$, or .016. Then we multiply this result by 100 to obtain the percentile rank, which is 1.6. This rank tells us the runner is below the 2nd percentile.

Now consider the Bay to Breakers race that attracts 50,000 runners to San Francisco. If you had finished 62nd out of 50,000, then the number of people who were behind you would be 49,938. Dividing this by the number of entrants gives .9988. When we multiply by 100, we get the percentile rank, which is 99.88. This tells us that finishing 62nd in the Bay to Breakers race is exceptionally good. A runner finishing 62nd would be in the 99.88th percentile.

Technical Box 2-1 presents the calculation of percentile ranks for the infant mortality rates from selected countries. Infant mortality is defined as the number of babies born alive who die before their first birthday per 1000 births. Before proceeding, we should point out that the meaning of this calculation depends on which countries are used in the comparison.

In this example, the calculation of the percentile rank is broken down into five steps and uses the raw data in the table. In Step 1 we arrange the data points in descending order. Japan has the lowest infant mortality rate of 4, Sweden is next with 6 years, and Ethiopia has the highest infant mortality rate at 133.

In Step 2 we determine the number of cases with worse rates than the case of interest. In this example, the case of interest is the United States. Therefore, we count the number of cases with worse rates than the United States. There are nine (Australia, Turkey, Saudi Arabia, Morocco, Zambia, Colombia, Zaire, Bolivia, Ethiopia). Each of these countries has an infant mortality rate greater than the 10 for the United States.

In Step 3 we determine the total number of cases. There are 16.

In Step 4 we divide the number of scores worse than the score of interest by the total number of scores:

$$\frac{9}{16} = .56$$

TECHNICAL BOX 2-1

Infant Mortality in Selected Countries, 1991

Country	Infant Mortality per 1000 Live Births
Australia	19
Bolivia	106
Colombia	86
Ethiopia	133
France	7
Israel	10
Italy	9
Japan	4
Morocco	69
Saudi Arabia	67
Spain	8
Sweden	6
Turkey	61
United States	*10*
Zaire	94
Zambia	76

Data from World Development Report, 1991, World Development Indicators, Oxford University Press, International Bank, 1991.

To calculate the percentile rank of infant mortality in the United States in comparison to that in selected countries, we use the following formula:

$$P_r = \frac{B}{N} \times 100$$

where P_r = the percentile rank

B = the number of cases with worse rates than the case of interest

N = the total number of cases

Steps

1. Arrange data in ascending order—the lowest score first, second lowest score second, and so on.

Country	Infant Mortality per 1000 Live Births
Japan	4
Sweden	6
France	7
Spain	8
Italy	9
Israel	10
United States	*10*
Australia	19
Turkey	61
Saudi Arabia	67
Morocco	69
Zambia	76
Colombia	86
Zaire	94
Bolivia	106
Ethiopia	133

$N = 16$, mean $= 47.81$, standard deviation $= 43.31$

2. Determine the number of cases with worse rates than the score of interest. There are nine countries in this sample with infant mortality rates greater than that in the United States.
3. Determine the number of cases in the sample. There are 16.
4. Divide the number of scores worse than the score of interest (Step 2) by the total number of scores (Step 3):

$$\frac{9}{16} = .56$$

5. Multiply by 100:

.56 × 100 = 56th percentile rank

Technically, the percentile rank is a percentage. Step 4 gives a proportion. Therefore, in Step 5 we transform this into a whole number by multiplying by 100:

$$.56 \times 100 = 56$$

Thus, the United States is in the 56th percentile.

The percentile rank depends absolutely on the cases used for comparison. In this example, we calculated that the United States is in the 56th percentile for infant mortality within this group of countries. If all the countries in the world had been included, the ranking of the United States would have been different.

Using this procedure, try to calculate the percentile rank for Colombia. The calculation is the same except that there are three countries with worse rates than Colombia (as opposed to nine worse than the United States). Thus, the percentile rank for Colombia is

$$\frac{3}{16} = .19 \times 100 = 19$$

or the 19th percentile. Now try France. You should get a percentile rank of 81.

V. *Percentiles*

Actual scores, not ranks

Percentiles are the specific scores or points within a distribution. Percentiles divide the total frequency for a set of observations into hundredths. They answer a different question from percentile ranks. Instead of indicating what percent of scores fall below a particular score, percentiles indicate the observed score that a particular percent of scores fall below.

Let us calculate the percentile and percentile rank for some of the data in Technical Box 2-1. As an example, look at Italy. The infant mortality rate in Italy is 9/1000. When calculating the percentile rank, we exclude the score of interest and count those below (in other words, Italy is not included in the count). There are 11 countries in this sample with infant mortality rates worse than Italy's. To calculate the percentile rank, we divide this number of countries by the total number of cases and multiply by 100:

$$P_r = \frac{B}{N} \times 100 = \frac{11}{16} \times 100 = .69 \times 100 = 69$$

Thus, we would say Italy is in the 69th percentile rank, or the 69th percentile in this example is 9/1000 live births.

Now let's take the example of Israel. This makes a good illustration because two countries have the same infant mortality rate (Israel and the United States). However, the calculation of percentile rank means that we look at the number of cases below the case of interest. In this example, there are nine countries in this group with infant mortality rates worse than Israel's (Australia, Turkey, Saudi Arabia, Morocco, Zambia, Colombia, Zaire, Bolivia, and

Ethiopia). Thus, the percentile rank for Israel is $9/16 \times 100 = 56$. The 56th percentile corresponds with the point or score 10 (or 10/1000 live births).

In summary, the percentile and the percentile rank are similar. The percentile gives the point in a distribution below which a specified percentage of cases fall. The percentile is in raw score units. The percentile rank gives the proportion of cases below the percentile.

When reporting percentiles and percentile ranks, you must carefully specify the population you are working with. Remember that a percentile rank is a measure of relative performance. When interpreting a percentile rank, you should always ask the question "Relative to what?" Suppose, for instance, that you finished in the 17th percentile in a swimming race (or fifth in a heat of six competitors). Does this mean that you are a slow swimmer? Not necessarily. It may be that this was a heat in the Olympic games, and the participants were the fastest swimmers in the world. An Olympic swimmer competing against a random sample of all people in the world would probably finish in the 99.99th percentile. The example for infant mortality rates depends on which countries in the world were selected for comparison. The United States actually does quite poorly when compared to European countries. However, the U.S. infant mortality rate looks much better in comparison to countries in the developing world.

VI. *Describing Distributions*

A. *Mean*

Statistics are used to summarize data. If you consider a set of scores, the mass of information may be too much to interpret all at once. That is why we need certain numerical conveniences to help summarize the information. An example of a set of scores that can be summarized is shown in Table 2-2 (see page 34). These scores are the amounts of rainfall in San Diego in the years 1967–1991. We signify the variable as X. A variable is a score that takes on different values. The amount of rain is a variable because different amounts of rain fell in different years.

The arithmetic average score in a distribution is called the **mean.** To calculate the mean, we total the scores and divide the sum by the number of cases. Usually we signify the number of cases by N. The capital Greek letter sigma (Σ) means summation. Thus, the formula for the mean, which we signify as $\overline{X}$, is

$$\overline{X} = \frac{\Sigma X}{N}$$

TECHNICAL BOX 2-2

Common Symbols

Some symbols will be used throughout this book, and it is important that you understand and learn to recognize them. $\overline{X}$ is the mean; it is pronounced X bar. Σ is the summation sign. It means sum, or add, scores together and is the capital Greek letter sigma. X is a variable that takes on different values. Each value of X_i represents a raw score, also called an obtained score.

In words, this formula says to total the scores and divide the sum by the number of cases. Using the information in Table 2-2, we find the mean by following these steps:

1. Obtain ΣX, or the sum of the scores:

$$11.04 + 8.04 + 11.68 + \cdots + 7.76 + 12.12 = 264.28$$

2. Find N, or the number of scores:

$$N = 25$$

3. Divide ΣX by N:

$$\frac{264.28}{25} = 10.57$$

Technical Box 2-2 summarizes common symbols used in basic statistics.

B. *Standard Deviation*

The standard deviation is an approximation of the average deviation around the mean. It will be described in more detail in the next section. The standard deviation for the amount of rainfall in San Diego is 3.72. In order to understand rainfall in San Diego, we need to consider at least two dimensions. First, there is the amount of rain that falls in a particular year. Second, we must consider how much variation there is from year to year in the amount of rain that falls. The calculation suggests that, on the average, the variation around the mean is about 3.72 inches.

Although it is very informative to know the mean of a group of scores, the mean does not give us all the desired information about the group of scores. As an illustration, look at the following sets of numbers.

Set 1	Set 2	Set 3
4	5	8
4	5	8
4	4	6
4	4	2
4	3	0
4	3	0

Calculate the mean of the first set. You should get 4. Now what is the mean of the second set? If you calculate correctly, you should get 4 again. Next, find the mean for Set 3. It is also 4. The three distributions of scores that appear very different have the same mean. Therefore, it is important to consider other characteristics of the distribution of scores besides the mean. The difference between Set 1, Set 2, and Set 3 is in variability. There is no variability in Set 1, a small amount in Set 2, and a lot in Set 3.

The variation we would like to consider here is similar to the average deviation around the mean. One way to do this is to subtract the mean from each score $(X - \overline{X})$. Statisticians often signify this with a lowercase x [$x = (X - \overline{X})$]. Then total the deviations. Try this for the data in Table 2-2. Did you get 0? You should have, and this is not an unusual example. In fact, the sum of the deviations around the mean will always equal 0. However, we do have an alternative: we can square all of the deviations around the mean in order to get rid of any negative signs. Then we can obtain the average squared deviation around the mean, which is known as the **variance.** The formula for the variance is

$$\sigma^2 = \frac{\Sigma(X - \overline{X})^2}{N}$$

where $(X - \overline{X})$ is the deviation of a score from the mean. The symbol σ is the lowercase Greek sigma; σ^2 is used as a standard description of the variance.

The variance is a very useful statistic and is commonly used in data analysis. The variance, however, shows the variable in squared deviations around the mean rather than in deviations around the mean. In words, the variance is the average squared deviation around the mean. In order to get it back into the units that will make sense to us, we need to take the square root of the variance.

The square root of the variance is the standard deviation (σ), and it is represented by the following formula:

$$\sigma = \sqrt{\frac{\Sigma(X - \overline{X})^2}{N}}$$

In words, the **standard deviation** is the square root of the average squared deviation around the mean. Although the standard deviation is not an average deviation, it gives a useful approximation of how much a typical score is above or below the average score.

The variance and the standard deviation have many advantages because of their mathematical properties. For example, knowing the standard deviation of a normally distributed batch of data allows us to make precise statements about the distribution. The formulas presented above are for computing the variance and the standard deviation of a population. That is why we use the lowercase Greek sigma (σ and σ^2). Technical Box 2-3 summarizes when Greek and Roman letters are used. Most often we use the standard deviation for a sample to estimate the standard deviation for a population. When we talk about a sample, we replace the Greek σ with a Roman letter S. Also, we divide by $N - 1$ rather than N:

$$S = \sqrt{\frac{\Sigma(X - \overline{X})^2}{N - 1}}$$

TECHNICAL BOX 2-3

Terms and Symbols Used to Describe Populations and Samples

	Population	Sample
Definition	All elements with the same definition	A subset of the population, usually drawn to represent it in an unbiased fashion
Descriptive characteristics	Parameters	Statistics
Symbols used to describe	Greek	Roman
Symbol for mean	μ	$\overline{X}$
Symbol for standard deviation	σ	S

In calculating the standard deviation, it is often easier to use the raw score equivalent formula, which is

$$S = \sqrt{\frac{\Sigma X^2 - \dfrac{(\Sigma X)^2}{N}}{N - 1}}$$

This calculation can also be done automatically by some minicalculators.

C. *Z Score*

One of the problems with means and standard deviations is that their interpretations are not clear. For example, if the mean of some set of scores is 57.6, that does not convey all of the information we would like. There are other metrics designed for a more exact interpretation. The Z score transforms data into standardized units that are easier to interpret. A Z score is the difference between a score and the mean, divided by the standard deviation:

$$Z = \frac{X - \overline{X}}{S}$$

In other words, a Z score is the deviation of a score X from the mean $\overline{X}$ in standard deviation units. If a score is equal to the mean, its Z score is 0. For example, suppose the score and the mean are both 6; then $6 - 6 = 0$. Zero divided by anything is still 0. If the score is greater than the mean, the Z score is positive; if the score is less than the mean, the Z score is negative.

Let's try an example. Suppose that $X = 6$, the mean $\overline{X} = 3$, and the standard deviation $S = 3$. Plugging these values into the formula, we get

$$Z = \frac{6 - 3}{3} = \frac{3}{3} = 1$$

Let's try another example. Suppose $X = 4$, $\overline{X} = 5.75$, and $S = 2.11$. What is the Z score? It is $-.83$:

$$Z = \frac{4 - 5.75}{2.11} = \frac{-1.75}{2.11} = -.83$$

This means that the score we observed (4) is .83 standard deviation below the average score, or that the score is below the mean but its difference from the mean is slightly less than the average deviation.

Center for Epidemiologic Studies Depression Scale (CES-D)

Instructions: Circle the number for each statement that best describes how often you felt or behaved this way DURING THE PAST WEEK.

	Rarely or none of the time (less than 1 day)	Some or a little of the time (1–2 days)	Occasionally or a moderate amount of the time (3–4 days)	Most or all of the time (5–7 days)
1. I was bothered by things that usually don't bother me.	0	 1	 2	 3
2. I did not feel like eating.	0	 1	 2	 3
3. I felt that I could not shake off the blues even with help from my family or friends.	0	 1	 2	 3
R **4.** I felt that I was just as good as other people.	0	 1	 2	 3
5. I had trouble keeping my mind on what I was doing.	0	 1	 2	 3
6. I felt depressed.	0	 1	 2	 3
7. I felt that everything I did was an effort.	0	 1	 2	 3
R **8.** I felt hopeful about the future.	0	 1	 2	 3
9. I thought my life had been a failure.	0	 1	 2	 3
10. I felt fearful.	0	 1	 2	 3
11. My sleep was restless.	0	 1	 2	 3
R **12.** I was happy.	0	 1	 2	 3
13. I talked less than usual.	0	 1	 2	 3
14. I felt lonely.	0	 1	 2	 3
15. People were unfriendly.	0	 1	 2	 3
R **16.** I enjoyed life.	0	 1	 2	 3
17. I had crying spells.	0	 1	 2	 3
18. I felt sad.	0	 1	 2	 3
19. I felt that people disliked me. .	0	 1	 2	 3
20. I could not get "going.".	0	 1	 2	 3

Example of depression in medical students—Center for Epidemiologic Studies Depression Scale (CES-D). The CES-D is a general measure of depression that has been used extensively in epidemiologic studies. The scale includes 20 items and taps dimensions of depressed mood, hopelessness, appetite loss, sleep disturbance, and energy level. Each year students at the University of California, San Diego School of Medicine, are asked to report how often they experienced a particular symptom during the first week of school on a four-point scale ranging from rarely or none of the time [0 to 1 days (0)] to most or all of the time [5 to 7 days (3)]. Four items on the CES-D are reversed scored. These are items 4, 8, 12, and 16. For these items, 0 is scored as 3, 1 is scored as 2, 2 as 1, and 3 as 0. The CES-D score is obtained by summing the circled numbers. Scores on the CES-D range from 0 to 60, with scores greater than 15 indicative of clinically significant levels of depressive symptomatology in adults.

Table 2-3

The Calculation of Mean, Standard Deviation, and Z Scores for CES-D Scores

Name	Test Score (X)	X^2	Z Score
John	14	196	.42
Carla	10	100	−.15
Fred	8	64	−.44
Monica	8	64	−.44
Eng	26	676	2.13
Fritz	0	0	−1.58
Mary	14	196	.42
Susan	3	9	−1.15
Debbie	9	81	−.29
Elizabeth	10	100	−.15
Sarah	7	49	−.58
Marcel	12	144	.14
Robin	10	100	−.15
Mike	25	625	1.99
Carl	9	81	−.29
Phyllis	12	144	.14
Jennie	23	529	1.70
Richard	7	49	−.58
Tyler	13	169	.28
Frank	1	1	−1.43
	$\Sigma X = 221$	$\Sigma X^2 = 3377$	

$$\bar{X} = \frac{\Sigma X}{N} = \frac{221}{20} = 11.05$$

$$S = \sqrt{\frac{\Sigma X^2 - \frac{(\Sigma X)^2}{N}}{N-1}} = \sqrt{\frac{3377 - \frac{(221)^2}{20}}{20-1}} = 7.01$$

Monica's Z score $= \dfrac{X - \bar{X}}{S} = \dfrac{8 - 11.05}{7.01} = -.44$

Marcel's Z score $= \dfrac{X - \bar{X}}{S} = \dfrac{12 - 11.05}{7.01} = .14$

Jennie's Z score $= \dfrac{X - \bar{X}}{S} = \dfrac{23 - 11.05}{7.01} = 1.70$

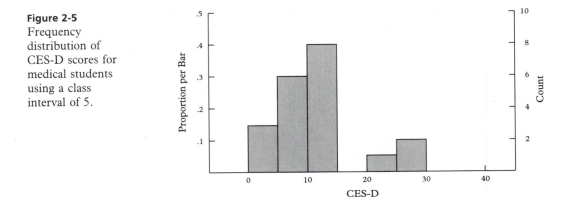

Figure 2-5
Frequency
distribution of
CES-D scores for
medical students
using a class
interval of 5.

Feel free to take the CES-D measure yourself. Calculate your score by summing the numbers you have circled. However, you must first reverse the scores on items 4, 8, 12, and 16. As you will see in Chapter 5, the CES-D does not have high validity for determining clinical depression. If your score is less than 15, the evidence suggests that you are not clinically depressed. If your score is high, this does not mean that you have a clinical depression problem. However, you may want to talk with your college counselor if you are feeling depressed.

Table 2-3 shows CES-D scores for a selected sample of medical students. You can use these data to practice calculating means, standard deviations, and Z scores.

Figure 2-5 provides a frequency distribution for the CES-D scores of medical students using a class interval of 5.

D. *Standard Normal Distribution*

Now we consider the standard normal distribution because it is of central importance to statistics and to psychological testing. First you should participate in a short exercise. Take any coin and flip it 10 times. Now repeat this exercise of 10 coin flips 25 times. Record the number of heads you observe in each group of 10 flips. When you are done, make a frequency distribution showing how many times you observed 1 head in your 10 flips, 2 heads, 3 heads, and so on.

Your frequency distribution might look like the example shown in Figure 2-6. The most frequently observed events are about equal numbers of heads and tails. As you go toward the 10 heads and 0 tails or the 10 tails and 0 heads, events are observed with less frequency. For example, there were no occasions in which fewer than 2 heads were observed and only 1 occasion in which more than 8 heads were observed. This is very much what we would expect from the

Figure 2-6
Frequency
distribution of the
number of heads
in 25 sets of 10
flips.

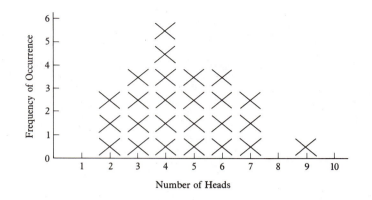

laws of probability. On the average, we would expect half of the flips to show heads and half to show tails if heads and tails are equally probable events. Although it is still possible to observe a long string of heads or tails, it is improbable. In other words, we will sometimes observe that the coin comes up heads in 9 out of 10 flips. The likelihood that this will happen, however, is quite small.

Figure 2-7 shows the theoretical distribution of heads in an infinite number of flips of the coin. This figure might look a little like the distribution from your coin-flipping exercise or the distribution shown in Figure 2-7. Actually this is a normal distribution, or what is known as a symmetrical binomial probability distribution.

On most occasions we refer to units on the x (or horizontal) axis of the normal distribution in Z score units. Any variable transformed into Z score units takes on special properties. First, Z scores have a mean of 0 and a standard deviation of 1. If you think about this for a minute, you should be able to figure out why this is true. Recall that the sum of the deviations around the mean is always equal to 0. The numerator of the Z score equation is the deviation around the mean, while the denominator is a constant. Thus, the mean of Z scores can be expressed as

$$\frac{\Sigma(X - \overline{X})/S}{N} \quad \text{or} \quad \frac{\Sigma Z}{N}$$

Because $\Sigma(X - \overline{X})$ will always equal 0, the mean of Z scores will always be 0.

In Figure 2-7 the standardized, or Z score, units are marked on the x axis. The numbers under the curve are the proportions of cases (in decimal form) we would expect to observe in each area. Multiplying these proportions by 100 yields percentages. For example, we see that 34.13% or .3413 of the cases fall between the mean and 1 standard deviation above the mean. Do not forget that 50% of the cases fall below the mean. Putting these two bits of information

Figure 2-7
The theoretical
distribution of the
number of heads
in an infinite
number of coin
flips.

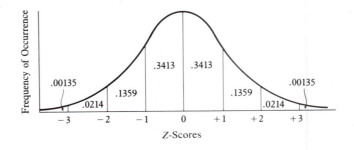

together, we can conclude that if a score is 1 standard deviation above the
mean, then it is at about the 84th percentile rank (50 + 34.13 = 84.13 to be
exact). A score that is 1 standard deviation below the mean would be about the
16th percentile rank (50 − 34.14 = 15.87). Thus, we can use what we have
learned about means, standard deviations, Z scores, and the normal curve to
transform raw scores, which have very little meaning to us, into percentile
scores, which are easier to interpret. These methods can be used only when the
distribution of scores is normal or approximately normal. Methods for nonnormal distributions are discussed in most statistics books under the heading
"nonparametric statistics."

Percentiles and Z scores. Appendix 1 contains two tables that relate Z scores to
proportions. Part I of the table gives percentile ranks associated with various Z
scores. These percentile ranks are the percentage of scores that fall below the
observed Z score. For example, the Z score −1.6 is associated with the percentile rank of 5.48. The Z score of 1.0 (third column) is associated with the
percentile rank of 84.13.

Part I of Appendix 1 is a simplified table. For more advanced use of Z
scores, you will need to use Part II, which gives the areas between the mean
and various Z scores. Standard scored values are listed in the column "Z." In
order to find the proportion of the distribution between the mean of the distribution and a given Z score, you must locate the entry indicated by a specific Z
score. Z scores are carried to a second decimal place in the columns that go
across the table. First, let us consider the second column of the table because it
is similar to Part I of Appendix 1. Take the Z score of 1.0. The second column
is labeled .00, which means that the second decimal place is also 0. The
number listed in the table is .3413. Since this is a positive number, it is above
the mean. We know that the area below the mean is .5. Thus, the total area
below a Z score of 1.0 is .5 + .3413 = .8413. In order to make this into a
percentile (as shown in Part I of the appendix), multiply by 100. This gives
84.13. Now try the example of a Z score of 1.64. To locate this value, find 1.6
in the first column. Then move your hand across the row until you get to the
number below the heading .04. The number should be .4495. Again, this is a
positive Z score, so the observed proportion must be added to the .5 that falls

below the mean. The proportion below 1.64 is .9495. Stated another way, 94.95% of the cases fall below a Z score of 1.64. Now try to find the percentile rank of cases that fall below a Z score of 1.10. If you are using the table correctly, you should obtain 86.43.

Now try $-.75$. You should be aware that this is a negative Z score, so the percentage of cases falling below the mean should be less than 50. There are no negative values in Part II of Appendix 1. For a negative Z score, there are several ways to obtain the appropriate area under the curve. The tables in Appendix 1 give the area from the mean to the Z score. For a Z score of $-.75$, we know that the areas between the mean and the Z score is .2734. This is found by entering the table in the row labeled .7 and then moving across the row until you get to the figure in that row below the heading .05. There you should find the number .2734. We know that .5 of the cases fall below the mean. Thus, for a negative Z score, we can obtain the proportion of cases falling below the score by subtracting .2734, the tabled value listed in the appendix, from .5. In this case, the result is

$$.5 - .2734 = .2266$$

Sometimes finding the percentile ranks associated with negative Z scores can be tricky. Therefore, it is often desirable to use Part I of Appendix 1 to see if you are in the right ballpark. This table gives both negative and positive Z scores but does not give the detail associated with the second decimal place. Look up $-.7$ in Part I. The percentile rank is 24.20. Now consider a Z score of $-.8$. That percentile rank is 21.19. Thus, you know that a Z score of $-.75$ should be associated with a percentile rank between 21.19 and 24.20. In fact, we have calculated that the actual percentile rank is 22.66.

Practice with Appendix 1 until you are confident you understand how it works. Do not hesitate to ask your professor or teaching assistant if you are confused. This is a very important concept that you will need throughout the rest of the book.

Let's take one more example from Table 2-2 (the table of rainfall amounts in San Diego). California had a dry year in 1990. The newscasters frequently commented that it was a very unusual year. The question is whether or not the amount of rainfall obtained in 1990 was unusual given what we know about rainfall in general. In order to evaluate this, we calculate the Z score for rainfall. According to Table 2-2, there were 7.76 inches of rainfall in 1990. The mean for rainfall is 10.57 inches and the standard deviation is 3.72. Thus, the Z score is

$$\frac{7.76 - 10.57}{3.72} = -.76$$

Next we need to determine where a Z score of $-.76$ falls within the Z distribution. According to Appendix 1, a Z score of $-.76$ is equal to the 22.36th percentile (50 − 27.64). Thus, the low rainfall year in 1990 was unusual; given all years, it was in about the 22nd percentile. However, it was not that unusual. We estimate that there would be less rainfall in approximately 22% of all years.

We can also turn the process around. Instead of using Z scores to find the percentile ranks, we can use the percentile ranks to find the corresponding Z scores. To do this we need to look in Part II of Appendix 1 under percentiles and find the corresponding Z score. For example, suppose we wish to find the Z score associated with the 90th percentile. When you enter Part II of Appendix 1, look for the value closest to the 90th percentile. This can be a little tricky because of the way the table is structured. Since the 90th percentile is associated with a positive Z score, you are actually looking for the area above the 50th percentile. So, you should look for the entry closest to .4000 (.5000 + .4000 = .9000). The closest value to .4000 is .3997, which is found in the row labeled 1.2 and the column labeled .8. This tells us that a person who obtains a Z score of 1.28 is at about the 90th percentile in the distribution.

Let us return to the example of CES-D scores for medical students. Monica had a Z score on the CES-D of −.44. Using Appendix 1, we learn that she was in the 33rd percentile (obtained as .50 − .1700 = .33 × 100 = 33). Marcel, with his Z score of .14, was in the 56th percentile, and Jennie, with a Z score of 1.70, was in the 96th percentile. We might have few worries about Monica and Marcel. However, it appears that Jennie is more depressed than 96% of her classmates and may need to talk to someone.

An example close to home. One of the difficulties in grading students is that performance is usually rated in terms of raw scores, such as the number of items a person gets correct on an examination. You are probably familiar with the experience of having a test returned to you with some number that makes little sense to you. For instance, the professor comes into class and hands you your test with a 72 on it. You must then wait patiently while he or she draws the distribution on the board and tries to put your 72 into some category that you understand, such as "B+."

An alternative way of doing things would be to give you feedback about your performance as a Z score. To do this, your professor would subtract the average score (mean) from your score and divide by the standard deviation. If your Z score was positive, you would immediately know that your score was above average; if it was negative, you would know your performance was below average.

Suppose that your professor tells you in advance that you will be graded on a curve system according to the following rigid criteria. If you are in the top 15% of the class, you will get an "A" (85th percentile or above); between the 60th and the 84th percentiles, you will get a "B"; between the 20th and the 59th percentiles, you will get a "C"; between the 6th and the 19th percentiles, you will get a "D"; and in the 5th percentile or below, you will not pass. Using Appendix 1, you should be able to find the Z scores associated with each of

Table 2-4

Z Score Cutoffs for a Grading System

Grade	Percentiles	Z Score Cutoff
A	85–100	1.04
B	60–84	.25
C	20–59	−.84
D	6–19	−1.56
F	0–5	Less than −1.56

these cutoff points for normal distributions of scores. Try it on your own, and then consult Table 2-4 to see if you are correct.

Looking at Table 2-4, you should be able to determine what your grade would be in this class on the basis of your *Z* score. If your *Z* score is 1.04 or greater, you would receive an "A"; if it were greater than .25 but less than 1.04, you would get a "B"; and so on. This system assumes that the scores are normally distributed.

Now let us try an example that puts a few of the concepts together. Suppose you get a 60 on a social psychology examination. You learned in class that the mean for the test was 55.70 and that the standard deviation was 6.08. If your professor uses the grading system that was just described, what would your grade be?

To solve this problem we must first find your *Z* score. The formula for a *Z* score is:

$$Z = \frac{X - \overline{X}}{S}$$

So your *Z* score would be

$$Z = \frac{60 - 55.70}{6.08} = \frac{4.30}{6.08} = .707$$

Looking at Table 2-4, we find that .707 is greater than .25 (the cutoff for a "B") but less than 1.04 (the cutoff for an "A"). Now let us find your exact standing in the class. To do this we need to look again at Appendix 1. Because the table gives *Z* scores only to the second decimal, we round .707 to .71. Looking at the appendix, we find that 76.11% of the scores fall below a *Z* score of .71. This means that you would be in approximately the 76th percentile, or you would have performed better on this examination than approximately 76 out of every 100 students.

E. *McCall's* T

There are a variety of other systems by which we can transform raw scores to give them more intuitive meaning. One system was established in 1939 by W. A. McCall, who originally intended to develop a system to derive equal units on mental quantities. He suggested that a random sample of 12-year-olds be tested and that the distribution of their scores be obtained. Then percentile equivalents were to be assigned to each raw score, showing the percentile rank in the group for the persons who obtained that raw score. After this had been accomplished, the mean of the distribution would be set at 50, to correspond with the 50th percentile. In McCall's system, called **McCall's *T*,** the standard deviation was set at 10.

In effect, what McCall generated was a system that is exactly the same as standard scores (*Z* scores), except that the mean in McCall's system is 50 rather than 0 and the standard deviation is 10 rather than 1. Indeed, a *Z* score can be transformed to a *T* score by applying the linear transformation

$$T = 10Z + 50$$

In words, you can get from a *Z* score to McCall's *T* by multiplying the *Z* score by 10 and adding 50. It should be noted that McCall did not originally intend to create an alternative to the *Z* score. He wanted to obtain one set of scores that could then be applied in other situations without standardizing the entire set of numbers.

There is nothing magical about the mean of 50 and the standard deviation of 10. It is a simple matter to create systems such as standard scores with any mean and standard deviation you like. If you want to say that you got a score 1000 points higher than a person who was 1 standard deviation below you, you could devise a system with a mean of 100,000 and a standard deviation of 1000. If you had calculated *Z* scores for this distribution, you would obtain this with the transformation

$$NS \text{ (for new score)} = 1000Z + 100,000$$

In fact, you can create any system you desire. To do so, just multiply the *Z* score by whatever you would like the standard deviation of your distribution to be and then add the number you would like the mean of your new distribution to be.

An example of a test that was developed using standardized scores is the Scholastic Aptitude Test (SAT). When this test was created in 1941, the developers decided to make the mean score 500 and the standard deviation 100. Thus, they multiplied the *Z* scores for those who took the test by 100 and added 500. Since the test has been in use, the basic scoring system has not been changed.

F. *Quartiles and Deciles*

The terms *quartiles* and *deciles* are frequently used when tests and test results are discussed. The two terms refer to divisions of the percentile scale into groups. The quartile system divides the percentage scale into four groups, whereas the decile system divides the scale into ten groups.

Table 2-5

Transformation of Percentile Scores into Stanines

Percentage of Cases	Percentiles	Stanines
4	1–4	1
7	5–11	2
12	12–23	3
17	24–40	4
20	41–60	5
17	61–77	6
12	78–89	7
7	90–96	8
4	97–100	9

Quartiles are points that divide the frequency distribution into equal fourths. The first quartile is the 25th percentile, the second quartile is the median, or 50th, percentile, and the third quartile is the 75th percentile. These are abbreviated Q_1, Q_2, and Q_3, respectively. One-quarter of the cases will fall below Q_1, one-half will fall below Q_2, and three-quarters will fall below Q_3. The **interquartile range** is the interval of scores bounded by the 25th and 75th percentiles. In other words, the interquartile range is bounded by the range of scores that represents the middle 50% of the distribution.

Deciles are similar to quartiles except that they use points that mark 10% rather than 25% intervals. Thus, the top decile, or D_9, is the point which 90% of the cases fall below. The next decile (D_8) marks the 80th percentile, and so forth.

Another system was developed in the U.S. Air Force during World War II and is known as the **stanine system** (see Technical Box 2-4). This system converts any set of scores into a transformed scale, which ranges from 1 to 9. Actually the term *stanine* comes from "standard nine." The scale is standardized to have a mean of 5 and a standard deviation of approximately 2. It has been suggested that stanines had computational advantages because they require only one column on a computer card (Anastasi, 1976). Table 2-5 shows how percentile scores are converted into stanines.

TECHNICAL BOX 2-4

Making Standard Units More Precise

Many authors have contested the U.S. Air Force stanine system because it does not have a standard deviation of exactly 2. In 1958, Henry Kaiser of the University of California at Berkeley revised the stanine system by introducing minor modifications in the percentile cutoffs. In Kaiser's revised system, the standard deviation is exactly 2.

In addition to the stanine scale, similar systems have been proposed. For example, one early variant was the Sten scale, which had 5 units above and 5 units below the mean on a 10-point scale (Canfield, 1951). Another version is the *c* scale, which has 11 points and a standard deviation of 2 (Guilford & Fruchter, 1973).

As you can see in Table 2-5, for every 100 scores, the lowest 4 (or bottom 4% of the cases) fall into the first stanine. The next 7 (or 7% of the cases) fall into the second stanine, and so on. Finally, the top 4 cases fall into the top stanine. Using what you have learned about *Z* scores and the standard normal distribution, you should be able to figure out the stanine for a score if you know the mean and the standard deviation of the distribution the score comes from. For example, suppose that Igor received a 48 on his normally distributed chemistry midterm. The mean in Igor's class was 42.6, and the standard deviation was 3.6. First we must find Igor's *Z* score. We do this by using the formula

$$Z = \frac{X - \overline{X}}{S} \quad \text{so} \quad Z = \frac{48 - 42.6}{3.6} = 1.5$$

Now we need to transform Igor's *Z* score into his percentile rank. To do this we use Appendix 1. Part I shows that a *Z* score of 1.5 is in approximately the 93rd percentile (middle column) and falls into the 8th stanine.

Actually you would rarely go through all these steps to find a stanine. There are easier ways of doing this, and there are computer programs that do it automatically. However, working out stanines the long way will help you become familiar with a variety of concepts covered in this chapter, including (1) standard scores, (2) means, (3) standard deviations, and (4) percentiles.

Let us review the five steps to go from raw scores to stanines:

1. Find the mean of the raw scores.
2. Find the standard deviation of raw scores.
3. Transform raw scores to *Z* scores.
4. Transform *Z* scores to percentiles (using Appendix 1).
5. Use Table 2-5 to convert percentiles into stanines.

Remember, in practice you probably would use a computer program to obtain the stanines.

VII. *Norms*

Norms refer to the performance by a defined group on a particular test. There are many ways to express norms, and we have discussed some of these under the headings of *Z* scores, percentiles, and means. The norms for a test are based on the distribution of scores obtained by some defined sample of individuals. The mean is a norm, and the 50th percentile is a norm. Norms are used to give information about performance relative to what has been observed in a standardization sample.

Much has been written about norms and their inadequacies. Much of this material will be discussed in later chapters in relation to particular tests. In this section, we will cover only the highlights. Whenever you see a norm for a test, you should ask how it was established. Norms are obtained by administering the test to a sample of people and obtaining the distribution of scores for that group.

For example, you might develop a measure of anxiety associated with taking tests in college. After establishing some psychometric properties for the test, you administer the test to normative groups of college students. The scores for these groups of students might then serve as the norms. For example, it might be found that for the normative groups of students, the average score was 19. Then, when your friend Alice comes to take the test and obtains a score of 24, the psychologist using the test might conclude that Alice is above the average in test anxiety.

The SAT, as indicated earlier, has norms. The test was administered to millions of high school seniors from all over the United States. By creating distributions of scores for this normative group, it was possible to obtain a distribution to provide meaning for particular categories of scores. For example, in the national sample, a person who scored 650 on the verbal portion of the SAT was at the 93rd percentile of high school seniors. However, if you took the test after 1941 and scored 650, it did not mean that you were at the 93rd percentile of the people who took the test when you did. Rather it meant that you would have been at the 93rd percentile if you had been in the group the test had been standardized on. However, if the normative group was a representative sample of the group to which you belonged (and there is every reason to believe it is), then it is reasonable to assume that you were in approximately the 93rd percentile of your own group.[2]

A. *Age-Related Norms*

Certain tests have different normative groups for particular age groups. Most IQ tests are of this sort. We will talk about IQ tests in more detail in Chapter 10. When the Stanford-Binet IQ test was originally created, distributions of the performance of random samples of children were obtained for various age groups. When applying an IQ test, the tester's task is to determine the mental age of the person being tested. This is accomplished through various exercises that help locate the age level norm at which a child is performing.

B. *Tracking*

One of the most common uses of age-related norms is for growth charts used by pediatricians. Consider the question "Is my son tall or short?" The answer will usually depend on a comparison of your son to other boys of the same age. Your son would be very tall if he was 5 feet at age 8 but very short if he was only 5 feet at age 18. Thus the comparison is usually with persons of the same age.

---

[2] Based on the American Testing Program Guide for 1989–1991, College Board of the Educational Testing Service, Princeton, New Jersey.

Figure 2-8
Tracking chart for
boys' physical
growth from birth
to 36 months.
(*Adapted from the
National Center for
Health Statistics:
NCHS Growth
Charts. Health
Resources
Administration,
Rockville,
Maryland, June
1976.*)

BOYS: BIRTH TO 36 MONTHS
PHYSICAL GROWTH
NCHS PERCENTILES*

NAME _____   RECORD # _____

Provided as a
service of
Ross Laboratories

* Adapted from: National Center for Health Statistics: NCHS Growth Charts,
1976. Monthly Vital Statistics Report. Vol. 25, No. 3, Supp. (HRA) 76-1120.
Health Resources Administration, Rockville, Maryland, June, 1976.
Data from The Fels Research Institute, Yellow Springs, Ohio.

© 1976 ROSS LABORATORIES

Beyond this rather obvious type of age-related comparison, child experts have discovered that children at the same age level tend to go through different growth patterns. Children who are small infants often remain small and continue to grow at a slower pace. Pediatricians must know more about a child than just age. They must know what percentile the child is in within a given age category. For a variety of physical characteristics, children tend to stay at about their same percentile level relative to other children in their age group as they grow older. This tendency to stay at about the same level relative to one's peers is known as **tracking**. Height and weight are good examples of physical characteristics that track. Figures 2-8 and 2-9 show the expected rates of growth for boys and girls in terms of height and weight. Notice that the children who were the largest babies are expected to remain the largest as they get older.

A pediatrician would use the charts to determine the expected course of growth for a child. For example, if a 3-month-old boy came into the office and weighed 13.2 pounds (6 kilograms), the doctor would locate the child as the center line on the bottom half of Figure 2-8. By age 36 months, the child would be expected to weigh just under 33 pounds. The tracking charts are very useful to doctors because they help determine whether the child is going through some unusual growth pattern. A boy who weighed 13 pounds at age 3 months might come under scrutiny if at age 36 months he weighed only 28 pounds. This might be normal for 3-year-olds in a different track, but the doctor might want to examine a child who started out larger to determine why the child did not stay in his track.

An example of a child going out of his or her track is shown in Figure 2-10. There is some concern that children who are fed a fat-restricted diet experience stunted growth (Kaplan & Toshima, 1992). The consequences of a slightly restricted vegetarian diet are mild if they exist at all. However, very restricted diets may have some consequences for growth. For instance, Pugliese et al. (1983) studied 24 adolescents who had voluntarily undergone severe caloric restrictions because they wanted to lose weight. These youths were not diagnosed as having anorexia nervosa, but they consumed only a small percentage of the calories recommended for their age. Figure 2-10 shows the growth pattern for one of these children. As the figure suggests, the child was growing normally until age 9. At that point, very restricted dieting began. Within a few years, growth was interrupted. The arrow in the figure shows the point at which psychotherapy began. After this point, normal feeding resumed, and growth started once again. However, at age 18, the child was still below the 5th percentile in height and weight. Given normal tracking, she should have been at about the 50th percentile.

Although the tracking system has worked well for medicine, it has stirred considerable controversy when it has been applied to education. Some people believe that there is an analogy between the rates of physical growth and the rates of intellectual growth. Just as there are some slow growers who eventually will be shorter adults, some researchers believe that there are slow learners who will eventually know less as adults. Furthermore, it has been suggested that the

Figure 2-9
Tracking chart for
girls' physical
growth from birth
to 36 months.
(*From the
National Center for
Health Statistics:
NCHS Growth
Charts. Health
Resources
Administration,
Rockville,
Maryland, June
1976.*)

GIRLS: BIRTH TO 36 MONTHS
PHYSICAL GROWTH
NCHS PERCENTILES*

NAME_____ RECORD #_____

Provided as a
service of
Ross Laboratories

* Adapted from: National Center for Health Statistics: NCHS Growth Charts,
1976. Monthly Vital Statistics Report. Vol. 25, No. 3, Supp. (HRA) 76-1120.
Health Resources Administration, Rockville, Maryland, June, 1976.
Data from The Fels Research Institute, Yellow Springs, Ohio.
© 1976 ROSS LABORATORIES

Figure 2-10
Growth description with severe dietary restriction. The scales represent percentile standards for height and weight, and the plotted values are for the clinical case. (*From Publiese et al., 1983, p. 514; reprinted by permission of* The New England Journal of Medicine, 309, 513–518, 1983.)

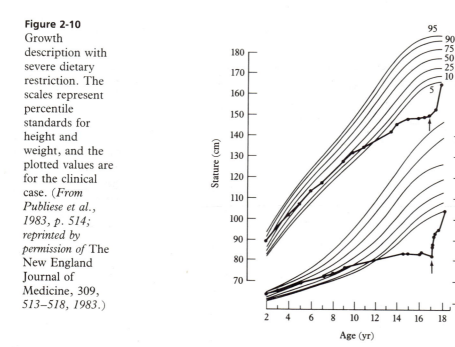

rates at which children learn differ. Thus, children are separated early in their educational careers and placed in classrooms that correspond with these different tracks. Many educators have attacked the tracking system because it unfairly discriminates against some children. Because psychological tests are used to place children in these tracks, the tests have come under severe scrutiny and attack. We will return to this controversy in Chapter 20.

C. *Criterion-Referenced Tests*

The purpose of establishing norms for a test is to determine how a test taker does in comparison to others. A test that compares each person to a norm is called **norm referenced.** This use of tests has been objected to by many because it forces competition among people. Young children exposed to many norm-referenced tests as early as elementary school get caught up in a never-ending battle to perform better than average. In addition to the function of ranking people according to performance, tests can play an important role in identifying problems and suggesting new directions for individualized programs of instruction. During the last two decades there has been a growing interest in tests that are used to determine whether students know specific information. These tests do not compare students with one another, they compare each student's performance with a criterion or an expected level of performance (Linn, 1980).

A **criterion-referenced test** is one that describes the specific types of skills, tasks, or knowledge that the test taker can demonstrate. For example, a criterion-referenced test might include items that test addition, subtraction, multiplication, long division, and short division skills. The results of the test might demonstrate that a particular child can add, subtract, and multiply but has difficulty with both long and short division. The results of the test would not be used to make comparisons between the child and other members of his or her class. Instead, they would be used to design an individualized program of instruction that focuses on division. Thus, the criterion-referenced testing movement emphasizes the diagnostic use of tests. The tests are diagnostic in the sense that they can be used to identify problems that can be remedied.

Summary

In this chapter we discussed some basic rules for translating observations of behavior and mental processes into numbers. The use of number systems is important for all scientific exercises in order to gain precision. Measures of psychological processes are represented by one of four types of scale. A *nominal scale* is a system that simply assigns numbers to categories. This type of scale has none of the properties of a numbered scale. An *ordinal scale* has the property of magnitude and allows us to rank objects, but it does not have the property of equal intervals or an absolute 0. An *interval scale* can describe the distances between objects because it has the property of equal intervals in addition to the property of magnitude. The *ratio scale* has an absolute 0 in addition to equal intervals and magnitude. Any mathematical operation is permissible with a ratio scale.

In order to make sense out of test scores, we have to examine the score for an individual relative to the scores of others. To do this requires that we create a distribution of test scores. There are several ways of displaying the distribution of scores, including frequency distributions and frequency polygons. We also need statistics to describe the distribution. The *mean* is the average score, the *variance* is the averaged squared deviation around the mean score, and the *standard deviation* is the square root of the variance. Using these statistics, we can tell a lot about a particular score by relating it to characteristics of a well-known probability distribution known as the standard normal distribution.

Norms are used to relate a score to a particular distribution for a subgroup of a population. For example, norms are used to describe where a child is on some measure relative to other children of the same age. In contrast, *criterion-referenced tests* are used to document specific skills rather than to compare people.

In summary, this chapter reviewed basic statistical methods for describing scores on one variable. In Chapter 3, we will discuss statistical methods for showing the relationship between two or more variables.

Chapter 3

Correlation and Regression

Learning Objectives

When you have completed this chapter,[1] you should be able to:

- Express the extent to which two measures are associated.
- Explain what a scatter diagram is and how it is used.
- Define a positive correlation and a negative correlation.
- Discuss some of the differences between correlation and regression.
- Tell how a regression line describes the relationship between two variables.
- Discuss under what circumstances you would use the point biserial correlation, the phi coefficient, and the tetrachoric correlation.
- Outline the procedure you would use to predict one score from the linear combination of several scores.
- Explain factor analysis and how it is used.

A banner headline in an issue of the *National Enquirer* read "FOOD CAUSES MOST MARRIAGE PROBLEMS." The article talked about "Startling Results of Studies by Doctors and Marriage Counselors." Actually the headline was not based on any systematic study. Rather, it used the opinions of some physicians and marriage counselors who felt that high levels of blood sugar are related to low energy levels, which in turn cause marital unhappiness.

Unfortunately, the *National Enquirer* did not report enough data for us to evaluate the hypothesis. We feel comfortable concluding that an association between diet and divorce has not been established. Before we are willing to accept the magazine's conclusion, we must ask many questions. This chapter

---

[1] Portions of this chapter are taken from *Basic Statistics for the Behavioral Sciences* by R. M. Kaplan (Newton, Mass.: Allyn & Bacon, 1987).

focuses on one of the many issues raised in the report—the level of association between variables.[2]

The *Enquirer* tells us that diet and unhappiness are associated, but it does not tell us to what extent. Is the association greater than we would expect by chance? Is it a strong or weak association?

Lots of things seem to be related. For example, life stress is associated with heart disease, training is associated with good performance in athletics, overeating is associated with indigestion. People are always telling us that things are associated. For some events the association is obvious. For example, the angle of the sun in the sky and the time of day are associated in a very predictable way. This is because time was originally defined by the angle of the sun in the sky. Other associations are less obvious. The association between performing well on the Scholastic Aptitude Test and obtaining good grades in college is one example.

Sometimes we do not know whether events are meaningfully associated with one another. If we do conclude that events are associated in some fundamental way, it is important to have a precise index of the degree. This chapter discusses statistical procedures that allow us to make precise estimates of the degree to which variables are associated. These methods are very important, and we will refer to them frequently in the remainder of this book. The indexes of association used most frequently in testing are correlation, regression, and multiple regression.

I. *The Scatter Diagram*

Before presenting the measures of association, we will look at visual displays of the relationship between variables. In Chapter 2, we concentrated on univariate distributions of scores. These involve only one variable; each person has only one score. This chapter considers statistical methods for studying bivariate distributions, which have two scores for each individual. For example, when we study the relationship between test scores and classroom performance, we are dealing with a bivariate distribution. Each person has a score on

---

[2] There were many other problems with the *National Enquirer* report. The observation was based on the clinical experiences of some health practitioners who found that many couples who came in for counseling had poor diets. One major oversight was that there was no control group of people who were not having marriage problems. We do not know from the study whether couples with problems have poor diets in greater proportions than people in general. Another problem is that neither diet nor marital happiness was measured in a systematic way. Thus, we are left with subjective opinions about the levels of these variables. Finally, we do not know the direction of the causation: does diet cause unhappiness or does unhappiness cause poor diet? Another possibility is that some other problem (such as stress) may cause both poor diet and unhappiness.

Figure 3-1
A scatter diagram. The circled point shows a person who had a score of 21 on X and 14 on Y (see the text). The line expresses the regression that describes the best linear relationship between X and Y.

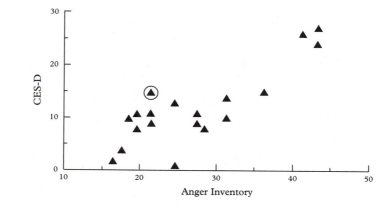

the test and a score for classroom performance. We must average the scores over all the individuals to know whether these two variables are associated.

A **scatter diagram** is a picture of the relationship between two variables. An example of a scatter diagram is shown in Figure 3-1, which relates scores on a measure of anger for medical students to scores on the CES-D. The axes in the figure represent the scales for two variables. Values of X for the anger inventory are shown on the horizontal axis and values of Y (in this example CES-D) on the vertical axis. Each point on the scatter diagram shows where a particular individual scored on both X and Y. For example, one person had a score of 14 on the CES-D and a score of 21 on the anger inventory. This point is circled in the figure. It can be located if we find 21 on the x axis and then go straight up to the level of 14 on the y axis. Each point indicates the scores for X and Y for one individual. As you can see, the figure presents a lot of information. Each point represents the performance of one person who has been assessed on two measures.

The next sections present methods for summarizing the information in a scatter diagram by finding the straight line that comes closest to more points than any other line. One of the reasons that it is important to examine the scatter diagram is because the relationships between X and Y are not always best described by a straight line. For example, Figure 3-2 shows the hypothetical relationship between levels of antidepressant medication in the blood of depressed patients and the number of symptoms they report. However, the relationship is systematic. Patients who have too little or too much medication experience more symptoms than those who get an intermediate amount. The methods of linear correlation or linear regression that will be presented in this chapter are not appropriate for describing nonlinear relationships such as that illustrated in Figure 3-2.

Figure 3-2
A scatter diagram
showing a
nonlinear
relationship.
(*From Kaplan &
Grant, 1993.*)

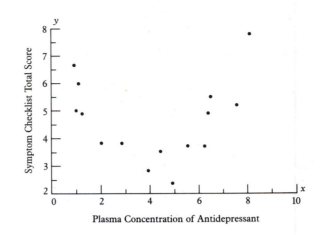

Plasma Concentration of Antidepressant

II. *Correlation*

In correlational analysis we ask whether two variables covary. In other words, does Y get larger as X gets larger? For example, does the patient feel dizzier when we increase the dose of a drug? Do people get more diseases when they are under more stress? Correlational analysis is designed primarily to examine linear relationships between variables. Although we can use correlational techniques to study nonlinear relationships, that is beyond the scope of this book.[3]

A **correlation coefficient** is a mathematical index that describes the direction and magnitude of a relationship. Figure 3-3 shows three different types of relationships between variables. Part (a) of the figure demonstrates a *positive correlation*. This means that high scores on Y are associated with high scores on X, and low scores on Y correspond to low scores on X. Part (b) shows *negative correlation*. When there is a negative correlation, higher scores on Y are associated with lower scores on X, and lower scores on Y are associated with higher scores on X. This might describe the relationship between barbiturate use and amount of activity. The higher the drug dose, the less active patients are. Part (c) of Figure 3-3 shows no correlation, or a situation in which the variables are not related. Here scores on X do not give us information about scores on Y. An example of this sort of relationship is the lack of correlation between shoe size and IQ.

There are a variety of ways to calculate a correlation coefficient. All involve pairs of observations: for each observation on one variable, there is an observa-

[3] Readers interested in methods for studying nonlinear relationships should review Pedhauzer (1982).

Figure 3-3
Three hypothetical relationships: (a) positive correlation, (b) negative correlation, (c) no correlation.

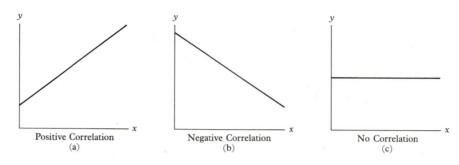

tion on one other variable for the same person.[4] Table 3-1 shows a set of observations on two variables. The first set of observations are the numbers of games won by the 13 teams in the American Football Conference. Each of these teams plays 16 games during the season. The second set of observations are the average salaries for players on the teams. It is widely speculated that there is a systematic relationship between the amount that football owners are willing to pay for exceptional athletes and the number of games their franchise teams win. There are many ways to calculate a correlation coefficient, and these methods are all mathematically equivalent. Before we present methods for calculating the correlation coefficient, we first discuss regression. Regression is the basic method on which correlation is based.

III. *Regression*

A. *The Regression Line*

Correlation is used when we are interested in assessing the magnitude and direction of a relationship. A related technique, known as *regression*, is used to make predictions about scores on one variable from a knowledge of scores on another variable. These predictions are obtained from the regression line. The **regression line** is the best-fitting straight line through a set of points in a scatter diagram. It is found by using the principle of least squres, which minimizes the squared deviation around the regression line.

The mean is the point of least squares for any single variable. This means that the sum of the squared deviations around the mean will be less than it is around any value other than the mean. The regression line is the running mean or the line of least squares in two dimensions or in the space created by two

---

[4] The pairs of scores do not always need to be for a person. They might also be for a group, an institution, a team, and so on.

Table 3-1
Games Won and Average Salaries for Teams in the American Football Conference

Team	X, Games Won	Y, Salary*	X²	Y²	XY
Los Angeles	8	240	64	57,600	1920
New York	10	234	100	54,756	2340
New England	11	223	121	49,729	2453
Cleveland	12	207	144	42,849	2484
Denver	11	193	121	37,249	2123
Miami	8	193	64	37,249	1544
Seattle	10	192	100	36,864	1920
San Diego	4	191	16	36,481	764
Kansas City	10	189	100	35,721	1890
Cincinnati	10	167	100	27,889	1670
Buffalo	4	165	16	27,225	660
Houston	5	153	25	23,409	765
Pittsburgh	6	149	36	22,201	894
	$\Sigma X = 109$	$\Sigma Y = 2496$	$\Sigma X^2 = 1007$	$\Sigma Y^2 = 489{,}222$	$\Sigma XY = 21{,}427$

From *Los Angeles Times*, January 18, 1987, part 3, p. 3.
* Average salaries are expressed in thousands of dollars.

variables. Consider the situation shown in the scatter diagram in Figure 3-1. For each level of X (or point on the X scale) there is a distribution of scores on Y. In other words, we could find a mean of Y when X is 3, another mean of Y when X is 4, and so on. The least squares method in regression finds the straight line that comes as close to as many of these Y means as possible. In other words, it is the line for which the squared deviations around the line are at a minimum.

The formula for a regression line is

$$Y' = a + bX \quad \leftarrow \text{ Raw score or actual value of } X$$

Predicted value of Y Intercept   Regression coefficient

To use the regression equation, we must define some of the terms. The term on the left of the equation is Y'. This is the predicted value of Y. When we create the equation, we use observed values of Y and X. The equation is the result of the least squares procedure and shows the best available relationship between

Figure 3-4
The regression
equation. The
slope is the
amount of
increase on the *y*
axis divided by
the range of
scores on the *x*
axis. The
intercept is the
value of *Y* when
X is 0.

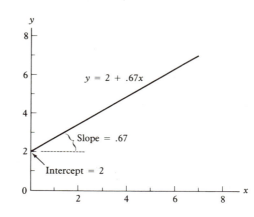

$$y = 2 + .67x$$

Slope = .67

Intercept = 2

X and *Y*. When the equation is available, we can take a score on *X* and plug it into the formula. What results is a predicted value of *Y*.

The most important term in the equation is the *regression coefficient*, or *b*. It is the slope of the regression line. The regression coefficient can be expressed as the ratio of the sums of squares for the covariance to the sums of squares for *X*. It can be defined by the following formula:

$$b = \frac{N(\Sigma XY) - (\Sigma X)(\Sigma Y)}{N\Sigma X^2 - (\Sigma X)^2}$$

The **slope** describes how much change is expected in *Y* each time *X* increases by one unit. For example, Figure 3-4 shows a regression line with a slope of .67. In this figure, the difference between 1 and 2 in units of *X* is associated with an expected difference of .67 in units of *Y* (for *X* = 1, *Y* = 2.67 and for *X* = 2, *Y* = 3.34; 3.34 − 2.67 = .67). The regression coefficient is sometimes expressed in different notation. For example, the Greek *β* is often used for a population estimate of the regression coefficient.

The **intercept,** *a,* is the value of *Y* when *X* is 0. In other words, it is the point at which the regression line crosses the *y* axis. This is shown in Figure 3-4. It is easy to find the intercept when we know the regression coefficient. The intercept is found by using the following formula:

$$a = \overline{Y} - b\overline{X}$$

B. *The Best-Fitting Line*

Correlational methods require us to find the best-fitting line through a series of data points. In Figure 3-4, a regression line is shown. This line is based on a series of observations for particular individuals. Each individual had actually obtained a score on X and on Y. Let's take the example of someone who obtained a score of 4 on X and 6 on Y. The regression equation gives a predicted value for Y that is denoted as Y'. Using the regression equation, we can calculate Y' for this person. It is

$$Y' = 2 + .67X$$

so

$$Y' = 2 + .67(4)$$
$$= 4.68$$

If that person received a score of 6 on Y, the regression equation predicts that he would have a score of 4.68. The difference between the observed and predicted score $(Y - Y')$ is called the **residual.** The best-fitting line keeps residuals to a minimum. In other words, it minimizes the deviation between observed and predicted Y scores. Since residuals can be positive or negative and will cancel to 0 if averaged, the best-fitting line is most appropriately found by squaring each residual. Thus, the best-fitting line is obtained by keeping these squared residuals as small as possible. This is known as the *principle of least squares.* Formally, it is stated as

$$\Sigma(Y - Y')^2 \quad \text{is at a minimum}$$

An example showing how to calculate a regression equation is given in Technical Box 3-1. Whether or not you become proficient at calculating regression equations, you should learn to interpret them in order to be a good consumer of research information.

TECHNICAL BOX 3-1

Calculation of a Regression Equation (Data from Table 3-1)

$$\textbf{Formulas} \quad b = \frac{N(\Sigma XY) - (\Sigma X)(\Sigma Y)}{N\Sigma X^2 - (\Sigma X)^2}$$
$$a = \overline{Y} - b\overline{X}$$

Steps
1. Find N by counting the number of pairs of observations.

$$N = 13$$

2. Find ΣX by summing the X scores.

   $8 + 10 + 11 + \cdots + 6 = 109$

3. Find ΣY by summing the Y scores.

   $240 + 234 + 223 + \cdots + 149 = 2496$

4. Find ΣX^2. Square each X score and then sum them.

   $64 + 100 + 121 + \cdots + 36 = 1007$

5. Find ΣY^2. Square each Y score and then sum them.

   $57,600 + 54,756 + 49,729 + \cdots + 22,201 = 489,222$

6. Find ΣXY. For each pair of observations multiply X by Y. Then sum the products.

   $(8 \times 240) + (10 \times 234) + (11 \times 223) + \cdots + (6 \times 149) = 1920 + 2340 + 2453 + \cdots + 894 = 21,427$

7. Find $(\Sigma X)^2$ by squaring the result of Step 2.

   $109^2 = 11,881$

8. Find $(\Sigma Y)^2$ by squaring the result of Step 3.

   $2496^2 = 6,230,016$

9. Find $N\Sigma XY$ by multiplying the results of Steps 1 and 6.

   $13 \times 21,427 = 278,551$

10. Find $(\Sigma X)(\Sigma Y)$ by multiplying the results of Steps 2 and 3.

    $109 \times 2496 = 272,064$

11. Find $N\Sigma XY - (\Sigma X)(\Sigma Y)$ by subtracting the result of Step 10 from the result of Step 9.

    $278,551 - 272,064 = 6487$

12. Find $N\Sigma X^2$ by multiplying the results of Steps 1 and 4.

    $13 \times 1007 = 13,091$

13. Find $N\Sigma X^2 - (\Sigma X)^2$ by subtracting the result of Step 7 from that of Step 12.

    $13,091 - 11,881 = 1210$

14. Find b by dividing the result of Step 11 by that of Step 13.
    $$\frac{6487}{1210} = 5.36$$

(continued)

(continued)

15. Find $\overline{X}$ by dividing Step 2 by Step 1.

$$\frac{109}{13} = 8.38$$

16. Find $\overline{Y}$ by dividing Step 3 by Step 1.

$$\frac{2496}{13} = 192.00$$

17. Find $b\overline{X}$ by multiplying the results of Steps 14 and 15.

$$5.36 \times 8.38 = 44.92$$

18. Find a by subtracting the results of Step 17 from Step 16.

$$192 - 44.92 = 147.08$$

19. The resultant regression equation is

$$Y = a + bX = 147.08 + (5.36)X$$

The regression equation created in Technical Box 3-1 allows us to estimate how much an owner may need to pay in order to achieve a certain win record. For example, suppose that an owner has a team that won seven games. Using the equation, we can estimate the expected average salary that would be required for players given this record; that is,

$$147.08 + (5.36)(7) = 184.6$$

The equation says that the average salary should be $184.6 (thousand) or approximately $185,000. Now suppose that the team owner would like his team to win 12 games, and he wants to know how much additional money he may need to pay the average player. Using the equation, we find

$$147.08 + (5.36)(12) = 211.4$$

The equation suggests that the average salary for a team winning 12 games should be more than $211,000. According to the equation, the difference between the 12-game winners and the 7-game winners is about $27,000 per player. If there are 45 players on the team, the owner might expect to pay approximately $1,215,000. Of course, correlation does not necessarily imply causation. The owner cannot say for sure that greater investment *causes* his team to win more games.

Correlation is a special case of regression in which the scores for both variables are in standardized, or Z, units. Having the scores in Z units is a nice convenience because it eliminates the need to find the intercept. In correlation, the intercept is always 0. Furthermore, the slope in correlation is easier to interpret because it is in a standardized unit. An example of how to calculate a correlation coefficient for the data in Table 3-1 is given in Technical Box 3-2. In the calculation of the correlation coefficient, we can bypass the step of changing all the scores into Z units. This gets done as part of the calculation process. You may notice that Steps 1–13 are identical for calculating regression (Technical Box 3-1) and correlation (Technical Box 3-2). Technical Box 3-3 gives a theoretical discussion of correlation and regression.

The **Pearson product moment correlation** coefficient, which is mentioned in Technical Box 3-3, is a ratio used to determine the degree of variation in one variable that can be estimated from knowledge about variation in the other variable. The correlation coefficient can take on any value from -1.0 to 1.0.

TECHNICAL BOX 3-2

Calculation of a Correlation Coefficient (Data from Table 3-1)

$$\text{Formula} \quad r = \frac{N\Sigma XY - (\Sigma X)(\Sigma Y)}{\sqrt{[N\Sigma X^2 - (\Sigma X)^2][N\Sigma Y^2 - (\Sigma Y)^2]}}$$

Steps

1. Find N by counting the number of pairs of observations.

   $N = 13$

2. Find ΣX by summing the X scores.

   $8 + 10 + 11 + \cdots + 6 = 109$

3. Find ΣY by summing the Y scores.

   $240 + 234 + 223 + \cdots + 149 = 2496$

4. Find ΣX^2. Square each X score and then sum them.

   $64 + 100 + 121 + \cdots + 36 = 1007$

5. Find ΣY^2. Square each Y score and then sum them.

   $57{,}600 + 54{,}756 + 49{,}729 + \cdots + 22{,}201 = 489{,}222$

6. Find ΣXY. For each pair of observations multiply X by Y. Then sum the products.

   $(8 \times 240) + (10 \times 234) + (11 \times 223) + \cdots + (6 \times 149) = 1920 + 2340 + 2453 + \cdots + 894 = 21{,}427$

7. Find $(\Sigma X)^2$ by squaring the result of Step 2.

   $109^2 = 11{,}881$

(continued)

(continued)

8. Find $(\Sigma Y)^2$ by squaring the result of Step 3.

   $2496^2 = 6{,}230{,}016$

9. Find $N\Sigma XY$ by multiplying the results of Steps 1 and 6.

   $13 \times 21{,}427 = 278{,}551$

10. Find $(\Sigma X)(\Sigma Y)$ by multiplying the results of Steps 2 and 3.

    $109 \times 2496 = 272{,}064$

11. Find $N\Sigma XY - (\Sigma X)(\Sigma Y)$ by subtracting the result of Step 10 from the result of Step 9.

    $278{,}551 - 272{,}064 = 6487$

12. Find $N\Sigma X^2$ by multiplying the results of Steps 1 and 4.

    $13 \times 1007 = 13{,}091$

13. Find $N\Sigma X^2 - (\Sigma X)^2$ by subtracting the result of Step 7 from that of Step 12.

    $13{,}091 - 11{,}881 = 1210$

14. Find $N\Sigma Y^2$ by multiplying the results of Steps 1 and 5.

    $13 \times 489{,}222 = 6{,}359{,}886$

15. Find $N\Sigma Y^2 - (\Sigma Y)^2$ by subtracting the result of Step 8 from that of Step 14.

    $6{,}359{,}886 - 6{,}230{,}016 = 129{,}870$

16. Find $\sqrt{[N\Sigma X^2 - (\Sigma X)^2][N\Sigma Y^2 - (\Sigma Y)^2]}$ by multiplying Steps 13 and 15 and then taking the square root of the product.

    $\sqrt{1210 \times 129{,}870}$

17. Find

    $$r = \frac{N\Sigma XY - (\Sigma X)(\Sigma Y)}{\sqrt{[N\Sigma X^2 - (\Sigma X)^2][N\Sigma Y^2 - (\Sigma Y)^2]}}$$

    by dividing the results of Step 11 by Step 16.

    $$\frac{6487}{12{,}535.66.} = .52$$

Table 3-2 gives the raw data for CES-D and anger inventory scores for medical students. Try to find the regression of anger upon CES-D and the correlation between these two measures. The correct answer is $r = .82$.

Table 3-2
CES-D
Correlation
Example

X, Anger Inventory	Y, CES-D	X^2	Y^2	XY	Predicted	Residual
21	14	441	196	294	7.31	6.69
21	10	441	100	210	7.31	2.69
21	8	441	64	168	7.31	.69
27	8	729	64	216	11.35	−3.35
43	26	1849	676	1118	22.14	3.86
24	0	576	0	0	9.33	−9.33
36	14	1296	196	504	17.42	−3.42
17	3	289	9	51	4.61	−1.61
31	9	961	81	279	14.05	−5.05
19	10	361	100	190	5.96	4.04
19	7	361	49	133	5.96	1.04
24	12	576	144	288	9.33	2.67
27	10	729	100	270	11.35	−1.35
41	25	1681	625	1025	20.79	4.21
18	9	324	81	162	5.29	3.71
24	12	576	144	288	9.33	2.67
43	23	1849	529	989	22.14	.86
28	7	784	49	196	12.03	−5.03
31	13	961	169	403	14.05	−1.05
16	1	256	1	16	3.94	−2.94

Step 1: $N = 20$
Step 2: $\Sigma X = 531$
Step 3: $\Sigma Y = 221$
Step 4: $\Sigma X^2 = 15,481$
Step 5: $\Sigma Y^2 = 3377$
Step 6: $\Sigma XY = 6800$
Step 7: 281,961
Step 8: 48,841
Steps 9, 10, 11: $20(6800) - (531)(221) = 18,649$
Steps 12, 13: $20(15,481) - (531)(531) = 27,659$
Step 14: $b = .67$
Step 15: $\overline{X} = 26.55$
Step 16: $\overline{Y} = 11.05$
Steps 17, 18: $a = 6.85$
Step 19: CES-D $= -6.85 + .67(\text{anger})$
For correlation:
Step 16: 22,741.93
Step 17 correlation: .82

TECHNICAL BOX 3-3

A More Theoretical Discussion of Correlation and Regression

The difference between correlation and regression is analogous to the difference between standardized scores and raw scores. In correlation we look at the relationship between variables when each one is transformed into standardized scores. In Chapter 2, standardized, or Z, scores were defined as $(X - \overline{X})/S$. In correlation, both variables are in Z scores, so they both have a mean of 0. In other words, the mean for the two variables will always be the same. As a result of this convenience, the intercept will always be 0 (when X is 0, Y is also 0) and will drop out of the equation. The resulting equation for translating X into Y then becomes $Y = rX$. In other words, the predicted value of Y equals X times the correlation between X and Y. If the correlation between X and Y is .80 and the standardized (Z) score for the X variable is 1.0, the predicted value of Y will be .80. Unless there is a perfect correlation (1.0 or -1.0), scores on Y will be predicted to be closer to the Y mean than scores on X. A correlation of .80 means that the prediction for Y is 80% as far from the mean as the observation for X. A correlation of .50 means that the predicted distance between the mean of Y and the predicted Y is half of the distance between the associated X and the mean of X.

One benefit of using the correlation coefficient is that it has a reciprocal nature. The correlation between X and Y will always be the same as the correlation between Y and X. For example, if the correlation between drug dose and activity is .68, the correlation between activity and drug dose is .68. Regression is used to transform scores on one variable into estimated scores on the other. We often use regression to predict raw scores on Y on the basis of raw scores on X. For instance, we might seek an equation to predict a student's grade point average on the basis of Scholastic Aptitude Test score. Because regression uses the raw units of the variables, the reciprocal property does not hold. The coefficient describing the regression of X on Y is usually not the same as the coefficient describing the regression of Y on X.

The term *regression* was first used in 1885 by an extraordinary British intellectual named Sir Francis Galton. Galton was found of describing social and political changes that occur over successive generations. He noted that extraordinarily tall men tended to have sons who were a little shorter than they and that unusually small men tended to have sons closer to the average height (but still shorter than average). Over time, individuals with all sorts of unusual characteristics tended to produce offspring who were closer to the average. Galton thought of this as regression toward mediocrity. This idea became the basis for a statistical procedure that describes how scores tend to regress toward the mean. If a person had been extreme on X, regression would predict that he or she would be less extreme on Y. Karl Pearson developed the first statistical models of correlation and regression in the late 19th century.

Statistical Definition of Regression

Regression analysis is used to show how change in one set of scores is related to change in another set of scores. In psychological testing, we often use regression to determine whether changes in test scores are related to changes in performance. Do people who score higher on tests of manual dexterity perform better in dental school? Can IQ scores measured during high school predict monetary income 20 years later? Regression analysis and related correlational methods tell us the degree to which these variables are linearly related. In addition, they give us an equation that estimates scores on a criterion (such as dental school grades) on the basis of scores on a predictor (such as manual dexterity).

In Chapter 2, we introduced the concept of variance. You might remember that *variance* was defined as the average squared deviation around the mean. We used the term *sum of squares* for the sum of squared deviations around the mean. Symbolically, this is

$$\Sigma(X - \overline{X})^2$$

The variance is the sum of squares divided by $N - 1$. The formula for this is

$$S_X^2 = \frac{\Sigma(X - \overline{X})^2}{N - 1}$$

We also gave some formulas for the variance of raw scores. The variance of X can be calculated from raw scores using the formula

$$S_X^2 = \frac{\Sigma X^2 - \frac{(\Sigma X)^2}{N}}{N - 1}$$

If there is another variable, Y, we can calculate the variance using a similar formula:

$$S_Y^2 = \frac{\Sigma Y^2 - \frac{(\Sigma Y)^2}{N}}{N - 1}$$

To calculate regression we need a term for the *covariance*. This tells us how much two measures covary, or vary together. To understand covariance, let's look at the extreme case of the relationship between two identical sets of scores. In this case, there will be a perfect association. We know that we can create a new score that exactly repeats the scores on any one variable. If we create this new twin variable, it will covary perfectly with the original variable. Regression analysis attempts to determine how similar the variance between two variables is by dividing the covariance by the average variance from each variable.

To calculate the covariance, we need to find the sum of cross products, which is defined as

$$\Sigma XY = \Sigma(X - \overline{X})(Y - \overline{Y})$$

and the raw score formula, which is often used for calculation, is

$$\Sigma XY - \frac{(\Sigma X)(\Sigma Y)}{N}$$

(continued)

(continued)

The covariance is the sum of cross products divided by $N - 1$.

Now look at the similarity of the formula for the covariance and the formula for the variance:

$$S_{XY}^2 = \frac{\Sigma XY - \frac{(\Sigma X)(\Sigma Y)}{N}}{N - 1}$$

$$S_X^2 = \frac{\Sigma X^2 - \frac{(\Sigma X)^2}{N}}{N - 1}$$

Try substituting X for Y in the formula for the covariance. You should get

$$\frac{\Sigma XX - \frac{(\Sigma X)(\Sigma X)}{N}}{N - 1}$$

If you replace ΣXX with ΣX^2 and $(\Sigma X)(\Sigma X)$ with $(\Sigma X)^2$, you will see the relationship between variance and covariance:

$$\frac{\Sigma X^2 - \frac{(\Sigma X)^2}{N}}{N - 1}$$

In regression analysis we examine the ratio of the covariance to the average of the variances for the two separate measures. This gives us an estimate of how much variance in one variable we can determine by knowing about the variation in the other variable.

As you can see from Technical Boxes 3-1 and 3-2, calculations of the correlation coefficient and the regression can be long and difficult. You may be able to avoid the many computational steps by using a calculator. Many inexpensive pocket calculators are preprogrammed for correlation and regression. When you buy a calculator, it is worthwhile to choose one with these functions.

C. *Testing the Statistical Significance of a Correlation Coefficient*

One of the most important questions in evaluating a correlation is whether it is larger than would be expected by chance. In other words, we hope to determine whether the association between two variables is significantly different from 0. Correlation coefficients can be tested for statistical significance using the t distribution. The formula for calculating the t value is

$$t = r \sqrt{\frac{N - 2}{1 - r^2}}$$

The significance of the t value, where df $= N - 2$ (df means degrees of freedom) and N is the number of pairs, can then be obtained by using Appendix 2.

Let's take one example of a correlation of .37 based on 50 pairs of observations. Using the formula, we obtain

$$t = .37 \sqrt{\frac{48}{.86}}$$

$$= .37(7.47)$$

$$= 2.76$$

Now, suppose we had stated the null hypothesis that the association between these two variables is not significantly different from 0. This would be tested against the alternative hypothesis that the association between the two measures is significantly different from 0 in a two-tailed test. A significance level of .05 is used. Formally, then, the hypothesis and alternative hypothesis are

$$H_0: \quad r = 0$$

$$H_1: \quad r \neq 0$$

Using the formula, we obtain a t value of 2.76 with 48 degrees of freedom. According to Appendix 2, this t value is sufficient to reject the null hypothesis. Thus, we conclude that the association between these two variables was not due to chance.

There are also statistical tables that give the critical values for r. One of these tables is included as Appendix 4. The table lists critical values of r for both the .05 and the .01 alpha levels according to degrees of freedom. For the correlation coefficient, df $= N - 2$. Suppose, for example, that you want to determine whether a correlation coefficient of .45 is statistically significant for a sample of 20 subjects. The degrees of freedom would be 18 $(20 - 2 = 18)$. According to Appendix 4, the critical value for the .05 level is .444 with 18 df. Since .45 exceeds .444, you would conclude that the chances of finding a correlation as large as the one observed by chance alone would be less than 5 in 100. However, the observed correlation is less than the criterion value for the .01 level (that would require .561 with 18 df).

D. *How to Interpret a Regression Plot*

Regression plots are pictures that show the relationship between variables. A common use of regression is to determine the **criterion validity** of a test, or the relationship between a test score and some well-defined criterion. The association between a test of job aptitude and the criterion of actual performance on the job is an example of criterion validity. The problems we deal with in studies of criterion validity require us to predict some criterion score on the basis of a predictor or test score. Suppose that you want to build a test to predict how enjoyable someone will turn out to be as a date. If you selected your dates randomly and had no information about them in advance, you might be best off just using normative information.

You might expect that the distribution of enjoyableness of dates is normal. Some people are just not fun for you to go out with, whereas others are exceptionally enjoyable. However, the great majority of the people are some fun but not excessively so and fall between these two extremes. Figure 3-5 shows what a frequency distribution for enjoyableness of dates might look like. As you can see, the highest point, which shows where dates are most frequently classified, is the location of the average date.

If you had no other way of predicting how much you would like your dates, the safest prediction would be to pick this middle level of enjoyableness because it is one observed most frequently. This is called *normative* because it uses information gained from representative groups. Knowing nothing else about an individual, we can make an educated guess that a person will be average in enjoyableness because past experience has demonstrated that the mean, or average, score is also the one observed most frequently. In other words, knowing about the average date gives you some information about what to expect from a particular date. But it is doubtful that you would really want to choose dates this way. You probably would rather use other information such as the person's educational background, attitudes, and hobbies to predict whether that person would be enjoyable for you to spend an evening with.

Figure 3-5
Hypothetical distribution of the enjoyableness of dates. Few dates are extremely enjoyable or extremely unenjoyable. The greatest number fall about in the middle.

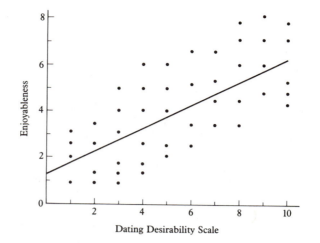

Figure 3-6

Hypothetical relationship between dating desirability and the enjoyableness of dates. Each point summarizes the dating desirability score and the enjoyableness rating for a single subject. The line was derived from a mathematical procedure to come as close to as many points as possible.

Most people do use some system to help them make important personal choices. These systems, however, are never perfect. Thus, you are left with something that is not perfect but is still better than using just normative information. In regression studies we develop equations that help us describe more precisely where tests fall between being perfect predictors and being no better than just using the normative information. This is done by graphing the relationship between test scores and the criterion. Then a mathematical procedure is used to find the straight line that comes as close to as many of the points as possible.

Figure 3-6 shows the points on hypothetical scales of dating desirability and the enjoyableness of dates. The line through the points is the one that minimizes the squared distance between the line and the data points. In other words, the line is the one straight line that summarizes more about the relationship between dating desirability and enjoyableness than any other straight line.

Figure 3-7 shows the hypothetical relationship between a test score and a criterion. Using this figure, you should be able to find the predicted value on the criterion variable by knowing the score on the test or the predictor. Here is how you read the graph. First pick a particular score on the test, say 8. Find 8 on the axis of the graph with the label "Test Score" (horizontal axis). Now draw a line straight up until you hit the slanted line on the graph. This is the regression line. Now make a 90-degree left turn and draw another line until it hits the other axis of the graph, which is labeled "Criterion Score." The dashed line in Figure 3-7 shows the course you should take. Now read the number on the criterion axis where your line has stopped. This score of 7.4 on the criterion

Figure 3-7
Predicted
relationship
between a test
score and a
criterion. The
dotted line shows
how you should
have obtained a
predicted criterion
score of 7.4 from
the test score of 8.

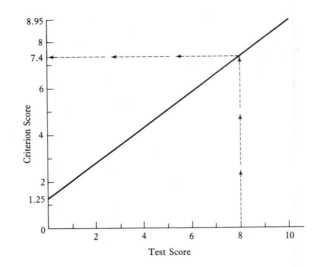

variable is the score you would expect to obtain on the basis of information you gained by using the test.

Notice that the line in Figure 3-7 is not at a 45 angle and that the two variables are measured in the same units. If it were at a 45 angle, the test would be a perfect (or close to perfect) forecaster of the criterion. However, this is almost never the case in practice. Now do the same exercise you did for the test score of 8 with test scores from the extremes of the distributions. Try the scores 0 and 10. You will find that the score of 10 for the test gives a criterion score of 8.95, and the test score of 0 gives a criterion score of 1.25. Notice how far apart 0 and 10 are on the test. Now look at how far apart 1.25 and 8.95 are on the

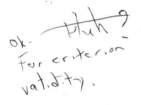

Figure 3-8
Regression lines
with different
standardized
slopes.

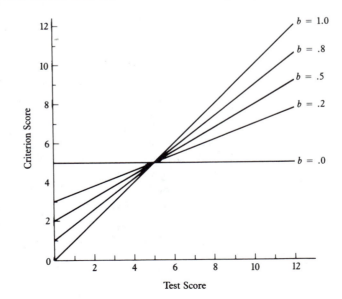

criterion. You can see that using the test as a predictor is not as good as perfect prediction, but it is still better than using the normative information. If we had used only the normative information, we would have predicted that all scores would be the average score on the criterion. And if there were perfect prediction, the distance between 1.25 and 8.95 on the criterion would be the same as the distance between 0 and 10 on the test.

Figure 3-8 shows a variety of different regression slopes. Notice that the higher the standardized regression coefficient, the steeper the line. Now look at the regression line that has a slope of 0. It is parallel to the axis for the test score and perpendicular to the line for the criterion. A regression line like this shows that the test score tells us nothing about the criterion beyond the consensus information.

Try an example. Take a test score of 11. Just as you did before, draw a line straight up from this score until you hit the regression line for a slope of 0. Now draw the line at a 90-degree angle to the left until you hit the criterion score axis. The score should be 5.5. Now do the same thing for a test score of 3. Did you get the same predicted criterion score? You should have. In fact, any test score will give you the same predicted criterion score, and that score will always be the average score on the criterion. The slope of 0 tells you that the test and the criterion are unrelated and that your best bet under these circumstances is to predict the average score on the criterion.

Take some time and try finding the predicted score on the criterion for test scores of 11 and 3. Do it for several of the different slopes shown in Figure 3-8. Notice that the steeper the slope of the regression line, the farther apart are the predicted scores on the criterion. Table 3-3 shows the predicted scores for all the different slopes. You can use it to check your answers.

When the regression lines have slopes of 0 or nearly 0, it is best not to take any chances in forecasting the criterion. Instead you should depend on the normative information and guess the mean of Y. As the slope becomes steeper, we are more prepared to take some chances and estimate that there will be differences in criterion scores.

Table 3-3
Expected Criterion Scores for Two Test Scores When Predicted from Regression Lines with Different Slopes

Test Score	Slope	Predicted Criterion Score
11	1.0	11.00
3	1.0	3.00
11	.8	9.90
3	.8	3.50
11	.5	8.25
3	.5	4.25
11	.2	6.60
3	.2	5.00
11	.00	5.50
3	.00	5.50

It is instructive to think about Figure 3-8 as we reflect on the meaning of psychological tests. For example, if SAT scores have a slope of .5 for predicting grades in college, this means that the SAT-performance relationship is defined by the line labeled "$b = .5$" in Figure 3-8. Using this sort of information, college administrators can forecast that there will be some differences in college performance that might be predicted from SAT scores. However, because the slope is not steep, those predictions are somewhere between perfect prediction and what they would get if they used the consensus information.

IV. *Other Correlation Coefficients*

The Pearson product moment correlation is only one of many types of correlation coefficient. It is the one most commonly used because most often we want to find the correlation between two continuous variables. Continuous variables can take on any values over a range of values. Height, weight, and intelligence are examples of continuous variables. However, there are situations where we want to find the correlations between variables that are scaled in other ways.

for ranks

Spearman's rho is a method of correlation that is used to find the association between two sets of ranks. The rho coefficient (ρ) is easy to calculate and is often used when the individuals in a sample can be ranked on two variables but their actual scores are not known or are very nonnormal in distribution.

There is a whole family of correlation coefficients that involve dichotomous variables. Dichotomous variables have only two levels. Examples are yes/no, correct/incorrect, and male/female. Some dichotomous variables are called *true dichotomous* because they naturally form two categories. For example, gender is a true dichotomous variable and has two levels: male and female. Other dichotomous variables are called *artificial dichotomous* because there was originally an underlying continuous scale that was forced into a dichotomy. Passing or failing a bar examination is an example of such an artificial dichotomy. (Actually, many scores can be obtained, but the examiners decide to consider only pass and fail.) The types of correlation coefficients used to find the relationship between dichotomous and continuous variables are shown in Table 3-4.

continuous/
artificial
dichotomy)

continuous/
true dichotomous

2 dichotomous

The **biserial correlation** expresses the relationship between a continuous variable and an artificial dichotomous variable. For example, the biserial correlation might be used to assess the relationship between passing or failing the bar examination (artificial dichotomous variable) and grade point average in law school (continuous variable). If the dichotomous variable had been "true" (such as gender), we would use the *point biserial correlation*. For instance, the point biserial correlation would be used to find the relationship between gender and grade point average. When both variables are dichotomous and at least one of the dichotomies is "true," the association between them can be estimated using the *phi coefficient*. For example, the relationship between passing or

Table 3-4

Appropriate Correlation Coefficients for Relationships Between Dichotomous and Continuous Variables*

Variable Y	Variable X		
	Continuous	**Artificial Dichotomous**	**True Dichotomous**
Continuous	Pearson *r*	Biserial *r*	Point biserial *r*
Artificial dichotomous	Biserial *r*	Tetrachoric *r*	Phi
True dichotomous	Point biserial *r*	Phi	Phi

* The entries in the table suggest which type of correlation coefficient is appropriate given the characteristics of the two variables. For example, if variable Y is continuous and variable X is true dichotomous, you would use the point biserial correlation.

failing the bar examination and gender (male or female) could be estimated using the phi coefficient. If both dichotomous variables are artificial, we might use a special correlation coefficient known as the *tetrachoric correlation*. Among these special correlation coefficients, the point biserial, phi, and Spearman's rho coefficients are probably used most often. The formulas for calculating these correlations are given in Technical Box 3-4.

TECHNICAL BOX 3-4

Formulas for Spearman's Rho, the Point Biserial Correlation, and the Phi Coefficient

$$\text{Spearman's rho formula:} \quad \rho = 1 - \frac{6\Sigma d_i^2}{N^3 - N}$$

where ρ = Spearman's rho coefficient

d_i = a subject's rank order on variable 2 minus his or her rank order on variable 1

N = the number of paired ranks

When used: To find the association between pairs of observations, each expressed in ranks.

$$\text{Point biserial correlation formula:} \quad r_{\text{pbis}} = \left[\frac{\overline{Y}_1 - \overline{Y}}{S_y} \right] \sqrt{\frac{P_x}{1 - P_x}}$$

where r_{pbis} = the point biserial correlation coefficient

X = a true dichotomous (two-choice) variable

Y = a continuous (multilevel) variable

(continued)

(continued)

$\overline{Y_1}$ = the mean of Y for subjects having a "plus" score on X

$\overline{Y}$ = the mean of Y for all subjects

S_y = the standard deviation for Y scores

P_x = the proportion of subjects giving a "plus" score on X

When used: To find the association between a dichotomous (two-choice) variable and a continuous variable. For the true dichotomous variable, one of the two choices is arbitrarily designated as a "plus" response.

Phi coefficient formula: $\phi = \dfrac{P_c - P_x P_y}{P_x(1 - P_x)\, P_y(1 - P_y)}$

where ϕ = the phi coefficient

P_c = the proportion in the "plus" category for both variables

P_x = the proportion in the "plus" category for the first variable

P_y = the proportion in the "plus" category for the second variable

When used: To find the association between two dichotomous (two-category) variables. A dichotomous variable might be yes/no or on/off. In each case, one of the two choices is arbitrarily chosen as a "plus" response. When you use phi, one of the variables must be "true" dichotomy (if both were "artificial," the tetrachoric correlation would be more appropriate).

V. *Terms and Issues in the Use of Correlation*

When you use correlation or read studies that report correlational analysis, you will need to know the terminology. Some of the terms and issues you should be familiar with are *residual, standard error of estimate, coefficient of determination, coefficient of alienation, shrinkage, cross validation, correlation-causation problem,* and *third variable.* Following are brief discussions of these terms and concepts.

Residual. A regression equation gives a predicted value of Y' for each value of X. In addition to these predicted values, there are observed values of Y. The difference between the predicted and the observed values is called the **residual.** Symbolically, the residual is defined as $Y - Y'$.

Consider the example of the CES-D. Earlier we calculated the regression equation that predicted CES-D scores from scores on the anger inventory. The equation suggested that predicted CES-D = $-6.85 + .67 \times$ anger. Let's take the example of a person who had an anger score of 19 and an observed CES-D score of 7. The predicted CES-D score is

$$-6.85 + (.67 \times 19) = 5.88$$

In other words, the person had an observed score of 7 and a predicted score of 5.88. The residual is

$$7 - 5.88 = 1.12^5$$

In regression analysis the residuals have certain properties. One important property is that the sum of the residuals always equals 0 $[\Sigma(Y - Y') = 0]$. In addition, the sum of the squared residuals is the smallest value according to the principle of least squares $[\Sigma(Y - Y')^2 = \text{smallest value}]$.

Standard error of estimate. Once we have obtained the residuals, we can find their standard deviation. However, in creating the regression equation, we have found two constants (a and b). Thus, we must use two degrees of freedom rather than one, as is usually the case in finding the standard deviation. The standard deviation of the residuals is known as the **standard error of estimate,** which is defined as

$$S_{yx} = \sqrt{\frac{\Sigma(Y - Y')^2}{N - 2}}$$

The standard error of estimate is a measure of the accuracy of prediction. Prediction is most accurate when the standard error of estimate is relatively small. As it becomes larger, the prediction becomes less accurate.

Coefficient of determination. The square of the correlation coefficient is known as the **coefficient of determination.** This value tells us the proportion of the total variation in scores on Y that we know as a function of information about X. For example, if the correlation between the SAT score and performance in the first year of college is .40, the coefficient of determination is .16. This means that we can explain 16% of the variation in first-year college performance by knowing SAT scores. In the CES-D and anger example, the correlation is .82. Therefore, the coefficient of determination is .67, suggesting that 67% of the variance in CES-D can be accounted for by the anger score.

Coefficient of alienation. The **coefficient of alienation** is a measure of non-association between two variables. This is calculated as $\sqrt{1 - r^2}$, where r^2 is the coefficient of determination. For the SAT example, the coefficient of alienation is $\sqrt{1 - .16} = \sqrt{.84} = .92$. This means that there is a high degree of non-association between SAT scores and college performance. In the CES-D and anger example, the coefficient of alienation is $\sqrt{1 - .67} = .57$.

---

[5] Note: There is a small discrepancy between 1.12 and the 1.04 for the example in Table 3-2. The difference is due to rounding error.

Shrinkage. Many times a regression equation is created on one group of subjects and then used to predict the performance of another group. One of the problems with regression analysis is that it takes advantage of chance relationships within a particular sample of subjects. Thus, there is a tendency to overestimate the relationship, particularly if the sample of subjects is small. **Shrinkage** is the amount of decrease observed when a regression equation is created for one population and then applied to another. Formulas are available to estimate the amount of shrinkage to expect given the characteristics of variance, covariance, and sample size (F. M. Lord, 1950; McNemar, 1969; Uhl & Eisenberg, 1970).

An example of shrinkage is when a regression equation is developed to predict first-year college grade point average on the basis of Scholastic Aptitude Test scores. Although the proportion of variance in grade point average might be fairly high for the original group, we can expect to account for a smaller proportion of the variance when the equation is used to predict grade point average in the next year's class. This decrease in the proportion of variance accounted for is the shrinkage.

Cross validation. The best way to ensure that proper references are being made is to use the regression equation to predict performance in a group of subjects

---

FOCUSED EXAMPLE 3-1

The Danger of Inferring Causation from Correlation

A recent newspaper article discussed the stressfulness of a variety of occupations. A total of 130 job categories were rated for stressfulness by examining Tennessee hospital and death records for evidence of stress-related diseases such as heart attacks, ulcers, arthritis, and mental disorders. The 12 highest and the 12 lowest jobs are listed in the table to the right.

The article advises readers who want to remain healthy to avoid the "most stressful" job categories. However, the evidence may not warrant the advice offered in the article. Although it is quite possible that certain diseases are associated with particular occupations, this does not necessarily mean that holding the jobs causes the illnesses. There are a variety of other explanations. For example, people with the propensity for

Most Stressful	*Least Stressful*
1. Unskilled laborer	1. Clothing sewer
2. Secretary	2. Garment checker
3. Assembly-line inspector	3. Stock clerk
4. Clinical lab technician	4. Skilled craftsperson
5. Office manager	5. Housekeeper
6. Foreperson	6. Farm laborer
7. Manager/administrator	7. Heavy-equipment operator
8. Waitress/waiter	8. Freight handler
9. Factory machine operator	9. Child care worker
10. Farm owner	10. Factory package wrapper
11. Miner	11. College professor
12. House painter	12. Personnel worker

other than the ones on which the equation was created. Then a standard error of estimate can be obtained for the relationship between the values predicted by the equation and those observed. This process is known as **cross validation.**

The correlation-causation problem. Just because two variables are correlated, it does not necessarily mean that one has caused the other (see Focused Example 3-1). For example, because there is a correlation between the number of hours spent viewing television and aggressive behavior, it does not mean that excessive viewing of television causes aggression. This relationship could mean that an aggressive child might prefer to watch a lot of television.

Third variable explanation. There are other possible explanations for the observed relationship between television viewing and aggressive behavior. One is that some third variable causes both excessive viewing of television and aggressive behavior. For example, poor social adjustment might explain both. Thus, the apparent relationship between viewing and aggression actually might be the result of some variable that is not included in the analysis and may be unknown. We usually refer to this external influence as a **third variable.**

heart attacks and ulcers might be more likely to select jobs as unskilled laborers or secretaries. Thus, the direction of causation might be that a health condition causes job selection rather than the reverse. Another possibility is a third variable explanation. Some other factor might cause the apparent relationship between job and health. For example, a certain income level might cause both stress and illness. It is well known that poor people have lower health status than wealthy people. It is possible that impoverished conditions might cause a person to accept certain jobs and also to have more diseases.

These three possible explanations are diagrammed in the right-hand column. An arrow shows a causal connection.

In this example we are *not* ruling out the possibility that job causes illness. In fact, it is quite plausible. However, because the nature of the evidence is correlational, it cannot be said with certainty that job causes illness.

$Job \rightarrow Illness$	$Illness \rightarrow Job$	*Economic Status*
		$\swarrow \searrow$
		Job Illness
Job causes illness	Tendency toward illness causes people to choose certain jobs	Economic status (third variable) causes job selection and illness

VI. *Multivariate Analysis (Optional)*

Multivariate analysis considers the relationship among combinations of three or more variables. For example, the prediction of success in the first year of college from the linear combination of SAT verbal and SAT quantitative scores is a problem for multivariate analysis. However, the field of multivariate analysis is a technical one and requires an understanding of linear and matrix algebra. Therefore, a detailed discussion of multivariate analysis is beyond the scope of this book.

On the other hand, multivariate analysis is common to the testing field. It will be important for you to have a general idea of what the different methods entail. This section will familiarize you with some of the multivariate analysis terminology. It should help you identify the situations in which some of the different multivariate methods are used. Several references are available in case you would like to learn more about the technical details (Cliff, 1987; Tabachnick & Fidell, 1989).

A. *General Approach*

Multivariate methods have advantages for the study of behavior because they permit us to examine the relationships among many variables. The correlational techniques we presented thus far in the chapter describe the relationship between only two variables. For example, they might consider the relationship between stress and illness. In order to understand more fully the causes of illness, we need to consider many potential factors in addition to stress. Multivariate analysis allows us to study the relationship between many predictors and an outcome. In addition, the methods allow us to study the relationship among the predictors.

Multivariate methods differ in the number and kind of predictor variables they utilize. They are the same in that they all transform groups of variables into linear combinations. A linear combination of variables is a weighted composite of the original variables. The weighting system combines the variables in order to achieve some goal. Multivariate techniques differ according to the goal they are trying to achieve.

A linear combination of variables looks like this:

$$Y' = a + b_1X_1 + b_2X_2 + b_3X_3 + \cdots + b_kX_k$$

where Y' is the predicted value of Y, a is a constant, X_1 to X_k are variables and there are k such variables, and the b's are regression coefficients. If you feel anxious about such a complex-looking equation, there is no need to panic. Actually, this equation describes something similar to what was presented in the section on regression. The difference is that instead of relating Y to X, we are now dealing with a linear combination of X's. The whole right side of the equation creates a new composite variable by transforming a set of predictor variables.

B. *An Example Using Multiple Regression*

Variables that are "important" in this combination are associated with larger standardized regression coefficients. An example using multiple regression might help illustrate this concept. Suppose we want to predict success in law school from three variables: undergraduate grade point average (GPA), rating by former professors, and age. This type of multivariate analysis is called **multiple regression,** and the goal of the analysis is to find the linear combination of the three variables that provides the best prediction of law school success. We find the correlation between the criterion (law school GPA) and some composite of the predictors (undergraduate GPA plus professor rating plus age). The combination of the three predictors, however, is not just the sum of the three scores. Instead, we program the computer to find a specific way of adding the predictors together that will make the correlation between the composite and the criterion as high as possible. A weighted composite might look something like this:

$$\text{law school GPA} = .80(Z \text{ scores of undergraduate GPA})$$
$$+ .24(Z \text{ scores of professor ratings})$$
$$+ .03(Z \text{ scores for age})$$

This example suggests that undergraduate GPA is given more weight in the prediction of law school GPA than the other variables. The undergraduate GPA is multiplied by .80, whereas the other variables are multiplied by much smaller coefficients. Age is multiplied by only .03, which is very close to no contribution. Because any number multiplied by 0 is 0, you can see that age almost drops out of the equation. This is because .03 times any Z score for age will give a number that is nearly 0 and, in effect, we would just be adding 0 to the composite.

The reason for using Z scores for the three predictors is that the coefficients in the linear composite are greatly affected by the range of values taken on by the variables. GPA is measured on a scale from 0 to 4.0, whereas the range in age might be 21 to 70. In order to compare the coefficients to one another, we need to transform all of the variables into similar units. This is accomplished by using Z scores (see Chapter 2). When the variables are expressed in Z units, the coefficients, or weights for the variables, are known as standardized regression coefficients (sometimes called B's and betas). There are also some cases in which we want to use the variables in their natural units. For example, we sometimes want to find an equation we can use to estimate someone's predicted level of success on the basis of personal characteristics, and we do not want to bother changing these characteristics into Z units. When we do this, the weights in the model are called *raw regression coefficients* (sometimes called b's).

Before moving on, we should caution you about interpreting regression coefficients. In addition to being a reflection of the relationship between a particular variable and the criterion, the coefficients are affected by the relationship among the predictor variables. You need to be very careful when the predictor variables are highly correlated with one another. Two predictor variables that are highly correlated with the criterion will not both have large regression coefficients if they are highly correlated with one another. For example, suppose that undergraduate GPA and the professors' rating are both highly correlated with law school GPA. However, these two predictors also are highly correlated with each other. In effect, the two measures seem to be of the same thing (which would not be surprising because the professors assigned the grades). So professors' rating may get a lower regression coefficient because some of its predictive power is already taken into consideration through its association with undergraduate GPA. We can only be confident in interpreting regression coefficients when the predictor variables do not overlap. They may do so when the predictors are uncorrelated.

C. *Discriminant Analysis*

Multiple regression is appropriate when the criterion variable is continuous. However, there are many cases in testing when the criterion is a set of categories. For example, we often want to know the linear combination of variables that differentiates passing from failing. When the task is to find the linear combination of variables that provides a maximum discrimination between categories, the appropriate multivariate is **discriminant analysis.** An example of discriminant analysis involves attempts to determine whether a set of measures predicts success or failure on a particular performance evaluation. Many tests had been given previously, and discriminant analysis is used to find the linear combination of these tests that best separates success from failure. Sometimes we want to determine the categorization in more than two categories. To accomplish this we use *multiple discriminant analysis.*

Discriminant analysis has many advantages in the field of test construction. For example, one approach to test construction is to identify two groups of people who represent two distinct categories on some trait. For example, two groups of children might be classified as "language disabled" and "normal." Then a variety of items would be presented, and discriminant analysis would be used to find the linear combination of items that best accounts for differences between the impaired and the nonimpaired children. With the use of this information, new tests could be developed to help diagnose language impairment. Furthermore, learning about the differences between impaired and nonimpaired children might provide insight into the nature of the problem and eventually lead to better treatments.

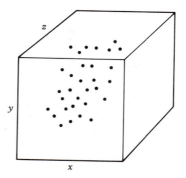

Figure 3-9

A three-dimensional scatter plot might be represented by this box. In addition to plotting points on the x and y axes, we must locate them in relation to a third z axis. Although it is hard to show more than two dimensions on a flat page, you can think of a three-dimensional figure as a box.

D. *Factor Analysis*

Discriminant analysis and multiple regression analysis are techniques that find linear combinations of variables that maximize the prediction of some criterion. Factor analysis is used to study the interrelationships among a set of variables without reference to a criterion. Factor analysis might best be thought of as a data reduction technique. When we have responses to a large number of items or a large number of tests, it is often desirable to reduce all this information to more manageable chunks. In Figure 3-1 we presented a two-dimensional scatter diagram. The task in correlation is to find the best-fitting line through the space created by these two dimensions. As we add more variables in multivariate analysis, we increase the number of dimensions. For example, a three-dimensional plot is shown in Figure 3-9. You can use your imagination to visualize what a larger set of dimensions would look like. Some people claim they can visualize more than three dimensions, while others feel they cannot. In any case, consider that points are plotted in the space created in these many dimensions.

In factor analysis, we first create a matrix that shows the correlation between every variable and every other variable. Then we find the linear combinations of the variables that describe as much of the interrelationships between the variables as possible. These linear combinations of the variables are called *principal components*, and the goal in creating them is to describe as much of the association between the variables as possible. We can find as many principal components as there are variables. However, each principal component is extracted according to mathematical rules that make it independent or uncorrelated with all of the other principal components. The first component will be the most successful in describing the variation among the variables, and each succeeding component will be somewhat less successful. Thus, we often decide

---

FOCUSED EXAMPLE 3-2

The Factors of Trust

Rotter (1967) described a scale for the measurement of interpersonal trust. Trust was defined as "an expectancy held by an individual or a group that the word, promise, verbal or written statement of another individual or group can be relied upon" (p. 651). However, since the publication of the original trust article, several authors have reported that trust seems to be composed of several independent factors (Chun & Campbell, 1974; Kaplan, 1973; Wright & Tedeschi, 1975). The method used to draw these conclusions was factor analysis. In each case, the items were given to a large group of people, and the results were subjected to factor analysis. This procedure reduced the many items down to a smaller number of factors. The factors are linear combinations of the original items. Then item loadings, which are the correlations of the original items with the factors, were studied in order to name the factors. The following table shows the loadings of the items on three of the factors (from Kaplan, 1973).

Once the factor loadings have been obtained, the researcher must attempt to name the factors by examining which items load highly on them. In this case, an item was used to help interpret a factor if its item loading on the factor was greater than .35 or less than −.35. In the Kaplan study (1973), three factors of trust were found.

Factor I: Institutional trust. This represented trust toward major social agents in society. It included items regarding the competence of politicians, such as "This country has a dark future unless we can attract better people into politics" (−.67). Many of the items conveyed the idea of misrepresentation of public events by either the government or the mass media. For example, some items with high loadings were "Most people would be horrified if they knew how much news the public hears and sees is distorted" (−.69) and "Even though we have reports in newspapers, radio, and TV, it is hard to get objective accounts of public events" (−.67).

Factor II: Sincerity. Items loading highly on sincerity tended to focus on the perceived sincerity of others. These items include "Most idealists are sincere and usually practice what they preach" (.62) and "Most people answer public opinion polls honestly" (.58). Nearly all the items with high loadings on the second factor began with the word "most." Because of this loose wording, it would be possible for people to agree with the items because they believe in the sincerity of most people in a given group but still feel little trust for the group because of a few "rotten eggs." Thus, a woman could believe most car repairers are sincere but still service her own car because she fears victimization by overcharging.

Factor III: Caution. This contained items that expressed fear that some people will take advantage of others. For example, items stated that "In dealing with strangers, one is better off being cautious until they have provided evidence that they are trustworthy" (.74) and "In these competitive times you have to be alert or someone is likely to take advantage of you" (.53). Note that caution appears to be independent of perceived sincerity.

The data imply that generalized trust may be composed of several dimensions. The trust scale may prove to be a valuable tool for clinicians and researchers. Their purposes may be better served, however, if they focus on specific components of trust rather than the generalized case.

Item number	Item	Loading factor		
		I	*II*	*III*
A. *Items with high loadings on institutional factor*				
4.	This country has a dark future unless we can attract better people into politics.	−.67	−.12	−.06
5.	Fear of social disgrace or punishment rather than conscience prevents most people from breaking the law.	−.54	.02	−.06
13.	The United Nations will never be an effective force in keeping world peace.	−.41	.09	−.21
16.	The judiciary is a place where we can all get unbiased treatment.	.37	.23	.00
19.	Most people would be horrified if they knew how much news the public hears and sees is distorted.	−.69	.18	.28
21.	Most elected public officials are really sincere in their campaign promises.	.44	.17	−.02
24.	Even though we have reports in newspapers, radio, and TV, it is hard to get objective accounts of public events.	−.67	−.08	.00
28.	If we really knew what was going on in international politics, the public would have more reason to be more frightened than it now seems to be.	−.49	.01	.24
33.	Many major national sports contests are fixed in one way or another.	−.55	−.04	.28
B. *Items with high loadings on sincerity factor*				
1.	Hypocrisy is on the increase in our society.	.09	−.52	.08
12.	Most students in school would not cheat even if they were sure of getting away with it.	.29	.45	.07
27.	Most experts can be relied upon to tell the truth about the limits of their knowledge.	.20	.66	.20
34.	Most idealists are sincere and usually practice what they preach.	.12	.62	−.20
38.	Most repair persons will not overcharge even if they think you are ignorant of their specialty.	.11	.48	−.35
44.	Most people answer public opinion polls honestly.	.04	.58	.16
C. *Items with high loadings on caution factor*				
2.	In dealing with strangers, one is better off being cautious until they have provided evidence that they are trustworthy.	−.22	−.03	.74
7.	Using the honor system of *not* having a teacher present during examinations would probably result in increased cheating.	.13	.08	.45
32.	In these competitive times you have to be alert or someone is likely to take advantage of you.	−.12	−.01	.53
42.	A large share of the accident claims filed against insurance companies are phony.	−.07	−.14	.57

Adapted from Rotter (1967).

to examine only a few components that account for larger proportions of the variation. Technically, principal components analysis and true factor analysis differ in how the correlation matrix is created. However, principal components are often called factors.

Once the linear combinations or principal components have been found, we can find the correlation between the original items and the factors. These correlations are called *factor loadings*. The expression "item 7 loaded highly on factor I" means there is a high correlation between item 7 and the first principal component. By examining which variables load highly on each factor, you can help determine the meaning for the factors. Focused Example 3-2 shows how the meanings of various factors in a scale on interpersonal trust are evaluated.

Factor analysis is a complex and technical method, and there are many options the user must learn about. For example, users frequently use methods that help them get a clearer picture of the meaning of the components by transforming the variables in a way that pushes the factor loadings toward the high or the low extreme. These transformation methods involve rotating the axes in the space created by the factors, and they have therefore been labeled *methods of rotation*. There are many options for methods of rotation, and there are other options about the characteristics of the matrix that originally is entered into the analysis. If you are interested, there are several books that discuss factor analysis methods in great detail, including H. H. Harmon's *Modern Factor Analysis* (1967) and R. L. Gorsuch's *Factor Analysis* (1974).

Summary

This chapter began with a discussion of a claim made in the *National Enquirer* that poor diet causes marital problems. Actually there was no specific evidence that diet *causes* the problems—only that diet and marital difficulties are associated. However, the *Enquirer* failed to specify the exact strength of the association. The rest of the chapter was designed to help you be more specific than the *Enquirer* article was by learning to specify associations with precise mathematical indexes known as *correlation coefficients*.

First, we presented pictures of the association between two variables, which are called *scatter diagrams*. Second, we presented a method for finding a linear equation to describe the relationship between two variables. This regression method uses the data in raw units. The results of regression analysis are two constants: a *slope* describing the degree of relatedness between the variables and an *intercept* giving the value of the Y variable when the X variable is 0. When both of the variables are in standardized or Z units, the intercept is always 0 and it drops out of the equation. In this unique situation, we solve for only one constant, which is r, or the *correlation coefficient*.

When using correlational methods, we must take many things into consideration. For example, correlation does not mean the same thing as causation. In the case of the *National Enquirer* article, the observed correlation between diet and problems in marriage may mean that diet causes the personal difficulties. However, it may also mean that marriage problems cause poor eating habits or that some *third variable* causes both diet habits and marital problems. In addition to the difficulties associated with causation, we must always consider the strength of the correlational relationship. The *coefficient of determination* describes the percentage of variation in one variable that is known on the basis of its association with another variable. The *coefficient of alienation* is an index of what is not known from information about the other variable.

A *regression line* is the best-fitting straight line through a set of points in a scatter diagram. The regression line is described by a mathematical index known as the regression equation. The *regression coefficient* is the ratio of covariance to variance and is also known as the slope of the regression line. The regression coefficient describes how much change is expected in the Y variable each time the X variable increases by one unit. Other concepts discussed are the *intercept* (the value of Y when X is 0), the *residual* (the difference between the predicted value given by a regression equation and the observed value), and the *standard error of estimate* (the standard deviation of the residuals obtained from the regression equation).

The field of *multivariate analysis* involves a complicated but important set of methods for studying the relationships among many variables. *Multiple regression* is a multivariate method for studying the relationship between one criterion variable and two or more predictor variables. A similar method known as *discriminant analysis* is used to study the relationship between a categorical criterion and two or more predictors. *Factor analysis* is another multivariate method for reducing a large set of variables down to a smaller set of composite variables.

Correlational methods are the most commonly used statistical techniques in the testing field. The concepts presented in this overview will be referred to throughout the remainder of this book.

Chapter 4

Reliability

Learning Objectives

When you have completed this chapter, you should be able to:

- Tell what measurement error is and how it interferes with scientific studies in psychology.

- Given that reliability is the ratio of true variability to observed variability, explain what this tells us about a test with a reliability of .30, .60, or .90.

- Describe how test-retest reliability is assessed.

- Explain the difference between test-retest reliability estimates and split-half reliability estimates.

- Discuss how the split-half method underestimates the reliability of a short test and what can be done to correct this problem.

- Know the easiest way to find the average reliability.

- Define coefficient alpha and tell how it differs from other methods of estimating reliability.

- Discuss how high a reliability coefficient must be before you would be willing to say the test is "reliable enough."

- Explain what can be done to increase the reliability of a test.

- Tell how the reliability of behavioral observations is assessed.

In the gymnastics competition at an international meet, a young Romanian woman received an 8.9 for the first portion of her routine. As she reappeared for the second portion, the television commentator said, "The 8.9 rating for her first routine does not accurately represent her ability. This young woman is clearly a 9.5 performer." With this remark, the commentator indicated a discrepancy between the gymnast's score for the first routine and her true ability, a common occurrence in the measurement of many different human abilities. For example, after an examination students sometimes feel that, although they know the material, the actual questions did not allow them to display their real knowledge. And actors sometimes complain that the five-minute sample of their performance in an audition is not an adequate measure of their talents.

Discrepancies between true ability and measurement of ability constitute errors of measurement. In psychological testing, we do not attach a negative connotation to the word *error*. It does not imply that a mistake has been made. Rather we acknowledge that there always will be some inaccuracy or error in our measurements. Our task is to find the magnitude of this error and to develop ways to minimize it. This chapter is about the conceptualization and assessment of measurement error. We call the chapter "Reliability" because tests that are relatively free of measurement error are deemed to be reliable. Tests that have relatively greater measurement error are considered to be unreliable.

I. *History and Theory of Reliability*

A. *Conceptualization of Error*

Students who major in physical science have chosen to study phenomena that are relatively easy to calibrate. Many physical qualities are simple to measure, and the instrumentation used to measure them is quite precise. If you want to measure the width of this book, for example, you need only apply a ruler and record the number of inches or centimeters.

In psychology, we have many problems that make the measurement task more difficult. First, we rarely are interested in measuring simple qualities such as width. Instead, we usually go after more complex traits such as intelligence or aggressiveness. These attributes cannot be seen or touched. Furthermore, there are no rigid yardsticks that can be used to measure such characteristics. We are forced to use "rubber yardsticks," which may stretch to overestimate our measurements on some occasions and shrink to give underestimates on others (Nunnally, 1982). A builder would not be able to get by with a rubber yardstick, and psychologists must assess their measuring instruments to determine how much rubber is in them. A psychologist attempting to understand human behavior on the basis of very unreliable tests is like a carpenter trying to build a house with a rubber measuring tape that never records the same length for the same piece of board.

As you will learn from this chapter, the theory of measurement error is very well developed within psychology. As a result, we are very sophisticated about the assessment of reliability and we are concerned that our measurements be dependable. This is not to say that measurement error is unique to psychology. In fact, serious measurement error is known to occur in most physical, social, and biological sciences. For example, measures of the gross national product (economics) and blood pressure (medicine) are known to be less reliable than well-constructed psychological tests. However, the concern with reliability has been a particular obsession for psychologists. This is evidence of the advanced scientific status of psychology.

B. *Spearman's Early Studies*

Psychology owes its advanced development of reliability assessment to the early work of British psychologist Charles Spearman. The basic notion of sampling error was introduced almost 250 years ago (DeMoivre, 1733), and the product moment correlation (see Chapter 3) was developed by Karl Pearson and published in 1896 (Pearson, 1896). Reliability theory puts these two concepts together in the context of measurement. Spearman, who was a contemporary of Pearson, actually worked out most of the basics of contemporary reliability theory and published his work in a 1904 article entitled "The Proof and Measurement of Association Between Two Things." Because the *British Journal of Psychology* did not begin until 1907, Spearman was forced to publish his work in the *American Journal of Psychology*. Spearman's work was absorbed quickly in the United States. The article was published in the January issue and came to the attention of measurement pioneer Edward L. Thorndike, who that very year was writing the first edition of *An Introduction to the Theory of Mental and Social Measurements* (1904).

Thorndike's book, though an early 20th-century work, is remarkably sophisticated, even by contemporary standards. Since 1904, many developments on both sides of the Atlantic Ocean have led to further refinements in the assessment of reliability. Most important among these is a 1937 article by G. F. Kuder and M. W. Richardson, in which several new reliability coefficients were introduced. Later L. J. Cronbach and his colleagues (Cronbach et al., 1972; Cronbach, 1989) made a major advance by developing methods for evaluating many sources of error in behavioral research. Reliability theory continues to be developed. In recent years, sophisticated mathematical models have been developed to quantify "latent" variables based on multiple measures (Bentler, 1990, 1991).

C. *Basics of Test Score Theory*

Classical test score theory assumes that each person has a true score that would be obtained if there were no errors in measurement. However, because our measuring instruments are imperfect, the score we observe for each person may differ from the person's true ability or characteristic. The difference between the **true score** and the score we observe results from **measurement error.** In symbolic representation, we can say that the observed score (*X*) has two components; a true score (*T*) and an error component (*E*):

$$X \quad = \quad T \quad + \quad E$$

$$\downarrow \qquad\quad \downarrow \qquad\quad \downarrow$$

Observed   True   Error
score   score

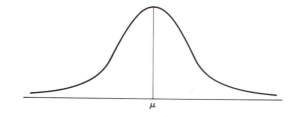

Figure 4-1
Distribution of observed scores for repeated testing of the same person. The mean of the distribution is the estimated true score, and the dispersion represents the distribution of random errors.

Or we can say that the difference between the score we obtain and the score we are really interested in is equal to the error of measurement:

$$X - T = E$$

A major assumption in classical test theory is that errors of measurement are random. Although systematic errors are acknowledged in most measurement problems, they are less likely to force an investigator to make the wrong conclusions. A carpenter who always misreads a tape measure by 2 inches (or makes a systematic error of 2 inches) would still be able to cut boards to be the same length. Using the rubber-yardstick analogy, we would say that this carpenter works with a ruler that is always stretched to be 2 inches too long. Classical test theory deals with rubber-yardstick problems in which the ruler stretches and contracts in a random way.

Using a rubber yardstick, we would not get the same score on each measurement. Instead, we would get a distribution of scores like that shown in Figure 4-1. Each observed score in the distribution is made up of two components: a true score component (T) and an error component (E). Basic sampling theory tells us that the distribution of random errors is bell shaped. Thus, the center of the distribution should represent the true score, and the dispersion around the mean of the distribution should display the distribution of sampling errors. This tells us that any one application of the rubber yardstick may or may not tell us the true score, but through repeated applications, we can estimate the true score by finding the mean of the observations.

Figure 4-2 shows three different distributions. In the left distribution, there is a great dispersion around the true score. In this case, you might not want to depend on a single observation because it might be quite far from the true score. The right distribution in Figure 4-2 displays a situation in which the dispersion around the true score is very small. In this case, most of the observa-

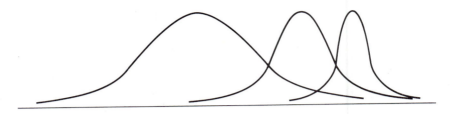

Figure 4-2
Three distributions of observed scores. The left distribution is the one in which the error is the greatest, and the right distribution has the least error.

tions actually are very close to the true score, and it might be more accurate to draw conclusions on the basis of fewer observations.

The dispersions or distributions around the true score in Figures 4-1 and 4-2 tell us how much error there is in the measure. Classical test theory assumes that the true score for an individual will not change with repeated applications of the same test. Because of random error, however, repeated applications of the same test can produce different scores. Random error is responsible for the distribution of scores shown in Figures 4-1 and 4-2. Theoretically, the standard deviation of the distribution of errors for each person tells us about the magnitude of measurement error. Although this theory deals with the distribution of errors for only a single person, we usually assume that the distribution of random errors will be the same for all persons. Thus, classical test theory uses the standard deviation of errors as the basic measure of error. Usually we call this the **standard error of measurement** and write it symbolically as:

$$\sigma_{meas}$$

The rubber-yardstick analogy may be useful in helping you understand this concept. Suppose you have a table that is 30 inches high. If you measured the height of the table using a steel yardstick, you probably would always find it to be the same height: 30 inches. However, now you try to measure the table with the rubber yardstick. The first time you try, the stick has stretched and you record 28 inches. The next time, you discover the stick has shrunk, and it gives you 32 inches for the height of the table. Now we are in trouble because repeated applications of the yardstick do not always give us the same information about the height of the table.

There is one way out of this situation. If we assume that the yardstick stretches and shrinks in a random fashion, then we can say that the distribution of scores given by the yardstick will be normal. Most scores will be close to the actual or true score, and we would expect scores that are greatly different from the true score to occur less frequently. Thus, it would be rare to observe a score as low as 5 inches or as high as 53 inches. The mean of the distribution of scores from repeated applications of the rubber yardstick would be an estimate of the true height of the table. The standard deviation would be the standard error of measurement. Remember from Chapter 3 that the standard deviation tells us something about the average deviation around the mean. The standard error of measurement tells us, on the average, how much a score varies from the true score. In practice, the standard deviation of the observed score and the reliability of the test are used to estimate the standard error of measurement. We will return to this concept after reviewing methods for estimating reliability.

II. *Models of Reliability*

Federal government guidelines require that a test be reliable before it can be used to make employment decisions. This is a very wise procedure, and in this section we hope to justify the need for high standards of reliability. Most reliability coefficients are correlations; however, it is sometimes more useful to define reliability as its mathematically equivalent ratio. It can be shown that the reliability coefficient is the ratio of the variance of the true scores on a test to the variance of the observed scores:

$$R = \frac{\sigma_T^2}{\sigma_X^2}$$

where R = the theoretical reliability of the test

σ_T^2 = the variance of the true scores

σ_X^2 = the variance of the observed scores

We have used the Greek σ^2 instead of S^2 to symbolize the variance because the equation describes theoretical values in a population rather than those actually obtained from a sample. The ratio of true score variance to observed score variance can be thought of as a percentage. In this case, it is the percentage of the observed variation (σ_X^2) that is attributable to variation in the true score. If we subtract this ratio from 1.0, we will have the percentage of variation attributable to random error.

Consider the situation in which the reliability is estimated to be .60. This tells us that 60% of the variation is associated with true variation among people who took the test. The remaining 40% of the variation is random. Suppose you are given a test that will be used to select people for a particular job and the reliability of the test is .40. When the employer gets the test back and begins comparing applicants, 40% of the variation or difference among the people will be explained by real differences among people, and 60% must be ascribed to random or chance factors. Now you can see why the government needs to insist on high standards of reliability.

A. *Sources of Error*

There may be many reasons why an observed score is different from a true score. There may be situational factors such as loud noises in the room while the test is being administered. The room may be too hot, or it may be too cold. The health status of the test takers also could affect test scores. For example, you may know how hard it is to do well on an examination when you have a cold or are just feeling depressed. Reliability assessment deals with these factors indirectly by using time sampling. The test is given at different times, and each test administration is considered an independent sample. The most common use of time sampling is for **test-retest reliability.** With this method the same group of people is tested at two different times with the same test. Then the correlation between these two samples is used as an estimate of reliability. The test-retest method is best suited for time-related sources of error. Time-related error is only one of many sources of error, and reliability theory is better equipped to evaluate errors that are internal to the test. Studies that evaluate internal problems in a test are best understood in terms of a domain sampling model (see Section D). Methods are available to assess each of these types of errors.

B. *Time Sampling: Test-Retest Method*

Test-retest reliability estimates are used to evaluate the error associated with administering a test at two different times. This type of analysis is of value only if we are measuring "traits" or characteristics of individuals that are believed not to change over time. We usually assume that an intelligence test measures a general ability that is not transient. Therefore, if we administer an IQ test at two points in time and get different scores, it might be concluded that the lack of correspondence is due to random measurement error. Usually we do not assume that a person got smarter or less so.

Some tests might not be appropriate for test-retest evaluation because they measure some characteristic that is constantly changing. In Chapter 16, we will discuss the Rorschach inkblot test and note that its value seems to be to tell the clinician how the client is functioning at a particular time. Thus, differences between Rorschach scores at two times could reflect one of two things: (1) there may have been a change in the true score being measured or (2) there may have been measurement error. This tells us that the test-retest method is appropriate only for the measurement of stable traits.

Test-retest reliability is relatively easy to evaluate. All you need to do is administer the same test on two well-specified occasions and then find the correlation between scores from the two administrations. Using the correlational methods presented in Chapter 3, you should have little difficulty calculating the correlation between the two test administrations to estimate test-retest reliability.

As is often the case, you need to consider many other details in addition to the methods for calculating the test-retest reliability coefficient. Being a good consumer and user of the information gained from these mechanical exercises requires some careful thought. One thing you always should consider is the possibility of a carry-over effect. This effect occurs when the first testing session influences scores from the second session. This happens when test takers remember their answers from the first time they took the test. Suppose we ask someone the trivia question "Who were the downstairs neighbors in the old television program 'I Love Lucy'"? Then we ask the same question two days later. Response on the second occasion might be influenced by hearing the question only two days earlier. When there are carry-over effects, the test-retest correlation usually overestimates the true reliability.[1]

A similar problem is what is known as the practice effect. Some skills improve with practice. Thus, when a test is given a second time, test takers score better because they have sharpened their skills by having taken the test the first time. Asking people trivia questions about old television programs might stimulate them to think more about the old shows or may actually give them some of the information. This sometimes happens on tests of manual dexterity: experience taking the test can improve dexterity skills. As a result, scores on the second administration are usually higher than they were on the first administration.

Because of these problems, the time interval between testing sessions must be selected and evaluated carefully. If the two administrations of the test are very close in time, there is a greater risk of carry-over and practice effects. However, as the time between testing sessions increases, many other factors intervene and serve as possible alternative explanations of the differences between scores from the two testing sessions. For example, if a test is given to children at ages 4 and 5 and the scores from the two administrations of the test correlate at .43, we are left with alternative explanations. The low correlation might mean that (1) the test has poor reliability, (2) children change on this characteristic between ages 4 and 5, or (3) some combination of low reliability and change in the children is responsible for the .43 correlation. Most test-retest evaluations do not allow us to choose among these alternatives.

When you find a test-retest correlation in a test manual, you should pay careful attention to the interval between the two testing sessions. A well-evaluated test will have many retest correlations associated with different time intervals between testing sessions. Most often you want to to be assured that the test is reliable over the time interval of your own study. You also should consider what events occur between the original testing and the retest. For

---

[1] Carry-over problems are of concern only when the changes over time are random. In cases where the changes are systematic, carry-over effects do not harm the reliability. An example of a systematic carry-over is when everyone's score improves exactly five points. In this case, no new variability occurs. Random carry-over effects occur when the changes are not predictable from earlier scores.

example, activities such as reading a book, participating in a course of study, or watching a TV documentary can alter the test-retest reliability estimate.

Sometimes poor test-retest correlations do not mean that a test is unreliable; instead, they suggest that the characteristic under study has changed. One of the problems with classical test theory is that it assumes that behavioral dispositions are constant over time. For example, if I am an aggressive person, it is assumed that I will be aggressive all of the time. However, some authors have suggested that important behavioral characteristics, such as motivation, fluctuate over time. In fact, important variables such as health status are expected to vary (Guyatt, Walter & Norman, 1987; Kaplan, 1992). In classical test theory these variations are assumed to be error. However, advanced theories of motivation predict these variations, and test theorists have been challenged to develop models to account for these systematic variations (Atkinson, 1981; McClelland, 1985; Pattishall, 1992).

C. *Error Associated with the Use of Particular Items*

Another concern in building a reliable test is that the test scores not represent any one particular set of items. If you are making a test for some particular characteristic, you might choose many different items to represent this construct. For example, if you are developing a test to determine spelling ability, many different words could be chosen for inclusion in the spelling test. One form of reliability analysis is to determine the error variance attributable to the selection of one particular set of items. Parallel test forms reliability is used for this purpose.

Parallel forms reliability is used to compare two equivalent forms of a test. Two forms of a test are constructed according to the same rules, but the two forms have different items. The term *parallel forms* is used because the tests are constructed in the same way and should measure the same attribute. The two forms are parallel because they use different items; however, the rules used to select items of a particular difficulty level are the same.

When two forms of the test are available, it is possible to compare performance on one form versus the other. Some textbooks refer to this process as *equivalent forms reliability*, whereas others call it simply *parallel forms.* Sometimes the two forms are administered to the same group of people on the same day. The Pearson product moment correlation coefficient (see Chapter 3) is used as an estimate of the reliability. When both forms of the test are given on the same day, the only sources of variation are random error and the difference between the forms of the test. (The order of administration is usually counterbalanced to avoid practice effects.) Sometimes the two forms of the test are given at different times. In this case, error associated with time sampling is also included in the estimate of reliability.

The use of two parallel or equivalent forms of a test provides one of the most rigorous assessments of reliability commonly in use. Unfortunately, the use of parallel forms occurs in practice less often than is desirable. Often test developers find it burdensome to develop two forms of the same test, and practical constraints make it difficult to retest the same group of individuals on a second occasion. Instead, many test developers prefer to estimate the reliability based on a single form of the same test.

D. *The Domain Sampling Model*

The domain sampling model considers the problems of using a limited number of items to represent some larger domain. For example, suppose we want to evaluate your spelling ability. The best technique would be to systematically go through an English dictionary, have you spell each word, and determine the percentage you spell correctly. However, it is unlikely that you would have time available for this. Instead, we need to find a way to evaluate your spelling without having you spell every word. To accomplish this evaluation, we use a sample of words. Remember that what we are really attempting to evaluate is how well you can spell, which would be determined by your percentage correct if you had been given all the words in the English language. This percentage would be your "true score." Our task in reliability analysis is to estimate how much error we will make by using the score from the shorter test as an estimate of your true ability.

Theoretically, this model conceptualizes reliability as the ratio of the variance of the observed score on the shorter test and the variance of the long-run true score. The measurement we consider in the domain sampling model is the error introduced by using a sample of items (or words in this case) rather than the entire domain.[2] As the sample gets larger, it will be more and more representative of the domain. As a result, the greater the number of items, the higher the reliability. We will show you exactly how a larger number of items increases reliability in a later section of this chapter.

When tests are constructed, each item is a sample of the ability or behavior under study. Long tests have many such samples, and short tests have very few. However, we assume that each item is an equal representation of the studied ability.

Reliability can be estimated from the correlation of the observed test score with the true score.[3] This would be easy to find if we could obtain true scores. However, finding the true scores is not practical and is rarely possible. In the example presented above, finding the true score would involve testing people on all of the words in the English language.

---

[2] The term *domain* is used to describe a very large collection of items. Some authors prefer the term *universe* or *population* to describe the same concept (Nunnally, 1978).

[3] As Allen and Yen (1979) point out, there are at least six alternative interpretations of the reliability coefficient. The interpretation we offer here is the one most commonly used.

Because true scores are not available, our only alternative is to estimate what they would be. Under the assumption that items are randomly drawn from a given domain, each test or group of items should yield an unbiased estimate of the true score. Because of sampling error, however, different random samples of items might give different estimates of the true score. The distribution of these estimates should be random and normally distributed. If we create many tests by sampling from the same domain, we should get a normal distribution of unbiased estimates of the true score. In order to estimate reliability, we can create many randomly parallel tests by drawing repeated random samples of items from the same domain. In the spelling test example, we would draw several different lists of words randomly from the dictionary and consider each of these samples to be an unbiased test of spelling ability. Then we would find the correlation between each of these tests with all of the other tests. The correlations then would be averaged.[4]

In practice we rarely develop randomly parallel tests because test items are seldom selected at random. In fact, the items usually are selected for a particular purpose. However, the same general strategy is often used to select items for the different parallel forms of the test. Selecting the items by this nonrandom process does not greatly affect estimates of reliability. Another problem is that it is uncommon in practice to have more than two forms of a test. Instead of evaluating the average correlation between a test and all of its randomly parallel forms, we typically evaluate the correlation between the test and the one other form we have created. As a result, the estimates of reliability used in practice may be less dependable than desired.

TECHNICAL BOX 4-1

The Unbiased Estimate of Reliability

Test theorists have demonstrated mathematically that an unbiased estimate of the reliability of a test is given by the square root of the average correlation between a test and all other randomly parallel tests from the domain. Symbolically,

$$r_{1t} = \sqrt{\bar{r}_{1j}}$$

where 1 = scores on test 1

t = the true score for the ability of interest

r_{1j} = the average correlation between test 1 and all other randomly parallel tests

As we learned in Chapter 3, product moment correlation coefficients always take on values between -1 and 1. When we are estimating reliability, the correlation always

---

[4] Technically, it is inappropriate to average correlation coefficients. The appropriate method is to use Fisher's r to Z' transformation to convert the correlations into approximate Z scores. Then the Z' scores are averaged, and the mean Z' is transformed back into a correlation (Silver & Dunlap, 1987).

will be positive. When a number is less than 1.0, its square root always will be larger than itself. Thus, the correlation between two randomly parallel tests will be smaller than the estimated correlation between one of the tests and the true score according to the formula. For example, if the correlation between two randomly parallel tests is .64, the estimated reliability of the test will be $\sqrt{.64} = .80$. This is built into the estimation of reliability because it would be impossible for a test to correlate more highly with any other test than it would correlate with its own true score. Thus, the correlation between two randomly parallel tests would be expected to be less than the correlation of either test with the true score.

In practice we do not always have two forms of a test. More often we are stuck with only one test form, and we must estimate the reliability for this single group of items. There are different methods for assessing the different sources of variation within a single test. One method is to evaluate the internal consistency of the test by dividing it into subcomponents. Another method is to examine the error variance that might be introduced by readministering the test at different points in time. This is known as the *test-retest method* (see section B above).

Internal consistency: split-half method. In **split-half reliability,** a test is given and divided into halves that are scored separately. We then compare the results of one half of the test with the results of the other. The two halves of the test can be created in a variety of ways. If the test is long, the best method is to randomly divide the items into two halves. However, for ease in computing scores for the different halves, some people prefer to calculate a score for the first half of the items and another score for the second half. Although it is convenient, this method can cause problems when items on the second half of the test are more difficult than items on the first half. If the items get progressively more difficult, you might be better advised to use the odd-even system, whereby a subscore is obtained for the odd-numbered items in the test and another subscore is found for the even-numbered items.

To estimate the reliability of the test, we could find the correlation between the two halves. However, this would be an underestimate because each subtest is only half as long as the full test. As we discussed earlier, test scores gain reliability as the number of items increases. An estimate of reliability based on two half-tests would be deflated because each half would be less reliable than the whole test. The correlation between the two halves of the test would be a reasonable estimate of the reliability of half of the test. In order to correct for half-length, the Spearman-Brown formula can be applied. It allows you to estimate what the correlation between the two halves would have been if each half had been the length of the whole test:

$$R = \frac{2r}{1 + r}$$

see p127

where R is the estimated correlation between the two halves of the test if each had had the total number of items, and r is the correlation between the two halves of the test.[5] For example, when the CES-D is divided into two equal parts, the correlation between the two halves of the test (for medical students) is .78. According to the formula, the estimated reliability would be

$$R = \frac{2(.78)}{1 + .78} = \frac{1.56}{1.78} = .876$$

The effect of using the Spearman-Brown formula is to increase the estimate of reliability. The left-hand column in Table 4-1 shows several estimates of reliability that are not corrected using the Spearman-Brown procedure. The middle column shows the same values after they have been corrected. The right-hand column shows the amount of change the correction introduces. As you can see, the Spearman-Brown procedure has a substantial effect, particularly in the middle ranges of the scale.

There are some circumstances in which the Spearman-Brown correction is not advisable. One of these is when the two halves of the test have unequal variances. When the halves do not appear to be equivalent, L. J. Cronbach's (1951) coefficient alpha (α) can be used. The alpha coefficient, which is a general reliability coefficient, provides the lowest estimate of reliability that can be expected. If alpha is very high, you might assume that the reliability of the test is acceptable. This means that the lowest boundary of reliability is still very high; the reliability will not drop below alpha. An alpha level that is low, on the other hand, gives you less information. Because the alpha coefficient marks only the lower bound for the reliability, the actual reliability may still be high. Thus, if the variances for the two halves of the test are unequal, coefficient alpha can be used to confirm that a test has substantial reliability; however, it cannot tell us that a test is unreliable. (Technical Box 4-2 provides an example.) The formula for coefficient alpha is

$$\alpha = \frac{2[\sigma_x^2 - (\sigma_{y1}^2 \sigma_{y2}^2)]}{\sigma_x^2}$$

where α = the coefficient alpha for estimating split-half reliability

σ_x^2 = the variance for scores on the whole test

$\sigma_{y1}^2, \sigma_{y2}^2$ = the variances for the two separate halves of the test

When the variances for the two halves of the test are equal, the Spearman-Brown coefficient and coefficient alpha give the same results. Under other specific circumstances, both procedures may underestimate the true reliability (see Allen & Yen, 1979).

---

[5] There are different forms of the estimation formula, as will be shown later in the chapter.

Table 4-1

Estimates of
Split-Half
Reliability Before
and After
Correction for
Half-Length
Using the
Spearman-Brown
Formula

Before Correction	After Correction	Amount of Change
.05	.09	.04
.15	.26	.11
.25	.40	.15
.35	.52	.17
.45	.62	.17
.55	.71	.16
.65	.79	.14
.75	.86	.11
.85	.92	.07
.95	.97	.02

TECHNICAL BOX 4-2

Using Coefficient Alpha to Estimate Split-Half Reliability When the Variances for the Two Halves of the Test Are Unequal

Formula: $R = \dfrac{2[S_x^2 - (S_{y1}^2 + S_{y2}^2)]}{S_x^2}$

Data: $S_x^2 = 11.5$
$S_{y1}^2 = 4.5$
$S_{y2}^2 = 3.2$

Steps

1. Find the variance for the whole test.

   $S_x^2 = 11.5$

2. Add together the variances for the two halves of the test.

   $S_{y1}^2 = 4.5$ $S_{y2}^2 = 3.2$ $4.5 + 3.2 = 7.7$

3. Find $S_x^2 - (S_{y1}^2 + S_{y2}^2)$ by subtracting the result of Step 2 from that of Step 1.

   $11.5 = 7.7 = 3.8$

4. Find $2[S_x^2 - (S_{y1}^2 - S_{y2}^2)]$ by multiplying the result of Step 3 times 2.

   $2(3.8) = 7.6$

5. Find alpha by dividing the results of Step 4 by Step 1.

   $\dfrac{7.6}{11.5} = .66$

General measures of internal consistency. In addition to the split-half technique, there are many other methods for estimating the internal consistency of a test. Many years ago, G. F. Kuder and M. W. Richardson (1937) greatly advanced reliability assessment by developing methods for evaluating reliability within a single administration of a test. Their approach does not depend on some arbitrary splitting of the test into halves.

Decisions about how to split tests into halves cause many potential problems for split-half reliability. The two halves of the test may have different variances. The split-half method also requires that each half of the test be scored separately, and this can create additional work. The Kuder-Richardson technique avoids these problems because it is a general method that simultaneously considers all of the possible ways of splitting the items.

KR$_{20}$. The formula for calculating the reliability of a test in which the items are dichotomous, scored 0 or 1 (usually for right or wrong), is known as the **Kuder-Richardson 20,** or *KR*$_{20}$ or *KR* 20. The formula came to be labeled this way because it was the 20th formula presented in the famous article by Kuder and Richardson (the *K* and *R* are obtained from the authors' initials). The formula is

$$KR_{20} = R = \frac{N}{N-1}\left(\frac{S^2 - \Sigma pq}{S^2}\right)$$

where KR_{20} = the reliability estimate (R)

N = the number of items on the test

S^2 = the variance of the total test score

p = the proportion of people getting each item correct (this is found separately for each individual item)

q = the proportion of people getting each item incorrect. For each item, q equals $1 - p$.

Σpq = the sum of the products of p times q for each item on the test

Although we will not go through the mathematical derivations of the KR_{20}, studying the components of the formula may give you a better understanding of how it works. First, you will recognize the term S^2 from Chapter 2. This is the variance of the test scores. The variance term appears twice in the formula: once on the top of the right portion in the equation and once on the bottom of the right portion. The other term in the right portion is Σpq. This is the sum of the product of the proportion of people passing each item times the proportion of people failing each individual item. It can be shown that the product pq is the variance for an individual item. Thus Σpq is the sum of the individual item variances.

Now let's think about conditions that would make the term on the right side of the equation either large or small. First, consider the situation in which the variance (S^2) is equal to the sum of the variances of the individual items.

Symbolically, this would be $S^2 = \Sigma pq$. In this case, the right-hand term in the formula would be 0 and, as a result, the estimate of reliability would be 0. This tell us that in order to have nonzero reliability, the variance for the total test score must be greater than the sum of the variances for the individual items. This will happen only when the items are measuring the same thing.

The only situation that will make the sum of the item variance less than the total test score variance is when there is covariance between the items. Covariance occurs when the items are correlated with one another. The greater the covariance, the smaller the Σpq term will be. When the items covary, they can be assumed to measure the same general trait, and the reliability for the test will be high. As Σpq approaches 0, the right side of the equation approaches 1.0. The other factor in the formula is an adjustment for the number of items in the test. This will allow the estimate of reliability to be higher for longer tests. (Technical Box 4-3 provides an example.)

In addition to the KR_{20}, Kuder and Richardson presented a special case of the reliability formula that does not require the calculation of the p's and q's for every item. Instead, an approximation of the sum of the pq products is used, and this approximation is the mean test score. This was the next formula presented in the famous Kuder-Richardson article and was labeled Formula 21. Thus, it has become known as the KR_{21}. The KR_{21} procedure rests on several important assumptions. The most important is that all of the items are of equal difficulty, or that the average difficulty level is 50%. Difficulty is defined as the percentage of test takers who pass the item. In practice, these assumptions are rarely met, and it is usually found that KR_{21} formula underestimates the split-half reliability:

$$KR_{21} = \frac{N}{N-1}\left[1 - \frac{\overline{X}\left(1 - \frac{\overline{X}}{N}\right)}{S^2}\right]$$

where all terms are as previously defined.

TECHNICAL BOX 4-3

The Calculation of Reliability Using KR₂₀

$$\textbf{Formula:} \quad KR_{20} = \frac{N}{N-1}\left(\frac{S^2 - \Sigma pq}{S^2}\right)$$

Data: NS = number of test takers = 50

N = number of items = 6

S^2 = variance (Step 6) = 2.8

(continued)

(continued)

Item	Number of Test Takers Responding Correctly	p (from Step 2)	q (from Step 3)	pq (from Step 4)
1	12	.24	.76	.18
2	41	.82	.18	.15
3	18	.36	.64	.23
4	29	.58	.42	.24
5	30	.60	.40	.24
6	47	.94	.06	.06

$\Sigma pq = 1.10$
(from Step 5)

Steps

1. Determine the number of test takers NS.

   $NS = 50$

2. Find p by dividing the number of people responding correctly to each item by the number of people taking the test (Step 1). This is the level of difficulty.

   $\dfrac{12}{50} = .24 \qquad \dfrac{41}{50} = .82 \qquad \cdots$

3. Find q for each item by subtracting p (the result of Step 2) from 1.0. This gives the proportion responding incorrectly to each item.

   $1.0 - .24 = .76 \qquad 1.0 - .82 = .18 \qquad \cdots$

4. Find pq for each item by multiplying the results of Steps 2 and 3.

   $(.24)(.76) = .18 \qquad (.82)(.18) = .15 \qquad \cdots$

5. Find Σpq by summing the results of Step 4 over the N items.

   $.18 + .15 + .23 + .24 + .24 + .06 = 1.1$

6. Find S^2, which is the variance for the test sources. To do this you need the scores for each individual in the group. The formula for the variance is

   $$S^2 = \frac{\Sigma X^2 - \left[\dfrac{(\Sigma X)^2}{NS}\right]}{NS - 1}$$

   In this example $S^2 = 2.8$.

7. Find $S^2 - \Sigma pq$ by subtracting the results of Step 5 from Step 6.

   $2.8 - 1.1 = 1.7$

8. Find $(S^2 - \Sigma pq)/S^2$ by dividing the results of Step 7 by Step 6.

   $\dfrac{1.7}{2.8} = .607$

9. Find N or the number of items.

$$N = 6$$

10. Find $N/(N - 1)$ by dividing the results of Step 9 by Step 9 minus 1.

$$\frac{6}{5} = 1.2$$

11. Find KR_{20} by multiplying the results of Steps 8 and 9.

$$(1.2)(.607) = .73$$

Alpha. Mathematical proofs have demonstrated that the KR_{20} formula gives the same estimate of reliability that would be obtained if you took the mean of the split-half reliability estimates obtained by dividing the test in all possible ways (Cronbach, 1951). You can see that the Kuder-Richardson procedure is very general and is usually more valuable than a split-half estimate of internal consistency. However, there are still cases in which the KR_{20} formula is not appropriate for evaluating internal consistency. These situations occur when a test has items that are not scored as "right" or "wrong." The KR_{20} formula requires that you find the proportion of people who got each item "correct."

There are many types of tests for which there are no right or wrong answers. This is typically the case for personality and attitude scales. For example, on an attitude questionnaire, you might be presented with a statement such as "I believe extramarital sexual intercourse is immoral." You must indicate whether you strongly disagree, disagree, are neutral, agree, or strongly agree. None of these choices is incorrect, and none is correct. Rather, your response indicates where you stand on the continuum between agreement and disagreement. In order to extend the Kuder-Richardson method for use with this sort of item, Cronbach developed a formula that could be used to estimate the internal consistency of tests where the items are not scored as 0 or 1 (right or wrong). In doing so, Cronbach developed a more general reliability estimate, which he called **coefficient alpha,** or α. The formula for coefficient alpha is[6]

$$R = \alpha = \left(\frac{N}{N - 1} \right) \left(\frac{S^2 - \Sigma S_i^2}{S^2} \right)$$

As you may notice, this looks very similar to the KR_{20} formula. The only difference is that Σpq has been replaced by ΣS_i^2. This new term, S_i^2, is for the

---

[6] Although this formula appears different from the formula for coefficient alpha from the section "Internal consistency: split-half method," the equations are mathematically equivalent.

variance of the individual items. The summation sign, Σ, informs us that we are to sum the individual item variances. S^2 is for the variance of the total test score. The only real difference is the way the variance of the items is expressed. Actually coefficient alpha is a more general reliability coefficient than KR_{20} because S_i^2 can describe the variance of items whether or not they are in a right/ wrong format. Thus, coefficient alpha is the most general case of internal consistency reliability.

All the measures of internal consistency evaluate the extent to which the different items on a test measure the same ability or trait. They will all give low estimates of reliability if the test is designed to measure several traits. Using the domain sampling model, we define a domain that represents a single trait or characteristic, and each item is an individual sample of this general characteristic. When the items do not measure the same characteristic, the test will not be internally consistent.

One popular method for dealing with the situation in which a test apparently measures several different characteristics is to perform factor analysis (see Chapter 3). This can be used to divide the items into subgroups, each internally consistent; however, the subgroups of items will not be related to one another. Factor analysis can help a test constructor build a test that has submeasures for several different traits. When factor analysis is used correctly, these subtests will be internally consistent (highly reliable) and independent of one another. For example, factor analysis might be used to divide a group of items on interpersonal communication into two subgroups. One might be assertiveness items, and the other subgroup might be aggressiveness items. The reliability of the aggressiveness and the assertiveness subscales might be quite high. However, the correlation between assertiveness and aggressiveness scores would be quite low. The nature of the factor analysis method ensures these characteristics. Thus, factor analysis is of great value in the process of test construction.

E. *Reliability of a Difference Score*

There are some applications of psychological testing when you will need to calculate a difference score, which is created by subtracting one test score from another. This might be the difference between performance at two points in time—for example, when you test a group of children before and after they have experienced a special training program. Or it may be the difference between measures of two different abilities. This might occur when you want to know whether a child is doing better in reading than in math. Whenever comparisons between two different attributes are being made (such as reading versus math), it is necessary to make the comparison in Z, or standardized, units (see Chapter 2).

Difference scores create a host of problems that make them more difficult to work with than single scores. In order to understand the problems, we must refer back to the definition of an observed score as composed of both true score (T) and error (E). In a difference score, the E, or error portion, is expected to be larger because it absorbs error from both of the scores used to create the difference score. Furthermore, the T, or true score portion, might be expected to be smaller because whatever is common to both measures is canceled out when the difference score is created. As a result of these two factors, the reliability of a difference score is expected to be lower than the reliability of either score on which it is based. If two tests measure exactly the same trait, the score representing the difference between them is expected to have a reliability of 0.

As was previously mentioned, it is most convenient to find difference scores by first creating Z scores for each measure and then finding the difference between them (score 2 $-$ score 1). The reliability of scores that represent the difference between two standard scores (or Z scores) is given by the formula

$$R = \frac{\frac{1}{2}(r_{11} + r_{22}) - r_{12}}{1 - r_{12}}$$

where r_{11} = the reliability of the first measure

r_{22} = the reliability of the second measure

r_{12} = the correlation between the first and the second measures

Using this formula, you can calculate the reliability of a difference score for any two tests for which the reliabilities and the correlation between them are known. For example, suppose that the correlation between two measures is .70 and the reliabilities of the two measures are .90 and .70, respectively. The reliability of the difference between these two measures is

$$R = \frac{\frac{1}{2}(.90 + .70) - .70}{1 - .70}$$

$$= \frac{.10}{.30}$$

$$= .33$$

As this example demonstrates, the reliability of the difference score between tests with reliabilities as high as .90 and .70 is only .33. The situation in which the reliability of the difference score is lower than the average reliabilities of the two initial measures is not unusual. In fact, it occurs in all cases except when the correlation between the two tests is 0.

The low reliability of a difference score should be a matter of concern to the practicing psychologist and education researcher. Because of their poor reliabilities, difference scores cannot be depended on for interpreting patterns.

For example, it may be difficult to draw the conclusion that a patient is more depressed than schizophrenic on the basis of an MMPI (see Chapter 13) profile that shows a lower depression than schizophrenia score. Any differences between these two scales must be interpreted cautiously because the reliability of the score that represents the difference between the two scales can be expected to be low. The difficulties associated with using difference scores have been well studied. In a widely cited article, L. J. Cronbach and L. Furby (1970) demonstrated that there are many pitfalls associated with using difference scores to measure change. For example, it appears impossible to make a meaningful interpretation of the difference between scores on the same children that are taken at the beginning and at the end of a school year. Measuring the "change" that occurred during that school year requires the use of sophisticated experimental designs in which children are randomly assigned to experimental and control conditions.

Although reliability is often difficult to calculate, computer programs that do much of the work are now available. Technical Box 4-4 describes one such program.

TECHNICAL BOX 4-4

Reliability is difficult to calculate by hand. However, in the modern era, reliability calculations can be performed very efficiently with standardized computer programs. One of the most common statistical programs for calculating reliability is part of the Statistical Package for the Social Sciences (SPSS, 1990). The SPSS program calculates several different types of reliability. A summary of an analysis performed by SPSS is given here. The data for this analysis come from the CES-D example. However, instead of using the subsample of 20 medical students as in Chapter 3, we used an entire class of 117 medical students. The first column in the table gives the item number. The second column lists the mean of the CES-D if an item was deleted. Unfortunately, the program is unable to make the adjustment for the CES-D in which 20 points are subtracted from each score. This adjustment has no impact on the statistical properties of the CES-D (i.e., it does not affect the correlation with other variables); however, it does affect the mean. The table tells us that if the first item of the CES-D was eliminated, the mean score for the CES-D would be 28.5983. Remember that the CES-D has an adjustment in which 20 points are subtracted, so the mean would be 8.5983. The second column in the table shows that the mean CES-D score is relatively unaffected by the elimination of any particular item. The third column in the table gives the scale variance if the item was deleted. We will not attempt to interpret that in this exercise. The fourth column gives the corrected item-total correlation. This column describes the correlation between any particular item and the total test score minus the item. Notice that the item-test correlation for item 2 is relatively low (.1689). This means that item 2 is a relatively poor item because it is unrelated to the total test score. Item 2 is "I did not feel like eating: my appetite was poor." Item 18, on the other hand, had a high correlation with the total score. Item 18 is "I enjoy life" and it was scored in the reverse direction. This item is conceptually close to the total score of the CES-D.

The column labeled "Squared Multiple Correlation" gives the proportion of variance in each item that can be explained by the other items. For example, about 35% of the variance in item 1 (.3520) can be explained by its relationship to the other items on the scale. For item 20, about 51% of the variance (.5096) can be explained through its associations with other items. These values are obtained by performing a multiple regression analysis in which each item is predicted from the combination of all the other items.

The final column in the table is the alpha for the total test if the particular item was deleted. As the numbers suggest, the alpha for the scale remains approximately the same if any single item is left out.

The computer summary also provides summary statistics for different methods of calculating reliabilities. It gives the alpha coefficient and a more complex standardized item alpha. The program is also capable of calculating different types of reliability. For example, the program was asked to calculate the split-half reliability. The printout shows that the correlation between the two halves of the test is .7807. The Spearman-Brown correction adjusts this reliability to .8768. Another method of split-half reliability that performs the correction automatically is called the Guttman split-half method. This gives a reliability of .8760. The program also calculates the alpha coefficient for the first and the second halves of the tests separately.

R E L I A B I L I T Y   A N A L Y S I S   -   S C A L E   (C E S-D)

ITEM-TOTAL STATISTICS

	SCALE MEAN IF ITEM DELETED*	SCALE VARIANCE IF ITEM DELETED	CORRECTED ITEM-TOTAL CORRELATION	SQUARED MULTIPLE CORRELATION	ALPHA IF ITEM DELETED
1	28.5983	48.3286	.4884	.3520	.8671
2	28.9145	51.9237	.1689	.2528	.8773
3	28.7521	48.0329	.5290	.4813	.8655
4	28.8547	49.0908	.3800	.3736	.8715
5	28.4957	48.9073	.3793	.2736	.8718
6	28.4872	46.1830	.7330	.6876	.8577
7	28.6581	47.9338	.5768	.5180	.8639
8	28.8974	49.2825	.5321	.4468	.8661
9	29.1368	52.3604	.2585	.2270	.8734
10	28.6325	49.4241	.3896	.3216	.8707
11	28.6752	50.4626	.2880	.2533	.8743
12	28.6496	47.6089	.6275	.5927	.8622
13	28.6325	49.4586	.3781	.3367	.8712
14	28.2991	46.5735	.5958	.5930	.8628
15	28.8205	49.7175	.4466	.3494	.8685
16	28.7778	47.7605	.6068	.5635	.8629
17	28.9145	50.8375	.3372	.2737	.8717
18	28.6154	47.5663	.6525	.5671	.8615
19	28.8718	49.5610	.5209	.4631	.8666
20	28.7009	48.1080	.6074	.5096	.8632

(continued)

(continued)

```
Alpha Method

RELIABILITY COEFFICIENTS     20 ITEMS

ALPHA =   .8734           STANDARDIZED ITEM ALPHA =    .8739

Split-Half Method

RELIABILITY COEFFICIENTS     20 ITEMS

CORRELATION BETWEEN FORMS =   .7807    EQUAL LENGTH SPEARMAN-BROWN =      .8768

GUTTMAN SPLIT-HALF =          .8760    UNEQUAL-LENGTH SPEARMAN-BROWN =    .8768

ALPHA FOR PART 1 =            .7424    ALPHA FOR PART 2 =                 .8031

  10 ITEMS IN PART 1                    10 ITEMS IN PART 2


*NOTE--The CES-D uses a correction in which 20 is subtracted from each score.
This correction is not reflected in the computer program.  So, for example, the
mean if item 1 was deleted would be 8.5983, not 28.5983.
```

F. *Reliability of Criterion-Referenced Tests*

Variations of the methods for assessing the reliability of randomly parallel tests have been developed specifically for criterion-referenced tests (Millman, 1979). One procedure requires two equal-length samples of items to be randomly drawn from the same domain (Lord, 1978). There also is a technique that can be used to evaluate the reliability of a criterion-referenced test made up of only one sample of items (Subkoviak, 1980). If you are interested in estimating the reliability of a criterion-referenced test, excellent tables that outline the steps can be found in the article by J. Millman (1979).

III. *Reliability in Behavioral Observation Studies*

Psychologists with behavioral orientations usually prefer not to use psychological tests. Instead, they favor the direct observation of behavior. To measure aggression, for example, they would record the number of times a child hits or kicks another child. Observers would tabulate the number of observable responses in each category. Thus, there would be a score for "hits," another score for "kicks," and so on.

Some people feel that behavioral observation systems are so simple that they are free from psychometric problems. Unfortunately, this is not the case. In practice, behavioral observation systems are frequently unreliable. The unreliability results from discrepancies between true scores and the scores recorded by the observer. For example, there may be a difference between the actual number of times a child hits or kicks and the number of behaviors the observer reports for these categories. There may be many reasons for these discrepancies. For instance, errors commonly occur when an observer misses certain events or when time sampling is done. Because it is sometimes impossible to monitor behavior continuously, it is common to take samples of behavior at certain time intervals. Under these circumstances, sampling error must be considered.

Sources of error introduced by time sampling are similar to those with sampling items from a large domain. When each time sample is thought of as an "item," these problems can be handled using sampling theory and methods such as alpha reliability.

The problem of error associated with different observers, however, presents some unique difficulties. In order to assess these problems, we need to estimate the reliability of the observers. There are at least three different ways this can be done.

The most common method for evaluating the reliability of observers is to record the percentage of times two or more observers agree. Unfortunately, this method is not the best one for at least two reasons. First, percentage agreement does not take into consideration the level of agreement that would be expected by chance alone. For instance, if two observers are recording whether a particular behavior either occurred or did not occur, they would have a 50% likelihood of agreeing by chance alone. Thus, a method for assessing the reliability of judges should include an adjustment for the level of agreement to be expected by chance. Second, percentages are not appropriate for mathematical manipulation. It is not technically appropriate to average percentages. Indexes like standardized, or Z, scores are manipulable and are better suited for the task of reliability assessment.

After reviewing several approaches, D. P. Hartmann (1977) concluded that the kappa statistic is best suited for assessing the level of agreement among several observers. The kappa statistic was introduced by J. Cohen (1960) as a measure of agreement between two judges who each rate a set of objects using nominal scales. The method was extended by J. L. Fleiss (1971) to consider the agreement between any number of observers. The calculation of kappa is beyond the scope of this presentation; interested readers can find the procedures in Fleiss (1971). An approximation of the coefficient for the agreement between two observers is also given by the phi coefficient, which was discussed in Chapter 3.

IV. *Connecting Sources of Error with Reliability Assessment Method*

Table 4-2 relates sources of measurement error to the methods used to assess reliability. Remember that *reliability* is a generic term. Different methods of reliability assessment are used to describe different sources of measurement

Table 4-2
Sources of Measurement Error and Methods of Reliability Assessment

Source of Error	Example	Method	How Assessed
Time sampling	Same test given at two points in time	Test-retest	Correlation between scores obtained on the two occasions
Item sampling	Different items used to assess the same attribute	Alternate forms/ parallel forms	Correlation between equivalent forms of the test that have different items
Internal consistency	Consistency of items within the same test	1. Split-half	1. Corrected correlation between two halves of the test
		2. KR_{20}	2. See Technical Box 4-3
		3. Alpha	3. See Technical Box 4-2
Observer differences	Different observers record the same behavior	Adjusted agreement	Kappa statistic

FOCUSED EXAMPLE 4-1

Summary of Guidelines for Reliability

The American Psychological Association, American Educational Research Association, and National Council on Measurement in Education suggest several standards for reliability.* Some of these standards are summarized as follows:

Primary Standards

1. Reliability estimates should be provided for each score, subscore, or combination of scores.
2. The procedures used in the study from which the reliability estimate was obtained should be described in detail. This should include the

exact numbers of participants and statistical descriptions of these people.
3. The exact statistical methods for obtaining the reliability estimate should be reported.
4. If statistical adjustments are made in the calculation of a reliability coefficient, both the adjusted and unadjusted coefficients should be reported.
5. When alternate forms of a test are given to the same sample of individuals on two separate occasions, the order of administration and the interval between test administrations should be reported. In addition, the rationale for choosing that interval should be described. Means and standard deviations for both forms should be reported, along with standard errors of measurement and the estimate of alternative forms of reliability.
6. Estimates of the internal consistency of a test

---

* Standards not applicable to basic psychometrics are not listed here.

error. Each of these has a different meaning. As suggested in Table 4-2, one source of measurement error is time sampling. The same test given at different points in time may produce different scores, even if it is given to the same test takers. This source of error is typically assessed using the test-retest method. Another source of error is item sampling. The same construct or attribute may be assessed using a wide pool of items. For example, no one item is used to assess human intelligence. Yet, different items that are used to measure this general construct may not always give the same reflection of the true ability. This sort of error is assessed using alternate forms or parallel forms reliability. Typically, the correlation between two forms of a test are created by randomly sampling a large pool of items believed to assess a particular construct is used as an estimate of this type of reliability.

The internal consistency of a test refers to the intercorrelations among items within the same test. If the test is designed to measure a single construct and all items are equally good candidates to measure that attribute, then there should be a high correspondence between the items. This internal consistency is evaluated using split-half reliability, the KR_{20} method, or coefficient alpha. Another source of measurement error occurs when different observers record the same behavior. Even though they have the same instructions, different

obtained with measures such as KR_{20} or alpha should not be interpreted as substitutes for alternative form reliability or estimates of stability of a measure over the course of time.

7. Some measures yield inflated estimates of reliability. For example, split-half coefficients used on speeded tests often overestimate the reliability of a test. These procedures should not be used on speeded tests.

8. In some tests, the judgmental process may affect the scores—for example, when judges rate the performance of a worker. When these judgments can affect a score, the interrater or interobserver agreement should be reported.

Conditional and Secondary Standards

9. When it is expected that different populations may have different reliabilities, separate reliability estimates should be reported for each of these groups (for example, if it is expected that the reliability would differ between men and women, blacks and whites, and so on). A reliability coefficient for each separate group should be given.

10. When tests are used in a decision process and there is a cut score, or a score at which those below fail or are not selected, the standard error of measurement at that critical score should be reported.

11. When a test is used to divide people into two groups (pass/fail or accept/reject), the percentage of test takers who are classified in the same way on two different occasions or with alternate forms of the test should be reported.

Adapted from American Educational Research Association et al. (1985, pp. 13–18).

judges observing the same event may record different numbers. This source of error is evaluated using an adjusted index of agreement, such as the kappa statistic.

As you can see, the term *reliability* refers to several different methods used to assess different sources of error. Sometimes different sources of error occur in the same situation. For example, there may be error associated with item sampling and additional error associated with time sampling. The wise consumer of testing materials must always take into consideration the potential sources of error when evaluating reliability information. A joint committee of the American Education Research Association, the American Psychological Association, and the National Council on Measurement in Education (1985) proposed standards for manuals describing educational or psychological tests. A summary of the standards for the reporting of information about reliability is presented in Focused Example 4-1.

V. *Using Reliability Information*

Now that you have learned about reliability theory and methods for estimating reliability, it will be worthwhile to review some practical aspects of reliability assessment. Different levels of reliability are required for different situations.

A. *Standard Errors of Measurement and the Rubber Yardstick*

Earlier in this chapter, we introduced the theoretical concept of the standard error of measurement using as an analogy the rubber yardstick. Remember that psychologists working with unreliable tests are like carpenters working with rubber yardsticks that stretch or contract and misrepresent the true length of a board. However, not all of these rubber yardsticks are equally inaccurate. Similarly, not all psychological tests are equally inaccurate. The standard error of measurement allows us to estimate the degree to which a test provides inaccurate readings; that is, it tells us how much "rubber" there is in our measurement. The larger the standard error of measurement, the less certain we can be about the accuracy with which an attribute is measured. Conversely, small standard errors of measurement tell us that an individual score is probably close to the measured value. Some textbooks refer to the standard error of measurement as the standard error of a score. In order to calculate the standard error of measurement, we need to use the standard deviation and the reliability coefficient. The formula for this calculation is

$$S_m = S \sqrt{1 - R}$$

where S_m = the standard error for the measurement

S = the standard deviation of the scores

R = the reliability coefficient

For example, suppose that an IQ test has a mean for a particular sample of 100, with a standard deviation of 14. You are particularly interested in a person with a score of 106. The reliability of the test is .89. Plugging these values into the formula, we find

$$S_m = 14 \sqrt{1 - .89} = 4.64$$

Standard errors of measurement are used to create confidence intervals around specific observed scores. You may want to review the concept of a confidence interval from your introductory statistics textbook. Briefly, we never know whether an observed score is the "true" score. However, we can form intervals around an observed score and use statistical procedures to estimate the probability that the true score falls within a certain interval. Common intervals used in testing are the 68% interval, the 95% interval, and the 99% interval. These intervals are created using Z scores (see Chapter 2). Let's suppose that we wish to create the 95% confidence interval for this specific IQ test. The 95% confidence interval is associated with the Z score of 1.96. The upper bound of the confidence interval is equal to the mean plus $1.96 S_m$ or, in this example,

$$106 + 1.96(4.64) = 115.09$$

The lower bound of the interval is equal to the mean minus

$$1.96 \times S_m$$

So, in this example, the lower bound would be

$$106 - 1.96(4.64) = 96.91$$

Although we do not know the true score for a person who received the mean score of 106, we can be 95% confident that the true score falls within the interval mounted by 96.9 and 115.1. As you can see, however, the scores of 96 and 115 on an IQ test (see Chapters 11 and 12) are quite different. Tests with more measurement error include more "rubber." In other words, the larger the standard error of measurement, the larger will be the confidence interval. When confidence intervals are very wide, our ability to make precise statements is greatly diminished.

B. *How Reliable Is Reliable?*

People often ask how high a reliability coefficient must be before it is "high enough." The answer depends on the use of the test. It has been suggested that reliability estimates in the range of .70 and .80 are good enough for most purposes in basic research. In many research studies, we attempt to gain only approximate estimates of whether two variables are related. In a research setting, it may be appropriate to estimate what the correlation between two variables would have been if the measures had been more reliable. If the results look promising, it then may be appropriate to spend the extra time and money necessary to make the research instruments more reliable. It even has been argued that it would be a waste of time and effort to refine research instruments beyond a reliability of .90. Although the higher reliability is desirable, it may not be worth the added burden and costs (Nunnally, 1982).

In clinical settings, high reliability is extremely important. When tests are used to make important decisions about someone's future, you must be certain to minimize any error in classification. Thus, a test with a reliability of .90 might not be good enough. For a test used to make a decision that affects some person's future, you should attempt to find a test with a reliability greater than .95.

C. *What to Do About Low Reliability*

Often test constructors want their tests to be used in applied settings, but analysis reveals that the test reliability is inadequate. Fortunately, psychometric theory does offer some options. Two of the most common approaches are to increase the length of the test and to throw out items that run down the reliability. Another procedure is to estimate what the true correlation would have been if the test did not have measurement error.

Increase the number of items. According to the domain sampling model, each item in a test is an independent sample of the trait or ability being measured. The larger the sample, the more likely it is that the test will be representative of the true characteristic. In the domain sampling model, the reliability of a test increases as the number of items increases. Thus, one way to increase the reliability of a test is to increase the number of items.

A medical example will help clarify why longer tests are more reliable. Suppose that you go to the doctor with indigestion. It is in your best interest for the doctor to make a reliable judgment about the etiology of your problem. How comfortable would you feel if the doctor asked only one question to provide a diagnosis? You probably would feel more comfortable if the doctor asked numerous questions. In general, people feel that the more information a doctor obtains by asking questions and performing tests, the more reliable the diagnosis will be. This same situation applies to psychological tests.

A decision to increase the number of items in a test might result in a long and costly process. When new items are added, the test must be reevaluated, and it may turn out to be below an acceptable level of reliability. In addition, adding new items can be very costly and can make a test so long that few people would be able to sit through it. Fortunately, there are procedures that can be used to estimate how many items will have to be added in order to bring a test to an acceptable level of reliability. This is accomplished by applying the Spearman-Brown prophecy formula. In the section on split-half reliability, we introduced the Spearman-Brown formula. This application requires a different form.

The **prophecy formula** for estimating how long a test must be in order to achieve a desired level of reliability is another case of the general Spearman-Brown method for estimating reliability. Algebraic manipulations of the general formula can be used to turn it around and solve for the length needed for any desired level of reliability. The formula is

See p. 109

$$N = \frac{r_d(1 - r_o)}{r_o(1 - r_d)}$$

where N = the number of tests of the current version's length that would be needed to have a test of the desired level of reliability

r_d = the desired level of reliability

r_o = the observed level of reliability based on the current version of the test

Consider the example of the 20-item CES-D test that had a reliability for medical students of .87. We would like to bring the reliability up to .95. Putting these numbers into the prophecy formula, we get

$$N = \frac{.95(1 - .87)}{.87(1 - .95)} = \frac{.124}{.044} = 2.82$$

These calculations tell us that we would need 2.82 tests the length of the current 20-item test to bring the reliability up to the desired level. In order to find the number of items that would be required for the test, we must multiply the number of items on the current test by N from the preceding formula. In the example, this would give $20 \times 2.82 = 56.4$. So the test would have to be expanded from 20 to about 56 items in order to achieve the desired reliability of .95. This assumes that the added items come from the same pool as the original items and that they have the same psychometric properties.

The decision to expand a test from 20 to 56 items must depend on economic and practical considerations. The test developer first must ask whether the increase in reliability is worth the extra time, effort, and expense required to achieve this goal. If the test is to be used for personnel decisions, it may be dangerous to ignore any effort that will enhance the reliability of the test. On the other hand, if the test is to be used only to get an idea of whether two variables are associated, the expense of extending it may not be worth the effort and cost.

When the prophecy formula is used, certain assumptions are made that may or may not be valid. One of these assumptions is that the probability of error in items added to the test is the same as that for the original items in the test. However, there may be some occasions in which adding many items brings about new sources of error. For instance, if the test becomes very long, fatigue might become a major source of error.

As an example of a situation in which it may not be worthwhile to attempt to increase the reliability of a test, consider a 40-item test that has a reliability of .50. We would like to bring the reliability up to .90. Using the prophecy formula, we get

$$N = \frac{.90(1 - .50)}{.50(1 - .90)} = \frac{.90(.50)}{.50(.10)} = \frac{.45}{.05} = 9$$

These figures tell us that the test would have to be nine times its present length in order to have a projected reliability of .90 (9 × 40 = 360 items long). Creating a test 360 items long would be very expensive, and validating it would require a considerable time investment for both test constructors and test takers. Beyond these problems, there might be new sources of error in the 360-item test that would not have been a problem for the shorter measure. For example, many errors may occur on the longer test simply because people get tired and bored during the long process of answering 360 questions. There is no way of taking these factors into account using the prophecy formula.

Factor and item analysis. The reliability of a test is dependent on all of the items being measures of the same underlying characteristic. Although we always intend to create tests in this way, it often happens that some items are not measures of this same construct. Leaving these items in the test reduces the reliability. The reliability estimates we have discussed in this chapter depend on high intercorrelations among the items. In order to ensure that the items are measuring the same thing, two approaches are suggested. One is to perform factor analysis (see Chapter 3 and also Fidell & Tabachnick, 1989; Pedhauzer, 1982). Tests are most reliable if they are unidimensional. This means that one factor should account for considerably more of the variance than any other factor. Items that do not load on this factor might be considered for elimination.

Another related approach is to examine the correlation between each item and the total score for the test. This is a form of item analysis (see Chapter 6) and is often called **discriminability** analysis. When the correlation between the performance on a single item and the total test score is low, the item is probably measuring something different from the other items on the test. It also might mean that the item is so easy or so hard that people do not differ in their response to it. In either case, the low correlation indicates that the item drags down the estimate of reliability and that it would be worthwhile to exclude it.

Correction for attenuation. Low reliability is a real problem in psychological research and practice because it reduces the chances of finding significant correlations between measures. We know that if a test is unreliable, information obtained with it is of little or no value. Thus, we say that potential correlations are attenuated, or diminished, by measurement error.

Fortunately, measurement theory does allow us to estimate what the correlation between two measures would have been if they had not been measured with error. These methods "correct" for the attenuation in the correlations caused by the measurement error. In order to use the methods, one needs to know only the reliabilities of two tests and the correlation between them. The **correction for attenuation** is

$$\hat{r}_{12} = \frac{r_{12}}{\sqrt{r_{11}r_{22}}}$$

where $\hat{r}_{12}$ = the estimated true correlation between tests 1 and 2

r_{12} = the observed correlation between tests 1 and 2

r_{11} = the reliability of test 1

r_{22} = the reliability of test 2

Suppose, for example, that the correlation between the CES-D and ratings of clinical skill was .34; the reliabilities of the tests were .87 and .70 for the CES-D and the clinical skill tests, respectively. The estimated true correlation between depression and clinical skill would be

$$\frac{.34}{\sqrt{(.87)(.70)}} = \frac{.34}{\sqrt{.609}} = \frac{.34}{.78} = .44$$

As the example shows, the estimated correlation increases from .34 to .44 when the correction is used.

Sometimes one measure meets an acceptable standard of reliability but the other one does not. In this case, we would want to correct for the attenuation caused only by the one unreliable test. To do this we use the formula

$$\hat{r}_{12} = \frac{r_{12}}{\sqrt{r_{11}}}$$

where $\hat{r}_{12}$ = the estimated true correlation

r_{12} = the observed correlation

r_{11} = the reliability of the variable that does not meet our standard of reliability

For example, suppose we want to estimate the correlation between the CES-D score and grade point average in medical school. The reliability of the CES-D test is .75, which is not quite as good as we would like, but medical school GPA is assumed to be measured without error. Using the fallible depression test, we observed the correlation to be .53. Plugging these numbers into the formula, we get

$$\frac{.53}{\sqrt{.75}} = \frac{.53}{.87} = .61$$

This informs us that correcting for the attenuation caused by the CES-D test would increase our observed correlation from .53 to .61.

Summary

Measurement error is common in all fields of science. Psychological and educational specialists, however, have devoted a great deal of time and study to measurement error and its effects. Tests that are relatively free of measurement error are considered to be reliable, and tests that contain relatively large measurement error are considered to be unreliable. The basics of contemporary theories and methods of reliability were worked out in the early part of this century by Charles Spearman. Test score and reliability theories have gone through continual refinements.

When we evaluate *reliability,* we must first specify the source of measurement error we are trying to evaluate. If we are concerned about errors that result from the test's being given at different times, we might consider the *test-retest method,* in which test scores obtained at two different points in time are correlated. On other occasions, we are concerned about errors that arise because we have selected a small sample of items to represent a larger conceptual domain. To evaluate this type of measurement error, we would use a method that assesses the internal consistency of the test, such as the *split-half method.* The KR_{20} and alpha methods are general methods for estimating the internal consistency of a test.

The standard of reliability for a test depends on the situation in which the test will be used. In some research settings it may not be worth the extra time and money required to bring a test up to an exceptionally high level of reliability. On the other hand, very strict standards for reliability are required when a test is to be used for making decisions that will affect people's lives. When a test has unacceptably low reliability, the test constructor might wish to boost the reliability by increasing the test length or by using factor analysis to divide the test into homogeneous subgroups of items. In research settings, it is sometimes possible to deal with the problem of low reliability by estimating what the correlation between tests would have been if there had been no measurement error. This procedure is called *correction for attenuation.*

Recently there has been increased interest in evaluating the reliability of behavioral observations. The percentage of items observers agree upon is not the best index of reliability for these studies because it does not take into consideration how much agreement is to be expected by chance alone. Correlation-like indexes such as kappa or phi are better suited to estimate reliability in these behavioral studies.

Reliability is one of the basic foundations of behavioral research. If a test is not reliable, it will not be possible to demonstrate that it has any meaning. In the next chapter, we will focus on how the meaning of tests is defined.

Chapter 5

Validity

Learning Objectives

When you have completed this chapter, you should be able to:

- Determine the relationship between establishing test validity and the use of the scientific method.

- Explain why it is inappropriate to refer to so-called face validity as a form of validity.

- List the categories of validity recognized in the booklet *Standards for Educational and Psychological Testing*.

- Tell how the strategy for establishing content validity differs from that used to obtain evidence for other types of validity.

- Discuss the difference between predictive and concurrent criterion validity.

- Relate the concept of the coefficient of determination (from Chapter 3) to the interpretation of the validity coefficient in criterion validity.

- Tell how to interpret the results of a test that, for example, had a validity coefficient of .35 for predicting success on a particular job.

- List some of the issues that should be taken into consideration when interpreting a validity coefficient.

- Know when construct validation is appropriate.

- Select some hypothetical construct and describe how you would go about developing a measure for it.

The case of Willie Griggs was argued before the U.S. Supreme Court in October 1970. Griggs and 12 other black laborers were employees of the Dan River Steam Station of the Duke Power Company in Draper, North Carolina. Griggs and the others involved in the lawsuit were classified as laborers by the company, and their primary work assignment was sweeping and cleaning. The men would have preferred to be promoted to the next higher classification level, which was coal handler. However, the company required a passing score on a general intelligence test for that promotion. Of the 95 employees at the power station, 14 were black. Among the 14 black workers, 13 were assigned to sweeping and cleaning duties. The major obstacle for the men who wanted to move up in the company was their performance on the test.

Because the test appeared to render ineligible a much higher proportion of black employees than white employees, the power company was sued for engaging in discriminatory employment practice. The central issue in the lawsuit was the meaning of the test scores. The power company managers argued that using the test "would improve the overall quality of the work force." They suggested that they did not intend to discriminate on the basis of race and that the test helped them find the employees who were the most capable.

In the course of the court battle, the power company was required to show why the test had meaning for the particular jobs within their establishment. In other words, the company had to prove that the test had a specific meaning for particular jobs such as laborer or coal handler. On hearing the arguments, the Supreme Court decided that the tests were unrelated to measuring job capability. They ruled that the tests served as "built-in head winds" for minority groups and had no meaning for the purpose of hiring or promoting workers to the classification of coal handler. The decision has been reaffirmed and eventually became the basis of the Civil Rights Bill of 1991 (see Chapter 21).

As a result of the *Griggs* v. *Duke Power* decision, employers have been forced to provide evidence that a test used for the selection of employees or for promotion purposes has a specific meaning. In the field of testing, we refer to this meaning as **validity.** The meaning of a test is defined by very specific evidence, and there are very specific methods used to acquire this information. The meaning of a test is established by this evidence and not by the word of a psychologist. Just as in a legal court proceeding, a psychologist must obey specific rules of evidence in establishing that a test has a particular meaning for a specific purpose. In this chapter, we will review the rules of evidence most frequently employed. Some court cases similar to the one involving Willie Griggs will be discussed in Chapter 21.

I. *Learning to Ask about the Validity Evidence*

Psychologists and other professionals continually attempt to convince the public that their discipline is meaningful. In the case of psychological tests, certain segments of the public may have been convinced to become overly trusting. After you read this chapter, we hope that you will be able to determine when test results are meaningful and when they are questionable.

A. *The Definition of Validity*

Validity can be defined as the agreement between a test score or measure and the quality it is believed to measure. Over the years, psychologists have created many subcategories of validity, and different definitions of validity began to blossom. In time, it became hard to determine whether psychologists who referred to different types of validity were really talking about something different. Validity defined the meaning of tests and measures, yet the term *validity* itself was beginning to lose its meaning. In 1985, a joint committee of the American Education Research Association, the American Psychological Association, and the National Council on Measurement in Education published a booklet entitled *Standards for Educational and Psychological Testing*. We will refer to this booklet frequently because it provides a sensible set of guidelines for psychological tests that have won approval by major professional groups.

The joint committee set aside numerous other definitions of validity and instead suggested that validity is the evidence for inferences that are made about a test score. There are three types of evidence: (1) construct-related, (2) criterion-related, and (3) content-related. Other textbooks may use other headings for validity, but these can all be subsumed under the three categories suggested by the joint committee. For example, what have been called *concurrent* validity and *predictive* validity are really subcategories of criterion validity. *Empirical* validity and *statistical* validity also are synonyms for criterion validity. *Convergent* validity and *discriminant* validity are really types of evidence for construct validity. And, *trait* validity and *factorial* validity sometimes also are considered symptoms for construct validity.

It is important to emphasize that categories for grouping different types of validity are convenient; however, the use of categories does not imply that there are distinct forms of validity. Sometimes we have been overly rigorous about making distinctions among categories when, indeed, different categories conceptually overlap (Anastasi, 1986).

B. *Nature of Evidence*

Obtaining data in validity studies is like gathering evidence for a court trial. Some psychologists have made the analogy between psychological inquiry and the legal system. One of the similarities is that we always begin by assuming that there is no reason to believe a measure is valid. Evidence for validity comes from showing the association between the test and other variables. The rules strictly forbid saying there is a relationship without some proof. This is similar to the legal notion of innocent until proven guilty. Proof of guilt must be persuasive. In a similar manner, we must have convincing proof that there is a relationship between two variables before we are justified in touting the connection.

II. *Types of Validity*

The Joint Committee on Educational and Psychological Tests uses three types of validity evidence: content, criterion, and construct. Each of these will be discussed below. In addition, we will comment on what some call *face validity*.

The joint committee refused to recognize face validity as a legitimate category because it is not technically a form of validity. However, the term needs to be mentioned because it is commonly used in the testing literature.

A. *Face Validity*

Face validity is the mere appearance that a measure has validity. Sometimes psychologists report exactly what they observe and do not try to generalize. When they do, they are depending on face validity. They assume that the measures have meaning themselves and that no other generalizations are necessary. In many behavioral studies, this type of validity is just fine. For example, if you are interested in bar-pressing behavior in rats and observe the bar press, no generalizations are necessary. The observed bar-press response is exactly what you want to talk about. Indeed, the face validity is all that is needed to make the point. On the other hand, implying that the bar-press response means something—for instance, that it is predictive of later feeding behavior—requires some evidence that feeding is really predictable from bar pressing. In other words, you are now using bar pressing as a real basis for inference, and so you need real validity evidence.

We are not suggesting that face validity is unimportant. In many settings, it is crucial to have a test that "looks like" it is valid. These appearances can help motivate test takers because they can see that the test is relevant. For example, suppose you had developed a test to screen applicants for a training program in accounting. Items that ask about balance sheets and ledgers might make applicants more motivated than items about fuel consumption. However, both types of items might be testing the same arithmetic reasoning skill. We often say a test has face validity if the items are reasonably related to the perceived purpose of the test.

B. *Content-Related Validity*

How many times have you studied for an examination and known almost everything, yet the professor is able to come up with some strange items that do not seem to represent the content of the course? If this has happened, you may have encountered a test with poor content validity. A test or measure possesses **content validity** to the extent that it provides an adequate representation of the conceptual domain it is designed to cover. For example, if you are being tested on the first six chapters of this book, the test you take is content valid to the extent that the items on the test adequately represent the information in the chapters.

Traditionally, content validity has been of greatest concern in educational testing. If you have a test in history, the concern has been that scores on the test represent your comprehension of the history you are expected to know. Many factors can limit performance on history tests and therefore make the professor's inferences about your knowledge less valid. These factors could include characteristics of the items (such as vocabulary some students do not understand) and the sampling of items (such as the selection of items that do not represent the information the test is supposed to evaluate).

It is difficult to separate content validity from other types of validity. In fact, many psychologists have commented that the boundaries between content and other forms of validity are not clearly defined (Anastasi, 1986; Cronbach, 1985, 1989; Ebel, 1977; Landy, 1986; Lawshe, 1985; Messick, 1988; Tenopyr, 1984; Wainer & Brown, 1988). However, there are some unique features of the content validation strategy. Aside from face validity, content validity is the only type of validity for which the evidence is logical rather than statistical. Actually, content validation involves inferences about the test scores (Tenopyr, 1984). In content validation we attempt to determine whether the test has been constructed adequately. (See Focused Example 5-1.) For example, we ask whether the items were chosen to be a fair sample of the content area. Establishing the content validity of a test requires good logic, intuitive skills, and perseverance. The test constructor must be careful and willing to continually revise the items.

Often test scores reflect many factors in addition to what we assume the test should measure. For example, your professor may assume that your score on a psychology examination represents the proportion of items you know how to answer correctly. However, it may be that you knew how to answer many more of the items correctly but that other factors interfered. For example, many students do poorly on tests because of anxiety (see Chapter 19) or reading problems. A slow reader may get a low score on an examination because he or she did not have adequate time to read through all of the questions. Thus, content validity must consider all of the other factors that might influence performance. These considerations are necessary in order to make accurate generalizations about what the test score really means. Chapter 8 will present a more detailed discussion of this problem.

FOCUSED EXAMPLE 5-1

Challenging the Professor

Most professors have had the experience of having the content validity of their tests challenged. The challenge is usually by a student who complains, "Your test did not give me an opportunity to demonstrate what I know" or "You assigned Chapters 1 through 5, but nearly all of the items came from Chapters 1 and 2—how can you evaluate whether we know anything about the other material we were supposed to read?" In the process of creating good and fair tests, professors should continually face this sort of questioning and attempt to create tests that will not evoke legitimate criticism. Good judgment is always required in test development: we can never get around the need for rational judgment (Ebel, 1977).

C. *Criterion-Related Validity*

Folklore includes stories about fortune tellers who can look into crystal balls and see the future. Much to our dismay, we do not believe that anyone has been able to manufacture a crystal ball that tells exactly what the future will hold. Instead of turning to fortune tellers with crystal balls, people who need to know about the future have frequently turned to psychologists. We want to know how well someone will do on a job or which students we should select for our graduate program or who is most likely to get a serious disease. The problem is that, while we want to know how well someone will do in the future, we need that information now. We depend on psychological testing to forecast future behavior.

The assessment of criterion validity tells us just how good the tests are in serving these predictive purposes. A measure achieves **criterion validity** to the extent that it corresponds to an accurate measure of interest. The reason for assessing criterion validity is that the test or measure is to serve as a "stand-in" for the measure we are really interested in.

Predictive and concurrent validity. The forecasting function of tests is actually a type or form of criterion validity that is known as **predictive validity.** Predictive validity is used for the purpose of forecasting. For example, the SAT has predictive validity as a college admissions test if it accurately forecasts how well high school students will do in their college studies. The SAT, including its quantitative and verbal subtests, is the predictor variable, and the college grade point average is the criterion. The purpose of the test is to predict the likelihood of succeeding on the criterion—that is, achieving a high grade point average in college. A valid test for this purpose would make the task of college admissions committees much easier because they would have some feeling in advance about which students would succeed. Unfortunately, many tests do not have exceptionally impressive prediction records, and we must search continually for better ways to predict outcomes.

Another type of criterion validity is concurrent validity. Studies of **concurrent validity** assess the simultaneous relationship between the test and the criterion. For example, we often look at the relationship between an employment screening test and performance on the job. The measures are actually taken at the same point in time because the test is designed to predict how well the person will do right away. In the case of employment screening tests, an employer might have to hire the person in order to evaluate how well he or she does on the criterion of job performance. Studies on concurrent validity are used to estimate how well the person will do on the job if he or she was hired now.

Job samples provide a good example of the use of concurrent validity. Industrial psychologists often have to select employees on the basis of limited information. One method that has gained popularity in recent years is to test potential employees on a sample of behaviors that are representative of the tasks that will be required of them. For example, J. E. Campion (1972) found that the most effective ways to select maintenance mechanics was to obtain samples of their mechanical work. Because these samples were shown to correlate well with performance on the job, the samples alone could be used for the selection and screening of applicants. Impressive results support the use of

---

FOCUSED EXAMPLE 5-2

Validation of a Self-Report Measure of Depression

In Chapters 2, 3, and 4, we offered some data on depression based on the Center for Epidemiologic Studies Depression Scale (CES-D). The CES-D is a general measure of depressive symptoms that has been used extensively in epidemiologic studies (Weissman et al., 1977). The scale includes 20 items and taps dimensions of depressed mood, feelings of guilt and worthlessness, appetite loss, sleep disturbance, and energy level. These items are assumed to represent all of the major components of depressive symptomatology. Sixteen of the items are worded negatively, whereas the other four are worded positively to avoid the possibility of patterned responses. The respondents are asked to report how often they experienced a particular "symptom" during the past week on a four-point scale: 0 (rarely or none of the time—less than 1 day), 1 (some or a little of the time—1 to 2 days), 2 (occasionally or a moderate amount of the time—3 or 4 days), and 3 (most or all of the time—5 to 7 days). The responses to the four positive items are reverse scored and then the total sum of the responses is derived. Scores on the CES-D scale can range from 0 to 60, with scores greater than 18 suggestive of clinically significant levels of depression.

Validity studies have demonstrated that the CES-D is highly correlated with other measures of depression. For example, one validity study demonstrated significant correlations with the more complete Beck Depression Inventory. The CES-D, however, was designed for studies of nonpsychiatric populations (Gottlib & Cine, 1989). A series of studies have demonstrated that the CES-D is associated with clinical diagnoses of de-

pression; however, the CES-D is a better screening instrument than a diagnostic tool. P. N. Lewinsohn and L. Teri (1982) demonstrated that scores of less than 16 on the CES-D were highly associated with clinical judgments of nondepression. Conversely, scores of 17 or greater had only a moderate hit rate for psychiatric diagnoses of depression.

Since the CES-D has only moderate validity for the evaluation of clinical depression, more complex methods are required for clinical evaluations. It has been suggested that as many as 3% of the population experience major depressive problems at any time. The American Psychiatric Association, in its *Diagnostic and Statistical Manual of Mental Disorders*, third edition (DSM-III-R) (APA, 1980), suggests that the diagnosis of major depressive disorder involves three components:

1. A clinician identifies a series of specific symptoms.
2. The symptoms are present for at least two weeks.
3. The diagnosis is not ruled out for another reason.

These judgments require the active involvement of a trained psychiatrist or psychologist. Most measures of depression cannot be used to make these complex judgments.

M. Zimmerman and W. Coryell (1987) offered a 22-item self-report scale that can be used to diagnose major depressive disorder. They suggest that the scale may give an accurate estimate of the work samples for selecting employees in a variety of areas, including motor skills (Asher & Sciarrino, 1974) and work in the petroleum industry (Dunnette, 1972).

According to contemporary standards for equal employment opportunity, tasks used to test potential new employees must be demonstrated to be relevant

prevalence of these problems in the general population. Thus, researchers can estimate the proportion of the general population that suffers from depression without the expense of having a psychiatrist or psychologist interview large samples. Zimmerman and Coryell call their measure the Inventory to Diagnose Depression (IDD). The IDD includes 22 items. For each item, the person records a score of 0, which represents no disturbance, through 4, indicating that the symptom is present. The numbers 1, 2, and 3 suggest different gradations of the symptom. For example, the IDD item about insomnia includes the following choices:

0 = I am not sleeping less than usual.
1 = I occasionally have slight difficulty sleeping.
2 = I clearly don't sleep as well as usual.
3 = I sleep about half my normal amount of time.
4 = I sleep less than two hours per night.

The IDD also considers whether the symptoms have been present for less than or more than two weeks. Some of the depressive symptoms considered by the IDD are decreased energy, decreased interest in sex, guilt, weight gain, anxiety, irritability, and weight loss.

Although the IDD seems to measure the concept of depression (face validity), systematic evidence obtained in validity studies is required. In other words, we need to ask "What is the evidence that self-reports on this scale actually measure depression?"

The first step in establishing the validity of the IDD was to demonstrate that it was related to other measures designed to assess depression. For example, it was shown to be significantly correlated with the Hamilton Rating Scale for Depression in 234 adults ($r = .80$), the Beck Depression Inventory in 234 adults ($r = .87$), and the Carroll Depression Scale in 105 adults ($r = .81$). In addition, reports of the experience of specific symptoms on the IDD were systematically related to clinicians' judgments of individual symptoms for the same patients.

In another study, first-degree relatives of patients with psychiatric disorders were interviewed using a highly structured system known as the diagnostic interview schedule. The system uses a computer program to generate diagnoses for specific disorders. In the study of 394 cases, the IDD gave the same diagnostic classification of depression as the more complex interview in 97.2% of the cases. There were some cases in which the detailed interview identified cases not detected by the IDD. However, the estimates of the rates of major depression assessed with the IDD are quite similar to those found in major studies of the general population.

There are many other measures of depression in addition to the IDD. However, most of these are not designed to make the specific diagnosis of major depressive disorder. Discriminant evidence for validity demonstrates the advantage of the IDD in comparison to other approaches. In particular, other measures do not feed directly into the DSM-III R classification system.

to actual job performance. D. E. Thompson and T. A. Thompson (1982) reviewed 26 federal court decisions in which the validity of tests used to screen employees had been challenged. Considering the judgments in the various cases, it is clear that the job-related test must focus on tasks, should be in a written form, and must include several different data sources with large samples. In other words, the courts are requiring good scientific evidence that a test used to screen employees is valid for inferring how job candidates will perform when employed (Zedeck & Cascio, 1984). See Focused Example 5-2.

Another use of concurrent validity occurs when a person might not know how he or she would respond to the criterion measure. For example, the Strong-Campbell Interest Inventory (SCII) uses patterns of interest among persons who are satisfied with their careers as criteria (Campbell, 1977). Then the patterns of interest for people taking the tests are matched to these criteria for various occupations.

Validity coefficient. The relationship between a test and a criterion is usually expressed as a correlation. This correlation is called a *validity coefficient,* and it tells the extent to which the test is valid for making statements about the criterion.

□◇ **FOCUSED EXAMPLE 5-3**

Nader's Raid on the Educational Testing Service

Ralph Nader, an aggressive attorney and consumer advocate, has earned a solid reputation over the years for his attacks on giant corporations, including automobile manufacturers and food producers. The Nader approach is to "expose" to the public the misdeeds of the corporations. Early in 1980, Nader released the results of his six-year investigation of the Educational Testing Service (ETS)—America's largest test producer. At the time the report was released, Nader called a press conference and exclaimed, "What this report makes clear is that ETS's claims to measure aptitude and predict success are false and unsubstantiated and can be described as a specialized kind of fraud."

What Nader disputed was the predictive validity of ETS tests such as the SAT and the Graduate Record Examination (GRE). The data used by Nader and his team of researchers were no differ-

ent from those used by ETS officials; however, the way Nader chose to interpret the data was very different. ETS has consistently reported that the SAT, for example, accounts for a small but significant percentage of the variance in first-year college grade point averages. Nader did not interpret the results in terms of percentage of variance as typically explained in the field of psychometrics. Instead, he reported the percentage of cases the test successfully predicted according to his own criteria. On the basis of this approach, he concluded that the test predicted successfully in only 12% of the cases. However, Nader's calculations were not based on an appropriate statistical model (Kaplan, 1982, 1985d).

On the basis of his interpretation of the data, Nader suggested that there should be more regulation of the testing industry. Referring to ETS, he

Not all validity coefficients are the same value, and there are no hard and fast rules about how large the coefficient must be in order to be meaningful. In practice, it is rare to see a validity coefficient larger than .60, and validity coefficients in the range of .30 to .40 are commonly considered high. A coefficient is statistically significant if the chances of obtaining its value by chance alone are quite small: usually less than 5 in 100. For example, suppose that the SAT had a validity coefficient of .40 for predicting grade point average at a particular West Coast university. Because this coefficient is likely to be statistically significant, we can say that the SAT score tells us more about how well people will do in college than we would know by chance.

There are many reasons why college students differ in their academic performance. You probably could easily list a dozen. Because there are so many factors that contribute to college performance, it would be too much to expect that the SAT could explain all of the variation. The question we must ask is "How much of the variation in college performance will we be able to predict on the basis of SAT scores?"

The validity coefficient squared is the percentage of variation in the criterion that we can expect to know in advance because of our knowledge of the test scores. Thus, we will know .40 squared, or 16%, of the variation in college

explained, "They have assumed a rare kind of corporate power, the power to change the way people think about their own potential, and through the passive acceptance of their test scores by admissions officers, to decide who will be granted and who will be denied access to education and career opportunities" (from *APA Monitor*, 1980, 11(2): 1–7).

It is clear that Nader uncovered an important problem, yet it is not certain that the Educational Testing Service deserves all of the blame. ETS does put out its own guidelines for the use of the SAT and other tests. These booklets, which are designed to be read by college admissions officers, clearly acknowledge the limitations of the tests. For example, college administrators are told that the test accounts for a small but significant percentage of the variation in college performance, and they are advised to look at other criteria in addition to test scores. Thus, much of the problem lies with admissions committees and with college administrators who passively accept SAT scores as the ultimate predictor of college performance.

Those administrators who know how to interpret the evidence for predictive validity do not make the sort of error Nader warned about. However, if school officials have used the SAT to select students, they did so to learn about the 16% of the variation between students that could be predicted before any students were admitted. It is important to realize that accounting for small percentages of the variance in some criterion under different circumstances is very useful for people making decisions. Obviously, college administrators feel that the small bit of information they get from SAT scores aids them in selecting the right students for their institutions.

performance because of the information we have from the SAT test. This is the coefficient of determination that was discussed in Chapter 2. The remainder of the variation in college performance is actually the greater proportion: 84% of the total variation is still unexplained. In other words, when students arrive at college, most of the reasons why they perform differently will still be a mystery to college administrators and professors. See Focused Example 5-3.

There are many circumstances in which using a test may not be worth the effort if it contributes only a few percentage points to the understanding of variation in a criterion. Actually low validity coefficients (.30 to .40) sometimes can be very useful even though they may explain only about 10% of the variation in the criterion. For example, Dunnette (1967) demonstrated how a simple questionnaire used for military screening could save taxpayers $4 million every month even though the validity was not remarkably high. (And this analysis was done before the days of high inflation. If it had been done today, the estimated savings would be far more!) F. J. Landy, J. L. Farr, and R. Jacobs (1982) found that a performance evaluation and feedback system with a validity of .30 could translate into increased earnings of $5.3 million in

---

FOCUSED EXAMPLE 5-4

The Cholesterol Test: Predictive Validity

The concept of predictive validity applies to medical tests as well as to psychological measures. One of the major issues in contemporary public health is the relationship between cholesterol levels and death from heart disease. Systematic studies have demonstrated that high levels of cholesterol in the blood are predictive of early death from heart disease and stroke. To learn more about these problems, physicians take samples of blood and examine the cholesterol level. In order to evaluate this information, it is important to consider the relationship between the test (blood cholesterol level) and the criterion (premature death). Although this relationship has been established in many studies, the level of association is actually quite low. Some studies show the relationship to be in the range of .1, or to account for about 1% of the variance in mortality. In order to lower blood cholesterol levels, dietary changes are often advocated. Those with high levels of blood cholesterol are advised to eat foods that are low in saturated fats and cholesterol. However, some systematic studies have failed to find strong, statistically significant relationships between these dietary habits and mortality rates (Stallones, 1983). The low validities for dietary habits predicting mortality suggest that these measures tell us very little about what can be predicted for a particular individual. However, heart disease is a very serious problem for the general population. Each year, more than 600,000 Americans die of these problems. Thus, even weak associations help explain a significant number of cases. As a society, if we reduce blood cholesterol levels, there will be a significant reduction in the number of deaths. The low correlation between these cholesterol tests and heart disease suggests that we will not be able to say precisely which specific individuals will benefit. However, the small but significant statistical relationship tells us that there is some predictive value of cholesterol tests that is important (Kaplan, 1984, 1985c, 1988a, 1990).

one year. There also are some circumstances in which a validity coefficient of .30 or .40 means almost nothing. In Chapter 7, we will show how validity coefficients are translated into specific decision models and how industrial psychologists use information about test validity to save money.

Evaluating validity coefficients. In order to be an informed consumer of information about tests, you should learn to review carefully any information offered by a test developer. Not all validity coefficients of .40 have the same meaning. Thus, there are a few things you should watch out for in evaluating this information. We will cover some of these issues here and go into more depth on this topic in Chapter 7.

In its booklet *Standards for Educational and Psychological Testing*, the joint committee of the American Education Research Association, the American Psychological Association, and the National Council on Measurement in Education (1985) lists several issues to be concerned about when interpreting validity coefficients. Here are some of its recommendations.

Look for changes in the cause of relationships. You should always be aware that the conditions of a validity study are never exactly reproduced. For example, if you are taking the GRE in order to gain admission to graduate school, the conditions under which you take the test may not be exactly the same as those in the studies that established the validity of the GRE. Many things may change, including the way grades are assigned in graduate school and the population taking the test.

The logic of criterion validation presumes that the causes of the relationship between the test and the criterion will still be in effect when the test is in use. In most circumstances, this will be the case, yet there may be circumstances in which the relationship changes. For example, a test might be used and shown to be valid for selecting supervisors in industry; however, the validity study may have been done at a time when all of the employees were men. The test may be valid to select supervisors for male employees. Later the company might have hired female employees, and the test may no longer be valid for selecting supervisors because it may not take into consideration the abilities necessary to supervise a sexually mixed group of employees.

What does the criterion mean? Another element to look out for when evaluating validity coefficients is the meaning of the criterion. Criterion validity studies mean nothing at all unless the criterion is valid and reliable. Some test constructors attempt to correlate their tests with other tests with unknown validity. A meaningless group of items that correlates well with another meaningless group of items is still meaningless.

For applied research, the criterion should relate specifically to the use of the test. The intent of the SAT is to predict performance in college, and so the appropriate criterion is grade point average, which is a measure of college performance. If any other inferences are to be made on the basis of the SAT, additional evidence to support these inferences is required. For example, if you want to say that the SAT tells you something about adaptability, evidence must be obtained on the relationship between the SAT and some measure of adaptability.

Review the subject population in the validity study. Another reason to be cautious of validity coefficients is that the validity study might have been done on a population that is not representative of that to which inferences will be made. For example, there is some debate about whether the validity coefficients for intelligence tests that are based primarily on samples of white students are accurate when they are used to test black students (Cleary, 1968; Educational Testing Service, 1991; Oakland & Parmelee, 1985; Sattler, 1989; Temp, 1971; Thorndike, 1971). We will review this problem in detail in Chapter 20.

When tests are used in industrial settings, validity studies can be seriously jeopardized by attrition. Those who do poorly on the job drop out or get fired and are not available to be studied when it comes time to do the job assessment. If there was a group that did well on the test but failed on the job, it might not be represented and could be systematically eliminated from the study because the workers were already off the job by the time the assessment came around.

Be sure the sample size was adequate. Another problem to look out for is a validity coefficient based on a very small number of cases. Sometimes a proper validity study cannot be done because there are too few people to study. A common practice is to do a small validity study with the people you have around. Unfortunately, a small study can be quite misleading. A correlation obtained from a small sample cannot be depended on as can a correlation obtained from a large sample. This is particularly true for multiple correlation and multiple regression. The smaller the sample, the more likely the correlation will capitalize on chance variation in the data. Thus, a validity coefficient based on a small sample may have a greater tendency to be artificially inflated.

A good validity study will present some evidence for cross validation. A cross-validation study assesses how well the test actually does in forecasting for an independent group of subjects. In other words, the initial validity study assesses the relationship between the test and the criterion, whereas a cross-validation study checks how well this relationship holds for an independent group of subjects. The larger the sample size in the initial study, the better the likelihood that the relationship will cross validate.[1]

Never confuse the criterion with the predictor. At the university where we work, one department required students to meet a certain cutoff score on the GRE before they could be admitted to the program. Occasionally, the department admits a student who did not get the cutoff score, but then it requires the student to meet the minimum GRE score before it confers a degree. The logic behind this policy represents a clear misunderstanding of the test and its purpose.

---

[1] Correct cross-validation methodology requires that the raw score weights from the original sample be applied to the validation sample. The use of standard score or standardized weights is not appropriate because the means and standard deviations for the validation sample may be different from those in the original sample (Dorans & Drasgow, 1980).

In this case, the GRE is the predictor, and success in graduate school is the criterion. The only reason for using the test in the first place is to help select students who have the highest probability of success in the program. Many students in this program have already succeeded on the criterion (success in the program). Before the university would acknowledge that the students indeed had succeeded, they had to go back and demonstrate that they would have been predicted to do well on the criterion. This reflects a clear confusion between predictor and criterion.

This example also demonstrates that the GRE is not a valid predictor of success among those provisionally accepted into this program. Indeed, most of the students who were given provisional admission because of low GRE scores succeeded by completing the program. The only reason for using the test is to forecast who is likely to finish. When the students succeed in completing the requirements for their degrees, there is no longer any need for the test. This calls into question the rationale for using the test at all.

Check for restricted range on both predictor and criterion. A variable has a "restricted range" if all scores for that variable fall very close together. For example, the grade point averages of graduate students in Ph.D. programs tend to fall within a limited range of the scale—usually above 3.5 (on a 4-point scale). The problem this creates is that correlation depends on variability. If all the people in your class have a grade point average of 4.0, it is not possible to predict variability in graduate school grade point average. Correlation requires that there be variability in both the predictor and the criterion.

One of the major problems with the GRE is that it does not correlate well with graduate school grade point average. R. E. Ingram (1980) did a detailed review of studies on the value of the GRE as a predictor of success in graduate school. He found that among all of the published studies, the verbal portion of the GRE significantly predicted graduate school grade point average in only 25% of the studies and the quantitative portion predicted this same criterion in only 12.5% of the studies. The Educational Testing Service now disputes these findings. However, according to their documents, the average correlation between GRE verbal and first-year psychology graduate school GPA is .28. The correlation between GRE quantitative and first-year grade point average is .29. The validity coefficient for the analytic portion of the GRE is .38 (*GRE Guide*, 1990).

There are at least three explanations for Ingram's findings. First, the GRE may not be a valid test for selecting graduate students. Second, those students who are admitted to graduate school represent such a restricted range of ability that it is not possible to find significant correlations. Those students with low GRE scores are never admitted to graduate school and, therefore, never get into the study. Third, grades in graduate school often represent a restricted range. Once admitted, students in graduate programs are usually given all "A's" and "B's." A grade of "C" is usually considered a failing grade.

Review evidence for validity generalization. Criterion-related validity evidence obtained in one situation may not generalize to other similar situations. *Generalizability* refers to the evidence that the findings obtained in one situation can be generalized or applied to other situations. This is not a matter of judgment but rather an issue of empirical study. In other words, we must prove that the results obtained in a validity study are not situation specific. There are many reasons why results may not generalize. For example, there may be differences in the way the predictor construct is measured or in the type of job or curriculum involved; in the actual criterion measure; between groups of people who take the test; or in the time period, year, or month when the test is administered. Because of these problems, we cannot always be certain that the validity coefficient reported by a test developer will be the same for our particular situation. An employer, for example, might use a work sample test based on information reported in the manual, yet the situation in which he or she uses the test may be different from the situations of the original validation studies. When using the test, the employer might be using different demographic groups or different criterion measures and may be predicting performance on a similar but different task. Generalizations from the original validity studies to these other situations should be made only on the basis of new evidence.

Consider differential prediction. Predictive relationships may not be the same for all demographic groups. There may be circumstances in which the validity for men is different from the validity for women. Or the validity of the test may be questionable because it is used for a group whose native language is different from English, yet the test was validated for those who always spoke only English. Under these circumstances, separate validity studies for different groups may be necessary. This issue will be discussed in more detail in Chapter 20.

A validity study that demonstrates that a test has a high correlation with another test is meaningless unless the other test has some established meaning. Correlations between two tests, both with unknown validity, tell us only that something that does not have any established meaning is related to something else with no established meaning.

Although criterion validity is very common in psychological and educational research, there are some instances in which it simply does not apply. By definition, the criterion must be a superior, more accurate measure of the phenomenon if it is to serve as the "gold standard." If a criterion exists, only greater practicality or less expense justifies the use of concurrent measures as proxies or substitutes for the criterion. If the criterion is not a superior measure, then failure of correspondence by any new measure may be a defect in the criterion itself. For example, studies on the validity of measures of general health have been hindered because a clear criterion of health has never been defined (Kaplan, 1990). The development of a health index helped define the meaning of the term *health*. Often work on a psychological test involves the simultaneous development of a concept and the instrumentation to measure the concept. This cannot be accomplished by criterion validity studies. Instead, we need a more involved approach known as *construct validation*.

D. *Construct-Related Validity*

Before 1950, most social scientists considered only criterion and content forms of validity. By the mid-1950s, investigators concluded that no clear criteria existed for most of the social and psychological characteristics they wanted to measure. Developing a measure of intelligence, for example, was difficult because no one could say for certain what intelligence was. Criterion validity studies would require that a specific criterion of intelligence be established against which tests could be compared. The problem was that there was no criterion for intelligence. Intelligence is actually a hypothetical construct we cannot touch or feel. A *construct* is defined as something constructed by mental synthesis.

In contemporary psychology, we often want to measure intelligence, love, curiosity, or mental health. All these are constructs that are not clearly defined, and there is no established criterion against which we can compare the accuracy of our test. These are the truly challenging problems in measurement.

Construct validity is established through a series of activities in which a researcher simultaneously defines some construct and develops the instrumentation to measure it. This process is required when "no criterion or universe of content is accepted as entirely adequate to define the quality to be measured" (Cronbach & Meehl, 1955, p. 282). Construct validation involves assembling evidence about what a test really means. This is done by showing the relationship between a test and other tests and measures. Each time a relationship is demonstrated, one additional bit of meaning can be attached to the test. Over a series of studies, the meaning of the test gradually begins to take shape. Construct validation is an ongoing process, similar to amassing support for a complex scientific theory. No single set of observations provides crucial or critical evidence, yet over time many observations gradually clarify what the test means. An example of construct validation is given in Focused Example 5-5.

Years ago, D. T. Campbell and D. W. Fiske (1959) introduced an important set of logical considerations for developing tests with construct validity. They distinguished between two types of evidence that are essential for a meaningful test: convergent and discriminant. In order to argue that a test has meaning, a test constructor is advised to be armed with as much evidence as possible for these two types of validity. We will present the basic logic of the Campbell and Fiske approach here. For those who desire a more detailed presentation, the 1959 reference is recommended.

Convergent evidence. When a measure correlates well with other tests that are believed to measure the same construct, **convergent evidence** for validity is obtained. This sort of evidence shows that measures of the same construct "converge," or narrow in, on the same thing. In many ways, convergent evidence for construct validity is like criterion validity. In each case, scores on the test are related to scores on some other measure. In the case of convergent evidence for construct validity, however, there is no criterion to define what you are attempting to measure. Criterion validity is fine for situations in which you are attempting to predict performance on a particular variable, such as success in graduate school. Here the task is well defined, and all you need to do is find the items that are good predictors of this graduate school criterion. In

---

FOCUSED EXAMPLE 5-5

The Meaning of Love

An interesting example of construct validation comes from the work of Zick Rubin (1970, 1973), who noted that love has been one of the most discussed issues of all time. Throughout history, men and women have written and sung about love more than about any other topic. The index to Bartlett's *Familiar Quotations* shows that references to love are second only to citations to "man" (with "love" cited 769 times and "man" cited 843 times). All of this preoccupation with love, however, has not led to a better understanding of its true meaning. Perhaps it is something we can feel but not necessarily understand well enough to describe in a definite way.

In the mid-1970s, there was a famous trial in Los Angeles in which singer Mischelle Triola Marvin sued actor Lee Marvin for half of his earnings while the couple lived together. A major issue in the trial was the couple's unmarried status during the period in which the earnings occurred. During the trial, Lee's attorney questioned the actor about the extent to which he loved Mischelle while they lived together. Unfortunately, there is no scale on which the actor could rate his love. If he had been asked his height, he could have used the scale of inches. But love? How could he put that into a number? However, the actor did resort to a gas-tank analogy. He said his love for the singer was like when you are driving your car and you look over at your gas gauge and find it "about half full." That is about how much he loved Mischelle— about half a tank. If there had been a measure of love, he would not have needed to use such a crude analogy (Rubin, 1979).

The first step in the development of Rubin's love scale was to create a list of items that represented all the different things people might call love. This was not an easy task because all of us have different romantic ideals. In order to create a measure of love, Rubin had to condense conventional wisdom about loving and liking into sets of statements to which people could respond on a scale. The scale presented statements, and subjects could respond by indicating the extent to which they agreed or disagreed on a 5-point scale (where 1 is for strong disagreement and 5 is for strong agreement).

Collecting the statements or any other original set of items for construct validation is not easy because you never know which items eventually will be relevant to the construct you are attempting to measure. Building the love scale was particularly difficult in this regard. In order to prepare his measure, Rubin read extensively about love.

Elizabeth Barrett Browning wrote, "How do I love thee? Let me count the ways." Indeed, after reading the many diverse views of love, Rubin hardly knew where to begin counting. Because this was a study in construct validity, however, it was important that Rubin considered counting. Construct validity requires that there be content validity. Content validity in turn requires that the domain of inference (in this case love) be fully represented by the items. All of the ways that love is defined by different people must be included in this collection.

Rubin began his study with his sets of statements that people could respond to on a scale ranging from disagreement to agreement. Some of the items were intended to measure love, whereas others were supposed to tap liking. Next he gave construct validity, there is no well-defined criterion, and the meaning of the test comes to be defined by the variables it can be shown to be associated with.

An example of the need to obtain construct validation evidence comes from studies by R. M. Kaplan, J. W. Bush, and C. C. Berry (1976), who attempted to define and measure the construct *health*. Health is a complex concept involv-

the pool of items to 198 students from the University of Michigan. Each of the items had a blank in which a name could be filled in. The students responded to the questions twice, one time filling in the name of their lover and another time filling in the name of a friend. Then the items were subjected to factor analysis. This is a method for reducing a large number of items or variables into smaller and more manageable composites of items called factors (see Chapter 3).

In the love scale, three factors were obtained: (1) attachment (for example, "If I were lonely, my first thought would be to seek out _____"), (2) caring ("If _____ were feeling bad, my first duty would be to cheer him/her up"), and (3) intimacy ("I feel that I can confide in _____ about virtually everything"). The items on the liking scale focused on favorable aspects of the other person along such dimensions as adjustment, maturity, good judgment, and intelligence.

The data from these scales were subjected to several statistical procedures that helped discriminate between the responses of lovers and friends and eventually led to the establishment of two measures: a love scale and a liking scale. Now that measures of liking and loving were available, it was necessary to determine whether they were really measuring what they were supposed to. One study using dating couples suggested that loving and liking were not necessarily related. There was a modest relationship between scores on the two scales, which was weaker for women than for men. This suggested, especially for women, that it is possible to love someone whom you may not particularly like.

There are several indications that the love scale really was measuring "love." For example, men and women scored higher on the love scale when they filled in the names of their lovers than when they filled in the name of a same-sex friend. There also was a substantial correlation between love scale scores and estimates of the likelihood of marriage. The greater the love score, the more probable marriage was considered to be.

Finally, some of the dating couples were separated into strong love (high love scores) and weak love (low love scores) groups. From behind a one-way mirror, the researchers noted how much eye contact the lovers had with one another. Strong lovers, it was observed, spent more time simply gazing into one another's eyes than did weak lovers. When paired with a strong opposite-sex lover from another couple, mutual eye contact was no greater than it was for people who were weak lovers.

In summary, Rubin began his study of love with neither a clear definition of love nor a method of measuring it. Through a series of structured exercises, he gradually came to have a better grasp of the construct. For example, he discovered that lovers mark some items differently than couples who are just friends. He also discovered that "love" may have at least three independent components. Once the basic scale was developed, each new application defined a new meaning. For instance, one study showed that the scale predicts how much time lovers will spend gazing into each other's eyes. Thus, in future applications of the love scale, we would expect couples who score as strong lovers (for one another) to spend more time in mutual gaze.

ing many facets. Because of the complexity of the health concept, no single measure can serve as the criterion against which a measure of health can be assessed. This situation requires studies in construct validation. Some of the construct validation studies were used to demonstrate the convergent validity of the measure of health the authors call a *health index*.

Convergent evidence is obtained in one of two ways. The first is by showing that a test measures the same things as other tests used for the same purpose. The second is by demonstrating specific relationships that could be expected if the test is really doing its job. Studies on the health index included both types of evidence. In demonstrating the meaning of the health index, the authors continually asked themselves, "If we were really measuring health, what relationships would we expect to observe between the health index and other measures?" The simplest relationship is between health index scores and the way people rate their own health status. This relationship was strong and clearly showed that the index captured some of the same information individuals used to evaluate their own health. However, a good measure must go beyond this simple bit of validity evidence because self-ratings are unreliable. If they were not, we would use self-perceived health status as the index of health because it is easier than using the health index.

In construct validity no single variable can serve as the criterion. Thus, other studies were used to show a variety of other relationships. For example, it was shown that people who scored as less healthy on the health index also tended to report more symptoms and chronic medical conditions. It also was hypothesized that health status would be related to age, and it was observed that these two variables were indeed systematically related. Older persons in the sample tended to have a lower health status.

The researchers also evaluated specific hypotheses that were advanced on the basis of some theoretical notion about the construct. In the health index studies, the authors reasoned, "If the index really measures health, then we would expect that people who score low on the measure should visit doctors more often." A study confirmed that they do indeed, and this provided evidence for one more inference. Also, certain groups (such as disabled persons) should have lower average scores on the index than other groups (such as nondisabled persons). Again, a study confirmed this hypothesis (Kaplan, Bush & Berry, 1976).

In another series of studies, investigators argued that a health index should correlate with specific physiological measures representing disease states. In one study, for example, patients with chronic lung diseases took measures of lung function. These measures were more strongly correlated with the general health index than they were with a variety of other physiological and social variables (Kaplan, Atkins & Timms, 1984). Other studies demonstrated that the measures were related to clinical indicators of arthritis, AIDS, and cystic fibrosis (Kaplan et al., 1989). If a health index really measures health, then treatments designed to improve health should be reflected by changes in the measure. In one study, patients with arthritis were subjected to a new treatment that was believed to remedy their condition. The general health index demonstrated the significant improvements caused by the treatment (Bombardier et al., 1986). In other studies, the measure was also shown to be related to improvements in conditions such as diabetes (Kaplan et al., 1987), obesity (Lakotas, 1987), and several other conditions (Kaplan, 1993).

Thus, in a series of studies the number of meanings that could be given to the health index was gradually expanded. Yet convergent validity does not constitute all of the evidence necessary to argue for the meaning or construct validity of a psychological test or measure. We also must have discriminant evidence for construct validity.

Discriminant evidence. Science can be very conservative. It confronts scientists with difficult questions such as "Why should we believe your theory if we already have a theory that seems to say about the same thing?" An eager scientist may answer this question by arguing that his or her theory is distinctive and better. In testing we have a similar dilemma. Why should we create a new test if there is already one available to do the job? Thus, one type of evidence a person needs in test validation is proof that the test measures something unique. For example, if a health index measures the same thing as self-rated health, number of symptoms, and number of chronic medical conditions, why do we need it in addition to all these other measures? The answer is that the measure taps something other than the tests used in the convergent validity studies. This demonstration of uniqueness is called **discriminant evidence.** Some authors call this same evidence *divergent validation.*

In the health index example, there may be many different measures that can be used to measure health. Discriminant evidence for validity comes from studies documenting that one health measure might be more responsive to clinical treatment than a variety of other measures (Bombardier et al., 1986).

By providing evidence that a test measures something different from other tests, we also provide evidence that we are measuring some unique construct. Calling an old construct by a new name always should be avoided. Discriminant evidence indicates that the measure does not represent a construct other than the one for which it is devised.

As this discussion implies, construct validity actually subsumes all the activities used in other types of validation studies. In construct validation, for example, content validation is an essential step. Furthermore, convergent and discriminant studies actually correlate the tests with many different criteria. Thus, there is a similarity between construct and criterion validity. Some psychologists argue that construct validity actually is the only major category of validity that need concern us and that others might be thought of as subcategories of construct validity (Anastasi, 1986; Landy, 1986; Messick, 1988; Tenopyr, 1984). According to testing pioneer Lee Cronbach, it may not be appropriate to continue to divide validity into three parts. Cronbach maintains, "All validation is one, and in a sense all is construct validation" (1980, p. 99).

Table 5-1
How Reliability
Affects Validity*

Reliability of Test	Reliability of Criterion	Maximum Validity (Correlation)
1.0	1.0	1.00
.8	1.0	.89
.6	1.0	.77
.4	1.0	.63
.2	1.0	.45
.0	1.0	.00
1.0	.5	.71
.8	.5	.63
.6	.5	.55
.4	.5	.45
.2	.5	.32
.0	.5	.00
1.0	.0	.00
.8	.0	.00
.6	.0	.00
.4	.0	.00
.2	.0	.00
.0	.0	.00

* The first column shows the reliability of the test. The second column displays the reliability of the validity criterion. The numbers in the third column are the maximum theoretical correlations between tests given the reliability of the measures.

Criterion-referenced tests. The procedures for establishing the validity of a criterion-referenced test are quite similar to those for studying the validity of any other test. As you may recall from Chapter 2, criterion-referenced tests have items designed to match certain specific instructional objectives. For example, if the objective for some educational program is for children to be able to list 75% of the countries in Europe, the criterion-referenced test could ask that the countries be listed. Children who listed 75% of the countries would pass the test. They would be evaluated against this specific criterion rather than on the basis of how they perform relative to other students. Validity studies for the criterion-referenced tests would compare scores on the test to scores on other measures that are believed to be related to the test. Some specific procedures for evaluating the validity of a criterion-referenced test have been discussed in more technical articles (see Cronbach, 1971; Hambleton, 1980; Millman, 1974).

E. *Relationship Between Reliability and Validity*

Attempting to define the validity of a test will be a futile effort if the test is not reliable. Theoretically, a test should not correlate more highly with any other variable than it correlates with itself. The maximum validity coefficient

Figure 5-1
Division of total
variation on a
performance
measure as a
function of
validity and
reliability. Many
sources of
variation are
reflected in a test
score.

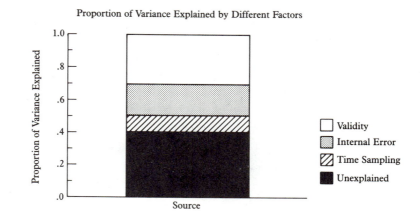

Proportion of Variance Explained by Different Factors

(R_{12max}) between two variables is equal to the square root of the product of their reliabilities, or $R_{12max} = \sqrt{R_{11}R_{22}}$, where R_{11} and R_{22} are the reliabilities for the two variables.

Because validity coefficients are not usually expected to be exceptionally high, it is possible that a modest correlation between the true scores on two traits may be missed if the test for each of the traits was not highly reliable. Table 5-1 shows the maximum validity you would expect to find given various levels of reliability for two tests. Sometimes it is not possible to demonstrate that a reliable test has meaning. In other words, it is possible to have reliability without validity. However, it is logically impossible to demonstrate that an unreliable test is valid.

Reliability and validity are related concepts. Figure 5-1 divides the total variation of a test score into different parts. The example used is a test with a validity coefficient of .40. If we consider the total variability on some measure, such as college performance, about 16% of the variation might be explained by performance on a predictor test. There is also variation in the score, part of which is explained by measurement error. As noted in Chapter 4, this error might be related to time sampling, internal consistency, item sampling, and so forth. The figure hypothetically shows these relationships. Finally, some of the variability is "unexplained" or explained by factors of which we are unaware.

Summary

Validity is a basic idea in measurement and in the science of psychology. Although we have emphasized the validity of psychological tests, the ideas we discussed apply equally to all measures. To make any inference, a good scientist must have substantiating data.

Once a test is "validated," many psychologists mistakenly think it can be used for all purposes. The mistake is that tests are used to support many different inferences. Actually, there should be as many validity studies as there are inferences about the scores (Cronbach, 1971). Anytime we claim that a test score means something different, we need a new validity study. Validity really refers to the things that are said on the basis of the test scores and not to the tests themselves (Landy, 1986).

This suggests that acquiring evidence about the meaning of tests should be an ongoing process. The more a test or a measure is used, the more we learn about what it means. According to two well-known applied psychologists, "Test users should never feel that they know enough about the behavioral meaning of their selection methods" (Dunnette & Borman, 1979, p. 484).

Chapter 6

Building a Test

Learning Objectives

When you have completed this chapter, you should be able to:

- Describe two types of item formats commonly used in objective classroom examinations.

- Know whether or not you should guess on a multiple-choice examination when you are not sure of the correct answer.

- Explain the types of measurement problems the Likert format is used for.

- Discuss what sorts of problems you might encounter if you used a 10-point category scale to rate the abilities of a group of similar individuals.

- Set the level of item difficulty needed for a test that discriminates well among individuals.

- Describe the process of assessing item discriminability.

- Define an item characteristic curve and tell how it is used.

- Draw an item characteristic curve for an item that discriminates well at high levels of performance but not at low levels.

- Explain how item characteristic curves can be used to find items that are unfair to students who "overstudied."

- Discuss some of the limitations of item analysis for tests designed to find specific learning problems.

At this point in your studies, you are probably an experienced test taker. Over the years you have had experience taking numerous tests. Most of these have been classroom exercises; however, you also have been exposed to standardized tests such as the SAT or the Iowa Test of Basic Skills.

As an experienced test taker, you also may have become an experienced test critic. After taking a test, most students are willing to render an opinion: to judge whether it was a fair test or a good test. When you feel that the test was bad, you might ask yourself "How could the test have been better?" In this chapter, we will give some of the basics for creating test items. In the next chapter, we will discuss how to choose and use published tests.

I. *Item Writing*

When a professor announces that there will be a test, one of the first questions is "What kind of test?" Will it be a true/false test, a multiple-choice test, an essay test, or a test in which one must fill in the blanks? Not all tests are in the same format. As you will learn in Part 2 of this book, personality and intelligence tests require all sorts of different responses. After defining the objectives and purpose of the test, the test constructor must determine the type of response he or she wants to require. In part this choice is determined by the purpose of the test. For example, if it is a test that requires right or wrong answers, the task will usually be true/false, multiple choice, matching, or essay.

A. *Item Formats*

The type of test you probably have experienced most is one in which you are given credit for a specific response. In classroom situations, credit is often given for the selection of the "correct" alternative for each test item, and only one alternative is scored as correct. True/false and multiple-choice examinations use this system. Similar formats are used for many other purposes, such as evaluating attitudes, determining knowledge about traffic laws, or deciding whether someone has characteristics associated with a particular health condition. The simplest test of this type uses a dichotomous format.

The dichotomous format. The **dichotomous format** offers two alternatives for each item. Usually a point is given for the selection of one of the alternatives. The most common example of this format is the true/false examination. This test presents students with a series of statements. The student's task is to determine which statements are true and which are false. There are many virtues of the true/false test, including ease of construction and ease of scoring, but the method has also become popular because a teacher can easily construct a test by copying lines out of a textbook. The lines that are copied verbatim are designated as "true." Other statements are altered, so that they are no longer true.

   The advantages of true/false items include their obvious simplicity, ease of administration, and quick scoring. However, there are also disadvantages. For example, true/false items encourage students to memorize material, and it is often possible for students to perform well on a test that covers materials they do not really understand. Another problem is that the chance of getting any item correct by chance alone is 50%. Thus, in order for a true/false test to be reliable, it requires many items.

The dichotomous format is not unique to true/false or educational tests. Many personality tests require responses in a dichotomous format. This may be true/false, or it may be in some other two-choice format such as yes/no. Personality test constructors often prefer this type of format because it requires absolute judgment. For example, in response to an item such as "I often worry about my sexual performance," persons are not allowed to be ambivalent—they must respond true or false. Dichotomous items have many advantages for personality tests with many subscales. One is that they make the scoring of the subscales easy. All that is necessary is to count the number of items a person endorses from each subscale.

Although the true/false format is popular in educational tests, it is not used as frequently as the multiple-choice test, which represents the polychotomous format.

The polychotomous format. The **polychotomous format** is similar to the dichotomous format except that each item has more than two alternatives. Typically, a point is given for the selection of one of the alternatives, and no point is given for selecting any other choice. The multiple-choice examination is the polychotomous format you have encountered most often because it is a popular method of measuring academic performance in large classes. Multiple-choice tests are easy to score, and the probability of obtaining a correct response by chance is lower than it is for true/false items. A major advantage of this format is that it takes very little time for test takers to respond to a particular item because they do not have to write. Thus, the test can cover a large amount of information in a relatively short time.

When taking a multiple-choice examination, your task is to determine which of several alternatives is "correct." All choices that are not correct are called **distractors.** As we will demonstrate in the section on item analysis, the choice of distractors is very important.

Because most students are familiar with multiple-choice tests and related formats such as matching, there is no need to elaborate on their description. However, it is worthwhile to consider some of the issues in the construction and scoring of multiple-choice tests. One question is "How many distractors should a test have?"

Psychometric theory suggests that the items will be more reliable if there are a large number of distractors. In other words, adding more distractors should increase the reliability of the items. However, in practice, adding distractors may not actually increase the reliability because it is difficult to find good ones. The reliability of an item is not enhanced by distractors that are never selected. Studies have shown that it actually is rare to find items for which more than three or four distractors operate efficiently. Ineffective distractors actually may hurt the reliability of the test because they are time consuming to read and can limit the number of items that can be included in a test. After a careful review of the distractor problem, A. G. Wesman (1971) concluded that item writers should try to find three or four good distractors for each item. Well-chosen distractors are an essential ingredient of good items.

Another issue is the scoring of multiple-choice examinations. Suppose you bring your roommate to your sociology test, and he or she fills out an answer sheet without reading the items. Will your roommate get any items correct? The answer is yes—by chance alone. If each item has four choices, the test taker would be expected to get 25% correct. If the items had three choices, a 33.33% correct rate would be expected. Because test takers get some "correct" answers simply by the luck of guessing, a correction for guessing is sometimes used. The formula to correct for guessing is

$$\text{corrected score} = R - \frac{W}{n - 1}$$

where R = the number of right responses

 W = the number of wrong responses

 n = the number of choices for each item

Omitted responses are not included; they provide neither credit nor penalty. For example, suppose that your roommate randomly filled out the answer sheet to your sociology test. The test had 100 items, each with four choices. By chance, his or her expected score would be 25 correct. Let's assume that he or she got exactly that (if the test was filled out randomly, we might not get exactly 25, which is the average random score). The expected score corrected for guessing would be

$$R - \frac{W}{n - 1} = 25 - \frac{75}{4 - 1} = 25 - \frac{75}{3} = 25 - 25 = 0$$

In other words, when the correction for guessing is applied, the expected score is 0.

A question frequently asked by students is "Should I guess on multiple-choice items when I don't know the answer?" The answer depends on how the test will be scored. If a correction for guessing is not used, the best advice is "guess away." By guessing, you have a chance of getting the item correct. You do not have this chance if you do not attempt the item. However, if a correction for guessing is used, random guessing will do you no good. Some speeded tests are scored so that the correction for the guessing formula includes only the items that were attempted; that is, those that were not attempted are not counted either right or wrong. In this case, random guessing and leaving the items blank have the same expected effect.

How about cases when you don't know the right answer but are able to eliminate one or two of the alternatives? How many times have you had it down to two alternatives but couldn't figure out which of the two was correct? In this case, it is advisable to guess. The correction formula assumes that you are equally likely to respond to each of the four categories. For a four-choice item, it would estimate your chance of getting the item correct by chance alone to be one in four. However, if you can eliminate two alternatives, the chances are actually one in two. This gives you a slight advantage over the correction formula. Recently, new mathematical methods have been introduced to summarize information in multiple-choice tests. These methods summarize the mean, the reliability as calculated from the binomial distribution, and a guessing threshold. The guessing threshold describes the chances that a low-ability testing taker will obtain each score. The newer methods are highly technical and are beyond the scope of this text. In summary, the techniques are derived from the first three moments of the test score distribution. Mathematically inclined readers interested in the methods should consult Carlin and Rubin (1991).

True/false and multiple-choice formats are common to educational and achievement tests in which each item has one correct choice and one or more incorrect alternatives. Similar formats are found on personality tests in which a yes or a no response might indicate that a person either endorses or does not endorse a particular item. For example, frequently used personality inventories such as the Minnesota Multiphasic Personality Inventory (MMPI) or the California Psychological Inventory (CPI) present subjects with a long list of statements to which one responds either "True" or "False" (see Chapter 14).

Other personality and attitude measures do not deem any response "right." Rather, they attempt to quantify characteristics of the response. These formats include the Likert format, the category scale, and the Q-sort. Some of these formats will be discussed in more detail in Chapter 14. We should also mention the essay format. This is commonly used in classroom evaluation. Furthermore, the Educational Testing Service announced in 1991 that it would be developing a writing sample as a component of its testing programs. Essay exams can be evaluated using the same principles as structured tests. For example, the validity of the test can be established through correlations with other tests. The reliability of the scoring procedure should be assessed by determining the association between two scores provided by independent scorers. In practice, however, the psychometric properties of essay exams are rarely evaluated.

The Likert format. One popular format for attitude and personality scales requires that a respondent indicate the degree of agreement with a particular attitudinal question. This technique is called the **Likert format** because it was used as part of R. Likert's (1932) method of attitude scale construction. A scale using the Likert format consists of a series of items such as "I am afraid of heights." Instead of asking for a yes/no reply, five alternatives are offered: strongly disagree, disagree, neutral, agree, and strongly agree. This format is especially popular in attitude measurement. For example, it is possible to determine the extent to which people endorse statements such as "The government should not regulate private business."

Responses in Likert format can be subjected to factor analysis. This makes it possible to find groups of items that go together. A similar technique that uses an even greater number of choices is the category format.

The category scale. Ten-point rating scales have become commonplace. When asked for an evaluation of many things, people are requested to rate them on a 10-point scale. The scale need not have exactly 10 points; it can have either more or fewer categories. Rating scales of this sort are called **category scales.**

Although the 10-point scale is very common to psychological research and to everyday conversation, there is still controversy about when and how it should be used. We recently encountered a college basketball coach who rates the quality of upcoming high school players on a 10-point rating scale. It is assumed that this rating provides a reliable estimate of the players' abilities.

FOCUSED EXAMPLE 6-1

The Effect of Context on Value Ratings

The numbers we assign when using rating scales are sometimes influenced by the context or the background against which objects are rated. In one experiment, college students were asked to rate how immoral they believed certain acts to be. The students were divided into two groups. One group rated the items that typically represented "mild" actions (List 1), and the other group rated items that typically represented more severe actions (List 2). The numbers on the right represent average ratings by a large number of college students. If you study the two lists, you will discover that six items are included on both lists. These are marked with asterisks. However, these items are judged more leniently when they are included with items on List 2. This experiment shows that the numbers we assign when using rating scales are affected by context (Parducci, 1968).

List 1

Registering in a hotel under a false name.	1.68
Bawling out servants publicly.*	2.64
Contributing money to a cause in which you do not believe in order to escape criticism.	3.03
Keeping a dime you find in a telephone booth.	1.08
Publishing under your own name an investigation originated and carried out without remuneration by a graduate student working under you.*	3.95
Failing to pay your bus fare when the conductor overlooks you.	2.36
Playing poker on Sunday.	1.17
Failing to put back in the water lobsters that are shorter than the legal limit.*	2.22
Cheating at solitaire.	1.53
Fishing without a license.	2.27
Habitually borrowing small sums of money from friends and failing to return them.*	2.93
Stealing towels from a hotel.	2.58
Stealing a loaf of bread from a store when you are starving.	1.79
Poisoning a neighbor's dog whose barking bothers you.*	4.19
Lying about your whereabouts to protect a friend's reputation.	1.60
Wearing shorts on the street where it is illegal.	1.59

However, experiments have shown that responses to items on 10-point scales are affected by the groupings of the items being rated. For example, if coaches are asked to rate the abilities of a group of 20 very talented players, they may tend to make fine distinctions among them and use many of the categories on the 10-point scale. A particular player who is rated as a 6 when he was on a team with many outstanding players might be rated as a 9 if he were judged with a group of poorly coordinated players (Parducci, 1968, 1982). When given a group of objects to rate, subjects have a tendency to spread their responses evenly across the 10 categories (Stevens, 1966).

Recent experiments have shown that this problem can be avoided if the endpoints of the scale are clearly defined and the subjects are frequently reminded of the definitions of the endpoints. For example, instead of asking coaches to rate the ability of basketball players on a 10-point scale, they might

Pocketing the tip the previous customer left for the waitress.*	3.32
Getting your own way by playing on people's sympathies.	2.90

List 2

Using guns on striking workers.	3.82
Bawling out servants publicly.*	2.39
Stealing ten dollars from an impecunious acquaintance.	3.79
Selling to a hospital milk from diseased cattle.	4.51
Publishing under your own name an investigation originated and carried out without remuneration by a graduate student working under you.*	3.47
Spreading rumors that an acquaintance is a sexual pervert.	3.91
Having a sane person committed to a mental hospital in order to get rid of him.	4.46
Failing to put back in the water lobsters that are shorter than the legal limit.*	1.82
Having sexual relations with a sibling (brother or sister).	3.72
Putting your deformed child in the circus.	3.81
Habitually borrowing small sums of money from friends and failing to return them.*	2.37
Having incestuous relations with your parent.	3.88
Murdering your mother without justification or provocation.	4.79
Poisoning a neighbor's dog whose barking bothers you.*	3.65
Testifying falsely against someone for pay.	4.07
Teaching adolescents to become dope addicts.	4.51
Pocketing the tip the previous customer left for the waitress.*	2.46
Sending another person to take a civil service exam for you.	3.39

From Parducci (1968). Reprinted by permission.

* Items followed by an asterisk appear on both lists.

be shown films depicting the performance of a player rated as 10 and other films of what was meant by 1. Under these circumstances, the subjects are less likely to offer a response that is affected by other stimuli in the group (Kaplan & Ernst, 1983).

People often ask "Why use a 10-point scale instead of a 13-point scale or a 43-point scale?" As it turns out, this has been a matter of considerable study. Some have argued that the optimal number of points is around seven (Symonds, 1924), whereas others have suggested that the optimal number of categories should be three times this number (Champney & Marshall, 1939). As is often the case, the number of categories required depends on the fineness of the discrimination subjects are willing to make. If the subjects are unconcerned about something, they will not make fine discriminations, and a scale with just a few categories will do about as well as a scale that has many. However, when people are very involved with some issue, they will tend to use a greater number of categories. For most rating tasks, however, a 10-point scale seems to provide enough discrimination. N. H. Anderson (1992) has found that a 10-point scale provides substantial discrimination among objects for a wide variety of stimuli.

Checklists and Q-sorts. One format common in personality measurement is the adjective checklist (Gough, 1960). With this method, a subject is given a long list of adjectives and asked to indicate whether each one is characteristic of himself or herself. Adjective checklists can be used for describing either oneself or someone else. (See Focused Example 6-1.) For example, in one study at the University of California at Berkeley, raters checked the traits they thought were characteristic of a group of 40 graduate students. Half these students had been designated by their instructors as exceptional in originality, and the other half had been characterized as low in originality. The results demonstrated that the adjectives chosen to describe members of these two groups differed. The highly original students were characterized most often by the traits "adventurous," "alert," "curious," "quiet," "imaginative," and "fair-minded." In contrast, the low-originality students were seen as "confused," "conventional," "defensive," "polished," "prejudiced," and "suggestible."

The adjective checklist requires subjects to endorse or not endorse self-descriptive adjectives, and it allows only these two choices. A similar technique known as the *Q-sort* increases the number of categories. The Q-sort can be used to describe oneself or to provide ratings of others (Stephenson, 1953). With this technique, a subject is given statements and asked to sort them into nine piles. For example, Block (1961) gave observers 100 statements about personal characteristics. The statements were sorted into piles indicating the degree to which they appeared to be accurate about some particular person. If you were using this method, you might be asked to rate your roommate. You would be given a set of 100 cards. Each card would have a statement on it, such as the following:

Figure 6-1
The California
Q-sort. The
numbers of items
distributed in the
nine piles of the
California Q-sort
approach a
normal
distribution.

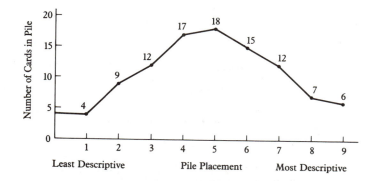

Has a wide range of interests.

Is productive; gets things done.

Is self-dramatizing; is histrionic.

Is overreactive to minor frustrations; is irritable.

Seeks reassurance from others.

Appears to have a high degree of intellectual capacity.

Is basically anxious.

If a statement really hit home, you would place it in pile 9. Those that were not at all descriptive would be placed in pile 1. Most of the cards are usually placed in piles 4, 5, and 6. The frequency of items placed in each of the categories usually looks like a bell-shaped curve (see Figure 6-1). The items that end up in the extreme categories usually say something interesting about the person.

B. *Other Possibilities*

The item formats we have discussed are only a few of many possibilities. If you are interested in learning more about item writing and item formats, you might check some classic references (Edwards, 1957; Guilford, 1954; Torgerson, 1958).

Unfortunately, there is no simple recipe for item writing. Several people have studied the issue carefully and have contributed many useful suggestions (Ebel, 1972; Sax, 1989; Stanley & Hopkins, 1972; Wesman, 1971). If you need to write test items, you should consult these sources. However, writing good items remains an art rather than a science. There is no substitute for using precise language, knowing the subject matter, being familiar with the level of examinees, and using your imagination (Wesman, 1971). Once the items are written and have been administered, there are item analysis techniques that can be used to evaluate them.

II. *Item Analysis*

A good test has good items. But what are good items? How many times have you been in a class in which students launched a full-scale battle over particular items in a multiple-choice test? Good tests with good items are hard to create. Good test making requires careful attention to the principles of test construction. **Item analysis** is a general term for a set of methods used to evaluate test items. It is one of the most important aspects of test construction. Although there are many techniques of item analysis, the basic methods involve assessment of item difficulty and item discriminability.

A. *Item Difficulty*

For a test that measures achievement or ability, **item difficulty** is defined by the number of people who get a particular item correct. For example, if 84% of the people taking a particular test get item 24 correct, then the difficulty level for that item is .84. Some people have suggested that these proportions are not really indicators of item "difficulty" but rather that they measure item "easiness." The higher the proportion of people who get the item correct, the easier the item (Allen & Yen, 1979).

How hard should items be in a good test? This depends on the uses of the test and the types of items. The first thing a test constructor needs to determine is the probability that an item can be answered correctly by chance alone. A true/false item could be answered correctly half of the time if people just guessed randomly. Thus, a true/false item with a difficulty level of .50 would not be a good item. A multiple-choice item with four alternatives could be answered correctly 25% of the time. Therefore, we would require difficulty greater than 25% for an item to be reasonable in this context. Other obvious limits are the extremes of the scale. An item that is answered correctly by 100% of the respondents is of little value in a test because it does not discriminate among individuals.

The optimum difficulty level for items is usually about halfway between 100% of the respondents getting the item correct and the level of success expected by chance alone. Thus, the optimum difficulty level for a four-choice multiple-choice item is about .625. To arrive at this value, we take the 100% success level (1.00) and subtract from it the chance performance level (.25). Then we divide the result by 2 to find the halfway point and add this value to the expected chance level. The steps are outlined here.

Step 1. Find half of the difference between 100% success and chance performance.

$$\frac{1.00 - .25}{2} = \frac{.75}{2} = .375$$

But see next pg.

Step 2. Add this value to the probability of performing correctly by chance.

$$.375 + .25 = .625$$

Midway point   Optimum item difficulty

In most tests we do not want to have all of the items of equal difficulty. Instead, it is preferable to have items that represent a variety of difficulty levels. This is important because a good test discriminates at a variety of different levels. For example, a professor who wants to determine how much students in the class have studied might like to discriminate between students who have not studied at all and those who have studied just a little. Furthermore, the professor might want to discriminate between students who have studied just a little and those who have studied a fair amount. Finally, he or she might want to distinguish those students who have studied more than average from those who have worked and studied exceptionally hard. In other words, the professor needs to make a variety of different discriminations. In order to accomplish this, items at many different levels of difficulty are required.

For most tests, items in the difficulty range of .30 to .70 tend to maximize information about the differences among individuals. However, some tests require a concentration of more difficult items. For example, if a test is to be used to select medical students and only a small number of qualified applicants can be accepted, a test with more difficult items will make finer discriminations. Conversely, a test used to select students for educable mentally retarded classes should have a greater concentration of easier items in order to make fine discriminations among individuals who ordinarily do not perform well on tests (Allen & Yen, 1979). In constructing a good test, you also must give some consideration to human factors. For example, items answered correctly by all students will have poor psychometric qualities, but they may help the morale of the students who take the test. A few easier items may help keep test anxiety in check, which in turn adds to the reliability of the test.

Item difficulty is only one way test items can be evaluated. Another way is to examine the relationship between performance on particular items and performance on the whole test. This is known as **discriminability.**

B. *Discriminability*

In the last section we discussed the analysis of item difficulty. These procedures are used to determine the proportion of people who succeed on a particular item. Another way to examine the value of items is to ask "Who gets this item correct?" Assessment of **item discriminability** is used to determine whether the people who have done well on particular items have also done well on the whole test. There are a variety of ways to evaluate the discriminability of test items.

The extreme group method. This method compares people who have done very well with others who have done very poorly on a test. For example, you might find the students with test scores in the top third and those in the bottom third of the class. Then you can find the proportion of people in the higher group and the proportion of people in the lower group who got each item correct. The difference between these proportions is the discrimination index. Technical Box 6-1 demonstrates this method.

Higher index = higher discriminability

TECHNICAL BOX 6-1

Finding the Item Discrimination Index by Using the Extreme Group Method

Step 1. Identify a group of students that have done well on the test—for example, those in the 67th percentile and above. Also identify a group that have done poorly—for example, those in the 33rd percentile and below.

Step 2. Find the proportion of students in the high group and the proportion of students in the low group that got each item correct.

Step 3. For each item subtract the proportion of correct responses for the low group from the proportion of correct responses for the high group. This gives the item discrimination index (d_i).

Example

Item Number	*Proportion Correct for Students in the Top Third of Class* (P_t)	*Proportion Correct for Students in the Bottom Third of Class* (P_b)	*Discriminability Index* $(d_i = P_t - P_b)$
1	.89	.34	.55
2	.76	.36	.40
3	.97	.45	.52
4	.98	.95	.03
5	.56	.74	−.18

In this example items 1, 2, and 3 appear to discriminate reasonably well. Item 4 does not discriminate well because it is too easy; the level of success is high for both groups. Item 5 appears to be a bad item because it is a "negative discriminator." This sometimes happens on multiple-choice examinations when overprepared students find some reason to disqualify the response keyed as "correct."

The point biserial method. Another way to examine the discriminability of items is to find the correlation between performance on the item and performance on the total test. You might remember from Chapter 3 that the correlation between a dichotomous (two-category) variable and a continuous variable is called a *point biserial correlation*. The point biserial correlation between an item and a total test score is

$$r_{pbis} = \left[\frac{\overline{Y}_1 - \overline{Y}}{S_y} \right] \sqrt{\frac{P_x}{1 - P_x}}$$

where r_{pbis} = the point biserial correlation or index of discriminability

$\overline{Y}_1$ = the mean score on the test for those who got item 1 correct

$\overline{Y}$ = the mean score on the test for all persons

S_y = the standard deviation of the exam scores for all persons

P_x = the proportion of persons getting the item correct (from Allen & Yen, 1979)

For example, suppose that 58% of the students in a psychology class gave the correct response to item 15 on their midterm exam. The mean score on the whole test for these students who got item 15 correct was 57.6, and the mean score for the entire class was 54.3. The standard deviation on the test was 9.7. In order to calculate the discriminability of item 15 by the point biserial method, you would enter this information into the formula:

$$\left(\frac{57.6 - 54.3}{9.7} \right) \sqrt{\frac{.58}{.42}} = .34 \times \sqrt{1.38} = (.34)(1.17) = .40$$

In other words, the correlation between succeeding on item 15 and total test performance is .40.

On tests with only a few items there is a problem with using the point biserial correlation because performance on the item contributes to the total test score. For example, if a test has six items, there is bound to be a positive correlation between getting a particular item correct and the total test score because one sixth of the total score is performance on that item. In order to compensate for this problem, it is sometimes advisable to exclude the item from the total test score. For the six-item test, we might look at the point biserial correlation between passing item 1 and the test score derived from items 2–6. In other words, the item we are evaluating (item 1) is excluded from the total test score.

The point biserial correlation (r_{pbis}) between an item and the total test score is evaluated in very much the same way as the extreme group discriminability index. If this value is negative or of low magnitude, the item should be eliminated from the test. The closer the value of the index is to 1.0, the better the item. It should be noted that very easy items, such as those answered correctly by 90% or more, usually do not appear to be good items on the discriminability index. If 90% of test takers get an item correct, there is too little variability in performance for a substantial correlation with the total test score.

C. *Pictures of Item Characteristics*

A valuable way to learn about items is to graph their characteristics. This can be accomplished with the **item characteristic curve.** A graph can be prepared for particular items in which the total test score is plotted on the *x*, or horizontal, axis and the proportion of examinees who get the items correct is plotted on the *y*, or vertical, axis. The total test score is used as an estimate of the amount of the "trait" possessed by individuals. Because we can never measure traits directly, the total test score is the best approximation we have. Thus, the relationship between performance on the item and performance on the test gives some information about how well the item is tapping the information we are interested in.

Drawing the item characteristic curve. In order to draw the item characteristic curve, you need to define discrete categories of test performance. If the test has been given to large numbers of persons, you can have a category for each test score (65, 66, 67, and so on). However, if the test has been given to a smaller group, you might use a smaller number of class intervals (such as 66–68, 69–71). Once you have arrived at these categories, you need to determine what proportion of the people within each category got each item correct. For example, if you are looking at item 34, you must determine what proportion of the people with a total test score of 65 got the item correct, what proportion of the people with a total test score of 66 got item 34 correct, and so on. Once this series of breakdowns has been obtained, a plot of the proportions of correct responses to an item by total test scores is created. Examples of these graphs are shown in Figures 6-2 to 6-6.

Figure 6-2 shows the item characteristic curve for a "good" test item. The gradual positive slope of the line demonstrates that the proportion of people who pass the item gradually increases as test scores increase. This means that the item successfully discriminates at all levels of test performance. The curve shown in Figure 6-3 illustrates an item that discriminates very well between people at the lower level of performance. However, all of the people who scored above average on the test got this item correct; thus, it did not provide much discrimination in the higher ranges of performance.

Figure 6-4 shows a variety of item characteristic curves. The items shown in the figure are each sensitive in a particular range. Figures 6-5 and 6-6 show item characteristic curves for poor items. The flat curve in Figure 6-5 indicates that test takers at all levels of ability were equally likely to get the item correct. Figure 6-6 demonstrates a particularly troublesome problem. The item characteristic curve gradually rises, showing that the item is sensitive to most levels of

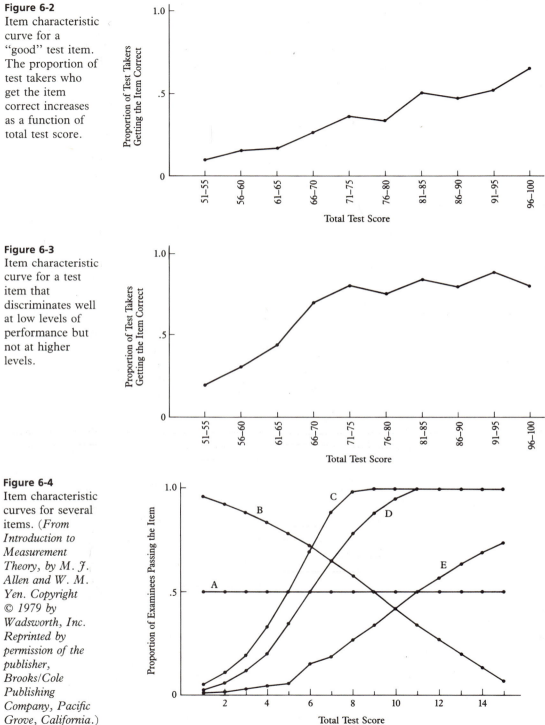

Figure 6-2
Item characteristic curve for a "good" test item. The proportion of test takers who get the item correct increases as a function of total test score.

Figure 6-3
Item characteristic curve for a test item that discriminates well at low levels of performance but not at higher levels.

Figure 6-4
Item characteristic curves for several items. (*From Introduction to Measurement Theory, by M. J. Allen and W. M. Yen. Copyright © 1979 by Wadsworth, Inc. Reprinted by permission of the publisher, Brooks/Cole Publishing Company, Pacific Grove, California.*)

Figure 6-5
An item characteristic curve for a poor item. People with different test scores were equally likely to get the item correct.

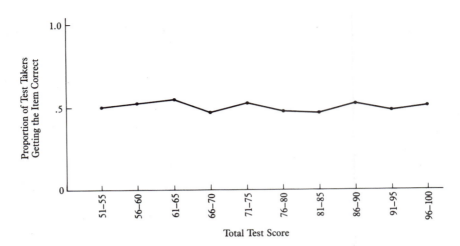

performance. Then it turns down for persons at the highest levels of performance. This suggests that those with the best overall performance on the test did not have the best chances of getting the item correct. This can happen on multiple-choice examinations when one of the alternatives is "none of the above." Students who are exceptionally knowledgeable in the subject area are sometimes able to rule out all of the choices and choose the "none of the above" alternative even though one of the alternatives had actually been designated as correct.

Another convenient picture of item characteristics is shown in Figure 6-7. This graph plots the item numbers within the space created by difficulty on one axis and discriminability (in this case point biserial correlation between item passage and test score) on the other axis. Item 12 has been circled on the graph so that you can identify it. Of all respondents, 46% got this item correct, and its

Figure 6-6
Another example of a problem item. Sometimes test takers who "know too much" will rule out the alternative designated as correct.

Figure 6-7
Items from a 30-item test are plotted on a graph with discriminability on one axis
and difficulty on the other. Each number of the graph represents a test item: 1 is for
item 1 and so on. The shaded area represents items above a discriminability level of
.30 and between 30% and 70% in difficulty level. These items would be the best
candidates to include in the final version of the test. Item 12 (circled) was passed by
46% of the respondents and was correlated .60 with total test score. Thus, it should
be retained.

discriminability level is .60. Thus, the location of item 12 on the graph is
adjacent to 46 on the difficulty axis and to .60 on the discriminability axis.
Earlier in the discussion we noted that "good" items usually fall within the
range of .30 and .70 on item difficulty. Thus, these boundaries represent the
region with acceptable levels of difficulty and discriminability. The shaded
region within these boundaries represents the region in which acceptable levels
of difficulty and discriminability are achieved. Thus, items for the final version
of the test should be selected from this area.

Item response theory. The new approaches to item analysis have generated a
new model of psychological testing. According to classical test theory, a score is
derived from the sum of an individual's responses to various items. The items
are sampled from a larger domain representative of a specific trait or ability.
Newer approaches to testing based on item analysis consider the chances of
getting particular items right or wrong. These approaches, now known as *item
response theory* (IRT), make extensive use of item analysis (Cascio, 1987; Traub
& Lam, 1985). According to this approach, each item on a test has its own item
characteristic curve. The curve describes the probability of getting each particular item right or wrong given the ability of the test takers. With the computer,

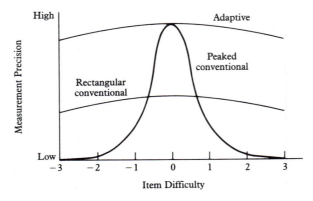

Figure 6-8
Measurement precision as a function of trait level for adaptive, peaked, and rectangular conventional tests. Adaptive tests based on item response theory (IRT) have higher precision across the range of ability levels. (*From "Adaptive Testing by Computer" by D. J. Weiss, in Journal of Consulting and Clinical Psychology, 1985, 53, p. 775.*)

items can be sampled, and the specific range of items where the test taker begins to have difficulty can be identified. From this approach, an ability judgment can be made without subjecting the test taker to all of the test items.

There are various approaches to the construction of tests using item response theory. Some of the approaches use the two dimensions shown in Figure 6-7: difficulty and discriminability. Other approaches add a third dimension for the probability of getting a correct response for test takers with very low levels of ability. Still other approaches use only the difficulty parameter. All of the approaches are similar in that they grade items in relation to the probability that those who do well or poorly on the exam have different levels of performance.

Item characteristic curves can be averaged to create a test characteristic curve, which gives the proportion of responses expected to be correct for each level of ability (Guion & Ironson, 1983).

Perhaps the most attractive advantage of tests based on item response theory is that they are easily adapted for computer administration. The computer can rapidly identify the specific items required to assess a particular ability level. When this approach is used, test takers do not have to suffer the embarrassment of attempting multiple items that are beyond their level of ability. Conversely, they do not need to waste their time and effort on easy items that are far below their capability. In addition, each test taker may get different items to answer. This greatly reduces the chances that someone can successfully cheat from a neighbor. It has been suggested that computer-adapted testing will increase efficiency by 50% or more by reducing the amount of time each test taker spends responding to items (Weiss, 1985).

Figure 6-8 shows the measurement precision associated with conventional and computer-adapted tests. Most conventional tests have the majority of their items at or near an average level of difficulty. This is described as the "peaked conventional" portion of the figure. The precision of the test is very good for those at average ability levels. However, those with very low or very high ability levels are not well assessed by this type of test. An alternative approach, labeled "rectangular conventional" in Figure 6-8, requires that test items be selected so that there is a wide range in level of difficulty. These items are pretested and selected to cover equally the span from very easy to very difficult. The problem with this approach is that only a few items of the test are appropriate for individuals at each ability level. In addition, many test takers spend much of their time responding to items that are either considerably below their ability level or so difficult that they are unable to solve them. As a result, as shown in Figure 6-8, measurement precision is constant across the range of test-taker abilities but relatively low for all people.

The supporters of item response theory believe the solution to this problem lies in computer-adaptive testing. The computer samples items and determines the range on the ability continuum that best represents each test taker. Then testing time is spent focusing on the specific range that challenges the respondent. Items are identified that have a 50% probability of a correct response (assuming no guessing) for each individual. This results in a measurement instrument of equally high precision for all test takers.

Many critics have asserted that computer-adaptive testing using item response theory is not feasible. However, a variety of computer-adaptive tests are now available, and there is growing enthusiasm for this approach (Weiss, 1985). Presently, computers are used in many different aspects of psychological testing (Fowler, 1985).

Internal criteria. One persistent problem in item analysis has been our continued dependence on internal criteria against which to evaluate items. By *internal criteria* we mean total test score. The examples we have just given demonstrate how to compare performance on an item with performance on the total test. Similar procedures can be used to compare performance on an item with performance on an external criterion. For example, if you were building a test to select airplane pilots, you might want to evaluate how well individual items predict success in pilot training or flying performance. The advantages of using external rather than internal criteria against which to validate items were outlined by L. Guttman (1950) more than 40 years ago. Nevertheless, external criteria are rarely used in practice (Linn, 1980).

D. *Items for Criterion-Referenced Tests*

In Chapter 2, we briefly mentioned the concept of criterion-referenced testing. The traditional use of tests requires that we determine how well someone has done on a test by comparing the person's performance to the performance of

Figure 6-9
Frequency polygon used to evaluate a criterion-referenced test.

others. For example, the meaning of Jeff's 67 on a geography test is interpreted by his percentile rank in the geography class. Another way of evaluating Jeff's performance is to ask how much he learned in comparison to how much he "should have" learned. Jeff is no longer in competition with everyone else. Instead, we have defined what Jeff needs to do in order to be considered knowledgeable about a certain unit. Grades are determined by how much Jeff knows rather than whether or not he knows more than someone else.

A *criterion-referenced test* is one that compares performance to some clearly defined criterion for mastery. This approach is very popular in individualized instruction programs. For each student a set of objectives is defined. These objectives state exactly what the student should be able to do after an educational experience. For example, an objective for a junior high school algebra student might be to solve linear equations with two unknowns. The criterion-referenced test would be used to determine whether this objective had been achieved. After demonstrating this knowledge, the student can move ahead to another objective. Many educators regard criterion-referenced tests as diagnostic instruments. When a student does poorly on some items, the teacher knows that the individualized education program needs more focus in that particular problem area.

There are many problems in the development of criterion-referenced tests. The first step involves clearly specifying the objectives. This is done by writing clear and precise statements about what the learning program is attempting to achieve. These are usually stated in terms of something the student will be able to do. For example, an objective for a unit in high school civics might be to understand the operation of municipal government. Test items that assess the attainment of this objective might ask about the taxation powers of local governments, the relation of municipal to state government, and so on.

To evaluate the items in the criterion-referenced test, the test should be given to two groups of students—one that has been exposed to the learning unit and one that has not. Figure 6-9 shows what the distribution of scores would look like. The frequency polygon looks like a V. The scores on the left side of the V are probably those from students who have not experienced the unit. Scores on the right represent those who have been exposed to the unit. The bottom of the V is called the *antimode,* and it is the least frequent score. This point divides those who have been exposed to the unit from those who have not been exposed. This is usually taken as the cutting point. When people get scores higher than the antimode, we assume that they have met the objective of the test. When they get lower scores, we assume they have not met the objective. In Figure 6-9 the cutting score is 5.

Criterion-referenced tests have many advantages for newer approaches to education. One growing area in which they have been useful is computer-assisted instruction. For example, a large program created by the American Institutes for Research and the Westinghouse Learning Corporation involved students obtaining much of their education by interacting with a computer terminal. Each student works at his or her own pace on an individualized program of instruction. After the student is exposed to the program, a criterion-referenced test is used to evaluate progress. Students who pass the test can move on to the next unit. Students who do not pass can repeat some of the instruction until they pass. Some people feel this approach to education maximizes individual potential (Flanagan, 1971).

E. *Limitations of Item Analysis*

The growing interest in criterion-referenced tests has posed some new questions about the adequacy of our item analysis procedures. The major problem is that statistical methods for item analysis tell the test constructor which items do a good job of separating students; however, they do not help the students learn. Young children do not care as much about how many items they missed as they do about what they are doing wrong (Davis, 1979). Many times a child will make very specific errors and will continue to make these same mistakes until discovering why he or she is making the mistakes.

For example, an achievement test might ask a fourth-grade student to add .40 and .30. One of the multiple-choice alternatives would be .07 because item analysis had demonstrated that this was a good distractor. The child who selected .07 would not receive a point on the item and also might continue to make similar errors. Although the data are available to give the child feedback on the "bug" in his or her thinking, there is nothing in the testing procedure that initiates this guidance (Linn, 1980). One study involving 1300 fourth-, fifth-, and sixth-graders found that 40% of the children made the same type of error when given problems of a particular kind (Brown & Burton, 1978). Some researchers in educational measurement now appear to be moving toward testing programs that diagnose in addition to assessing (Bloom, 1980; Davis, Jockusch & McKnight, 1978; Linn, 1980). Tests can have different purposes. In the past, we have placed too much emphasis on ranking students and not enough on discovering specific weaknesses or gaps in knowledge.

Summary   There is an art and a science to test construction. Writing good items is a complex and demanding task. The first step involves deciding what sort of information you are trying to obtain. True/false items may be used if you are attempting to evaluate absolute judgment. A similar format that is used to evaluate whether or not test takers know "the right information" is the multiple-choice format, in which a correct choice must be selected among several alternatives. With these types of formats, the test constructor always must consider the probability that someone will get an answer correct by chance.

Many formats are available for tests that do not have right or wrong answers. The Likert format is popular for attitude scales. Statements are presented, and respondents can check the degree to which they agree or disagree with the statements on a 5-point scale. A similar format is the category-scaling method, in which ratings are obtained on a scale with defined endpoints. The familiar 10-point scale is an example of a category scale. Unfortunately, category scales are subject to some bias when the endpoints are not clearly defined. Checklists and Q-sorts are among the many item formats used in personality research. These methods require a person to make judgments about whether certain items are descriptive of them or of other people.

Once test items have been created, they can be administered to groups of individuals and the values of the items can be systematically assessed. One method of item analysis requires evaluation of item difficulty. *Difficulty* is usually assessed by examining the number of persons who get each item correct. In addition to difficulty analysis, test constructors usually examine the correlation between getting any item correct and the total test score. This correlation is used as an index of *discriminability*.

Another way to learn about the value of items is by drawing a picture of the *item characteristic curve*. For example, the proportion of people who get an item correct can be plotted as a function of the total test score. Better items are those for which the probability of getting the item correct is highest among those with the highest test scores.

Criterion-referenced tests require a different approach to test construction. With criterion-referenced tests, a person's knowledge is evaluated against what he or she is expected to know rather than against what others know. To evaluate items in criterion-referenced tests, performance for those who would be expected to know the material is compared with performance of others who would not be expected to have mastered the information.

Chapter 7

Selection and Decision Analysis

Learning Objectives

When you have completed this chapter, you should be able to:

- Discuss the proper methods for selecting a meaningful test.
- Identify the first consideration in determining whether it is worthwhile to administer a test.
- Explain the meaning of base rates in personnel selection.
- Identify three methods that have been developed to estimate the amount of information a test gives beyond what is known by chance.
- Define incremental validity.
- Discuss the significance of utility and decision theory.
- Explain the problem with utility theory equations.
- List several sources that contain valuable information about psychological tests.

There are literally thousands of psychological tests. Some of these may be valuable, while others are useless. As a student of psychology, you will need to learn how to be a good consumer of testing materials.

Table 7-1 presents two sets of items from two "tests." One set is from the Experiential World Inventory. The other set is from the writings of columnist and humorist Art Buchwald. Both sets of items appear to be ridiculous, yet one set purportedly has a purpose other than to provide humor. Can you tell which test is which?

Just because the promoters of a personality test known as the Experiential World Inventory argue that their measure is valuable, you do not have to accept their opinion. Instead, you must carefully evaluate the information yourself. Do items that ask about drinking blood have more meaning than those that ask about being bored by thoughts of death? The answer depends on the evidence the test constructors have to support the meaning of their test. In

Table 7-1
Items from Two
Personality Scales

Set 1	Set 2
The sight of blood no longer excites me.	Animals often try to fool me.
It makes me furious to see an innocent man escape the chair.	I feel like killing untidy people.
When I was a child, I was an imaginary playmate.	I sometimes taste sound.
I am bored by thoughts of death.	Someone is making copies of me.
I become homicidal when people try to reason with me.	I sometimes think other people's thoughts.
I don't like it when somebody is rotten.	I am afraid somebody may cut off my nose.
Most of the time I go to sleep without saying goodbye.	Old men are indecent.
Frantic screams make me nervous.	I am someone else.
	I would like to drink blood.
	I feel that my ideas may turn into insects.

From "Objective Personality Tests and Measures" by L. R. Goldberg. Reproduced, with permission, from the *Annual Review of Psychology*, Vol. 25. © 1974 by Annual Reviews, Inc. (Set 1 is from Art Buchwald's column, and set 2 is from the Experiential World Inventory.)

the case of the Experiential World Inventory, there is little reason to believe that scores on this test are more meaningful than the scores on a test created by Art Buchwald, a test he created only for comedy.

This chapter will review methods for selecting a meaningful test. These methods assess whether the test results will provide useful information.

I. *The Test Manual*

Before you use a test, many decisions must be made. Tests are categorized as proprietary and nonproprietary. A *proprietary* test is one that is the property of the test developer or, in many cases, of a publishing company. A proprietary test is protected by copyright laws, and a user must pay for the privilege of using it. The items on proprietary tests are protected and generally kept restricted. For example, unless you are a professional psychologist, you probably would not have access to the items from widely used tests such as the Minnesota Multiphasic Personality Inventory or the Stanford-Binet intelligence scales. *Nonproprietary* tests are not protected by copyright in the same way. Most often they are distributed by the test developer or are published in journals. For example, the Internal-External Locus of Control Scale (Rotter, 1966), one of the most widely used measures in personality research, was published in an academic journal. Most users of this scale simply copy the items from the article and pay no royalty to a publisher. However, before you use test items in a written publication, you should check with the publisher. The June/July 1981 *APA Monitor* reported that *Boston Magazine* was required to pay psychologist Zick Rubin $5000 for using his love questionnaire without permission (Foltz, 1981).

Testing is a large and profitable business that has not been controlled. In many ways the use of psychological tests is similar to the use of prescription

Table 7-2
Checklist of
Questions That
Should Be
Answered in the
Test Manual

Standardization Sample
1. How many subjects were used to establish the reliability, validity, and norms for the test?
2. What were the demographic and personal characteristics of these subjects? Are they similar to those of the group you will give the test to?

Reliability
1. What methods were used to estimate the reliability of the test?
2. Is the reliability high enough for your purposes (usually .90 or above for tests used to make decisions about individuals and .70 or above for research purposes)?

Validity
1. Is there evidence that the test is meaningful for *your purposes*?
2. What specific criteria was the test validated against?

Scoring
1. Are scoring keys available?
2. If the test can be scored by machine, how much does it cost and what sort of report is offered?

Practical Considerations
1. How long does it take to administer the test?
2. Does the test require reading? If so, is it at the right level for the people you will test?
3. How much training is required for the test administrator? How can the training be obtained?

drugs. Although there are no toxic effects from the tests, it is possible that people can be unnecessarily hurt when they are classified improperly by the tests. In order for a new drug to get on the market, it must be tested and meet the standards of the Food and Drug Administration (FDA). There is no equivalent agency that monitors the standards for psychological tests. In place of a federal bureau responsible for overseeing psychological tests, a joint committee of the American Education Research Association, the American Psychological Association, and the National Council for Measurement in Education (1985) created standards and published them in a booklet entitled *Standards for Educational and Psychological Testing*. The short booklet provides a clear set of standards for test developers and users and defines the minimum information necessary for a test manual.

Most commercial test users find proprietary tests best suited for their purposes. If you were to use a proprietary test, you would need to be a qualified test administrator who has had appropriate training and experience. To decide whether the test was suited for your purpose, you would need to consult the test manual.

The test manual gives all of the basic information needed to administer a test, to score it, and to make sense out of the results. If a test manual is constructed according to the *Standards* defined by the joint committee, it will answer most of the questions you have about validity, reliability, and norms. Because we covered these topics in earlier chapters, you should have a good feel for the meaning of norms and the minimum standards for reliability and validity. When evaluating a test, you should ask a series of questions; these are summarized in the checklist in Table 7-2.

For many industrial applications, other factors also must be considered. One important criterion is the amount of information the test gives beyond what is known without it. This can be derived from an analysis of base and hit rates.

II. *Base Rates and Hit Rates*

A test always should provide more information than you would get by chance. Thus, tests must be evaluated in terms of how much they contribute beyond what would be known without them. Many times tests are used to place individuals into one of two categories. For example, on the basis of an employment test, a candidate is deemed acceptable or unacceptable. In a medical setting, a test may be used to decide whether or not a person has a tumor in a certain area of the brain. Because tests are not always exactly accurate, the possibility of making an error in assigning someone to a category must be evaluated.

If a test is used to make a dichotomous (two-choice) decision, a cutoff score usually is used. Values above this score might go into the plus category, and values below it might go into the minus category. The plus category might be used to indicate that the person is suitable for the job or that he or she has the tumor. The score marking the point of decision is called the *cutting score*. Establishing a cutting score does not necessarily mean that the decisions will be correct. Sometimes a person will score above the cutting score but will perform as though he or she should not have. For example, suppose that a person scores above the cutting score for an employment test but later fails on the job. This suggests that the test has not done its job. Tests can be evaluated by how well they sort people into the right categories.

By using cutting scores, we can divide people into two categories—for example, accept/reject or positive diagnosis/negative diagnosis. For the purpose of illustration, we will use a test that determines which people to hire for a particular job. Those who score above the cutting score might be labeled "acceptable," and those who score below might be called "unacceptable." In addition to the scores on the test, it is essential to have some data on how people really do on the job. To do this, the employer must define some criterion for deciding whether job performance has been acceptable or unacceptable. Using these two sets of categories, we can construct a chart such as that shown in Table 7-3. There are four cells in this table. Two of the four cells are labeled "Hit" because the test has made the correct prediction. *Hits* occur when (1) the test predicts that the person will be unacceptable and indeed he or she fails, or (2) the test indicates that the person is acceptable and he or she does turn out to be successful. *Misses* occur when the test makes an inaccurate prediction. The **hit rate** is the proportion of cases in which a test accurately predicts success or failure.

Table 7-3
Hits and Misses
for Predicting a
Dichotomous
Outcome Using a
Cutting Score

Performance on the Job	Decision on the Basis of Cutting Score	
	Acceptable	Unacceptable
Success	Hit	Miss
Failure	Miss	Hit

Many times a test does not need to have a good hit rate because the rate of predicting success on the job is high without the test. For example, it might be possible to predict who will do well in law school on the basis of information other than scores on the Law School Admissions Test (LSAT). College grades might be used. Success on the criterion in this case might be passing the bar examination on the first attempt. The pass rate not using the LSAT would be called the **base rate.** The real value of a test comes from a comparison of the hit rate when the test is used with the base rate without the test. In other words, the hit rate must tell us how much information a test contributes to the prediction of success beyond what we would know by just examining the proportion of people who succeed.

For example, suppose the LSAT has a hit rate of 76% for predicting who will pass the bar examination in a certain state. However, 85% of the people who take the test for the first time in that state pass. The LSAT in this case tells us less than the available information. There may be other circumstances in which the hit rate is very low but the base rate is even lower. For example, suppose you need to select people for a position that will involve world-class competition. Under the circumstances very few people could be expected to do well—say only 3% would be expected to succeed. If a test could be developed that had a 10% hit rate, it might be considered of value.

Another problem to consider with regard to hit and miss rates is the relative costs. Sometimes a miss is very costly. Medical situations provide good examples of costly misses. Consider the costs of concluding on the basis of a test that a tumor is benign (not cancerous) when it is really malignant (cancerous). The cost of this sort of miss is that the life of the patient is seriously endangered. In a psychological application, there may be grave consequences of concluding that someone is not suicidal because he or she is below the cutoff score when there is, in fact, suicide potential. The cost of this sort of miss is that a preventable suicide may occur. These cases are **false negatives.** If the cost of a false negative is high, it may be of value to lower the cutting score. With a lower cutting score, the test will make more errors, but the errors will not be so potentially dangerous.

The other type of miss is the **false positive.** An example of a false-positive situation is one in which someone is selected for a job on the basis of a test. Once on the job, the person does poorly and gets fired. Sometimes there are high costs associated with this type of error. For instance, time and money might be invested to train a person who eventually is unable to do the job. In

Table 7-4
Hypothetical
Example of Hits
and Misses, with
83% Accuracy
and 80%
Detection*

		Test Result		
		Brain Damage	**Normal**	**Total**
	Brain Damage	A 8	B 2	10
Actual	**Normal**	C 15	D 75	90
	Total	23	77	100

A = hit   A + B = base rate

B = false negative

C = false positive

D=hit

A/(A + B) = detection rate (sensitivity)

D/(C + D) = specificity

(A + D)/(A + B + C + D) = accuracy rate

* We are grateful to Dr. Frank M. Rosekrans, Eastern Washington University, for suggesting this example.

addition, job failure is harmful for the person and might be a blow to self-esteem and self-confidence. If the costs of a false positive are high, it may be of value to raise the cutting score.

A few examples may help clarify the concepts of hits and misses for different base rates. Table 7-4 presents a medical example in which a test is used to determine whether a patient has brain damage. In a validation study, an expensive radiological procedure is used to confirm whether the patient actually has brain damage. On the basis of the test results, we conclude that the patient has brain damage or is normal. The test suggests that 23 of 100 patients have brain damage, while the other 77 are normal. The table also shows the actual number of patients who have brain damage or are normal. In reality, 10 of the 100 have damage, while 90 are normal. There are two types of hits in Table 7-4. For the 10 patients who actually have brain damage, 8 are detected by the tests. In other words, the test has a detection rate of 80%. In addition, the test says that 75 individuals are normal who, it is confirmed, are actually normal. Both of these cases are hits because the test produces the correct result. There are 83 cases in 100 when the test produces an accurate conclusion; that is, the test has 83% accuracy.

There are also two types of misses. In two cases, the test suggested that a person was normal when he or she actually had brain damage. In addition, there were 15 cases in which the test suggested that a person had brain damage when, in fact, he or she was normal. Cases in which the test suggests the person is normal when, in fact, he or she has a problem are called *false negatives*. The test is negative but, in actuality, the negative conclusion is false. There are two

Table 7-5
Hypothetical
Example of Hits
and Misses, with
40% Accuracy
and 44%
Detection*

| | | Test Result | | |
		Brain Damage	Normal	Total
	Brain Damage	A 40	B 50	90
Actual	**Normal**	C 10	D 0	10
	Total	50	50	100

A = hit   A + B = base rate

B = false negative

C = false positive

D = hit

A/(A + B) = detection rate (sensitivity)

D/(C + D) = specificity

(A + D)/(A + B + C + D) = accuracy rate

* We are grateful to Dr. Frank M. Rosekrans, Eastern Washington University, for suggesting this example.

such cases in this example. Cases in which the test suggests there is a problem when there really is no problem are called *false positives*. There are 15 cases in this example. A false positive occurs when we come to the incorrect conclusion that there is a problem.

The cells in Table 7-4 are labeled A, B, C, and D. Cells A and D are hit cells. The sum of these cells divided by the sum of all cells (A + B + C + D) is the accuracy rate. Cell B is a false negative, and cell C is a false positive. Cell A divided by the sum of A + B is the detection rate.

The example in Table 7-4 suggests that the test is relatively good at detecting brain damage. One of the reasons the test works well in this situation is that the base rate for brain damage is relatively low. In actuality, only 10% of the patients have this problem, and the test detects 80% of the cases.

Now consider the example in Table 7-5. In this case, a test is used on a population with a very high base rate for brain damage (90%). The test suggests that 50 of 100 people have brain damage when, in fact, 90 of 100 people have the problem. The test is accurate in 44% (40/90 = .44) of the cases. In this example, there are only 10 false positives. These are cases where the test says there is a problem but the person is really normal. The test has a high false-negative rate. In these cases, the test reports normal when, in reality, the person does have a problem. Finally, the table suggests that the test never concludes that someone is normal when he or she does not have a problem.

Using cutting scores to find hits and misses is an issue in criterion validity (see Chapter 5). Many years ago, H. C. Taylor and J. T. Russell (1939) demonstrated how to relate validity coefficients to accuracy rates in selection.

A. *Taylor-Russell Tables*

The decision to use a test must depend on what is gained by it. In Chapter 5, we reviewed the concept of criterion validity and showed that tests with significant predictive or concurrent validity coefficients did better than chance in forecasting performance on a criterion. However, knowing that a test is better than chance is not good enough for making choices about whether it will be of value in some applications. In the last section, we presented the concept of base rates and noted that a worthwhile test must provide more information than would be known from the base rates.

In 1939, Taylor and Russell developed a method for evaluating the validity of a test in relation to the amount of information it contributes beyond the base rates. The method for assessing the value of tests is neatly summarized in a series of tables that have come to be known as the **Taylor-Russell tables.** To use the tables you must have the following information:

F O C U S E D   E X A M P L E   7 - 1

The Mammography Controversy

Medical tests are not unlike psychological tests. They have validity and reliability and can be assessed in relation to their hit rates and miss rates. One interesting controversy involves the use of mammography to screen women for breast cancer. Mammography has clearly been shown to be a valuable medical test for women age 50 and older. However, there is some controversy for women who are younger than 50. The reason for this controversy is related to the base rates and the rates of false positives and false negatives.

Breast cancer is very much related to age. Although the American Cancer Society argues that one in nine women will develop breast cancer, these tumors are much more common among older women than among younger women (see Figure 7-1). For women in their twenties, breast cancer is an extremely rare disease. In fact, 100,000 mammograms would have to be performed in order to find one such woman with breast cancer. This suggests that for younger women the base rate for breast cancer is very low (1/100,000). This has become somewhat of a controversy because the popular media have lodged a campaign attempting to increase the use of mammography for all women. If we pay for mammography from public funds and the cost of a mammogram is $100, it would cost about $10 million to detect one case. Of course, any investment would be valuable if it saved lives. However, analyses of studies of breast cancer suggest that the rare case of breast cancer detected in young women results in no better chance of survival than a case left undetected. However, this is a matter of considerable debate in the medical community.

The related concern for performing mammography in younger women is that breast tissue in young women is denser than it is in older women. As a result, there is a significant number of false positives in younger women. It has been estimated that one younger woman in three who gets repeated mammograms will have a false positive that requires further medical tests or biopsies (Miller, 1991).

What does this tell us? Clearly, mammography has been shown to be a valuable medical test

1. *Definition of success*. For each situation in which the test is to be used, success on the outcome must be defined. This could be that the patient lived, that the person succeeded on the job, or that the student did well in college. Success must be defined clearly by dichotomizing some outcome variable. For example, first-year grade point averages above 2.3 might be defined as success in college and those below might be defined as failures. Or salespersons who achieve average monthly sales over $5000 might be deemed successful, and those who sell less than $5000 might be thought of as unsuccessful.

2. *Determination of base rate*. The percentage of persons who would succeed if there were no testing or screening procedure must be determined.

3. *Definition of selection ratio*. The **selection ratio** must be defined. This is the percentage of applicants selected or admitted.

for older women, but for younger women, those in their twenties and early thirties, the picture may be different. There is a very low base rate for the problem, and there are significant risks of false- positive results. Of course, women with risk factors for breast cancer, such as a strong family history of the condition, may still benefit from routine screening.

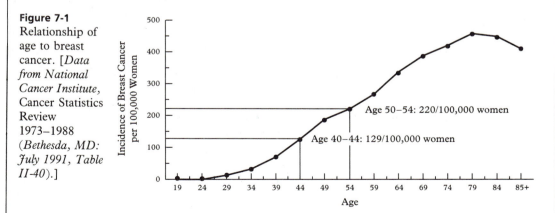

Figure 7-1 Relationship of age to breast cancer. [*Data from National Cancer Institute,* Cancer Statistics Review 1973–1988 (*Bethesda, MD: July 1991, Table II-40*).]

Table 7-6
Taylor-Russell Table for a Base Rate of .60

Validity (ρ_{XY})	Selection Ratio										
	.05	.10	.20	.30	.40	.50	.60	.70	.80	.90	.95
.00	.60	.60	.60	.60	.60	.60	.60	.60	.60	.60	.60
.05	.64	.63	.63	.62	.62	.62	.61	.61	.61	.60	.60
.10	.68	.67	.65	.64	.64	.63	.63	.62	.61	.61	.60
.15	.71	.70	.68	.67	.66	.65	.64	.63	.62	.61	.61
.20	.75	.73	.71	.69	.67	.66	.65	.64	.63	.62	.61
.25	.78	.76	.73	.71	.69	.68	.66	.65	.63	.62	.61
.30	.82	.79	.76	.73	.71	.69	.68	.66	.64	.62	.61
.35	.85	.82	.78	.75	.73	.71	.69	.67	.65	.63	.62
.40	.88	.85	.81	.78	.75	.73	.70	.68	.66	.63	.62
.45	.90	.87	.83	.80	.77	.74	.72	.69	.66	.64	.62
.50	.93	.90	.86	.82	.79	.76	.73	.70	.67	.64	.62
.55	.95	.92	.88	.84	.81	.78	.75	.71	.68	.64	.62
.60	.96	.94	.90	.87	.83	.80	.76	.73	.69	.65	.63
.65	.98	.96	.92	.89	.85	.82	.78	.74	.70	.65	.63
.70	.99	.97	.94	.91	.87	.84	.80	.75	.71	.66	.63
.75	.99	.99	.96	.93	.90	.86	.81	.77	.71	.66	.63
.80	1.00	.99	.98	.95	.92	.88	.83	.78	.72	.66	.63
.85	1.00	1.00	.99	.97	.95	.91	.86	.80	.73	.66	.63
.90	1.00	1.00	1.00	.99	.97	.94	.88	.82	.74	.67	.63
.95	1.00	1.00	1.00	1.00	.99	.97	.92	.84	.75	.67	.63
1.00	1.00	1.00	1.00	1.00	1.00	1.00	1.00	.86	.75	.67	.63

From ''The Relationship of Validity Coefficients to the Practical Effectiveness of Tests in Selection: Discussion and Tables'' by H. C. Taylor and J. T. Russell. *Journal of Applied Psychology*, 1939, *23*, 565–578. Copyright 1939 by the American Psychological Association.

4. *Determination of validity coefficient.* Finally, a validity coefficient for the test is required. That is usually the correlation of the test with the criterion.

The Taylor-Russell tables give the likelihood that a person selected on the basis of the test score will be successful. There is a different table for each base rate. Table 7-6 is a Taylor-Russell table for a base rate of .60.

To use the table find the row representing the validity of the test that would be used for selection. Then find the column associated with the proportion of people who can be selected. The number in the body of the table associated with a particular row and a particular column gives you an estimate of the percentage of people who could be expected to succeed when they are selected on the basis of the test.

For example, suppose that you are put in charge of deciding who will be admitted to a program to train teachers in secondary education. The first thing you must do is decide on a definition of success. After meeting with a committee, you may decide that success will be defined as completing the program and obtaining a satisfactory performance evaluation in student teaching. By studying records, you determine that when no selection procedure was used, 60% of the applicants to the program succeeded on this task. Thus, the base rate would be 60%, and the Taylor-Russell table for a base rate of .60 would be used. You then consider using the Graduate Record Examination (GRE) to select people for your program because you can accept only 70% of the applicants. A study is done, and it is determined that the correlation between GRE scores and success (completing the program and obtaining a satisfactory evaluation in student teaching) is .30. This is the validity of the test for predicting the criterion.

In order to estimate how many people would be expected to succeed if they are selected on the basis of GRE scores, we must enter the Taylor-Russell table (Table 7-6) for a base rate of .60. Find the row associated with the .30 validity and move across the table until you are in the column for a selection ratio of .70 (the percentage of applicants you can admit to your program). You should arrive at the number .66, which is the proportion of applicants you would expect to be successful if the selection was on the basis of the GRE. This analysis tells us that 66% of those selected on the basis of GRE scores can be expected to be successful and 60% of those selected at random can be. Should the GRE be required for admittance to your program? To answer this question, you must decide whether the increment of 6% associated with the use of the test is worth the extra effort and expense of requiring it.

Looking at Table 7-6, you can see that tests will be more valuable in some situations than in others. For example, a test is most useful when the validity of the test is high and the selection ratio is low. This is clear from an inspection of the lower left-hand portion of Table 7-6. Conversely, when the validity is low and the selection ratio is high (the upper right-hand portion of the table), the test will be of little value. When the test has no validity (see the first row of the table), using the test will be no better than selecting applicants by chance. Similarly, when nearly everyone is selected (last column), there is little reason to use a test.

Whenever a selection procedure is used, you always should remember that some qualified applicants will be turned away. The use of rational selection procedures should help make the system more fair by decreasing the number of qualified applicants not selected. One way to evaluate the selection procedure is to show the ratio of people selected by the test who then succeed and the ratio of those who would have succeeded but were not selected.

Suppose that you are the personnel manager for a company and that you can choose 30 of 100 applicants for a job. In order to make this decision, you have results of a test with a validity of .70. You also know that the base rate for success on the job is .60. Using the Taylor-Russell table for a base rate of .60, you find that 91% of those selected on the basis of the test would be expected to

Table 7-7
What Would
Happen to 100
Applicants If 30
People Were
Selected on the
Basis of a Test
with a Validity of
.70 for a Job with
a 60% Base
Success Rate?

	Decision		
Performance	**Select**	**Reject**	**Total**
Success*	27	33	60
Failure	3	37	40
Total	30	70	100

* Success ratio given selection = 27/30 = .90 (actually
.91 without rounding, see Table 7-6). Success ratio given
rejection = 33/70 = .47.

succeed on the job. Because you can select 30 people, this would imply that approximately 27 of them would be expected to succeed and 3 would be expected to fail (91% of 30 = 27.3).

When you decide to hire 30 of the applicants, you also are deciding not to hire 70 people. It is important to realize that not all of the 70 people would fail if they were selected. In fact, many of them will be capable people who have been "misdiagnosed" by the testing procedure. In order to justify your use of the test, it would be your responsibility to explain why your selection procedure is worthwhile, even though it turns down some people who would have succeeded and selects some who fail.

Table 7-7 shows what would happen to all of the 100 applicants. A total of 30 would be accepted and 70 would be rejected (the selection ratio equals .30). However, because the base rate for success is .60, 60 of the 100 applicants would have succeeded on the job and 40 would have failed. The Taylor-Russell table tells us that 91% of those selected on the basis of the test will succeed. This translates into 27 of the 30 selected (.9 × 30 = 27.3), and it also implies that only about 3 of the 30 selected will fail.

Among the 60 people who would have succeeded, only 27 could be selected. This means that 33 people who would have been good choices were rejected. However, among the 40 people who would have failed, an estimated 37 would be in the rejected group. We already know from the Taylor-Russell table that about 91% of those selected by the test would be expected to succeed. Using Table 7-7, we also can calculate the proportion of those rejected on the basis of the test who would be expected to succeed. This comes to 33/70 = .47. Although the procedure leads to the rejection of many capable applicants, it can be defended as rational because the proportion of those succeeding is much higher among those who are selected by the procedure than among those rejected by the procedure.

The Taylor-Russell tables can also be used to show the futility of certain types of assessment procedures. For example, M. A. McDaniel (1989) suggested that routine background information may be useful in predicting employee success. In his study, McDaniel used information on school suspension, drug use, quitting school, participation in social clubs, school grades, contacts with the legal system, and socioeconomic status to predict success in the military service. The criterion for succeeding in the military service was not being discharged for being unsuitable. The study demonstrated that most of the background variables predicted unsuitability discharges. However, the validity coefficients were very low. The highest validity coefficient was about .15. Let us assume that the selection ratio for the armed services is about .9. In other words, nine out of every ten applicants are admitted to the military service. Let us also assume the base rate of success of 60%. (Actually in the McDaniel study the base rate was about 85%, but assuming 60% allows us to do this exercise with Table 7-6.) When we use the Taylor-Russell table for a validity of .15 and a selection ratio of .90, we find that the proportion who succeed in military service goes to .61. Using only base rate information, we would have predicted that 60% succeed. The information on dropping out of school improves this prediction to only 61%! The low validity for the background information is the reason for this negligible improvement. Although background information may be useful, it may provide only a minimum of information about future success.

B. *Utility Theory and Decision Analysis*

The use of Taylor-Russell tables requires that the criterion be a dichotomous variable. However, success usually is measured on a more refined numerical scale. By considering it as only a dichotomous variable, we ignore much of the information available to the analyst. For example, instead of considering whether or not someone failed on a job, it seems more reasonable to use a continuum of performance as the criterion. Developments since the publication of the Taylor-Russell tables have attempted to define levels of success rather than considering either success or failure. These formulations are based on utility theory (Brogden, 1946, 1949; Cronbach & Gleser, 1965; Schmitt & Robertson, 1990).

Although the use of decision and utility theory can be of great advantage to the industrial psychologist, the equations used to calculate the value of test information are quite complex. Furthermore, the equations require certain information that is hard to estimate. For example, in order to use the equations, you must estimate the dollar value associated with different levels of performance on the job. For most jobs this is difficult to estimate (Dunnette & Borman, 1979). F. Schmidt and J. E. Hunter (1983) demonstrated that 40% of the average salary can be used as a rough estimate of the standard deviation of the output. They presented mathematical arguments showing that the 40% rule produces reasonable estimates in most cases. Several other approaches have been suggested to resolve this problem, although progress has been slow (Cascio & Ramos, 1986; Eaton, Wing & Mitchell, 1985). Raju and co-workers (1989) developed a new approach to utility assessment that did not require an estimate of the dollar value for performance. They proposed that the value of each individual can be estimated from the total value of his or her compensation package. This approach simplifies the calculations and produces results similar to other methods. In summary, the utility methods hold great promise for making rational personnel decisions, yet the difficulty in applying utility formulations has prevented their widespread use. More theoretical work is needed because different procedures can sometimes lead to different decisions (Weekley et al., 1985). However, studies do demonstrate financial advantages for companies that select employees on the basis of these formal models (Burke & Doran, 1989). An example of utility calculations is given in Focused Example 7-2.

C. *Incremental Validity*

Validity defines the inferences that can be made on the basis of a score or measure (see Chapter 5). Evidence that a test is valid for particular inferences does not necessarily mean that the test is valuable. Even though a test is reliable and valid, the decision to use one must depend on some additional considerations. For example, does the test give you more information than would be expected if it were not used? What information can the test provide beyond

---

FOCUSED EXAMPLE 7-2

How Much Money Can Be Saved Through Valid Selection?

A major issue in business and industrial psychology is how to get the most productivity out of employees. Tests are often used in employment settings to select employees who have the greatest chance of being productive. Some industrial psychologists, however, may have failed to realize just how much economic value can be gained from effective selection procedures. Although L. J. Cronbach and G. C. Gleser (1965) developed methods for evaluating the cost-effectiveness of testing many years ago, their technique was not frequently used because it required estimation of the standard deviation of the dollar value of employee performance. However, newer methods have been developed to estimate this quantity. As a result, it is possible to determine how much money is saved by using a valid selection procedure.

One study on the use of these decision models concerned the selection of computer programmers using the Programmer Aptitude Test (PAT). The PAT is a fairly good predictor of the job performance of programmers and has a validity coefficient of .76. In a series of analyses, it was shown that the use of the PAT, in place of less valid selection procedures, saves considerable money. For example, the U.S. government employs about 17,000 computer programmers. A comparison was made for the dollar savings of using the PAT instead of an alternative procedure with a validity for predicting success on the job of only .20. Twenty percent of the applicants could be selected. The analysis demonstrated that the savings to the government could be $1.2 billion. If this example is expanded to the economy as a whole, the impact of what is already known? This added bit of information gained through using the test is known as *incremental validity.*

The sections on base and hit rates and on Taylor-Russell tables considered problems in incremental validity. Methods were presented for evaluating what a test contributed beyond what was known from base rates. The assessment of incremental validity is not necessarily limited to comparisons with base rates. A particularly important aspect of incremental validity is the determination of how much information a test contributes beyond some simpler method for making the same prediction.

Most of the examples given in the preceding sections concerned tests used for selection purposes. However, the same rules and methods apply for tests used for the evaluation of personality or in the practice of clinical psychology.

Recent research on the prediction of behavior in particular situations has yielded some simple but startling results. Although it is difficult to predict behavior on the basis of reports by trained clinical psychologists (Meehl, 1954), people are remarkably good at predicting their own behavior (Bem & Allen, 1974; Bem & Funder, 1978; Bandura, 1992). We can learn a lot about whether a person will be able to perform a particular behavior by simply asking.

Frequently, expensive and time-consuming psychological tests are given in order to make predictions about future behavior. Before exerting this effort, it

using the PAT for one year would be $10.78 billion. According to this analysis, the gains in productivity associated with using a valid selection procedure are much greater than previously realized (Schmidt et al., 1979).

Although this analysis is very encouraging, there is at least one problem with the application to programmers. At present, there are more jobs for programmers than there are trained people to fill them. Thus, for the entire economy, the selection ratio cannot be 20%. In fact, nearly 100% of the qualified programmers find work. Gains realized by those who employ the best qualified programmers are offset by losses to those who employ the less qualified applicants.

In another analysis, J. E. Hunter and R. F. Hunter (1984) considered the consequences of substituting less valid predictors for the selection of employees for entry-level government jobs. They argued that the most valid predictors of performance on the job were ability and work sample tests, which have validities of .53. If a good but less valid predictor involving job tryouts (validity of .44) was used, losses in productivity would be $3.12 billion per year. However, selecting employees on the basis of age, which has only a low correlation with job performance ($r = -.01$), would result in losses of $15.89 billion per year. Of course, employers need to take into consideration many factors when making employment decisions. For example, selection on the basis of test performance alone may have adverse consequences for minority group members.

is worthwhile to ask what the tests are adding beyond what would be known if the information was obtained in some simpler manner. For example, J. L. Holland and R. C. Nichols (1964) attempted to find the characteristics that distinguished high school students with high accomplishments from those with less notable credits. They found that a 15-item scale about what activities the students preferred discriminated between the groups as well as a battery of complex personality tests.

Other studies have attempted to determine how a person will be rated by peers on the basis of variety of tests and self-ratings. The results often demonstrate that simple gross self-ratings are as good at predicting how someone will be rated by peers as are complex personality tests that make inferences about underlying traits (Hase & Goldberg, 1967). Furthermore, self-predictions are no less accurate in forecasting who will go under a hypnotic trance than are complex hypnotizability scales (Melei & Hilgard, 1964). Personality tests have been of little value in predicting whether snake phobics will learn to approach a snake after therapy; however, self-predictions have been found to be shockingly accurate (Bandura, 1977, 1992).

These examples are not given to convince you that personality tests are meaningless. As you will see in Chapters 14–17, personality measures make many valuable and important contributions. However, test users always should ask themselves whether they can gain the same information with a simpler or less expensive method or with one that will cause less strain for the subject. Tests should be used when they provide a significant increment in information over what would be obtained with simpler methods. In order to ensure that testing is a worthwhile use of time and resources, you must carefully select your testing materials.

III. *Locating Information about Published Tests*

When choosing a test for a particular purpose, it is important that you carefully research your options. There are a variety of reference books you should be able to find in the library that provide information about the tests. Each of these books refers you to other journal articles that summarize specific evaluations of the test. In order to get a general overview of the test, seven references are of particular value: *Tests in Print III* (Mitchell, 1983); *The Mental Measurements Yearbook* (Conoley & Kramer, 1989); *Tests: A Comprehensive Reference for Assessment in Psychology, Education, and Business* (Sweetland & Keyser, 1991); *Test Critiques* (Keyser & Sweetland, 1985); *Measures of Personality and Social Psychological Attitudes* (Robinson, Shaver & Wrightsman, 1991); *Unpublished Experimental Mental Measures* (Goldman & Osbourne, 1985); and the *Handbook of Psychiatric Rating Scales* (Research and Education Association, 1981).

A. *Tests in Print III*

This exhaustive reference book summarizes information on most of the tests in the English language. The book lists the following information: the title of the test, who the test is designed for, when the test was developed (copyright date), the acronym for the test (or the set of letters the test is often called by, such as SAT), what subtests are available, whether or not there is a test manual, problems in updating the test materials, the authors of the test, the publisher of the test, the country in which the test was published, and cross references to *The Mental Measurements Yearbook* and *Personality Tests and Reviews* along with references to relevant journal articles. If you do not know the name of a test, you can locate it by content using this source.

B. *The Mental Measurements Yearbook*

This book is a classic collection of 569 test reviews. It was begun in 1938 by Oscar K. Buros (1978). After his death in 1978, arrangements were made for the series to be taken over by the University of Nebraska Press, which produced the first publication in 1985 and the second in 1989. The MMY, as it is often called, provides comprehensive reviews of testing materials by hundreds of noted psychologists and education specialists. Each review comments on the evidence for the validity and reliability of a test. Often the reviews are quite critical, and the reviewer critiques the meaning of the available data. More than 1880 references for journal articles reviewing the tests are also given. There are several sourcebooks made up of selected subsections of the MMY. *Vocational Tests and Reviews* (Buros, 1975c) consists of the vocational sections of the seventh MMY and *Tests in Print III*. Similarly, *Personality Tests and Reviews* (Buros, 1975b) is made up of the sections on personality tests, and *Intelligence Tests and Reviews* (Buros, 1975a) includes the intelligence testing sections.

The tenth edition of the *Mental Measurement Yearbook* was published in 1989. It includes a bibliography of 396 commercially available tests, 569 reviews of tests by well-qualified measurement experts, bibliographies and references about the specific tests, their construction, validity, and so forth. The tenth edition focuses on tests that are new or were revised after 1985. The book includes a test title index with extensive cross referencing, a classified subject index, a directory of publishers that provides information on how to obtain tests, and other indexes that allow the search for test information by author names, test names, test acronyms, and types of score. In addition, the tenth edition includes the *Mental Measurement Database*, which is an on-line computer service.

The most common type of test reviewed in the *Mental Measurement Yearbook* is a vocation test (25%). The next most common type is a personality test. Table 7-8 summarizes the major types of test classifications in 16 major categories.

Table 7-8
Tests by Major
Classifications,
from the *Mental
Measurements
Yearbook*, 10th
Edition

Classification	Number	Percentage
Vocations	100	25.3
Personality	72	18.2
Miscellaneous	43	10.9
Developmental	31	7.8
Intelligence and scholastic aptitude	28	7.1
English	24	6.1
Reading	24	6.1
Speech and hearing	22	5.6
Education	20	5.1
Achievement	12	3.0
Mathematics	9	2.2
Social studies	3	.8
Fine arts	2	.5
Foreign languages	2	.5
Sensory-motor	2	.5
Neuropsychological	2	.5
Total	396	100.00

From Conoley & Kramer (1989, p. x).

The MMY also helps identify which tests are cited most frequently. Table 7-9 provides this summary. Among all tests, the Wide Range Achievement Test—Revised (see Chapter 12) is the most commonly cited.

C. *Tests: A Comprehensive Reference for Assessment in Psychology, Education, and Business*

The excellent tradition begun by Buros has been continued in a series of new volumes. *Tests: A Comprehensive Reference for Assessment in Psychology, Education, and Business* (Sweetland & Keyser, 1991) provides descriptive information on more than 3500 tests from 467 publishers. These tests are divided into three categories: psychology, education, and business. The volume describes the format for tests, provides a statement of purpose for each, and describes the relevant information on cost, available data, and scoring. Information is also provided on computer scoring, and indexes allow the easy location of the author, publisher, and other relevant information.

D. *Test Critiques*

In 1985, a new volume by Keyser and Sweetland was published as a supplement to their comprehensive reference for tests (Sweetland & Keyser, 1983), which had omitted important psychometric information on reliability, validity,

Table 7-9
Number of
References for the
Ten Most
Frequently Cited
Tests

Name of Test	Number of References
Wide Range Achievement Test—Revised	161
Stanford-Binet Intelligence Scale, Fourth Edition	89
Multiple Affect Adjective Check List, Revised	84
Bayley Scales of Infant Development	80
California Achievement Tests, Forms E and F	68
Personality Research Form, 3rd Edition	68
Iowa Tests of Basic Skills, Forms G and H	45
Metropolitan Achievement Tests, Sixth Edition	45
Myers-Briggs Type Indicator	42
Woodcock Reading Mastery Tests—Revised	38

From Conoley & Kramer (1989, p. xii).

and normative development. As noted in Chapters 4 and 5, it is difficult to evaluate the merits of a test without knowing this information. *Test Critiques* (Keyser & Sweetland, 1985) provides detailed reviews on different topic areas. For example, experts critique tests of achievement and aptitude, educational development, gerontology, intelligence, and so on. Some critiques focus on specific tests, while others cover broader areas such as attitude survey tests.

E. *Measures of Personality and Social Psychological Attitudes*

This reference is particularly valuable for people interested in measures of personality and social attitudes. The reference, edited by J. P. Robinson, P. R. Shaver, and L. S. Wrightsman (1991), includes 12 edited chapters that cover a wide range of measures of personality, depression, coping, and other psychological processes. The book provides evaluative information about the measures and establishes criteria for a good measure. It also gives samples of the items for some of the measures.

F. *Unpublished Experimental Mental Measures*

Not all measures are published. *Unpublished Experimental Mental Measures* (Goldman & Osbourne, 1985) describes measures that have not been published. By 1985, there were four volumes covering several thousand measures. Each entry is accompanied by a brief summary of research relevant to the measure. Unfortunately, the volumes did not get wide circulation and they are difficult to find in some college libraries.

G. *Handbook of Psychiatric Rating Scales*

Developed by the Research and Education Association, the *Handbook of Psychiatric Rating Scales* (1981) describes a wide variety of rating scales that are used in psychiatric research. For each of the rating scales, the book gives a general description and background; desribes the types of patients for whom the scale might be used, the sources of items used in testing, and the reliability and validity of the scale; and provides a list of related references. The book is very useful for those interested in measures for clinical research.

Summary

Making a selection among the many published tests has become a technical skill. One of your first considerations should always be whether it is worthwhile to administer this test. How much information does the test give beyond what is known without the test? In personnel selection, the *base rate* is the probability of succeeding without any selection procedure. A variety of methods have been developed to estimate the amount of information a test gives beyond what is known by chance. This depends on the validity of the test, the percentage of people being selected, and the proportion of people expected to succeed if no selection test is used. *Taylor-Russell tables* can be used for this purpose. When the outcome is defined more precisely than just success or failure, utility and decision theories are sometimes used. However, the application of the utility theory equations is fairly difficult in most circumstances.

Because there are so many tests available, a wise test consumer will carefully review published information on the test before making a decision. Valuable sourcebooks on testing information are *Tests in Print III; The Mental Measurements Yearbook; Tests: A Comprehensive Reference for Assessment in Psychology, Education, and Business; Test Critiques; Measures for Psychological Assessment* (Chun, Cobb & French, 1975); *Measures of Personality and Social Psychological Attitudes; Unpublished Experimental Mental Measures*; and the *Handbook of Psychiatric Rating Scales*.

Chapter 8

Test Administration

Learning Objectives

When you have completed this chapter, you should be able to:

- Know whether the majority of the research evidence shows that white examiners impede the intelligence test performance of black children.

- Discuss how the relationship between the examiner and the test taker can have an impact on test scores.

- Discuss an expectancy effect and how it might affect a test score.

- Examine the relationship between reinforcing particular responses and test performance.

- Outline some of the advantages of computer-assisted test administration.

- List what characteristics of the state of the subject should be considered when evaluating a test score.

- Know what problems you would need to consider in training your observers if you were in charge of a behavioral observation study.

In the last six chapters, we discussed many topics related to test construction. Now we are ready to make the transition to using psychological tests. Before we move on to the section on applications, however, there is one final methodological issue that needs to be covered: the administration of tests.

Test scores are influenced by many factors. When we obtain scores, there is a tendency to think that the observed score is really representative of the true ability or trait we are trying to measure. In Chapter 4, we reviewed the concept of reliability and introduced measurement error, which is the difference between the true score and the observed score. Reliability theory is most concerned with random sources of error. In the actual application of tests, many other sources of error must be considered, including effects of the testing situation, of tester characteristics, and of test taker characteristics.

I. *The Examiner and the Subject*

A. *The Race of the Tester*

The effects of the race of the tester have generated considerable attention because of concern about bias. Some groups feel that their children should not be tested by anyone except a member of the same race. For example, there has been concern that black children receive lower test scores when they are tested by white examiners. Although the effects of racial bias in test administration are discussed very frequently, the exact impact has been studied in relatively few experimental studies. The effects of the examiner's race have been reviewed on several occasions by J. M. Sattler (1970, 1973a, 1973b, 1973c, 1982, 1988). After very careful consideration of the problem and occasional reanalysis of the data, Sattler concluded that there is little evidence that the race of the examiner has much effect on intelligence test scores.

The most common finding in studies of this type is that the race of the examiner has nonsignificant effects on test performance for both black and white children. These results occurred for both the Stanford-Binet scale and the Peabody Picture Vocabulary Test (Costello & Dickie, 1970; Miller & Phillips, 1966). A similar study with older children (black sixth-graders) failed to show differences between the children when they were given the Stanford-Binet by a black examiner and by a white one (Caldwell & Knight, 1970).

This same result also has been obtained for group intelligence tests. Scores of black and white fourth-, fifth-, and sixth-graders were not found to be significantly influenced by having a trained black or white examiner give the Lorge-Thorndike Group Intelligence Test (Lipsitz, 1969). Although a few studies have shown an effect attributed to the race of the examiner, they are clearly in the minority. In fact, these effects have been found in only 4 of 29 studies (Sattler, 1979a). J. M. Sattler and J. Gwynne (1982) refer to the belief that white examiners impede the test performance of black children as a myth widely held but unsupported by scientific studies.

One of the reasons so few studies show effects of the examiner's race on the results of IQ tests is that the procedures for properly administering an IQ test are so specific. Anyone who gives the test should be doing so according to a very strict procedure. In other words, well-trained black and white test administrators should be acting in an almost identical fashion. Deviation from this procedure might produce differences in performance associated with the race of the examiner. For example, in the next sections we will show how very subtle (nonverbal) cues can affect test scores. Even though most standardized tests have a very strict administration procedure, there are numerous ways the examiner can communicate a hostile or friendly atmosphere, a hurried or relaxed manner, or an inquisitorial or therapeutic role. These effects may not be a function of the race of the examiner per se but may be reflected in strained relationships between members of different ethnic groups.

Sattler (1973c) has shown that there are some situations in which information is affected by the race of the examiner. Thus, examiner effects might be expected to be greatest when examiners are given more discretion about the use of the tests. In one study in which a small effect of the examiner's race was found, the examiners were paraprofessionals rather than psychologists. In this study, white examiners obtained higher scores from white children, whereas scores for black or white children were comparable when tested by black examiners (Abramson, 1969). However, after a detailed review of the literature, Sattler (1988) concluded that the effects of test administrators' race are negligible.

B. *The Examiner-Test Taker Relationship*

Test scores can be affected by the behavior of the examiner and his or her relationship to the test taker. One variable that may affect test scores is rapport. In one study, first- through seventh-grade children were given the WISC (Wechsler Intelligence Scale for Children) intelligence test (see Chapter 11) under one of two conditions. Half the children were given the test under enhanced rapport conditions, in which the examiner used friendly conversation and verbal reinforcement during the test administration. The other children took the test under a neutral rapport condition. For these children, the examiner never initiated conversation or used reinforcement (Feldman & Sullivan, 1960). There was little effect of the examiner's rapport on the scores of the younger children (just through third grade). However, average IQ scores for the fifth- through ninth-grade students were higher for those who had received the test under the enhanced rapport condition (mean IQ = 122) than for the children who had taken the test with a neutral administrator (mean IQ = 109). This difference (122 − 109) is almost a full standard deviation.

Another study compared scores obtained by examiners who made approving comments (such as "good" or "fine") with those obtained by examiners who used disapproving comments ("I thought you could do better than that") or neutral comments. Children who took the test under a disapproving examiner received lower scores than those who had been exposed to a neutral or an approving examiner (Witmer, Bornstein & Dunham, 1971). For younger children a familiar examiner may make a difference. In one study, 137 children took a reading test. For half of the children there was a familiar proctor, whereas for the other half the proctor was unfamiliar. Reading scores were significantly lower when the proctor was unfamiliar (DeRosa & Patalano, 1991).

Enough studies have accumulated on examiner-test taker relationships that a quantitative review of the literature has been performed. D. Fuchs and L. S. Fuchs (1986) reviewed 22 different studies that involved 1489 children. Averaging across studies, they found that test performance was about .28 standard deviation, or about 4 IQ points, higher when the examiner was familiar with the test taker. In those studies involving children from lower socioeconomic classes, the effect was larger. In these cases, familiarity accounted for about 7.6 IQ points. The review raises some important concerns, demonstrating as it does that familiarity with the test taker, and perhaps preexisting notions about the test taker's ability, can either positively or negatively bias test results.

In most testing situations, examiners should not attempt to have a particular rapport with different test takers. However, rapport might be influenced by very subtle processes such as the level of performance expected by the examiner.

C. *Expectancy Effects*

A well-known line of research in psychology has shown that data obtained in experiments sometimes can be affected by what an experimenter expects to find. Robert Rosenthal and his colleagues at Harvard University contributed a large number of experiments on the effects of experimenter **expectancy.** Because these studies are so well known, many have come to label the effects of experimenter expectancy the **Rosenthal effect.** In a typical experiment, Rosenthal employs a large number of student experimenters to help collect data on a task such as rating human faces for success or failure. Half the student experimenters are led to believe that the average response will be toward the success side of the scale, and the other half are led to expect that the average response will be on the failure side. The results of these experiments consistently demonstrate that the subjects actually provide data that confirm the experimenter's expectancies. However, the magnitude of the effects is small—about a 1-point difference on a 20-point scale (Rosenthal, 1966).

The experimenter's influence is not limited to human subjects. Other experiments have demonstrated that rats expected to be "maze bright" will learn to run through a maze more quickly than rats expected to be "maze dull." All of the rats are from the same litter, but the experimenter is told to expect a difference (Rosenthal & Fode, 1963).

Several authors have challenged the Rosenthal experiments, claiming that they are based on unsound statistical procedures or faulty design (Barber & Silver, 1968; Elashoff & Snow, 1971; Thorndike, 1968). Rosenthal acknowledges some problems in his early work and has greatly improved his own skills as a methodologist (Rosenthal & Rosnow, 1991). After reviewing many studies, he still maintains that there is an expectancy effect in some situations.

Two aspects of the expectancy effect are important with regard to the use of standardized tests. First, the expectancy effects observed in Rosenthal's experiments were obtained when all the experimenters followed a standardized script. Although gross forms of bias are possible, Rosenthal argues that the expectancy effect results from very subtle uses of nonverbal communication between the experimenter and the subject. The experimenter may not even be aware of his or her role in the process. The second point to consider with regard to the expectancy effect is that it has a very small, subtle effect on scores. Furthermore, Rosenthal reports that it occurs in some situations but not in others. Determining whether test scores are affected by expectancy requires careful studies for the particular tests being used.

In intelligence testing, the expectancy effect can have several different impacts. One type of influence is on scoring. In a series of experiments, graduate students with some training in intelligence testing were asked to score ambiguous responses from certain intelligence tests. Sometimes they were told that the responses had been given by persons who were "bright," and other times the responses were attributed to "dull" persons. The students tended to give more credit to responses purportedly from bright test takers (Sattler, Hillix & Neher, 1970; Sattler & Winget, 1970). Other studies have demonstrated that the expectancy effect can occur even if the responses are not ambiguous (Egeland, 1969; Simon, 1969).

A variety of interpersonal and cognitive process variables have been shown to affect the judgment of others (Arkes, 1991). These biases may also affect the scoring of tests. For example, D. Donahue and J. M. Sattler (1971) demonstrated that students who scored the WAIS intelligence test were more likely to give credit for selected items to examinees they liked or perceived to be warm. Thus, examiners must be aware that their relationships with examinees can affect their objectivity on certain types of tests.

Studies in which expectancies have been created for test administrators (giving rather than just scoring tests) have yielded somewhat inconsistent results. Some have shown that there is a significant expectancy effect (Hersh, 1971; Larrabee & Kleinsaser, 1967; Schroeder & Kleinsaser, 1972), whereas other studies have not demonstrated the expectancy effect (Dangel, 1970; Ekren, 1962; Gillingham, 1970; Saunders & Vitro, 1971).

Many studies have attempted to find subtle variables that affect test responses. For example, N. B. Rappaport and D. P. McAnulty (1985) presented tape-recorded responses to people scoring IQ tests. The children on the tape recording gave the same response with or without an accent. There was no difference between these two conditions.

In reviewing these studies, Sattler (1988) noted that studies that showed an expectancy effect tended to have an administrator test only two children (one under a high and one under a low expectancy condition). The studies that did not find an expectancy effect tended to have more subjects tested by each test administrator. The studies that used more samples of each tester's behavior should produce more reliable estimates of the expectancy effect, and these were the ones where the effect was least often observed. Therefore, the studies that failed to show an expectancy effect may be more credible.

Even though the results of studies on expectancy effects are often inconsistent, it is important to pay careful attention to the potentially biasing effect of expectancy. Even Rosenthal's harshest critics do not deny the possible biasing effect of expectancy. Thus, it is always important to do as much as you can to eliminate the possibility of experimenter or test administrator bias.

D. *Effects of Reinforcing Responses*

Because there is such a well-known effect of reinforcement on behavior, it is very important to administer tests under controlled conditions. J. M. Sattler and F. Theye (1967) reviewed the literature on procedural and situational variables in testing and found that an inconsistent use of feedback can damage the reliability and validity of test scores.

Several studies have shown that reward can have an important effect on test performance. For example, incentives can help improve performance on IQ tests for specific subgroups of children. In one study, 6- to 13-year-olds were given tokens that could be exchanged for money each time they gave a correct response on the WISC verbal scale. This incentive was effective in improving performance for lower-class white children but not effective for middle-class children or lower-class blacks (Sweet, 1969).

The incentive need not necessarily be monetary. Many studies have shown that children will work very hard to obtain praise such as "You are doing well" (Eisenberger, 1970, 1972). Several studies have shown that the effects of verbal reinforcement or praise are about as strong as monetary rewards or candy (Cohen, 1970; Quay, 1971; Sattler, 1991; Tiber & Kennedy, 1964). The results of these studies, however, are sometimes complicated. For instance, one study found that girls increased their accuracy on the WISC block design subtest when given any type of reinforcement for a correct response. Boys increased in accuracy only when given chips that could be exchanged for money. However, girls decreased in speed when given reinforcement, and boys increased in speed only when given verbal praise (Bergan, McManis & Melchert, 1971).

There is some evidence that black children do not respond as well to verbal reinforcers as they do to tangible rewards such as money or candy (Schultz & Sherman, 1976). However, black psychologist Francis Terrell and his colleagues (Terrell, Taylor & Terrell, 1978) suggest that this is because the verbal reinforcement often given to the black children is not culturally relevant. To demonstrate their point, they administered the WISC-R intelligence test to lower socioeconomic black second-graders and gave one of four types of feedback for each correct response. One-quarter of the children were given no feedback at all about whether or not they had made a correct response. One group received verbal praise, and another group was given candy. The final group was given culturally relevant verbal praise. For example, after each correct response, the black test administrator remarked "Nice job, Blood" or

"Nice job, little Brother." Using culturally relevant feedback boosted IQ a remarkable 17.6 points, whereas giving feedback that was not culturally relevant had very little effect (about 3 points). Tangible rewards boosted performance about 11 points. This result is most unusual in light of several previous studies that show only minor effects of reinforcement. Certainly more attention needs to be devoted to the effects of culturally relevant rewards.

Some of the most potent effects of reinforcement have been shown in attitudinal studies. In survey research, the answer given by a respondent is not necessarily right or wrong. Instead, it is an expression of how someone feels about something. Repeated studies have demonstrated that the content of responses in interview studies is affected by the way an interviewer responds (Cannell & Henson, 1974). One of the most interesting demonstrations of this was a study in which respondents in a household survey were asked if they suffered from certain physical symptoms. For half of the subjects, the interviewer gave an approving nod each time a symptom was reported. For the other half, the interviewer remained expressionless. The number of symptoms reported increased significantly when approval was given for reporting a symptom. In a similar study, two symptoms that no one should report were added to the list. These were "Are your intestines too long?" and "Do the ends of your hair itch?" A greater proportion of people reported that they experienced these symptoms if they have been reinforced for reporting other symptoms.

Reinforcement and feedback guide the examinee with regard to which response should be given. Another way to demonstrate the potency of reinforcement involves misguiding the subject. A variety of studies have demonstrated that random reinforcement destroys the accuracy of performance and decreases the motivation to respond (Eisenberger, Kaplan & Singer, 1974; Koller & Kaplan, 1978). It is how you might feel if the grades you received were totally random. The effects of random feedback have been shown to be rather severe, causing a condition of low motivation for responding, depression, and inability to solve problems. This condition is known as *learned helplessness* (Abramson, Metalsky & Alloy, 1989; Seligman, 1975).

Because of the potency of reinforcement for performance, very strict control over the use of feedback by test administrators should be followed (see Technical Box 8-1). Because different test takers make different responses, it is not possible to ensure that advantages due to reinforcement will be the same for all people. As a result, most test manuals and interviewer guides insist that no feedback be given.

It is important to give tests under standardized conditions because situational variables can affect test scores. The *Standards for Educational and Psychological Testing* published by the American Psychological Association and other professional groups (1985) emphasize that the directions for the administration of tests should be clearly spelled out in a test manual. These directions should be in sufficient detail to be duplicated in all situations in which the test is given. A good test manual will give the test examiner very detailed and strict instructions that include the exact words to be read to the test takers. Furthermore, it should spell out which questions are to be expected and how they are to be answered.

TECHNICAL BOX 8-1

The Incentive Scoreboard

As noted in the text, there is a predominant belief that reinforcement can affect test performance. Therefore, methods are typically implemented to standardize reinforcement during testing procedures. However, as in most areas of psychology, there is some inconsistency in the literature. J. M. Sattler (1988) reviewed 34 different studies that evaluated the effect of incentives, which included praise, candy, and money as well as social reinforcement and reinforcement with tokens. The subjects in these experiments included normal and handicapped children of various ethnic groups. By tallying the results of these studies, Sattler observed that (1) 14 studies found that incentives or feedback did not affect performance, (2) 13 studies found mixed results, and (3) 7 studies found that reinforcement either improved or hindered performance.

There appeared to be no clear and consistent difference between the studies that showed a positive and a negative effect of token and social reinforcement. One of the issues raised by research on incentive effects is what the results imply for test interpretation. If a child's IQ score of 110 can be boosted to 120 with reinforcement for correct responses, does this mean the child is likely to do better in school? The validity of the test is based on a standardized administration procedure, and it is not clear that enhancing IQ scores with reinforcement would enhance the validity of the test.

Inexperienced test administrators often do not fully appreciate the importance of standardization in administration. If you are giving tests or supervising others who are given this responsibility, you must take into consideration that the test may not be reliable or valid if you deviate from the specified instructions.

There are a few occasions that require deviation from standardized testing procedures. J. M. Sattler (1988) acknowledges that special considerations must be given for the blind who cannot read portions of the test, and O. J. Kaplan (1979) discusses special considerations for testing the aged. However, many widely used tests have now developed special standardized methods for testing these special populations. In order to assure that tests are given under standardized conditions, some examiners prefer to give instructions through a tape recorder. Others have opted for computer-assisted test administration.

E. *Computer-Assisted Test Administration*

Computer technology is having an impact on many fields. Testing and test administration are not exceptions. Today most colleges and many grade schools have interactive computer capabilities. Easy access to computers allows the administration of a test through interaction with a computer (Gianetti et al., 1976).

Interactive testing involves the presentation of test items through a computer terminal or personal computer and the automatic recording of test responses. The computer also can be programmed to instruct the test taker and to provide some instruction when parts of the testing procedure are not clear. As early as 1970 L. J. Cronbach recognized the value of computers as test administrators. These are some advantages of computers:

Excellence of standardization

Individually tailored sequential administration

Precision of timing responses

Release of human testers for other duties

Patience

Control of bias

Since the publication of the first edition of this book in 1982, there has been an explosion of computer technology in testing. Today, many of the major psychological tests are available for use on a personal computer. This development has many advantages, including the possibility of "tailored" tests. With such tests, the items may be ordered according to level of difficulty. If the test taker gets several items correct at a certain level of difficulty, the program logic might jump that person ahead to items of greater difficulty. Through this process, the program eventually can identify the ability level without relying on the subjective biases of the examiner (Recase, 1977).

Computer-assisted test administration does not necessarily depend on a structured order of test items. Indeed, one advantage of this approach is that the items can be given in any order or in a unique random order for every test taker. The computerized approach does offer many advantages for unique testing situations. Computers are objective and cost-effective. Furthermore, they allow more experimental control. For example, if you want to exactly limit the amount of time any one item can be studied, the computer can easily be programmed to flash the items on the screen for specific durations. The computer-assisted method also makes it impossible for test takers to look ahead at other sections of the test or go back to sections that already have been completed (Groth-Marmat & Shumaker, 1989; Lautenschlager & Flaherty, 1990). Comparisons of test scores obtained with computer-assisted or paper-and-pencil administration have not tended to show large differences between the methods (Ward et al., 1989), yet the computer method ensures standardization and control and also reduces scoring errors. It was once thought that people would rebel against interactions with machines. However, newer evidence suggests test takers actually find that interactions with computers are more enjoyable than using paper-and-pencil tests (Rosenfeld et al., 1989).

There have been a few serendipitous findings on computer-assisted test administrations. One of the most interesting concerns the use of computers to interview potentially suicidal persons. Many psychologists and psychiatrists believe that people in trouble always must be interviewed by a warm, caring, and empathetic person. These therapists would be appalled if someone experiencing an emotional crisis was interviewed by an electronic computer terminal. However, one study demonstrated that people will divulge more personal information to a machine than they will to a human interviewer. Apparently, many people are secretive about their thoughts and feelings and would rather discuss them anonymously.

Not all observers endorse the rapid development of computerized test administration. For example, J. D. Matarazzo (1986) suggested that computer-generated test reports in the hands of an inexperienced psychologist cannot replace clinical judgment. In such cases, computerized reports may actually be harmful because they may be misinterpreted. Other problems are that computerized scoring routines can have errors or be poorly validated, and such problems are often difficult to detect within the software. D. E. Hartman (1986b) speculated that there will be consumer liability cases involving software products. Groth-Marmat and Schumaker (1989) outlined a number of problems that have been caused by faulty computerized testing systems. For example, some programs have untested claims of validity, and computerized reports might be based on an obsolete data base. A clinical psychologist who lets the computer do too much of the thinking may be open to misinterpreting test responses. With the growth in computerized testing, new guidelines may be necessary to regulate the industry.

F. *Subject Variables*

A final variable that may be a serious source of error is the state of the subject. It is well known that motivation and anxiety can greatly affect test scores. For example, studies have shown that many college students suffer from a serious debilitating condition known as **test anxiety.** Test-anxious students often have difficulty focusing attention on the test items and might be distracted by other thoughts such as "I am not doing well" or "I am running out of time." Test anxiety is a very important problem in testing and an important area of contemporary research. Therefore, we will cover this topic in detail in Chapter 18.

It may seem obvious that test scores are affected by illness. When you have a cold or the flu, you might not perform as well as when you are feeling well. Many variations in health status are known to affect performance in behavior and in thinking (Kaplan, 1990). In fact, medical drugs are now evaluated according to their effects on the cognitive process (Spilker, 1990). The measurement of the effects of health status on functioning will be discussed in more detail in Chapter 19.

There has been some debate about whether normal hormonal variations affect test performance. It has been reported that healthy women experience variations in their perceptual and motor performance as a function of phase of the menstrual cycle. In the middle of each monthly cycle, women may have enhanced performance on tests of speeded motor coordination in comparison to their performance during menstruation. However, these same women may perform more poorly on tests of perceptual and spatial abilities during midcycle than during the menses (Hampson & Kimura, 1988). More recent studies, reported by Kimura at the 1991 neurosciences meetings, suggest that men also vary in test performance as a function of variations in male sex hormones.

II. *Behavioral Assessment Methodology*

Measurement goes beyond the application of psychological tests. Many applications of assessment procedures involve the observation of behavior. For example, personnel psychologists often obtain work samples as a way of estimating job performance. The work samples require the performance of tasks in environments similar to the actual work setting. During performance of the tasks, systematic observations of behavior are made. Some applied psychologists believe that work samples provide the most valid indication of actual work performance (Green & Wing, 1988). Behavioral observation methods are also becoming increasingly important in clinical psychology (Bellack & Hersen, 1988; Hersen, Kazdin & Bellack, 1991; Tryon, 1991). The increasing use of behavioral observation methodology has been accompanied by many new problems. As we have seen in this chapter, minor variations in standard test administration procedures can have an effect on test scores. However, most of these problems can be overcome by adhering very closely to standard test administration procedures. In behavioral observation studies, the observer has a more active role in recording the data and, as a result, is much more likely to make errors. Some of the problems include reactivity, drift, and expectancies (Kazdin, 1977).

A. *Reactivity*

The reliability of observers in behavioral observation studies is usually assessed in selected sessions in which an experimenter "observes the observers." In other words, someone looks over the observer's shoulder to determine whether he or she is properly recording. Studies have shown that the time when the reliability and accuracy are highest is when someone is checking on the observers. This increase in reliability is called **reactivity** because it is a reaction to being checked. In one study, observers rated behavior recorded on a videotape under one of two conditions. First, the observers were told that their ratings would be checked against a standard for accuracy. Later, the observers were told there was no standard. However, there actually was a standard against which the accuracy of both conditions was checked. The data demonstrated that accuracy dropped by 25% when the observers were led to believe their observations would not be evaluated (Reid, 1970). Indeed, many studies have demonstrated that accuracy and interrater agreement decrease when observers believe their work is not being checked (Harris & Lahey, 1982; Kent et al., 1977; Taplin & Reid, 1973).

In order to deal with this problem, some experimenters resort to covert operations. For example, the experimenter might randomly check up on the performance of the observers without their knowledge. In general, one always should be cautious in interpreting reports on interrater reliability. Often the estimate of rater reliability is based on assessment during training. When observers are not observed themselves (when they are actually collecting data), their accuracy can be expected to drop.

B. *Drift*

When observers are trained in behavioral observation methods, they are given extensive feedback and coaching. After they leave the training sessions, it is assumed that they will continue to perform on the job as they did in training. However, studies show that observers have a tendency to **drift** away from the strict rules they followed in training and to adopt their own idiosyncratic definitions of behavior (O'Leary & Kent, 1973; Reid & DeMaster, 1972). One of the most common problems is called the *contrast effect*. This is the tendency to rate the same behavior differently when repeated observations are made in the same context. Standards may shift, resulting in biased ratings of behavior. This can affect performance ratings or ratings of potential employees in interviews (Maurer & Alexander, 1991). The drift may not always be peculiar to the individual observer. Sometimes when many observers work together on the same job, they seem to drift away from the original definitions of the behavior, but they do it as a group (O'Leary & Kent, 1973). The occurrence of observer drift and contrast effects suggests that observers should be periodically retrained. Frequent meetings with the observers should be held at which there are discussions about the use of the observation methods. These meetings can eliminate some of the difficulties (Bellack & Hensen, 1988).

C. *Expectancies*

The literature on observer expectancies is similar to that on test examiner expectancies. As noted earlier, Rosenthal has accumulated some evidence that the expectancies of experimenters can affect the results of behavioral experiments. Some of the Rosenthal experiments show an effect of experimenter expectancies, whereas others do not. Similarly, some studies show that test administrator expectancies can affect scores on individual IQ tests, whereas other studies do not (Sattler, 1988).

The same sort of inconsistent picture appears for studies on behavioral observation. Some studies have shown that behavioral observers will observe the behavior they expect (Azrin et al., 1961; Scott, Burton & Yarro, 1967). On the other hand, some very thorough studies do not demonstrate an expectancy effect (Kent et al., 1974; Redfield & Paul, 1976). Expectancies have been more consistently shown to cause bias in the behavioral observation when observers are given reinforcement for recording a particular behavior (O'Leary, Kent & Kanowitz, 1975).

The impact of expectancy is very subtle. It probably has some minor biasing effect on behavioral data. The finding that expectancy bias occurs significantly in some studies but not others is consistent with the notion that there is a minor but potentially damaging effect of expectancy. In order to avoid this sort of bias, observers should not be informed about what behavior to expect.

D. *Problems in Rating Accuracy*

Most people are confident that they can accurately make judgments about other people. For example, it is common for people to feel they can figure out whether someone else is lying. Different people use different cues in their attempts to catch a liar. For example, when U.S. Supreme Court Justice Clarence Thomas was up for confirmation by the U.S. Senate, he was accused

AP/WIDE WORLD PHOTOS

of sexually harassing a former employee. Both Thomas and his accuser were interviewed by a congressional committee and the hearings were broadcast to the American public. Thomas denied the allegations, but views differed as to whether it was he or his accuser who was lying.

Systematic studies show that most people do remarkably poorly in detecting a liar. Many of these studies are done using videotapes in which someone is either lying or telling the truth. Not only do average people do poorly in detecting deception, but so do people in most professions who have the obligation of detecting these problems. For example, one study evaluated U.S. Secret Service agents, Central Intelligence Agency (CIA) agents, Federal Bureau of Investigation (FBI) investigators, employees of the National Security Agency, employees of the Drug Enforcement Agency, police officers, judges, and psychiatrists. Evaluation of the data suggested that only Secret Service agents performed better than chance in detecting deception (Ekman & O'Sullivan, 1991).

The detection of lying and being honest has become a major industry. For example, despite substantial evidence questioning their value, lie detector tests are commonly given. In addition, a new industry of "psychological services" has created commercial tests to evaluate the honesty and integrity of employees for prospective employees. On the basis of the tests, people were being fired from jobs or denied employment. The American Psychological Association decided to investigate this issue. After a comprehensive review of the literature, they found that there was substantial variability among the tests in the way they substantiated claims of validity and utility. However, many of the test publishers were unable to produce any evidence for the validity and reliability of their measures. Instead, they simply claimed that the evidence exists and that it could not be released because of "proprietary interests." Although some of the better tests did have evidence for predictive validity, the APA Task Force questioned the construct validity. Over all, the commission was very concerned that an industry that proposed to test for honesty could itself benefit from greater openness and honesty about the evidence supporting its techniques (Goldberg et al., 1991).

E. *Statistical Control of Rating Errors*

Many efforts to improve the accuracy of raters have produced discouraging results. Attempts to increase rater reliability through extended training have been particularly frustrating for many researchers and applied psychologists because training is expensive and time consuming. Some psychologists have argued that halo or leniency errors can be controlled statistically. (The halo effect is the tendency to ascribe positive attributes independently of the behavior that is observed.) This is accomplished through a method known as *partial correlation*. Here, the correlation between two variables is found while variability in a third variable is controlled.

As an example of the method, one study evaluated 537 supervisory ratings of middle-level managers. Each manager was rated on 15 specific attributes and 1 overall performance rating. Then the variance associated with the overall performance rating was separated from the other ratings. By using this method, the variance attributable to the halo effect was reduced and the discriminant validity of the method for rating performance was improved (Landy et al., 1980). Rater characteristics may play an important role in the accuracy of evaluations. Those with greater cognitive abilities and high spatial aptitudes may make more accurate ratings. Sometimes more critical raters tend to produce scores that are more accurate. However, we need more research on factors associated with rater accuracy. This is critically important because accurate performance evaluations provide the basis for employee selection and advancement (Borman & Hallman, 1991).

Summary

Standardized test administration procedures are a necessity. Extensive research in social psychology has clearly demonstrated that situational factors can affect scores on mental and behavioral tasks. These effects, however, can be very subtle and may not be observed in all studies. For example, a few studies have shown that the race of the examiner has an impact on scores on standardized intelligence tests. However, the majority of the studies do not find that the examiner's race has an impact. Similarly, the examiner's rapport and expectancies may influence scores on some but not all occasions. Direct reinforcement of specific responses (something that should not be done in most testing situations) does have an acknowledged impact.

In order to reduce some of the effects of the examiner, there has been an increasing interest in computer-assisted test administration. Computers can administer and score most tests with great precision and with minimum bias. This mode of test administration is expected to become more common in the near future.

Test scores also are affected by the state of the subject. For example, some students suffer from debilitating test anxiety that seriously interferes with performance.

The use of behavioral observation raises some of the same problems as test administration. In behavioral observation an observer records the responses of others, whereas in traditional test taking the subject records his or her own behavior. A common problem in behavioral observation is *reactivity*, in which the observer is most accurate only when he or she thinks someone is checking the work. A second problem is *drift*, in which observers gradually come to ignore the procedure they were taught and adopt their own observation method. A third problem is *expectancy*, or the tendency for observations to be affected by what the observer expects to observe. The magnitude of these effects is probably small, but the potential bias they introduce is serious enough that precautions should be taken.

PART II

CHAPTER 9
Interview Techniques

CHAPTER 10
Tests of Mental Ability:
The Binet Scale

CHAPTER 11
The Wechsler Intelligence Scales

CHAPTER 12
Other Individual Tests of Ability

CHAPTER 13
Group Ability Tests:
Intelligence, Achievement,
and Aptitude

CHAPTER 14
Tests for Choosing Careers

CHAPTER 15
Structured Personality Tests

CHAPTER 16
Projective Personality Tests

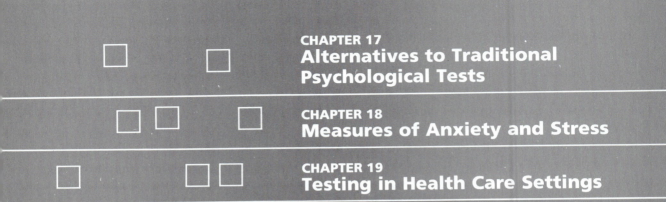

CHAPTER 17
Alternatives to Traditional Psychological Tests

CHAPTER 18
Measures of Anxiety and Stress

CHAPTER 19
Testing in Health Care Settings

Introduction to
Part II: Applications

Although psychology began as a strictly scientific discipline, today there are more positions for appliers of psychological knowledge than for strictly scientific pursuits, as is evident from an examination of employment announcements in the *APA Monitor*. Indeed, many students associate psychology more with its applications in clinical, counseling, educational, and industrial settings than with its scientific base. Furthermore, it seems as though an increasing number of students enter applied psychology. Perhaps the interest in applied aspects of psychology reflects a need to find relevance in the educational process. Nevertheless, because applied psychology depends on psychology's scientific base, a thorough knowledge of scientific principles is essential for a good understanding of any applied branch of psychology, and psychological tests are no exception.

In Chapters 2–8, we stressed scientific knowledge and the principles underlying psychological tests. Part II on applications continues the emphasis on scientific findings, major principles, and basic concepts. However, consistent with the current interest, Part II also provides an in-depth discussion of applied aspects of testing. Our decision to present this material on the application of some of the most used tests is based primarily on student interest. It also meets the need for an understanding of tests by the increasing numbers of nonpsychologists who make use of tests. Thus, the application section provides an overview of many of the most important and highly used psychological tests and also a good introduction for those who may directly or indirectly make use of tests in professional activities.

In the first eight chapters, certain key terms and distinctions were introduced and subsequently reviewed to facilitate learning and offer you the opportunity to study the material from a variety of perspectives. In this section we will not only introduce some new terms and distinctions but also review some of the earlier presented concepts. Your success in mastering the application of psychological testing will depend on your attainment of a firm understanding of several basic ideas and distinctions. Through repetition and presentation of these basic concepts in a variety of contexts, we hope to establish them in your long-term store of knowledge.

I. *The Issue of Test Use*

A little knowledge can be a dangerous thing because, without a proper perspective, there is always the danger of the misuse or improper application of facts. Because psychological and educational tests can be extremely powerful tools, the danger of their misuse is great. Therefore, in learning about the application of tests, one has a responsibility to be cautious and to remain within the boundaries of one's training and experience. Indeed, of all the issues and controversies involving tests, the issue of the uses of tests is perhaps the most critical from an ethical and moral standpoint.

In our society, especially as it functions today, decisions are constantly made that affect the lives of countless individuals. Most people eventually find themselves grouped, categorized, selected, or rejected (for example, for college or a job). We are not saying this decision process is good or bad; it is simply a reality of contemporary life. By now you are well aware that tests often are used as aids to this decision process. One important issue facing both professional persons and the public is whether tests should play a role in the inevitable decision process.

Given that psychological and educational tests are imperfect instruments, what role do you feel tests should play in making decisions? The American Education Research Association, American Psychological Association, and National Council on Measurement in Education (1985) noted in their *Standards for Educational and Psychological Testing* that some people believe that because tests may be biased or lacking in accuracy, no test should be used until alternative tests are developed. In defense of tests, it was argued that the basic issue is not so much test quality as test use (also see APA, 1974). We concur with this argument.

Any test can be misused—regardless of its fairness, lack of bias, and psychometric adequacy. As previously indicated, decisions are going to be made whether or not tests are used. Thus, it seems more relevant to ask whether tests can be fairly and appropriately used as an aid in the decision process. The elimination of tests will not solve the problems inherent in the decision-making process. Bias or potential bias would not be eliminated because people can be just as biased, if not more so, as tests. Thus, in solving the problems of the decision process, we must look beyond tests per se (Reschly, 1981; Snyderman & Rothman, 1987).

Testing continues to flourish despite heavy attacks from both the public and professionals. This seems to indicate that many decision makers consider tests useful. Again, it is not the tests but how they are used that is of central importance. Tests themselves are neither good nor bad, but unless they are properly used, tests can be extremely harmful to individuals as well as to society. Thus, the real problem for test users and the public is to ensure that tests are *properly used* (for example, see Novick, 1981).

To make proper use of a test, a tester must have a complete understanding of it. This involves knowledge of the **standardization sample** and the procedures for administering the test. According to the *Standards for Educational and Psychological Testing* (1985), a test manual must describe the standardization sample and the methods for administering the test. The procedure outlined in the test manual, when followed, is known as a **standard administration** of the test. If the test is not administered according to the procedure specified in the test manual, then it is not appropriate to compare the resulting test data to the standardization sample (which was given a standard administration). Furthermore, the importance of comparing a test result to an appropriate standardization sample cannot be overemphasized. If the standardization sample is made up of exclusively middle-class, white Americans, then the validity of the test for other populations is clearly highly questionable. Thus, the validity of such tests for other populations cannot simply be assumed.

In Chapters 4 and 5, you learned about the different types of reliability and validity. In making proper use of tests, however, it is not sufficient to ask "Is this test reliable?" or "Is this test valid?" A test may have an extremely high level of internal consistency, as indicated by high split-half reliability coefficients, and such reliability would provide support for the test. However, a test that is internally consistent is not necessarily reliable over time. Thus, in making appropriate use of a test, one cannot feel comfortable just because the test manual reports that the test is "highly reliable" or "highly valid." One also must know whether the test has the type of reliability and the type of validity appropriate for one's purposes. If results are needed that are stable across time, for example, you would expect to find evidence of test-retest reliability. Test users therefore must ask, "Does this test have the type of reliability and validity for the purposes for which it is to be used?" If the answer is "no," then the test should not be used.

To understand a test means to know (1) the characteristics of its standardization sample, (2) the types and quality of its reliability and validity, (3) the reliability and validity of comparable tests, (4) the scoring procedures, (5) the method of administration, (6) the limitations, and (7) the strengths. Information about all these areas should be available in the test manual. One also should know the basic concepts covered in this book.

Even if one understands a test completely, it still is vulnerable to misuse unless the tester is trained in its proper use and has had experience with the test, preferably under supervision by an expert. In the absence of the recommended experience, the test user should state the limitations of the results and caution anyone who might use the test score.

State licensing laws and professional ethical codes are designed to protect the public from abuses that result from test misuse. Licensing laws attempt to prevent tests from being used by people other than those who are qualified by training and experience. Ethical codes of such organizations as the American Medical Association and American Psychological Association furthermore prohibit even highly trained specialists from using procedures beyond their competency. Despite these safeguards, however, the responsibility for proper test use must be shared by all concerned. Teachers, counselors, and others who do not actually administer tests but do make use of test results have a responsibility to understand the appropriate uses and limitations of any test they use. In the absence of such knowledge, test results should be viewed cautiously. For example, if a high school counselor encounters a result based on a new test, the result should not be used until all the necessary information about the test has been obtained. The counselor must be satisfied that the result can be appropriately applied to the person for whom it is being used.

In addition to precautions on the part of the examiner and anyone else who uses test scores, the public or consumer of tests must share in the burden of ensuring that tests are properly used and not misused. This means that we should become as informed as possible about tests that are used in decisions affecting our lives. One major intent of this book is to provide the consumers of tests as well as the users of tests with sufficient information to become responsible, informed participants in the pervasive field of testing.

II. *Concepts and Distinctions*

In making the proper use of tests, you should be familiar with some important concepts, definitions, and distinctions. We now discuss a test battery, in which results from two or more tests are used together and often in conjunction with other (nontest) sources of data. We also make a distinction between testing and assessment.

A. *A Test Battery*

In reading Part II, you no doubt will quickly conclude that although they are useful in applied settings, even the best available tests leave much to be desired in terms of scientific, or what we will refer to as *psychometric*, adequacy. However, as in medicine, psychological practitioners must make daily decisions on the basis of existing technology. Because of the need for psychological services, practitioners do not have the luxury of waiting until conclusive evidence is published before applying existing technology. On the other hand, all psychologists are rooted to a scientific perspective. Those who use psychological tests, therefore, usually have a scientific orientation. They are acutely aware of the limitations of the existing technology but often find themselves forced to use the best of what is available.

To deal with their frequently divergent needs for tests that are useful in professional settings and scientifically sound, psychologists have come up with better ways of using the existing tools. One method involves the concept of a test battery. A **test battery** is a collection of tests whose scores are used together in appraising an individual. In using a test battery, the practitioner refuses to accept the validity of a single bit of isolated information. On the contrary, the modern practitioner bases his or her decisions on a variety of data sources. In the test battery, a single test score is used in conjunction with other tests and other sources of information, not in isolation. These sources of information may include an interview, direct observations, input from others such as the person's peers or relatives, and records of past performance. In using a test battery in conjunction with other sources of information, the test user integrates a wide variety of findings. This helps to reduce potential errors and avoid the pitfalls that can occur when only isolated bits of information are used.

B. *Testing Versus Assessment*

The terms *testing* and *assessment* often are confused. The goal of **assessment** is to evaluate an individual so that he or she can be described in terms of current functioning and also so that predictions can be made concerning future functioning. Psychological assessment involves the classification of behavior into categories measured against a normative standard. Tests are used in the assessment process. Thus, not all assessment procedures can be called tests. In the strictest sense, an assessment procedure is called a test only when its procedures for administration, scoring, and interpretation are standardized, there is a **normative sample**, and there is evidence in support of its reliability and validity.

A tool useful in the assessment process may or may not qualify as a test. Indeed, many psychologists have concluded that certain so-called tests would be more appropriately labeled assessment tools because, although they are useful to practitioners in evaluating an individual's functioning, they do not meet the requirements of a test. In Part II, we call many procedures tests that others might prefer to call assessment techniques. For many of the procedures, especially measures of personality, opinion is divided concerning whether or not the term *test* is appropriate. Thus, where we use the term *test* to describe a particular procedure, your instructor might prefer a term such as *technique* or *assessment tool*.

III. *Criteria for Selection of Tests*

In view of the large number of available tests, it was no easy matter to decide which to include and which to omit. We thought you might be interested in the major guidelines we used in selecting tests for Part II and for deciding how much detail to include about each test.

A. Ability Tests

It was not our purpose to discuss every test of human ability that has ever been used or even all of those that currently exist. *The Mental Measurements Yearbooks* (for example, Buros, 1972, 1978; Mitchell, 1985) and other sources discussed in earlier chapters are designed for this purpose. Our goal is to help you understand the principles underlying individual and group ability tests so that you will know what to look for in selecting and evaluating them.

In order to include as many tests as possible and to present them in a readable context, our general format is as follows: We briefly describe each test, classify it according to use, provide a general discussion of its psychometric properties, and then attempt to note its major limitations and strengths. For the more important tests, we also include some of the major recent research findings. Students who require more specific or detailed information should consult *The Mental Measurements Yearbooks*, the actual test manual, the psychological abstracts, and other sources listed in Chapter 7.

Our primary criterion for selecting a test for discussion demanded that the test illustrate an important concept, a unique property, or an important principle. Whenever more than one test was available to illustrate a specific concept or application, we generally included only the most important for discussion. To evaluate importance, we considered how much the test is actually used as revealed in studies of test usage (Lubin, Larsen & Matarazzo, 1984; Lubin, Wallis & Paine, 1971; Piotrowski, Sherry & Keller, 1985; Polyson, Peterson & Marshall, 1986; Sundberg, 1961; Wade & Baker, 1977). These have used questionnaire data completed by users of tests to determine the frequency of a test's use in applied settings.

In evaluating importance, we also consulted *The Mental Measurements Yearbooks* to determine the number of references to any given test. This number of references provided a rough index of the interest the test has generated in the research community. As a final gauge of importance, we surveyed the literature and determined which tests have been discussed by experts in books and reviews exclusively devoted to ability tests, such as J. M. Sattler's (1988) text on testing the intelligence of children. We avoided any test in which, in our judgment, the psychometric characteristics were poor; however, any exclusion on our part does not mean a test is psychometrically unsound. Finally, tests of historical value or significance often were included.

It was not hard to ascertain which intelligence tests are most used. Without question, the most frequently used ones are the Stanford-Binet intelligence scale and the family of tests known as the Wechsler intelligence scales. Furthermore, more research has been conducted with these two scales than with any other ability test (Buros, 1974; Mitchell, 1985). Together, the Stanford-Binet intelligence scale and the Wechsler intelligence scales account for about half the research done with intelligence tests of any kind and about half the individual ability tests administered in the United States. Furthermore, the principles of all intelligence tests can be easily illustrated in an analysis of the evolution of the Stanford-Binet scale and the Wechsler intelligence scales, which we refer to as the "major" intelligence scales. Therefore, in order to achieve the necessary depth for understanding while avoiding the encyclopedic approach, we devote one chapter to the Stanford-Binet scale (Chapter 10) and another to the Wechsler intelligence scales (Chapter 11). These two chapters provide the foundation for understanding all other ability tests, which are discussed in Chapters 12 and 13.

B. *Approach to Personality Tests*

Our approach to personality tests concentrates on principles, as does our approach to ability tests. Our discussions of ability and personality tests both contain sections in which great detail is presented. We realize that absorbing such detail can be a burden. However, with a detailed knowledge of a relatively few of the most highly used and researched tests, you will acquire a basis for comparing all other tests. What we have tried to do is present each of the major types and kinds of personality tests with sufficient detail to give you a basis to compare and evaluate new tests or any of the many personality tests not included in our discussion. You will see a clear-cut emphasis on the Minnesota Multiphasic Personality Inventory (MMPI), which is the most frequently referenced structured personality test (and the most referenced of all personality tests), as well as an emphasis on the Rorschach inkblot test, the most frequently referenced projective personality test (Buros, 1972, 1978; Mitchell, 1985).

Summary

In this brief transition to Part II, we have provided an introduction to the *applications* of psychological tests, and we have discussed the use of test results. Our position, consistent with the *Standards* of the American Education Research Association, American Psychological Association, and National Council on Measurement in Education and with expert opinion, is that the major problem today with tests is not their quality or soundness but the way test results are used (Snyderman & Rothman, 1987). Although new and better tests are most welcome, the real challenge is to ensure that the available tests are used properly.

One important way of making appropriate use of psychological tests is to use them in a battery. A *test battery* does not rely on a single bit of information; rather, data from two or more tests are combined with other sources of information, such as an interview. In the next chapter, you will be exposed to the major concepts underlying several types of interviews, including employment and clinical. Because the interview plays such an important role in so many decisions and complements standard tests so well, the importance of an interview as an adjunct to the testing process cannot be overemphasized.

In addition to the issue of test use and the concept of a test battery, we explained our rationale for selecting the tests that are discussed in Part II. For the most part, we have included the most highly used and referenced ability and personality tests. You will find an in-depth discussion on a few tests, but these are tests for which thousands of references exist. We have assumed that with a thorough knowledge of a select group of especially important tests and a more general knowledge of a wide variety of other widely used tests, you will acquire the skills you need to evaluate tests.

Chapter 9

Interview Techniques

Learning Objectives

When you have completed this chapter, you should be able to:

- Explain the difference between a structured and an unstructured interview.

- Discuss the importance of setting the proper tone for the interview.

- Describe the role of the attitude of the interviewer in the interview process.

- Identity some of the characteristics of effective interviewing.

- List which types of statements tend to keep the interaction flowing or elicit self-exploration in the interviewee.

- Explain the effects of understanding statements on interviewee responses.

- Identify the various sources of error in the interview.

- Appreciate the role of cultural, ethnic, and socioeconomic factors in the interview process.

- Explain how interview skills are acquired and developed.

John was being considered for a high-level public relations position with his firm in the computer industry. The job duties would require him to interact with a wide variety of people, ranging from heads of state and corporation presidents to rank-and-file employees and union officials. In addition, the position would involve making formal policy statements for release to the press. Any poorly phrased statement or inappropriate reaction on his part could result in adverse publicity, which could cost the firm millions of dollars. The application process therefore involved an elaborate testing procedure. Included were two lengthy interviews. The first was with the firm's personnel selection officer; the second was with the firm's clinical psychologist. (See Figure 9-1.)

Knowing the importance of first impressions (Lyman, Hatlelid & Macundy, 1981), John was careful to appear neat and well groomed. In his first

Figure 9-1
An interview.

interview, the personnel officer read from a form as she conducted the interview, which went something like this:

Officer: I've read your application form and have gone over your qualifications. Would you now please outline your educational experiences, beginning with high school?

John: I graduated from high school in June of 1980 with a major in history and social studies. I began attending college in September of 1980. I graduated in June of 1984 with a major in psychology and minor in business management. I then entered the university's graduate program in business. I obtained my master's degree in business administration.

Officer: What is your work history? Begin with your first full-time employment.

John described his work history. The personnel officer then continued a series of questions, which John systematically answered. The questions went something like this:

How do your education and experience relate to the job for which you are applying?

What educational experiences have you had that might help you function on the job for which you are applying?

What employment experiences have you had that might help you function on the job for which you are applying?

Identify any deficiencies in your educational and work experiences.

What educational and work experiences have you had that might impair your ability to function on the job for which you are applying?

The interview continued in a similar manner. With each question, the personnel officer attempted to relate John's educational and work experiences to the particular job duties he was hoping to assume. For her final question the personnel officer asked, "Why do you believe you would make a good candidate for this position?"

John felt good about his interview with the personnel officer. He thought the questions were clear and straightforward, and he was pleased by his answers. The next day he appeared for his interview with the clinical psychologist. Unlike the personnel officer, the psychologist conducted the interview without using written interview questions. This second interview, which was quite different from the first, went something like this:

Psychologist: John, why don't you tell me a little bit about yourself?

John: Where do you want me to begin?

Psychologist: Oh, it doesn't matter. Just tell me about yourself.

John: I graduated from high school in June of 1980. I majored in history and social studies.

Psychologist: Yes, I see.

John: I then attended college and finally graduate school. My master's degree should help me to assume the duties of the new position.

Psychologist: You feel that your master's degree is a useful asset in your application.

John: Yes, my graduate experiences taught me how to work with others.

Psychologist: With these graduate experiences, you learned the art of working with other people.

John: Well, I guess I didn't learn it all in graduate school. I've always managed to get along well with others.

Psychologist: As far as you can tell, you work pretty well with people.

John: That's right. As the oldest of three children, I've always had responsibility for supervising others. You know what I mean?

Psychologist: Being the oldest, you were given extra responsibilities as a child.

John: Not that I resented it. Well, maybe sometimes. It's just that I never had much time for myself.

Psychologist: And having time for yourself is important to you.

John: Yes, of course it is. I guess everybody needs some time alone.

Psychologist: As a person who deals with others all day long, you must treasure those few moments you have to yourself.

John: I really do. Whenever I get a chance I like to drive up to the lake all by myself and just think.

Psychologist: These moments are precious to you.

The interview continued like this for about an hour. After it was over, John wasn't sure how he had done. Think about the two interviews. In what ways were they alike? How did they differ? As you contemplate your answers, you will soon realize that there is more than one type of interview and that interviews can differ considerably.

The first interview with the personnel officer was highly structured. The interviewer read from a printed set of questions. The personnel officer's interview was no doubt **standardized.** Thus, all applicants for the position were asked the same questions in the same sequence. The second interview, by contrast, was **unstructured** and therefore unstandardized. The clinical psychologist didn't appear to have any specific or particular questions in mind, and the sequence of questions followed from John's statements. Each applicant, no doubt, would be asked different questions, depending on his or her responses.

Can you identify other differences between the two interviews? The first was narrow and restricted. It focused on two specific areas: John's education and work experiences. The second was broad and unrestricted. It touched on a variety of areas, although the focus of the interview was clearly John himself. The first interview was *directive*. The personnel officer directed, guided, and controlled the course of the interview. The second interview was *nondirective*. The clinical psychologist let John determine the direction of the interview. When John talked about his master's degree, the psychologist discussed this. When John talked about being the oldest of three children, this became the focus of the psychologist's response. Furthermore, unlike the personnel officer, the psychologist rarely asked questions. Instead, the psychologist tended to comment or reflect on John's previous statement. Last, but perhaps most important, John's interview with the personnel officer can best be described as an **employment** or **selection interview;** it was designed to elicit information pertaining to John's qualifications and capabilities for particular employment duties. The second interview, on the other hand, can best be described as a **diagnostic interview;** it was designed to elicit information concerning John's emotional functioning. His qualifications were clearly not an issue in the second interview. Rather, in conducting a diagnostic interview, the clinical psychologist was interested in John's feelings, thoughts, attitudes, and the like, which might impede or facilitate John's ability to function competently.

I. *The Interview as a Test*

In many respects, an interview is like a test (see Table 9-1). Like any psychological or educational test, an interview is a method for gathering data or information about an individual. This information is then used to describe the

Table 9-1
Similarities
Between an
Interview and a
Test

Method for gathering data
Used to make predictions
Can be evaluated in terms of reliability
Can be evaluated in terms of validity
Can be group or individual
Can be structured or unstructured

individual, make future predictions, or both. Like tests, interviews can be evaluated in terms of standard psychometric qualities such as reliability and validity. Furthermore, there are several types of interview procedures, depending on the type of information that is sought and the goals of the interviewer.

Like any test, the interview involves an interaction between two or more people. Some interviews proceed like individually administered tests in which the interviewer interacts with a single individual at a time. In other interviews, such as the family interview, a single interviewer interacts with two or more individuals at the same time, just as in a group test. Like all tests, an interview has a definite purpose. Furthermore, just as the person who administers a test must take responsibility for the test administration process, so the interviewer must assume responsibility for the conduct of the interview.

Many tests, such as the Thematic Apperception Test (TAT), cannot be properly used without adequate interview data. The interview, on the other hand, is often the only or most important source of data. Good interviewing skills may be one of the most important tools for functioning in today's society. Not only is interviewing the chief method for data collection in clinical psychiatry (Mackinnon & Michels, 1971; Stevenson, 1971), but interviewing also is used in all health-related professions including general medicine and nursing. Interviewing is an essential testing tool in subspecialties such as clinical, industrial, counseling, school, and correctional psychology.

Interviewing is a tool in social work, vocational and guidance counseling, marriage and family counseling, and so on. Parole boards conduct parole interviews. In addition, interviewing is an essential tool of the researcher. Business people and managers use interviewing to evaluate employees as well as potential clients. Interviewing also is a primary tool of the courtroom attorney. Indeed, interview skills are important in most professions involving people. Contractors or architects must possess sufficient interviewing skills to determine exactly what their customers want them to do. Interviewing also plays a role in everyday life, such as when a parent questions a group of children to find out who is responsible for a broken window. In beginning new relationships on a positive note, one must possess a degree of interviewing skill. Given its broad application, no introductory text on psychological tests could be complete without reference to the interview.

II. *Reciprocal Nature of Interviewing*

Interactive in activity

Although there are many types and purposes of interviews, some factors are common to all interviews. First, all interviews involve mutual or shared interaction (Wiens, 1976). The participants are interdependent and influence each other (Heller, 1971, pp.145–148). The transactional or reciprocal nature of the interview process is illustrated in a study by K. Heller, J. D. Davis, and R. A. Myers (1966). They found that if one of the participants in the interview increased his or her activity level, the activity level of the other participant also increased. Similarly, a reduction in activity by one of the interview participants was associated with a reduction in the activity of the other. A similar finding was reported by J. D. Matarazzo and colleagues (1968). Thus, the participants in an interview have a profound effect on each other.

in mood

In addition to influencing each other's activity, the mood of one of the participants in an interview influences the mood of the other. Heller (1971), for example, reported that when professional actors responded with anger (hostility) to even highly trained, experienced interviewers, the interviewers responded in kind; that is, they became angry themselves and directed this back toward the actors. The phenomenon observed by Heller is generally known as **social facilitation** (see Bandura, 1986). Social facilitation means we tend to act like the models around us. If the interviewer is tense, anxious, defensive, and aloof, the interviewee tends to respond in kind. Thus, if the interviewer wishes to create conditions of openness, warmth, acceptance, comfort, calmness, and support, he or she must exhibit these qualities.

Social facilitation is one of the most important concepts underlying the interview process. Because the participants in an interview influence each other, obviously the good interviewer must provide a relaxed and safe atmosphere. Through social facilitation, the interviewee eventually begins to feel relaxed and safe. However, although participants in an interview influence each other, the good interviewer remains in control and sets the tone of the interview. If the interviewer reacts to the interviewee's tension and anxiety with more tension and anxiety, then a tense situation will rapidly develop. By remaining calm, confident, in control, and self-assured, the interviewer has a calming effect on the interviewee. In our experience, even potentially violent prison inmates or disturbed psychotic persons become manageable when the interviewer sets the proper tone.

III. *Principles of Effective Interviewing*

Setting the tone to facilitate the proper attitudes (for example, relaxation and openness) in the person being interviewed is just one factor in effective interviewing. There are other principles that also seem to be common to effective interviewing. Naturally, specific interview techniques and approaches vary depending on such factors as the type of interview (for example, employment versus diagnostic) and the goals of the interviewer (for example, description versus prediction). Thus, there are no hard and fast rules that apply to all interview situations. However, there are some principles that aid in the conduct of almost any interview. We present some of these principles because they will increase your understanding of the factors and processes that underlie the interview. Knowledge of these principles also should help you acquire interview skills of your own.

A. *The Proper Attitudes*

As L. E. Tyler (1969) noted, good interview behavior is actually more a matter of attitude than skill. Experiments in social psychology have shown that interpersonal influence (that is, the degree to which one person can influence another) is related to interpersonal attraction (that is, the degree to which there is a shared feeling of understanding, mutual respect, similarity, and the like) (Baglan, 1981; Cialdini, 1985). Attitudes generally related to good interviewing skills include warmth, genuineness, acceptance, understanding, openness, honesty, and fairness. D. P. Saccuzzo (1975), for example, studied the initial psychotherapy interviews of first-year clinical psychology graduate students. Patients and therapists both responded to a questionnaire. Their task was to rate the quality of the interview and indicate the topics, concerns, problems, and feelings of the patient as well as the feelings of the therapist.

Although the patients' feelings and concerns were important, the most important factor in the patients' evaluations of the quality of the interview was their perceptions of the interviewer's feelings. The session was given a good evaluation by both interview participants when the patient saw the interviewer as warm, open, concerned, involved, committed, and interested, irrespective of the type or severity of the problem or what was talked about. On the other hand, independent of all other factors, when the interviewer was seen as cold, defensive, uninterested, uninvolved, aloof, and bored, the session was rated poorly. To appear effective and establish rapport, the interviewer must display the proper attitudes.

B. *Responses to Avoid*

In a "stress interview" the interviewer may deliberately induce discomfort or anxiety in the interviewee. As a rule, however, making interviewees feel uncomfortable tends to place them on guard, and guarded or anxious interviewees tend to reveal little information about themselves. However, one purpose of the stress interview is to determine how well an individual functions in a stressful, uncomfortable, or demanding situation. Thus, the purpose of the interview dictates the type of responses to use or avoid. If the goal is to elicit as much information as possible, or if one wishes the interview to be considered satisfactory by the interviewee, then certain responses should be avoided. Responses that should generally be avoided because of their disruptive or limiting effect on the interview process include *judgmental* or *evaluative statements*, *probing statements*, *hostility*, and *false reassurance*.

Judgmental or evaluative statements are particularly likely to inhibit the interviewee. Being judgmental means evaluating the thoughts, feelings, or actions of another. When we use such terms as *good, bad, excellent, terrible, disgusting, disgraceful*, and *stupid*, we are being evaluative. When we make an **evaluative statement,** we are judging the other person. This tends to put the person on guard because it communicates "I don't approve of this aspect of you." In placing the person on guard, we limit his or her ease in revealing important information. Thus, unless the goal of the interview is to determine how a person responds to being evaluated or to apply stress by responding with strong disapproval or displeasure, evaluative or judgmental statements generally should be avoided in good interview behavior.

Also to be avoided, unless necessary for a specific purpose or type of interview, are **probing statements.** These demand more information than the interviewee has been willing to provide voluntarily. The most common way to phrase a probing statement is to ask a question that begins with "Why?" As A. N. Wiens (1976) noted, asking "Why?" tends to place the person on the defensive. When we ask "Why?" as in "Why did you stay out so late?" we are demanding that the person explain his or her behavior. Such a demand obviously has a judgmental quality. Furthermore, in probing we may induce the interviewee to reveal something he or she is not yet ready to reveal. If this happens, the interviewee will probably feel anxious and thus not very well disposed to revealing additional information.

In some circumstances, probes are appropriate and necessary. When dealing with children, for instance, it is often necessary to ask questions in order to elicit meaningful information. Highly anxious or withdrawn individuals may also need a probe in order to get beyond a superficial interchange. In such circumstances it is important to use the probe wisely, by avoiding "Why?" statements and replacing them with "Tell me" or "How?" statements, as illustrated in Table 9-2.

The **hostile response** directs anger toward the interviewee. Clearly such responses should be avoided unless one has a specific purpose, such as determining how an interviewee responds to anger.

The **reassuring response** attempts to comfort or support the interviewee, such as "Don't worry. Everything will be all right." Reassurance may sometimes be appropriate, but false reassurance almost always should be avoided. For example, imagine a friend of yours flunks out of college, loses her job, and gets kicked out of her home by her parents. You are lying to this person when you say, "Don't worry; no problem; it's okay." This is false reassurance, and it

Table 9-2
Effective Probing
Statements

Poor	Better
Why did you yell at him?	1. Tell more more about what happened.
	2. How did you happen to yell at him?
	3. What led up to the situation?
Why did you say that?	1. Can you tell me what you mean?
	2. I'm not sure I understand.
	3. How did you happen to say that?
Why can't you sleep?	1. Tell me more about your sleeping problem.
	2. Can you identify what prevents you from sleeping?
	3. How is it that you are unable to sleep?

does nothing to help your friend except perhaps make her realize that you are not going to assist. The fact is that what has happened to your friend is terrible and will require specific action on her part to prevent even more disastrous developments. Naturally, you should not overwhelm your friend with all the facts at once, but she needs to come to grips with the situation in manageable doses before taking the necessary steps to constructively solve the problem. The person who gives false reassurance usually knows this, and so does the person who receives it. (See Figure 9-2.)

C. *Effective Responses*

Knowing what types of responses to avoid, how does one go about conducting an effective interview? One major general principle of effective interviewing is to keep the interaction flowing. The interview is a two-way process. First one person speaks, then the other, and so on. Furthermore, in general, the interviewer uses a minimum amount of effort to keep the interaction flowing. As long as the interviewee's verbalizations are relevant to the purpose of the interview, the interviewer listens with interest by maintaining face-to-face contact.

Except in structured interviews or for a particular purpose, an effective way to initiate the interview process involves the use of an **open-ended question.** This is one that usually cannot be answered specifically, as opposed to a **closed-ended question,** which can. Examples of open-ended questions are "Tell me a little bit about yourself." "Tell me about what interests you," and "What is it that brings you here to see me?" Examples of closed-ended questions are: "Do you like sports?" "Are you married?" and "How old are you?"

A closed-ended question brings the interview to a dead halt and thus violates the principle of keeping the interaction flowing. In the example at the beginning of the chapter, even the personnel officer's opening statement was

Figure 9-2
Responses to
avoid in an
unstructured
interview.

sufficiently open-ended to permit a variety of responses, depending on the interviewee. Where one individual might provide every minute detail of his or her education, for example, a second might simply include major events. In degree, however, the clinical psychologist's opening statement—"Why don't you tell me a little bit about yourself?" was even more open-ended. John could have replied with just about anything.

Open-ended questions give the interviewee wide latitude in choosing the topics that he or she feels are important. Except for highly specific structured interviews, we usually can learn a lot more about people when they tell us what they think is important than when we try to guess by asking a series of unrelated closed-ended questions. The open-ended question requires the interviewee to produce something spontaneously, as opposed to the closed-ended question, which generally requires the person to recall something (Wiens, 1976). Table 9-3 presents some closed-ended questions along with corresponding open-ended questions.

Flexibility is needed in conducting an interview. Except for structured interviews, most interviews cannot be conducted in precisely the same way. In therapeutic or diagnostic interviews, the interviewer usually follows only general guidelines in conducting the interview. The goal of such interviews is to get to know the person as well as possible in order to understand him or her and make predictive statements about future behavior.

D. *Responses to Keep the Interaction Flowing*

After asking the open-ended question, the interviewer, as a rule, lets the interviewee respond without being interrupted; that is, the interviewer should remain quiet and listen. Unless the interview is structured, once the interviewee's response dies down, the interviewer usually responds in a way that will keep the interaction flowing. A closed-ended question at this point would naturally bring the interview to a halt and should be avoided. Instead, the interviewer should follow the principle of using the minimum effort to keep the interview flowing. Therefore, after the initial response to the open-ended question has been completed, the interviewer could appropriately use a transitional phrase such as "Yes," "I see," or "And." These transitional phrases imply that the interviewee should continue talking about the same topic. In John's interview with the clinical psychologist, for example, John stated, "I graduated from high school in June of 1980. I majored in history and social studies." The

Table 9-3
Open- and
Closed-Ended
Questions

Closed-Ended	Open-Ended
Do you like sports cars?	What kind of cars do you like?
Do you like baseball?	What kinds of recretional activities do you prefer?
Are you having a problem?	Tell me about your problems.
Is your father strict?	Describe your father.
Would you like to vacation in Hawaii?	What are your favorite vacation spots?

clinical psychologist simply responded with a transition, "Yes, I see." John then continued to elaborate on his response.

Sometimes the transitional phrase fails to have the desired effect. When this occurs, it is the interviewer's turn to respond again. The interviewer should make a response relevant to what has just been communicated. In other words, the interview is thematic; it does not jump from one unrelated topic to another as it might if the interviewer were asking a series of questions. The theme in John's interview with the clinical psychologist involved John. Although the topics did change from John's education to his feeling about being the oldest of three children, John himself remained the central focus. The psychologist accomplished this by making statements that were relevant to what John was saying.

To make a response relevant to what has been communicated, the interviewer may use any of the following types of statements: verbatim playback, paraphrasing, restatement, summarizing, clarifying, and understanding. You can view these statements as being on a continuum ranging from a statement that is totally interchangeable with the interviewee's response to a response that adds to or goes beyond it.

In a verbatim playback, the interviewer simply repeats the interviewee's last response. For example, in his interview with the clinical psychologist, John stated, "I majored in history and social studies." The psychologist replied with the transitional phrase "Yes, I see." A verbatim playback, "You majored in history and social studies," would have been equally effective. In either case, John most likely would continue to elaborate on his previous response. Thus, like the transitional phrase, the verbatim playback generally leads to an elaboration of the interviewee's previous response.

Closely related to the verbatim playback in terms of eliciting elaborations are paraphrasing and restatement responses, which are both interchangeable with the interviewee's response. A paraphrase tends to be more similar to the interviewee's response than the restatement, but both serve to capture the meaning of the interviewee's response. When John said, "My master's degree should help me assume the duties of the new position," the psychologist replied with a restatement: "You feel that your master's degree is a useful asset in your application." A paraphrase might have taken the form: "You feel that your master's degree will be an important aid in tackling the responsibilities of the new position." In his restatement, the psychologist introduced "useful asset" to restate John's attitude toward his master's degree. The paraphrase, on the other hand, simply replaced "important aid" for "help" and "tackling the responsibilities" for "assuming the duties." Neither statement, however, added anything to John's.

Summarizing and clarification statements tend to go just beyond the interviewee's response, thus adding to it. In summarizing, the interviewer pulls together the meaning of several interviewee responses. To John's last statement in the example, the psychologist could have replied with a summarizing statement such as "As a youth you never had much time to yourself because you were responsible for taking care of the two younger children. Today you enjoy those few moments you have to be alone. Whenever you get a chance to be alone you drive to the lake all by yourself and just think." Notice that this summarizing statement involves verbatim playback, paraphrasing, and restating. With these three types of statements, the psychologist summarizes an entire sequence of responses.

The clarification statement, as its name implies, serves to clarify the interviewee's response. When John stated, "Not that I resented it. Well, maybe sometimes. It's just that I never had much time for myself," the psychologist attempted to clarity what John was trying to say. It was not that John resented the extra responsibilities; rather, he simply wanted some time to be alone. Thus, the psychologist clarified John's statement by saying, "And having time for yourself is important to you."

The clarification statement—like summarizing, paraphrasing, restatement, and verbatim playback—remains very close to the meaning of the interviewee's response. These responses are either interchangeable with the interviewee's own response or add slightly to it. Each of these responses communicates or facilitates a degree of understanding. At the lowest level, the verbatim playback communicates that the interviewer at least heard the communication. The restatement, paraphrase, and summarizing responses go a bit further and communicate that the interviewer has a good idea of what the interviewee is trying to communicate.

Even more powerful is the **empathy** or **understanding response.** This response communicates that the interviewer understands how the interviewee must feel. When the psychologist stated, "These moments are precious to you," he was not simply paraphrasing or restating what John had said. Instead, the psychologist was communicating that he understood how John felt about having time to himself. (See Table 9-4 for a summary of responses that keep the interview flowing.)

Many students have considerable difficulty seeing the value of understanding and other statements that stay close to the interviewee's response. Some

Table 9-4
Responses to
Keep the
Interaction
Flowing

Response	Definition or Example
Transitional phrase	"Yes," "I see," "Go on"
Verbatim playback	Repeats interviewee's exact words
Paraphrasing and restatement	Repeats interviewee's response using different words
Summarizing	Pulls together the meaning of several responses
Clarification	Clarifies the interviewee's response
Empathy	Communicates understanding

students consider such statements to be artificial and weak because of their noncommittal quality. However, the rationale for such responses is based on the well-known and well-documented finding that when we communicate to a person that we understand, that person will talk about or explore himself or herself at deeper and deeper levels (Rogers, 1980; Truax & Mitchell, 1971). Accurate empathy elicits self-exploration. Consider the following example:

Psychologist:	What's been happening today, Bill? (*open-ended question*)
Bill:	My physics teacher yelled at me in front of the whole class.
Psychologist:	That's embarrassing. (*understanding*)
Bill:	Not only that, she seems to pick on me all the time.
Psychologist:	That must make you angry. (*understanding*)
Bill:	Yeah, I guess so. It seems like she's always finding fault with my work. No matter what I do, she just doesn't like it.
Psychologist:	That is really frustrating, Bill. You just can't seem to please her. (*understanding*)
Bill:	The other day we had an exam and I got an "F." I checked my answers with Tom, and mine were the same as his. Yet I got an "F" and Tom got a "B."
Psychologist:	Hey, that doesn't seem fair. (*clarification and understanding*)
Bill:	You bet it isn't fair. But when I tried to talk to her about it, she refused to listen.
Psychologist:	That's scary. (*understanding*)
Bill:	It sure is. If I get one more "F," I'll be kicked out of school.
Psychologist:	This is really serious. (*clarification*)
Bill:	Yeah. If I get kicked out of school, I couldn't face my parents or friends.
Psychologist:	This whole thing has really got you upset. (*understanding*)

Certainly, the psychologist's responses are not the only ones that could have been used. However, you should note how the psychologist, in providing a series of understanding responses, was able to "uncover" the real source of Bill's anguish. The feelings Bill expressed ranged from embarrassment to anger to fear of being kicked out of school and finally to fear of how his friends and family would view his failure.

Let's consider other possible responses the psychologist could have made to Bill's initial statement "My physics teacher yelled at me in front of the whole class." The psychologist could have replied: (1) "Why did she do that?" With this probing statement, Bill is forced to defend himself or explain why it happened. He would have to go over the circumstances that preceded the incident, which actually leads away from Bill's real feelings and concerns. (2) "Why did you let her do that to you? That wasn't very smart of you." This evaluative statement places Bill on the defensive and has the further disadvantage of criticizing him and possibly hurting his feelings. Given this type of reaction from the psychologist, Bill could in no way feel safe in exploring his real feelings. (3) "That woman is always yelling at somebody. You should report her to the chairperson." With this off-the-cuff advice, the psychologist again removes himself from Bill's real concerns. Now the two might spend the rest of their time together weighing the pros and cons of reporting Bill's physics teacher. Still worse, Bill might impulsively follow the advice and get into real trouble if he cannot substantiate his claims. (4) "Don't worry. That physics teacher yells at everyone. It doesn't mean a thing." With this false reassurance, Bill no longer is free to express his real concern. The psychologist has already dismissed the whole matter as insignificant.

In short, understanding responses that stay close to the content and underlying feeling provided by the interviewee permit the individual to explore the situation out loud and at deeper and deeper levels. In general, unstructured interviewing is an uncovering process. Questions, evaluations, reassurances, and the like—unless specifically called for, as in a structured interview—generally allow only a superficial coverage of the individual. As a rule, the problem in interviewing is to obtain verbal information from the interviewee. One good way of accomplishing this is by responding with facilitative statements. The facilitative interview provides a positive atmosphere. It begins with an open-ended question followed by understanding statements that capture the meaning and feeling of the interviewee's communication. See Figure 9-3 for an exercise in keeping the interaction flowing.

E. *Measuring Understanding*

Understanding statements can be further appreciated by an analysis of measures of understanding. Attempts to measure understanding or empathy originated with Carl Rogers's pioneering research into the effects of client-centered therapy (Rogers, 1959a, 1961b; Walker, Rablen & Rogers, 1960). It culmi-

Figure 9-3
Exercise in
keeping the
interaction
flowing.

Directions: Below is a list of statements, each followed by two possible replies. Select the one that would tend to keep the interaction flowing.

1. I hate school.
☐   a. It sounds like you're fed up with school.
☐   b. What's wrong with school?

2. My dad is a jerk.
☐   a. Why don't you just tell him to "chill out"?
☐   b. You're angry with your dad.

3. Most people are liars.
☐   a. Don't be so negative.
☐   b. You feel that most people can't be trusted.

4. We were ahead until the last minute of the game.
☐   a. That's disappointing.
☐   b. Why didn't you win?

5. She stood me up again.
☐   a. If I were you, I wouldn't ask her out again.
☐   b. It hurts to be treated like that.

6. I hope I passed that test.
☐   a. You're worried about how you did on the test.
☐   b. Don't worry. I'm sure you passed.

Answers: 1. a; 2. b; 3. b; 4. a; 5. b; 6. a

Notes:
1b is a probing statement.
2a is advice.
3a is advice.
4b is a probing statement.
5a is advice.
6b is false reassurance.

5 empathy levels in responses

nated in a five-point scoring system (Truax & Carkhuff, 1967, pp. 46–58), which was subsequently revised (Carkhuff & Berenson, 1967). Each of the levels in this five-point system represents a degree or level of empathy. The levels range from a response that bears little or no relationship to the previous statement to a response that captures the precise meaning and feeling of the statement. The highest level of empathy, level five, has relevance primarily for therapeutic interviews. Levels four and three represent various degrees of true empathy or understanding and may be used in all types of unstructured or semistructured (that is, partially structured) interviews. The lowest levels, one and two, have no place in a professional interview and should be avoided. Low-level responses, however, occur frequently in everyday conversations. We discuss these levels to illustrate how understanding can be measured.

Level-one responses. Level one responses bear little or no relationship to the interviewee's response. According to R. R. Carkhuff and B. C. Berenson (1967), these responses "do not attend to or detract significantly" from the interviewee's responses. A level one conversation might proceed as follows:

Jennifer: Jason, look at my new dress.
 Jason: I sure hope it doesn't rain today.
Jennifer: See, it's red with blue stripes.
 Jason: If it rains, my baseball game might get canceled.
Jennifer: I really love this dress; it's my favorite.
 Jason: It's sure going to tick me off if that game gets canceled.

The two might as well be talking to a tape recorder.

Level-two responses. The level two response communicates some awareness of the meaning of a statement, but only at a superficial level. The individual who makes a level two response never quite goes beyond his or her own limited perspective. Level two responses subtract from the communication; for example:

Jennifer: Boy, I feel good. I just got a beautiful new dress.
 Jason: I feel bad. It's probably going to rain.
Jennifer: I'll wear this dress to your baseball game.
 Jason: If it rains, there won't be a game.

Here the conversation is related, but only tangentially. Neither person is really aware of what is going on in the other.

Level-three responses. A level three response is interchangeable with the interviewee's statement. According to Carkhuff and Berenson (1967), level three is the minimum level of responding to facilitate the interaction and to be of help to the interviewee. Responses at levels one and two can actually be detrimental to a person in need of help and are clearly nonfacilitative.

Level-four and -five responses. Level four and five responses not only provide accurate empathy but also go beyond the statement given. In a level four response, the interviewer adds "noticeably" to the interviewee's response. In a level five response, the interviewer adds "significantly" to the response (Carkhuff & Berenson, 1967). We recommend that interviewers learn to respond at levels three and four to maximize self-exploration and the uncovering process in unstructured and semistructured interviews. In the example with Jennifer and Jason, a level four interchange might proceed as follows:

Jennifer: I just got a new dress.
 Jason: You feel glad because you like new clothes.

Jennifer: This one is beautiful; it has red and blue stripes.
Jason: You really love that new dress. It is a nice addition to your wardrobe.

Active listening. An impressive array of research has accumulated that documents the power of the understanding response (Patterson, 1974; Rogers, 1980; Truax & Mitchell, 1971). This type of responding, which is sometimes called *active listening*, is the foundation of good interviewing skills for many different types of interviews.

IV. *Types of Interviews*

The previously discussed guides provide a general format for conducting an interview. The specifics vary, however, depending on the goal, purpose, and theoretical orientation of the interviewer. We can distinguish, for example, among five types of interviews: the evaluation interview, the structured clinical interview, the case history interview, the mental status examination, and the employment or selection interview.

A. *Evaluation or Assessment Interview*

According to M. P. Maloney and M. P. Ward (1976), the purpose of the evaluation interview is to assist in the evaluation of the individual. This type of interview is similar to what A. N. Wiens (1976) referred to as the "assessment interview." Maloney and Ward's conception of an evaluation interview provides guides similar to those presented in this chapter for effective interviewing. This similarity is not surprising because both methods are based on the impressive body of literature previously cited that shows that accurate understanding leads to self-exploration. Thus, Maloney and Ward recommend beginning with an open-ended question, with the interviewer "listening, facilitating, and clarifying" during the initial phases of the interview. In addition, Maloney and Ward recommend that the powerful tool of confrontation be included in the process.

The confrontation response is usually most appropriate in therapeutic interviews, but it is a technique that the experienced interviewer should have at his or her disposal. A **confrontation** is a statement that points out a discrepancy or inconsistency. R. R. Carkhuff (1969) distinguishes among three types: (1) a discrepancy between what the person is and what he or she wants to become, (2) a discrepancy between what the person says about himself or herself and what he or she does, and (3) a discrepancy between the person's perception of himself or herself and the interviewer's experience.

The problem with the confrontation is that it may induce anxiety by bringing conflicts or inconsistencies into a person's awareness when he or she may not be ready to handle them. We therefore strongly recommend that the beginning student leave confrontation for the more experienced practitioner.

Direct questions can be used toward the end of the interview to fill in any needed details or gaps in the interviewer's knowledge. For unstructured or semistructured interviews, we advocate the use of direct questions whenever (1) the data can be obtained in no other way, (2) time is markedly limited and the interviewer is in need of relatively specific information, or (3) the interviewee cannot or will not cooperate with the interviewer. The open-ended, facilitative technique does not work well for nonverbal, intellectually limited, and uncooperative subjects. It also doesn't work well with children, for whom direct questioning and careful observation are needed (Wood, 1982). For these subjects, it is exceedingly difficult to get the interview off the ground. Thus, direct questioning becomes an absolute necessity. Finally, at the end of an interview, direct questions should be used as a clean-up procedure to fill in missing details.

B. *Structured Clinical Interviews*

A relatively recent development in interviewing has been the proliferation of structured clinical interviews (Standage, 1989). Structured interviews, as has been indicated, provide a specific set of questions to be presented in a particular order. Terms are operationally defined (Spiker & Ehler, 1984). In addition, there is usually a carefully specified set of rules for probing so that, as in a standardized test, all interviewees are handled in the same manner. Structured interviews lend themselves to scoring procedures, so that norms can be developed and applied. Typically, cutoff scores are used so that a particular score indicates the presence or absence of a given condition.

The development of structured clinical interviews followed the evolution of the *Diagnostic and Statistical Manual of Mental Disorders* (DSM). First published in 1952, revised in 1968, 1980, and 1987, and scheduled to be revised again in 1993, the DSM attempts to classify mental disorders into specific, definable categories. Prior to the 1980 DSM-III, however, the definitions for mental disorders were poorly defined. The result was a very low reliability in psychiatric diagnosis.

The DSM-III attempted to overcome the lack of reliability in psychiatric diagnosis by providing a specific set of criteria for each category of mental disorder. Table 9-5, for example, shows the diagnostic criteria for an obsessive-compulsive disorder.

With specifiable criteria for mental disorders it was possible to develop a specific set of questions to determine whether or not a person met those criteria. Such questionnaires were quickly developed and circulated even while prepublication drafts of the DSM-III were being written in the late 1970s. The Schedule of Affective Disorders (Endicott & Spitzer, 1978) was among the

Table 9-5
Diagnostic
Criteria for an
Obsessive-
Compulsive
Disorder

A. Either obsessions or compulsions

Obsessions
1. Recurrent and persistent ideas, thoughts, impulses, or images that are experienced as intrusive and senseless.
2. The person attempts to ignore or suppress such thoughts or impulses or to neutralize them with some other thought or action.
3. The person recognizes that the obsessions are the product of his or her own mind.

Compulsions
1. Repetitive, purposeful, and intentional behaviors that are performed in response to an obsession, or according to certain rules or in a stereotyped fashion.
2. The behavior is designed to neutralize or to prevent discomfort or some dreaded event or situation.
3. The person recognizes that his or her behavior is excessive or unreasonable.

B. The obsessions or compulsions cause marked distress, are time consuming (take more than an hour a day), or significantly interfere with the person's normal routine, occupational functioning, or usual social activities.

From *Diagnostic and Statistical Manual of Mental Disorders, Third Edition, Revised* (DSM-III-R). Washington, D.C.: American Psychiatric Association, 1987.

earliest of the major structured clinical interviews. Its purpose was to provide a diagnosis for more than 20 different disorders.

More recently, R. L. Spitzer and colleagues have developed a comprehensive interview specifically for making diagnoses from the DSM-III-R, called the Structural Clinical Interview for the DSM-III-R, or the SCID (Spitzer et al., 1990a). Table 9-6 provides an example of the SCID used to diagnose obsessive-compulsive disorder. Notice that the interview formula is quite specific, allows for a specific scoring system, and makes clear-cut provisions for unclear responses.

Today there are countless structured interviews for just about every imaginable problem (Sattler, in press). Interviews are available to assess disorders in children: the Diagnostic Interview Schedule for Children, or DISC (Costello et al., 1984), and the Child Assessment Schedule, or CAS (Hodges, 1985); to assess personality disorders: the Structured Clinical Interview for DSM-III-R—Personality Disorders, or SCID-II (Spitzer et al., 1989b); and to do preliminary screening of mental illness in jails: the Referral Decision Scale, or RDS (Teplin & Schwartz, 1989).

As we have emphasized, structured interviews have the advantage of reliability at the sacrifice of flexibility. They are especially useful in research when an investigator wants to document and define a specific group. For example, if you plan to study obsessive-compulsive disorder, then you need subjects who fall into this category, and there is no better way to document that you have such subjects than to conduct a structured clinical interview. Of course, if you don't know what you're looking for, a structured interview that covers more than 20 diagnoses could become quite a lengthy task. Such interviews require

Table 9-6
SCID 9/1/89 Version Obsessive-Compulsive Disorder   Anxiety Disorders

Obsessive-Compulsive Disorder	Obsessive-Compulsive Disorder Criteria				
	A. Either obsessions or compulsions:				
Now I would like to ask you if you have ever been bothered by thoughts that didn't make any sense and kept coming back to you even when you tried not to have them? (What were they?)	Obsessions: (1), (2), (3), and (4):	?	1	2	3
	(1) Recurrent and persistent ideas, thoughts, impulses, or images that are experienced, at least initially, as intrusive and senseless, e.g., a parent's having repeated impulses to hurt a loved child, a religious person's having recurrent blasphemous thoughts				
(What about awful thoughts, like actually hurting someone even though you didn't want to, or being contaminated by germs or dirt?)	NOTE: DO NOT INCLUDE BROODING ABOUT PROBLEMS (SUCH AS HAVING A PANIC ATTACK) OR ANXIOUS RUMINATIONS ABOUT REALISTIC DANGERS.				
When you had these thoughts, did you try hard to get them out of your head? (What would you try to do?)	(2) The person attempts to ignore or suppress such thoughts or to neutralize them with some other thoughts or action	?	1	2	3
IF UNCLEAR: Where did you think these thoughts were coming from?	(3) The person recognizes that the obsessions are the product of his or her own mind, not imposed from without (as in thought insertion)	?	1	2	3
	(4) If another Axis I disorder is present, the content of the obsession is unrelated to it, i.e., the ideas, thoughts, impulses, or images are not about food in the presence of an Eating Disorder, about drugs in the presence of a Psychoactive Substance Use Disorder, or guilty thoughts in the presence of a Major Depression	?	1	2	3

OBSES-
SIONS

DESCRIBE:

Obsessive-Compulsive Disorder	Compulsions: (1), (2), and (3):				
Was there ever anything that you had to do over and over again and couldn't resist doing, like washing your hands again and again, or checking something several times to make sure you'd done it right?	(1) Repetitive, purposeful, and intentional behaviors that are performed in response to an obsession, or according to certain rules, or in a stereotyped fashion	?	1	2	3
IF YES: What did you have to do? (What were you afraid would happen if you didn't do it?) (How many times did you have to _____? How much time did you spend each day _____?)	(2) The behavior is designed to neutralize or prevent discomfort or some dreaded event or situation; however, either the activity is not connected in a realistic way with what it is designed to neutralize or prevent, or it is clearly excessive	?	1	2	3
IF UNCLEAR: Do you think that you (DO COMPULSIVE BEHAVIOR) more than you should? (Do you think [COMPULSION] makes sense?)	(3) The person recognizes that the behavior is excessive or unreasonable (this may no longer be true for people whose obsessions have evolved into overvalued ideas)	?	1	2	3

COMPULSIONS

DESCRIBE:

IF NEITHER OBSESSIONS NOR
COMPULSIONS, CHECK HERE AND
GO TO *GENERALIZED ANXIETY
DISORDER* _____ .

What effect did this (OBSESSION
OR COMPULSION) have on your
life? (Did _____ bother
you a lot?)

(How much time do you spend
[OBSESSION OR COMPULSION])?

(Did anyone in your family, or your
friends, have to go out of their
way because of your [OBSESSION
OR COMPULSION]?)

B. The obsessions or compulsions cause marked
distress, are time-consuming (take more than an
hour a day), or significantly interfere with the
person's normal routine, occupational functioning,
or usual social activities or relationships with others

DESCRIBE:

?   1   2   3

GO TO
GAD,

OBSESSIVE COMPULSIVE DISORDER CRITERIA A
AND B ARE CODED "3"

1   3

GO TO   OBSES-
GAD,   SIVE
             COMPUL-
             SIVE
             DISOR-
             DER

CHRONOLOGY

IF UNCLEAR: During the past
month, did the (OBSESSIONS OR
COMPULSIONS) have any effect on
your life or bother you a lot?

Has met criteria for Obsessive Compulsive Disorder
during past month (criteria A and B)

?   1   3

When were you last bothered by
(ANY OBSESSIONS OR COMPUL-
SIONS)?

Number of months prior to interview when last
had symptoms of Obsessive-Compulsive Disorder

___ ___ ___

PAST FIVE YEARS
During the past five years, how
much of the time have (ANY
OBSESSIONS OR COMPULSIONS)
had an effect on your life or bothered you a lot?

Would you say . . . [CODE
DESCRIPTIONS]?

Approximate percentage of time during past five
years that any symptoms of Obsessive-Compulsive
Disorder were present

1   Not at all (0%)

2   Rarely (e.g., 5–10%)

(continued)

Table 9-6
(continued)

Obsessive-Compulsive Disorder	Obsessive-Compulsive Disorder Criteria		
	3 A significant minority of the time (e.g., 20–30%)		
	4 About half the time		
	5 A significant majority of the time (e.g., 70–80%)		
	6 Almost all the time (e.g., 90–100%)		
	7 Unknown		
How old were you when the (OBSESSIONS OR COMPULSIONS) first had any effect on your life or bothered you a lot?	Age at onset of Obsessive-Compulsive Disorder (criteria A and B) (CODE 99 IF UNKNOWN)	—	—

From Spitzer et al. (1990a). Copyright 1990 American Psychiatric Press, Inc. Reprinted by permission of the American Psychiatric Association.

? = inadequate information   1 = absent or false   2 = subthreshold   3 = threshold or true

the cooperation of the interviewee, which is not always easy to obtain when the interviewee is a disturbed mental patient or in acute distress.

A major limitation of the structured interview is that it relies exclusively on the respondent. It assumes that the respondent is honest and capable of accurate self-observation. It assumes that the respondent will provide frank, candid answers, even to embarrassing questions. As we discuss in Chapter 15 on objective personality tests, such assumptions cannot always be considered valid. In forensic settings in particular, it is very difficult to accept the validity of an interviewee's response at face value. After all, if a person is pleading insanity and faces a death sentence, what assurances do we have that he's telling the truth when he says, "Yes, I hear voices all the time." On a less obvious level, an interviewee may simply be trying to impress the interviewer or dramatize her plight by endorsing symptoms that aren't really present. Thus, although structured interviews may be a valuable source of information, the results from such procedures must be interpreted cautiously.

C. *Case History Interview*

An interview that begins with an open-ended question followed by level three and four responses can yield a wealth of data about an individual. The interviewer obtains an in-depth description of those factors most important to the interviewee. However, case history data may or may not be revealed, depending on their relevance to central issues in the interviewee's life. To obtain a complete *case history*—that is, a biographical sketch—specific questioning is often necessary. Case history data may include a chronology of major events in the person's life, a work history, a medical history, and a family history. A family history does not have to be detailed, but it should include a complete listing of the ages and genders of each member of the immediate family. It also is important to note whether any family members including parents, grandparents, uncles, aunts, and siblings have had difficulties similar to those experienced by the interviewee. This is because many conditions occur more frequently in families than in the general population.

In obtaining the history, the interviewer often takes a developmental approach and examines major events in the infancy, early childhood, primary school, secondary school, young adult, mature adult, and older adult years. M. P. Maloney and M. P. Ward (1976) offer the useful suggestion of beginning with an open-ended question in each major category of the case history and completing the details of each category before going on to the next. For example, the interviewer may say, "Tell me about your work record." After the work history is clarified, another category such as medical history can be explored.

The purpose of obtaining a case history is to know and understand the background of individuals. It is only from an understanding of the individual that we can interpret a test score. To this end, in addition to the above-mentioned factors in a case history, it is important to attempt to uncover information pertaining to religious preference, premarital and marital experiences, hobbies, education, accomplishments, and habits. Life-style information such as smoking behavior, use of alcohol, exercise patterns, and current stressors can also be useful. If a child is the focus of the interview, then information about the child as well as the parent should be obtained.

Case history interviews are relatively easy to computerize (Nurius, 1990). In a computerized interview, the interview is presented via computer rather than by a human interviewer. Naturally, such interviews are highly structured. They do, however, possess some flexibility through structured branching, in which algorithms are written so that branching is contingent on an examinee's responses. For example, the interviewee may be asked, "Do you smoke?" If the answer is "no," the program goes to the next main question. If the answer is "yes," however, the questioning branches into a number of other questions about smoking such as "How many cigarettes do you smoke per day?" "How long have you been smoking?" and "Have you ever tried to quit?" Still another branch may be entered that relates to previous efforts to quit, such as "How many times have you tried to quit?" See Table 9-7 for an example of part of a branching algorithm.

Computerized interviews have the advantage of nearly perfect interviewer reliability. However, unlike a human interviewer, the computer cannot respond to facial expressions and similar nonverbal cues, so in some situations valuable information is lost.

Table 9-7
Part of a
Branching
Algorithm for a
Computerized
Interview

---

1. Have you ever used tobacco?
   If No, go to 2.
   If Yes, answer a–d.

   a. At what age did you first start smoking?
   b. About how many cigarettes did you smoke on the average?
   c. Have you ever tried to quit?
      If No, go to d.
      If Yes, answer i–iii.

      i. When was the first time you tried to quit?
      ii. To what extent were you able to reduce the number of cigarettes you smoked each day?
      iii. How many times have you tried to quit?

   d. Identify any stressors that seem to cause you to smoke more.

2. Have you ever used alcohol?
   If No, go to 3.
   If Yes, answer a–e.

D. *Mental Status Examination*

The mental status examination is an important tool in psychiatric and neurological examinations. It is a special type of interview used primarily to diagnose psychosis, brain damage, and other major mental health problems. The purpose of the mental status examination is to evaluate a person suspected of having neurological or emotional problems in terms of variables known to be related to these problems.

Among the areas covered in the mental status examination are the person's appearance, attitudes, and general behavior. The interviewer also is alert to the emotions emitted by the interviewee. For example, is there one dominant emotion that fluctuates little? Is there an absence of emotion (that is, a flat affect)? Are the emotions appropriate? Do the emotions fluctuate widely? Also evaluated in the mental status examination are the person's thought processes. Intelligence can be evaluated by such factors as speed and accuracy of thinking, richness of thought content, ability to interpret proverbs, memory, and judgment. Especially important in the assessment of schizophrenia, a major form of psychosis involving loss of contact with reality, is the quality of the person's thought processes. This can be assessed through an analysis of thought content. For example, is there anything unusual or peculiar about the person's thoughts? Is the person preoccupied with any particular idea? Are the person's ideas realistic?

Other important areas evaluated in the mental status examination are the person's ability to direct and deploy attention. Is the person distracted? Can he or she attend to a task for as long as necessary for successful completion? Sensory factors also are considered. Is the person seeing things that aren't there? What is the accuracy of the person's perceptions? A number of guides for conducting mental status exams are available (see, for example, MacKinnon, 1980; Sands, 1972).

As a student, you must keep in mind that to make proper use of the mental status examination, one must have a broad understanding of the major mental disorders and the various forms of brain damage. There is no room for amateurs or self-appointed practitioners when a mental status examination is needed. However, knowledge of those areas covered in the mental status examination can be of use to interviewers who are interested in knowing the important variables in observing and evaluating another human being.

E. *Employment Interview*

The purpose of the employment interview is to aid in selection and promotion decisions in business and industry. It generally has been given its own special place in the psychological literature. A number of important articles and books are exclusively devoted to the employment (selection) interview.

The first extensive review of the employment interview was provided by R. Wagner (1949), who reviewed about 100 studies. He severely criticized most of the available studies, however, emphasizing that much of the literature consisted of contradicting opinions and how-to formulas. Following Wagner's call for more and better studies, E. C. Webster (1964) presented a series of important experimental investigations into the nature of the employment interview. Two independent reviews of the literature on the employment interview were subsequently published in the mid-1960s (Mayfield, 1964; Ulrich & Trumbo, 1965). Both reviews began where Wagner (1949) had left off. O. R. Wright (1969) then reviewed the literature between 1964 and 1969. More recently, the relevant literature has been examined by N. Schmitt (1976), R. D. Arvey and J. E. Campion (1982), and S. Zedeck, A. Tziner, and S. E. Middlestadt (1983) (also see Dougherty, Ebert & Callender, 1986).

These reviews have revealed some extremely valuable information about interviews in general and the employment interview in particular. It is interesting that the reviewers almost unanimously recommended a structured format for the employment interview. A number of studies clearly pointed to the superiority of structured interviews for enabling interviewers to reach agreement concerning their employment decisions based on interviews. Thus, the loss of flexibility in structured interviews can be balanced by increases in reliability. A meta-analytic investigation of the literature found that structured interviews produced mean validity coefficients twice as high as did unstructured interviews (Wiesner & Cronshaw, 1988). As we will see later when we discuss sources of error in the interview, researchers who have studied the employment interview have often found less than satisfactory results (Balzer, Rohrbaugh & Murphy, 1983; Zedeck, Tziner & Middlestadt, 1983), although recent reviews have been more encouraging (Harris, 1989). In this section we briefly touch on what interviewers look for in employment interviews and on methods of presenting oneself in an interview.

It has long been known that the employment interview often involves a search for negative or unfavorable evidence about a person rather than a search for favorable evidence (Webster, 1964). If a negative is found, the person probably will not be hired unless there are a considerable demand for workers and very few individuals available to fill open positions. In one study reported by E. C. Webster (1964), it was noted that as few as one unfavorable impression was followed by final rejection in 90% of the cases. This rejection rate, however, dropped to 25% when early impressions were favorable. Webster (1964) and others caution employment interviewers against forming an early bias that might result in rejecting a competent individual. Despite widespread knowledge of Webster's cautions, interviewers continue to look for errors when making personnel decisions (Dreher, Ash & Hancock, 1988).

Negative factors that commonly lead to the rejection of candidates include poor communication skills, lack of confidence or poise, low enthusiasm, nervousness, and failure to make eye contact (Nykodym & Ruud, 1985; Nykodym & Simonetti, 1981). Positive factors include the ability to express oneself, self-confidence and poise, enthusiasm, the ability to sell oneself, and aggressiveness (Baehr, 1987).

Can you increase your chances of presenting yourself favorably in a job interview? With the tightening of the job market in many sectors of the economy, this is not an idle question. And, as R. C. Heimberg, K. E. Keller, and T. Peca-Baker (1986) noted, competent performance in job interviews is widely regarded as one of the most important factors in obtaining employment. Thus, a number of approaches have been recommended for prospective employees who wish to improve their interview performance and tip the balance in their favor (Baron, 1986).

A good first impression is one of the most important factors in a successful job interview. To make a good first impression, research studies have revealed the value of having a professional style of dress and good grooming (Cash, 1985; Dipboye, Arvey & Terpstra, 1977), projecting an aura of competence and expertise (Baron, 1986; Price & Garland, 1983), and transmitting an impression of friendliness or personal warmth through nonverbal cues (Imada & Hakel, 1977). But going too far with these tactics can sometimes backfire.

R. A. Baron (1986) arranged to have female confederates pose as applicants for an entry-level management position. The women either did or did not engage in two different tactics of self-presentation. Some wore perfume; others did not. In addition, some attempted to convey friendliness through nonverbal behaviors including a high level of eye contact with the interviewer, an informal, friendly posture (such as leaning forward at predetermined points), and frequent smiling. Interviewees in the neutral cue condition refrained from these nonverbal behaviors. The results revealed that when used alone, either perfume or positive nonverbal behaviors produced enhanced ratings for the applicants. When used together, however, these tactics produced negative reactions among interviewers, probably because they caused the applicant to be perceived as manipulative (Baron, 1986). Thus, while it is important to put your best foot forward in an interview, you must be careful not to overdo it.

V. *Developing Interviewing Skills*

One controversy in the field of interviewing concerns whether or not interviewing skills can be learned and acquired (Wiens, 1976). The general consensus at this time is that interviewing skills can be acquired (Latham, 1987). To acquire such skills, you should familiarize yourself with research and theory on the interview. By understanding the principles and underlying variables in the interview, you will have taken the first step toward the acquisition of interviewing skills..

A second factor in acquiring interviewing skills is supervised practice. It is still true that experience is the best teacher. No amount of book learning can compare to having one's taped interview analyzed by an experienced interviewer.

A third factor in the acquisition of interviewing skills has to do with the principles for learning such skills. As a student, you must make a conscious effort to apply the principles learned from books and supervisors. For example, you must continually try to apply the principles involved in keeping the interaction flowing. In addition, you must continually ask yourself questions such as "What does this person mean? Am I communicating that I understand? Is the person exploring at deeper levels? What is being communicated nonverbally?"

In the initial phase of learning any new skill, it almost seems as though you must attend to a hundred things at once—an impossible task. However, if you make a persistent effort, gradually you will begin to respond appropriately by habit. Thus, experienced interviewers automatically attend to the person's appearance, nonverbal communications, emotional tone, and so on. They do so not because they are endowed with special abilities, but because they trained themselves to do so. With practice many behaviors can be completed almost automatically. This is true for many of the skills of successful interview behavior.

VI. *Sources of Error in the Interview*

In making appropriate use of the interview, you must develop an awareness of the various sources of error or potential bias in interview data. In acquiring a knowledge of these sources of error, you can try to compensate for their negative effects. Furthermore, in acquiring this knowledge, you will develop a better awareness of the limitations inherent in judging human beings on the basis of the interview.

A. *Interview Validity*

Many sources of interview error can be attributed to the extreme difficulty we have in making accurate, logical observations and judgments. Suppose, for example, in his first day of teaching a fifth-grade class, a teacher observes that one child follows all the rules and directions but a second child just cannot seem to stay out of trouble. If that teacher is not careful, he might develop a bias in his judgments of both these children. He might see the first child as good even if she breaks the rules for several weeks in a row. On the other hand, he might see the second child as bad even if she follows the rules for the rest of the school term. Similarly, a child may turn in a composition replete with grammatical and spelling errors. This child may have just had a bad day. However, even if his or her next paper is relatively free of errors, the teacher will have a tendency to look for them and to view the child as weak in grammar. Furthermore, the teacher may see the child as weak in other areas just on the basis of his early impression of the child's grammatical skills.

E. L. Thorndike (1920) labeled this tendency to judge specific traits on the basis of a general impression the "halo effect." Thorndike became aware of the halo effect when he noticed that ratings of behavioral tendencies (that is, traits) based on interview data tended to correlate more highly than could be reasonably expected.

Thus, there appears to be a human tendency to generalize in our judgments on the basis of a single, limited experience (Cooper, 1981). In the interview, halo effects occur when the interviewer forms a favorable or unfavorable early impression. The early impression then biases the remainder of the judgment process. Thus, with an early favorable impression or positive halo, the interviewer will have difficulty seeing the negatives. Similarly, with an early unfavorable impression or negative halo, the interviewer will have difficulty seeing the positives. In short, halo effects impair objectivity and must be consciously avoided by the effective interviewer.

Similar to the halo effect is the tendency to judge on the basis of one outstanding characteristic. H. L. Hollingworth (1922) first called this error tendency "general standoutishness." One prominent characteristic can bias the interviewer's judgments and prevent an objective evaluation. In an early paper, H. E. Burtt (1926) noted the tendency of interviewers to make unwarranted inferences from personal appearance. A well-groomed, attractive individual might be rated higher in intelligence than a poorly groomed, unattractive individual, even though the latter is more intelligent than the former. It remains widely recognized that physical appearance can play a major role in how a job applicant is perceived and rated (Gilmore, Beehr & Love, 1986).

Another potential source of error in the interview can be found in cross-ethnic, cross-cultural, and cross-class interviewing (Sattler, 1970, 1973b, 1977).

Table 9-8

Suggestions for Handling Cross-Ethnic, Cross-Cultural, and Cross-Class Interviews

- **Increase Cultural Awareness**
  Try to become sensitive to cultural, social class, and ethnic differences. Study the culture, language, and traditions of groups you are likely to have contact with as an interviewer.

- **Know Yourself**
  Examine your own stereotypes and prejudices. What are your preconceived notions about individuals from races, cultures, and socioeconomic groups other than your own?

- **Be Flexible**
  Try to suspend your preconceived notions. Be willing to accept a perspective other than your own.

- **Look Beyond Yourself**
  Try to appreciate the interviewee's perspective. Put yourself in the interviewee's shoes. Look for ways to circumvent potential difficulties.

After Sattler (1988, p. 462).

In the international business community, ignorance of cultural differences is becoming increasingly apparent. Japanese and Arabs consider direct eye contact a sign of aggression. The Japanese person avoids eye contact as a sign of deference and respect. In middle-class America, by contrast, direct eye contact is expected as a sign of honesty and sincerity. Unless we understand and take cultural differences into account, it is easy to send the wrong message or misinterpret the intentions of others. Even within the United States there are cultural differences that, if not understood, may lead to bias in the interview process. For example, whereas middle-class whites generally look at a speaker while listening, many African-Americans tend to look away while listening. These differences in style may lead a white interviewer to believe she is not being listened to, or an African-American to feel like he is being unduly scrutinized (Sattler, 1988, p. 461). Although reviews of the literature have failed to provide a framework from which to understand bias in the personnel selection process (Ralston, 1988), J. M. Sattler (1988) has offered a number of suggestions for handling cross-ethnic, cross-cultural, and cross-class interviews. Table 9-8 summarizes some of these suggestions.

Sources of error such as cultural distortions can reduce the validity of interview data. Recall that validity tells us about the meaning of test scores. Errors that reduce the objectivity of the interviewer produce inaccurate judgments, thus biasing the validity of the evaluation. These error tendencies perhaps explain why the predictive validity of interview data varies so widely. R. Wagner (1949), for example, reported studies that attempted to correlate judgments from interview data with such factors as grades, intelligence, and performance on standardized tests. The correlations ranged from .09 to .94, with a median of .19. Studies reviewed by L. Ulrich and D. Trumbo (1965) revealed a similar range of predictive validity coefficients, with correlations as low as −.05 and as high as .72 when ratings based on interview data were correlated with a variety of indices such as job performance. R. E. Carlson and colleagues (1971) reported similar findings, as have R. D. Arvey and J. E. Campion (1982). A more recent review by M. M. Harris (1989) suggested

Interaction of interview and test data

higher and more consistent coefficients in the .70s, especially when structured interviews are used.

Although the validity of interview data can be questioned, the interview does provide a wealth of unique data. The safest approach is to consider interview data as tentative: a hypothesis or a set of hypotheses to be confirmed by other sources of data. Interview data may be of dubious value without the support of more standardized procedures. Results from standardized tests, on the other hand, are often meaningless if not placed in the context of case history or other interview data. The clear and simple conclusion is that the two go together, each complementing the other. Both are essential in the process of evaluating human beings.

B. *Interview Reliability*

Recall that reliability refers to the stability, dependability, or consistency of test results. For interview data, the critical questions about reliability have centered around interinterviewer agreement (agreement between two or more interviewers). As with the validity studies, reliability coefficients for interinterviewer agreement vary widely. R. Wagner (1949), for example, found a range of reliability coefficients from .23 to .97 (median .57) for ratings of traits (enduring behavioral tendencies). The range of coefficients for ratings of overall ability was even wider ($-.20$ to .85; median. 53). Ulrich and Trumbo's (1965) review reported similar findings.

Again, reliability runs twice as high for structured as for unstructured interviews (Harris, 1989). Webster (1964) argued that one reason for fluctuations in interview reliability is that different interviewers look for different things, a sentiment echoed by others (Schmitt, 1976; Zedeck, Tziner & Middlestadt, 1983). Thus, whereas one interviewer might focus on strengths, another might focus on weaknesses. The two interviewers would disagree because their judgments are based on different aspects of the individual. To enhance interrater reliability in interviewer behavior, J. C. Callender and T. W. Dougherty (1983) recommend that interviewers be trained to evaluate very specific dimensions. Such an approach has, in fact, been shown to have merit (Dougherty, Ebert & Callender, 1986; Dreher, Ash & Hancock, 1988).

As we have noted, agreement among interviewers varies for different types of interviews. The research suggests that a highly structured interview in which specific questions are asked in a specific order can produce highly stable results (Harris, 1989). For example, if we ask a person his or her name, date of birth, parents' names, and the addresses of all residences within a particular time span and then ask the same questions a year later, results should be nearly identical. Reliability would be limited only by the memory and honesty of the interviewee and the clerical capabilities of the interviewer. Although this is an extreme example, it should be clear that highly structured interviews that ask a set of specific questions in a specific order should produce fairly dependable results. The problem is that such structure can limit what can be obtained from the interview, thus defeating the purpose of interviews designed to provide a broad range of data.

Unstructured or semistructured interviews frequently provide data that cannot be obtained from other sources (Wiens, 1976). However, the dependability of such results is clearly limited. The same question may not be asked twice, or it may be asked in a different way. Thus, interviewers readily acknowledge the limited reliability of interview data.

VII. *Research Approaches to the Study of Interviewing*

The interview has been studied from a wide variety of perspectives. Our purpose in this section is to provide you with a few of the major approaches that have been taken in research attempts to understand the interview process.

A. *Nonverbal Communication*

Interviewees communicate through both verbal and nonverbal means. Nonverbal methods of communication include such factors as facial expressions, body posture, body movements, and tone quality of the voice. All these factors have been studied and, as we have seen, play an important role in the interview process. Consider the case where a friend of yours has just received some bad news. You ask, "Are you all right?" She hangs her head low and in a quiet voice says, "Yeah, I'm okay." Actually, her nonverbal behavior indicates she is *not* all right. Indeed, when there is a discrepancy between verbal and nonverbal behaviors, the odds are that the nonverbal behavior is the more accurate reflection of a person's feelings. People lie, distort, and color their communications much less often in their nonverbal than in their verbal communication.

Excellent analyses of nonverbal behavior in the interview situation have been conducted (Ekman & Friesen, 1968; Rasmussen, 1984). P. Ekman and W. V. Friesen (1968) discussed the assumptions that underlie studies of nonverbal behavior. Among these assumptions are that nonverbal behavior (1) communicates emotions, (2) provides clues as to how the verbal discourse should be interpreted, and (3) is less affected than verbal behavior by attempts to censor communication. One of the findings reported by Ekman and Friesen is that experts (Dittmann, 1962) as well as naive judges (Ekman, 1965a, b) can reliably judge emotion (that is, affect) from nonverbal behavior. The implication is that it is possible to reliably evaluate nonverbal communication. Another interesting finding reported by Ekman and Friesen has to do with the activity of the person's feet. In a case study, these authors found evidence suggesting that the movement of the interviewee's feet can reflect anger, annoyance, and irritation. Even more revealing are the movements of the hands, which may reflect how the person feels about himself or herself (Ekman & Friesen, 1968). Such findings tend to support S. Freud's (1905) statement, "If his lips are silent, he chatters with his fingertips; betrayal oozes out of him at every pore."

One of the most interesting developments in the field of nonverbal communication was the introduction of the Profile of Nonverbal Sensitivity (PONS) test (Rosenthal et al., 1980). The PONS test provides quantitative indices of a person's abilities to accurately decode nonverbal cues given by another person who is shown in a film. The test provides scores for accuracy in reading facial expressions, body movements, posture, and voice tones. Extensive validity studies support the use of the PONS test for evaluating and training professionals who are involved in therapeutic interviews. For example, among six samples of counselors, psychotherapists, and advanced students in these fields, supervisor ratings of therapeutic skill correlated with nonverbal sensitivity as measured by the PONS test. In other studies, it has been shown that physicians' accuracy in the body movement and posture portion of the PONS test was significantly correlated with favorable ratings of the doctors by their patients (DiMatteo, 1979).

B. *Quantitative Aspects of Interview Behavior*

Other major areas of focus in interview research include the analysis of silence (Matarazzo et al., 1968); the analysis of acoustical properties of speech such as pitch, frequencies, intensities, and timbre (Matarazzo & Wiens, 1972); and the timing of verbal interactions (Wiens, Matarazzo & Saslow, 1965). All these factors have been found to be related to the communication process. Findings have been so encouraging that some investigators have proposed models in which computers could be programmed to analyze the meaning of interview data based on quantitative characteristics such as length of silences, pitch, tone quality, and body movements (Jaffe, 1968). Although computers have yet to reach a level of sophistication to conduct such analyses (Nurius, 1990), clearly the potential is there.

Summary

In a *structured interview*, the interviewer asks a specific set of questions. In the structured *standardized* interview, these questions are printed. The interviewer reads the questions in a specific order or sequence. In the *unstructured interview*, there are no specific questions or guidelines for the interviewer to follow. Thus, each unstructured interview is unique. Unstructured interviews provide considerable flexibility but at the expense of stability of interview data.

An *interview* is an interactive process. The participants (interviewer and interviewee) influence each other. Good interviewers set the tone of the interview by maintaining a warm, open, confident atmosphere.

Good interviewing is a matter of attitude. A study by D. P. Saccuzzo (1975) showed that interviewees give positive evaluations to interviewers when the interviewer is seen as warm, genuine, accepting, understanding, open, committed, and involved. Poor evaluations are given when the opposite attitudes and feelings were exhibited by the interviewer. Good interview behavior involves developing the proper attitudes and displaying them during the interview.

Good interviewing also involves avoiding statements that are judgmental, probing, evaluative, or hostile. An unstructured interview should begin with an *open-ended question*—that is, one that cannot be answered "yes" or "no" or with a short, specific response. The process of interviewing then involves facilitating the flow of communication. *Closed-ended questions*, which can be answered with a "yes" or "no" or a specific response, usually bring the interview to a halt and typically should be reserved for instances where less directive procedures fail to produce the desired information.

Transitional phrases such as "I see" help keep the interview flowing. Statements that communicate understanding or are interchangeable with the interviewee's responses tend to elicit self-exploration at increasingly deeper levels. These responses include verbatim playback, paraphrasing, restatement, summarizing, clarification, and understanding.

Efforts to assess the quality of understanding statements have led to a five-point scale system developed by Truax, Carkhuff, and co-workers. A large body of knowledge has shown that understanding statements are extremely powerful in helping the interviewee uncover and explore underlying feelings. Some types of interviews are the evaluation or assessment interview, the structured clinical interview, the case history interview, the mental status examination, and the employment interview.

There are two primary sources of error in the interview: those pertaining to the validity or meaning of interview data and those pertaining to the dependability or reliability of interview data. The tendency to draw general conclusions about an individual based on the limited data of a first impression limits the meaning and accuracy of interview data. Such tendencies have been labeled the "halo effect" and "standoutishness." Cultural distortions can also bias interview data and lead to inaccurate conclusions. Furthermore, predictive validity coefficients for interview data vary widely. The reliability of interview data has been measured primarily in terms of agreement among interviewers on variables such as intelligence, overall ability, and traits. The more structured the interview, the more interviewers agree. Thus, like predictive validity coeffficients, reliability coefficients for interview data vary widely. Training tends to enhance reliability coefficients.

Interviewing skills are developed by acquiring knowledge about good interview behavior and principles, supervised practice, and a conscious effort to form the right habits. However, the interview is fallible. Interview data can best be seen as the complement of other sources of data.

Chapter 10

Tests of Mental Ability: The Binet Scale

Learning Objectives

When you have completed this chapter, you should be able to:

- Explain how Binet and other psychologists have defined *intelligence*.
- Identify Binet's two guiding principles of test construction.
- Describe the concept of age differentiation.
- Describe the concept of mental age (MA).
- Describe the intelligence quotient (IQ) concept.
- Define deviation IQ.
- Discuss the fourth edition of the Stanford-Binet Intelligence Scale.

Three 8-year-old children, Fred, Maria, and Dale, were being evaluated for a special program for the gifted in a magnet school for which children from all over the city are bussed. Those who qualify for the gifted program are placed in a special, accelerated program where the student-teacher ratio is 15 to 1 rather than the usual 25 to 1 in the normal classroom. The gifted program also has special funds for enrichment programs such as field trips and hands-on exposure to computers. To qualify, a child must score three standard deviations above the mean on the Stanford-Binet Intelligence Scale: Fourth Edition (Thorndike, Hagen & Sattler, 1986). (See Figure 10-1.)

Since the Stanford-Binet is standardized, all three children are exposed to identical conditions. The test begins with a set of vocabulary items. On the first item, the child is asked to name a pictured object. Then the child is asked to define words like *quarter*, *sailor*, and *borrow* at the lower end of difficulty and *predilection* at the upper end. In fact, there are some 14 different tasks, including one that requires the child to reproduce bead patterns by finding them in photographs (bead memory) and others that ask the child to predict the next two numbers in a series like 9, 8, 7, -, -.

Figure 10-1
Materials of the
Stanford-Binet.
(*Photo by Rick
Ingram*)

As it turned out, only Dale scored high enough on the test to be placed in the gifted program. Now, given that all children were exposed to the same set of tasks, can we rest assured that the procedure was fair and that Dale was indeed the most intelligent of the three? As a critical thinker, you of course cannot give an unqualified yes to the question. You need much more information.

To begin, to say that one person is more intelligent than a second, we must be prepared to define *intelligence*. Unfortunately, of all the major concepts in the field of testing, intelligence is one of the most elusive; there is little agreement concerning its definition.

Alfred Binet, one of the original authors of the test that bears his name, defined intelligence as "the tendency to take and maintain a definite direction; the capacity to make adaptations for the purpose of attaining a desired end; and the power of autocriticism" (cited in Terman, 1916, p. 45). Later on in the chapter we will look more closely at Binet's definition of intelligence. C. E. Spearman (1923), by contrast, defined intelligence as the ability to educe either relations or correlates. According to Freeman (1955), intelligence is "adjustment or adaptation of the individual to his total environment" and "the ability to learn" and "the ability to carry on abstract thinking" (pp. 60–61). And J. P. Das (1973) defined intelligence as "the ability to plan and structure one's behavior with an end in view" (p. 27). More recently, H. Gardner (1983) defined intelligence in terms of the ability "to resolve genuine problems or difficulties as they are encountered" (p. 60); while R. J. Sternberg (1986, 1988) defined intelligence in terms of "mental activities involved in purposive adaptation to, shaping of, and selection of real-world environments relevant to one's life" (p. 33).

As you can surmise from these definitions, a test that examines one's ability to define words and remember bead patterns certainly does not meet the standards of all or even most definitions. But let's assume for the purpose of argument that the Stanford-Binet scale is a valid measure of intelligence, however defined. Is it then safe to say that the evaluation procedure for Fred, Maria, and Dale was fair? Again, we cannot answer unequivocally.

Maria, a Mexican-American, was born of Spanish-speaking parents, neither of whom finished high school. Her father spent most of his life working as a tomato picker. Fred, an African-American, came from a family of ten children. As with Maria, neither of Fred's parents completed high school. Although Fred's father worked long, hard hours as a machine operator on an assembly line, the family was very poor. Dale's parents, by contrast, were well-to-do and well educated. His mother was a clinical psychologist, his father a prominent attorney.

The fact is, there is a correlation between socioeconomic background and scores on standardized intelligence tests such as the Stanford-Binet. Examination of the test manual for the fourth edition of the Stanford-Binet shows that the average score for children of college graduates is more than 10 points *above* the mean, whereas that for children of parents with less than high school educations is about 6 points below the mean. Similar differences occur depending on the occupation of the parents. Thus, many have charged that intelligence tests are biased, especially against ethnic minorities and the poor. Ironically, as you will see, intelligence tests were initially developed in order to eliminate subjectivity in the evaluation of childrens' ability.

What do you think of when someone mentions intelligence testing? For many people, the topic arouses strong feelings and sometimes strong personal biases, even among experts (Snyderman & Rothman, 1987). Proponents hold that intelligence tests provide a universal and objective standard of competence and potential (Brim, 1965; Jackson, 1980). Critics charge that intelligence tests not only are biased against certain racial and economic groups but also are used by those in power to maintain the status quo (Gould, 1981; Owen, 1985). In fact, intelligence tests have been under attack almost from their inception (Haney, 1981; Snyderman & Rothman, 1987).

Intelligence testing began with the decision of a French minister of public instruction around the turn of the century. The minister's decision was one that some might criticize today: to create a procedure for identifying intellectually limited individuals so they could be removed from the regular classroom and be given special educational experiences. This decision provided the force behind the development of modern intelligence tests and all the heated controversy presently associated with them (Hebb, 1981).

In 1904, the French minister officially appointed a commission to implement his decision. The commission was given a definite assignment: to recommend a procedure for identifying so-called subnormal (intellectually limited) children. One member of this commission was Alfred Binet, who had demonstrated his qualifications for the job by his earlier research on human abilities (Binet, 1890a, b). The task of the commission was indeed formidable. No one doubted that human beings were capable of incredible accomplishments, which were obviously a reflection of intelligence. Nor was there much doubt that differences existed among individuals in their level of intelligence. But how was one to define intelligence?

Binet had few guideposts. A study by C. Wissler (1901) indicated that simple functions such as reaction time, sensory acuity, and the like failed to discriminate well among individuals of high and low scholastic ability. Therefore, Binet looked for complex, rather than simple, processes in his struggle to understand human intelligence. However, unlike today, there were few available definitions of intelligence. Binet's first problem was to decide what he wanted to measure—that is, to define intelligence.

Binet, as we have seen, defined intelligence as "the tendency to take and maintain a definite direction; the capacity to make adaptations for the purpose of attaining a desired end; and the power of autocriticism" (cited in Terman, 1916, p. 45). Beginning with this definition, Binet and his colleagues developed the world's first intelligence test.

In this chapter, we examine the test that Binet and his colleagues developed as well as its many subsequent revisions. In its present form, the Binet scale bears little resemblance to the original. Because the principles used to construct the various versions of the Binet test are illustrative of major approaches to intelligence tests, however, our discussion will cover much of what comprised the past scales as well as the new scale. We will highlight various changes that took place in the evolution of the Binet scale, examine the most recent version, and also consider some basic issues pertaining to the nature of human intelligence.

I. *Binet's Principles of Test Construction*

In choosing a definition, Binet took the necessary first step in developing a measure of intelligence. However, he was still faced with the problem of deciding exactly what he wanted to measure. Binet believed that intelligence, as he defined it, expressed itself through the judgmental, attentional, and reasoning facilities of the individual (Binet & Simon, 1905). He therefore decided to concentrate on finding tasks related to these three facilities.

In developing tasks to measure judgment, attention, and reasoning, Binet used trial and error as well as experimentation and hypothesis-testing procedures. He was guided by two major concepts that to this day provide the underlying principles to the Binet scale and all of its many revisions and offshoots: age differentiation and general mental ability. These principles, which perhaps represent Binet's most profound contribution to the study of human intelligence, provided the foundation for subsequent generations of human ability tests.

A. *Principle 1: Age Differentiation*

Age differentiation refers to the simple fact that older children can be differentiated or distinguished from younger children by their greater capabilities. For example, whereas most 9-year-olds can tell that a 50-cent coin is worth more than a quarter, a quarter is worth more than a dime, and so on, most 5-year-olds cannot. In employing the principle of age differentiation, Binet searched for tasks that could be completed by between 66.67% and 75% of the children of a particular age group and also by a smaller proportion of younger children but a larger proportion of older ones. Thus, Binet eventually assembled a set of tasks that could be completed by an increasingly larger proportion of children with increasing age.

Using these tasks, he was able to estimate the mental ability of a child in terms of his or her completion of tasks designed for the average child of a particular age, regardless of the child's actual or chronological age. A particular 5-year-old child might be able to successfully complete tasks that the average 8-year-old could complete. On the other hand, another 5-year-old might not be capable of completing even those tasks that the average 3-year-old could complete. With the principle of age differentiation, it became possible to determine the equivalent age capabilities of a child independent of chronological age. This equivalent age capability was eventually called *mental age*. If a 6-year-old completed tasks appropriate for the average 9-year-old, then the 6-year-old had demonstrated that he or she had capabilities equivalent to those of the average 9-year-old. With capabilities equivalent to the 9-year-old, the 6-year-old had a mental age of 9.

B. *Principle 2: The Concept of General Mental Ability*

Binet was also guided in his selection of tasks by his decision to measure only the total product of the various separate and distinct elements of intelligence—that is, "general mental ability." With the concept of general mental ability, Binet freed himself from the burden of identifying each element or independent aspect of intelligence. He also was freed from ascertaining the relative contribution of each element to the whole. Binet's decision to measure general mental ability was based on practical considerations. The search for tasks could then be restricted to anything related to the total or the final product of intelligence. The value of any particular task could be judged in terms of its correlation with the combined result (total score) of all other tasks. Tasks with low correlations could be eliminated, and tasks with high correlations retained.

Figure 10-2

Spearman's model of intelligence. According to the model, intelligence can be viewed in terms of one general underlying factor (g) and a large number of specific factors ($S_1, S_2, \ldots, S_n$). Thus, intelligence can be viewed in terms of g (general mental ability) and S (specific factors). Spearman's theory was consistent with Binet's approach to constructing the first general intelligence test.

The notion of general mental ability was previously propounded by Sir Francis Galton (1869) in his classic work, *Hereditary Genius: An Inquiry into Its Laws and Consequences* (see Chapter 1). An independent of Binet, in Great Britain, Charles Spearman (1904a, 1927) advanced the notion of a general mental ability factor underlying all intelligent behavior (see Thorndike, 1990). According to Spearman's theory, intelligence consists of one general factor (g) plus a large number of specific factors (see Figure 10-2). Spearman's notion of general mental ability, which he referred to as psychometric g (or simply g), was based on his observation, and the well-documented phenomenon, that when a set of diverse ability tests are administered to large, unbiased samples of the population, almost all the correlations are positive. This phenomenon is termed *positive manifold*. Positive manifold, according to Spearman, was due to the fact that all tests, no matter how diverse, are influenced by g. For Spearman, g could best be conceptualized in terms of mental energy.

To understand how a single general factor can underlie all intelligent behavior, consider the analogy of a central power station for a large metropolitan city. The same station provides the power for lights of all sizes and types. Although some individual lights may be brighter or better than others, all depend on power from the central power source. Reduce the output from the central source, and all lights are affected.

To support the notion of g, Spearman developed a statistical technique called **factor analysis.** Factor analysis is a method for reducing a set of variables or scores to a smaller number of hypothetical variables called *factors*. Through factor analysis, it is possible to determine how much variance a set of tests or scores has in common. This common variance represents the g factor. The g in a factor analysis of any set of mental ability tasks is represented in the first unrotated factor in a principal components factor analysis. Spearman found that as a general rule, about half the variance in a set of diverse mental ability tests is represented in the g factor.

A major implication of the concept of general intelligence is that a person's intelligence can best be represented by a single score—the score that presumably reflects the shared variance underlying performance on a diverse set of tests. True, performance on any given individual task can be attributed to *g* as well as to some specific or unique variance (just as the luminance of a light depends on the central power source as well as the individual qualities of the light). However, if the set of tasks is large and broad enough, the role of any given task can be reduced to a minimum. Differences in unique ability due to the specific task tend to cancel each other, and overall performance comes to depend more heavily on the general factor. Such was the reasoning underlying the development of the Binet scale as well as all its subsequent revisions.

(handwritten margin note: Spearman's S-factors (specific))

II. *The Early Binet Scales*

Using the principles of age differentiation and general mental ability, Binet and another appointee of the French minister of public instruction, T. Simon, collaborated to develop the first version of what was eventually to be called the Stanford-Binet Intelligence Scale. The first version was called the 1905 Binet-Simon Scale. The original Binet scale was limited compared to present-day applications of intelligence tests. Its purpose was restricted to identifying mentally defective children in the Paris school system.

A. *Nature of the 1905 Binet-Simon Scale*

The 1905 Binet-Simon Scale was an individual intelligence test consisting of 30 items presented in an increasing order of difficulty. Item 4, for example, tested the subject's ability to recognize food (for example, to discriminate between chocolate and wood). Item 14 required subjects to define familiar objects such as a fork. The most difficult item, 30, required subjects to define and distinguish between paired abstract terms (for example, *sad* and *bored*). Binet proposed that item 9, which required subjects to name designated objects in a picture, was the approximate limit of the average 3-year-old.

In Binet's time, three levels of intellectual deficiency were designated by terms no longer in use today because of the derogatory connotations they have acquired for the general public. *Idiot* was used to describe the most severe form of intellectual impairment, *imbecile* to designate moderate levels of impairment, and *moron* for the mildest level of impairment. Binet believed that the ability to follow simple directions and imitate simple gestures (item 6 on the 1905 scale) was the upper limit of adult idiots. The ability to identify parts of the body or simple objects (item 8) would rule out severe intellectual impairment in an adult. The upper limit for adult imbeciles was item 16, which required the subject to state the differences between two common objects such as wood and glass.

Figure 10-3
Schematic summary of the evolution of the Binet scale: 1905 scale.

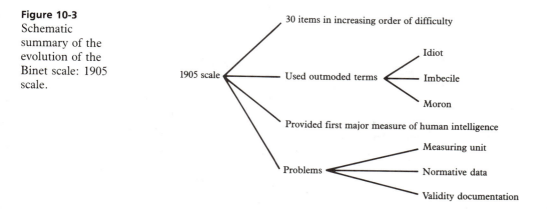

The collection of 30 tasks of increasing difficulty in the Binet-Simon scale provided the first major measure of human intelligence. It was a scientific breakthrough. Binet had solved two major problems of test construction: he determined exactly what he wanted to measure and he developed items for this purpose. He fell short, however, in several other areas of measurement. The 1905 Binet-Simon Scale lacked an adequate measuring unit to express results, adequate normative data, and evidence to support its validity. The classifications Binet used (idiot, imbecile, and moron) can hardly be considered adequate for expressing results and, as Binet himself was aware, little had been done to document the scale's validity. Furthermore, norms for the 1905 scale were based on only 50 children who had been considered normal based on average school performance. See Figure 10-3.

B. *The 1908 Scale*

Binet was interested in producing a sound scientific instrument rather than defending his position at the expense of progress. He therefore made a major effort to deal with the limitations of the 1905 scale in his second major revision. In the 1908 scale, Binet and Simon retained the principle of age differentiation. Indeed, the 1908 scale was an age scale, which means items were grouped according to age level rather than simply increasing difficulty, as in the 1905 scale.

The notion of an age scale is important because it provided a model for innumerable tests that continue to be used in educational settings. However, the age scale format also involved a serious limitation. When items are grouped according to age level, it is difficult, if not impossible, to determine how a child performed on one particular class of tasks relative to another. For example, is the child's performance exceptionally strong on quantitative items? The age scale format does not lend itself to this type of analysis. The limitations of the age scale format were considered so great that in the most recent revision of the

Table 10-1
Sample Items
from the 1908
Binet-Simon Scale

Age Level Three (Five Items)
1. Point to various parts of face.
2. Repeat two digits forward.

Age Level Four (Four Items)
1. Name familiar objects.
2. Repeat three digits forward.

Age Level Five (Five Items)
1. Copy a square.
2. Repeat a sentence containing ten syllables.

Age Level Six (Seven Items)
1. State age.
2. Repeat a sentence containing 16 syllables.

Age Level Seven (Eight Items)
1. Copy a diamond.
2. Repeat five digits forward.

Age Level Eight (Six Items)
1. Recall two items from a passage.
2. State the differences between two objects.

Age Level Nine (Six Items)
1. Recall six items from a passage.
2. Recite the days of the week.

Age Level Ten (Five Items)
1. Given three common words, construct a sentence.
2. Recite the months of the year in order.

Age Level 11 (Five Items)
1. Define abstract words (for example, *justice*).
2. Determine what is wrong with absurd statements.

Age Level 12 (Five Items)
1. Repeat seven digits forward.
2. Provide the meaning of pictures.

Age Level 13 (Three Items)
1. State the differences between pairs of abstract terms.

Binet scale (Thorndike, Hagen & Sattler, 1986), the age scale format was abandoned.

In the 1908 scale, the standardization sample was increased more than fourfold. The new sample consisted of 203 Paris schoolchildren. Items were grouped by age, and the criterion for the inclusion of an item at any particular age level was that it must have been successfully passed by two-thirds to three-fourths of a representative group of children at that age. Table 10-1 provides a sample of some of the items included at each age level.

Despite its limitations, the 1908 Binet scale was a clear improvement over the 1905 scale. However, Binet had done little to meet one persistent criticism: the verbal/language emphasis of the scale. The scale provided many tasks in a variety of areas. As an individual test, it required 30 to 85 minutes of professional time to administer to a single person. Yet for all this time and effort, the scale produced only one score, which was almost exclusively related to verbal, language, and reading ability. Binet's rationale for providing only one score was based on the notion of general mental ability, for which a single score was appropriate as well as logically consistent. Unfortunately, however, Binet made little effort to diversify the range of abilities tapped. As a result, the scale remained heavily weighted on language, reading, and verbal skills at the expense of other factors such as the integration of visual and motor functioning

Figure 10-4
Schematic summary of the evolution of the Binet scale: 1908 scale.

1908 scale
— Retained principle of age differentiation
— Used age scale format
— Introduced concept of mental age

mental age

(for example, eye-hand coordination). It was not until the 1986 revision that these problems were seriously addressed.

Perhaps the major improvement in the 1908 scale was the introduction of the concept of mental age. Here Binet attempted to solve the problem of expressing the results in adequate units. A subject's mental age was based on his or her performance compared to the average performance of individuals in a specific chronological age group. In simple terms, if a 6-year-old can perform the tasks that can be done by two-thirds to three-fourths of the representative group of 8-year-old children, then this child has a mental age of 8. A 10-year-old who can do no more than pass items that two-thirds to three-fourths of the representative group of 5-year-olds can pass is said to have a mental age of 5.

To summarize, the 1908 Binet-Simon scale introduced two major concepts: the age scale format and the concept of mental age. However, even though both concepts eventually were abandoned, they found widespread use and application in a host of new tests as well as in subsequent revisions of the Binet. See Figure 10-4.

III. *Terman's Stanford-Binet Intelligence Scale*

Binet and Simon again revised their intelligence scale in 1911, but this third version contained only minor improvements. By this time, the potential utility of the Binet scale had been recognized throughout Europe and in the United States. In the United States, for example, H. H. Goddard published a translation of the 1905 Binet-Simon scale in 1908, and he published a version of the 1908 scale in 1911 (Herrnstein, 1981). Other Americans subsequently published a variety of versions of the Binet scale. These included R. M. Yerkes's 1915 and 1923 versions, J. P. Herring's 1922 version, and F. Kuhlmann's 1912, 1922, and 1930 versions. However, it was the 1916 Stanford-Binet version, developed under the direction of L. M. Terman, that flourished and became, for quite some time, the dominant intelligence scale in the world.

In this section, we continue our analysis of the evolution of the Binet scale. First, we examine Terman's 1916 version of the scale and see how the concept of mental age was incorporated into the intelligence quotient (IQ) concept. Then we look at the 1937 and 1960 revisions before we move on to the modern Binet.

Figure 10-5
Schematic
summary of the
evolution of the
Binet scale: 1916
scale.

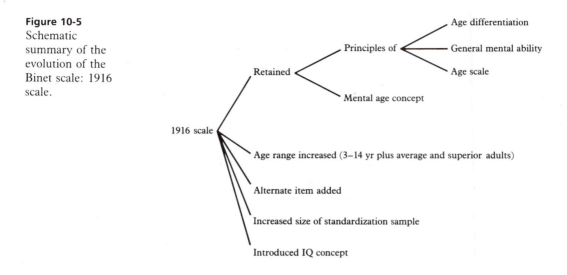

A. *The 1916 Stanford-Binet Intelligence Scale*

In developing the 1916 Stanford-Binet version, Terman relied heavily on Binet's earlier work. The principles of age differentiation, general mental ability, and the age scale were retained. The mental age concept also was retained. The 1916 revision included 59 items from the previous Binet-Simon scales, four tasks from existing American tests, and many originally constructed tasks (Terman, 1916). See Figure 10-5.

Terman's 1916 revision increased the size of the standardization sample. Unfortunately, the entire standardization sample of the 1916 revision consisted exclusively of native-born white children from California. Thus, although the standardization sample was markedly increased, it was far from representative. In fact, given that geographic location may affect test performance (Lewandowski & Saccuzzo, 1976; Saccuzzo & Lewandowski, 1976), this sample cannot even be considered representative of white native-born Americans. Nevertheless, the increased sample size was a step in the right direction and was clearly an improvement over the meager 50 and 203 individuals of the 1905 and 1908 Binet-Simon versions.

B. *The Intelligence Quotient (IQ) Concept*

The 1916 scale provided the first significant application of the now outdated **intelligence quotient** (IQ) concept. The IQ concept that, as R. J. Herrnstein (1981) noted, had been recommended by W. Stern (1912) used a subject's mental age in conjunction with his or her chronological age to obtain a ratio

Table 10-2
The Intelligence
Quotient Concept

Child 1:
Chronological age (*CA*): 6 years
Mental age (*MA*): 6 years

$$IQ = \frac{MA}{CA} \times 100 = \frac{6}{6} \times 100 = 100$$

Child 2:
Chronological age (*CA*): 6 years
Mental age (*MA*): 3 years

$$IQ = \frac{MA}{CA} \times 100 = \frac{3}{6} \times 100 = 50$$

Child 3:
CA = 6; *MA* = 12; IQ = 200

Adult 1:
CA = 50; *MA* = 16

$$IQ = \frac{16}{16} \times 100 = 100$$
$\leftarrow$ (the maximum *CA*)

---

score. This ratio score presumably reflects the subject's rate of mental development. Table 10-2 illustrates how IQ is determined.

In calculating IQ, the first step is to determine the subject's chronological age. To obtain this, we need only know his or her birthday. In the second step, the subject's mental age is determined by his or her score on the scale. Finally, to obtain the IQ, the chronological age (*CA*) is divided into the mental age (*MA*) and the result is multiplied by 100 to eliminate fractions:

$$IQ = \frac{MA}{CA} \times 100$$

As you can see in Table 10-2, when *MA* is less than *CA*, the IQ is below 100. In this case, the subject was said to have slower than average mental development. When the converse occurs—that is, when *MA* exceeds *CA*—the subject was said to have faster than average mental development.

The IQ score altered the nature of the measuring unit that was used to express the results. However, as will be seen, the method may have actually been a step backward, and the *MA/CA* method of calculating IQ scores was ultimately abandoned. The 1916 scale had a maximum possible mental age of 19.5 years; that is, if every group of items was passed, a mental age score of 19.5 would result. Given this limitation in the magnitude of the mental age, anyone older than 19.5 would have an IQ of less than 100 even if all items were passed. Therefore, a maximum limit on the chronological age had to be set. Because it was believed at the time of the 1916 revision that mental age ceased to improve after 16 years of age, 16 was used as the maximum chronological age.

C. *The 1937 Scale*

The 1937 scale extended the age range down to the 2-year-old level. The mental age range was increased because new tasks were added. This increased the maximum possible mental age to 22 years, 10 months. Scoring standards and instructions were improved to reduce ambiguities, enhance the standardization of administration, and increase interscorer reliability. Furthermore, a number of performance items, which required the subject to do things like copy designs, were added in an effort to deal with criticisms concerning the scale's emphasis on verbal skills.

The standardization sample was markedly improved. Whereas the 1916 norms were restricted to Californians, the new subjects for the 1937 Stanford-Binet standardization sample came from 11 states spread across a variety of regions in the United States. Subjects were selected according to their fathers' occupations. In addition to improvements in its representativeness, the standardization sample was substantially increased. Unfortunately, the standardization sample included only whites and an excess of urban versus rural subjects (Terman & Merrill, 1937). Nevertheless, this improved sample represented a desirable trend. The 3184 individuals included in the 1937 standardization sample represented more than a threefold increase from the 1916 scale and was more than 63 times larger than the original sample of the 1905 scale.

Perhaps the most important improvement in the 1937 version was the inclusion of an alternate equivalent form. Forms L and M were designed to be equivalent in terms of both difficulty and content. With two equivalent forms, the psychometric properties of the scale could be readily examined.

D. *Psychometric Properties of the 1937 Scale*

Subjects in the 1937 standardization sample were tested on both forms within one day to one week after the initial testing. Results were extremely impressive, with a correlation of greater than .91 for unselected cases (Terman & Merrill, 1937). As Q. McNemar (1942) noted, however, reliability coefficients were higher for older subjects. Thus, results for younger individuals were not as stable as those for older ones. Reliability figures also varied as a function of IQ level, with higher reliabilities in the lower IQ ranges (that is, less than 70) and poorer reliability coefficients at the higher IQ ranges. The lowest reliabilities occurred in the younger age groups at the higher IQ ranges. These findings with the 1937 Binet apply generally to all modern intelligence tests: scores are most unstable for younger children in the highest IQ ranges.

Along with the differing reliabilities, each age group in the standardization sample produced its own unique standard deviation of IQ scores. This differential variability in IQ scores as a function of age created the single most important problem in the 1937 scale. More specifically, despite the great care that was taken in selecting the standardization sample, different age groups showed significant differences in the standard deviation of IQ scores. As reported by L. M. Terman and M. A. Merrill (1937), the standard deviation in the IQ scores at age 6 was approximately 12.5. The standard deviations at ages $2\frac{1}{2}$ and 12, on the other hand, were 20.6 and 20.0, respectively. Because of these discrepancies in the standard deviations at different age levels, IQs at one age level were not equivalent to IQs at another. This concept is elaborated on in Focused Example 10-1.

Despite some problems related to reliability, the validity of the 1937 scale was strongly supported. Clearly, the scale had content validity. Examination of its content reveals that the subject engages in everything from simple manipulation of objects to complex abstract reasoning. The 1937 Stanford-Binet scale also had well-documented predictive validity. In one sense, however, the scale's high level of predictive validity is a mixed blessing. The high correlations between the 1937 scale and school success (Terman & Merrill, 1953; Watson, 1951) suggest that the scale is largely a measure of scholastic aptitude, academic achievement, verbal ability, and reading skills. However, the evidence in support of the scale is not limited to predictive validity. Biserial correlational analysis revealed a sizable correlation between each item and the total test score (Terman & Merrill, 1937). That is, each item contributed substantially to the total test score, just as the concept of general mental ability demanded. Because more items were passed with increasing age, the concept of age differentiation and thus the construct validity of the scale also were supported. Finally, factor analytic studies supported the validity of the scale. See Figure 10-6.

FOCUSED EXAMPLE 10-1

Differential Variability in IQ Scores

Recall our discussion of standard deviations and percentiles in Chapter 2. A score that is two standard deviations above the mean is approximately at the 98th percentile. Therefore, if the mean IQ is 100, a 6-year-old, where the standard deviation is 12.5, would need an IQ of 125 to be two standard deviations above the mean. Being two standard deviations above the mean, this child would be at about the 98th percentile. However, at 12 years of age, where the standard deviation is 20, the same child would need an IQ of 140 to be two standard deviations above the mean and in the 98th percentile. Thus, a child at age 6 who obtained an IQ of 125 would be two standard deviations above the mean and in the 98th percentile. If this same child obtained an IQ of 125 at age 12, he or she would be only 1.25 standard deviations above the mean (remember, the standard deviation at age 12 is 20) and thus at only about the 89th percentile. Thus, in the 1937 scale, an IQ at one age range was not comparable to an IQ at another age range in terms of percentiles.

Figure 10-6
Schematic summary of the evolution of the Binet scale: 1937 scale.

E. *The 1960 Stanford-Binet Revision*

Twenty-three years after the 1937 revision, the test originated by Binet in 1905 was again revised. The 1960 revision consists entirely of items from Forms L and M of the 1937 scale. Terman and Merrill (1960) argued that the purpose of having an alternate form had been served. Reliabilities and standard error of measurement had been determined, and the scale more than met rigorous psychometric standards. However, by 1960 many of the items had become outdated, and experience revealed a number of scoring and test administration ambiguities.

The goal of the 1960 revision was to create a single instrument by selecting the best from the two forms of the 1937 scale. Tasks that showed an increase in the percentage passing with an increase in age—the major criterion and guiding principle for all versions of the Binet scale—were given the highest priority. Also given priority were tasks that correlated highly with scores as a whole—the second major guiding principle of the Binet scale. In addition, instructions for scoring and test administration were improved, and IQ tables were extended from age 16 to 18 (Terman & Merrill, 1960). Perhaps most important, the problem of differential variation in IQs was solved by using the deviation IQ concept.

One persistent problem in measuring human intelligence has been finding an adequate unit for expressing results. In 1908, the concept of mental age was introduced, only to be extended by the intelligence quotient (IQ) concept in the 1916 revision. The IQ concept was retained in the 1937 revision; however, as noted earlier, standard deviations of IQs obtained by the formula IQ = MA/CA × 100 were not always the same at all age levels in the standardization sample. As a result of this variability in standard deviations, an IQ at one age level was not comparable (that is, did not have the same meaning or percentile standing) to an identical IQ obtained at a different age level (see Focused Example 10-1).

The IQ concept is also limited in that an individual's MA gradually ceases to increase as maturity is reached. As a result, the IQ concept is limited to the point where increases in chronological age no longer produce equivalent increases in mental age. This point begins at about 16 years of age, depending on the type of item. Furthermore, the IQ concept does not take into account possible declines in MA that may occur during aging. In an effort to deal with the limitations of the intelligence quotient (IQ), the 1960 Binet scale revision incorporated D. Wechsler's (1939) deviation IQ methodology.

The deviation IQ, as it is used in the Stanford-Binet scale, is simply a standard score with a mean of 100 and a standard deviation of 16. With the mean set at 100 and assigned to scores at the 50th percentile, the deviation IQ was ascertained by evaluating the standard deviation of mental age for a representative sample at each age level. New IQ tables were then constructed that corrected for differences in variability at the various age levels. In correcting for these differences in variability, the 1960 IQ tables produced IQs that were comparable from one age level to another (Terman & Merrill, 1960). The deviation IQ method eliminated one major problem of the intelligence quotient concept. With the deviation IQ, scores finally could be directly compared across age groups. Thus, scores could be interpreted in terms of standard deviations and percentiles with the assurance that IQ scores for every age group corresponded to the same percentile. Today, the deviation IQ method is considered the most precise way of expressing results on an intelligence test.

The 1960 revision did not include a new normative sample or restandardization. The investigators argued that psychometric data accumulated on the 1937 scale could be transformed to the 1960 scale (Terman & Merrill, 1960). We might describe the scale's psychometric qualities by the term *inherited validity*. In fact, the work that has been reported does tend to confirm the assumption that the psychometric characteristics of the 1937 scale were inher-

Figure 10-7
Schematic summary of the evolution of the Binet scale: 1960 scale.

ited by the 1960 scale (Brittain, 1968; Share, Webb & Koch, 1964). However, the assumption of inherited psychometric properties has not gone uncriticized (Fraser, 1965). M. Berger (1970), in particular, charged that the deviation IQs of the 1960 revision were based on data obtained with the 1937 scales. As Berger correctly noted, the 1960 ratio IQs may not have the same properties (distribution statistics) as those observed in the 1937 scale. Thus, the IQs and *MA*s of the 1960 revision may be limited in accuracy. See Figure 10-7.

Criticisms of the 1960 revision were met by positive action rather than by defensive arguments. By 1972, a new standardization group consisting of a representative sample of 2100 children (about 100 at each Stanford-Binet age level) had been obtained for use with the 1960 revision (Thorndike, 1973). Unlike all previous norms, the 1972 norms included nonwhites. For many, however, the general improvements in the 1960 revision, even with the new 1972 norms, were not enough. By 1986, a new and drastically revised version of the Binet scale was published (Thorndike, Hagen & Sattler, 1986).

IV. *The Modern Binet Scale*

Our discussion of the evolution of the Binet scale has illustrated many of the major concepts that dominated intelligence testing from its inception to the present. The modern fourth edition of the Stanford-Binet scale continues a tradition of innovation and incorporation of central psychometric and theoretical concepts. In this section, we examine the modern Binet scale, which its authors claim was needed because of cultural and social changes and new research in cognitive psychology. First, we consider the basic model that guided the development of the modern Binet. Next, we compare the modern Binet to its predecessors and look at what was retained, what was changed, and what was added. Then we consider the test itself—the various subtests and summary scores and procedures for administration. We also examine the scale's psychometric properties. Finally, we attempt a tentative evaluation of this latest edition in the long, distinguished line of Binet scales. See Figure 10-8.

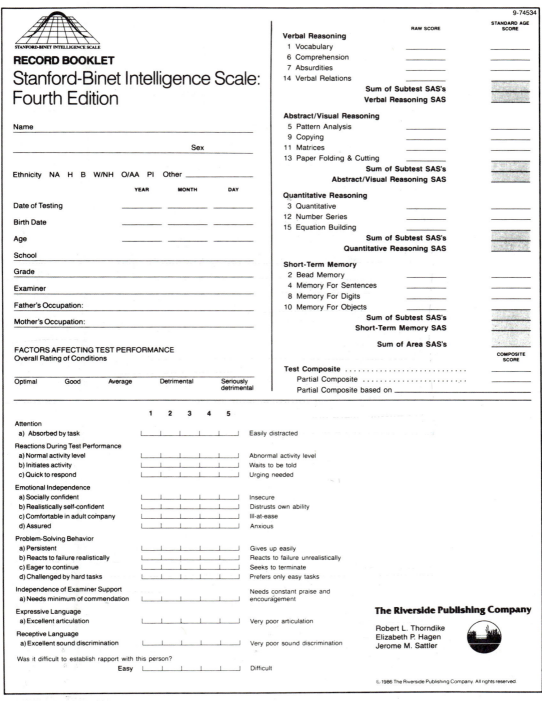

Figure 10-8

Cover page of Stanford-Binet Intelligence Scale. (*Courtesy of The Riverside Publishing Company*.)

Figure 10-9
Three-level
hierarchical model
of the modern
Binet. (*Adapted
from Figure 2.1 in
Thorndike, Hagen
& Sattler, 1986,
p. 9.*)

A. *Model of the Modern (1986) Binet Scale*

The model for the modern Binet is far more elaborate than the Spearman model that best characterized the original versions of the scale. It is based on the three-level hierarchical model shown in Figure 10-9. At the top of the hierarchy is *g*—general intelligence, which reflects the common variability of all tasks. At the next level are three group factors. *Crystallized abilities* reflect learning—the overlay of experience on original potential. *Fluid abilities* are those that are inborn, or biologically given (Horn & Cattell, 1966). *Short-term memory* refers to one's memory during short intervals—the amount of information that can be retained briefly after a single, short presentation. In addition, crystallized ability is subdivided into two subcategories: verbal reasoning and quantitative reasoning. (By referring to Figure 10-9, you can discern which subtests are associated with each of the four major content areas.)

The model of the modern Binet represents an attempt to place an evaluation of *g* in the context of a multidimensional model, which attempts to evaluate specific abilities. The impetus for a multidimensional model stemmed from the work of L. L. Thurstone (1938), who argued that, contrary to Spearman's notion of intelligence as a single process, intelligence could best be conceptualized as a number of independent factors, or "primary mental abilities." Years of painstaking work ultimately revealed evidence for group abilities factors that were relatively, but not totally, independent. The group factors were correlated, and from them a *g* factor could be extracted, as in the hierarchical model of the modern Binet.

B. *Characteristics of the 1986 Revision*

The 1986 revision attempted to retain all the strengths of the earlier revisions while eliminating the weaknesses. This was no easy task. In an effort to continue to provide an overall measure of general mental ability, the authors of the 1986 revision decided to retain the wide variety of content and task characteristics of earlier versions. However, to avoid having this wide content unevenly distributed across age groups, the age scale format was eliminated. In place of

Table 10-3
The 15 Tests of
the Modern Binet

1. *Vocabulary (46 items)*

   For the first 14 items a picture of an object is presented and the subject must name the object. Each of 32 words is then presented orally and the subject is asked to provide a definition. Words similar to those used on the actual tests are *truck* and *cryptic.*

2. *Bead memory (42 items)*

   The subject is asked to reproduce a pattern of beads on a stick or by locating them in a photograph.

3. *Quantitative (40 items)*

   The subject is asked to solve quantitative problems such as What is the area of a rectangle that is 3 feet by 5 feet?

4. *Memory for sentences (42 items)*

   The subject must repeat orally presented sentences of increasing length.

5. *Pattern analysis (42 items)*

   The subject must reproduce a design drawn on a card with blocks.

6. *Comprehension (42 items)*

   The subject must answer questions dealing with social situations or involving judgment; for example, Why do we limit the president's term of office?

7. *Absurdities (32 items)*

   The subject must identify a problem or incongruity in a picture, such as someone trying to drive a car without a steering wheel.

8. *Memory for digits (26 items)*

   The subject must repeat strings of digits forward and backward (e.g., repeat 3, 6, 9, 8, 1).

9. *Copying (28 items)*

   The subject must copy geometric designs (e.g., line, circle, triangle) shown on a card.

10. *Memory for objects (14 items)*

    The subject must recall a series of pictured objects in the order in which they were presented.

11. *Matrices (26 items)*

    The subject must complete the pattern in a matrix, such as:

A	B
C		DEFGH

12. *Number series (26 items)*

    The subject must predict which two numbers appear next in a series, such as:

    $$\frac{1}{3}, \frac{1}{4}, \frac{1}{5}, \underline{\quad}, \underline{\quad}$$

13. *Paper folding and cutting (18 items)*

    The subject must choose among five alternatives to match how a folded, cut piece of paper looks when unfolded.

14. *Verbal relations*

    The subject must indicate how the first three items are alike and how they are different from a fourth item; for example, How are a peach, banana, and plum alike and different from a loaf of bread?

15. *Equation building*

    The subject must arrange numbers and mathematical symbols (e.g., $+$, $\times$, $\div$, $=$) into an equation; for example, $4 = \underline{\quad} \div 2$.

Figure 10-10
The four major
content areas of
the modern Binet
and associated
tests.

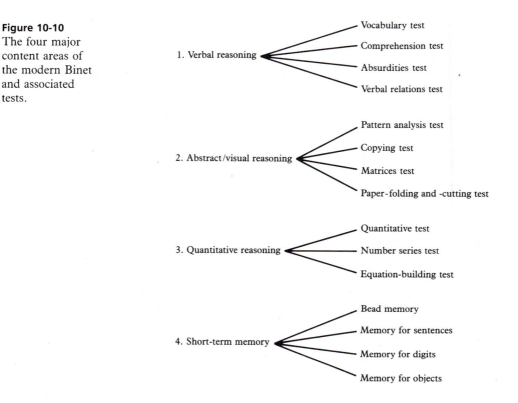

1. Verbal reasoning
- Vocabulary test
- Comprehension test
- Absurdities test
- Verbal relations test

2. Abstract/visual reasoning
- Pattern analysis test
- Copying test
- Matrices test
- Paper-folding and -cutting test

3. Quantitative reasoning
- Quantitative test
- Number series test
- Equation-building test

4. Short-term memory
- Bead memory
- Memory for sentences
- Memory for digits
- Memory for objects

the age scale, items of the same content were placed together into any one of 15 separate tests. For example, all vocabulary items were placed together in one test; all matrices items were placed together in a second. (See Table 10-3 for a list of tests.)

Placing together items of similar content permits the calculation of specific scores for each of the 15 tests. Thus, in addition to an overall score that presumably reflects *g*, it is possible to obtain scores related to each specific content area. In addition, each of the specific 15 tests can be grouped into one of four content areas, as illustrated in Figure 10-10.

In administering the modern Binet, one must determine where to begin each specific test. This is accomplished by using the individual's score on the vocabulary test in conjunction with the person's chronological age. Since the scale purports to measure intelligence in individuals aged 2 years through adult, obviously all items in any given test will not be appropriate for all subjects. The test format is *adaptive*: each individual is tested with a range of tasks best suited to his or her ability (Thorndike, Hagen & Sattler, 1986). What one must do is establish a **basal age** for each test: the lowest level or point where two consecutive items of approximately equal difficulty are passed. Testing then proceeds within each test until a **ceiling** is reached: the point at

Figure 10-11
Characteristics of
the modern (1986)
Binet.

which at least three out of four items are missed. The concept of age differentiation is retained in that within each test, items are presented in order of increasing difficulty roughly according to their ability to discriminate different age groups.

The modern Binet scale retains the use of standard scores. Raw scores on each of the 15 tests can be converted to a *standard age score* with a mean of 50 and a standard deviation of 8. The grouping of individual tests into content areas permits the calculation of four area content scores, each with a mean of 100 and standard deviation of 16. A composite score reflective of general mental ability and based on the tests given to an individual is also calculated. The mean of this composite is also 100 (SD = 16) as in the deviation IQ of the 1960 version. See Figure 10-11.

C. *Psychometric Properties of the Modern Binet*

The modern Binet was constructed with exceptional diligence. It continues the tradition of its predecessors in providing a state-of-the-art model for intelligence tests in terms of its psychometric standards, theoretical foundation, and empirical support. Items were subjected to two separate field trials, each followed by careful revision and fine tuning. Items were also extensively reviewed for fairness and to identify and eliminate sources of bias or imbalance in ethnic or gender representation.

The standardization sample consisted of more than 5000 subjects in 47 states and the District of Columbia. The sample was stratified on the basis of geographic region, community size, ethnic group, age, and gender (based on the 1980 census).

Table 10-4
Median
Reliabilities
(KR_{20}) of the
Modern Binet
Across Age
Groups

	Median Reliability, KR_{20}
Verbal reasoning area	.97*
Vocabulary	.87
Comprehension	.89
Absurdities	.87
Verbal relations	.91
Abstract/visual reasoning area	.96*
Pattern analysis	.92
Copying	.87
Matrices	.90
Paper folding and cutting	.94
Quantitative reasoning area	.96*
Quantitative	.88
Number series	.90
Equation building	.91
Short-term memory area	.93*
Bead memory	.87
Memory for sentences	.89
Memory for digits	.83
Memory for objects	.73
Composite	.98

Based on Table 5.2 in Thorndike, Hagen & Sattler (1986, p. 41).
* All area scores are based on the maximum number of tests for any given area.

Overall, the reliability of the modern Binet is quite good. Data on the internal consistency as well as test-retest reliabilities are reported in the manual as a function of age range. Internal consistency estimates are based on the Kuder-Richardson formula, KR_{20}, which calculates the highest reliability from all possible half-splittings of the data. In order to use this formula, it was assumed that all items below the basal were passed and all items above the ceiling were failed. As the authors of the manual note, this procedure is not very conservative and most likely leads to slightly inflated (at best, the upper bounds) reliability.

Table 10-4 shows the median reliability coefficients across age groups for individual tests, area scores, and the composite. Examination of the table reveals that the reliabilities of area scores and the composite are well above the .90 minimum that most experts believe a test should have if it is to be used to make decisions about individuals. Coefficients for individual tests, however, often fall below this minimum or are right on the borderline. Given that these coefficients represent the upper bounds of reliability, the need for caution in using individual test scores is evident.

Table 10-5

Correlation of the Composite of the Modern (1986) Binet with More Established Measures of Intelligence

Measure	Correlation
Stanford-Binet Form L-M (1972)	.81
Wechsler Intelligence Scale for Children, Revised	
Verbal IQ	.78
Performance IQ	.73
Full-scale IQ	.83
Wechsler Preschool and Primary Scale of Intelligence	
Verbal IQ	.78
Performance IQ	.71
Full-scale IQ	.80
Wechsler Adult Intelligence Scale, Revised	
Verbal IQ	.90
Performance IQ	.85
Full-scale IQ	.91
Kaufman Assessment Battery for Children	
Sequential processing	.84
Simultaneous processing	.82
Mental processing composite	.89
Achievement	.89

Based on data from Thorndike, Hagen & Sattler (1986, pp. 60–68).

Test-retest reliability data were obtained from a sample of 57 5-year-olds and 55 8-year-olds. The average interval between the two testings was about 16 weeks. The figures were somewhat disappointing except for the composite, which yielded reliabilities of .91 and .90 for the 5- and 8-year-olds, respectively. Although most of the coefficients for individual tests were in the low .80s or high .70s, a few low coefficients emerged. For instance, test-retest reliabilities for the quantitative and copying tests in the 8-year-old group were .28 and .46, respectively.

The technical manual reports three types of evidence in support of the validity of the modern Binet: (1) the intercorrelations and factor structure of the 15 specific tests, (2) the correlation of test scores with other measures purporting to measure intelligence, and (3) the performance of children designated as intellectually gifted or intellectually dull by other measures. We briefly discuss each type of evidence.

Correlational and factor analytic procedures reported in the test manual generally supported the validity of the modern Binet. Each of the 15 tests received substantial loadings on the *g* factor (range of .79 for number series to .51 for memory for objects). In addition, four group factors corresponding to the four area composites emerged from a factor analysis of the intercorrelation matrix, thus supporting the general model on which the modern Binet is based.

The modern Binet correlates well with other intelligence measures. Illustrative correlations with the composite score of the modern Binet and other tests reported in the technical manual are as follows: Stanford-Binet Form L-M (1972)—.81; Wechsler Intelligence Scale for Children, Revised (WISC-R), full-scale IQ—.83; Wechsler Preschool and Primary Scale of Intelligence

(WPPSI), full-scale IQ—.80; Wechsler Adult Intelligence Scale, Revised (WAIS-R), full-scale IQ—.91; and Kaufman Assessment Battery for Children (K-ABC), standard scores—.82–.89. The relatively low correlation between the modern Binet and Form L-M is attributable to the high verbal emphasis of Form L-M. As the technical manual notes, students with exceptional verbal skills but only above-average skills in other cognitive areas receive a bonus on Form L-M that they would not get with the modern (fourth edition) Binet (Thorndike, Hagen & Sattler, 1986). For samples of learning-disabled children, the modern Binet composite correlates .79 with Form L-M, .87 with the Wechsler Intelligence Scale for Children, full-scale IQ, and .66 with the Kaufman Assessment Battery for Children.

Table 10-5 shows the correlations of the composite score of the modern Binet with more established measures of intelligence. The correlations are quite high.

D. *Research on the Modern Binet*

To date, there have been about 25 published articles pertaining to the modern Binet. Many of these studies have examined the factor structure. G. J. Boyle (1989), for example, noted the presence of several inconsistent factor loadings for which no reasonable explanation could be provided. Using different techniques of factor analysis, Boyle (1989, 1990) and later Thorndike (1990) found that the initially reported inconsistent factor loadings were essentially artifacts of the particular factor analytic procedures used, thus supporting the validity of the modern Binet. Nevertheless, the four-factor hierarchical model underlying the Binet has yet to be fully confirmed empirically (Glutting, 1989; Kline, 1989). Determining whether the four-factor theory is viable, or in need of modification, is a major topic of current investigation (McCallum, 1990).

Another major portion of the published studies on the modern Binet have correlated the Binet with other more established standardized intelligence tests. In general, the conclusions have supported the results provided in the manual. H. Carvajal and K. Weyand (1986) report a correlation of .78 between the composite score of the modern Binet and the full-scale IQ Wechsler Intelligence Scale for Children, Revised. For the Wechsler Preschool and Primary Scale of Intelligence, Carvajal, Hardy, Smith, and Weaver (1988) report a correlation of .587 between the overall composite of the modern Binet and full-scale IQ. Both of these studies are limited, however, in that they are based on small samples of 20 or less. A study comparing the Modern Binet composite and the full-scale IQ of the Wechsler Adult Intelligence Scale, Revised (WAIS-R) for 15 adults found that the mean WAIS-R score was 13.8 points lower than that of the Stanford-Binet composite (Templer, Schmitz & Corgiat, 1985). This may be because the WAIS-R has an entire performance scale (for more on the Wechsler Intelligence Scale, see Chapter 11). The composite score of the Binet has correlated in the .50s to .70s for a variety of other standardized tests such as the Peabody Picture Vocabulary Test, Revised, Columbia Mental Maturity Scales, and McCarthy Scales of Children's Abilities (see Chapter 12) (Carvajal et al., 1987; Carvajal, Karr, Hardy & Palmer, 1988).

A few studies have attempted to compare the modern Binet with other tests (McCallum & Karnes, 1987; Phelps, 1989). A survey of 856 school psychologists by S. H. Chattin and B. A. Bracken (1989) is an example of this work. They surveyed the membership of the National Association of School Psychologists from its 1986 directory concerning four commonly used individual IQ tests: the Kaufman Assessment Battery for Children (see Chapter 12), the McCarthy Scales of Children's Abilities (see Chapter 12), the Wechsler Intelligence Scale for Children, Revised (see Chapter 11), and the modern fourth edition of the Stanford-Binet. The school psychologists were asked to rate each of the four tests in terms of ease of administration, interpretation, and usefulness. The Wechsler Intelligence Scale for Children, Revised was by far the most favorably rated on all dimensions. Unfortunately, the modern Binet consistently received the lowest ratings. The authors attribute the low ratings for the modern Binet in part to its newness and in part to its relative complexity and difficulty of administration (Chattin & Bracken, 1989). They are quick to point out, however, that all four of the measures surveyed are very well constructed and useful.

E. *Evaluation of the Modern Binet*

It has been said that a camel is a horse made by committee; the modern Binet may be such an animal. In many ways it is cumbersome, and from the standpoint of test administration, it's a nightmare. One must obtain basals and ceilings for all 15 tests. The examiner must estimate where to begin each test from the vocabulary and age of the subject. The value of having specific test scores is somewhat lessened by the borderline or less than satisfactory reliabilities these tests yield.

Although items were evaluated for fairness and possible bias, there is a consistent trend, as in all previous versions of the Binet, toward an increase in the mean scores as the educational level of the parents increases. Thus, Binet scores remain tied to socioeconomic factors. Moreover, three ethnic groups— Hispanics, Asians, and African-Americans—have distinctive patterns of mean scores, indicating that performance on the modern Binet interacts with race.

On the positive side, the area and composite scores possess more than adequate reliability. Together, these scores provide a wealth of knowledge concerning general intelligence as well as four specific areas of considerable interest in the evaluation of giftedness, learning disability, and mental retardation. Overall, the modern Binet is a well-constructed instrument. Though far from perfect, it meets the highest standards for a modern psychological test.

Summary
Binet defined *intelligence* as the capacity (1) to find and maintain a definite direction or purpose, (2) to make adaptations—that is, strategy adjustment if necessary to achieve that purpose, and (3) for self-criticism so that necessary adjustment in strategy can be made.

Binet's two major principles of test construction were age differentiation and general mental ability. *Age differentiation* refers to the fact that with increasing age, children develop increasing capabilities. Thus, older children have greater capabilities than younger ones.

Mental age is a unit of measure for expressing the results of intelligence tests. The concept was introduced in the second revision of the Binet scale in 1908. A subject's mental age is based on his or her performance compared to the average performance of individuals in a specific chronological age group. For example, if a 6-year-old child can perform tasks that can be done by the average 8-year-old, then the 6-year-old child is said to have a mental age of 8.

The *intelligence quotient* (IQ), like mental age, is a unit of measure for expressing the results of intelligence tests. Introduced in the Terman 1916 Stanford-Binet revision of the Binet scale, the intelligence quotient (IQ) is a ratio score. Specifically, the IQ is the ratio of a subject's mental age (as determined by his or her performance on the intelligence scale) and chronological age. This ratio is then multipled by 100 to eliminate fractions.

The deviation IQ, as it is used in the Stanford-Binet scale, is a standard score with a mean of 100 and a standard deviation of 16.

The most recent revision of the Binet scale, the fourth edition, was released in 1986. The modern Binet consists of 15 individual tests, each of which is grouped into one of four major content areas.

Chapter 11

The Wechsler Intelligence Scales

Learning Objectives

When you have completed this chapter, you should be able to:

- Identify the major motivation for the development of the Wechsler scales.
- Briefly describe the point and performance scale concepts.
- List the verbal and performance subtests of the WAIS-R and briefly describe the function purportedly measured by each subtest.
- Explain the declining age standard on the WAIS-R.
- Tell how IQ scores are determined on the WAIS-R.
- Describe the reliability of the WAIS-R.
- Describe the validity of the WAIS-R.
- Identify some of the major advantages and disadvantages of the WAIS-R.
- Briefly describe the WISC-III and WPPSI-R.

Susan's family had just moved from a small rural town to a large metropolis on the East Coast. At age 9, she was still shy around strangers and lacked confidence. Her attempt to adjust to a new school was a disaster. Because she started in the middle of the school term, all the other children seemed way ahead of her. She felt hopelessly behind. To make matters worse, she had an unusually strong fear of failure. Rather than make an error, she would remain silent even if she knew an answer. With all her negative experiences in the new school, she began to develop a poor attitude toward school tasks and avoided them. Eventually, she was referred to the school psychologist for testing. To Susan, this referral was the school's way of punishing her for not doing her homework. Fearful, upset, and angry, she made up her mind not to cooperate with the psychologist.

When the time finally came for her appointment, Susan began to cry. The principal was called in to accompany her to the psychologist's office. All the psychologist's attempts to comfort Susan did little to reduce her fear and anxiety. Finally, the psychologist decided to begin the testing. He started with a relatively simple task that required Susan to repeat digits. The psychologist stated, "I'm going to say some numbers. Listen, because when I'm through, I want you to say them as I do." He began the first set of digits and stated in a soft, clear voice, "Six, three, one." Susan did not even respond. She had been staring blankly at the walls and did not listen to what the psychologist had said. The psychologist attracted her attention and said, "Now say what I say: four, two, seven." This time Susan heard, but again she remained silent.

Now think for a moment. How many different factors were involved in the psychologist's ostensibly simple request to repeat three digits forward? To comply with this request, Susan would have had to direct her attention to the words of the psychologist, possess adequate hearing, and understand the instructions. She would also have had to cooperate, make an effort, and be capable of repeating what was in her mind. Certainly her familiarity with numerals—that is, her previous learning and experience—could influence her performance. If the children in her new school had more exposure to numerals than she, then they would have an advantage over her in this regard. Furthermore, her lack of confidence, negative attitude toward school, fear of failure, and shyness all played a role in her performance. A more confident, less fearful child with positive attitudes toward school would have a clear advantage over Susan. Thus, in addition to memory, many nonintellective factors (for example, attitude, experience, and emotional functioning) play an extremely important role in a person's ability to perform a task even as "simple" as repeating three digits forward.

Both Binet and Terman were aware of the influence of nonintellective factors on results from intelligence tests. However, David Wechsler is perhaps one of the most influential advocates of the role of nonintellective factors in these tests. In the fourth edition of his book *The Measurement and Appraisal of Adult Intelligence*, Wechsler stated, "Factors other than intellectual ability, for example, those of drive and incentive, are involved in intelligent behavior" (1958, pp. vii–viii).

In the highly influential fifth revision of Wechsler's (1958) book, J. D. Matarazzo added to Wechsler's statement on the role of nonintellective factors in IQ testing: "Although the IQ is the best single measure of intelligence, it is neither the only nor a complete measure of it. It [IQ] is a function of other factors besides sheer intellectual ability" (1972, p. 132). Wechsler (1981) subsequently reasserted the importance of nonintellective factors but warned that "no amount of drive will develop a dullard into a mathematician."

I. *The Wechsler Intelligence Scales*

The role of nonintellective factors is apparent in the intelligence scales that bear the name of Wechsler. Just two years after the Binet scale's monumental 1937 revision, its supremacy as a measure of human intelligence was challenged by

Wechsler's contribution to human intelligence testing, the Wechsler-Bellevue Intelligence Scale. With so many different and varied abilities associated with intelligence, many of which were affected or influenced by a unique set of nonintellective factors, Wechsler objected to the single score offered by the 1937 Binet scale. In constructing his own intelligence test, Wechsler deviated considerably from many of the central concepts in the Binet scale.

Wechsler (1939) capitalized on the inappropriateness of the Binet scale as a measure of the intelligence of adults. The Binet scale items were selected for use with children, not adults. Thus, Wechsler concluded that the Binet items lacked validity when answered by adults. As a result, examiner–subject rapport was often impaired in Binet scale testing with adults. Wechsler (1939) further noted that the Binet scale's emphasis on speed, with timed tasks scattered throughout the scale, tended to unduly handicap older adults. Furthermore, mental age norms were clearly not applicable to adults. In addition, Wechsler criticized the Binet scale because it did not consider possible deterioration in intellectual performance with increasing age.

A. *Advances in Intelligence Testing: Point and Performance Scale Concepts*

Many of the differences between the Wechsler and the 1937 Binet scales are quite profound. Two of the most critical differences are (1) Wechsler's use of the point scale concept rather than an age scale and (2) Wechsler's inclusion of a performance scale.

The point scale concept. Recall that since its 1908 and subsequent revisions through 1960, the Binet scale grouped items by age level. Each age level included a group of tasks that could be passed by two-thirds to three-fourths of the individuals at that age level. In the **age scale** format, the arrangement of items has nothing to do with their content. At a particular year level, there might be one task related to memory, a second related to reasoning, and a third related to skill in using numerical data. Another year level might also include a task related to memory but then include other tasks related to concentration or language skills. Thus, various types of content are scattered throughout the scale. Furthermore, subjects do not receive a specific amount of points or credit for each task completed. For example, if a Binet scale subject was required to pass three out of four tasks in order to receive credit for a particular test, then passing only two tasks would produce no credit at all for that test.

In a **point scale,** credits or points are assigned to each item. An individual receives a specific amount of credit for each item passed. The Binet scale, including the 1986 modern Binet, does not afford such credit. For example, on the modern Binet, a ceiling is reached whether the individual is correct on three out of four or on all four items at two consecutive levels. The individual who gets three items correct obtains the same score as the one who gets all four correct. Thus, although the modern Binet abandoned the age scale concept (see Chapter 10), it did not go so far as to adopt the point scale concept.

[handwritten in margin] Wechsler: multiple scores

[handwritten in right margin] Binet inappropriate for adults

Figure 11-1
Advantages of
Wechsler's scale.

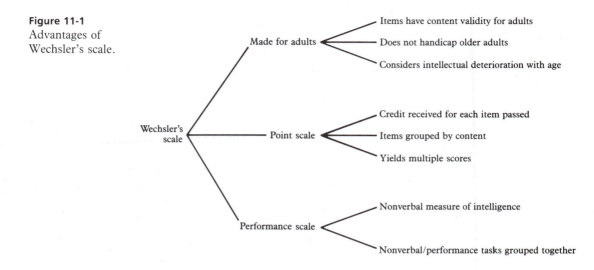

An inherent advantage of the point scale is that it makes it easy to group items of a particular content together, which is exactly what Wechsler did. The effect of such groupings was so powerful that a similar concept was used in the revision of the 1986 modern Binet scale. By arranging items according to content and assigning a specific number of points to each item, Wechsler was able to construct an intelligence test that yielded not only a total overall score like the 1937 Binet but also scores for each content area. Thus, with the point scale concept, Wechsler was able to devise a test that permitted an analysis of the individual's ability in a variety of content areas (for example, judgment, vocabulary, and range of general knowledge).

The performance scale concept. The 1937 Binet scale has been persistently and consistently criticized for its emphasis on language/verbal skills. In dealing with this problem, Wechsler included an entire scale that provided a measure of nonverbal intelligence: a **performance scale.** In addition to its advantage as a measure of adult intelligence and its ability to yield separate scores for various functions, Wechsler's approach thus had a third major advantage over the Binet scale. The performance scale consists of tasks that require a subject to do something (for example, copy symbols or point to a missing detail) rather than to simply answer questions. See Figure 11-1.

Although the 1937 Binet scale contained some performance tasks, these tended to be concentrated at the early age levels. Furthermore, the results of a subject's response to a performance task on the Binet scale were extremely difficult to separate from the results of verbal tasks. Thus, it was not possible on the Binet scale to determine the precise extent to which a subject's response to a performance task increased or decreased the total score. The Wechsler scale, however, included two separate scales. The verbal scale provided a

NAME _____ AGE _____ SEX _____

MARITAL STATUS _____ HANDEDNESS _____

OCCUPATION _____ EDUCATION _____

PLACE OF TESTING _____

TESTED BY _____

REFERRED BY _____

REASON FOR REFERRAL _____

WAIS-R® EXPANDED RECORD FORM

	Year	Month	Day
Date Tested	____	____	____
Date of Birth	____	____	____
Age	____	____	____

TABLE OF SCALED SCORE EQUIVALENTS*

Scaled Score	RAW SCORE											Scaled Score
	VERBAL SUBTESTS						PERFORMANCE SUBTESTS					
	Information	Digit Span	Vocabulary	Arithmetic	Comprehension	Similarities	Picture Completion	Picture Arrangement	Block Design	Object Assembly	Digit Symbol	
19	—	28	70	—	32	—	—	—	51	—	93	19
18	29	27	69	—	31	28	—	—	—	41	91-92	18
17	—	26	68	19	—	—	20	20	50	—	89-90	17
16	28	25	66-67	—	30	27	—	—	49	40	84-88	16
15	27	24	65	18	29	26	—	19	47-48	39	79-83	15
14	26	22-23	63-64	17	27-28	25	19	—	44-46	38	75-78	14
13	25	20-21	60-62	16	26	24	—	18	42-43	37	70-74	13
12	23-24	18-19	55-59	15	25	23	18	17	38-41	35-36	66-69	12
11	22	17	52-54	13-14	23-24	22	17	15-16	35-37	34	62-65	11
10	19-21	15-16	47-51	12	21-22	20-21	16	14	31-34	32-33	57-61	10
9	17-18	14	43-46	11	19-20	18-19	15	13	27-30	30-31	53-56	9
8	15-16	12-13	37-42	10	17-18	16-17	14	11-12	23-26	28-29	48-52	8
7	13-14	11	29-36	8-9	14-16	14-15	13	8-10	20-22	24-27	44-47	7
6	9-12	9-10	20-28	6-7	11-13	11-13	11-12	5-7	14-19	21-23	37-43	6
5	6-8	8	14-19	5	8-10	7-10	8-10	3-4	8-13	16-20	30-36	5
4	5	7	11-13	4	6-7	5-6	5-7	2	3-7	13-15	23-29	4
3	4	6	9-10	3	4-5	2-4	3-4	—	2	9-12	16-22	3
2	3	3-5	6-8	1-2	2-3	1	2	1	1	6-8	8-15	2
1	0-2	0-2	0-5	0	0-1	0	0-1	0	0	0-5	0-7	1

SUMMARY

	Raw Score	Scaled Score	Age-Scaled Score¹
VERBAL SUBTESTS			
Information	____	____	____
Digit Span	____	____	____
Vocabulary	____	____	____
Arithmetic	____	____	____
Comprehension	____	____	____
Similarities	____	____	____
Verbal Score		____	
PERFORMANCE SUBTESTS			
Picture Completion	____	____	____
Picture Arrangement	____	____	____
Block Design	____	____	____
Object Assembly	____	____	____
Digit Symbol	____	____	____
Performance Score		____	

¹Scaled score equivalents of raw scores for a specific age range(see Manual, Table 21). Not to be used for determination of IQ.

*Clinicians who wish to draw a profile may do so by locating the examinee's raw scores on the table above and drawing a line to connect them. See Chapter 4 in the Manual for a discussion of the significance of differences between scores on the subtests.

	Scaled Score	IQ	Percentile Rank	Classification
Verbal Score	____†	____	____	____
Performance Score	____‡	____	____	____
Full Scale Score	____	____	____	____

†Prorated from 5 subtests, if necessary.
‡Prorated from 4 subtests, if necessary.

Figure 11-2
WAIS-R Expanded Record Form. (*Wechsler Adult Intelligence Scale-Revised.*
Copyright © 1981, 1955 by The Psychological Corporation. Reproduced by permission. All rights reserved.)

measure of verbal intelligence, and the performance scale provided a measure of nonverbal intelligence.

The concept of a performance scale was far from new. Prior to the development of the Wechsler scale, several performance tests were available as a supplement or alternative to the verbally weighted Binet scale (such as the Leiter International Performance Scale, which is discussed in Chapter 12). However, Wechsler's new scale offered the possibility of a direct comparison of an individual's verbal and nonverbal intelligence. Thus, both verbal and performance scales were standardized on the same sample, and results for both scales were expressed in comparable units.

A performance scale attempts to overcome (to the extent possible) biases caused by language, cultural, and educational factors in measuring intelligence. Furthermore, if verbal tasks provide a useful context in which to observe behavior, then tasks that require the subject to do something can offer an even richer and more varied context in which to observe a subject's approach to problem solving. Indeed, performance tasks tend to require a longer interval of sustained effort, concentration, and attention than most verbal tasks. Therefore, despite their relative insensitivity to language, educational, and cultural factors, performance tasks are generally more vulnerable to emotional disorders (Rapaport, Gill & Schafer, 1968). With a performance and a verbal scale, Wechsler went a long way toward resolving one of the major problems in the 1937 Binet scale. See Figure 11-2.

B. *From the Wechsler-Bellevue Intelligence Scale to the WAIS-R*

But poorly standardized

Despite his conceptual improvements, Wechsler's first effort to measure adult intelligence, the Wechsler-Bellevue scale (Wechsler, 1939), was poorly standardized. Its normative sample consisted of a nonrepresentative sample of 1081 whites from the eastern United States (primarily New York residents). By 1955, however, Wechsler had revised the Wechsler-Bellevue scale into its modern form, the Wechsler Adult Intelligence Scale (WAIS), which was revised in 1981 (Wechsler, 1981). The WAIS-R is based on the 1970 census and a representative sample of 1880 individuals distributed over nine age groups who were tested between 1976 and 1980.

II. *Scales and Subtests of the WAIS-R*

Like Binet, Wechsler defined intelligence as the capacity to act purposefully and to adapt to the environment. Intelligence is, he stated, "the aggregate or global capacity of the individual to act purposefully, to think rationally and to deal effectively with his environment" (Wechsler, 1958, p. 7). Wechsler be-

Table 11-1
WAIS-R Subtests

Subtest	Major Function Measured
Verbal Scales	
Information	Range of knowledge
Comprehension	Judgment
Arithmetic	Concentration
Similarities	Abstract thinking
Digit span	Immediate memory, anxiety
Vocabulary	Vocabulary level
Performance Scales	
Digit symbol	Visual-motor functioning
Picture completion	Alertness to details
Picture arrangement	Planning ability
Block design	Nonverbal reasoning
Object assembly	Analysis of part-whole relationships

lieved that intelligence comprised specific elements that could be individually defined and measured; however, these elements were seen as interrelated— that is, not entirely independent. This is why he used the term *global* or *aggregate*. Wechsler's definition implies that intelligence comprises a number of specific interrelated functions or elements and that general intelligence is the result of the interplay of these elements. Theoretically, by measuring each of the elements, we can measure general intelligence by summing the individual's capacities on each element. Thus, Wechsler made an effort to measure separate abilities, which Binet had avoided in his decision to adopt the concept of general mental ability. In creating the WAIS-R, Wechsler identified 11 elements or functions, 6 related to verbal intelligence and 5 to nonverbal intelligence. Table 11-1 lists these 11 subtests and the basic function they purportedly measure (Rapaport, Gill & Schafer, 1968; Sattler, 1982; Wechsler, 1958; Zimmerman, Woo-Sam & Glasser, 1973).

A. *The Verbal Subtests*

The six verbal subtests are (1) information, (2) comprehension, (3) arithmetic, (4) similarities, (5) digit span, and (6) vocabulary. Each of these is briefly discussed here.

The information subtest. College students typically find the information subtest a relatively easy and fun task. As in all Wechsler subtests, items are presented in order of increasing difficulty. Item 6 asks something like "Name four famous U.S. presidents." In all, there are 29 items. Item 22 asks something like "How many members are there in the U.S. Congress?" Like all

Figure 11-3
Information
subtest:
intellective and
nonintellective
components.
(Based on factor
analytic and
logical analyses of
intellective and
nonintellective
components in the
information
subtest.)

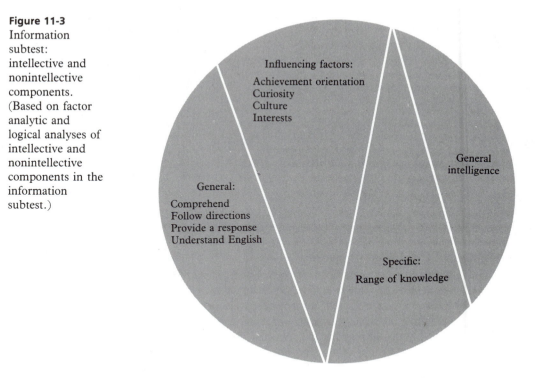

Influencing factors:
Achievement orientation
Curiosity
Culture
Interests

General
intelligence

General:
Comprehend
Follow directions
Provide a response
Understand English

Specific:
Range of knowledge

Wechsler subtests, the information subtest involves both intellective and nonintellective components. These components include the ability to comprehend instructions, follow directions, and provide a response. Although purportedly a measure of the subject's range of knowledge, factors such as curiosity and interest in the acquisition of knowledge tend to influence test scores. Figure 11-3 illustrates how a score on the information subtest can be parceled into components.

The comprehension subtest. Like the information subtest, the comprehension subtest is given without any specific preparatory instructions. The examiner simply reads each question and waits for the response. The comprehension subtest has three types of questions. The first places the subject in a situation and asks what should be done in that situation. For example, a person might be asked something like "What should you do if you find an injured person lying in the street?" The second type of question asks the subject to provide a logical explanation for some rule or phenomenon such as "Why do we bury the dead?" The third type of question asks the subject to define proverbs such as "A stitch in time saves nine." Previous learning and scholastic aptitude play a far smaller role in the comprehension subtest than in the information subtest;

Figure 11-4
Arithmetic
subtest:
intellective and
nonintellective
components.

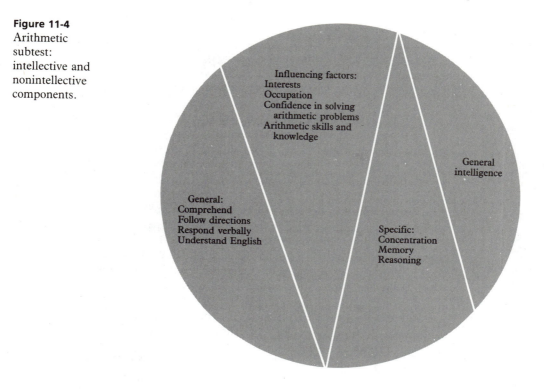

generally, the comprehension subtest measures common sense. In addition, emotional difficulties frequently reveal themselves on this subtest and lower the person's score. For example, a psychopathic individual might respond to the question concerning what to do if you find an injured person as follows: "Tell them I didn't do it." A phobic neurotic might respond, "Make sure I don't get any blood on myself." A schizophrenic might say, "Run!" In each case the person's emotional disturbance interferes with his or her judgment and results in an inappropriate response.

The arithmetic subtest. The arithmetic subtest contains 14 relatively simple problems. The ninth most difficult item is as easy as this: "A person with $17.50 spends $7. How much does he have left?" Obviously, you need not be a mathematician to figure this one out; however, you must be able to retain the figures in memory while manipulating them. In a few cases, such as in retarded or educationally deprived subjects, arithmetic skills sometimes play a significant role. Generally, however, concentration, motivation, and memory are the major factors underlying performance. Figure 11-4 illustrates some of the intellective and nonintellective components for the arithmetic subtest as revealed by factor analytic and logical analyses.

The similarities subtest. The similarities subtest consists of 14 paired items of increasing difficulty. The subject's task is to identify the similarity between the items in each pair. The subject may be asked, for example, "In what way are a horse and a cow alike?" Many of the early, easier items are so well known that responses simply reflect previously learned associations (Zimmerman, Woo-Sam & Glasser, 1973). However, the more difficult items—for example, "In what way are an ant and a rose alike?"—definitely require the subject to think at an abstract level. This subtest measures the subject's ability to see the similarity between apparently dissimilar objects or things.

The character of a person's thought processes can be seen in many cases. For example, schizophrenic persons tend to give concepts that have meaning only to them—that is, idiosyncratic concepts. An idiosyncratic response to the hypothetical horse and cow item might be "Both are places to hide." Such a response has meaning only to the schizophrenic person, who may further explain, "My favorite hiding place is on my uncle's farm." Brain-injured and mentally retarded individuals tend to have difficulty thinking abstractly. The character of their thought processes is concrete. A concrete response is highly specific, such as "A cow and a horse both have four legs."

The digit span subtest. The digit span subtest requires the subject to repeat digits, read at the rate of one per second, forward and backward. In terms of intellective factors, the digit span subtest measures short-term auditory memory. As with other Wechsler subtests, however, nonintellective factors (for example, attention) often influence the results. For example, a large body of literature has shown that anxiety in the test situation impairs performance on the digit span subtest (Boor & Schill, 1968; Edwards, 1966; Hodges & Spielberger, 1969).

The vocabulary subtest. The ability to define words is not only one of the best single measures of intelligence but also the most stable and least deteriorating aspect of intelligence (Rapaport, Gill & Schafer, 1968). Vocabulary tests are included on nearly every individual test involving verbal intelligence. The relative stability of the vocabulary scale is one of its most important features. If an individual has shown deterioration (that is, lowered performance compared to a higher level at some earlier time) because of emotional factors or brain damage, vocabulary is one of the last subtests to be affected. For example, the poor concentration of schizophrenic persons lowers their performance on arithmetic or digit span tasks long before vocabulary is negatively affected. Whereas mild concentration difficulties lower optimal performance on arithmetic and digit span tasks, such difficulties generally do not affect vocabulary until they become quite severe. Because the vocabulary subtest provides an estimate of general verbal intelligence that is relatively stable and independent of deterioration, it can be used to evaluate baseline intelligence (that is, what a person's intellectual capacity probably was prior to an emotional illness, brain injury, or trauma).

Figure 11-5
A WAIS-R pattern. (*Wechsler Adult Intelligence Scale—Revised. Copyright © 1981, 1955 by The Psychological Corporation. Reproduced by permission. All rights reserved.*)

Scaled score	Information	Digit span	Vocabulary	Arithmetic	Comprehension	Similarities	Picture completion	Picture arrangement	Block design	Object assembly	Digit symbol	Scaled score
			Verbal tests						Performance tests			
19	—	28	70	—	32		—	—	51	—	93	19
18	29	27	69	—	31	28	—	—	—	41	91-92	18
17	—	26	68	19	—	—	20	20	50	—	89-90	17
16	28	25	66-67	—	30	27	—	—	49	40	84-88	16
15	27	24	65	18	29	26	—	19	47-48	39	79-83	15
14	26	22-23	63-64	17	27-28	25	19	—	44-46	38	75-78	14
13	25	20-21	60-62	16	26	24	—	18	42-43	37	70-74	13
12	23-24	18-19	55-59	15	25	23	18	17	38-41	35-36	66-69	12
11	22	17	52-54	13-14	23-24	22	17	15-16	35-37	34	62-65	11
10	19-21	15-16	47-51	12	21-22	20-21	16	14	31-34	32-33	57-63	10
9	17-18	14	43-46	11	19-20	18-19	15	13	27-30	30-31	53-56	9
8	15-16	12-13	37-42	10	17-18	16-17	14	11-12	23-26	28-29	48-52	8
7	13-14	11	29-36	8-9	14-16	14-15	13	8-10	20-22	24-27	44-47	7
6	9-12	9-10	20-28	6-7	11-13	11-13	11-12	5-7	14-19	21-23	37-43	6
5	6-8	8	14-19	5	8-10	7-10	8-10	3-4	8-13	16-20	30-36	5
4	5	7	11-13	4	6-7	5-6	5-7	2	3-7	13-15	23-29	4
3	4	6	9-10	3	4-5	2-4	3-4	—	2	9-12	16-22	3
2	3	3-5	6-8	1-2	2-3	1	2	1	1	6-8	8-15	2
1	0-2	0-2	0-5	0	0-1	0	0-1	0	0	0-5	0-7	1

Table of scaled score equivalents — Raw score

B. *Raw Scores, Scaled Scores, and the Verbal IQ*

The six verbal subtests make up the verbal scale of the WAIS-R. Each subtest produces a raw score—that is, a total number of points. The information subtest, as we have seen, contains 29 items. Each is scored 1 or 0. The highest possible raw score on information is 29. The maximum possible raw score on vocabulary, on the other hand, is 70. Clearly, a raw score of 29 on information is not comparable to a raw score of 29 on vocabulary.

To deal with the lack of comparability of raw scores for the individual subtests, the raw scores for each subtest are converted to a standard or **scaled score** with a mean of 10 and a standard deviation of 3. On the WAIS-R, a raw score for any given subtest yields the same scaled score regardless of age because norms for WAIS-R scaled scores were based on a reference sample of 500 cases ranging between 20 and 34 years of age selected from the standardization sample. For a given subject, the scaled score on one subtest can be directly compared to any other score. For example, a scaled score of 10 is at the 50th percentile for all subtests. Thus, a person's relative strength on any subtest can be directly compared to his or her strength on any other. This feature of the WAIS-R opens the possibility of pattern analysis, in which a person's pattern of weaknesses and strengths can be related to particular problems. Figure 11-5 illustrates a possible WAIS-R pattern.

Figure 11-5 indicates that the subject obtained an average scaled score on every subtest except arithmetic and block design. In pattern analysis, an effort is made to determine what type of problem would lower performance on these subtests. It is assumed that the person's other (average) subtest scores indicate that he or she is capable of average performance in all areas. The relatively low scores on arithmetic and block design are assumed to reflect deterioration. Because these scores are both related to abstract thinking (verbal and nonverbal, respectively), the question is "What type of problem would cause deterioration in abstract thinking?" In answering this question, the tester may gain insights into the nature of the person's problem.

To obtain the verbal IQ, the scaled scores on each of the six verbal subtests are summed. This sum is then compared to the standardization sample of the person's age group. You should note that the same scaled score sum produces different IQs depending on age. For example, a sum of 60 yields a verbal IQ of 97 in the 25–34 age group, but this same sum yields a verbal IQ of 109 in the

FOCUSED EXAMPLE 11-1

The Declining Age Standard

One of the important debates within psychology has centered around the question "Does intelligence decrease in the later years of life?" Analysis of the WAIS standardization had indicated that scores rise until the late 20s or 30s and then decline until about age 60. After age 60, there seemed to be a relatively sharp decline in intelligence (Doppelt & Wallace, 1955). However, the WAIS was standardized cross-sectionally. This means a different sample of subjects was tested at each age level. In contrast to the cross-sectional method is the longitudinal method, in which the same subjects are tested at various points in time. Obviously, the longitudinal method provides far greater control over important variables than the cross-sectional one.

When the same individuals are tested several times over a long period of time (longitudinal method), there is control over educational opportunities (more colleges are available today than were available 40 years ago), cultural experiences,

technological advances (for example, the availability of home computers), and a host of other factors. Furthermore, a longitudinal study precludes the possibility of inadvertently having unusually bright (or limited) individuals at one particular age group, which would bias the results. However, a longitudinal study requires many years to complete. In standardizing the WAIS, Wechsler could not afford to take the same group of adults and test them at various points in their lives over a 50-year span. However, recent evidence from longitudinal studies has indicated that intelligence actually does not decline as dramatically as indicated by an analysis of Wechsler's cross-sectional normative sample. In fact, the evidence indicates that, except in certain abnormal conditions and just prior to death (Rinn, 1988), intelligence remains fairly stable throughout the life span (Matarazzo, 1972).

The reason for the dramatic differences between a verbal IQ for a scaled score sum of 60 in

70–74 age group for the WAIS-R. The reason older subjects require a lower scaled score sum to produce the same or even higher IQ as middle-aged subjects is discussed in Focused Example 11-1. Tables are provided in the manual so that, given the person's age and summed scaled scores, the IQ can be looked up. The verbal IQ for each age level is a deviation IQ with a mean of 100 and a standard deviation of 15.

C. *The Performance Subtests*

The five performance subtests of the WAIS-R are digit symbol, picture completion, block design, picture arrangement, and object assembly. Each of these is discussed here.

The digit symbol subtest. The digit symbol subtest requires the subject to copy symbols. In the upper part of the standard WAIS-R form for recording responses are the numbers 1 through 9. Under each number is a symbol (see Figure 11-6). After completing a short practice sample, the subject is given 90 seconds to copy as many symbols as possible. The subtest measures such factors as ability to learn an unfamiliar task, visual-motor dexterity, degree of

the 25–34 age group (IQ = 97) and the verbal IQ for a sum of 60 in the 70–74 age group (IQ = 109) is that WAIS and WAIS-R norms are based on cross-sectional data. The decline in intelligence in the later years of life indicated by the cross-sectional data is reflected in the IQ conversions for a particular age group. The average sum of the verbal subtest scaled scores in the WAIS cross-sectional standardization sample, for example, was about 48 in the 70–74 age range. The average sum in the 25–34 age range, however, was 61. Therefore, in order to obtain a verbal IQ of 100, someone in the 70–74 age range would need a sum of scaled scores of 48, whereas someone in the 25–34 age range would need a sum of 61. This phenomenon is known as the *declining age standard*.

By using age-matched norms, it was possible to avoid penalizing aging adults. If intelligence did in fact decline with age and all subjects were compared to the performance of adults at their peak, as in the Binet scale, then younger subjects would obtain consistently higher IQ scores than older subjects. A subject who showed no more decline in intelligence above and beyond the normal aging process would still manifest substantial reductions in IQ score. Unless corrected for, the end result would be that few elderly would obtain even average scores and most would fall in the below average or retarded ranges. However, inasmuch as the longitudinal data show that intelligence does not decline significantly throughout the life span, the declining age standard actually has the reverse of its intended effect when subjects tested 20 or 30 years ago are retested and evaluated in terms of cross-sectional norms. An adult tested at 34 years of age in 1955 would actually gain 5 to 10 IQ points if tested in 1982. As J. D. Matarazzo (1972) noted, the age norms of the WAIS score require periodic updating, which is one reason the WAIS was revised in 1981.

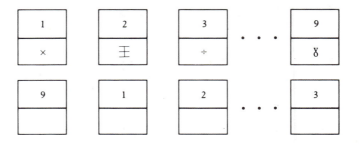

Figure 11-6
Digit symbol: an illustrative example. The top row contains divided boxes with a number in the upper half and a mark underneath. The bottom row contains divided boxes with numbers on top but no marks. The subject's task is to supply the appropriate mark in the lower half of the bottom row.

persistence, and speed of performance (Zimmerman, Woo-Sam & Glasser, 1973). Naturally, the subject must have adequate visual acuity and appropriate motor capabilities to complete this subtest successfully.

The picture completion subtest. In the picture completion subtest, the subject is shown a picture in which some important detail is missing, such as a horse without a tail. The subject is asked to tell which part is missing (Wechsler, 1955); however, credit can be obtained by simply pointing to the missing part. As in all five WAIS-R performance subtests, picture completion is timed: the subject is given 20 seconds to locate the missing detail. As simple as this task seems from a test administration standpoint, the importance of an experienced examiner becomes clear in a close examination. If the subject points, the examiner must ascertain that the right detail has been identified. In addition, the experienced examiner will not immediately go to the next item if 20 seconds have elapsed but the subject has not yet responded. If the subject appears to be contemplating a response, the examiner will generally permit a response, even though no credit can be obtained beyond the time limit. An experienced examiner knows that it is unwise to force a subject to struggle over a picture when it is clear that he or she has no idea of the answer. Discretion is necessary in giving this, as well as other, WAIS-R performance subtests.

The block design subtest. Block design tasks have long been included in non-verbal measures of intelligence (Arthur, 1930; Kohs, 1923). Materials for the design subtest include nine blocks. Some sides are all red, some are all white, and others are red on one half and white on the other. The materials also include a booklet with pictures of the blocks arranged according to a specific design or configuration. The subject is asked to arrange the blocks into the designs in increasing difficulty. The block design subtest requires the subject to reason, analyze spatial relationships, and integrate visual and motor functions. The input information (that is, pictures of designs) is visual, but the response (output) is motor. The subtest provides an excellent measure of nonverbal concept formation or abstract thinking (Rapaport, Gill & Schafer, 1968).

The picture arrangement subtest. The picture arrangement subtest also requires the subject to notice relevant details. In addition, the subject must be able to plan adequately and notice cause-and-effect relationships (Zimmerman, Woo-Sam & Glasser, 1973). The subtest consists of ten items, each of which contains a series of related pictures such as those found in most comic strips. The pictures are placed in a mixed-up order, and the subject is asked to put them in the right order so that they tell a story. Because the individual must find the logical sequence of events, the subtest taps nonverbal reasoning ability. Because some of the items involve social or interpersonal content, it has been suggested that the subtest also taps the ability to accurately interpret social situations (Sattler, 1982; Zimmerman, Woo-Sam & Glasser, 1973).

The object assembly subtest. Object assembly consists of four puzzles (four cut-up objects) that the subject is asked to put together as quickly as possible. The subtest measures the ability of the subject to see part-whole relationships and involves "visual analysis and its coordination with simple assembly skills" (Zimmerman, Woo-Sam & Glasser, 1973).

D. *Performance IQs*

As with the verbal subtests, the raw scores for each of the five performance subtests are converted to scaled scores based on the 500 cases in the 20–34 age group of the standardization sample. The mean and standard deviation are the same as for the verbal subtests—10 and 3, respectively. The performance IQ is obtained by summing the scaled scores on the five performance subtests and comparing this score to the appropriate age group. The performance IQ, like the verbal IQ, is a deviation IQ with a mean of 100 and a standard deviation of 15.

E. *Full-Scale IQs*

The full-scale IQ follows the same principles of the verbal and performance IQs. It is obtained by summing the scaled scores of the six verbal subtests with the five performance subtests and comparing the subject to his or her appropriate age group. Again, a deviation IQ with a mean of 100 and a standard deviation of 15 is obtained. Table 11-2 shows the conversions of IQ to percentile ranks for the verbal, performance, and full-scale IQs. As inspection of the table indicates, IQs between 45 and 67 are all in the 1st percentile. An IQ of 80 is at the 9th percentile; an IQ of 110 is at the 75th percentile; and so on.

Table 11-2
Percentile Rank
(PR) Equivalents
for Verbal,
Performance, and
Full-Scale IQs*

IQ	PR	IQ	PR	IQ	PR
45	1	80	9	115	84
46	1	81	10	116	86
47	1	82	12	117	87
48	1	83	13	118	88
49	1	84	14	119	90
50	1	85	16	120	91
51	1	86	18	121	92
52	1	87	19	122	93
53	1	88	21	123	94
54	1	89	23	124	95
55	1	90	25	125	95
56	1	91	27	126	96
57	1	92	30	127	96
58	1	93	32	128	97
59	1	94	34	129	97
60	1	95	37	130	98
61	1	96	40	131	98
62	1	97	42	132	98
63	1	98	45	133	99
64	1	99	47	134	99
65	1	100	50	135	99
66	1	101	53	136	99
67	1	102	55	137	99
68	2	103	58	138	99
69	2	104	61	139	99
70	2	105	63	140	99
71	3	106	66	141	99
72	3	107	68	142	99
73	4	108	70	143	99
74	4	109	73	144	99
75	5	110	75	145	99
76	5	111	77	146	99
77	6	112	79	147	99
78	7	113	81	148	99
79	8	114	82	149	99
				150	99

* Wechsler Adult Intelligence Scale-Revised. Copyright
© 1981, 1955 by The Psychological Corporation.
Reproduced by permission. All rights reserved.

III. *Interpretive Features of the WAIS-R*

The WAIS-R provides a rich source of data that often furnishes significant cues in the diagnosis or evaluation of emotionally disordered states. Of particular significance in evaluating persons in disordered states is the comparison of verbal and performance IQs and analysis of the pattern of subtest scores (Guertin et al., 1966, 1971).

A. *Verbal-Performance IQ Comparisons*

In providing a measure of nonverbal intelligence in conjunction with a verbal IQ, the WAIS-R offers an extremely useful opportunity not offered by the early Binet scales. First, the inclusion of the performance IQ aids in the interpretation of the verbal IQ (Sattler, 1988). Assume, for example, that a subject obtains a verbal IQ (VIQ) in the retarded ranges (such as VIQ = 60). If the performance IQ is also approximately 60, then results with the verbal IQ have been confirmed, and we have a good indication that the individual is, in fact, intellectually retarded. Remember, however, that a diagnosis of mental retardation should never be made on the basis of IQ alone. The individual must show significant deficits in adaptive functioning as well as a full-scale IQ below 70. Suppose, however, that the performance IQ exceeded 100, but the verbal IQ was 55. Then we have a case where the individual is at least average in his or her nonverbal skills but three standard deviations below the mean in the verbal area. Even though the full-scale IQ might still fall within the retarded range, it is quite unlikely that such a person is mentally retarded. Instead, language, cultural, or educational factors might account for the differences in the two IQs.

In one study of verbal versus performance IQs, Saccuzzo, Johnson, and Russell (1992) examined approximately 5000 gifted children from four ethnic backgrounds: African-American, Caucasian, Filipino, and Hispanic. Results showed that even though all children had IQs of 125 or greater, the nature of the verbal-performance discrepancy, if any, depended on ethnic background. The African-American and Caucasian groups had higher verbal than performance IQs. The reverse was found for the Filipinos, who had significantly higher performance IQs. No differences were found between the verbal and performance IQs for the Hispanics. Results such as these indicate that it is not appropriate to make sweeping generalizations about the meaning of a verbal versus performance IQ discrepancy. When considering any test sign, you must take the ethnic background of the individual into account.

B. *Pattern Analysis*

The 11 separate subtest scores of the WAIS-R offer an opportunity for pattern analysis. In pattern analysis, relatively large differences between subtest scaled scores are evaluated. Wechsler (1958) believed that certain patterns of scores might be related to certain types of emotional problems. He reasoned that different types of emotional problems might have differential effects on the subtests. Hysterics (called conversion disorders), for example, use denial and repression—that is, put things out of awareness as a defense mechanism. Therefore, they should show lapses in their long-term store of knowledge, which might be reflected in a relatively low score on the information subtest. Schizophrenia involves poor concentration and impaired judgment, which might be reflected in relatively low scores on arithmetic and comprehension. Wechsler (1958) provided a host of patterns tentatively proposed to have diagnostic significance.

Following Wechsler's (1958) proposed patterns, many investigators empirically studied the potential validity of pattern analysis (Guertin et al., 1966, 1971; Guertin et al., 1962). The results were inconclusive and contradictory. Indeed, G. H. Frank (1970) surveyed the literature relevant to the diagnostic and personality implications of the WAIS. He concluded that the available research was so poorly controlled that the best thing to do would be to forget the work that had been done and start all over again from scratch.

Following Frank's criticisms of the literature and all but dismissal of the potential of pattern analysis, D. G. Lewandowski and D. P. Saccuzzo (1975, 1976) and Saccuzzo and Lewandowski (1976) listed a number of methodological considerations that must be followed in order to fairly answer the questions concerning the validity of pattern analysis. These authors argued that although the validity may be dubious, the question has yet to be satisfactorily resolved. They further suggested that the question concerning validity might be resolved if appropriate methodological rigor is used in the design of relevant studies. The purpose of Lewandowski and Saccuzzo (1975) and Saccuzzo and Lewandowski (1976) was to illustrate how their methodological considerations might be applied to validate a specific Wechsler intelligence scale pattern for a particular disordered state. These authors failed to confirm many of Wechsler's (1958) hypotheses concerning the meaning of certain subtest patterns, which had been based on his examination of the standardization sample. However, they found that a definite, reliable pattern of subtest scores could be associated with individuals who had been incarcerated for delinquency. This work was subsequently cross-validated and confirmed by T. Wickham (1978).

Although the issue of the validity of pattern analysis has yet to be resolved, clinical practitioners continue to interpret Wechsler subtest patterns. The hypothetical cases that follow illustrate what WAIS-R scores might mean to a clinician.

C. *Hypothetical Case Studies*

Consider the following example of a 16-year-old high school junior who obtained a "D" average despite a previously stable "B" average. Standard achievement tests found his reading and arithmetic grades appropriate. His scaled scores were as shown in Table 11-3 (remember, the mean is 10 and the standard deviation is 3).

The previously stable "B" average indicates that this individual is probably of at least average intelligence. The rapid decline in his grades, however, suggests some dramatic change or shift in functioning. His scaled score of 11 on vocabulary is above the mean. Because vocabulary is a relatively stable measure of IQ, the scaled score of 11 also indicates this individual's IQ of 93 is likely to be an underestimate of his intelligence. Assuming that this individual's typical scaled score performance would be about 11, as reflected in his

Table 11-3
Scaled Scores

Verbal Scales	Performance Scales
Information: 11	Digit symbol: 4
Comprehension: 9	Picture completion: 10
Arithmetic: 7	Book design: 5
Similarities: 11	Picture arrangement: 11
Digit span: 5	Object assembly: 6
Vocabulary: 11	
Scaled score sum: 54	Scaled score sum: 36
Verbal IQ: 104*	Performance IQ: 83*
Sum of scaled scores for verbal and performance scales: 90	
Full-scale IQ: 93*	

* According to Table 20 provided in the WAIS-R manual
(Wechsler, 1981, pp. 92–93).

scaled score on vocabulary and confirmed by his scaled scores on information and similarities, we find evidence for deterioration in his judgment (comprehension), concentration (arithmetic), and immediate memory (digit span) in the verbal areas. We also find deterioration in his visual motor speed and integration (digit symbol), nonverbal reasoning (block design), and ability to see part-whole relationships (object assembly) in the performance areas.

When we consider all the areas of impairment, as indicated by relatively low-scaled scores, we must hypothesize the possibility of some type of brain injury or tumor because these impair performance on all the subtests in which the subject has shown evidence of deterioration. With the possibility of a brain tumor, both a medical examination and additional tests are necessary.

In the absence of evidence to the contrary, the clinician would strongly suspect that the subject's shift in grades may be due to a brain injury or tumor. However, the clinician would consider other possibilities as well. Environmental or situational factors could lead to impairment on the various WAIS-R subtests. For example, the subject may have become involved with drugs, so this possibility must be examined. Furthermore, the pathology of schizophrenia may cause similar decrements in performance. Therefore, signs of peculiar behavior or other symptoms of schizophrenia should be ruled out by an interview and perhaps a projective test (see Chapter 16). Ruling out situational, environmental, or schizophrenic factors, the examiner might interview to determine whether the subject has suffered a recent blow to the head. If these possibilities prove to be negative, the subject should be immediately referred for a neurological examination by an appropriate medical specialist.

In considering this illustration, as well as the one that follows, it is important not to lose your perspective. Remember that the validity of pattern analysis is still questionable. Saccuzzo and Lewandowski (1976) found a pattern for acting-out behavior that was later substantiated by Wickham (1978). However, the evidence in support of the validity of most patterns, for reasons that will be

Table 11-4
Scaled Scores for
a Slow Learner

Verbal Scales	Performance Scales
Information: 3	Digit symbol: 12
Comprehension: 7	Picture completion: 11
Arithmetic: 4	Block design: 13
Similarities: 11	Picture arrangement: 10
Digit span: 10	Object assembly: 12
Vocabulary: 8	
Scaled score sum: 43	Scaled score sum: 58
Verbal IQ: 89	Performance IQ: 112
Sum of scaled scores for verbal and performance scales: 101	
Full-scale IQ: 99	

discussed more fully in the pages ahead, is still questionable. Our illustrations are designed to give you a flavor of the approach that is taken by many practicing psychologists. Most real-life examples, however, are nowhere near as clearcut as our hypothetical example.

As you no doubt have observed, the above analysis resulted in several speculations, and the clinician exercised the usual caution in interpreting and using the results. For our next example, we present a pattern very much like the one that Saccuzzo and Lewandowski (1976) and Wickham (1978) found in acting-out delinquents. The figures are based on the WAIS rather than the WAIS-R.

In this example, we have the scaled scores of a 16-year-old girl with chronic school problems. She was identified as a slow learner in the earlier grades, and she reads far below her grade level. Her scores are shown in Table 11-4.

The subject is nearly one standard deviation above the mean in her performance IQ, and all of her subtests in the performance area are at or greater than the mean. Clearly, she is not lacking intellectual potential. Thus, her verbal IQ of 89 is very likely an underestimate of her intellectual capacity. Furthermore, she obtains an above-average score on similarities, a noneducationally related measure of abstract thinking skills. Her major areas of weakness are in the subtests related to academic achievement, information, and arithmetic. In addition, she shows some impairment in her judgment. Her verbal IQ thus appears to be lowered due to her lack of motivation for academic achievement and poor judgment. Her pattern of subtest scores is one typically found in poor readers and delinquents.

IV. *Psychometric Properties of the WAIS-R*

The WAIS-R does well in both reliability and validity. Here is a summary of these qualities.

A. *Reliability*

Reliability coefficients for the WAIS-R have been impressive and attest to the internal and temporal reliability of the verbal, performance, and full-scale IQs. When the split-half method is used for all subtests except digit span[1] and digit symbol,[2] the average coefficients across age levels are .97 for the full-scale IQ and the verbal IQ and .93 for the performance IQ (Wechsler, 1981). Test-retest coefficients reported in the manual are only slightly lower.

The Wechsler (1981) WAIS-R manual reports an overall standard error of measurement of 2.53 for the full-scale IQ, 2.74 for the verbal IQ, and 4.14 for the performance IQ. As you may recall from our discussion of correlation and reliability (see Chapter 4), all tests possess a certain degree of measurement error. The standard error of measurement (SEM) is the standard deviation of the distribution of error scores. Theoretically, an error score is the difference between the score one would obtain by giving the test and the individual's true score given a perfect measuring instrument. In practice, the SEM is based on the reliability coefficient, given by the formula

$$SEM = S\sqrt{1 - r_{xx}}$$

where S is the standard deviation of the test scores and r_{xx} is the reliability coefficient.

In practice, the SEM can be used to form a confidence interval within which an individual's true score is likely to fall. More specifically, we can determine the probability that an individual's true score will fall within a certain range a given percentage of the time. To be roughly at the 68% level, an obtained score must be within the range of one SEM. The 95% confidence interval is approximately two SEMs.

Using this information, we can see that the smaller SEM for the verbal and full-scale IQs means that we can have considerably more confidence that an obtained score represents an individual's true score than we can for the performance IQ. Thus, given a full-scale IQ of 110, we can assume that 95% of the time the subject's true score would fall at ±5.06 (two SEMs), or approximately between 105 and 115. Given a performance IQ of 110, however, the 95% confidence range would be ±8.28, or roughly 102 to 118.

Test-retest reliability coefficients for the 11 subtests have tended to vary widely. For data presented by Wechsler (1981), coefficients for most subtests run in the low .90s or high .80s. However, some of the coefficients are in the .60s. These relatively low coefficients again indicate the potential hazards of pattern analysis. If the individual subtests are not stable, then clearly patterns would also lack stability, thus limiting the potential validity of pattern interpretation.

---

[1] For digit span, digits forward are compared to digits backward.

[2] For digit symbol, a parallel form is used to estimate reliability.

Table 11-5
Correlations of the
WAIS-R with the
WAIS and the
WISC-R*

Scale	N	r_{12}
WAIS	72	
Verbal IQ		.91
Performance IQ		.79
Full-scale IQ		.88
WISC-R	80	
Verbal IQ		.89
Performance IQ		.76
Full-scale IQ		.88

Data from Tables 17 and 18 of the
WAIS-R manual (Wechsler, 1981).
* For groups of individuals tested with
both scales.

Perhaps you can now understand why the validity of pattern analysis is questionable and difficult to document. The dependability of pattern analysis depends on subtest intercorrelation as well as the separate reliabilities of the subtests. As the subtest intercorrelations increase and the reliabilities of individual subtests decrease, pattern analysis becomes increasingly dubious (Saccuzzo et al., 1981).

B. *Validity*

The validity of the WAIS-R rests primarily on studies done with earlier versions of the test, the Wechsler-Bellevue (1939) and WAIS (1955). About 80% of the WAIS-R items come from the WAIS (Wechsler, 1981). In general, the WAIS has been shown to correlate at between .40 and .80 with a host of other measures that purport to measure intelligence.

Table 11-5 shows the correlations between the WAIS-R and the WAIS as well as the Wechsler Intelligence Scale for Children, Revised (WISC-R). Inspection of the table reveals an extremely high degree of shared variability between the WAIS-R and both the WAIS and WISC-R.

In addition to being correlated with other Wechsler scales, the concurrent

Figure 11-7
Idealized factor analysis of the WAIS-R. Verbal IQ consists primarily of information, comprehension, similarities, vocabulary, and arithmetic. Performance IQ consists primarily of the five performance subtests. Memory consists primarily of digit span and arithmetic.

validity of the WAIS-R has been supported by numerous studies that have correlated scores on the WAIS-R with those from other tests of ability (Fowles & Tunick, 1986; Retzlaff, Sligner & Gibertini, 1986), tests of achievement (Ryan & Rosenberg, 1983), and formal education (Matarazzo & Herman, 1984). In general, the correlations range between .43 and .94 (see Sattler, 1988, p. 224), with a median coefficient in the high .60s.

Factor analytic studies have supported the construct validity of Wechsler's intelligence scales. What typically emerges is a general second-order factor corresponding to *g* and two or three group factors corresponding to the verbal IQ, the performance IQ, and memory, sometimes called freedom from distractibility (Cohen, 1957; Silverstein, 1982). (See Figure 11-7.)

V. *Evaluation of the WAIS-R*

The WAIS-R is extensively used as a measure of adult intelligence. It is well constructed and its primary measures, the verbal, performance, and full-scale IQs, are highly reliable. As with the modern Binet, the reliability of the individual subtests makes analysis of subtest patterns dubious, if not hazardous, for the purpose of making decisions about individuals. Yet making such conclusions is commonplace. As we have noted, such analysis may be useful for generating hypotheses, but extreme caution is called for.

The strong correlations between the WAIS-R and WAIS, which was correlated highly with the older Wechsler-Bellevue test, are somewhat of a mixed blessing. Clearly, the WAIS-R is very much the same test as the old Wechsler-Bellevue of 1939, with minor modifications. Thus, the WAIS-R relies on the theories and data of the 1920s and 1930s. It does not incorporate, as attempted by the modern Binet, notions of intellectual functioning in the mushrooming area of cognitive psychology. Moreover, the WAIS-R does not allow for the idea of multiple intelligences, an important concept. According to one modern theory, there are at least seven distinct and independent intelligences—linguistic, body-kinesthetic, spatial, logical-mathematical, musical, intrapersonal, and interpersonal (Gardner, 1983). The view of intelligence reflected in the WAIS-R leaves little room for such ideas.

Another problem with the WAIS-R is its weakness in measuring extreme IQs. The lowest possible IQ one can obtain ranges from 45 to 50, depending on the age range. A 65-year-old who fails every single item would obtain a verbal IQ of 53, a performance IQ of 60, and a full-scale IQ of 50. What is worse, the test manual indicates that scores below 70 reflect "mental retardation," as if mental retardation can be diagnosed solely on the basis of an IQ test, which it should never be.

In evaluating the WAIS-R, one must also be concerned with the issue of bias. Is the WAIS-R fair to racial and cultural minorities? We will consider this question in greater detail when we consider the downward extension of the WAIS-R, the WISC-III.

VI. *Downward Extensions of the WAIS-R: The WISC-III and WPPSI-R*

WAIS - adults

WISC III - 6 - 16/11/30

WPPSI-R - 4 - 6½

Most of the basic ideas of the WAIS-R apply to its downward extension, the WISC-III, which was first published in 1949, revised in 1974, and most recently revised in 1991. The WISC-III measures intelligence from ages 6 through 16 years, 11 months, 30 days. The basic ideas of the WAIS-R also apply to the Wechsler Preschool and Primary Scale of Intelligence, Revised (WPPSI-R). The WPPSI-R, first published in 1967 and revised in 1989, measures intelligence in children from 4 to 6½ years old. Basic ideas that apply to all Wechsler scales and that have already been discussed in the section on the WAIS-R will not be discussed again here, nor will the details previously provided on the WAIS-R. If you understand the WAIS-R, then you should have little difficulty with the WISC-III and WPPSI-R. Therefore, only the major distinguishing features of these Wechsler scales are presented.

A. *The WISC-III*

The Wechsler Intelligence Scale for Children, third edition (WISC-III), is the latest version of Wechsler Intelligence Scale for Children. The original form of the WISC-III is based on Form II of the Wechsler-Bellevue scale. Its purpose was to provide a point scale measure of intelligence for children between the ages of 6 years and 16 years, 11 months. Whereas the WAIS-R contains 11 subtests, all of which are used in the calculation of IQ scores, the WISC-III contains 13 subtests, three of which are supplementary. Within the WISC-III verbal scale are information, comprehension, arithmetic, similarities, and vocabulary subtests. Digit span is a supplementary subtest. Within the WISC-III performance scale are picture completion, picture arrangement, block design, object assembly, and coding (which parallels digit symbol on the WAIS-R) subtests. The supplementary tests are a series of mazes through which the child is asked to traverse with a pencil and a symbol search, which consists of paired groups of symbols. In the symbol search subtest, each pair contains a target group and a search group. The child scans the two groups and indicates whether or not a target symbol appears in the search group. These subtests, with the exception of mazes and symbol search, parallel the corresponding WAIS-R subtests in content and functions measured. Items are arranged in order of difficulty and are grouped by content. (See Figure 11-8.)

One of the major differences between the WAIS-R and WISC-III has to do with termination of a subtest administration. In general, the WISC-III terminates a subtest administration after a fewer number of consecutive errors than does the WAIS-R. This is to prevent younger or duller subjects from experi-

Information (30 questions)

How many legs do you have?
What must you do to make water freeze?
Who discovered the North Pole?
What is the capital of France?

Similarities (17 questions)

In what way are pencil and crayon alike?
In what way are tea and coffee alike?
In what way are inch and mile alike?
In what way are binoculars and microscope alike?

Arithmetic (18 questions)

If I have one piece of candy and get another one, how
  many pieces will I have?
At 12 cents each, how much will 4 bars of soap cost?
If a suit sells for 1/2 of the ticket price, what is the cost of
  a $120 suit?

Vocabulary (32 words)

ball   poem
summer   obstreperous

Comprehension (17 questions)

Why do we wear shoes?
What is the thing to do if you see someone dropping his
  packages?
In what two ways is a lamp better than a candle?
Why are we tried by a jury of our peers?

Digit Span

Digits Forward contains seven series of digits, 3 to 9
  digits in length (Example: 1-8-9).
Digits Backward contains seven series of digits, 2 to 8
  digits in length (Example: 5-8-1-9).

Picture Completion (26 items)

The task is to identify the essential missing part of the
picture.
A picture of a car without a wheel.
A picture of a dog without a leg.
A picture of a telephone without numbers on the dial.
An example of a Picture Completion task is shown below.

Picture Arrangement (12 items)

The task is to arrange a series of pictures into a meaningful sequence.

Block Design (11 items)

The task is to reproduce stimulus designs using four or
nine blocks. An example of a Block Design item is shown
below.

Object Assembly (4 items)

The task is to arrange pieces into a meaningful object. An
example of an Object Assembly item is shown below.

Coding

The task is to copy symbols from a key (see below).

Mazes

The task is to complete a series of mazes.

Note. The questions resemble those that appear on the WISC-R
but are not actually from the test. Chapter 7 describes each subtest in more detail.

Figure 11-8
WISC-III–like items. (*Simulated items similar to those in the Wechsler Intelligence
Scales for Adults and Children. Copyright 1949, 1955, 1974, 1981 and 1989 by The
Psychological Corporation. Reproduced by permission. All rights reserved.*)

encing too many failures and to reduce administration time, which usually takes about an hour.

The verbal scales of the WISC-III. The information subtest of the WISC-III contains items such as "Who was the first president of the United States?" Some items, however, are more difficult, such as "Who was the first person who sailed around the world?" Like its counterpart of the WAIS-R, the WISC-III comprehension subtest puts the subject in a situation or asks a question that requires common sense in order to measure judgment. A WISC-III comprehension item might ask, "What should you do if you were the first person to see a house on fire?" As in the WAIS-R, the early items of the arithmetic subtest are fairly simple. Later items, however, can be difficult even for adults, such as "27 is three-fourths of what number?" As in the WAIS-R, the similarities subtest contains items that require the subject to state the similarity between two objects or things, such as brick and wood. The vocabulary and digit span subtests are identical in format to their counterparts on the WAIS-R.

The performance scales of the WISC-III. As in the verbal subtests, the regular performance subtests of the WISC-III parallel those of the WAIS-R. Indeed, the formats for picture completion, picture arrangement, block design, object assembly, and coding (called digit symbol on the WAIS-R) are nearly identical. The major difference between the WAIS-R and WISC-III on the performance scale is the content, which is geared toward children on the WISC-III. The only WISC-III subtests not included on the WAIS-R are mazes, a supplementary subtest that measures planning ability and perhaps general intelligence, and symbol search, which is also a supplementary subtest.

Standardization of the WISC-III. The WISC-III standardization sample consisted of 2200 children selected to be representative of the 1988 U.S. census. The sample was stratified using age, gender, race (black, Hispanic, white, other), geographic region, parent occupation, and urban–rural residence as variables. It contained 100 boys and 100 girls at each age from 6 through 16 years. (See Figure 11-9.)

[handwritten margin note: Well standardized]

Raw scores and scaled scores. In scoring the WISC-III, scaled scores are calculated from raw scores on the basis of norms at each age level. This procedure differs from that for the WAIS-R, where scaled scores are obtained from a representative sample at only one age level. However, as for the WAIS-R, the mean scaled score is set at 10 and the standard deviation at 3. Scaled scores are summed for verbal, performance, and full-scale IQs. These totals are then compared against a single table of standard scores with a mean of 100 and a standard deviation of 15 for each of the three IQs—verbal, performance, and full scale.

WISC-III™

Characteristics of the Standardization Sample

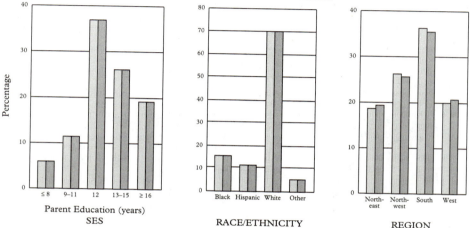

Percentage of the population based on the 1988 U.S. Census.

Percentage in the WISC-III norm sample.

These graphs show demographic characteristics of the WISC-III norm sample compared with those of the U.S. population. The total number sampled was 2,200 children between ages 6 and 16, with equal numbers of males and females.

Parent Education (years)
SES

RACE/ETHNICITY

REGION

Figure 11-9
Characteristics of the WISC-III standardization sample. (*Wechsler Intelligence Scale for Children: Third Edition. Copyright © 1989 by The Psychological Corporation. All rights reserved. Reproduced by permission.*)

Interpretation: Hypothetical case studies. Interpretation of the WISC-III also parallels that of the WAIS-R. Consider the following example. A 7-year-old, white, English-speaking boy who is having school problems obtains the scaled scores shown in Table 11-6. This child showed deficiencies in all areas measured by the WISC-III. In no case did he obtain a scaled score that was as high as even one standard deviation below the mean. This child is consistently impaired in all areas, and so his full-scale IQ of 54, more than two standard deviations below the mean, is clearly indicative of mental retardation. Thus, the WISC-III is consistent with mental retardation. However, additional data (for example, a medical examination and a history of social functioning) would be necessary if the diagnosis of mental retardation is to be made (Malgady et al., 1980).

Consider another example of a 9-year-old, white, English-speaking girl who is having school difficulties (see Table 11-7). Although this child has verbal and full-scale IQs that are both two standard deviations below the mean and thus in the mentally retarded range according to the WISC-III manual, analysis of her profile pattern indicates average or better performance in three areas: information, picture completion, and coding. Her average or better capabilities in these areas would make a diagnosis of mental retardation highly suspect and premature. However, the wide variability in subtests, known as

Table 11-6
Scaled Scores for
a Boy Having
School Problems

Verbal Scales	Performance Scales
Information: 4	Picture completion: 5
Comprehension: 5	Picture arrangement: 2
Arithmetic: 3	Block deisgn: 6
Similarities: 0	Object assembly: 6
Vocabulary: 1	Coding: 4
Scaled score sum: 13	Scaled score sum: 23
Verbal IQ: 53	Performance IQ: 62
Sum of scaled scores for verbal and performance scales: 36	
Full-scale IQ: 54	

subtest scatter, indicates her performance is below what she might have accomplished at some previous time. This lowered performance from previous levels suggests deterioration. Her major areas of weakness in the verbal areas are judgment (comprehension subtest), concentration (arithmetic subtest), and abstract thinking (similarities subtest). Her adequate scores on coding and block design, however, indicate no apparent brain damage or visual motor difficulties. One possible hypothesis in this case is that emotional difficulties are responsible for this child's school problems.

Reliability of the WISC-III. When the WISC-III was revised in 1991, it was intended to maintain the general properties of its predecessors, the most recent being the Wechsler Intelligence Scale for Children-Revised (WISC-R). Indeed, the psychometric properties of the WISC-III are quite similar to those of the WISC-R. Reliability coefficients for the WISC-III, as for the WISC-R, were obtained as for the WAIS-R subtests. Split-half reliabilities for full-scale, verbal, and performance IQs average .96, .95, and .91, respectively; standard errors of measurement average 3.20, 3.53, and 4.54, respectively. Test-retest reliability coefficients are only slightly below those obtained using the split-half method.

Reliability coefficients for individual subtests are somewhat less impressive, with most in the .70s and .80s. As with the Binet scales, reliability coefficients are poorer for the younger groups. Test-retest coefficients tend to run in the high .80s to low .90s for the three IQs.

WISC-III validity. The correlation between the WISC-III and other Wechsler scales is rather good. Because the WISC-III overlaps with both the WAIS-R for 16-year-olds and the downward extension of the WISC-III (the WPPSI-R for 6-year-olds), the WISC-III could be correlated with both the WAIS-R and the WPPSI-R. All coefficients were in the .70s and .80s. The manual also reported correlations with the WISC-III and the Stanford-Binet scale, with the majority of coefficients in the .60s and .70s for individual subtests and in the .80s to low .90s for the three IQs.

Table 11-7
Scaled Scores for
a Girl Having
School Problems

Verbal Scales	Performance Scales
Information: 10	Picture completion: 11
Comprehension: 1	Picture arrangement: 3
Arithmetic: 2	Block deisgn: 9
Similarities: 5	Object assembly: 1
Vocabulary: 8	Coding: 10
Scaled score sum: 26	Scaled score sum: 34
Verbal IQ: 70	Performance IQ: 78
Sum of scaled scores for verbal and performance scales: 60	
Full-scale IQ: 71	

B. *Evaluation of the WISC-III*

The WISC-III shares many of the strengths of the WAIS-R, but it also suffers from the same weaknesses. Prominent among these are its underlying model of intelligence, its poor treatment validity for academically impaired children, and problems of bias toward certain cultural and racial groups. We will touch briefly on each of these problems.

As with the WAIS-R, the model of intelligence of the WISC-III does not reflect recent developments in cognitive science and theories of multiple intelligences. Cognitive science has emphasized analysis in terms of components of information processing (Hunt, 1980) and abilities such as executive processes (Sternberg, 1984), organizing skills (Das, 1987), and metacognition (see Sternberg, 1985; Sternberg & Gardner, 1982). The WISC-III's only attempt to incorporate any of these concepts is in the supplemental symbol search subtest. In fact, the changes that have been made in the various revisions of this test have been disappointingly minimal.

Another problem with the WISC-III is its questionable usefulness for enhancing remedial intervention for children who show specific academic deficiencies. Like the WISC-R, it lacks treatment validity (Witt & Gresham, 1985). Specific deficits on the WISC-III do not necessarily suggest specific treatments. And although the WISC-III predicts school achievement for children regardless of ethnic background, the issue of the clear superiority in IQ scores for Caucasians when compared with African-American and other culturally different groups has not been confronted in the most recent 1991 revision. The result is a selection bias. Black children are overselected for mentally retarded classes and underselected for gifted programs. The issue of test bias is as controversial as it is complex. Because of the selection bias of standardized intelligence tests such as the WISC, standardized tests were banned in California as a means of determining mental retardation and special education placement for African-American children. (For more on test bias, see Chapter 20.)

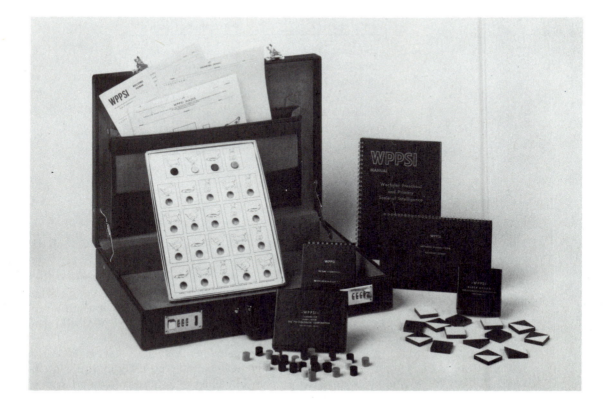

Figure 11-10
Wechsler
Preschool and
Primary Scale of
Intelligence.
(*Courtesy of The
Psychological
Corporation.*)

C. *The Wechsler Preschool and Primary Scale of Intelligence (WPPSI-R)*

In 1967, Wechsler published a scale for use with children 4 to 6½ years of age. The WPPSI was revised in 1985 and became the WPPSI-R. It parallels the WAIS-R and WISC-III in format, in the method of determining reliabilities, and in subtests. Only three unique subtests are included: (1) animal pegs, an optional test that is timed and requires the child to place a colored cylinder into an appropriate hole in front of an animal; (2) geometric design, a perceptual motor task in which the child must select a matching design from four choices or, for the more advanced items, copy a geometric design shown on a printed card; and (3) sentences, a second optional test of immediate recall in which the child is asked to repeat sentences presented orally by the examiner. Reliability coefficients are comparable to those obtained with the other Wechsler scales except for the performance IQ at the 7-year-old level. Validity studies, however, have a rather wide range of correlation coefficients (.07 to .92) reported in the manual for a variety of measures from the Stanford-Binet scale, where the correlations are at the upper level, to motor scales, where the correlations are low.

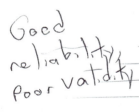

Good reliability, poor validity [handwritten annotation]

Most of the support for the WPPSI-R is based on earlier studies with the WPPSI. The manual reports coefficients of .82, .85, and .87 for the performance, verbal, and full-scale IQs, respectively, when the WPPSI and WPPSI-R are correlated. Factor analyses of the WPPSI-R subtests reported in the manual have resulted in a two-factor solution, supporting an interpretation in terms of separate performance and verbal abilities (Webster, 1989). Independent analyses have confirmed and supported the two-factor solution for the WPPSI-R (Gyurke, Stone & Beyer, 1990; LoBello & Gulgoz, 1991).

A major advantage of the WPPSI-R over many other tests of very young children is that it measures the same abilities that will be appraised later on, assuming, of course, that the WISC-III and WAIS-R will be used at the later date. Typically, as we will see in Chapter 12 in which infant intelligence is discussed, there is a low correlation between tests given at very young ages and those given to the same children at school age. This low correlation can be attributed, in large part, to the fact that the tests used at earlier ages do not measure the same functions as those emphasized later on.

The WPPSI-R was standardized on a stratified sample, which means that individuals were selected in proportion to their numbers in the population based on the 1986 census using the following variables: age, gender, geographic region, urban–rural, color (white/nonwhite), and parent's occupation. A total of 1700 children were included in the standardization sample. Overall, the WPPSI-R is a very well-constructed test. Its strengths and weaknesses are similar to those we have discussed for the WAIS-R and WISC-III.

Summary

Motivation for the development of the Wechsler scales began with the search for a more appropriate measure of adult intelligence than that provided by the 1937 Binet scale. The first product of this effort was the Wechsler-Bellevue scale.

In a *point scale,* a specific number of credits or points is assigned to each item. A *performance scale* measures nonlanguage intelligence, as opposed to a *verbal scale,* which measures language/verbal intelligence. On a performance scale, the subject is required to do something other than answer questions.

The six verbal subtests of the WAIS-R and the functions they purportedly measure are as follows:

1. Information: range of knowledge
2. Comprehension: judgment
3. Arithmetic: concentration
4. Similarities: abstract thinking
5. Digit span: immediate memory, anxiety
6. Vocabulary: vocabulary level

The five performance subtests of the WAIS-R and the functions they purportedly measure are as follows:

1. Digit symbol: visual-motor functioning
2. Picture completion: alertness to details
3. Picture arrangement: planning ability
4. Block design: nonverbal reasoning
5. Object assembly: analysis of part–whole relationships

The WAIS-R uses a declining age standard. This means that elderly subjects must obtain fewer correct responses in order to achieve the same IQs as young adults. The declining age standard resulted from the cross-sectional nature of the standardization sample. This sample, which involved testing different subjects of differing ages at about the same time, suggested that intelligence declined with age. However, longitudinal studies, which test the same subjects at varying intervals across the life span, have indicated that intelligence remains relatively stable over the life span. The implication is that the norms must be periodically revised, as they were in 1981 with the WAIS-R.

Three IQ scores can be obtained from the WAIS-R: verbal IQ, performance IQ, and full-scale IQ. The verbal and performance IQs are obtained by converting the raw score of each subtest to a standard score of 10 with a standard deviation of 3. The *scaled scores* are then summed separately for the verbal and performance IQs. Each of the IQs can be determined from a table, which converts the summed scaled scores to a standard score with a mean of 100 and a standard deviation of 15. To obtain the full-scale IQ, the scaled scores for the verbal and performance IQs are summed. This sum is again compared to a table of norms, which converts it to a standard score (mean = 100; SD = 15).

The reliability coefficients of the WAIS-R are excellent for verbal, performance, and full-scale IQs, in terms of both temporal stability and internal consistency. Reliabilities for the individual subtests, however, vary widely.

Evidence for the validity of the WAIS-R comes from a variety of sources. The WAIS-R correlates well with other tests purporting to measure intelligence. Factor analytic studies also support the validity of the WAIS-R.

Among the major advantages of the WAIS-R are that it (1) is appropriate for adults, (2) uses deviation IQs, (3) has strong evidence of reliability and validity, (4) uses a point scale, (5) includes a performance scale, and (6) offers the possibility of pattern analysis.

Among the disadvantages of the WAIS-R are that (1) it has poor reliability for the individual subtests, (2) it is a poor measure of extreme (high and low) levels of intelligence, and (3) it does not take into account recent empirical and theoretical advances, especially those in cognitive science.

The WISC-III is a downward extension of the WAIS-R for measuring children's intelligence. First published in 1949, the WISC was revised in 1974. The last revision, the WISC-III, was done in 1991.

The WPPSI-R is a downward extension of the WISC-III for measuring intelligence in very young children (4 to 6½ years). It was published in 1967 and revised in 1989.

Chapter 12

Other Individual Tests of Ability

Learning Objectives

When you have completed this chapter, you should be able to:

- Identify the advantages and disadvantages of the alternative individual ability tests compared to the Binet and Wechsler scales.

- List six differences among the alternative individual ability tests.

- Discuss the strengths and weaknesses of the Bayley Scales of Infant Development compared to other measures of infant intelligence.

- Identify some of the purposes of the Columbia Mental Maturity Scale.

- Explain the major theory behind tests of learning disability.

- Explain the main idea behind testing for brain damage.

- List three possible reasons for errors on the Bender Visual Motor Gestalt Test.

- Describe the general reaction among reviewers to the Torrance Tests of Creative Thinking.

- Identify a major problem with the Wide Range Achievement Test, revised.

For assessing general intelligence in relatively normal individuals, the Binet and Wechsler scales are exceptionally good instruments. As we have noted, however, both scales have serious limitations. For instance, the standardization samples do not include individuals with sensory, physical, or language handicaps. How, then, can we fairly evaluate the performance on the Binet scale of someone who has been blind for life? What about individuals who are unable to speak? Clearly, there are numerous instances where a score on the major scales would be either impossible to obtain or seriously biased against the individual. Thus, a number of individual tests have been created to meet special problems, measure specific abilities, or address the specific limitations of the Binet and Wechsler scales.

I. *General Features of Alternative Individual Ability Tests*

Before beginning our discussion of specific tests, some general comments are in order. As you will see, there is quite an array of individual ability tests; however, most were designed primarily to provide an alternative to the Binet and Wechsler scales. It is instructive to compare the general features of the alternative individual tests with those of the Binet and Wechsler scales.

A. *Alternative Individual Ability Tests Compared with the Binet and Wechsler Scales*

Recalling the information in Chapters 10 and 11 on the Binet and Wechsler scales, you may find it instructive to consider individual ability tests, particularly individual intelligence tests, as they compare with these two important scales. Although most individual intelligence tests other than the Binet and Wechsler scales are newer and less well established than the two major scales, these factors alone do not explain why no other individual intelligence test is used as much as these two major scales (Lubin, Wallis & Paine, 1971; Lubin et al., 1985). Despite the limitations of the Binet and Wechsler scales, none of the alternatives is clearly superior from a psychometric standpoint. Some of the alternative individual intelligence tests are weaker in terms of the representativeness or quality of the standardization sample. Some are less stable, and most are more limited in their documented validity. Some have inadequacies in the test manual, such as unclear or poorly standardized administration instructions, and others provide insufficient information about psychometric adequacy, appropriate uses, and limitations. Some of the alternatives compare poorly on all counts. Except for their advantages for specific purposes, perhaps none of the alternatives can be considered better than the two major scales when all relevant factors are considered.

Though usually weaker in psychometric properties, many of the alternatives to the major scales are not as reliant on a verbal response as are the Binet and Wechsler verbal scales. Many require the subject only to point or to make any response indicating "yes" or "no" and thus are not so dependent on the complex integration of visual and motor functioning. Like the Wechsler scales, most of the alternatives contain a performance scale or subscale. Indeed, it was the dearth of performance tasks in the Binet scale that helped to stimulate the development of many alternative individual tests of ability.

In providing a performance component (many alternatives are exclusively performance scales), alternatives to the Binet scale, and even to the Wechsler in some cases, have particular relevance for special populations. In many respects, the alternatives to the major intelligence scales were developed to fill in gaps in the applicability of the major scales. Some were designed for special

Table 12-1

Comparison of
General Features
of Alternatives
with the Wechsler
and Binet Scales

Disadvantages of Alternatives

 Weaker standardization sample

 Less stable

 Less validity documentation

 Limitations in test manual

 Not so psychometrically sound

 IQ scores *not* interchangeable with Binet or Wechsler

Advantages of Alternatives

 Can be used for specific populations and special purposes

  Sensory limitations

  Physical limitations

  Language limitations

  Culturally deprived

  Foreign born

  Non-English speaking

 Not so reliant on verbal responses

 Not so dependent on complex visual-motor integration

 Useful for screening, supplement, and reevaluations

 Can be administered nonverbally

 Less variability due to scholastic achievement

populations, such as individuals with sensory limitations (for example, the deaf) or physical limitations (for example, the paralyzed or partially paralyzed). Others were designed to evaluate those with language limitations, such as the culturally deprived, certain brain-damaged individuals, and foreign-born or non-English-speaking individuals. Still others were designed to assess learning disabilities.

Because the tests were designed for special populations or purposes, the existence of alternatives is justifiable. However, their specificity often limits the range of functions or capabilities that they can measure. Thus, the greater specificity of some alternatives may be considered a weakness as well as a strength. Although the alternatives may be much more suitable for special populations than are the major scales, an IQ score based on one of the alternatives, with rare exceptions, cannot be used interchangeably with a score from one of the major scales. The alternatives are generally most appropriate when used for their own unique purposes. In addition, the alternatives are often useful as a supplement for results obtained with one of the major scales, for screening purposes, for follow-up or reevaluations, or when insufficient time is available to administer one of the major scales.

Because they are designed for special populations, some alternatives can be administered totally without verbal instructions (for example, through panto-mime or chalkboard instructions). A few of the alternatives can be administered and scored without a single word being spoken. Furthermore, most are less related to reading ability than is the Binet scale, and a few are almost totally independent of reading ability. As a consequence, the scores from many alternatives contain less variability due to scholastic achievement than either the Binet or the Wechsler scale, both of which correlate strongly with scholastic achievement. See Table 12-1 for a summary of alternative tests versus the major scales.

B. *Alternatives Compared with Each Other*

To construct and publish a useful test, it is necessary to develop a better (for example, a more psychometrically sound) method than is currently available. One may develop a test to measure some factor not being tapped by any existing measure or provide a test for a particular group for which existing procedures have proved to be inadequate. If there are no specific advantages in a new test, most examiners would probably stay with the more established test (see Hooper, Conner & Umansky, 1986). This is true even if they are given a choice between a more established test in which they have experience and an equally sound new test for the same purpose. Therefore, most alternatives tend to differ from each other in some important way. Alternatives to the major scales that do no more than attempt to measure abilities in the same way, only better, have met with little success.

In comparing individual intelligence tests other than the Binet and Wechsler scales, we find that some are restricted to very young children, others are for older children and adolescents, and still others are for both children and adults. Thus, one difference among the alternatives to the major scales is the targeted age range. A second important difference concerns what is measured. Some of the alternatives attempt to measure language or vocabulary skills through nonverbal techniques, some purport to measure nonverbal or nonlanguage intelligence, and others are most strongly related to perceptual-motor skills. Alternatives also differ in the type of score that results. Some produce only a single score as in the older Binet scales. Others, however, produce several scores, as in the Wechsler scales. Another difference among the alternatives is the type of response required of subjects. As previously indicated, whereas some present the items in a multiple-choice format, requiring that the subject choose or point to a correct alternative, others simply require the subject to indicate "yes" or "no" by whatever means possible.

There are still other important differences among the alternative individual tests of human ability. Some require simple motor skills, whereas others demand more complex motor behavior. A few sample a wide range of abilities; most are quite narrow in the range of abilities sampled. Still another difference concerns the target population (for example, the deaf, blind, physically handicapped, learning disabled, language impaired, and foreign-born). Furthermore, some provide timed tasks, whereas others do not. Some claim to have

Table 12-2
Summary of
Differences
Among Individual
Ability Tests
Other Than the
Binet and
Wechsler Scales

Difference	Definition or Example
Age range	Different tests are designed for specific age groups
What is measured	Verbal intelligence, nonverbal intelligence, and so on
Type of score	Single score versus multiple scores
Type of skill required	Simple motor, complex motor, and so on
Range of abilities sampled	Single specific ability versus a wide range of abilities
Target population	Deaf, blind, learning disabled, and so on
Timing	Some are timed; others are not
Personality versus ability	Some claim to have relevance for personality and clinical diagnoses as well as ability
Examiner skill and experience	Some require far less examiner skill and experience to administer and interpret than others

significance for personality and clinical diagnoses; others are exclusively related to an ability.

Another difference is the amount of examiner skill and experience necessary for administration. Whereas some tests require as much skill and experience as do the Binet or Wechsler scales, others require only minimal examiner skill and could probably be administered by a trained paraprofessional under the supervision of an experienced professional. To facilitate memory and to avoid confusing the various tests in this chapter, you are advised to compare and contrast the various procedures to the Binet and Wechsler scales and to each other in terms of the major properties of tests. Table 12-2 summarizes the major distinguishing features of the alternatives.

II. *Specific Alternative Individual Ability Tests*

The earliest individual ability tests were typically designed for specific purposes or populations. One of the first, the Seguin Form Board Test (Seguin, 1866), actually preceded the Binet. Seguin's test was of the performance variety and produced only a single score. It consisted of a simple form board with objects of various shapes placed in appropriately shaped holes (such as squares or circles). The Seguin Form Board Test was used primarily to evaluate mentally retarded adults and emphasized speed of performance. A version of the Seguin Form Board Test is still available. Quite a while after the development of the Seguin test, the Healy-Fernald Test (1911) was developed as an exclusively nonverbal test for adolescent delinquents. Although it produced only a single score, the Healy-Fernald test provided several types of tasks, rather than just one as in the Seguin Form Board task, and there was less emphasis on speed. Then H. A. Knox (1914) developed a battery of performance tests for non-English-speaking adult immigrants to the United States. The test was one of the first that could be administered without language. Speed was not emphasized.

In sum, early individual ability tests other than the Binet scale were designed for specific populations, produced a single score, had nonverbal performance scales, and gradually decreased the emphasis on speed from the earliest to the more recent tests. These early procedures demonstrated the feasibility of constructing individual nonverbal performance tests that could provide an alternative to the verbally dependent Binet scale, could be administered without verbal instructions, and could be used with children as well as adults.

A. *Infant Scales*

An important category of alternative individual tests of ability attempts to measure intelligence in infants and young children. Four such tests are discussed here.

Brazelton Neonatal Assessment Scale (BNAS). The BNAS is an individual test for newborn infants between 3 days and 4 weeks of age (Brazelton, 1973, 1984). It purportedly provides an index of a newborn's competence. Developed by a Harvard pediatrician, the Brazelton scale produces 47 scores, 27 behavioral items and 20 elicited responses (Buros, 1978). These scores are obtained in a variety of areas, including neurological, social, and behavioral aspects of a newborn infant's functioning. Factors such as reflexes, responses to stress, startle reactions, cuddliness, motor maturity, ability to habituate to sensory stimuli, and hand-mouth coordination are all assessed. Reviews of the Brazelton scale have been favorable. A. M. Sostek (1978, p. 208) stated that the Brazelton has "the greatest breadth of the available neonatal examinations," and an earlier review described it as "rigorous" (Wolkind, 1974).

The Brazelton scale has found wide use as a research tool and as a diagnostic tool for special purposes (Beal, 1991). The scale has been used for such purposes as assessing the characteristics of drug-addicted neonates (Strauss et al., 1975) and evaluating the effects of low birth weight on premature infants (Als et al., 1976). It has been used to study the effects of cocaine use in pregnancy (Chasnoff, Burns & Burns, 1987), prenatal alcohol exposure (Coles, Smith & Falek, 1987), and environmental agents (Tronic, 1987). Researchers have also used the scale to study parent–infant attachment (Beal, 1991) and high-risk neonates (Emory, Tynan & Dave, 1989). Reviews of the relevant literature have been highly enthusiastic (Als, 1984; Als et al., 1979).

Despite the enthusiasm for the scale, it has a number of significant drawbacks. No norms are available. Thus, although examiners and researchers can state that one infant scored higher than another in a particular area, there is no standard sample against which to compare test results. In addition, more re-

Figure 12-1
Schematic
summary of the
Brazelton
Neonatal
Assessment Scale.

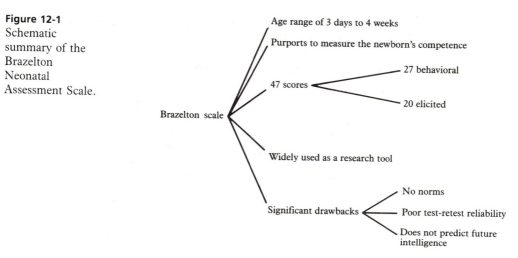

search is needed concerning the meaning and implication of scores (see Beal, 1991). The scale purportedly aids in assessing the infant's role in the mother–infant social relationship, and, presumably, high scores are associated with high levels of intelligence. Like most infant intelligence measures, however, the Brazelton scale has poorly documented predictive and construct validity. The scale has not been shown to be of value in predicting later intelligence (Tronick & Brazelton, 1975). Furthermore, despite relatively good interrater reliability for trained examiners, with coefficients ranging from .85 to .90 (Sostek, 1978), the test-retest reliability (that is, reliability over time) leaves much to be desired. As for all measures of intelligence prior to age 8, when development is rapid and uneven, test-retest reliability coefficients for the Brazelton scale are typically poor and unstable. See Figure 12-1.

In conclusion, although the Brazelton scale may have considerable merit as a research tool, as an individual test of infant intelligence it leaves much to be desired. Its lack of norms is a serious shortcoming, and its failure to predict future intelligence leaves us wondering what the scale is really measuring. In fairness to the Brazelton, the scale is extremely well constructed. Moreover, as we will see, all infant ability tests based on sensorimotor functioning have proven ineffective in predicting later intelligence except in the lowest ranges (Fagan, 1985; McCall, Hogarty & Hurlburt, 1972).

Gesell Developmental Schedules (GDS). The Gesell Developmental Schedules—also known as the Gesell Maturity Scale, the Gesell Norms of Development, and the Yale Tests of Child Development (see Buros, 1974)—are one of the oldest and most established infant intelligence measures. First published in 1925 (Gesell, 1925), the Gesell scale has been subjected to extensive research and refinement (Williamson et al., 1990). One of the leading infant intelligence measures from the 1930s through the 1960s, the Gesell scale continues to be used by those interested in assessing infant intelligence (Bernheimer & Keogh, 1988; Hooper, Conner & Umansky, 1986). However, as we will see, the Gesell scale suffers from a number of psychometric weaknesses.

The Gesell Developmental Schedules purport to provide an appraisal of the developmental status of individuals from $2\frac{1}{2}$ to 6 years of age. In the most recent version (Knobloch & Pasamanick, 1974), behavior is divided into five general areas: gross motor, fine motor, adaptive, language, and personal-social. Development is examined in each of the five areas at ages 4, 16, 28, and 40 weeks and at 12, 18, 24, 36, 48, and 60 months.

One reason for the popularity of the Gesell scale is that its use is based on normative data from a carefully conducted longitudinal study of early human development (see Gesell et al., 1940). The idea behind procedures that are based on developmental data is that human development unfolds in stages or in sequences over time. Gesell and colleagues obtained normative data concerning these various stages in the maturational process. With data on when specific developmental milestones manifest themselves (for example, when the infant first rolls from back to stomach unassisted, when the child first utters words, or when the child learns to walk), it becomes possible to compare the rate of development of any infant or young child to established norms. If the individual shows behavior or responses associated with a more mature level of development than typically found for his or her chronological age, then it can be assumed that the child is ahead in development compared with others of the same age. Accelerated development can be related to high intelligence.

In the Gesell scale, an individual's **developmental quotient** (DQ) is determined according to a test score, which is evaluated by assessing the presence or absence of behavior associated with maturation. The DQ score concept parallels the mental age (MA) concept. Thus, the Gesell produces an intelligence quotient (IQ) score similar to that of the Binet scale. The formula for IQ in the Gesell scale is as follows:

$$IQ = \frac{\text{developmental quotient}}{\text{chronological age}} \times 100$$

or more simply,

$$IQ = \frac{DQ}{CA} \times 100$$

Normative data for the Gesell scale were obtained from a sample of 107 American-born Caucasian infants (49 boys, 58 girls) whose parents were of northern European descent and who were judged to be normal. Any student who has studied this text will readily and immediately recognize the lack of representativeness of this sample. However, these infants were carefully studied. Beginning at 4 weeks of age, they were examined at two-week intervals until the 8th week of life. From the 8th through the 56th weeks, they were examined at four-week intervals (12th, 16th, 20th, and so on). The sample was examined again at $1\frac{1}{2}$ and 2 years of age and also at yearly intervals between ages 2 and 6.

A. Gesell and colleagues (see, for example, Gesell & Amatruda, 1947) believed the Gesell scale could be used for a wide variety of purposes in addition to estimating intelligence from patterns and rates of development. They believed the scale could be used for assessing normal, subnormal, and superior infants and young children. The scale was also thought to have value in assessing developmental deviations, neurological impairment, personality organization, and emotional or temperamental characteristics (Gesell & Amatruda, 1941).

Despite years of extensive use and some updating, the Gesell scale continues to fall short of acceptable psychometric standards. The standardization sample is inadequate. Despite efforts to add to the original 107 subjects (Knobloch & Pasamanick, 1974), the sample consists predominantly of individuals of northern European descent living in the northeastern part of the United States. The manual and book that come with the test offer no evidence of reliability or validity. The test directions are vague, and there are questions concerning the scoring procedures (Naglieri, 1985). In support of the validity of the Gesell, a study of 61 very low-birth-weight infants with no obvious cognitive, motor, or sensory defects were compared to a control group of normal-birth-weight infants (Williamson et al., 1990). The low-birth-weight babies had lower scores across all major areas as measured by the Gesell scale. Moreover, the Gesell scale apparently picked up deficits not found by conventional means. Although the Gesell does not predict later intelligence except at the low end of scores, scores at these lower ends are highly reliable (Bernheimer & Keogh, 1988). See Figure 12-2.

In conclusion, Gesell's concept of empirically determining developmental sequence norms in evaluating infants and young children is logical and promising. When first constructed, the Gesell scale was nothing short of a breakthrough in infant ability testing. The use of a nonrepresentative sample in its initial development, furthermore, was not at all unusual. However, since its early construction, little has been done to improve the Gesell scale according to today's more rigorous standards for a standardization sample. Although the Gesell scale may be of value to the highly trained and experienced examiner in providing a standard format for observing behavior, the available empirical data indicate that it is not highly accurate for predictive purposes except at the low ranges. The scale does appear to be of value, however, in uncovering subtle deficits in infants.

Bayley Scales of Infant Development (BSID). As with many infant tests, the underlying idea of the Bayley Scales of Infant Development is the same as that for the pioneer in infant testing, the Gesell scale. Like the Gesell, the Bayley bases its assessments on normative maturational developmental data. Published only four years before the Brazelton scale, the Bayley scale was the

Figure 12-2
Schematic
summary of the
Gesell
Developmental
Schedules.

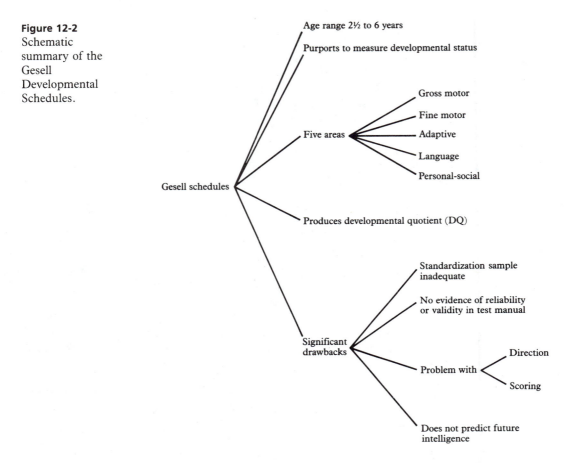

product of 40 years of study (Bayley, 1969). It was designed for infants between 2 and 30 months of age; it produces two main scores (mental and motor) and 30 ratings of behavior. To assess mental functions, the Bayley scale uses measures such as the infant's response to a bell, the ability to follow an object with the eyes, and, in older infants, the ability to follow oral instructions. The heart of the Bayley scale is the motor scale because a major underlying assumption is that later mental functions are dependent on motor development (Bayley, 1969).

Unlike the Gesell and Brazelton scales, the standardization of the Bayley scale is excellent. With a normative sample of 1262 infants between 2 and 30 months of age divided into subgroups by gender, race, socioeconomic status, rural versus urban area, and geographic region according to the 1960 census, the Bayley scale is the best standardized test of its kind available to date.

Like the Stanford-Binet scale, raw scores on the Bayley scale are converted to standard scores with a mean of 100 and a standard deviation of 16. Given the

Figure 12-3
Bayley Scales of
Infant
Development.
(*Courtesy of The
Psychological
Corporation.*)

care and effort that Bayley put into its development, the positive reviews of the Bayley scale (for example, by Damarin, 1978a) comes as no surprise. In addition to its exemplary standardization, the median split-half reliability coefficients are about .88 for the mental scale and .84 for the motor scale, with ranges from the low .80s to low .90s for the mental scales and ranges from the high .60s to low .90s for the motor scales (Bayley, 1969).

Research interest in the Bayley scale continues to grow (Hooper, Conner & Umansky, 1986; van Baar, 1990). Nevertheless, more validity studies are needed. In terms of construct validity, Bayley (1969) reported that the performance scale increases with increasing chronological age. She also reported correlations clustering in the high .40s and high .50s for the mental scale and Stanford-Binet IQs for preschoolers at three age levels: 24, 27, and 30 months. However, the manual presents no data on either the validity of the motor scale or the predictive validity of the mental scale. Moreover, the preponderance of available research casts considerable doubt on Bayley's (1969) basic assumption concerning the relationship between motor behavior and later mental functions. In fact, there is no relationship between the two prior to 18 months (Fagan, 1985; Hooper, Conner & Umansky, 1986). After 18 months of age, there is a small, statistically significant relationship that increases gradually at the older age ranges (McCall, 1979). In favor of the Bayley scale, it does predict mental retardation (Self & Horowitz, 1979). Infants who score two standard deviations below the mean on the Bayley have a high probability of testing in

Figure 12-4
Schematic
summary of the
Bayley Scales of
Infant
Development.

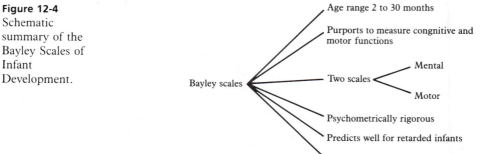

the retarded ranges later in life (Ames, 1967; Simon & Bass, 1956). However, for infants who score within the normal ranges, there is, as mentioned above, no more than low correlation (roughly .10 to .50) between Bayley's scores and those obtained from standard intelligence tests (such as the WISC-R and Binet scale) if the individual is retested during childhood (Bayley, 1949; Hindley, 1965; McCall, 1979). Like the Brazelton, the Bayley is widely used in research (Atkinson, 1990a; Sloman, Bellinger & Krentzel, 1990). A major research use is to assess infants of drug-using mothers (e.g., van Baar, 1990) and other at-risk infants (Wasik et al., 1990). See Figure 12-4.

In conclusion, the Bayley is the most psychometrically sound test of its kind (Self & Horowitz, 1979). The question is whether tests of this type can predict future intelligence. The available research indicates that although the Bayley may be a good predictor for handicapped populations, it does not predict well within the normal ranges.

Cattell Infant Intelligence Scale (CIIS). Another noteworthy infant ability test is the Cattell Infant Intelligence Scale (CIIS), which is also based on normative developmental data. Designed as a downward extension of the Stanford-Binet scale for infants and preschoolers between 2 and 30 months of age, the Cattell scale purports to measure intelligence in infants and young children (Cattell, 1940). Patterned after the 1937 Binet in an age scale format, the Cattell scale contains five test items for each month of age between 2 and 12 months and five items for each two-month interval between 12 and 36 months of age. The items are similar to those on other infant tests such as the Gesell scale. Tasks for infants include attending to a voice and following objects with the eyes. Tasks for young children involve form board procedures and the manipulation of common objects. The ability to follow oral instructions becomes an increasingly important factor with increasing age.

The Cattell Infant Intelligence Scale, which was revised in 1960, uses the Binet scale administration and scoring procedures. If a young child passes an item at the 30-month level, the examiner is instructed to immediately begin at Level III of the Stanford-Binet scale. However, scores are expressed in items of mental age (MA) and intelligence quotient (IQ) rather than in terms of deviation IQs as in the modern Stanford-Binet scale.

For examiners who require a Gesell-type developmental infant test with a standardization that is more adequate than the Gesell scale, the Cattell Infant Intelligence Scale is among the most popular options (Damarin, 1978b; Hooper, Conner & Umansky, 1986). In fact, in his review of the Cattell scale, Damarin found little difference between the types of tasks used in the Bayley scale and those in the Cattell scale. However, the Cattell scale is obviously the older scale; it was copyrighted nearly three decades before the Bayley scale. Unfortunately, being an older, more established instrument is no advantage for the Cattell Infant Intelligence Scale. Normative data for the Cattell scale compare unfavorably with those of the Bayley scale in several respects. In addition to being outdated and more than four times smaller, the Cattell scale sample is based primarily on children of parents from the lower and middle classes and therefore is not representative of the general population.

Because its normative data are considerably weaker than those of the Bayley scale, it seems appropriate to ask whether the Cattell Infant Intelligence Scale has any advantages over its more recent competitor, the Bayley scale. In answering this question, we find that evidence in support of the reliability and validity of the two instruments is similar. If time is limited, the Cattell scale may be preferable because it takes only about half as long to administer. However, it produces only a single score rather than the two scores and 30 observations of the Bayley scale. Thus, its shorter administration time is balanced by more limited results. Furthermore, as a downward extension of the Stanford-Binet scale, the Cattell scale seems to be in need of updating in that the former no longer uses the intelligence quotient for calculating scores. Thus, IQ scores from the Cattell scale may not be comparable to deviation IQs on the Binet scale. Moreover, the modern Binet scale is drastically different from the form on which the Cattell is based. In one of the few recently published studies involving the Cattell scale compared to the Bayley, scores derived from the Bayley were superior to those obtained from the Cattell in predicting Stanford-Binet IQs (Atkinson, 1990b). See Figure 12-5.

In sum, the Cattell scale has remained relatively unchanged for more than 45 years. From a psychometric standpoint, it is unsatisfactory. Reliability coefficients vary widely, with many being less than acceptable (see Hooper, Conner & Umansky, 1986). Moreover, it is unclear what the scale measures; it does not predict future intelligence for infants in the normal ranges.

See Table 12-3 for a summary of the properties of infant scales.

Recent developments in infant intelligence testing. Recent efforts to evaluate infant intelligence have attempted to look beyond indices of sensorimotor development (Bendell-Estroff et al., 1989). J. F. Fagan (1985), for example, has cogently argued for attempting to evaluate skills such as memory and abstraction, since these are skills on which later intelligence will be evaluated. The work of Fagan and colleagues has shown that such skills can be evaluated as

Figure 12-5
Schematic
summary of the
Cattell Infant
Intelligence Scale.

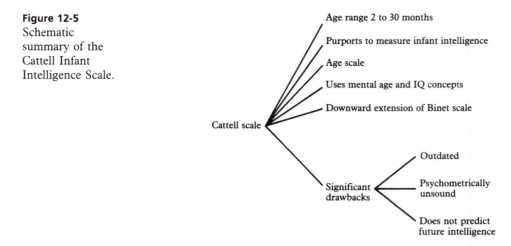

early as the first day of life because from birth infants demonstrate memory skills (for instance, they are able to recognize which of two targets they have seen before). Fagan's approach, which stems from his work in cognitive science, appears to hold the best promise as of this writing for developing procedures that some day will be able to predict future intelligence from infant behavior.

In support of Fagan, researchers have found that measures of visual recognition memory are predictive of IQ in infants. In one study (Bendell-Estroff et al., 1989), a measure of visual recognition memory taken at 3 months of age predicted later IQ, whereas the Bayley scale, taken on the same infants, did not. The future of infant testing appears to be in the developing cognitive sciences.

B. *Major Tests for Young Children*

In this section we discuss two major individual tests that have been specifically developed to evaluate intelligence in young children: the McCarthy Scales of Children's Abilities (MSCA) and the Kaufman Assessment Battery for Children (K-ABC).

McCarthy Scales of Children's Abilities (MSCA). A product of the early 1970s, the McCarthy Scales of Children's Abilities (MSCA) measure ability in children between $2\frac{1}{2}$ and $8\frac{1}{2}$ years old. It picks up just about where the Bayley scale leaves off. Overall, the McCarthy scale is a carefully constructed individual test of human ability. In fact, were it not for its relatively meager validity data, the McCarthy scale might well have reached the status of the Wechsler scale (WPPSI-R), which overlaps with the McCarthy scale's age range. Indeed, the

Table 12-3
Summary of
Infant Scales

Scale	Age Range	Standardization Sample	Psychometric Properties
Brazelton	3 days–4 weeks	None	Good interrater reliability, poor test-retest reliability
Gesell	2½–6 years	107 Caucasians	Little evidence, some support for construct validity
Bayley	2–30 months	1262 infants	Very good split-half reliability
Cattell	2–30 months	285 infants	Little evidence, some support for construct validity

General: For children younger than 18 months, these measures do not correlate significantly with IQ later in life. After 18 months, there are significant but small and clinically not useful correlations. Correlations tend to increase with the age of the infant at the time of testing.

Major alternative: Tests of memory, particularly visual memory and abstraction. Such tests do correlate with IQs in later life, even for infants tested in the first several days after birth.

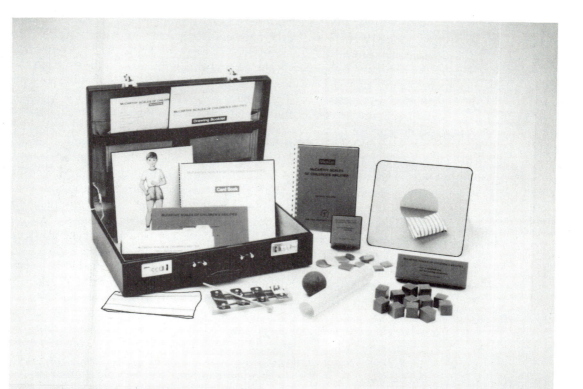

Figure 12-6
McCarthy Scales of Children's Abilities. (*Courtesy of The Psychological Corporation.*)

McCarthy scale seems to offer some advantages over the WPPSI-R and even the Binet scale for the $2\frac{1}{2}$–$8\frac{1}{2}$ year age range. Unfortunately, because of McCarthy's death (she died before the test was even published), the task of strengthening the McCarthy scale falls to interested researchers.

On the positive side, the McCarthy scale produces a pattern of scores as well as a variety of composite scores. Its battery of 18 tests samples a wide variety of functions long held to be related to human intelligence. Of the 18 scales, 15 are combined into a composite score known as the **general cognitive index** (GCI), a standard score with a mean of 100 and a standard deviation of 16. Presumably, the index reflects how well the child has integrated prior learning experiences and adapted them to the demands of the scales. It is not unreasonable to assume that McCarthy believed that the general cognitive index reflected intelligence and that her definition of intelligence must have included something like the ability to integrate past learning and adapt it to the solution of new problems. Sattler (1978), for example, argued that the definition of McCarthy's general cognitive index is similar to definitions of the intelligence quotient (IQ) and most likely was meant as a substitute for the IQ concept.

The 15 tests that make up the general cognitive index are divided into three scales: verbal (five tests), perceptual-performance (seven tests), and quantitative (three tests). Two additional scales can be derived by combining the three tests not included in the general cognitive index with two from the perceptual-performance scale to produce a motor scale. Combining all four memory-related tests from the general cognitive index produces a memory scale. In all, the McCarthy scale contains six overlapping scales, including the general cognitive index. (See Figure 12-7.)

The psychometric properties of the McCarthy scale are relatively good. Although the six scales were grouped by McCarthy on the basis of her experience and knowledge with the aim of obtaining a set of scales with diagnostic potential (that is, the scales were grouped by nonempirical methods), factor analytic studies have tended to produce strong support for her groupings. A factor analysis of the standardization data by A. S. Kaufman (1975a), for example, resulted in four factors roughly corresponding to the general cognitive index, verbal, memory, and motor scales.

The standardization sample, though somewhat dated, meets modern standards of rigor. The 1032 children in this sample were stratified along lines of race, geographic region, father's occupation, and urban–rural residence according to the 1970 U.S. census. Boys and girls were evenly distributed, and at least 100 children were included in each of the age groupings, which consisted of ten separate groupings for each half-year interval from $2\frac{1}{2}$ through $8\frac{1}{2}$.

Raw scores for each of the 18 tests are weighted by a factor of .5, 1, or 2 and then summed in the appropriate combinations to yield composite raw scores for each of the six scales except the general cognitive index. The composite raw score for the index is obtained from the composite scores on the verbal, perceptual-performance, and quantitative scales. These raw scores are

Figure 12-7
Schematic
overview of the
general cognitive
index of the
McCarthy scales.

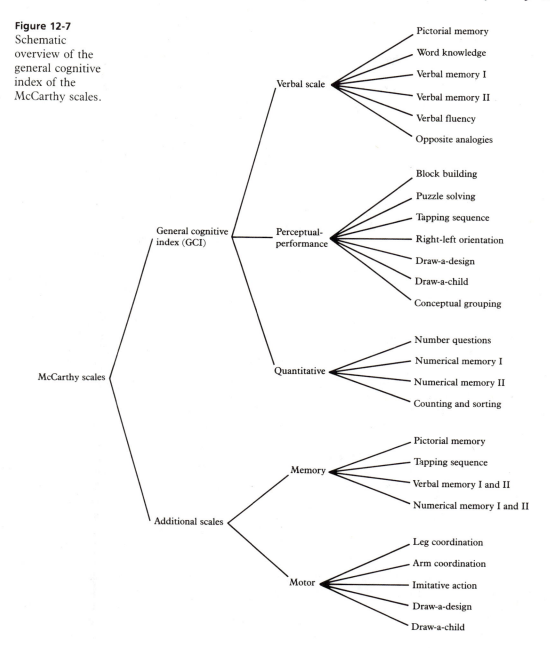

then converted into standard scores with a mean of 50 and a standard deviation of 10 (Silverstein, 1978). Norms are available for each of the ten age groups. Thus, subjects can be compared to members of their own age group.

Reliability coefficients for the McCarthy scale are very good. These coefficients were determined by the split-half method unless the procedure was inappropriate; then the test-retest procedure was used.

Reliability coefficients of the ten age groups for the general cognitive index tend to run in the low .90s. Coefficients for the other five scales range from the high .70s to high .80s. Temporal stability (that is, test-retest) coefficients are also good, with coefficients in the .90s for the general cognitive index and with median coefficients in the mid .90s for the other five scales. Thus, the six scales of the McCarthy scale hold their own when compared to the three Wechsler IQs (VIQ, PIQ, and FSIQ).

Validity data are also encouraging. Although concurrent validity data are limited, correlations with the Stanford-Binet scale (Form L-M) and the WPPSI are quite good. The general cognitive index correlates at .81 with the Binet IQ and at .71 with the WPPSI full-scale IQ. Additional validity coefficients based on small samples are provided in the manual and by T. V. Hunt (1978).

The McCarthy scale has been used in a variety of research studies (Mitchell et al., 1991). B. H. Wasik and co-workers (1990) used the McCarthy scale to evaluate the effects of early intervention in at-risk children. Children who received educational day care and family support were found to have significantly higher scores than a control after 6 months of intervention. Two studies have used the McCarthy scale to document the adverse effects of certain prenatal environments. For example, children of mothers who quit smoking during pregnancy had significantly higher McCarthy scores than children of those who did not (Sexton, Fox & Hebel, 1990). Low-birth-weight children were also found to have lowered scores on the McCarthy scale when compared to normal-weight controls (Smith & Knight-Jones, 1990). In another study, A. J. McMichael and colleagues (1988) attempted to evaluate the effects of environmental exposure to lead on childrens' abilities. Exposed children were found to suffer deficits in the perceptual-performance and memory areas. Finally, R. R. Valencia (1988) reviewed the literature pertaining to the use of the McCarthy scales with Hispanic children. The available studies, including a number of unpublished doctoral dissertations and articles in Spanish, indicate that the McCarthy scale has clear promise as a useful psychoeducational assessment tool for English-speaking Mexican-American children (Valencia, 1988).

In sum, the McCarthy scale is psychometrically sound. Its six scores permit pattern analysis and possible diagnostic interpretation. The available studies are supportive of its validity, and its promise as an assessment tool for Mexican-American children is encouraging.

Kaufman Assessment Battery for Children (K-ABC). A product of the early 1980s, the Kaufman Assessment Battery for Children (K-ABC) is an individual ability test for children between $2\frac{1}{2}$ and $12\frac{1}{2}$ years of age. The K-ABC consists of

Figure 12-8
Schematic
overview of the
Kaufman
Assessment
Battery for
Children.

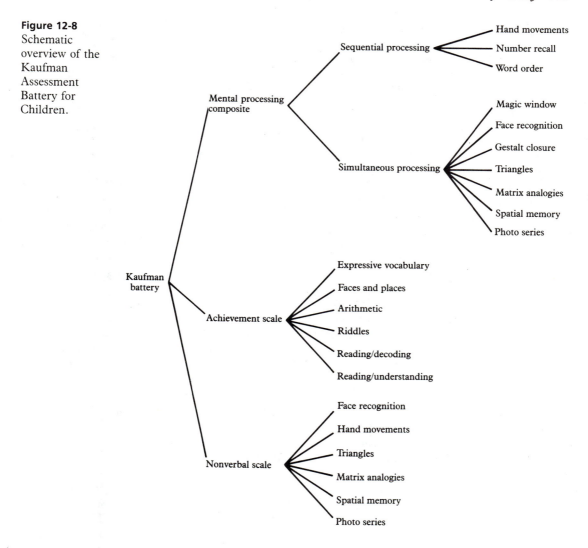

16 subtests, which are combined into five global scales called sequential processing, simultaneous processing, mental processing composite (a combination of sequential and simultaneous processing), achievement, and nonverbal. Figure 12-8 presents a schematic overview of the structure of the K-ABC. As the figure shows, the mental processing composite consists of the sequential processing and simultaneous processing scales, each of which has specific subtests. The achievement scale is independent of the mental processing composite. The nonverbal scale consists of those subtests that can be administered in pantomime and responded to physically.

The K-ABC, as its stated purposes and intentions in the test manuals reveal (Kaufman & Kaufman, 1983a, b), is quite ambitious. It is intended for psychological, clinical, minority group, preschool, and neuropsychological assessment and also for research. In addition, the manual states that the test is intended for the psychoeducational evaluation of learning disabled and other exceptional children and educational planning and placement. Later, we will examine the extent to which the K-ABC succeeds in meeting its lofty goals, but first we examine some of its basic underlying concepts.

The K-ABC purports to measure intelligence through its three mental processing scales: sequential processing, simultaneous processing, and mental processing. Theoretically, the K-ABC is based on the combination of several theoretical approaches (see Kaufman, 1984). These approaches include the neuropsychological model of brain functioning of the renowned Russian neuroscientist, Aleksandr Luria (1966); the theory of split brain functioning of the American Nobelist, Roger Sperry (1968); and the theories of information processing, most notably, that of cognitive scientist, Ulric Neisser (1967). In the work of these and other scientists, the Kaufmans noted a major distinction between two types of higher brain processes, which they refer to as the *sequential-simultaneous distinction* (Kaufman, 1984). Sequential processing takes place in serial. It refers to the child's ability "to solve problems by mentally arranging input in sequential or serial order" (Kaufman, Kaufman & Kaufman, 1985, p. 250). Examples of sequential processing are number and word order recall. Items are presented one at a time and thus must be dealt with sequentially, rather than all at once. In contrast to sequential processing, simultaneous processing takes place in parallel. It refers to a child's ability to "synthesize information (from mental wholes) in order to solve a problem" (Kaufman, Kaufman & Kaufman, 1985, p. 250).

The sequential-simultaneous distinction of the K-ABC is one of the test's most distinguishing characteristics (Kamphaus & Reynolds, 1984; Rothlisberg & Dean, 1989). It is important to note, however, that Kaufman and Kaufman (1983b) do not claim to provide a pure measure of either sequential or simultaneous processing with the K-ABC. Instead, they selected tasks that from a rational analysis appeared to distinguish one type of processing from the other.

A major intent of providing separate measures of simultaneous and sequential processing is to identify the child's unique strengths and personal problem-solving strategies. Such information can presumably be used to develop educational and remedial intervention strategies for a child (Gunnison, 1984; Majovski, 1984).

In addition to its sequential-simultaneous distinction, the K-ABC provides an independent achievement score. This provision of independent and comparable scores for both intelligence and achievement in the same test is a major advantage of the K-ABC in comparison to the Binet and Wechsler scales. In addition, the K-ABC's nonverbal scale provides a measure of ability specifically designed to be as fair as possible to children with language handicaps.

The K-ABC is well constructed and psychometrically sound (see Mehrens,

1984). It was standardized on a sample of 2000 children stratified according to age (100 at each half-year between $2\frac{1}{2}$ and $12\frac{1}{2}$), gender, geographic region, race (black, white, Hispanic, other), parent education, community size, and educational placement (regular class versus special) according to the 1980 census. Learning disabled, mentally retarded, and gifted and talented children selected approximately in proportion to their numbers in the general population were also included. Finally, supplementary norms based on 496 black and 119 white children are available.

Raw scores for each of the 16 subtests can be converted to standard scores with a mean of 10 (SD = 3). The global scales can be converted to standard scores (mean = 100, SD = 15), percentiles, and age-equivalent norms.

Split-half reliabilities for the individual subtests are, on the average, slightly lower than for the individual subtests of the WISC-R and specific tests of the modern Binet. Coefficients range from .72 (magic window) to .88 (number recall) for preschool children and from .71 (Gestalt closure) to .85 (matrix analogies) for school-age children. Split-half coefficients for the global scales range from .86 (simultaneous processing) to .93 (achievement) for preschool children and from .89 (sequential processing) to .97 (achievement) for school-age children. Thus, as with other major ability tests, reliability is lower for younger children. Test-retest coefficients are just slightly lower than those obtained by the split-half method.

Considerable attention is given to the question of validity in the K-ABC test manual. Factor analytic studies support its sequential-simultaneous and mental processing (intelligence)–achievement distinctions. The mental processing composite correlates at .61 with the Stanford-Binet (Form L-M) IQ and at .70 with the WISC-R full-scale IQ. Correlation coefficients between the achievement scale and the Binet and WISC-R IQ measures are even higher. More recent concurrent validity studies with the modern Binet (fourth edition) have tended to produce slightly higher coefficients (Smith, Martin & Lyon, 1989). The global scales have a range of correlations of .36 to .84 with a variety of standard group achievement tests and correlate at about .50 with reading ability (Kaufman & Kaufman, 1983b).

The K-ABC intelligence estimates tend to show smaller (about 8 points) black-white differences than either the WISC-R or Binet scales, in which whites typically show about a 15-point difference (see Jensen, 1985). Thus, it tends to be less biased against minorities (Nolan, Watlington & Willson, 1989). However, the K-ABC also tends to underestimate the scores of gifted children (compared to the Binet Form L-M and the WISC-R), and therefore its validity for evaluating giftedness is questionable (McCallum, Karnes & Oehler-Stinnett, 1985). On the other hand, the K-ABC may be more valid than the WISC-R for Navajo children (Naglieri, 1984). However, its ability to discriminate among at-risk preschoolers functioning in the lower IQ ranges is questionable (Bloom et al., 1988).

Since its publication in April 1983, the K-ABC has generated considerable interest. Reactions have varied widely, however. In summarizing the strengths of the K-ABC, Kaufman, Kaufman, and Kaufman (1985, p. 268) point to its strong theoretical orientation, separate intelligence and achievement scales, separate nonverbal scale, limited oral instructions and limited verbal responding, colorful and interesting items, inclusion of sociocultural norms, and empirical documentation of smaller black–white, Hispanic–white, and Native American–white differences on the K-ABC compared to other tests. These strengths are acknowledged by independent reviewers (Aiken, 1987; Anastasi, 1984).

Criticism of the K-ABC has been harsh. According to A. R. Jensen (1984), the smaller white–minority differences on the K-ABC are attributable to its poorer predictive validity for school achievement and its less effective measurement of general intelligence (*g*) than the Binet and WISC-R. Other critics point to the K-ABC's imperfect match with its theoretical foundation and disproportionate contribution of the simultaneous and mental processing composites (Bracken, 1985). In addition, the K-ABC is highly visual in nature, which limits its use for visually handicapped children, and it is poor in testing at the extremes of intelligence (Aiken, 1987, pp. 225–226). Moreover, the neuropsychological model that underlies the sequential-simultaneous distinction is poorly supported at best and at worst inaccurate and outmoded (Herbert, 1982).

Perhaps the most severe criticism of the K-ABC has come from R. J. Sternberg (1984), who charges that the K-ABC manual misrepresents the support for the theory underlying the K-ABC and maintains that the test suffers from a noncorrespondence between its definition and its measurement of intelligence. Sternberg found that empirical support for the theory underlying the K-ABC is questionable. Sternberg also noted, as did Jensen (1984), an overemphasis on rote learning at the expense of measurement of the ability to learn.

Although, on the whole, the criticisms of the K-ABC are valid, it is important to see them in perspective. First, many of the same criticisms (such as lack of correspondence between definition and measurement of intelligence) also apply to the K-ABC's major competitors. Even the very best available instruments have shortcomings and limitations, and although the underlying theory of the K-ABC has yet to be fully established, there is at least some guiding theoretical structure. As a replacement for the WISC-III and Binet scales, the K-ABC leaves much to be desired because it does not predict academic achievement as well as these tests. However, the K-ABC is the best alternative or supplement for special specific questions and educational assessment to date.

C. *General Individual Ability Tests for Handicapped and Special Populations*

In addition to tests for infants and young children, a number of alternatives are specifically designed to provide a more valid measure of intellectual functioning than the Binet and Wechsler scales for cases in which the major scales may be biased or inappropriate. Each of these general individual ability tests for handicapped and special populations contains unique strengths and limitations.

Columbia Mental Maturity Scale, third edition (CMMS). A variety of sensory and physical limitations often make a valid administration of the Binet, Wechsler, or even many of the major alternative scales (such as the McCarthy scale) quite impossible. Therefore, for children suffering from physical limitations (for example, cerebral palsy), speech impairments, language limitations, or hearing loss, instruments are needed that do not create negative bias. One such instrument is the Columbia Mental Maturity Scale, third edition (CMMS), which evaluates ability in normal and variously handicapped children from 3 through 12 years of age. When used for individuals with special needs, the test often provides a more suitable measure of intelligence than do the more established scales (Kamhi, Minor & Mauer, 1990).

The most recent version of the Columbia scale was revised in the early 1970s (Burgemeister, Blum & Lorge, 1972). One of its distinguishing characteristics is that it requires neither a verbal response nor fine motor skills. Purported to be a measure of general reasoning ability, the Columbia scale requires the subject to discriminate similarities and differences by indicating which drawing does not belong on a 6-by-9-inch card containing three to five drawings, depending on the level of difficulty. The task, then, is multiple-choice in nature.

The 1972 edition of the Columbia scale contains 92 different cards grouped into eight overlapping levels, or scales, according to chronological age. Testing begins at a scale commensurate with the child's age. Some advantages of the Columbia scale are its relative independence of reading skills, ease of administration and scoring, and the clarify of its test manual (Egeland, 1978). Subjects are not timed, so pressure is minimal.

One problem with earlier versions of the Columbia scale was its poor standardization sample. However, the 1972 standardization sample is quite impressive. It consists of 2600 children divided into 13 levels from 3 years 6 months to 9 years 11 months. Each level contains 200 children, and the sample is stratified according to the U.S. population in terms of the major important variables including gender, race, geographic region, and parent occupation.

Raw scores from the Columbia scale can be converted to a standard score with a mean of 100 and a standard deviation of 16, which is known as the *age deviation score* (ADS). The age deviation score can be expressed in terms of percentiles. Raw scores can also be converted to mental age equivalents. As is typically found in the better or more recent tests, the child is compared to his or her own age group (that is, the 200 children at his or her age group in the standardization sample).

The Columbia scale manual contains data on both split-half and test-retest reliability for various age groupings in the standardization sample. The scale is internally as well as temporarily consistent for short intervals. Coefficients range between .85 and .90 for both split-half and test-retest reliabilities.

Although we have seen great strides in terms of minimum acceptable normative and reliability requirements in individual tests of ability, typical validity requirements appear to be weaker. The Columbia scale, like so many other individual ability tests, could benefit greatly from additional validity documentation. The available validity data reported in the manual and elsewhere have been encouraging; however, sufficient data do not exist for a complete evaluation. The highest correlate of the 1972 edition is the 1959 edition of the Columbia scale. Thus, the newer scale overlaps considerably with the older scale, with a correlation of about .84 according to the manual. The Columbia scale's correlation with the Binet scale (Form L-M), as reported in the manual, is .67. Correlations with group ability tests are similar.

The Columbia scale has one important difficulty of which all its users should be aware. The scale is highly vulnerable to random error. A young child can obtain a score of 82 simply on chance alone, and a score in the average ranges can be obtained with just a few lucky guesses (Kaufman, 1978). Theoretically, if 100 apes were administered the lower levels of the Columbia scale, an alarming number might obtain scores in the average ranges for human beings.

In conclusion, the Columbia scale is a well-standardized, reliable instrument useful in assessing ability for a variety of sensory, physical, and language handicapped individuals. Because of its multiple-choice nature, however, and consequent vulnerability to chance variance, results should be used with caution. When used with subjects for whom the major scales would be appropriate, the Columbia scale might best be seen as a screening device. The importance and value of the Columbia scale can be found in its relevance to a variety of special populations. Even for these populations, however, the Columbia scale might be more safely used in conjunction with those Wechsler or K-ABC subtests that can be given, depending on the disability of the child involved. If the child can point, for example, Wechsler's picture completion subtest can be given in conjunction with the Columbia scale as an additional check on the accuracy of the results. If the child is physically handicapped but can speak, then some of the Wechsler verbal subtests can be used with the Columbia scale to support results.

Peabody Picture Vocabulary Test, revised (PPVT-R). Similar to the Columbia scale in several respects is the Peabody Picture Vocabulary Test, revised (PPVT-R), developed by Dunn (1959, 1965) and Dunn and Dunn (1981). Although the age range of $2\frac{1}{2}$ through 18 years and adults is considerably wider than for the Columbia scale, both are multiple-choice tests that require a subject to indicate only "yes" or "no" in some manner. Primarily for the physically or language handicapped, the PPVT-R cannot be used with the deaf because the subject must be able to hear the instructions. However, the test has been used in research with the deaf to evaluate their ability to define words (Krinsky, 1990). The test purports to measure hearing or **receptive vocabulary,** presumably providing a nonverbal estimate of verbal intelligence. It has utility as a screening instrument or as a supplement to other measures in evaluating learning (McGivern et al., 1991), linguistic (Bayles, 1990), and a variety of other special problems (Knotek, Bayles & Kaszniak, 1990). Though untimed, the PPVT-R can be administered in 20 minutes or less, and it requires no reading ability. Two forms (L and M) are available. Each form has 175 plates, each containing four numbered pictures. The subject's task is to indicate which of the four pictures is best related to a word read by the examiner. Items are arranged in increasing order of difficulty, and administration entails determination of a basal and ceiling performance as in the modern Binet scale. The number of incorrect responses is subtracted from the ceiling to produce a total score. This total score can then be converted to a standard score (mean = 100, SD = 15), percentile rank, stanine, or age-equivalent score.

The Peabody test was standardized in 1979 on a national sample of 4200 individuals aged $2\frac{1}{2}$ to 18 and 800 adults aged 19 to 40. The sample was stratified by gender, race, parent occupation, geographic location, and community size according to the 1970 census. Reliability coefficients range from .71 to .81 for internal consistency estimates, from .52 to .90 for test-retest estimates, and from .71 to .91 for alternate form estimates. There is no direct evidence of predictive validity reported in the manual, although the PPVT-R does correlate with the older PPVT (Dunn, 1959), which has been shown to have correlations with the Binet and Wechsler scales ranging from the low .20s to low .90s. In addition, a number of studies have investigated the validity of the Peabody test for specific uses.

The PPVT-R tends to underestimate Wechsler or Binet IQs for retarded (Prout & Sheldon, 1984) as well as for gifted children (Hayes & Martin, 1986). Research has supported its use for adults referred to the California State Department of Rehabilitation (Stevenson, 1986) and for adults with developmental handicaps (Groenweg, Conway & Stan, 1986). It should be noted, however, that the manual advises caution when using the test with adults. Moreover, even where its use is supported, the Peabody test tends to underestimate the IQ score (Stevenson, 1986). The PPVT-R should never be used as a substitute for a Wechsler or Binet IQ, since it evaluates only receptive vocabulary and not problem solving, abstract thinking, and other functions tapped by the major IQ tests.

In conclusion, the Peabody test has a number of positive attributes and some negative ones. On the positive side are its ease of administration and utility for certain handicapped groups. On the negative side, its tendency to underestimate IQ scores, in conjunction with the problems inherent in the multiple-choice format, indicate that the Peabody test cannot be used in place of the major ability scales (that is, the Binet and Wechsler scales). It should be used for general screening purposes and evaluation of receptive vocabulary.

Figure 12-9
Leiter
International
Performance
Scale. (*Courtesy of
Stoelting Co.*)

Leiter International Performance Scale (LIPS). Whereas the Columbia and Peabody tests measure verbal aspects of intelligence, the Leiter International Performance Scale (LIPS) is strictly a performance scale whose intent is to provide a nonverbal alternative to the Stanford-Binet scale for the age range of 2 to 18 years. (See Figure 12-9.) First developed in the 1930s and last revised in 1948, the Leiter scale has experienced a recent decrease in interest among researchers, although it finds rather frequent use in clinical settings. The Leiter scale purports to provide a nonverbal measure of general intelligence by sampling a wide variety of functions from memory through nonverbal reasoning. It can be administered without the use of language, and it requires no verbal response from subjects.

Presumably, it can be applied to a rather large range of handicapped individuals, particularly the deaf and language-disabled. Like the Peabody test and the Columbia scale, the Leiter scale is untimed. Patterned after the old Binet scale, the 54 tests of the Leiter scale are arranged in an age scale format at yearly intervals from 2 through 18. Despite its many positive features and utility for subjects who cannot or will not provide a verbal response, the Leiter scale has some noteworthy problems. It was published during a time when it was common to construct a test and leave the job of psychometric documentation to users and general researchers. The Leiter manual fails to include information routinely found in modern test manuals. However, the Leiter scale's validity documentation is extremely good, with a range of criterion validity coefficients from .52 to .92 (median .83).

We agree with Sattler (1988) that the Leiter scale merits consideration as an aid to clinical diagnosis in handicapped children. As with other tests discussed in this chapter, however, we must encourage the test user to exercise caution in interpreting Leiter test results because more research is needed into the meaning of test scores (Mask & Brown, 1984). It is hoped that interested researchers will see the need for additional investigations into the properties of the Leiter scale. In addition, a careful standardization of the Leiter scale would be most welcome.

D. *Broad-Range Individual Ability Tests: Child Through Adult*

Whereas the tests discussed in the previous sections tend to apply to a specific population or age group, broad-range individual ability tests can usually be used with individuals of all ages. In addition, these tests are designed to estimate intelligence in both normal and a wide variety of special populations.

Porteus Maze Test (PMT). Another popular but poorly standardized nonverbal performance measure of intelligence is the Porteus Maze Test (PMT), which has been one of the more important individual ability tests since it was first published at about the time of World War I. As its name implies, the Porteus Maze Test consists of maze problems. Like the Leiter scale, the Porteus test can be administered without verbal instruction and thus can be used for a variety of special and handicapped populations. Supporting the Porteus test is a large body of empirical findings reported in various editions of *The Mental Measurements Yearbook*. These findings add construct validity to the test.

The Porteus test has no manual. Furthermore, its standardization sample is quite old (Doctor, 1972). Despite its problems, however, the Porteus test, like so many other tests discussed in this chapter, meets an important need in providing a measure of ability for a variety of handicapped groups for whom the Binet and Wechsler scales are inappropriate. And like many similar tests, a restandardization would greatly improve the quality of the Porteus test.

Other broad-range tests. The widespread use and interest in tests such as the Peabody, Leiter, and Porteus are clearly an indication of the need for strictly nonverbal or performance measures of intelligence, especially for the handicapped. Therefore, it is unfortunate that so many of the available instruments are in need of restandardization and additional reliability or validity documentation. Clearly, more work is needed to improve the status of ability tests for handicapped individuals. Other procedures—such as the Columbia scale, the Quick Test (Ammons & Ammons, 1962), the Pictorial Test of Intelligence (French, 1964), and the Slosson Intelligence Test (Slosson, 1963)—may offer some hope, but these also have limitations similar to those of the tests discussed thus far.

Much can be said for the Quick Test, except that the standardization sample is not representative of the general population. The Slosson test also is useful as a quick measure of intelligence, but it is heavily dependent on language skills. The Pictorial Test of Intelligence is almost as sound as the Columbia scale and can be used for similar purposes. In general, the Columbia scale and the Pictorial Test of Intelligence are perhaps the most strongly supported general ability measures for a broad range of handicaps. Each of the tests for the handicapped, however, has its own unique advantages and disadvantages. All should be interpreted with caution and subjected to additional research investigation.

III. *Individual Tests of Ability for Specific Purposes*

The tests discussed below are the best examples, according to our criteria, of individual ability tests for a variety of specific abilities such as learning ability and memory. Our discussion is far from complete, but it does focus on important or instructive instruments. Students interested in encyclopedic coverage should consult *The Mental Measurements Yearbook*.

A. *Learning Disabilities*

One of the most important areas in education involves the study of specific learning disabilities. A major idea behind the notion of learning disabilities is that a child may be average in intelligence but fail in school because of a specific deficit or disability that prevents learning (Coplan & Gleason, 1990). Of the major tests designed specifically to assess learning disabilities, none is more illustrative of the theory of learning disabilities and has generated more interest than the controversial Illinois Test of Psycholinguistic Abilities (ITPA).

Based on modern concepts of human information processing, the ITPA assumes that failure to respond correctly to a stimulus can result not only from a defective output (that is, response) system but also from a defective input or information-processing system. Consistent with information-processing theory (for example, see Haber, 1969), the Illinois test assumes that a human response to an outside stimulus can be viewed in terms of discrete stages or processes. Stage 1, the input stage, involves the reception of incoming environmental information by the senses. Thus, the information must first be received by the senses before it can be analyzed. During Stage 2 of processing, input information is analyzed or processed. Finally, having processed the information, the individual must make a response—the final stage of processing. See Figure 12-10.

Assuming that a learning disability can occur at any of these three levels of processing, the Illinois test theorizes that the child may be impaired in one or more specific sensory modalities. Input information may be visual, auditory, or tactile. The Illinois test provides three subtests that measure the individual's ability to receive input information in terms of visual, auditory, or tactile input independently of processing and output factors. Three additional subtests are available that provide independent measures of processing in each of these

Figure 12-10
Information-Processing
Model
(Three-Stage
Model)

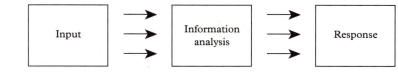

three sense modalities, and other subtests provide independent measures of motor and verbal output.

By providing relatively independent measures for each of these areas, the Illinois test purports to have value in isolating the specific site of a learning disability. For example, a child may receive age-appropriate scores for all three input and all three processing subtests but may have an unusually low score on

Table 12-4
Description of
Illinois Test of
Psycholinguistic
Abilities (ITPA)
Subtests

Subtest	Description
Auditory Reception	Measures ability to understand spoken words. Example: "Do chairs eat?"
Visual Reception	Measures ability to gain meaning from familiar pictures. Example: Match picture stimulus with picture from same category.
Auditory Association	Measures ability to relate concepts presented orally. Example: Verbal-analogies test (e.g., "Grass is green, sugar is _____."
Visual Association	Measures ability to relate concepts presented visually. Example: Relate a pictorial stimulus to its conceptual counterpart (e.g., bone goes with dog).
Verbal Expression	Measures ability to express concepts verbally. Example: Describe common objects verbally.
Manual Expression	Measures ability to demonstrate knowledge of the use of objects pictured. Example: Express an idea with gestures (e.g., "Show me what to do with a hammer").
Grammatic Closure	Measures ability to use proper grammatical forms to complete statement. Example: "Here is a dog. Here are two _____."
Visual Closure	Measures ability to identify common objects from an incomplete visual presentation. Example: Locating specific objects in a scene filled with distracting stimuli.
Auditory Sequential Memory	Measures ability to reproduce orally a sequence of digits from memory. Example: Repeating digits.
Visual Sequential Memory	Measures ability to reproduce sequences of geometrical forms from memory. Example: Placing geometric shapes in proper sequence from memory.
Auditory Closure	Measures ability to complete a word when only fragments of it are orally presented. Example: "Listen. Tell me who I am talking about. DA / Y. Who is that?"
Sound Blending	Measures ability to synthesize into words syllables spoken at half-second intervals. Example: "What word is D—OG?"

Note. The two supplementary subtests are Auditory Closure and Sound Blending.
Reprinted by permission of Jerome M. Sattler, Publisher, P.O. Box 151677, San Diego, Calif. 92115. Copyright 1988.

motor (but not verbal) output. This result would indicate that, although the child is able to receive and process information as well as others do, he or she has trouble in expression through the motor areas. The child's problem can thus be localized to motor output, and the treatment can focus on enhancing motor skills. However, if the problem involves auditory processing, then this area becomes the focus.

Designed for use with children aged 2 through 10, the Illinois test has found widespread use and interest among educators, psychologists, learning disability specialists, and researchers (Crisco, Dobbs & Mulhern, 1988). This popularity, however, cannot be attributed to its psychometric qualities (Bell, 1990). Not only is the Illinois test one of the most difficult individual ability tests to administer, but the manual presents no reliability or validity data. Although normative data are provided, the exact nature of the normative sample is difficult to ascertain from the manual—a problem that has been severely criticized (Lumsden, 1978). In fact, the Illinois test has been criticized on a variety of grounds, including inadequate validity, excessively low reliabilities for individual subtests, and failure to provide normalized standard scores. Moreover, because it was normed on middle-class children and contains culturally loaded content, the ITPA is not appropriate for use with lower socioeconomic children or disadvantaged minority groups. The reviews of both Lumsden (1978) and Wiederholt (1978) conclude that the test should not be used in the assessment of learning disabilities. We concur with this judgment; our presentation here is to illustrate the information-processing approach.

A much better test for evaluating learning disabilities is the Woodcock-Johnson Psycho-Educational Battery (Woodcock, 1977). The Woodcock-Johnson was designed as a broad-range individually administered test to be used in educational settings. It assesses three areas of functioning through 27 tests as follows: cognitive ability (12 tests), achievement (10 tests), and interest (5 tests). By comparing a child's score on cognitive ability with his or her score on achievement, it is possible to evaluate possible learning problems. Such problems are defined in terms of a major discrepancy (usually two standard deviations) between cognitive ability (intelligence) and achievement. If a child is at the mean for cognitive ability (i.e., 50th percentile) and is two standard deviations below the mean in achievement (i.e., 2.2 percentile), a learning disability can be suspected and it indicates the need for a more in-depth evaluation.

The 12 tests of cognitive ability of the Woodcock-Johnson are picture vocabulary, spatial relations, memory for sentences, concept formation, analogies, and a variety of quantitative problems. The tests of achievement cover letter and word recognition, reading comprehension, proofing, calculation, science, social science, and humanities. Finally, the tests of interest level cover reading interest, math interest, language interest, physical interest, and social interest. Scores can be converted to percentile ranks. These ranks, in turn, can be converted to a standard score with a mean of 100 and a standard deviation of 15, or a mean of 50 and a standard deviation of 10.

The Woodcock-Johnson has relatively good psychometric properties. The standardization sample included more than 4700 persons representative of the U.S. population in terms of gender, race, occupational status, geographic region, and urban versus nonurban status. Many of the specific tests have split-half reliabilities in the .80s and .90s, with a range of .57 to .96 when both split-half and test-retest reliabilities are considered. However, factor analytic studies have failed to support the validity of the structure. Factor analysis of the standardization sample yielded only two factors: a verbal factor that accounted for nearly 70% of the variance and a smaller nonverbal/visual-spatial factor (McGrew, 1986).

The field of learning disability assessment is relatively new and so are tests in this area. As a result, with the possible exception of the K-ABC, new tests of learning disabilities are in the same stage as early intelligence instruments. When judged by modern standards for individual ability tests, especially those that purportedly measure intelligence, these tests compare unfavorably in a variety of respects.

For learning disability tests, three conclusions seem warranted. First, test constructors should attempt to respond to the same criticisms that led to changes in the Binet and Wechsler scales and ultimately to the development of the K-ABC. Second, much more empirical and theoretical research is needed. Finally, users of learning disabilities tests should take great pains to understand the weaknesses of these procedures and not overinterpret results. The ITPA should not be used to make decisions that might affect the future of a child. The Woodcock-Johnson is much more suitable but should be used carefully.

B. *Visiographic Tests*

Visiographic tests require a subject to copy various shapes. Tests of the ability to copy designs have achieved a central position in neuropsychological testing because of their sensitivity to many different kinds of brain damage (Lezak, 1976). In this section we briefly describe three such tests. Then in Chapter 19 we will discuss neuropsychological testing in greater detail.

Benton Visual Retention Test (BVRT). Tests for brain damage are based on the concept of psychological deficit, in which a poor performance on a specific task is related to or caused by some underlying deficit. By knowing the underlying function or ability measured by a specific psychological test, the test examiner can relate a poor performance on that test to this underlying function (Downey et al., 1991). Such is the idea behind the Benton Visual Retention Test (BVRT), which assumes that visual memory ability is easily impaired by brain damage. Thus, a deficit on a visual memory task is consistent with possible brain damage or brain diseases such as Alzheimer's (Rebok, Brandt & Folstein, 1990).

Figure 12-11
Designs similar to
those on the
Benton Visual
Retention Test

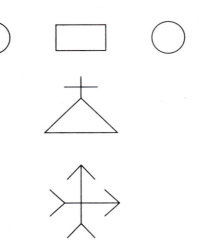

Designed for individuals aged 8 and older, the Benton test consists of geometric designs that are briefly presented and then removed (see Figure 12-11). The subject is asked to reproduce the designs from memory. The responses are scored according to criteria in the manual. The subject loses points for mistakes and omissions and gains points for correct or partially correct responses. Norms are then available to evaluate scores. As the number of errors increases, the subject approaches the organic (brain-damaged) range.

Bender Visual Motor Gestalt Test (BVMGT). Also used in the assessment of brain damage and similar to the Benton test is the Bender Visual Motor Gestalt Test (BVMGT). The Bender test has a variety of uses and is among the most popular individual tests. It consists of nine geometric figures (such as a circle and a diamond) that the subject is simply asked to copy (see Figure 12-12). A number of specific errors have been identified for each design, and the Bender test is scored according to the number of errors the subject makes. Developmental norms are available that describe the number of errors associated with children aged 5 through 8 (see Koppitz, 1964). By age 9, any child of normal intelligence can copy the figures with only one or two errors. Therefore, anyone over 9 who cannot copy the figures may be suffering from some type of deficit.

Research on the Bender test (see Koppitz, 1964) has shown that errors can occur for individuals whose mental age is less than 9 (for example, because of low intelligence), individuals with brain damage, and individuals with emotional problems. Errors associated with brain damage have been identified, and a variety of scoring systems for brain damage are available. However, the reliability of such systems has been questioned (Howell, 1985; Wagner & Flamos, 1988).

Figure 12-12
The figures of the Bender Visual Motor Gestalt Test. (*From The Bender Visual Motor Gestalt Test by L. Bender, 1962. Reprinted with permission from The American Orthopsychiatric Association.*)

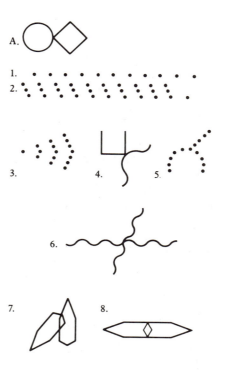

Memory-for-Designs Test (MFD). Another simple drawing test involving perceptual-motor coordination is the Memory-for-Designs Test (MFD). Requiring only a ten-minute administration, the Memory-for-Designs Test can be used for individuals $8\frac{1}{2}$ to 60 years of age. Empirical data have tended to support its use as an indicator of brain injury (Graham & Kendall, 1960) and brain disease (Strauss & Brandt, 1990; Teng et al., 1989). As with the Benton test, the subject attempts to draw a briefly presented design from memory. Drawings are scored from 0 to 3, depending on how they compare with representative sample drawings from normal controls and persons with varying degrees of brain injury. A raw score total based on all 15 drawings can then be corrected for age and intelligence by reference to a table. This corrected score can then be evaluated against a relatively large (825) normative sample.

Reported split-half reliability indices are quite good (.92), and test-retest indices range from .81 to .90 (Graham & Kendall, 1960). Like so many psychological tests, additional validity documentation of the Memory-for-Designs Test is needed. The studies that are available, however, have been quite supportive (Goldstein, Canavan & Polkey, 1988; Mandes & Gessner, 1988).

Evaluation of individual perceptual motor drawing tests of brain damage.
Like all psychological tests of brain damage used in isolation, the Benton,
Bender, and Memory-for-Designs tests have been criticized because of their
limitations in reliability and validity documentation. However, all three can be
used as screening devices. An excessive number of errors on any of these
procedures provides a signal for the examiner that more in-depth testing or a
medical evaluation may be necessary.

C. *Creativity: Torrance Tests of Creative Thinking (TTCT)*

The 1960s and 1970s saw a growing interest in the assessment of a previously
overlooked ability: creativity. Like learning disability tests, most creativity
tests are still in the early stages of development. One of the better, more
established, and more popular of these creativity tests is known as the Torrance
Tests of Creative Thinking (TTCT).

Like many other creativity tests, the Torrance tests measure a variety of
areas or aspects of creative thinking (for example, fluency, flexibility, originality, and elaboration). Scores on the TTCT can be obtained in each of these
areas. However, like individual ability tests for the handicapped and tests of
learning disability, the TTCT does not quite meet the standards of the Binet
and Wechsler scales in terms of standardization, reliability, and validity. Reliability studies have varied widely (for example, correlations of .35 to .73 for a
three-year period), and validity studies have tended to be varied as well as
inconclusive (Hattie, 1980). Reviewers typically suggest that more work is
needed (Baird, 1972; Thorndike, 1972). Unlike some creativity tests, the
TTCT was conservatively presented as a research tool, but little has been done
to prevent it from being used in applied settings. On the positive side, a
number of research studies have supported the utility of the Torrance tests as
an unbiased indicator of giftedness (Esquivel & Lopez, 1988; Torrance, 1970,
1977).

In sum, the Torrance tests are typical of creativity tests. Applied practitioners demand such a tool for their work, and, though inconsistent, available
data reflect the tests' merit and fine potential. As with so many other tests,
however, more work is needed. Results from the new creativity tests must be
viewed as tentative and with caution.

D. *Individual Achievement Tests: Wide Range Achievement Test, Revised (WRAT-R)*

We have discussed the widely made distinction between intelligence and
achievement. As you know, tests of intelligence presumably measure potential
capability, whereas achievement tests presumably measure what the person has

actually acquired or done with that potential. Although scores from intelligence tests and achievement tests often overlap, discrepancies sometimes are found between purported measures of intelligence and measures of achievement. Such discrepancies may occur if a person of average potential has not made full use of that potential. Such a person would tend to score higher on a general ability test than on a specific achievement test, especially if the general ability test minimizes the effects of learning and the achievement test is highly specific. Similarly, a person may score average on a general intelligence test but—because of a high level of interest, motivation, or special training—score above average on achievement. Thus, despite the overlap between intelligence and ability tests, comparisons of achievement and intelligence test data can sometimes be extremely revealing.

Most achievement tests are group tests, and these will be discussed in the next chapter. Perhaps the most popular and widely used individual achievement test is the Wide Range Achievement Test, revised (WRAT-R), which purportedly permits an estimate of grade-level functioning in reading, spelling, and arithmetic. It can be used for children aged 5 and older and has two levels for each of the three achievement areas.

Revised in 1984, the Wide Range Achievement Test is easy to administer. It also is highly popular (Wasserman et al., 1991). The WRAT-R has been used to assess the effects of low birth weight (Saigal et al., 1991), diabetes (Hosey et al., 1990), and attention deficit disorder (Ackerman, Dykman & Gardner, 1990). However, although it may have research and clinical uses, test users must again be cautioned about the many problems of the WRAT-R.

N. Reid (1986) criticizes the WRAT-R on a number of grounds. As Reid notes, there is confusion about what the WRAT-R really measures because the validity of the test is poorly documented. According to Reid (1986), although the WRAT-R has possible clinical and research applications, it is unsuitable for general use.

Other reviewers are equally pessimistic (Reynolds, 1986). J. C. Witt (1986) believes that the WRAT-R contains some of the worst characteristics of the testing industry. According to Witt, using the scores derived from the norms of the WRAT-R as roughly equivalent to a child's academic achievement is like performing inner ear surgery with a chainsaw. This criticism of the WRAT-R norms is well founded. For example, average readers in the 11th grade (50th percentile) score about two years behind when compared with individuals for the test's norms. Such individuals might be inappropriately labeled "reading disabled."

The problems with the Wide Range Achievement Test, revised, underscore our repeated warning for caution in the use of test results. All test users should learn as much as they can about the tests they use. Statements from the test publishers or distributors of tests, and even statements in the test manuals, always must be carefully examined. In Chapter 13, we will discuss a number of very sound group achievement tests.

Summary

The number of individual ability tests is almost overwhelming. Most of these tests are for highly specific purposes, and their strength lies in their specificity. Table 12-2 summarized some of the major differences among the various individual tests of ability. Of the infant and preschool scales, the Bayley Scales of Infant Development are the most psychometrically sound. The McCarthy Scales of Children's Abilities appear to be promising tests for measuring intelligence in young children, but more work is needed. The K-ABC is a new test of considerable value, but it has been strongly criticized. Overall, general ability tests for handicapped and special populations should be used cautiously. Among the tests of ability for the handicapped, the Columbia Mental Maturity Scale, third edition, is one of the most promising.

Learning disability tests are based on information-processing theory. These tests are relatively new, so their results should be viewed with caution. These tests, like creativity tests, have a long way to go if they hope to reach the standards of the Binet and Wechsler scales. A number of useful drawing tests such as the Bender, the Benton, and the Memory-for-Designs are all excellent economical screening devices for brain damage. These tests attempt to measure an ability related to brain functioning. From a deficit, brain damage is inferred. The Bender Visual Motor Gestalt Test, in addition to being a screening device for brain damage, can be used to measure intellectual and emotional functioning. Finally, although achievement and intelligence tests often overlap, a comparison between the two can be useful. One of the major individual achievement tests is the Wide Range Achievement Test, revised. This test, however, can lead to incorrect conclusions because of a number of serious problems, including poor norms.

Chapter 13

Group Ability Tests: Intelligence, Achievement, and Aptitude

Learning Objectives

□ □ □

When you have completed this chapter, you should be able to:

- Compare group and individual ability tests.
- Identify the major characteristics of group tests.
- List four general rules for using results from group ability tests.
- Evaluate the adequacy of the available group ability tests for use in kindergarten through 12th grade.
- Identify and evaluate two major group ability tests for college entrance.
- Identify and evaluate two major group ability tests for graduate school entrance.
- Identify some of the advantages of the Goodenough-Harris Drawing Test.
- Identify some group ability tests widely used in business and industry.

With individual tests a single person can, in effect, be placed under a microscope and analyzed in minute detail. Group tests can place a whole nation under the microscope. Consider, for example, the reading proficiency of 9-year-olds in the United States. According to data collected by the National Assessment of Education Progress (NAEP) and the Educational Testing Service (ETS), only about one in six 9-year-old children in the United States can read well enough to search for specific information, interrelate ideas, and make generalizations (Educational Testing Service Policy Information Report, 1991).

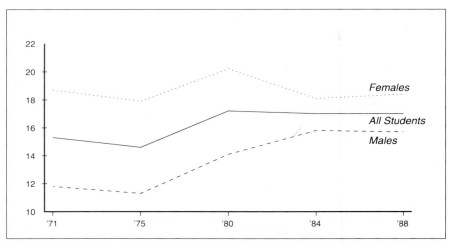

Figure 13-1
Percentage of 9-year-olds at or above level 250 on the NAEP Reading Scale. (*From "Performance at the Top: From Elementary Through Graduate School," p. 5. Copyright © 1991 by Educational Testing Service. Reprinted by permission of Educational Testing Service, the copyright holder.*)

Figure 13-1 shows the results of a national testing program to assess academic achievement in the United States. The figure presents a graph of the percentage of 9-year-olds at or above Level 250 on the NAEP reading scale, which evaluates a reader's ability to use intermediate skills and search for, locate, and organize information. As the figure shows, there have been only small changes between 1971 and 1988 in the percentage of 9-year-old children who can read at Level 250, which is considered a middle level.

The microscope of national testing programs can also be used to examine racial and ethnic differences in achievement, as well as those pertaining to geographic location and other variables. Consider, for example, Figure 13-2. As the figure shows, in 1988 there were substantial ethnic differences in the reading levels of 9-year-olds. In addition, children in the central United States and in the Northeast scored considerably higher than those in the Southeast and West. It is no surprise that reading achievement was correlated with parent education, as illustrated in the bar graph on the far right of Figure 13-2.

As we saw in Chapter 1, the role of group tests in the lives of individuals is growing. The White House has released a plan for the national testing of every American child in the 4th, 8th, and 12th grades. Results from such tests may affect funding, educational approaches, and the futures of millions of young Americans. It behooves us all to understand these tests, whose influence over our lives appears to be growing by leaps and bounds.

In this chapter, we examine many of the group tests that are used on a daily basis in schools, colleges, graduate and professional schools, the civil service,

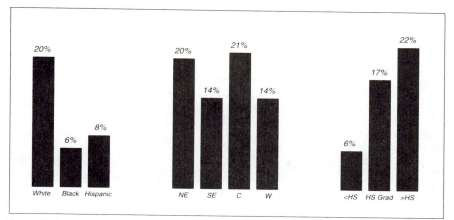

Figure 13-2

Percentage of 9-year-olds at or above level 250 on the NAEP Reading Scale by Race/Ethnicity, Region, and Parent Education, 1988. (*From "Performance at the Top: From Elementary Through Graduate School," p. 5. Copyright © 1991 by Educational Testing Service. Reprinted by permission of Educational Testing Service, the copyright holder.*)

the military, business and industry. Before discussing specific tests, we compare group and individual tests and also reexamine the distinction among achievement, aptitude, and intelligence.

I. *Comparison of Group and Individual Ability Tests*

Individual tests, you will recall, require a single examiner for a single subject. The examiner provides the instructions according to a standardized procedure stated in the test manual. The subject responds, and the examiner records the response verbatim. The examiner then evaluates and scores the subject's responses. This scoring process usually involves considerable skill. In contrast, group tests can be administered to more than one person at the same time by a single examiner. The examiner may read the instructions and impose time limits. Subjects record their own responses, which usually are choices between two or more alternatives. Scoring is typically objective and requires no skill on the part of the examiner, who simply adds the number of correct responses and in some cases subtracts a certain percentage for incorrect responses.

In addition to differences in whether a single person or a group of individuals is tested at once, who records the response (examiner or subject), and the objectivity of scoring, there is still another important difference between group and individual tests. In most individual tests, the examiner takes the responsibility for eliciting a maximum performance. If a problem exists that might inhibit a maximum performance—for example, if a subject is frightened, ner-

Table 13-1
Individual Versus
Group Tests

Individual Tests	Group Tests
One subject is tested at a time.	Many subjects are tested at a time.
Examiner records response.	Subjects records own response.
Scoring requires considerable skill.	Scoring is straightforward and objective.
Examiner attempts to elicit maximum performance.	There are no safeguards.

vous, uncooperative, or unmotivated—the examiner takes responsibility for neutralizing this problem. In an individual test, the examiner may encourage guessing—for example, by saying in a warm, friendly, supportive tone, "Sure you know that. Just guess."

Those who use the results of group tests must assume the subject was cooperative and motivated. Subjects are not praised for responding, as they are on individual tests, and there are no safeguards to prevent a person from receiving a low score for reasons other than low ability, such as lack of motivation, lack of cooperation, or emotional upset. As a result of this lack of safeguards, low scores on group tests are often difficult to interpret. With high scores, especially very high scores, it is logical to assume that the subject was motivated and has mental abilities commensurate with the obtained score. Low scores, however, may have been due to low ability, lack of interest, inadequate motivation, clerical errors in recording responses, or a host of other factors. Table 13-1 compares individual and group tests.

A. *Advantages of Individual Tests*

A major advantage of individual tests is that they can provide a wealth of information about a subject above and beyond the test score. Individual tests allow examiners to observe behavior in a standard situation. Because the instructions and methods of administration are as identical as possible, the situation in which subjects take an individual test is typically the same. Therefore, differences observed in behavior and attitudes are most likely a reflection of differences in the individuals taking the test. One person may respond quickly and enthusiastically when correct but become hesitant or withdrawn following failure. Another person may react to failure by trying harder and may actually do better in the face of frustration and failure.

After examiners have gained experience with an individual test and know how to use it properly, they have the opportunity to observe different reactions from individuals placed in the same situation. Experienced examiners eventually develop internal norms. They have an idea of how most subjects react to a certain task or situation and can easily identify unusual reactions. The opportunity to observe behavior in a standard situation can be invaluable to an examiner trying to understand the unique attributes of a person and in adequately interpreting the meaning of a test score.

Table 13-2
Unique
Advantages of
Individual and
Group Tests

Individual Tests
Provide information beyond the test score
Allow the examiner to observe behavior in a standard setting
Allow unique interpretation of test scores

Group Tests
Are cost-efficient
Minimize professional time for administration and scoring
Require less examiner skill and training
Have more objective and reliable scoring procedures
Have a very broad application

By providing the opportunity to observe behavior under standardized conditions, individual tests add a whole new dimension to the information that can be obtained from an interview. Some subjects will not talk, and some cannot talk for a variety of reasons. How is the examiner to gain an understanding of such individuals? Information provided by friends or relatives cannot be relied on because they are rarely objective and usually are not trained in observing human behavior. Simply observing the person in a natural setting may provide some useful information, but then the examiner has nothing with which to compare these observations. Thus, by allowing observations of behavior under standard conditions, individual tests provide an invaluable opportunity for the examiner to get information beyond what can be obtained in an interview.

B. *Advantages of Group Tests*

Group tests also have unique advantages. Group tests are cost-efficient in that they minimize the amount of professional time necessary for administration and scoring, involve less expensive materials, and usually require less skill in and training of examiners than do individual tests. Scoring for group tests is more objective and hence typically more reliable than the subjective scoring of many individual tests. Group tests can be used with large numbers of individuals, and, when combined with data from other sources, group test results can yield information as useful and meaningful as that obtained from individual tests.

Whereas individual tests find their greatest application in the assessment and diagnosis of psychological or medical problems in the clinical situation, the application of group tests is far broader. Group tests are used in schools at every level from kindergarten through college and graduate school. They are also extensively used by the military, in industry, and for a variety of research problems. Group test results can be used for screening and selection purposes; to assess mental, vocational, or special abilities; to assess mastery of a particular discipline or subject area; and to assess interests and aptitudes for specific occupations or job duties.

If the benefits of individual observation and unique interpretation of test scores are minimal for the examiner's purpose or if many individuals must be tested in a limited time with limited personnel, then group tests, administered with care and interpreted with an understanding of their properties, strengths, and limitations, can be extremely valuable tools. Table 13-2 lists the advantages of individual and group tests.

II. *General Features of Group Tests*

A. *Characteristics of Group Tests*

Generally speaking, group tests can be characterized as paper-and-pencil or booklet-and-pencil tests because the only materials required are a printed booklet of test items, a test manual, a scoring key, an answer sheet, and a pencil. Most group tests are of the multiple-choice variety, where the subject must select one alternative from as many as eight possible responses. Some group tests also require a free response, such as completing a sentence or design.

There are by far more group than individual tests, and, like individual tests, group tests vary among themselves in many respects. One major difference is whether the test is primarily verbal (thus requiring reading or language skills), primarily nonverbal, or combines verbal and nonverbal tasks. Some group tests group items by type (for example, all verbal analogy problems are in the same section, with items arranged in order of increasing difficulty). A test of this kind is ideally suited for producing a variety of scores such as those obtained from the Wechsler scales. Other group tests present different tasks arranged in no particular or systematic order. A test of this kind typically produces a single score related to general ability. Group test scores can be converted to a variety of units. Most produce percentiles or some type of standard score, but a few produce ratio or deviation IQs.

B. *Selecting Group Tests*

In selecting a group test, one should remember that there are a sufficient number of psychometrically adequate group tests for most purposes. Therefore, the test user need never settle for any tests but those whose psychometric soundness has been well documented. This is especially true for ability tests used in the schools.

In view of the ready availability of psychometrically sound instruments, we will not discuss poorly standardized or marginally reliable tests. However, as with our discussion of individual tests, our treatment of group tests is not comprehensive. Therefore, tests that are not included in our discussion are not necessarily psychometrically unsound instruments. Our criteria for the selection of tests parallel our criteria for the selection of individual tests. We were especially influenced by *The Mental Measurements Yearbooks*. We gave highest priority to established, highly used tests that continue to generate interest among researchers and practitioners. If several tests are similar in design, construction, and purpose, we generally include only the one or two most highly referenced in *The Mental Measurements Yearbooks*. However, we also include tests that illustrate concepts or meet specific needs. Finally, we include a few recent tests as well as tests of historical value.

C. *Using Group Tests*

Overall, the tests included in our discussion are about as reliable and well standardized as the best individual tests. However, as for some individual tests, validity data for some group tests are weak, meager, contradictory, or all three. Therefore, all users of group tests must be careful in interpreting and making use of test scores. These tests should not be seen as a simple solution to the decision-making process; rather, their main value arises when they are used in conjunction with other data.

Test use is an especially important issue for group tests because the results from these procedures are probably used by more people than the results from individual tests. Therefore, for the thousands of teachers, educators, school administrators, personnel staff in industry, counselors, and others who routinely have access to results from group tests, we have a few suggestions.

Use results with caution. Never consider scores in isolation or as absolutes. Try to include the test score as only one bit of data, to be tentatively accepted unless not confirmed by other data. Be especially careful in using these tests for prediction, except for predicting relatively limited factors over a brief time. Avoid overinterpreting test scores or attributing to test scores more value than is warranted by their limitations.

Be especially suspicious of low scores. Users of group tests must of necessity assume that subjects understand the purpose of testing and want to do well and are equally rested and free of emotional problems. Many group tests also require reading ability as well as an interest in solving test problems. When any of these assumptions and requirements are not met, an artificially low score can result.

Consider wide discrepancies a warning signal. When an individual exhibits wide discrepancies either between two or more test scores or between a test score and behavior or other sources of data, all may not be well with the individual (assuming the discrepancy is not the result of a clerical error). The discrepancy may reflect emotional problems or severe stress. For example, a child with high test scores may obtain poor grades because of emotional upset. Or a child with good grades may obtain a poor test score because of a crisis, such as a death in the family.

When in doubt, refer. With low scores, wide discrepancies, or sufficient reason to doubt the validity or fairness of a test result, the safest course is to refer the subject for individual testing by a competent professional. Given the reasons for the referral, a professional trained in individual test use can generally ascertain the cause of the problem and provide the unique interpretation called for in such cases. It is well to know one's limitations. It is often dangerous as well as reckless to take on a responsibility that is appropriate for a trained specialist.

III. *Group Tests in the Schools: Kindergarten through 12th Grade*

The purpose of these tests is to measure educational achievement in school children. Before proceeding to a discussion of the specific tests, it might be useful to refresh our memories on the nature of achievement tests and how they are different from aptitude tests.

A. *Achievement Tests Versus Aptitude Tests*

Achievement: Assessing what has been Learned.

Achievement tests attempt to assess what one has learned following a specific course of instruction. As we saw in Chapter 1, the first achievement tests used in the schools were of the essay variety. Such essay tests were rapidly replaced in the 1930s by standardized achievement tests such as the Stanford Achievement Test, which is still in use today. Standardized achievement tests were more cost-effective than their essay counterparts. The scoring of such tests was also far more objective and reliable. However, like their predecessors, standardized achievement tests had as their goal the evaluation of a student's knowledge after a standard course of training. They represented the endpoint or terminal evaluation of performance and helped reveal how much a student had learned. A major feature of such tests is that their validity is determined primarily by content validation procedures. Such tests are considered valid if they adequately sample the domain of the construct (e.g., math, science, or history) being assessed.

Aptitude: potential to Learn

Achievement tests, as we learned in Chapter 1, are typically distinguished from aptitude tests, which attempt to evaluate a student's potential for learning rather than how much a student has already learned. As opposed to achievement tests, aptitude tests evaluate a wide range of experiences obtained in a variety of ways. They evaluate the effects of unknown and uncontrolled experiences. The validity of an aptitude test is judged primarily on its ability to predict future performance. Thus, such tests rely heavily on criterion-oriented validity studies. Table 13-3 lists contrasting characteristics of achievement and aptitude tests.

Table 13-3
Achievement
Tests Versus
Aptitude Tests

Achievement Tests
1. Evaluate the effects of a known or controlled set of experiences
2. Evaluate the end product of a course of training
3. Rely heavily on content validation procedures

Aptitude Tests
1. Evaluate the effects of an unknown, uncontrolled set of experiences
2. Evaluate the potential to profit from a course of training
3. Rely heavily on predictive criterion validation procedures

A third type of ability test is, of course, the intelligence test. Intelligence tests, as we have seen, measure general capacity. Like aptitude tests, intelligence tests attempt to predict future performance. However, intelligence tests attempt to predict generally and broadly, as opposed to aptitude tests, which typically attempt to predict potential in a specific area such as math, science, or music.

Clearly, as we have stressed, achievement, aptitude, and intelligence are highly interrelated. What one has learned is related to general intelligence, specific aptitude, motivation, and a host of other factors. And what one has learned (achievement) can be used to predict future success, just as an algebra achievement test might be used to predict success (aptitude) in a geometry course.

In our discussion of group tests, we consider all three types of tests. Our discussion begins with achievement tests. Then we consider group intelligence tests used in the school system. Subsequently, we examine tests used to measure scholastic aptitude.

B. *Group Achievement Tests*

As previously indicated, the Stanford Achievement Test (SAT) is one of the oldest of the standardized achievement tests that are widely used in the school system (Gardner et al., 1982). Published by the Psychological Corporation, the Stanford Achievement Test is a well-normed, criterion-referenced test with exemplary psychometric documentation. It evaluates achievement in 1st through 9th grades in the following areas: spelling, reading comprehension, word study and skills, language arts, social studies, science, mathematics, and listening comprehension. Figure 13-3 shows an example of the scoring output for the Stanford Achievement Test. Two related tests, the Stanford Early School Achievement Tests: Second Edition (SESAT) and the Stanford Test for Academic Skills: Second Edition (TASK), are used to extend the grade range covered from K through 13th. Together, all three tests are referred to as the Stanford Achievement Series.

Another well-standardized and psychometrically sound group measure of achievement is the Metropolitan Achievement Test (MAT), which measures

Figure 13-3
Example of a
score report for
the Stanford
Achievement
Test. (*Reproduced
by permission from
the Score Report
for the Stanford
Achievement Test,
7th Edition.
Copyright © 1982
by Harcourt Brace
Jovanovich, Inc.
All rights reserved.*)

STANFORD

ACHIEVEMENT TEST SERIES, EIGHTH EDITION
HITH OTIS-LENNON SCHOOL ABILITY TEST, SIXTH EDITION

TEACHER:	CESTERO	
SCHOOL:	NEWTOWN ELEM	
DISTRICT:	NEWTOWN	

C 1988
NORMS:
GRADE: 04   SPRING
TEST DATE: LEVEL:
03/89   FORM:

STANFORD   OLSAT
GRADE 04   GRADE 04
NATIONAL   NATIONAL
INTERMED 1 E
J   1

STUDENT SKILLS ANALYSIS
FOR
A ANDREW D ARCANGEL

TESTS	NO. OF ITEMS	RAW SCORE	SCALED SCORE	NATL PR-S	LOCAL PR-S	GRADE EQUIV	AAC RANGE
Total Reading	94	63	628	52-5	51-5	4.9	MIDDLE
Vocabulary	40	32	655	75-6	71-6	6.3	HIGH
Reading Comp.	54	31	611	37-4	33-4	4.0	MIDDLE
Total Math	118	70	615	42-5	58-5	4.5	MIDDLE
Concepts of No.	34	20	618	44-5	60-6	4.6	MIDDLE
Computation	44	21	594	25-4	39-4	3.8	LOW
Applications	40	29	635	59-5	70-6	5.4	MIDDLE
Total Language	60	45	638	57-5	63-6	5.4	MIDDLE
Lang Mechanics	30	20	616	36-4	34-4	4.1	MIDDLE
Lang Expression	30	25	662	74-6	78-7	8.5	HIGH
Spelling	40	22	615	37-4	35-4	4.2	MIDDLE
Study Skills	30	16	606	30-4	38-4	3.3	LOW
Science	50	36	642	79-7	84-7	7.3	HIGH
Social Science	50	34	627	63-6	61-6	5.6	MIDDLE
Listening	45	36	660	90-8	85-7	8.3	HIGH
Using Information	70	43	619	41-5	46-5	4.3	MIDDLE
Thinking Skills	101	67	627	61-6	65-6	5.4	MIDDLE
Basic Battery	387	252	623	49-5	54-5	4.7	MIDDLE
Complete Battery	487	322	627	54-5	56-5	5.2	MIDDLE

NATIONAL GRADE PERCENTILE BANDS

1   10   30   50   70   90   99

E

OTIS-LENNON SCHOOL ABILITY TEST		RAW SCORE	SAI	AGE PR-S	AGE NCE	SCALED SCORE	NATL GRADE PR-S	NATL GRADE NCE
Total		72	35	105	62-6	56.4	598	49-5	49.5
Verbal	**F**	36	15	102	55-5	52.6	588	36-4	42.5
Nonverbal		36	20	108	69-6	60.4	608	59-5	54.8

1   10   30   50   70   90   99

G
AGE   9 YRS   8 MOS

READING GROUP
Comprehension

LANGUAGE ARTS GROUP
Study Skills

MATHEMATICS GROUP
Computation

COMMUNICATIONS GROUP
Reading

CONTENT CLUSTERS	**H** RAW SCORE/ NUMBER OF ITEMS	BELOW AVERAGE	AVERAGE	ABOVE AVERAGE
Reading Vocabulary	32/ 40		✓	
Synonyms	21/ 24		✓	✓
Context	4/ 8		✓	✓
Multiple Meanings	7/ 8		✓	✓
Reading Comprehension	31/ 54		✓	
Recreational	14/ 18	✓		
Textual	7/ 18	✓		
Functional	10/ 18		✓	
Literal	10/ 21		✓	
Inferential	18/ 26		✓	
Critical	3/ 7		✓	
Concepts of Number	20/ 34		✓	
Whole Numbers	8/ 16		✓	
Fractions	1/ 4		✓	
Decimals	3/ 3			✓
Operations and Properties	8/ 11		✓	
Mathematics Computation	21/ 44		✓	
Add and Subtract/Whole Nos	8/ 12		✓	
Multiplication/Whole Numbers	6/ 12	✓		
Division/Whole Numbers	4/ 10		✓	
Add and Subtract/Decimals	3/ 6		✓	
Add and Subtract/Fractions	0/ 4	✓		
Mathematics Applications	29/ 40		✓	
Problem Solving	16/ 22		✓	
Graphs and Charts	4/ 6		✓	
Geometry/Measurement	9/ 12		✓	

CONTENT CLUSTERS	RAW SCORE/ NUMBER OF ITEMS	BELOW AVERAGE	AVERAGE	ABOVE AVERAGE
Language Mechanics	20/ 30		✓	
Capitalization	6/ 7			✓
Punctuation	5/ 11	✓		
Applied Grammar	9/ 12		✓	
Language Expression	25/ 30		✓	
Sentence Correctness	16/ 20		✓	
Sentence Effectiveness	9/ 10		✓	
Spelling	22/ 40		✓	
Study Skills	16/ 30		✓	
Library/Reference Skills	9/ 17		✓	
Information Skills	7/ 13		✓	
Science	36/ 50			✓
Physical Science	11/ 16		✓	
Biological Science	13/ 20		✓	
Earth/Space Science	12/ 14			✓
Social Science	34/ 50		✓	
Geography	10/ 13		✓	
History	6/ 8		✓	
Political Science	5/ 10		✓	
Economics	7/ 10		✓	
Psych/Sociol/Anthro	6/ 9		✓	
Listening	36/ 45			✓
Vocabulary	11/ 15			✓
Listening Comprehension	25/ 30			✓
Using Information	43/ 70		✓	
Thinking Skills	67/101		✓	

Scores based on Normative Data Copyright © 1988 by Harcourt Brace Jovanovich, Inc. All rights reserved.
COPY 01   PROCESS NO. 18904271-8909-00038-1

Copyright ©1991 by Harcourt Brace Jovanovich, Inc.
All rights reserved. Printed in the United States of America.

Actual size 8 ½" × 11".
Simulated data.

THE PSYCHOLOGICAL CORPORATION®
HARCOURT BRACE JOVANOVICH, INC.

achievement in reading by evaluating vocabulary, word recognition, and reading comprehension. An example of a reading item follows:

Jennifer ――――――― to play house.
Pick the word that best completes the sentence.

A. wood   **B.** book   **C.** likes   **D.** hopes

The MAT also measures mathematics by evaluating number concepts (e.g., measurement, decimals, factors, time, money), problem solving (e.g., word problems), and computation (addition, subtraction, multiplication, division). For example, a child might be presented with this item:

Jason had four candy bars. He gave one to Mary and one to Bill. Which number sentence below shows how many candy bars he had left?

A. $4 - 2 = \square$ **B.** $4 + 2 = \square$ **C.** $2 + 2 = \square$ **D.** $2 - 2 = \square$

Spelling is evaluated on the MAT in a normal spelling test format in which the student is asked to spell an orally dictated word presented in a sentence. Language skills are evaluated with a grammar test as well as a measure of alphabetizing skills. Science knowledge is evaluated in items such as the following:

A thermometer is used to measure ――――――――――.
(Mark the best answer.)

A. light   **B.** dark   **C.** temperature   **D.** planets

Finally, the MAT has a number of social studies items. Students are tested on their knowledge of geography, economics, history, political science, anthropology, sociology, and psychology; for example:

Paris is in ―――――――――.
(Mark the best answer.)

A. England   **B.** Spain   **C.** Canada   **D.** France

The most recent version of the MAT was standardized in 1985 on more than 250,000 students. The sample was stratified by school size, public versus nonpublic school affiliation, geographic region, socioeconomic status, and ethnic background. Reliabilities of the total scores run in the high .90s, while those for the five major content areas range between .90 and .96.

The Stanford Achievement Test and Metropolitan Achievement Test are the state of the art in achievement testing. Their psychometric documentation is outstanding. The tests are reliable and normed on very large samples. They sample a variety of school subjects and cover all grade levels.

C. Group Tests of Mental Abilities (Intelligence)

In this section, we discuss four group tests of mental abilities: the Kuhlmann-Anderson, the Henmon-Nelson, the Cognitive Abilities Test, and the Developing Cognitive Abilities Test.

Kuhlmann-Anderson Test, Eighth Edition (KAT). The Kuhlmann-Anderson Test (KAT) is a group intelligence test with eight separate levels for all grades, kindergarten through 12th grade. Each level of the KAT contains several tests, with a variety of items on each test. As with most multilevel batteries that cover multiple levels or age (grade) ranges, KAT items are primarily nonverbal at lower levels, requiring minimal reading and language ability. However, whereas most multilevel batteries become increasingly verbal with increasing age or grade level, the KAT remains primarily nonverbal throughout. Thus, the KAT not only is suited to young children but also can be useful for those who might be handicapped in following verbal procedures.

The results of the most recent (eighth) edition of the KAT can be expressed in verbal, quantitative, and total scores. At some levels, total scores can be expressed as deviation IQs. Scores at other levels can be expressed as percentile bands. A **percentile band** is like a confidence interval. It provides the range of percentiles that are likely to represent a subject's true score. It is created by forming an interval that is one standard error of measurement above and below the obtained score and then converting the resulting values to percentiles.

The overwhelming majority of reviews have praised the KAT for its construction, standardization, and other excellent psychometric qualities. Normative data have been continually improved and are based on more than 10,000 representative subjects. Reliability coefficients are quite good, with split-half coefficients running in the low .90s and test-retest coefficients ranging from the low .80s to low .90s. Validity is also well documented. The KAT correlates highly with a variety of ability tests and, in particular, has an impressive correlation with the Stanford-Binet (Form L-M). In one study with an earlier edition, the KAT was found to correlate almost perfectly with the Stanford-Binet when measurement errors were taken into account (Dearborn & Rothney, 1941).

In sum, the KAT is an extremely sound, sophisticated group test. Its nonverbal items make it particularly useful for special purposes. However, its impressive validity and reliability also make it one of the group ability tests of choice for all grade levels.

Henmon-Nelson Test (H-NT). A second well-standardized, highly used, and carefully constructed test for all grade levels is the Henmon-Nelson Test (H-NT) of mental abilities. Whereas the KAT contains eight levels, the H-NT is broken down into four levels by grade (kindergarten through 2, 3–6, 6–9, 9–12). Although it produces only a single score that is believed to reflect general intelligence, two sets of norms are available. One set is based on raw score distributions by age, the other on raw score distributions by grade. Raw scores can be converted into deviation IQs as well as percentiles. The availability of only a single score has been a continued source of controversy (see Lefever, 1959). However, a single score is consistent with the purpose of the test, which is to obtain a relatively quick measure of general intelligence (it takes approximately 30 minutes to complete the 90 items).

As with the KAT, normative data for the H-NT are based on a large sample. Current normative data are representative of the U.S. population according to the 1970 census. In fact, the standardization of the H-NT is one of the best found in any test. Subjects were selected from 250 schools on the basis of clustering and randomizing procedures to ensure representativeness.

As in the other tests for school-age individuals, most of the reliability coefficients, both split-half and test-retest, reported in the manual run in the .90s. Furthermore, the H-NT correlates well with a variety of intelligence tests (median .76, range .50–.84) as well as with achievement test scores (median .79, range .64–.85). Correlations with grades, though not as high, are quite impressive, with a median coefficient of .60.

In sum, the H-NT is an extremely sound instrument. It can help predict future academic success in a relatively brief time (30 minutes). It should be noted, however, that the H-NT has some important limitations when used as the sole screening instrument for selecting giftedness or identifying learning disabilities in minority, culturally diverse, and economically disadvantaged children.

By providing only a single score related to Spearman's *g* factor, the H-NT does not consider multiple intelligences. After the items were selected, no special effort was made to check for content bias, either by judges or by statistical analysis. The manual presents no specific data pertaining to the norms for specific racial/ethnic or socioeconomic groups, nor was the test specifically designed to be used for culturally diverse children. Indeed, the manual specifically calls for caution when using the H-NT for individuals who are known to be from an educationally disadvantaged subculture. It also advises caution when extreme scores (below 80 or above 130) are obtained. Consistent with these cautions, research suggests that the H-NT tends to underestimate Wechsler full-scale IQ scores by 10 to 15 points for certain populations (Watson & Klett, 1975). A major problem with the H-NT is its relatively low ceiling. For example, to achieve an IQ of 130, a ninth-grade child would have to answer about 85 of the items correctly. This leaves only five items to discriminate all those above 130.

Cognitive Abilities Test (COGAT). In terms of its reliability and validity, the 1982 edition of the Cognitive Abilities Test (COGAT) is comparable to the H-NT. Unlike the H-NT, however, the COGAT provides three separate scores: verbal, quantitative, and nonverbal. Reliabilities (KR_{20}) for the verbal score are in the high .90s; for the quantitative, the low .90s; and for the nonverbal, the high .90s.

Item selection of the COGAT is superior to that of the H-NT in terms of selecting minority, culturally diverse, and economically disadvantaged children. Unlike the H-NT, the COGAT was specifically designed for poor readers, the poorly educated, and persons for whom English is a second language.

The test authors of the COGAT took special steps to eliminate irrelevant sources of test difficulty, especially those pertaining to cultural bias. All items were reviewed to eliminate items with content that might be biased for or against any particular group. Statistical tests were then performed to eliminate items that might predict differentially for white and minority students. To eliminate the effect of test-taking skills, extensive practice exercises are used as part of the test administration.

The COGAT manual provides data concerning the percentage of racial/ethnic representation in its national standardization sample. Its standardization sample of 1984 included 94 public school districts and 71 nonpublic schools or school systems. Three stratification variables were used to ensure representativeness: geographic region, enrollment size, and socioeconomic status determined from the 1980 census. An effort was also made to ensure that the racial/ethnic composition of the standardization sample was representative of the national racial/ethnic composition. For grades 1 through 8, weighted racial/ethnic data are as follows: black 10.8%, Hispanic 6.9%, Asian 1%, Native American .6%, white 80.8%. For grades 9 and 10, the weighted scores are: black 13.1%, Hispanic 5.3%, Asian 1%, Native American .4%, white 80.2%.

The COGAT has advantages over the H-NT in its selection of minority, culturally diverse, and economically disadvantaged children. Moreover, research has revealed that the COGAT is a sensitive discriminator for giftedness (Harty, Adkins & Sherwood, 1984) and a good predictor of future performance (Henry & Bardo, 1990).

On the negative side, each of the three subtests of the COGAT requires 32 to 34 minutes of actual working time, which the manual recommends be spread out over two or three days. The manual claims that the tests are primarily "power tests" but provides no data to support this claim. Despite the apparent strength of the norms, uncertainty remains as to whether they are, in fact, representative. For example, when a selected community declined to participate in the norming process, a second, third, fourth, or, in some cases, fifth choice was needed to find a replacement. No data are provided regarding the frequency and magnitude of this type of sampling bias. A more serious potential drawback can be found in the information presented in the manual regarding ethnic group means. The standard age scores (SAS—normalized standard scores with a mean of 100 and standard deviation of 16) averaged about 15 or more points lower for black students (compared to whites) on the verbal battery and quantitative batteries. Hispanic students also tended to score lower than white students across the test batteries and grade levels (see Ansorge, 1985).

Developing Cognitive Abilities Test (DCAT). Compared to the H-NT and COGAT, available information on the Developing Cognitive Abilities Test (DCAT) is meager. Like its counterparts, the DCAT is designed to predict academic performance or, more specifically, to provide "a measure of characteristics and ability that contribute to academic performance" (p. 3). The unique feature of the DCAT is that it measures two dimensions of ability: (1) a traditional dimension that includes verbal, quantitative, and spatial abilities; and (2) a dimension based on Bloom's taxonomy of educational objectives. Reliability coefficients are within acceptable limits for the total score (low .90s) but are marginal for the verbal score (mid .80s) and questionable for the quantitative (mid .70s) and spatial (high .70s) scores. There is a ceiling problem for the higher grade levels. The technical manual provides rather limited evidence of the test's validity (see Fox, 1985).

Standardization of the DCAT involved 51 public school districts and 13 nonpublic school systems—a total of 28,656 students. In the sampling procedure, the nation was divided into four geographic areas with proportionate representation. The socioeconomic levels of the participating districts were slightly biased in favor of above-average districts, however. Racial/ethnic data reveal a relatively low percentage of Hispanics (2.9%), with blacks being 11.0%, Asians .6%, whites 85.2%, and other .3%. According to the manual, the test was written with a "sensitive concern" to provide an unbiased treatment of minority groups and women. A statistical item bias analysis was used. According to the authors, "the degree of bias produced by all forms and levels of the DCAT fall within acceptable limits." No data are presented to support this contention, however.

D. *Summary of Group Tests in the Schools*

The SAT, MAT, KAT, H-NT, COGAT, and DCAT are all sound, viable instruments. The SAT and MAT provide outstanding measures of achievement. A particular strength of the KAT in evaluating intelligence is its set of nonverbal items. The H-NT provides a quick estimate of *g* (general intelligence) for most children but is not as valid as the COGAT for assessing minority or culturally diverse children. Each test should be used only by those who have a knowledge of its particular properties, strengths, and limitations.

IV. *College Entrance Tests*

Three of the most widely used and well-known entrance tests are the College Board Scholastic Aptitude Test, the Cooperative School and College Ability Tests, and the American College Test.

A. *College Board Scholastic Aptitude Test (SAT)*

The College Board Scholastic Aptitude Test (SAT) leads all other group tests in relevant published research and exceeds all individual ability tests in this regard except for the Binet and Wechsler tests. Many of you have taken the SAT or a similar college entrance test and are perhaps interested in finding out more about it. Indeed, the SAT or a related test has probably played at least some role in deciding your future (see, for example, Hargadon, 1981).

In use since 1926, the SAT is given yearly to some 1.5 million students at 5000 centers. Rather than being an achievement or intelligence test, the SAT purports to predict the potential for higher education of high school seniors at the upper ability levels—thus, the term *aptitude* in its name.

The SAT produces two main scores: a verbal (SAT-V) and a mathematical (SAT-M) score. In addition, two other scores are obtained: one from a test of standard written English (TSWE) and a second from an experimental test. The SAT-V is composed of carefully selected and analyzed items involving sentence completion, identification of opposites, use of analogies, and paragraph comprehension. The SAT-M covers arithmetic, algebra, and geometry. (See Figure 13-4.) The SAT-V and SAT-M are each administered in two 30-minute sections (one hour total for the SAT-M and one hour for the SAT-V). They both correlate in the high .60s, with a definite increasing relationship between the two over the last few decades (ETS, 1991). Presumably, this increasing correlation reflects a decreasing emphasis on specific knowledge; however, the math section tends to be "wordy" (Wallace, 1972) and so the relationship may be due in part to a verbal influence in the math section.

The SAT is one of the most stable tests of any kind. The five-option, multiple-choice tasks are scored by a formula that adjusts for guessing. Test-retest, internal consistency, and alternative forms reliability coefficients consistently range from the high .80s to low .90s.

In addition to documenting stability, researchers have put much work into validity documentation. Validity data have not been as spectacular as reliability data, although the results are quite good. Predictive validity coefficients for freshman grades do, however, vary widely depending on one's major. Such variability is, of course, no surprise, since colleges are differentially selective and therefore differentially restrict the range of ability. The lowest coefficients are in the .10s and the highest coefficients are in the low to mid .60s. Median and modal coefficients, which run from the low to high .30s, are only modest.

Verbal Items (Analogies)

Directions: Each question below consists of a related pair of words or phrases, followed by five lettered pairs of words or phrases. Select the lettered pair that best expresses a relationship similar to that expressed in the original pair.

1. YAWN : BOREDOM :: (A) dream : sleep (B) anger : madness (C) smile : amusement (D) face : expression (E) impatience : rebellion
2. SUBMISSIVE : LED :: (A) wealthy : employed (B) tolerant : indulged (C) humble : humiliated (D) incorrigible : taught (E) inconspicuous : overlooked
3. SONG : REPERTOIRE :: (A) score : melody (B) instrument : artist (C) solo : chorus (D) benediction : church (E) suit : wardrobe
4. FAMINE : STARVATION :: (A) deluge : flood (B) drought : vegetation (C) war : treaty (D) success : achievement (E) seed : mutation

Verbal Items (Antonyms)

5. GOOD: (A) sour (B) bad (C) red (D) hot (E) ugly
6. SUBSEQUENT: (A) primary (B) recent (C) contemporary (D) prior (E) simultaneous
7. FERMENTING: (A) improvising (B) stagnating (C) wavering (D) plunging deeply (E) dissolving
8. DEPRESS: (A) force (B) allow (C) clarify (D) elate (E) loosen

Mathematics Items

9. In a restaurant where the sales tax on a $4.00 lunch is $0.24, what will be the sales tax due on a $15.00 dinner?

(A) $0.60
(B) $0.75
(C) $0.90
(D) $1.20
(E) $1.74

10. 1st Row   0 1 0
    2nd Row   0 1 1 0
    3rd Row   0 1 2 1 0
    4th Row   0 1 3 3 1 0
    5th Row   0 1 4 6 4 1 0
    6th Row

The nonzero numbers above form a triangular array. Beginning with the second row, each nonzero number in a row is the sum of the two numbers nearest to it in the row immediately above. If a sixth row is added in this fashion, what will be the sum of all the numbers in the sixth row?

(A) 8   (B) 10   (C) 16   (D) 32   (E) 64

11. If x is a positive integer and $x^2 + x = n$, which of the following could be the value of n?

(A) 14
(B) 15
(C) 18
(D) 23
(E) 30

12.

If one more of the lit signals on the rear of the car above were out, what per cent of all the rear signals would then be lit?

(A) 25%   (B) 33⅓%   (C) 50%
(D) 66⅔%   (E) 75%

Figure 13-4
Sample items from the verbal and mathematical sections of the Scholastic Aptitude Test. Answers are as follows: 1 (c), (2) (e), 3 (e), 4 (a), 5 (b), 6 (d), 7 (b), 8 (d), 9 (c), 10 (d), 11 (e), 12 (c). (SAT questions selected from *"Taking the SAT: A Guide to the Scholastic Aptitude Test and the Test of Standard Written English,"* College Entrance Examination Board (1981, 1982). *Reprinted by permission of Educational Testing Service, the copyright owner.*)

Figure 13-5
Percentage of students scoring 600 or above on the SAT, 1972–1990. *(From "Performance at the Top: From Elementary Through Graduate School," p. 23. Copyright © 1991 by Educational Testing Service. Reprinted by permission of Educational Testing Service, the copyright holder.)*

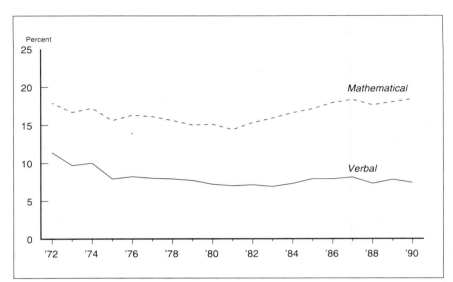

predictive ✗
Validity

However, as many have noted, when combined with the high school record, the SAT can be extremely useful in predicting freshman college grades (Payne et al., 1990). Typical validities are .57 for the high school record, with a multiple correlation on the order of .65 (Donlon, 1984, pp. 144–147). However, the actual validity varies greatly, depending on the college or university.

The psychometric soundness of the SAT is based on years of experience, statistical analyses of the results from tens of thousands of administrations, and careful item selection. Although present norms are based on a relatively old sample consisting of more than 10,000 students who took the test in 1941, the psychometric adequacy of the SAT is perhaps better documented than that for any other ability test. Separate norms as a function of various demographic variables (gender, race) are not available, but evidence shows the test is equally valid for all groups (see Wallace, 1972).

When compared with the original norms, the scores of modern users of the SAT tend to be about 20 points lower for both SAT-V and SAT-M. In accounting for this decline, professionals have pointed to the larger, more diverse pool of students and a dilution of substance and softening of high school standards (Hanford, 1986).

While overall scores have declined, there was a steady decline in the percentage of high scores (scores over 600) between the late 1970s and the early 1980s. Since 1981, however, the percentage of high scores (600 or above) in math has increased steadily from 14% to 18% in 1990 (see Figure 13-5). As Figure 13-5 also shows, the percentage of high scores for the verbal test has increased only from 7% in 1983 to 8% in 1987, and more recently it has fluctuated.

Critics of the SAT claim that the test is outmoded and call for better procedures (Morgan, 1984). A major weakness of the SAT as well as other major college entrance tests is relatively poor predictive power in discriminating the grades of students who score in the middle ranges (total scores between 900 and 1200). It is not uncommon for a student at the mean on the SAT to have a higher college grade point average than a student who scores a standard deviation above the mean on both sections, perhaps because factors such as motivation, determination, personality, emotional stability, and home and social life also influence freshman grades. In other words, test scores and high school performance records aren't the only determinants of college success. Another weakness is that the number of English or math units a student has does not correlate significantly with his or her SAT-V or SAT-M score (Sinha, 1986). This may be due to the effects of coaching (that is, training courses that expose students to questions like those on the actual test and attempt to develop good test-taking skills).

Despite its critics, the SAT is a sound instrument. There is much to be said for its value as a predictor of grades during the early years of college when it is used in conjunction with other sources of data such as the high school record. The psychometric adequacy of the SAT may be the highest possible for any such test, and the SAT is likely to play a role in college entrance decisions for some time to come, despite attacks from the public and the decline in average SAT scores.

B. *Cooperative School and College Ability Tests (SCAT)*

Second to the SAT in terms of usage is the Cooperative School and College Ability Tests (SCAT), developed in 1955. In addition to the college level, the SCAT covers three precollege levels beginning at the fourth grade. The SCAT purports to measure school-learned abilities as well as the individual's potential to undertake additional schooling.

Although the SCAT is well designed and constructed, H. L. Butcher (1972) questions the representativeness of the SCAT standardization sample. Psychometric documentation of the SCAT, furthermore, is neither as strong nor as extensive as that of the SAT. Another problem is that little empirical data are provided to support the major assumption that previous success in acquiring school-learned abilities can predict future success in acquiring such abilities. Even if this assumption were accurate—and it probably is—grades, which also reflect school-learned abilities, should provide about as much information as the SCAT, especially at the college level. In view of these considerations, we concur with Butcher (1972) that additional evidence on the SCAT would be highly desirable. Also, despite its reasonably good correlation with

Figure 13-6

A sample student profile from ACT. (*Copyright 1991 by The American College Testing Program. All rights reserved. Reproduced with permission.*)

the SAT, we see little advantage of the SCAT over the SAT for predicting college success.

C. *The American College Test (ACT)*

The American College Test (ACT) is another popular and widely used college entrance (aptitude) test. In some states (for instance, Alabama), most students take the ACT. The ACT produces specific content scores and a composite. The content scores are in English, mathematical usage, social studies reading, and natural science reading. In expressing results, the ACT makes use of the Iowa Test of Educational Development (ITED) Scale. Scores on this scale can vary between 1 and 36, with a standard deviation of 5 and a mean of 16 for high school students and a mean of 19 for college aspirants. Figure 13-6 shows a sample profile report for the ACT.

The ACT is comparable to the SAT in terms of predicting college GPA alone or in conjunction with high school GPA. In fact, the correlation between the two tests is quite high (high .80s) (Pugh, 1968). However, internal consistency coefficients are not as strong in the ACT, with coefficients in the mid .90s for the composite and in the high .70s to high .80s for the four content scores.

V. *Graduate School Entrance Tests*

If you plan to go to graduate school, then you very likely will be required to take a graduate school entrance test. The two most widely used are the Graduate Record Examination Aptitude Test and the Miller Analogies Test.

A. *Graduate Record Examination Aptitude Test (GRE)*

The Graduate Record Examination Aptitude Test, better known as the GRE, is one of the most commonly used tests for graduate school entrance. Almost any student who wishes to pursue graduate work in psychology, as well as in many other disciplines, is likely to be confronted with the GRE. Offered throughout the year at designated examination centers, which are located mostly at universities and colleges, the GRE purports to be a measure of general scholastic ability. It is most frequently used in conjunction with grade point average, letters of recommendation, and other academic factors in the highly competitive graduate school selection process. The GRE contains a general section that produces verbal (GRE-V), quantitative (GRE-Q), and analytic (GRE-A) scores. In addition to this general test, which is used for all college majors, the GRE contains an advanced section that measures achievement in at least 20 majors, such as psychology, history, and chemistry (see Figures 13-7, 13-8, and 13-9[1]).

In some respects, the GRE parallels the SAT. With a standard mean score of 500 and a standard deviation of 100, as in the original standardization sample of the SAT-V, the verbal section covers reasoning, identification of opposites, use of analogies, and paragraph comprehension. The quantitative section covers arithmetic reasoning, algebra, and geometry as in the SAT-M. However, the normative sample for the GRE is only about one-fifth the size of the SAT

---

[1] Figures 13-7, 13-8, and 13-9 are previously administered GRE questions selected from the GRE's General Test. Reprinted by permission of Educational Testing Service, the copyright owner.

Figure 13-7
GRE verbal
ability sample
items. (*GRE test
items in Figures
13-7, 13-8, and
13-9 selected from
GRE General Test
administered
December, 1991.
Reprinted by
permission of
Educational
Testing Service, the
copyright owner.*)

Directions: Each sentence below has one or two blanks, each indicating that something has been omitted. Beneath the sentence are five lettered words or sets of words. Choose the word or set of words for each blank that *best* fits the meaning of the sentence as a whole.

1. From observing the ------ of those about me during the flag raising, I concluded that patriotism, if not actually on the decline, is at least in a state of ------.

   (A) irreverence..amelioration   (B) absorption..atrophy   (C) lassitude..rampancy   (D) allegiance..decadence   (E) apathy..dormancy

2. Long before there was a European or American civilization, the Greeks demonstrated the ------ of war, fighting chiefly among themselves until their great city-states became the ------ of lesser folk.

   (A) imbecility..bane   (B) grandeur..scapegoats   (C) transience..paragons   (D) futility..prey   (E) profitability..allies

   · · ·

Directions: In each of the following questions, a related pair of words or phrases is followed by five lettered pairs of words or phrases. Select the lettered pair that best expresses a relationship similar to that expressed in the original pair.

8. Apprentice:Master ::   (A) novice:expert   (B) specimen:scientist   (C) doctor:psychiatrist   (D) teacher:dean   (E) musician:orchestra

9. Pursuit:Capture ::   (A) flight:siege   (B) competition:prize   (C) fugitive:posse   (D) courtship:ambush   (E) stampede:migration

sample (about 2000 college seniors tested at 11 colleges in 1952). The psychometric adequacy of the GRE is also less spectacular than that of the SAT, both in the reported coefficients of validity and reliability and in the extensiveness of documentation. Nevertheless, the GRE is a relatively sound instrument.

The stability of the GRE based on Kuder-Richardson and odd-even reliability is adequate, with coefficients only slightly lower than those of the SAT. However, the predictive validity of the GRE is far from convincing. Independent studies of the GRE vary from those that find moderate correlations between the GRE and grade point average to those that find no or even a negative relationship between the two. Although it can be said that high GRE scorers tend to complete graduate school more often than low scorers for certain programs, general predictive studies have proved somewhat discouraging.

Those who aspire to go to graduate school might be asking at this point, "With its limitations, why is it that the GRE has such a critical effect on my chances for going to graduate school and on my future career?" Indeed, many graduate school hopefuls have asked this question. One answer is that many schools have developed their own local norms and psychometric documentation and are able to use the GRE, either independently or in conjunction with

Figure 13-8
GRE quantitative ability sample items.

Numbers:	All numbers used are real numbers.
Figures:	Position of points, angles, regions, etc. can be assumed to be in the order shown; and angle measures can be assumed to be positive.
	Lines shown as straight can be assumed to be straight.
	Figures can be assumed to lie in a plane unless otherwise indicated.
	Figures that accompany questions are intended to provide information useful in answering the questions. However, unless a note states that a figure is drawn to scale, you should solve these problems NOT by estimating sizes by sight or by measurement, but by using your knowledge of mathematics (see Example 2 below).

Directions: Each of the questions 1–15 consists of two quantities, one in Column A and one in Column B. You are to compare the two quantities and choose

A if the quantity in Column A is greater;
B if the quantity in Column B is greater;
C if the two quantities are equal;
D if the relationship cannot be determined from the information given.

Note: Since there are only four choices, NEVER MARK (E).

Common Information: In a question, information concerning one or both of the quantities to be compared is centered above the two columns. A symbol that appears in both columns represents the same thing in Column A as it does in Column B.

	Column A	**Column B**	**Sample Answers**
Example 1:	2×6	$2 + 6$	● Ⓑ Ⓒ Ⓓ Ⓔ

Examples 2-4 refer to $\triangle PQR$.

	Column A	**Column B**	**Sample Answers**
Example 2:	PN	NQ	Ⓐ Ⓑ Ⓒ ● Ⓔ (since equal measures cannot be assumed, even though PN and NQ appear equal)
Example 3:	x	y	Ⓐ ● Ⓒ Ⓓ Ⓔ (since N is between P and Q)

Figure 13-9
GRE analytical ability sample items.

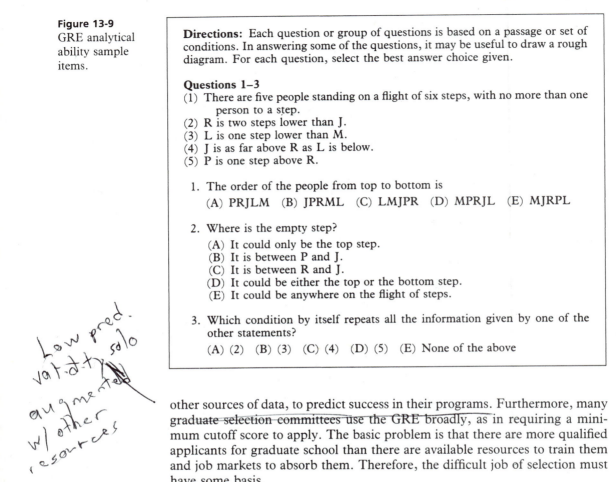

Directions: Each question or group of questions is based on a passage or set of conditions. In answering some of the questions, it may be useful to draw a rough diagram. For each question, select the best answer choice given.

Questions 1–3
(1) There are five people standing on a flight of six steps, with no more than one person to a step.
(2) R is two steps lower than J.
(3) L is one step lower than M.
(4) J is as far above R as L is below.
(5) P is one step above R.

1. The order of the people from top to bottom is
   (A) PRJLM   (B) JPRML   (C) LMJPR   (D) MPRJL   (E) MJRPL

2. Where is the empty step?
   (A) It could only be the top step.
   (B) It is between P and J.
   (C) It is between R and J.
   (D) It could be either the top or the bottom step.
   (E) It could be anywhere on the flight of steps.

3. Which condition by itself repeats all the information given by one of the other statements?
   (A) (2)   (B) (3)   (C) (4)   (D) (5)   (E) None of the above

other sources of data, to predict success in their programs. Furthermore, many graduate selection committees use the GRE broadly, as in requiring a minimum cutoff score to apply. The basic problem is that there are more qualified applicants for graduate school than there are available resources to train them and job markets to absorb them. Therefore, the difficult job of selection must have some basis.

Graduate schools also frequently complain that grades are no longer good predictors of scholastic ability because of *grade inflation*—the phenomenon of rising average college grades despite declines in average SAT scores. Thus, many people claim that a "B" today is equivalent to a "C" 15 or 20 years ago, and that an "A" today is equivalent to a "B" then. This grade inflation has led to a corresponding restriction in the range of grades, which may, in part, explain the low predictive validity coefficient for the GRE. Another reason for reliance on GRE scores is that the Freedom of Information Act grants students the right to examine their files, including letters of recommendation. The argument is that professors and other sources of student recommendations cannot be open or candid, knowing the student may someday read the letter. Thus, as the validity of grades and letters of recommendation becomes more questionable, greater reliance is being put on test scores. Fair or not, this is the reality. However, students with relatively poor GRE scores need not feel devas-

Figure 13-10
GRE score trends, 1981–1990. (*From "Performance at the Top: From Elementary Through Graduate School," p. 33. Copyright © 1991 by Educational Testing Service. Reprinted by permission of Educational Testing Service, the copyright holder.*)

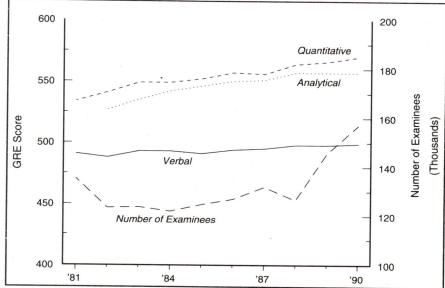

tated and can take heart in the knowledge that their score is not necessarily predictive of success in graduate school.

Nevertheless, the definite trend of GRE scores is upward. As Figure 13-10 illustrates, quantitative scores were up 36 points between 1981 and 1990, from a mean of 534 to a mean of 570. During this same period, analytical scores increased from a mean of 527 to a mean of 557, up 30 points. The verbal mean rose a modest 8 points, from 491 to 499. These increases are particularly impressive because they occurred during a time of a substantial increase in the numbers of students taking the GRE, from 135,339 in 1981 to 157,023 in 1990.

One trend in graduate selection in psychology has been the consideration of nontraditional factors such as research experience and publications. D. P. Saccuzzo and R. Schulte (1978), for example, surveyed American Psychological Association approved and nonapproved clinical and nonclinical psychology programs and found that the most important consideration beyond grades and GRE scores was research experience and professional publications. Although apparently rare according to their results, research publications can do more to enhance a new application or previously rejected application for graduate study than can retaking the GRE, taking additional courses to improve grades, or even obtaining a master's degree. The message is clear. Students who believe themselves to be more capable than their undergraduate grades and GRE scores indicate simply must demonstrate this capability through research endeavors.

Another issue to consider is whether to study for the GRE. In addition to study books and guides, many courses are offered to those who hope to in-

Figure 13-11
MAT sample
items. (*From the
Miller Analogies
Test. Copyright
© 1988 by The
Psychological
Corporation.
Reproduced by
permission. All
rights reserved.*)

Look at the first sample analogy below. **Pain** is the right answer because **pain** is related to PLEASURE as DARK is related to LIGHT. On the **Answer Sheet** mark c for the first sample to show that choice **c. pain** is the right answer. The diagram at the right shows you how to mark on your **Answer Sheet**.

SAMPLES

1. LIGHT : DARK :: PLEASURE : (*a.* picnic, *b.* day, *c.* pain, *d.* night)
2. LEAVE : DEPART :: (*a.* stay, *b.* go, *c.* home, *d.* come) : REMAIN
3. STAPLE : (*a.* clamp, *b.* paper, *c.* glue, *d.* food) :: NAIL : WOOD
4. (*a.* 4, *b.* 5, *c.* 7, *d.* 6) : 12 :: 12 : 24

**How to Mark
on Answer Sheet**

Choose the proper word **in the parentheses** in Sample 2 and mark the corresponding letter in the proper place on **your Answer Sheet**. Do the same thing in the third and fourth samples.

crease their chances of success (see Anastasi, 1981). Some of these courses are offered through recognized universities, but there are no restrictions on who can offer them or on how much students are charged. Students can pay more than $600 for such courses. Unfortunately, no published data support the value of such courses or study guides. Certainly, you should attempt to prepare as much as possible for this important exam; however, be advised that many of those who offer study programs have not yet bothered to document their value.

B. *Miller Analogies Test (MAT)*

A second major graduate school entrance test is the Miller Analogies Test (MAT). Like the GRE, the MAT is designed to measure scholastic aptitudes for graduate-level studies. However, unlike the GRE, the MAT is a strictly verbal test. It requires the student to discern in 50 minutes logical relationships for 100 varied analogy problems ranging in difficulty to the most difficult items found on any test (see Figure 13-11). Knowledge of specific content and a wide vocabulary are extremely useful in this endeavor. However, the most important factor appears to be the ability to see relationships as well as a knowledge of the various ways analogies can be formed (by sound, number, similarities, differences, and so forth). The MAT is used in a variety of specializations and fields, and special norms are available for various fields.

Odd-even reliability data for the MAT are adequate, with reported coefficients in the manual in the high .80s. Unfortunately, as with the GRE, predictive validity support for the MAT is lacking. Despite a substantial correlation with the GRE (coefficients run in the low .80s), validity coefficients reported in the manual for grades vary considerably from sample to sample and are only modest (median in the high .30s). Generally, the psychometric adequacy of the MAT is reasonable when compared with ability tests in general, but GRE scores and grade point average remain its primary correlates. Furthermore, the MAT is not predictive of research ability, creativity, and other factors important to graduate school and professional performance. However, as an aid in discriminating among graduate school applications and adults at the highest level of verbal ability, the MAT is an excellent device.

VI. *Nonverbal Group Ability Tests*

As we noted in our discussion of individual tests that do not require the use of language, nonverbal tests are needed for evaluating individuals who are either handicapped or limited in the verbal/language realm. Like their individual test counterparts, nonverbal group tests may be performance tests, which require the subject to do something (draw, solve maze problems), or they may be paper-and-pencil tests, which provide printed nonverbal relationship items and instruct the subject to select the best of two or more multiple-choice responses. Some nonverbal group tests can be administered without the use of language.

A. *Raven Progressive Matrices (RPM)*

The Raven Progressive Matrices (RPM) test is one of the best known and most popular nonverbal group test. Only the SAT, Wechsler, and Binet tests are referenced more in *The Mental Measurements Yearbook*. The RPM may be group or individually administered and covers an age range from 5 years through elderly adults. Instructions are simple and, if necessary, the RPM can be administered by demonstration without the use of language. The RPM consists exclusively of one of the most common type of stimuli in nonverbal tests of any kind—matrices (see Figure 13-12). The 60 matrices of the standard RPM are graded in difficulty. Each contains a logical pattern or design with a missing part. The subject's task is to select the appropriate design from up to eight alternative choices. The test can be used with or without a time limit, and research supports the RPM as a measure of general intelligence, or Spearman's *g* factor (Paul, 1985). In fact, the Raven may be the best single measure of *g*

Figure 13-12
Sample
Progressive
Matrices items.
(*Reprinted by
permission of J. C.
Raven, Ltd.*)

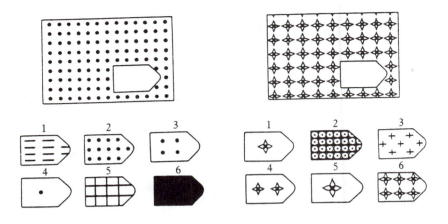

available, as shown by a multidimensional scaling by B. Marshalek, D. F. Lohman, and R. E. Snow (1983). See Figure 13-13.

The RPM, a product of England, was originally designed to assess military recruits independently of educational factors. For years, the lack of adequate U.S. norms for the RPM and weaknesses in the manual were sources of criticism. In spite of these limitations, the RPM and PM-like tests flourished. The versatility of matrices in ability testing can be seen in their wide application for such groups as young children, the culturally deprived, and the language-handicapped. Analysis of available reliability studies shows a rather respectable range of coefficients, from the high .70s to low .90s (see Bortner, 1965). Early studies also revealed a fairly high correlation between the RPM and the Stanford-Binet ($r = .60$) (Keir, 1949), Wechsler performance IQ ($r = .70$), and Wechsler verbal IQ ($r = .58$) (Hall, 1957).

More recently, the manual for the Raven has been updated along with the publication of an impressive set of norms (Raven, 1986, 1990). With these new norms, it is possible to compare the performance of children from major cities around the world. Thus, a major criticism of the Raven has finally been corrected and in a rather marvelous way.

A major advantage of the Raven is that it appears to minimize the effects of language and culture. For example, whereas Hispanics and African-Americans typically score about 15 points lower on the Wechsler and Binet scales than Caucasians (see Chapters 10 and 11), there is only about a seven- or eight-point difference with the Raven. Thus, the Raven tends to cut in half the selection bias that occurs when the Binet or Wechsler is used. Consequently, it has great utility for use in selecting disadvantaged African-American and Hispanic children for giftedness (Saccuzzo, in press). Moreover, unlike the Kaufman, which also has a reduced African-American-Caucasian and Hispanic-Caucasian discrepancy (see Chapter 12), the Raven, as we have seen, is actually a better measure of general intelligence than the Wechsler scales. With its new world-

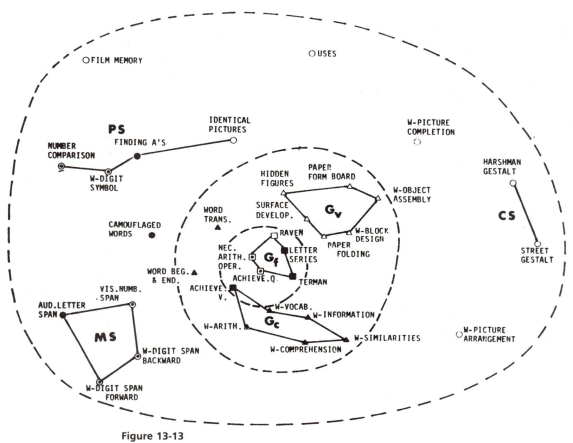

Figure 13-13
Marshalek, Lohman, and Snow's radix analysis of the Raven. (*Courtesy of Richard Snow.*)

wide norms and updated test manual, the Raven holds promise as one of the major players in the testing field in the 21st century.

B. *Goodenough-Harris Drawing Test (G-HDT)*

A remarkable nonverbal intelligence test that can be either group or individually administered is the Goodenough-Harris Drawing Test (G-HDT). The G-HDT is one of the simplest, quickest, easiest to administer, and least expensive of all ability tests. A pencil and white unlined paper are the only needed materials. The subject is instructed to draw a picture of a whole man and to do the best job possible. The G-HDT was standardized by determining those characteristics of human figure drawings that differentiated subjects in various age groups. More than 70 scoreable items were discerned. Subjects get credit for each item included in their drawings. As a rule, each detail is given one point. For example, if only a head is included with no facial features, then the subject receives only one point. Points are added for additional details, such as facial features and clothing.

The G-HDT was originally standardized in 1926 and was restandardized in 1963 (Harris, 1963). Scoring of the G-HDT follows the principle of age differentiation—older children tend to get more points because of the greater accuracy and detail of their drawings. Thus, mental ages can be determined by comparing scores with those of the normative sample. Raw scores can be converted to standard scores with a mean of 100 and a standard deviation of 15. Split-half, test-retest, and interscorer reliability coefficients are good, with ranges in the high .60s to low .90s for both old and revised forms (Dunn, 1972). Scores begin leveling off at about age 14 or 15 (Anastasi, 1972b), so the use of the G-HDT is restricted primarily to children, and the test works best with younger children (Scott, 1981). Correlations with the Stanford-Binet (Form L-M) have ranged from .36 to .74 (Dunn, 1972).

Because of their ease of administration and short administration time, the G-HDT and other human-figure drawing tests are used extensively in test batteries (Lubin, Wallis & Paine, 1971). Relatively recent representative norms and good validity documentation allow the examiner to obtain a quick rough estimate of a child's intelligence. However, the G-HDT is most appropriately used in conjunction with other sources of information in a battery of tests; results based on G-HDT data alone can be quite misleading.

C. *IPAT Culture Fair Intelligence Test*

All cultures tend to reinforce certain skills and activities at the expense of others. One purpose of nonverbal and performance tests is to remove factors related to cultural influences so that pure intelligence, independent of learning, culture, and the like, can be measured. Experience and empirical research have shown that such a test has yet to be developed (see Olmedo, 1981). Indeed, many doubt whether such an accomplishment is even within the realm of possibility (Tannenbaum, 1968), although the Raven probably comes as close to this goal as any test.

The IPAT Culture Fair Intelligence Test was designed to eliminate language influences in an ability test and to provide an estimate of intelligence that is relatively free of cultural influence. Although it is no more successful in this regard than any other such attempt, the popularity of the Culture Fair Intelligence Test reflects the strong desire among users for a test that reduces cultural factors as much as possible.

Constructed in the 1940s under the direction of R. B. Cattell, the Culture Fair Intelligence Test is a paper-and-pencil procedure that covers three levels (ages 4–8 and mentally defective adults, ages 8–12 and randomly selected adults, and high school age and superior adults). Two parallel forms are available. Standardization varies according to age level. Kuder-Richardson reliabilities are only in the .70s, with substantially lower test-retest coefficients. The test has been correlated with a wide variety of other tests with mixed results. Correlations with the Wechsler and Binet tests are quite good, with a range of .56 to .85 (Tannenbaum, 1968). Also in support of the Culture Fair Intelligence Test is the finding that normative data from Western European countries, the United States, and Australia are comparable. Thus, if one wishes to estimate intelligence in a Western European or Australian individual, the Culture Fair Intelligence Test is probably the instrument of choice. However, the norms are becoming outdated and more work is needed if the Culture Fair Test is to compete with the Raven.

VII. *Group Tests for Specific Purposes*

There are an almost uncountable number of group tests for an endless variety of purposes. In addition to group tests used to assess intelligence, academic aptitude, and factors relevant to personnel and occupation selection, there is an endless variety of tests for specific populations. The Black Intelligence Test of Cultural Homogeneity (BITCH), for example, is designed to be a culture-fair intelligence test for blacks (see Chapter 20). The Barranquilla Rapid Survey Intelligence test (BRSI) purports to measure intelligence in Spanish-speaking persons. Inasmuch as intelligence tests for specific groups are new and poorly documented, we mention them here only to make you aware of the richness and variety of available tests.

A. *Tests for Use in Industry: Wonderlic Personnel Test (WPT)*

Business and industry make extensive use of tests, especially as an aid in making decisions concerning employment, placement, and promotion. One widely used such test is the Wonderlic Personnel Test (WPT). Based on a popular instrument, the Otis Self-Administering Tests of Mental Ability, the WPT is a quick (12-minute) test of mental ability in adults. Normative data are available on more than 50,000 adults 20 to 65 years old. Five forms, whose intercorrelations range from .82 to .94, are available. Odd-even reliability coefficients are also excellent, with a range of .88 to .94 reported in the manual. The main drawback of the WPT is its meager validity documentation, although those studies that are available tend to be supportive (Dodrill & Warner, 1988; Kennedy et al., 1989). Moreover, the WPT is a quick, stable, paper-and-pencil intelligence test with extensive norms. It is widely used for employee-related decisions in industry but has its greatest value when local validity data are available. In the absence of local data, test scores must be interpreted with some caution.

B. *Tests for Assessing Occupational Aptitude*

The number and variety of group ability tests for measuring aptitude for various occupations are staggering. The General Aptitude Test Battery (GATB), for example, is a reading ability test that purportedly measures aptitude for a variety of occupations.

The GATB was developed and used by the U.S. Employment Service for making employment decisions in government agencies. It attempts to measure a wide range of aptitudes from general intelligence (*g*) through finger and manual dexterity. The GATB also produces scores for motor coordination, form perception (awareness of relevant details and ability to compare and discriminate various shapes), and clerical perception (for example, the ability to proofread). Scores are also available for verbal, numerical, and spatial aptitudes.

The GATB was originally standardized in 1952 on a sample of 4000 people believed to be representative of the working population of the United States in 1940. The sample was stratified according to gender, education, occupation, and geographic location and ranged in age from 18 to 54. The mean education level of the sample of 11.0 years reveals that the GATB is most appropriate for noncollege graduates. Moreover, with rapidly changing times and the advent of high technology, the GATB may be out of date (see, for example, Avolio & Waldman, 1990).

A more serious problem for the GATB is the concern that the test may not be fair to racial and ethnic minority groups (Science Agenda, Jan./Feb. 1991). As of this writing, the Department of Labor has plans to discontinue using the GATB until additional research is completed.

In measuring potential ability (aptitude) for specific vocations, a number of fine tests are available. The Differential Aptitude Test (DAT) is especially useful in assessing clerical competence, such as clerical speed and accuracy and grammar. The Bennett Mechanical Comprehension Test and the Revised Minnesota Paper Form Board Tests are two popular measures of mechanical ability. The Accounting Orientation Test has shown some promise in measuring accounting skills. To assess business skills and readiness for graduate study in business, there is the Admission Test for Graduate Study in Business. There are also special ability tests for advanced study in dentistry (for example, the Dental Admission Testing Program), law (for example, the Law School Admission Test), and medicine (for example, the Medical College Admission Test).

C. *Armed Services Vocational Aptitude Battery (ASVAB)*

Designed for the Department of Defense, the Armed Services Vocational Aptitude Battery (ASVAB) is administered to more than 1.3 million students each year. A multiple aptitude battery, the ASVAB was designed for use with students in grades 11 and 12 and in postsecondary schools. The test yields scores that are used in both educational and military settings. In the military services, ASVAB results are used to identify students who potentially qualify for entry into the military and for assignment to various military occupational training programs.

The ASVAB consists of ten subtests: general science, arithmetic reasoning, word knowledge, paragraph comprehension, numeral operations, coding speed, auto and shop information, mathematics knowledge, mechanical comprehension, and electronics information. These subtests are grouped into various composites, including three academic composites—academic ability, verbal, and math; four occupational composites—mechanical and crafts, business and clerical, electronics and electrical, health and social; and an overall composite reflecting general ability.

The psychometric characteristics of the ASVAB are excellent. The most recent form of the test was normed on a nationally representative group of nearly 12,000 men and women between the ages of 16 and 23 who took the ASVAB-8a between July and October 1980.

Blacks, Hispanics, and economically disadvantaged whites were oversampled and then weighted to represent the national population distribution for all groups. Reliability coefficients for composite scores based on the Kuder-Richardson formula (KR_{20}) are excellent, ranging from .84 to .92 for women and .88 to .95 for men. The test manual and supporting documents strongly support the ASVAB as a valid predictor of performance during training for a variety of military and civilian occupations.

Recently, the military has been involved in presenting the ASVAB via microcomputer rather than in the traditional paper-and-pencil format. Through this new computerized format, subjects can be tested adaptively, meaning that the questions given each person are based on his or her unique ability. Briefly, adaptive testing of ability involves presenting an item of a known level of difficulty and then presenting either a more difficult or a less difficult item, depending on whether the subject is correct. The procedure cuts testing time almost in half and is far less fatiguing than the complete test. Preliminary results have supported computerized adaptive testing in U.S. Army recruiting (Sands & Gade, 1983), and the procedure may become a normal part of the military testing procedure by the 21st century.

Summary

Group ability tests are available for just about any purpose, and there appears to be no end to the construction of this type of test. Relative ease in scoring and administration gives group ability tests a major advantage over individual tests, and, in many cases, the results from group tests are as stable and valid as those from individual tests. However, low scores, wide discrepancies between two group test results, or wide discrepancies between a group test result and some other indicator such as grades should be a reason for exercising caution in interpreting results. When in doubt, users of group ability tests should refer the problem to a competent professional who can administer an individual ability test.

The public school system makes the most extensive use of group ability tests. Indeed, many sound tests exist for all levels from kindergarten through 12th grade. College and graduate school entrance tests also account for a large proportion of the group ability tests used in the United States.

In addition to their use in the educational system, a considerable number of group ability tests play an important role in personnel decisions. Some ability tests have been developed for personnel selection in business and industry. Other group ability tests can be used by vocational counselors to assess ability for certain occupations. Still other group ability tests measure aptitude for advanced or professional training. In viewing group ability tests, one gets the impression that there is almost no limit to the scope and applicability of psychological tests.

Chapter 14

Tests for Choosing Careers

Learning Objectives

When you have completed this chapter, you should be able to:

- Describe the use of the criterion-keying method in the development of the SVIB.
- List some of the criticisms of the SVIB.
- Describe how the SCII improved on the SVIB.
- Describe how the KOIS differs from the SVIB and the SCII.
- Outline some of the controversial issues in interest measurement.
- Compare the approaches to career placement taken by Osipow, Super, and Roe.
- State why it is important to study the characteristics of work environments.
- Discuss several ways in which work environment can affect behavior.
- List several methods of job analysis.
- Describe the template-matching method of assessment.

At age 35, Harry found himself faced with a dilemma. He had studied hard for many years to become a dentist, but what he had suspected for many years was becoming obvious: he really did not like dentistry. Although Harry had chosen dentistry as an occupation, he had not given detailed consideration to what the practice of dentistry was like before making a commitment to the field.

Harry could trace his interest in becoming a dentist to an experience he had during his childhood. As a young boy, he liked to play golf. While on the course one day, Harry met a dentist who explained that the practice of dentistry was lucrative and that it still allowed practitioners enough time to play golf and engage in other activities. Harry was a good student, and the encounter with the golfer-dentist made him think that dentistry would afford him the ideal life style. Harry liked his science classes when he entered college, and he continued to be an outstanding student. After four years at a state university, he was accepted by a good dental school.

In dental school, Harry began to question his career choice. Two things were apparent by the end of his third year. First, he did not really enjoy doing dental work. He found himself uneasy when his patients fussed in the chair, and he disliked subjecting people to the discomfort associated with some dental procedures. Second, Harry discovered that he was not interested in the same things as were other people in the field of dentistry.

After completing dental school, Harry did a brief tour of duty in the Air Force as a dentist. When he left the service, he decided he wanted to get away from dentistry for a while and he enrolled in art school. However, despite his dislike for dentistry, he returned to the practice because of the large personal and financial investment he had already made in the profession. Dentistry paid well, and it was difficult to give it up; retraining in a field of more interest to him would be difficult and costly. During the ten years following dental school, Harry quit and reentered his dental practice on three separate occasions. Throughout the entire experience, he remained unhappy with his choice of profession.

Although Harry is a fictitious name, this story is true, and it recounts the lives of many people in many careers who feel they have made the wrong choice. Some of the misery talented people like Harry have experienced could have been avoided with proper career counseling and guidance. In this chapter, we examine the contribution of psychological tests to the selection of and preparation for a career.

The term *career* denotes adventure to many people. As a noun it means swift course, and as a verb, it means to go swiftly or wildly. The Latin root is *carrus,* "chariot." Thus, the term for today's rat race of the work world has its roots in the exciting chariot races of the Romans (Super & Hall, 1978). Careers can indeed be exciting and the essence of life if they are properly selected. They can also lead to misery and unhappiness if they are not carefully chosen, as in the example of Harry. Psychological tests can be helpful in selecting the right career. The first step in the identification of an appropriate career path is the evaluation of interests.

I. *Measuring Interests*

If you want to enter a career that will be satisfactory to you, it is important to identify your interests. Some people need little help in finding work that interests them; however, others can benefit from the guidance given by a psychological test. In the more than 60 years since the introduction of interest inventories, millions of people have received feedback about their own interests in order to help them make wise career choices.

The first interest inventory was introduced in 1921 and was called the Carnegie Interest Inventory. By the time *The Mental Measurements Yearbook* was published for the first time in 1939, it found 15 different interest measures to discuss (Datta, 1975). The two most widely used interest tests were introduced relatively early. The Strong Vocational Interest Blank was first released in 1927, and the Kuder Preference Survey made its appearance in 1939. Today there are more than 80 interest inventories in use; however, the Strong (now called the Strong-Campbell Interest Inventory) remains the most widely used test in research and practice.

A. *The Strong Vocational Interest Blank*

Shortly after World War I, psychologist E. K. Strong, Jr., and some of his colleagues began to carefully examine the activities that were liked and disliked by members of different professions. During the course of their study, they came to realize that people in different professional groups had different patterns of interests. To some extent, you might expect this because people tend to choose lines of work that are of interest to them. Carpenters might be expected to be interested in woodworking, and painting might be of more interest to an artist than to a salesperson. However, Strong and his colleagues also found that people in the same line of work had similar hobbies, liked the same types of entertainment, and read the same types of books and magazines.

With this research as a base, Strong set out to develop a test that would match the interests of a subject to the interests and values of a criterion group of people who were happy in the careers they had chosen. This procedure is called *criterion keying,* or the *criterion-group approach* (see Chapter 15 for a discussion of this approach). The test that was created with this method was called the Strong Vocational Interest Blank (SVIB).

In the early studies, groups of individuals from many professions and occupations responded to approximately 400 items dealing with likes and dislikes related to these occupations and to leisure activities. The Strong procedure then determined whether the interests of new subjects were similar to those of the criterion groups.

In the revised 1966 version of the SVIB, the 399 items were related to 54 occupations for men. A separate form was available for 32 different occupations for women. Items in the SVIB were weighted according to how frequently an interest occurred in a particular occupational group as opposed to how frequently it occurred in the general population. Raw scores were converted to standard scores, with a mean of 50 and a standard deviation of 10. Each criterion group used in the construction of the SVIB contained about 300 persons, which made for a good normative sample. Numerous reliability studies produced impressive results, with odd-even and short-term test-retest figures generally running between the low .80s and low .90s. Long-term (20-year) test-retest coefficients ran in the respectable .60s. Validity data indicated that the SVIB was good for predicting job satisfaction (for example, Strong & Campbell, 1966).

One of the most interesting findings to emerge from the hundreds of published studies using the SVIB is that patterns of interest remain relatively stable over a long period of time. Strong made a practice of asking a group of Stanford University students who took the test in the 1930s to take the test again as they grew older. These studies showed that interests remain relatively stable over a period as long as 22 years. Of course, most people did modify their interests slightly over this period, and a few people made complete turnabouts; nevertheless, the great majority remained consistent.

Studies with the SVIB also showed that interest patterns are fairly well established by age 17. For example, Stanford students who were premedical majors and eventually became physicians scored high on the physician scale of the SVIB. When recontacted throughout life, they tended to remain high on that scale (Tyler & Walsh, 1979). Other studies showed some instability of interests during adolescence, with the patterns becoming stable by the time of the senior year in high school (Hansen & Campbell, 1985).

Despite the widespread acceptance and use of the SVIB, disenchantment with the test began to mount in the late 1960s and early 1970s. Critics cited a sex bias in the scales because different tests were used for men and women. Others complained about the lack of theory associated with the test.

B. *The Strong-Campbell Interest Inventory*

In 1974, psychologist D. P. Campbell published a new version of the SVIB, which he called the Strong-Campbell Interest Inventory (SCII). The SCII was Campbell's (1974) response to the shortcomings of the SVIB. Items from both the men's and women's forms of the SVIB were merged into a single form that included scales devoid of sex bias. For example, the scales for waiter and waitress were merged, and items that referred to gender (for example, salesman) were appropriately modified.

Table 14-1
Holland's Six
Personality
Factors

Factor	Interest Pattern
Realistic	Enjoys technical material and outdoor activities
Investigative	Is interested in science and the process of investigation
Artistic	Enjoys self-expression and being dramatic
Social	Is interested in helping others and in activities involving other people
Enterprising	Is interested in power and political strength
Conventional	Likes to be well organized and has clerical interests

Adapted from Holland (1985b).

Table 14-2

Summary of the Seven Parts of the Strong-Campbell Interest Inventory

Section	Name	Number of Items	Examples of Items
1	Occupations	131	Actor/actress, criminal lawyer, freelance writer, office clerk, x-ray technician
2	School subjects	36	Algebra, art, economics, literature, zoology
3	Activities	51	Cooking, taping a sprained ankle, watching an open-heart operation
4	Amusements	39	Fishing, boxing, listening to religious music, skiing, attending lectures
5	Types of people	24	Military officers, ballet dancers, very old people
6	Preference between two activities	30	Being an airline pilot or being an airline ticket agent, taking a chance or playing safe, reading a book or watching television
7	Your characteristics	14	Wins friends easily, can prepare successful advertisements, has patience when teaching others

Adapted from Hansen & Campbell (1985).

The SVIB had been attacked because it lacked a theoretical orientation. In the development of the SVIB, Strong had focused on the match between the interests of a subject and those of people who enjoyed working in various fields. However, he shied away from providing a theoretical explanation for why certain types of individuals liked working in some fields and disliked employment in others. In the SCII, Campbell incorporated J. L. Holland's (1975) theory of vocational choice. After many years of study, Holland postulated that interests are an expression of personality and that people can be classified into one or more of six categories according to their interests. These categories are listed in Table 14-1. One detailed study using all 437 occupation titles from the Bureau of the Census demonstrated that Holland's system is better able to describe work activities, general training requirements, and occupational rewards than are a variety of competing vocational classification systems (Gottfredson, 1980). Holland's work came to the attention of Campbell because the six personality factors in Holland's theory were quite similar to the patterns of interest that emerged from many years of research with the SVIB. In addition, the factors postulated by Holland could be used for either men or women. Thus, Holland's theory and his six personality factors became incorporated into the SCII (Tyler & Walsh, 1979).

The SCII in its current form is divided into seven parts, which are summarized in Table 14-2. The test, which still retains the core of the SVIB, now has 325 items, to which a person responds "like," "dislike," or "indifferent."

Various agencies provide automated scoring services for the SCII, and most of them summarize several different scores for each profile. The first score is a summary of general themes, which are based on Holland's six personality types (see Table 14-1). For example, the profile might provide information about the general types of activities the person enjoys, the kinds of people the person might work well with, and the most suitable general occupational environment.

The second score summary given in a report is for the administrative indices. These are of less personal importance to the test taker but are needed in order to ensure that errors were not made in the administration, scoring, or processing of the test.

The third set of scores provides a summary of the person's basic interests. For example, they suggest whether the person was high, low, or about average in preference for science, mechanical activities, and athletics. This information is reported in standardized **T scores** (see Chapter 2). (Remember that *T* scores have a mean of 50 and a standard deviation of 10. Thus, a *T* score of 60 would be one standard deviation above the mean or in approximately the 84th percentile.)

The final set of summary scores given in the SCII profile is for the occupational scales. These scales occupy most of the space on the SCII profile. The profile shows the person's score for each of 124 occupations, which are broken into six general occupational themes. The scoring for the occupational scales differs from the scoring for the general theme and basic interest scales because the occupational scale compares the test taker's score with the scores of people working in the various professions. The general theme and basic interest scales compare the test taker's score with those of people in general. If you took the SCII, for each scale you would be assigned a score indicating the degree of similarity—very dissimilar, dissimilar, average, similar, or very similar—between your interests and the interests of people who are happy in their chosen occupations. Many of the occupations are divided so that different criterion groups are provided for men and women. For example, if your score was in the "very similar" category for the occupation social worker (for female), this finding would suggest that your interests were very similar to those of women who had been employed as social workers and had enjoyed the profession.

Several systems provide computerized reports for SCII profiles. Focused Example 14-1 shows the interpretive report for a 39-year-old woman college professor named Jean A. As you can see, the report provides much information about her interests as well as about the meaning of the SCII.

Eleven years ago, when the first edition of this book was published, Jean A., who was then a psychology graduate student, also completed the SCII. She was then 28 years old and had not started her professional career. Table 14-3 compares her SCII profiles at ages 28 and 39. As the table shows, the general profile remains very similar. During this 11-year interval, Jean A. completed her Ph.D. degree, held three different jobs, and had two children.

FOCUSED EXAMPLE 14-1

SCII Profile for Jean A.

```
                 REALISTIC            INVESTIGATIVE
                    36                      58
                    Low             * Moderately high
                                  *   *
                                *       *          ARTISTIC
                              *           *           47
                            *               *    Moderately low
         CONVENTIONAL     *                   *
             44          *                     *
          Average         *                   *
                            *               *
                              *           *
                                *       *            SOCIAL
                                  *   *                46
                    37          * * *               Average
                 ENTERPRISING
                    Low
```

These six themes are arranged in a hexagon with the themes most similar to each other falling next to each other and those most dissimilar falling directly across the hexagon from each other. Types adjacent to one another on the hexagon, such as Realistic and Investigative, or Social and Enterprising, have more in common with one another than do types diametrically opposed to each other on the hexagon, such as Realistic and Social or Investigative and Enterprising.

Your highest General Occupational Theme: Investigative

You expressed preferences in Investigative areas, particularly mathematics, physical sciences, and medical and biological sciences. These areas include occupations in research, mathematics, statistical analysis, and measurement; sciences that study physical objects and the chemical composition of substances; medicine; and sciences that deal with living beings and life processes.

Investigative types tend to view themselves as persistent, self-controlled, analytical, scholarly, and achievement-oriented.

(continued)

(continued)
You often prefer to work independently on ambiguous and theoretical tasks.

You probably like to work with numbers, symbols, words, and ideas. You may already have computational and numerical skills. And, you may want to work in a medical setting.

Occupationally, your interests are like the following Investigative type(s):

Computer programmer   Systems analyst
Medical technologist   Research & development manager
Science teacher   Physical therapist
Respiratory therapist   Pharmacist
Dietitian   Optometrist
Physician   Mathematician
Geographer   College professor
Psychologist   Sociologist

You probably enjoy spending your leisure time participating in complex activities that require learning many new facts, theories, and principles, such as astronomy, computer science, sailing, or skiing. Your approach to both your avocation and your vocation will be analytical.

Your preferences indicate an interest in athletics, which may refer to participation in sports as either a competitor or as a spectator or sports fan.

The following are your strongest Basic Interest Area(s):

Science   Mathematics
Medical science   Teaching
Athletics

You may wish to think about your basic areas of interest to determine if the interests are related to vocational possibilities, or recreational and avocational activity.

You have interests similar to people in the following occupation(s):

Research & development manager
Pharmacist
Optometrist
Geographer
Psychologist
Investments manager

Physical therapist
Dietitian
Physician
College professor
Marketing executive
Accountant

You have interests moderately similar to people in the following occupation(s):

Computer programmer
Medical technologist
Respiratory therapist
Sociologist
Nurse, RN
Recreation leader

Systems analyst
Science teacher
Mathematician
Speech pathologist
Dental hygienist
Mathematics teacher

You have interests that are very dissimilar to people in the following occupation(s):

Art teacher
Public relations director
Minister
Buyer

Interior decorator
English teacher
Realtor
Business education teacher

Your score on the College Professor scale suggests that you may want to work in an academic environment, teaching adults and associating with colleagues who have intellectual interests.

Of course, Occupational Scale scores only evaluate how similar your interests are to people already in the occupation. The scores give no indication of your ability or probability of success. Therefore, consider your abilities as well as your interests as you explore career possibilities.

Modified and reproduced by special permission of the Publisher, Consulting Psychologists Press, Inc., Palo Alto, CA 94303 from *Strong Interest Inventory of the Strong Vocational Interest Blanks Interpretive Report* by Edward K. Strong, Jr. and David P. Campbell. Copyright 1985 by The Board of Trustees of the Leland Stanford Junior University. All rights reserved. Further reproduction is prohibited without the Publisher's written consent.

Table 14-3
SCII results for
Jean A.

Theme	Age 28	Age 39
Investigative	58	58
Artistic	51	51
Social	45	46
Enterprising	42	37
Conventional	37	44
Realistic	36	36

Similarity Scores	Age 28	Age 39
High Similarity		
Physician	58	53
Optometrist	52	47
Psychologist	50	47
College professor	49	50
Low Similarity		
Librarian	32	27
Beautician	28	31
Flight attendant	27	31
Army officer	27	25

C. *The 1985 SCII Revision*

A new version of the SCII was released in the spring of 1985. Although the testing materials (that is, test booklets and answer sheets) did not change, the SCII profile was expanded to include 207 occupational scales, 144 of which have been developed since 1977. In the new revision, every occupational criterion group is represented by a national sample. In addition, special precautions were taken to rule out potential difficulties in interpretation. For example, one criticism of the SCII has been that members of the criterion groups were older than those who would be just entering the work force. In the revised SCII, younger and older members of each criterion group were compared to determine whether the interests and values of the recent entrants to the work force differed from those of workers who had been on the job for many years. The new SCII also includes male and female norms for nearly every occupation.

Now 202 of the 207 scales are sex-matched. This means that there are 101 occupational scales with male norms and there are separate norms for these same 101 scales. Thus, occupations such as carpenter, geographer, and medical illustrator have separate norms for male and female test takers. There are still four occupations (dental assistant, dental hygienist, home economics teacher, and secretary) for which there is no male scale and one scale (agribusiness manager) for which there is no female scale. The new SCII also provides scales for men in general (MIG) and women in general (WIG) (Hansen & Campbell, 1985). In summary, the 1985 revision eliminates some of the few remaining problems of this sound psychological test.

D. *The Kuder Occupational Interest Survey*

Although the SCII is probably the most widely used interest inventory today, many other interest inventories compete for large shares of the market. The Kuder Occupational Interest Survey (KOIS) ranks second in popularity. It is one of several interest scales that grew out of the original Kuder Preference Survey published in 1939. Throughout the years, the Kuder has always been an alternative to the SVIB-SCII and has always advertised its unique features.

The KOIS presents the test taker with 100 triads (sets of three) of alternative activities. For each triad, the test taker selects the most preferred and the least preferred alternatives. Scoring of the KOIS scales gives the same information yielded by the earlier Kuder Preference Surveys—data on ten general occupational interests (for example, outdoor interests versus social service interests). However, in its current form (Kuder, 1979), the KOIS examines the similarity between a test taker's interests and the interests of people employed in different occupations in a manner very similar to that of the SCII. One of the distinguishing features of the KOIS is that it has a separate set of scales for college majors. Thus, in addition to suggesting which occupational group might be best suited to a test taker's interests, the KOIS may also provide direction with regard to the selection of a major.

A series of new scales have been added to the KOIS to emphasize nontraditional occupations for men and women. Examples of these new scales are architect (female norms), journalist (female norms), and film/television producer/director (male norms) (Zytowski, 1985).

Although each test taker is evaluated with regard to the norms for many occupational and college major groups, the KOIS provides a summary of an individual's highest scores by signaling them with an asterisk. Table 14-4 shows one of these summaries. The scores are rank-ordered in the table. Those toward the top are for the vocations in which this test taker showed the highest interest. The higher the score, the greater the similarity between the test taker and people who are actually engaged in that line of work or who are enrolled in that college major. A score higher than .45 is typically obtained by about 80% of the people in the actual vocation or college major. Most students will have some scores above this level and they may want to pay particular attention to them. For example, the scores in Table 14-4 suggest that the woman has interests that resemble those of women working in professional jobs and in computer programming.

Recent studies show that the psychometric properties of the KOIS are very good. Short-term reliabilities tend to be high (between .80 and .95), and increasing evidence indicates that scores remain stable for as long as 19 years

Table 14-4 Summary Report for Kuder Occupational Interest Survey

Report of Scores			Kuder Occupational Interest Survey						Form DD	
Name Student One			Female				99991		Date 01/20/81	

Occupational Scales

OCCUPATIONAL SCALES	Norms M	Norms F
>COMPUTR PROGRAMR	.60*	
>DENTIST	.57*	
SOC WORKR,SCHOOL	.57*	
>ARCHITECT	.56*	
>PHYSICIAN	.56*	
>FILM/TV PROD/DIR	.55*	
>PHYS THERAPIST	.54*	
ENGINEER		.53
>ACCT.CERT PUBLIC		.52
>COMPUTR PROGRAMR	.52*	
>FILM/TV PROD/DIR	.52*	
>PSYCHIATRIST	.52*	
>PSYCH, CLINICAL	.52*	
STATISTICIAN	.52*	
>AUDIOL/SP PATHOL		.51
>PSYCHOLOGIST		.51
>PSYCH, CLINICAL		.51
>AUDIOL/SP PATHOL	.51*	
>OPTOMETRIST	.51*	
>ARCHITECT	.50*	
PEDIATRICIAN	.50*	
PHOTOGRAPHER	.50*	
>PHYS THERAPIST	.50*	
PODIATRIST	.50*	
PSYCH,INDUSTRIAL	.50*	
ELEM SCHL TCHR	.49*	
>NURSE	.49*	
PSYCHOLOGY PROF	.49*	
>SOC WORKER,PSYCH	.49*	
OCCUPA THERAPIST		.48
>SOC WORKER,PSYCH		.48
>DENTIST	.48*	
MATHEMATICIAN	.48*	
PSYCH,COUNSELING	.48*	
DIETITIAN, ADMIN		.47
CHEMIST	.47*	
>LAWYER	.47*	
>JOURNALIST		.46

Occupational Scales (Continued)

Occupational Scales (Continued)	Norms M	Norms F
ENG,HEAT/AIR CON	.43	
METEOROLOGIST	.43	
>SOC WORKER,GROUP		.42
AUTO SALESPERSON	.42	
>COUNSELOR,HI SCH	.42	
ENGINEER, ELEC	.42	
ENG.MINING/METAL	.42	
TRAVEL AGENT	.42	
>VETERINARIAN	.42	
>X-RAY TECHNICIAN	.42	
STENOGRAPHER		.41
ENGINEER, CIVIL	.41	
RADIO STATON MGR	.41	
DENTAL ASSISTANT		.40
ENGINEER, INDUS	.40	
>FLORIST	.40	
>LIBRARIAN	.40	
PLANT NURSRY WKR	.40	
>FLORIST		.39
BUYER	.39	
CLOTHIER, RETAIL	.39	
>JOURNALIST	.39	
>MATH TCHR,HI SCH	.39	
PERSONNEL MANAGR	.39	
TV REPAIRER	.39	
>COUNSELOR,HI SCH		.38
SECRETARY	.38	
FORESTER	.38	
>LIBRARIAN	.37	
>MATH TCHR,HI SCH	.37	
RELIGIOUS ED DIR	.37	
MINISTER		
REAL ESTATE AGT	.37	
SCHOOL SUPT	.37	
BEAUTICIAN		.36
PRIMARY SCH TCHR	.35	
PRINTER		
HOME DEMONST AGT		.34

College Major Scales

College Major Scales	Norms M	Norms F
>BIOLOGICAL SCI	.64*	
>PSYCHOLOGY	.64*	
HEALTH PROFES	.59*	
>MATHEMATICS	.59*	
>ART AND ART EDUC	.58*	
>BIOLOGICAL SCI	.58*	
>FOREIGN LANGUAGE	.57*	
>FOREIGN LANGUAGE		.57
>MUSIC & MUSIC ED	.57*	
>PSYCHOLOGY	.57*	
DRAMA		.56
>HISTORY		.56
>POLITICAL SCI	.56*	
PREMED/PHAR/DENT	.56*	
>SOCIOLOGY	.56*	
>ART AND ART EDUC		.55
PHYSICAL SCIENCE	.55*	
>ENGLISH		.54
SOCIAL SCI, GENL		.54
HOME ECON EDUC		.54
>MUSIC & MUSIC ED	.54*	
>PHYSICAL EDUC		.54
AIR FORCE CADET	.54*	
ARCHITECTURE	.53*	
>MATHEMATICS	.53*	
>SOCIOLOGY		.52
>ELEMENTARY EDUC	.52*	
>ELEMENTARY EDUC		.51
NURSING		.51
>ENGLISH		.49
>HISTORY		.49
LAW-GRAD SCHOOL		.49
MILITARY CADET		.49
>POLITICAL SCI		.48

College Major Scales (Continued)	Norms M	Norms F
>SCIENCE TCHR, HS		.46
>SOCIAL CASEWORKR		.46
>INTERIOR DECORAT	.46*	
OSTEOPATH	.46*	
PHARMACIST	.46*	
>SCIENCE TCHR, HS	.46*	
>SOCIAL CASEWORKR	.46*	
>INTERIOR DECORAT	.45	
>LAWYER	.45	
NUTRITIONIST	.45	
>BANKER	.44	
DIETITIAN,SCHOOL	.44	
HOME EC TCHR COL	.44	
>INSURANCE AGENT	.44	
SOC WORKER,MEDIC	.44	
>X-RAY TECHNICIAN	.44	
>ACCT,CERT PUBLIC	.44	
>BOOKSTOR MANAGER	.44	
ENGINEER, MECH	.44	
PHARMACEUT SALES	.44	
>PHYSICIAN	.44	
>SOC WORKER,GROUP	.44	
>BOOKSTOR MANAGER	.43	
DEAN OF WOMEN	.43	
>NURSE	.43	

College Major Scales (Continued)	Norms M	Norms F
>VETERINARIAN		.34
>INSURANCE AGENT	.34	
YMCA SECRETARY	.34	
>BANKER	.33	
>BOOKKEEPER	.33	
BANK CLERK		.32
>BOOKKEEPER		.31
BLDG CONTRACTOR	.31	
COUNTY AGRI AGT	.31	
PLUMBING CONTRAC	.31	
POSTAL CLERK	.31	
DEPT STORE SALES		.30
OFFICE CLERK		.30
SUPERVSR,INDUSTR	.30	
ELECTRICIAN	.29	
WELDER	.29	
BRICKLAYER	.28	
PAINTER, HOUSE	.28	
POLICE OFFICER	.28	
AUTO MECHANIC	.27	
>FARMER	.27	
TRUCK DRIVER	.27	
MACHINIST	.25	
PLUMBER	.24	
CARPENTER	.22	

College Major Scales (Continued)	Norms M	Norms F
ENGINEERING,CHEM	.47	
ENGINEERING,ELEC	.47	
>PHYSICAL EDUC	.47	
BUS ED COMMERC		.46
ECONOMICS	.46	
ENGINEERING,MECH	.46	
ENGINEERING,CIVIL	.44	
BUS ACCT AND FIN	.43	
BUS & MARKETING	.43	
BUS MANAGEMENT	.43	
FORESTRY	.43	
ANIMAL HUSBANDRY	.42	
AGRICULTURE	.39	
TCHG CATH SISTER		.38

	V	52	
M .42	S	.49	
MBI .30	F	.42	
W .45	D	.53	
WBI .34	MO	.40	

Your scores are reported to you in rank order, on all scales. They show to what extent the choices you marked were like those typical of satisfied people in the occupations and college majors listed. Your top scores are followed by an asterisk (*). (For additional information and for an alphabetical list of scales, see the other side of this report.) > INDICATES TWIN SCALES, WITH SCORES IN M AND F COLUMNS.

©1979, 1970, 1968, 1965. Science Research Associates, Inc. All rights reserved. Printed in the United States of America. 7-3870

From "Report of Scores," in *Kuder Occupational Interest Survey, Form DD.* © 1979, 1970, 1968, 1965 Science Research Associates, Inc. Reprinted by permission of CTB Macmillan/McGraw-Hill.

(Zytowski, 1976). One study on the predictive validity of the KOIS showed that half of a group of adults who had been given an early version of the KOIS while they were high school students were working in fields that the high school KOIS suggested they enter. Predictive validity for the college major scales was even better. There was closer correspondence between interests and the occupation a person was working in for those who had completed college. A college degree provides more freedom than does a high school diploma in finding work that is personally desirable (Zytowski, 1976).

Other studies on the KOIS reveal that high school students report greater confidence in their knowledge of themselves when they are given KOIS results than when they are not. But knowing the results of the KOIS did not make the high school students more confident or more satisfied with their career plans, except when the students expressed a special interest in learning about the test results (Zytowski, 1977). Even though the KOIS has been less thoroughly studied than the SVIB-SCII, a growing amount of evidence indicates that it may be quite useful for guidance decisions for high school and college students. New refinements published in 1985 reflect continuing development of this measure (Zytowski, 1985).

E. *The Minnesota Vocational Interest Inventory*

One criticism of the SCII and the KOIS has been that they emphasize professions that require college and professional training. Although an increasing number of Americans eventually obtain a college degree, most workers still do not graduate from college. The Minnesota Vocational Interest Inventory (MVII) is designed for men who are not oriented toward college and emphasizes skilled and semiskilled trades (Clark, 1961; Clark & Campbell, 1965). The MVII is modeled after the SVIB scales and has nine basic interest areas, including mechanical interests, electronics, and food service, as well as 21 specific occupational scales, including those for plumber, carpenter, and truck driver. The MVII has been used extensively by the military and by guidance programs for non-college-bound individuals.

F. *The Career Assessment Inventory*

A more modern interest inventory for nonprofessionally oriented adults than the MVII is the Career Assessment Inventory (CAI). Developed by Charles B. Johansson, the CAI is written at the sixth-grade reading level and is designed for the 80% of Americans who have fewer than four years of postsecondary education. The CAI provides information similar to that yielded by the SCII. Each test taker is evaluated on Holland's six occupational theme scales: realistic, investigative, artistic, social, enterprising, and conventional. The second portion of the CAI report describes basic interests. Each test taker is evaluated in 22 specific areas, including carpentry, business, and food service. The third section of the report is a series of occupational scales. Scores for the 89 occupational scales on the CAI were obtained by using a criterion-keying method. The interests of the test takers are matched to the interests of truck drivers, secretaries, waitresses, and so forth.

Validity and reliability studies reported in the test manual suggest that the CAI has desirable psychometric properties. Scores tend to be quite stable, and people who find employment in occupations for which they have expressed strong interest tend to remain at their jobs and find more satisfaction with work than do those who have low scores for those occupations. The test developer also took special pains to be certain that the CAI was culturally fair and that sex bias was avoided. In many ways, the CAI has become the workingperson's SCII (Johansson, 1976; Johansson & Johansson, 1978).

G. *The Self-Directed Search*

Most interest inventories require professional or computer-automated scoring. In addition, they typically require interpretation by a trained counselor. J. L. Holland developed the Self-Directed Search (SDS) to be a self-administered, self-scored, and self-interpreted vocational interest inventory. The SDS attempts to simulate the counseling process by allowing the respondent to list occupational aspirations, indicate occupational preferences in six areas, and rate abilities and skills in these areas. Then the test taker can score his or her own inventory and calculate six summary scores, which can be used to obtain codes that reflect the highest areas of interest. The SDS is linked to an occupational finder. In the 1985 edition of the system, the individual is able to locate 1156 occupations and to match his or her own interest codes to corresponding occupational choices.

The SDS includes 228 items. Sixty-six of the items describe activities, which have six scales with 11 items each. In addition, another 66 items are used to assess competencies, with six scales of 11 items each. Occupations are evaluated in six scales of 14 items each. Self-estimates are obtained in two sets of six ratings. Studies have demonstrated that respondents are accurate in scoring their own tests. Validity studies show that there is a moderate, but not high, association between SDS categories and stated vocational aspirations (Holland, 1985b).

Another approach similar to the self-directed search is to allow subjects to interact with a computer-assisted guidance system. One study analyzed "dialogue" used in interactions with the computer. The analysis suggests that most people do not do comprehensive searches. They seek information on only some alternatives. The larger the number of choices, the smaller the number explored. This is not unexpected, since most people need to simplify information and gather it very selectively (Gati & Tikotzki, 1989).

Despite the common and enthusiastic use of interest inventories, several problems have repeatedly surfaced, including faking, sex bias, and mismatches between abilities and interests.

H. *Eliminating Sex Bias in Interest Measurement*

The use and development of interest inventories have not been acceptable to all members of society. In particular, advocates of women's rights justifiably pointed out that the early interest inventories contributed to the discrimination against women (Birk, 1974; Diamond, 1979; Peoples, 1975; Tittle, 1983). The Association for Evaluation in Guidance appointed a Commission on Sex Bias in Measurement, which concluded that interest inventories contributed to the policy of guiding young men and women into sex-typed careers. The interest inventories were much more likely to direct women into work roles that are traditional for women, such as nursing, clerical service, and elementary school teaching. The SVIB, which was the major interest inventory at the time of the commission report, had separate forms for men and for women. Careers on the women's form, it was noted, tended to be lower in status and to command lower salaries (Harmon et al., 1973).

In response to these criticisms, the SCII began using the same forms for both men and women. However, in the 1977 SCII manual, D. P. Campbell (1977) noted that Strong (who is no longer alive) may have felt that using the same norming tables for both men and women would have harmed the validity of the test. A unisex interest inventory, according to Strong, ignores the social and statistical reality that men and women have different interests. In other words, knowing the sex of the test taker tells us a lot about his or her interests. Nevertheless, the new SCII has made major efforts to reduce sex bias.

We must emphasize that the new SCII has reduced but not eliminated sex bias. Although the basic interest and general theme portions of the SCII compare a respondent's responses to those from a combined male/female reference group, the occupational scales are normed separately for men and women. Furthermore, the interpretive comments that are provided by most scoring services are geared toward the test taker's gender (Minton & Schneider, 1980). We anticipate that the value of using the same or different norms for men and women will be a matter of continuing controversy and debate. The current versions of both the SCII and the KOIS reflect the growing concern about sex bias (Hansen & Campbell, 1987).

I. *Aptitudes and Interests*

Extensive research on interest inventories reinforces an important but often overlooked point: interest inventories measure interests; they do not measure the chances that people will be successful in the jobs that they find interesting.

The norm groups for the Strong inventories consist of people who are successful enough in various fields to remain working in them for defined periods of time. However, degree of success is not defined. If you obtain a high score for a particular occupation, you have interests that are similar to the people working in that field. Self-rated satisfaction with chosen careers does appear to be higher for those whose interests match those of others working in the field. But repeated studies have emphasized that chances of succeeding in that job depend on aptitudes and abilities.

II. *Measuring Personal Characteristics for Job Placement*

Interests are just one of the many factors that must be considered in career planning and placement. Career choices depend on matches between people and jobs. Employers want to find the right person for the job, and job hunters continually seek that one job that is just right for their personal skills and interests. Thus, psychologists and vocational guidance specialists look at job placement from many different perspectives. Some focus on the person and his or her characteristics, others attend to the work environment, while still others concentrate on unique combinations of persons and situations. To begin, let's look at some of the theories and measurement methods that focus on the person.

A. *Trait Factor Approach: Osipow's Vocational Dimensions*

Samuel Osipow has been a leading figure in the field of counseling psychology for many years. Like Holland's method of trait assessment, Osipow's (1983) approach to career guidance is to give extensive tests covering personality, abilities, interests, and personal values in order to learn as much about a person's traits as possible. This approach involves the administration of an extensive battery of tests, including many of the ones we have covered in the last several chapters (Purdue pegboard, see Fleishman & Quaintance, 1984; Seashore Measure of Musical Talents, see Lezak, 1983; SCII; KOIS). The results from this large battery of tests were factor analyzed (see Chapter 3) to find common factors or traits that characterize different occupational groups. People requiring guidance are given the battery of tests in order to learn about their traits. Then the counselor matches their traits to the traits that characterize the different occupations.

Osipow's approach has been used extensively in research and practice and has undoubtedly helped many people find their occupational niches. However, the approach has also come under fire for overemphasizing the person and

Table 14-5

Stages in Super's
Developmental
Vocational
Maturity Model

Stage	Age Range
Crystallization	14–18
Specification	18–21
Implementation	21–24
Stabilization	25–35
Consolidation	35 and up

paying too little attention to the work environment. Furthermore, some critics suggest that Osipow's system focuses too much on a single point in time and does not attend sufficiently to the process by which someone reaches a career decision (Tyler & Walsh, 1979).

B. *The Career Maturity Inventory: Super's Development Theory*

Many theories of career choice draw on stage theories from life-span developmental psychology, which is the study of personal development throughout the life cycle (Osipow, 1987). Noted counseling psychologist Donald Super (1953) proposes that individuals go through five developmental stages that are relevant to their career choices and aspirations. Table 14-5 summarizes the stages. Super believes that people enter careers in order to express themselves. Activities in the world of work are expressions of the worker's self-concept. The developmental stages define the vocational behavior that is expected of an individual during given portions of the life cycle. The correspondence between vocational behavior and the expected behavior for that age period is called *vocational maturity*.

Several tests measure vocational maturity. The best known and most widely used of these is the Vocational Maturity Inventory (VMI), which later became the Career Maturity Inventory (CMI) (Crites, 1973). This test provides scores for vocational maturity, attitude, self-knowledge or vocational competence, choosing a job, problem solving, occupational information, and looking ahead. Most of the psychometric data on the CMI are impressive. In particular, the vocational competence portion is well constructed, and data obtained with it seem to demonstrate the expected properties. For example, high school students do show an expected year-to-year increase in scores on the vocational competence scale. This is the result that would be expected as the students become more vocationally mature (Crites, 1974). Unfortunately, some problems with the CMI still remain; for example, it appears that 12th-graders score as less vocationally mature than do 11th-graders, which is inconsistent with the notion that students should become more vocationally mature with age (Crites, 1973).

Table 14-6
Examples of
Career Fields for
Individuals Rated
on Roe's Continua

	High on Orientation to Purposeful Communication	**High on Orientation to Resource Utilization**
High on Orientation to Interpersonal Relations	Arts and entertainment; uses tastes	Business contacts; uses persuasive techniques
High on Orientation to Natural Phenomena	Science; uses "laws"	Technology; uses mechanics

Adapted from Roe & Klos (1969).

C. *The California Occupational Preference Survey: Roe's Career-Choice Theory*

Anne Roe, who is another major theorist in counseling psychology, believes that career choice is the result of the type of relationship a person has had with his or her family during childhood. After extensive research on the personalities of scientists who had entered different fields of study, Roe came to the conclusion that some people are interested primarily in other people, whereas other people are not. Children reared in a warm and accepting environment, according to Roe, become people-oriented adults, whereas those exposed to a cold and aloof environment at home become more interested in things than in other people (Roe & Klos, 1969; Roe & Siegelman, 1964).

Roe's theory identifies person or nonperson orientation as the major factor in career choice. Those who are people oriented seek careers in which they will have contact with others. They may find careers in service areas, the arts, or entertainment. Individuals who are not person oriented may prefer occupations that minimize interpersonal relationships, such as those in science or technology or those involving outdoor activities. In an elaboration of the theory, A. Roe and D. Klos (1969) classified occupational roles according to two independent continua. The first had orientation to purposeful communication at one extreme and orientation to resource utilization at the other. The second had orientation to interpersonal relations at one extreme and orientation to natural phenomena at the other. Table 14-6 summarizes the vocations that fall within the space created by these two continua. Placement in a particular job within a field depends on the ability and training of the individual.

To measure the characteristics described in Roe's theory, R. R. Knapp and his associates developed the California Occupational Preference Survey (COPS). This test requires respondents to indicate on a four-point scale the degree to which they like or dislike 168 different occupational activities. The COPS gives scores in six different fields: aesthetic, business, linguistic, scientific, service, and technical. Scores are also given for professional versus skilled orientation as well as for outdoor versus clerical orientation. (The COPS has been expanded to become the California Preference System Inventory, which includes nine occupational clusters.) Reliabilities for the COPS have been reported to be in the .90s. Normative data have been reported for 512 high school males and 589 high school females.

D. *Are There Stable Personality Traits?*

Imagine that you have the responsibility for hiring employees for a large business and you want to do everything you can to convince your supervisors that you have done a good job. You want to make certain decisions about the personalities of the people you interview, and you need to communicate this information to the people who will supervise the employees. For example, you might ask whether they have the traits of kindness, honesty, trustworthiness, reliability, and dedication. We often believe knowledge of such personality traits provides us with a convenient way of organizing information about others, for describing how they have behaved in the past, and for making predictions about how they will act in the future (Bradbury & Fincham, 1990; Higgins & Bargh, 1987; Jones & Nisbett, 1971; Kelly, 1967).

Much of the study of personality has been devoted to creating categories of traits, developing methods for measuring them, and finding out how groups of traits cluster together. Indeed, the very concept of personality assumes that the characteristics of a person are stable over time. If Richard is a hard-working person, we expect him to work hard in many different situations. Although we commonly use trait names in this way to describe other people, the evidence that personality characteristics are stable is a little shaky. For example, W. Mischel (1984) has shown that personality traits are simply not good predictors of how people will behave in particular situations. In a classic, well-argued attack on trait theorists, Mischel (1968) demonstrated that knowing how someone scores on measures of psychological traits sometimes gives little better than chance insight into how the person will act in any situation. Thus, trait theorists were forced to retreat and rethink their assumptions.

Another problem for traditional trait theories is raised by research on a relatively new approach to personality and social psychology known as *attribution theory*. Originally, attribution theory considered only how people make judgments about others; however, there has been an enormous expansion of interest in attribution theory. Research in this area now covers all aspects of how people attempt to understand the causes of events in their lives.

The ideas behind attribution theory were first presented by F. Heider (1944, 1958) and were made popular in the late 1960s. Attribution theorists suggest that events in a person's environment can be caused by one of three sources: persons, entities (things or some aspect of the environment), and times (situations) (Kelly, 1967). To determine which of these (or which combination) has caused an event, an observer uses three criteria: distinctiveness, consensus, and consistency. For example, if we are looking for an explanation of why John is unhappy with his job today, we need to ask whether it has to do with something that happened on the job this particular day (distinctiveness), whether others in the same situation also dislike the job (consensus), or whether John is unhappy on all workdays (consistency).

Attribution theory is thus less concerned with predicting behavior in particular situations than it is with studying how individuals make judgments about the causes of behavior. Some researchers have suggested that the selection of an explanation for behavior depends on the role played by the person offering the judgment. The person making the judgment acts like a scientist in using all data to come to the best conclusion (Weiner, 1991). When we are observers and are making judgments about other people, we tend to use dispositional, or trait, explanations; however, we do not use trait explanations for our own behavior (Forsterling, 1988). When we are the actors in a situation, we see our own behavior in terms of the situation. In other words, we describe others in terms of traits, but we explain our own behavior in terms of situations. Why is there a difference between the attributions of actors and observers? E. E. Jones and R. E. Nisbett (1971) suggest that we know more about ourselves than we know about others. By searching our memory, we can remember behaving in many different situations. However, when we make judgments about others, we do not have as much information about how situations caused them to act differently. Yet we may be able to identify with others when they tell us that situations have influenced their behavior. For example, juries may be forgiving of a criminal defendant who claims to have been influenced by a situation and makes a confession (Weiner et al., 1991).

To summarize, Mischel and the attribution theorists feel that psychologists have devoted too much attention to personality traits and not enough attention to situations. Thus, they recommend attention to the effect of situations on behavior.

III. *Measuring Characteristics of the Work Setting*

To study the influence of situations, we need methods to describe and measure them. These methods are described in this section.

A. *The Social-Ecology Approach*

Ecology is the branch of biology that studies the relationship between living organisms and their environments. Organisms must adapt to the physical environment in order to survive. Similarly, environments can have an impact on the social lives of their inhabitants. Thus, psychologists have recently come to recognize the importance of studying people within their natural environments and of analyzing the impact physical environments have on social behavior (Wicker, 1979). As environmental psychologist Daniel Stokols (1978, p. 253) proclaims, "At a time when environmentalists and economists are proclaiming that 'small is beautiful,' the research literature on human behavior in relation to its environmental settings continues to expand at a staggering rate." This field of study is called *environmental psychology*. A similar area is *ecological psychology*, which focuses on events that occur in a behavioral setting. We refer to these topics of study together as **social ecology** (Stokols, 1992). One of the most important areas in social ecology is the study of behavioral settings.

Each day, you participate in a variety of behavioral settings. For example, your psychological testing class is a behavioral setting. The program for this setting might include a lecturer who comes to deliver a prepared talk to a group of students. The lecturer might arrive two to three minutes late and enter a room in which students are enjoying conversation with one another. However, after the arrival of the lecturer, the room grows quiet and, as the presentation begins, attention is focused on the speaker. Physical arrangements in the room facilitate this social interaction. For example, the chairs face the front of the room, and there is a chalkboard available for the lecturer's use. R. G. Baker has made the study of behavioral settings his life work. For many years, he and his colleagues described the publicly available behavioral settings in two small towns; Oskaloosa, Kansas, and Leyburn, England. Each of these towns included many behavioral settings such as card games, court sessions, and special businesses. Barker's work involved documenting each setting by describing how long interactions lasted, who participated, the genders of the people in the setting, and so on (Barker, 1979; Barker & Schoggen, 1973; Schoggen, 1979; Wicker, 1979).

The study of behavioral settings reveals a great deal about the social rules of the environment. For example, in both small towns (Oskaloosa and Leyburn), women spent less time in public behavioral settings than did men. The studies also confirmed what many feminists have been saying all along—that women are limited to certain settings. For example, women in both towns were observed most often in such behavioral settings as churches and schools. They were often found in settings that favored social talking and less often in business and government settings.

Behavioral settings are truly self-regulating ecologies. When a component of the system is missing, the activities in the program are changed to correct the imbalance. For example, if there are no chairs in your psychological testing class, students will probably go out looking for them in order to bring the situation into balance. If someone in the class makes too much noise, social forces will come into operation to eliminate the disruption (Wicker, 1979). Thus, in order to avoid social condemnation, you must act according to the rules for that behavioral setting. A catcall during psychology class might bring you strange and rejecting looks because it is out of place. Yet in the behavioral setting of a rock concert, it is perfectly appropriate. Social adjustment requires that you know the rules of many social behavioral settings and that you follow them.

The study of behavioral settings also involves examining the relationship between work satisfaction and the requirements of the job. A. W. Wicker and S. L. Kirmeyer (1976) used this approach in a study of coping behavior among rangers in Yosemite National Park. During the summer, the workload for the rangers varies greatly because of the different numbers of people entering the behavioral setting. When the workload increases, the rangers feel more challenged and needed on the job and also use more strategies to cope with their jobs. By the end of the summer, when the workload is the heaviest, the challenge of heavy crowds is no longer associated with job satisfaction. Instead, the rangers are less able to cope and they feel physically and emotionally drained. In order to understand the relationship between work setting and satisfaction, many aspects of the ecology must be considered, including the workload, coping strategies, and the duration of work overload. It also requires making a precise description of the work environment.

There are many applications of the social ecology approach in clinical and health psychology. For example, it has been demonstrated that characteristics of the work environment can influence health-damaging behaviors such as smoking and lack of exercise. Restructuring the environment may modify these dangerous behaviors (Johansson et al., 1991). Considerable work has gone into characterizing family environments and the interaction between spouses. The social environment may have an impact on cigarette smoking, diet, and other health behaviors (Cohen & Lichtenstein, 1990; Ewart, 1991).

B. *Classifying Environments*

How do different environments affect your behavior? Are you able to work better when the sun is out? Do you get more tired and irritable on hot days? Most of social psychology is based on the premise that behavior is influenced by situations. Some of the early work in the field of environmental psychology involved building classification systems for various situations (Holahan, 1986). You might think of this as similar to the work done by many early personality psychologists who built elaborate systems to classify personality types (for example, aggressive, masculine). The environmental psychologists built elaborate systems to classify the characteristics of environments that had been shown to affect individual or group behavior.

Table 14-7 shows a classification system created by R. H. Moos (1973). It includes six characteristics of environments and gives some examples. Many studies demonstrate that the characteristics of the people in your environment affect your behavior. The likelihood that a high school girl will begin to smoke, for example, can be greatly influenced by the number of other girls who already smoke or who approve of smoking (Pierce et al., 1992). Over the years, Moos and his colleagues have developed many different measures to evaluate the characteristics of environments. A summary of these scales is shown in Table 14-8.

Moos's work on measuring the characteristics of environments is important for the field of vocational psychology because it demonstrates how personal

Table 14-7	Characteristics	Examples
Six Characteristics of Environments	Ecological dimensions	Architectural design, geographic location, weather conditions
	Behavioral settings	Office, home, store
	Organizational structure	Percentage of women in the student body, number of people per household, average age of group
	Characteristics of inhabitants	Proportion of students who date, drink, or vote
	Psychosocial and organizational climate	Work pressure, encouragement of participation, orientation toward helping with personal problems
	Functional or reinforcing properties	Is aggression reinforced on the football field; is it reinforced at home?

Adapted from Moos (1973).

characteristics of the work environment affect job choice and worker satisfaction. For example, workers are more satisfied with work environments that promote quality interactions between workers and supervisors than they are with environments in which these relationships are kept more distant. The quality of the relationship between workers and supervisors also enhances productivity (Moos, 1986c). Some evidence also indicates that workers in supportive work environments are less likely to develop disabilities caused by stress on the job than are workers in nonsupportive environments (Holahan & Moos, 1986). A pleasant work environment is also good for business. Bank customers who perceive bank employees as being friendly and supportive are less likely to withdraw their money to switch banks than are customers who dislike the social environment of the bank (Moos, 1986a).

Moos and Lemke (1986) have expanded the work on characterization of the environment to create a multiphasic environmental assessment procedure (MEAP). One use of this approach is to describe sheltered care settings, including skilled nursing homes and other housing situations for older adults. The complex approach includes evaluation of the settings according to physical and architectural features, policy and program information, resident and staff information, physical attractiveness and other characteristics, and a general environment scale. Each of these features has many subscales. For example, policy and program information includes how selective the home is in admitting new patients, how clearly its policies are specified, how much control residents have over policies, and so on. The resident and staff information includes the ratio of staff members to residents, the resident activity level, and the functional abilities of the residents. Figure 14-1 describes the physical and architectural resources of two nursing homes: Pacific Place and Bella Vista. As the figure shows, the homes are very similar on some variables such as community accessibility and safety features. However, Bella Vista receives a much

Table 14-8
Summary of
Scales Used to
Evaluate Different
Environments

Type of Environment	Scale	Reference
Treatment	Ward Atmosphere Scale	Moos (1987a)
	Community Oriented Programs Environment Scale	Moos (1987b)
Institutional	Correctional Institutions Environment Scale	Moos (1987c)
Educational	University Residence Environment Scale	Moos (1987d)
	Classroom Environment Scale	Moos and Truckett (1986)
Community	Work Environment Scale	Moos (1986a)
	Group Environment Scale	Moos (1986b)
	Family Environment Scale	Moos and Moos (1986)

better score for social recreational activities, whereas Pacific Place receives a better score for orientational aids. Using this sort of information, one can quantitatively measure the characteristics of a work or home environment (Moos & Lemke, 1984a).

In sum, behavioral settings and social environments are coming to be recognized as important factors in job and personal satisfaction. The study of

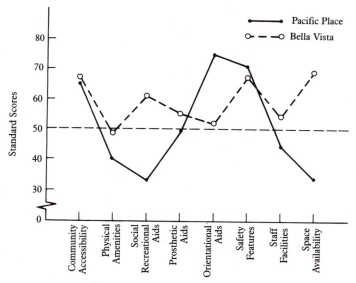

Figure 14-1
Physical and architectural resources profile for two nursing homes. (*From the Multiphasic Environmental Assessment Procedure (MEAP) Manual by R. H. Moos and S. Lemke, p. 22. Copyright 1984 by the Social Ecology Laboratory, Stanford University School of Medicine, Palo Alto, California. Reproduced with permission.*)

Table 14-9
Job Checklist for
Research
Assistant*

Activity	Frequency of Occurrence				
	Per Hour	Per Day	Per Week	Per Month	Per Year
Photocopying		1			
Typing			2		
Attending meetings				1	
Meeting with subjects			3		
Ordering supplies				1	
Writing reports					1

* The assistant would be expected to photocopy materials once per day, type twice per week, meet with subjects three times per week, and so on.

work environments is a relatively new area that we expect to blossom in the coming decade.

C. *Job Analysis*

In addition to knowing how to classify work environments, the industrial psychologist needs to be able to describe and measure characteristics of the job. Employers often want to describe the activities of their work place to determine what type of personnel is needed or why some employees are unhappy working in the setting. There are many available methods for doing so. S. Zedeck and M. R. Blood (1974) summarize the five basic methods: checklists, critical incidents, observations, interviews, and questionnaires.

Checklists are used by job analysts to describe the activities and working conditions that are usually associated with a job title. An example of a checklist for a research assistant in behavioral research is shown in Table 14-9. The first column of the checklist shows the activities associated with the job title, and the other columns list the frequency of occurrence of these activities. The task for the job analyst is simply to record how frquently each activity occurs for persons in this job classification.

Checklists have been criticized because they do not provide an integrated picture of the job situation, nor do they provide information about specific behaviors. In contrast to Moos's environment scales, checklists are less predictive of whether someone will like a particular job environment.

Critical incidents are observable behaviors that differentiate successful from unsuccessful employees. The critical-incident method was developed by J. C. Flanagan (1954). By acquiring specific descriptions of the behaviors of successful employees and their unsuccessful counterparts, one can learn something about the differences between the two groups. An example of a critical incident that might describe a successful employee is "always arrives at meetings on time." A critical incident describing an unsuccessful employee might be "leaves work area disorganized."

Observation is another method for learning about the nature of the job. As we discussed in Chapter 8, information gathered through observation methods can sometimes be biased because people change their behavior when they know they are being watched. In order to avoid this problem, the participant-observation method is sometimes used. A participant-observer is someone who participates in the job and functions as though he or she were one of the workers.

Interviews can also be used to find out about the job. The difficulty with interviews is that some workers may give an interviewer information that is different from what they would give another employee because they are uncomfortable or fear that what they say may be held against them. Another problem is that an interviewer who is unfamiliar with the job may not ask the right questions. Some methods that may help you get more information out of an interview were discussed in Chapter 9.

Questionnaires are commonly used to find out about job situations, but we do not recommend using them unless special precautions are taken. Many employers favor questionnaires because they are inexpensive. However, the employer may never know whether the respondent understood the questions, and the type of information gained is limited to the specific questions. A more serious problem is that there is a selective return rate in questionnaire studies. Employees who feel very favorable or very unfavorable toward the company are more likely to complete the questionnaire and return it.

The task of constructing methods of job analysis is extremely difficult (Hakel, 1986). E. A. Fleishman and M. K. Quaintance (1984) reviewed the methodological issues in developing taxonomies for job analysis and found that characterization of jobs is often done poorly. Job analysis faces many of the same challenges as creating other tests and performance instruments.

IV. *Measuring the Person-Situation Interaction*

Two different perspectives have been presented in this chapter. First, we reviewed research and methods from counseling psychology that emphasized the importance of persons' characteristics or traits in their career satisfaction. Then we discussed the characteristics of work situations and how they may affect people.

To a growing number of psychologists, whether traits or situations are more important in determining behavior is a "pseudo-question" (Anastasi, 1986; Endler, 1973; McFall & McDonell, 1986; Sarason, Sarason, & Pierce, 1990). It is meaningless to ask whether trait or situation is more important in explaining behavior when it is clear that behavior is always a joint function of characteristics of the person and characteristics of the situation. This position is

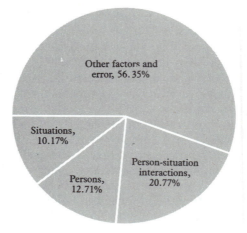

Figure 14-2

Factors influencing behavior. A pie is divided according to the proportion of variation in behavior accounted for by trait, situation, and the interaction between trait and situation. The interaction is greater than either of the other two sources of influence. However, unexplained or error variance is much greater than any other factor. (*Adapted from data in Bowers, 1973.*)

a compromise between trait and situational approaches to personality assessment. It acknowledges the importance of personality characteristics as well as the role of situations (Endler, 1973; Endler & Hunt, 1968; Endler & Magnusson, 1976; Magnusson & Endler, 1977). The interactionists support their position by reporting the proportion of variance in behavior that is explained by person, by situation, and by the interaction between person and situation. You might think of this as a pie divided to represent all the different influences on human behavior. Figure 14-2 shows the pie. One slice represents the proportion of the variation attributable to personality traits. Another slice represents the proportion of the variation caused by situational influences. A third slice is for the interaction between situational influences and dispositional, or trait, influences. This interaction is caused by unique combinations of traits and situations. For example, an interaction might describe how Harry reacts to being a dentist. This cause is different from the characteristics of Harry (in all situations) or the effects of performing the role of a dentist. Careful studies that apply a statistical method known as *analysis of variance* have separated the proportion of variance attributable to each of these factors. As shown in Figure 14-2, the interaction accounts for a larger portion of the variance in behavior than does either the person or the situation (Endler et al., 1991).

Although it is revealing that unique combinations of persons and situations explain more of the variation than does either influence by itself, the interaction position still explains only some of the people some of the time (Bem & Allen, 1974). As Figure 14-2 shows, the largest slice of the pie represents *error vari-*

ance, the proportion of the total not explained by the three sources of influence. After reviewing many studies on the influences of person and situation, I. G. Sarason, R. E. Smith, and E. Diener (1975) concluded that none of the three sources account for an impressive share of the variation when compared with the amount of variation left unexplained. Although the interaction is a better predictor than either the trait or the situation, it is only slightly better. Thus, the need was still present for measurement methods that could be used to predict more of the people more of the time.

D. J. Bem and D. C. Funder (1978) introduced a descriptive system that could be used to take advantage of our ability to predict our own behavior in particular situations. They call their approach the *Template-Matching Technique.* The system attempts to match personality to a specific template of behavior. For example, consider how to answer the question "Should Tom become an insurance salesperson?" Assuming you know nothing about Tom, perhaps the best way to guide him would be to describe how several hypothetical people might react to working in this job. You might say, for example, that people who are shy may have difficulty approaching new customers or that people with families may not like insurance sales because of the irregular work hours. Now Tom can predict his own reaction to the job by matching his characteristics with the set of templates you have provided for him.

Along the same lines, D. J. Bem and D. C. Funder (1978, p. 486) propose that "situations be characterized as sets of template-behavior pairs, each template being a personality description of an idealized type of person expected to behave in a specified way in that setting." The probability that a particular person will behave in a particular way in a situation is a function of the match between his or her characteristics and a template. For example, if Tom's personality characteristics matched the template for those who hated being insurance salespersons, he might be best advised to avoid that career.

The template-matching idea arose from research in personality and social psychology, and is not often discussed in other areas of psychology. However, the person-situation interaction resembles what educational psychologists call the *aptitude-treatment interaction* (Snow, 1991). Furthermore, the template-matching idea is quite similar to a popular theory of career choice that J. L. Holland (1985a) proposes. Holland suggests that there are six clusters of personality and interest traits; these are the same six clusters represented as the six general themes on the SCII (see Table 14-1). Holland contends that there are six vocational environments corresponding to these traits and that people will be happiest if they are able to match their personal characteristics to the characteristics of the work environment (Holland, 1975; Holland & Gottfredson, 1976). For example, an investigative individual will be most content if he or she can work in an investigative field such as science. The idea of matching traits to situations is intuitively appealing. The concept of "different strokes for different folks" seems like a good way to structure our search for the right job, the right apartment, or the right psychotherapist. However, there are some problems. First, there are an enormous number of combinations of persons and situations. For example, predicting how 10 personality types will perform in 20 different work environments produces $10 \times 20 = 200$ unique combinations. Most real-life decisions require many more factors. One of the most important problems with the interaction concept is illustrated by research on psychotherapy. Studies have shown that the effectiveness of psychotherapy is often weaker than expected. When challenged by these results, therapists argue that weak results might be expected because therapies must be tailored to the specific personalities of clients. Some people will do well in behavior therapy, whereas others will have better success with a more cognitive approach. However, research has typically failed to identify consistent personalities that respond to particular treatments. When these interactions are found, they tend not to be replicated by other studies (Smith & Sechrest, 1991). As a result we must go back to the theoretical drawing board for new insights into the selection of treatment for unique individuals.

In general, career satisfaction depends on an appropriate match between person and job. The developing technology for finding job-person matches holds great promise for the field of career counseling and guidance testing.

Summary

In the beginning of this chapter we presented the real-life case of Harry, a dentist who felt he had made the wrong career choice. Harry's problem might have been avoided through proper interest testing and career counseling. Several methods for assessing vocational interests are available. The best known of these is the SVIB, an empirically keyed test that matched the interests of male and female test takers with those of people who were satisfied with their career choices. Although it was among the most widely used tests in the history of psychology, the SVIB was harshly criticized for its sexist and atheoretical orientation. A new version, the SCII, responds to these criticisms by including male and female keys in the same form and by embracing Holland's theory of occupational themes.

The KOIS is the next most frequently used interest test. In contrast to earlier versions, the present KOIS provides occupational scores similar to those given by the SVIB. A unique feature of the KOIS is that it provides scores for college majors. Other occupational interest measures are also available, including the MVII and the CAI, which are designed for use with non-college-oriented individuals.

Several prominent counseling psychologists have proposed that career placement be guided by personality traits. Osipow used multivariate statistics to identify clusters of interests and abilities that characterized those in different occupations. Super and Crites favored a developmental perspective, suggesting that career satisfaction is related to vocational maturity. Roe believed that different approaches to child-rearing produced some individuals who were people oriented and others who were thing oriented. People-oriented individuals find their way into people-oriented careers, and those who are not oriented toward people gain more satisfaction from work that involves less contact with people.

In 1968, Mischel demonstrated that personality measures may not always be accurate in predicting behavior in particular situations. At about the same time, many attribution theorists began demonstrating that people explain the behavior of others by using personality traits; however, when asked about their own behavior, they tend to attribute cause to the situation. These ideas gave rise to the development of measures to assess the characteristics of social environments and work settings.

Out of these new developments grew a new perspective on personality. This was the interactional perspective, which emphasized that all behavior is the product of both personal characteristics and the situation in which the behavior occurs. The interactional perspective gave rise to new assessment techniques such as the Template-Matching Technique, which attempts to predict behavior by finding the optimal match between characteristics of persons and aspects of the situation.

Chapter 15

Structured Personality Tests

Learning Objectives

When you have completed this chapter, you should be able to:

- Identify the major characteristics of a structured personality test.

- Identify the underlying assumption of the first structured personality test (the Woodworth Personal Data Sheet).

- Identify the assumptions of early structured personality tests based on the logical-content strategy.

- Briefly discuss the strategy used in construction of the MMPI and MMPI-2.

- Describe the K and F scales on the MMPI and MMPI-2.

- Identify strengths and weaknesses of the MMPI and MMPI-2.

- Explain how factor analysis is used in the construction of structured personality tests.

- Briefly describe the Cattell 16PF.

- Briefly describe the EPPS and explain the meaning of an ipsative score.

In his junior year in college, Mike went to the university counseling center. He wanted help in finding a direction in life. To aid him in his quest, a psychologist suggested that he respond to a long list of items known as the California Psychological Inventory (CPI). The CPI is a structured personality test that provides a list of statements and asks the subject to respond "true" or "false" to each. The statements were something like these: "I like to read mystery stories." "I am usually alert to my environment." "I would rather follow others than be the leader." "I like to solve difficult problems." "My father is a good man." It took Mike about an hour to respond to the 462 items.

A week later, he returned for an interpretation of his test scores. The psychologist told Mike that the test indicated he was highly effective in dealing with other individuals; his response pattern was similar to that produced by individuals who make effective leaders. The CPI also indicated that Mike was able to control his desires and impulses and express them effectively and appropriately.

How did the psychologist decide that Mike's responses to certain items reflected specific traits and characteristics (such as leadership ability and control of impulses)? How accurate were the psychologist's interpretations? Did the interpretations really reflect Mike's characteristics? How stable are the results? Can we expect that after ten years the CPI will still indicate that Mike has leadership qualities? We explore these and other questions in this chapter on the structured personality tests.

Tests came into existence in an effort to solve the problems that face modern societies. Tests of mental ability were created to distinguish those with subnormal mental abilities from those with normal abilities in order to enhance the education of both groups. However, there is far more to being human than having normal or subnormal mental capabilities. It is not enough to know that a person is high or low in such factors as speed of calculation, memory, range of knowledge, and abstract thinking. To make full use of information about a person's mental abilities, it is also important to know how that person uses these abilities. All the mental abilities in the world are useless in a totally withdrawn individual who sits in the corner of a room all day. But even modest mental abilities can go far in a high-energy individual who is organized, persistent, determined, and highly motivated and who relates well to others. These nonintellective aspects of human behavior are typically distinguished from mental abilities and are referred to as *personality characteristics*.

Personality can be defined as the relatively stable and distinctive patterns of behavior that characterize an individual and his or her reactions to the environment. Structured personality tests attempt to evaluate personality traits, personality types, personality states, and other aspects of personality, such as self-concept. **Personality traits** refer to relatively enduring dispositions—tendencies to act, think, or feel in a certain manner in any given circumstance—that distinguish one individual from another. **Personality types** refer to general descriptions about people, such as the avoiding types, who A. Adler (1933/1964) described as individuals of low social interest and low activity who cope by avoiding situations. **Personality states** refer to emotional reactions that vary from one situation to another. Finally, **self-concept** refers to a person's self-definition or, according to C. R. Rogers (1959a), an organized and relatively consistent set of assumptions that a person has about himself or herself. In this chapter, we focus on personality traits, with some discussion of personality types and self-concept. In Chapter 18, we will examine personality states and compare and contrast personality traits and personality states.

Even prior to the development of the first Binet scale, A. Binet had hypothesized that a person's pattern of intellectual functioning might reveal information about personality factors (Binet & Henri, 1895, 1896). Subsequent investigators agreed with Binet's hypothesis (Hart & Spearman, 1912; Terman, 1916; Thorndike, 1921; Webb, 1915), and the hypothesis continues to find support (Eysenck, 1967; Frank, 1970, 1976; Wechsler, 1943, 1958, 1981). However, specific tests of human personality were not developed until World War I created a need to distinguish people on the basis of emotional functioning. Thus, the impetus for the development of measures of functioning above and beyond mental abilities came from a need to separate groups on the basis of emotional well-being.

Like the early developers of tests of mental ability, early developers of personality tests were traveling in uncharted territory. Imagine yourself faced with the task of measuring some aspect of human behavior. How would you begin? You could observe and record a person's behavior. This approach, however, would not have helped early investigators because their problem was to find a way of identifying emotionally unstable military recruits. The volume of applicants for military service in the United States during World War I was so great that it became impossible to successfully use the one available method of the time, the psychiatric interview. A measure of emotional functioning was needed to evaluate large numbers of people and to screen out those unfit for military service. To meet this need, psychologists used the self-report questionnaire. **Self-report questionnaires** provide a list of statements and require subjects to respond in some way to each, such as marking "true" or "false" to indicate whether the statement applies to them.

The general procedure in which the subject is asked to respond to a written statement is known as the **structured,** or objective, method of personality assessment, as distinguished from the projective method (to be discussed in Chapter 16). As their name implies, structured measures of personality are characterized by structure and lack of ambiguity. A clear and definite stimulus is provided, and the requirements of the subject are evident and specific. An example of a structured personality test item is "Respond 'yes' or 'no' to the statement 'I am happy.'" In contrast, a projective test item may provide a picture on an inkblot and ask, "What might his be?" In a projective personality test, the stimulus is ambiguous and the subject has few guidelines about what type of response is required.

I. *Strategies of Structured Personality Test Construction*

Many approaches to or strategies of test construction have been tried during the evolution of structured personality tests.

A. *Overview of the Strategies*

Like measures of mental ability, efforts to measure nonintellective personality factors evolved through a number of phases. New features were added as

Figure 15-1
Overview of
strategies for
structured
personality test
construction.

problems with the old approaches became evident. In the realm of structured personality testing, a number of approaches or strategies have been tried. There is some disagreement concerning how these strategies should be classified, what they should be called, and even how many distinctly different strategies exist (Ben-Porath & Butcher, 1991; Gynther & Gynther, 1976). At the broadest level, the strategies are empirical or nonempirical (deductive). Each of these two major strategies can be further divided into two major substrategies. Empirical strategies may use either the method of criterion groups or the method of factor analysis. Deductive strategies may be of either the logical-content variety or the theoretical variety. These four types of strategies will be discussed more or less in the order in which they came to prominence in the field of structured personality testing. In addition, we will discuss procedures that combine two or more strategies. Figure 15-1 provides an overview of the strategies.

Deductive strategies use reason and deductive logic to determine the meaning of a test response, and empirical strategies use statistical or experimental methods or both. For the deductive strategies, in the logical-content method, items are selected on the basis of simple face validity; in the theoretical approach, test construction is guided by a particular psychological theory. For the empirical strategies, in the criterion-group approach, items are selected to distinguish a group of individuals with certain characteristics, known as the criterion group, from a control group; the factor analytic approach uses the statistical technique of factor analysis to determine the meaning of test items.

B. *Deductive Strategies*

The two deductive strategies are the logical-content and theoretical approaches.

Logical-content strategy. The logical-content strategy, as its name implies, uses reason and deductive logic in the development of personality measures. This strategy has also been referred to as the content approach (Maloney & Ward, 1976), the intuitive approach (Goldberg, 1974), and the rational approach (Wiggins, 1973). In the most general use of this strategy, the test designer tries to logically deduce the type of content that should measure the characteristic to be assessed. For example, if you want to measure eating behavior, it makes sense to include statements such as "I frequently eat between meals." Statements that have no direct logical relevance to eating behavior, such as "I enjoy solving complex puzzles," would not be included in tests that use the logical-content strategy. The principal distinuishing characteristic of the logical-content strategy is that it assumes that the test item describes the subject's personality and behavior. If a person marks "true" for the statement "I am outgoing," then it is assumed that he or she is outgoing. Initial efforts to measure personality used the logical-content approach as the primary strategy.

Theoretical strategy. The theoretical strategy, as its name implies, begins with a theory concerning the nature of the particular characteristic to be measured. As in the logical-content approach, an attempt is then made to deduce items. In the theoretical approach, however, items must be consistent with the theory. If the theory hypothesizes that personality can be broken down into six major areas, then an effort is made to develop items that tap each of these six areas. In addition to being guided by theoretical concerns, rather than simply selecting any item that seems to measure a particular characteristic, theoretical strategies demand that every item in a scale be related to the characteristic that is being measured. Thus, the theoretical approach attempts to create a homogeneous scale and, to this end, may use statistical procedures such as item analysis.

C. *Empirical Strategies*

Empirical strategies rely on data collection and statistical analyses to determine the meaning of a test response or the nature of personality. These strategies retain the self-report features of the deductive strategies in that subjects are asked to respond to items that are descriptive of their own views, opinions, and feelings. However, empirical strategies attempt to use experimental research to empirically determine the meaning of a test response or the major dimensions of personality or both.

Criterion-group strategy. The criterion-group strategy, sometimes known as the contrasted-group method (Goldberg, 1972b), the external strategy (Goldberg, 1974), or even the empirical strategy (Maloney & Ward, 1976), begins with a known or criterion group. The criterion group is one that possesses a certain characteristic, such as a group of individuals known to be aggressive or a group known to be schizophrenic. Test constructors select and administer a group of items to all individuals in this criterion group as well as to a control group from the normal population. They then attempt to locate items that distinguish the criterion and control groups. This procedure always involves the use of an external criterion—a group known to possess certain characteristics—and involves contrasting the criterion and control groups. Thus, the terms *contrasted-group* and *external-criterion* strategy are frequently used interchangeably with the term *criterion-group strategy*.

Hypothetically, suppose that a group of aggressive individuals marks "true" to items such as "I am not aggressive," "I like to attend concerts," and "I would rather read than write" significantly more often than do individuals in a normal control comparison group. These items can then be included on an aggression scale. When new subjects endorse a large proportion of items on the aggression scale, we may hypothesize that they are aggressive because they endorsed the same items that distinguished aggressive individuals from control individuals. The content of the items is of little consequence. What is important is that aggressive individuals marked "true" to these items, and this endorsement discriminated the aggressive individuals from the control group. As J. S. Wiggins (1973, p. 394) notes, depressed individuals respond "false" significantly more than normals to the statement "I sometimes tease animals." There is no logical or rational reason for this response. It is important to remember that the actual content or face validity of an item in the criterion-group strategy is of little importance. Instead, the approach attempts to determine which items discriminate the criterion and control groups.

Once distinguishing items have been determined for one sample of subjects representing the criterion group, the next step is to cross-validate the scale by checking its discriminating power for an independent criterion sample—individuals also known to possess the characteristics to be measured—against a control group. If the scale significantly distinguishes the two groups, then it is said to have been *cross-validated*. Once a scale has been developed, data from the normal controls can be used to obtain standard scores. It can then be determined how far above or below the mean of the normal group each new subject scores in standardized units. Thus, a subject's score on each scale can be converted to percentiles (see Chapter 2).

After a scale has been constructed and cross-validated, the third step in the criterion approach is to conduct additional research in order to empirically ascertain what it means when subjects endorse a large number of items on a particular scale (for example, McGrath & O'Malley, 1986; Svanum & Dallas, 1981). An independent group that scores two standard deviations above the mean on an aggression scale, for example, may be studied intensely to determine how they describe themselves, how others describe them, the characteristics of their family background, and so on. Hence, when a person scores two standard deviations above the mean on a particular scale, it is known that the items endorsed by this individual were those that distinguished a criterion group from a control group and that high scores on this scale tend to be obtained by individuals who possess certain characteristics as indicated by empirical research.

Factor analytic strategy. The factor analytic strategy uses the statistical procedure of factor analysis to empirically derive the basic dimensions of personality. As you will recall from Chapter 3, factor analysis is a technique for boiling down or reducing data to a small number of descriptive units or dimensions. A test, for example, may have two scales that correlate highly, such as hostility and aggression. The correlation between the two means that they overlap in what they measure; that is, they share common variance. Both, for example, may be related to characteristics of a paranoid personality, a personality problem characterized in part by aggression and hostility. The same test may also have two other scales, suspicion and defensiveness, variables also associated with the paranoid personality. These two scales may correlate not only with each other but also with the hostility and aggression scales. Thus, all four scales may overlap, or share common variance. If it can be shown that a substantial proportion of the variability in all four scales is related to some common factor, then a factor analyst could argue that the test actually has only one scale, which is related to the paranoid personality.

Factor analysts begin with an empirical data base consisting of the intercorrelation of a large number of items or tests. They then factor analyze these intercorrelations, typically in such a manner as to find the minimum number of vectors of common variance to account for as much of the variability in the data as possible. They then attempt to label these factors by ascertaining what the items related to a particular factor have in common.

II. *Criteria Used in Selecting Tests for Discussion*

There are far too many structured personality tests to adequately discuss them all even in a book devoted exclusively to the subject, let alone in a single chapter. (We prefer the term *tests* for general purposes, although for specific procedures other terms like *inventories, techniques, scales,* and *assessment procedures* are often preferred.) However, all available structured personality tests can be classified according to whether they use one or some combination of the four strategies discussed above: logical-content, theoretical, criterion-group, and factor analytic. We selected the tests included in the discussion that follows because they illustrate each of the major strategies and because of their (1) widespread use as indicated by surveys of psychological test usage in the United States (Lubin, Larson & Matarazzo, 1984; Lubin, Wallis & Paine, 1971; Polyson, Peterson & Marshall, 1986); (2) interest to the research community as determined by the number of references listed in the personality sections of *The Mental Measurements Yearbooks*; and (3) historical value as determined by the introduction of new concepts in structured personality testing. In selecting these criteria, we were guided by those used by Gynther and Gynther (1976) in their excellent overview of structured personality tests.

III. *The Logical-Content Strategy*

We begin our discussion with the first personality test ever developed—the Woodworth Personal Data Sheet. We then present two examples of early logical-content tests. The Mooney Problem Checklist is a relatively recent example of the logical-content approach.

A. *Woodworth Personal Data Sheet*

The first personality inventory ever, the Woodworth Personal Data Sheet, was developed during World War I and published in its final form after the war (Woodworth, 1920). Its purpose was to identify military recruits who were likely to break down in combat. Prior to the Woodworth, military recruits were screened in psychiatric interviews; however, because of a shortage of psychiatrists, adequate interviewing of all applicants became impossible. This need for alternative screening methods was the impetus for the development of tests of personality.

The final form of the Woodworth contained 116 questions to which the individual responded "yes" or "no." The items were selected from lists of symptoms known to be related to emotional disorders and from the questions asked by psychiatrists in their screening interviews. In effect, the scale was a paper-and-pencil psychiatric interview. The Woodworth consisted of questions similar to these: "Do you drink a fifth of whiskey a day?" "Do you wet the bed at night?" "Do you frequently daydream?" "Do you usually feel in good health?" "Do you usually sleep soundly at night?" The Woodworth yielded a single score, which provided a single global measure of functioning. Only those recruits who reported many symptoms were subsequently given an interview. In this way, the military was able to concentrate its efforts on the most likely candidates for rejection from service on the basis of emotional problems.

Although its items were selected through the logical-content approach, the Woodworth had two additional features. First, items that were endorsed by 25% or more of a normal sample in the scored direction were excluded from the test. This technique tended to reduce the number of false positives—that is, subjects identified as risks by the test who were not actually risks and would most likely be cleared in an actual interview. Second, only those symptoms that occurred twice as often in a previously diagnosed neurotic group as in normals were included in the first version of the test.

The success of the Woodworth in solving the problem of mass screening provided a stimulus for the development of a host of structured tests (inventories) aimed at measuring personality characteristics. These tests borrowed items from each other, particularly the Woodworth, and used a variety of methods for clustering and scoring items. However, all were alike in that they assumed that test items could be taken at face value; that is, they assumed the face validity of a test response.

B. *Early Multidimensional Logical-Content Scales*

Two of the better known early tests developed by using the logical-content strategy were the Bell Adjustment Inventory and the Bernreuter Personality

Inventory. The Bell Adjustment Inventory attempted to evaluate the subject's adjustment in a variety of areas such as home life, social life, and emotional functioning. The Bernreuter Personality Inventory could be used for subjects as young as 13 or 14 years old and included items related to six personality traits such as introversion, confidence, and sociability. The Bell and the Bernreuter were both first published in the 1930s, and both, in contrast to the Woodworth, produced more than one score. These multidimensional procedures were the forerunners of many modern tests, which yield multiple scores rather than a single overall index.

C. *Mooney Problem Checklist*

Few modern tests rely extensively on the logical-content method of test construction. Perhaps the most recent important example is the Mooney Problem Checklist, which was published in 1950. The Mooney contains a list of problems that reoccurred in clinical case history data and in the written statements of problems submitted by approximately 4000 high school students. It is like the Woodworth in that in clinical practice subjects who check an excessive number of items are considered to have difficulties. The major interpretive procedure is to assume the face validity of a test response. Thus, if a subject checks an item related to finances, it is assumed that the person is having financial difficulties.

D. *Criticisms of the Logical-Content Approach*

Psychologists involved in the development of the Woodworth and the plethora of subsequent tests satisfied an important need. These tests proved extremely useful as screening devices and methods of obtaining information about a person without the necessity of an extensive interview. Before long, however, the weaknesses of the logical-content strategy became evident.

In assuming that test items can be interpreted at face value, the logical-content strategy also assumes that the subject takes a normal approach to the test, complies with the instructions, reads each item, and answers as honestly as possible. Even assuming the validity of these assumptions, subjects may not be capable of objectively evaluating their own behavior in the area covered by the test item (for example, "I never drink too much alcohol"). And even if subjects are capable of accurate self-evaluation, they still may not interpret the test item in the same way as the test constructor or test user, which is also an implicit assumption of the logical-content strategy.

A. Ellis (1946) argued that none of the above assumptions is necessarily true and that assuming they are is certain to produce errors. Indeed, structured personality tests based on the logic of face validity were so sharply criticized (Landis, 1936; Landis, Zubin & Katz, 1935; McNemar & Landis, 1935) that the entire structured approach to personality was all but discarded until it was finally rescued by the introduction of a new conceptualization in personality testing, the empirical criterion-group strategy (Dahlstrom, 1969a).

IV. *The Criterion-Group Strategy*

Just when the development of an adequate structured personality test seemed nothing more than a pipe dream, the Minnesota Multiphasic Personality Inventory (MMPI) introduced a number of innovations in the construction of structured personality tests. The main idea—assume nothing about the meaning of a subject's response to a test item—though not entirely new, was the only possible way of meeting objections from critics of structured personality tests based on face validity. Since the logical-content approach had been beaten to death because of its many assumptions, developers of the MMPI argued that the meaning of a test response could be determined only through empirical research. In this section, we discuss the MMPI as well as its most recent offspring, the MMPI-2.

A. *Minnesota Multiphasic Personality Inventory*

The Minnesota Multiphasic Personality Inventory (MMPI and MMPI-2) is a true-false self-report questionnaire. Statements are typically of the self-reference type, such as "I like good food" and "I never have trouble falling to sleep." The subject is asked to mark "true" or "false" for each statement as it applies to himself or herself. The heart of the test consists of its validity scales, clinical scales, and content scales. The validity scales provide information concerning the person's approach to testing, such as whether an attempt was made to fake bad by endorsing more items of pathological content than could be justified by any person's actual problems or whether an attempt was made to fake good by avoiding pathological items. The clinical scales were designed to identify psychological disorders such as depression and schizophrenia. Today, the clinician uses the pattern of scores, codebooks that provide extensive research summaries on the meaning of test scores, formulas, and clinical judgment to assess the meaning of the clinical scales. Content scales consist of groups of items related to a specific content area that have been empirically related to that content area, such as the anger scale whose content contains references to irritability, hot-headedness, and other symptoms of anger-control problems. Subjects obtain a raw score on each scale based on the number of items they marked in the scored direction. Raw scores are then converted to standardized scores, which are called *T scores*, with a mean of 50 and a standard deviation of 10.

Purpose. Like the Woodworth, the purpose of the MMPI and MMPI-2 is to assist in distinguishing normal from abnormal groups. Specifically, the test was

Figure 15-2
An MMPI profile sheet. (*Reproduced by permission of University of Minnesota Press.*)

designed to aid in the diagnosis or assessment of the major psychiatric or psychological disorders, and, for the most part, it continues to be used for this purpose. The test can be used with persons 14 years of age or older. The MMPI requires at least a 6th-grade reading ability; the MMPI-2 an 8th-grade reading ability. Great care must be taken to make sure the individual can read at the appropriate level and has an IQ within normal limits (see Focused Example 15-1).

Original development of the scales. Beginning with a pool of 1000 items selected from a wide variety of sources, including case histories, psychological reports, textbooks, and existing tests, the original authors of the test, S. R. Hathaway, a psychologist, and J. C. McKinley, a physician, selected 504 items that were judged to be relatively independent of one another. The scales were then determined empirically by presenting the items to criterion and control groups in order to find those items that distinguished the groups.

The criterion groups used in the development of the original version of the MMPI consisted of psychiatric inpatients at the University of Minnesota Hospital. These psychiatric patients were divided into eight groups according to their psychiatric diagnoses. The original pool of psychiatric patients had 800 persons, but this number was substantially reduced in order to find homogeneous groupings with sufficient agreement on diagnoses. The final eight criterion groups each consisted of about 50 patients: hypochondriacs—individuals preoccupied with the body and fears of illness; depressed patients; hysterics—

□ ◇ FOCUSED EXAMPLE 15-1

Reading the MMPI

In one interesting case that we had the opportunity to observe, a 16-year-old girl was being detained by the juvenile court. Her mother reported her to the police, stating she could not be controlled. A few hours before her preliminary hearing, the judge requested psychological testing to aid in the assessment process. A psychology intern, who was inexperienced with the MMPI, was the only professional staff member available, and he tried to carry out the judge's orders himself by administering a quick MMPI. The intern warned the girl of the validity scales, stating that he could tell if she tried to fake. When she was presented with the test booklet, the girl groaned, stating, "This test is too hard." The intern assured her not to worry, that there were no right or wrong answers. "Oh, I hope I pass," the girl said. "I'm not good at tests."

She finished moments before the time of her court hearing, after taking more than 3 hours rather than the usual 1–2 hours required to complete the MMPI. The intern immediately scored it and found that she had marked nearly half of the 64 items in the scored direction on the F scale, one of the validity scales containing highly pathological content. Since the average for the general population on this scale is four items in the scored direction, with an average of eight items in the scored direction for adolescents, the girl's endorsement of 30 items clearly indicated she had not taken a normal approach to testing and suggested to the intern that she had faked by deliberately endorsing pathological items in order to appear disordered.

In court the judge asked the intern what the results showed. "I can't tell," said the intern, "because she tried to fake." "Did you fake?" asked the judge. "No sir," said the girl, "I swear I didn't." The judge told her to go back and take the test again.

Irate, the intern again warned the girl not to fake. "Oh, I hope I pass," she moaned. "Just answer truthfully and you'll pass," said the intern. She completed the test, and the intern immediately scored it. The results were almost identical to those for the previous testing. The intern rushed into the testing room and scolded the girl for faking again. "I knew I'd flunk that test," she said. "It was too hard for me." Finally, it dawned on the intern to question whether she could read the test. A reading test revealed that she could read at only the fourth-grade level. Most of the items were therefore incomprehensible to her. The embarrassed intern was forced to go back into court and explain what had happened. No doubt he never again made the mistake of administering the MMPI when the subject's reading level was in doubt.

primarily individuals who showed a physical problem with no physical cause, such as hysterical blindness; psychopathic deviates—delinquent, criminal, or antisocial individuals; paranoids—individuals who showed symptoms including poor reality testing (for example, delusions in which they falsely believed that people were plotting against them); psychasthenics—individuals with a neurotic disorder characterized by excessive doubts and unreasonable fears; schizophrenics—individuals with a psychotic disorder involving dramatic symptoms such as hallucinations (see things that aren't there) and thinking problems such as illogical reasoning; and hypomanics—individuals with a disorder characterized by hyperactivity and irritability. (See Table 15-1.)

Those in the criterion groups were then compared to about 700 controls consisting primarily of relatives and visitors of the patients, excluding mental patients in the University of Minnesota Hospital. The use of this control group was perhaps the greatest source of criticism for the original MMPI. Clearly, there is little basis for calling the relatives of patients in a large city university hospital representative of the general population, although the control group was augmented by other subjects such as a group of recent high school graduates. The MMPI-2, as we will see, has a large and fairly representative control sample.

Despite its weakness, the original control group did provide a reference sample against which the criterion groups could be compared. After an item analysis was conducted, items that separated the criterion from the control group were included on one or more of the eight scales. To cross-validate the scales, independent samples of the criterion and control groups were administered the items. To qualify as cross-validated, a scale had to distinguish the criterion group from the control group at the .05 level of significance.

Table 15-1
Original Criterion Groups for the MMPI

Hypochondriacs	Patients suffering from overconcern of bodily symptoms; express conflicts through bodily (somatic) symptoms.
Depressives	Patients with depressed mood, loss of appetite, loss of interest, suicidal thoughts, and other depressive symptoms.
Hysterics	Immature individuals who overdramatize their plight and may exhibit physical symptoms for which no physical cause exists.
Psychopathic deviates	Individuals who are antisocial and rebellious; exploit others without remorse or anxiety.
Paranoids	Individuals who show extreme suspicions, hypersensitivity, and delusions.
Psychasthenics	Individuals plagued by excessive self-doubts, obsessive thoughts, anxiety, and low energy.
Schizophrenics	Disorganized, highly disturbed individuals out of contact with reality and having difficulties with communication, interpersonal relations, sensory abnormalities (e.g., hallucinations), or motor abnormalities (e.g., catonia).
Hypomanics	Individuals in a high-energy, agitated state with poor impulse control, inability to sleep, and poor judgment.

Table 15-2
Original Validity
Scales of the
MMPI

Lie scale (L)	15 rationally derived items included in both the MMPI and MMPI-2 designed to evaluate a naive attempt to present oneself in a favorable light. The items reflect personal weaknesses such as "I never lose control of myself when I drive." Most people are willing to admit to these weaknesses. People who score high on this scale are unwilling to acknowledge minor flaws.
Infrequency scale (F)	Of the original 64 items from the MMPI that were developed to detect deviant response patterns, 60 were retained for the MMPI-2. These are items that are scored infrequently (less than 10%) by the normal population. An example of an F-scale-like item is "I am aware of a special presence which others cannot perceive." High scores on the F scale invalidate the profile.
K scale	30 items included on both the MMPI and MMPI-2 that detect attempts to deny problems and present oneself in a favorable light. People who score high on this scale are attempting to project an image of self-control and personal effectiveness. Very high scores on this scale invalidate the profile.

In addition to the eight scales described above, two content scales were added: the masculinity-feminity (MF) scale, which contained items differentially endorsed by men and women, and the social-introversion (Si) scale, which was developed by L. E. Drake (1946) to identify extroverted individuals. These latter two scales plus the eight scales described above constitute the original ten clinical scales of the MMPI.

Because the logical-content approach had been criticized for its many assumptions, S. R. Hathaway and J. C. McKinley developed validity scales to measure test-taking attitude and to assess whether the subject took a normal, honest approach to the test (see Table 15-2). The L, or lie, scale was rationally designed to detect individuals who attempted to present themselves in an overly favorable way.

The K scale served the same purpose, but it was empirically constructed. In deriving the K scale, Hathaway and McKinley compared the MMPI scores of nondisturbed individuals showing normal patterns with the MMPI scores of individuals who were known to be disturbed but who produced normal MMPI patterns in that they showed no scales that deviated significantly from the mean. The K scale thus attempts to locate those items that distinguished normal from abnormal groups when both groups marked the test in such a way as to produce a normal pattern. It was assumed that pathological groups would produce normal patterns because of defensiveness, a tendency to hide or deny psychological problems, and that this defensiveness could be determined by comparing these individuals to nondisturbed normals.

The F scale, designed to detect individuals who attempted to fake bad, consists of those items endorsed by less than 10% of the control group. Of the 64 items on the F scale, most of which contain pathological content such as "Odd odors come to me at times," the average number of items endorsed in the scored direction is four. Clearly, anyone who marks a lot of these items is taking an unusual approach to the test. Thus, high F scores bring the validity of the whole profile into question.

Finally, although it is referred to as a validity scale, the "cannot say" scale consists simply of the items to which the subject failed to respond either "true" or "false." If as few as 10% of the items are omitted, the entire profile becomes invalid. As a result, many present-day clinicians discourage the subject from omitting items because providing the option produces little useful information and can easily lead to a completely invalid profile.

Initial interpretations. For all the scales, the control group provided the reference for which standard scores were determined. McCall's T, with a mean of 50 and a standard deviation of 10, was used to compute standard scores. Subjects with T scores of 50 were thus at the mean of the control sample; T scores of 70, two standard deviations above the mean, were considered significantly elevated for the MMPI. With the new norms for the MMPI-2, T scores of 65 are now considered significant.

The original approach taken in MMPI interpretation was simple and straightforward. Because the scales significantly discriminated the criterion from control groups and withstood the test of cross-validation, most users assumed that individuals with characteristics similar to those of a criterion group would have significant elevation on the appropriate scale. Schizophrenics, for example, would show significant elevation on the schizophrenia scale, hysterics would show elevation on the hysteria scale, and so on. Unfortunately, this turned out to be a false assumption. Experience with the MMPI rapidly revealed that only a relatively small number of disturbed subjects showed elevation on only a single scale. More often, elevation was found in two, three, four, or even all the scales. Thus, there was a problem: What did the test mean when someone showed elevation on the hysteria, psychopathic deviate, schizophrenia, and hypomania scales? There is no such thing as a hysterical psychopathic hypomanic schizophrenic!

To deal with multiple-scale elevations, clinicians made use of pattern, or configural, analysis, which the test authors had originally suggested (Hathaway & McKinley, 1943). This change led to an avalanche of studies and proposals for identifying clinical groups on the basis of patterns of MMPI scores (Henrichs, 1964; Meehl & Dahlstrom, 1960; Taulbee & Sisson, 1957). However, early investigations (Garfield & Sineps, 1959; Loy, 1959) as well as more recent studies (Fowler & Coyle, 1969; Meikle & Gerritse, 1970) revealed the futility of this approach. Either the rules were so complex that only an extremely small portion of the profiles met the criteria, like the Gilberstadt and Duker (1965) rules, or the rules led to diagnoses that were no more accurate than those made by untrained nonprofessionals (Meehl, 1954, 1956, 1957; Meehl & Rosen, 1955). Led by Paul Meehl, clinicians subsequently began to look at the highest two scales.

Meehl's extension of the empirical approach. Pointing to the possible advantages of analyzing the two highest scales that are elevated, known as the *two-point code,* Meehl (1951) began to emphasize the importance of conducting research on individuals who showed specific two-point codes and other configural patterns in order to empirically determine the meaning of MMPI elevations. Thus, the validity of the MMPI was extended by finding homogeneous profile patterns and determining the characteristics of individuals who show these patterns. In other words, new criterion groups were established, consisting of individuals grouped on the basis of similarities in their MMPI profiles. In this approach, the characteristics of a criterion group, consisting of subjects who showed elevation on two scales (for example, the psychopathic deviate and hypomania scales), could be empirically determined. The difference in approach meant that MMPI configural patterns, rather than psychiatric diagnosis, became the criterion for the selection of homogeneous criterion groups.

Because the original idea of the contrasted-group method was extended by using criterion groups based on MMPI patterns and then studying these groups, we use the term *criterion-group strategy* rather than *contrasted-group strategy* to describe the MMPI and related tests. The more recent approach does not attempt to distinguish the criterion group from a control group. Instead, the characteristics of the criterion groups are evaluated through empirical means such as peer ratings, physician ratings, and demographic characteristics. The upshot has been numerous studies describing the characteristics of individuals who show certain MMPI patterns.

In conjunction with his proposed extension of the empirical approach to personality assessment, Meehl and others (Hathaway, 1947; Welsh, 1948) began to advocate a change in the names of the scales. Since elevation on the schizophrenia scale did not necessarily mean the person was schizophrenic, the use of such a name was awkward as well as confusing. They therefore suggested that the scales be identified by number rather than name. Table 15-3 lists the scales by their number. Only clinical scales were given numbers; validity scales retained their original names.

With the use of numbers, MMPI patterns could be given a numerical code. For each of the two most commonly used coding systems (Hathaway, 1947; Welsh, 1948), the clinical scales are listed in rank order from highest T score to lowest. A symbol is then used to indicate the level of elevation. In Welsh's (1948) system, for example, T scores of 90 (four standard deviations above the mean) and greater are designated by $\star$; T scores between 80 and 89 are designated by ”; T scores between 70 and 79, by ’; T scores between 60 and 69, by –; and so on for each ten-point interval down to # placed to the right of T scores below 29. For example, the code 13$\star$ 2” 7’ 456890– means that Scales 1 and 3 have T scores above 90, Scale 2 above 80, Scale 7 above 70, and the remaining scales between 60 and 69. This pattern is referred to as a one-three two-point pattern or, more simply, a 13 code, based on the two highest scales.

Table 15-3
Original MMPI Scales

Symbol Currently in Use	Old Name	Number of Items in Scale*	Common Interpretation of Elevation
Validity Scales			
L	Lie scale	15	Naive attempt to fake good
K	K scale	30	Defensiveness
F	F scale	64	Attempt to fake bad
Clinical Scales			
1	Hypochondriasis	33	Physical complaints
2	Depression	60	Depression
3	Hysteria	60	Immaturity
4	Psychopathic deviate	50	Authority conflict
5	Masculinity-femininity	60	Masculine or feminine interests
6	Paranoia	40	Suspicion, hostility
7	Psychasthenia	48	Anxiety
8	Schizophrenia	78	Alienation, withdrawal
9	Hypomania	46	Elated mood, high energy
0	Social introversion	70	Introversion, shyness

* Because of item overlap, the total number of items here is 654.

Note: The validity scales (L, K, and F) determine the individual's approach to testing (normal or honest, fake bad or fake good). Of the ten clinical scales, two were developed rationally (5 and 0). The remaining eight scales were developed through the criterion-group method. Numerous interpretive hypotheses can be associated with each MMPI scale; however, the meaning of any MMPI scale depends on the characteristics of the subject (age, race, sex, socioeconomic status, education, IQ, and so forth).

The restandardization: MMPI-2. Beginning in 1982, a major effort was made to update and restandardize the MMPI. The result was the MMPI-2 (Butcher et al., 1989). The purpose of the revision was to update and expand the norms, revise items that were out of date, awkward, sexist, or problematic, and broaden the item pool to extend the range of constructs that could be evaluated. At the same time, the goal was to retain all the features of the original MMPI, including the original validity and clinical scales. A final goal was to develop a separate form for adolescents. All of these goals were accomplished in masterful fashion.

All 550 of the original items were retained. Of these, 82 were modified and another 154 were added. Research presented in the manual (Ben-Porath & Butcher, 1989) as well as more recently published studies (Graham, Timbrook & Ben-Porath, in press) have indicated that the item rewording did not alter the psychometric properties of the items.

In developing new norms, the MMPI project committee, which consisted of James Butcher of the University of Minnesota, Grant Dahlstrom of the University of North Carolina, Jack Graham of Kent State University, and Auke Tellegen of the University of Minnesota, selected 2900 subjects from seven geographic areas of the United States: California, Minnesota, North Carolina,

Figure 15-3
An MMPI-2 profile sheet. (*Reproduced by permission of University of Minnesota Press.*)

Ohio, Pennsylvania, Virginia, and Washington. Of these, 300 were eliminated due to incomplete or invalid profiles, resulting in a final sample of 2600 men and women. Potential subjects for the restandardization were initially identified by telephone and then contacted by letter. Testing centers were set up in major cities to make personal contact and arrange for the testing. The goal was to obtain a sample that reflected the demographic characteristics of the 1980 census. However, because participation was completely voluntary, the final sample was more educated and had greater economic means than the general population.

A major feature of the MMPI-2 is the inclusion of additional validity scales. On the original MMPI, all the F items are in the first 370 items and appeared on the front of the answer sheet. The MMPI-2 expanded the F scale to the back of the scoring sheet as well. The F_B (Back F) score provides a check on validity and cooperation throughout the test and permits a confirmation of F scores obtained in the first half of the test. Two additional validity scales, the

Variable Response Inconsistency Scale (VRIN) and the True Response Inconsistency Scale (TRIN), are included to evaluate response styles. VRIN attempts to evaluate random responding. The scale consists of matched pairs of items that have similar content. Each time the pairs are marked in opposite directions, a point is scored on the scale. The TRIN attempts to measure acquiescence—the tendency to agree or mark true irrespective of content. This scale consists of matched pairs of items with opposite content.

The additional 154 items of the MMPI-2 permit the evaluation of a number of content areas (Butcher et al., 1990). The MMPI-2 contains 15 content scales including HEA (health concerns) and TPA (Type A), which evaluates for the hard-driving, irritable, impatient Type A personality type. (For more on the Type A personality, see Chapter 18.) Other MMPI-2 content scales include FAM (family problems), which evaluates family disorders and possible child abuse, and WRK (work interference), which examines behaviors or attitudes likely to interfere with work performance.

Psychometric properties. The psychometric properties of the MMPI and MMPI-2 are comparable; the newer version maintains strong continuity with the original. For example, the factor structures of the new and original versions are highly similar.

Median split-half reliability coefficients for both the original MMPI and the MMPI-2 run in the .70s, with some coefficients as high as .96 but others much lower. Median test-retest coefficients range from the low .50s to the low .90s (median .80s). Although these coefficients are not as solid as those for the major ability tests such as the Binet and Wechsler, they are as high or better than those reported in any other comparable test. Moreover, when looking at the basic higher-order factor structure, the MMPI and MMPI-2 are extremely reliable, with coefficients running in the high .90s.

Although the reliability of the MMPI is generally adequate, there are some notable problems that have not been dealt with. For example, because of the way in which scales were originally constructed, many items are on more than one scale, and some items are on as many as six. Scale 8, which has more items than any other scale (78 items), contains only 16 unique items (Dahlstrom, Welsh & Dahlstrom, 1972, p. 232). This problem of item overlap was not confronted in the MMPI-2 revision because the goal was to retain all of the original scales.

Perhaps as a result of item overlap, *intercorrelations among the clinical scales* are extremely high. For example, Scales 7 and 8 correlate between .64 and .87 depending on the sample studied (Butcher et al., 1989; Dahlstrom & Welsh, 1960). This high intercorrelation among the scales has led to a number of factor analytic studies (Block, 1965; Dahlstrom & Welsh, 1960; Dahlstrom, Welsh & Dahlstrom, 1972, 1975; Welsh, 1956), which consistently show that two factors account for most of the variance in the ten original MMPI scales. These factors have been variously labeled throughout the literature (for instance, as negative or positive affectivity and as constraint; see Finn, 1986). Because of the high intercorrelations among the scales and the results of factor analytic studies, the validity of pattern analysis is questionable.

Another problem with the MMPI and MMPI-2 is the *imbalance in the way items are keyed*. Many individuals approach structured tests with a *response style*, or bias, which is a tendency to mark an item in a certain way irrespective of content. One of these tendencies is **acquiescence,** the tendency to agree with or to endorse an item as true. Given the possibility of response tendencies, one would expect an equal number of items in the keyed direction for the categories "true" and "false." Not so; all the items on the L scale and 29 of the 30 items on the K scale are keyed false. Scales 7, 8, and 9 are keyed on a 3 : 1 true-false ratio. The VRIN and TRIN scales of the MMPI-2 referred to earlier allow the examiner to evaluate response tendencies and represent a clear positive step toward overcoming this imbalance.

Major works devoted to the MMPI and MMPI-2 strongly emphasize the importance of taking into account the *demographic characteristics* of the subjects in interpreting profiles (Butcher, 1990; Butcher et al., 1990; Dahlstrom & Welsh, 1960; Dahlstrom, Welsh & Dahlstrom, 1972; Graham, 1990; Hathaway & McKinley, 1967). This advice is indeed warranted in that most of the studies have shown that age (Butcher et al., in press, 1992), gender (Butcher et al., 1989; Webb, 1970), race (Butcher, 1990; Gynther, 1972; Strauss, Gynther & Wallhermfechtel, 1974), place of residence (Erdberg, 1969), and other demographic factors such as intelligence, education, and socioeconomic status (Butcher, 1990; Butcher et al., 1990; Gynther & Shimkunas, 1965; Thumin, 1969) are all related to the MMPI and MMPI-2 scales. This overwhelming evidence supporting the covariation between demographic factors and the meaning of MMPI and MMPI-2 scores clearly shows that two exact profile patterns can have quite different meanings depending on the demographic characteristics of each subject.

The major source of *validity* for the MMPI and MMPI-2 comes from the multitude of research studies that describe the characteristics of particular profile patterns. Volume II of the revised MMPI handbook (Dahlstrom, Welsh & Dahlstrom, 1975) cites approximately 6000 studies, with the number of new studies increasing every year. In conjunction with this older base, there is a mushrooming literature devoted to the MMPI-2, with the number of studies published or in press already in the hundreds. This body of research provides ample evidence for the construct validity of the MMPI.

A number of studies, for example, have related MMPI response patterns to alcoholism (Greene et al., in press; McMahon et al., 1991). For example, evidence indicates that the MMPI and MMPI-2 might be useful in the early detection of individuals who later become alcoholics (Hoffman, Loper & Kammeier, 1974; Kammeier, Hoffman & Loper, 1973; Loper, Kammeier & Hoffman, 1973). The items of the original MMPI were administered to a group of men while they were still in college. The response patterns of those individuals who later became alcoholics were compared to those of a control group who did not become alcoholics. Results showed that the subjects who eventually became alcoholics had significantly higher scores on one validity scale (F) and two clinical scales (4 and 9). Thus, these scales may be related to characteristics that contribute or lead to alcoholism in men. It is interesting that the response pattern of those in the alcoholic group was the same as their retest pattern after they had become alcoholics.

Indeed, the range of problems for which the MMPI has been shown to be of value spans everything from eating disorders (Shisslak, Pazda & Crago, 1990), posttraumatic stress syndrome (Litz et al., in press), prediction of surgical outcome in chronic low-back-pain patients (Turner, Herron & Weiner, 1986), and prediction of delinquent behavior (Lindgren et al., 1986), to prediction of women at risk for child abuse (Egeland, Butcher & Ben-Porath, in press). Of course, not all MMPI studies report positive results (Levenson et al., 1986), but the vast majority attest to its utility and versatility.

Current status. The restandardization of the MMPI has eliminated the most serious drawback of the original version: the inadequate control group. With its already widespread use and acceptance, the future of the MMPI appears to be extremely bright. And with the addition of 154 new items, we are sure to see many new applications. In addition, the newer items can be added to the original scales when appropriate to increase their reliability as well as their predictive validity. It is unlikely that the MMPI will soon be replaced as the premiere structured personality test. However, as things have currently evolved, the MMPI and MMPI-2 are really two different tests despite efforts to incorporate all the old into the new.

B. *California Psychological Inventory*

The California Psychological Inventory (CPI) (Gough, 1957, 1969, 1987) is second only to the MMPI in popularity as a structured personality test constructed primarily by the criterion-group strategy. For 11 of the 20 CPI scales in the 1987 revision, criterion groups (for example, males versus females; homosexual males versus heterosexual males) were contrasted to produce measures of personality that were categorized into three themes: (1) introversion-extroversion, (2) conventional versus unconventional in following norms, and (3) self-realization and sense of integration.

In contrast to the MMPI, the CPI attempts to evaluate personality in normally adjusted individuals. The test contains 18 scales, each of which is grouped into one of four classes. Class I scales measure poise, self-assurance, and interpersonal effectiveness. Individuals who score high on the scales in this class tend to be active, resourceful, competitive, outgoing, spontaneous, and self-confident. They are also at ease in interpersonal situations. Individuals who score high on Class II scales, which evaluate socialization, maturity, and responsibility, tend to be conscientious, honest, dependable, calm, practical, cooperative, and alert to ethical and moral issues. Class III scales measure achievement potential and intellectual efficiency. High scores in this class tend to indicate organized, efficient, sincere, mature, forceful, capable, and well-informed persons. Class IV scales examine interest modes. High score tend to be responsive to the inner needs of others and flexible in their social behavior.

More than a third of the 462 items are almost identical to items in the MMPI, and many others are quite similar to MMPI items (Megargee, 1972). However, the test does more than share items with the MMPI (Furnham & Henderson, 1982). Like the MMPI, the CPI shows considerable intercorrelation among its scales. Factor analytic studies have shown that only two factors in the CPI, associated with internal controls (Class 2 scales) and interpersonal effectiveness (Class 1 scales), account for a large part of the variance (Megargee, 1972). Also like the MMPI, true-false scale keying is often extremely unbalanced. Furthermore, reliability coefficients are similar to those reported for the MMPI (Megargee, 1972). Short-term test-retest coefficients range from .49 to .90 depending on the sample; long-term coefficients range from .38 to .77 (Megargee, 1972). The method used to establish some criterion groups for the CPI has been questioned. For example, for some of the scales, subjects were placed in criterion groups on the basis of ratings by friends. Nevertheless, the psychometric properties of the CPI must be considered adequate by today's standards because they are comparable to those of most widely used personality tests.

The CPI is commonly used in research settings to examine everything from the personality of nursing students (Houldin & Forbes, 1990) to Type A behavior (Haemmerlie & Beamish, 1990). In one study, 112 women were tested as college seniors in the late 1950s and then retested in the late 1980s at the age of 43. Women who scored high in traditional role behavior for the 1950s and did not enter the work force tended to suffer severe changes in psychological and physical health by age 43. Traditional women who entered the work force seemed to cope better with changing times and showed much less distress.

The advantage of the CPI is that it can be used with normal subjects. The MMPI is generally not appropriate with normal subjects, and the meaning of nonelevated profiles is not well established. Therefore, if the intent is to assess normal individuals for interpersonal effectiveness and internal controls, the CPI is a good candidate for the measure. Furthermore, as with the MMPI, a considerable body of literature has focused on the CPI. Each new piece of literature extends the utility of the test and adds to its construct validity. Therefore, the future of the CPI as a measure of normal personalities has good potential despite its limitations.

V. *The Factor Analytic Strategy*

Structured personality tests, as they exist today, share one common set of assumptions. These assumptions, simply stated, are that humans possess characteristics or traits that are exhibited across situations (are stable), vary from individual to individual, and can be measured. Nowhere are these assumptions better illustrated than in the factor analytic strategy of test construction.

As you will recall, factor analysis is a statistical procedure for reducing the redundancy in a set of intercorrelated scores. For example, one major technique of factor analysis, the principal-components method (Hotelling, 1933), finds the minimum number of common factors that can account for an interrelated set of scores. As noted in the previous section, two factors can account for most of the variance in both the CPI and the MMPI, which suggests that these tests are actually measuring only two unique components and that all scales are related to these two components.

The advantages of factor analysis are quite evident. However, prior to the advent of the high-speed computer, even simple factor analyses required several weeks or even months of tedious arithmetic operations on a hand calculator. Therefore, the development of the factor analytic strategy awaited the technological refinement of computers. One individual, R. B. Cattell, has distinguished himself in using the factor analytic strategy of structured personality assessment; his work is the focus of this section.

A. *Guilford's Pioneer Efforts*

One usual strategy in validating a new test is to correlate the scores on the new test with the scores on other tests that purport to measure the same entity. J. P. Guilford's approach was related to this procedure; however, instead of individually comparing one test to a series of other tests, Guilford and his associates determined the interrelationship (intercorrelation) of a wide variety of tests and then factor analyzed the results in an effort to find the major underlying dimensions common to all personality tests. If the results from existing personality tests could be reduced to only a few factors, then items that correlated highly with these factors could be used in a new test that would capture the major dimensions of personality.

The result of the initial attempt to apply this strategy was a series of inventories, which Guilford and his associates published in the 1940s (the STDCR, Guilford, 1940; the GAMIN, Guilford & Martin, 1943; the Temperament Survey, Guilford & Zimmerman, 1949). These procedures were ultimately collapsed into a single scale—the Guilford-Zimmerman Temperament Survey (Guilford & Zimmerman, 1956).

The Guilford-Zimmerman Temperament Survey reduces personality to ten dimensions, each of which is measured by 30 different items (Guilford, 1959). The ten dimensions are general activity, restraint, ascendance (leadership), sociability, emotional stability, objectivity, friendliness, thoughtfulness, personal relations, and masculinity. The test presents a list of statements, most of which are self-statements as in the MMPI, and the subject's task is to indicate "yes" or "no" for each statement. Three validity, or verification, keys are included to detect falsification and to evaluate the validity of the profile, as in the MMPI. Standard scores were obtained from college group reference samples, and split-half reliabilities are good, ranging from .75 to .85. However, this first major factor analytic structured personality test failed to catch on, perhaps because it was overshadowed by the MMPI and because of the arbitrary, subjective way of naming factors. The Guilford-Zimmerman Temperament Survey is now primarily of only historical interest.

B. *Cattell's Contribution*

Rather than attempt to uncover the major dimensions of personality by intercorrelating personality tests, R. B. Cattell began with all the adjectives applicable to human beings in order to empirically determine and measure the essence of personality. Beginning with a monumental catalog of all the adjectives (trait names) in an unabridged dictionary that apply to humans, G. W. Allport and H. S. Odbert (1936) reduced their list to 4504 "real" traits. Adding to the list traits found in the psychological and psychiatric literature, Cattell then reduced the list to 171 items that he believed accounted for the meaning of all items on the original list. College students rated their friends on these 171 terms, and the results were intercorrelated and factor analyzed. The 171 terms were reduced to 36 dimensions, which were called *surface traits* (Cattell, 1957). Subsequent investigation by factor analysis finally produced 16 distinct factors that accounted for all the variables. Thus, Cattell had reduced personality to 16 basic dimensions, which he called *source traits*. Table 15-4 lists these source traits.

The product of Cattell's marathon task was the Sixteen Personality Factor Questionnaire, better known as the 16PF (Cattell, 1949), which was subsequently revised based on continued factor analysis (Cattell, Eber & Tatsuoka, 1970). Consistent with the factor analytic strategy, items that correlated highly with each of the 16 major factors, or source traits, were included, and those with relatively low correlations were excluded.

Great care was taken in the standardization of the 16PF. Separate norms were provided for men alone, women alone, and men and women combined for each of three groups: U.S. adults, college students, and high school seniors. Thus, nine sets of norms are available. To further deal with the covariation of structured personality test data and demographic variables that plagues the MMPI, the 16PF provides age corrections for scales that change significantly with age. Six forms of the test are available: two parallel forms for each of three levels of vocabulary proficiency, ranging from newspaper-literate adults through the educationally disadvantaged. For the educationally disadvantaged, a tape-recorded (oral) form is also available. Norms for the various forms are based on more than 15,000 subjects representative of geographic area, population density, age, family income, and race according to figures provided by the U.S. census.

Unlike the MMPI and CPI, the 16PF contains no item overlap, and keying is balanced among the various alternative responses. Short-term test-retest

Table 15-4
The Primary
Source Traits
Covered by the
16PF Test

Factor	Low Sten Score Description (1–3)	High Sten Score Description (8–10)
A	*Cool,* **reserved, impersonal, detached, formal, aloof** Sizothymia*	*Warm,* **outgoing, kindly, easygoing, participating, likes people** Affectothymia
B	*Concrete-thinking,* **less intelligent** Lower scholastic mental capacity	*Abstract-thinking,* **more intelligent, bright** Higher scholastic mental capacity
C	*Affected by feelings,* **emotionally less stable, easily annoyed** Lower ego strength	*Emotionally stable,* **mature, faces reality, calm** Higher ego strength
E	*Submissive,* **humble, mild, easily led, accommodating** Submissiveness	*Dominant,* **assertive, aggressive, stubborn, competitive, bossy** Dominance
F	*Sober,* **restrained, prudent, taciturn, serious** Desurgency	*Enthusiastic,* **spontaneous, heedless, expressive, cheerful** Surgency
G	*Expedient,* **disregards rules, self-indulgent** Weaker superego strength	*Conscientious,* **conforming, moralistic, staid, rule-bound** Stronger superego strength
H	*Shy,* **threat-sensitive, timid, hesitant, intimidated** Threctia	*Bold,* **venturesome, uninhibited, can take stress** Parmia
I	*Tough-minded,* **self-reliant, no-nonsense, rough, realistic** Harria	*Tender-minded,* **sensitive, overprotected, intuitive, refined** Premsia
L	*Trusting,* **accepting conditions, easy to get on with** Alaxia	*Suspicious,* **hard to fool, distrustful, skeptical** Protension
M	*Practical,* **concerned with "down-to-earth" issues, steady** Praxernia	*Imaginative,* **absent-minded, absorbed in thought, impractical** Autia
N	*Forthright,* **unpretentious, open, genuine, artless** Artlessness	*Shrewd,* **polished, socially aware, diplomatic, calculating** Shrewdness
O	*Self-assured,* **secure, feels free of guilt, untroubled, self-satisfied** Untroubled adequacy	*Apprehensive,* **self-blaming, guilt-prone, insecure, worrying** Guilt proneness
Q_1	*Conservative,* **respecting traditional ideas** Conservatism of temperament	*Experimenting,* **liberal, critical, open to change** Radicalism
Q_2	*Group-oriented,* **a "joiner" and sound follower, listens to others** Group adherence	*Self-sufficient,* **resourceful, prefers own decisions** Self-sufficiency
Q_3	*Undisciplined self-conflict,* **lax, careless of social rules** Low integration	*Following self-image,* **socially precise, compulsive** High self-concept control
Q_4	*Relaxed,* **tranquil, composed, has low drive, unfrustrated** Low ergic tension	*Tense,* **frustrated, overwrought, has high drive** High ergic tension

* Titles in roman type are the technical names for the factors and are explained more fully in the *Handbook.*
Source: From the *Administrator's Manual for the 16 Personality Factor Questionnaire,* copyright © 1972, 1979, 1986 by the Institute for Personality and Ability Testing, Inc. Reproduced by permission.

correlation coefficients for the 16 source traits are impressive, with a range of .65 to .93 and a median coefficient of .83. Long-term test-retest coefficients, however, which range from .21 to .64, are not so impressive, and most such coefficients reported in the literature are lower than those reported for the MMPI and MMPI-2 (Schuerger, Tait & Tavernelli, 1982). Also a bit disappointing are the correlations between the various forms, which range from a low of .16 to a high of .79, with median coefficients in the .50s and .60s, depending on which forms are correlated. Moreover, despite the method used for deriving the factors, the 16 source traits of the 16PF do intercorrelate, with some correlations as high as .75 (Cattell, Eber & Tatsuoka, 1970). To deal with this overlap, the 16 factors themselves were factor analyzed, which resulted in four second-order factors. Scores can be obtained for these second-order factors. Analysis of the psychometric properties of the 16PF thus reflects the effort Cattell and his colleagues have made in attempting to provide a psychometrically sound instrument.

Other important features of the test are its provision of a parallel inventory for ages 12 to 18, the Jr. Sr. High School Personality Questionnaire, and still another parallel extension for use with children aged 8 to 12, the Children's Personality Questionnaire. Cross-cultural studies have been conducted in Western Europe, Eastern Europe, the Middle East, Australia, and Canada (Gynther & Gynther, 1976). Furthermore, various research investigations have supported the validity of Cattell's personality test (Cattell, Eber & Tatsuoka, 1970). To extend the test to the assessment of clinical populations, items related to psychological disorders have been factor analyzed (Cattell & Bolton, 1969; Delhees & Cattell, 1971a), resulting in 12 new factors in addition to the 16 needed to measure normal personalities. These new factors were then used to construct a clinical instrument, the Clinical Analysis Questionnaire (CAQ) (Delhees & Cattell, 1971b).

Despite the care that has gone into the 16PF, its research base and use pale when compared with those of the MMPI. The fact is, neither clinicians nor researchers have found the 16PF to be as useful as the MMPI. Moreover, the claims of the 16PF to have identified the basic source traits of the personality are simply not true. Factor analysis is one of many ways of constructing tests. Factor analysis will identify only those traits about which questions are asked and it has no more claim to uniqueness than any other method. However, the 16PF remains an exemplary illustration of the factor analytic approach to structured personality testing.

C. *Problems with the Factor Analytic Strategy*

One major criticism of factor analytic approaches is the subjective nature of naming factors. To understand this problem, it is necessary to understand that each score on any given set of tests or variables can be broken down into three components: common variance, unique variance, and error variance. *Common variance* is the amount of variance a particular variable holds in common with other variables. It results from the overlap between what two or more variables are measuring. *Unique variance* is highly specific and refers to factors uniquely measured by the variable. In other words, unique variance refers to some construct measured only by the variable in question. *Error variance* is variance attributable to error. Factor analytic procedures generally identify sources of common variance at the expense of unique variance. Thus, important factors may be overlooked when the data are categorized solely on the basis of blind groupings by computers. Furthermore, all the computer can do is identify the groupings. The factor analyst must determine what factors these groupings measure, and there are no definite criteria or rules for naming factors. If five items such as daring, outgoing, determined, excitable, and fearless load high on a factor, what should this factor be called? In factor analysis, your name for this factor has about as much validity as anybody else's.

VI. *The Theoretical Strategy*

To avoid the potential disagreement and biases that stem from factor analytic approaches, structured personality tests guided in their construction by theory have been proposed. In this approach, items are selected to measure the variables or constructs specified by a major theory of personality. After the items have been selected and grouped into scales, a construct validity approach is taken. Presumably, predictions are made concerning the nature of the scale, and if the predictions hold up, the scale is supported.

A. *Edwards Personal Preference Schedule*

One of the most well-known examples of a structured personality test developed using the theoretical strategy is the Edwards Personal Preference Schedule (EPPS) (Edwards, 1954, 1959). (Again, we use the term *test* in the general sense. According to Edwards, the EPPS is not a test in the strict sense of the word because there are no right or wrong answers.) At one time, the EPPS was used widely in counseling centers (Lubin, Wallis & Paine, 1971), and it has been widely researched (Gynther & Gynther, 1976, p. 247). Today, the test is not used extensively. However, in addition to illustrating the theoretical strategy, the EPPS illustrates some interesting concepts in personality test construction, such as the concept of ipsative scores, which we will discuss later.

The theoretical basis for the EPPS is the need system proposed by H. A. Murray (1938), which has probably been the most influential theory in personality test construction to date. Among the human needs proposed by Murray are the need to accomplish (achievement), the need to conform (deference), and the need for attention (exhibition). In developing the EPPS, Edwards selected 15 needs from Murray's list and constructed items with content validity for each of these needs (see Table 15-5).

Having selected items based on theory, Edwards was able to avoid the blind, subjective, and atheoretical approaches of other strategies. However, he was still faced with the perpetual problems of response styles and biases, problems the MMPI had dealt with by including special scales to detect faking or unusual test-taking approaches. Edwards was especially concerned with faking and social desirability, the tendency to say good things about yourself or to mark items that you believe will be approved by the examiner, irrespective of accuracy.

To deal with these sources of bias, Edwards attempted to rate each of his items on social desirability. He then formed pairs of items that were roughly comparable in social desirability and required subjects to select the one item in the pair that was more characteristic of their likes or feelings. Subjects cannot simply provide the socially desirable or expected response because both items in the pair are presumably equal on social desirability. There is also not much point in faking—that is, selecting the less characteristic item. In addition, there is no problem of balancing scored items, such as is presented by the true-false imbalance of the MMPI.

As a further check on the validity of EPPS results, Edwards included a consistency scale with 15 pairs of statements repeated in identical form. In other words, of the 210 pairs of statements, only 195 are different. The 15 pairs that occur twice are presented more or less randomly throughout the test. With this format, the number of times a subject makes the identical choice can be converted to a percentile based on normative data. The approach is analogous to the VRIN and TRIN scales of the MMPI-2. The EPPS also permits an analysis of within-subject consistency, which consists of the correlation of odd and even scores in the 15 scales.

Norms for the EPPS were based on more than 1500 college men and women and approximately 9000 adults from the general population selected from urban and rural areas in 48 states. Separate normative data are available for each of these two groups as well as for high school students. For a given raw score on each of the 15 scales, a percentile can be obtained immediately from the profile sheet.

To better understand the EPPS, you should bear in mind that in constructing it, Edwards listed items for each of the scales and then paired them with items from the other 14 scales. When subjects make a choice, they are selecting between one of two needs. In other words, in each choice, a subject is selecting one need at the expense of another. With this procedure, it becomes possible to express the selection of items on one scale relative to the selection of items on another in order to produce an **ipsative score.** Ipsative scores present results in relative terms rather than as absolute totals. The implication is that two individuals with identical relative, or ipsative, scores may differ markedly in the absolute strength of a particular need. Ipsative scores compare the individual

Table 15-5

List and
Description of
Murray's
Psychogenic
Needs

Need	Description
Abasement	To submit passively to external force. To accept injury, blame, criticism, punishment. To surrender. To become resigned to fate. To admit inferiority, error, wrong-doing, or defeat. To confess and atone. To blame, belittle, or mutilate the self. To seek and enjoy pain, punishment, illness, and misfortune.
Achievement	To accomplish something difficult. To master, manipulate, or organize physical objects, human beings, or ideas. To do this as rapidly and as independently as possible. To overcome obstacles and attain a high standard. To excel one's self. To rival and surpass others. To increase self-regard by the successful exercise of talent.
Affiliation	To form friendships and associations. To greet, join, and live with others. To cooperate and converse sociably with others. To love. To join groups.
Aggression	To overcome opposition forcefully. To fight. To revenge an injury. To attack, injure, or kill another. To oppose forcefully or punish another.
Autonomy	To get free, shake off restraint, break out of confinement. To resist coercion and restriction. To avoid or quit activities prescribed by domineering authorities. To be independent and free to act according to impulse. To be unattached, unconditioned, irresponsible. To defy convention.
Blamavoidance	To avoid blame, ostracism, or punishment by inhibiting asocial or unconventional impulses. To be well-behaved and obey the law.
Counteraction	Proudly to refuse admission of defeat by restriving and retaliating. To select the hardest tasks. To defend one's honor in action.
Defendance	To defend oneself against blame or belittlement. To justify one's actions. To offer extenuations, explanations, and excuses. To resist "probing."
Deference	To admire and support a superior other. To praise, honor, or eulogize. To yield eagerly to the influence of an allied other. To emulate an exemplar. To conform to custom.
Dominance	To influence or control others. To persuade, prohibit, dictate. To lead and direct. To restrain. To organize the behavior of a group.
Exhibition	To make an impression. To be seen and heard. To excite, amaze, fascinate, entertain, shock, intrigue, amuse, or entice others.
Harmavoidance	To avoid pain, physical injury, illness, and death. To escape from a dangerous situation. To take precautionary measures.
Infavoidance	To avoid humiliation. To quit embarrassing situations or to avoid conditions that may lead to belittlement; the scorn, derision, or indifference of others. To refrain from action because of the fear of failure.
Nurturance	To nourish, aid, or protect a helpless other. To express sympathy. To "mother" a child.
Order	To put things in order. To achieve cleanliness, arrangement, organization, balance, neatness, tidiness, and precision.
Play	To relax, amuse oneself, seek diversion and entertainment. To "have fun," to play games. To laugh, joke, and be merry. To avoid serious tension.
Rejection	To snub, ignore, or exclude another. To remain aloof and indifferent. To be discriminating.
Sentience	To seek and enjoy sensuous impressions.
Sex	To form and further an erotic relationship. To have sexual intercourse.
Succorance	To seek aid, protection, or sympathy. To cry for help. To plead for mercy. To adhere to an affectionate, nurturant parent. To be dependent.
Understanding	To analyze experience, to abstract, to discriminate among concepts, to define relations, to synthesize ideas.

From *Explorations in Personality*, edited by Henry A. Murray. Copyright © 1938 by Oxford University Press, Inc.; renewed 1966 by Henry A. Murray. Reprinted by permission of the publisher.

against himself or herself and produce data that reflect the relative strength of each need for that person; each person thus provides his or her own frame of reference (see Mullins, Weeks & Wilbourn, 1978).

Although only short-term (one-week) test-retest reliability figures are presented in the manual, the coefficients, which range from .74 to .88, are quite respectable for personality test data. Split-half reliabilities, which range from .60 to .87 as reported in the manual, though not so impressive, are generally satisfactory. Furthermore, intercorrelations among the scales are lower than for either the MMPI or 16PF, ranging between −.34 and .46.

The EPPS has a number of interesting features. Its forced-choice method, which requires subjects to select one of two items rather than to respond "true" or "false" ("yes" or "no") to a single item, is an interesting solution to the problem of faking and other sources of bias. Because each subject provides his or her own frame of reference, the relative strength of needs as well as the internal consistency for each individual subject can be determined. Item content follows established theoretical lines. The 15 identical pairs aid in the evaluation of the validity of the profile. Norms are based on large samples and are available for adults from the general population as well as for high school and college students. Ipsative scores based on these norms can be converted to percentiles. Reliability data generally are adequate for the short term, and the 15 scales of the EPPS have lower intercorrelations than do the scales of the major tests developed by using factor analytic and criterion-group strategies. Last, but not least, the test is among the most researched of the personality inventories and is used widely in applied settings.

Despite its impressive features and extensive use and the widespread interest it has engendered, the EPPS has not been well received by reviewers. J. A. Radcliffe (1965), L. J. Stricker (1965), and A. B. Heilbrun (1972) have all been critical. Part of the problem is that studies have shown that, like other structured personality tests, the EPPS can be faked in spite of its forced-choice procedure (Dicken, 1959). Other data raise questions concerning the test's ability to adequately control social-desirability effects (Feldman & Corah, 1960; Wiggins, 1966). The appropriateness of converting ipsative scores, which are relative, to normative percentiles is also questionable. Gynther and Gynther (1976) believe the major problem with the EPPS is the rather meager data in support of its validity. Although a number of studies have attempted to discriminate among a variety of groups (for example, smokers versus nonsmokers) with the EPPS, the EPPS has a "paucity" of nontest correlates (Gynther & Gynther, 1976), and little is being done to correct the problem.

Since the first attempts at test construction, the trend has been gradual improvement following criticism and the identification of problems. The EPPS seems to have originated in this spirit, and it is unfortunate that efforts are not being made to improve it. Many more validity studies are needed (Stricker, 1965), and new norms are long overdue (Cooper, 1990).

B. *Personality Research Form and Jackson Personality Inventory*

Other attempts to use the theoretical strategy in constructing a structured personality test are the Personality Research Form (PRF) (Jackson, 1967) and the Jackson Personality Inventory (JPI) (Jackson, 1976a, b.) Like the EPPS, the PRF and JPI were based on H. A. Murray's (1938) theory of needs. However, unlike Edwards, the constructors of these tests developed specific

Jackson Personality Inventory

PROFILE SHEET: MALE

Name _____ Age _____ Form Administered _____

Date Tested _____ Other Information _____

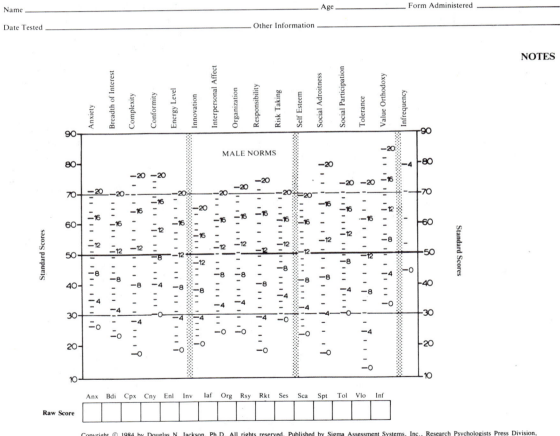

Copyright © 1984 by Douglas N. Jackson, Ph.D. All rights reserved. Published by Sigma Assessment Systems, Inc., Research Psychologists Press Division, P.O. Box 610984, Port Huron, MI 48061-0984. Published simultaneously in Canada.

Figure 15-4
Jackson Personality Inventory profile sheets. (*Reprinted with permission of Sigma Assessment Systems, Inc., P.O. Box 610984, Port Huron, MI 48061-0984, copyright 1976.*)

definitions of each need. In this way, items for each scale could be as independent as possible, an important consideration in creating homogeneous scales. To further increase the homogeneity of scales, more than 100 items were tentatively written for each scale and were administered to over 1000 college students. Biserial correlational analysis then located the items that correlated highest with the proposed scale while showing relatively low correlations with other scales, particularly social desirability. In other words, strict definitional standards and statistical procedures were used in conjunction with the theoreti-

Jackson Personality Inventory

PROFILE SHEET: FEMALE

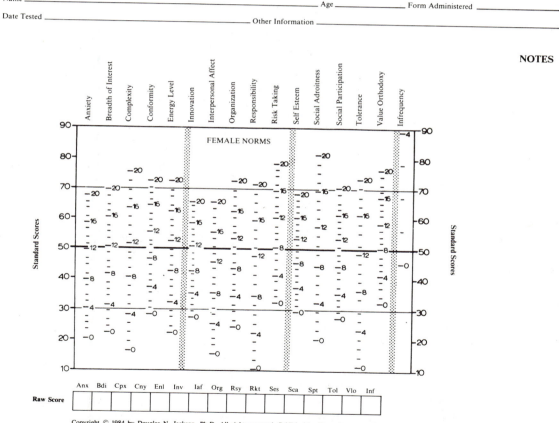

Copyright © 1984 by Douglas N. Jackson, Ph.D. All rights reserved. Published by Sigma Assessment Systems, Inc., Research Psychologists Press Division, P.O. Box 610984, Port Huron, MI 48061-0984. Published simultaneously in Canada.

Table 15-6
Trait Descriptions
for the Jackson
Personality
Inventory

Scale	Trait
Anxiety	Tendency to worry over minor matters
Breadth of interest	Curiosity; inquisitiveness
Complexity	Preference for abstract versus concrete thought
Conformity	Compliance; cooperativeness
Energy level	Energy; enthusiasm
Innovation	Originality; imagination
Interpersonal affect	Ability to identify with others
Organization	Planfulness; systematic versus disorganized
Responsibility	Responsibility; dependability
Risk taking	Reckless and bold versus cautious and hesitant
Self-esteem	Self-assured versus self-conscious
Social adroitness	Skill in persuading others
Social participation	Sociable and gregarious versus withdrawn loner
Tolerance	Broad-minded and open versus intolerant and uncompromising
Value orthodoxy	Moralistic and conventional versus modern and liberal
Infrequency	Validity of profile

cal approach. This use of a combination of procedures is the latest trend in personality test construction.

To aid in the assessment of validity, a scale analogous to the F scale of the MMPI was constructed. Like the MMPI F scale, the PRF and JPI infrequency scales consist of items with low endorsement rates for a standard sample. Thus, high rates of endorsement on this scale throw doubt on the validity of the results. A social desirability scale similar to the K scale of the MMPI is also included in the PFR. Two sets of parallel forms (four forms in all) as well as a form based on the best items from other forms were developed for the PFR. The JPI has one form consisting of 320 true/false items and 16 scales for use with high school students through college students and adults. The PFR, as its name implies, is primarily for research purposes. The JPI is for use on normal individuals to assess various aspects of personality including interpersonal, cognitive, and value orientations. See Figure 15-4 for profile sheets for the Jackson Personality Inventory.

Items for the PFR and JPI are balanced in true-false keying. Unlike the scales of the MMPI, the PRF and JPI scales have no item overlap. Furthermore, the scales are relatively independent, with most intercorrelation coefficients at $\pm .30$ (Gynther & Gynther, 1976). See Table 15-6.

The internal consistency coefficients reported in the test manuals are extremely good, with a range of .80 to .94. Factor analytic studies have supported the validity of the tests (Jackson, 1970). Furthermore, many studies have supported the construct validity of the tests (Mungas, Trontel & Weingardner, 1981; Murray-Jobsis, 1991; Trott & Morf, 1972) as well as their predictive validity (Kusyszyn, 1968).

Clearly, the PRF and JPI possess sound psychometric properties, which perhaps accounts for the preponderance of favorable reviews (Anastasi, 1972a; Kelly, 1972; Wiggins, 1973). In any case, by combining theory with rigorous statistical procedures, these tests appear to have established a new trend in the construction of structured personality tests. As with other structured personality tests, however, the PRF has yet to challenge the MMPI and MMPI-2 in terms of use (both clinical and research) and status.

C. *Temperament: The Myers-Briggs Type Indicator*

The Myers-Briggs Type Indicator developed by Isabel Myers and Katherine C. Briggs is a theoretically constructed test based on Carl Jung's theory of psychology types (Myers, 1976, 1977; Myers & Briggs, 1943/1962). Jung had theorized that there are four main ways in which we experience or come to know the world: *sensing*, knowing through our sensory systems of sight, hearing, touch, and so on; *intuition*, guessing about what underlies sensory inputs; *feeling*, focusing on the emotional aspect of experience; and *thinking*, abstract thought or reasoning. Jung argued that we must strive for balance in the four modes, but each person, he believed, tended to emphasize one over the other. In addition, Jung believed that all individuals could be distinguished in terms of the dimension introversion versus extroversion. The purpose of the Myers-Briggs test is to determine where people fall on the introversion-extroversion dimension and on which of the four modes they rely.

In line with Jung's theory, the underlying assumption of the Myers-Briggs Type Indicator is that people have specific preferences in the way they construe their experiences. These preferences, moreover, are believed to underlie our interests, needs, values, and motivation.

The most recent norms for the Myers-Briggs test are based on more than 2000 males and females in grades 4 through 12 spanning three public and four private schools (Myers, 1976). Reliability for the test is adequate, with split-half figures ranging in the .70s and .80s. The Myers-Briggs test appears to hold special promise in predicting vocational preference when used in conjunction with interest and ability tests (Lowman, 1991).

D. *Self-Concept*

A number of personality tests have evolved from a theoretical strategy to evaluate self-concept—the set of assumptions a person has about himself or herself. Theoretically, what you believe to be true about yourself will have a strong impact on your behavior. If you believe you are honest, then you will tend to act in conformity with this belief. If you believe you are effective with others, you are more likely to assume a leadership role than if you believe you are ineffective. The extent to which you use your leadership skills or other abilities is influenced by your self-concept.

Many tests have been developed to evaluate self-concept. The Tennessee Self-Concept Scale is a formal paper-and-pencil test designed to measure self-concept data. Several adjective checklists are also available in which a list of adjectives is presented and subjects are asked to indicate which apply to them.

Gough's Adjective Checklist, for instance, contains 350 adjectives in alphabetical order (Gough, 1960; Gough & Heilbrun, 1980). The Piers-Harris Children's Self-Concept Scale contains 80 self-statements (e.g., "I like my looks") and requires a "yes" or "no" response to evaluate self-concept in children.

A novel approach to the assessment of self-concept is based on Carl Rogers's theory of the self. According to Rogers, the self is organized to remain consistent. When new experiences are consistent with a person's self-concept, they are easily integrated. Experiences inconsistent with the self-concept tend to be denied or distorted. For example, if you view yourself as honest and moral and find yourself looking at another student's exam during the pressure of a difficult test, you might try to distort the experience by thinking your classmate purposefully flashed her paper in front of your eyes.

To evaluate self-concept, Rogers uses a Q-Sort technique, in which a person is given a set of cards with self-concept-related self-statements such as "I am a good person." The individual then sorts the cards in piles from least to most personally descriptive. The person is asked to make two sorts of the cards. The first describes who the person really is (real self). The second describes what the person believes he or she should be (ideal self). As Rogers's theory predicts, large discrepancies between the real and ideal selves reflect poor adjustment and low self-esteem (Rogers, 1961b).

VII. *Combination Strategies*

The clear-cut modern trend is to use a mix of strategies. Indeed, almost all of the tests we have examined use factor analytic methods regardless of their strategy of scale development. In this final section, we briefly discuss two newer tests that rely on a combination of strategies in scale development: the Millon Clinical Multiaxial Inventory and the NEO Personality Inventory.

A. *The Millon Clinical Multiaxial Inventory*

The Millon Clinical Multiaxial Inventory (MCMI) is a structured inventory designed to evaluate personality disorders. There are two versions, both of which continue to be the subject of research and debate (Streiner & Miller, 1989; Wetzler, 1990). The manual for the MCMI was published in 1983 (Millon, 1983). Following some controversy concerning whether the MCMI provided a good measure of personality disorders as defined by the American Psychiatric Association's (1980) *Diagnostic and Statistical Manual of Mental Disorders,* third edition (DSM-III), T. Millon (1985) wrote that the MCMI was never intended to be such a measure. A few years later, the MCMI-II was published (Millon, 1987). The MCMI-II added two new scales to the original 20 and attempted to accommodate itself to the personality disorders of the revised version of the DSM-III, the DSM-III-R. In the MCMI-II, Millon also replaced 45 of the original items and introduced a weighting scheme, whereby certain items were given greater weight based on earlier validity studies.

The purpose of the MCMI-II is to help the clinician make a diagnosis on Axis II of the DSM-III-R. These disorders are pervasive and stable patterns of behaving that are deeply ingrained and influence the individual's thinking, feeling, and acting in a wide range of situations. Controversy continues concerning how much better the MCMI-II is than the original MCMI. However, the test is in widespread use and follows Millon's highly influential theory of personality disorders.

According to Millon's theory (1969), personality disorders are rooted in how an individual deals with dependency needs. Detached individuals give up on having their dependency needs met and so avoid or are indifferent to others. Dependent individuals either passively submit to others or try to actively obtain reassurance and support by dramatic displays. Ambivalents cannot decide whether they want to rely on themselves or others, and their moods and behaviors often fluctuate. Independents trust no one and rely on themselves to satisfy dependency needs.

The MCMI-II, like the MCMI, is comparable to other personality tests in terms of reliability. It is also supported by a wide variety of validity studies. Its primary use is for clinical populations; it is not intended for normal subjects.

Development of the items and scales followed Millon's personality theory (see Millon, 1969). However, the final item pool and scale composition were refined through a variety of internal consistency methods and external criterion checks. In using a variety of approaches, the MCMI-II represents the latest trend in personality test construction.

B. *The NEO Personality Inventory*

One of the newest major personality inventories is the NEO Personality Inventory (Costa & McCrae, 1985), which used both factor analysis and theory in item development and scale construction. The NEO is quite ambitious and attempts to provide a multipurpose inventory for predicting interests, health and illness behavior, psychological well-being, and characteristic coping styles.

Based on their review of extensive factor analytic studies and personality theory, the authors of the NEO identified three broad domains: neuroticism (N), extraversion (E), and openness (O). Within each domain are six specific facets. Neuroticism (N) is defined primarily by anxiety and depression. In fact,

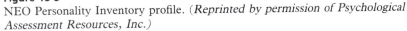

PSYCHOLOGICAL ASSESSMENT RESOURCES, INC.   P.O. Box 98 / Odessa, Florida 33556

PAR   Copyright · 1985 by Paul T. Costa, Jr. and Robert R. McCrae. All rights reserved. Not to be reproduced in whole or in part by any process without written permission of Psychological Assessment Resources, Inc.

Printed in U.S.A.

1 2 3 4 5 6 7 8 9

Figure 15-5
NEO Personality Inventory profile. (*Reprinted by permission of Psychological Assessment Resources, Inc.*)

the six facets of this domain are anxiety, hostility, depression, self-consciousness, impulsiveness, and vulnerability (to describe people who don't feel safe). Extraversion (E) refers to the degree of sociability or withdrawal a person tends to exhibit. The six facets of extraversion are warmth, gregariousness, assertiveness, activity, excitement-seeking, and positive emotions. Finally, openness refers to the breadth of experience to which a person is amenable. Its six dimensions are fantasy, aesthetics, feelings (openness to feelings of self and others), actions (willingness to try new activities), ideas (intellectual curiosity), and values. Figure 15-5 is a profile from the NEO Personality Inventory.

Guided by personality theory and factor analytic findings, the authors of the NEO took a rational approach in constructing items. For each of the 18 facets, 14 items were written. Seven were positively worded and seven were negatively worded to create a balance. Subjects respond on a five-point Likert scale format from "strongly disagree" to "strongly agree." Initial items were then refined using a variety of statistical procedures.

Data presented in the manual support the NEO Personality Inventory. Factor analytic studies support the grouping of three major areas and associated facets. Reliabilities for the three domains are in the high .80s to low .90s for both internal consistency and test-retest reliability. Reliabilities of the individual facets are lower, as is true of all major personality tests. Preliminary predictive and concurrent validity studies have been encouraging, with coefficients ranging into the .80s.

The NEO Personality Inventory reflects modern trends in personality test construction in relying on theory, logic, and liberal use of factor analysis and statistical approaches in test construction. It appears to be exceptionally promising for a wide range of characteristics. The research that will no doubt soon follow should further enlighten us as to its strengths and limitation.

Summary   Structured personality tests are self-report procedures that provide statements to which the subject must either respond "true" or "false" ("yes" or "no") or choose the most characteristic of two or more alternatives. These tests are highly structured and provide a definite, unambiguous stimulus for the subject. Scoring is straightforward and usually involves summing the number of items marked in a scored direction.

The original pressure to develop personality tests came from the demands created by World War I for a screening instrument to identify emotionally unstable recruits who might break down under the pressures of combat. The initial structured personality instrument, the Woodworth Personal Data Sheet, was based on a logical-content strategy in which items were interpreted in terms of face validity.

Not long after their appearance, tests based on the logical-content strategy fell into disrepute. The problem with these tests was the numerous assumptions underlying them. Included in these assumptions were that the subject complies with the instructions and provides an honest response; that the subject understands the items and is an accurate observer capable of evaluating his or her own behavior and responding in a nondefensive manner; and that the subject, test constructor, and test interpreter all define the questions in the same way. A review by A. Ellis (1946) seriously questioned all these assumptions.

The first major advance in structured personality assessment came with the MMPI, which used a strategy involving criterion groups. In this criterion-group strategy, groups who had known characteristics were contrasted with a control population. Items that distinguished the criterion group were included in a scale that was then cross-validated on an independent sample of criterion and control subjects. The MMPI revitalized structured personality tests. It made no assumptions about the meaning of a subject's response to a test item but rather attempted to empirically discern its meaning. In the criterion-group strategy, the content of the item is irrelevant. If a subject marks "true" to the statement "I hear loud voices when I'm alone," it is not assumed that he or she really does hear loud voices when alone.

In addition to its advantages over logical-content tests in avoiding assumptions, the MMPI had the feature of validity scales. The two most important MMPI validity scales are the K scale, which measures social desirability, and the F scale, which consists of 64 infrequently endorsed items to pick out subjects who take an unusual or unconventional approach to testing. Theoretically, excessively high scores on the validity scales can be used to identify biased results, thus avoiding the problems of faking and social desirability inherent in the logical-content approach.

Despite its extensive use, the widespread interest in it by researchers, and a recent restandardization (the MMPI-2), the MMPI does have problems, including item overlap among the scales, an imbalance in true-false keying, high intercorrelation among the scales, and lack of generalizability across demographic variables.

The factor analytic strategy of test construction has been used in an effort to overcome some of the problems inherent in the criterion strategy. Factor analytic strategies attempt to find areas of common variance in order to locate the minimum number of variables or factors that account for a set of intercorrelated data. R. B. Cattell has been the most important representative of this approach.

Using the factor analytic approach to find the common variance of all trait-descriptive terms in the dictionary, Cattell reduced an original pool of more than 4000 items to 16 and created the 16PF. Great care was taken to provide adequate norms. Nine separate normative samples based on demographic variables, plus an age-correction scale, are available. Also available are three sets of parallel forms for individuals of varying levels of vocabulary proficiency.

The EPPS has found its primary use in counseling centers. It employs a forced-choice strategy that requires subjects to choose the more applicable of two statements. *Ipsative scores*, which use the subject as his or her own frame of reference, express results in terms of the relative strength of a need.

A number of tests have been developed with the theoretical strategy. Among these are the Myers-Briggs Type Indicator, which measures temperament, and the Q-Sort technique, which measures self-concept.

The modern trend is to use a combination of strategies in scale construction. This approach is used in the Millon Clinical Multiaxial Inventory and the NEO Personality Inventory.

Chapter 16

Projective Personality Tests

Learning Objectives

When you have completed this chapter, you should be able to:

- Define the projective hypothesis.

- Identify five individuals who played a dominant role in the development of the Rorschach.

- Describe the Rorschach stimuli.

- Briefly describe Rorschach administration and scoring.

- List the pros and cons of the Rorschach.

- Describe the Holtzman.

- Describe the TAT stimuli.

- Briefly describe TAT administration.

- Identify the factors that should be considered in evaluating the TAT.

- List some of the major similarities and differences between the Rorschach and the TAT.

A few years ago the wife of an army sergeant sued him for divorce after 14 years of marriage. The wife claimed that her husband was "mentally unstable and deranged." She accused him of beating her, often for no apparent reason. The sergeant went to a psychologist to "prove" his sanity. In addition to an interview, an ability test (the Wechsler Adult Intelligence Scale-Revised), and an objective personality test (the Minnesota Multiphasic Personality Inventory-2), the psychologist administered the Rorschach inkblot test. The Rorschach is one of the best known and most widely used of the projective personality tests. According to the psychologist's evaluation, the Rorschach indicated that the sergeant was free of unusual or bizarre thought processes. The psychologist concluded that, based on the Rorschach and other test results, the sergeant was mentally stable, contrary to his wife's claims.

The matter went to court; the psychologist was called to the witness stand. The cross-examination by the wife's attorney proceeded as follows:

Attorney: Based on the Rorschach and other tests, you concluded that this man is mentally stable.

Psychologist: I did.

Attorney: What is the Rorschach?

Psychologist: The Rorschach is a projective psychological test that contains ten cards with inkblots on them. Five of the inkblots are black and gray; two are black, gray, and red; and the remaining three are composed of a variety of pastel colors of various shades.

Attorney: How do you administer a Rorschach?

Psychologist: The subject—that is, the person taking the test—is shown each of the cards, one at a time. The subject is required to state what the inkblot might be.

Attorney: You mean to say that you can tell whether a person is sane or insane by the way he or she interprets ten black, gray, and variously colored inkblots?

Psychologist: That is correct.

Attorney: Your honor, this is ridiculous. For 14 years, a man beats his wife for no apparent reason, but the psychologist says he's normal because he passed an inkblot test!

You should keep in mind that this example is not representative of the uses of the Rorschach. The Rorschach, as we will see, plays an important role in clinical assessment. The example is meant to illustrate why feelings about the Rorschach run so high.

Projective tests, such as the Rorschach, are among the most controversial and misundertood psychological tests (Blatt, 1990; Meloy & Singer, 1991). The Rorschach has been vigorously attacked on a variety of scientific and statistical grounds (Eysenck, 1959; Jensen, 1965; Knutson, 1972). Yet, in B. Lubin, H. R. Wallis, and C. Paine's (1971) survey of psychological test usage in the United States, the Rorschach was reported to be used in 91% of the 251 clinical settings surveyed. And things have not changed much (Lubin, Larsen & Matarazzo, 1984). The Rorschach is used extensively in clinical settings, and it is widely taught in doctoral training programs for clinical psychologists (Meloy & Singer, 1991; Piotrowski, 1984; Piotrowski, Sherry & Keller, 1985; Ritzler & Alter, 1986). Why are there such widespread use and acceptance of projective tests like the Rorschach in spite of severe attacks from prominent researchers and psychometricians? To answer this question, we need to take a look at the rationale for and the nature of projective tests.

I. *The Projective Hypothesis*

The primary rationale underlying projective tests is the **projective hypothesis.** Numerous definitions have been advanced for the projective hypothesis, with credit for the most complete analysis commonly given to L. K. Frank (1939). Simply stated, the projective hypothesis proposes that when people attempt to understand an ambiguous or vague stimulus, their interpretation of that stimulus reflects their needs, feelings, experiences, prior conditioning, thought processes, and so forth. When a frightened little boy looks into a dark room and sees a huge shadow that he interprets as a monster, he is projecting his fear onto the shadow. The shadow itself is neutral; it is neither good nor bad, fearsome nor pretty. What the child really sees is a reflection of the inner workings of his mind.

The concept of projection is not new. J. E. Exner (1976) notes, for example, that Leonardo da Vinci used ambiguous figures to evaluate young art students. Leonardo presented potential students with an ambiguous figure and presumably evaluated their imaginations according to the quality of the artistic form the students created from it. The concept of projection is also reflected in Shakespeare's "Nothing is either good or bad, but thinking makes it so."

Although what the subject finally sees in a stimulus is assumed to be a reflection of personal qualities or characteristics, some responses may be more revealing than others. If, for example, you say that a round figure is a ball, you provide a relatively straightforward interpretation of the stimulus. The stimulus itself is low on ambiguity; it is round and shaped like a ball. In viewing this stimulus, a high percentage of people probably see, though not necessarily report, a ball. Even this simple response, however, can reveal a lot about you. Your response indicates that you are accurate in your perception of simple objects in the external environment and are willing to provide a conventional response. Suppose, however, you said that this same stimulus looked like a square peg in round hole. Assuming the stimulus is actually round and contains no lines or shapes resembling a square peg, your perception of the stimulus does not conform to its actual property (roundness). Thus, your perceptions in general may not be accurate. Your response may also indicate that you are unwilling to provide the obvious, conventional response. Or your response may indicate that you perhaps feel out of place, like a square peg in a round hole.

In understanding projective tests, you should realize from the start that absolute, definite conclusions should never be drawn from any single response to an ambiguous stimulus. The examiner may only hypothesize what a test response means. Even the same response to the same stimulus may have several possible meanings depending on the characteristics of the people who make the response. Many factors can influence your response to a stimulus on a projective test. Your response, for example, may reflect a recent experience or an early experience of which you are unaware (Lindzey, 1952). It may reflect something you have witnessed (a bloody murder) or something you imagine (flunking out of college) rather than something you have actually experienced (Lindzey, 1952). It may reflect your day-to-day problems, such as an argument with your boyfriend or girlfriend. With all these possible factors influencing a response, it is little wonder that the validity of projective tests is difficult to document. The interpretation of projective tests requires highly trained, experienced practitioners. Even a highly trained expert, however, can easily draw the wrong conclusions, and often even the most experienced experts disagree among themselves. As in the example at the beginning of the chapter, the experts claim that they can use projective tests to draw valid conclusions. Researchers, however, remain unconvinced.

II. *The Rorschach Inkblot Test*

As an example of a psychological test based on the projective hypothesis, the Rorschach has few peers. For many years, the Rorschach was without question the dominant personality test discussed in *The Mental Measurements Yearbooks* in both research citations and clinical use. Indeed, no general discussion of psychological tests is complete without reference to the Rorschach.

A. *Historical Antecedents*

Like most concepts, the notion of using inkblots to study human functioning did not simply appear out of thin air. More than 25 years before the birth of Herman Rorschach, the originator of the test that bears his name, J. Kerner (1857) noted that individuals frequently report idiosyncratic or unique personal meanings when viewing inkblot stimuli. The wide variety of possible responses to inkblots makes them valuable in studying individuals. Indeed, the idea of using inkblots to assess personality functioning was proposed by A. Binet (Binet & Henri, 1896) when Rorschach was only 10 years old. Several investigators then supported Binet's position concerning the potential value of inkblots for investigating human personality (Dearborn, 1897; Kirkpatrick, 1900), and their support led to the publication of the first set of standardized inkblots by G. M. Whipple (1910). Rorschach receives credit for finding an original and important use for inkblots: identifying psychological disorders. Rorschach's investigation of inkblots began in around 1911 and culminated in 1921 with the publication of his famous book *Psychodiagnostik*. A year later, he suddenly and unexpectedly died of a serious illness at the early age of 37.

Like many unconventional ideas, Rorschach's work was initially viewed with suspicion and even disdain. The sole psychiatric journal of Rorschach's homeland, Switzerland, did not even review *Psychodiagnostik* (Allison, Blatt & Zimet, 1968). In fact, there were only a few foreign reviews of the book, and these tended to be critical. When David Levy first brought Rorschach's test to the United States from Europe, he found a cold, unenthusiastic response. American psychologists judged the test to be scientifically unsound, and psychiatrists found little use for it. Nevertheless, the use of the test gradually increased, and eventually it became quite popular.

Five individuals have played dominant roles in the use and investigation of the Rorschach. One of these, Samuel J. Beck, was a student of Levy's. Beck was especially interested in studying certain patterns or, as he called them, "configurational tendencies" in Rorschach responses (Beck, 1933). Beck, who died in June 1980, eventually wrote several books on the Rorschach and influenced generations of Rorschach practitioners (Beck, 1944, 1945, 1952). A second dominant person was Marguerite Hertz. Hertz, like Beck, stimulated considerable research on the Rorschach during the years when the test first established its foothold in the United States (Hertz, 1937, 1938). Bruno Klopfer, who emigrated to the United States from Germany, published several key Rorschach books and articles and played an important role in the early development of the Rorschach (Klopfer & Davidson, 1944; Klopfer & Kelley, 1942). Zygmunt Piotrowski (1947, 1964) and David Rapaport (Rapaport, Gill & Schafer, 1945, 1946) came somewhat later than Beck, Hertz, and Klopfer. Like the three who preceded them, both Piotrowski's and Rapaport's influences continue to be felt to this day. As J. E. Exner (1976, p. 75) notes, the development of the Rorschach can be attributed primarily to the efforts of these five individuals. Like most scholars, however, the five often disagreed. Their disagreements are the source of many of the current problems with the Rorschach. Each expert developed a unique system of administration, scoring, and interpretation. They all found disciples willing to accept their biases and to use their systems.

B. *Stimuli, Administration, and Interpretation*

Rorschach constructed each stimulus card by dropping ink onto a piece of paper and folding it. The result was a unique, bilaterally symmetrical form on a white background. After apparently experimenting with thousands of such blots, Rorschach selected ten. Five were black and gray, two contained black, gray, and red, and three contained pastel colors of various shades. An example of a Rorschach card is shown in Figure 16-1.

The Rorschach is an individual test. In the administration procedure, each of the ten cards is presented to the subject with minimum structure. After some preliminary remarks concerning the purpose of testing, the examiner hands the first card to the subject and asks something like "What might this be?" No restriction is placed on the type of response permitted, and no clues are given concerning what is expected. If the subject asks for guidance or clarification, the examiner gives little information. If, for example, the subject asks, "Do I use the whole thing or just part of it?" the examiner replies, "As you like" or "Whatever you choose." Anxious subjects or individuals who are made uncomfortable by unstructured situations frequently ask questions, attempting to find out as much as possible before committing themselves. The examiner, however, may not give any cues that might reveal the nature of the response that is expected. Furthermore, in view of the finding that the examiner may inadvertently reveal information or reinforce certain types of responses through facial expressions and other forms of nonverbal communication (E. Lord, 1950), Exner (1974) advocates an administration procedure in which the examiner sits next to the subject rather than face to face.

Figure 16-1
A Rorschach-type image is created by dropping ink onto a piece of paper and folding it. This is a reproduction of an actual card from the Rorschach.

Notice that the examiner is nonspecific and, to a large degree, vague. This lack of clear structure or direction with regard to demands and expectations is a primary feature of all projective tests. The idea is to provide as much flexibility as possible so that the subject's response is a reflection of the subject. If the examiner inadvertently provides too many guidelines, then the response may simply reflect the subject's tendency to perform as expected or to provide a socially desirable response, as discussed in Chapter 15. Therefore, an improper administration that provides too much structure invalidates the results. Interpretations from such administrations are dubious.

Each card is administered twice. During the free-association phase of the test, the examiner presents the cards one at a time and asks, "What might this be?" If the subject gives only one response to the first card, the examiner may say, "Some people see more than one thing here." The examiner usually makes this remark only once. If the subject rejects the card—that is, states that he or she sees nothing—the examiner may reply, "Most people do see something here. Just take your time." The examiner records every word and even every sound made by the subject verbatim. In addition, the examiner records how long it takes a subject to respond to a card (reaction time) and the position of the card when the response is made (upside down, sideways).

The purpose of the second phase of the Rorschach administration, the inquiry, is to allow the examiner to score the subject's responses. Responses are scored according to at least five dimensions, including location (where the perception was seen), determinant (what determined the response), form quality (to what extent the response matched the stimulus properties of the ink-blot), content (what the perception was), and frequency of occurrence (to what extent the response was popular or original; popular responses occur once in every three protocols on the average). A complete discussion of these special

[handwritten margin note: Scored on: location determinant form quality content]

scoring categories is beyond the scope of this text. For more information on scoring and interpretation, you are referred to Exner's (1974) Rorschach textbook and to Exner and Weiner (1981).

In scoring for location, the examiner must determine where the subject's perception is located on the inkblot. To facilitate determining this location, a small picture of each card, known as the location chart, is provided. If necessary, on rare occasions, an examiner may give a subject a pencil and ask the subject to outline the perception on the location chart. In scoring for location, the examiner notes whether the subject used the whole blot (W), a common detail (D), or an unusual detail (Dd). Location may be scored for other factors as well, such as for the *confabulatory response* (DW). In the confabulatory response, the subject overgeneralizes from a part to the whole. We will discuss this response in detail later on.

A summary of a subject's location choices can be extremely valuable. The examiner may, for example, determine the number and percentage of W, D, and Dd responses. This type of information, in which scoring categories are summarized as a frequency or percentage, is known as the *quantitative*, structural, or statistical aspect of the Rorschach as opposed to the *qualitative* aspects, which pertain to the content and sequence of responses. Normal subjects typically produce a certain balance of W, D, and Dd responses. When a subject's pattern deviates from the typical balance, the examiner begins to suspect problems. However, no one has been able to demonstrate that a particular deviation is linked to a specific problem. A substantial deviation from what is typical or average may suggest a number of possibilities. It alerts the examiner to the possibility that the protocol may be invalid. Or the subject may be original or unconventional and thus fail to respond according to the typical pattern. Or the subject may have a perceptual problem such as occurs with certain types of brain damage or severe emotional problems. It is interesting that the relative proportion of W, D, and Dd location choices varies with maturational development. L. B. Ames, R. W. Metraux, and R. N. Walker (1971), for example, note that W responses occur most frequently in the 3- to 4-year-old group. As the child grows older, the frequency of W responses gradually decreases until young adulthood. Thus, adult protocols with a preponderance of W responses may suggest immaturity or low mental age.

Like other quantitative aspects of the Rorschach, location patterns and frequencies have been studied in a large number of experimental investigations. These investigations provide information concerning the meaning of various response patterns and thus contribute to the construct validity of the Rorschach. Unfortunately, many of the results of the studies conflict with the opinions of experts. Furthermore, many studies that support the validity of the Rorschach have not been successfully replicated. The ability to form W responses, for example, has been linked to intelligence. Presumably, the W response requires an ability to organize the entire inkblot into a single, meaningful percept, and this organization process requires intelligence. However, because W responses are related to intelligence only for specific cards, there is a low correlation (about .40) between the number of W responses and IQ

(Abrams, 1955; Holzberg & Belmont, 1952; Lotsoff, 1953; McCandless, 1949; Wishner, 1948).

Having ascertained the location of a response, the examiner must determine what it was about the inkblot that led the subject to see that particular percept. This factor is known as the *determinant*. One or more of at least four properties of an inkblot may determine or lead to a response: its form or shape, its perceived movement, its color, and its shading. If the subject uses only the form of the blot to determine a response, then the response is scored F and is called a pure form response. Responses are scored for form when the subject justifies or elaborates a response by statements such as "It looks like one," "It is shaped like one," "Here are the head, legs, feet, ears, and wings." In all these examples, the response is determined exclusively on the basis of shape. In addition to form, a perception may be based on movement, color, shading, or some combination of these factors. These other determinants can be further subdivided. Movement may be human (M), such as two people hugging; animal (FM), such as two elephants playing; or inanimate (m), such as sparks flying.

As with location, the presence (or absence) of each determinant as well as the relative proportion of the various determinants can be related to a number of hypotheses and empirical findings (Exner, 1986; Georgoff, 1991). Consider

FOCUSED EXAMPLE 16-1

Expert Interpretation of the Rorschach

Rorschach experts resolutely maintain that, if properly used, the Rorschach can be an invaluable tool. Scientists remain unconvinced. In our judgment, the key issue revolves around test use. As we have stated, Rorschach interpretations should be viewed only as tentative hypotheses. Those hypotheses that can be confirmed by other sources of data can be seen as having more validity than those that cannot be confirmed. When the Rorschach is rigidly or blindly interpreted, the scientists' disdain becomes justified. When the Rorschach is interpreted cautiously and in conjunction with other sources of data, however, a highly trained expert may astound even the most critical scientist.

One of us had a predoctoral internship at a Veterans Administration Hospital in which Marguerite Hertz, one of the five original Rorschach experts, was a consultant. Every second Thursday

of the month, Hertz would interpret an actual Rorschach protocol presented by one of the interns or staff members. Her interpretations were so detailed and exact that we, as scientists inexperienced with the Rorschach, doubted the validity of her interpretations. When other interns or the staff psychologists agreed with everything Hertz said, we became even more skeptical. We thought they were just awed by Hertz's reputation and were afraid to challenge this spirited woman.

When our turn came to present a Rorschach, we used the protocol of a patient we had been seeing in psychotherapy for several months. We knew this patient very well. We fully expected Hertz to make errors in her interpretation. We were determined to point these out to the group, thus exposing the group's error in accepting Hertz's previous interpretations. We were the movement response. Most Rorschach experts agree that whether and how a subject uses movement can be most revealing. The meaning of movement, however, is unclear because of disagreements among experts and contradictory or unclear experimental findings. Many experts believe the movement response is related to motor activity and impulses. Numerous movement responses, for example, may suggest high motor activity or strong impulses. The ratio of M (human movement) to FM (animal movement) responses has been linked by some experts to a person's control and expression of internal impulses. In addition, like many other quantitative aspects of the Rorschach, the movement category varies with development. Ames, Metraux, and Walker (1971), for example, found more FM than M responses from children than from adults. Thus, a high proportion of FM responses in an adult may indicate immaturity or a primitive capacity to deal with impulses. As you think about these inferences, however, you should keep in mind that they are no more than hypotheses. An examiner who blindly accepts one interpretation of a particular quantitative aspect can be making a big mistake. Certainly one who blindly accepts a particular interpretation of a Rorschach pattern is ignoring the available literature. Focused Example 16-1 illustrates the value of using highly trained experts to interpret Rorschach patterns.

Making sure the determinant can be identified is the most difficult aspect

shocked, however, when Hertz was able to describe this patient after reading only the first four or five responses and examining the quantitative summary of the various scoring categories and ratios. Within 25 minutes, Hertz not only told us what we already knew but also began to tell us things we hadn't seen that were obviously true once pointed out. This experience was most unsettling. Having started with a strong bias against the Rorschach, we could not dismiss what Hertz had done without concluding that there must be some value in it.

Later, we found that Hertz's secret was her experience. She had given or studied so many Rorschachs that she had an intuitive feeling for the meaning of a particular pattern. After having seen the Rorschach patterns of dozens, if not hundreds, of disturbed individuals, she could easily identify a

problem. Indeed, her knowledge and experience were so broad that she could even distinguish among specific types of disturbances based on the Rorschach.

We still feel the scientific status of the Rorschach leaves much to be desired. However, our experiences with the Rorschach, which include direct observation of interpretations from prominent experts, have led us to reconsider its value. If experts can make accurate interpretations, then it may be premature to reject the Rorschach without more experimental investigations. However, until the experts can specify the exact processes underlying correct interpretations from the Rorschach, the criticism from scientists will continue, as Hertz herself (1986), who has repeatedly called for innovation and rigorous research, acknowledges.

of Rorschach administration. Because of the difficulties of conducting an adequate inquiry and the present lack of standardized administration procedures, there are wide variations among examiners in the conduct of the inquiry. It has been known for years that examiner differences influence the subject's response (Gibby, Miller & Walker, 1953). As a result of this problem, much of the Rorschach literature is confounded by differences in administration and scoring alone. This is one of the reasons why good experimental investigations of the Rorschach are rare (Lewandowski & Saccuzzo, 1976).

Scoring content, however, is a relatively simple matter. Most authorities list content categories such as human (H), animal (A), and nature (N). An inquiry is generally not necessary to determine content.

Similarly, most experts generally agree on the so-called populars, those responses that are frequently given for each card. Furthermore, Exner's (1974) comprehensive system, which includes as populars only those responses that occur once in three protocols on the average, provides a standardized method for scoring populars.

Scoring form quality, the extent to which the percept matches the stimulus properties of the inkblot, is difficult. Some experts argue that if the examiner can also see the percept, then the response has adequate form quality. If the examiner cannot see it, then the response has poor form quality and is scored F−. Obviously, such a subjective system is grossly inadequate because scoring for form quality may then depend on the intelligence, imagination, skill, and even psychological state of the examiner. Exner's (1974) comprehensive system, which uses the usual frequency of the occurrence of various responses in evaluating form quality, is more objective and thus more scientifically acceptable than the method based on the examiner's ability to see the percept.

Table 16-1 summarizes our discussion of Rorschach scoring. The discussion has obviously been incomplete, but perhaps you now have an idea of how a projective test can be scored to yield quantitative data. These quantitative data, in turn, are important because they permit the accumulation of norms for particular groups. If subjects deviate from the typical or expected performance, then the examiner must determine the reason underlying the deviation. This process often leads to valuable information about the individual (Exner et al., 1982; Smith et al., 1991).

Rorschach scoring is obviously difficult and complex. The purpose of the preceding discussion is to familiarize you with some of the many possibilities. Use of the Rorschach requires advanced graduate training. You should not attempt to score or use a Rorschach without formal and didactic graduate instruction and supervised experience. Without this detailed training, you might make serious errors because the procedure is so complex.

In addition to the quantitative aspects, Rorschach protocols may be evaluated for nonquantitative, or qualitative, features, including the specific content as well as an analysis of the sequence of responses. One important aspect of a qualitative interpretation is an evaluation of content that is reported frequently by emotionally disturbed, retarded, or brain-damaged individuals but infre-

Table 16-1
Summary of
Rorschach
Scoring

I. Location
Definition: Where on the blot was the percept seen (located)?
*Types:** 1. Whole (W). The whole inkblot was used.
2. Common detail (D). A common or well-defined part of the inkblot was used.
3. Unusual detail (Dd). An unusual or poorly defined part of the inkblot was used.

II. Determinant
Definition: What feature of the inkblot determined the response?
*Types:** 1. Form (F). The shape or outline of the blot determined the response ("because the inkblot looked like one").
2. Movement (M, FM, m). Movement was seen ("two animals walking up a hill").
3. Color (C). Color played a role in determining the response ("a brown bear," "pink clouds").
4. Shading (T). Texture or shading features played a role in determining the response ("a furry bear because of the shading").

III. Form Quality
Definition: To what extent did the percept match the stimulus properties of the inkblot?
*Types:** 1. F+ or +. Percept matched stimulus properties of the inkblot in an exceptionally good way.
2. F. Percept matched stimulus properties of the inkblot.
3. F− or −. Percept matched the stimulus properties of the inkblot poorly.

IV. Content
Definition: What was the percept?
*Types:** 1. Human (H).
2. Animal (A).
3. Nature (N).

V. Popular-original
Definition: How frequently is the percept seen in normative samples? (Popular responses are seen in about one of every three protocols.)

---

* This list is incomplete and does not cover the entire range of possibilities. The information given is designed to illustrate quantitative scoring of a projective test.

quently by the normal population. Such responses can be used to discriminate normal from disordered conditions. Confabulatory (DW) responses illustrate the value of qualitative interpretations. In the DW response, the subject overgeneralizes from a part to a whole: "It looked like my mother because of the eyes. My mother has large piercing eyes just like these." Here the subject sees a detail—"Large piercing eyes"—and overgeneralizes so that the entire inkblot looks like his or her mother. Although one such response has no clear or specific meaning, when a subject makes a number of confabulatory responses, a disordered state becomes increasingly likely. These responses are infrequently given by the normal population yet are often given by brain-damaged, mentally retarded, or emotionally disturbed individuals. Naturally, the examiner must evaluate interviews, the case history, the presenting problem, and results from other tests before accepting the validity of a qualitative analysis of a Rorschach protocol. A problem arises when the examiner or a researcher tries to use a single Rorschach feature to predict or define a specific disordered state (see Focused Example 16-2).

◻ ◇　　　　F O C U S E D　E X A M P L E　1 6 - 2

The Danger of Basing Rorschach Interpretations on Insufficient Evidence

We had the opportunity to become involved in a forensic case in which an individual claimed that the negligence of a large company in sealing pipes together caused a gas leak that resulted in brain damage. This individual consulted an attorney, who sent him to a psychologist. The psychologist administered a Rorschach test. Based on her findings, the psychologist concluded that the person was brain damaged and thus had a legitimate case. The company called us and asked whether the Rorschach could be used to diagnose or identify

brain damage. We replied that certain Rorschach patterns may be consistent with brain damage but that you can't prove a person is brain damaged simply on the basis of Rorschach results.

Lawyers for the company brought in the psychologist's report and a copy of the Rorschach protocol. The person suspected of brain damage provided only six responses, far fewer than the 22 to 32 responses typically found for the ten Rorschach cards. The protocol was as follows:

	Free Association	Inquiry	Scoring
Card 1	A bat	Here are the wings; there is the head	W F A P

Discussion

The W indicates the whole inkblot was used in the percept. The F indicates that only the form or shape (not color, movement, or shading) deter-

mined the response. The A stands for animal content. The P indicates this response is a popular (that is, one that is commonly given).

Card 2	I don't know.	No, I still don't.	Rejection

Discussion

When the subject fails to provide a response, this is known as a rejection. Some examiners present the card again in the inquiry and ask, "Now do you see

anything?" A rejection could indicate a number of things. The typical or classical interpretation of a rejection is guardedness or defensiveness.

Card 3	I don't know. (Q) No, I don't see anything.	I said I don't know.	Rejection

Discussion

The (Q) indicates the examiner questioned the subject further, thus attempting to elicit a re-

sponse. Notice the defensive quality in the subject's response during the inquiry.

Card 4	A gorilla	All of it; big feet, head, body	W F A
Card 5	A moth	Whole thing; wings, feelers, head	W F A P
Card 6	I don't know.	No, nothing	Rejection
Card 7	A bird without a head	Wings, but no head (Q) All of it	W F–A

Discussion

The F– indicates a poor correspondence between the response, bird, and the stimulus properties of

the inkblot. Bird is an unusual response to this inkblot.

	Free Association	*Inquiry*	*Scoring*
Card 8	Animals, maybe rats try-ing to steal something	Just two animals on the sides	D F A P

Discussion

The two animals were formed from two common details (D). It was scored P since this response is a popular (that is, frequently occurring).

Card 9	I don't know.	No, it doesn't look like anything to me.	Rejection
Card 10	Nothing, wait, looks like a bug here	Just a bug, legs, pinchers, head	D F Insect

The psychologist who conducted this Rorschach administration stretched the interpretation, in our judgment, when she claimed this person was brain damaged. The argument presented was that a small number of responses, a preponderance of W responses, a lack of determinants other than form, and misperception (the poor form quality response to card 7) were all consistent with brain damage. Because the protocol contained qualities commonly found in the protocols of brain-damaged individuals, the psychologist argued that she had found evidence for brain damage.

We looked at this Rorschach protocol and concluded that its information alone could in no way be considered sufficient evidence for brain damage. First, a small number of responses in it-self cannot be attributed to any single factor. A small number of responses can be found in re-tarded, depressed, and extremely defensive individuals as well as in those who are brain damaged. Second, the small number of responses led to an imbalance in the proportion of W to D responses. Data on the typical ratio of W to D responses are based on protocols with 20 to 30 responses. With only six responses, all bets are off. You can't say anything about the balance with so few responses. And, in any case, there is no clear evidence that brain-damaged persons give a preponderance of W responses. Third, the one F− response proves nothing. A single F− response does not necessarily indicate anything in particular, let alone brain damage or disturbed perceptions. On the contrary, the subject gave three popular responses, indicating he was capable of accurate perceptions. How else could he see things that are so commonly seen by others? Fourth, the lack of determinants other than form can have several possible interpretations. The significance of the exclusive use of form in this protocol is dubious, however, in view of the small number of responses. A protocol with 30 responses, all determined exclusively by form, would have quite a different meaning. Notice how the total number of responses can influence or alter the meaning of Rorschach data. The Rorschach places no limit on the number of possible responses.

We suggested that other tests be used to evaluate brain damage in this individual. Taking a conservative approach, we did not deny that this person was brain damaged. We simply stated that the Rorschach in no way documented the presence of brain damage. The person in question, however, dropped his suit after our analysis was communicated to his attorney and psychologist.

C. *Psychometric Properties*

Evaluating the Rorschach on classical psychometric properties (standardization, norms, reliability, validity) has proved exceptionally difficult, and this
attempt to document or refute the adequacy of the Rorschach has produced one
of the greatest divisions of opinion within the entire field of psychology. Time
and again scientific psychologists have evaluated the available empirical data
and concluded that the Rorschach is inadequate when judged by traditional
standards. Yet despite these negative evaluations, the Rorschach has flourished
in clinical settings (Lubin, Larsen & Matarazzo, 1984; Lubin, Wallis & Paine,
1971).

In evaluating the Rorschach, you should keep in mind that there is no
universally accepted method of administration. Some examiners provide
lengthy introductions and explanations; others provide almost none. Most of
the experts state that the length, content, and flavor of administrative instructions should depend on the subject. Yet empirical evidence indicates that the
method of providing instructions and the content of the instructions influence a
subject's response to the Rorschach (Goetcheus, 1967). Given the lack of standardized instructions, comparisons of the protocols of two different examiners
are tenuous at best. There is no scientifically legitimate excuse for this lack of
standardization, which contributes to the inherent difficulties in validating the
Rorschach. Suppose, for example, it is hypothesized that the total number of
responses to a Rorschach is related to the level of defensiveness. Even if an
adequate criterion measure of defensiveness could be found, if examiner instructions influence the number of responses, one examiner might obtain an
average of 32 responses, whereas a second might obtain 22, independent of
defensiveness. If protocols from both examiners are averaged in a group, any
direct relationship between number of responses and defensiveness can easily
be masked or distorted. Until a universally accepted method of Rorschach
administration is used, researchers must standardize the Rorschach administration procedures themselves or risk confounding their results.

In addition to nonuniform administration, Rorschach scoring procedures
are not standardized. One system scores for human movement whenever a
human is seen, whereas another has elaborate and stringent rules for scoring
human movement. The former system obviously finds much more human
movement than does the latter, even when the same test protocols are evaluated. Without standardized scoring it is extremely difficult to determine the
frequency, consistency, and meaning of a particular Rorschach response. One
result of unstandardized Rorschach administration and scoring procedures is
that reliability investigations have produced varied and inconsistent results
and, even when reliability is shown, validity is questionable. Moreover, scoring as well as interpretation procedures do not enjoy criterion-related validity
and are not linked to any theory, which limits the evaluation of construct
validity.

Researchers must also share in the responsibility for the contradictory and inconclusive findings that permeate the Rorschach literature. Many research investigations of psychological tests such as the Rorschach have failed to control important variables like race, sex, age, socioeconomic status, and intelligence. If a particular variable such as race influences test results, as the research indicates (see Lewandowski & Saccuzzo, 1976; Saccuzzo, in press), then studies that fail to control for race may lead to false conclusions. Other problems attributable to the research rather than to the psychometric properties of the Rorschach are lack of relevant training experience in those who score the protocols, poor statistical models, and poor validating criteria (Blatt, 1975; Meloy & Singer, 1991; Parker, 1983).

Whether the problem is lack of standardization, poorly controlled experiments, or both, there is little agreement regarding the scientific status of the Rorschach (Aronow, Reznikoff & Rauchway, 1979; Blatt, 1990). As O. K. Buros (1970, p. xxvi) notes, "This vast amount of writing and research has produced astonishingly little, if any, agreement among psychologists regarding the specific validities of the Rorschach." In brief, the meaning of the thousands of published Rorschach studies is still debatable. For every supportive study, there appears to be a negative or damaging one. See Table 16-2.

Traditional belief, especially among opponents of the Rorschach, is that the Rorschach is unreliable. Indeed, when one views individual studies in isolation, especially those published prior to 1985, the results appear confusing. For every study reporting internal consistency coefficients in the .80s and .90s, one can find another with coefficients of .10 or even .01. Two recent developments, however, show a much brighter picture: the use of meta-analysis to analyze Rorschach reliability and validity and new approaches to the evaluation of the Rorschach's internal consistency.

Meta-analysis is a statistical procedure in which the results of numerous studies are averaged in a single, overall investigation. In a meta-analysis of Rorschach reliability and validity, K. Parker (1983) found an overall internal reliability coefficient of .83 based on 530 statistics from 39 papers published between 1971 and 1980 in the *Journal of Personality Assessment*, the major outlet for research on projective techniques. Moreover, when one uses the Kuder-Richardson formula (which examines all possible ways of splitting the test in two) to calculate internal consistency coefficients rather than the more traditionally used odd-even procedure, Rorschach reliability coefficients are markedly increased. In one study, E. E. Wagner and co-workers (1986) compared the split-half coefficients using the odd-even and the Kuder-Richardson technique for 12 scoring categories. When the odd-even technique was used, coefficients ranged between $-.075$ and $+.785$, which reflects the general findings in the literature through the mid-1980s. However, when the Kuder-Richardson procedure was used, which is common for evaluating the major ability tests, the coefficients ranged from .55 to .88, with a mean of .77. Thus, results from both meta-analysis and application of Kuder-Richardson techniques reveal a higher level of Rorschach reliability than has generally been attributed to the test.

Table 16-2
Summary of
Arguments for
and Against the
Rorschach

Against	In Favor
1. Lacks a universally accepted standard of administration, scoring, and interpretation.	1. Lack of standardized procedures is a historical accident that can be corrected.
2. Evaluations of data are subjective.	2. Test interpretation is an art, not a science; all test interpretation involves a subjective component.
3. Results are unstable over time.	3. A new look at the data reveals that the Rorschach is much more stable than is widely believed.
4. Is unscientific.	4. Has a large empirical base.
5. Is inadequate by all traditional standards.	5. Available evidence is biased and poorly controlled and has therefore failed to provide a fair evaluation.

Clearly, the final word on the Rorschach has yet to be spoken. Far more research is needed, but unless practitioners can agree on a standard method of administration and scoring, the researcher's hands will be tied. Fortunately for the Rorschach, the first steps toward an adequate evaluation have already been taken. In a heroic effort, J. E. Exner (1974) distilled the best elements of the various Rorschach systems and proposed a comprehensive system that provides standard administration procedures that were developed and refined on the basis of empirical analysis. Likewise, scoring has been designed to increase interscorer reliability. Normative frequency tables based on empirical investigations are available to aid in evaluating quantitative factors. Although additional work is still needed, Exner and his colleagues are improving the psychometric qualities of the Rorschach. Interpretive suggestions are based on experimental investigations rather than on theoretical dogma or personal bias. If Exner's goal of providing a standard administration and scoring system can be realized, the 21st century may find the Rorschach elevated to a position unimaginable 20 years ago. In any event, both opponents as well as proponents still have a long way to go before the psychological community will be able to achieve a consensus on this most controversial test (Hertz, 1986; Piotrowski, 1984). As Rorschach expert and recipient of the Society for Personality Assessment Distinguished Contributor Award Sidney J. Blatt stated, it is best to view the Rorschach "as an experimental procedure that systematically presents an individual with ambiguity and allows us to observe and study how the individual constructs meaning from relative ambiguity" (1990, p. 401).

III. *An Alternative Inkblot Test: The Holtzman*

Among the prime problems of the Rorschach, from a psychometric viewpoint, are its variable number of responses from one subject to another, lack of standard procedures, and lack of an alternative form. To meet these difficulties while maintaining the advantages of the inkblot methodology, the Holtzman Inkblot Test was created (Holtzman et al., 1961). In the Holtzman, the subject is permitted to give only one response per card. Administration and scoring procedures are standardized and carefully described. An alternative form is available that correlates well with the original test stimuli. Interscorer as well as split-half reliabilities are comparable to those found for objective personality tests (Gamble, 1972).

Both forms, A and B, of the Holtzman contain 45 cards. Each response may be scored on 22 dimensions. Many of these dimensions are similar to those found in the Rorschach and include location, determinant, and content. Responses may also be scored for such factors as anxiety and hostility. For each scoring category or variable, norms are presented for several samples ranging from 5-year-olds through adults. Given the psychometric advantages of the Holtzman, it is interesting that the test hasn't even begun to challenge the Rorschach's popularity.

K. R. Gamble (1972) reviewed the literature on the Holtzman and concluded that there were insufficient data to adequately compare the Holtzman to the Rorschach. The main difficulty with the Holtzman appears to be its validity (Gamble, 1972; Zubin, 1972). The few available validity studies are hardly impressive. As Zubin (1972) notes, those studies that show a positive relationship between the Holtzman and various criterion measures are based on qualitative rather than quantitative features. Thus, the available supportive evidence is highly subjective and depends on examiner skill rather than formal interpretive standards. In short, the Holtzman cannot, at this time, be considered any more useful than the Rorschach, despite its superior psychometric features. Nevertheless, the Holtzman is a relatively young test compared with the Rorschach, and it is still too early to judge its clinical utility relative to the Rorschach (Leichsenring, 1990, 1991).

IV. *The Thematic Apperception Test*

The Thematic Apperception Test (TAT) is a product of U.S. psychology that is comparable to the Rorschach in many ways, including its importance and psychometric problems. It was introduced in 1935 by Christina Morgan and Henry Murray of Harvard University. As with the Rorschach, use of the TAT grew rapidly after its introduction, but its psychometric adequacy was (and still is) seriously questioned (Keiser & Prather, 1990). Unlike the Rorschach, however, the TAT has been relatively well received by the scientific community. The TAT differs from the Rorschach in that it is based on H. A. Murray's (1938) theory of needs (see Chapter 15), whereas the Rorschach is basically atheoretical. The TAT and the Rorschach differ in other respects as well. The TAT authors were conservative in their evaluation of the TAT and scientific in their outlook. The TAT was not oversold as was the Rorschach, and no extrav-

Table 16-3
A Comparison of
the Rorschach
and TAT

Rorschach	TAT
Rejected by scientific community	Well-received by scientific community
Atheoretical	Based on Murray's (1938) theory of needs
Oversold by extravagent claims	Conservative claims
Purported diagnostic instrument	Not purported as diagnostic
Primarily clinical use	Clinical and nonclinical uses

agant claims were made. Unlike the Rorschach, the TAT was not billed as a diagnostic instrument—that is, a test of disordered emotional states. Instead, the TAT was presented as a measurement instrument for evaluating human personality characteristics. See Table 16-3.

The TAT has also distinguished itself from the Rorschach in that its nonclinical uses are just as important as its clinical uses. Indeed, the TAT is one of the most important techniques used in personality research (for example, Atkinson, 1981; Cramer & Blatt, 1990; McClelland et al., 1953; Turner, 1970). As stated, the TAT is based on Murray's (1938) theory, which distinguishes 28 human needs, including the needs for sex, affiliation, and dominance. Many of these needs have been extensively studied in personality research by using the TAT. Murray's need for achievement—"the desire or tendency to do things as rapidly and/or as well as possible" (1938, p. 164)—alone has generated countless studies involving the TAT. A review of the relevant literature by R. C. Birney (1968) cites well over 100 studies on this one need, most of them by D. C. McClelland (1951a, 1951b, 1958, for example). The TAT measure of the achievement need has been related to factors such as parental perceptions, parental expectations, and parental attitudes toward their children. Need achievement is also related to the standards you as a student set for yourself (for example, academic standards). The higher your need for achievement, the more you are likely to study and ultimately achieve a high economic and social position in society. Studies such as those on the achievement motive have increased the construct validity as well as the scientific respectability of the TAT.

A. *Stimuli, Administration, and Interpretation*

The TAT is more structured and less ambiguous than the Rorschach. TAT stimuli consist of pictures that depict a variety of scenes. There are 30 pictures and one blank card, for a total of 31 test stimuli. Specific cards are designed for males; others for females. Some of the cards are appropriate for older subjects; others are for young subjects. A few of the cards are appropriate for all subjects. Card 1, for example, can be given to any subject. It shows a boy, neatly dressed and groomed, sitting at a table on which is a violin. In his description of Card 1, Murray stated that the boy is "contemplating" the violin. According

Figure 16-2
Card 12F from the Thematic Apperception Test. This card often gives the subject a chance to express attitudes toward a mother or daughter figure. Sometimes attitudes toward marriage and aging also emerge. (*Reprinted by permission of the publishers from Henry A. Murray,* Thematic Apperception Test, *Cambridge, Mass.: Harvard University Press, Copyright © 1943 by the President and Fellows of Harvard College, © 1971 by Henry A. Murray.*)

to experts such as L. Bellak (1986), Card 1 of the TAT tends to reveal a person's relationship toward parental figures.

Other TAT cards tend to elicit other kinds of information. Card 4 is a picture of a woman "clutching the shoulders of a man whose face and body are averted as if he were trying to pull away from her" (Bellak, 1975, p. 51). This card elicits information concerning male-female relationships. Bellak (1975, 1986) and others (Rapaport, Gill & Schafer, 1945, 1946) provide a description of the TAT cards along with the information each card tends to elicit. This knowledge is essential in TAT interpretation. Figure 16-2 shows Card 12F, which sometimes elicits conflicting emotions about the self. Other feelings may also be elicited.

Standardization of administration and especially scoring procedures are about as poor, if not worse, for the TAT as for the Rorschach. Most examiners typically state something like "I am going to show you some pictures. I want you to tell me a story about each picture. Tell me what led up to the story, what is happening, what the characters are thinking and feeling, and what the outcome will be." In the original design of the test, 20 cards were to be administered to each subject, 10 cards in each of two separate one-hour sessions. In actual practice, however, only 10 or 12 cards are typically used (Bellak, 1975, p. 47). As with the Rorschach and almost all other individually administered tests, the examiner records the subject's responses verbatim. The examiner also records the reaction time—the time interval between the initial presentation of a card and the subject's first response. By recording reaction time, the examiner can determine whether the subject has difficulty with any particular card. Because each card is designed to elicit its own themes, needs, and conflicts, an abnormally long reaction time may indicate a specific problem. If, for example, the reaction time substantially increases for all cards involving heterosexual relationships, then the examiner may hypothesize that the subject is experiencing difficulty in this area.

There are by far more interpretive and scoring systems for the TAT than for the Rorschach. In his excellent review of the TAT literature, B. I. Murstein (1963, p. 23) states, "There would seem to be as many thematic scoring systems as there were hairs in the beard of Rasputin." Murstein summarizes most of the major methods of interpretation for the TAT, grouping them into quantitative and nonquantitative methods. Unlike the quantitative aspects of the Rorschach, which are considered to be extremely important by most examiners, the quantitative methods of TAT interpretation are rather unpopular (Westen, 1991). Most TAT examiners find the available scoring systems overly elaborate, complex, and time consuming. They therefore tend to use only nonquantitative methods of interpretation.

Almost all methods of TAT interpretation take into account the hero, needs, press, themes, and outcomes. The hero is the character in each picture with whom the subject seems to identify. In most cases, the story revolves around one easily recognizable character. If a number of characters seem to be important, the character most like the storyteller is selected as the hero. Of particular importance are the motives and needs of the hero. Most systems, including Murray's original, consider the intensity, duration, and frequency of each need to be indicators of the importance and relevance of that need. In TAT interpretation, *press* refers to the environmental forces that interfere with or facilitate satisfaction of the various needs. Again, factors such as frequency, intensity, and duration are used to judge the relative importance of these factors. The frequency of various themes (for example, depression) and outcomes (for example, failures) is also a prime indicator of their importance.

To understand the potential value of the TAT in evaluating personality characteristics, you should realize that quite different responses to the same card are elicited from different individuals. For example, for Card 1, in which a boy is contemplating a violin, one subject may say, "This boy's mother has just reminded him to practice the violin. The boy hates the violin and is wondering what he can do to make his practice session less boring. As he daydreams, his mother scolds him, so he picks up the violin and plays, resenting every minute." Another subject may respond, "The boy has just come home from school and is getting ready to practice the violin. He hopes to become a great violin player someday but realizes he's just an average, ordinary person. He picks up the violin and plays, dreaming about success." A third story may go as follows: "It's violin practice again and the boy is fed up. Do this, do that; his parents

Table 16-4
Lindzey's
Assumptions for
TAT
Interpretation

Primary assumption

In completing an incomplete or unstructured situation, the individual may reveal his or her own characteristics (strivings, dispositions, conflicts).

Other assumptions

1. The storyteller ordinarily identifies with one person in the drama. The characteristics (wishes, strivings, conflicts) of this imaginary person may reflect those of the storyteller.
2. The storyteller's characteristics may be represented indirectly or symbolically.
3. All stories are not of equal importance.
4. Themes directly related to stimulus material are less likely to be significant than those unrelated to stimulus material.
5. Recurrent themes (those that show up in three or four different stories) are particularly likely to mirror the characteristics of the storyteller.
6. The stories may reflect momentary characteristics of the storyteller (those aroused by temporary environmental factors) as well as enduring characteristics.
7. Stories may reflect events from the past that the storyteller has only observed or witnessed. However, the selection of these stories suggests that the events may still be a reflection of the storyteller's own characteristics.
8. Group membership or sociocultural factors may also be reflected in the stories.
9. Dispositions and conflicts that are inferred from the storyteller's creations may be unconscious and thus may not always be reflected directly in overt behavior or consciousness.

Adapted from Lindzey (1952).

are always trying to live his life. This time he fixes them. He picks up the violin, smashes it, and goes out to play baseball.''

Think about these three different stories. Because the stimulus was the same in each case, differences in the stories must in some way reflect differences in the storytellers. The primary issue is exactly what is revealed in these stories. Many years ago, G. Lindzey (1952) analyzed a number of assumptions underlying the TAT. Table 16-4 lists these major assumptions. Although there were problems with many of the studies cited by Lindzey, positive evidence was found to support these assumptions, whose validity holds to this day (Keiser & Prather, 1990; Westen, 1991). By understanding these assumptions, you can get an idea of the complexity of TAT interpretation.

Although Lindzey's analysis was conducted some time ago, many TAT practitioners are guided by the assumptions listed in Table 16-4. The primary assumption—in completing an incomplete or unstructured situation, the individual may reveal his or her own strivings, dispositions, and conflicts—provides a rationale and support for projective tests in general. Most of the other nine assumptions, however, pertain specifically to the TAT. As these assumptions indicate, although a story is a reflection of the storyteller, a multitude of factors may influence the story. Therefore, all TAT experts agree that a complete interview and a case history must accompany any attempt to interpret the TAT. No matter how careful and thorough such an interview, however, final conclusions and interpretations are still based on many factors, including the skill and experience of the examiner.

B. *Psychometric Properties*

Many experts consider the TAT to be psychometrically unsound. With the unstandardized procedures for administration, scoring, and interpretation, it is easy to understand why psychometric evaluations have produced inconsistent, unclear, and conflicting findings. Division of opinion is so wide that, whereas one expert finds impressive evidence of intrinsic validity (Harrison, 1965), others have found TAT validity to be almost nil (Varble, 1971). Not only is the interpretation of the TAT subjective, but analysis of the TAT literature is also a matter of subjective interpretation. In other words, as with the Rorschach, two experts can look at the same research data and draw different or even opposite conclusions. It should be no surprise, then, that for almost every positive empirical finding there is a countering negative empirical finding.

An analysis of existing results does reveal that when specific variables are studied, such as the achievement need, respectably high reliability figures are found (Exner, 1976; Murstein, 1963). Test-retest reliabilities appear to fluctuate, however, and to diminish as the interval between the two testing sessions increases. S. S. Tomkins (1947), for example, found that a test-retest correlation coefficient of .80, obtained after a two-month interval, diminished to .50 after a ten-month interval for an independent sample. The median test-retest correlation across studies is only about .30 (Kraiger, Hakel & Cornelius, 1984; Winter & Stewart, 1977). However, J. W. Atkinson (1981) has argued that the validity of the TAT does not depend on test-retest reliability. Split-half reliabilities have been consistently poor. It should be noted, however, that many TAT proponents do not consider the split-half method appropriate because each card is designed to produce its own theme and content. What is needed is a study with Kuder-Richardson reliabilities, as has recently been done with the Rorschach. Agreement among interpreters varies considerably, with correlations ranging from the low .30s to the .90s, with the greatest agreement among similarly trained examiners (Harrison & Rotter, 1945; Mayman & Kutner, 1947).

Validity studies have produced even less clear findings. Most experts agree that the TAT has content validity for evaluating human personality; however, criterion validity has been difficult to document. In an early but often cited study, R. Harrison (1940) found that his own inferences based on TAT stories correlated at .78 with hospital records for specific variables. And he reported that he was 75% correct in diagnosing patients into major categories, such as psychotic versus neurotic, using TAT data. K. B. Little and E. S. Shneidman (1959) found, however, that when 12 specialists for each of four tests (TAT, Make-a-Picture Story, Rorschach, MMPI) were asked to match the judgments of a group of criterion judges who had conducted extensive interviews with each of the subjects, not only was there little agreement between the test judges and the criterion judges, but also of the four tests the TAT fared poorest, having both the lowest reliability and the poorest predictive validity. More recent studies also report discouraging reliability coefficients (Singh, 1986).

As we review the psychometric properties of the TAT, we find that, like the Rorschach, the TAT has a number of significant problems. In spite of these problems, however, the TAT continues to find widespread application in clinical as well as research settings. As with the Rorschach, the most pressing need appears to be establishing standardized administration and scoring procedures. Until such standardization is achieved, the TAT will continue to fare poorly according to traditional psychometric standards.

V. *Alternative Apperception Procedures*

An alternative thematic apperception test (Ritzler, Sharkey & Chudy, 1980; Sharkey & Ritzler, 1985) has been constructed by selecting pictures from the *Family of Man* photo-essay collection (Museum of Modern Art, 1955). According to the authors of this long overdue attempt to update the TAT methodology, the new procedure can be scored quantitatively. It provides a balance of positive and negative stories and a variety of action and energy levels for the main character. In comparison, the TAT elicits predominantly negative and low-energy stories (Ritzler, Sharkey & Chudy, 1980). Preliminary results with this new procedure, known as the Southern Mississippi TAT (or SM-TAT), have been encouraging. These results indicate that the SM-TAT preserves many of the advantages of the TAT while providing a more rigorous and modern methodology than that offered by the TAT. Naturally, more research is needed, but the authors of this new attempt to modernize the TAT are to be applauded.

The versatility and usefulness of the TAT approach are illustrated not only by attempts such as that of Ritzler, Sharkey, and Chudy (1980) to update the test but also by the availability of special forms of the TAT for children and other special forms for the elderly. The Children's Apperception Test (CAT) was created to meet the special needs of children aged 3 through 10 (Bellak, 1975). The CAT stimuli contain animal rather than human figures as in the original TAT. The Gerontological Apperception Test uses stimuli in which one or more elderly individuals are involved in a scene with a theme relevant to the concerns of the elderly, such as loneliness and family conflicts (Wolk & Wolk, 1971). The Senior Apperception Technique is an alternative to the Gerontological Apperception Test and is parallel in content (Bellak, 1975; Bellak & Bellak, 1973).

VI. *Nonpictorial Projective Procedures*

Projective tests need not necessarily involve the use of a pictorial stimulus. Words or phrases sometimes provide the stimulus, as in the Word Association

Test and the Incomplete Sentence Test. Or a subject can be asked to create or draw something, as in the Draw-A-Man Test. In our final section, we briefly describe each of these procedures.

A. *Word Association Test*

Imagine yourself comfortably seated in a psychologist's examining office. Your task is simple, or at least it seems so. The psychologist says a word and you say the first word that comes to mind. The test begins. The first word is "hat." You reply "coat," the most common response of college students according to Rapaport, Gill, and Schafer (1968). The test goes on as follows:

Lamp

Love

Father

Paper

Masturbation

Chair

Breast

Car

Penis

Suicide

Do some of these words arouse any feelings in you? Words like *love, mother, breast,* and *masturbation* do in many people. The purpose of word association tests is to infer possible disturbances and areas of conflict from an individual's response to words.

The use of word association tests dates back to F. Galton (1879) and was first used on a clinical basis by Carl Jung (1910) and G. H. Kent and A. J. Rosanoff (1910). Kent and Rosanoff were the first to attempt to standardize word association procedures. They developed a list of 100 standard words and presented them to a sample of 1000 normal adults who were partially stratified by geographic location, education, occupation, age, and intelligence. An objective scoring system was developed and the Kent-Rosanoff word association test enjoyed moderate popularity in the 1920s and 1930s.

Rapaport, Gill, and Schafer (1968) subsequently developed a 60-item word association test. The range of words covered familial, household, oral, anal, aggressive, and phobic content. Responses were quantified by collecting norms on college students and schizophrenics, although interpretations were clearly psychoanalytic in nature.

Interest in word association techniques dropped considerably after Rapaport, Gill, and Schafer (1968) concluded that the procedures did not live up to their clinical promise. Although the techniques are still in use today (deGroot, 1988; Pons, 1989), they play only a limited role in clinical and counseling settings.

B. *Sentence Completion Tests*

Another family of projective techniques involving words is incomplete sentence tests. These tests provide a stem that the subject is asked to complete; for example:

1. I am_____

2. I enjoy_____

3. What annoys me_____

4. It pains me to_____

5. Men_____

6. Dancing_____

7. Sports_____

As with all projective techniques, the individual's response is believed to be a reflection of that person's needs, conflicts, values, and thought processes. In clinical use the test also gives a person the opportunity to provide information that may have been too embarrassing to present in a face-to-face verbal interview. Clinicians look for recurring themes of conflict and pathological content.

A number of incomplete sentence techniques are available with scoring procedures. Among the most widely used of these is the Rotter Incomplete Sentence Blank (Rotter & Rafferty, 1950). The Rotter provides 40 stems, each of which is scored on a seven-point system. In general, short sentences with some humor and positive content get the highest scores—for example, "Men have their advantages and disadvantages." Long complex sentences with negative or depressed content receive the lowest scores—for example, "Men who I can't stand and would like to sometimes kill and do away with really know how to make a person feel crazy all the time."

Sentence completion procedures are used widely in clinical as well as research settings. A relatively recent addition to this family of tests is the Incomplete Sentence Task of Lanyon and Lanyon (1980). Sentences are scored on a three-point scale (0, 1, 2), and norms are available as a function of age and gender. The initial reviews of Lanyon and Lanyon's incomplete sentence test have been positive and encouraging (Cundick, 1985; Dush, 1985).

C. *Figure Drawing Tests*

Another category of projective tests is the expressive techniques, in which the subject is asked to create something, usually a drawing. In the Draw-A-Person Test (Machover, 1949), the subject, most often a child, is asked to draw the picture of a person. Later the child is asked to tell a story about the person. A similar technique is the House-Tree-Person Test (Buck, 1948), in which the subject is asked to draw the picture of a house, tree, and person and then make up a story about it. In the Kinetic Family Drawing Test (Burns & Kaufmann, 1970, 1972), the subject is asked to draw a picture of his or her family.

Projective drawing tests are scored on a number of dimensions, including absolute size, relative size, omissions, and disproportions. For example, in drawing her family, a young child may omit herself. It might then be assumed that the child feels alienated from the family. In drawing a house-tree-person, the child might draw himself in the house looking out, perhaps reflecting a feeling of being isolated or trapped.

If there is a tendency to overinterpret projective test data without sufficient empirical foundation, then projective drawing tests are among the worse offenders. Although experienced clinicians can gain insights into an individual through a skillful and cautious interpretation, there is a tendency to go too far in what can be inferred. For instance, in the Draw-A-Person Test, a clinician is advised to interpret a large head as indicating an overconcern with matters of intellectual functioning or even brain damage according to one system (Machover, 1949). Although figure drawing tests have a place in a test battery, great caution is called for in their use until rigorous research can document the valid inferences that can be made from them.

Summary

According to the *projective hypothesis,* interpretations of an ambiguous or vague stimulus reflect the subject's own needs, feelings, experiences, prior conditioning, thought processes, and so forth.

The Rorschach is the preeminent projective test. Five individuals played a dominant role in its development: Beck, Hertz, Klopfer, Piotrowski, and Rapaport. Rorschach stimuli consist of ten black, gray, red, and various pastel inkblots. These stimuli were formed by dropping ink onto a piece of paper and folding the paper.

Rorschach administration involves two phases. During the free-association phase, the examiner presents each card with a minimum of structure. During the second phase—the inquiry—the examiner presents each card again to obtain sufficient information for scoring purposes. The five major Rorschach scoring categories are location (where), determinant (why), content (what), popular-original (frequency of occurrence), and form quality (correspondence of percept to stimulus properties of the inkblot).

The Rorschach is highly controversial. On the negative side, it has been attacked for its lack of standardized methods for administration, scoring, and interpretation. It has been criticized because interpretations are subjective and results are unstable over time. With the exception of recent reliability studies, the weight of scientific evidence has been generally unfavorable. On the positive side, efforts are being made to establish standardized procedures. In the hands of an expert, the Rorschach can reveal a wealth of information about a single individual. Unfavorable scientific evidence is disputable.

The Holtzman is a recently developed alternative to the Rorschach. The Holtzman overcomes much of the scientific criticism of the Rorschach, but the value and importance of this relatively new procedure have not yet been determined.

The TAT is another projective test; it enjoys wide research as well as clinical use. The TAT stimuli consist of 30 pictures depicting a variety of scenes and one blank card. Card 1, for example, shows a scene in which a boy, neatly dressed and groomed, is sitting at a table on which is a violin. The boy is contemplating the violin. Specific cards are suited for adults, children, males, and females. In administering the TAT, the examiner requests the subject to make up a story. The story should include the events that led up to the scene, what the characters are thinking and feeling, and the outcome.

Like the Rorschach, the TAT has strong supporters but also has been attacked on a variety of scientific grounds. Though not psychometrically sound by traditional standards, the TAT is in widespread use. Like the Rorschach, it is capable of providing a wealth of information about a single individual.

Some of the similarities between the TAT and Rorschach are as follows: They are both individual projective tests for measuring human functioning and personality characteristics. Both are poorly standardized for administration, scoring, and interpretation. Reliability coefficients for both tests vary widely. Both are highly criticized, yet both are used extensively and adopted enthusiastically by practitioners. Both provide a rich source of information about a single individual. And both are supported by a wide body of empirical findings.

Some of the differences between the TAT and Rorschach are as follows: The Rorschach stimuli are inkblots; the TAT stimuli depict scenes. Thus, TAT stimuli are more meaningful than Rorschach stimuli. The TAT is based on Murray's (1938) theory of needs; the Rorschach is atheoretical. Formal scoring and quantitative features are important in the Rorschach but are of little significance in the TAT. The TAT finds extensive use in research as well as in clinical settings; the Rorschach is primarily a clinical tool. TAT interpretation is guided by a variety of assumptions, which were listed and explored by Lindzey (1952). Rorschach interpretation still depends on the opinion of experts and on research surveys such as those described in Exner's (1974) Rorschach textbook.

A number of nonpictorial projective tests are available, including word association tests and incomplete sentence tests. Expressive techniques require a person to make something, such as draw a picture of a person or of one's family.

Chapter 17

Alternatives to Traditional Psychological Tests

Learning Objectives

When you have completed this chapter, you should be able to:

- Identify the differences between behavioral and traditional assessment procedures.
- Identify the difference between the beliefs underlying traditional tests and the beliefs underlying behavioral tests.
- Briefly describe behavioral assessment based on operant conditioning.
- Identify the main difference between behavioral self-report techniques and traditional self-report techniques.
- List four types of behavioral self-report techniques.
- Briefly describe the functional, or behavior-analytic, approach to behavioral assessment.
- Explain how cognitive-behavioral assessment differs from other types of behavioral assessment.
- List four types of cognitive-behavioral assessment.
- Describe a cognitive functional analysis.
- Briefly describe psychophysical assessment.
- Describe two major ways in which computers play a role in testing.

A high school teacher once contacted us regarding her 7-year-old son. At the age of 4, the boy had suffered from an illness in which he was unable to eat solid food for 25 days because it made him gag. If he managed to swallow, he became extremely nauseous. Ever since he recovered from the illness, he had been reluctant to eat all but a few select foods. His usual menu was cold cereal for breakfast, a peanut butter sandwich for lunch, and plain spaghetti for dinner. He refused to eat meat or vegetables of any kind. His parents tried everything, but nothing worked. The mother was concerned that the boy was not developing properly. She had taken him to a pediatrician who told her that unless something could be done to get the boy to eat, he would have to be hospitalized. The physician suggested psychiatric intervention and gave the boy one month to improve.

After explaining the presenting problem, the mother asked us whether we could administer a test that might explain why the child wasn't eating. A school psychologist had suggested to her that psychological tests might be useful in facilitating the treatment process. If we could understand why the boy wasn't eating, perhaps this information would aid in the treatment. During our interview, we discovered that the boy had been in psychiatric treatment when he was 5. The treatment had lasted about one year with little improvement. Partly because of this previous failure and partly because of her desperation, the mother insisted we do some testing. As we thought about the various tests we might use, we could see little value in using any of the traditional tests for this presenting problem.

We did administer the Wechsler Intelligence Scale for Children-Revised (WISC-R) and found that the boy had above average intelligence (full-sale IQ = 115). In achievement, as measured by the Wide Range Achievement Test, the boy was functioning about half a grade level above his present grade placement in both reading and arithmetic. Thus, intellectual and achievement factors could not account for the problem; the ability tests yielded little information in this case. Personality tests were more revealing than the ability tests but, unfortunately, were not very useful. We administered the Children's Apperception Test (see Chapter 16), and our interpretation confirmed our suspicion that the boy's eating problem originated with the trauma he had suffered when he was unable to eat solid foods. In simple terms, the boy had a fear of eating.

Knowing why the boy wasn't eating certainly wasn't much help. One of the weaknesses of the traditional tests we had used in this case is that they provide little information concerning possible treatment approaches. When we explained the situation to the mother, she pleaded, "Isn't there any other type of test you can give him? Isn't there a test that might also indicate what type of treatment would be most effective?" Thanks to advances within scientific psychology, we were able to answer "yes."

We told the mother that a relatively new approach to testing had been developed by psychologists in the specialty based on learning principles known as behavior modification, or behavior therapy. Collectively, these nontraditional testing techniques are known as *behavioral assessment*. "Please try these new procedures," she said. "I don't care if they are new and perhaps untested," she continued, "if they might help, by all means use them."

Would you be willing to try a new, nontraditional testing procedure? If so, you are not alone. Traditional psychological tests may be extremely valuable in the hands of highly trained experts, but they still fall short on several grounds.

The traditional tests that we have discussed thus far offer little information concerning treatment approaches. As a rule, these traditional procedures also provide little information concerning how a person might behave in a particular situation. Even if these traditional procedures do explain the reason behind a particular symptom, this information is often of little value to the overall treatment process. Thus, in addition to limitations in reliability, validity, norms, and the like, traditional psychological tests have been criticized on other grounds. The result has been an explosion of alternative approaches.

I. *The Status of Traditional Psychological Tests and an Overview of the Alternatives*

In 1953, L. Shaffer conducted a survey asking clinical psychological practitioners to rank order their primary responsibilities. The practitioners ranked psychological testing first among all their duties. Only 14 years later, R. R. Holt wrote, "Diagnostic testing today is in a funk" (1967, p. 44). A number of authors have explored the reasons for this dramatic decline in the role and status of psychological testing (Lewandowski & Saccuzzo, 1976; Saccuzzo, 1976). In addition to the unreliability and poorly documented validity of many traditional procedures, many psychologists rejected traditional tests because of their lack of grounding in the psychological sciences and their poor relationship to treatment.

The psychologists' aversion to traditional testing procedures was paralleled by attacks from the public. As noted by D. Rapaport, M. M. Gill, and R. Schafer (1968), books written for the general public strongly attacked psychological tests during the interval between Shaffer's (1953) survey and Holt's (1967) assessment of the status of testing. In summarizing the general spirit of these attacks, Rapaport, Gill, and Schafer provided this statement: "Although their instruments are unscientific and invalid, psychologists are reading our minds, invading our privacy, imposing a yoke of conformity on employees, and stifling originality in school children, driven by morbid sexual curiosity and the cynical pursuit of money" (1968, p. 32). These accusations led to an inquiry by the Senate Subcommittee on Constitutional Rights and the House Subcommittee on Invasion of Privacy (Dahlstrom, 1969b). Although neither of these subcommittees succeeded in documenting deliberate and widespread misuse of tests (Brayfield, 1965), public attacks against testing continued. There was, for example, a call for a moratorium on all tests until improved procedures were developed (APA, 1974). Hardly a year goes by without some major challenge to psychological tests (National Commission on Testing and Public Policy, 1990).

In response to these criticisms, psychologists began to develop testing techniques based on the psychological sciences, on principles and concepts

Table 17-1
Categories of
Alternatives to
Traditional
Testing
Procedures

Behavioral assessment
Operant conditioning techniques
Self-report techniques
Kanfer and Saslow's behavior-analytic technique
Cognitive techniques
Psychophysiological techniques
Community assessment procedures
Psychophysical and signal detection procedures

developed in psychological laboratories. Grounded in psychological findings and theories, these tests, though relatively new, provide genuine alternatives to traditional testing procedures.

The alternatives fall into three main categories (see Table 17-1). The first, and by far the largest, category is generally referred to as behavioral assessment, which can be broken down into the subcategories of procedures based on operant conditioning, self-report techniques, Kanfer and Saslow's behavior-analytic (or functional) approach, cognitive techniques, and psychophysiological techniques. The second category consists of community assessment procedures. The third category is newly emerging psychophysical and signal detection procedures. We discuss each of these procedures in the sections that follow.

II. *Behavioral Assessment Procedures*

Traditional testing procedures are based on a medical model. According to this model, the overt manifestations of a disordered psychological condition (for example, overeating or undereating) are only symptoms—surface expressions of an underlying cause. Disordered behavior is believed to be caused by some underlying characteristic such as an early traumatic experience. In the example at the beginning of this chapter, the boy's avoidance of food was, in a sense, caused by the trauma of an illness in which solid food made him nauseous. Treatment in the medical model is based on the idea that, unless the cause of a symptom is removed, a new symptom may develop. Thus, one major function of traditional psychological tests is to ascertain the hypothetical underlying causes of disordered behaviors.

In behavioral assessment, by contrast, the behaviors, cognitions, or physiological responses that define a disordered condition are considered the real problem. If the person eats too much, then the problem is simply overeating and not some hypothetical underlying cause. The overeating may, in fact, have been caused by some early experience, just as in the 7-year-old boy. However,

	Traditional Assessment	Behavioral Assessment
Target	Underlying cause	Disordered behavior
Symptoms	Superficial	Focus of treatment
Assessment	Indirect; not related to treatment	Direct; related to treatment
Theory	Medical model	Behavioral model
Goal	Determine cause of symptoms	Analyze disordered behavior

Table 17-2
Traditional Versus
Behavioral
Assessment

in behavioral assessment, the eating behavior becomes the direct target of treatment. Therefore, the testing procedure evaluates eating behavior.

You shouldn't think that behavioral assessment denies, ignores, or negates the causes of psychological disorders. On the contrary, certain techniques of behavior assessment include an evaluation of the factors that precede, coexist with, and follow (maintain) disordered behavior (Haynes, 1990, 1992). These may be environmental factors (for example, working conditions, home situation), thought processes (for example, internal dialogue), or both. Thus, behavioral assessment often includes an evaluation of the internal and external factors that lead to and maintain disordered behavior as well as an evaluation of the behavior itself (Bellack & Hersen, 1988).

Behavioral assessment is more direct than traditional psychological tests. All the major reviewers of the distinction between traditional and behavioral assessment agree that behavioral assessment is characterized by fewer inferential assumptions and remains closer to observables (Goldfried, 1976; Haynes, 1992; Mischel, 1968). Through behavioral assessment, it might be found, for example, that just prior to eating, the 7-year-old boy in our example says to himself, "I don't want to eat; it will make me sick." Subsequently, the boy refuses to eat. As he leaves the dinner table, his mother might say, "That's OK, honey, you don't have to eat." The boy's self-statement, "I don't want to eat," precedes the disordered behavior. His avoidance of food is the core of the disorder. His mother's comment, plus the boy's relief that he doesn't have to eat, reinforces or maintains the disorder. In behavioral assessment, preceding and subsequent factors are analyzed and the focus is on behavioral change. The treatment process thus involves an attempt to alter the disordered behavior (for example, increasing the frequency of eating behavior). Treatment may also involve modification of the internal dialogue before and after the boy eats and modification of the mother's behavior so that she no longer reinforces avoidance of food and instead reinforces eating.

In traditional procedures, the boy's failure to eat would be viewed as only a symptom. Testing would be aimed at determining the cause of this symptom (the early trauma of the illness he had when he was 4), and treatment would be directed at the cause rather than at the behavior itself. Presumably, by giving the boy insight into the causes of his behavior, a psychologist could get the boy to understand why he wasn't eating. When he achieved this understanding, he would no longer need to avoid eating. Table 17-2 compares traditional and behavioral assessment.

Table 17-3
Steps in a
Behavioral
Assessment

Step 1: Identify critical behaviors.
Step 2: Determine whether critical behaviors are excesses or deficits.
Step 3: Evaluate critical behaviors for frequency, duration, or intensity (that is, obtain a baseline).
Step 4: If excesses, attempt to decrease frequency, duration, or intensity of behaviors; if deficits, attempt to increase behaviors.

It is beyond the scope of this text to debate the pros and cons of the behavioral and medical models. Our goal is to help you understand the differences between the two. Suffice it to say that behavioral testing procedures have added a whole new dimension to the field of psychological testing.

A. *Procedures Based on Operant Conditioning*

In operant conditioning, we observe the behaviors of an individual. After the individual has made a response, we can do something to the individual to alter the probability of the recurrence of the response. We may present something positive or remove something negative following the response to increase the rate of recurrence, or we may present something aversive or remove something positive preceding the response to reduce the rate of recurrence. In behavioral assessment based on operant conditioning, our first task is to identify the critical response or responses involved in the disorder. We can then evaluate these critical responses for frequency, intensity, or duration. This evaluation establishes the baseline (usual rate of occurrence) for the particular behavior. According to an early system developed by F. H. Kanfer and G. Saslow (1969), if the behaviors occur too frequently, they are called behavioral *excesses*. If they occur too infrequently, they are called behavioral *deficits*. Obviously when there is a behavioral excess, treatment is aimed at reducing the frequency, intensity, or duration of the behavior in question. When there is a behavioral deficit, treatment is aimed at increasing the frequency, intensity, or duration of the behavior. Table 17-3 outlines the steps in behavioral assessment based on operant conditioning.

After attempting to increase or decrease the behavior (treatment intervention), psychologists observe the effect of the intervention on the behavior in question relative to the baseline. If the goal was to decrease the behavior, then there should be a decrease relative to the baseline. If the critical behavior remains at or above baseline levels, then the intervention has failed.

In the example at the beginning of this chapter with the 7-year-old boy, we decided to use behavioral assessment based on operant conditioning. The critical behavior was obvious: frequency of eating. Furthermore, the critical behavior was a deficit; that is, the boy wasn't eating enough. To evaluate the critical behavior, Step 3, we asked the boy's mother to record the amount and kind of food that the boy ate each day. Using standard calorie references, we converted the amount of food the boy ate into calories. The baseline looked something

Figure 17-1
Baseline of eating.

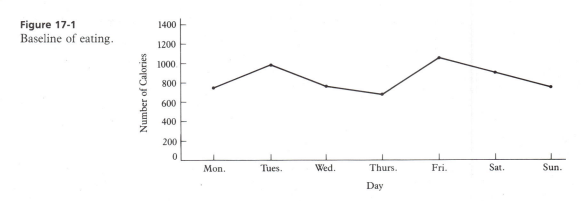

like the graph in Figure 17-1. The boy was eating an average of about 800 calories a day, with a range of 600 to 1000 calories on any given day. This number of calories is too few to prevent a small, gradual weight loss.

Because the behavior was a deficit, the goal was to increase the boy's frequency of eating. For our intervention, we used a reward system based on points. The plan was that the boy be given points for everything he ate. The more he ate, the more points he could get. Following each meal, his mother recorded the number of points that he received as well as the cumulative total. She posted this record on a bulletin board in the boy's room so he could observe his own progress. She also posted a chart that we had worked out with her and the boy. The chart listed toys and other rewards that he could trade for points. For example, he could exchange 10 points for a package of baseball cards any time he wanted. He could also save his points for bigger prizes. For 350 points he could get a miniature pinball machine he had been wanting, and so on. In the treatment procedure, his mother recorded exactly what he ate each day just as she did during the pretreatment assessment in which the baseline was obtained. This record was then converted into calories, and each week we made a graph of his day-to-day calorie intake.

The intervention proved highly effective. Within one week, the boy had earned about 200 points and was well on the way to securing a pinball machine. The graph for this first week of treatment is shown in Figure 17-2. As the graph indicates, the boy doubled his average intake of calories to about 1600 (range 1400 to 1800). Thus, his intake of calories was far above baseline following the intervention. Assessment continued throughout the treatment and also provided feedback concerning the effects of the treatment. In the second week, the boy's consumption of calories fell below the dramatic increases of the first week, but it never fell below baseline levels. In six weeks, the boy gained about 8 pounds. He had earned just about every toy he had ever wanted. At this point his mother became concerned that he might gain too much weight or that she might go broke paying for rewards. After consultation with us, she terminated the point system. Following termination, there was a substantial drop in his

Figure 17-2
Eating behavior during the first week of intervention.

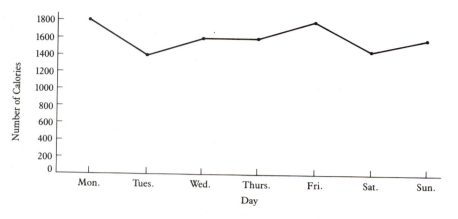

eating behavior for three or four days, but then it increased to about normal levels for his age.

Apparently, the boy's parents had developed a different attitude about his eating behavior. So did the boy. Everybody concerned now knew the boy could eat without negative consequences. The parents refused to permit the boy to get away without eating, and the boy no longer had an excuse not to eat. Although the therapy never attempted to get at an original or hypothetical underlying cause of the behavior, the boy was in every sense cured. He wasn't hospitalized, and his eating behavior was adequate six months following treatment. His mother complained that he was still a finicky eater, but his weight was within normal limits.

The operant approach can be used to solve a variety of problems including smoking cessation, increasing studying time, and losing weight. In each case, you first calculate a baseline. Then you implement an intervention. Finally, you observe the effects of your intervention on the baseline. If you feel you don't study enough, you can try the approach yourself. To assess your study behavior, record the number of minutes you study each day for one week. This is your baseline. Then decide on a reward you can give yourself. Every day record how long you study. Give yourself the reward whenever you study longer than 75% of the average time for your baseline. See whether this procedure doesn't increase the time you spend studying.

B. *Self-Report Techniques*

In our example, the frequency of the 7-year-old boy's disordered eating behavior was recorded by his mother because the assessment process required that someone observe the boy. Not all problems, however, can be so easily and readily observed (Allen, Iacono & Danielson, in press; Mitchell, 1979). Furthermore, when a patient or relative of the subject does the observing and recording, the practitioner must depend on the skill, accuracy, and honesty of the well-meaning but untrained relative. Thus, in the ideal situation, the practitioner or a trained assistant takes the responsibility for observing the individual to be assessed. The practitioner directly observes and records specific problem behaviors in a variety of situations and notes the factors that precede and maintain these behaviors. Naturally, like any observer, the practitioner must make himself or herself as inconspicuous (unobtrusive) as possible so as not to interfere with or influence the subject. Unfortunately, it is difficult, time consuming, and often unrealistic for a trained professional to follow a subject around recording behaviors, and in most cases it is difficult for the observer to avoid influencing the subject. Indeed, it has long been known that the mere presence of an observer may alter the behavior of an individual (Polansky et al., 1949).

One attempt to deal with the problems inherent in obtaining observational data is the self-report technique (Maisto, McKay & Connors, 1990). The typical self-report is a list of statements about particular situations. The subject's task may be either to respond "true" or "false" to each statement or to circle a number (1 to 5, 1 to 7, for example) to indicate the importance or relevance of the statement. Table 17-4 gives examples of the types of statements used. Self-report techniques assume that the person's responses reflect individual differences and are measures of some other observable phenomenon (Tasto, 1977). If, for example, one person circles 5 for fear of snakes and another person circles 1, we would assume that direct observation of these two individuals in the presence of snakes would reveal different, measurable responses. The person who circled 5 might scream and run. The person who circled 1 might simply ignore the snake. Thus, a person's response is assumed to be related to a behavior that can actually be observed. In place of direct observation, the practitioner accepts the face validity of the subject's responses.

Behavioral assessment has concentrated on phenomena such as fear, and this concentration illustrates the major distinction between behavioral self-report procedures and traditional self-report procedures. Behavioral self-report procedures focus on situations that lead to particular response patterns. Traditional procedures focus on relatively enduring internal characteristics of the individual (personality traits) that lead to particular response patterns. In the behavioral approach, situations are seen as the primary determinant of behavior. In the traditional approach, characteristics that the person brings to a situation (for example, traits) are seen as the primary determinant of behavior. Thus, in the behavioral approach, a person is not simply fearful and therefore fearful no matter what the situation; a person is fearful only in certain circumstances or situations because these circumstances elicit fear in that person.

The Fear Survey Schedule. The Fear Survey Schedule (FSS) is the oldest and most researched of the behavioral self-report procedures. It has been in clinical and experimental use since the 1950s and continues to be used for a variety of

Table 17-4
Examples of a
Behavioral
Self-Report

Circle 1 if the item elicits no fear
     2 if the item elicits some fear
     3 if the item elicits a little fear
     4 if the item elicits a lot of fear
     5 if the item elicits extreme fear

Worms	1	2	3	4	5
Bats	1	2	3	4	5
Psychological tests	1	2	3	4	5
Dogs	1	2	3	4	5
Snakes	1	2	3	4	5
Highways	1	2	3	4	5
Men	1	2	3	4	5

Circle true or false as the item applies to you.

I like to talk when in a group.	True	False
I relate easily to persons of the opposite sex.	True	False
I like to walk in dark places.	True	False
I like to give speeches to large groups.	True	False
I feel most comfortable with strangers.	True	False
I feel most comfortable with family.	True	False
I feel most comfortable with friends.	True	False
I like to be the leader in a group.	True	False
I would rather follow than lead in a group.	True	False

purposes (Matias & Turner, 1986). Since the FSS was introduced into the literature by D. A. Akutagawa (1956) as a 50-item test, it has undergone a variety of changes, and various versions have from 50 to 122 items (Lawlis, 1971), with ratings of fear on either five- or seven-point scales. Items are typically related to situations that involve fear and avoidance behaviors, such as fear of open places, fear of snakes, fear of dead animals. Subjects rate each item according to the degree to which they experience that particular fear. Items on the FSS have been derived both from clinical observation of actual cases (Wolpe & Lang, 1964) and from experimental investigations in laboratory settings (Geer, 1965). The FSS attempts to identify those situations that elicit fear and thus avoidance. Once these situations are identified, treatment can be aimed at helping the person to deal with these situations, thus reducing fear.

Social avoidance and depression. Since the introduction of the FSS, behavioral practitioners have developed numerous other self-report techniques to measure a variety of problems. D. Watson and R. Friend (1969) attempted to measure anxiety in society situations with their 28-item true-false Social Avoidance Distress (SAD) scale and 30-item Fear of Negative Evaluation (FNE) scale. B. L. Lubin (1965) published a Depression Adjective Check List (DACL) to assist in the behavioral treatment of depression. In Lubin's depression scale, subjects indicate whether each of 32 adjectives "applies to me" or "does not apply to me." Eight forms are available. A recent tendency has been to combine two or more measures into a single, more effective one (see Blanchard et al., 1986).

Assertiveness. Many individuals have difficulty speaking up for themselves, and often when they finally do speak up, they are aggressive. Suppose someone cuts in front of you in a long line to see a popular movie. Assertiveness experts might suggest that you calmly and firmly inform this person of the location of the end of the line. If you encounter resistance, you calmly explain that everyone has been waiting in line and that the only polite and appropriate thing for the intruder to do is to go to the end of the line. Many people, however, have difficulty acting appropriately in this type of situation. They may stew inside or go to the other extreme and display aggression, such as striking the intruder or throwing a temper tantrum.

A number of behavioral practitioners have constructed measures of assertiveness. Table 17-5 illustrates the type of item found in a behavioral assessment self-report questionnaire for assertiveness, such as the Assertive Behavior Survey Schedule (ABSS). If you were taking the ABSS, you would indicate the responses you would make in specific situations in which assertiveness is indicated. You would also be asked to speculate on the consequences of assertiveness for you. Thus, the ABSS can help determine whether you can be assertive if necessary, situations in which you might have difficulty being assertive, and your personal attitude toward assertiveness.

The availability of many other assertiveness questionnaires illustrates the importance this topic has in behavioral assessment. Another approach was developed by S. A. Rathus (1973). The Rathus Assertiveness Schedule (RAS) consists of 30 items that subjects rate on a six-point scale depending on the extent to which the item applies to them. R. M. McFall and D. B. Lillesand (1971) developed still another assertiveness procedure, the 35-item Conflict Resolution Inventory (CRI). The CRI describes a series of unreasonable requests and asks whether the subject would refuse each request. For example, a fellow classmate who missed the last lecture asks you to recopy your notes, neatly of course, and bring them to his house that night so he can study for the exam scheduled for the next day. Would you comply? What would you say to this person? How would you feel about your response?

Self-report battery. J. R. Cautela and D. Upper (1976) have proposed the use of a self-report battery that incorporates many of the commonly used self-

Table 17-5
Sample Questions
from a Behavioral
Assertiveness
Questionnaire

I. Suppose you were in the following situations. How would you respond? Indicate by circling number 1, 2, or 3.

   A. You have ordered filet mignon for you and your date at an expensive restaurant. You wanted yours cooked rare. The waiter brings it well done. What would you do?

      1. Tell the waiter to bring you another, cooked the way you wanted it.

      2. Complain to the waiter, but eat what he had brought for you anyway.

      3. Say nothing.

   B. You are at a bank. You've been waiting in line for nearly 10 minutes. Finally, you reach the head of the line. A man with a large briefcase comes from the outside and steps right in front of you. What would you do?

      1. Tell him to go to the end of the line.

      2. Tell him there is a long line, but let him go in front of you anyway.

      3. Say nothing.

II. In those situations in which you say nothing, what are you afraid of? (Check the best answer.)

   A. Being yelled at ( )

   B. Being beat up ( )

   C. Being embarrassed ( )

   D. Being rejected ( )

   E. Violating a personal or religious belief ( )

   F. Expending excessive energy ( )

Adapted from Cautela and Upper (1976, pp. 97–98).

report techniques, such as a variety of behavioral self-rating checklists and the FSS. The battery contains three types of scales. Primary scales request general information such as historical data. These scales assess general needs. Secondary scales are designed to yield information about the need for specific techniques such as relaxation or assertiveness training. Tertiary scales require a highly specific response. These scales are designed to yield information about specific problems such as alcohol and drug abuse, overeating, and inappropriate sexual behavior (Cameron & Evers, 1990).

Evaluation of self-report procedures. Obviously, any practitioner with a problem to assess can simply devise and publish a self-report device. Indeed, there appears to be no shortage of such practitioners. Unfortunately, little psychometric data, if any, are ever presented to aid in an evaluation of these devices. The little information that is presented usually is based on poorly controlled correlational studies with highly variable results (Maisto, McKay & Connors, 1990).

The lack of psychometric data on behavioral self-report measures may be the result of the relative newness of these procedures. This lack, however, may also reflect a feeling of many behavioral practitioners that their techniques are fundamentally different from traditional procedures and therefore need not be judged by the same criteria. Nevertheless, in their use of self-report techniques, behavioral psychologists appear to be repeating history and reinventing the wheel. In introducing their self-report battery, for example, Cautela and

Upper (1976) do not hesitate to admit that the prototypes of current self-report techniques are tests such as the Woodworth Personal Data Sheet, which was discussed in Chapter 15. Early paper-and-pencil structured personality tests, which were finally abandoned in the 1930s, are indeed difficult to distinguish from many present-day self-report procedures. Both implicitly assume that a test response can be interpreted on the basis of face validity. Thus, all the problems of interpretation in terms of face validity (subject capacity and willingness to be truthful, response bias, poor reliability, poor validity, lack of norms) generally apply to current behavioral self-report techniques.

Unfortunately, only one of the currently available self-report techniques, the FSS, has been subjected to anything close to an adequate psychometric analysis, and the results are not at all encouraging. In fact, the FSS may be worse than the Rorschach in meeting traditional psychometric standards. D. L. Tasto (1977) lists at least seven different forms of the FSS, with little agreement as to which one is best. No standardized administration procedure exists, and there is little agreement as to how the FSS should be scored or interpreted. The generalizability of the FSS is questionable because most of the studies with the procedure have used primarily college students as subjects. Reliability studies have shown that the FSS is internally consistent, with split-half reliability coefficients exceeding .90 (Geer, 1965; Hersen, 1971). However, test-retest reliability studies have produced varied and inconsistent results (Braun & Reynolds, 1969; Suinn, 1969a). Almost no norms are available. Efforts to provide evidence of the validity of the FSS by correlating it with traditional measures of anxiety, such as the Taylor Manifest Anxiety Scale, have produced correlations as high as .80 (Lang & Lazovik, 1963) and as low as .39 (Geer, 1965). However, it has been shown that fear questionnaire data can aid in a differential diagnosis among various types of anxiety disorders (Oei, Moylan & Evans, 1991).

Clearly, behavioral practitioners have a long way to go before behavioral self-report procedures can be offered as anything more than idiosyncratic clinical tools. However, when used in conjunction with other sources of data, such as psychophysiological recordings and direct observation, self-report data can provide useful information in clinical as well as research settings. Indeed, the modern trend is to use self-report data in conjunction with more direct observations and physiological recordings (Haynes, 1991, 1992; Matias & Turner, 1986).

C. *Kanfer and Saslow's Functional Approach*

In our discussion of behavioral assessment procedures based on operant conditioning, we mentioned Kanfer and Saslow's (1969) original concepts of behavioral deficits and excesses. Now we would like to discuss this approach in detail because it goes beyond the principles of operant conditioning. Indeed, Kanfer and Saslow are among the most important pioneers in the field of behavioral assessment.

Kanfer and Saslow's method of behavioral assessment provides an alternative to the traditional diagnostic labeling of the medical model (neurotic, psychotic, and so forth). These authors propose what they call a *functional (behavior-analytic) approach* to assessment. Rather than labeling people schizophrenic or neurotic, this approach focuses on behavioral excesses and deficits. As previously indicated, a *behavioral excess* is any behavior or class of behaviors described as problematic by an individual because of excesses in its frequency, intensity, duration, or because of its inappropriateness. The functional approach adheres to the underlying assumptions of the learning approach to the study of disordered behavior. This approach assumes that normal and disordered behavior both develop according to the same laws and differ only in extremes. Taking a shower, for example, is a normal behavior. What about taking two showers a day? Clearly, the laws that govern the acquisition of the behaviors involved in taking one shower are the same as those for taking two showers. What about eight showers a day? Consider three hour-long showers a day, or showers taken within minutes after company comes for an unexpected visit. Behavior is abnormal only because of excessive frequency, intensity, duration, or inappropriateness. Similarly, most of us blow off steam by yelling every now and then. However, if you yell every 30 seconds at an extreme intensity and you keep on yelling for up to half an hour, especially when you go to the public library, then your yelling behavior is clearly extreme and maladaptive.

Behavioral deficits are classes of behaviors described as problematic because they fail to occur with sufficient frequency, with adequate intensity, in appropriate form, or under socially expected conditions (Kanfer & Saslow, 1969). Lack of assertiveness, for example, may be viewed as a behavioral deficit. Again, the behavior, or lack of it, is not by itself a disorder. If, for example, a gang of high school dropouts drive their motorcycles into the parking spot you were prepared to pull into, then it may not be too wise to say, "That's my spot; there's another around the block." Finding another parking spot yourself is probably far more adaptive behavior.

Besides isolating behavioral excesses and deficits, a functional analysis involves other procedures, including clarifying the problem and making suggestions for treatment. In the traditional approaches, knowing a person has a particular disorder or conflict does little to suggest treatment strategies. However, when behavioral excesses are identified, efforts can be made to reduce the intensity, frequency, and so forth, of these behaviors. When behavioral deficits are identified, efforts can be made to provide new behaviors or increase the frequency of existing behaviors.

D. *Cognitive-Behavioral Assessment Procedures*

Whereas behavioral assessments based on operant conditioning, self-reports, and Kanfer and Saslow's functional analysis are relatively established, cognitive-behavioral assessment is a new and exciting development. The more established techniques of behavioral assessment, in general, concentrate on overt behavior and the situations that lead to particular behavioral patterns. Cognitive-behavioral assessment, however, evaluates the thinking patterns and other processes that are believed to lead to behavior, including beliefs, expectations, and statements that the person makes to himself or herself (self-statements). As with other areas of behavioral assessment, treatment interventions and the testing processes are linked.

A major pillar of cognitive behavioral assessment is A. T. Beck's (1967, 1976) Cognitive Model of Psychopathology. The model is based on the notion of schemas, which are cognitive frameworks or organizing principles of thought. For example, in your first impression of an individual, you create a schema of that person. In your subsequent interactions with that person, you add to or subtract from that original schema. Moreover, the original schema influences your subsequent perceptions. For instance, if you originally pegged the person as a nerd, then you are likely to label subsequent behavior accordingly. According to Beck, schemas serve to organize prior experience, guide the interpretations of new experiences, and shape expectancies and predictions. Beck's theory holds that dysfunctional schemas predispose an individual to develop psychopathology (Beck et al., 1991).

To evaluate negative schemas, Beck and colleagues have developed the Dysfunctional Attitude Scale (DAS) (Weissman, 1979; Weissman & Beck, 1978). The purpose of the DAS is to identify beliefs that might interact with a stressor to produce psychopathology. Such a belief may be that it is impossible to find happiness without being loved by another or that turning to someone else for advise or help is an admission of weakness. The subject is provided with a list of statements such as "Others can care for me even if they know all my weaknesses" and is asked to respond on a seven-point Likert scale ranging from "totally agree" to "totally disagree." The validity of the scale is supported by a variety of factor analytic data (Beck et al., 1991; Cane et al., 1986).

In a discussion and review of cognitive-behavioral assessment, P. C. Kendall and G. P. Korgeski (1979) discuss several different types: thought sampling, assessing imagery, assessing beliefs, and assessing self-statements. We briefly discuss each of these procedures. In the thought-sampling approach, there is an effort to obtain a random sample of a person's thoughts. E. Klinger (1978), for example, provides the individual with a portable beeper, which goes off at varying intervals. When it does, the individual records his or her thoughts at the moment using a Thought Sampling Questionnaire (TSQ). The TSQ allows the individual to rate inner experience on a variety of variables including vividness and controllability. E. Klinger, S. Barta, and T. Mahoney (1976) have shown that people spend more time thinking about their current concerns than about other subjects. Therefore, the TSQ presumably provides a measure of the person's most important and pressing current concerns (Kendall & Korgeski, 1979, p. 4).

The ability to visualize or imagine is essential in many techniques of behavior therapy. Therefore, a number of procedures have been developed to assess how well an individual can visualize. M. Hiscock (1978) examined these various procedures. Unfortunately, Hiscock's review reveals a very poor correlation among the various measures of imagery. Thus, far more work is needed in this area if the behavioral tests of imagery are to achieve respectable levels of validity.

According to the social learning viewpoint, human behavior is often determined by beliefs and expectations rather than by what may be true in reality. If, for example, your instructor announces that there is to be an exam in the third week of classes, you will do most of your studying for it the day or two before if you are like most students. Suppose, however, you miss the class just before the announced exam. And suppose that a "friend" of yours plays a trick on you. He telephones and tells you the exam has been canceled. If you believe him and therefore expect that there will be no exam, will you study as hard as you would have before (if at all)? It's unlikely. The exam will still be given (reality), but your behavior is different because you believe the exam has been canceled. In view of the importance of beliefs and expectations in determining behavior, a number of behavioral tests have been developed to measure them. R. A. Jones (1968), for example, developed a 100-item Irrational Beliefs Test (IBT) to measure irrational beliefs (for example, the belief that you must always succeed to be worthwhile).

The IBT has found widespread use in clinical as well as research settings, and considerable attention has been devoted to it in recent years (Deffenbacher et al., 1986; Ellis, 1985; Lohr & Bonge, 1982). The IBT requires subjects to indicate their level of agreement or disagreement with each of the 100 items on a five-point scale (for example, "I frequently worry about things over which I have no control"). Half of the items indicate the presence of a particular irrational belief; the other half, its absence.

The reliability of the IBT appears to be similar to that of structured personality tests, with test-retest coefficients for short intervals (two weeks or less) ranging from .48 to .90 for individual scales and .88 for the full scale. The validity documentation of the IBT is weak and questionable (Smith & Zurawski, 1983), although the IBT does appear to be related to both anxiety and depression (Cook & Peterson, 1986; Deffenbacher et al., 1986). Given the current interest in cognitive approaches to therapy, it is likely that there will be considerable use of the IBT and similar procedures in the years ahead.

What people say to themselves also influences behavior. If you tell yourself that you can't learn statistics, then you are likely to avoid statistics. Furthermore, when confronted with a difficult statistics problem, you are likely to give up easily. If you tell yourself you like statistics, however, you probably look forward to studying statistics. When you confront a difficult statistics problem, you are likely to take your time and systematically figure out the answer. Self-statements have been shown to be influential in behaviors as diverse as assertiveness (Schwartz & Gottman, 1976) and coping behavior in cardiac patients (Kendall et al., 1979). It is interesting that positive and negative self-statements don't function in the same way. Apparently, negative self-statements do far more harm than positive self-statements do good. Thus, treatment generally involves identifying and then eliminating negative self-statements rather than increasing positive self-statements. Try to become aware of your own self-statements for a moment. What do you say to yourself as you go about your daily activities? The odds are, if you are making a lot of negative self-statements, you are hindering your personal efficiency and ability to cope.

One of the most important examples of the cognitive-behavioral assessment approach is D. Meichenbaum's (1976) technique called *cognitive functional analysis*. The premise underlying a cognitive functional analysis is that what a person says to himself or herself plays a critical role in behavior. The cognitive functional analyst is thus interested in internal dialogue such as self-appraisals and expectations. Again, what do you say to yourself about yourself as you go about your daily activities? Do you constantly criticize or belittle yourself? Or do you always reassure yourself of your capabilities? Research clearly indicates these self-statements influence your behavior and even your feelings (Meichenbaum, 1976).

Meichenbaum's cognitive functional analysis is an extension of previously discussed behavioral assessment procedures. Like other forms of behavioral assessment, cognitive functional analysis is concerned with ascertaining the environmental factors that precede behavior (environmental antecedents) as well as the environmental factors that maintain behavior (environmental consequences). In addition, however, a cognitive functional analysis attempts to ascertain the internal or cognitive antecedents and consequences for the behavioral sequence (the internal dialogue). What does the person say to himself or herself prior to, during, and following behavior? What is said prior to the behavior may influence what is done. What is said during the behavior may influence the manner in which the behavior manifests itself. What is said following the behavior may influence its probability of recurrence (Meichenbaum & Turk, 1976).

If thoughts influence behavior, then modifying thoughts can lead to modifications in behavior. That is, to the extent that thoughts play a role in eliciting or maintaining a behavioral sequence, modification of the thoughts underlying the sequence should lead to behavioral changes. If, for example, the thought "I must have a cigarette" is consistently associated with the behavioral sequence involved in smoking, then changing that thought to "My lungs are clean, I feel healthy, and I have no desire to smoke" should modify the person's pattern of smoking behavior.

Paralleling Meichenbaum's technique of cognitive functional analysis are procedures and devices that allow a person to test himself or herself. These procedures are typically known as *self-monitoring devices*. Because behavioral practitioners value the role and responsibility of the individual in the therapeutic process, they have developed a wide variety of these devices. In the simplest case, an individual is required to record the frequency of a particular behavior—that is, to monitor it so that he or she becomes aware of the behavior. To monitor your smoking behavior, simply count the number of cigarettes you

Table 17-6
Summary of
Cognitive-
Behavioral
Procedures

Scale or Technique	Author	Goal
Dysfunctional Attitude Scale (DAS)	Beck and colleagues	Evaluates negative schemas
Thought Sampling Questionnaire (TSQ)	Klinger	Samples thoughts randomly
Irrational Beliefs Test (IBT)	Jones	Measures irrational beliefs
Cognitive functional analysis	Meichenbaum	Analyzes internal dialogue

smoke each day. To monitor your weight, weigh yourself each morning and record the number of pounds.

Some self-monitoring procedures are quite sophisticated (Mahoney, 1974). For example, a mechanical counter marketed to the general public can be attached to the jaw in order to count the number of bites a person takes when eating. The idea is to take fewer bites each day, even if it's only one fewer than the day before. Presumably, this procedure will ultimately result in a lower intake of food and eventually weight loss. Related to mechanical counters are timing devices that permit an assessment of how long a person engages in an activity. In one method, the subject is required to plug in a clock every time he or she studies, thus recording total study time. The goal is to increase this length of time, either by increasing the length of individual study sessions or by increasing the total study time within a specific period. These self-monitoring assessment tools are limited only by the imagination of the practitioner. N. H. Azrin and J. Powell (1968) developed an electronic device attached to a cigarette case. The device counts the number of times the case is opened. Treatment is aimed at opening the case fewer times each day. Naturally, it is easy to cheat with these devices, but to think of this possibility is to miss the point of these procedures. These devices help people help themselves by increasing awareness through feedback. You test yourself. If you cheat, you cheat yourself. See Table 17-6.

E. *Psychophysiological Assessment Procedures*

Seen as a variant of behavioral assessment by some and as an independent category by others, psychophysiological methods of assessment utilize such indicators as heart rate, blood pressure, galvanic skin response (GSR), and skin temperature to assess psychological problems (Haynes, 1991; Iacono, 1991). In essence, psychophysiological assessment procedures attempt to quantify physiological responses. This quantification is then translated into psychological factors (Steptoe & Johnston, 1991). Thus, physiological data are used to draw inferences concerning the psychological state of the individual (Fredrikson, 1991). As S. N. Haynes (1991) states, "A fundamental tenet of [psychophysiological assessment] is that social, behavioral, cognitive, and emotional phenomena are often a function of, and are often reflected in, physiological processes" (p. 307).

The feasibility of psychophysiological assessment received support in an early study conducted by A. F. Ax (1953). Ax demonstrated that the fear response was related to specific physiological changes such as increases in blood pressure and skin conductance levels. He found that he could distinguish fear and anger based on physiological data. Ax's early work, which has subsequently been supported (see Ekman, Levenson & Friesen, 1983; Turpin, 1991), had interesting implications. For instance, it suggested the possibility of assessing abnormally chronic and intense anger or fear through strictly physiological methods. This type of assessment would be a quantum leap from traditional procedures, which depend on a voluntary response from the subject. In addition, as with other methods of behavioral assessment, psychophysiological assessment has direct implications for treatment (Haynes, 1992).

The polygraph and related devices that measure blood pressure, heart rate, and galvanic skin response (GSR) have been the primary tools of the psychophysiological assessment specialist. However, imaginative researchers continue to add to this hardware. For example, psychophysiologists have been particularly interested in measuring sexual response and sexual arousal in men and women.

Measures of sexual arousal make use of the fact that it is directly related to the flow of blood into the penis in men and into the vagina in women (Masters & Johnson, 1966). Using this knowledge, researchers have developed measures of sexual arousal in both men and women. In men, for example, penile erection can be measured by the penile transducer (Baxter, Barbaree & Marshall, 1986; Zuckerman, 1971), a device that encircles the penis. As erection occurs, an electrical signal is generated, and this signal can then be recorded. The procedure can be used to determine the type of stimuli (pictures, fantasies, men, women, and so forth) that lead to arousal in men as well as the strength of the male sexual response. The penile transducer and related devices are much more objective than are traditional tools. Again, however, this type of assessment is still in the exploratory stages and thus far from perfected.

Support for psychophysiological assessment has come from investigations that have revealed a systematic covariation between measurable physiological processes and cognitive processes (Iacono, 1991; Jennings, 1986). For example, S. Ahern and J. Beatty (1979) found that more intelligent subjects show smaller task-evoked pupillary dilations than less intelligent subjects (as evaluated by their scores on the Scholastic Aptitude Test). These results reveal physiological differences in individuals with differing mental abilities. In other studies, Beatty and colleagues (for example, Geiselman, Woodward & Beatty, 1982) used measures of heart rate variability and skin conductance to evaluate processing intensity, the amount of effort or energy devoted to a cognitive task. Presumably, brighter individuals expend less of their total available processing resources in solving a difficult problem, either because they have greater resources or because they make more efficient use of them.

Psychophysiological hardware seems to hold considerable promise for raising the scientific respectability of psychological testing. Problems still remain, however, and considerably more research and development are needed. One of the most serious problems in psychophysiological assessment concerns artifacts. For instance, movement by the person may result in recording a physiological response that did not occur. In many cases, furthermore, direct measurement is difficult if not impossible. In measuring brain-wave patterns, for example, electrodes are placed on the head, whereas the electrical current measured actually comes from the brain. Thus, the skull distorts the electrical impulse measured by the recording device. There are other problems as well, including the long-known effect of initial values (Wilder, 1950). According to the concept of initial values, the strength of a response is influenced by the absolute prestimulus strength. Is an increase in heart rate from 60 to 85 beats per minute or an increase from 110 to 125 beats per minute the stronger response? Obviously, one must take initial values into account in evaluating the strength, intensity, and significance of a physiological response. Another problem, which has been seen throughout our discussion of tests, is that demographic factors such as age, gender, and ethnicity influence psychophysiological responses (Anderson & McNeilly, 1991). Thus, cultural, ethnic, economic, gender, and other variables must always be considered in taking any kind of assessment. In spite of these problems, psychophysiological procedures appear to hold great promise for the future of psychological testing.

III. *Computers and Psychological Testing*

A major development has been the application and use of computers in testing (Farrell, 1989, 1992a). Computers can be used in one of two major ways. They can be used to create new tasks and perhaps measure abilities that cannot be tapped by traditional procedures. In addition, computers can be programmed to administer, score, and even interpret traditional tests. In this last section on alternatives to traditional procedures, we briefly discuss each of these two recent applications of computers to the testing field.

A. *Psychophysical and Signal Detection Procedures*

An early impetus for using computers to generate tasks that cannot be presented through traditional methods came from the application of psychophysical and signal detection procedures. In these procedures, a signal is presented and the subject is required to report whether he or she saw it. Many variations in presenting a signal are possible. The examiner can vary the strength of the signal, use more than one signal and require the subject to guess which one has been presented, or follow the signal with noise or another signal to determine the effects of one signal on another.

```
Target:              T   or   A

                         X
Mask:                X   X
                         X
```

Figure 17-3
Target and mask in signal detection. In signal detection experiments, the target and mask are presented to the same visual area in close temporal succession. The minimum interval between presentation of the target and presentation of the mask at which the mask no longer interferes with processing of the target is used to evaluate the information-processing speed.

D. P. Saccuzzo and colleagues (Saccuzzo, 1977, 1981; Saccuzzo & Braff, 1981, 1986; Saccuzzo et al., 1979; Saccuzzo & Miller, 1977; Saccuzzo & Schubert, 1981) suggest that psychological disorders can be evaluated, and perhaps detected in their early stages, by psychophysical methods. In a series of studies beginning with Saccuzzo, Hirt, and Spencer (1974), Saccuzzo has provided considerable evidence that the severe psychological disorder of schizophrenia may be related to the speed with which information is transferred throughout the nervous system. If schizophrenia does in fact develop because of slow processing by the individual, then it would seem sensible to use a direct measure of processing speed to assess schizophrenia rather than indirect procedures such as the Rorschach.

Indeed, information-processing speed can be assessed by flashing two stimuli in brief succession on a microcomputer screen or a tachistoscope. If a stimulus, such as the letter T, is presented and then terminated, the information is first registered by the nervous system. After the information is registered, it theoretically enters a brief perceptual memory system, which U. Neisser (1967) calls *iconic storage*. The person does not become consciously aware of the stimulus until it is transferred to the higher brain centers, where it is compared with previous learning. The rate of this transfer of information is the speed of information processing (Saccuzzo, Hirt & Spencer, 1974).

If a stimulus is presented, terminated, and then followed by a second, noninformational stimulus, such as a random pattern, the second and first stimuli may integrate in the visual system. Only this unidentifiable composite will then be transferred to the higher brain centers. Obviously, if this occurs, the individual is not able to identify the originally presented T. However, if the T is transferred to the higher centers before the noninformational stimulus is presented, the person is able to identify the letter. By finding the minimum interval between presentation of the letter and presentation of the noninformational stimulus at which the noninformational stimulus no longer interferes with processing of the letter, it becomes possible to estimate how long it took the letter to reach the higher centers (Saccuzzo & Miller, 1977). Thus, the speed of information processing can be determined by finding this minimum interval. (See Figure 17-3.)

Saccuzzo and colleagues have shown that schizophrenic persons can be distinguished from normal persons and others (for example, neurotic persons) on the basis of information-processing speed (see Saccuzzo, 1986). Normal persons require a much shorter interval to avoid the effects of the noninformational stimulus. For example, Saccuzzo, Hirt, and Spencer (1974) showed that normal persons and hospitalized nonschizophrenic persons reached maximum performance with only a 150-millisecond interval between presentation of the letter and presentation of a second, noninformational stimulus. The schizophrenic persons, however, required an interval of 300 milliseconds to reach maximum performance. This finding suggests that schizophrenic persons process information more slowly than normal persons do and that schizophrenic persons can be distinguished from normal persons on the basis of the length of the interval between the two stimuli required for maximum performance. This approach, which is only in its infancy, offers a variety of advantages over other procedures: scoring can be simplified, administration can be easily standardized, and the effects of the examiner can be minimized.

Psychophysical and signal detection procedures have also been applied to ability testing (Jensen, 1982; Nettelbeck, 1982). Reaction time and backward masking tasks (in which a briefly presented informational target stimulus is followed by a noninformational noise stimulus, known as a mask) are used to measure the speed, capacity, or efficiency of information processing (Saccuzzo, Larson & Rimland, 1986). The general idea is that better or faster information-processing capabilities are the underlying difference among individuals who differ in psychometric intelligence (Hunt, 1980; Jensen, 1986).

Support for a relationship between information-processing capabilities and individual differences in intelligence has come from choice reaction time studies in which the individual is required to make a rapid response to two or more alternative choices (Jensen, 1979; Jensen & Munro, 1979; Lunneborg, 1978; Smith & Stanley, 1983). When parameters such as median reaction time, slope of reaction time as a function of the number of choices, and intraindividual standard deviations of reaction time performance are used, large differences emerge between groups of retarded persons and persons with normal IQs as well as between groups of vocational college students and university students (Jensen, 1980, 1982). However, results differ across samples (Lunneborg, 1978). Although the correlations vary widely, with estimates ranging from the high .60s to the low .20s, the correlations are almost always in the expected direction (Jensen, 1982).

The visual paradigm for studying the relationship between information processing and intelligence, in which the subject must respond to a visual stimulus, parallels the backward masking approach used by Saccuzzo and colleagues to study schizophrenia. The subject is required to discriminate between two briefly exposed target stimuli, such as identifying which of two lines presented to the right and left of central fixation is longer (see Figure 17-4). The targets are then followed by a spatially overlapping, noninformational mask (for example, two uniform lines that completely superimpose the

Stimulus: _____ ● _____

Mask: _____

Figure 17-4
Stimuli used in signal detection studies of intelligence. The stimulus and mask are presented in close temporal succession. The subject's task is to estimate which line is longer.

lines of the target stimulus). Extensive literature indicates that the mask limits the time the informational impulse is available for processing in the nervous system (Felsten & Wasserman, 1980). Speed of processing, or inspection time (Vickers, Nettlebeck & Willson, 1972), can be evaluated by systematically varying the exposure duration of the target and estimating the minimum duration needed for criterion accuracy (Brand, 1981; Lally & Nettelbeck, 1977; Nettelbeck & Lally, 1976) or by keeping the stimulus duration constant and varying the interval between target and mask (Saccuzzo et al., 1979; Saccuzzo & Marcus, 1983).

Numerous studies have reported a statistically significant (nonchance) difference between mentally retarded and nonretarded (average IQ) individuals in their speed of visual information processing as evaluated in a backward masking paradigm (Saccuzzo et al., 1979; Saccuzzo & Michael, 1984). Such differences occur in spite of wide variations in the nature of the stimuli, method of stimulus presentation, and technique used to estimate visual processing speed (Saccuzzo & Michael, 1984). In addition, there are clear-cut developmental differences, with the general finding of a direct relationship between chronological and/or mental age and performance (Blake, 1974; Liss & Haith, 1970; Saccuzzo et al., 1979). Finally, the evidence supports a significant relationship between degrees of normal intelligence and visual information processing. As in reaction time studies, however, correlations vary widely, and the magnitude of the relationship remains highly controversial (Mackintosh, 1981; Nettelbeck, 1982).

Recently, the reaction time and backward masking tasks have been adapted for presentation by inexpensive personal computers, such as the Apple II and IBM PC (see Brand, 1981; Saccuzzo, Larson & Rimland, 1986; Saccuzzo & Larson, 1987). With the standard programs available, it seems possible that results from psychophysical and signal detection procedures can be readily verified by independent investigators. Thus far the findings seem to indicate a clear-cut, but modest, relationship between information-processing capabilities and intelligence. In their present state of development, however, such procedures are no substitute for traditional tests. If they eventually prove to be a valid substitute, the objectivity of assessment may be markedly enhanced.

B. *The Computerization of Traditional Tests*

Another major application of computers is the computerization of traditional tests. A number of studies have shown that presentation of traditional test content by computer does not appreciably reduce reliability or validity (Greaud & Green, 1986; Lee, Moreno & Sympson, 1986).

As R. D. Fowler (1985) notes, computers began to be applied to psychological testing almost as soon as they were available. However, the increase in application of computer technology to traditional testing has been all but geometric during the 1980s and 1990s. Currently, there are numerous programs for administering, scoring, and even interpreting a host of personality tests, including the MMPI and Rorschach (see Butcher, Keller & Bacon, 1985; Fowler, 1985).

Of course, the new developments in computerized testing are not without controversy and problems (Hofer & Green, 1985). Although computers may be able to score and even administer traditional tests without reducing reliability or validity, interpretations based on a computer program must be approached with great caution (Moreland, 1985). If the clinicians who use such reports are not adequately trained to recognize errors and be cognizant of the limitations of computerized test interpretations, great harm can come to consumers of psychological testing services. Again, cautious optimism and far more empirical research are called for.

C. *Computerization of Behavioral Assessment*

More recently, computers have been used in behavioral assessment. A. D. Farrell (1992b), for instance, identifies seven major applications of computers to behavioral assessment: (1) collecting self-report data, (2) coding observational data, (3) directly recording behavior, (4) training, (5) organizing and synthesizing behavioral assessment data, (6) analyzing behavioral assessment data, and (7) supporting decision making. As Farrell notes, the computerization of behavioral self-report tests, such as those discussed earlier in the chapter, would be a relatively simple endeavor. Once computerized, such questionnaires could be easily administered and immediately scored by the computer, thus saving valuable professional time.

According to Farrell (1992b), a number of factors continue to impede the widespread use of computers in behavioral assessment. Perhaps first among these is lack of acceptance by practitioners. Many practitioners simply have no experience with computers and so avoid them, although attitudes seem to be changing in a favorable direction (Farrell, 1989). Another obstacle to the use of computers in behavioral assessment involves evelution of software (Farrell, 1992b). Apparently vendors are reluctant to make their products available for review; consequently, potential users do not have sufficient information to evaluate the quality of the software. Despite such obstacles, it seems inevitable that the future will see a greater use of computers in all areas of assessment.

Summary

Behavioral procedures differ from traditional tests in that they are more direct, have fewer inferential assumptions, and remain closer to observables. Traditional tests are based on the medical model, which views the overt manifestations of psychological disorders merely as symptoms of some underlying cause. This underlying cause is the target of the traditional procedures. Behavioral tests are based on the belief that the overt manifestations of psychological disorders are more than mere symptoms. Although these overt manifestations may be caused by some other factor, they, rather than a hypothetical cause, are the targets of behavioral tests.

In behavioral assessment based on operant conditioning, the first task is to identify the critical response or responses involved in a disorder. These critical responses are then evaluated for frequency, intensity, or duration. The resulting data provide the baseline for the particular behaviors. Once a baseline is obtained, an intervention is introduced. The effect of this intervention on the baseline is then observed.

Self-report techniques of behavioral assessment focus on situations that lead to particular response patterns; traditional procedures focus on determining the internal characteristics of the individual that lead to particular response patterns. Furthermore, more than traditional procedures, the behavioral procedures purport to be related to observable phenomena. Four major types of behavioral self-report techniques are the FSS, the ABSS, the DACL, and the self-report battery.

Kanfer and Saslow (1969) developed the functional, or behavior-analytic, approach to behavioral assessment. Rather than labeling people as schizophrenic or neurotic, this approach focuses on behavioral deficits and behavioral excesses. A behavioral excess is any behavior described as problematic because of excesses in its frequency, intensity, duration, or because of its inappropriateness; a behavioral deficit is the opposite (occurs too infrequently, for example).

Behavioral assessment based on operant conditioning, self-reports, and functional analyses concentrates on overt behaviors and the situations that lead to particular behavioral patterns. Cognitive-behavioral assessment, by contrast, evaluates thinking patterns and thinking processes that lead to certain behavior, including beliefs and expectations. Kendall and Korgeski (1979) discuss several approaches to cognitive-behavioral assessment, including thought sampling, assessing imagery, assessing beliefs, and assessing self-statements.

One of the most important examples of the cognitive-behavioral assessment approach is Meichenbaum's (1976) technique, cognitive functional analysis. The premise underlying cognitive functional analysis is that what a person says to himself or herself plays a critical role in determining behavior. A cognitive functional analysis ascertains the environmental factors that precede behavior as well as those that maintain behavior. In addition, a cognitive functional analysis attempts to ascertain the internal or cognitive antecedents and consequences for a behavioral sequence.

Of the alternatives to traditional psychological tests, behavioral assessment is by far the most important and most extensively developed. However, an important recent development has been the application of computers to testing. Computers can be used to present new tasks or traditional task content. In the psychophysical and signal detection approaches, computers are used to present tasks that cannot be given by traditional means. The subject is required to make a visual discrimination or to respond rapidly to a stimulus in an effort to measure information-processing capabilities.

Chapter 18

Measures of Anxiety and Stress

Learning Objectives

When you have completed this chapter, you should be able to:

- List the three major types of situations that cause stress.
- Define anxiety and describe how it is usually expressed.
- Describe the difference between state anxiety and trait anxiety.
- Describe the type of anxiety the Taylor Manifest Anxiety Scale was designed to measure.
- Name the first test designed to measure test anxiety.
- Discuss some of the different theoretical orientations that underlie the different test-anxiety measures.
- Describe treatments that can be used to reduce test anxiety.
- Describe the strengths and weaknesses of two different approaches for the assessment of life stress.
- Discuss why it is important to measure coping.
- Discuss the relationship between measures of coping, life stress, and social support.

It is the day of your final exam. You have studied hard and you have every reason to expect an "A." As you enter the classroom, you have a stiff feeling in the back of your neck. Your hands sweat as you get out your pencil. Finally, the long, complicated instructions are over, the materials are distributed, and it is time to work. Yet despite all your preparation, the test does not go the way you had hoped. Instead of concentrating on the task of test taking, you worry about not doing well or you think about running out of time. When it is all over, you feel cheated. You knew the material well, but your grade on the exam does not reflect your knowledge.

If this story describes a situation you have experienced, you have company. Although there are no good figures, this experience is typical for thousands of students and other test takers each year. Test anxiety is a common problem among college students and a major factor in diminishing the validity of tests.

Test anxiety is also an important and active area in psychological research. There are a good many theories (Wine, 1980) about the relationship of anxiety to performance, and these theories have led to the development of a variety of specific test-anxiety scales and measures (see Sarason, 1980). In this chapter, we review the general concepts of anxiety and stress, and then we review in some detail the theory and measurement of anxiety and stress.

I. *Stress and Anxiety*

Stress is a response to situations that involve demands, constraints, or opportunities (Sarason & Sarason, 1980). During our lifetimes all of us will experience some psychological stress. The extent to which it bothers us at different times in our lives, however, is different for each of us. For some people, stress is a debilitating problem that interferes with virtually every aspect of their lives. For others, stress causes problems in particular situations. For still others, stress helps them accomplish important goals. The study of psychological stress has gained an increasingly central position within psychological and biomedical sciences. It has become clear that psychological stress can interfere with performance on mental and academic tests (Sarason et al., 1990), and it is increasingly apparent that stress is a major factor in the disease process. Some medical investigators now believe that stress is involved in 50% to 80% of all illnesses.

Psychological stress has three components: frustration, conflict, and pressure. Frustration occurs when the attainment of a goal is blocked. It may take different forms, but the principle remains the same. If, after being a premed student for four years, you are rejected by all major medical schools, frustration is likely to result. Or if you want to get into a concert and are refused entrance, you may become frustrated. In each case, something or someone has blocked the attainment of a goal. Conflict is a type of stress that occurs when a choice must be made between two or more important goals. For example, you must decide between going to law school and going to graduate school in psychology. The final type of stress is pressure to speed up activities. External pressure occurs when your professor assigns a lot of extra reading right before the midterm exam; internal pressure occurs when no such reading is assigned but you take it on yourself because it fits your style and aspirations (Coleman, 1973).

Exposure to stressful situations can cause an observable reaction known as anxiety. **Anxiety** is an unpleasant emotional state marked by worry, apprehension, and tension. When you are anxious, your autonomic nervous system becomes activated: your heart beats fast, your pulse rate goes up, your hands tend to sweat. The amount of anxiety you experience depends, in part, on the intensity of the stress-producing stimulus as you perceive it. It results from your evaluation of the situation (Spielberger, 1972): How potentially harmful is the situation for you? How threatening? How dangerous?

II. *General Measures of Anxiety*

A. *The State-Trait Anxiety Inventory*

Actually, there are two types of anxiety. Anxiety as described in the preceding paragraph is **state anxiety,** an emotional reaction that varies from one situation to another. **Trait anxiety** is a personality characteristic, reflecting the noticeable differences among the frequencies and intensities of people's emotional reactions to stress; it is a characteristic of the person and not of the situation confronted. Interest in these two types of anxiety led Charles D. Spielberger to develop the state-trait anxiety theory, which in turn led to the development of the State-Trait Anxiety Inventory (STAI). The STAI provides two separate scores: one for state anxiety (A-State) and another for trait anxiety (A-Trait). The STAI A-Trait scale consists of 20 items. Subjects indicate how they generally feel about each item on a four-point scale. A similar set of items is used to evaluate the A-State.

There is good evidence for the validity and the reliability of the STAI. Test-retest reliabilities range from .73 to .86 for the trait scale. The state scale, which is supposed to be inconsistent over time, indeed has low test-retest reliability (.16 to .54). As we noted in Chapter 5, validity defines the range of inferences that can be made on the basis of a score or a measure. Validity studies have shown that the STAI can be used to make several important and useful generalizations. For example, concurrent validity studies have shown that the STAI trait scale correlates well with other measures of trait anxiety. C.D. Spielberger, R. L. Gorsuch, and R. E. Lushene (1970) report a variety of studies in which the STAI trait scale was correlated with the Taylor Manifest Anxiety Scale, which is discussed later. It was also associated with another trait-anxiety scale known as the IPAT Anxiety Scale (Cattell & Scheier, 1961) for the same groups of college students and psychiatric patients. The correlations with the Taylor and the IPAT ranged from .75 to .85, which are quite impressive and suggest that these three scales are, for the most part, measuring much of the same psychological dimension. Other scales that attempt to measure trait anxiety do not do so well. One example is the Affect Adjective Checklist developed by M. Zuckerman (1960). It correlated only moderately with other tests designed to measure trait anxiety. In this case, the concurrent validity correlations ranged from .41 to .57 (Spielberger, Gorsuch & Lushene,

1970). Overall, the STAI seems to measure the same thing as other scales that purport to assess trait anxiety.

In order for us to give a test a positive recommendation, we must go beyond the observation that it correlates well with other tests that supposedly measure the same thing. At least two other conditions must be met. First, we must show that the test measures something that the other tests do not. This is discriminant evidence for construct validity (see Chapter 5). If a new test does just what the old tests could already do, there is no need to develop a new test. Second, the test must be shown to have meaning beyond what is known through its relationships to other tests. Just because a test correlates with other tests does not mean that it is valid for the inferences we want to make. It is possible that the other tests are themselves meaningless.

A good example of a validity study for the STAI is reported by Spielberger and co-workers (1975). This study took advantage of the natural anxiety associated with the anticipation of surgery. Patients who were scheduled to undergo surgery were given the STAI before and after the medical procedure. Patients who had undergone major surgery showed less state anxiety after they had been told they were recovering well than they did before the operation. This finding demonstrates that state anxiety fluctuates with the situation—just as the test constructors say it will. Trait anxiety was not affected by the situation; it remained the same before and after surgery. People high in trait anxiety simply continued to respond in an anxious way, even in situations that evoked little or no anxiety among people low in trait anxiety. Each component of the STAI thus appears to measure what it is supposed to measure. And the two components are clearly assessing different aspects of anxiety.

Over the course of several decades, studies have continually supported the value of the STAI. More recent factor analysis studies have continued to show the two-factor structure. For example, a study involving 205 patients with panic disorder confirmed that state and trait anxiety are two different dimensions, even among people with fairly serious emotional problems (Oei, Evans & Crook, 1990).

Other multidimensional measures. Although the STAI continues to be the most widely used multidimensional measure, several others are now available. For example, Endler et al. (1991) produced the Endler Multidimensional Anxiety Scales (EMAS). These measures are based on a long-standing research program by Norman Endler from York University in Canada. The four factors of the EMAS are based on factor analysis of responses by more than 2000 subjects. The first scale is social evaluation trait anxiety. This measures an individual's predisposition to react to situations that are perceived as being evaluative. Physical danger is the second subscale. This scale measures the fear of being physically damaged or hurt. The third subscale, entitled ambiguous anxiety, describes situations that are ambiguous, new, or uncertain. The final subscale is called daily routines. This is related to anxiety associated with routines in daily life (Endler et al., 1991; Endler & Parker, 1990).

Other recent developments emphasize a larger number of dimensions. For example, F. Koksal and K. G. Power (1990) have developed a Four Systems Anxiety Questionnaire (FSAQ), which emphasizes more recent research that identifies four separate components of anxiety. The first component is somatic, which is reflected in physiological signs such as increased heart rate or sweating. The second two components are cognitive. Cognitive components of anxiety often include two aspects: awareness of one's own irrationality and negative self-statements. The fourth dimension represents feelings about anxiety or the affective-emotional component. The FSAQ separates the cognitive and feeling components into different dimensions. The final component is behavioral, which describes alterations in behaviors as a function of anxiety.

The FSAQ was administered to 218 first-year university students. In addition, a group of 54 anxiety patients from a psychology clinic and 14 agoraphobic (afraid to go outside) patients were evaluated. The analysis demonstrated that a behavioral treatment improved the behavioral dimension for agoraphobic patients. Treatment also had an impact on feelings but did not affect the cognitive component. University students and anxiety patients differed on all four dimensions. Measures such as the FSAQ help us redefine the construct of anxiety. Separating feeling from cognitive components may help clinical psychologists identify the appropriate treatments for people who suffer from anxiety.

B. *The Taylor Manifest Anxiety Scale*

The Taylor Manifest Anxiety Scale grew out of a different tradition within psychology. Janet Taylor was a student (and later wife and widow) of the famous learning psychologist Kenneth Spence. Originally, Taylor was interested in the conditioning of the eyelid response. In eyelid-conditioning experiments, puffs of air are administered to the eyelids in order to cause a blinking response. Over a series of trials, subjects learn to anticipate the puff, and the blink comes to precede rather than follow the air puff. The observation that stimulated the development of the Taylor Manifest Anxiety Scale was that some individuals learned to anticipate the air puff more rapidly than others. Manifest anxiety refers to the effect of anxiety on the performance of a learned task.

According to Spence's learning theory, the performance of a response is partially a function of motivation. In this case, the motivation is anxiety. Thus, Taylor needed to measure anxiety. She began by selecting items from the MMPI (see Chapter 15) that described anxiety states. A partial list of these items and the answers that indicate high anxiety are presented in Table 18-1. Taylor reasoned that her list of items about these rather private events tapped an inferred drive state (Taylor, 1953). When she divided subjects into groups high and low on manifest anxiety, she found that the rate of anticipatory eye blinking was greater for the high-anxiety subjects than for the low-anxiety

Table 18-1

Ten Items from
the Taylor
Manifest Anxiety
Scale

I have very few headaches. (False)
I cannot keep my mind on one thing. (True)
I frequently notice my hand shakes when I try to do something. (True)
I practically never blush. (False)
I have nightmares every few nights. (True)
I sweat very easily even on cool days. (True)
I have a great deal of stomach trouble. (True)
I am usually calm and not easily upset. (False)
I am happy most of the time. (False)
I have been afraid of things or people that I know could not hurt me. (True)

From Taylor (1953, p. 286). Copyright 1953 by the American Psychological Association. Reprinted by permission.

subjects. This experiment demonstrates both the validity of the scale for learning experiments and the plausibility of Taylor's hypothesis about eyelid conditioning and anxiety (Taylor, 1951).

In recent years, the Taylor scale has been found to be of less value because anxiety research has often required more specific measures. Anxiety is no longer regarded as a global trait; rather, there has been a growing tendency to consider specific types of anxiety and to use specific measures. One type of anxiety that has attracted an enormous amount of research attention is test anxiety.

III. *Measures of Test Anxiety*

Few topics in contemporary psychology are as well studied as test anxiety. Test anxiety affects large numbers of students at most levels of the educational system. Most readers of this book have experienced some form of test anxiety. For some, this may have been a debilitating form of test anxiety that interfered with performance on an exam.

We discuss research on test anxiety in more detail than research on other topics for three reasons. This topic is relevant to many college students, test-anxiety research is relevant to many major psychological theories, and test anxiety is a factor that may interfere with performance on all sorts of tests.

Test anxiety has been the object of a lot of theoretical research within psychology for more than 40 years. Much of this research was stimulated by a theory of test anxiety proposed by George Mandler and Seymour Sarason (1952). These theorists described test anxiety as a drive, or motivational state, that could become manifest in two different types of responding—task relevant and task irrelevant. Task-relevant responses are directed toward accomplishing the task at hand. They direct the energy associated with the test situation toward the goal of achieving a good grade. These responses may actually reduce anxiety. The major difficulty for students with test-anxiety problems is with task-irrelevant responses. In a test-taking situation, these students begin to respond in a way that interferes with their performance on the test. Usually, they begin thinking in self-oriented ways; they entertain thoughts such as "I am going to fail." Because they entertain these thoughts at the expense of devoting attention to the items on the test, the result is often a disappointing performance.

Although Mandler and Sarason were from the same theoretical persuasion as Taylor, they concluded that the Taylor Manifest Anxiety Scale was too general as a measure of test anxiety. They decided instead to develop a specific measure of test anxiety and called their product the Test Anxiety Questionnaire. Over the years, people have discovered some inadequacies with this questionnaire and have transformed it into other measures such as the Test Anxiety Scale (Sarason, 1958), the Liebert-Morris Emotionality and Worry Scales (Liebert & Morris, 1967), and the Test Anxiety Inventory (Spielberger, Anton & Bedell, 1976). Others have used different sources of items to construct tests such as the Achievement Anxiety Test (Alpert & Haber, 1960) and the Suinn Test Anxiety Behavior Scale (Suinn, 1969b). In the following sections, we review some of these test-anxiety measures.

A. *The Test Anxiety Questionnaire*

The Test Anxiety Questionnaire (TAQ) is the grandfather of all test-anxiety measures. It was the outgrowth of the Mandler and Sarason (1952) test-anxiety theory. The theory distinguishes between two different drives, or motivational states, that operate in test-taking situations. One is the learned task drive, which is the motivation to emit responses relevant to the task at hand. The other is the learned anxiety drive, which has two components: task-relevant responses and task-irrelevant responses. Mandler and Sarason developed a 37-item questionnaire (the TAQ) that assesses a person's predisposition to think or act in a way that interferes with the completion of a task. In other words, they attempted to build a measure to assess the task-irrelevant responses in the learned-anxiety-drive portion of their theory. Some of the items from the TAQ are presented in Table 18-2. You might check the items to see whether they describe the way you feel during testing situations. Responses to the TAQ items are obtained on a 15-centimeter graphic scale. On the scale, the endpoints and the midpoint are identified. For example, a student is asked whether he or she avoids intelligence tests more or less than other students avoid them. The endpoints of the scale are "more often than other students" and "less often than other students." The midpoint is simply labeled "midpoint."

The reliability of the TAQ is very good. Early studies using a group of 100 Yale students demonstrated that the split-half reliability was .99, and a coefficient of .82 was obtained in a test-retest study over a six-week period. Some validity evidence showed that students who were high in test anxiety actually did more poorly on intellectual tasks than did students who were low in test anxiety (Mandler & Sarason, 1952).

Table 18-2

Some of the
Questions Used in
the Test Anxiety
Questionnaire

4. If you know that you are going to take a group intelligence test, how do you feel *beforehand*?

I..I..I
Feel very confident   Midpoint   Feel very unconfident

9. While taking a group intelligence test, to what extent do you perspire?

I..I..I
Perspire not at all   Midpoint   Perspire a lot

17. Before taking an individual intelligence test, to what extent are you (or would you be) aware of an "uneasy feeling"?

I..I..I
Am not aware of it at all   Midpoint   Am very much aware of it

24. In comparison to other students, how often do you (would you) think of ways of avoiding an individual intelligence test?

I..I..I
More often than other students   Midpoint   Less often than other students

26. When you are taking a course examination, to what extent do you feel that your emotional reactions interfere with or lower your performance?

I..I..I
Do not interfere with it at all   Midpoint   Interfere a great deal

From Mandler and Sarason (1952). Copyright 1952 by the American Psychological Association. Reprinted by permission.

B. *The Test Anxiety Scale*

One of the early criticisms of the TAQ was that it dealt with state anxiety rather than trait anxiety. The first revision of the TAQ began to consider individual or personality differences in test anxiety. In 1958, Irwin Sarason, the brother of Seymour Sarason (the original codeveloper of test-anxiety theory), rewrote the TAQ items in a true/false format to create the 21-item Test Anxiety Scale (TAS). Irwin Sarason agreed with the earlier theory that test anxiety produced interfering responses during test-taking situations, but he also recognized personality differences between people who were high or low in test anxiety. He believed that less test-anxious people respond to test-taking situations by increasing their effort and attention toward the problem they are working on. Highly test-anxious persons react to the threatening situation by making self-oriented and personalized responses, often criticizing themselves rather than working on the test problems.

As you can see, the focus on the test-anxiety problem shifts from the situation in the TAQ to the person in the TAS. Although the TAS and the TAQ are quite similar and are indeed highly correlated, one measure assesses anxiety associated with situations, whereas the other determines which persons are highly test anxious.

Since the introduction of the TAS, Sarason has accumulated convincing evidence that there is a meaningful distinction between more and less test-anxious individuals. For example, there is a difference in the way they respond to instructions. In some experiments, the experimenter intentionally gives instructions that are stress producing—for example, by telling the students that they are expected to finish in a limited time or by telling them that the test they are taking correlates well with measures of intelligence. For subjects who score low on the TAS, these instructions may actually help. Usually less test-anxious students score better under stress-producing conditions. The opposite seems to be true for the more test-anxious group. These individuals tend to do better when the instructions are neutral or reassuring rather than stress producing (Paul & Eriksen, 1964; Sarason, 1958, 1959, 1961, 1975). These studies are valuable for at least two reasons. First, they show that the TAS does make meaningful distinctions between people. Second, they suggest that differences in school performance may be associated with personality characteristics other than intelligence.

Furthermore, the research gives specific hints about the nature of test anxiety. Only the more test anxious say negative things to themselves instead of thinking about the problems on the test. This interference with thought has been found to be most severe for test-anxious people while they are working on difficult tasks (Sarason & Palola, 1960).

Some studies demonstrate that students who score high and low on the TAS also use information in different ways. Those with low scores on the TAS tend to increase their efforts when they are told they have not done well. In other words, if they do not do well, they may try to do better. Given the same feedback, test-anxious persons plunge into themselves instead of plunging themselves into the task (Mandler & Sarason, 1952; Marlett & Watson, 1968; Sarason, 1975).

The differences between more and less test-anxious individuals can also be detected in the way they respond to neutral feedback. After they have been given neutral feedback, students who score high on the TAS tend to respond as though they had just been given bad news, and they do not have much faith in their future success. Those who score low on the TAS tend to be optimistic about their future performance after they have been given neutral feedback (Meunier & Rule, 1967).

Some studies have even shown that when test-anxious individuals are placed in situations in which they will be evaluated (like describing themselves orally for half an hour), they attend most to negative references to themselves. They may not expect others to evaluate them well, and they actively search their environment for information to prove to themselves that this is true. For example, if someone leaves the room during a test, a test-anxious subject may interpret the behavior as an indication that he or she is not working fast enough (Sarason, 1975).

Research using the TAS is among the most extensive in the test-anxiety literature, and it confirms the validity of the TAS as a personality measure. The research shows that poor performance on tests may result from a combination of two factors: being a test-anxious person and being in a situation that arouses anxiety. When they come to an anxiety-arousing testing situation, highly test-anxious individuals may not be able to focus on the task at hand, which in this case is performing well on the test. Instead, they may have to contend with many interfering thoughts such as "My mind's a blank" or "I really feel stupid." Those of you who have had this experience know how distressing it can be. When you should be concentrating on calculating the statistics problem or picking the correct multiple-choice alternative, you begin instead to think that you are running out of time or that you are going to fail.

You may also experience some physiological changes: your heart rate may speed up, your mouth may get dry, you may begin to sweat, you may get an upset stomach or a stiff neck. Recognizing these physical side effects of test taking, some researchers have proposed that these emotional responses be measured separately.

C. *Other Measures of Test Anxiety*

A number of other measures of test anxiety are commonly used in research and practice. R. M. Liebert and L. W. Morris (1967) suggested that test anxiety has two different components: emotionality and worry. Emotionality is the physical response to test-taking situations. It is associated with accelerated heart rate, muscle stiffness, and so on. Worry is the mental preoccupation with failing and with the personal consequences of doing poorly. The Liebert-Morris scales tap these two components separately.

Spielberger, Anton, and Bedell (1976) also created a test-anxiety scale that has both emotionality and worry factors. Spielberger's 20-item Test Anxiety Inventory conceptualizes test anxiety in terms of state and trait. According to Spielberger, worry is a trait that is more consistent over the course of time. Different people worry different amounts about tests. The manner in which arousal is expressed in particular situations is emotionality. Thus, this theory proposes that the emotional component is a state, or situational, aspect. Systematic studies have confirmed that emotionality and worry are independent dimensions of test anxiety. Furthermore, these two dimensions have been observed in both males and females. Females score significantly higher than males on the emotionality components but not on the worry components (Everson, Millsap & Rodriguez, 1991; Zeidner, 1990).

Another approach to the measurement of test anxiety was proposed by R. Alpert and R. N. Haber (1960). Their Achievement Anxiety Test (AAT) is a 19-item scale that gives scores for two different components of anxiety: facilitating anxiety and debilitating anxiety. Debilitating anxiety is similar to the anxiety that all the other scales attempt to measure. The debilitating anxiety scale measures the extent to which anxiety interferes with performance on tests. The novel component of the AAT is facilitating anxiety, a state that can motivate performance. This type of anxiety gets you worried enough to study hard. If you are not anxious at all, you may not be motivated enough to gear up for the exam. Thus, facilitating anxiety is helpful, and debilitating anxiety is harmful.

IV. *Treatments for Test Anxiety*

Throughout this chapter, we have stressed that test anxiety can be a debilitating problem for many college students. If you have problems with test anxiety, you may gain some comfort from knowing that clinical psychologists have sharpened their skills for dealing with test anxiety. The most successful approaches have been those that use some form of behavior modification. The most popular treatments are systematic desensitization (Wolpe, 1969) and cognitive behavior modification. In systematic desensitization, a student systematically learns to relax and then experiences the thought of successively more threatening situations. Cognitive behavior modification combines systematic desensitization with training in which a student learns to say positive things to himself or herself (Meichenbaum, 1972; Kaplan, McCordick & Twitchell, 1979). For example, the student may learn to relax muscles in order to combat

---

FOCUSED EXAMPLE 18-1

Test Anxiety and the Funny Test

Perhaps the most unusual treatment for test anxiety was reported by R. E. Smith and several of his colleagues (1971). These psychologists were aware that some students in their classes had difficulties with test anxiety. They were also aware of several theories that suggest that a good laugh may help alleviate anger and anxiety. Smith and his colleagues used the TAS to determine which of their students were low and which were high in test anxiety. Then half the students in each group were given a funny version of their midterm. The other half were given a serious version. For comparison, some items on each version of the test were identical.

In the funny version, one-third of the items were intended to be humorous. For example, one of the items about abnormal behavior read:

Claiming to be a slot machine, Julius has been standing against a wall in a Las Vegas casino for six years making bell-like sounds and occasionally complaining that he is being tilted. Which other member of Julius's family is most likely to exhibit bizarre behavior? Alternatives: (a) his mother; (b) his sister; (c) his identical twin; (d) it is impossible to make a probability statement.

The results demonstrated that the humorous items did help relieve some of the test anxiety. On the serious version of the test, the highly anxious students did not do as well as those who did not experience much test anxiety. However, on the test with some funny items, the differences between high and low test-anxious students disappeared.

emotional responses during a test and then may also learn to make self-statements such as "I am not going to let this get to me" or "Just relax; I'm in control; concentrate on the exam."

The success of these approaches depends to some extent on the measures used to evaluate them. For example, systematic desensitization is quite effective when it is evaluated by changes in the TAQ, the TAS, or the AAT. However, systematic desensitization and most other therapies are less effective if the measure used is an increase in grade point average. When combined with training in study skills, however, systematic desensitization again appears to be effective even when the measure is grade point average (Allen, 1972; Anton, 1976; Smith, 1977; Spielberger, Anton & Bedell, 1976).

Thus, test-anxious college students may need help not only in reducing their test anxiety but also in improving their study skills. Additional benefits appear when a self-talk component is added to the study skills-desensitization treatment package. Thus, clinical psychologists now are beginning to feel that they have the technology to help college students cope with the debilitating effects of test anxiety. Furthermore, these new approaches appear to effect improvements in classroom performance in addition to positive changes in scores on anxiety inventories (McCordick et al., 1981; Meichenbaum, 1977; Meichenbaum & Butler, 1980). Other methods have also been shown to be valuable. For example, both relaxation exercises and regular physical activity may reduce test anxiety among college students (Topp, 1989). Focused Example 18-1 describes a different approach to treating test anxiety.

V. *Measures of Life Stress*

The research on the relationship between stress and illness requires measures of stressful life events. Table 18-3 shows a very early measure called the Survey of Recent Events (SRE), which lists events that may have occurred in a person's life. This instrument is commonly used in psychiatric research (Holmes & Rahe, 1967; Rahe, 1972). The SRE was designed on the assumption that specific life events have a cumulative impact on well-being. In Table 18-3, each of the events is associated with a life change unit (LCU) value. These are social values that need to be measured. It is easy to see that all the events listed in the table represent life changes, but obviously each life event change cannot be counted as having the same effect. Getting a traffic ticket cannot be considered as disrupting as getting a divorce.

To determine how much weight each of the events has, the investigators had people of different social backgrounds rate the degree of turmoil, upheaval, and social readjustment each of the events causes. Each event was rated in comparison to the life change of getting married, which was arbitrarily assigned the score of 50. For example, people were asked to give a number to the readjustment required by the death of a spouse (if the amount of readjust-

Table 18-3
Values of Life
Change Events*

	LCU Values
Family	
Death of spouse	100
Divorce	73
Marital separation	65
Death of close family member	63
Marriage	50
Marital reconciliation	45
Major change in health of family	44
Pregnancy	40
Addition of new family member	39
Major change in arguments with spouse	35
Son or daughter leaving home	29
In-law troubles	29
Spouse starting or ending work	26
Major change in family get-togethers	15
Personal	
Detention in jail	63
Major personal injury of illness	53
Sexual difficulties	39
Death of a close friend	37
Outstanding personal achievement	28
Start or end of formal schooling	26
Major change in living conditions	25
Major revision of personal habits	24
Changing to a new school	20
Change in residence	20
Major change in recreation	19
Major change in church activities	19
Major change in sleeping habits	16
Major change in eating habits	15
Vacation	13
Christmas	12
Minor violations of the law	11
Work	
Being fired from work	47
Retirement from work	45
Major business adjustment	39
Changing to different line of work	36
Major change in work responsibilities	29
Trouble with boss	23
Major change in working conditions	20

Table 18-3
(*continued*)

	LCU Values
Financial	
Major change in financial state	38
Mortgage or loan over $10,000	31
Mortgage foreclosure	30
Mortgage or loan less than $10,000	17

From Rahe (1972, pp. 250–265).

* Scoring directions: Mark the changes that may have happened in your life within the last six months. Add up the life change unit (LCU) values associated with each of the events you have checked. People who experience the most life changes also experience the most illness (see text).

ment necessitated by marriage is 50). Remarkably, there is little disagreement about these values among raters who differ in age, gender, marital status, education, social class, race, and creed. In addition, there was substantial agreement among people from different cultures. Swedes, Danes, Japanese, and North Americans appeared to regard the impact of life changes in similar ways.

Once the scoring system had been developed, it was possible to create life stress scores and to compare these scores to the amounts of illness contracted (Komaroff, Masuda & Holmes, 1968). A variety of studies demonstrated that there is a small but significant correlation between the life change score for the last six months and the probability of developing an illness. In one study conducted with U.S. Navy personnel, life stress scores were obtained for entire crews before their vessels were sent out to sea. After six months, the sailors and their health records were examined. It was observed that sailors who were in the top 10% in life change scores were twice as likely to become ill as sailors in the bottom 10%. Life crises may have weakened the immune system and made the sailors easier targets for disease.

The relationship between stress and illness continues to be documented in a wide variety of studies (Zales, 1985), including studies on heart disease (Rosenman & Chesney, 1985) and cancer (Biondi & Pancheri, 1985). Recent research is beginning to illuminate the relationship between stress and illness. For example, M. Irwin and co-workers (1987) have demonstrated how two aspects of the immune system (natural killer cell activity and t-cell subpopulations) are affected by bereavement. Women who recently lost a husband had more severe depressive symptoms and lower ratios of helper to suppressor t-cells. Newer evidence has suggested that these same biochemical changes can be induced by a brief (12-minute) stressful mental arithmetic exam (Naliboff et al., 1991). These biochemical events are associated with impaired immunity.

There continues to be debate about the effect of life stress on illness (Kaplan, 1990). However, there is at least some evidence that serious health outcomes are related to the inability to cope with stress. For example, H. J.

Eysenck (1990) has shown that inability to cope with stress, which often results in feelings of hopelessness, helplessness, and desperation, may predict death from serious disease such as cancer. Certainly, this is an area that will continue to attract research attention.

The Survey of Recent Events has been criticized by G. W. Brown, M. N. Bhrolchain, and T. Harris (1975) because the weighting system and interview format are arbitrary and not applicable across all groups of people. Brown and Harris (1978) proposed an alternative method that requires personal interviews to determine when life events occurred and how much ongoing difficulty these events pose in people's lives. It has been argued that Brown's interview method is more appropriate for studies of the elderly (Wilkinson, James & Davies, 1985). S. J. Wilkinson and colleagues (1986) have shown that the test-retest reliability for the Brown scale is indeed adequate for elderly populations. Another approach based on a similar criticism of the SRE is the Life Experiences Survey.

A. *Life Experiences Survey*

The SRE was based on the assumption that specific life events have a cumulative impact on well-being, that the degree of impact is the same for any individual, and that a mean societal evaluation of the desirability or undesirability of an event is appropriate for any individual. For example, the desirability of pregnancy would be determined by the mean scale value that a community assigned to this event, and the mean value would be applied to any woman who became pregnant within some defined time interval. I. G. Sarason, J. H. Johnson, and J. M. Siegel (1978) note that this is not a palatable assumption. A positive pregnancy test may be received as good news by some women and as a disaster by others. Life change measures, they argue, must allow for individual differences in reactions to stress.

A similar assumption in the life stress literature is that positive and negative life events both contribute to probabilities of poor future functioning. This assumption, which is evident from theories of stress, has been so widely accepted that few investigators have attempted to separate positive and negative life events.

I. G. Sarason and B. R. Sarason (1985a) showed the importance of these points by presenting data from a new Life Experiences Survey (LES). The measure includes 47 events that may be appropriate for any subjects and an additional section with 10 items specifically designed for students. The subject's task is to indicate which events have occurred within a specific time period and to record the perceived impact of the event on a scale ranging from -3 for extremely negative to $+3$ for extremely positive. Separating those events with negative weights from those with positive weights yields two separate scores for negative and positive events.

Validity data suggest that the LES negative score correlates with depression, external locus of control, state and trait anxiety, and low grade point average. These variables were not correlated with positive life events. In addition, the LES showed good discriminant validity. To evaluate discriminant validity, estimates of SRE life change units and LES scores were obtained for the same group of subjects, and it was observed that the SRE tended not to correlate as highly with a variety of different measures as did the LES. The LES performed better than the SRE because it allowed individuals to express the extent to which different events bothered them as individuals. For example, with the SRE, any person who had been fired from a job would get the same score. The LES allows the respondent to specify how stressful the event was.

A variety of new measures have been created to record perceived stress. For example, S. Cohen, T. Karnarack, and R. Mermelstein (1983) developed a measure that focuses on the perceived stressfulness of various events. Respondents are asked how often they felt upset because something had happened to them, how often they felt stressed or nervous, how often they felt they could not cope with what was happening, how often they felt angered by things that were happening beyond their control, how often they found themselves thinking about things they had to accomplish, and how often they felt difficulties were piling so high that they could not overcome them.

Some research also shows that it is not just major life events that cause problems. Instead, daily irritations pile up. A. D. Kanner and colleagues (1981) have begun to measure the minor "hassles" in daily life. In addition, they record the small pleasures that may make life more bearable. Some research has demonstrated that daily hassles are better predictors of poor health than are major life events (DeLongis et al., 1982). Thus, it may be the minor irritations that are difficult to cope with. Conversely, small uplifts may improve the ability to cope. Although research on daily hassles has attracted a lot of attention, it is less clear that there is a strong association between hassles and health. For example, among students, daily stress does not predict variations in mental health measures (Johnson & Bornstein, 1991). In the next section, we examine measures of coping with stress.

B. *Measures of Coping*

Measuring the stressfulness of one's environment may not be adequate for an understanding of the relationship between stress and poor health. Different people confronted with the same stressful situation may respond quite differently. In a study by H. Feifel, S. Strack, and V. T. Nagy (1987), the coping styles of two different patient groups were compared. Some of the patients had life-threatening illnesses such as cancer or heart attacks. The comparison group had non-life-threatening illnesses such as skin problems or arthritis. The coping styles were different for the two groups. In particular, those with life-threatening illnesses used confrontation more frequently. It is interesting that acceptance and resignation were not used often by either group. Several measures have been developed to assess the ways people cope with stress (Dupue & Monroe, 1986; Folkman & Lazarus, 1980). One of these measures, the Ways of Coping Scale (Lazarus & Folkman, 1984; Lazarus et al., 1985), is a 68-item checklist. Individuals are presented with thoughts and actions that may be used to deal with stressful situations, and respondents check whether or not they use these strategies. The scale includes seven subscales for problem solving, growth, wishful thinking, advice seeking, minimizing threat, seeking support, and self-blame. Studies using this scale have suggested that the seven subscales can be divided into problem-focused and emotion-focused strategies for dealing with stressful situations. Problem-focused strategies involve cognitive and behavioral attempts to change the course of the stress. In other words, these are active methods of coping. Emotion-focused strategies do not attempt to alter the stressor but instead focus on ways of dealing with the emotional responses to stress.

A related measure is the Coping Inventory (Horowitz & Wilner, 1980), which is a 33-item measure that was derived from clinical interview data. There are three categories of items. The first set describes activities and attitudes people may use to avoid stress. The second category involves items that characterize strategies for working through stressful events. The third set of items considers socialization responses. The respondent indicates whether or not each of these strategies would be helpful for coping with a specific stressful event. These measures and related tests, such as the coping resources inventory (Hammer & Marting, 1985), have been very useful in research on both adults and adolescents. For example, one study demonstrated that coping resources predict lower rates of both psychological and physical symptoms independent of stressful life events. In other words, having good coping capabilities is important whether or not you are under stress (Zeidner & Hammer, 1990).

C. *Measures of Social Support*

Over the last few years, health psychologists have devoted considerable effort to the study of social support. Social support and social resources appear to be significant buffers for stressful life events and moderators of psychological and physical well-being (Sarason & Sarason, 1985b; Turner, 1981). Family, friends, and other social contacts may aid in reducing emotional distress and problems resulting from injuries or other disabilities. Several lines of research suggest that those confronted with serious life events may cope better if they have friends or family to help them absorb shock.

Although definitions vary, most measures of social support include both tangible (financial assistance and physical aid) and intangible (encouragement and guidance) support. Social support has been shown to help mediate stressful life events, speed recovery from illness, and increase the likelihood that a person will follow the advice of his or her doctor. However, there are many inconsistent findings in the literature, and it is difficult to resolve discrepancies because measures of social support vary widely from study to study. When C. A. Heitzmann and R. M. Kaplan (1988) reviewed 26 measures for evaluating social support, they looked for reliability coefficients greater than .80 and documented validity. Correlations between various social support and criterion measures were simulated in order to demonstrate the consequences of choosing a measure with low reliability.

According to the review, few social support measures had adequate documentation of reliability. In addition, documentation of validity was available for only some measures. Evidence for discriminant validity was almost never presented. Perhaps the best example of a social support measure has been presented by I. G. Sarason and co-workers (1983). This measure, known as the Social Support Questionnaire (SSQ), includes 27 items, each with two parts. For each item the respondent must (1) list the people who can be counted on for support in given circumstances and (2) indicate the overall level of satisfaction with these supports. The SSQ yields two scores: the number (N) score for each item is the number of supports the person lists. The satisfaction (S) score ranges from 1 for very dissatisfied to 6 for very satisfied for each of these items. The mean number of persons someone can count on is averaged across the 27 items to get a mean N score, and the satisfaction ratings are also averaged across the items to get a mean satisfaction score.

Sarason and colleagues (1983) conducted a series of studies to determine the reliability and validity of their measure. Based on a normative sample of 602 undergraduate college students, coefficient alpha for satisfaction (S) was .94 and for number (N) was .97. Test-retest correlations over a four-week period were .90 for N and .83 for S. These results indicate that the SSQ is a very stable instrument with high internal consistency. Validity data were based on a number of comparisons between the SSQ and other measurement techniques. A sample of 277 undergraduate students were given the SSQ, the Multiple Affect Adjective Check List (MAACL), and the Lack of Protection scale (LP). There were significant negative correlations between the SSQ-N and SSQ-S and measures of emotional discomfort as tapped by the MACCL. Likewise, items on the LP that deal with recollections of separation anxiety in childhood also correlated negatively with the SSQ.

The interest in social support continues to grow as does the number of measures. Most of the newer measures attempt to identify multiple factors of social support. For example, a new Multidimensional Scale of Perceived Social Support (MSPSS) has been introduced to separate support obtained from family, friends, and significant others (Zimet et al., 1990). The psychometric properties of some of the new measures are improved over the earlier ones. However, this continues to be a field that requires rigorous research investigation.

Comment on theory. This chapter emphasizes the measurement of stress and anxiety. The complex theory that links stress to illness and to performance is beyond the scope of a book on psychological testing, yet measurement is central for the evaluation of these theoretical models. For example, the same levels of stress may cause mental health symptoms for some people but not for others. This may be because stress activates a mental disorder (Monroe & Simons, 1991) or because some people have better social relationships to help them buffer the stress. Evaluating these theories is difficult. For instance, mental health symptoms may bias the report of life stress. New theories about the role of stress in the development of physical and mental problems may stimulate a better understanding of the role of stress in depression or other forms of psychopathology (Monroe & Simons, 1991). Ultimately, research and theory development should stimulate better measures and clinical interventions.

Summary

Test anxiety is a fact of life for many students. In this chapter, we reviewed some of the existing research on the theory and measurement of test anxiety. Research on test anxiety was an outgrowth of general theories of learning. Early studies by Taylor identified anxiety as a motivational state that could be measured with a short scale. Using the scale, she was able to relate anxiety to a general theory that had previously depended primarily on evidence from animal studies. Later developments divided anxiety into state and trait components.

Eventually specific test-anxiety theories were proposed, and test anxiety became an area of study in itself. As test-anxiety theory developed, many scales were devised to measure test-anxiety problems. Different theories emphasized that test anxiety is a general motivational state, is a personality trait, or is related both to situations and to the characteristics of the test taker. In other words, there are many different theories of test anxiety and many different ways of measuring it. Recent developments in psychotherapy hold great promise for the successful treatment of test anxiety.

In recent years, there has been considerable interest in the measurement of life stress. The Survey of Recent Events (SRE) is a list of occurrences that could cause disruption in an individual's life. The events are weighted by the perceived amount of readjustment that would be required to cope with them. Studies have linked scores on these measures with the onset of illness. However, a variety of critiques have demonstrated that the SRE has weaknesses. The Life Experiences Survey (LES) is an alternative approach that allows each individual to weight the amount of readjustment required by particular events in their own lives. The LES may be a superior measure of life stress. Future research will be required to learn more about the relationship among life stress, perceived disruption, and health outcomes. The measurement of health outcomes will be described in more detail in Chapter 19.

In addition to measures of test anxiety and life stress, a variety of measures are available to quantify adaptation to stressful situations. These include measures of coping and measures of social support. Not all individuals faced with the same stresses have the same reactions. Measures of social support and coping help explain why some people are better able to adapt to stressful situations than are others.

Chapter 19

Testing in Health Care Settings

Learning Objectives

When you have completed this chapter, you should be able to:

- Describe at least two important situations in which psychological tests are used in health care.
- Define the term *clinical neuropsychology*.
- Discuss the use of neuropsychological instruments in both childhood and adulthood.
- Describe the Halstead-Reitan test battery.
- Describe the Luria-Nebraska test battery.
- Discuss the advantages of the California Verbal Learning Test.
- Differentiate psychometric and decision theory approaches to quality of life measurement.
- Describe the Sickness Impact Profile.
- Discuss the advantages and disadvantages of measures such as the Index of Activities of Daily Living, the Karnofsky Performance Status, and the McMaster Health Index Questionnaire.
- Discuss the concept of a quality-adjusted life-year.

Today more than 5% of all psychologists are directly employed by hospitals, medical centers, and clinics, and projections indicate that this figure will increase in the future. One of the major functions of psychologists in these settings is to use and interpret measurement instruments. Although we are not able to discuss the wide variety of measures used in medical settings, we focus on two areas that have experienced rapid development in the last few years: neuropsychological assessment and quality of life assessment.

I. *Neuropsychological Assessment*

A. *Clinical Neuropsychology*

Linda was an intelligent, extremely cooperative 7-year-old when she was hit by a car in a tragic accident. She was unconscious for only a short time and appeared to show a rapid physical recovery from the accident. However, by the time one year had passed, her parents had become very concerned about behavioral changes they had observed after the accident. She had become very introverted, did not interact well with others, and seemed anxious, prone to temper tantrums, frustrated, and unable to take criticism. The doctor who had originally examined Linda referred her to a neurologist, who was unable to find anything abnormal in her CAT scans and EEG tests. Unable to determine the source of her difficulties, the neurologist referred Linda to a specialized psychologist trained in neuropsychological assessment. The psychologist discovered that Linda's visual functioning and her ability to talk were superior; however, she had difficulties in auditory functioning and in the ability to write down phonemes she had heard. Furthermore, tests showed that she had done very well on things she had learned before the accident but that she had lost the ability to discriminate among the sounds of letters that were closely related to one another. This in turn caused a great deal of strain and created her belief that she was stupid and unable to keep up with other children. The test that helped identify Linda's specific problem is called the Luria-Nebraska Neuropsychological Battery. After discovering that Linda's problem was very specific, her teachers designed a special education program to adapt learning materials to a visual approach and to avoid auditory presentations. Her parents were also able to adapt to their child's problem once they realized its nature. Given this support and the reduced pressure, Linda's introversion, sensitivity to criticism, and frustration decreased. Over time, as her injuries healed, she returned to normal (Golden, 1981).

The case of Linda shows the importance of a rapidly expanding new field known as **clinical neuropsychology.** Clinical neuropsychology is a scientific discipline that focuses on psychological impairments of the central nervous system and their remediation. One formal definition of neuropsychology is the application of methods from experimental and clinical psychology to the analysis of cognitive and behavioral problems that are caused by injury, disease, or abnormal development of the brain (Levin et al., 1989). The activities of neuropsychologists include identification, description, multivariate quantification, and treatment of diseases of the brain and spinal cord. Clinical neuropsychology is a multidisciplinary endeavor that overlaps with neurology, psychiatry, and psychometric testing in the following ways: Neuropsychology and neurology both focus on sensations and perceptions and on motor movements. Neuropsychology and psychiatry both study mood and adaptations to psychosocial situations. Finally, neuropsychology and psychometrics both use psychological tests. Neuropsychology is different from these other clinical disciplines because it is finely specialized, focusing on attention, memory, learning, language and communication, spatial integration, and cognitive flexibility. In summary, neuropsychology is a field of study that actively attempts to relate brain dysfunction and damage to observable and measurable behavioral problems (Crockett, Clark & Kalonoff, 1981; Grant & Adams, 1986).

Clinical neuropsychology has developed rapidly over the last few decades. In 1970, neuropsychology was viewed as a new field characterized by rapid growth (Parsons, 1970). During the 1970s and early 1980s, there was an explosion of research in neuropsychology and the rapid development of a practice specialty. Currently, neuropsychology has formally joined the ranks of other neurosciences. Neuropsychologists use powerful measurement techniques and have developed many procedures for identifying the relationship between brain problems and behavior problems (Chelune & Edwards, 1981). The activities of neuropsychologists are extremely varied and require some complex technology. An exploration of this important new discipline in any depth would require a review of neuroanatomy and other topics in neuroscience, which we will not discuss owing to space limitations. Instead, we describe some current activities of active neuropsychological research and practice. The interested reader should consult Filskov and Boll (1981), Satz and Fletcher (1981), Hynd and Obrzut (1981), Lezak (1983), and Grant and Adams (1986).

Neuropsychologists are very specialized. Some focus on the study of brain dysfunction in children (Fletcher, Levin & Satz, 1989; Pirozzolo et al., 1981), whereas others work with adults (Heaton & Pendleton, 1981) or older adults (Albert, 1981; Kaszniak, 1986; Welsh et al., 1991). Most of the work in neuropsychology is directed at the assessment of brain dysfunction, but some neuropsychologists are actively developing interventions for those who suffer brain injuries or related problems (Diller & Gordon, 1981). Neuropsychologists also study the impact of mental illness (Caine, 1986; Goldstein, 1986) as well as alcohol abuse (Grant, 1987) or serious diseases such as the Acquired Immune Deficiency Syndrome (AIDS) (Grant & Heaton, 1991) on cognitive processes. Neuropsychologists differ in the methods they apply. Some prefer to use batteries of psychological tests, whereas others prefer specific tasks derived from experimental psychology (Delis et al., 1991; Satz & Fletcher, 1981).

B. *Developmental Neuropsychology*

The study of brain dysfunction in childhood is extremely important. Neuropsychological problems are apparent in speech and reading disorders. These disorders, known as *learning disabilities,* account for problems in significant numbers of young children. **Dyslexia** is a specific reading disorder characterized by reading backwardness (Rutter, 1978). Unfortunately, it is difficult to estimate the exact number of children affected by dyslexia because different studies apply different definitions. Nevertheless, federal law now requires that children with specific disabilities be given individualized instruction programs and special attention. Thus, the identification of a learning disability such as dyslexia means that considerable attention will be devoted to the child, which involves enormous public expense. In other words, learning disabilities represent major public health problems. Therefore, considerable effort has been devoted to defining subcategories of learning disabilities, developing procedures to identify them, and instituting methods for helping children overcome these problems (Fletcher, Levin & Satz, 1989; Rourke & Gates, 1981; Rourke et al., 1986; Rutter, 1978).

Other clinical neuropsychologists have been busy identifying the cognitive consequences of early brain lesions. For example, studies have shown that high-risk infants show poor performance on tests of verbal ability, coordination, visual-spatial ability, and the like by the time they are $3\frac{1}{2}$ years old (Francis-Williams, 1974). Other studies focus on recovery from accidents and trauma. For example, a few years after children have been in accidents involving head injuries, neurological tests often show no remaining problems. Nevertheless, neuropsychological tests of intellectual abilities often show that these functions remain somewhat impaired (Fuld & Fisher, 1977). In summary, developmental neuropsychologists are actively working toward an understanding of brain-behavior relationships in children. They have created extensive diagnostic procedures for identifying different learning disabilities, including articulation disorders, speech disorders, and dyslexia. Furthermore, they have attempted to link specific medical problems such as birth complications and prematurity to later intellectual function. Finally, they have attempted to identify the cognitive consequences of early brain disease and injury.

Developmental neuropsychology is a difficult field because several levels of assessment are necessary. Figure 19-1 shows a model that is used by neuropsychologists in the development of rehabilitation plans. The first step requires the application of formal tests to determine the nature of the problem. The second step requires an assessment of the environment. For example, demands of the school environment and other academic expectations must be taken into consideration. The third and fourth steps require the formulation of treatment plans. These plans involve a prediction of the short- and long-term consequences of the brain problem and the chances that intervention will make a difference. The fifth level of assessment concerns the availability of resources. For example, is there a family member who can assist in treatment? Are there facilities and therapists in the community? The sixth step requires the development of a realistic treatment plan that considers the information gained in Steps 1–5. Even though the neuropsychologist may not deliver the treatment, he or she may remain involved in evaluating progress made in the course of clinical care. When treatment is not achieving its objectives, modifications may be suggested (Step 7) (Fletcher, Levin & Satz, 1989).

As suggested by Figure 19-1, the neuropsychologist has many complex and important tasks that require the administration and interpretation of assessment devices.

Figure 19-1
The process of
habilitation
requires at least
seven steps:
assessment of the
child (1) and the
environment (2),
predictions about
short- and
long-term
outcomes (3),
development of an
ideal plan (4),
assessment of
resources available
(5), and
development of a
realistic
intervention plan
(6). The entire
process requires
ongoing
assessment (7).
(*From Fletcher,
Levin & Satz,
1989, p. 517.
Reprinted by
permission of
Guilford
Publications.*)

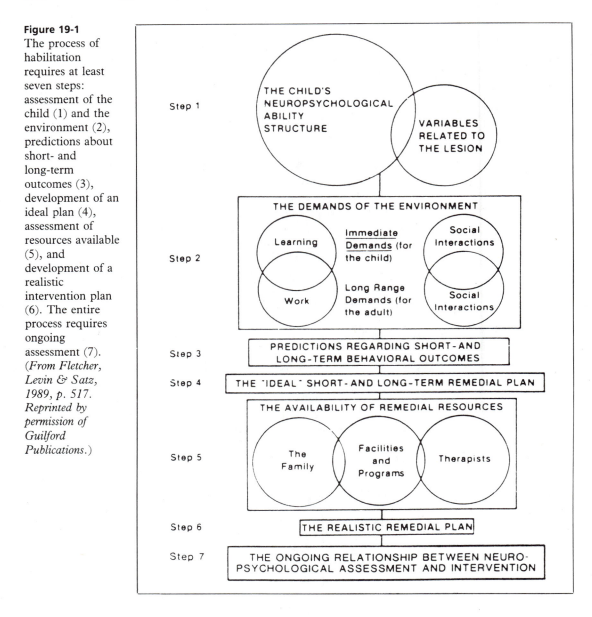

C. *Adult Neuropsychology*

There are many different approaches to identifying the consequences of brain
injury in adults. Perhaps the two best known approaches involve administration of the psychological test batteries, Halstead-Reitan and Luria-Nebraska.
Each of these test batteries is discussed briefly.

Halstead-Reitan Neuropsychological Battery. In 1935, Ward Halstead opened a laboratory to study the impact of impairments of brain function on a wide range of human abilities. Some of Halstead's observations were formal, while others involved observations in work and social settings. The formal observations were obtained through modifications of existing psychological tests. Over time, Halstead realized that determining inadequacy in brain function required a very wide range of tests that measured characteristics and abilities beyond those targeted by existing psychological tests. In 1944, Halstead was joined in his neuropsychological laboratory by his first graduate student, Ralph M. Reitan. Halstead and Reitan worked together until 1950, when Reitan received his Ph.D. Reitan's contribution was to add several tests to the assessment procedures. The full battery includes many psychological tests and sometimes requires 8 to 12 hours to administer. In addition, patients assessed by the Halstead-Reitan procedures often receive the full Minnesota Multiphasic Personality Inventory (MMPI) to evaluate their emotional state in response to a medical situation.

The full Halstead-Reitan Neuropsychological Battery is available in different versions for children and adults. A summary of the components in the adult battery is given in Table 19-1.

A large number of studies validate the Halstead and Reitan procedures (Reitan, 1986). Most of the studies show that performance on specific subtasks of the Halstead-Reitan battery is associated with dysfunction in one of the two hemispheres of the brain. For example, tactile, visual, and auditory problems on one side of the body reflect damage in the opposite hemisphere of the brain. Difficulty on the right side of the body indicates a problem in the left side of the brain (Wheeler & Reitan, 1962). Later studies by Reitan (1968) demonstrated that the battery is able to locate tumors or lesions in the right or left hemisphere of the brain and in the front or back portion of the brain in a significant number of cases. By studying performance in a systematic way, neuropsychologists have been able to provide important information about the location and the impact of brain problems (Reitan & Wolfson, 1985).

Luria-Nebraska Neuropsychological Battery. A different approach to neuropsychological assessment is found in the work of A. R. Luria, who has been recognized for many years as an expert on the functions of the human brain (Luria, 1966, 1973). Luria's theory and methods differ from those applied by Halstead, Reitan, and others. The most important concepts in Luria's theory are that the brain is a functional system and that many areas within the system coordinate to produce observable behavior. Other researchers attempted to find specific areas within the brain that are responsible for particular behaviors. Luria differed because he did not acknowledge any single area in the brain as solely responsible for any particular behavior. Instead, Luria used the brain as a functional system, with a limited number of brain areas involved in each behavior. Each area in the functional system might be considered a link in a

Table 19-1
Components
of the
Halstead-Reitan
Neuropsychology
Battery for Adults

Test	Description
Halstead category test	This test is a learning experiment for current learning skills, mental efficiency, and abstract concept formation.
Tactual test (time, memory, localization)	The patient is required to put variously shaped blocks into holes of the same shape. The test assesses several abilities, including motor speed and tactual and kinesthetic psychomotor performance, as well as memory.
Rhythm test	Thirty pairs of rhythm beats are presented, and the patient is asked to identify which pairs are the same and which are different. The task measures auditory perception, concentration, and attention.
Speech-sounds perception test	Sixty nonsense words are presented on a tape recorder. After hearing each word, the patient must choose the word from among four alternatives presented visually. The test measures auditory-verbal perception, auditory-visual coordination, and some aspects of language and concentration.
Finger oscillation test	The patient is required to tap the index finger as rapidly as possible, alternating hands on consecutive trials. The test is used to analyze motor speed and right-left hand preference.
Related Procedures	The following tests are often given in conjunction with the Halstead-Reitan battery.
Trail-making test	This test requires patients to connect numbers and letters as rapidly as possible. The test measures speed, visual scanning, and ability to process information in sequence.
Strength-of-grip test	A mechanical device (the hand dynamometer) is used to measure the strength of grip in each hand.
Sensory-perceptual examination	In a variety of sensory modalities, such as touch, hearing, and vision, the patient is given information on one side of the body and then on the other side. The test is used to determine whether stimuli presented on one side of the body are perceived when presented alone and also to determine whether competition with other stimulation reduces the perception of the stimulus.

From Saccuzzo and Kaplan (1984, pp. 226–227).

chain. Each link is necessary, and if any link is injured, there will be a breakdown in the total system.

Luria also introduced the concept of *pluripotentiality*—that is, any one center in the brain can be involved in several different functional systems (Golden, 1981). For example, one center in the brain may be involved in both visual and tactile senses. Luria also felt that multiple systems might be responsible for the same behavior. Thus, if a child has an injury that affects one system, another system may take over.

In practice, Luria applied his theory clinically to make intuitive judgments about deficits in functional systems. Since Luria did not use a standardized procedure, the amount of time he spent testing individuals varied greatly. In addition, it was difficult for others to repeat the exact steps Luria had used to

Table 19-2
Subsections of
Luria-Nebraska
Neuropsychological
Battery

Item	Description
Motor functions	Examines basic and complex motor skills. Some items ask patients to perform fine tasks with the right and left hand and with the eyes open or closed. Other items involve mouth, tongue, and speech movements.
Rhythm	Evaluates rhythm and pitch skills. Patients are asked to reproduce melodic sounds such as from the song "Home on the Range." They are also to identify soft and loud sounds and musical patterns.
Tactile	Evaluates a variety of kinesthetic (movement) and tactile (touch) abilities. Patients are blindfolded and asked to identify where they have been touched. Then a variety of shapes and letters are written on the back of the patient's hand, and the patient is asked to identify them. In addition, the patient is asked to identify common objects such as quarters, keys, paper clips, and so on.
Visual	Investigates visual and spatial skills. Patients are asked to identify objects through pictures and through progressively more difficult items. They are asked to put pieces together or identify objects in overlapping sketches.
Receptive speech	Tests patient's ability to understand the spoken language. Items range from simple phonemes to comprehension of complex sentences.
Expressive speech	Estimates patient's ability to express speech orally. The word sounds range from "see" to "Massachusetts" to "episcopal."
Writing	Identifies basic writing skills including simple spelling, copying letters and words, and writing names.
Reading	Similar to writing section. It tests whether patients can identify individual letters and read symbols, words, sentences, and stories.
Arithmetic skills	Tests a variety of simple numeric and algebraic abilities.
Memory	Assesses verbal and nonverbal memory skills. Items range from very simple recall to complex memorization tasks.
Intellectual processes	Evaluates intellectual level using items similar to those on traditional intelligence tests.

From Saccuzzo and Kaplan (1984, p. 230).

reach conclusions about particular patients. Reitan (1976b) criticized Luria on the grounds that Luria's opinion was the only known evidence for the validity of the tests.

Although Luria's procedures were widely regarded as important, they did not meet the psychometric standards of many American psychologists. In order to face these criticisms, Golden (1981) developed a standardized version of Luria's procedures. Because Golden worked at the University of Nebraska, the test has become known as the Luria-Nebraska Neuropsychological Battery. The battery includes 269 items that can be administered in about $2\frac{1}{2}$ hours. The items are divided into 11 subsections; these subsections are listed in Table 19-2. A similar test for children has also been developed (Plaisted et al., 1983).

The inventory is scored by finding a standardized performance level for each of the 11 subtests. In addition, three more scores are reported. First, there

Figure 19-2
Profile of a patient
tested with the
Luria-Nebraska
Battery. (*From
Golden, 1981.
Copyright © 1981
by John Wiley &
Sons, Inc.
Reprinted by
permission of John
Wiley & Sons,
Inc.*)

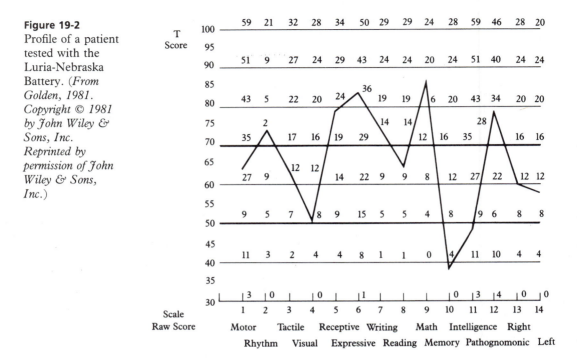

is a pathogenomonic scale, which consists of 32 items found in previous studies
to be highly sensitive to brain dysfunction. The other two scores are used to
identify whether dysfunction is in the right or the left hemisphere of the brain.
They are taken from the sections of the battery that independently test the
function of the right or left side of the body. A variety of studies (summarized
by Golden, 1981) have demonstrated that the Luria-Nebraska Battery is capable of making fine distinctions in neuropsychologic functions. Many of these
studies used the battery to estimate the area of the brain that has been damaged
by a tumor or lesion. In many of these studies, confirmation of localization is
made by surgery, angiogram, or CAT scan. In one study, the Luria-Nebraska
Battery was able to localize problems in 22 of 24 right-hemisphere cases and 29
of 36 left-hemisphere cases (Golden, 1981). Since the Luria-Nebraska Battery
is new, a final evaluation of its effectiveness cannot be made at this time. Some
evaluations are very encouraging, whereas others fail to show that these tests
give significantly more information than IQ tests (Carr, Sweet & Rossini,
1986). Statistical methods for interpreting results are continually improving
(Reynolds, 1982; Webster & Dostrow, 1982); nevertheless, the approach still
has some serious critics (Spiers, 1982).

An example of a profile from a patient tested with the Luria-Nebraska
Battery is shown in Figure 19-2. The two dark horizontal lines in the figure
represent the normal ranges for performance on the various subtests. Scores

above the top dark line indicate significant problem areas. As the figure shows, there is significant impairment for the person who took this test in both expressive and receptive language, and there are also some problems in the areas of arithmetic and writing. There were no problems on the visual memory scales. Neuropsychologists have learned that memory problems are associated with damage in the temporal lobe of the brain. Thus, the good performance on memory rules out a temporal lobe problem. Receptive and expressive language abilities seem to be localized more in the left than the right side of the brain. The difficulties seen in this profile in the language areas imply that there is a problem in the left side of the brain. Comparing the profile with information acquired in other studies, the neuropsychologists estimated that there was damage in the left side of the brain in the parietal-occipital area (or the area of the brain toward the back of the left side). A neurological report confirmed that the patient had had a stroke that had damaged the left parietal-occipital section.

Using information from neuropsychological test batteries, clinical neuropsychologists are able to evaluate damage and suggest programs for rehabilitation. Despite important improvements in the Luria-Nebraska Battery, several methodological questions still remain. After a detailed review of the test and the standardization procedures, Lezak (1983) concluded that caution must be exercised in the use of the measure. She stated, "the examiner must be extremely cautious about drawing conclusions based on the scores and indices of this battery as presently constituted." Some neuropsychologists prefer to use specific experimental tasks in addition to test batteries.

D. *California Verbal Learning Test (CVLT)*

Most psychological tests evaluate performance by summing the number of correct responses. For many years, psychologists have known that people can get a wrong response for different reasons. More than half a century has passed since H. Werner (1937) objected to the use of global scores based only on the number of right or wrong items. Instead, Werner favored tests that assess how problems are solved in addition to the overall level of achievement.

Modern cognitive psychology has identified many levels of human information processing (Squire & Butters, 1984). Contemporary cognitive psychology suggests that performance on any task is determined by many different factors. It is not enough to know that there is an impairment in cognitive functioning. Instead, we need to know which aspects of the human information-processing system are defective and which aspects are functioning well. This information is essential in designing rehabilitation strategies for patients who have selective problems.

The California Verbal Learning Test (CVLT) is a new approach to clinical neuropsychology that builds on research in psychological testing, cognitive psychology, and computer science (Delis et al., 1987). The major emphasis of the test is to determine how errors are made in learning tasks. In other words, the intent is to identify different strategies, processes, and errors associated with specific deficits. The test attempts to link memory deficits identified in populations with known neurological problems to impaired performance on specific tasks. The CVLT assesses a variety of different variables, including levels of recall and recognition, semantic and serial strategies, serial position effects, learning rates across trials, consistency of item recall across trials, degree of vulnerability to proactive and retroactive interference, retention of information over short and long delays, and learning errors in recall and recognition.

In one component of the CVLT, the subject is asked to imagine that he or she is going to go shopping. Then the subject is given a list of items to buy. The examiner lists 16 items verbally at a pace of about one word per second. The respondent is asked to repeat the list. This process is repeated through a series of five trials.

Performance on these tasks is analyzed in a variety of different ways. For example, learning across trials gives the test taker considerable information. Those who are very anxious may perform poorly on the first trial but improve as the task is repeated (Lezak, 1983). However, adults with limited learning capacity may do relatively well on early trials but reach a plateau where repeated trials are not associated with improved performance. Adults with limited learning capacity may also have inconsistent recall across trials. This can happen when they abandon one strategy and adopt another. Studies have demonstrated that inconsistent recall across trials is characteristic of patients with amnesia caused by frontal lobe pathology.

The CVLT also includes other features derived from experimental cognitive psychology. For example, after five trials of exposure to the 16-word lists, a second interference list of 16 words is given. Subjects are tested immediately and after a 20-minute delay for free recall, cued recall, and recognition of the first list.

Another unique feature of the CVLT is that it can be administered either in a paper-and-pencil form or with a microcomputer. Versions for both the IBM PC and the Apple are available. The computer does not replace but rather works to assist the psychologist test administrator. In the computer-assisted form of the test, the examiner can enter responses directly into the computer using a single key or a light pen to touch the words on a monitor screen. This greatly facilitates and speeds the scoring process.

The validity of the CVLT has been evaluated in several studies. For example, it has been shown that the test correlates with other measures such as the Wechsler memory scale (Delis et al., 1987). In addition, factor analysis studies of the CVLT suggest that there are independent factors for learning strategy, acquisition rate, serial position, discriminability, and learning performance. These constructs correspond to empirical findings from modern cognitive psychology. The diversity of deficits identified by the CVLT could not be identified using more traditional psychometric tests (Delis et al., 1987).

Figure 19-3
Long-delay recall
on CVLT in three
patient groups.
(*Adapted from
Delis et al., 1991.*)

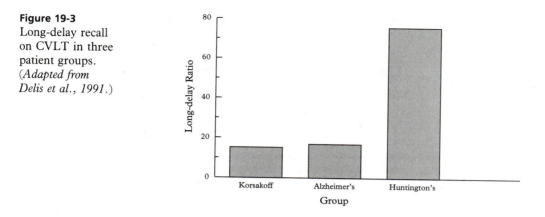

The CVLT has been used to compare patients with Alzheimer's disease, Korsakoff syndrome, and Huntington's disease. Alzheimer's disease is a serious neurological disorder that causes loss of short-term memory. Korsakoff's syndrome is an organic brain disorder, often associated with long-term alcohol use, that also results in the loss of short-term memory. Finally, Huntington's disease is an inherited disorder that emerges in adulthood and is also associated with memory loss. Although all three organic brain problems are associated with memory loss, the nature of the deficit may be different. For example, patients with Alzheimer's disease and Huntington's disease may score about the same on measures of recall in memory tests but may differ in measures of forgetting. Studies of brain pathology show that these two diseases affect different parts of the brain. An advantage of the CVLT is that it allows a more precise evaluation of the nature of the problems.

When representative groups of patients from these three diagnostic groups are compared on the CVLT, those with Alzheimer's disease and with Korsakoff's syndrome appeared very similar. They have comparable scores for recall, learning and forgetting, semantic clustering, and several other cognitive factors. However, each of these groups performed at a lower level than patients with Huntington's disease on measures of retention, intrusion errors, and recognition. Figure 19-3 shows an example of this finding. The figure compares CTLV scores for long-delay savings for the three patient groups. Long-delay savings require that subjects learn a list of words. Then, after a long delay, they are given a free recall test. The results are reported as a ratio of all responses given to correct for the fact that different subjects give different numbers of responses. The figure shows that Huntington's patients have significantly higher recall than those in the other two groups. These findings are consistent with the neuroanatomy of the illnesses. Huntington's disease is a subcortical dementia, while Alzheimer's disease is associated with cortical lesions. The CLTV may be helpful in identifying the location of the organic problem; however, the results may be less useful in differentiating Korsakoff's syndrome from Alzheimer's disease (Delis et al., 1991).

In summary, clinical neuropsychology is an emerging and important area in psychological testing. It is linked closely to basic research in neuroscience and in cognitive psychology. We expect that clinical neuropsychology will continue to experience rapid development over the next few decades.

II. *Quality of Life Assessment*

Health is probably more important to us than any other issue. Studies on the preference for different states of being sometimes exclude ratings of health because everyone rates health as more important than anything else they can obtain in life. Despite the almost universal feeling that health is important, the definition of health status has remained somewhat ambiguous. Considering many different definitions of health, we find two common themes. First, there is agreement that premature mortality is undesirable, so one aspect of health is the avoidance of death. The health status of nations is often evaluated in terms of their mortality rates or infant mortality rates. (Infant mortality is the number of children who die before one year of age per thousand live births.)

Second, in addition to length of life, quality of life is also very important. Disease and disability are of concern because they affect either our life expectancy or our life quality. A serious illness, for example, might terminate our lives prematurely. Cancer and heart disease are the two major causes of premature death in the United States. In addition, these diseases or disabilities can make life less desirable. A person with heart disease may have restrictions on daily living activities and may be unable to participate in social activities or to work. All diseases and disabilities may have some impact on quality of life. A cold, for example, may interfere with your ability to concentrate or attend school. The cold, however, is of relatively brief duration and affects your life for only a limited time. A more serious disease may affect the quality of your life for a longer period of time.

Within the last few years, medical scientists have come to realize the importance of quality of life measurement. Many major diseases, including arthritis, heart disease, and diabetes, are evaluated in terms of the degree to which they affect life quality and life expectancy. Treatments for these conditions can also be evaluated by the amount of improvement they produce in quality of life. The Food and Drug Administration now considers quality of life data in their evaluations of new products. In the remainder of this chapter, we review several approaches to quality of life measurement.

A. *What Is Health-Related Quality of Life?*

Numerous new quality of life measurement systems have evolved during the last 20 years and represent various traditions in measurement. At least two different conceptual approaches have been presented in recent articles. One approach grows out of the tradition of health status measurement. In the late 1960s and early 1970s, the National Center for Health Services Research funded several major projects to develop general measures of health status. All the projects were guided by the World Health Organization's (WHO) definition of health status, which states that "health is a complete state of physical, mental, and social well-being and not merely absence of disease" (WHO, 1948). The projects resulted in a variety of assessment tools, including the Sickness Impact Profile (Bergner et al., 1981), the Quality of Well-being Scale (Kaplan & Anderson, 1990), the McMaster Health Index Questionnaire (Chambers, 1988), the SF-36 (Ware, 1991), and the Nottingham Health Profile (McEwen, 1992). Many of the measures examined the effect of disease or disability on performance of social role, ability to interact in the community, and physical functioning. Some of the systems have separate components for the measurement of social and mental health.

Other authors refer to quality of life as something that is independent of health status. For instance, M. J. Follick and co-workers (1988) suggest that quality of life represents a broader outcome than traditional measures of symptoms and mortality. S. H. Croog and colleagues (1986) used a wide variety of outcome measures, collectively referring to these as quality of life. The measures included the patients' subjective evaluation of well-being, physical symptoms, sexual function, work performance and satisfaction, emotional status, cognitive function, social participation, and life satisfaction. Other investigators, including Hunt and McEwen (1983), regard quality of life as subjective appraisals of life satisfaction. In summary, a wide variety of different dimensions have all been described as quality of life. There is no agreement about which dimensions should be assessed in research studies, but a consideration of recurrent themes in the methodologic literature can assist in evaluating existent instruments.

There are two major approaches to quality of life assessment: a psychometric approach and a decision theory approach. The psychometric approach attempts to provide separate measures for the many different dimensions of quality of life. Perhaps the best known example of the psychometric tradition is the Sickness Impact Profile (SIP). The SIP is a 136-item measure that yields 12 different scores. The scores are displayed in a format similar to an MMPI profile.

The decision theory approach attempts to weight the different dimensions of health in order to provide a single unitary expression of health status. Supporters of this approach argue that psychometric methods fail to consider that different health problems are not of equal concern. One hundred runny noses are not the same as 100 missing legs (Bush, 1984). In an experimental trial using the psychometric approach, it is not uncommon to find that some aspects of quality of life improve while others get worse. For example, a medication might reduce high blood pressure but also be associated with headaches and impotence. It is argued that the quality notion is the subjective evaluation of observable or objective health states. The decision theory approach attempts to provide an overall summary measure of quality of life that integrates subjective function states, preferences for these states, morbidity, and mortality.

B. *Common Methods for the Measurement of Quality of Life*

A variety of methods have been proposed to measure quality of life, but it is not possible here to review and critique all of these methods. Instead, some of the more widely used methods are presented. Readers interested in more detailed reviews should consult Spilker (1990) or Walker and Rosser (1992).

Some of the more commonly used assessment methods are the Sickness Impact Profile (SIP), the Index of Activities of Daily Living scales, the Karnofsky Performance Status, the McMaster Health Index Questionnaire, the SF-36, the Quality of Well-being Scale, and the Nottingham Health Profile.

Sickness impact profile. The Sickness Impact Profile (SIP) is one of the best known and widely used quality of life measures and is a general measure applicable to any disease or disability group. Furthermore, the SIP has been successfully used with a variety of different cultural subgroups.

The SIP includes 136 items, divided into 12 categories, that describe the effect of sickness on behavioral function. Each of the 12 categories is clustered into three groups: independent categories, physical, and psychosocial. Independent categories include sleep and rest, eating, work, home management, and recreation and pastimes. Physical categories include ambulation, mobility, and body care and movement. The psychosocial categories are social interaction, alertness behavior, emotional behavior, and communication. Table 19-3 shows the categories for the SIP and gives sample items.

Each SIP item has been evaluated by an independent group of judges on a 15-point scale of dysfunction. The judges' ratings determine the weighting of each item in the SIP scoring. The respondent does not consider the judges' weightings in deciding to endorse an item. The overall SIP percent score is obtained by separating the items endorsed by the respondent, summing their scale values, and dividing by the sum of all values for all items on the SIP. Then this proportion is multiplied by 100 to compute a total percent impaired score. Similarly, scores are obtained for each category. Percent scores for each category can be plotted on a graphic display that looks similar to an MMPI profile. A variety of studies attest to the reliability and validity of the SIP for various patient groups and clinical applications (see Bergner et al., 1981). An example of an application of the SIP in cardiovascular disease is shown in Figure 19-4. The figure compares 50 patients with angina (chest pain) against 50 healthy volunteers. Angina patients have more impairment in all categories.

Table 19-3

Sickness Impact Profile Categories and Selected Items

Dimension	Category	Items Describing Behavior Related to:	Selected Items
Independent categories	SR	Sleep and rest	I sit during much of the day.
			I sleep or nap during the day.
	E	Eating	I am eating no food at all; nutrition is taken through tubes or intravenous fluids.
			I am eating special or different food.
	W	Work	I am not working at all.
			I often act irritable toward my work associates.
	HM	Home management	I am not doing any of the maintenance or repair work around the house that I usually do.
			I am not doing heavy work around the house.
	RP	Recreation and pastimes	I am going out for entertainment less.
			I am not doing any of my usual physical recreation or activities.
Physical	A	Ambulation	I walk shorter distances or stop to rest often.
			I do not walk at all.
	M	Mobility	I stay within one room.
			I stay away from home only for brief periods of time.
	BCM	Body care and movement	I do not bathe myself at all but am bathed by someone else.
			I am very clumsy in body movements.
Psychosocial	SI	Social interaction	I am doing fewer social activities with groups of people.
			I isolate myself as much as I can from the rest of the family.
	AB	Alertness behavior	I have difficulty reasoning and solving problems, for example, making plans, making decisions, learning new things.
			I sometimes behave as if I were confused or disoriented in place or time, for example, where I am, who is around, directions, what day it is.
	EB	Emotional behavior	I laugh or cry suddenly.
			I act irritable and impatient with myself, for example, talk badly about myself, swear at myself, blame myself for things that happen.
	C	Communication	I am having troiuble writing or typing.
			I do not speak clearly when I am under stress.

From Bergner et al. (1981). Reprinted by permission.

Figure 19-4
Differences
between angina
patients and
healthy adults for
various SIP
categories.

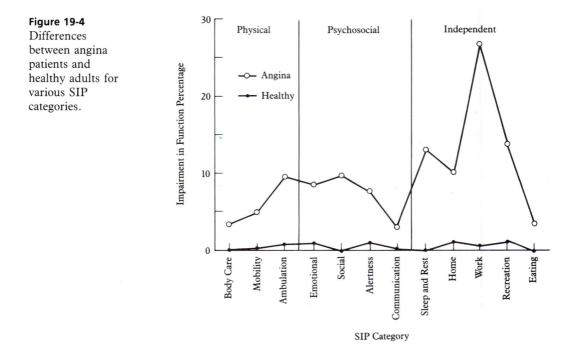

Although angina has less impact on body care, mobility, and eating, work and recreation are most seriously affected (Vandenburg & Vogler, 1985).

Index of Activities of Daily Living. Perhaps the oldest general quality of life measure is the Index of Activities of Daily Living (ADL), which was contributed by S. T. Katz and his associates (1963). Katz argued very early that the major impact of disease and disability was on function and ability to perform role activities in everyday life.

The ADL is most commonly used in studies of the elderly. The system includes six subscales for bathing, dressing, toileting, transfer, continence, and feeding. These categories are listed in Table 19-4. For each category, a judgment is made as to whether the person is independent or dependent. For the category of bathing, people are judged to be independent if they need assistance only in bathing a single part of the body or can bathe themselves. They are judged to be dependent if they need assistance in bathing more than one part of the body. Once a judgment of dependence or independence is obtained for each of the six categories, an overall grade is assigned. To receive the top grade, or grade A, the person must be independent in all six categories. Grade B is assigned for those who are independent in all but one of these functions. The bottom grade, G, is assigned to those who are dependent in all six functions. Several reliability and validity studies for the ADL have been reported

Table 19-4
Definitions and
Grades for the
Katz Index of
Activities of Daily
Living

Index of Independence in Activities of Daily Living

The Index of Independence in Activities of Daily Living is based on an evaluation of the functional independence or dependence of patients in bathing, dressing, going to the toilet, transferring, continence, and feeding. Specific definitions of functional independence and dependence appear below the index.

A   Independent in feeding, continence, transferring, going to toilet, and bathing

B   Independent in all but one of these functions

C   Independent in all but bathing and one additional function

D   Independent in all but bathing, dressing, and one additional function

E   Independent in all but bathing, dressing, going to toilet, and one additional function

F   Independent in all but bathing, dressing, going to toilet, transferring, and one additional function

G   Dependent in all six functions

Other   Dependent in at least two functions, but not classifiable as C, D, E, or F

    Independence means without supervision, direction, or active personal assistance, except as specifically noted below. This is based on actual status and not on ability. A patient who refuses to perform a function is considered as not performing the function, even though he is deemed able.

Bathing (sponge, shower, or tub)

Independent: assistance only in bathing a single part (as back or disabled extremity) or bathes self completely

Dependent: assistance in bathing more than one part of body; assistance in getting in or out of tub or does not bathe self

Dressing

Independent: gets clothes from closets and drawers; puts on clothes, outer garments, braces; manages fasteners; act of tying shoes is excluded

Dependent: does not dress self or remains partly undressed

Going to toilet

Independent: gets to toilet; gets on and off toilet; arranges clothes, cleans organs of excretion (may manage own bedpan used at night only and may or may not be using mechanical supports)

Dependent: uses bedpan or commode or receives assistance in getting to and using toilet

Transfer

Independent: moves in and out of bed independently and moves in and out of chair independently (may or may not be using mechanical supports)

Dependent: assistance in moving in or out of bed and/or chair; does not perform one or more transfers

Continence

Independent: urination and defecation entirely self-controlled

Dependent: partial or total incontinence in urination or defecation; partial or total control by enemas, catheters, or regulated use of urinals and/or bedpans

Feeding

Independent: gets food from plate or its equivalent into mouth (precutting of meat and preparation of food, as buttering bread, are excluded from evaluation)

Dependent: assistance in act of feeding (see above); does not eat at all or parental feeding

From Katz et al. (1963). Copyright 1963, American Medical Association.

(Katz et al., 1970). Despite its many important applications in studies of aging, the ADL has been criticized because it does not make distinctions toward the well end of the quality of life continuum. A. L. Stewart and co-workers (1978) have suggested that nearly 80% of the noninstitutionalized population have no gross functional limitations and would obtain the top score in the ADL system. However, other population surveys have demonstrated that more than 50% of the population experiences one or more symptoms on a given day (Kaplan, Bush & Berry, 1976). Most of these symptoms cause minor irritation but do not cause the type of dysfunction detected using ADL measures. For example, chest pain, shortness of breath, and dizziness would not be recorded by the ADL scales in cases where they did not disrupt major role activities. Given the wide array of behaviors and symptoms that are relevant to life quality, the ADL has some significant limitations. Other measures are required in order to make discriminations among impaired individuals who are toward the healthy end of the functioning continuum.

Karnofsky Performance Status. Often in quality of life assessment, general measures are tailored for use with a specific disease category. For example, a measure will be designed to assess the effect of arthritis on quality of life. In cancer research, however, a different trend seems to have occurred. One general quality of life measure, known as the Karnofsky Performance Status (KPS), has found widespread use in cancer research, but it has not been used for populations other than cancer patients. The term *quality of life* first appeared as a heading in the *Index Medicus* in 1977. A. Grieco and C. J. Long (1984) reviewed the 45 studies listed in the *Index Medicus* that used quality of life measures. Among those cited, the Karnofsky Performance Status was used in about 18% of the studies. However, because of the diversity of outcome measures used in the studies, the KPS was actually used more often than any other technique. Yet, all studies that used the KPS involved cancer patients.

The KPS is a simple rating form that requires a physician, an observer, or even the patient to assign a percentage score. The scores range from 0 for dead to 100 for normal with no complaints and no evidence of disease. Each 10-point interval is labeled with a description. For example, 90% is associated with "ability to carry out normal activity, with minor signs or symptoms of disease." Fifty percent is labeled "requires considerable assistance and frequent medical care."

Among the advantages of the KPS is that it is easy to use and attempts to relate disease or disability to daily functioning. However, it has several deficiencies. First, it has apparently never been published, and guidelines for its use are not available. Use of the KPS requires subjective judgments, and there are not adequate data to suggest that these judgments can be made reliably. For example, T. A. Hutchinson, N. F. Boyd, and A. R. Feinstein (1979) found interrater agreement to be only .29 to .34. J. W. Yates, B. Chalmer, and F. P. McKegney (1980) reported more positive results, with a correlation of .69 between nurses' and social workers' ratings of cancer patients. Even this higher estimate, however, is less than what would be acceptable for research or clinical practice. Despite its poor reliability, the KPS has been shown to correlate with survival in lung cancer (Hyde et al., 1973; Stanley, 1980).

Grieco and Long (1984) revised the KPS in an attempt to improve its psychometric profile. They attempted to make the assessment more objective by using behaviorally oriented procedures. The revised procedure includes three components: (1) a structured interview, (2) a review of the medical chart, and (3) a supplemental interview with persons closely associated with the patient. Using trained observers, Grieco and Long were able to boost the interrater reliability to .96 and to demonstrate the validity of the KPS by showing its correlation with other established quality of life scales and its ability to discriminate between different patient groups.

In summary, the KPS is an interesting approach that has found widespread use in cancer research. It has the advantages of brevity and ease of administration. In a carefully controlled study, adequate reliability was obtained. However, the scores on the KPS are somewhat arbitrary, and it is not clear how the KPS deals with the transition between health states over time. Another difficulty with the system is that it depends most often on a clinical judgment of functional status. E. Nelson and co-workers (1983) have shown that there are serious discrepancies between the functional status as reported by patients and that reported by their doctors. Physicians tend to miss much of the dysfunction and may systematically underestimate the impact of illness on the quality of life. The work of Grieco and Long is very important and may lead to substantial improvements in the KPS.

The McMaster Health Index Questionnaire. A similar approach has been developed by Larry Chambers and colleagues at McMaster University in Hamilton, Ontario. The measure this group has developed is known as the McMaster Health Index Questionnaire (MHIQ). In developing their questionnaire, a multidisciplinary group of specialists in internal medicine, family medicine, psychiatry, epidemiology, statistics, and social science reviewed existing health status questionnaires. Their goal was to develop an instrument that conforms with the World Health Organization's definition of health as "not merely the absence of disease or infirmity" (WHO, 1948). Similar to the SIP, the MHIQ has separate scales. For example, some of the physical health items were taken from the Index of Activities of Daily Living Scale (Katz et al., 1970). The emotional function items were adapted or taken verbatim from a variety of sources, including the Social Readjustment Rating Scale (Holmes & Rahe, 1967). This resulted in an original questionnaire of 172 items.

After validation testing, the pool of items was reduced to 59. The criteria for selection of the final items included association with observed functional changes before and after patients entered the hospital and correlation with ratings by family physicians. Later studies validated the MHIQ against a variety of other quality of life measures such as the Lee Index of Functional Capacity, the Spitzer Quality of Life Index, and the Bradburn Psychological

Well-Being Scale. The MHIQ is a self-administered questionnaire, and validity studies have demonstrated that these self-reports correlate significantly with ratings by external observers. In one study, it was demonstrated that the physical function portion of the index changes in response to therapies designed to affect physical function. The physical function portion of the MHIQ has adequate but not impressive reliability. In one study of patients in a physiotherapy clinic, the MHIQ was administered twice within a one-week period. The physiotherapists reported that functional status should not change over the short interval in this patient population. Using test-retest assessment, the interclass correlation coefficients were .53, .70, and .48 for the physical, emotional, and social function portions of the MHIQ, respectively. Another study evaluated the internal consistency of the MHIQ as assessed by KR_{20} coefficients. For the physical, emotional, and social function indices, the coefficients were .76, .67, and .51, respectively. Although these levels of reliability may be acceptable for group comparisons for large clinical trials, they are less than optimal. Low reliability, causing attenuation in correlations between variables, may reduce the chances of detecting important relationships. Unfortunately, many predictors of quality of life are also measured with substantial error. For instance, some measures of social support have reliabilities of around .50.

An example may help clarify the consequences of low reliability. Suppose that the reliability of a social support measure was .50 and we wish to show its association with the physical health portion of the MHIQ, which also has a reliability of approximately .50. Furthermore, suppose that the true correlation between these two constructs is .50. Because of attenuation due to measurement error, the observed correlation would be .25. For a sample size of 50, this would not be statistically significant. In other words, many problems in health psychology require the detection of moderate relationships with moderate sample sizes. For instruments with reliabilities in the .50 range, there will be attenuation in correlations, and the detection of important relationships may be missed.

SF-36. Another commonly used measure is the Medical Outcome Study Short Form-36 (SF-36). The SF-36 grew out of work by the RAND Corporation and the Medical Outcomes Study (MOS) (Stewart & Ware, 1992). Originally, it was based on the measurement strategy from the RAND Health Insurance Study. The MOS attempted to develop a very short, 20-item instrument known as the Short Form-20 or SF-20. However, the SF-20 did not have appropriate reliability for some dimensions. The SF-36 includes eight health concepts. Limitations in physical activities, limitations in social activities, limitations in usual role, pain, general mental health (psychological distress and well-being), limitations in usual role due to emotional problems (vitality, energy, and fatigue), and general health perceptions. The SF-36 can be either administered by a trained interviewer or self-administered. It has many advantages; for example, it is brief and there is substantial evidence for its reliability and validity. The SF-36 can be machine scored and has been evaluated in large population studies.

Despite the many advantages of the SF-36, there are also some disadvantages. For example, the SF-36 does not have age-specific questions and it is unclear whether it is equally appropriate at each level of the age continuum. The items for older retired individuals are the same as those for children (Stewart & Ware, 1992). Nevertheless, the SF-36 has become perhaps the most commonly used behavioral measure in contemporary medicine.

Nottingham Health Profile. One of the other major approaches is the Nottingham Health Profile (NHP), which has been particularly influential in the European community. The NHP has two parts. Part one includes 38 items divided into six categories: sleep, physical mobility, energy, pain, emotional reactions, and social isolation. Items within each of these sections are rated in terms of relative importance. Items are rescaled in order to allow them to vary between 0 and 100 within each section.

Part two of the NHP includes seven statements related to the areas of life most affected by health: employment, household activities, social life, home life, sex life, hobbies and interests, and holidays. In the second portion of the NHP, the respondent indicates whether or not a health condition has affected his or her life in these areas. The NHP has been used in a substantial number of studies and there is considerable evidence for its reliability and validity.

There are many attractive features of the NHP. The scale is consumer based and arises from definitions of health offered by individuals in the community. Furthermore, the NHP was designed to use language that is easily interpretable by people in the community and to conform to minimum reading requirements. Substantial testing has been performed on the NHP. The major difficulty with the NHP is that it does not provide relative importance weightings across dimensions. As a result, it is difficult to compare the dimensions directly with one another (McEwen, 1992).

Decision theory approaches. Within the last few years, there has been a growing interest in using quality of life data to help evaluate the cost/utility or cost-effectiveness of health care programs. Cost studies have gained in popularity because health care costs have grown so rapidly in recent years. Not all health care interventions are equally efficient in returning benefit for the expended dollar. Objective cost studies might guide policymakers toward an optimal and equitable distribution of scarce resources. Cost-effectiveness analysis typically quantifies the benefits of a health care intervention in terms of years of life, or quality-adjusted life-years (QALYs). Cost/utility is a special use of cost-effectiveness that weights observable health states by preferences or utility judgments of quality (Kaplan & Anderson, 1990). In cost/utility analysis, the benefits of medical care, behavioral interventions, or preventive programs are expressed in terms of well-years.

If a man dies of heart disease at age 50 and we expected him to live to age 75, it might be concluded that the disease was associated with 25 lost life-years. If 100 men died at age 50 (and also had a life expectancy of 75 years), we might conclude that 2500 (100 men × 25 years) life-years had been lost. Yet death is not the only outcome of concern in heart disease. Many adults suffer myocardial infarctions that leave them somewhat disabled over long periods of time. Although they are still alive, the quality of their lives has diminished. Quality-adjusted life-years take into consideration the quality of life consequences of these illnesses. For example, a disease that reduces quality of life by one-half will take away .5 QALY over the course of each year. If the disease affects two people, it will take away one year (2 × .5) over each year period. A medical treatment that improves quality of life by .2 for each of five individuals will result in the equivalent of 1 QALY if the benefit is maintained over a one-year period. This system has the advantage of considering both benefits and side effects of programs in terms of the common QALY units.

The need to integrate mortality and quality of life information is clearly apparent in studies of heart disease. Consider the case of hypertension. People with high blood pressure may live shorter lives if they are untreated. Thus, one benefit of treatment is to add years to life. However, for most patients, high blood pressure is not associated with symptoms for many years. Conversely, the treatment for high blood pressure may cause a variety of symptoms. In the short run, patients who take medication may experience more symptoms than those who avoid it. If a treatment is evaluated only in terms of changes in life expectancy, the benefits of the program will be overestimated because side effects are not taken into consideration. On the other hand, considering only current quality of life will underestimate the treatment benefits, since information on mortality (death) is excluded. In fact, considering only current function might make the treatment look harmful because the side effects of the treatment might be worse than the symptoms of hypertension. A comprehensive measurement system may take into consideration side effects and benefits and provide an overall estimate of the benefit of treatment (Russell, 1986).

Although there are several different approaches for obtaining quality-adjusted life-years, most of them are similar (Kaplan, 1990). The approach that we prefer involves several steps. First, patients are classified according to objective levels of functioning. These levels are represented by the scales of mobility, physical activity, and social activity. Once observable behavioral levels of functioning have been classified, a second step is required to place each individual on the 0 to 1 scale of wellness. This is required to describe where a person lies on the continuum between optimum function and death.

Most traditional measures used in medicine and public health consider only whether a person is dead or alive. In other words, all people who are alive get the same score. Yet we know that there are different levels of wellness, and there is a need to score these levels. To accomplish this, the observable health states are weighted by quality ratings for the desirability of these conditions. Human value studies have been conducted to place the observable states onto a preference continuum, with an anchor of 0 for death and 1.0 for completely well (Kaplan, Bush & Berry, 1976). Studies have shown that the weights are highly stable over a one-year period and that they are consistent across diverse groups of raters (Kaplan, 1993). Finally, it is necessary to consider the duration of stay in various health states. Having a cough or a headache for one day is not the same as having the problem for one year. A health measure must take these durations into consideration. Using the duration information, it is possible to describe health-related quality of life in terms similar to years of life. For example, one year in a state that has been assigned the weight of .5 is equivalent to .5 of a quality-adjusted life-year.

This system has been used to evaluate many different health care programs. For example, it was used to demonstrate that a new medication for patients with arthritis produced an average of .023 QALY per year, whereas a new medication for AIDS produced nearly .46 of these units per year. However, the benefit of the arthritis medication may last as long as 20 years, ultimately producing .023 × 20 years = .46 year. The AIDS treatment produced a benefit for only one year, so its total effect was .46 × 1 year = .46 year. In other words, the general system allows the benefits of these two very different treatments to be compared (Kaplan et al., 1989).

Summary

In this chapter, we considered two broad areas relevant to testing in medical settings. First, we reviewed clinical neuropsychology. This remarkable new area of investigation has generated new research and clinical opportunities for psychologists. Neuropsychology involves the application of tests to evaluate the status of the central nervous system. Some of the more common approaches are the Halstead-Reitan battery and the Luria-Nebraska battery. Each of these approaches is based on different principles of cognitive psychology. A newer approach, the California Verbal Learning Test, attempts to evaluate brain function by considering not only errors but also how people make errors.

Another major area for the application of tests in medical settings involves health status and quality of life assessment. The goals of health care are to help people live longer and to live higher quality lives before their deaths. The quantification of life quality, however, is difficult. Two approaches to this type of assessment use psychometric methods and decision theory methods. Psychometric methods include the Sickness Impact Profile, the Index of Activities of Daily Living, the MOS Short Form 36, the McMaster Health Index Questionnaire, and the Karnofsky Performance Status. Decision theory approaches include methods for estimating the value of the equivalent of a life-year. We expect that the fields of psychological measurement and medical measurement will continue to merge over the next few decades.

PART III

Issues

CHAPTER 20
Test Bias

CHAPTER 21
Testing and the Law

CHAPTER 22
The Future of Psychological Testing

Chapter 20

Test Bias

Learning Objectives

When you have completed this chapter, you should be able to:

- Discuss some of the current controversies surrounding the use of intelligence tests.

- Give some of the arguments for and against the belief that the content of standardized tests is biased in favor of white, middle-class children.

- Explain how criterion validity studies, which review the slopes and intercepts of regression lines, are used in the study of test bias.

- Discuss some of the problems with popular tests such as the Chitling Test and the BITCH.

- List the components of the SOMPA and some of its advantages and disadvantages.

- Describe how different social, political, and ethical viewpoints are represented by different definitions of test fairness.

- Discuss some of the opportunities for developing improved predictors for minority-group members.

- Describe some of the problems with the criteria commonly used to evaluate standardized tests.

- Describe how differences in test scores can be used to justify efforts to change the social environment.

- Using the information from this chapter and from other sources, write an essay for or against the use of standardized tests for minority children.

Psychological testing is not a field without controversy. Since the early 1970s, serious and emotional debates have flourished about the meaning of tests for the placement and classification of individuals. This chapter reviews the issue of test bias, which is at the heart of the controversy. The issue is so controversial that it has inspired some court evaluations of the meaning of tests for minority-group members.

Although test bias is unmistakably an emotional issue, we should not give the impression that it is the first controversy about mental testing. Controversy has surrounded mental testing since test reports began in 1905, and the issues have been debated on and off since the 1920s (Cronbach, 1975b; Haney, 1981).

I. *Why Is the Issue Controversial?*

A basic tenet of U.S. society is that all persons are created equal. This cornerstone of political and social thought is clearly defended in the Constitution. Yet all individuals are not treated equally, and the history of social action is replete with attempts to remedy this situation. Psychological tests are among the many practices that counteract the idea that all people are the same. Tests are designed to measure differences among people, and often the differences that tests measure are in desirable personal characteristics such as intelligence and aptitude. Test scores that demonstrate differences among people may suggest to some that people are not created with the same basic abilities.

The most aggravating problem is that certain ethnic groups, on the average, score differently on some psychological tests. The most controversial case concerns intelligence tests. On the average, black Americans score 15 points lower than white Americans on standardized IQ tests. (See Chapter 11 for the meaning of IQ scores.) This difference is equal to about one standard deviation. Nobody disagrees that the two distributions overlap greatly and that there are some blacks who score as high as the highest whites. There are also some whites who score as low as the lowest blacks. Yet only about 15% to 20% of the black population score above the average white score, and only about 15% to 20% of the white population score below the average black score. Figure 20-1 shows the overlap between these two populations.

This is not a debatable issue. If you were to administer the Stanford-Binet or the Wechsler scale (see Chapter 11) to large random samples of black and white Americans, you would most likely get the same results. The dispute has not been over whether these differences exist but over where the responsibility for the differences lies. Many have argued that the differences are due to environmental factors (Kamin, 1974; Rosenthal & Jacobson, 1968; Turkheimer, 1991; Zuckerman, 1990), while others have suggested that the differences are biological (Eysenck, 1991; Jensen, 1969, 1972; Munsinger, 1975; Rushton, 1991). We will not discuss the environmental versus the biological debate because this is a technical issue that is independent of the problems with tests.

II. *Test Fairness and the Law*

The U.S. government has attempted to establish clear standards for the use of psychological tests. Regulation of tests comes in many forms, including executive orders, laws created by legislative bodies, and actions by the courts. The

Figure 20-1
IQ distributions
for black and
white Americans.
Although the
distributions
overlap, the
means are
different. Only
about 15% to 20%
of the black
population score
above the white
mean. The IQs
were measured
using the
Stanford-Binet
scale. (*From
Kennedy, Van de
Riet & White,
1963. Reprinted by
permission.*)

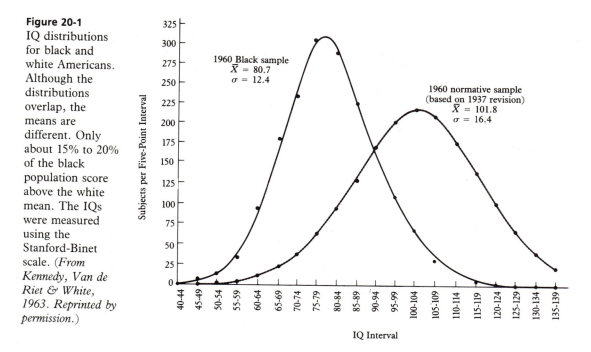

most important legal development was the passage of the 1964 Civil Rights
Act. Title VII of this act created the Equal Employment Opportunity Commission (EEOC). In 1970, **EEOC guidelines** were published for employee selection procedures. In 1978, the EEOC released a new document entitled *Uniform
Guidelines on Employee Selection Procedures*. These are the major guidelines for
the use of psychological tests in education and in industry.

The 1978 guidelines are stricter, more condensed, and less ambiguous
about the allowable uses of psychological test scores than were the 1970 guidelines. The original act clearly prohibited discrimination in employment on the
basis of race, color, religion, gender, or national origin. However, the 1978
guidelines made it clear that any screening procedure, including the use of
psychological tests, may be viewed as having an **adverse impact** if it systematically rejects substantially higher proportions of minority than nonminority
applicants. When any selection procedure does so, the employer must demonstrate that the procedure has validity for the inferences the employer wants to
make. These criteria for the validity of a selection procedure are similar to
those discussed in Chapter 5. However, the guidelines are specific about the
acceptable criteria for the use of a test; we will review these criteria in detail in
Chapter 21. The guidelines have been adopted by a variety of federal agencies,
including the Civil Service Commission, the Department of Justice, the Department of Labor, and the Department of the Treasury. The Office of Federal
Contract Compliance has the direct power to cancel government contracts held

by employers who do not comply with these guidelines. The guidelines became the focus of several political controversies in 1991. For example, when Clarence Thomas was nominated for a position on the U.S. Supreme Court, he was challenged because of his enforcement of the guidelines while he was the head of the EEOC. President George Bush also opposed some aspects of the guidelines. In fact, he had planned to relax these standards in the 1991 Civil Rights Bill; however, last-minute political pressure successfully encouraged Bush to leave the guidelines unchanged.

III. *The Traditional Defense of Testing*

In this chapter, we focus on a central issue: are standardized tests as valid for blacks and other minority groups as they are for whites? All the types of validity we discussed in Chapter 5 come into play when the issue of test bias is considered (Cole, 1981). Some psychologists argue that the tests are differentially valid for blacks and whites. Because the issue of **differential validity** is so controversial and so emotionally arousing, it has forced psychologists to think carefully about many issues in test validation. Differences among ethnic groups on test performance do not necessarily indicate that the test is biased. The question is whether the test has different meanings for different groups. In psychometrics, validity defines the meaning of a test.

A. *Content Validity*

In 1968, *Newsweek* magazine published an article on cultural fairness in testing. The article listed several items from the general information portion of the Stanford-Binet scale that might be problematic for persons with disadvantaged backgrounds. Test constructors and users were accused of being biased because some children have never had the opportunity to learn about some of the items, and other items may be answered differently (but still correctly) by members of different ethnic groups.

Many researchers also argue that scores on intelligence tests are affected by language skills that are inculcated as part of a white, middle-class upbringing but that are foreign to inner-city children (Castenell & Castenell, 1988; Kagan, Moss & Siegel, 1963; Lesser, Fifer & Clark, 1965; Mercer, 1971; Pettigrew, 1964; Scarr-Salapatek, 1971). Because they are unfamiliar with the language, some children have no chance of doing well on standardized IQ tests. For example, an American child is not likely to know what a shilling is, but a British child probably does. Similarly, the American child would not be expected to know where one puts the petrol; we assume that only a British child would understand this term. Some psychologists argue that asking an inner-city child about opera is just as unfair as asking an American child about petrol. In both cases, the term is not familiar to the child (Hardy et al., 1976).

R. L. Flaugher (1978) considered the accusations about bias in psychological tests and concluded that many perceived problems are based on misunderstandings. Many people feel that a fair test is one that asks questions they can answer. By contrast, a biased test is one that does not ask about things a test taker knows. Flaugher argued that the purpose of aptitude and achievement tests is to measure performance on items sampled from a wide range of information. Test developers are not particularly concerned about individual items. Instead, they are interested in performance on the test, and they make judgments about this performance based on correlations between the tests and external criteria. Many test critics focus attention on specific items. For example, D. Owen (1985), in his popular book, *None of the Above: Behind the Myth of Scholastic Aptitude,* reported that famous people like Nicholas von Hoffman and William F. Buckley had difficulty with specific items on the SAT and LSAT examinations. He also asserted that some items on standardized tests are familiar only to those with a middle-class background. Test developers are indifferent to the opportunities people have to learn the information on the tests. The meaning they eventually assign to the tests comes from correlations of test scores with other variables.

However, some research evidence suggests that the linguistic bias in standardized tests does not cause the observed differences (Scheuneman, 1987). L. C. Quay (1971) administered the Stanford-Binet test to 100 children in an inner-city Head Start program. Half of the children were given a version of the test that used black dialect, while the others were given the standard version. The results demonstrated that the advantage produced by having the test in black dialect translates into less than a one-point increase in test scores. This finding is consistent with other research findings demonstrating that black children can comprehend standard English about as well as they can comprehend nonstandard black dialect (Clarizio, 1979a; Copple & Succi, 1974). This finding does not hold for white children, who seem to be functional only in the standard dialect.

Systematic studies have failed to demonstrate that biased items in well-known standardized tests are responsible for the differences in scores between ethnic groups (Flaugher, 1978). One approach has been to find people who have expertise in judging the unfairness of particular items. Once these unfair items have been eliminated, the test should be less biased. Unexpectedly, the many attempts to purify tests using this approach have not yielded positive results. In one study, 16% of the items in an elementary reading test were eliminated after experts reviewed them and labeled them as potentially biased toward the majority group. However, when the new version of the test, which had the bad items "purged," was used, the differences between the majority and the minority school populations were no smaller than they had been when the original form of the test was used (Bianchini, 1976).

Another approach to the same problem is to find classes of items that are most likely to be missed by members of a particular minority group. If a test is biased against that group, there should be significant differences between minority and nonminority groups on certain categories of items. These studies are particularly important because if they identify certain types of items that discriminate between groups, these types of items can be avoided on future tests. Again, the results have not been encouraging; studies have not been able to clearly identify categories of items that discriminate between groups (Wild et al., 1989). The studies do show that groups differ on certain items, but it has not been clear whether these are real or chance differences. When groups are compared on large numbers of items, some differences will occur for chance reasons.

Differential item functioning (DIF) analysis. Another approach to the analysis of test bias has been developed by the Educational Testing Service (ETS, 1991). The ETS creates and administers a variety of aptitude tests, including the Graduate Record Examination (GRE), the Scholastic Aptitude Test (SAT), the Law School Admissions Test (LSAT), and several others. In each of these testing programs, there are significant differences in performance between white test takers and those of other racial/ethnic groups on verbal and analysis measures. On quantitative measures, Asian-Americans tend to have higher scores than do the white groups. On the Graduate Records Examination, men and women score equivalently on verbal and analytic measures. Men, however, obtain higher scores on the quantitative measures.

Differential item functioning (DIF) analysis attempts to identify items that are specifically biased against an ethnic/racial or gender group. The analysis first equates groups on the basis of overall score. For example, it would find subgroups of test takers who obtain equivalent scores. These might be groups of men and women who obtain scores of about 500 on the verbal portion of the GRE. Using these groups, it evaluates differences in performance between men and women on particular items. Items that differ significantly between the groups are thrown out and the entire test is rescored.

A final approach to this problem is to find items that systematically show differences among ethnic groups. Then these items are eliminated, and the test is rescored. In one study, 27 items from the SAT were eliminated because they were the specific items on which ethnic groups differed. Then the test was rescored for everyone. Although it seems this procedure should have eliminated the differences between the two groups, it actually had only slight effects because the items that differentiated the groups tended to be the easiest items in the set. When these items were eliminated, the test was harder for everyone (Flaugher & Schrader, 1978).

There is at least some evidence that test items depicting people do not accurately portray the distribution of genders and races in the population. L. S. Zores and P. B. Williams (1980) reviewed the WAIS, WISC-R, Stanford-Binet, and Slosson Intelligence test items for race and gender characterization and found that white male characterization occurred with disproportionate frequency. Nevertheless, it has not yet been established that the frequency with which different groups are pictured in items is relevant to the issue of test bias. Various studies have failed to demonstrate that there is serious bias in item content. Most critics argue that the verbal content of test items is most objectionable because it is unfamiliar to minority groups. However, J. D. Scheuneman (1981) reviewed the problem and concluded that verbal material in tests is usually closer to the life experiences of blacks than is nonverbal material. Studies that manipulate gender bias by creating neutral, male, and female items demonstrate little effect on the performance differences between male and female test takers (McLarty, Noble & Huntley, 1989).

Other statistical models have been used to evaluate item fairness. In these studies, which use different populations and different methods of analysis, little evidence has been produced of bias in test items (Gotkin & Reynolds, 1981). However, different models may identify different items as biased. In one comparison, G. H. Ironson and N. J. Sebkovial (1979) applied four different methods to analyze item bias in the National Longitudinal Study test battery. Three differential statistical methods identified many of the same items as biased in evaluating 1691 black high school seniors in contrast to 1794 white 12th-graders. However, there was little agreement between these item evaluations and the bias items selected by a method proposed by D. R. Green and J. F. Draper (1972).

How do biased test items affect the differential validity of a test? In one theoretical example, 25% of the items on a test were presumed to be so biased that minority test takers would be expected to perform at chance level. Despite random performance, according to this simulation, there would be only slight and perhaps undetectable differences in validity coefficients for minority- and majority-group members (Drasgow, 1982). However, this result may be artificial and dependent on an unusual use of the term *test bias* (Dobko & Kehoe, 1983). Using a more general definition of test bias and biased items, they suggested that failure to find differences in validity coefficients is consistent with the belief that the tests are equally valid for members of different ethnic and racial groups.

Although most studies fail to support hypotheses about item bias (Scheuneman, 1987), the role of item bias remains poorly understood. For example, students who are test wise may be better able to answer questions that are irrelevant to the knowledge base being assessed. Since test-wise students tend to get other items correct, item analysis may incorrectly identify the irrelevant items as useful. These problems magnify the differences between high-achieving and low-achieving students (Masters, 1988).

In summary, studies have not supported the popular belief that items have different meanings for different groups; however, we must continue to scrutinize the content of tests. On some occasions, careful reviews of tests have turned up questionable items. Many tests are carelessly constructed, and every effort should be taken to purge items that have the potential for being biased.

Figure 20-2
A sample
regression plot.
The slope of the
line shows the
relationship
between a test and
a criterion. The
steeper the slope
of the line, the
better the
prediction of the
criterion score.

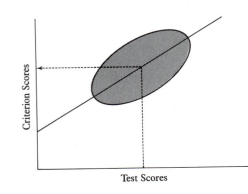

B. *Criterion Validity*

Each night on the evening news, the weatherperson forecasts the conditions for the next day. We come to depend on these forecasts if they have a history of being accurate. In evaluating the weather report, we are making a subjective assessment of validity. In a similar way we evaluate tests by asking whether they forecast future performance accurately. Standardized tests such as the SAT have been evaluated and found to be satisfactory in predicting performance during the first year of college. These tests clearly do not give us all the information we need for perfect prediction; yet they do give us enough information that we should pay attention to them.

College administrators who use the test scores are faced with difficult problems. On the average, minority applicants have lower test scores than nonminority applicants. At the same time, most universities and colleges are attempting to increase their minority enrollments. Because minority applicants are considered as a separate category, it is appropriate to ask whether the tests have differential predictive power for the two groups of applicants.

As we mentioned in Chapter 5, the criterion validity of a test is assessed by the coefficient of correlation between the test and some criterion. The higher the correlation, the more confident we are about making predictions. If college grades are the criterion (the variable we are trying to forecast), the validity of a test such as the SAT is represented by the correlation between the SAT score and first-year college grades. If students who score well on the SAT do well in college and students who score poorly on the SAT get lower grades, then the test might be considered valid for aiding in the decision of admitting college students.

In Chapter 3, we reviewed the interpretation of regression plots as they relate to the validity of psychological tests. Plots like the one in Figure 20-2 were shown, and we explained how to obtain a predicted criterion score from a test score. This was done by finding the test score on the horizontal axis of the graph and drawing a line directly upward until it hits the regression line. Then

Figure 20-3
A single regression slope can predict performance equally well for two groups. However, the means for the two groups differ.

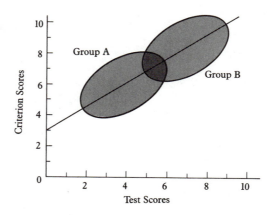

the line was drawn directly over to the left until it came to the vertical axis. This gave the predicted criterion score. The only difference between Figure 20-2 and Figure 3-8 is that we have added an ellipse around the regression line. This ellipse is called an **isodensity curve.** It is used to encircle a specified portion of the cases that constitute a particular group.

Figure 20-3 shows a regression line that represents two groups equally well. Group A appears to be performing less well than Group B on both the test (predictor) and the criterion scores. You can demonstrate this for yourself by selecting some points from the test scores for Group A and finding the expected scores on the criterion. By repeating this exercise for a few points in Group B, you will find that Group A is expected to do more poorly on the criterion because it did more poorly on the test. However, for both Group A and Group B, the relationship between the test score and performance on the criterion is the same. Thus, Figure 20-3 shows there is little evidence for test bias.

Figure 20-4 represents a different situation. Here there is a separate regression line for each group. The slopes of the two lines are the same, and that is why the two lines are parallel. However, the *intercepts,* or the points where the regression lines cross the vertical axis, differ. If you pick a particular test score, you get one expected criterion score if you use regression line A and another expected criterion score if you use regression line B. For a test score of 8, the expected criterion score from regression line A is 6, whereas the expected criterion score from regression line B is 10. The broken line in Figure 20-4 is based on a combination of regression lines A and B. Now try finding the predicted score for a test score of 8 from this combined (broken) regression line. You should get 8. Thus, the combined regression line actually overpredicts performance on the criterion for Group A and underpredicts performance for Group B. According to this example, the use of a single regression line produces discrimination in favor of Group A and against Group B.

This situation seems to fit the use of the SAT and GRE (Cleary, 1968; Jensen, 1984; Kallingal, 1971; Pfeifer & Sedlacek, 1971; Reynolds, 1986;

Figure 20-4
Regression lines
with equal slopes
but different
intercepts.

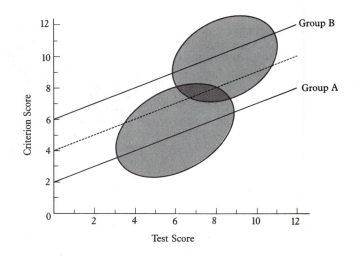

Schneider & Briel, 1990; Temp, 1971). Each of these studies showed that the relationship between college performance and SAT scores was best described by two separate regression equations. Using a combined regression equation, which is common in practice, overpredicts how well minority students will do in college and tends to underpredict the performance of majority-group students. In other words, it appears that the SAT used with a single regression line yields biased predictions and that the bias is in favor of minority groups and against majority-group students.

Since the lines in Figure 20-4 are parallel, the slopes of the lines are the same for both groups. The equal slopes suggest equal predictive validity. Most standardized intelligence, aptitude, and achievement tests do confirm the relationships shown in the figure (Reschly & Sabers, 1979; Reynolds, 1980; Reynolds & Nigl, 1981). Thus, there is little evidence that tests such as the SAT predict college performance differently for different groups or that IQ tests have different correlations with achievement tests for black, white, or Hispanic children. This finding has been reported for the SAT (Temp, 1971), preschool tests (Reynolds, 1980), and IQ tests such as the WISC-R (Reschly & Sabers, 1979). Whether separate or combined regression lines are used depends on different definitions of bias. (We return to this issue later in the chapter. As we will see, the interpretation of tests for assessing different groups can be strongly influenced by personal and moral convictions.) It is worth noting that the situation shown in Figure 20-4 is independent of differences in mean scores. The differences in mean scores in the figure are equal to the differences between the two regression lines.

Some studies have shown that these problems are not specific to American culture. Psychometric aptitude tests are currently used by all Israeli universities. Israeli society is made up of a wide variety of cultural and ethnic groups. As in the United States, there is interest in determining whether or not aptitude

Figure 20-5
Regression lines with different slopes suggest that a test has different meanings for different groups. This is the most clear-cut example of test bias.

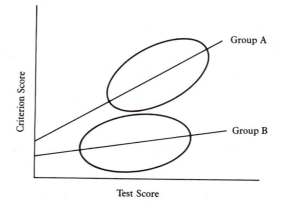

tests include biases against specific ethnic or cultural groups. In a study of 1538 Israeli college student candidates of varying ethnic backgrounds, the predictive validity of the test was the same across groups even though there were mean differences among the groups (Zeidner, 1987).

A third situation outlined by T. A. Cleary and co-workers (1975) is shown in Figure 20-5. In this figure, there are two regression lines, but the lines are no longer parallel. The coefficient for one group is different from the coefficient for the other group. In the situation presented in Figure 20-4, each group was best represented by its own regression line. Using a common regression line causes error in predicting the scores for each group. However, the situation depicted in Figure 20-4 is not hopeless, and indeed some psychologists feel that this situation is useful because it may help increase the accuracy of predictions (Cleary, 1968). However, Figure 20-5 demonstrates a more hopeless situation. The test is differentially valid for the two groups, meaning that the test has an entirely different meaning for each group. Although empirical studies have rarely turned up such a case, there are some known examples of differential slopes (Mercer, 1979). An example of differential validity might be a test designed to predict performance in a mechanical training program. This test might predict performance much better for men than for women. Some women would score poorly on the test because they had less previous experience with mechanical concepts. However, when taking the course, women would easily acquire this information and perform well. Thus, the test would provide relatively little information about how women would perform in the program, but it would predict how men would perform. Furthermore, poor test performance by a man would indicate that he might never learn mechanical concepts, given that these men had been previously exposed to this information. An extensive discussion of differential validity is presented by Bartlett and O'Leary (1969). Focused Example 20-1 illustrates the application of both content and criterion validity.

FOCUSED EXAMPLE 20-1

Scoring the WISC-R for Inner-City Children

The WISC-R requires that a test administrator follow a rigid protocol in allowing credit for certain types of responses. Over the years, many people have questioned whether these scoring procedures should be so stringent. In particular, they have suggested that some children may be giving an appropriate response for the subculture they are familiar with even though that response may not be given credit. A large study conducted in the inner portion of Baltimore (the Johns Hopkins Child Development Study) favors this conclusion (Hardy et al., 1976).

As part of the Johns Hopkins study, 200 children from the inner city of Baltimore were given selected questions from the WISC-R. For this study, however, the standard WISC-R scoring instructions were abandoned, and an attempt was made to understand the reasoning behind the children's answers. For example, this WISC-R question was given: "What would you do if you were sent to buy a loaf of bread, and the grocer said he did not have anymore?" The WISC-R scoring instructions state that that correct answer is "Go to another score." Among the 200 children in the study, 61 gave an incorrect response. However, when the examiners probed the children about their responses, they discovered that many of the children had given replies that were reasonable considering their circumstances. For instance, the rigid WISC-R scoring procedures do not allow credit for the response "Go home." Yet many of the inner-city children explained that there were no other stores near their homes and they were not allowed to go away from home without permission. Others reported that they used family credit to shop and would need to go home to get money if they had to go to another store. In each of these cases, the researchers suggested that the children had given correct and reasonable responses to the question, given their own circumstances (Hardy et al., 1976).

Other psychologists emphasize the need for strict scoring procedures if intelligence tests are to be reliable. Standardization implies that all children take the test with the same set of rules. Beyond this objection, the methodology of the Johns Hopkins study has been called into question. J. M. Sattler (1979b) carefully reviewed the study and found a variety of methodological problems. In particular, there was no control group of children who were not from the inner city. Thus, it is not possible to determine whether children in general would have benefited from a more liberal interpretation of the criteria for a correct answer. There is abundant evidence that permitting a tester to exercise judgment about the reasonableness of a response results in higher scores for children from many different walks of life. Under most circumstances, this procedure does not result in greater validity for the test (Sattler, 1988).

Another of Sattler's objections is that the study may have had serious rater bias. It is quite likely that the psychologists who tested the inner-city children knew that the study was on test bias and that their interpretations of a reasonable response were influenced by a subjective predisposition.

Ultimately, a test is evaluated by its criterion validity. How well does it do its job in predicting performance on some criterion of interest? It has been argued that any scoring procedure is valid if it enhances the relationship between a test and a criterion (Barrett & Depinet, 1991). In the Johns Hopkins study, no information was offered about the benefits of a liberal scoring system for the criterion validity of the test (Hardy et al., 1976). Thus, different scoring procedures may make the scores of inner-city children higher, but it remains to be determined whether the revised procedures would make the tests more meaningful (Sattler, 1979b). Most studies on criterion validity suggest that IQ tests are not differentially meaningful for different groups of children (Barrett & Depinet, 1991; Hall, Huppertz & Levi, 1977; Hartigan & Wigdor, 1989; Hartlage & Steele, 1977; Henderson et al., 1973; Lamp & Traxler, 1973; Lunemann, 1974; Palmer, 1970; Valencia & Lopez, 1992).

IV. *Other Approaches to Testing Minority-Group Members*

To many American psychologists the defense of psychological tests has not been totally satisfactory. Although some consider the defense of the tests to be strong enough, others emphasize that we must try to find selection procedures that will end all discriminatory practices and protect the interests of minority-group members. Those who do not think that the tests are fair suggest one of two alternatives: outlaw the use of psychological tests for minority students (Williams, 1974) or develop psychological assessment strategies that suit minority children. Advocates of the first alternative have launched a legal battle to restrict the use of tests. This battle is discussed in detail in Chapter 22. In this section, we review various approaches to the second alternative. In particular, we look at four different assessment approaches: the Chitling Test, the Black Intelligence Test of Cultural Homogeneity, and the System of Multicultural Pluralistic Assessment. Each of these approaches is different, yet they are all based on one common assumption: minority children have not had the opportunity to learn how to answer items on tests that reflect traditional, white, middle-class values.

A. *Ignorance Versus Stupidity*

In a California trial about the use of testing in public schools, *Larry P.* v. *Wilson Riles*, the judge made an abrasive but insightful comment. Both sides in the case agreed that minority children perform more poorly on standardized tests. The major issue debated by the witnesses was the meaning of the scores. One side argued that the scores reflect the underlying trait of intelligence. In other words, the tests allegedly measure how smart a child is. Witnesses for the other side suggested that the tests measure only whether the child has learned the appropriate responses needed to perform well on the test. This position claims that the tests do not measure how smart the child is but only whether the child has been exposed to the information on the test. After hearing the testimony for the different points of view, the judge commented that the issue was really one of ignorance versus stupidity. Although this comment appears insensitive and racist, it deserves reflection. There are two potential explanations for why some children do more poorly on standardized tests than other children. One explanation is that they are less intelligent. Put bluntly, this would be the stupidity explanation. The other explanation is that some children do more poorly because they are ignorant. In other words, they simply have not learned the right responses for a particular test. If ignorance is the explanation, then differences in IQ scores are of less concern because they can be changed. The stupidity explanation is more damning because it implies that the lower test scores obtained by black students are a product of some deficit that cannot be easily changed.

The term *ignorance* implies that differences can easily be abolished. Just as some minority children are ignorant about how to answer items that might predict success in white, middle-class culture, so could white, middle-class children be labeled ignorant about how to succeed in the world of an inner-city child. This proposition is illustrated by the Chitling Test.

B. *The Chitling Test*

Many years ago, animal psychologists talked about higher and lower animals. The higher animals were considered to be intelligent because they could do some of the same things humans can do, and the lower animals were considered to be unintelligent because they could not perform like humans. However, in 1969 a famous article by W. Hodos and C. B. G. Campbell changed the thinking of many students of animal behavior. Hodos and Campbell argued that all animals are equally intelligent for the environments in which they live. We cannot compare the intelligence of a rat with that of a cat because a rat is adapted to a rat's environment and a cat is adapted to a cat's environment. Both animals are best suited to survive in the environment they occupy.

The same insight seems not to have permeated the world of human affairs. Because of poverty and discrimination, minority and nonminority children grow up in different environments. To be successful in each of these environments requires different skills and knowledge. A psychological test may consider survival in only one of these environments, and this is usually the white, middle-class environment. Thus, using one of these tests for impoverished children is analogous to testing a cat on a task designed to determine how well a rat is adapted to a rat's environment.

The Chitling Test was developed by black sociologist Adrian Dove to demonstrate that there is a body of information about which the white middle class is ignorant. Dove named his effort the Dove Counterbalance General Intelligence Test, but it has become known as just the Chitling Test (Dove, 1968). A major aim in developing the Chitling Test was to show that blacks and whites are just not talking the same language.

Some of the items from the Chitling Test are listed in Table 20-1. Try to answer the questions and tally up your scores. Many of you may not do too well because you have not been exposed to black, mid-1960s culture. Minority-group members who have grown up in a ghetto in this era should clearly outperform you. On this test, a white, middle-class student would probably score as culturally deprived.

However, we must caution you about the meaning of the test. At present, no more than face validity has been established. No body of evidence demonstrates that the test successfully predicts performance on any important criterion. If we want to predict which students will do well in college, the Chitling

Table 20-1
Selected Items
from the Dove
Counterbalance
General
Intelligence Test
(the Chitling
Test)*

1. A "handkerchief head" is: (a) a cool cat, (b) a porter, (c) an Uncle Tom, (d) a hoddi, (e) a preacher.
2. Which word is most out of place here? (a) splib, (b) blood, (c) gray, (d) spook, (e) Black.
3. A "gas head" is a person who has a: (a) fast-moving car, (b) stable of "lace," (c) "process," (d) habit of stealing cars, (e) long jail record for arson.
4. "Bo Diddley" is a: (a) game for children, (b) down-home cheap wine, (c) down-home singer, (d) new dance, (e) Moejoe call.
5. If a pimp is uptight with a woman who gets state aid, what does he mean when he talks about "Mother's Day"? (a) second Sunday in May, (b) third Sunday in June, (c) first of every month, (d) none of these, (e) first and fifteenth of every month.
6. If a man is called a "blood," then he is a: (a) fighter, (b) Mexican-American, (c) Negro, (d) hungry hemophile, (e) Redman or Indian.
7. What are the "Dixie Hummingbirds"? (a) part of the KKK, (b) a swamp disease, (c) a modern gospel group, (d) a Mississippi Negro paramilitary group, (e) deacons.
8. T'Bone Walker got famous for playing what? (a) trombone, (b) piano, (c) "T-flute," (d) guitar, (e) "hambone,"

From Dove (1968). Copyright 1968 by Newsweek, Inc. All rights reserved. Reprinted by permission.
* The correct answers are: 1 (c), 2 (c), 3 (c), 4 (c), 5 (e), 6 (c), 7 (c), and 8 (d).

Test will be of no benefit. In fact, standardized tests predict performance for both minority and nonminority students, and the Chitling Test predicts performance for neither group. It may well be that the Chitling Test will turn out to be a valid test for inferring how streetwise someone is. Yet we must await validity evidence before we can make any generalizations. Dove described his efforts to develop an intelligence test as "half serious." But we have seen that the test does identify an area of content on which the races differ and blacks outperform whites.

C. *The Black Intelligence Test of Cultural Homogeneity*

Some psychologists regard most achievement and intelligence tests as instruments of racism. Most racist actions are felt to be illogical and emotional. However, the use of intelligence tests is seen as a subtle and thus more dangerous racist move because the tests are supported by scientific validity studies (Garcia, 1981). Robert Williams, a well-known black psychologist, has labeled this phenomenon *scientific racism* (1974). Williams (1974, p. 34) views IQ and standardized achievement tests as "nothing but updated versions of the old signs down South that read 'For Whites Only.'"

Of particular interest to Williams and his colleagues is the assessment of the ability to survive in the black community. Indeed, they feel that assessment of survival potential with a survival quotient (SQ) is more important than assessment of IQ, which indicates only the likelihood of succeeding in the white community. As a beginning, Williams developed the Black Intelligence Test of Cultural Homogeneity (BITCH), which asks respondents to define 100 vocabulary words relevant to Afro-American culture. The words came from the *Afro-American Slang Dictionary* and from Williams's personal experience interacting with black Americans. Black persons obtain higher scores than their white counterparts on the BITCH. When Williams administered the BITCH to 100 16- to 18-year-olds from each group, the average score for black subjects was 87.07 (out of 100). The mean score for the whites was significantly lower (51.07). Williams argues that traditional IQ and achievement tests are nothing more than culture-specific tests that assess how much white children know about white culture. The BITCH is also a culture-specific test, but one on which black subjects outperform whites.

Although the BITCH does tell us a lot about the cultural loading in intelligence and achievement tests, it has received mixed reviews. The reliability data reported by Williams show that the BITCH is quite reliable for black test takers (standard error less than 3 points on the 100-point scale) and acceptably reliable for white test takers (standard error about 6). (Conventional tests have similar reliabilities for both groups; see Oakland & Feigenbaum, 1979.) However, little convincing validity data on the BITCH are available. Although the test manual does report some studies, the samples are small and not representative of any clearly defined population (Cronbach, 1978). The difficulty is that we cannot determine whether the BITCH does predict how well a person will survive on the streets, how well he or she will do in school, in life, or in anything else. To support the conclusion that the BITCH is an intelligence test, we must have some evidence. The test does assess word association, but it seems to give no information on reasoning abilities.

More studies are needed to determine whether the BITCH does what it is supposed to do. One of the rationales for the test is that it will identify children who have been unfairly assigned to classes for the educable mentally retarded (EMR) on the basis of IQ scores. In one study, P. A. Long and J. J. Anthony (1974) attempted to determine how many black EMR children would be reclassified if they were retested with the BITCH. Among a small and limited sample of 30 black EMR high school students from Gainesville, Florida, all the students who performed poorly on the WISC also performed below the first percentile on the BITCH. Using the BITCH served to reclassify none of the students. However, this was just one small and nonrepresentative study. In its present state, the BITCH can be a valuable tool for measuring white familiarity with the black community. When white teachers or administrators are sent to schools that have predominantly black enrollments, the BITCH may be used to determine how much they know about the culture. Furthermore, the BITCH may be used to assess the extent to which a black person is in touch with his or her own community. As L. J. Cronbach (1978) notes, people with good abstract reasoning skills may function poorly if they are unfamiliar with the community in which they live. Similarly, people with poor reasoning skills may get along just fine if they are familiar with the community.

D. *The System of Multicultural Pluralistic Assessment*

No assessment technique covered in this book challenges our traditional beliefs about testing as much as the System of Multicultural Pluralistic Assessment (SOMPA) (Mercer, 1979). This system, developed by sociologist Jane Mercer, has been adopted by several states. Before we discuss the SOMPA and the evaluations of it, it is instructive to review Mercer's beliefs about the social and political implications of testing.

Mercer feels that our beliefs about what is fair and what knowledge exists are related to the social structure. She agrees with sociologist K. Mannheim (1936) that members of the politically dominant group provide the interpretation of events within a society and they do so from their own perspective. The traditional psychometric literature on IQ tests provides a scientific rationale for the dominant group to keep minority-group members in their place by demonstrating that the minority-group members do not have the language and knowledge skills to perform well in a white cultural setting. The feedback given to the minority groups is not that they are ignorant about the rules for success in another culture (just as the dominant group would be in a minority culture) but that they are stupid and unlikely to succeed. Mercer emphasizes that we must take into consideration that some individuals are working from a different knowledge base.

It is not possible to give a complete description of the SOMPA here. The system is complex, and many technical issues have been raised about its validity and its applicability (Brown, 1979a, 1979b; Clarizio, 1979a, 1979b; Goodman, 1977, 1979; Mercer, 1979; Oakland, 1979; Oakland & Parmelee, 1985; Taylor, Sternberg & Partenio, 1986).

One important philosophical assumption underlies the development of the SOMPA—that all cultural groups have the same average potential. Any differences among cultural groups are assumed to be caused by differences in access to cultural experiences. Those who do not perform well on the tests are not well informed about the criteria for success that are usually set forth by the dominant group. However, within groups that have had the same cultural experiences, not all individuals are expected to be the same, and assessment of these differences is a better measure of ability than is assessment of differences among cultural groups.

Mercer (1972) has been concerned about the consequences of labeling a child as mentally retarded. She has convincingly argued that many children are incorrectly identified as retarded and that they suffer severely as a result of this inaccurate branding. In particular, she is distressed that classes for EMR students have disproportionate numbers of minority children. Mercer maintains that some minority students score low on the traditional tests because they are ignorant about the ways of the dominant culture, and they are not in any way mentally retarded. Another reason for misclassification is medical problems. Thus, a fair system of evaluation must include medical assessment. It must also include the assessment of children relative to other children who have had similar life experiences. The basic point of divergence between the SOMPA and earlier approaches to assessment is that the SOMPA attempts to integrate three different approaches to assessment: medical, social, and pluralistic.

One of the most consistent findings in the field of public health is that members of low-income groups have more health problems than do those who are economically better off. The *medical* component of the SOMPA system asks "Is the child an intact organism?" (Mercer, 1979, p. 92). The rationale for this portion is that medical problems can interfere with a child's performance on mental measures and in school.

The *social-system* component attempts to determine whether a child is functioning at a level that would be expected by social norms. For example, does the child do what is expected by family members, peer groups, or the community? Mercer feels that test users and developers typically adopt only a social-system orientation. For example, if a test predicts who will do well in school, it is forecasting behavior that is expected by the dominant social system. Mercer emphasizes that the social-system approach is a narrow one because only the dominant group in society defines the criteria for success (Reschly, 1981).

The *pluralistic* component of the SOMPA recognizes that different subcultures are associated with different life experiences. Only within these subgroups do individuals have common experiences. Thus, tests should assess individuals against others in the same subculture. It is important to recognize the distinction between the criteria for defining deviance in the pluralistic model and in the social-system model. The social-system model uses the norms of society as the criteria, whereas the pluralistic model uses the norms within a particular group.

The SOMPA attempts to assess children relative to each of these models. The medical portion of the SOMPA package includes physical measures such as tests of vision, hearing, and motor functioning. The social-system portion is similar to most assessment procedures. The entire WISC-R is given and evaluated according to the regular criteria. Finally, the pluralistic portion also uses WISC-R scores but evaluates them against those for groups that have similar social and cultural backgrounds. In other words, the WISC-R scores are adjusted for socioeconomic background. These adjusted scores are known as **estimated learning potentials** (ELPs). An example of a SOMPA profile is shown in Figure 20-6.

The major dispute between Mercer and her many critics is over the validity of the SOMPA. Mercer (1979) points out that a test itself is not valid or invalid, but the inferences that are made on the basis of the test scores are. She insists that ELPs cannot be validated in the same way as are other test scores. (Validating a test by predicting who will do well in school is appropriate only for the social-system model.) Mercer argues that the criteria for evaluating the

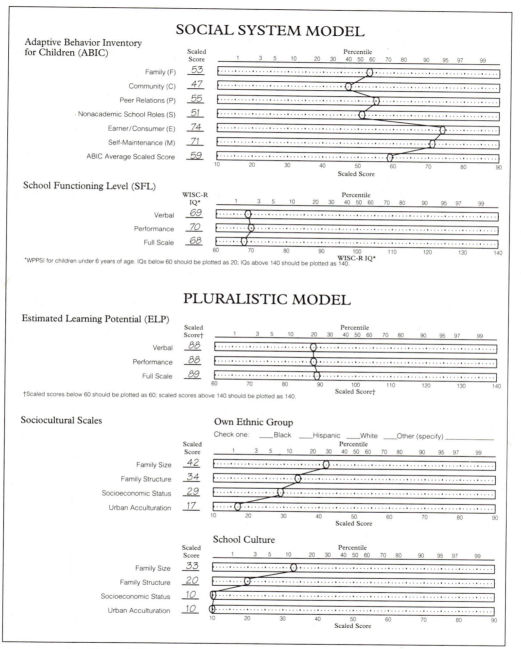

Figure 20-6
Sample SOMPA profile. (*From the* System of Multicultural Pluralistic Assessment. *Copyright © 1978 by The Psychological Corporation. Reproduced by permission. All rights reserved.*)

ELPs must be different. She states that the appropriate validity criterion for ELPs should be the percentage of variance in WISC-R scores that is accounted for by sociocultural variables. Many SOMPA critics (Brown, 1979a; Clarizio, 1979b; Goodman, 1979; Oakland, 1979), however, feel that a test should always be validated by demonstrating that it predicts performance. The correlation between ELPs and school achievement is around .40, whereas the correlation between the WISC-R and school achievement is around .60 (Oakland, 1979). Thus, ELPs are a poorer predictor than WISC-R scores of school success. Mercer refutes these critics by arguing that the test is not designed to identify which children will do well in school. Its purpose is to determine which children are mentally retarded. This can be done only by comparing children with others who have had the same life experiences.

Accepting Mercer's argument may produce a quota system for EMR classes. Using ELPs should make the proportions of ethnic groups in EMR classes more representative than they now are. Because several states have adopted the SOMPA, we may soon be able to determine the ultimate effect of the system. There is no question that it will identify many fewer minority children as EMR students. This may please some taxpayers because the costs of educating EMR students are higher than average. Yet we still do not know whether children no longer considered EMR students will benefit. Mercer's (1972) research suggests that a big part of the battle is just getting more children labeled as normal. Her critics retaliate by suggesting that the effects of labeling are weak and inconsequential. They argue that no matter what these children are called, they will need some special help in school.

V. Suggestions for Solutions

This chapter has been about problems associated with the finding of ethnic differences in test scores. We have presented many different arguments from many different perspectives. In the following pages, we offer some solutions; however, we must warn you that the different solutions depend on different social and political beliefs about the definition of bias.

A. Ethical Concerns and the Definition of Test Bias

It is difficult to define the term *test bias*. Different authors have different views (Barrett & Depinet, 1991; Cole, 1981; Darlington, 1978; Flaugher, 1978; Hunter & Schmidt, 1976). These different definitions represent commitments to underlying ethical viewpoints about the way various groups ought to be treated. J. E. Hunter and F. L. Schmidt (1976) identify three ethical positions that set the tone for much of the debate: unqualified individualism, the use of quotas, and qualified individualism. All these positions are concerned with the use of tests to select people either for jobs or for training programs (including college).

Supporters of *unqualified individualism* would use tests to select the most qualified individuals they could find. In this case, users of tests would be indifferent to the race or gender of applicants. The goal would be to predict those who would be expected to perform best on the job or in school. According to this viewpoint, a test is fair if it finds the best candidates for the job or for admission to school. If race or gender was a valid predictor of performance over and above the information in the test, the unqualified individualist would see nothing wrong with considering this information in the selection process.

A quite different ethical approach to selection is to use *quotas*. Quota systems explicitly recognize race and gender differences. If the population of a state is 20% black, then supporters of a quota system might argue that 20% of the new medical students in the state-supported medical school should also be black. Selection procedures are regarded as biased if the actual percentage of applicants admitted is different from the percentage in the population; each group should have a fair share of the representation (Gordon & Terrell, 1981). This fair-share selection process gives less emphasis than the testing process to how well people in the different groups are expected to do once they are selected (Darlington, 1971; Hunter & Schmidt, 1976; Thorndike, 1971).

The final moral position considered by Hunter and Schmidt might be viewed as a compromise between unqualified individualism and a quota system. *Qualified individualism,* like unqualified individualism, embraces the notion that the best qualified persons should be the ones selected. But unqualified individualists also take information about race, gender, and religion into consideration if it helps to predict performance on the criterion. Not to do so results in underprediction of performance for one group and overprediction of performance for another group. Qualified individualists, however, recognize that, although failing to include group characteristics (race, gender, and religion) may lead to differential accuracy in prediction, this differential prediction may counteract known effects of discrimination. It may, for example, lead to underprediction of the performance of the majority group and overprediction of the performance of the minority group. The qualified individualist may choose not to include information about personal characteristics in selection because ignoring this information may serve the interests of minority-group members.

Each of these ethical positions can be related to a particular statistical definition of test bias, and we now turn to these definitions. Table 20-2 shows several different models of test bias based on different definitions of fairness. All these models are based on regression lines, as we discussed. The models discussed in Table 20-2 are relevant to tests that are used for selection purposes, including job-placement tests and tests used to select students for college or for advanced-degree programs.

The regression model described in Table 20-2 (see also Cleary, 1968) represents the unqualified individualism position. The result of this approach is that a large number of majority-group members may be selected. This approach maintains that an employer or a school should be absolutely color and gender blind. The reason for considering ethnicity or gender is to improve the prediction of future performance. This approach has been favored by business because it ensures the highest productivity of employees selected by the procedure.

At the other extreme is the quota system. To achieve fair-share representation, separate selection procedures are developed. One procedure, for example, is used to select the best available black applicants, and another procedure is used to select the best available nonblack applicants. If a community has 42% black residents, the first procedure would be used to select 42% of the employees, and the other procedure would be used to select the other 58%.

The difficulty with the quota system is that it may lead to greater rates of failure among some groups. Suppose that a test had been devised to select telephone operators and that the test did indeed predict who would succeed on the job. However, the test selected 70% women and only 30% men. The quota system would encourage the use of separate cutoff scores so that the proportion of men selected would approach 50%. But because the women scored higher on the average, they would perform better on the job, resulting in a higher rate of failure among the men. Thus, although quota systems often aid in increasing the selection of underrepresented groups, they also make it likely that the underrepresented groups will experience failure.

Table 20-2 shows two other models (Cole, 1973; Darlington, 1971; Thorndike, 1971). These models represent compromises between the quota and the

FOCUSED EXAMPLE 20-2

Quotas in the Civil Rights Act of 1991

The difference between unqualified individualism and quota systems became a central issue in the 1991 Civil Rights Bill. The bill never mentioned the word *quota;* however, the structure of the bill emphasized selection systems that would support affirmative action and increase the percentage of minority-group members in federal jobs. President George Bush initially refused to support the bill and accused the Democratic Congress of pushing discriminatory quotas. Bush favored an unqualified individualism position and emphasized that many prominent minority-group members had achieved success without special programs. During the 1980s, President Ronald Reagan had appointed a director of the Equal Employment Opportunities Commission (EEOC) who had, in effect, also supported unqualified individualism over quota systems. During that era, the EEOC failed to act on a substantial number of adverse selection cases. In the fall of 1991, newspapers reported that President Bush would add language to the bill that would halt the use of quota selection systems. However, last-minute lobbying by civil rights groups persuaded the president to leave undisturbed the federal policies encouraging affirmative action. (For more details, see Chapter 21.)

Table 20-2
Different Models of Test Fairness

Model	Reference	Use of Regression	Rationale	Effect on Minority Selection	Effect on Average Criterion Performance
Regression	Cleary (1968)	Separate regression lines are used for different groups. Those with the highest predicted criterion scores are selected.	This is fair because those with the highest estimated level of success are selected.	Few minority-group members selected	Good performance on criteria
Constant ratio	Thorndike (1971)	Points equal to about half of the average difference between the groups are added to the test scores of the group with the lower score. Then a single regression line is used, and those with the highest predicted scores are selected.	This is fair because it better reflects the potential of the lower-scoring group.	Some increase in the number of minority-group members selected	Somewhat lower
Cole/ Darlington	Cole (1973), Darlington (1971, 1978)	Separate regression equations are used for each group, and points are added to scores of those from the lower group to ensure that those with the same criterion score have the same predictor score.	This is fair because it selects more potentially successful persons from the lower group.	Larger increase in the number of minority-group members selected	Lower
Quota	Dunnette and Borman (1979)	The proportion of persons to be selected from each group is predetermined. Separate regression equations are used to select those persons from each group who are expected to perform highest on the criterion.	This is fair because members of different subgroups are selected based on their proportions in the community.	Best representation of minority groups	About the same as for the Cole/ Darlington model

Based on Dunnette and Borman (1979).

unqualified individualism points of view. In each of these cases, there is an attempt to select the most qualified persons, yet there is some adjustment for minority-group members. When persons from two different groups have the same test score, these procedures give a slight edge to the person from the lower group and put the person from the higher group at a slight disadvantage. Although these approaches have been attacked for being based on faulty logic (Hunter & Schmidt, 1976, 1978), plausible defenses have been offered. The effect of these procedures is to increase the number of persons selected from underrepresented groups. However, these procedures also reduce the average performance score on the criterion. We cannot tell you which of these approaches is right and which is wrong. That decision depends on your own values and judgment about what is fair.

Despite these problems and controversies, surveys show that psychologists and educational specialists generally have positive attitudes about intelligence and aptitude tests. In one survey of 1020 experts selected from the American Educational Research Association, the National Council on Measurement in Education, the American Psychological Association, the American Sociological Association, and the Behavior Genetics Association, experts agreed that there were some sociocultural biases in the tests (Snyderman & Rothman, 1987). However, these experts generally agreed that the tests were valid for predictive purposes. Their major concerns were the interpretation and application of test results by elementary and secondary schools.

B. *Improving the Use of Selection Devices*

We have contended that the observed differences between minority and non-minority groups on standardized tests are a problem. Sometimes a problem stimulates us to think differently; in the words of famous entrepreneur Henry Kaiser: "A problem is an opportunity in work clothes." Another reason for the differences in test scores may be that different strategies for solving problems characterize different subcultures. Knowing how groups differ in their approaches to problem solving can be of benefit for two reasons. First, it can help us learn important things about the relationship between socialization and problem-solving approaches. This information can guide the development of pluralistic education programs (Castaneda & Ramirez, 1974). Second, knowing more about the ways different groups approach problems can lead to the development of improved predictors of success for minority groups (Goldman, 1973; Sternberg, 1991).

Along these lines, R. D. Goldman (1973) has proposed the differential process theory, which maintains that for many tasks, different strategies may lead to an effective solution. According to this theory, strategies—the ways people go about solving problems (Frederiksen, 1969; Sternberg, 1985)—mediate between abilities and performance.

An example of a differential process at work is that black college students (on the average) tend to score higher on the verbal subtest of the SAT than they do on the quantitative subtest. White students (on the average) score about the same on both subtests. As the result of socialization experiences, it is possible that black students structure the task of getting through school differently; they develop their verbal skills rather than their quantitative abilities. This result may also reflect differences in the opportunity to learn proper quantitative skills because of unequal educational opportunity. In any case, black students tend to choose college majors that emphasize their verbal abilities. It may thus be appropriate to build specific tests that predict how well these students will do in the majors they choose. These tests could deemphasize quantitative skills if they are shown to be unrelated to success for these particular majors. In other words, the test would be validated for the specific majors chosen by black students.

C. *Developing Different Criteria*

Criterion validity is the correlation between the test and the criterion. But what are the criteria used to validate the tests for assessing the potential of children? Most of these tests are simply valid predictors of how well children will do on other standardized tests. In other words, most standardized tests are evaluated against other standardized tests. The difficulty is that the criterion may be the test dressed in different clothes. For example, an intelligence test may be evaluated to determine how well it predicts performance on a standardized achievement test. This test is measuring not native ability but achievement. Differences in scores on this test between minority and nonminority groups are therefore due to the opportunity to learn rather than the ability to learn. This is recognized by the Educational Testing Service, which requests special care in interpreting SAT and GRE scores for students who have had "an educational and cultural experience somewhat different from that of the traditional majority" (*GRE Guide*, 1991, p. 14).

If we do not accept standardized tests as a criterion against which tests can be evaluated, how can we determine the meaning of the tests? There is considerable debate about whether classroom grades should be allowed as the criterion. Supporters of the use of classroom grades claim that these grades are the only independent measure of how well the child is doing. It is no surprise, they maintain, that there is a correlation between IQ tests and scores on standardized achievement tests because both measure a similar domain of content. However, they argue that IQ tests do not predict classroom grades for minority children and, therefore, are not valid for minority youngsters. The support for this position comes from studies like one by R. D. Goldman and L. Hartig (1976). In this study, scores on the WISC were found to be unrelated to teacher ratings of classroom performance for minority children. For the nonminority children, there was a significant relationship between IQ and teacher ratings. If the criterion becomes classroom grades rather than another standardized test, the IQ test appears valid for nonminority but not for minority children.

Supporters of the use of the tests do not want classroom grades to be the criterion for three reasons. First, teacher-assigned grades are unstandardized and are open to subjective bias (Sattler, 1979a). For example, teachers have been known to reward effort more than ability (Weiner & Kukla, 1970). Second, there are few available studies in which grades have been used as the criterion. Third, the most frequently cited study (Goldman & Hartig, 1976) is open to other explanations. In this study, the teachers rated the classroom performance of nearly all the minority children as poor. These low ratings resulted in little variance on the criterion measure. As we learned in Chapter 3, any variable for which there is no variability cannot correlate well with other variables.

The problem with criterion measures becomes even more apparent for measures used with adults. We know, for example, that the Medical College Admission Test (MCAT) predicts success in medical school. Yet, as Focused Example 20-3 demonstrates, it does not predict who will be a successful doctor. Similarly, the Law School Admission Test (LSAT) predicts performance in law school, yet there is little evidence that it predicts who will be a good attorney. The professional school admission tests may be weeding out candidates who

---

FOCUSED EXAMPLE 20-3

Evaluating the Medical College Admission Test

The ultimate goal in medical practice is the successful diagnosis and treatment of patients. Thus, the selection of medical students should proceed with this objective in mind. However, the MCAT is designed to predict only how well students will do in medical school. Studies do show that the MCAT is an adequate predictor of medical school grades. But how meaningful are medical school grades?

The importance of medical school grades has been a matter of some debate. For example, one study that considered measures of physician success in practice found that grades were unassociated with measures of real-life performance (Loughmiller et al., 1970). In another study of 217 physicians who were practicing in Utah, 76 measures of doctor performance were taken. Among more than 1000 correlations between grades and performance on these measures,

97% were nearly 0. On the basis of these results, the criteria for admission to medical school were seriously questioned (Taylor et al., 1965). Although tests may predict medical school grades, it is unclear whether grades or the tests give us much information about who will be a successful doctor.

After students graduate from medical school, they must face selection into medical residency programs to obtain training in their specialty areas. In order to select the best residents, specialty training programs have typically used test scores and personal interviews. These interviews and tests are very important because they determine where a physician will get training and which physicians will gain entry into the most prestigious programs. Studies suggest that programs are increasingly relying on academic test performance for entry into these programs. In addition, most resident prowould not do so well on the narrowly defined criterion of medical school or law school grades. In doing so, they may be eliminating people who are potentially better doctors and lawyers than those who are admitted. Imagine, for example, that an Anglo and a Hispanic doctor are trained equally well in the science of medical care and that both are practicing in a public hospital in a Hispanic neighborhood. The Hispanic doctor will more likely be effective because he or she understands the culture and the language of the patients and thus is better at understanding specific complaints and symptoms. The Anglo doctor may do a poorer job at diagnosing the problems. The MCAT would have done its job poorly by focusing on the short-term criterion of medical school grades. More work is needed to develop measures that are good predictors of the long-range goal of clinical success (Altmaier et al., 1991).

D. *Changing the Social Environment*

It is not hard to determine that majority and minority children grow up in different social environments. You can learn this by reading any sociology textbook or by getting in your car and driving to the nearest inner-city ghetto. Given this disparity in environment, it is not surprising that tests favor the majority. Many critics of tests seem to hold the tests responsible for inequality

grams require interviews. During the interview process, prospective specialists are evaluated on their personality characteristics, professional maturity, enthusiasm and energy, and interpersonal rapport. Detailed studies have evaluated the relationship between these cognitive (test performance) and noncognitive (interview) predictors of success in the residency program. The studies have produced consistent results: traditional tests and interviews are terrible predictors of success as a physician (Altmaier et al., 1990, 1991; Wood et al., 1990).

Why are these predictors inadequate? One explanation is that the practice of medicine is very complicated. Physicians need more than test score knowledge. The tests often evaluate the physicians' understanding of the basic biological constructs but may not tap into their motivation, ability to interact with people, or judgment. Although interviews are designed to capture some of these characteristics, personal interviews are notoriously poor at identifying the appropriate information (see Chapter 10). In order to target some of these abilities, newer approaches use techniques of job analysis and analysis of specific skills that may be required in the practice of medicine. These studies identify specific behavioral skills related to lack of confidence, conscientiousness, interpersonal skills, curiosity, and a variety of other behaviors. Each of these was linked to specific behavioral incidents that could be self-reported. The early analysis suggests that these techniques successfully predict performance in the residency programs as evaluated by senior physicians and patients (Wood et al., 1990). In the future, we expect more use of behavioral-based measures for the selection of medical residents.

of opportunity (Flaugher, 1978). One view of test scores is that they are an accurate reflection of the effects of social and economic inequality (Green, 1978).

To understand this argument, we must consider the purpose of testing. In educational settings, tests such as the SAT, the GRE, or even IQ tests are usually considered to be tests of aptitude: they measure some trait that is inborn and unlikely to change if the person is put in a different environment. But most experts now agree that the tests are measuring not aptitude but

Table 20-3
For and Against
the Use of Tests

Against	For
The Stanford-Binet was standardized on only 1000 children and 400 adults. None of these people were black (Gurie, 1976).	Although the tests were not standardized on minority-group members, they have now been used to test millions of children of all races. The tests appear to have the same validity for minority students as they do for majority students. Therefore, neglecting to include minorities in the original validation studies was not relevant (Barrett & Depinet, 1991).
The use of intelligence tests can have a damaging social impact. For example, differences in IQ between different ethnic groups were used to limit immigration of certain groups into the United States during the early years of the 20th century (Kamin, 1974).	Examination of the Congressional Record covering the debates about the 1924 Immigration Act failed to uncover discussion of intelligence test data or claims that the mean IQ of Americans would decline if the immigration of certain groups was allowed (DuBois, 1972a).
If a teacher just thinks some children have higher IQs, the actual test scores of those children will improve (Rosenthal & Jacobson, 1968).	Studies documenting the effects of self-fulfilling prophecies and teacher expectations overinterpreted their original data, contained some results that are statistically impossible, and cannot be depended on (Elashoff & Snow, 1971; Snow, 1969; Thorndike, 1968).
Minority children can only be damaged by the continued use of psychological tests.	Psychological tests can be used to identify the most capable members of each group. Without the tests, people will be selected on the basis of personal judgment, which might be more racist than the tests (Cronbach, 1975b).
The validity of IQ tests was documented using other standardized tests as the criterion rather than measures of classroom performance (Mercer, 1979).	The objective tests are better validity criteria than classroom performance, which is more subjective. Teachers may grade on the basis of effort rather than ability (Sattler, 1979a).
Most test administrators are white; the scores of black children would improve if they were tested by black examiners (Forrester & Klaus, 1964; Pasamanick & Knobloch, 1955).	Some studies do indeed show that the race of the examiner is an important factor. However, most studies do not. Among 28 different studies on the effects of the examiner's race, 24 fail to show that the race of the examiner has a significant impact on scores (Sattler, 1979a).

achievement. The scores can be changed with proper nurturing. Verbal and numerical abilities are acquired through experience. Thus, low test scores should not be viewed as insurmountable problems; they can be improved.

Much of what has been said in this chapter is consistent with the view that tests do point out differences between minority and nonminority students. Furthermore, systematic attempts to show that this problem is the fault of the tests have not been convincing. Many minority students do well on the tests, and the tests accurately predict that these students will do well on the criterion. A black student and a white student who both achieve a score of 1100 on the SAT are predicted to do equally well in college, and studies show that indeed they do perform at about the same level.

Blaming the tests for observed differences between groups may be a convenient way to avoid a much larger problem. No one has suggested that the tuberculin test is unfair because it demonstrates that poor people have the disease more often than wealthy people do. Public health officials have correctly concluded that some people live in environments that predispose them to the disease. Getting rid of scales that identify underweight children will not cure malnutrition (Flaugher, 1978). Although measuring intelligence may not be the same as testing for tuberculosis or measuring weight, the analogy may be worth considering.

If unequal access to adequate education and to stimulating experiences results in differences in test scores, it would be more useful to change the social environment than to continuously bicker about the tests. The tests may only be the bearers of bad news. By documenting how severe the problem is, the tests may be telling us that overcoming this problem will be expensive, will be difficult, and may take many years. Blaming the tests for a problem that they did not cause seems to be shortsighted and nonproductive (Elliot, 1988).

Summary

In this chapter, we examined two sides of the issue of test bias. A summary of some of the arguments for and against the use of tests is given in Table 20-3. As the table shows, there are strong differences of opinion about the value of intelligence and aptitude tests for minority-group members. As a result of the challenge to traditional tests, new approaches such as the Chitling Test, the BITCH, and the SOMPA have been developed. Among these, the SOMPA is clearly the most sophisticated. All of these new approaches are based on the assumption that social groups do not differ in their average potential. These approaches have been challenged because they do not have the same sort of validity evidence as is available for the traditional tests.

Part of the debate about test bias results from different moral views about what is fair. Some have argued that a testing and selection program is fair if it selects the best-suited people, regardless of their social group. This approach may lead to overrepresentation of one group. Another moral position supports selection procedures that select members from different racial and ethnic groups according to their proportions in the general population. A third moral position is a compromise between the preceding two.

Although test bias is sure to remain an area of considerable controversy, there are some positive potential solutions. For example, tests might be evaluated against outcome criteria that have relevance for minority-group members.

A current raging controversy is over the nature of differences in test performance. One group believes the differences are genetic or biological in origin (Hernstein, 1982; Rushton, 1991; Vandenburg & Vogler, 1985), while another group believes the differences result from differences in the social environment (Kamin, 1974; Olmedo, 1981; Zuckerman, 1990). Some people believe there is evidence for both genetic and environmental explanations (Turkheimer, 1991). The social-environment explanation (Gould, 1981) seems to be the more popular. If we accept this view, differences in test performance might suggest to us that we need to escalate our efforts to wipe out inequality. If we endorse the genetic position, we are acknowledging that little can be done to equalize performance among different groups.

Chapter 21

Testing and the Law

Learning Objectives

When you have completed this chapter, you should be able to:

- Describe the bases on which the federal government can regulate the use of psychological tests.
- Describe the EEOC guidelines and their importance.
- Describe how the New York Truth in Testing Law affects the use of psychological tests.
- Discuss the impact of PL 94-142.
- Discuss the importance of *Hobson* v. *Hansen*.
- Describe the issue in *Diana* v. *State Board of Education* and how it differs from the major issue in *Larry P.* v. *Wilson Riles*.
- Compare and contrast the decisions in *Larry P.* v. *Wilson Riles* and *Parents in Action on Special Education* v. *Hannon*.
- Discuss the importance of *Regents of the University of California* v. *Bakke*.
- Describe how the courts are involved in the use of personnel tests.
- Discuss the events that led to the Civil Rights Act of 1991.

In 1969, the California Department of Education began requiring the use of standardized IQ tests to diagnose retardation. Students who scored below 85 on the WISC or the Stanford-Binet were sent to special classes for the educable mentally retarded (EMR). Larry P. was one of approximately 6000 black children who were assigned to EMR classes on the basis of the tests. However, a few years later, Larry P. and five of his black schoolmates were retested by black psychologists, who reported higher IQ scores. On the basis of these new, higher test scores, Larry and the others were placed back in the regular school track.

Larry P.'s battle was not as simple as being retested to gain an appropriate placement. Instead, a class-action lawsuit was filed on behalf of the six black children (representing the class of all similar students). This case challenged the right of the state to use IQ tests for classroom placement, arguing that the tests were racially discriminatory and therefore violated both the California Constitution and the 14th Amendment to the U.S. Constitution, which guarantees equal protection under the law.

It took until 1977 for the case to be heard in the U.S. District Court. After hearing and reviewing more than 11,000 pages of testimony by psychologists and interested parties, Judge Robert Peckham released a 131-page opinion in October 1979 forbidding the placement of black children in EMR classes on the basis of standardized test scores. Thus, the ultimate decision about the use of psychological tests was made not by trained psychologists, professional educators, or interested citizens but rather by the courts.

The same year the decision in Larry P.'s case was released, the state of New York passed a Truth in Testing Law, and a similar bill was introduced on the floor of the U.S. House of Representatives. In addition, a Florida judge ruled that black students who did not receive all their education in integrated schools could not be denied a high school credential on the basis of a minimum

---

FOCUSED EXAMPLE 21-1

What Is a Law?

As common as it is for each of us to refer to laws, many people are confused about what exactly constitutes the law. Most people think of law only as statutes. *Statutes* are the rules written by legislative bodies at any level of government. Before proposed statutes become law, they are called *bills* or *propositions*.

In addition to statutes, *constitutions* have the force of law. In the United States there is a federal Constitution, and each state has its own constitution. In lawsuits (or litigation) it is frequently argued that a policy violates a constitutional rule or principle. The U.S. Constitution is considered the supreme law of the land because any federal, state, or local law is invalid if it is judged to conflict with the Constitution. State or local laws that are inconsistent with a state constitution can also be declared invalid.

Statutes and constitutions are typically worded in general terms. Frequently, they give authority to a specific agency to write *regulations*. For all intents and purposes, these regulations are also laws. For example, the Civil Rights Act of 1964 (a statute) created the Equal Employment Opportunity Commission (EEOC), which wrote guidelines for fair employment practices; these guidelines are regulations. Although these regulations were not created by any elected officials, they are laws that must be adhered to.

The final form of law is *judicial opinion*. Statutes, constitutions, and regulations must be applied to the specific facts. Thus, courts of law are frequently called on to interpret the law in view of a given factual situation. In doing so, the courts offer opinions that consider specific cases against the background of statutes, constitutions, and regulations. Once a court offers an opinion on a specific case, the opinion becomes law. For example, in the case of *Larry P.* v. *Wilson Riles*, a judge rendered the opinion that IQ tests could not be used to place black children in EMR classes. This opinion is the law in California unless a higher court reverses the U.S. District Court opinion (Wing, 1976).

competence test. By the end of the 1970s, the use of psychological tests had become a major legal issue. The focus was broadened to employment testing in the 1980s and early 1990s. These courtroom and legislative battles over the appropriate use of psychological tests set the stage for the many current conflicts over testing.

In this chapter, we review some of the major legal issues concerning the use of psychological tests. We begin by covering some of the basic laws that regulate the use of tests, and then we report on how the courts have interpreted some of these laws. Focused Example 21-1 discusses the meaning of the word *law*.

I. *Laws Governing the Use of Tests*

A. *Federal Authorities*

Many people commonly believe that the federal government has unlimited authority to regulate almost any activity. Actually, the circumstances under which the federal government can regulate are limited. Until fairly recently, the most commonly used authority for regulation was interstate commerce.

Interstate commerce. The Constitution gives most of the power to the states. Each state has its own constitution, which generally defines the relationship between the state and its citizens. It is up to the states to make policies for the recognition of other administrative units, such as cities and counties, that exist within the states. The Constitution does not directly recognize cities, counties, or school districts. The only restriction on the states' authority to pass laws is that no state can pass or enforce a law that is inconsistent with the Constitution.

The federal government is charged with regulating interstate commerce because each state has only that authority necessary to attend to its own affairs. Interstate commerce is business activity involving two or more states. For example, a test that is developed by a New Jersey company and shipped (over state lines) to be administered for profit in Kansas clearly involves interstate commerce. Some legal authorities now believe that interstate commerce involves almost all activities. Thus, the federal government can regulate many activities under the umbrella of interstate commerce.

The regulation of interstate commerce is clear and direct. Federal agencies such as the Federal Trade Commission create specific policies to regulate specific products and activities. Congress also devotes much of its energy to the creation of laws that regulate specific business activities. These extensive and well-documented policies represent direct regulation. The other form of government regulation—the power to regulate through the control of spending—is indirect.

Control of spending. The U.S. government is a big spender—so big, in fact, that virtually all major American business institutions depend to some extent on federal revenues. This spending gives the federal government considerable leverage. It can withhold money whenever federal authorities consider it just to do so. In effect, the government has the right to say "Do it our way or we will not pay."

This policy is straightforward for cases in which the government is a customer and needs to regulate the product it is purchasing. For example, when the federal government is paying for the development of a test, it has the right to withhold payment unless the work is done according to government standards. However, this power is frequently exercised in an indirect manner. For example, the government has standards for equality in employment, and it has the authority to ask that institutions conform to this standard. The government can say in effect "Conform to our employment guidelines or we will not pay you to develop a test."

Most school districts are happy to receive federal funds to implement certain programs; however, they may not be enthusiastic about implementing other policies. For example, a district may have a school lunch program for underprivileged children, and it may enthusiastically support this program. The government may then ask the district to build ramps for handicapped children, however, and the district may not want to follow through. There is no criminal penalty for deciding not to build the ramps; however, the government has the authority to withhold the funds for the desired program (lunches) unless there is compliance with the government's request (ramps).

Virtually all public and most major private institutions can be regulated in this way because of their dependence on federal contracts and grants. And institutions in the private sector that do not depend as heavily on federal funds can be regulated through interstate commerce. Government regulation is thus difficult to escape.

Guidelines of the Equal Employment Opportunity Commission. One of the major ways in which the government exercises its power to regulate testing is through interpretations of the 14th Amendment to the Constitution. The 14th Amendment guarantees all citizens due process and equal protection under the law. However, specifying the conditions under which due process and equal protection are afforded has taken a long time. Gradually, the way in which these principles are implemented has been carefully refined. The clearest statement from the federal government has been with regard to employee testing and personnel procedures.

During the presidency of Lyndon Johnson, Congress enacted the Civil Rights Act of 1964, one of the century's most important pieces of legislation. Title VII of the act and its subsequent amendments created an Equal Employment Opportunity Commission (EEOC). In 1970, the EEOC released a set of guidelines that defined fair employee-selection procedures. In 1978, the guidelines were revised and simplified, published as the *Uniform Guidelines on Em-*

ployee Selection Procedures, and jointly adopted by the EEOC, the Civil Service Commission, and the Departments of Justice, Labor, and the Treasury. These guidelines thus affect most public employment and can also be imposed in institutions that receive government funds (Novick, 1981).

The intent of the guidelines is to prohibit discrimination. The document makes it clear that an employer cannot discriminate on the basis of race, color, gender, national origin, or religion. The guidelines are particularly concerned with selection procedures that might have *adverse impact.* Adverse impact is interpreted according to the four-fifths rule, which is one of the most controversial components of the guidelines. The **four-fifths rule** is stated as follows:

> A selection rate of any race, sex, or ethnic group which is less than four-fifths ($\frac{4}{5}$) (or 80%) of the rate for the group with the highest rate will generally be regarded by the federal enforcement agencies as evidence of adverse impact, while a greater than four-fifths rate will generally not be regarded by federal enforcement agencies as evidence of adverse impact.

This means that a selection procedure may be suspected of having adverse impact if it gives any homogeneous group of employees four-fifths or more of the jobs. For example, if an employer hires 90% of the white male applicants and only 20% of the black male applicants, the selection procedure violates the four-fifths rule. The employer then has to demonstrate that extenuating circumstances make the standards unreasonable. One of the most interesting problems with the four-fifths rule has been that efforts to recruit minorities reduce the percentage from that group that is hired. By recruiting members of many minority groups, an employer can hire a smaller percentage of those recruited. Active recruiting may result in selection of a smaller percentage of minority-group members. Thus, the rule, which was designed to protect minority-group members, may discourage the aggressive recruiting of these groups. The EEOC acknowledges these problems and has developed exceptions for particular circumstances. The authorization of these exceptions for specific individual cases is left up to the EEOC and, in many cases, will be left to the courts (McCormick & Ilgen, 1980).

The guidelines are explicit and include many careful definitions of terms such as *validity.* Whenever a psychological test or other selection device is employed and its use results in adverse impact (or overselection in one group), extensive evidence for the validity of the selection procedure must be presented. Much of the text of the EEOC guidelines is devoted to a discussion of the minimum requirements for the validity of a selection procedure. In essence, the guidelines parallel the discussion presented in Chapter 5. Technical Box 21-1 gives the EEOC requirements for criterion validity.

If prospective employees feel they have been treated unfairly, they can file complaints with the EEOC. The EEOC regional and district offices handle about 70,000 complaints each year. The EEOC also gathers information. Any organization with more than 100 employees must complete a form each year that describes the number of women and members of four different minority

TECHNICAL BOX 21-1
EEOC Guidelines for Criterion Validity

Technical standards for criterion-related validity studies—(1) *Technical feasibility.* Users choosing to validate a selection procedure by a criterion-related validity strategy should determine whether it is technically feasible (as defined in section 16) to conduct such a study in the particular employment context. The determination of the number of persons necessary to permit the conduct of a meaningful criterion-related study should be made by the user on the basis of all relevant information concerning the selection procedure, the potential sample, and the employment situation. Where appropriate, jobs with substantially the same major work behaviors may be grouped together for validity studies, in order to obtain an adequate sample. These guidelines do not require a user to hire or promote persons for the purpose of making it possible to conduct a criterion-related study.

(2) *Analysis of the job.* There should be a review of job information to determine measures of work behavior(s) or performance that are relevant to the job or group of jobs in question. These measures or criteria are relevant to the extent that they represent critical or important job duties, work behaviors, or work outcomes as developed from the review of job information. The possibility of bias should be considered both in selection of the criterion measures and their application. In view of the possibility of bias in subjective evaluations, supervisory rating techniques and instructions to raters should be carefully developed. All criterion measures and the methods for gathering data need to be examined for freedom from factors which would unfairly alter scores of members of any group. The relevance of criteria and their freedom from bias are of particular concern when there are significant differences in measures of job performance for different groups.

(3) *Criterion measures.* Proper safeguards should be taken to ensure that scores on selection procedures do not enter into any judgments of employee adequacy that are to be used as criterion measures. Whatever criteria are used should represent important or critical work behavior(s) or work outcomes. Certain criteria may be used without a full job analysis if the user can show the importance of the criteria to the particular employment context. These criteria include but are not limited to production rate, error rate, tardiness, absenteeism, and length of service. A standardized rating of overall work performance may be used where a study of the job shows that it is an appropriate criterion. Where performance in training is used as a criterion, success in training should be properly measured and the relevance of the training should be shown either through a comparison of the content of the training program with the critical or important work behavior(s) of the job(s) or through a demonstration of the relationship between measures of performance in training and measures of job performance. Measures of relative success in training include but are not limited to instructor evaluations, performance samples, or tests. Criterion measures consisting of paper-and-pencil tests will be closely reviewed for job relevance.

(4) *Representativeness of the sample.* Whether the study is predictive or concurrent, the sample subjects should insofar as feasible be representative of the candidates normally available in the relevant labor market for the job or group of jobs in question, and should insofar as feasible include the races, sexes, and ethnic groups normally available in the relevant job market. In determining the representativeness of the sample in a

concurrent validity study, the user should take into account the extent to which the specific knowledges or skills which are the primary focus of the test are those which employees learn on the job.

Where samples are combined or compared, attention should be given to see that such samples are comparable in terms of the actual job they perform, the length of time on the job where time on the job is likely to affect performance, and other relevant factors likely to affect validity differences; or that these factors are included in the design of the study and their effects identified.

(5) *Statistical relationships*. The degree of relationship between selection procedure scores and criterion measures should be examined and computed, using professionally acceptable statistical procedures. Generally, a selection procedure is considered related to the criterion, for the purposes of these guidelines, when the relationship between performance on the procedure and performance on the criterion measure is statistically significant at the .05 level of significance, which means that it is sufficiently high as to have a probability of no more than one (1) in twenty (20) to have occurred by chance. Absence of a statistically significant relationship between a selection procedure and job performance should not necessarily discourage other investigations of the validity of that selection procedure.

(6) *Operational use of selection procedures*. Users should evaluate each selection procedure to assure that it is appropriate for operational use, including establishment of cutoff scores or rank ordering. Generally, if other factors remain the same, the greater the magnitude of the relationship (e.g., correlation coefficient) between performance on a selection procedure and one or more criteria of performance on the job and the greater the importance and number of aspects of job performance covered by the criteria, the more likely it is that the procedure will be appropriate for use. Reliance upon a selection procedure which is significantly related to a criterion measure but which is based upon a study involving a large number of subjects and has a low correlation coefficient will be subject to close review if it has a large adverse impact. Sole reliance upon a single selection instrument which is related to only one of many job duties or aspects of job performance will also be subject to close review. The appropriateness of a selection procedure is best evaluated in each particular situation and there are no minimum correlation coefficients applicable to all employment situations. In determining whether a selection procedure is appropriate for operational use, the following considerations should also be taken into account: the degree of adverse impact of the procedure, the availability of other selection procedures of greater or substantially equal validity.

(7) *Overstatement of validity findings*. Users should avoid reliance upon techniques which tend to overestimate validity findings as a result of capitalization on chance unless an approriate safeguard is taken. Reliance upon a few selection procedures or criteria of successful job performance when many selection procedures or criteria of performance have been studied, or the use of optimal statistical weights for selection procedures computed in one sample, are techniques which tend to inflate validity estimates as a result of chance. Use of a large sample is one safeguard; cross validation is another.

(8) *Fairness*. This section generally calls for studies of unfairness where technically feasible. The concept of fairness or unfairness of selection procedures is a developing concept. In addition, fairness studies generally require substantial numbers of employees in the job or group of jobs being studied. For these reasons, the federal enforcement agencies recognize that the obligation to conduct studies of fairness imposed by the guidelines generally will be upon users or groups of users with a large number of

(continued)

(continued)
persons in a job class, or test developers; and that small users utilizing their own selection procedures will generally not be obligated to conduct such studies because it will be technically infeasible for them to do so.

(a) *Unfairness defined.* When members of one race, sex, or ethnic group characteristically obtain lower scores on a selection procedure than members of another group and the differences in scores are not reflected in differences in a measure of job performance, use of the selection procedure may unfairly deny opportunities to members of the group that obtains the lower scores.

(b) *Investigation of fairness.* Where a selection procedure results in an adverse impact on a race, sex, or ethnic group identified in accordance with the classifications set forth in section 4 above and that group is a significant factor in the relevant lab or market, the user generally should investigate the possible existence of unfairness for that group if it is technically feasible to do so. The greater the severity of the adverse impact on a group, the greater the need to investigate the possible existence of unfairness. Where the weight of evidence from other studies shows that the selection procedure predicts fairly for the group in question and for the same or similar jobs, such evidence may be relied on in connection with the selection procedure at issue.

(c) *General considerations in fairness investigations.* Users conducting a study of fairness should review the A.P.A. Standards regarding investigation of possible bias in testing. An investigation of fairness of a selection procedure depends on both evidence of validity and the manner in which the selection procedure is to be used in a particular employment context. Fairness of a selection procedure cannot necessarily be specified in advance without investigating these factors. Investigation of fairness of a selection procedure in samples where the range of scores on selection procedures or criterion measures is severely restricted for any subgroup sample (as compared to other subgroup samples) may produce misleading evidence of unfairness. That factor should accordingly be taken into account in conducting such studies and before reliance is placed on the results.

(d) *When unfairness is shown.* If unfairness is demonstrated through a showing that members of a particular group perform better or poorer on the job than their scores on the selection procedure would indicate through comparison with how members of other groups perform, the user may either revise or replace the selection instrument in accordance with these guidelines, or may continue to use the selection instrument operationally with appropriate revisions in its use to ensure compatibility between the probability of successful job performance and the probability of being selected.

(e) *Technical feasibility of fairness studies.* In addition to the general conditions needed for technical feasibility for the conduct of a criterion-related study, an investigation of fairness requires the following.

(i) An adequate sample of persons in each group available for the study to achieve findings of statistical significance. Guidelines do not require a user to hire or promote persons on the basis of group classifications for the purpose of making it possible to conduct a study of fairness, but the user has the obligation otherwise to comply with these guidelines.

(ii) The samples for each group should be comparable in terms of the actual job they perform, length of time on the job where time on the job is likely to affect performance, and other relevant factors likely to affect validity differences; or such factors should be included in the design of the study and their effects identified.

(f) *Continued use of selection procedures when fairness studies not feasible.* If a study of fairness should otherwise be performed, but is not technically feasible, a selection procedure may be used which has otherwise met the validity standards of these guidelines, unless the technical infeasibility resulted from discriminatory employment practices which are demonstrated by facts other than past failure to conform with requirements for validation of selection procedures. However, when it becomes technically feasible for the user to perform a study of fairness and such a study is otherwise called for, the user should conduct the study of fairness.

Source: From "EEOC Guidelines," Equal Employment Opportunity Commission, 1978.

groups employed in nine different job categories within the organization. The specific minority groups are black, Hispanic (Cuban, Spanish, Puerto Rican, or Mexican), Asian, and American Indian. After collecting these forms from 260,000 organizations, the EEOC can estimate broad patterns of discrimination. The EEOC is involved in hundreds of lawsuits concerning discrimination each year.

□ ◇   **F O C U S E D   E X A M P L E   2 1 - 2**

Content Validity and Sexual Harassment During a Paramedic Exam

The EEOC guidelines make it clear that questions asked on employment tests and during employment interviews must be relevant to performance on the job. However, not all agencies are in full compliance with this regulation, particularly with regard to job interviews. This noncompliance was a source of irritation to Sandra Buchanan when she appeared before the Los Angeles City Fire Department for an interview for a paramedic job. During the interview, she was asked as much about her sex life as she was about her four years of paramedic training and experience. For example, she was asked: "Have you ever had semipublic sex?" "Have you had sex on the beach?" "Have you had sex in a parked car?" "Have you ever exposed yourself indecently?" "Have you molested any children?" "Do you have any homosexual contacts?"

Ms. Buchanan was so disturbed by these questions that she filed a complaint with the Civil Service Commission. In the ensuing investigation, the fire department was asked to show how the questions about sex related to the paramedic job.

Its response was that the questions create stress and therefore give the department a chance to observe how a person handles himself or herself in stressful situations. The department also argued that it needed to delve deeply into the backgrounds of applicants because paramedics are entrusted with important responsibilities. One member of the fire department argued that the question on indecent exposure was necessary because "they have a dormitory situation that is quite different from other jobs; the nature of this job makes some of the questions job related that would not be related in other jobs."

The commission decided that the department had to reinterview Ms. Buchanan. It was instructed to review the questions and eliminate those that were not job related. It appeared that the commission agreed with Ms. Buchanan's attorney, who argued, "It is time that the city of Los Angeles stop asking 'How's your sex life?' and get back to the business of finding the most qualified person for the job of Los Angeles paramedic" (quoted from *Los Angeles Times*, June 29, 1979).

Although the validity requirements are specifically applicable to psychological tests, they also apply to other selection devices such as employment forms and interviews. See Focused Example 21-2 for an example. In addition, they apply to other job requirements, including educational and work-experience requirements. In summary, the EEOC guidelines provide clear, unambiguous regulations for the use of any assessment device in the selection of employees.

As you might expect, many employers were furious about the EEOC guidelines. They saw them as additional government interference with their conduct of business and as a means of inhibiting them from hiring the best person for a job. Although it is easy to sympathize with their concern about excessive bureaucratic red tape, historical evidence supports the implementation of the guidelines. The basic rationale for the EEOC guidelines was provided by the equal protection clause in the 14th Amendment to the Constitution. The 14th Amendment was ratified in the post–Civil War era, but the equal protection clause was not a major basis for public policy for nearly 100 years—until the court battles over school desegregation and the activities of the civil rights movement led to the passage of the 1964 Civil Rights Act. Even after the passage of this important law, employers did not follow fair employment practices. The specific EEOC guidelines were therefore necessary in order for the intent of the law to be realized. Without the specific guidelines, more than 100 years passed without employers recognizing the legal requirements of equal protection.

In 1980, the EEOC added specific guidelines on sexual harassment in the workplace. Sexual harassment was defined as unsolicited sexual advances, requests for sexual favors, or any other implicit or explicit conduct that might be interpreted as a condition of an individual's employment. The EEOC has ruled that a company is always liable for sexual harassment by supervisors even

---

□ ◇   F O C U S E D   E X A M P L E   2 1 - 3

Sexism in Other Countries

The fairness in employment policies that characterizes American and European countries is not observed throughout the world. Consider this advertisement placed in a 1985 Hong Kong newspaper:

OBEDIENT YOUNG SECRETARY
Very obedient young woman required by American Director of position as Secretary/Personal Assistant. Must be attractive and ea-

ger to submit to authority, have good typing and filing skills, and be free to travel. Knowledge of Mandarin an advantage. Most important, she should enjoy following orders without question and cheerfully accept directions. Send handwritten resume on unlined paper and recent photo to G.P.O. Box 6132, Hong Kong.

From Cascio (1987, p. 29).

when company officials are unaware of the problem. However, the Supreme Court overturned this policy in a 1986 decision. Nevertheless, the Supreme Court affirmed that sexual harassment is sexual discrimination and underscored the need for employers to eliminate any form of sexual harassment (Wermiel & Trost, 1986). When traveling abroad, some Americans are surprised by evidence of sexual discrimination and the sexist standards apparent in job-selection procedures. Consider the advertisement in Focused Example 21-3.

In November 1991, President George Bush signed the 1991 Civil Rights Bill. The bill essentially reaffirmed the EEOC guidelines. However, the bill was a reaction to a trend that had eroded the impact of these guidelines during the 1980s and early 1990s. We return to a discussion of the 1991 Civil Rights Bill later in the chapter.

B. *Specific Laws*

Other regulatory schemes attempt to control the use of tests. Two examples are the New York Truth in Testing Law of 1979 and the Education for All Handicapped Children Act of 1975.

Truth in testing laws. The New York Truth in Testing Law is one of the most controversial measures in the testing field. The New York law was motivated by an extensive investigation of the Educational Testing Service (ETS) by the New York Public Interest Research Group (NYPIRG). Other testing companies are affected by the law, but the New York law was written with ETS specifically in mind.

ETS was created by the College Entrance Examination Board, the American Council on Education, and the Carnegie Foundation in 1948. Its original and best-known mission was to create and administer aptitude tests such as the SAT. ETS is responsible for more than 300 testing programs, including the Graduate Management Admission Test (GMAT), the Graduate Record Examination (GRE), the Multi-State Bar Exam, and the Law School Admission Test (LSAT). The assets and income of the company are very substantial.

NYPIRG seemed upset by the wealth and success of ETS, yet what bothered NYPIRG more was the power ETS has. Each year several million persons take tests designed and administered by ETS, and the results of these tests have pronounced impacts on their lives (Brill, 1973; Kiersh, 1979; Levy, 1979). Many educational programs take the scores seriously. Students who score poorly on the LSAT, for example, may be denied entrance to law school, and this rejection may eventually affect many important aspects of their lives. Higher scores might have resulted in a higher income, more occupational status, and greater self-esteem for them.

In its investigation, NYPIRG became dissatisfied with the available information on test validity, the calculation of test scores, and the financial accounting of ETS. The Truth in Testing Law responds to these objections by requiring testing companies to (1) disclose all studies on the validity of a test, (2) provide a complete disclosure to students about what scores mean and how they were calculated, and (3) on request by a student, provide a copy of the test questions, the correct answers, and the student's answers.

The first two portions are essentially noncontroversial. The test developers argue that they do disclose all pertinent information on validity and they do release many public documents highlighting the strengths and weaknesses of their tests. We have written to ETS many times and have never been refused any report. Furthermore, ETS strongly encourages institutions that use its tests to perform local validity studies. Any of these studies can be published in scholarly journals (which are found in most college libraries) with no interference from ETS. However, NYPIRG provided some evidence that ETS and other testing companies have files of secret data that they do not make public because these data may reflect poorly on the product. The second aspect of the law was included because ETS sometimes reports index scores to schools without telling students how the index was calculated and the exact index value being reported.

The controversial third portion of the law may turn out to seriously decrease the value of testing programs. Requiring that the test questions be returned to students means that the same questions cannot be used in future versions of the test. Several problems have resulted from this policy. First, it decreases the validity of the test. With the items constantly changing, the test essentially becomes a new test each time the items change. As a result, it is impossible to accumulate a record of construct validity.

Second, it is difficult to equate scores across years. For example, a graduate school must often consider students who took the GRE in different years. Since the test itself is different each year, it is difficult to compare the scores of students who took the test at different times. Although the bill eventually adopted in New York did allow testing companies to keep some of the items secret for equating purposes, this practice falls short of being a satisfactory solution. Equating can be accomplished, but it has been difficult without increasing the chances of error.

Third, the most serious problem associated with the disclosure of test items was that it increased the costs to ETS and other testing companies. ETS did not absorb these inflated costs but passed them on to the consumer.

ETS does make booklets available to the public that present information on the scoring system, the validity, the reliability, and the standard error of measurement for each of their tests. Persons with no background in testing probably will not comprehend all this information. Each of you, after completing this testing course, will have little difficulty interpreting the manuals, but, as you know, it has taken you a long term of hard study to get to this point. The authors of the bills fail to recognize that the proper use of tests and test results is a technical problem that requires technical training in advanced courses such as psychological testing. After all, we do not expect people to be able to practice medicine without the technical training given in medical school. Surveys sug-

Table 21-1

Summary of the American Psychological Association's Statement on Testing Legislation

1. We recommend a "wait and see" period prior to enacting further legislation. The legislation enacted in New York and California has created a situation that can be viewed as a naturally occurring field experiment. A few years of studying this "experiment" are warranted before other legislation is passed or rejected.

2. We strongly support provisions encouraging the dissemination of information about test content, test purpose, validity, reliability, and interpretation of test scores. Test takers should have access to their individual results and interpretative information, especially where such test results are used for educational or employment decisions.

3. We oppose total disclosure of items from low-volume tests or tests where item domains are finite (for instance, measuring specific content areas).

4. We oppose disclosure of tests where interpretation is dependent upon a long history of research (for example, extensive norming); disclosure would result in loss of valid interpretation. This is particularly true of interest and personality measures.

5. In disclosure cases involving large-volume tests testing a broad domain, we recommend at a minimum that only items used to determine test performance be disclosed. Pretesting and equating items should be protected from disclosure.

6. Where disclosure is deemed desirable, we encourage examination of alternative methods of conveying this information to test takers, such as partial disclosure (disclosure of one test after several administrations) or making sample tests available for perusal at a secure location.

7. We urge that any personnel selection or licensing procedure in use should be subject to the same scrutiny as tests, provided that sample size is sufficient for meaningful statistical analyses.

From American Psychological Association Statement on Test Item Disclosure Legislation (August 1983).

gest that testing experts agree that test scores are misused by primary and secondary schools. In the hands of those who do not understand the limitations of tests, too much reliance may be placed on a test score (Snyderman & Rothman, 1987).

We must consider the ultimate impact of the truth in testing legislation. One side argues that the laws have made for a fairer and more honest testing industry. The other argues that students now have to pay a higher price for a poorer product. As a result of these laws, other tests are given on only a limited number of occasions and test items are not reused. The distribution of test items has required that tests are not as thoroughly validated prior to their use as they were 15 years ago, and this may result in greater error in selecting students. In addition, continuing the development of the tests has increased expense. Ultimately, students may need to pay more in order to take a lower quality test. In response to these concerns, ETS argues that the validity of its tests has not declined. In fact, it suggests that the concurrent validity of the tests is still significant (ETS, 1991).

The American Psychological Association has issued a statement expressing a conservative attitude toward truth in testing laws. This statement is summarized in Table 21-1.

The Education for All Handicapped Children Act of 1975. In 1975, Congress passed a law that is having a major impact on the use of psychological tests. PL 94-142 (the 142nd Public Law passed by the 94th Congress) guarantees a publicly financed education to all handicapped children. The law is detailed with regard to its major requirement—that an individually tailored education plan be developed for each handicapped child. The additional requirement that the educational characteristics of each handicapped child be assessed necessitates the use of tests. In particular, children may be identified for placement in programs funded through PL 94-142 by the use of psychological tests. For example, tests may be used to identify children for EMR classes, which receive funding under the law.

The law clearly specifies that the tests must be reliable, valid, and nondiscriminatory with regard to the non-English-speaking, the poor, members of minority groups, and the bilingual. A debate has erupted about which tests meet these criteria. Jane Mercer, the creator of the SOMPA (see Chapter 20), argues that her test meets the requirements of the law, whereas the WISC and Stanford-Binet scales do not. In fact, she suggests that the SOMPA system is the only test that conforms to the law (Mercer, 1979). Her critics interpret the law as requiring traditional tests such as the Stanford-Binet and WISC scales and assert that the SOMPA cannot be used under the law (Clarizio, 1979a; Sattler, 1979a).

II. *Some Major Lawsuits*

Legislation is not the only way to change policy; there are other options for those who have particular conflicts. One option that is being used with increasing frequency is litigation, or the lawsuit. Lawsuits are usually considered to be the last resort for resolving personal conflicts. For example, if you feel you have been wronged and you have been unable to persuade those who have offended you through other legal means, you may file a lawsuit. In doing so, you trust the court system to make a fair judgment about your case.

There have already been many lawsuits concerning the use of psychological tests, and we expect the number to increase in the years to come. Some of the most important of these lawsuits are discussed in this chapter. It is important to realize that each of these cases was complex and involved considerably more evidence than we can cite here.

A. *Early Desegregation Cases*

The 14th Amendment requires that all citizens be granted equal protection of the laws. At the end of the 19th century, it was being argued that segregated schools did not offer such protection. In the famous 1896 case of *Plessy* v. *Ferguson*,[1] the Supreme Court ruled that schools could remain segregated but

---

[1] 163 U.S. 537 (1896).

that the quality of the schools must be equal. This was the much-acclaimed separate-but-equal ruling.

Perhaps the most influential ruling in the history of American public school education came in the case of *Brown* v. *Board of Education*[2] in 1954. In the *Brown* case, the Supreme Court overturned the *Plessy* v. *Ferguson* decision and ruled that the schools must provide nonsegregated facilities for black and white students. In its opinion, the court raised several issues that would eventually affect the use of psychological tests.

The most important pronouncement of *Brown* was that segregation was a denial of equal protection. In coming to its decision, the court made extensive use of testimony by psychologists. This testimony suggested that black children could be made to feel inferior if the school system kept the two races separate.

The story of the *Brown* case is well known, but what is less often discussed is the ugly history that followed. Many school districts did not want to desegregate, and the battle over busing and other mechanisms for desegregation continues today in many areas. Many of the current arguments against desegregation are based on fear of children leaving their own neighborhoods or on the stress on children who must endure long bus rides. The early resistance to the *Brown* decision was more clearly linked to the racist belief of black inferiority.

B. *Stell* v. *Savannah-Chatham County Board of Education*[3]

The most significant reactionary court case occurred when legal action was taken to desegregate the school system of Savannah, Georgia, on behalf of a group of black children. The conflict began when the attorneys for two white children intervened. They argued that they were not opposed to desegregating on the basis of race but that black children did not have the ability to be in the same classrooms as whites. Testimony from psychologists indicated that the median IQ score for black children was 81, whereas that for white children was 101. Because there was such a large difference in this trait (which was assumed to be genetic), the attorneys argued that it could be to the mutual disadvantage of both groups to congregate them in the same schools. Doing so might create even greater feelings of inferiority among black children and might create frustration that would eventually result in antisocial behavior.

The court essentially agreed with this testimony and ruled that the district should not desegregate. The judge's opinion reflected his view of what was in the best interest of all of the children. Later, this decision was reversed by Judge Griffin Bell of the U.S. Court of Appeals for the Fifth Circuit. In doing

---

[2] 347 U.S. 483 (1954), 349 U.S. 294 (1955).

[3] 210 F. Supp. 667, 668 (S.D. Ga. 1963), rev'd 333 F.2d 55 (5th Cir. 1964), cert. denied, 379 U.S. 933 (1964).

so, the court used the precedent set forth by *Brown* as the reason for requiring the Savannah district to desegregate. It is important to note that the validity of the test scores, which were the primary evidence, was never discussed (Bersoff, 1979, 1981).

C. *Hobson* v. *Hansen*[4]

Stell was just one of many cases that attempted to resist the order set forth in the famous *Brown* desegregation case. Like *Stell*, many of these cases introduced test scores as evidence that black children were genetically incapable of learning or being educated in the same classrooms as white children. The courts routinely accepted this evidence. Given the current controversy over the use of psychological tests, it is remarkable that several years passed before the validity of the test scores became an issue.

The first major case to examine the validity of psychological tests was *Hobson* v. *Hansen*. The *Hobson* case is relevant to many current lawsuits. Unlike the early desegregation cases, it did not deal with sending black and white children to different schools. Instead, it concerned the placement of children once they arrived at a school. Although the courts had been consistent in requiring schools to desegregate, they tended to take a hands-off approach with regard to the placement of students in tracks once they arrived at their desegregated schools.

The *Hobson* case contested the use of group standardized ability tests to place students in different learning tracks. Julius W. Hobson was the father of two black children placed in a basic track by the District of Columbia School District. Carl F. Hansen was the superintendent for the district. Within the district, children were placed in honors, regular, general, and basic tracks on the basis of group ability tests. The honors track was designed to prepare children for college, while the basic track focused on skills and preparation for blue-collar jobs. Placement in the basic track makes it essentially impossible to prepare for a high-income, high-prestige profession.

The rub in *Hobson* was that racial groups were not equally represented among those assigned to the basic track. In effect, the tracking system served to racially segregate groups by placing black children in the basic track and white children in the other tracks. Psychological tests were the primary mechanism used to justify this separation.

The *Hobson* case was decided in 1967 by Judge Skelly Wright of the Federal District Court of Washington, D.C. Just two years before the decision, the Supreme Court had ruled that a group is not denied equal protection by "mere classification" (Bersoff, 1979). Nevertheless, Judge Wright ruled against the use of the tracking system when based on group ability tests. After

---

[4] 269 F. Supp. 401 (D.D.C. 1967).

extensive expert testimony on the validity of the tests for minority children, the judge concluded that the tests discriminated against them. An interesting aspect of the opinion was that it claimed that grouping would be permissible if it was based on innate ability. The judge asserted that ability test scores were influenced by cultural experiences, and that the dominant cultural group had an unfair advantage on the tests and thereby gained admission to the tracks that provided the best preparation for high-income, high-prestige jobs.

D. *Diana* v. *State Board of Education*[5]

The decision in *Hobson* v. *Hansen* opened the door for a thorough examination of the use of standardized tests for the placement of students in EMR tracks. The case of *Diana* has particular implications for the use of standardized tests for bilingual children. Diana was one of nine Mexican-American elementary-school children who had been placed in EMR classes on the basis of scores on the WISC or Stanford-Binet test. These nine children represented a class of bilingual children. They brought a class-action suit against the California State Board of Education, contending that the use of standardized IQ tests for placement in EMR classes denied equal protection because the tests were standardized only for whites and had been administered by a non-Spanish-speaking psychometrist. Although only 18% of the children in Diana's school district had Spanish surnames, this group made up nearly one-third of the enrollment in EMR classes.

When originally tested in English, Diana achieved an IQ score of only 30. However, when retested in Spanish and English, her IQ bounced to 79, which was high enough to keep her out of the EMR classes in her school district. Seven of the other eight plaintiffs also achieved high enough scores on retesting in Spanish to be taken out of the EMR classes.

When faced with this evidence, the California State Board of Education decided not to take the case to court. Instead, they adopted special provisions for the testing of Mexican-American and Chinese-American children. These provisions included the following: (1) If English was not the primary language, the children would be tested in their primary language. (2) Questions based on certain vocabulary and information that the children could not be expected to know would be eliminated. (3) The Mexican-American and Chinese-American children who had been assigned to EMR classes would be reevaluated with tests that used their primary language and nonverbal items. (4) New tests would be developed by the state that reflected Mexican-American culture and that were normed for Mexican-American children (Bersoff, 1979). Later studies confirmed that bilingual children do score higher when tested in their primary language (Bergan & Parra, 1979).

---

[5] C.A. No. C-70 37 RFP (N.D. Cal., filed Feb. 3, 1970).

The combination of the judgment in *Hobson* and the change in policy brought about by *Diana* forced many to seriously question the use of IQ tests for the assignment of children to EMR classes. However, these decisions were quite specific to the circumstances in the particular cases. *Hobson* dealt with group tests but did not discuss individual tests; yet individual tests are used more often than group tests to make final decisions for EMR placement. The ruling in *Diana* was limited to strictly bilingual children. These two cases were thus not relevant to black children placed in EMR classes on the basis of individual IQ tests. This specific area was left for the most important court battle of them all—*Larry P.* v. *Wilson Riles.*

E. *Larry P.* v. *Wilson Riles*[6]

In October 1979, Judge Robert Peckham of the Federal District Court for the Northern District of California handed down an opinion that declared that "the use of IQ tests which had a disproportionate effect on black children violated the Rehabilitation Act, the Education for All Handicapped Children Act, Title VI, and the 14th Amendment when used to place children in EMR classes." Attorneys for Larry P., one of six black elementary-school students who were assigned to EMR classes on the basis of IQ test results, had argued that the use of standardized IQ tests to place black children in EMR classes violated both the California constitution and the equal protection clause of the 14th Amendment (Opton, 1979), as well as those laws mentioned above.

The court first ruled in the case of *Larry P.* in 1972. It found that the school district had incorrectly labeled Larry as EMR and violated his right to equal educational opportunity. As a result, a preliminary injunction was issued that prohibited that particular school district from using IQ tests for EMR placement decisions. Later, the California Department of Education called for a temporary moratorium on IQ testing until another court opinion on the validity of the tests could be obtained (Opton, 1977). The *Larry P.* case came before the same court that had issued the preliminary injunction in order to obtain a ruling on test validity for black children.

During the trial, both sides geared up for a particularly intense battle. Wilson Riles was the black superintendent of public instruction in California; he had instituted many significant reforms that benefited minority children. Thus, it was particularly awkward to have a nationally recognized spokesperson for progressive programs named as the defendant in an allegedly racist scheme.

In defense of the use of tests, Riles and the state called many nationally recognized experts on IQ tests including Lloyd Humphreys, Jerome Sattler, Robert Thorndike, Nadine Lambert, and Robert Gordon. These witnesses

---

[6] 343 F. Supp. 1306 (N.D. Cal. 1972), aff'd 502 F.2d 963 (9th Cir. 1979).

presented rather extensive evidence that IQ tests, particularly the Stanford-Binet and the WISC (which were used to test Larry and the others), were not biased against blacks. Although the tests had not originally been normed for black populations, studies had demonstrated that they were equally valid for use with black and white children. (Many of the arguments that support the use of tests for all races are summarized in Chapter 20.) Yet, if the tests were not biased, then why did Larry and the others receive higher scores when they were retested by black psychologists? The defense argued that the black psychologists did not follow standard testing procedures and that IQ test scores are not changed when standardized procedures are followed.

Statements from special education teachers were also presented. The teachers argued that the children involved in the case could not cope with the standard curriculum and that they required the special tutoring available in the EMR classes. The children had not been learning in regular classes, and the schools investigated classes in which there was doubt about the placement. For all these children, the assignment to EMR classes was deemed appropriate (Sattler, 1979a).

The Larry P. side of the case also had its share of distinguished experts, including George Albee, Leon Kamin, and Jane Mercer. The arguments for Larry were varied. His lawyers argued that all humans are born with equal capacity and that any test that assigns disproportionate numbers of children from one race to an EMR category is racist and discriminatory. The witnesses testified that dominant social groups had historically used devices such as IQ tests to discriminate against less powerful social groups and that the school district had intentionally discriminated against black children by using unvalidated IQ tests. Specifically, the tests were used to keep blacks in dead-end classes for the mentally retarded, in which they would not get the training they needed to move up in the social strata. Furthermore, the plaintiffs suggested that labeling someone as EMR has devastating social consequences. Children who are labeled as EMR lose confidence and self-esteem (Mercer, 1973), and eventually the label becomes a self-fulfilling prophecy (Rosenthal & Jacobson, 1968). In other words, labeling a child as mentally retarded may cause the child to behave as though he or she really is mentally retarded.

The judge was clearly persuaded more by the plaintiffs than by the defense. He declared that the tests "are racially and culturally biased, have a discriminatory impact on black children, and have not been validated for the purpose of (consigning) black children into educationally dead-end, isolated, and stigmatizing classes." Furthermore, the judge stated that the Department of Education had "desired to perpetuate the segregation of minorities in inferior, dead-end, and stigmatizing classes for the retarded."

The effect of the ruling was a permanent discontinuance of IQ testing to place black children in EMR classes. The decision immediately affected all black California school children who had been labeled as EMR. More than 6000 of these children had to be reassessed in some other manner.

There are strong differences of opinion about the meaning of the *Larry P.* decision. Harold Dent, one of the black psychologists who had retested Larry P. and the other children, hailed the decision as a victory for black children:

> For more than 60 years psychologists have used tests primarily to justify the majority's desire to "track" minorities into inferior education and dead-end jobs. The message of *Larry P.* is that psychologists must involve themselves in the task mandated in the last sentence of the court's opinion: "this will clear the way for more constructive educational reform" [quoted in Opton, 1979].

Others did not share the belief that the *Larry P.* decision was a social victory. Nadine Lambert, who was an expert witness for the state, felt it was a terrible decision. On learning of it, she remarked, "I think the people who will be most hurt by it are the black children" (quoted in Opton, 1979). Banning the use of IQ tests opens the door to completely subjective judgments, which may be even more racist than the test results. Opponents of the *Larry P.* decision cite many instances in which gifted black children were assumed to be average by their teachers but were recognized as highly intelligent because of IQ test scores.

The *Larry P.* decision has been frequently cited in subsequent cases, some of which are actually remote from the issues in *Larry P.* For example, in the case of *Ana Maria R.* v. *California Department of Education*,[7] parental rights were terminated on the grounds that the mother was mentally retarded. However, the mother was Spanish-speaking, and *Larry P.* was cited as precedent that tests used for classification of mental retardation are discriminatory against blacks and Hispanics. In contrast to the case of *Ana Maria R.*, the factual situation in an Illinois case was quite similar to *Larry P.* That case is described in the following section.

F. *Parents in Action on Special Education* v. *Hannon*[8]

Just as the case of *Larry P.* was making headlines in California, a similar case came to trial in Illinois. The case was a class-action lawsuit filed on behalf of two black children (representing the class of all similar children) who had been placed in special classes for the educable mentally handicapped (EMH) on the basis of IQ test scores. Attorneys for the two student plaintiffs argued that the children were inappropriately placed in EMH classes because of racial bias in the IQ tests. They suggested that the use of IQ tests for black children violates the equal protection clause of the Constitution and many federal statutes.

---

[7] 96 U.S. 2040(c) (1976).

[8] USDC NI11; J. Grady pub. 7/7/80.

In their presentation to the court, the plaintiffs relied heavily on the *Larry P.* decision, which held that the WISC, the WISC-R, and the Stanford-Binet IQ tests are biased and inappropriate for the testing of minority children. However, Judge John Grady of the U.S. District Court came to exactly the opposite conclusion of Judge Robert Peckham, who had presided over the *Larry P.* case. Judge Grady found evidence for racial bias in the three major IQ tests to be unconvincing. In his opinion, he noted that the items objected to were only a fraction of the items on the entire test. For example, witnesses for the plaintiffs never mentioned whole subtests on the WISC and WISC-R, such as arithmetic, digit span, block design, mazes, coding, and object assembly. The judge noted that these subtests were not biased in favor of either black or white children because most youngsters of both groups would never have confronted problems of this type before. The items for which there were legitimate objections were too few to have an impact on test scores.

Thus, less than one year after the historic *Larry P.* case, another court concluded: "Evidence of racial bias in standardized IQ tests is not sufficient to render their use as part of classification procedures to place black children in 'educable mentally handicapped' classes violative of statutes prohibiting discrimination in federal funded programs." Focused Example 21-4 presents conflicting statements from the two judges in these cases.

G. *Crawford et al.* v. *Honig et al.*[9]

In 1986, the court modified the *Larry P.* court order to expand the intelligence testing ban to all black children. The California Department of Education and the public interest lawyers who represented Larry P. were successful in gaining an order from Judge Peckham to ban the use of standardized intelligence tests for black children for assignment to special education programs. However, black children could take intelligence tests to be considered for the state-supported gifted and talented education program (GATE).

After the 1986 strengthening of the *Larry P.* decision, several new problems arose. One of them is represented by the case of *Crawford* v. *Honig*. Some children do have special needs and may benefit from special education programs. Indeed, special education programs were never developed for punishment. The intention was to identify learning problems and to provide special assistance. Under the 1986 modification of the *Larry P.* decision, white, Hispanic, Asian-American, and Native American students can be evaluated with intelligence tests for placement in special education. However, these tests cannot be used for black children. In fact, these tests cannot be given to black children even if the families request them. Crawford was the child of a mixed racial couple. The mother was black and the father was not black. Recognizing that the child was having difficulties in school, the mother requested testing.

---

[9] C.A. No. C-89-0014-RFP.

FOCUSED EXAMPLE 21-4

Different Opinions from Different Judges

We often think that two judges looking at the same evidence will come to the same conclusion. However, many times judges differ sharply in their opinions. When confronted with different opinions from Judges Peckham (*Larry P.* v. *Wilson Riles*) and Grady (*Parents in Action on Special Education* v. *Hannon*), J. M. Sattler (1980) juxtaposed quotes from the two judges on selected issues in the cases. Below are some of the statements demonstrating that the judges viewed the issues differently.

Judge Robert Peckham

Judge John Grady

What are the functions of special classes for the educable mentally retarded or educable mentally handicapped?

"EMR classes are designed to separate out children who are *incapable* of learning in the regular classes. . . . Further, the curriculum was not and is not designed to help students learn the skills necessary to return to the regular instructional program. . . . Finally, consistent with the first two aspects of EMR classes, the classes are conceived of as 'dead-end classes.' Children are placed there, generally at about eight to ten years of age, because they are thought to be incapable of learning the skills inculcated by the regular curriculum. They are provided with instruction that deemphasizes academic skills in favor of adjustment, and naturally they will tend to fall farther and farther behind the children in the regular classes."

"The EMH curriculum is designed for the child who cannot benefit from the regular curriculum. It is designed for children who learn slowly, who have short attention spans, slow reaction time, and difficulty retaining material in both the short term and the long term. The curriculum also recognizes the difficulty an EMH child has in seeing similarities and differences, in learning by implication, in generalizing and in thinking abstractly. The curriculum thus involves much repetition and concrete teaching. Subjects are taught for short periods of time, in recognition of the children's short attention spans."

How much emphasis is given to the IQ in placing children in mentally retarded or educable mentally handicapped classes?

"The available data suggest very strongly that, even if in some districts the IQ scores were not always determinative, they were pervasive in the placement process. . . . Retardation is defined in terms of the IQ tests, and a low score in effect establishes a *prima facie* case of retardation."

"The IQ score is not the sole determinant of whether a child is placed in an EMH class. First, the score itself is evaluated by the psychologist who administers the test. The child's responses are recorded verbatim, and the significance of his numerical score is a matter involving judgment and interpretation. . . . The examiner who knows the milieu of the child can correct for cultural bias by asking the questions in a sensitive and intelligent way. . . . Finally, the IQ test and the psychologist's evaluation of the child in the light of that test are only one component of several which form the basis for an EMH referral."

Judge Robert Peckham

Was the issue of test validity important in the trial?

"If defendants could somehow have demonstrated that the intelligence tests had been 'validated' for the purpose of EMR placement of black children, those tests could have been utilized despite their disproportionate impact. . . . However, defendants did not make these showings."

Judge John Grady

"We do not address the broader questions of whether these IQ tests are generally valid as measures of intelligence, whether individual items are appropriate for that purpose, or whether the tests could be improved. Those questions are not involved in this case."

To what extent do socioeconomic factors account for the findings that Black children score lower than White children on intelligence tests?

"It is clear that socioeconomic status by itself cannot explain fully the undisputed disparities in IQ test scores and in EMR placements. . . . The insufficiency of the above explanation leads us to question the cultural bias of IQ tests. The first important inferential evidence is that the tests were never designed to eliminate cultural biases against Black children; it was assumed in effect that Black children were less 'intelligent' than Whites."

"It is uncontradicted that most of the children in the EMH classes do in fact come from the poverty pockets of the city. This tends to suggest that what is involved is not simply race but something associated with poverty. It is also significant that many Black children who take the tests score at levels high enough to preclude EMH placement. Plaintiffs have not explained why the alleged cultural bias of the tests did not result in EMH-level scores for these children. Plaintiffs' theory of cultural bias simply ignore the fact that some Black children perform better than most Whites. Nationally, 15 to 20 percent of the Blacks who take the tests score above the White mean of 100."

To what extent does Black children's use of nonstandard English affect their performance on intelligence tests?

"At the outset, it is undeniable that to the extent Black children speak other than standard English, they will be handicapped in at least the verbal component of the tests. . . . Dr. [Asa] Hilliard and other witnesses pointed out that Black children are more likely to be exposed to nonstandard English, and that exposure will be reflected in IQ scores."

"The evidence does not establish how the use of nonstandard English would interfere with performance on the Wechsler and Stanford-Binet tests. . . . Dr. [Robert J.] Williams testified that a Black child might say, 'John go to town' instead of 'John is going to town,' or 'John book' instead of 'John's book.' . . . What is unclear is how the use of such nonstandard English would handicap a child either in understanding the test items or in responding to them. . . . Moreover, responding to a test item in nonstandard English should not af-

(continued)

Citing *Larry P.*, the school denied the request because the child had been identified as black. However, the mother was told that if she changed the child's racial identification to match the father, testing would be permitted. The lawsuit that followed claimed that California Superintendent of Public Education Bill Honig and the California Board of Education violated Crawford's civil rights by denying a public service on the basis of race. The arguments in court suggested that a race-conscious testing policy promoted inequities and indignities. Eventually, the case was heard by Judge Peckham, the same judge who had issued the *Larry P.* ruling and the 1986 modification strengthening the original judgment. Crawford's case was vigorously opposed by the California Department of Education. However, since this 1991 case was

(continued)
Judge Robert Peckham

Judge John Grady

fect a child's score on the item, since the examiners are specifically instructed by the test manuals to disregard the form of the answer so long as the substance is correct. . . . But there are no vocabulary items on the IQ tests, so far as I can tell, which are peculiar to White culture."

To what extent do differences between Black culture and White culture affect Black children's performance on intelligence tests?

"To the extent that a 'Black culture'—admittedly a vague term—exists and translates the phenomenon of intelligence into skills and knowledge untested by the standardized intelligence tests, those tests cannot measure the capabilities of Black children. . . . On the basis of their different cultural background, which results particularly in lower scores on IQ tests, Black children are subjected to discrimination analogous to that borne by many San Francisco Chinese, who, because of their cultural background, could not communicate effectively in English. Certainly many Chinese-Americans would succeed in those schools even without remedial English. Nevertheless, the failure to provide English-language teaching foreclosed substantial numbers of students from any meaningful educational opportunity. This same result occurs from the use of IQ tests and a biased placement process."

"Dr. Williams did not explain how he relates the other characteristics of Black culture to performance on the tests. It is not clear, for instance, how the extended family as opposed to the nuclear family would pertain to performance on the tests. Like Dr. [Leon] Kamin's description of the racist attitudes of Goddard, Yerkes and Terman, Dr. Williams's description of Black culture has not been connected to the specific issue in this case. . . . Dr. Kamin's argument that the Black child does not obtain the same 'information,' and Dr. [George] Albee's argument that the Black child does not share in the dominant White culture, seem inapplicable to most items on all three of the tests in question. As already noted, many of the categories of test items have no precise counterpart in the experience of any children, of whatever race. Others have almost precise counterparts in the everyday experience of American children of all races. Any number of test items could be cited to illustrate this point."

not a class-action suit, it was uncertain whether or not the ruling would apply to all children. The plaintiffs petitioned the court to extend the judgment to all similar black children (Bredemeier, 1991). In September of 1992, Judge Peckham issued an order reversing the earlier ban on IQ tests for black students.

H. *Marshall* v. *Georgia*

One of the first major decisions that was contrary to the *Larry P.* judgment was *Marshall* v. *Georgia*. This was a class-action suit filed in 1981 on behalf of a group of black students in Georgia. The complaint was that the students had

Judge Robert Peckham

Judge John Grady

Generally, to what extent are intelligence tests racially biased?

"The answer, as should be clear from the earlier discussion of the history and biases of IQ tests, is that validation has been assumed, not established, for Blacks. The tests were developed and standardized in the United States on White, essentially middle-class groups."

"All but a few of the items on their face appear racially neutral. . . . I conclude that the possibility of the few biased items on these tests causing an EMH placement that would not otherwise occur is practically nonexistent."

Does the use of intelligence tests violate some provisions of Public Law 94-142 (Education for All Handicapped)?

"Defendants have failed to take the steps necessary to assure the tests' validity. They have committed a serious error that Title VII regulations warn against in the employment situation: 'Under no circumstances will the general reputation of a test, its author, or its publisher, or casual reports of test utility be accepted in lieu of evidence of validity.' Whether or not the tests in fact do what they are supposed to do, the law is that defendants must come forward and show that they have been validated for each minority group with which they are used. This minimal burden has not been met for diagnosing the kind of mental retardation justifying EMR placement."

"The requirement that 'materials and procedures' used for assessment be nondiscriminatory, and that no single procedure be the sole criterion for assessment, seems to me to contemplate that the process as a whole be nondiscriminatory. It does not require that any single procedure, standing alone, be affirmatively shown to be free of bias. The very requirement of multiple procedures implies recognition that one procedure, standing alone, could well result in bias and that a system of cross-checking is necessary."

From "Different Opinions for Different Judges: Judges Peckham (*Larry P.* v. *Wilson Riles*) and Grady (*Parents in Action for Special Education* v. *Hannon*)" by J. Sattler. In *American Psychological Association Monitor*, 1980, 11(11): 7–8. Copyright 1980 by the American Psychological Association. Reprinted by permission.

been disproportionately placed in classes for the educable mentally retarded (EMR) and were underrepresented in classes for learning disabilities (LD). The defendants in the case were 13 school districts, most in the state of Georgia. The key witness for the plaintiff was Robert Calfee, an educational psychologist from Stanford University. Calfee noted that racial differences were more important than socioeconomic status in accounting for differential performance in school. Through a series of complex analyses, Calfee concluded that the school experience itself was actually creating differences between groups. Thus, the practice of assigning students to groups was damaging. As a remedy, Calfee suggested that students be assigned to classrooms on a random basis.

The defense argued that, indeed, placement into certain classrooms did provide benefits for students. The court ultimately ruled that the grouping of students was to their benefit. Thus, they allowed the use of tests to separate students because these procedures ultimately resulted in better outcomes. The critical result of the decision was that the focus shifted to emphasize the ultimate benefit to students. One of the important issues in the case was the focus on curriculum-based assessment rather than IQ testing. Perhaps the most important difference between the *Marshall* decision and previous court cases was the judge's belief that test information could be used to structure interventions that would be helpful to the children (*Marshall et al.* v. *Georgia*, 1984, 1985; Reschly, Kicklighter & Mckee, 1988; Richley & Ward, 1991).

I. *Debra P.* v. *Turlington*[10]

Some people feel that a test is biased if it contains questions that particular test takers cannot answer. One 1979 lawsuit in Florida involved ten black students who had failed in their first attempt to pass Florida's minimum competence test, the State Student Assessment Test. Debra P. was one of the students, and the case took her name. In Hillsborough County, where the suit was filed, about 19% of the students in the public school system were black; however, black students constituted 64% of those who failed the test.

Minimum competence tests similar to the one used in Florida have been adopted by more than 30 states, and 19 states require the exam for graduation. If they meet other requirements, students who do not pass the exam are given a certificate of completion, which acknowledges that they attended high school but does not carry the same status as a high school diploma. Examples of items from a minimum competence test are shown in Table 21-2.

The Florida suit charged that the test should not be used for minority students when most of their education occurred before the schools were desegregated. Thus, the dispute was over whether the same test should be used for students who may have had unequal opportunities to learn in school. Attorneys for the students argued that their clients had been in inferior schools and had

---

[10] 474 F. Supp. 244 (M.D. Fla. 1979).

Table 21-2

Examples of Items from a Minimum Competence Test

Use the following table to answer question 1:

12 inches = 1 foot	1,760 yards = 1 mile
3 feet = 1 yard	5,280 feet = 1 mile

1. Sara needs to wrap string around 8 boxes. Each box needs a piece of string 72 inches long. How many yards of string does she need?
   A. 8 yards   B. 16 yards   C. 48 yards   D. 576 yards

2. The Florida sales tax on cars is 4%. The sticker price on a car including extras, title, transportation, and dealer preparation is $3,200. What is the total cost of the car including sales tax?
   A. $3,204   B. $3,212   C. $3,314   D. $3,328

3. The graph below shows the changes in the cost of coffee during a one-year period. According to this graph, how much did the cost of a pound of coffee change from April 1 to July 1?
   A. $.50   B. $1.00   C. $1.50   D. $2.50

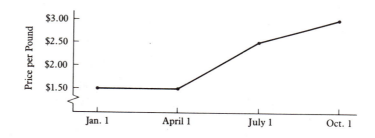

Chocolate Chip Cookies

1 cup brown sugar	2 eggs	1 tsp. salt
1 cup white sugar	1 tsp. baking soda	1 tsp. vanilla
1 cup shortening	2¼ cups flour	1 pkg. chocolate chips

Preheat oven to 350 degrees. In a medium-sized mixing bowl, combine sugar and shortening. Add vanilla and eggs. In another bowl sift together flour, salt, and baking soda. Add sifted ingredients to sugar and shortening mixture. Add chocolate chips. Mix all ingredients together and drop by teaspoon on a cookie sheet. Bake at 350 degrees for 10 minutes.

4. From the above recipe, what should be sifted with baking soda? A. vanilla and eggs   B. sugar and shortening   C. flour and salt   D. chocolate chips and salt

Answers to sample questions:
1. B   2. D   3. B   4. C

From *State Student Assessment Test. Part II: Answers to Your Questions.* Reprinted with permission of the State of Florida, Department of Education.

been the subjects of continued discrimination; thus, they should not be held to the standards for majority students, who had better opportunities.

Ralph D. Turlington was the commissioner of education and one of the defendants in the case. He argued that basic minimum standards must be applied in order to certify that students have enough information to survive in situations that require high school level sophistication. These standards, it was argued, must be absolute. Either students know the basic information or they do not. According to the commissioner, "To demand that a 12th-grade student with a 3rd-grade reading level be given a diploma is silly."

The Florida case illustrates the kind of lawsuit we might expect in the future. It pits two sides with reasonable arguments against each other. One side argues that minority children have worked hard in school under great disadvantage and cannot be expected to have learned the things majority children know. In recognition of their work, they deserve a diploma. The other side argues that there should be an absolute standard for basic information (Seligmann et al., 1979).

The court essentially sided with the commissioner. The judge did not challenge the validity of the test. However, he did suspend the use of the test for four years, after which all the students who had any part of their education in segregated schools would have graduated. Then, according to the opinion, the test could be used.

In a 1981 article, Lerner argued that minimum competence exams, such as the SSAT II used in the state of Florida, benefit both students and society. As an attorney, she found little legal justification for court involvement. However, the court reopened the *Debra P.* case the same year that Lerner's paper was published. This new consideration came after those students who had begun their education under a segregated system had graduated, and thus differences in performance could not be attributed to segregation. In the new evaluation, the U.S. District Court of Appeals considered the validity of the test. It stated that the test would violate the equal protection clause if "the test by dividing students into two categories, passers and failers, did so without a rational relation to the purpose for which it was designed, then the Court would be compelled to find the test unconstitutional."[11] However, in this case, the court concluded that the test did have adequate construct validity and that it could be used to evaluate functional literacy. In the same opinion, the court stressed that the test must reflect what is taught in school and that continual surveillance of test fairness is warranted.

J. *Regents of the University of California* v. *Bakke*[12]

Alan Bakke was an engineer in his thirties who decided to apply to the University of California, Davis, medical school in the early 1970s. Although Bakke

---

[11] 474 F. Supp. 260.

[12] 438 U.S. 265, 17 Fair Empl. Prac. Cas. (BNA) 1000 (1978).

had a high grade point average and good MCAT scores, he was denied admission. Bakke decided to investigate the matter. He discovered that his test scores were higher than those of minority students who had gained admission to the medical school under a special affirmative action program. Bakke eventually sued the university on the grounds that he had been discriminated against because he was not a minority-group member. The suit ended in the Supreme Court.

Although many arguments were presented in the *Bakke* case, one of the major ones concerned the use of test scores. Under the affirmative action program, the cutoff value for MCAT scores was higher for nonminority than for minority students. In defense of the special admissions program, it was argued that the tests were not meaningful (valid) for minority students. However, evidence was also presented that the tests were equally meaningful for both groups.

The Supreme Court ruling was not specific about the use of tests. The court ruled that the university had to admit Bakke and that it had denied him due process in the original consideration of the case. It also implied that the use of different cutoff scores was not appropriate. However, the court did acknowledge that race could be taken into consideration in selection decisions. This acknowledgement was interpreted by the EEOC as meaning that affirmative action programs based on numerical quotas could continue (Norton, 1978). However, the Bakke case was symbolic of a change in attitude about affirmative action programs.

President Ronald Reagan openly opposed selection goals and affirmative action and made a political issue out of "racial quotas." In the 1980s, Reagan appointed several people to key positions who agreed with his beliefs. For example, his assistant attorney general for civil rights, Bradford Reynolds, became an advocate for unqualified individualism (see Chapter 20). He argued for "color blind" equal opportunity in which skin color is not considered in selection decisions. According to Reynolds, selecting blacks with lower test scores to remediate past discrimination would be "borrowing the tools of the racist." He emphasized that government must "never support the use of quotas or any other numerical formulas" (Bearak & Lauter, 1991, p. A18). Many Reagan appointees held similar beliefs. Even the Reagan-appointed director of the EEOC stressed the importance of individual qualifications over racial identification. Thus, by the late 1980s and early 1990s, the mood toward affirmative action had changed. This mood change has most clearly affected personnel cases.

K. *Golden Rule Insurance Company et al. v. Washburn et al.*

In 1976, the Golden Rule Insurance Company of Lawrenceville, Illinois, sued the Educational Testing Service (ETS) and the Illinois Department of Insurance over "cultural bias" in the Illinois Insurance Licensing Examination. The examination was created by the ETS for the state of Illinois, which was why both defendants were in the suit. A 1978 study showed that 77% of white applicants passed the exam, while only 52% of blacks passed. The case was settled out of court. ETS made no admission of guilt but did agree to make changes in the test. The major change was to revise the way items are selected for the test. An expert committee of insurance officials and testing experts now oversee the selection of the items. Items are selected on the criterion that the proportions of correct answers for white and black test takers differ by no more than .15.

When the *Golden Rule* case was settled in 1984, civil rights experts predicted that there would be a major revision in the way insurance tests were administered in 22 other states. About 200,000 applicants for insurance li-

---

FOCUSED EXAMPLE 21-5

The Twists and Turns of University Affirmative Action Policies

Federal regulation of college admissions policies has taken many interesting twists and turns. Initially affirmative action policies were designed to guarantee that institutions of higher learning would be ethnically diverse. Indeed, most disciplinary actions have been taken because universities had not been successful in attracting an ethnically diverse student body. However, some institutions have been very successful. One example is the University of California, Berkeley, School of Law. The Berkeley Law School, known as Boalt Hall, has made very aggressive efforts to attract an ethnically diverse student body. In the class of 1996 (made up of students admitted in 1992), 39% of the students were from minority groups.

In September, 1992, Boalt Hall came under scrutiny for their admissions policies. The U.S. Department of Education's Office of Civil Rights argued that the university had engaged in policies that were not consistent with Title VI of the 1964 Civil Rights Act. In particular, it was claimed that the law school had violated the portions of the Civil Rights Act that prohibit discrimination on the basis of race, color, or national origin. The reason for this violation was that Boalt Hall set aside a portion of their entering class positions for minority students. Separate decision processes were made for minority and nonminority students. It was argued that discrimination was taking place and that those who were being discriminated against were Asians and to some extent Caucasians.

When faced with the complaint the university agreed to alter their admissions policies. They were required to report by 1994 the number of applicants in each racial and ethnic category and to list how many of these applicants were admitted. The university is also now required to show that they do not treat students from different racial and ethnic groups differently. Many academic leaders fear that the Boalt Hall agreement will seriously weaken efforts to attract an ethnically diverse student body. They argue that law school's affirmative action policies have improved the quality of justice by contributing to ethnic and racial diversity in the legal profession.

Reference: Merl, J., & Trombley, W. (1992). Law school's admissions plan unfair, U.S. finds. *Los Angeles Times*, September 29: A1, A26.

censes take these tests every year ("Insurance License Exams . . . ," 1984, p. 5). In 1985, a related case (*Allen* v. *Alabama State Board of Education*) followed similar lines of reasoning. However, in this case, a much more stringent rule was used. The Alabama State Board of Education agreed to use items for which the black/white proportion of correct answers differed by no more than .05. The *Golden Rule* case is important because it sets a new precedent within the testing industry. Although ETS admitted no guilt, it clearly agreed to revise its method of operation.

L. *Personnel Cases*

Most of the cases we have discussed involved educational tests. Several other important lawsuits have dealt with the use of tests in employment settings. Through a series of Supreme Court decisions, specific restrictions have been placed on the use of tests for the selection of employees. The most important of these cases are *Griggs* v. *Duke Power Company*,[13] *Albemarle Paper Company* v. *Moody*,[14] and *Washington* v. *Davis*.[15] The effect of these decisions has been to force employers to define the relationship between tests scores and job performance and to define the measure of job performance. However, none of the decisions denies that tests are valuable tools in the personnel field and that the use of tests can continue.

In Chapter 5, we mentioned the case of *Griggs* v. *Duke Power Company*. The case involved 14 black employees of the Duke Steam Plant in North Carolina who were concerned about their lack of opportunity. In the steam plant, few employees, either black or white, had graduated from high school. In 1966, the most a black employee could earn was $1.65 per hour, while whites started at $1.81. Furthermore, white men generally rose through the ranks of the company and became managers or supervisors. They had comfortable offices with bathrooms down the hall. Black men were assigned to clean the toilets in those bathrooms but were not allowed to use them. Instead, the company built a "colored" bathroom and placed it across the railroad tracks behind the coal pile. The leader of the black employees was Willie Boyd. He had learned about the EEOC and become acquainted with a civil rights leader who persuaded Willie and his co-workers to file a complaint. When they presented their complaint to the company, they were told that education and training were necessary for advancement. Yet few black or white employees had much educational background. In fact, only 15 white employees had finished high school. The company reacted by creating a test and telling the

---

[13] 401 U.S. 424(a) (1971).

[14] 442 U.S. 405 (1975).

[15] 96 U.S. 2040(c) (1976).

black employees that they needed to pass it in order to gain advancement. The test included 50 items such as this one:

> In printing an article of 24,000 words, a printer decides to use two sizes of type. With the larger type, a printed page contains 900 words. With the smaller type, a page contains 1200 words. The article is allotted 21 full pages in the magazine. How many pages must be in small type?

The test was difficult and none of the black employees passed it. However, neither did any of the white employees. The validity of the test became the central issue in the lawsuit that followed. Specifically, evidence was required on the relationship between the test and the job duties. Although Boyd was the leader of the group, the lawsuit was filed under the name of Willie Griggs, who was another one of the 14 janitors. Griggs was the youngest of the group with the least seniority and his name was put forth because he was the one with the least to lose. After 5 years the case worked its way to the U.S. Supreme Court, and the court ruled that employment tests must be valid and reliable. The *Griggs* case set the tone for the next two decades of civil rights action in the United States (Bareak & Louter, 1991).

In the 1988 Supreme Court case, *Watson* v. *Fort Worth Bank and Trust,*[16] it was argued that any procedure that appears to be discriminatory because of the ratio of minorities selected is in violation of the law. The case involved Clara Watson, a black woman employee of the Fort Worth Bank and Trust. Ms. Watson was passed over for promotion to a supervisory position. She filed suit and argued that blacks made up 13% of the bank's work force and 10% of Forth Worth's population. However, the bank had only one black supervisor. Thus, there was a misrepresentation in selection for higher jobs. The lower courts had rejected Watson's petition, arguing that statistical evidence for bias applied only to objective selection devices, such as psychological tests, and that subjective judgments could be defended when there was evidence of "business necessity." The Supreme Court disagreed, suggesting that employers could protect themselves from discrimination suits by adding just one subjective item to objective tests. The court affirmed that statistical selection ratios are sufficient evidence of adverse impact.

Sometimes trends in one direction spur reactions in another. The *Watson* case was among the first important civil rights cases that had been decided by a conservative group of Supreme Court justices picked by President Ronald Reagan. The Reagan Administration was unhappy with the trend set in earlier decisions and emphasized the "color blind" selection of employees. The next major case that came to the court was *Wards Cove Packing Company* v. *Antonio.*[17] The case concerned salmon canneries in Alaska. Most of the workers

---

[16] *Los Angeles Times*, June 30, 1988, Part 1, pp. 1, 16.

[17] 490, U.S. 642 (1989).

were nonskilled Filipinos and Eskimos who sliced up the fish during fishing season. These were the worst jobs in the company because they were unsteady and dirty. The employees claimed that the company was biased against them and kept them out of the better-paying skilled jobs such as machinery repair. The nine Supreme Court justices decided not to hear the case. Instead, they returned it to the lower courts. This decision was important because it reversed a central theme of the *Griggs* decision. In refusing to hear the case, the court noted that the burden of proof should be shifted from the employer to the employee. In other words, instead of requiring the employer to show that a psychological test is valid and reliable, the burden was shifted to the employee to demonstrate that it did not have these properties. This may seem like a minor point, but in practice it could have an enormous impact. Employers know how to interpret their own tests, financial records, and selection procedures. Requiring the plaintiff to discredit these procedures gives him or her an almost impossible task. Even the most skilled lawyers felt that the long fight for equal employment opportunity had been lost (Bareak & Louter, 1991b).

The *Wards Cove Packing Company* v. *Antonio* decision upset the Democratic-controlled 1991 Congress. Both the House and the Senate introduced new legislation. For example, the Senate enacted Senate Bill 45 of the 102nd Congress and stated specifically that the Supreme Court decision had weakened the scope and effectiveness of federal civil rights protection. In response to court actions, they felt that new and stronger legislation was required. The purposes of the 1991 Civil Rights Act are listed here:

1. Provide appropriate redress for intentional discrimination and unlawful harassment in the workplace.
2. Overrule proof burdens and the meaning of business necessity in *Wards Cove Packing Company* v. *Antonio* and codify the proof burdens and the meaning of business necessity used in *Griggs* v. *Duke Power Company*.
3. Confirm the basic aspects of the 1964 Civil Rights Act.
4. Provide a clear response to the Supreme Court decision.

The bill clarified that the burden of proof lies with the employer.

One provision of the 1991 Civil Rights Act deals specifically with test scores. Section 9 entitled "Prohibition Against Discriminatory Use of Test Scores" states, "It shall be an unlawful employment practice for a respondent in connection with the selection or referral of applicants or candidates for employment or promotion to adjust the scores of, use different cutoff scores, or otherwise alter the results of employment related tests on the basis of race, color, religion, sex, or natural origin." This aspect of the bill appears to outlaw the use of differential cutoff scores by race, gender, or ethnic background. The impact of this clause may be to shift away from the use of quotas.

The early 1990s saw the beginning of a new type of lawsuit. Affirmative action programs did not necessarily benefit all minority groups. For example, Asian students have historically done very well on college admissions tests such as the SAT. Some have argued that affirmative action programs systematically discriminate against some minority and majority students. In 1991, a California congressman requested an investigation of the University of California in San Diego (UCSD). The university admits about 60% of its freshman class according to grade point average and SAT scores. Admission to the university is extremely competitive, with most students being admitted having a nearly perfect grade point average and high SAT scores; however, 40% of the spots are reserved for students admitted under special considerations. These considerations include special achievements in fields such as music, athletics, or student government. In addition, the supplemental criteria can include race and ethnicity. Students admitted under the supplemental criteria are much more likely to be from traditionally underrepresented groups such as Latinos and Afro-Americans. The USCD case was initiated by a Filipino student who

---

FOCUSED EXAMPLE 21-6

Different Views of Affirmative Action

Blacks and Caucasians differ in their views of affirmative action. For example, a 1991 poll conducted by the *Los Angeles Times* suggested that nearly two-thirds of Caucasians felt that affirmative action was either adequate or had gone too far. One-third thought that it had not gone far enough. Among black respondents, 60% felt that it had not gone far enough.

It is acknowledged that, on average, blacks have less desirable jobs, income, and housing than do whites. Sixty-five percent of black respondents said that discrimination was the cause of this problem, while only 33% of Caucasians came to the same conclusion.

These data are shown in the accompanying figure. They suggest that there are important attitudinal differences between blacks and Caucasians that must become the focus of attention if we are to resolve these problems.

Percent stating affirmative action programs had gone too far, 1991

Percent stating discrimination is cause of problems for Blacks, 1991 was not admitted under either the standard or supplemental criteria. However, if all students had been admitted under the standard criteria, this student would probably have been admitted because both his grade point average and SAT scores were high. The congressman argued that Asian-Americans had been systematically denied admission because of their race. They did not receive extra consideration under the supplemental criteria because they were not underrepresented in the first 60% of students selected. On the other hand, their test scores and grade point averages were higher than other minority-group members who were selected under the special admissions policies.

Similar complaints were filed at other University of California campuses. The university's defense has been that it does not discriminate on the basis of race. Selection criteria are not iron clad. In other words, the university reserves the right to have some flexibility in its decision to select students. Ethnic diversity, they argue, is an appropriate goal for a public university.

◻ ◇   **F O C U S E D   E X A M P L E   2 1 - 7**

Coaching and the Bias in Aptitude Tests

One of the criticisms of standardized achievement tests is that coaching may improve performance. So widespread is the belief that coaching is helpful that SAT, LSAT, and GRE preparatory schools have become a big business. If coaching does improve performance on these tests, then they are not really aptitude tests but achievement tests. Those who believe that coaching works have accused the ETS of being biased and fraudulent because its tests do not measure pure aptitude.

One major problem with studies on coaching is that few of them include a proper control group. Thus, when students improve after coaching classes, it is not clear whether this was due to the coaching, their commitment to improve performance (as evidenced by enrollment in the course), or some other personality characteristic associated with taking a coaching course. The few studies with proper control groups show a very small but significant gain in performance as a function of obtaining coaching, but is the small gain worth the effort?

Systematic reviews of the coaching literature suggest that the more time spent in preparation for the test, the greater the increase in score. How-ever, the relationship is nonlinear. Small increases in preparation time result in some improvement in test performance, but as preparation time increases, lesser returns in performance are realized. According to S. Messick and A. Jungeblut (1981, p. 191), who completed the review, "the student contact time required to achieve average score increases much greater than 20 to 30 points (on a 200- to 800-point scale) for both the SAT-V and the SAT-M rapidly approaches that of full-time schooling."

Despite these studies, ETS critics still maintain that coaching is useful. D. Owen (1985), for example, suggests that coaching schools can improve scores by teaching skills in multiple-choice test taking. He cites one New York area test preparation course that has achieved success by teaching students to analyze the choices to a question. In some cases, students are able to improve their scores without even studying alternative choices and without referring to the questions. Owen rebuffs the ETS claim that coaching makes little difference. He is quick to point out that ETS itself sells (at a handsome price) its own version of coaching booklets.

The courts have also been asked to decide on issues of test administration. For example, an employee of the Detroit Edison Company was not promoted because of a low test score. In his defense, his union suggested that the low score might have been an error and requested a copy of the test to check the scoring. Detroit Edison did not want to release the test because it feared that the union would distribute the items to other employees. By a vote of five to four, the Supreme Court ruled on the side of Detroit Edison (*Detroit Edison Co.* v. *N.L.R.B.*[18]). It is interesting that in a major decision such as this, a single vote can make a difference in policy (Cronbach, 1980).

A 1982 Supreme Court decision (*Connecticut* v. *Teal*[19]) considered the issue of discrimination against an individual even when there has been no adverse impact. In this case, a written test unrelated to any specific job was used as an initial screening device. This screening device significantly reduced the number of blacks in the application pool. However, at the next step in the screening process, blacks who had passed the test had a better chance of being hired than whites. The end result was that the total number of blacks hired did not reflect an adverse impact.

On review of the situation, the U.S. Supreme Court ruled that Title VII protects individuals, not just the groups to which they belong. Thus, it ruled that black applicants had been discriminated against by the use of a test that did not have validity for the particular job. The court suggested that these individuals were not compensated just because other members of their minority group were given favorable treatment if they could pass the initial test. In other words, it is not defensible to argue that the end result is appropriate if particular individuals have been discriminated against. In more recent decisions, the court has upheld hiring goals that favor formerly underrepresented groups as interim relief for past discrimination while new and more valid selection procedures are being established (*United States* v. *City of Buffalo*, 1985). In one summary article, J. Hogan and A. M. Quigley (1986) reviewed all the cases involving physical standards used in employment decisions.[20] Physical tests, including height, weight, and physical strength, must be subjected to the same validity criteria as are psychological tests. It is expected that there will continue to be many lawsuits concerning these issues.

One of the major issues that has plagued job discrimination cases is the evidence that can be used to prove bias. Proof of discrimination has often been difficult. In blue-collar jobs, employers have defended their hiring practices on the basis of the validity of aptitude tests. Challenges were typically based on the test criterion validity and the ratio of minority applicants that the test selected. In contrast, decisions about the selection and advancement of people in white-collar jobs have been based on subjective impressions of job performance and interviews.

---

[18] 99 S. Ct. 1123 (1979).

[19] 102 S. Ct. 2525 (1982).

[20] 37 U.S. 628 (W.D.N.Y. 1985).

M. *A Critical Look at Lawsuits*

As surely as the sun rises, there will be more court battles over the use of psychological tests. The problems that we as pyshcologists are unable to resolve ourselves will eventually be turned over to someone else for a binding opinion. This procedure may not be in the best interest of the field of psychology or of the people whom the profession serves.

It is difficult to be an uncritical admirer of the courts. As B. Lerner (1979) notes, inconsistencies in court decisions are commonplace. Even worse, judges who make important decisions about the use of tests often have little background in psychology or testing. On completing this course, you should be better able to evaluate most of the evidence than some judges who ultimately make the decisions in courtrooms. Often judges obtain their entire education about testing during the course of a trial.

In the near future, we must grapple with many difficult issues. For example, many current social problems seem related to the differential distribution of resources among the races in American society. Changing the income distribution seems to be one of the only ways in which effective social change can occur. To accomplish this redistribution, we must get minority children in appropriate educational tracks, into professional schools, and into high-income positions. The courts have ruled that psychological tests are blocking this progress.

Psychologists themselves are not of one mind regarding the use of psychological tests. However, as we noted in Chapter 20, at least some researchers have come to a conclusion opposite that of the courts, which have given the issue a briefer evaluation. In the end, however, the courts have the power, and their judgment is the law.

Summary

With increasing frequency, tests are coming under legal regulation. One of the major sets of regulations has been provided by the EEOC. This commission, which was created by the Civil Rights Act of 1964, has issued strict guidelines for the use of tests. The guidelines clearly spell out the minimum criteria for validity and reliability of psychological measures. The role of the EEOC became the focus of considerable debate in the 1980s, and the power of the commission was questioned by two court decisions at the end of that decade. However, a new 1991 Civil Rights Bill reaffirmed commitment to affirmative action programs.

Tests have also come to be regulated by statute. The states of California and New York were among the first to pass truth in testing laws that place many requirements on commercial testing companies. These laws have required testing companies to disclose actual test items to test takers. In the past, test items were protected by copyright. Items on tests that are affected by these laws must now be rewritten frequently, and this procedure may have had a damaging effect on the reliability and the validity of the tests. In 1975, Congress passed PL 94-142, which outlined standards for the assessment of potential among handicapped children. This law continues to affect the use of tests in the education system.

Many lawsuits have had an impact on the use of tests. In *Stell* v. *Savannah-Chatham County Board of Education*, the court ruled that differences between blacks and whites in IQ scores could not be used as a justification for keeping the schools segregated. In *Hobson* v. *Hansen*, group tests were found to be inappropriate for the assignment of black children to EMR classes. The concern over IQ tests was extended in *Diana* v. *State Board of Education*. This case, which was settled out of court, established that IQ tests could not be used with bilingual children, and it stimulated the development of new methods of assessment for these children. The impact of each of these decisions was magnified in *Larry P.* v. *Wilson Riles*, in which tests were banned as a means of assigning black children to EMR classes. In 1980, a court apparently reversed this decision in the case of *Parents in Action on Special Education* v. *Hannon*. In *Debra P.* v. *Turlington*, a court ruled that a minimum competence test could be used only when the students had received their entire education in integrated schools.

The regulation of testing through statute (laws passed by legislators), regulation (rules created by agencies), and litigation (lawsuits) has only recently become common. In the future, we can expect more interactions between testing and the law.

Chapter 22

The Future of Psychological Testing

Learning Objectives

When you have completed this chapter, you should be able to:

- Explain why the question of whether people possess stable traits is an issue in the testing field.
- Explain the issue of actuarial versus clinical prediction.
- Identify human rights as they pertain to testing.
- Explain the problem of labeling.
- Explain the issue of divided loyalties.
- Identify some important responsibilities of test users and test constructors.
- Identify four important current trends in the testing field.
- Describe the future prospects of testing.

No one can predict the future with certainty. However, by examining current trends in conjunction with pressures and forces that are currently shaping the testing field, we can deepen our understanding of testing and venture a few educated guesses about the future. The future of testing will depend ultimately on numerous complex, interacting forces. Identifying each force individually tends to oversimplify reality. Therefore, you should recognize that the forces identified separately here do not operate in isolation but rather interact with one another in highly complicated ways.

I. *Pressures Shaping the Field of Testing*

The pressures currently shaping the testing field include professional issues, moral issues, ethical issues, and social issues.

A. *Professional Issues*

Three major professional issues play an especially important role in the current status and the future of psychological testing: theoretical concerns, the adequacy of tests, and actuarial versus clinical prediction.

Theoretical concerns. One of the most important considerations underlying tests is the dependability (reliability) of test results. Reliability places an upper limit on validity. According to the *Standards of Educational and Psychological Tests* of the American Psychological Association, the American Education Research Association, and the National Council on Measurement in Education (AERA et al., 1985; APA, 1974), a test that is totally unreliable (unstable) has no meaning. There may be exceptions to this rule (Atkinson, 1981), but current practice generally demands that tests possess some form of stability. As a corollary, whatever is being measured must itself have stability. When we say that a test has reliability, we are implying that test results are attributable to a systematic source of variance, which is stable itself. In other words, the test is presumed to measure a stable entity. There are various types of reliability, depending on the different purposes of the tests. Each test must possess the type of reliability that is appropriate for the uses to which it is put (AERA et al., 1985; APA, 1974).

Most existing tests measure what we assume is a stable entity—either the individual as he or she presently functions or some temporally stable characteristic of the individual. In measuring current functioning, we may say something like "the person is emotionally unstable" or "the person is out of contact with reality," or we may provide a diagnostic label such as "schizophrenic" or "neurotic." In describing current functioning, we imply that the person functions this way in a fairly stable, though perhaps short-term, manner, independent of the situation or environment. In other words, we assume that we can describe the person in absolute terms, as if in a vacuum, independent of external factors. Similarly, and even more strikingly, when we purport to measure a temporally stable characteristic of an individual, we are assuming that we are measuring an enduring quality that will manifest itself over time regardless of immediate or long-term external (situational, environmental, and so forth) factors. Again, we assume that what we are measuring exists in absolute terms—that is, in a vacuum or independent of external factors.

Whether we are measuring current functioning or a temporally stable characteristic, the assumption is always that the systematic source of variance measured by the test is due entirely to the person as opposed to some factor external to the person. When we purport to measure a stable characteristic of an individual and find less than perfect temporal reliability, we assume that the imperfections are due to test-related inadequacies, such as measurement error, or to minor fluctuating subject variables, such as fatigue. Thus, we assume that the characteristic or variable being measured is stable, that it exists, and that our ability to measure it is limited only by the adequacy of the test instrument. Therefore, the more accurate a test, the more stable the results should be.

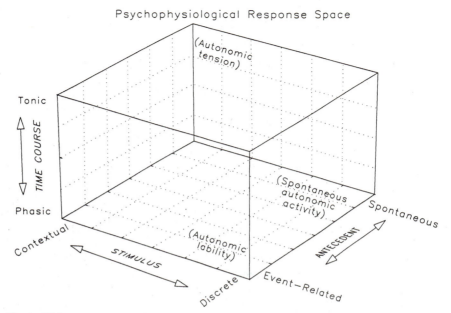

Figure 22-1

Dimensions of psychophysiological response space. One dimension represents the antecedent of the physiological event (event-related/spontaneous), a second dimension represents the nature of the stimulus (discrete/contextual), and a third represents the time course of the physiological event (tonic/phasic). Each of the pairs of terms in this figure represents endpoints on a continuum rather than narrowly and absolutely defined categories of activity. (*From Cacioppo, Berntson & Andrews, 1991. Copyright 1991 by the American Psychological Association. Reprinted by permission.*)

In simple terms, in using tests we assume that people possess stable characteristics (for example, intelligence) and stable response tendencies (for example, traits) that hold up across situations and exist independent of the environment. This assumption may be most unfortunate in view of the results of empirical investigations (Cacioppo, Berntson & Anderson, 1991; Rowe, 1987). Even the best tests have yet to achieve such temporal stability that differences over time can readily be attributed solely to measurement error or fluctuating subject variables. Hence, one of the main assumptions underlying tests—that humans possess stable characteristics and response tendencies independent of external factors—is not entirely correct. Moreover, the social environment has an impact on behavior, as illustrated in a model by Cacioppo, Bernston, and Anderson (1991) that shows the relationship between the psychological domain and the physiological domain. (See Figure 22-1.)

The trait question is relevant to psychology as a whole and to personality psychology in particular. Early formulations of human personality tended to view it as consisting of enduring and stable traits (behavioral dispositions). Freud and many of his followers, for example, believed that early experiences, memories, traumas, and anxieties often resulted in behavioral dispositions that persisted throughout life. Views such as Freud's, however, were challenged by those who saw human personality as changing rather than as fixed and stationary as well as by those who saw that situations and external factors also influence behavior.

Most tests discussed in this text are based on the assumption that human characteristics can be measured independent of the context in which these characteristics occur (the environment), a theory that not only is disputable but also has failed to find significant support (Bandura, 1986; Mischel, 1968). Psychological tests can be no better than the science of psychology that underlies them. As the science clarifies basic theoretical issues, changes in testing are to be expected so that tests will conform to the available knowledge. In the meantime, it must be acknowledged that perhaps the single most important theoretical assumption of tests—that human characteristics are stable and can be measured independent of the environment—is debatable.

Human behavior may be the result of long-term stable behavioral tendencies (traits); the external or internal environments that precede, coexist with, and follow behavior; or some other factor such as the interaction between traits and environments (Mischel, 1968; Rowe, 1987). Either our tests have a long way to go before they will be able to measure the precise determinants of human behavior, or, for predictive purposes, current conceptualizations and underlying assumptions of tests are not precise enough.

Based on our review of the psychometric qualities and the limits of mental ability and personality tests, we conclude that, although there is a basic core of stability, humans continually change. One explanation for the far from perfect temporal reliability of tests in general and the relatively poor long-term reliability of personality tests in particular is that as the individual adapts and adjusts to an ever-changing environment, the individual changes. Most definitions of intelligence include the ability to adapt or change according to circumstances.

A theory consistent with the available data would postulate that all normal humans possess the ability to adapt to changing circumstances. This ability is itself a combination of factors that can and do change. We can refer to these combined factors as the individual's *index of adjustment*, which we believe is correlated with scores on major ability tests in use today. An individual with a high index of adjustment can adapt more readily and perhaps find more effective solutions to environmental pressures than can those with a low index. However, reacting to the environment may not only change behavioral tendencies but also influence the index of adjustment. Repeated failures or consistent success, for example, may increase rigidity, which in turn can lower the index of adjustment. However, an extremely demanding environment, such as one that forces the individual to call on latent reserves, may increase the index. In this theory, ability and personality are always changing and can be measured only within the context in which they occur.

The point here is that all psychological tests are based on implicit theories of human functioning. Unfortunately, the validity of these theories and their underlying assumptions is far from proven. Furthermore, there is no consensus concerning either a definition of human intelligence or the essence of human personality, whether it be normal or abnormal. A revolution in psychological theory, therefore, could revolutionize psychological tests. In any case, today's tests are no better than the theories and assumptions that underlie them.

The adequacy of tests. A second professional issue in testing concerns the adequacy of existing tests. This entire book has been aimed at providing you with the knowledge needed to evaluate tests. To this end, the book is filled with statements about standardization, norms, scoring, interpretation, test design, reliability, and validity. Thus far, however, our discussion has been in relative terms; we have identified tests that are superior to other tests according to traditionally accepted psychometric standards. We have not established absolute external criteria against which to evaluate tests. Many psychologists as well as nonpsychologists have questioned whether even the best existing tests possess sufficiently sound psychometric qualities to warrant their use.

As we have noted, the real issue in testing is how tests are used. In support of this position, the APA (1974) argues that decisions are going to be made whether or not tests are used in the process. As convincing as this argument is, it is also true that it may be better to have no test at all than one that leads to an incorrect conclusion more often than it leads to a correct one. There may be, and no doubt are, situations in which all concerned would be better off without test results than they would be with them.

We are not advocating that all tests be eliminated until better ones are developed, but we do believe that the issue of the adequacy of tests should be viewed from all possible perspectives. Some tests, such as many individual and group ability tests, are generally adequate in reliability. However, just about any test could benefit from greater validity documentation. Clearly, the quality or adequacy of existing tests viewed in absolute rather than relative terms is a factor that must be considered when evaluating current and future trends in testing.

Actuarial versus clinical prediction. A third professional issue, which is related to the issue of the adequacy of tests, concerns the accuracy of predictions made by test users. Throughout this book we have argued that tests provide a standard setting in which behavior can be observed and that practitioners can use this situation in conjunction with experience and local norms to gain a greater degree of accuracy in their observations and decisions than would otherwise be possible. Certainly, users of psychological tests must feel this way or they simply would not waste their time with tests. However, can tests truly help in the assessment process, or are practitioners fooling themselves, repeating their errors and teaching their errors to students? Indeed, test users rarely, if ever,

Figure 22-2
Schematic
summary of
professional
issues.

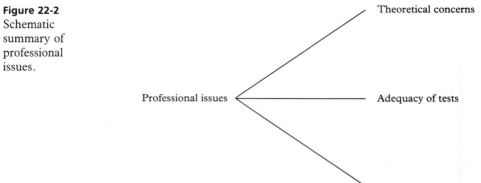

Professional issues — Theoretical concerns

Professional issues — Adequacy of tests

Professional issues — Actuarial vs. clinical prediction

receive feedback on the accuracy of their predictions and decisions based on tests.

Again, we do not know the answer, but the issue must be seen from all sides. The early work of P. E. Meehl (Meehl, 1954; Meehl & Rosen, 1955) and others (Little & Shneidman, 1959) drew attention to the limits of test data even in the hands of trained practitioners. In subsequent analyses, J. Sawyer (1966) and J. O. Sines (1970) reviewed a number of studies that compared an actuarial approach, in which test results were interpreted by using a set of rules, against a clinical approach, in which trained professionals interpreted test results. These reviews indicated that the set of rules was more accurate than the trained professional practitioners, even when the practitioners knew the rules. This research confirmed Meehl's (1954) earlier finding that trained practitioners could not improve on predictions based on statistical formulas. Other studies and analyses, however, indicate that the trained practitioner is a better predictor than actuarial formulas, especially when using data from a variety of sources including a test battery, interview, and case history (for example, Goldberg, 1970; Holt, 1970; Wiggins & Kohen, 1971). In either case, we again find professional disagreement at the most basic levels.

The issue of actuarial versus clinical prediction has reemerged in recent times with the proliferation of computerized test interpretations, which we briefly discussed in Chapter 17. Can a computer really accurately interpret a psychological test? Although the potential may be there, this potential has been far from realized owing to the many problems inherent in such interpretations (Moreland, 1985). As D. E. Hartman (1986b) notes, there are a number of potential abuses inherent in the use of computer software to interpret psychological tests. These include trivialization of assessment, use of software inappropriate to the client, inadequate contribution of the clinician to the assessment process, and, as we discussed here and in Chapter 17, whether the computer's interpretations can be as good (or better) than those of the clinician. See Figure 22-2.

B. *Moral Issues*

Professional issues alone will not determine the future of testing. The field is also being shaped by moral issues—human rights, labeling, and invasion of privacy. These moral issues are an extremely important influence in the testing field.

Human rights. Several different kinds of human rights are relevant to psychological testing. Among these is the right not to be tested (APA, 1974). Individuals who do not want to subject themselves to testing should not, and ethically cannot, be forced to do so. The APA (1974) also states that test takers have the right to know test scores and interpretations as well as the bases of any decisions that affect their lives. The position on the right to know is a change in policy that reflects current realities. In the past, guarding the security of tests was of paramount importance. The more recent position is that all precautions should be taken to protect test security but not at the expense of an individual's right to know the basis for detrimental or adverse decisions. Other human rights, some of which are only now being accepted on a widespread basis, are the right to know who will have access to test data and the right to have the confidentiality of test results protected. (This right to privacy is discussed below.)

Test users have a moral as well as an ethical obligation to protect human rights. Potential test takers have the responsibility of knowing and demanding their rights. The increasing awareness among test users and the public of the importance of human rights is an important factor currently shaping the testing field.

Labeling. In standard medical practice, a person's disease or disorder is first identified (diagnosed). Once diagnosed, the disease can be labeled, and standard medical intervention procedures can be implemented. It is no embarrassment to be diagnosed as having gallbladder or kidney disease. No one will avoid you or think less of you if you are given these labels. However, it is well known that certain medical diseases, such as AIDS, and many psychiatric labels can be extremely damaging (Smith, 1981). The public has little understanding of the label schizophrenia, for example. Therefore, someone with this label is vulnerable to being stigmatized, perhaps for life. Labels may also be detrimental in that many carry certain negative connotations. Chronic schizophrenia, for example, has no cure. Labeling someone a chronic schizophrenic may be a self-fulfilling prophecy. Because the disorder is incurable, nothing can be done. Because nothing can be done, why should one bother to help? Because no help is given, the person is a chronic case.

Still another problem with labels, which are unfortunately often justified by psychological tests as they are currently used, is a theoretical one. As T. S. Szasz (1961) originally noted, a medical label such as schizophrenia implies that a person is ill or diseased. Because no one can be blamed for becoming ill, a medical or psychiatric label implies that the person is not responsible for the condition. However, it may very well be that those who are labeled as psychiatrically disturbed must take responsibility for their lives in order to get better.

When we take responsibility for our lives, we believe that we can exercise some degree of control over our fates (after all, what is intelligence?) rather than simply being the victims of uncontrollable external forces. Individuals who feel a sense of control or responsibility for themselves should be able to tolerate more stress, frustration, and pain than those who feel like passive victims of external forces. Certainly, a person who feels responsible or in control makes a greater effort to alter negative conditions than one who does not.

Labels that imply a person is not responsible may therefore increase the risk that the person so labeled will feel like a passive victim. Thus, the labeling process may not only stigmatize the person but also lower tolerance for stress and make treatment more difficult. In view of the potentially negative effects of labels, the APA (1974) states that a person has the right not to be labeled and suggests that, rather than being labeled, the person be described.

Invasion of privacy. Still another moral issue concerns invasion of privacy. As we stated earlier, people have a right to privacy. When people respond to psychological tests, they have little idea what is being revealed, but they often feel that their privacy has been invaded and that this intrusion into their lives is not justified by the benefits. Public concern over this issue once became so strong that tests were investigated by the Senate Subcommittee on Constitutional Rights and the House Subcommittee on Invasion of Privacy. Neither of these subcommittees found evidence of deliberate and widespread misuse of tests (see Brayfield, 1965).

Again, there are two sides to the issue. W. G. Dahlstrom (1969b) argues that the issue of invasion of privacy is based on serious misunderstandings. He states that tests have been oversold and that the public doesn't realize their limitations. Psychological tests can't invade one's privacy because they are so limited that they are incapable of doing so. Another issue, according to Dahlstrom (1969b), is the ambiguity of the notion of invasion of privacy. It isn't necessarily wrong, evil, or detrimental to find out information about a person. The person's privacy is invaded when this information is used in inappropriate ways. But psychologists are morally, ethically, and often legally bound to maintain confidentiality and do not have to reveal any more information about a person than is necessary to accomplish the purpose for which testing was initiated. Furthermore, psychologists are bound to inform subjects of the limits of confidentiality, and subjects have the right not to be tested. As Dahlstrom (1969b) notes, subjects must cooperate in order to be tested. On the whole, those tested by today's procedures must be willing participants.

The ethical code of the APA (1981) includes the principle of confidentiality. This principle, which is guaranteed by law in most states that have laws governing the practice of psychology, means that personal information ob-

Figure 22-3
Schematic
summary of moral
issues.

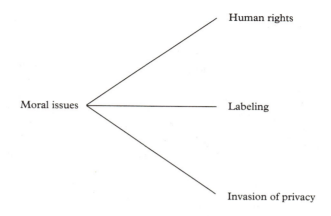

tained by the psychologist from any source is communicated only with the person's consent. However, there are exceptions, such as circumstances in which there is danger to the person or society or when certain records, including tests, are subpoenaed by the courts. Therefore, included in a person's right to know is the right to know the limits of confidentiality and to know that test data can be subpoenaed and used as evidence in a court of law. See Figure 22-3.

C. *Ethical Issues*

Ethical issues are closely related to professional and moral issues and indeed often cannot be easily separated from them. Two extremely important ethical issues are divided loyalties and the responsibilities of test users and test constructors.

Divided loyalties. D. N. Jackson and S. Messick (1967, chap. 69) argue that it has not been possible to formulate a coherent set of ethical principles that govern all legitimate uses of testing. They believe the core of the problem lies in divided loyalties—the often conflicting commitments of the psychologist who uses tests. One ethical principle is that the psychologist must protect the welfare and privacy of the client or consumer of tests. A conflict arises, however, when the welfare of the individual is at odds with the welfare of the institution that employs the psychologist. For example, a psychologist employed by an industrial firm to identify individuals who might break down under stress has a responsibility to the institution to identify such individuals as well as a responsibility to protect the rights and welfare of clients who are seeking employment with the firm. Thus, the psychologist's loyalty is divided. Similarly, the psychologist must maintain test security but also not violate the client's right to know the basis for an adverse decision. However, if the basis for an adverse decision is explained to one client, this information may leak out, and others with the same problem can then outsmart the test. Again, the test user is trapped between two opposing forces and principles.

The conflict is presently being resolved in this way: Ethically, psychologists must inform all concerned where their loyalty lies. They must tell clients or subjects in advance how tests are to be used and describe the limits of confidentiality. To the institution, they provide only the minimum information possible, such as "This subject has a low probability of breaking down under stress, and the probability that this conclusion is accurate is 68/100." Unnecessary or irrelevant personal information remains private and confidential.

In addition, test security is not as important as the person's right to know the basis of an adverse decision. Either the results are explained to the client or they are given to a representative of the client who is qualified to explain them (AERA et al., 1985). A law in the state of New York prohibits the distributors of standardized tests used in selection procedures (for example the SAT, the GRE, the MCAT) from keeping the items confidential. The implication of the law is that the person has the right to see the items missed. In other words, the dilemma of test security versus client welfare has been decided by the courts, and the decision clearly favors the client.

Responsibilities of test users and test constructors. A second ethical issue in testing concerns the responsibilities of test users. Because even the best test can be misused, the testing profession has become increasingly stringent and precise in outlining the ethics of responsible test use. According to the APA (1974), almost any test can be useful in the right circumstances, but even the best test, when used inappropriately, can be damaging to the subject. To reduce potential damage, the APA (1974) specifies that users of tests are responsible for knowing the reason for using the test, the consequences, and the procedures necessary to maximize effectiveness of the test and to minimize unfairness. Test users must thus possess sufficient knowledge to understand the underlying principles in the construction and supporting research of any test they administer. They must also know the psychometric qualities of the test being used as well as the literature relevant to the test. In addition, they are responsible for ensuring that interpretations based on the test are justified and that the test is properly used. In our judgment, a test user cannot claim ignorance ("I didn't realize normative data were not representative"). The test user is responsible for finding out all the necessary and pertinent information before using any test.

It is the test developer's responsibility to provide this information. Current standards for test use state that test constructors must provide a test manual with sufficient data to permit appropriate use of the test, including adequate validity and reliability data, clearly specified scoring and administration standards, and a clear description of the normative sample (AERA et al., 1985; APA, 1974). The standards also state that the test manual should warn against possible misinterpretation and identify necessary qualifications for responsible test use. Despite these guidelines, some new tests are still being published that do not meet specified standards. It is not unusual for a researcher to receive requests from test designers to investigate a newly developed test. These designers hope that others will conduct the necessary research to provide adequate psychometric documentation.

A test user has no excuse for employing an inadequately documented instrument that has damaging consequences. The test user must know enough to tell the difference between a test that meets present standards and one that does not. Jackson and Messick (1967, chap. 69) wisely suggest that the test user ask two questions whenever a test is proposed for a particular use. First, "Is the test any good as a measure of the characteristics it purports to measure?" This is a technical question; the answer lies in the psychometric qualities of the test, such as reliability and validity documentation. Second, "Should the test be used for this purpose?" The answer to this question is based on ethical and social values. It requires the test user to think about the effect of the test on the individual and on the individual's human rights. Thus, test constructors bear the responsibility for a poorly designed test or an inadequate test manual. However, the ultimate responsibility for the ethical use of tests rests with the test user.

D. *Social Issues*

In addition to professional, moral, and ethical issues, a number of social issues play an important role in the testing field. We discuss three of these social issues: dehumanization, the usefulness of tests, and access to psychological testing sources.

Dehumanization. One social issue in the testing field concerns the dehumanizing tendencies that lurk in the testing process. For example, as noted in Chapter 17, some corporations provide computerized analyses of the MMPI and other test results. Such technology tends to minimize individual freedom and uniqueness. With high-speed computers and centralized data banks, the risk that machines will someday make important decisions about our lives is always increasing. Thus, society must weigh the risks against the benefits of the growing application of modern technology to the testing field. This evaluation should be made now, or a situation may develop that nobody likes but that cannot be changed. If psychologists or the public allows test results to be stored and analyzed by computers, it may become extremely difficult to reverse this trend. Our society is founded on principles of individual rights and freedom. Any potential threat to these principles—such as computerized test interpretations—must be evaluated, and decisions concerning such issues should be made with an awareness of the potential risks as well as the benefits. Only when the benefits far outweigh the risks and the risks are minimized can the decision be socially acceptable.

Usefulness of tests. From a social perspective, it is not necessary to demand that all tests be perfect in all ways. Society often finds uses for tools that are initially crude but that become precise with research and development. To gain a perspective of the testing field, you should discriminate between something that it useful (something that works) and something that is true or correct. When Western society believed the sun revolved around the earth, the available formulas and principles were useful in that they led to some accurate predictions, even though the underlying theories were incorrect. This may also be the situation with testing as it is currently practiced. Our underlying theories and assumptions may be fundamentally incorrect and the resulting test instruments far from perfect. However, the tests may still be useful as long as they provide information that leads to better predictions and understanding than can otherwise be obtained. The point is that a test may be useful to society even if all the principles that underlie tests are totally incorrect.

Thus, the crucial social issue in testing is not whether tests are perfect but whether they are useful to society. Obviously, the answer to this question to date has been a strong but disputed "yes" (see Snyderman & Rothman, 1987). However, as new knowledge is gained, society must continually weigh the risks of tests against the benefits. The risks, of course, include the possible misuse of tests, which in turn may adversely affect the life of an individual or may discriminate systematically against a specific cultural group (see Henry, Bryson & Henry, 1990). The benefits include the potential for increased precision and fairness in the decision-making process. The issue is one that recurs, and the resolution will obviously have a profound effect on the field of testing.

Modern tests are and have been used by society on a wide scale. First the military, then the schools and psychiatric facilities, and finally business and industry have found important uses for psychological tests. Indeed, there appears to be no end to the proliferation of tests, despite criticisms and heated debates. If the pervasiveness of tests in our society is any indication of society's opinion of the usefulness of tests, then certainly society has found tests useful. Tests are currently serving a function in society, and as long as they continue to do so, they most likely will be used.

Access to psychological testing services. If tests are of value to society, who will have access to psychological testing services? Being tested can be quite an expense. It is not unusual for a practitioner in a large metropolitan area to command a fee of $1000 or more to administer a full battery of individual tests, score and interpret the findings, and produce a written report. Fees for neurological testing can be two to three times higher. Moreover, the cost of test materials continues to skyrocket. A WAIS-R kit cost $98 in 1983. In 1992, it cost more than $400, with further price increases in the works. Such high costs increase the cost of psychological assessments. As with many other commodities, the cost of testing places these services beyond the reach of many members of society. Yet, if a person's well-being depends on information from a psycho-

Figure 22-4
Schematic
summary of social
issues.

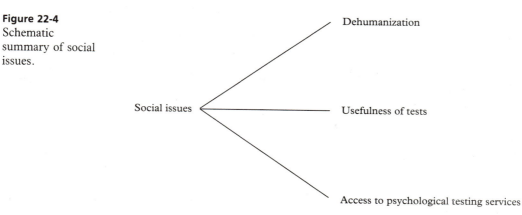

logical test battery, how will it be decided who will have access to testing and who will not?

As it stands now, the expensive test batteries for neurological and psychiatric assessment are available to those who can afford them and to those who have insurance that covers all or most of the expense. In California, developmentally disabled persons (for example, the mentally retarded) or those with suspected developmental disabilities have access to psychological testing services at regional centers throughout the state. Unless California laws are changed, anyone suspected of having a handicap that originated during the developmental years can request (or have someone request on his or her behalf) an evaluation that may include a medical examination and psychological testing. The service is free, regardless of income or socioeconomic status, and if a team of specialists finds the person developmentally disabled, additional services are available.

Anyone with a developmental disability in California may be eligible to receive Medi-Cal, which provides free medical services, including the services of a psychologist for psychotherapy and psychological testing. The individual may also be eligible for federal assistance such as Medicare and SSI, which provide cash benefits. Thus, current California and federal laws and policies help ensure that certain disabled persons will have access to psychological testing services. However, such guarantees are not available in all states, and only certain disabled persons are covered.

Some in our society have offered national health insurance as a possible solution to the general problem of providing adequate medical care to everyone. As of this writing, no program of national health insurance has been implemented, but talk about it continues. One of the controversies in proposals for national health insurance concerns the extent of mental health coverage and whether psychological services will be included. Presumably, if psychological testing services are included in a national health insurance program, then anyone who needs such services will have access to them. If not, then the availability of testing services may be substantially limited. In a sense, society will be making a judgment concerning the value of tests in its decision to include or not to include psychological testing services in a national health insurance program. Resources are clearly limited, and testing services may have to be included at the expense of some other needed service, or vice versa. See Figure 22-4.

II. *Current Trends*

Professional, moral, ethical, social, and even legal issues have interacted to produce today's trends in testing. These trends can be placed into four main categories: the proliferation of new tests; higher standards, improved technology, and increased objectivity; greater public awareness and influence; and computer applications.

A. *Proliferation of New Tests*

New tests keep coming out all the time and there seems to be no end in sight. If we count revised and updated tests, we find hundreds of new tests being published each year. The impetus for the development of these new tests comes from professional disagreement over the best strategies for measuring human characteristics, over the nature of these characteristics, and over theories about the causes of human behavior. [For example, see the discussion of the Kaufman Assessment Battery for Children (K-ABC) in Chapter 12.] The impetus also stems from public and professional pressure to use only fair, accurate, unbiased instruments. Finally, if tests are used, then the authors and publishers of tests stand to profit financially. As long as it is profitable to publish tests, new tests will be developed and marketed.

An examination of major reference books on tests indicates that the majority of new tests are based on the same principles and underlying theories as are the more established tests. Indeed, most newly developed tests justify their existence on the grounds that either they are psychometrically superior to the existing tests or they are more specific and thus more appropriate for particular problems. However, as we saw in Chapter 17, some of the newer tests, especially the most recent ones, are based on models, theories, and concepts that are fundamentally different from those on which the traditional, established tests are based. These nontraditional tests are based on modern concepts and theories from learning, social, physiological, and experimental psychology. Most of these newer tests are rooted in empirically derived data (Iacono, 1991).

The proliferation of nontraditional tests is related to two other current trends in testing. First, the development of these nontraditional tests reflects the increasing application and role of the science of psychology in testing

(Haynes, 1991). Even critics of testing must admit that the testing field has been characterized by a responsiveness to criticism and an honest and persistent effort to improve the quality of tests. The application of insights and empirical findings from psychological laboratories is a current trend that reflects this responsiveness.

Second, efforts are being made to integrate tests with other aspects of applied psychology. Many psychologists, especially behaviorally oriented psychologists (Haynes, 1992), have long been disillusioned by the poor relationship between clinical assessment, traditional tests, and subsequent treatment interventions. Most desirable would be tests whose results not only have a direct relationship to treatment but also can be used to assess the effectiveness of treatment. Psychologists are presently making an effort to devise such procedures, and their products add to the list of the many new tests that are published each year.

B. *Higher Standards, Improved Technology, and Increasing Objectivity*

In addition to a proliferation of new tests, various pressures and issues have led to still another current trend. The minimum acceptable standards for tests are becoming higher and more stringent. Before the APA (1974) clearly and specifically defined their responsibilities, test constructors had neither a uniform nor a widely accepted set of guidelines. As a result, the quality of newly published tests was quite variable. Now that published standards are available, test constructors no longer have to work in the dark. Already it is possible to see that an increasing percentage of new tests provide the information necessary for test users to make a fully informed choice in test selection and for maximizing the probability that the tests will be used properly.

Higher standards of test construction are encouraging better and more appropriate use of tests. The APA (1974) and the AERA (1985) standards have helped considerably by reemphasizing the critical importance of proper test use and by articulating the responsibilities of test users. More recently, a working group of the Joint Committee on Testing Practices sponsored by the American Association for Counseling and Development, the American Educational Research Association, the American Psychological Association, the American Speech-Language-Hearing Association, and the National Council on Measurement in Education has published a thorough document devoted to delineating the qualifications of test users (Eyde et al., 1988). This comprehensive guide clearly specifies the competencies needed to use various types of tests and will provide a beacon for some time to come. Moreover, as we indicated earlier, the ethics of testing have been modified in an effort to encourage the proper use of tests and to avoid misuse. Now that test users have a published set of standards, there is no excuse for misusing a test. Naturally, misuse and even abuse will never be entirely eliminated; however, the trend toward better and more appropriate use of existing tests is a most desirable one.

Related to higher standards is the improved technology currently being applied in the testing field. Those in the testing field now have at their disposal the benefits of the remarkable technology that has developed during the previous few decades (Farrell, 1992a, b; Haynes, 1992; Lowman, 1991; Matarazzo, 1990). Primarily because of advances in computer technology, statistical procedures such as factor analysis and item analysis can be performed with great ease. This technology contributes to the current trend toward better tests.

Also related to high standards is the trend toward increasing objectivity in test interpretation. Although we generally spoke in favor of projective tests such as the Rorschach, many practitioners have been displeased with the often subjective nature of the interpretation of projective tests. As a result, many practitioners have shown a tendency to rely heavily on objective data such as that provided by the MMPI and MMPI-2. This trend toward increased objectivity in testing can be seen readily by the shift in the relative proportion of references devoted to the Rorschach and the MMPI in *The Mental Measurements Yearbooks* and other sources (for example, Archer et al., 1992; Piotrowski, Sherry & Keller, 1985; Polyson, Peterson & Marshall, 1986).

Also reflecting the trend toward objectivity in testing is the continuing research interest on testing. In view of the tens of thousands, if not hundreds of thousands, of published studies directly or indirectly related to psychological tests, a casual observer might conclude that there is little else to be done. This conclusion is far from correct. Despite the thousands of published articles devoted to the MMPI and MMPI-2, for example, hundreds more creative and scientifically rigorous articles are published each year on these tests, not to mention the hundreds of other tests listed in *The Mental Measurements Yearbooks* and other resource books. As long as tests are anything but perfect, and in this regard they are a long way off, psychological researchers will no doubt continue to conduct investigations to facilitate the objective use of tests.

C. *Greater Public Awareness and Influence*

The current trend toward greater public awareness of the nature and use of psychological tests has led to the trend of increasing external influence on the practice of testing. This awareness and influence from outside of psychology have, furthermore, led to still other trends in psychological testing. At one time the public knew little about psychological tests; psychologists played an almost exclusive role in governing how tests were used. With the greater assertiveness on the part of the public during the 1980s and 1990s, the days when psychologists alone called the shots are gone forever. In our opinion, this is a desirable trend that has had a positive effect on the field.

Public awareness has led to the current trend toward an increased demand for psychological services, including testing services. Balancing this increased demand is the tendency toward restrictive legislative and judicial regulations and policies such as the judicial decision restricting the use of standard intelligence tests in diagnosing mental retardation. These restrictions originate in real and imagined public fears. In short, the public seems to be ambivalent about psychological testing, simultaneously desiring the benefits yet fearing the power the general public attributes to tests.

Perhaps the greatest benefit of increased public awareness of tests has been the increased insistence on safeguarding human rights. As more individuals share the responsibility of encouraging the proper use of tests by becoming informed of their rights and insisting on receiving them, the probability of misuse and abuse of tests will be reduced. The commitment of the field of psychology to high standards in ethics, morals, and human rights can be easily seen in the published ethical guidelines, position papers, and debates that have evolved during the relatively short period beginning in 1947 with the development of formal standards for training in clinical psychology (Shakow et al., 1947). Practitioners of psychology as well as their instructors and supervisors have a deep concern for social values and the dignity of the individual human being. However, the pressure of public interest in psychological tests has led psychological practitioners to even greater sensitivity to and awareness of their role and responsibility in safeguarding the rights and dignity of the individual. Increased concern for ensuring and protecting human rights is thus still another desirable current trend in the field.

Interrelated with all of these trends is the trend toward greater protection for the public. Nearly every state has laws that govern the practice of psychology, including laws about the use of psychological tests. Limiting testing to reduce the chance that unqualified persons will use psychological tests, sensitivity among practitioners to the rights of the individual, relevant court decisions, and a clearly articulated set of ethical guidelines and published standards for proper test use give the public significant protection against the inherent risks involved in testing. Thus, yet another desirable current trend in the field is increasingly greater protection and safeguards for the consumer of tests—the public.

D. *The Computerization of Tests*

Throughout this book we have discussed how computers are being applied to testing on a rapid and widespread basis. The computerization of tests is a major current trend, and computers, as we saw in Chapter 17, are being used in a number of different ways.

In adaptive computerized testing, different sets of test questions are administered, via computer, to different individuals depending on each individual's status on the trait being measured (Weiss, 1983, 1985). In ability testing, for example, the computer adapts the level of item difficulty depending on the subject's response. If the subject's answer is incorrect, an easier item is given; if the subject's answer is correct, a more difficult item can be selected. Such an approach individualizes a test and has the added advantage of reducing total testing time. Research is currently in progress that may some day lead to the conversion of the Armed Services Vocational Aptitude Battery, which is given to millions, to an adaptive computerized format (see Chapter 13).

Computers are also being used to administer, score, and even interpret psychological tests (see Chapter 17). In addition, as we saw in Chapter 17, computers are being used to generate tasks that cannot be presented by traditional methods. Through computer technology, it may be possible to tap a whole new range of abilities that have heretofore been beyond the scope of traditional tests. Objective personality tests such as the MMPI and MMPI-2 can be processed by a computer with a typed report as the final product. Each year, more programs are developed that score tests and produce written reports (Prince & Guastello, 1990). The use of the computer extends to all types of tests, including behavioral assessment (Farrell, 1992a, b).

III. *Future Trends*

Having analyzed the major relevant issues and forces in testing and identified current trends, we are now ready to venture a few guesses about what the future holds for the field. Certainly, we are reasonably safe in stating that the trends identified above will continue and become established as realities of the field. However, our predictions for the future are educated guesses based on limited knowledge.

A. *Prediction 1: Future Prospects for Testing Are Promising*

Our studies lead us to feel safe in concluding that testing has a promising future. Our optimism in this regard is based on the integral role testing has played in the development and recognition of psychology in general and of professional psychology in particular. Psychology gained its first real status from its role in the development of screening tests for the military in World War I. Later, psychologists' creativity and skill in the testing field during World War II were no doubt among the factors that ultimately led to government funding through the Veterans Administration to encourage the development of professional psychology. Indeed, this federal funding, which was first earmarked for psychology in 1945, played an important role in the birth of clinical psychology and formal training standards.

The central role played by testing in the development and recognition of psychology, however, is certainly not enough to ensure an important role for testing in the future. Despite discontent and division within psychology concerning the role and value of testing, psychological testing in the general sense remains one of the few unique functions of the professional psychologist. When one sees psychological testing as encompassing not only traditional uses but also new and innovative uses, such as in behavioral assessment, psychophysiology, evaluation research, organizational assessment, community assessment, and investigations into the nature of human functioning, one can understand just how important tests are to psychologists.

Thus, psychologists have a traditional and fundamental tie with tests and are the undisputed leaders in the field. We do not believe that attacks on and dissatisfaction with traditional psychological tests will suddenly compel psychologists to totally abandon tests, which would likely lead to the demise of testing. Instead, we predict that psychologists will continue to take the lead in this field to produce better and better tests, and that such a direction will be of benefit to both psychologists and the field.

In addition, tests are used in most of our institutions—schools, colleges, hospitals, industry, business, the government, and so forth—and new applications and creative uses continue to emerge. It is inconceivable that tests will suddenly disappear with nothing to replace them. If anything, current tests will continue to be used until they are replaced by still better tests, which of course may be based on totally new ideas. Tests as we know them today may gradually fade from the scene, but we believe psychological testing will not simply survive but instead flourish and thrive through the rest of this and the next century.

B. *Prediction 2: The Proliferation of New and Improved Tests Will Continue Unabated*

In conjunction with our prognostication of a promising future for psychological testing, we feel safe in predicting that the future will see the development of still more tests. In our evaluation of the status of intelligence tests (Chapters 10, 11, and 12), we presented our belief that currently available intelligence tests are far from perfect and that we have a long way to go before the ultimate in such tests is seen. Consistent with this belief, we believe the dominant role of the Stanford-Binet and Wechsler tests is far from secure. These two major intelligence scales are probably about as technically adequate as they will ever be. They can, of course, be improved through minor revisions to update test stimuli and to provide larger and even more representative normative samples with special norms for particular groups and through additional research to extend and support validity documentation. However, despite the changes in the modern Binet and the new WISC-III, the fundamental characteristics and underlying concepts are similar to the original scales.

During the next few decades, we will be most surprised if these two major intelligence scales are not challenged at least several times by similar tests whose justification will be superior standardization and normative data. However, if history is any indicator of what is to be, a true challenge can come only from a test based on original concepts and a more comprehensive theoretical rationale than that of the present scales. The Kaufman Assessment Battery for Children may be one such contender in its age range (see Chapter 12). We believe that the development of such a test is inevitable and only a question of time (see, for example, Sternberg, 1981). Just how soon such a test appears will, of course, depend primarily on need. Should a compelling need for such an instrument arise, then we will see it sooner rather than later.

In structured personality testing, the MMPI-2 appears to be destined to be the premier test of the 21st century. This favorable prediction for the MMPI-2 is a turnabout from the 1982 prediction made in the first edition of this book. We had not anticipated the innovative approach that Butcher and colleagues would take in restandardizing the MMPI. The restandardization, as we noted in Chapter 15, also deals with the major problem of the original MMPI: its inadequate normative sample. Thus, future prospects for the MMPI-2 are indeed bright.

Regarding *projective personality testing,* we believe that the Rorschach will achieve a new level of acceptance and respectability as the 21st century dawns. The Rorschach continues to be used on a wide scale in clinical settings, and it has few competitors. Computer programs that generate reports are available, just as they are for objective tests (Exner, 1980, 1986). The Holtzman Inkblot Test takes care of just about every psychometric criticism of the Rorschach, yet it still has not found widespread clinical use. Our view of the Rorschach is that it is fundamentally sound and will ultimately be vindicated because of the work of psychologists such as J. Exner and I. B. Weiner. Most likely, the Rorschach will never achieve the prominence it enjoyed during its heyday. In fact, relative to other personality tests, the Rorschach may show even further declines. However, only when the mysteries of schizophrenia are better understood and new ways to measure the pathology of schizophrenia are perfected will the Rorschach be seriously threatened.

The future of the TAT is more difficult to predict. The TAT is affixed to some of the main arteries of psychological theory, has an incredibly extensive research base, and is a prominent clinical tool. Unfortunately, the TAT stimuli are quite out of date. In a projective test, outdated stimuli are not a devastating weakness because projective stimuli are by nature ambiguous. Nevertheless, the TAT stimuli have been revised (Ritzler, Sharkey & Chudy, 1980), and so, like the Rorschach, the TAT may enjoy increased respectability as data are acquired on the latest version.

C. *Revolutionary Changes: "Perestroika" in School Testing*

Recently we attended a meeting on testing in Washington, D.C. Speaker after speaker, including the U.S. Secretary of Education, predicted changes in testing in our schools. Whereas some speakers emphasized national standardized tests, others rejected the idea. According to one speaker, there would soon be a

Table 22-1
Performance
Testing

Purchasing an Automobile
You are considering two used cars: a 1988 Ford Taurus priced at $3800 and a 1988 Honda Accord priced at $4100. How would you go about determining which is the best decision for you? Your task is to design and carry out a study to answer this question.

Grade level:	12th
Curriculum topics:	Computational skills: ability to work with money, ability to make relative judgments and comparisons, ability to analyze and write conclusions in a clear narrative form
Suggested length of time: In class: Out of class:	1–2 weeks 2 periods 4 periods

Based on the Connecticut Common Core of Learning Performance Assessment Project sponsored by the National Science Foundation.

"perestroika" in the field of testing in the schools. Performance tests, it was predicted, would replace standardized multiple-choice tests by the year 2000.

Panic is indeed raging in Washington, D.C., because of the poor performance of American school children compared to children from other industrialized nations including Japan, Korea, Canada, and the European Community nations. At the heart of this panic is how we evaluate school performance and measure progress.

A report of the National Commission on Testing and Public Policy (1990) made the following points:

1. "America must revamp the way it develops and utilizes human talent, and to do that, educational and employment testing must be restructured" [p. ix].

2. "Current testing, predominantly multiple choice in format, is overrelied upon, lacks adequate public accountability, sometimes leads to unfairness in the allocation of opportunities, and far too often undermines vital social policies" [p. ix].

3. "To help promote greater development of the talents of all our people, alternative forms of assessment must be developed and more critically judged and used, so that testing and assessment open gates of opportunity rather than close them off" [p. x].

The "new" assessment currently being called for by the National Education Association and others is performance testing. Performance testing, as we've seen, requires a subject to do something, rather than to provide a verbal response or fill in a blank. In performance testing in the schools, students would be asked to write essays, provide written responses to specified problems, or solve open-ended math problems (see Table 22-1).

Performance testing is multifaceted and includes such procedures as observing a foreign-language student having a conversation in the foreign language; requiring science students to conduct a real experiment; asking students to work together as a group and observing the interaction; and giving problems that have no answer or more than one correct answer and observing a student's approach. A related idea is the concept of a portfolio, which is a collection of samples of the student's work.

So we presently have two contrary positions, each purporting to be a solution to the problems in the U.S. school system: national standardized testing versus performance testing and portfolios. It is interesting to note that this battle is not new. As we saw back in Chapter 1, performance tests were replaced by standardized achievement tests in the 1930s because they were seen as more objective. Now, more than 60 years later, certain educators are calling for a return to the older method. Whichever force ultimately wins out, we are sure to see substantial change in how tests are used in the schools as the new century dawns.

D. *Prediction 3: Controversy, Disagreement, and Change Will Continue*

We feel quite safe in predicting continued controversy and disagreement in the testing field, which will no doubt produce further change. Disagreement and controversy are second nature to psychologists; it doesn't matter whether the topic is testing or animal learning. Because of disagreement, however, new data are sought, found, and ultimately produce some clarification of old controversies along with brand-new contradictions and battle lines (Jensen, 1988). This is the way of psychology. Therefore, it's not likely that psychologists will ever agree that any one test is perfect. As a consequence, change will be a constant characteristic of the field. We continue to be optimistic because we see the change as ultimately resulting in more empirical data, better theories, continuing innovations and advances, and higher standards.

Summary

Anything is possible, especially in a field as controversial as testing. Psychology is now better equipped in technique, methodology, empirical data, and experience than ever before, and the members of this new and expanding field, as a group, are relatively young. Therefore, it does not, on the one hand, seem unrealistic or overly optimistic to expect that the next 50 years will see advances equal to those of the last 50 years. On the other hand, psychology has come so far in the last 50 years that a comparable advance in the next 50 years could easily produce results unimaginable today. What happens to testing in the future will depend on the goals and objectives chosen by those in the field and by their persistence and creativity in accomplishing these goals.

Appendix 1

Areas of a Standard Normal Distribution

Part I
Percentiles
Associated with
Various Z Scores

Z	% Rank	Z	% Rank
−3.0	.13	0	50.00
−2.9	.19	.1	53.98
−2.8	.26	.2	57.93
−2.7	.35	.3	61.79
−2.6	.47	.4	66.54
−2.5	.62	.5	69.15
−2.4	.82	.6	72.57
−2.3	1.07	.7	75.80
−2.2	1.39	.8	78.81
−2.1	1.79	.9	81.59
−2.0	2.28	1.0	84.13
−1.9	2.87	1.1	86.43
−1.8	3.59	1.2	88.49
−1.7	4.46	1.3	90.32
−1.6	5.48	1.4	91.92
−1.5	6.68	1.5	93.32
−1.4	8.08	1.6	94.52
−1.3	9.68	1.7	95.54
−1.2	11.51	1.8	96.41
−1.1	13.57	1.9	97.13
−1.0	15.87	2.0	97.72
− .9	18.41	2.1	98.21
− .8	21.19	2.2	98.61
− .7	24.20	2.3	98.93
− .6	27.43	2.4	99.18
− .5	30.58	2.5	99.38
− .4	34.46	2.6	99.53
− .3	38.21	2.7	99.65
− .2	42.07	2.8	99.74
− .1	46.02	2.9	99.81
0	50.00	3.0	99.87

Part II
Areas Between Mean and Various Z Scores

Z	.00	.01	.02	.03	.04	.05	.06	.07	.08	.09
.0	.0000	.0040	.0080	.0120	.0160	.0199	.0239	.0279	.0319	.0359
.1	.0398	.0438	.0478	.0517	.0557	.0596	.0636	.0675	.0714	.0753
.2	.0793	.0832	.0871	.0910	.0948	.0987	.1026	.1064	.1103	.1141
.3	.1179	.1217	.1255	.1293	.1331	.1368	.1406	.1443	.1480	.1517
.4	.1554	.1591	.1628	.1664	.1700	.1736	.1772	.1808	.1844	.1879
.5	.1915	.1950	.1985	.2019	.2054	.2088	.2123	.2157	.2190	.2224
.6	.2257	.2291	.2324	.2357	.2389	.2422	.2454	.2486	.2517	.2549
.7	.2580	.2611	.2642	.2673	.2704	.2734	.2764	.2794	.2823	.2852
.8	.2881	.2910	.2939	.2967	.2995	.3023	.3051	.3078	.3106	.3133
.9	.3195	.3186	.3212	.3238	.3264	.3289	.3315	.3340	.3365	.3389
1.0	.3413	.3438	.3461	.3485	.3508	.3531	.3554	.3577	.3599	.3621
1.1	.3643	.3665	.3686	.3708	.3729	.3749	.3770	.3790	.3810	.3830
1.2	.3849	.3869	.3888	.3907	.3925	.3944	.3962	.3980	.3997	.4015
1.3	.4032	.4049	.4066	.4082	.4099	.4115	.4131	.4147	.4162	.4177
1.4	.4192	.4207	.4222	.4236	.4251	.4265	.4279	.4292	.4306	.4319
1.5	.4332	.4345	.4357	.4370	.4382	.4394	.4406	.4418	.4429	.4441
1.6	.4452	.4463	.4474	.4484	.4495	.4505	.4515	.4525	.4535	.4545
1.7	.4554	.4564	.4573	.4582	.4591	.4599	.4608	.4616	.4625	.4633
1.8	.4641	.4649	.4656	.4664	.4671	.4678	.4686	.4693	.4699	.4706
1.9	.4713	.4719	.4726	.4732	.4738	.4744	.4750	.4756	.4761	.4767
2.0	.4772	.4778	.4783	.4788	.4793	.4798	.4803	.4808	.4812	.4817
2.1	.4821	.4826	.4830	.4834	.4838	.4842	.4846	.4850	.4854	.4857
2.2	.4861	.4864	.4868	.4871	.4875	.4878	.4881	.4884	.4887	.4890
2.3	.4893	.4896	.4898	.4901	.4904	.4906	.4909	.4911	.4913	.4916
2.4	.4918	.4920	.4922	.4925	.4927	.4929	.4931	.4932	.4934	.4936
2.5	.4938	.4940	.4941	.4943	.4945	.4946	.4948	.4949	.4951	.4952
2.6	.4953	.4955	.4956	.4957	.4959	.4960	.4961	.4962	.4963	.4964
2.7	.4965	.4966	.4967	.4968	.4969	.4970	.4971	.4972	.4973	.4974
2.8	.4974	.4975	.4976	.4977	.4977	.4978	.4979	.4979	.4980	.4981
2.9	.4981	.4982	.4982	.4983	.4984	.4984	.4985	.4985	.4986	.4986
3.0	.4987	.4987	.4987	.4988	.4988	.4989	.4989	.4989	.4990	.4990

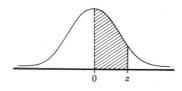

Standard score values are listed in the column headed "Z." To find the proportion of the total area occurring between the mean and any given Z score, locate the entry indicated by the Z score. For example, a Z score of $+1.85$ is located by reading across to the column for .05 from the value of 1.8 in the "Z" column. The value in the table is .4678. Since the total area above the mean is equal to .5000, this means that only .0322 of the area is beyond the Z score of $+1.85$.

Appendix 2

Publishers of Major Tests

Listed are the names and addresses of the publishers of major tests mentioned in this book.

Bayley Scales of Infant Development
Psychological Corporation
757 Third Avenue
New York, N.Y. 10017

Bender Visual Motor Gestalt Test
American Orthopsychiatric Association, Inc.
1790 Broadway
New York, N.Y. 10019

Bennett Mechanical Comprehension Test
Psychological Corporation
757 Third Avenue
New York, N.Y. 10017

Benton Visual Retention Test
Psychological Corporation
757 Third Avenue
New York, N.Y. 10017

California Psychological Inventory
Consulting Psychologists Press, Inc.
577 College Avenue
Palo Alto, Calif. 94306

Career Assessment Inventory
Interpretive Scoring Systems
4401 West 76th Street
Minneapolis, Minn. 55435

Cattell Infant Intelligence Scale
Psychological Corporation
757 Third Avenue
New York, N.Y. 10017

Children's Apperception Test
CPS, Inc.
P.O. Box 83
Larchmont, N.Y. 10538

Children's Personality Questionnaire
Institute for Personality and Ability Testing
1602 Coronado Drive
Champaign, Ill. 61820

Clinical Analysis Questionnaire (research edition)
Institute for Personality and Ability Testing
1602 Coronado Drive
Champaign, Ill. 61820

Cognitive Abilities Test
Houghton Mifflin
110 Tremont Street
Boston, Mass. 02107

Columbia Mental Maturity Scale
Harcourt Brace Jovanovich
757 Third Avenue
New York, N.Y. 10017

Cooperative School and College Ability Tests—
  Series II
Addison-Wesley Testing Service
2725 Sand Hill Road
Menlo Park, Calif. 94025

Culture Fair Intelligence Test
Institute for Personality and Ability Testing
1602 Coronado Drive
Champaign, Ill. 61820

Dental Admission Testing Program
Division of Educational Measurements
Council on Dental Education
American Dental Association
211 East Chicago Avenue
Chicago, Ill. 60611

Differential Aptitude Test
Psychological Corporation
757 Third Avenue
New York, N.Y. 10017

Edwards Personal Preference Schedule
Psychological Corporation
757 Third Avenue
New York, N.Y. 10017

Fear Survey Schedule
Educational and Industrial Testing Service
P.O. Box 7234
San Diego, Calif. 92107

General Aptitude Test Battery
U.S. Employment Service
North Capitol and H Streets N.W.
Washington, D.C. 20401

Gerontological (Senior) Apperception Test
CPS, Inc.
P.O. Box 83
Larchmont, N.Y. 10538

Gesell Developmental Schedules
Psychological Corporation
757 Third Avenue
New York, N.Y. 10017

Goodenough-Harris Drawing Test
Harcourt Brace Jovanovich
757 Third Avenue
New York, N.Y. 10017

Graduate Record Examination Aptitude Test
Educational Testing Service
Princeton, N.J. 08540

Guilford-Zimmerman Temperament Survey
Sheridan Psychological Services
P.O. Box 6101
Orange, Calif. 92667

Henmon-Nelson Tests of Mental Ability
  (1973 revision)
Houghton Mifflin
110 Tremont Street
Boston, Mass. 02107

Holtzman Inkblot Test
Psychological Corporation
757 Third Avenue
New York, N.Y. 10017

Illinois Test of Psycholinguistic Abilities
University of Illinois Press
Urbana, Ill. 61801

Jr. Sr. High School Personality Questionnaire
Institute for Personality and Ability Testing
1602 Coronado Drive
Champaign, Ill. 61820

Kuder Occupational Interest Survey
Science Research Associates, Inc.
259 East Erie Street
Chicago, Ill. 60611

Kuhlmann-Anderson Test (seventh edition)
Personnel Press
191 Spring Street
Lexington, Mass. 02173

Law School Admission Test
Educational Testing Service
Princeton, N.J. 08540

Leiter International Performance Scale
C. H. Stoelting Company
1350 South Kostner Avenue
Chicago, Ill. 60623

McCarthy Scales of Children's Abilities
Psychological Corporation
757 Third Avenue
New York, N.Y. 10017

Memory-for-Designs Test
Psychological Test Specialists
Box 1441
Missoula, Mont. 59801

Miller Analogies Test
Psychological Corporation
757 Third Avenue
New York, N.Y. 10017

Minnesota Multiphasic Personality Inventory
University of Minnesota
Minneapolis, Minn. 55455

Mooney Problem Checklist
Psychological Corporation
757 Third Avenue
New York, N.Y. 10017

Otis Self-Administering Tests of Mental Ability
Harcourt Brace Jovanovich
757 Third Avenue
New York, N.Y. 10017

Peabody Picture Vocabulary Test
American Guidance Service
Publisher's Building
Circle Pines, Minn. 55014

Personality Research Form
Research Psychologists Press
13 Greenwich Avenue
Goshen, N.Y. 10924

Pictorial Test of Intelligence
Houghton Mifflin
110 Tremont Street
Boston, Mass. 02107

Porteus Maze Test
Psychological Corporation
757 Third Avenue
New York, N.Y. 10017

Progressive Matrices
Psychological Corporation
757 Third Avenue
New York, N.Y. 10017

Quick Test
Psychological Test Specialists
Box 1441
Missoula, Mont. 59801

Revised Beta Examination
Psychological Corporation
757 Third Avenue
New York, N.Y. 10017

Revised Minnesota Paper Form Board Test
Psychological Corporation
757 Third Avenue
New York, N.Y. 10017

Rorschach Inkblot Test
Grune & Stratton, Inc.
757 Third Avenue
New York, N.Y. 10017

Scholastic Aptitude Test
Educational Testing Service
Princeton, N.J. 08540

Sixteen Personality Factor Questionnaire
Institute for Personality and Ability Testing
1602 Coronado Drive
Champaign, Ill. 61820

Stanford-Binet Intelligence Scale
Houghton Mifflin
110 Tremont Street
Boston, Mass. 02107

State-Trait Anxiety Inventory
Consulting Psychologists Press, Inc.
577 College Avenue
Palo Alto, Calif. 94306

Strong-Campbell Interest Inventory
Consulting Psychologists Press, Inc.
577 College Avenue
Palo Alto, Calif. 94306

System of Multicultural Pluralistic Assessment
Psychological Corporation
757 Third Avenue
New York, N.Y. 10017

Thematic Apperception Test
Harvard University Press
79 Garden Street
Cambridge, Mass. 02138

Torrance Tests of Creative Thinking
Personnel Press
191 Spring Street
Lexington, Mass. 02173

Wechsler Adult Intelligence Scale
Psychological Corporation
757 Third Avenue
New York, N.Y. 10017

Wechsler Intelligence Scale for Children-Revised
Psychological Corporation
757 Third Avenue
New York, N.Y. 10017

Wechsler Preschool and Primary Scale of
    Intelligence
Psychological Corporation
757 Third Avenue
New York, N.Y. 10017

Wide Range Achievement Test (revised edition)
Guidance Associates of Delaware
1526 Gilpin Avenue
Wilmington, Del. 19806

Wonderlic Personnel Test
E. P. Wonderlic & Associates
P.O. Box 7
Northfield, Ill. 60093

Appendix 3

Critical Values of *r* for α = .05 and α = .01 (*Two-Tailed Test*)

df*	α = .05	α = .01	df*	α = .05	α = .01
1	.99692	.999877	17	.456	.575
2	.9500	.99000	18	.444	.561
3	.878	.9587	19	.433	.549
4	.811	.9172	20	.423	.537
5	.754	.875	25	.381	.487
6	.707	.834	30	.349	.449
7	.666	.798	35	.325	.418
8	.632	.765	40	.304	.393
9	.602	.735	45	.288	.372
10	.576	.708	50	.273	.354
11	.553	.684	60	.250	.325
12	.532	.661	70	.232	.302
13	.514	.641	80	.217	.283
14	.497	.623	90	.205	.267
15	.482	.606	100	.195	.254
16	.468	.590			

* *df* are equal to $N - 2$, where *N* is the number of paired observations.

Reprinted with permission from Table IX.1, Percentage Points. Distribution of the Correlation Coefficient. When $\rho = 0$, *CRC Handbook of Tables for Probability and Statistics* (2nd ed.). Copyright 1968, CRC Press, Inc., Boca Raton, Florida.

Appendix 4

Critical Values of *t**

For any given *df*, the table shows the values of t corresponding to various levels of probability. Obtained t is significant at a given level if it is equal to or *greater than* the value shown in the table.

* Appendix 4 is taken from Table III of Ronald A. Fisher and Frank Yates, *Statistical tables for biological, agricultural and medical research*, published by Longman Group Ltd., London (previously published by Oliver and Boyd, Edinburgh), and by permission of the authors and publishers.

	Level of Significance for One-Tailed Test					
	.10	.05	.025	.01	.005	.0005
	Level of Significance for Two-Tailed Test					
df	.20	.10	.05	.02	.01	.001
1	3.078	6.314	12.706	31.821	63.657	636.619
2	1.886	2.920	4.303	6.965	9.925	31.598
3	1.638	2.353	3.182	4.541	5.841	12.941
4	1.533	2.132	2.776	3.747	4.604	8.610
5	1.476	2.015	2.571	3.365	4.032	6.859
6	1.440	1.943	2.447	3.143	3.707	5.959
7	1.415	1.895	2.365	2.998	3.499	5.405
8	1.397	1.860	2.306	2.896	3.355	5.041
9	1.383	1.833	2.262	2.821	3.250	4.781
10	1.372	1.812	2.228	2.764	3.169	4.587
11	1.363	1.796	2.201	2.718	3.106	4.437
12	1.356	1.782	2.179	2.681	3.055	4.318
13	1.350	1.771	2.160	2.650	3.012	4.221
14	1.345	1.761	2.145	2.624	2.977	4.140
15	1.341	1.753	2.131	2.602	2.947	4.073
16	1.337	1.746	2.120	2.583	2.921	4.015
17	1.333	1.740	2.110	2.567	2.898	3.965
18	1.330	1.734	2.101	2.552	2.878	3.922
19	1.328	1.729	2.093	2.539	2.861	3.883
20	1.325	1.725	2.086	2.528	2.845	3.850
21	1.323	1.721	2.080	2.518	2.831	3.819
22	1.321	1.717	2.074	2.508	2.819	3.792
23	1.319	1.714	2.069	2.500	2.807	3.767
24	1.318	1.711	2.064	2.492	2.797	3.745
25	1.316	1.708	2.060	2.485	2.787	3.725
26	1.315	1.706	2.056	2.479	2.779	3.707
27	1.314	1.703	2.052	2.473	2.771	3.690
28	1.313	1.701	2.048	2.467	2.763	3.674
29	1.311	1.699	2.045	2.462	2.756	3.659
30	1.310	1.697	2.042	2.457	2.750	3.646
40	1.303	1.684	2.021	2.423	2.704	3.551
60	1.296	1.671	2.000	2.390	2.660	3.460
120	1.289	1.658	1.980	2.358	2.617	3.373
∞	1.282	1.645	1.960	2.326	2.576	3.291

Code of Fair Testing Practices in Education

*Prepared by the Joint Committee
on Testing Practices*

The Code of Fair Testing Practices in Education states the major obligations to test takers of professionals who develop or use educational tests. The Code is meant to apply broadly to the use of tests in education (admissions, educational assessment, educational diagnosis, and student placement). The Code is not designed to cover employment testing, licensure or certification testing, or other types of testing. Although the Code has relevance to many types of educational tests, it is directed primarily at professionally developed tests such as those sold by commercial test publishers or used in formally administered testing programs. The Code is not intended to cover tests made by individual teachers for use in their own classrooms.

The Code addresses the roles of test developers and test users separately. Test users are people who select tests, commission test development services, or make decisions on the basis of test scores. Test developers are people who actually construct tests as well as those who set policies for particular testing programs. The roles may, of course, overlap as when a state education agency commissions test development services, sets policies that control the test development process, and makes decisions on the basis of the test scores.

The Code has been developed by the Joint Committee on Testing Practices, a cooperative effort of several professional organizations, that has as its aim the advancement, in the public interest, of the quality of testing practices. The Joint Committee was initiated by the American Educational Research Association, the American Psychological Association, and the National Council on Measurement in Education. In addition to these three groups, the American Association for Counseling and Development/Association for Measurement and Evaluation in Counseling and Development, and the American Speech-Language-Hearing Association are now also sponsors of the Joint Committee.

This is not copyrighted material. Reproduction and dissemination are encouraged. Please cite this document as follows:

Code of Fair Testing Practices in Education. (1988) Washington, D.C. Joint Committee on Testing Practices. (Mailing Address: Joint Committee on Testing Practices, American Psychological Association, 1200 17th Street, NW, Washington, D.C. 20036.)

The Code presents standards for educational test developers and users in four areas:

A. Developing/Selecting Tests
B. Interpreting Scores
C. Striving for Fairness
D. Informing Test Takers

Organizations, institutions, and individual professionals who endorse the Code commit themselves to safeguarding the rights of test takers by following the principles listed. The Code is intended to be consistent with the relevant parts of the *Standards for Educational and Psychological Testing* (AERA, APA, NCME, 1985). However, the Code differs from the Standards in both audience and purpose. The Code is meant to be understood by the general public; it is limited to educational tests; and the primary focus is on those issues that affect the proper use of tests. The Code is not meant to add new principles over and above those in the Standards or to change the meaning of the Standards. The goal is rather to represent the spirit of a selected portion of the Standards in a way that is meaningful to test takers and/or their parents or guardians. It is the hope of the Joint Committee that the Code will also be judged to be consistent with existing codes of conduct and standards of other professional groups who use educational tests.

A. *Developing/Selecting Appropriate Tests**

Test developers should provide the information that test users need to select appropriate tests.

Test users should select tests that meet the purpose for which they are to be used and that are appropriate for the intended test-taking populations.

Test Developers Should:

1. Define what each test measures and what the test should be used for. Describe the population(s) for which the test is appropriate.

2. Accurately represent the characteristics, usefulness, and limitations of tests for their intended purposes.

3. Explain relevant measurement concepts as necessary for clarity at the level of detail that is appropriate for the intended audience(s).

Test Users Should:

1. First define the purpose for testing and the population to be tested. Then, select a test for that purpose and that population based on a thorough review of the available information.

2. Investigate potentially useful sources of information, in addition to test scores, to corroborate the information provided by tests.

3. Read the materials provided by test developers and avoid using tests for which unclear or incomplete information is provided.

---

* Many of the statements in the Code refer to the selection of existing tests. However, in customized testing programs test developers are engaged to construct new tests. In those situations, the test development process should be designed to help ensure that the completed tests will be in compliance with the Code.

4. Describe the process of test development. Explain how the content and skills to be tested were selected.

5. Provide evidence that the test meets its intended purpose(s).

6. Provide either representative samples or complete copies of test questions, directions, answer sheets, manuals, and score reports to qualified users.

7. Indicate the nature of the evidence obtained concerning the appropriateness of each test for groups of different racial, ethnic, or linguistic backgrounds who are likely to be tested.

8. Identify and publish any specialized skills needed to administer each test and to interpret scores correctly.

4. Become familiar with how and when the test was developed and tried out.

5. Read independent evaluations of a test and of possible alternative measures. Look for evidence required to support the claims of test developers.

6. Examine specimen sets, disclosed tests or samples of questions, directions, answer sheets, manuals, and score reports before selecting a test.

7. Ascertain whether the test content and norms group(s) or comparison group(s) are appropriate for the intended test takers.

8. Select and use only those tests for which the skills needed to administer the test and interpret scores correctly are available.

B. *Interpreting Scores*

Test developers should help users interpret scores correctly.

Test users should interpret scores correctly.

Test Developers Should:

9. Provide timely and easily understood score reports that describe test performance clearly and accurately. Also explain the meaning and limitations of reported scores.

10. Describe the population(s) represented by any norms or comparison group(s), the dates the data were gathered, and the process used to select the samples of test takers.

11. Warn users to avoid specific, reasonably anticipated misuses of test scores.

12. Provide information that will help users follow reasonable procedures for setting passing scores when it is appropriate to use such scores with the test.

Test Users Should:

9. Obtain information about the scale used for reporting scores, the characteristics of any norms or comparison group(s), and the limitations of the scores.

10. Interpret scores taking into account any major differences between the norms or comparison groups and the actual test takers. Also take into account any differences in test administration practices or familiarity with the specific questions in the test.

11. Avoid using tests for purposes not specifically recommended by the test developer unless evidence is obtained to support the intended use.

12. Explain how any passing scores were set and gather evidence to support the appropriateness of the scores.

13. Provide information that will help users gather evidence to show that the test is meeting its intended purpose(s).

13. Obtain evidence to help show that the test is meeting its intended purpose(s).

C. *Striving for Fairness*

Test developers should strive to make tests that are as fair as possible for test takers of different races, gender, ethnic backgrounds, or handicapping conditions.

Test users should select tests that have been developed in ways that attempt to make them as fair as possible for test takers of different races, gender, ethnic backgrounds, or handicapping conditions.

Test Developers Should:

14. Review and revise test questions and related materials to avoid potentially insensitive content or language.

15. Investigate the performance of test takers of different races, gender, and ethnic backgrounds when samples of sufficient size are available. Enact procedures that help to ensure that differences in performance are related primarily to the skills under assessment rather than to irrelevant factors.

16. When feasible, make appropriately modified forms of tests or administration procedures available for test takers with handicapping conditions. Warn test users of potential problems in using standard norms with modified tests or administration procedures that result in noncomparable scores.

Test Users Should:

14. Evaluate the procedures used by test developers to avoid potentially insensitive content or language.

15. Review the performance of test takers of different races, gender, and ethnic backgrounds when samples of sufficient size are available. Evaluate the extent to which performance differences may have been caused by inappropriate characteristics of the test.

16. When necessary and feasible, use appropriately modified forms of tests or administration procedures for test takers with handicapping conditions. Interpret standard norms with care in the light of the modifications that were made.

D. *Informing Test Takers*

Under some circumstances, test developers have direct communication with test takers. Under other circumstances, test users communicate directly with test takers. Whichever group communicates directly with test takers should provide the information described below.

Under some circumstances, test developers have direct control of tests and test scores. Under other circumstances, test users have such control. Whichever group has direct control of tests and test scores should take the steps described below.

Test Developers or Test Users Should:

17. When a test is optional, provide test takers or their parents/guardians with information to help them judge whether the test should be taken, or if an available alternative to the test should be used.

Test Developers or Test Users Should:

19. Provide test takers or their parents/guardians with information about rights test takers may have to obtain copies of tests and completed answer sheets, retake tests, have tests rescored, or cancel scores.

18. Provide test takers the information they need to be familiar with the coverage of the test, the types of question formats, the directions, and appropriate test-taking strategies. Strive to make such information equally available to all test takers.

20. Tell test takers or their parents/guardians how long scores will be kept on file and indicate to whom and under what circumstances test scores will or will not be released.

21. Describe the procedures that test takers or their parents/guardians may use to register complaints and have problems resolved.

Note: The membership of the Working Group that developed the Code of Fair Testing Practices in Education and of the Joint Committee on Testing Practices that guided the Working Group was as follows:

Theodore P. Bartell
John R. Bergan
Esther E. Diamond
Richard P. Duran
Lorraine D. Eyde
Raymond D. Fowler
John J. Fremer
    Co-chair, JCTP and
    Chair, Code
    Working Group)

Edmund W. Gordon
Jo-Ida C. Hansen
James B. Lingwall
George F. Madaus
    (Co-chair, JCTP)
Kevin L. Moreland
Jo-Ellen V. Perez
Robert J. Solomon
John T. Stewart

Carol Kehr Tittle
    (Co-chair, JCTP)
Nicholas A. Vacc
Michael J. Zieky
Debra Boltas and
    Wayne Camara of
    the American Psy-
    chological Associa-
    tion served as staff
    liaisons.

Glossary

Achievement Previous learning.

Acquiescence The tendency to agree or to endorse a test item as true.

Adverse impact The effect of any test used for selection purposes if it systematically rejects substantially higher proportions of minority than majority job applicants.

Age differentiation Discrimination based on the fact that older children have greater capabilities than younger children.

Age scale A test in which items are grouped according to age level. (The Binet scale, for example, grouped into one age level items that two-thirds to three-quarters of a representative group of children at a specific age could successfully pass.)

Anxiety An unpleasant emotional state marked by worry, apprehension, and tension.

Aptitude Potential for learning a specific skill (for example, musical aptitude).

Assessment A procedure used to evaluate an individual so that he or she can be described in terms of current functioning and also so that predications can be made concerning future functioning. Tests are used in the assessment process.

Basal age In the Stanford-Binet intelligence scale, the highest year level at which the subject successfully passes all tests.

Base rate In decision analysis, the proportion of persons expected to succeed on a criterion if selected without a test.

Biserial correlation An index used to express the relationship between a continuous variable and an artificially dichotomous variable.

Category format A rating scale format that often uses the categories 1 to 10.

Ceiling In the Stanford-Binet intelligence scale, the year level at which all tests are failed.

Class interval The unit for the horizontal axis in a frequency distribution.

Closed-ended question In interviewing, a question that can be answered specifically (for example, "yes" or "no"). Such questions generally require the interviewee to recall something.

Coefficient alpha A generalized method for estimating reliability. Alpha is similar to the KR_{20}

formula, except it allows items to take on values other than 0 and 1.

Coefficient of alienation In correlation and regression analysis, the index of nonassociation between two variables.

Coefficient of determination The correlation coefficient squared; gives an estimate of the percentage of variation in Y that is known as a function of knowing X (and vice versa).

Concurrent validity A form of criterion validity in which the test and the criterion are administered at the same point in time.

Confrontation A statement that points out a discrepancy or inconsistency.

Construct validity A process used to established the meaning of a test through a series of studies. To evaluate construct validity, a researcher simultaneously defines some construct and develops the instrumentation to measure it. In the studies, observed correlations between the test and other measures come to define the meaning of the test. See also *convergent validity* and *discriminant validity*.

Content validity The extent to which the content of a test is representative of the conceptual domain it is designed to cover.

Convergent validity A form of construct validity in which evidence is obtained to demonstrate that a test measures the same attribute as do other measures that purport to measure the same thing.

Correction for attenuation Correction of the reduction in the estimated correlation between a test and another measure caused by low reliability. The correction for attenuation formula is used to estimate what the correlation would have been if the variables had been perfectly reliable.

Correlation coefficient A mathematical index used to describe the direction and the magnitude of a relationship between two variables. The correlation coefficient ranges between -1.0 and 1.0.

Criterion-referenced test A test that describes the specific types of skills, tasks, or knowledge of an individual relative to a well-defined mastery criterion. The content of criterion-referenced tests is limited to certain well-defined objectives.

Criterion validity The extent to which a test score corresponds to an accurate measure of interest. The measure of interest is called the criterion.

Cross-validation The process of evaluating a test or a regression equation for a sample other than the one used for the original studies.

Deciles Points that divide the frequency distribution into equal tenths.

Descriptive statistics Methods used to provide a concise description of a collection of quantitative information.

Developmental quotient In the Gesell Developmental Schedules, a test score that is obtained by assessing the presence or absence of behaviors associated with maturation.

Diagnostic interview An interview designed to elicit information concerning emotional functioning, including feelings, thoughts, and attitudes.

Dichotomous format A test item format in which there are two alternatives for each item.

Differential validity The extent to which a test has different meanings for different groups of people. For example, a test may be a valid predictor of college success for white students but not for black students.

Discriminability In item analysis, how well an item performs in relation to some criterion. For example, items may be compared according to how well they separate groups who score high and low on the test. The index of discrimination would then be the correlation between performance on an item and performance on the whole test.

Discriminant analysis A multivariate data analysis method for finding the linear combination of variables that best describes the classification of groups into discrete categories.

Discriminant validity A form of construct validity in which evidence is obtained to demonstrate that a test measures something unique and different from what other available tests measure.

Distractor An alternative on a multiple-choice exam that is not correct or for which no credit is given.

Drift The tendency for observers in behavioral studies to stray from the definitions they learned during training and to develop their own idiosyncratic definitions of behaviors.

Dyslexia A specific reading disorder characterized by reading backwardness.

EEOC guidelines A set of procedures created by the Equal Employment Opportunity Commission (EEOC) to ensure fairness in employment practices. The EEOC guidelines discuss the minimum requirements for the validity and reliability of the psychological tests that are used for employee selection.

Empathy response In interviewing, a statement that communicates understanding (also called an *understanding response*).

Employment interview An interview designed to elicit information pertaining to a person's qualifications and capabilities for particular employment duties.

Estimated learning potentials (ELPs) In the SOMPA system, WISC-R scores adjusted for the socioeconomic background of the children. ELPs take the place of IQ scores.

Evaluative statement A statement in interviewing that judges or evaluates.

Expectancy effect The tendency for what an experimenter or a test administrator expects to find to influence the results (also known as the Rosenthal effect for the psychologist who has studied this problem intensively).

Face validity The extent to which items on a test appear to be meaningful and relevant. Actually not a form of validity because face validity is not a basis for inference.

Factor analysis A set of multivariate data analysis methods for reducing large matrixes of correlations to fewer variables. The variables are linear combinations of the variables that were in the original correlation matrix.

False negative In test decision theory, a case in which the test suggests a negative classification, yet the correct classification is in the positive category.

False positive In test decision analysis, a case in which the test suggests a positive classification, yet the correct classification is in the negative category.

Four-fifths rule A rule used by federal agencies in deciding whether there is equal employment opportunity. Any procedure that results in a selection rate for any race, gender, or ethnic group that is less than four-fifths (or 80%) of the selection rate for the group with the highest rate is regarded as having an adverse impact.

Frequency distribution The systematic arrangement of scores on a measure to reflect how frequently each value on the measure occurred.

General cognitive index In the McCarthy Scales of Children's Abilities, a standard score with a mean of 100 and standard deviation of 16.

Group test A test that can be given to more than one person at a time by a single test administrator.

Hit rate In test decision analysis, the proportion of cases in which a test accurately predicts success or failure.

Hostile statement A statement in interviewing that reflects anger.

Human ability Behaviors that reflect either what a person has learned or the person's capacity to emit a specific behavior; includes *achievement*, *aptitude*, and *intelligence*.

Individual test A test that can be given to only one person at a time.

Inference A logical deduction (from evidence) about something we cannot observe directly.

Inferential statistics Methods used to make inferences from a small group of observations, called a sample. These inferences are then applied to a larger group of individuals, known as a population. Typically, the researcher wants to make statements about the larger group but cannot make all the necessary observations.

Intelligence General potential, independent of prior learning.

Intelligence quotient A unit for expressing the results of intelligence tests. The intelligence quotient is based on the ratio of the individual's mental age (MA) (as determined by the test) to actual or chronological age (CA): $IQ = MA/CA \times 100$.

Intercept The point on a two-dimensional graph on the y axis where x equals 0. In regression, this is the point at which the regression line intersects the y axis.

Interquartile range The interval of scores bounded by the 25th and the 75th percentiles.

Interval scale A scale that can be used to rank order objects and on which the units reflect equivalent magnitudes of the property being measured.

Interview A method of gathering information by talk, discussion, or direct questions.

Ipsative scores Test results presented in relative rather than absolute terms. Ipsative scores compare the individual against himself or herself. Each person thus provides his or her own frame of reference.

Isodensity curve An ellipse on a scatterplot (or two-dimensional scatter diagram) that encircles a specified proportion of the cases constituting particular groups.

Item analysis A set of methods used to evaluate test items. The most common techniques involve assessment of item difficulty and item discriminability.

Item characteristic curve A graph prepared as part of the process of item analysis. One graph is prepared for each test item and shows the total test score on the x axis and the proportion of test takers passing the item on the y axis.

Item difficulty A form of item analysis used to assess how difficult items are. The most common index of difficulty is the percentage of test takers who respond with the correct choice.

Item discriminability See *discriminability*.

Kuder-Richardson 20 A formula for estimating the internal consistency of a test. The KR_{20} method is equivalent to the average split-half correlation obtained from all possible splits of the items. For the KR_{20} formula to be applied, all items must be scored either 0 or 1.

Likert format A format for attitude scale items in which subjects indicate their degree of agreement to statements using these categories: strongly disagree, disagree, neither disagree nor agree, agree, strongly agree.

McCall's *T* A standardized score system with a mean of 50 and a standard deviation of 10. McCall's *T* can be obtained from a simple linear transformation of Z scores ($T = 10Z + 50$).

Mean The arithmetic average of a set of scores on a variable.

Measurement error The component of an observed test score that is not the true score or the quality you wish to measure.

Median The point on a frequency distribution marking the 50th percentile.

Mental age A unit for expressing the results of intelligence tests based on comparing the individual's performance on the test with the average performance of individuals in a specific chronological age group.

Multiple regression A multivariate data analysis method that considers the relationship between a continuous outcome variable and the linear combination of two or more predictor variables.

Multivariate analysis A set of methods for data analysis that considers the relationships between combinations of three or more variables.

Nominal scale A system of arbitrarily assigning numbers to objects. Mathematical manipulation of numbers from a nominal scale is not justified. For example, numbers on the backs of football players' uniforms are a nominal scale of measurement.

Normative sample A comparison group consisting of individuals who have been administered a test under standard conditions—that is, with the instructions, format, and general procedures outlined in the test manual for administering the test (also called a *standardization sample*).

Norm-referenced test A test that evaluates each individual relative to a normative group.

Norms A summary of the performance of a group of individuals on which a test was standardized. The norms usually include the mean and the standard deviation for the reference group and information on how to translate a raw score into a percentile rank.

Open-ended question In interviewing, a question that usually cannot be answered specifically. Such questions require the interviewee to produce something spontaneously.

Ordinal scale A scale that can be used to rank order objects or individuals.

Parallel forms reliability The method of reliability assessment used to evaluate the error associated with the use of a particular set of items. Equivalent forms of a test are developed by generating two forms using the same rules. The correlation between the two forms is the estimate of parallel forms reliability.

Pearson product moment correlation An index of correlation between two continuous variables.

Percentile band The range of percentiles that are likely to represent a subject's true score. It is created by forming an interval that is one standard error of measurement above and below the obtained score and converting the resulting values to percentiles.

Percentile rank The proportion of scores that fall below a particular score.

Performance scale A test that consists of tasks that require a subject to do something rather than to answer questions.

Personality test A test that measures overt and covert dispositions of the individual (the tendency that the individual will show a particular behavior or response in any given situation). Personality tests measure typical human behavior.

Point scale A test in which points (0, 1, or 2, for example) are assigned for each item. In a point scale, all items with a particular content can be grouped together.

Polychotomous format A format for objective tests in which three or more alternative responses are given for each item. This format is popular for multiple-choice exams.

Predictive validity The extent to which a test forecasts scores on the criterion at some future time.

Probing statement A statement in interviewing that demands more information than the interviewee has been willing to provide of his or her own accord.

Projective hypothesis The proposal that when a person attempts to understand an ambiguous or vague stimulus, his or her interpretation reflects needs, feelings, experiences, prior conditioning, thought processes, and so forth.

Projective test A test in which the stimulus or the required response or both are ambiguous. The general idea behind projective tests is that a person's interpretation of an ambiguous stimulus reflects his or her unique characteristics.

Prophecy formula A formula developed by Spearman and Brown that can be used to correct for the loss of reliability that occurs when the split-half method is used and each half of the test is one half as long as the whole test. The method can also be used to estimate how much the test length must be increased to bring the test to a desired level of reliability.

Psychological test A device for measuring characteristics of human beings that pertain to overt (observable) and covert (intraindividual) behavior. A psychological test measures past, present, or future human behavior.

Psychological testing The use of psychological tests. Psychological testing refers to all the possible uses, applications, and underlying concepts of psychological tests.

Quartiles Points that divide the frequency distribution into equal fourths.

Randomly parallel tests Tests created by successive random sampling of items from a domain or universe of items.

Ratio scale An interval scale with an absolute zero, or point at which there is none of the property being measured.

Reactivity The phenomenon that causes the reliability of a scale in behavior studies to be higher when an observer knows that his or her work is being monitored.

Reassuring statement In interviewing, a statement that tries to comfort or support.

Receptive vocabulary In the Peabody Picture Vocabulary Test, a nonverbal estimate of verbal intelligence; the ability to understand language.

Regression line The best-fitting straight line through a set of points in a scatter diagram.

Reliability The extent to which a score or measure is free of measurement error. Theoretically, reliability is the ratio of true score variance to observed score variance. This ratio can be estimated using a variety of correlational methods, including *coefficient alpha, KR₂₀, test-retest, parallel forms.*

Representative sample A sample (group) that is composed of individuals whose characteristics are similar to those for whom the test is to be used.

Residual The difference between predicted and observed values from a regression equation.

Response style The tendency to mark a test item in a certain way irrespective of content.

Rosenthal effect See *expectancy effect.*

Scaled score On the Wechsler tests, a standard score with a mean of 10 and a standard deviation of 3.

Scatter diagram A picture of the relationship between two variables. For each individual, a pair of observations is obtained, and the values are plotted in a two-dimensional space created by variables X and Y.

Selection ratio In test decision analysis, the proportion of applicants who are selected.

Self-report questionnaire A questionnaire that provides a list of statements about an individual and requires the subject to respond in some way to each, such as "true" or "false."

Shrinkage Many times a regression equation is created on one group and used to predict the performance on another group of subjects. This procedure tends to overestimate the magnitude of the relationship for the second group. The amount of decrease in the strength of the relationship from the original sample to the sample on which the equation is used is known as *shrinkage.*

Social ecology A relatively new field of study that deals with the relationship between environments and behavior, the description of behavioral settings, and other related topics.

Social facilitation Tendency of people to behave like the models around them.

Spearman's rho A method for finding the correlation between two sets of ranks.

Split-half reliability A method for evaluating reliability in which a test is split into halves. The correlation between the halves of the test, corrected for the shortened length of the halves, is used as an estimate of reliability.

Standard administration The procedures outlined in the test manual for administering a test.

Standard deviation The square root of the average squared deviation around the mean (or the variance). It is used as a measure of variability in a distribution of scores.

Standard error of estimate An index of the accuracy of a regression equation. It is equivalent to the standard deviation of the residuals from a regression analysis. Prediction is most accurate when the standard error of estimate is small.

Standard error of measurement An index of the amount of error in a test or measure. The standard error of measurement is a standard deviation of a set of observations for the same test.

Standardization sample A comparison group consisting of individuals who have been administered a test under standard conditions—that is, with the instructions, format, and general procedures outlined in the test manual for administering the test (also called a *normative sample*).

Standardized interview   An interview conducted under standard conditions.

Stanine system   A system for assigning the numbers 1 through 9 to a test score. The system was developed by the U.S. Air Force. The standardized stanine distribution has a mean of 5 and a standard deviation of approximately 2.

State anxiety   An emotional reaction to a situation. State anxiety varies from one situation to the next.

Stress   A response to situations that pose demands, place constraints, or give opportunities.

Structured personality test   A test that provides a statement, usually of the self-report variety ("I like rock and roll music"), and requires the subject to choose between two or more alternative responses ("true" or "false," for example). It is also sometimes known as an objective personality test.

Subtest scatter   On the Wechsler tests, the degree of subtest variability.

Taylor-Russell tables   A series of tables that can be used to evaluate the validity of a test in relation to the amount of information it contributes beyond what would be known by chance.

Test   A measurement device that quantifies behavior.

Test administration   The act of giving a test.

Test administrator   Person giving a test.

Test anxiety   Anxiety that occurs in test-taking situations.

Test battery   A collection of tests whose scores are used together in appraising an individual.

Test-retest reliability   A method for estimating how much measurement error is caused by time sampling, or administering the test at two different points in time. Test-retest reliability is usually estimated from the correlation between performances on two different administrations of the test.

Third variable   A variable that may account for the observed relationship between two other variables.

Tracking   The tendency to stay at about the same level of growth or performance relative to other peers who are the same age.

Trait   An enduring or persistent characteristic of an individual that is independent of situations.

Trait anxiety   A personality characteristic reflecting the differences among people in the intensity of their reaction to stressful situations.

True score   The score that would be obtained on a test or measure if there were no measurement error. In practice, the true score can be estimated, but it is not directly observed.

T score   On the MMPI, a standard score with a mean of 50 and a standard deviation of 10. (Also see McCall's T.)

Understanding response   In interviewing, a statement that communicates understanding (also called an *empathy response*).

Unstructured interview   An interview conducted without any specific or particular questions or sequences of questions.

Validity   The extent to which a test measures the quality it purports to measure. Types of validity include *content validity*, *criterion validity*, and *construct validity*.

Variance   The average squared deviation around the mean; the standard deviation squared.

References

Abrams, E. W. (1955). Predictions of intelligence from certain Rorschach factors. *Journal of Clinical Psychology, 11,* 81–94.

Abramson, L. Y., Metalsky, G. I., & Alloy, L. B. (1989). Helplessness depression: A theory based system of depression. *Psychological Review, 96,* 358–372.

Abramson, T. (1969). The influence of examiner race on first-grade and kindergarten subjects' Peabody Picture Vocabulary Test scores. *Journal of Educational Measurement, 6,* 241–246.

Ackerman, P. T., Dykman, R. A., & Gardner, M. Y. (1990). ADD students with and without dyslexia differ in sensitivity to rhyme and alliteration. *Jouranl of Learning Disabilities, 23,* 279–283.

Adler, A. (1933/1964). *Social interest: A challenge to mankind.* New York: Capricorn.

Ahern S., & Beatty, J. (1979). Pupillary responses vary during information-processing with scholastic aptitude test score. *Science, 205,* 1289–1292.

Aiken, L. R. (1987). *Assessment of intellectual functioning.* Newton, Mass.: Allyn and Bacon.

Akutagawa, D. A. (1956). *A study in construct validity of the psychoanalytic concept of latent anxiety and a test of projection distance hypothesis.* Unpublished doctoral dissertation, University of Pittsburgh.

Albert, M. S. (1981). Geriatric neuropsychology. *Journal of Consulting and Clinical Psychology, 49,* 835–850.

Allen, G. J. (1972). The behavioral treatment of text anxiety: Recent research and future trends. *Behavior Therapy, 3,* 253–262.

Allen, J. J., Iacono, W. G., & Danielson, K. (in press, 1992). The development and validation of an event-related potential memory assessment procedure: A methodology for prediction in the face of individual differences. *Psychophysiology, 29.*

Allen, M. J., & Yen, W. M. (1979). *Introduction to measurement theory.* Pacific Grove, Calif.: Brooks/Cole.

Allison, J., Blatt, S. J., & Zimet, C. N. (1968). *The interpretation of psychological tests.* New York: Harper & Row.

Allport, G. W., & Odbert, H. S. (1936). Trait-names, a psycholexical study. *Psychological Monographs, 47,* No. 1.

Alpert, R., & Haber, R. N. (1960). Anxiety in academic achievement situations. *Journal of Abnormal and Social Psychology, 61,* 207–215.

Als, H. (1984). Newborn behavioral assessment. In W. J. Burns & J. V. Lavigne, (eds), *Progress in pediatric psychology.* New York: Grune & Stratton.

Als, H., Tronick, E., Adamson, L., & Brazelton, T. B. (1976). The behavior of the full-term yet underweight newborn infant. *Developmental Medicine and Child Neurology, 18,* 599–602.

Als, H., Tronick, E., Lester, B. M., & Brazelton, T. B. (1979). Specific neonatal measures: The Brazelton neonatal behavioral assessment scale. In J. Osofsky (ed.), *Handbook of infant development.* New York: Wiley.

Altmaier, E. M., McGuinnes, S. G., Wood, P., Ross, R. R., Bartley, J., & Smith, W. L. (1990). Defining successful performance among pediatric residents. *Pediatrics, 85,* 139–143.

American Education Research Association, American Psychological Association, & National Council on Measurement in Education (1985). *Standards for educational and psychological testing.* Washington, D.C.: American Psychological Association.

American Psychiatric Association (1980). *Diagnostic and statistical manual of mental disorders* (3rd ed.). Washington, D.C.: American Psychiatric Association.

American Psychological Association (APA) (1954). *Psychology and its relations with other professions.* Washington, D.C.: American Psychological Association.

American Psychological Association (APA) (1974). *Standards for educational and psychological tests.* Washington, D.C.: American Psychological Association.

American Psychological Association (APA) (1981). Ethical principles of psychologists. *American Psychologist, 36,* 633–638.

Ames, L. B. (1967). Predictive value of infant behavior examination. In J. Hellmuth (ed.), *Exceptional infant. Vol. 1: The normal infant.* Seattle: Straub & Hellmuth.

Ames, L. B., Metraux, R. W., & Walker, R. N. (1971). *Adolescent Rorschach responses.* New York: Brunner/Mazel.

Ammons, R. B., & Ammons, C. H. (1962). The quick test (QT): Provisional manual. *Psychological Reports, 11,* 111–161.

Anastasi, A. (1972a). Personality research form. In O. K. Buros (ed.), *The seventh mental measurements yearbook* (vol. 1). Highland Park, N.J.: Gryphon Press.

Anastasi, A. (1972b). Review of the Goodenough-Harris Drawing Test. In O. K. Buros (ed.), *The seventh mental measurements yearbook* (vol. 1). Highland Park, N.J.: Gryphon Press.

Anastasi, A. (1976). *Psychological testing* (4th ed.). New York: Macmillan.

Anastasi, A. (1981). Coaching, test sophistication, and developed abilities. *American Psychologist, 36,* 1086–1093.

Anastasi, A. (1984). The K-ABC in historical and contemporary perspective. *Journal of Special Education, 18*(3), 357–366.

Anastasi, A. (1986). Evolving concepts of test validation. *Annual Review of Psychology, 37,* 1–15.

Anderson, N. B., & McNeilly, M. (1991). Age, gender, and ethnicity as variables in psychophysiological assessment: Sociodemographics in context.

Psychological Assessment: A Journal of Consulting and Clinical Psychology, 3, 376–384.

Anderson, N. H. (1991). Contributions to information integration theory. Hillsdale, N.J.: Erlbaum.

Ansorge, C. J. (1985). Review of the Cognitive Abilities Test, Form 3. In J. V. Mitchell (ed.), *The ninth mental measurements year book* (vol. 1). Highland Park, N.J.: Gryphon Press.

Anton, W. D. (1976). An evaluation of outcome variables in the systematic desensitization of test anxiety. *Behaviour Research and Therapy, 14,* 217–224.

Archer, R. P., Maruish, M., Imhof, E. A., & Piotrowski, C. (in press, 1992). Psychological test usage with adolescent clients: 1990 survey. *Professional Psychology: Research & Practice.*

Arkes, H. R. (1991). Costs and benefits from judgement errors: Implications for debiasing. *Psychological Bulletin, 110,* 486–489.

Aronow, E., Reznikoff, M., & Rauchway, A. (1979). Some old and new directions in Rorschach testing. *Journal of Personality Assessment, 43,* 227–234.

Arthur, G. (1930). *Arthur point scale of performance tests.* Chicago: Stoelting.

Arvey, R. D., & Campion, J. E. (1982). The employment interview: A summary and review of recent research. *Personnel Psychology, 35,* 281–322.

Asher, J. J., & Sciarrino, J. A. (1974). Realistic work sample tests: A review. *Personnel Psychology, 27,* 519–533.

Atkinson, J. W. (1981). Studying personality in the context of an advanced motivational psychology. *American Psychologist, 36,* 117–128.

Atkinson, L. (1990a). Intellectual and adaptive functioning: Some tables for interpreting the Vineland in combination with intelligence tests. *Journal of Mental Retardation, 95,* 198–203.

Atkinson, L. (1990b). Reliability and validity of ratio developmental quotients from the Cattell Infant Intelligence Scale. *Ameri-can Journal of Mental Retardation, 95,* 215–219.

Avolio, B. J., & Waldman, D. A. (1990). An examination of age and cognitive test performance across job complexity and occupational types. *Journal of Applied Psychology, 75,* 43–50.

Ax, A. F. (1953). The physiological differentiation between fear and anger in humans. *Psychosomatic Medicine, 15,* 433–442.

Azrin, N. H., & Powell, J. (1968). Behavioral engineering: The reduction of smoking behavior by a conditioning apparatus and procedure. *Journal of Applied Behavior Analysis, 1,* 193–200.

Azrin, N. H., Holz, W., Ulrich, R., & Goldiamond, I. (1961). The control of the content of conversation through reinforcement. *Journal of the Experimental Analysis of Behavior, 4,* 25–30.

Baehr, M. (1987). A review of employee evaluation procedures and a description of "high potential" executives and professionals *Journal of Business and Psychology, 1,* 172–202.

Baglan T. (1981). Effects of interpersonal attraction and type of behavior on attributions. *Psychological Reports, 48,* 299–304.

Baird, L. L. (1972). Review of the Torrance Tests of Creative Thinking. In O. K. Buros (ed.), *The seventh mental measurements yearbook* (vol. 1). Highland Park, N.J.: Gryphon Press.

Bandura, A. (1977). Self-efficacy: Toward a unifying theory of behavioral change. *Psychological Review, 84,* 191–215.

Bandura, A. (1986). *Social foundations of thought and action: A social cognitive theory.* Englewood Cliifs, N.J.: Prentice-Hall.

Bandura, A. (1992). Exercise of personal agency through the self-efficacy mechanism. In R. Schwarzer (ed.), *Self-efficacy: Thought control of action.* Washington: Hemisphere, 3–38.

Barber, T. X., & Silver, M. J. (1968). Fact, fiction, and the experimenter bias effect. *Psychological Bulletin Monograph Supplement, 70,* 1–29.

Bareak, B., & Lauter, D. (1991). 1991 rights bill a return to earlier path of bias redress. *Los Angeles Times.* November 5:A1, A18.

Barker, R. G. (1979). Settings of a professional lifetime. *Journal of Personality and Social Psychology, 37,* 2137–2157.

Barker, R. G., & Schoggen, P. (1973). *Qualities of community life.* San Francisco: Jossey-Bass.

Baron, R. A. (1986). Self-presentation in job interviews: When there can be "too much" of a good thing. *Journal of Applied Social Psychology, 16,* 16–28.

Barrett, G. V., & Depinet, R. L. (1991). A reconsideration of testing for confidence rather than for intelligence. *American Psychologist, 46,* 1012–1024.

Bartlett, C. J., & O'Leary, B. S. (1969). A differential prediction model to moderate the effects of heterogeneous groups in personnel selection and classification. *Personnel Psychology, 22,* 1–17.

Baxter, D. J., Barbaree, H. E., & Marshall, W. L. (1986). Sexual responses to consenting and forced sex in a large sample of rapists and nonrapists. *Behaviour Research & Therapy, 24,* 513–520.

Bayles, K. A. (1990). Language and Parkinson disease. *Alzheimer Disease and Associated Disorders, 4,* 171–180.

Bayley, N. (1949). Consistency and variability in the growth of intelligence from birth to 18 years. *Journal of Genetic Psychology, 75,* 165–196.

Bayley, N. (1969). *Manual: Bayley Scales of Infant Development.* New York: Psychological Corporation.

Beal, J. A. (1991). Methodological issues in conducting research on parent-infant attachment. *Journal of Pediatric Nursing, 6,* 11–15.

Beck, A. T. (1967). *Depression: Clinical, experimental, and theoretical aspects.* New York: Harper & Row.

Beck, A. T. (1976). *Cognitive therapy and the emotional disorders.* New York: International Universities Press.

Beck, A. T., Brown, G., Steer, R. A., & Weissman, A. N. (1991). Factor analysis of the Dysfunctional Attitude Scale in a clinical population. *Psychological Assessment: A Journal of Consulting and Clinical Psychology, 3*, 478–583.

Beck, S. J. (1933). Configurational tendencies in Rorschach responses. *American Journal of Psychology, 45*, 433–443.

Beck, S. J. (1944). *Rorschach's test. I: Basic processes.* New York: Grune & Stratton.

Beck, S. J. (1945). *Rorschach's test. II: A variety of personality pictures.* New York: Grune & Stratton.

Beck, S. J. (1952). *Rorschach's test. III: Advances in interpretation.* New York: Grune & Stratton.

Bell, T. K. (1990). Rapid sequential processing in dyslexic and ordinary readers. *Perceptual and Motor Skills, 71*, 1155–1159.

Bellack, A. S., & Hersen, M. (1988). *Behavioral assessment: A practical handbook.* (3rd ed.). New York: Pergamon Press.

Bellak, L. (1975). *The TAT, CAT, and SAT in clinical use* (3rd ed.). New York: Grune & Stratton.

Bellak, L. (1986). *The TAT, CAT, and SAT in clinical use* (4th ed.). New York: Grune & Stratton.

Bellak, L., & Bellak, S. S. (1973). *Manual: Senior Apperception Technique.* Larchmont, N.Y.: CPS, Inc.

Bem, D. J., & Allen, A. (1974). On predicting some of the people some of the time: The search for cross-situational consistencies in behavior. *Psychological Review, 81*, 506–520.

Bem, D. J., & Funder, D. C. (1978). Predicting more of the people more of the time: Assessing the personality of situations. *Psychological Review, 85*, 485–501.

Ben-Porath, Y. S., & Butcher, J. N. (1989). The comparability of MMPI and MMPI-2 scales and profiles. *Psychological Assessment: Journal of Consulting and Clinical Psychology, 1*, 1–3.

Ben-Porath, Y. S., & Butcher, J. N. (1991). The historical development of personality assessment. In C. E. Walker (ed.), *Clinical psychology: Historical and research foundations.* New York: Plenum.

Bendell-Estroff, D., Greenfield, D. B., Hogan, A. E., & Claussen, A. H. (1989). Early assessment of sensorimotor and cognitive development in high-risk infants. *Journal of Pediatric Psychology, 4*, 549–557.

Bentler, P. (1988). *Causal modeling.* Paper presented at the Health Services Research Methodology Conference, Tucson, Ariz., April 1987.

Bentler, P. M. (1990). Comparative fit indexes in structural models. *Psychological Bulletin, 107,*(2), 238–246.

Bentler, P. M. (1991). Modeling of intervention effects. *Nida Research Monograph, 107*, 159–182.

Bergan, A., McManis, D. L., & Melchert, P. A. (1971). Effects of social and token reinforcement on WISC block design performance. *Perceptual and Motor Skills, 32*, 871–880.

Bergan, J. R., & Parra, E. B. (1979). Variations in IQ testing and instruction and the letter learning and achievement of Anglo and bilingual Mexican-American children. *Journal of Educational Psychology, 71*, 819–826.

Berger, M. (1970). The third version of the Stanford-Binet (Forms L-M): Some methodological limitations and their practical implications. *Bulletin of the British Psychological Society, 23*, 17–26.

Bergner, M., Bobbitt, R. A., Carter, W. B., & Gilson, B. S. (1981). The Sickness Impact Profile: Development and final revision of a health status measure. *Medical Care, 19*, 787–788.

Bernheimer, L. P., & Keogh, B. K. (1988). Stability of cognitive performance of children with developmental delays. *American Journal of Mental Retardation, 92*, 539–542.

Bersoff, D. N. (1979). Regarding psychologists testily: Legal regulation of psychological assessment in the public schools. In B. Sales & M. Novick (eds.), *Perspectives in law and psychology. III: Testing and evaluation.* New York: Plenum.

Bersoff, D. N. (1981). Testing and the law. *Americal Psychologist, 36*, 1047–1057.

Bianchini, J. C. (1976). *Achievement tests and differentiated norms.* Paper presented at the U.S. Office of Education invitational conference on achievement testing of disadvantaged and minority students for educational program evaluation, Reston, Va., May.

Binet, A. (1890a). Perceptions d'enfants. *La Revue Philosophique, 30*, 582–611.

Binet, A. (1890b). Recherches sur les mouvements de quelques jeunes enfants. *La Revue Philosophique, 29*, 297–309.

Binet, A., & Henri, V. (1895). La physchologie individuelle. *L'Annee Psychologique, 2*, 411–463.

Binet, A., & Henri, V. (1896). La psychologie individuelle. L'Annee Psychologique, 3, 296–332.

Binet, A., & Simon, T. (1905). Methodes nouvelles pour le diagnostic du niveau intellectuel des anormaux. *L'Annee Psychologique, 11*,, 191–244.

Biondi, M., & Pancheri, P (1985). Stress, personality, immunity, and cancer: A challenge for psychosomatic medicine. In R. M. Kaplan & M. H. Criqui (eds), *Behavioral epidemiology and disease prevention.* New York: Plenum.

Birk, J. M. (1974). Interest inventories: A mixed blessing. *Vocational Guidance Quarterly, 22*, 280–286.

Birney, R. C. (1968). Research on the achievement motive. In E. F. Borgatta & W. W. Lambert (eds.), *Handbook of personality theory and research.* Chicago: Rand McNally.

Blake, J. (1974). Developmental changes in visual information processing under backward masking. *Journal of Experimental Influence of Cognitive Psychology* on *Testing and Measurement.* Hillsdale, N.J.: Erlbaum.

Blanchard, E. B., Gerardi, R. J., Kolb, L. C., & Barlow, D. H. (1986). The utility of the Anxiety Disorders Interview Schedule (ADIS) in the diagnosis of the post-traumatic stress disorder (PTSD) in Vietnam veterans. *Behaviour Research & Therapy, 24,* 577–580.

Blatt, S. J. (1975). The validity of projective techniques and their research and clinical contributions. *Journal of Personality Assessment, 39,* 327–343.

Blatt, S. J. (1990). The Rorschach: A test of perception or an evaluation of representation. *Journal of Personality Assessment, 55,* 394–416.

Block, J. (1961). *The Q-sort method in personality assessment and psychiatric research.* Springfield, Ill.: Thomas.

Block, J. (1965). *The challenge of response sets: Unconfounding meaning, acquiescence, and social desirability in the MMPI.* New York: Appleton-Century-Crofts.

Bloom, A. S., Allard, A. M., Zelko, F. A., Brill, W. J., Topinka, C. W., & Pfohl, W. (1988). Differential validity of the K-ABC for lower functioning preschool children versus those of higher ability. *American Journal of Mental Retardation, 93,* 273–277.

Bloom, B. S. (1980). The new direction in educational research: Alterable variables. *New Directions for Testing and Measurement, 5,* 17–30.

Bombardier, C., Ware, J., Russell, I. J., et al. (1986). Auranofin therapy in quality of life for patients with rheumatoid arthritis: Results of a multicenter trial. *American Journal of Medicine, 81,* 565–578.

Boor, M., & Schill, T. (1968). Subtest performance on the WAIS as a function of anxiety and defensiveness. *Perceptual and Motor Skills, 27,* 33–34.

Borman, W. C., & Hallman, G. L. (1991). Observational accuracy for assessors of work-sample performance: Consistency across task and individual differences correlate. *Journal of Applied Psychology, 76,* 11–18.

Bortner, M. (1965). Review of the Progressive Matrices Test. In O. K. Buros (ed.), *The sixth mental measurements yearbook.* Highland Park, N.J.: Gryphon Press.

Bowers, K. S. (1973). Situationalism in psychology: An analysis and critique. *Psychological Review, 80,* 307–336.

Boyle, G. J. (1989). Confirmation of the structural dimensionality of the Stanford-Binet Intelligence Scale [fourth edition]. *Personality and Individual Differences, 10,* 709–715.

Boyle, G. J. (1990). Stanford-Binet IV Intelligence Scale: Is its structure supported by Lisrel congeneric factor analyses? *Personality and Individual Differences, 11,* 1175–1181.

Bracken, B. A. (1985). A critical review of the Kaufman Assessment Battery for Children (K-ABC). *School Psychology Review, 14,* 21–35.

Bradbury, T. N. & Fincham, F. D. (1990). Attributions in marriage: Review and critique. *Psychological Bulletin, 107*(1), 3–33.

Brand, C. R. (1981). General intelligence and mental speed: Their relationship and development. In M. P. Friedman, J. P. Das, & N. O'Conner (eds.), *Intelligence and learning.* New York: Plenum.

Braun, P. R., & Reynolds, D. N. (1969). A factor analysis of a 100 item fear survey inventory. *Behaviour Research and Therapy, 7,* 399–402.

Brayfield, A. H. (ed.) (1965). Testing and public policy. *American Psychologist, 20,* 857–1005.

Brazelton, T. B. (1973). *Neonatal behavioral assessment scale.* Philadelphia: Lippincott.

Brazelton, T. B. (1984). *Neonatal behavioral assessment scale* (2nd ed.). Philadelphia: Lippincott.

Bredemeier, M. (1991). IQ test ban for blacks called unconstitutional. California *Associations of School Psychologists Today,* Nov/Dec. 22–23.

Brill, S. (1973). The secrecy behind the college boards. *New York Magazine.* (Reprinted by the NYG Corporation.).

Brim, O. G., Jr. (1965). American attitudes toward intelligence tests. *American Psychologist, 20,* 125–130.

Brittain, M. (1968). A comparative study of the use of the Wechsler Intelligence Scale for Children and the Stanford-Binet intelligence scale (Form L-M) with eight-year-old children. *British Journal of Educational Psychology, 38,* 103–104.

Brogden, H. E. (1946). On the interpretation of the correlation coefficient as a measure of predictive efficiency. *Journal of Educational Psychology, 37,* 65–76.

Brogden, H. E. (1949). When tests pay off. *Personnel Psychology, 2,* 171–183.

Brown, F. G. (1979a). The algebra works—but what does it mean? *School Psychology Digest, 8*(2), 213–218.

Brown, F. G. (1979b). The SOMPA: A system of measuring potential abilities? *School Psychology Digest, 8*(1), 37–46.

Brown, G. W., & Harris, T. (1978). *Social origins of depression.* London: Tabistock.

Brown, G. W., Bhrolchain, M. N., & Harris T. (1975). Social class and psychiatric disturbance among women in an urban population. *Sociology, 9,* 225–254.

Brown, J. S., & Burton, R. B. (1978). Diagnostic models for procedural bugs in basic mathematical skills. *Cognitive Science, 2,* 155–192.

Buck, J. N. (1948). The H-T-P technique as a qualitative and quantitative scoring manual. *Journal of Clinical Psychology, 4,* 317–396.

Burgemeister, B. B., Blum, L. H., & Lorge, I. (1972). *Columbia Mental Maturity Scale* (3rd ed.). New York: Harcourt Brace Jovanovich.

Burke, M. J., & Doran, L. I. (1989). A note on the economic utility of generalized validity coefficients. *Journal of Applied Psychology, 73,* 171–175.

Burns, R. C., & Kaufman, S. H. (1970). *Kinetic Family Drawings (K-F-D): An introduction to understanding through kinetic drawings.* New York: Brunner/Mazel.

Burns, R. C., & Kaufman, S. H. (1972). *Actions, styles, and symbols in Kinetic Family Drawings (K-F-D).* New York: Brunner/Mazel.

Buros, O. K. (1974). *Tests in print II.* Highland Park, N.J.: Gryphon Press.

Buros, O. K. (ed.) (1970). *Personality tests and reviews.* Highland Park, N.J.: Gryphon Press.

Buros, O. K. (ed.) (1972). *The seventh mental measurements yearbook* (2 vols.). Highland Park, N.J.: Gryphon Press.

Buros, O. K. (ed.) (1975a). *Intelligence tests and reviews.* Highland Park, N.J.: Gryphon Press.

Buros, O. K. (ed.) (1975b). *Personality tests and reviews* (vol. 2). Highland Park, N.J.: Gryphon Press.

Buros, O. K. (ed.) (1975c). *Vocational tests and reviews.* Highland Park, N.J.: Gryphon Press.

Buros, O. K. (ed.) (1978). *The eighth mental measurements yearbook* (2 vols.). Highland Park, N.J.: Gryphon Press.

Burtt, H. E. (1926). *Principles of employment psychology.* Boston: Houghton Mifflin.

Bush, J. W. (1984). Relative preferences versus relative frequencies in health-related quality of life evaluations. In N. K. Wenger, M. E. Mattson, C. D. Furberg, & J. Elinson (eds.), *Assessment of quality of life in clinical trials of cardiovascular therapies.* New York: LaJacq.

Butcher, H. L. (1972). Review of cooperative school and college ability tests: Series 2. In O. K. Buros (ed.), *The seventh mental measurements yearbook* (vol. 1). Highland Park, N.J.: Gryphon Press.

Butcher, J. N. (1989). *MMPI-2 users guide.* Minneapolis, Minn.: Natural Computer Systems.

Butcher, J. N. (1990). *MMPI-2 in psychological treatment.* New York: Oxford University Press.

Butcher, J. N., Aldwin, C. M., Levenson, M. R., & Ben-Porath, Y. S. (in press, 1992). Personality and aging: A study of the MMPI-2 among older men. *Psychology and Aging.*

Butcher, J. N. Graham, J. R., Dahlstrom, W. G., Tellegen, A. M., & Kaemmer, B. (1989). *MMPI-2 manual for administrators and scoring.* Minneapolis: University of Minnesota Press.

Butcher, J. N., Graham, J. R., Williams, C. L., & Ben-Porath, Y. S. (1990). *Development and use of the MMPI-2 Content Scales.* Minneapolis: University of Minnesota Press.

Butcher, J. N., Keller, L. S., & Bacon, S. F. (1985). Current developments and future directions in computerized personality assessment. *Journal of Consulting and Clinical Psychology, 53,* 803–815.

Cacioppo, J. T., Berntson, G. G., & Anderson, B. L. (1991). Physiological approaches to the evaluation of psychotherapeutic process and outcome, 1991: Contributions from social psychophysiology. *Psychological Assessment: A Journal of Consulting and Clinical Psychology, 3,* 321–336.

Caine, E. D. (1986). Neuropsychology of depression: The pseudodementia syndrome. In I. Grant & K. M. Adams (eds.), *Neuropsychological assessment of neuropsychiatric disorders.* New York: Oxford University Press.

Caldwell, M. B., & Knight, D. (1970). The effects of Negro and White examiners on Negro intelligence test performance *Journal of Negro Education, 39,* 177–179.

Callender, J. C., & Dougherty, T. W. (1983). *Effects of interviewer training on interview information, interviewer behavior, and interview ratings: A field investigation.* Proceedings of the Southwest Division of The Academy of Management, Houston.

Cameron, R., & Evers, S. E. (1990). Self-report issues in obesity and weight management: State of the art and future directions. *Behavioral Assessment, 12,* 91–106.

Campbell, D. P. (1974). *Manual for the SVIB-SCII Strong-Campbell Interest Inventory* (2nd ed.). Stanford, Calif.: Stanford University Press.

Campbell, D. P. (1977). *Manual for the Strong-Campbell Interest Inventory.* Stanford, Calif.: Stanford University Press.

Campbell, D. T., & Fiske, D. W. (1959). Convergent and discriminant validation by the multitrait-multimethod matrix. *Psychological Bulletin, 56,* 81–105.

Campion, J. E. (1972). Work sampling for personnel selection. *Journal of Applied Psychology, 56,* 40–44.

Cane, D. B., Olinger, L. J., Gotlib, I. H., & Kuiper, N. A. (1986). Factor structure of the Dysfunctional Attitude Scale in a student population. *Journal of Clinical Psychology, 42,* 307–309.

Canfield, A. A. (1951). The "sten" scale—a modified C-scale. *Educational and Psychological Measurement, 11,* 295–297.

Cannell, C. F., & Henson, R. (1974). Incentives, motives, and response bias. *Annals of Economic and Social Measurement, 3,,* 307–317.

Carkhuff, R. R. (1969). *Helping and human relations. I: Selection and training. II: Practice and research.* New York: Holt, Rinehart & Winston.

Carkhuff, R. R., & Berenson, B. C. (1967). *Beyond counseling and therapy.* New York: Holt, Rinehart & Winston.

Carlin, J. B., & Rubin, D. B. (1991). Summarizing multiple-choice tests using three information statistics. *Psychological Bulletin, 110,* 338–349.

Carlson, R. E., Thayer, P. W., Mayfield, E. C., & Peterson, D. A. (1971). Improvements in the selection interview. *Personnel Journal, 50,* 268–275.

Carr, M. A., Sweet, J. J., & Rossini, E. (1986). Diagnostic validity of the Luria-Nebraska Neuropsychological Battery—Children's revision. *Journal of Consulting and Clinical Psychology, 54,* 354–358.

Carroll, J. B., & Horn, J. L. (1981). On the scientific basis of ability testing. *American Psychologist, 36,* 1012–1020.

Carvajal, H., & Weyand, K. (1986). Relationships between scores on Stanford-Binet IV and Wechsler Intelligence Scale for Children—Revised. *Psychological Reports, 59,* 963–966.

Carvajal, H., Hardy, K., Harmon, K., Sellers, T. A., & Holmes, C. B. (1987). Relationships among scores on the Stanford-Binet IV, Peabody Picture Vocabulary Test-Revised, and Columbia Mental Maturity Scale. *Bulletin of the Psychonomic Society, 25*(4), 275–276.

Carvajal, H., Hardy, K., Smith, K. L., & Weaver, K. A. (1988). Relationships between scores on Stanford-Binet IV and Wechsler preschool and primary scale of intelligence. *Psychology in the Schools, 25.*

Carvajal, H., Karr, S. K., Hardy, K. M., & Palmer, B. L. (1988). Relationships between scores on Stanford-Binet IV and scores on McCarthy Scales of Children's Abilities. *Bulletin of the Psychonomic Society, 26*(4), 349.

Cascio, W. F. (1987). *Applied psychology in personnel management* (3rd ed.). Englewood Cliifs, N.J.: Prentice-Hall.

Cascio, W. F., & Ramos, R. A. (1986). Development and application of a new method for assessing job performance in behavioral economic terms. *Journal of Applied Psychology, 71,* 20–28.

Cash, T. F. (1985). The impact of grooming style on the evaluation of women in management. In M. Solomon (ed.), *The psychology of fashion.* New York: Lexington Press.

Castaneda, A., & Ramirez, M. (1974). *Cultural democracy, bicognitive development, and education.* New York: Academic Press.

Castenell, L. A., & Castenell, N. E. (1988). Norm-referenced testing in low-income black. *Journal of Counseling and Development, 67,* 205–206.

Cattell, J. M. (1890). Mental tests and measurements. *Mind, 15,* 373–380.

Cattell, J. M. (1930). Psychology in America. *Scientific Monthly, 30,* 114–126.

Cattell, P. (1940). *The measurement of intelligence of infants and young children.* New York: Psychological Corporation.

Cattell, R. B. (1949). *Manual for forms A and B: Sixteen Personality Factors Questionnaire.* Champaign, Ill.: Institute for Personality and Ability Testing.

Cattell, R. B. (1957). *Personality and motivation, structure and measurement.* Yonkers, N.Y.: World Book.

Cattell, R. B., & Bolton, L. S. (1969). What pathological dimensions lie beyond the normal dimensions of the 16 PF? A comparison of MMPI and 16 PF factor domains. *Journal of Consulting and Clinical Psychology, 33,* 18–29.

Cattell, R. B., & Scheier, I. H. (1961). *The meaning and measurement of neuroticism and anxiety.* New York: Ronald Press.

Cattell, R. B., Eber, H. W., & Tatsuoka, M. M. (1970). *Handbook for the Sixteen Personality Factor Questionnaire (16 PF).* Champaign, Ill.: Institute for Personality and Ability Testing.

Cautela, J. R., & Upper, D. (1976). The behavioral inventory battery: The use of self-report measures in behavioral analyses and therapy. In M. Hersen & A. S. Bellack (eds.), *Behavioral assessment.* New York: Pergamon Press.

Chambers, L. W. (1988). The McMaster Health Index Questionnaire. In S. R. Walker (ed.), *Quality of life: Assessment and application.* London: MTP Press.

Champney, H., & Marshall, H. (1939). Optimal refinement of the rating scale. *Journal of Applied Psychology, 23,* 323–331.

Chasnoff, I. J., Burns, K. A., & Burns, W. J. (1987). Cocaine use in pregnancy: Perinatal morbidity and mortality. *Neurotoxicology and Teratology, 9,* 291–293.

Chattin, S. H., & Bracken, B. A. (1989). School psychologists' evaluation of the K-ABC, McCarthy Scales, Stanford-Binet IV, and WISC-R. *Journal of Psychoeducational Assessment, 7,* 112–130.

Chelune, G. J., & Edwards, P. (1981). Early brain lesions: Ontogenetic-environmental considerations. *Journal of Clinical and Consulting Psychology, 49,* 777–790.

Chun, K, & Campbell, J. B. (1974). Dimensionality of the Rotter Interpersonal Trust Scale. *Psychological Reports, 35,* 1059–1070.

Cialdini, R. B. (1985). *Influence: Science and practice.* Glenview, Ill.: Scott, Foresman.

Clarizio, H. F. (1979a). In defense of the IQ test. *School Psychology Digest, 8*(1), 79–88.

Clarizio, H. F. (1979b). SOMPA—A symposium continued: Commentaries. *School Psychology Digest, 8*(2), 207–209.

Clark, K. E. (1961). *The vocational interests of nonprofessional men.* Minneapolis: University of Minnesota Press.

Clark, K. E., & Campbell, D. P. (1965). *Manual for the Minnesota Vocational Interest Inventory.* New York: Psychological Corporation.

Cleary, T. A. (1968). Test bias: Prediction of grades of Negro and White students in integrated colleges. *Journal of Educational Measurement, 5,* 115–124.

Cleary, T. A., Humphreys, L. G., Kendrick, S. A., & Wesman, A. (1975). Educational uses of tests with disadvantaged populations. *American Psychologist, 30,* 15–41.

Cliff, N. (1987). *Analyzing multivariate data.* San Diego: Harcourt, Brace, Jovanovich.

Cohen, I. (1970). The effects of material and non-material reinforcement upon performance of the WISC block design subtest by children of different social classes: A follow-up study. *Psychology, 7*(4), 41–47.

Cohen, J. (1957). The factorial structure of the WAIS between early adulthood and old age. *Journal of Consulting Psychology, 21*, 283–290.

Cohen, J. (1960). A coefficient of agreement for nominal scales. *Educational and Psychological Measurement, 20*, 37–46.

Cohen, S., & Lichtenstein, E. (1990). Partner behaviors that support quitting smoking. *Journal of Consulting and Clinical Psychology, 58*, 304–309.

Cohen, S., Kanarack, T., & Mermelstein, R. (1983). A global measure of perceived stress. *Journal of Health and Social Behavior, 24*, 385–396.

Cole, N. S. (1973). Bias in selection. *Journal of Educational Measurement, 10*, 237–255.

Cole, N. S. (1981). Bias in testing. *American Psychologist, 36*, 1067–1077.

Coleman, J. C. (1973). Life stress and maladaptive behavior. *American Journal of Occupational Therapy, 27*, 169–180.

Coleman, W., & Cureton, E. E. (1954). Intelligence and acheivement: The "jangle fallacy" again. *Educational and Psychological Measurement, 14*, 347–351.

Coles, C. D., Smith, I. E., & Falek, A. (1987). Prenatal alcohol exposure and infant behavior: Immediate effects and implications for later development. *Advances in Alcohol and Substance Abuse, 6*, 87–104.

Conoley, J. C., & Kramer, J. J. (1989). *Tenth mental measurements yearbook.* The Buros Institute of Mental Measurements, The University of Nebraska–Lincoln: University of Nebraska Press.

Cook, M. L., & Peterson, C. (1986). Depressive irrationality. *Cognitive Therapy and Research, 10*, 293–298.

Cooper, D. (1990). Factor structure of the Edwards Personal Preference Schedule in a vocational rehabilitation sample. *Journal of Clinical Psychology, 46*, 421–425.

Cooper, W. H. (1981). Ubiquitous halo. *Psychological Bulletin, 90*, 218–244.

Coplan, J., & Gleason, J. R. (1990). Quantifying language development from birth to 3 years using the Early Language Milestone Scale. *Pediatrics, 86*, 963–971.

Copple, C. E., & Succi, G. J. (1974). The comparative ease of processing standard English and Black nonstandard English by lower-class Black children. *Child Development, 45*, 1048–1053.

Costa, P. T., Jr., & McCrae, R. R. (1985). *The NEO Personality Inventory: Manual.* New York: Psychological Assessment Resources, Inc.

Costello, A. J., Edelbrock, C., Dulcan, M. K., Kalas, R., & Klaric, S. H. (1984). *Development and testing of the NIM# diagnostic interview schedule for children in a clinic population.* Final report (contract #RFP-08-81-0027). Center for Epidemiologic Studies, NIMH, Rockville, Md.

Costello, J., & Dickie, J. (1970). Leiter and Stanford-Binet IQ's of preschool disadvantaged children. *Developmental Psychology, 2*, 314.

Cramer, P., & Blatt, S. J. (1990). Use of the TAT to measure change in defense mechanisms following intensive psychotherapy. *Journal of Personality Assessment, 54*, 236–251.

Crisco, J. J., Dobbs, J. M., & Mulhern, R. K. (1988). Cognitive processing of children with Williams syndrome. *Developmental Medicine and Child Neurology, 30*, 650–656.

Crites, J. O. (1973). *Career Maturity Inventory: Theory and research handbook and administration and use manual.* Monterey, Calif.: CTB/McGraw-Hill.

Crites, J. O. (1974). The Career Maturity Inventory. In D. E. Super (ed.), *Measuring vocational maturity for counseling and evaluation.* Washington, D.C.: National Vocational Guidance Association.

Crockett, D., Clark, C., & Kalonoff, H. (1981). Introduction—overview of neuropsychology. In F. E. Filskov & T. J. Boll (eds.), *Handbook of clinical neuropsychology.* New York: Wiley.

Cronbach, L. J. (1951). Coefficient alpha and the internal structure of tests. *Psychometrika, 16*, 297–334.

Cronbach, L. J. (1971). Test validation. In R. L. Thorndike (ed.), *Educational measurement* (2nd ed.). Washington, D.C.: American Council on Education.

Cronbach, L. J. (1975). Five decades of public controversy over mental testing. *American Psychologist, 30*, 1–14.

Cronbach, L. J. (1978). Black Intelligence Test of Cultural Homogeneity: A review. In O. K. Buros (ed.), *The eighth mental measurements yearbook* (vol. 1). Highland Park, N.J.: Gryphon Press.

Cronbach, L. J. (1980). Validity on parole: How can we go straight? *New Directions for Testing and Measurement, 5*, 99–108.

Cronbach, L. J. (1985, June). *Construct validation after 30 years.* Paper presented at the University of Illinois, Department of Educational Psychology, Champaign, Ill.

Cronbach, L. J. (1989). Construct validation after thirty years. In R. Linn (ed.), *Intelligence: Measurement, theory, and public policy.* Urbana: University of Illinois Press.

Cronbach, L. J., & Furby, L. (1970). How we should measure "change"—or should we? *Psychological Bulletin, 74*, 68–80.

Cronbach, L. J., & Gleser, G. C. (1965). *Psychological tests and personnel decisions.* Urbana: University of Illinois Press.

Cronbach, L. J., & Meehl, P. E. (1955). Construct validity in psychological tests. *Psychological Bulletin, 52*, 281–302.

Cronbach, L. J., Gleser, G. C., Nanda, H., & Rajaratnam, N.

(1972). *The dependability of behavioral measures: Theory of generalizability for scores and profiles*. New York: Wiley.

Croog, S. H., Levine, S., Testa, M. A., Brown, D., Bulpitt, C. J., Jenkins, C. D., Klerman, G. L., & Williams, G. H. (1986). The effects of antihypertensive therapy on quality of life. *New England Journal of Medicine, 314,* 1657–1664.

Cundick, B. P. (1985). Review of Incomplete Sentences Task. *Ninth mental measurements yearbook* (Vol. 1), 681–682.

Dahlstrom, W. G. (1969a). Invasion of privacy: How legitimate is the current concern over this issue? In J. N. Butcher (ed.), *MMPI: Research developments and clinical applications*. New York: McGraw-Hill.

Dahlstrom, W. G. (1969b). Recurrent issues in the development of the MMPI. In J. N. Butcher (ed.), *MMPI: Research developments and clinical applications*. New York: McGraw-Hill.

Dahlstrom, W. G., & Welsh, G. S. (1960). *An MMPI handbook: A guide to use in clinical practice and research*. Minneapolis: University of Minnesota Press.

Dahlstrom, W. G., Welsh, G. S., & Dahlstrom, L. E. (1972). *An MMPI handbook. I: Clinical interpretation* (rev. ed.). Minneapolis: University of Minnesota Press.

Dahlstrom, W. G., Welsh, G. S., & Dahlstrom, L. E. (1975). *An MMPI handbook. II: Research applications* (rev. ed.). Minneapolis: University of Minnesota Press.

Damarin, F. (1978a). Review of Bayley Scales of Infant Development. In O. K. Buros (ed.), *The eighth mental measurements yearbook* (vol. 1). Highland Park, N.J.: Gryphon Press.

Damarin, F. (1978b). Review of Cattell Infant Intelligence Scale. In O. K. Buros (ed.), *The eighth mental measurements yearbook* (vol. 1). Highland Park, N.J.: Gryphon Press.

Dangel, H. L. (1970). *The biasing effect of pretest information on the WISC scores of mentally retarded children*. Doctoral dissertation, Pennsylvania State University. (University Microfilms No. 71–16, 588.)

Daniel, W. W. (1990). *Applied nonparametric statistics* (2nd ed.). Boston: PWS–Kent.

Darlington, R. B. (1971). Another look at "cultural fairness." *Journal of Educational Measurement, 8,* 71–82.

Darlington, R. B (1978). Cultural test bias: Comment on Hunter and Schmidt. *Psychological Bulletin, 85,* 673–674.

Das, J. P. (1973). Cultural deprivation and cognitive competence. In N. R. Ellis (ed.), *International review of research in mental retardation.* (vol. 6). New York: Academic Press.

Datta, L. (1975). Foreword. In E. E. Diamond (ed.), *Issues of sex bias and sex fairness in career interest measurement.* Washington, D.C.: National Institutes of Education.

Davis, R. B. (1979). *Error analysis in high school mathematics, conceived as information processing pathology.* Paper presented at the annual meeting of the American Educational Research Association, San Francisco.

Davis, R. B., Jockusch, E., & McKnight, C. (1978). Cognitive process in learning algebra. *Journal of Children's Mathematics Behavior, 2,* 1–320.

Dearborn, G. (1897). Blots of ink in experimental psychology. *Psychological Review, 4,* 390–391.

Dearborn, W. F., & Rothney, J. W. M. (1941). *Predicting the child's development.* New York: Sci-Art Publishers.

Deffenbacher, J. L., Swemer, W. A., Whisman, M. A., Hill, R. A., & Sloan, R. D. (1986). Irrational beliefs and anxiety. *Cognitive Therapy and Research, 10,* 281–292.

deGroot, A. M. (1988). Word association norms with reaction times. *Nederlands-Tiydschrift-voor-de-Psychologie-haar-Grensqebieden, 43,* 280–296.

Delhees, K. H., & Cattell, R. B. (1971a). The dimensions of pathology: Proof of their projection beyond the normal 16 PF source traits. *Personality, 2,* 149–173.

Delhees, K. H., & Cattell, R. B. (1971b). *Manual for the Clinical Analysis Questionnaire (CAQ)*. Champaign, Ill.: Institute for Personality and Ability Testing.

Delis, D. C., Freeland, J., Kramer, J. H., & Kaplan, E. (1988). Integrating clinical assessment with cognitive neuroscience: Construct validation of the California Verbal Learning Test. *Journal of Consulting and Clinical Psychology, 56,* 123–130.

Delis, D. C., Kramer, J. H., Kaplan, E., & Ober, B. A. (1987). *The California Verbal Learning Test,* research edition. San Diego: Harcourt Brace Jovanovich.

Delis, D. C., Massman, P. J., Butters, N., Salmon, D. P., Cermak, L. S., & Kramer, J. H. (1991). Profiles of demented and amnesic patients on the California Verbal Learning Test: Implications for the assessment of memory disorders. *Psychological Assessment: A Journal of Consulting and Clinical Psychology, 3,* 19–26.

DeLongis, A., Coyne, J. C., Dakof, G., Folkman, S., & Lazarus, R. S. (1982). Relationship of daily hassles, uplifts, and major life events to health status. *Health Psychology, 1,* 119–136.

DeMoivre, A. (1733). *Approximatio ad summam terminorum binomii $(a + b)^n$ in seriem expansi.* (Cited in Stanley, 1971.)

DeRosa, A., & Patalano, F. (1991). Effects of familiar proctor on fifth and sixth grade student's test anxiety. *Psychological Reports, 68,* 103–113.

Diamond, E. E. (1979). Sex equality and measurement practices. *New Directions for Test and Measurement, 3,* 61–78.

Dicken, C. F. (1959). Simulated patterns on the Edwards Personal Preference Schedule.

Journal of Applied Psychology, 43, 372–378.

Diller, L., & Gordon, W. A. (1981). Interventions for cognitive deficits in brain-injured adults. *Journal of Consulting and Clinical Psychology,* 49, 822–834.

DiMatteo, M. R. (1979). A socio-psychological analysis of physician-patient rapport: Toward a science of the art of medicine. *Journal of Social Issues,* 85(1), 12–33.

Dipboye, R. L., Arvey, R. D., & Terpstra, D. E. (1977). Sex and physical attractiveness of raters and applicants as determinants of resume evaluations. *Journal of Applied Psychology,* 62, 288–294.

Dittmann, A. T. (1962). The relationship between body movements and moods in interviews. *Journal of Consulting Psychology,* 26, 480.

Dobko, P., & Kehoe, J. F. (1983). On fair use of bias: A comment on Drasgow. *Psychological Bulletin,* 93, 604–608.

Doctor, R. (1972). Review of the Porteus Maze Test. In O. K. Buros (ed.), *The seventh mental measurements yearbook* (vol. 1). Highland Park, N.J.: Gryphon Press.

Dodrill, C. B., & Warner, M. H. (1988). Further studies of the Wonderlic Personnel Test as a brief measure of intelligence. *Journal of Consulting and Clinical Psychology,* 59, 145–147.

Donahue, D., & Sattler, J. M. (1971). Personality variables affecting WAIS scores. *Journal of Consulting and Clinical Psychology,* 36, 441.

Donlon, T. F. (ed.) (1984). *The College Board technical handbook for the Scholastic Aptitude Test.* New York: College Entrance Examination Board.

Doppelt, J. E., & Wallace, W. L. (1955). Standardization of the Wechsler Adult Intelligence Scale for older persons. *Journal of Abnormal and Social Psychology,* 51, 312–330.

Dorans, N. J., & Drasgow, F. (1980). A note on cross-validating prediction equations. *Journal*

of Applied Psychology, 65, 728–730.

Dougherty, T. W., Ebert, R. J., & Callender, J. C. (1986). Policy capturing in the employment interview. *Journal of Applied Psychology,* 71, 9–15.

Dove, A. (1968). Taking the Chitling Test. *Newsweek,* 72, 51–52.

Downey, J., Elkin, E. J., Ehrhardt, A. A., Meyer-Bahlburg, H. F., Bell, J. J., & Morishima, A. (1991). Cognitive ability and everyday functioning in women with Turner Syndrome. *Journal of Learning Disabilities,* 24, 32–39.

Drake, L. E. (1946). A social I. E. scale for the MMPI. *Journal of Applied Psychology,* 30, 51–54.

Drasgow, F. (1982). Biased test items and differential validity. *Psychological Bulletin,* 92, 526–531.

Dreher, G. F., Ash, R. A., & Hancock, P. (1988). The role of the traditional research design in understanding the validity of the employment interview. *Personnel Psychology,* 41, 315–327.

DuBois, P. H. (1966). A test-dominated society: China 115 B.C.–1905 A.D. In A. Anastasi (ed.), *Testing problems in perspective.* Washington, D.C.: American Council on Education.

DuBois, P. H. (1970). *A history of psychological testing.* Boston: Allyn and Bacon.

DuBois, P. H. (1972). Increase in educational opportunity through measurement. *Proceedings of the 1971 Invitational Conference on Testing Problems.* Princeton, N.J.: Educational Testing Service.

Dunn, J. A. (1972). Review of the Goodenough-Harris Drawing Test. In O. K. Buros (ed.), *The seventh mental measurements yearbook* (vol. 1). Highland Park, N.J.: Gryphon Press.

Dunn, L. M. (1959). *Peabody Picture Vocabulary Test manual.* Minneapolis, Minn.: American Guidance Service.

Dunn, L. M. (1965). *Expanded manual for the Peabody Picture Vocabulary Test.* Minneapolis,

Minn.: American Guidance Service.

Dunn, L. M., & Dunn, I. M. (1981). *Peabody Picture Vocabulary Test—Revised.* Circle Pines, Minn.: American Guidance Service.

Dunnette, M. D. (1967). The assessment of managerial talent. In F. R. Wickert & D. E. McFarland (eds.), *Measuring executive effectiveness.* New York: Appleton-Century-Crofts.

Dunnette, M. D. (1972). *Validity study results for jobs relevant to the petroleum refining industry.* Washington, D.C.: American Petroleum Institute.

Dunnette, M. D., & Borman, W. C. (1979). Personnel selection and classification systems. *Annual Review of Psychology,* 30, 477–525.

Dupue, R. A., & Monroe, S. M. (1986). Conceptualization and measurement of human disorder in life stress research: The problem of chronic disturbance. *Psychological Bulletin,* 99, 36–51.

Dush, D. M. (1985). Review of Incomplete Sentences Task. *Ninth mental measurements yearbook* (vol. 1), 682–683.

Eaton, N. K., Wing, H., & Mitchell, K. J. (1985). Alternative methods of estimating the dollar value of performance. *Personnel Psychology,* 38, 27–40.

Ebel, R. L. (1972). *Essentials of educational measurement.* Englewood Cliffs, N.J.: Prentice-Hall.

Ebel, R. L. (1977). Comments on some problems of employment testing. *Personnel Psychology,* 30, 55–63.

Educational Testing Service (1991). *Sex, race, ethnicity, and performance on the GRE General Test.* Graduate Record Examinations. Princeton, N.J.: Educational Testing Service.

Edwards, A. L. (1954). *Manual for the Edwards Personal Preference Schedule.* New York: Psychological Corporation.

Edwards, A. L. (1957). *Techniques of attitude scale construction.* New York: Appleton-Century-Crofts.

Edwards, A. L. (1959). *Edwards Personal Preference Schedule.*

New York: Psychological Corporation.

Edwards, G. A. (1966). Anxiety correlates of the WAIS. *California Journal of Educational Research, 17,* 144–147.

Egeland, B. R. (1969). Examiner expectancy: Effects on the scoring of the WISC. *Psychology in the Schools, 6,* 313–315.

Egeland, B. R. (1978). Review of Columbia Mental Maturity Scale. In O. K. Buros (ed.), *The eighth mental measurements yearbook* (vol. 1). Highland Park, N.J.: Gryphon Press.

Egeland, B., Butcher, J. N., & Ben-Porath, Y. S. (1992). MMPI-2 profiles of women at risk for child abuse. (Unpublished manuscript)

Eisenberger, R. (1970). Is there a deprivation-satiation function for social approval? *Psychological Bulletin, 74,* 255–275.

Eisenberger, R. (1972). Explanation of rewards that do not reduce tissue need. *Psychological Bulletin, 77,* 319–339.

Eisenberger, R., Kaplan, R. M., & Singer, R. D. (1974). Decremental and nondecremental effects of noncontingent social approval. *Journal of Personality and Social Psychology, 30,* 716–722.

Ekman, P. (1965a). Communication through nonverbal behavior: A source of information about an interpersonal relationship. In S. S. Tomkins & C. E. Izard (eds.), *Affect, cognition, and personality.* New York: Springer.

Ekman, P. (1965b). Differential communication of affect by head and body cues. *Journal of Personality and Social Psychology, 2,* 725–735.

Ekman, P., & Friesen, W. V. (1968). Nonverbal behavior in psychotherapy research. In J. Shlien, H. Hunt, J. D. Matarazzo, & C. Savage (eds.), *Research in psychotherapy* (vol. 3). Washington, D.C.: American Psychological Association.

Ekman, P., Levenson, R. W., & Friesen, W. V. (1983). Autonomic nervous system activity distinguishes among emotions. *Science, 221,* 1208–1210.

Ekman, P. N., & O'Sullivan, M. (1991). Who can catch a liar? *American Psychologists 46,* 913–920.

Ekren, U. W. (1962). *The effect of experimenter knowledge of subjects' scholastic standing on the performance of a task.* Unpublished master's thesis, Marquette University.

Elashoff, J., & Snow, R. E. (eds.) (1971). *Pygmalion revisited.* Worthington, Ohio: C. A. Jones.

Elliot, R. (1988). Tests, abilities, race, and conflict. *Intelligence, 12,* 333–350.

Ellis, A. (1946). The validity of personality questionnaires. *Psychological Bulletin, 43,* 385–440.

Ellis, T. E. (1985). The hopelessness scale and social desirability: More data and a contribution from the Irrational Beliefs Test. *Journal of Clinical Psychology, 41,* 634–639.

Emory, E. K., Tynan, W. D., & Dave, R. (1989). Neurobehavioral anomalies in neonates with seizures. *Journal of Clinical and Experimental Neuropsychology, 11,* 231–240.

Endicott, J., & Spitzer, R. L. (1978). A diagnostic interview: The schedule for affective disorders and schizophrenia. *Archives of General Psychiatry, 35,* 837–844.

Endler, N. S. (1973). The person versus the situation—a pseudo issue? A response to Alker. *Journal of Personality, 41,* 287–303.

Endler, N. S., & Hunt, J. McV. (1968). S-R inventories of hostility and comparisons of the proportions of variance from persons, responses, and situations for hostility and anxiousness. *Journal of Personality and Social Psychology, 9,* 309–315.

Endler, N. S., & Magnusson, D. (1976). *Interactional psychology and personality.* Washington, D.C.: Hemisphere.

Endler, N. S., & Parker, J. D. A. (1989). Multidimensional assessment of coping: A critical evaluation. *Journal of Personality and Social Psychology, 58,* 844–854.

Endler, N. S., & Parker, J. D. A. (1990). The analysis of a construct that does not exist: Misunderstanding the multidimensional nature of trait anxiety. *Educational and Psychological Measurement, 50,* 265–271.

Endler, N. S., Parker, J. D. A., Bagby, R. M., & Cox B. J. (1991). Multidimensionality of state and trait anxiety: Factor structure of the Endler multidimensional anxiety scales. *Journal of Personality and Social Psychology, 60,* 919–926.

Erdberg, S. P. (1969). *MMPI differences associated with sex, race, and residence in a Southern sample.* Unpublished doctoral dissertation, University of Alabama.

Esquivel, G. B., & Lopez, E. (1988). Correlations among measures of cognitive ability, creativity, and academic achievement for gifted minority children. *Perceptual and Motor Skills, 67,* 395–398.

Everson, H. T., Millsap, R. E., & Rodriguez, C. M. (1991). Isolating gender differences in test anxiety: A confirmatory factor analysis of the test anxiety inventory. *Educational and Psychological Measurement, 51,* 243–251.

Ewart, C. K. (1991). Social action theory for a public health psychology. *American Psychologist, 46,* 931–946.

Exner, J. E. (1974). *The Rorschach: A comprehensive system.* New York: Wiley.

Exner, J. E. (1976). Projective techniques. In I. B. Weiner (ed.), *Clinical methods in psychology.* New York: Wiley.

Exner, J. E. (1986). Some Rorschach data comparing schizophrenics with borderline and schizotypal personality disorders. *Journal of Personality Assessment, 50,* 455–471.

Exner, J. E., & Weiner, I. B. (1981). *The Rorschach: A comprehensive system. III: Assessment of children and adolescents.* New York: Wiley.

Exner, J. E., Gillespie, R., Viglione, D., & Coleman, M. (1982). Some intercorrelational data concerning Rorschach structural variables. *Journal of Personality Assessment, 46,* 32–37.

Eyde, L. D., Moreland, K. L., & Robertson, G. J., with Primoff, E. S., & Most, R. B. (December 1988). *Test user qualifications: A data-based approach to promoting good test use.* Washington, D.C.: American Psychological Association.

Eysenck, H. J. (1959). Review of the Rorschach. In O. K. Buros (ed.), *The fifth mental measurements yearbook.* Highland Park, N.J.: Gryphon Press.

Eysenck, H. J. (1967). Intelligence assessment: A theoretical and experimental approach. *British Journal of Educational Psychology, 37,* 81–98.

Eysenck, H. J. (1990). The prediction of death from cancer by means of personality stress questionnaire: Too good to be true. *Perceptual and Motor Skills, 71,* 216–218.

Eysenck, H. J. (1991). Raising IQ through vitamin and mineral supplementation: An introduction. *Personality and Individual Differences, 12,* 329–333.

Fagan, J. F. (1985). A new look at infant intelligence. In D. K. Detterman (ed.), *Current topics in human intelligence* (vol. 1). *Research methodology,* 223–246. Norwood, N.J.: Ablex.

Farrell, A. D. (1989). The impact of computers on professional practice: A survey of current practices and attitudes. *Professional Psychology: Research and Practice, 20,* 172–178.

Farrell, A. D. (in press, 1992a). Behavioral assessment with adults. In R. T. Ammerman & M. Hersen (eds.), *Handbook of behavior therapy with children and adults: A developmental and longitudinal perspective.* New York: Pergamon Press.

Farrell, A. D. (in press, 1992b). Computers and behavioral assessment: Current applications, future possibilities, and obstacles to routine use. *Behavioral Assessment.*

Feifel, H., Strack, S., & Nagy, V. T. (1987). Degree of life-threat and differential use of coping modes. *Journal of Psychosomatic Research, 31,* 91–99.

Feldman, M. J., & Corah, N. L. (1960). Social desirability and the forced choice method. *Journal of Consulting Psychology, 24,* 480–482.

Felsten, G., & Wasserman, G. S. (1980). Visual masking: Mechanisms and theories. *Psychological Bulletin, 88,* 329–353.

Filskov, F. E., & Boll, T. J. (1981). *Handbook of clinical neuropsychology.* New York: Wiley.

Finn, S. E. (1986). Structural stability of the MMPI in adult males. *Journal of Consulting and Clinical Psychology, 54,* 703–707.

Flanagan, J. C. (1954). The critical incident technique. *Psychological Bulletin, 51,* 327–358.

Flanagan, J. C. (1971). The PLAN system of individualizing education. *NCME Measurement in Education, 2(2),* 1–8.

Flaugher, R. L. (1978). The many definitions of test bias. *American Psychologist, 33,* 671–679.

Flaugher, R. L., & Schrader, W. B. (1978). *Eliminating differentially difficult items as an approach to test bias* (RB-78-4). Princeton, N.J.: Educational Testing Service.

Fleishman, E. A., & Quaintance, M. K. (1984). *Taxonomies of human performance: The description of human tasks.* Orlando, Fla.: Academic Press.

Fleiss, J. L. (1971). Measuring nominal scale agreement among many raters. *Psychological Bulletin, 76,* 378–382.

Fletcher, J., Levin, H. S., & Satz, P. (1989). Neuropsychological and intellectual assessment of children. In H. I. Kaplan & B. J. Sadock (eds.), *Comprehensive textbook of psychiatry, fifth edition, volume 1,* pp. 513–525. New York: Guilford Publications.

Folkman, S., & Lazarus, R. S. (1980). An analysis of coping in a middle aged community sample. *Journal of Health and Social Behavior, 21,* 219–239.

Follick, M. J., Gorkin, L., Smith, T., Capone, R. J., Visco, J., & Stabein, D. (1988). Quality of life post-myocardial infarction: The effects of a transtelephonic coronary intervention system. *Health Psychology, 7,* 169–182.

Foltz, D. (1981). Courts take psychologists' side in copyright, confidentiality fight. *APA Monitor,* June/July, 13.

Forrester, B. J., & Klaus, R. A. (1964). The effect of race of the examiner on intelligence test scores of Negro kindergarten children. *Peabody Papers in Human Development, 2,* 1–7.

Forsterling, F. (1988). *Attribution theory in clinical psychology.* New York: Wiley.

Fowler, R. D. (1985). Landmarks in computer-assisted psychological assessment. *Journal of Consulting and Clinical Psychology, 53,* 748–759.

Fowler, R. D., & Coyle, F. A. (1969). Collegiate normative data on MMPI content scales. *Journal of Clinical Psychology, 25,* 62–63.

Fowles, G. P., & Tunick, R. H. (1986). WAIS-R and Shipley estimated IQ correlations. *Journal of Clinical Psychology, 42,* 647–649.

Fox, L. H. (1985). Review of Developing Cognitive Abilities Test. In J. V. Mitchell (ed.), *The ninth mental measurements yearbook* (vol. 1). Highland Park, N.J.: Gryphon Press.

Francis-Williams, J. (1974). *Children with specific learning disabilities* (2nd ed.). Oxford, England: Pergamon Press.

Frank, G. H. (1970). The measurement of personality from the Wechsler tests. In B. A. Mahrer (ed.), *Progress in experimental personality research.* New York: Academic Press.

Frank, G. H. (1976). Measures of intelligence and conceptual thinking. In I. B. Weiner (ed.), *Clinical methods in psychology.* New York: Wiley.

Frank, L. K. (1939). Projective methods for the study of personality. *Journal of Psychology, 8,* 343–389.

Fraser, E. D. (1965). Review of the Stanford-Binet intelligence scale, third revision. In O. K. Buros (ed.), *The sixth mental measurements yearbook.* Highland Park, N.J.: Gryphon Press.

Frederiksen, C. (1969). Abilities transfer and information retrieval in verbal learning. *Multivariate Behavioral Research Monographs,* 1–82.

Fredrikson, M. (1991). Physiological responses to stressors: Implications for clinical assessment. *Psychological Assessment: A Journal of Consulting and Clinical Psychology, 3,* 350–355.

Freeman, F. S. (1955). *Theory and practice of psychological testing.* New York: Holt.

French, J. L. (1964). *Manual: Pictorial Test of Intelligence.* Boston: Houghton Mifflin.

Freud, S. (1953). Fragment of an analysis of a case of hysteria. In *The standard edition of the complete psychological works of Sigmund Freud* (vol. 7). London: Hogarth. (Originally published in 1905.)

Fuchs, D., & Fuchs, L. S. (1986). Test procedure bias: A meta-analysis of examiner familiarity effects. *Review of Educational Research, 56,* 243–262.

Fuld, P. A., & Fisher, P. (1977). Recovery of intellectual ability after closed head injury. *Developmental Medicine and Child Neurology, 19,* 495–502.

Furnham, A., & Henderson, M. (1982). Content analysis of four personality inventories. *Journal of Clinical Psychology, 38,* 818–825.

Galton, F. (1879). Psychometric experiments. *Brain, 2,* 149–162.

Galton, F. (1883). *Inquiries into human faculty and its development.* London: Macmillan.

Galton, R. (1869). *Hereditary genius: An inquiry into its laws and consequences.* London: Collins.

Gamble, K. R. (1972). The Holtzman Inkblot Technique: A review. *Psychological Bulletin, 77,* 172–194.

Garcia, J. (1981). The logic and limits of mental aptitude testing. *American Psychologist, 36,* 1172–1180.

Gardner, E. F., Rudman, H. C., Karlsen, B., & Merwin, J. C. (1982). *The Stanford Achievement Test: Seventh edition.* New York: Harcourt Brace Jovanovich.

Gardner, H. (1983). *Frames of mind: The theory of multiple intelligences.* New York: Basic Books.

Garfield, S. L., & Sineps, J. (1959). An appraisal of Taulbee and Sisson's "configurational analysis of MMPI profiles of psychiatric groups." *Journal of Consulting Psychology, 23,* 333–335.

Gati, I., & Tikotzki, Y. (1989). Strategies for collection and processing of occupational information in making career decisions. *Journal of Counseling Psychology, 36,* 430–439.

Geer, J. H. (1965). The development of a scale to measure fear. *Behaviour Research and Therapy, 3,* 45–53.

Geiselman, R. E., Woodward, J. A., & Beatty, J. (1982). Individual differences in verbal memory performance: A test of alternative information-processing models. *Journal of Experimental Psychology: General, 111,* 109–134.

Georgoff, P. B. (1991). The Rorschach with hospice cancer patients and surviving cancer patients. *Journal of Personality Assessment, 56,* 218–226.

Gesell, A. (1925). Monthly increments of development in infancy. *Journal of Genetic Psychology, 32,* 203–208.

Gesell, A., & Amatruda, C. S. (1941). *Developmental diagnosis: Normal and abnormal child development: Clinical methods and practical applications.* New York: Paul B. Hoebler.

Gesell, A., & Amatruda, C. S. (1947). *Developmental diagnosis: Normal and abnormal child development: Clinical methods and pediatric applications* (2nd ed.). New York: Paul B. Hoebler.

Gesell, A., Halverson, H. M.,

Thompson, H., Ilg, F. L., Castner, B. M., Ames, L. B., & Amatruda, C. S. (1940). *The first five years of life: A guide to the study of the preschool child.* New York: Harper & Row.

Gianetti, R. Z., Klinger, D. E., Johnson, J. H., & Williams, T. A. (1976). The potential for dynamic assessment systems using on-line computer technology. *Behavior Research Methods and Instrumentation, 8,* 101–103.

Gibby, R. G., Miller, D. R., & Walker, E. L. (1953). The examiner's influence on the Rorschach protocol. *Journal of Consulting Psychology, 17,* 425–428.

Gilberstadt, H., & Duker, J. (1965). *A handbook for clinical and actuarial MMPI interpretation.* Philadelphia: Saunders.

Gillingham, W. H. (1970). *An investigation of examiner influence on Wechsler Intelligence Scale for Children scores.* Doctoral dissertation, Michigan State University. (University Microfilms No. 70-20, 458.)

Gilmore, D. C., Beehr, T. A., & Love, K. G. (1986). Effects of applicant sex, applicant physical attractiveness, type of job on interview decisions. *Journal of Occupational Psychology, 59,* 103–109.

Glutting, J. J. (1989). Introduction to the structure and application of the Stanford-Binet Intelligence Scale—Fourth Edition. *Journal of School Psychology, 27,* 69–80.

Goddard, H. H. (1908). The Binet and Simon tests of intellectual capacity. *Training School, 5,* 3–9.

Goddard, H. H. (1911). A revision of the Binet scale. *Training School, 8,* 56–62.

Goetcheus, G. (1967). *The effects of instructions and examiners on the Rorschach.* Unpublished master's thesis, Bowling Green State University.

Goldberg, L. R. (1970). Man versus model of man: A rationale, plus some evidence for a method of improving on clinical inferences. *Psychological Bulletin, 73,* 422–432.

Goldberg, L. R. (1972b). Parameters of personality inventory construction and utilization: A comparison of prediction strategies and tactics. *Multivariate Behavioral Research Monographs, 7*(2).

Goldberg, L. R. (1974). Objective personality tests and measures. *Annual Review of Psychology, 25,* 343–366.

Goldberg, L. R., Grenier, J. R., Guion, R. M., Sechrest, L. B., & Wing, H. (1991). Questionnaires used in the prediction of trustworthiness in pre-employment selection decisions: An APA Task Force Report. *American Psychological Association, Science Directorate,* Washington.

Golden, C. J. (1981). A standardized version of Luria's neuropsychological tests: Quantitative and qualitative approach in neuropsychological evaluation. In F. E. Filskov & T. J. Boll (eds.), *Handbook of clinical neuropsychology.* New York: Wiley.

Goldfried, M. R. (1976). Behavioral assessment. In I. B. Weiner (ed.), *Clinical methods in psychology.* New York: Wiley-Interscience.

Goldman, B. A., & Osbourne, W. (1985). *Unpublished experimental mental measures* (Vol. 4). New York: Human Sciences Press, Inc.

Goldman, R. D. (1973). Hidden opportunities in the prediction of college grades for different subgroups. *Journal of Educational Measurement, 10*(3), 205–210.

Goldman, R. D., & Hartig, L. (1976). The WISC may not be a valid predictor of school performance for primary-grade minority children. *American Journal of Mental Deficiency, 80,* 583–587.

Goldman, R. D., & Hewitt, B. (1976). *Culture-free selection of professional school students.* Unpublished manuscript, University of California, Riverside.

Goldstein, G. (1986). The neuropsychology of schizophrenia. In I. Grant & K. M. Adams (eds.), *Neuropsychological assessment of neuropsychiatric disorders.* New York: Oxford University Press.

Goldstein, L. H., Canavan, A. G., & Polkey, C. E. (1988). Verbal and abstract designs paired associate learning after unilateral temporal lobectomy. *Cortex, 24,* 41–52.

Goodman, J. (1977). The diagnostic fallacy: A critique of Jane Mercer's concept of mental retardation. *Journal of School Psychology, 15,* 197–206.

Goodman, J. (1979). "Ignorance" versus "stupidity"—the basic disagreement. *School Psychology Digest, 8*(2), 218–223.

Gordon, E. W., & Terrell, M. D. (1981). The changed social context of testing. *American Psychologist, 36,* 1167–1171.

Gorsuch, R. L. (1974). *Factor analysis.* Philadelphia: Saunders.

Gotkin, T. D., & Reynolds, C. R. (1981). Factorial similarity of the WISC-R White and Black children from the standardization sample. *Journal of Educational Psychology, 73,* 227–231.

Gottfredson, L. S. (1980). Construct validity of Holland's occupational typology in terms of prestige, census, Department of Labor, and other classification systems. *Journal of Applied Psychology, 65,* 697–714.

Gottlib, I. H., & Cine, D. B. (1989). Self-report assessment of depression and anxiety. In P. C. Kendill & D. Watson (eds.), *Anxiety and depression: Distinctive and overlapping features.* San Diego: Academic Press, pp. 131–169.

Gough, H. G. (1957). *California Psychological Inventory manual.* Palo Alto, Calif.: Consulting Psychologists Press.

Gough, H. G. (1960). The adjective checklist as a personality assessment research technique. *Psychological Reports, 6,* 107–122.

Gough, H. G. (1969). *California Psychological Inventory, revised manual.* Palo Alto, Calif.: Consulting Psychologists Press.

Gough, H. G., & Heilbrun, A. B., Jr. (1980). *The Adjective Checklist manual (revised).* Palo Alto, Calif.: Consulting Psychologists Press.

Gould, S. J. (1981). *The mismeasure of man.* New York: Norton.

Graham, F. K., & Kendall, B. S. (1960). Memory-for-Designs test: Revised general manual. *Perceptual Motor Skills, 11,* 147–190.

Graham, J. R. (1990). *MMPI-2 in psychology treatment.* New York: Oxford University Press.

Graham, J. R., Timbrook, R. E., & Ben-Porath, Y. S. (in press). Code-type congruence between MMPI and MMPI-2. Separating fact from artifact. *Journal of Personality Assessment.*

Grant, I. (1987). Alcohol and the brain: Neuropsychological correlates. *Journal of Consulting and Clinical Psychology, 55,* 310.

Grant, I., & Adams, K. M. (1986). *Neuropsychological assessment of neuropsychiatric disorders.* New York: Oxford University Press.

Grant, I, & Heaton, R. K. (1990). Human immunodeficiency virus-type 1 (HIV-1) and the brain. *Journal of Consulting and Clinical Psychology, 58,* 22–30.

Grant, I, & Kaplan, R. M. (1988). Statistics and experimental design. In H. I. Kaplan & D. J. Sadock (eds.), *Comprehensive text book of psychiatry* (5th ed.). Baltimore: Williams & Wilkins.

GRE Guide (1990). Princeton, N.J.: Educational Testing Service.

GRE Guide (1991). Princeton, N.J.: Educational Testing Service.

Greaud, V. A., & Green, B. F. (1986). Equivalence of conventional and computer presentation of speeded tests. *Applied Psychological Measurement, 10,* 23–34.

Green, B. F. (1978). In defense of measurement. *American Psychologist, 33,* 664–670.

Green, D. F., Jr., & Wing, H. (1988). *Analysis of job performance measurement data: Report of a workshop.* Washington, D.C.: National Academy Press.

Green, D. R., & Draper, J. F. (1972). Exploratory studies of bias and achievement. *American*

Psychological Association, Honolulu, September.

Greene, R. L., Weed, N. C., Butchers, J. N., Arredondo, R., & Davis, H. G. (in press). A cross-validation of MMPI-2 Substance Abuse Scales. *Journal of Personality Assessment*.

Grieco, A., & Long, C. J. (1984). Investigation of the Karnofsky performance status as a measure of quality of life. *Health Psychology*, *3*, 129–142.

Groenweg, G., Conway, D. G., & Stan, E. A. (1986). Performance of adults with developmental handicaps on alternate forms of the Peabody Picture Vocabulary Test. *Journal of Speech and Hearing Disorders*, *51*, 259–263.

Groth-Marnat, G., & Shumaker, J. (1989). Computer-based psychological testing: Issues and guidelines. *American Journal of Orthopsychiatry*, *59*, 257–263.

Guertin, W. H., Ladd, C. E., Frank, G. H., Rabin, A. I., & Hiester, D. S. (1966). Research with the Wechsler Intelligence Scales for Adults: 1960–1965. *Psychological Bulletin*, *66*, 385–409.

Guertin, W. H., Ladd, C. E., Frank, G. H., Rabin, A. I., & Hiester, D. S. (1971). Research with the Wechsler Intelligence Scales for Adults: 1965–1970. *Psychological Record*, *21*, 289–339.

Guertin, W. H., Rabin, A. I., Frank, G. H., & Ladd, C. E. (1962). Research with the Wechsler Intelligence Scales for Adults: 1955–1960. *Psychological Bulletin*, *59*, 1–26.

Guilford, J. P. (1940). *An inventory of factors*. Beverly Hills, Calif.: Sheridan Supply.

Guilford, J. P. (1954). *Psychometric methods* (2nd ed.). New York: McGraw-Hill.

Guilford, J. P. (1959). *Personality*. New York: McGraw-Hill.

Guilford, J. P., & Fruchter, B. (1973). *Fundamental statistics in psychology and education* (5th ed.). New York: McGraw-Hill.

Guilford, J. P., & Martin, H. G. (1943). *The Guilford-Martin inventory of factors: GAMIN:*

Manual of directions and norms. Beverly Hills, Calif.: Sheridan Supply.

Guilford, J. P., & Zimmerman, W. S. (1949). *The Guilford Temperament Survey: Manual of instructions and interpretations.* Beverly Hills, Calif.: Sheridan Supply.

Guilford, J. P., & Zimmerman, W. S. (1956). Fourteen dimensions of temperament. *Psychological Monographs*, *70*, No. 10.

Guion, R. M., & Ironson, G. H. (1983). Latent trait theory for organizational research. *Organizational Behavior and Human Performance*, *31*, 54–87.

Gunnison, J. A. (1984). Developing educational intervention from assessments involving the K-ABC. *The Journal of Special Education*, *18*(3), 325–343.

Guthrie, R. V. (1976). *Even the rat was white: A historical view of psychology*. New York: Harper & Row.

Guttman, L. (1950). Relation of scalogram analysis to other techniques. In S. A. Stouffer et al. (eds.), *Measurement and prediction*. Princeton, N.J.: Princeton University Press.

Guyatt, G., Walter, S., & Norman, G. (1987). Measuring change over time: Assessing the usefulness of evaluative instruments. *Journal of Chronic Diseases*, *40*, 171–178.

Gynther, M. D. (1972). White norms and Black MMPIs: A prescription for discrimination? *Psychological Bulletin*, *78*, 386–402.

Gynther, M. D., & Gynther, R. A. (1976). Personality inventories. In I. B. Weiner (ed.), *Clinical methods in psychology*. New York: Wiley.

Gynther, M. D., & Shimkunas, A. M. (1965). Age, intelligence, and MMPI F scores. *Journal of Consulting Psychology*, *29*, 383–388.

Gyurke, J. S., Stone, B. J., & Beyer, M. (1990). A confirmatory factor analysis of the WPPSI-R. *Journal of Psychoeducational Assessment*, *8*, 15–21.

Haber, R. H. (1969). Perception

and thought: An information processing analysis. In J. I. Voss (ed.), *Approaches to thought*. Columbus, Ohio: Merrill.

Haemmerlie, F. M., & Beamish, P. (1990). The Jenkins Activity Survey and the CPI-Revised: Further evidence of adaptive and maladaptive Type A traits. *Journal of Clinical Psychology*, *46*, 573–581.

Hakel, M. D. (1986). Personnel selection and placement. *Annual Review of Psychology*, *37*, 351–380.

Hall, J. C. (1957). Correlation of a modified form of Raven's Progressive Matrices (1938) with the Wechsler Adult Intelligence Scale. *Journal of Consulting Psychology*, *21*, 23–26.

Hall, V. C., Huppertz, J. W., & Levi, A. (1977). Attention and achievement exhibited by middle and lower-class Black and White elementary school boys. *Journal of Educational Psychology*, *69*, 115–120.

Hambleton, R. K. (1980). Validation of criterion-referenced test score interpretations and standard setting methods. In R. A. Berk (ed.), *Criterion-referenced measurement: The state of the art*. Baltimore, Md.: Johns Hopkins University Press.

Hammer, A. L., & Marting, M. S. (1985). *Manual for the Coping Resources Inventory*. Palo Alto, Calif.: Consulting Psychologists Press.

Hampson, E., & Kimura D. (1988). Reciprocal effects of hormonal fluctuations on human motor and perceptual-spatial skills. *Behavioral Neuroscience*, *102*, 456–459.

Haney, W. (1981). Validity, vaudeville, and values: A short history of social concerns over standardized testing. *American Psychologist*, *36*, 1021–1034.

Hanford, G. H. (1986). The SAT and statewide assessment: The distinction between measurement and evaluation. *Vital Speeches of the Day*, *LII*(24), 765–768.

Hansen, J. C., & Campbell, D. P. (1985). *Manual for the SVIB-*

SCII (4th ed.). Stanford, Calif.: Stanford University Press.

Hardy, J. B., Welcher, D. W., Mellits, E. D., & Kagan, J. (1976). Pitfalls in the measurement of intelligence: Are standardized intelligence tests valid for measuring the intellectual potential of urban children? *Journal of Psychology, 94,* 43–51.

Hargadon, F. (1981). Test and college admission. *American Psychologist, 36,* 1112–1119.

Harman, H. H. (1967). *Modern factor analysis* (2nd ed.). Chicago: University of Chicago Press.

Harmon, L. W., Cole, N., Wysong, E., & Zytowski, D. G. (1973). AMEG commission report on sex bias in interest measurement. *Measurement and Evaluation in Guidance, 6,* 171–177.

Harris, D. B. (1963). *Children's drawings as measures of intellectual maturity: A revision and extension of the Goodenough Draw-a-Man Test.* New York: Harcourt, Brace, & World.

Harris, F. C., & Lahey, B. B. (1982). Subject reactivity in direct observational assessment: A review and critical analysis. *Clinical Psychology Review, 2,* 523–538.

Harris, M. M. (1989). Reconsidering the employment interview: A review of recent literature and suggestions for future research. *Personnel Psychology, 42,* 691–726.

Harrison, R. (1940). Studies in the use and validity of the Thematic Apperception Test with mentally disordered patients. II: A quantitative validity study. III: Validation by blind analysis. *Character and Personality, 9,* 122–133, 134–138.

Harrison, R. (1965). Thematic apperceptive methods. In B. Wolman (ed.), *Handbook of clinical psychology.* New York: McGraw-Hill.

Harrison, R., & Rotter, J. B. (1945). A note on the reliability of the Thematic Apperception Test. *Journal of Abnormal and Social Psychology, 40,* 97–99.

Hart, B., & Spearman, C. (1912). General ability, its existence and nature. *British Journal of Psychology, 5,* 51–84.

Hartigan, J, & Wigdor, A. (1989). Fairness in employment testing. *Science, 245,* 14.

Hartlage, L. C., & Steele, C. T. (1977). WISC and WISC-R correlates of academic achievement. *Psychology in the Schools, 14,* 15–18.

Hartman, D. E. (1986a). Artificial intelligence or artificial psychologists? Conceptual issues in clinical microcomputer use. *Professional Psychology: Research and Practice, 17,* 528–534.

Hartman, D. E. (1986b). On the use of clinical psychology software: Practical, legal, and ethical concerns. *Professional Psychology: Research and Practice, 17,* 473–475.

Hartmann, D. P. (1977). Considerations in the choice of interobserver reliability estimates. *Journal of Applied Behavior Analysis, 10,* 103–116.

Harty, H., Adkins, D. M., & Sherwood, R. D. (1984). Predictability of giftedness indentification indices for two recognized approaches to elementary school gifted education. *Journal of Educational Research, 77,* 337–342.

Hase, H. D., & Goldberg, L. R. (1967). Comparative validity of different strategies of constructing personality inventory scales. *Psychological Bulletin, 67,* 231–248.

Hathaway, S. R. (1947). A coding system for MMPI profiles. *Journal of Consulting Psychology, 11,* 334–337.

Hathaway, S. R., & McKinley, J. C. (1943). *Manual for the Minnesota Multiphasic Personality Inventory.* New York: Psychological Corporation.

Hathaway, S. R., & McKinley, J. C. (1967). *Minnesota Multiphasic Personality Inventory, revised manual.* New York: Psychological Corporation.

Hattie, J. (1980). Should creativity tests be administered under test-like conditions? An empirical study of three alternative conditions. *Journal of Educational Psychology, 72,* 87–98.

Hayes, F. B., & Martin, R. P. (1986). Effectiveness of the PPVT-R in the screening of young gifted children. *Journal of Psychoeducational Assessment, 4,* 27–33.

Haynes, S. N. (1990). Behavioral assessment of adults. In A. Goldstein & M. Hersen (eds.), *Handbook of psychological assessment* (2nd ed.), pp. 423–467. New York: Pergamon Press.

Haynes, S. N. (1991). Clinical application of psychophysiological assessment: An introduction. *Psychological Assessment: A Journal of Consulting and Clinical Psychology, 3,* 307–308.

Haynes, S. N. (in press, 1992). Behavioral assessment. In M. Hersen, A. Kazdin, & A. Bellack (eds.), *The clinical psychology handbook* (2nd ed.). New York: Pergamon Press.

Healy, W., & Fernald, G. M. (1911). Tests for practical mental classification. *Psychological Monographs, 13,* No. 2.

Hearst, E. (1979). One hundred years: Themes and perspectives. In E. Hearst (ed.), *The first century of experimental psychology.* Hillsdale, N.J.: Erlbaum.

Heaton, R. K., & Pendleton, M. G. (1981). Use of neuropsychological tests to predict adult patients' everyday functioning. *Journal of Consulting and Clinical Psychology, 49,* 807–821.

Hebb, D. O (1981). Reply irrelevant? *American Psychologist, 36,* 423–424.

Heider, F. (1944). Social perception and phenomenal causation. *Psychological Review, 51,* 358–374.

Heider, F. (1958). *The psychology of interpersonal relations.* New York: Wiley.

Heilbrun, A. B., Jr. (1972). Edwards Personal Preference Schedule. In O. K. Buros (ed.), *The seventh mental measurements yearbook* (vol. 1). Highland Park, N.J.: Gryphon Press.

Heimberg, R. C., Keller, K. E., & Peca-Baker, T. (1986). Cognitive assessment of social-evaluative anxiety in the job interview: Job Interview Self-Statement Schedule. *Journal of Counseling Psychology, 33,* 190–195.

Heitzmann, C. A., & Kaplan, R. M. (1988). Assessment of measures for measuring social support. *Health Psychology, 7,* 75–109.

Heller, K. (1971). Laboratory interview research as an analogue to treatment. In A. E. Bergin & S. L. Garfield (eds.), *Handbook of psychotherapy and behavior change.* New York: Wiley.

Heller, K., Davis, J. D., & Myers, R. A. (1966). The effects of interviewer style in a standardized interview. *Journal of Consulting Psychology, 30,* 501–508.

Henderson, N. B., Fay, W. H., Lindemann, S. J., & Clarkson, Q. D. (1973). Will the IQ test ban decrease the effectiveness of reading prediction? *Journal of Educational Psychology, 65,* 345–355.

Henrichs, T. (1964). Objective configural rules for discriminating MMPI profiles in a psychiatric population. *Journal of Clinical Psychology, 20,* 157–159.

Henry, P., & Bardo, H. R. (1990). Relationship between scores on developing cognitive abilities test and scores on medical college admissions test for nontraditional premedical students. *Psychological Reports, 67,* 55–63.

Henry, P., Bryson, S., & Henry, C. A (1990). Black student attitudes toward standardized tests. *College Student Journal, 23,* 346–354.

Herbert, W. (1982). Intelligence tests: Sizing up a newcomer. *Science News, 122,* 280–281.

Hernstein, R. J. (1981). Try again, Dr. Albee, *American Psychologist, 36,* 424–425.

Hernstein, R. J. (1982). IQ testing and the media. *Atlantic Monthly,* August, 68–74.

Herring, J. P. (1922). *Herring revision of the Binet-Simon tests.* Yonkers, N.Y.: World Book.

Hersen, M. (1971). Fear scale norms for an in-patient population. *Journal of Clinical Psychology, 27,* 375–378.

Hersen, M., Kazdin, A. E., & Bellack, A. S. (1991). *The clinical psychology handbook* (2nd ed.). New York: Pergamon Press.

Hersh, J. B. (1971). Effects of referral information on testers. *Journal of Consulting and Clinical Psychology, 37,* 116–122.

Hertz, M. R. (1937). Discussion on "Some recent Rorschach problems." *Rorschach Research Exchange, 2,* 53–65.

Hertz, M. R. (1938). Scoring the Rorschach inkblot test. *Journal of Genetic Psychology, 52,* 16–64.

Hertz, M. R. (1986). Rorschach bound: A 50-year memory. *Journal of Personality Assessment, 50,* 396–416.

Higgins, E. T., & Bargh, J. A. (1987). Social cognition and social perception. *Annual Review of Psychology, 38,* 369–425.

Hindley, C. B. (1965). Stability and change in abilities up to 5 years: Group trends. *Journal of Child Psychology and Psychiatry, 6,* 85–99.

Hiscock, M. (1978). Imagery assessment through self report: What do imagery questionnaires measure? *Journal of Consulting and Clinical Psychology, 46,* 223–230.

Hodges, K. (1985). *Manual for the child assessment schedule (CAS).* Unpublished manuscript, University of Missouri, Columbia.

Hodges, W., & Spielberger, C. (1969). Digit span: An indication of trait or state anxiety? *Journal of Consulting and Clinical Psychology, 33,* 430–434.

Hodos, W., & Campbell, C. B. G. (1969). Scala naturae: Why there is no theory in comparative psychology. *Psychological Review, 76,* 337–350.

Hofer, P. J., & Green, B. I (1985). The challenge of competence and creativity in computerized psychological testing. *Journal of Consulting and Clinical Psychology, 53,* 826–838.

Hoffman, H., Loper, R. G., & Kammeier, M. L. (1974). Identifying future alcoholics with MMPI alcoholism scales. *Quarterly Journal of Studies on Alcohol, 35,* 490–498.

Hogan, J., & Quigley, A. M. (1986). Physical standards for employment and the courts. *American Psychologist, 41,* 1193–1217.

Holahan, C. J. (1986). Environmental psychology. *Annual Review of Psychology, 37,* 381–407.

Holahan, C. J., & Moos, R. H. (1986). Personality, coping, and family support in stress resistance: A longitudinal analysis. *Journal of Personality and Social Psychology, 51,* 389–395.

Holland, J. L. (1975). *Manual for the Vocational Preference Inventory.* Palo Alto, Calif.: Consulting Psychologists Press.

Holland, J. L. (1985a). *Making vocational choices* (2nd ed.). Englewood Cliffs, N.J.: Prentice-Hall.

Holland, J. L. (1985b). *The self-directed search, professional manual.* Odessa, Fla.: Psychological Assessment Resources.

Holland, J. L., & Gottfredson, G. D. (1976). Using a typology of persons and environments to explain careers: Some extensions and clarifications. *Counseling Psychologist, 6,* 20–29.

Holland, J. L., & Nichols, R. C. (1964). Prediction of academic and extracurricular achievements in college. *Journal of Educational Psychology, 55,* 55–65.

Hollingworth, H. L. (1922). *Judging human character.* New York: Appleton-Century-Crofts.

Holmes, T. S., & Rahe, R. H. (1967). The Social Readjustment Rating Scale. *Journal of Psychosomatic Research, 11,* 213–218.

Holt, R. R. (1967). Diagnostic testing: Present status and future prospects. *Journal of Nervous and Mental Disease, 141,* 444–464.

Holt, R. R. (1970). Yet another look at clinical and statistical prediction: Or, is clinical psychology worthwhile? *American Psychologist, 25,* 337–349.

Holtzman, W. H., Thorpe, J. S.

Swartz, J. D., & Herron, E. W. (1961). *Inkblot perception and personality*. Austin: University of Texas Press.

Holzberg, J. D., & Belmont, L. (1952). The relationship between factors on the Wechsler-Bellevue and Rorschach having a common psychological rationale. *Journal of Consulting Psychology, 16*, 23–30.

Hooper, S. R., Conner, R. E., & Umansky, W. (1986). The Cattell Infant Intelligence Scale: A review of the literature. *Developmental Review, 6*, 146–164.

Horn, J. L., & Cattell, R. B. (1966). Refinement and test of the theory of fluid and crystallized intelligence. *Journal of Educational Psychology, 57*, 253–276.

Horowitz, M. J., & Wilner, N. (1980). Life events, stress, and coping. In L. Poon (ed.), *Aging in the eighties*. Washington, D.C.: American Psychological Association.

Hosey, G. M., Freeman, W. L., Stracqualursi, F., & Gohdes, D. (1990). Designing and evaluating diabetes education material for American Indians. *Diabetes Educator, 16*, 407–414.

Hotelling, H. (1933). Analysis of a complex statistical variable into principal components. *Journal of Educational Psychology, 24*, 417–441, 498–520.

Houldin, A. D., & Forbes, E. J. (1990). Nursing students' personalities as measured by the California Psychological Inventory: Participants vs nonparticipants in a program of research. *Psychological Reports, 67*, 1119–1122.

Howell, K. W. (1985). Review of the Watkins-Bender Gestalt Scoring System. In J. V. Mitchell (ed.), *The ninth edition mental measurements yearbook* (vol. 1). Highland Park, N.J.: Gryphon Press.

Hunt, E. (1980). Intelligence as an information-processing concept. *British Journal of Psychology, 71*, 449–474.

Hunt, T. V. (1978). Review of McCarthy Scales of Children's Abilities. In O. K. Buros (ed.), *The eighth mental measurements yearbook* (vol. 1). Highland Park, N.J.: Gryphon Press.

Hunter, J. E., & Hunter, R. F. (1984). Validity and utility of alternative predictors of job performance. *Psychological Bulletin, 96*, 72–98.

Hunter, J. E., & Schmidt, F. L (1976). Critical analysis of statistical and ethical implications of various definitions of test bias. *Psychological Bulletin, 83*, 1053–1071.

Hunter, J. E., & Schmidt, F. L. (1978). Bias in defining test bias: Reply to Darlington. *Psychological Bulletin, 85*, 675–676.

Hutchinson, T. A., Boyd, N. F., & Feinstein, A. R. (1979). Scientific problems in clinical scales as demonstrated in the Karnofsky Index of Performance Status. *Journal of Chronic Diseases, 32*, 309–312.

Hyde, L., Wolf, J., McCracken, S., & Yesner, R. (1973). Natural course of inoperable lung cancer. *Chest, 64*, 309–312.

Hynd, T. W., & Obrzut, J. E. (1981). *Neuropsychological assessment and the school-age child: Issues and procedures*. New York: Grune & Stratton.

Iacono, W. G. (1991). Psychophysiological assessment of psychopathology. *Psychological Assessment. A Journal of Consulting and Clinical Psychology, 3*, 309–320.

Imada, A. S., & Hakel, M. D. (1977). Influences of nonverbal communication and rater proximity on impressions and decisions in simulated employment interviews. *Journal of Applied Psychology, 62*, 295–300.

Ingram, R. E. (1980). *The GREs: Are we weighing them too heavily in graduate psychology admissions?* Unpublished manuscript. University of Kansas.

Insurance license exams will be revised. (1984, November 29). *Los Angeles Times*, Part I, p. 5.

Ironson, G. H., & Sebkovial, N. J. (1979). A comparison of several methods for assessing item bias. *Journal of Educational Measurement, 16*, 209–225.

Irwin, M., Daniels, M., Bloom, E. T., Smith, T. L., & Weiner, H. (1987). Life events, depressive symptoms, and immune function. *American Journal of Psychiatry, 144*, 437–441.

Jackson, D. N. (1967). *Personality Research Form Manual*. Goshen, N.Y.: Research Psychologists Press.

Jackson, D. N. (1970). A sequential system for personality scale development. In C. D. Spielberger (ed.), *Current topics in clinical and community psychology* (vol. 2). New York: Academic Press.

Jackson, D. N. (1976a). *Jackson Personality Inventory*. Goshen, N.Y.: Research Psychologists Press.

Jackson, D. N. (1976b). *Manual for the Jackson Personality Inventory*. Goshen, N.Y.: Research Psychologists Press.

Jackson, D. N., & Messick, S. (eds.) (1967). *Problems in human assessment*. New York: McGraw-Hill.

Jackson, E. W. (1980). Identification of gifted performance in young children. In W. C. Roedell, N. E. Jackson, & H. B. Robinson (eds.), *Gifted young children*. New York: Teachers College Press.

Jaffe, J. (1968). Computer assessment of dyadic interaction rules from chronographic data. In J. Shlien, H. Hunt, J. D. Matarazzo, & C. Savage (eds.), *Research in psychotherapy* (vol. 3). Washington, D.C.: American Psychological Association.

Jennings, J. R. (1986). Bodily changes during attention. In M. G. H. Coles, E. Donchin, & S. W. Porges (eds.), *Psychophysiology: Systems, processes, and applications*. New York: Guilford Press.

Jensen, A. R. (1965). Review of the Rorschach. In O. K. Buros (ed.), *The sixth mental measurements yearbook*. Highland Park, N.J.: Gryphon Press.

Jensen, A. R. (1969). How much can we boost IQ and scholastic achievement? *Harvard Educational Review, 39*, 1–23.

Jensen, A. R. (1972). *Genetics and education*. New York: Harper & Row.

Jensen, A. R. (1979). g—Outmoded theory or unconquered frontier? *Creative Science and Technology, 2* 16–29.

Jensen, A. R. (1980). *Bias in mental testing*. New York: Free Press.

Jensen, A. R. (1982). Reaction time and psychometric "g." In H. J. Eysenck (ed.), *A model for intelligence*. New York: Springer-Verlag.

Jensen, A. R. (1984). The Black-White difference on the K-ABC: Implication for future tests. *Journal of Special Education, 18,* 377–408.

Jensen, A. R. (1985). The nature of black-white differences on various psychometric tests: Spearman's hypothesis. *The Behavioral and Brain Sciences, 8,* 193–263.

Jensen, A. R. (1986). The "g" beyond factor analysis. In J. C. Conoley, J. A. Glover, & R. R. Ronnings (eds.), *The influence of cognitive psychology on testing and measurement*. Hillsdale, N.J.: Erlbaum.

Jensen, A. R. (1991). Spearman G and the problem of educational equality. *Oxford Review of Education, 17,* 169–187.

Jensen, A. R., & Munro, E. (1979). Reaction time, movement time, and intelligence. *Intelligence, 3,* 121–126.

Johansson, C. B. (1976). *Manual for the Career Assessment Inventory*. Minneapolis, Minn.: National Computer Systems.

Johansson, C. B., & Johansson, J. C. (1978). *Manual supplement for the Career Assessment Inventory*. Minneapolis, Minn.: National Computer Systems.

Johansson, G., Johnson, J. V., & Hall, E. M. (1991). Smoking and sedentary behavior as related to work organization. *Social Science and Medicine, 32*(7), 837–846..

Johnson, J. G., & Bornstein, B. F. (1991). Does daily stress independently predict psychopathology? *Journal of Social and Clinical Psychology, 10,* 58–74.

Jones, E. E., & Nisbett, R. E. (1971). *The actor and observer: Divergent perceptions of the causes of behavior*. Morristown, N.J: General Learning Press.

Jones, R. A. (1968). *A factored measure of Ellis' irrational belief system with personality and maladjustment correlates*. Unpublished doctoral dissertation, Texas Technological College.

Jung, C. G. (1910). The association method. *American Journal of Psychology, 21,* 219–269.

Kagan, J., Moss, H. A., & Siegel, I. E. (1963). Psychological significance of styles of conceptualization. *Monographs of the Society for Research in Child Development, 28* (2, Serial No. 86), 73–124.

Kaiser, H. F. (1958). A modified stanine scale. *Journal of Experimental Education, 26,* 261.

Kallingal, A. (1971). The prediction of grades for Black and White students at Michigan State University. *Journal of Educational Measurement, 8,* 263–265.

Kamhi, A. G., Minor, J. S., & Mauer, D. (1990). Content analysis and intratest performance profiles on the Columbia and the TONI. *Journal of Speech and Hearing Research, 33,* 375–379.

Kamin, L. J. (1974). *The science and politics of IQ*. Hillsdale, N.J.: Erlbaum.

Kammeier, M. L., Hoffman, H., & Loper, R. G. (1973). Personality characteristics of alcoholics as college freshmen and at time of treatment. *Quarterly Journal of Studies on Alcohol, 34,* 390–399.

Kamphaus, R. W., & Reynolds, C. R. (1984). Development and structure of the Kaufman Assessment Battery for Children. *The Journal of Special Education, 18*(3), 213–228.

Kanfer, F. H., & Saslow, G. (1969). Behavioral diagnosis. In C. M. Franks (ed.), *Behavior therapy: Appraisal and status*. New York: McGraw-Hill.

Kanner, A. D., Coyne, J. C., Schaeffer, C., & Lazarus, R. S. (1981). Comparison of two modes of stress measurement: Daily hassles and uplifts versus major life events. *Journal of Behavioral Medicine, 4,* 1–39.

Kaplan, O. J. (1979). Psychological testing in seniles. In O. J. Kaplan (ed.), *Psychopathology and aging*. New York: Academic Press.

Kaplan, R. M. (1973). Components of trust: Note on use of Rotter's scale. *Psychological Reports, 33,* 13–14.

Kaplan, R. M. (1982). Nader's raid on the Educational Testing Service: Is it in the best interest of the consumer? *American Psychologist, 37,* 15–23.

Kaplan, R. M. (1984). The connection between clinical health promotion and health status: A critical overview. *American Psychologist, 39,* 755–765.

Kaplan, R. M. (1985). The controversy related to the use of psychological tests. In B. B. Wolman (ed.), *Handbook of Intelligence: Theories, measurements, and applications*. New York: Wiley.

Kaplan, R. M. (1987). Basic statistics for the behavioral sciences. Newton, Mass.: Allyn and Bacon.

Kaplan, R. M. (1988a). New health promotion indicators: The general health policy model. *Health Promotion, 3,* 35–49.

Kaplan, R. M. (1988b). The value dimension in studies of health promotion. In S. Spacapan & S. Oskamp (eds.), *The Social Psychology of Health*. Beverly Hills: Sage.

Kaplan, R. M. (1990). Behavior as the central outcome in health care. *American Psychologist, 45,* 1211–1220.

Kaplan, R. M. (1992). A quality-of-life approach to health resource allocation. In M. A. Strosberg, J. M. Wiener, R. Baker & I. A. Fein (eds.), *Rationing America's medical care: The Oregon plan and beyond*. Washington, D.C.: The Brookings Institution.

Kaplan, R. M. (1993). *The hippocratic predicament*. San Diego: Academic Press.

Kaplan, R. M., & Anderson, J. P. (1990). The general health policy model: An integrated approach. In B. Spilker (ed.), *Quality of life assessments in clinical trials*. New York: Raven Press, pp. 131–149.

Kaplan, R. M., Anderson, J. P., Wu, A. W., Mathews, W. C., Kozin, F., & Orenstein, D. (1989). The quality of well-being scale: Applications in AIDS, cystic fibrosis, and arthritis. *Medical Care, 27*(Suppl 3), S27–S43.

Kaplan, R. M., & Ernst, J. (1983). Do category rating scales produce biased preference weights for a health index? *Medical Care, 21*, 193–207.

Kaplan, R. M., & Toshima, M. T. (1992). Does a reduced fat diet cause retardation in child growth? *Preventive Medicine, 21*, 33–52.

Kaplan, R. M., Atkins, C. J., & Timms, R. M. (1984). Validity of a quality of well-being scale as an outcome measure in chronic obstructive pulmonary disease. *Journal of Chronic Diseases, 37*, 85–95.

Kaplan, R. M., Bush, J. W., & Berry, C. C. (1976). Health status: Types of validity for an index of well-being. *Health Services Research, 11*, 478–507.

Kaplan, R. M., Hartwell, S. H., Wilson, D. K., & Wallace, J. P. (1987). Effects of diet and exercise interventions upon control and quality of life in non-insulin-dependent diabetes mellitus. *Journal of General Internal Medicine, 2*, 220–228.

Kaplan, R. M., McCordick, S., & Twitchell, M. (1979). Is it the cognitive or the behavioral component which makes cognitive behavior modification effective in test anxiety? *Journal of Counseling Psychology, 26*, 371–377.

Kaszniak, A. W. (1986). The neuropsychology of dementia. In I. Grant & K. M. Adams (eds.), *Neuropsychological assessment of neuropsychiatric disorders*. New York: Oxford University Press.

Katz, S. T., Downs, H., Cash, H., & Grotz, R. (1970). Progress and development of an index of EDL. *Gerontologist, 10*, 20–30.

Katz, S. T., Ford, A. D., Moskowitz, R. W., Jackson, B. A., & Jaffe, M. W. (1963). Studies of illness in the aged: The index of ADL. *Journal of the American Medical Association, 185*, 914–919.

Kaufman, A. S. (1975). Factor structure of the McCarthy Scales of Children's Abilities. *Educational and Psychological Measurement, 35*, 641–656.

Kaufman, A. S. (1978). Review of Columbia Mental Maturity Scale. In O. K. Buros (ed.), *The eighth mental measurements yearbook* (vol. 1). Highland Park, N.J.: Gryphon Press.

Kaufman, A. S. (1984). K-ABC and controversy. *The Journal of Special Education, 18*(3), 409–444.

Kaufman, A. S., & Kaufman, N. L. (1983a). *K-ABC administration and scoring manual*. Circle Pines, Minn.: American Guidance Service.

Kaufman, A. S., & Kaufman, N. L. (1983b). *K-ABC interpretive manual*. Circle Pines, Minn.: American Guidance Service.

Kaufman, A. S., Kaufman, R. W., & Kaufman, N. L. (1985). The Kaufman Assessment Battery for Children (K-ABC). In C. S. Newmark (ed.), *Major psychological assessment instruments*. Newton, Mass.: Allyn and Bacon.

Kazdin, A. E. (1977). Artifact, bias, and complexity of assessment: The ABC's of reliability. *Journal of Applied Behavior Analysis, 10*, 141–150.

Keir, G. (1949). The Progressive Matrices as applied to school children. *British Journal of Psychology* (statistical section 2), 140–150.

Keiser, R. E., & Prather, E. N. (1990). What is the TAT? A review of ten years of research. *Journal of Personality Assessment, 55*, 800–803.

Kelley, T. L (1927). *Interpretation of educational measurements*. Yonkers, N.Y.: World Book.

Kelly, E. L (1972). Personality Research Form. In O. K. Buros (ed.), *The seventh mental measurements yearbook* (vol. 1). Highland Park, N.J.: Gryphon Press.

Kelly, H. H. (1967). Attribution theory in social psychology. In D. Levine (ed.), *Nebraska Symposium on Motivation*. Lincoln: University of Nebraska Press.

Kendall, P. C., & Korgeski, G. P. (1979). Assessment and cognitive-behavioral interventions. *Cognitive Therapy and Research, 1*, 1–21.

Kendall, P. C., Williams, S., Pechacek, T. F., Graham, L. G., Shisslak, C. S., & Herzoff, N. (1979). Cognitive-behavioral and patient education interventions in cardiac catheterization procedures: The Palo Alto medical psychology project. *Journal of Consulting and Clinical Psychology, 47*, 49–58.

Kennedy, R. S., Baltzley, D. R., Turnage, J. J., & Jones, M. B. (1989). Factor analysis and predictive validity of microcomputer-based tests. *Perceptual and Motor Skills, 69*, 1059–1074.

Kennedy, W. A., Van de Riet, V., & White, J. C., Jr. (1963). A normative sample of intelligence and achievement of Negro elementary school children in the Southeast United States. *Monographs of the Society for Research in Child Development, 28*(6, Serial No. 90).

Kent, G. H., & Rosanoff, A. J. (1910). A study of association in insanity. *American Journal of Insanity, 67*, 37–96, 317–390.

Kent, R. N., Kanowitz, J., O'Leary, K. D., & Cheiken, M. (1977). Observer reliability as a function of circumstances of assessment. *Journal of Applied Behavior Analysis, 10*, 317–324.

Kent, R. N., O'Leary, K. D., Diament, C., & Dietz, A. (1974). Expectation biases in observational evaluation of therapeutic change. *Journal of*

Consulting and Clinical Psychology, 42, 774–780.

Kerner, J. (1857). Klexographien (Pt. VI). In R. Pissin (ed.), *Kerners Werke*. Berlin: Bong.

Keyser, D. J., & Sweetland, R. C. (eds.) (1985). *Test critiques* (vol. 1). Kansas City, Mo.: Test Corporation of America.

Kiersh, E. (1979). Testing is the name, power is the game. *The Village Voice*, January 15.

Kirkpatrick, E. A. (1900). Individual tests of school children. *Psychological Review, 7*, 274–280.

Kline, R. B. (1989). Is the Fourth Edition Stanford-Binet a four-factor test? Confirmatory factor analyses of alternative methods for ages 2 through 23. *Journal of Psychoeducational Assessment, 7*, 4–13.

Klinger, E. (1978). Modes of normal conscious flow. In K. S. Pope & J. L. Singer (eds.), *The stream of consciousness: Scientific investigations into the flow of human experience*. New York: Plenum.

Klinger, E., Barta, S., & Mahoney, T. (1976). Motivation, mood, and mental events: Patterns and implications for adaptive processes. In G. Serban (ed.), *Psychopathology of human adaptation*. New York: Plenum.

Klopfer, B., & Davidson, H. H. (1944). Form level rating: A preliminary proposal for appraising mode and level of thinking as expressed in Rorschach records. *Rorschach Research Exchange, 8*, 164–177.

Klopfer, B., & Kelley, D. (1942). *The Rorschach technique*. Yonkers, N.Y.: World Book.

Knobloch, H., & Pasamanick, B. (1974). *Gesell and Amatruda's developmental diagnosis: The evaluation and management of normal and abnormal neuropsychologic development in infancy and early childhood* (3rd ed.). New York: Harper & Row.

Knotek, P. C., Bayles, K. A., & Kaszniak, A. W. (1990). Response consistency on a semantic memory task in persons with dementia of the Alzheimer type.

Brain and Language, 38, 465–475.

Knox, H. A. (1914). A scale based on the work at Ellis Island for estimating mental defect. *Journal of the American Medical Association, 62*, 741–747.

Knutson, J. F. (1972). Review of the Rorschach. In O. K. Buros (ed.), *The seventh mental measurements yearbook* (vol. 1). Highland Park, N.J.: Gryphon Press.

Kohs, S. C. (1923). *Intelligence measurement: A psychological and statistical study based upon the block-design tests*. New York: Macmillan.

Koksal, F., & Power, K. G. (1990). Four Systems Anxiety Questionnaire (FSAQ): A self-report measure of somatic, cognitive, behavioral, and feeling components. *Journal of Personality Assessment, 54*, 534–545.

Koller, P. S., & Kaplan, R. M. (1978). A two-process theory of learned helplessness. *Journal of Personality and Social Psychology, 36*, 1077–1083.

Komaroff, A. L., Masuda, M., & Holmes, T. H. (1968). The Social Readjustment Rating Scale: A comparative study of Negro, Mexican, and White Americans. *Journal of Psychosomatic Research, 12*, 121.

Koppitz, E. M. (1964). *The Bender Gestalt test for young children*. New York: Grune & Stratton.

Kraepelin, E. (1912). *Lehrbuch der psychiatrie*. Leipzig: Barth.

Kraiger, K., Hakel, M. D., & Cornelius, E. T., III. (1984). Exploring fantasies of TAT reliability. *Journal of Personality Assessment, 48*, 365–370.

Krinsky, S. G. (1990). The feeling of knowing in deaf adolescents. *American Annals of the Deaf, 135*, 389–395.

Kuder, G. F. (1979). *Manual, Kuder Occupational Interest Survey, 1979 revision*. Chicago: Science Research Associates.

Kuder, G. F., & Richardson, M. W. (1937). The theory of the estimation of reliability. *Psychometrika, 2*, 151–160.

Kuhlmann, F. (1912). A revision

of the Binet-Simon system for measuring intelligence of children. *Journal of Psycho-Asthenics Monograph Supplement, 1*(1), 1–41.

Kuhlmann, F. (1922). *A handbook of mental tests*. Baltimore, Md.: Warwick & York.

Kusyszyn, I. (1968). Comparison of judgmental methods with endorsements in the assessment of personality traits. *Journal of Applied Psychology, 52*, 227–233.

Lakotis, L. (1987). *Quality of life and depression for patients undergoing gastric restriction surgery*. Unpublished master's thesis, San Diego State University.

Lally, M., & Nettelbeck, T. (1977). Intelligence, reaction time, and inspection time. *American Journal of Mental Deficiency, 82*, 273–281.

Lamp, R. E., & Traxler, A. J. (1973). The validity of the Slosson Intelligence Test for use with disadvantaged Head Start and first grade children. *Journal of Community Psychology, 1*, 27–30.

Landis, C. (1936). Questionnaires and the study of personality. *Journal of Nervous and Mental Disease, 83*, 125–134.

Landis, C., Zubin, J., & Katz, S. E. (1935). Empirical evaluation of three personality adjustment inventories. *Journal of Educational Psychology, 26*, 321–330.

Landy, F. J. (1986). Stamp collecting versus science: Validation as hypothesis testing. *American Psychologist, 41*, 183–192.

Landy, F. J., Farr, J. L., & Jacobs, J. W. (1982). Utility concepts in performance measurement. *Organizational Behavior and Human Performance, 30*, 15–40.

Landy, F. J., Vance, R. J., Barnes-Farrell, J. L., & Steele, J. W. (1980). Statistical control of halo error in performance ratings. *Journal of Applied Psychology, 65*, 501–506.

Lang, P. J., & Lazovik, A. D. (1963). Experimental desensitization of a phobia. *Journal of Abnormal and Social Psychology, 66*, 519–525.

Lanyon, B. P., & Lanyon, R. I. (1980). *Incomplete Sentences Task: Manual.* Chicago: Stoelting.

Larrabee, L. L., & Kleinsaser, L. D. (1967). *The effect of experimenter bias on WISC performance.* Unpublished manuscript. St. Louis, Mo.: Psychological Associates.

Latham, V. M. (1987). Interviewee training: A review of some empirical literature. *Journal of Career Development, 14,* 96–107.

Lautenschlager, G. J., and Flaherty, V. L. (1990). Computer administration of questions: More desirable or more social desirability? *Journal of Applied Psychology, 75,* 310–314.

Lawlis, G. F. (1971). Response styles of a patient population on the Fear Survey Schedule. *Behaviour Research and Therapy, 9,* 95–102.

Lawshe, C. L. (1985). Inferences from personnel tests and their validities. *Journal of Applied Psychology, 70,* 237–238.

Lazarus, R. S., & Folkman, S. (1984). *Stress, appraisal, and coping.* New York: Springer-Verlag.

Lazarus, R. S., Delongis, A., Folkman, S., & Gruen, A. (1985). Stress and adaptational outcomes: The problem of confounded measures. *American Psychologist, 40,* 770–779.

Lee, J. A., Moreno, K. E., & Sympson, J. B. (1986). The effects of mode of test administration on test performance. *Educational and Psychological Measurement, 46,* 467–473.

Lefever, D. W. (1959). Review of the Henmon-Nelson Test of Mental Ability, revised edition. In O. K. Buros (ed.), *The fifth mental measurements yearbook.* Highland Park, N. J.: Gryphon Press.

Leichsenring, F. (1990). Discriminating borderline from neurotic patients: A study with the Holtzman Inkblot Technique. *Psychopathology, 23,* 21–26.

Leichsenring, F. (1991). Primary process thinking, primitive defensive operations and object relations in borderline and neurotic patients. *Psychopathology, 24,* 39–44.

Lerner, B. (1979). Tests and standards today: Attacks, counterattacks, and responses. *New Directions in Testing and Measurement, 1*(3), 15–31.

Lerner, B. (1981). The minimum competence testing movement: Social, scientific, and legal implications. *American Psychologist, 36,* 1057–1066.

Lesser, G. S., Fifer, G., & Clark, D. H. (1965). Mental abilities of children from different social-class and cultural groups. *Monographs of the Society for Research in Child Development, 30* (4, Serial No. 102).

Levenson, H., Olkin, R., Herzoff, N., & DeLancy, M. (1986). MMPI evaluation of erectile dysfunction: Failure of organic vs. psychogenic decision rules. *Journal of Clinical Psychology, 42,* 752–754.

Levin, H. S., Benton, A. L., Fletcher, J. N., & Satz, P. (1989). Neuropsychological and intellectual assessment of adults. In H. I. Kaplan & B. J. Sadock (eds.), *Comprehensive textbook of psychiatry, fifth edition, volume 1,* pp. 496–512.

Levy, S. (1979). E.T.S. and the "coaching" cover-up. *New Jersey Monthly, 3*(5), 4–7.

Lewandowski, D. G., & Saccuzzo, D. P. (1975). Possible differential WISC patterns for retarded delinquents. *Psychological Reports, 37,* 887–894.

Lewandowski, D. G., & Saccuzzo, D. P. (1976). The decline of psychological testing: Have traditional procedures been fairly evaluated? *Professional Psychology, 7,* 177–184.

Lewinsohn, P. N., & Teri, L. (1982). Selection of depressed and non-depressed subjects on the basis of self-report data. *Journal of Consulting and Clinical Psychology, 50,* 590–591.

Lezak, M. D. (1976). *Neuropsychological assessment.* New York: Oxford University Press.

Lezak, M. D. (1983). *Neuropsychological assessment* (2nd ed.). New York: Oxford University Press.

Liebert, R. M., & Morris, L. W. (1967). Cognitive and emotional components of test anxiety: A distinction and some initial data. *Psychological Reports, 20,* 975–978.

Likert, R. (1932). A technique for the measurement of attitudes. *Archives of Psychology,* No. 40.

Lindgren, S., Harper, D. C., Richman, L. C., & Stehbens, J. A. (1986). "Mental imbalance" and the prediction of recurrent delinquent behavior. *Journal of Clinical Psychology, 42,* 821–825.

Lindzey, G. (1952). The Thematic Apperception Test: Interpretive assumptions and related empirical evidence. *Psychological Bulletin, 49,* 1–25.

Linn, R. L. (1980). Test design and analysis for measurement of educational achievement. *New Directions for Testing and Measurement, 5,* 81–92.

Lipsitz, S. (1969). *Effect of the race of the examiner on results of intelligence test performance of Negro and White children.* Unpublished master's thesis, Long Island University.

Liss, P. H., & Haith, M. M. (1970). The speed of visual processing in children and adults: Effects of backward and forward masking. *Perception and Psychophysics, 8,* 396–398.

Little, K. B., & Shneidman, E. S. (1959). Congruencies among interpretations of psychological test and anamnestic data. *Psychological Monographs, 73*(6, Whole No. 476).

Litz, B. T., Penk, W. E., Walsh, S., Hyer, L., Blake, D. D., Marx, B., Keane, T. M., & Bitman, D. (1991). Similarities and differences between Minnesota Multiphasic Personality Inventory (MMPI) and MMPI-2: Applications to the assessment of post-traumatic steps disorder. *Journal of Personality Assessment, 57,* 238–253.

LoBello, S. G., & Gulgoz, S. (1991). Factor analysis of the Wechsler Preschool and Primary

Scale of Intelligence-Revised. *Psychological Assessment: A Journal of Consulting and Clinical Psychology, 3*, 130–132.

Loftus, E. F. (1991). The glitter of everyday memory . . . and the gold. *American Psychologist, 46*, 19–26.

Lohr, J. M., & Bonge, D. (1982). The factorial validity of the Irrational Beliefs Test: A psychometric investigation. *Cognitive Therapy and Research, 6*, 225–230.

Long, P. A., & Anthony, J. J. (1974). The measurement of retardation by a culture-specific test. *Psychology in the Schools, 11*, 310–312.

Loper, R. G., Kammeier, M. L., & Hoffman, H. (1973). MMPI characteristics of college freshman males who later became alcoholics. *Journal of Abnormal Psychology, 82*, 159–162.

Lord, E. (1950). Experimentally induced variations in Rorschach performance. *Psychological Monographs, 64* (10, Whole No. 316).

Lord, F. M. (1950). *Efficiency of prediction when a regression equation from one sample is used in a new sample* (Research Bulletin 50-40). Princeton, N.J.: Educational Testing Service.

Lord, F. M. (1978). *A prediction interval for scores on a parallel test form* (Research Bulletin RB-78-5). Princeton, N.J.: Educational Testing Service.

Lotsoff, E. (1953). Intelligence, verbal fluency and the Rorschach test. *Journal of Consulting Psychology, 17*, 21–24.

Loughmiller, G. C., Ellison, R. L., Taylor, C. W., & Price, P. B. (1970). Predicting career performances of physicians using the biographical inventory approach. *Proceedings of the American Psychological Association, 5*, 153–154.

Lowman, R. L. (1991). *The clinical practice of career assessment.* Washington, D.C.: American Psychological Association.

Loy, D. L. (1959). The validity of the Taulbee-Sisson MMPI scale pairs in female psychiatric groups. *Journal of Clinical Psychology, 15*, 306–307.

Lubin, B., Larsen, R., & Matarazzo, J. (1984). Patterns of psychological test usage in the United States: 1935–1982. *American Psychologist, 39*, 451–454.

Lubin, B., Larsen, R. M., Matarazzo, J. D., & Seever, M. (1985). Psychological test usage patterns in five professional settings. *American Psychologist, 40*, 857–861.

Lubin, B., Wallis, H. R., & Paine, C. (1971). Patterns of psychological test usage in the United States: 1935–1969. *Professional Psychology, 2*, 70–74.

Lubin, B. L. (1965). Adjective checklists for measurement of depression. *Archives of General Psychiatry, 12*, 57–62.

Lumsden, J. (1978). Review of Illinois Test of Psycholinguistic Abilities. In O. K. Buros (ed.), *The eighth mental measurements yearbook* (vol. 1). Highland Park, N.J.: Gryphon Press.

Lunemann, A. (1974). The correlational validity of I.Q. as a function of ethnicity and desegregation. *Journal of School Psychology, 12*, 263–268.

Lunneborg, C. (1978). Some information-processing correlates of measures of intelligence. *Multivariate Behavioral Research, 13*, 153–161.

Luria, A. R. (1966). *Higher cortical functions in man.* New York: Basic Books.

Luria, A. R. (1973). *The working brain.* New York: Basic Books.

Lyman, B., Hatlelid, D., & Macundy, C. (1981). Stimulus-person cues in first-impression attraction. *Perceptual and Motor Skills, 52*, 59–66.

Machover, K. (1949). *Personality projection in the drawings of the human figure: A method of personality investigation.* Springfield, Ill.: Thomas.

MacKinnon, R. A. (1980). Psychiatric interview. In H. I. Kaplan, A. M. Freedman, & B. J. Sadock (eds.), *Comprehensive textbook for psychiatry, Vol III.* Baltimore: Williams & Wilkins.

MacKinnon, R. A., & Michels, R. (1971). *The psychiatric interview in clinical practice.* Philadelphia: Saunders.

Mackintosh, N. J. (1981). A new measure of intelligence. *Nature, 289* (No. 5798), 529–530.

Magnusson, D., & Endler, N. S. (1977). Interactional psychology: Present status and future prospects. In D. Magnusson & N. S. Endler (eds.), *Personality at the crossroads: Current issues in interactional psychology.* Hillsdale, N.J.: Erlbaum.

Mahoney, M. J. (1974). *Cognition and behavior modification.* Cambridge, Mass.: Ballinger.

Maisto, S. A., McKay, J. R., & Connors, G. J. (1990). Self-report issues in substance abuse: State of the art and future directions. *Behavioral Assessment, 12*, 117–134.

Majovski, L. V. (1984). The K-ABC: Theory and implications for child neuropsychological assessment and research. *The Journal of Special Education, 18*(3), 257–268.

Malgady, R., Barcher, P. R., Davis, J., & Towner, G. (1980). Validity of the vocational adaptation rating scale: Prediction of mentally retarded workers' placement in sheltered workshops. *American Journal of Mental Deficiency, 84*, 633–640.

Maloney, M. P., & Ward, M. P. (1976). *Psychological assessment: A conceptual approach.* New York: Oxford University Press.

Mandes, E., & Gessner, T. (1988). Differential effects on verbal-performance achievement levels on the WAIS-R as a function of progressive error rate on the Memory for Designs Test (MFD). *Journal of Clinical Psychology, 44*, 795–798.

Mandler, G., & Sarason, S. B. (1952). A study of anxiety and learning. *Journal of Abnormal and Social Psychology, 47*, 166–173.

Mannheim, K. (1936). *Ideology and utopia.* London: Kegan, Paul, Trench, Trubner.

Marchall et al. v. Georgia. US District Court for the Southern

District of Georgia, CV482-233, June 28, 1984, Affd (11th cir no 84-8771), Oct. 29, 1985.

Marlett, N. J., & Watson, D. (1968). Test anxiety and immediate or delayed feedback in a test-avoidance task. *Journal of Personality and Social Psychology, 8,* 200–203.

Marshalek, B., Lohman, D. F., & Snow, R. E. (1983). The complexity continuum in the Radex and hierarchical models of intelligence. *Journal of Intelligence, 7,* 107–127.

Mask, N., & Brown, C. E. (1984). Comparison of the WISC-R and the Leiter International Performance Scale with average and above-average students. *Journal of Clinical Psychology, 40,* 303–305.

Masters, B. N. (1988). Item discrimination: One more is worse. *Journal of Educational Measurement 25,* 15–29.

Masters, W., & Johnson, V. (1966). *Human sexual response.* Boston: Little, Brown.

Matarazzo, J. D. (1972). *Wechsler's measurement and appraisal of adult intelligence* (5th ed.). Baltimore: Williams & Wilkins.

Matarazzo, J. D. (1986). Computerized clinical psychological test interpretations: Unvalidated plus all mean and no sigma. *American Psychologist, 41,* 14–24.

Matarazzo, J. D. (1990). Psychological assessment versus psychological testing: Validation from Binet to the school, clinic, and court room. *American Psychologist, 45,* 999–1017.

Matarazzo, J. D. (1991). Psychological assessment is reliable and valid: Reply to Ziskin and Faust. *American Psychologist, 46,* 882–884.

Matarazzo, J. D., & Herman, D. O. (1984). Relationship of education and IQ in the standardization sample. *Journal of Consulting and Clinical Psychology 52,* 631–634.

Matarazzo, J. D., & Wiens, A. N. (1972). *The interview: Research on its anatomy and structure.* Chicago: Aldine-Atherton.

Matarazzo, J. D., Wiens, A. N.,

Matarazzo, R. G., & Saslow, G. (1968). Speech and silence behavior in clinical psychotherapy and its laboratory correlates. In J. Shlien, H. Hunt, J. D. Matarazzo, & C. Savage (eds.), *Research in psychotherapy* (vol. 3). Washington, D.C.: American Psychological Association.

Matias, R., & Turner, S. M. (1986). Concordance and discordance in speech anxiety assessment. The effects of demand characteristics on the tripartite assessment method. *Behavior Research & Therapy, 24,* 537–545.

Maurer, T. J., & Alexander, R. A. (1991). Contrast effects in behavioral measurement: An investigation of alternative process explanations. *Journal of Applied Psychology, 76,* 3–10.

Mayfield, E. C. (1964). The selection interview: A re-evaluation of published research. *Personnel Psychology, 17,* 239–260.

Mayman, M., & Kutner, B. (1947). Reliability in analyzing TAT stories. *Journal of Abnormal and Social Psychology, 42,* 365–368.

McCall, R. (1980). *Fundamental statistics for psychology* (3rd ed.). New York: Harcourt Brace Jovanovich.

McCall, R. B. (1979). The development of intellectual functioning in infancy and the prediction of later IQ. In J. D. Osofsky (ed.), *Handbook of infant development.* New York: Wiley.

McCall, R. B., Hogarty, P. S., & Hurlburt, N. (1972). Transitions in infant sensorimotor development and the prediction of childhood IQ. *American Psychologist, 27,* 728–748.

McCall, W. A. (1939). *Measurement.* New York: Macmillan.

McCallum, R. S. (1990). Determining the factor structure of the Stanford-Binet: Fourth Edition—the right choice. *Journal of Psychoeducational Assessment, 8,* 436–442.

McCallum, R. S., & Karnes, F. (1987). Comparison of intelligence tests: Responses of gifted pupils to the Stanford-Binet

Intelligence Scale (4th ed.), the British Ability Scales, and the Wechsler Intelligence Scale for Children-Revised. *School Psychology International, 8,* 133–139.

McCandless, B. B. (1949). The Rorschach as a predictor of academic success. *Journal of Applied Psychology, 33,* 43–50.

McClelland, D. C. (1951a). Measuring motivation in phantasy: The achievement motive. In H. Guetzkow (ed.), *Groups, leadership, and men.* Pittsburgh, Pa.: Carnegie University Press.

McClelland, D. C. (1951b). *Personality.* New York: William Sloane Associates.

McClelland, D. C. (1958). Methods of measuring human motivation. In J. W. Atkinson (ed.), *Motives in fantasy, action, and society.* New York: Van Nostrand Reinhold.

McClelland, D. C. (1985). How motives, skills, and values determine what people do. *American Psychologist, 40,* 812–825.

McClelland, D. C., Atkinson, J. W., Clark, R. A., & Lowell, E. L (1953). *The achievement motive.* New York: Appleton-Century-Crofts.

McCordick, S., Kaplan, R. M., Smith, S., & Finn, M. B. (1981). Variations in cognitive behavior modification for test anxiety. *Psychotherapy: Theory, Research & Practice, 18,* 170–178.

McCormick, E. J., & Ilgen, D. (1980). *Industrial psychology* (7th ed.). Englewood Cliffs, N.J.: Prentice-Hall.

McDaniel, M. A. (1989). Biographical constructs for predicting employee suitability. *Journal of Applied Psychology, 74,* 964–970.

McEwen, J. (1992). The Nottingham Health Profile. In S. R. Walker & R. M. Rosser (eds.), *Quality of life assessment: Key issues for the 1990s.* Dordreht, The Netherlands: Kluwer Academic Publishers.

McFall, R. M., & Lillesand, D. B. (1971). Behavior rehearsal with modeling and coaching in assertion training. *Journal of Abnormal Psychology, 77,* 313–323.

McFall, R. M., & McDonell, A. (1986). The continuous search for units of analysis in psychology: Beyond persons, situations, and their interactions. In R. O. Nelson & S. C. Hays (eds.), *Conceptual foundations of behavioral assessment.* New York: Guilford Press.

McGivern, R. F., Berka, C., Langlais, M. L., & Chapman, S. (1991). Detection of deficits in temporal pattern discrimination using the seashore rhythm test in young children with reading impairments. *Journal of Learning Disabilities, 24,* 58–62.

McGrath, R. E., & O'Malley, W. B. (1986). The assessment of denial and physical complaints: The validity of the HY Scale and associated MMPI signs. *Journal of Clinical Psychology, 42,* 754–760.

McLarty, J. R., Noble, A. C., & Huntley, R. M. (1989). Effects of item wording on sex bias. *Journal of Educational Measurement, 26,* 285–293.

McMahon, R. C., Davidson, R. S., Gersh, D., & Flynn, P. (1991). A comparison of continuous and episodic drinkers using the MCMI, MMPI, and ALCEVAL-R. *Journal of Clinical Psychology, 47,* 148–159.

McMichael, A. J., Baghurst, P. A., Wigg, N. R., Vimpani, G. V., Robertson, E. F., & Roberts, R. J. (1988). Port Pirie Cohort Study: Environmental exposure to lead and children's abilities at the age of four years. *New England Journal of Medicine, 319,* 468–475.

McNemar, O. W., & Landis, C. (1935). Childhood disease and emotional maturity in the psychopathic woman. *Journal of Abnormal and Social Psychology, 30,* 314–319.

McNemar, Q. (1942). *The revision of the Stanford-Binet scale.* Boston: Houghton Mifflin.

McNemar, Q. (1969). *Psychological statistics* (4th ed.). New York: Wiley.

Meehl, P. E. (1951). *Research results for counselors.* St. Paul, Minn.: State Department of Education.

Meehl, P. E. (1954). *Clinical versus statistical prediction: A theoretical analysis and a review of the evidence.* Minneapolis: University of Minnesota Press.

Meehl, P. E. (1956). Wanted—a good cookbook. *American Psychologist, 11,* 263–272.

Meehl, P. E. (1957). When shall we use our heads instead of the formula? *Journal of Counseling Psychology, 4,* 268–273.

Meehl, P. E., & Dahlstrom, W. G. (1960). Objective configural rules for discriminating psychotic from neurotic MMPI profiles. *Journal of Consulting Psychology, 24,* 375–387.

Meehl, P. E., & Rosen, A. (1955). Antecedent probability and the efficiency of psychometric signs, patterns or cutting scores. *Psychological Bulletin, 52,* 194–216.

Megargee, E. I. (1972). *The California Psychological Inventory Handbook.* San Francisco: Jossey-Bass.

Mehrens, W. A. (1984). A critical analysis of the psychometric properties of the K-ABC. *The Journal of Special Education, 18*(3), 297–310.

Meichenbaum, D. (1972). Cognitive modification of test-anxious college students. *Journal of Consulting and Clinical Psychology, 39,* 370–380.

Meichenbaum, D. (1976). A cognitive-behavior modification approach to assessment. In M. Hersen & A. S. Bellack (eds.), *Behavioral assessment.* New York: Pergamon Press.

Meichenbaum, D. (1977). *Cognitive-behavior modification.* New York: Plenum.

Meichenbaum, D., & Butler, L. (1980). Toward a conceptual model for the treatment of test anxiety: Implications for research and treatment. In I. G. Sarason (ed.), *Test anxiety: Theory, research, and applications.* Hillsdale, N.J.: Erlbaum.

Meichenbaum, D., & Turk, D.

(1976). The cognitive-behavioral management of anxiety, anger, and pain. In P. Davidson (ed.), *Behavioral management of anxiety, depression and pain.* New York: Brunner/Mazel.

Meikle, S., & Gerritse, R. (1970). MMPI cookbook pattern frequencies in a psychiatric unit. *Journal of Clinical Psychology, 26,* 82–84.

Melei, J. P., & Hilgard, E. R. (1964). Attitudes toward hypnosis, self predictions, and hypnotic susceptibility. *International Journal of Clinical and Experimental Hypnosis, 12,* 99–108.

Meloy, J. R., & Singer, J. (1991). A psychoanalytic view of the Rorschach Comprehensive System "Special Scores." *Journal of Personality Assessment, 56,* 202–217.

Mercer, J. R. (1971). Sociocultural factors in labeling mental retardates. *Peabody Journal of Education, 48,* 188–203.

Mercer, J. R. (1972). *Anticipated achievement: Computerizing the self-fulfilling prophecy.* Paper presented at the meeting of the American Psychological Association, Honolulu, September.

Mercer, J. R. (1973). *Labeling the mentally retarded: Clinical and social system perspective on mental retardation.* Berkeley: University of California Press.

Mercer, J. R. (1979). In defense of racially and culturally non-discriminatory assessment. *School Psychology Digest, 8*(1), 89–115.

Messick, S. (1988). Validity. In R. L. Linn (ed.), *Educational measurement.* New York: Macmillan.

Messick, S., & Jungeblut, A. (1981). Time and method in coaching for the SAT. *Psychological Bulletin, 89,* 191–216.

Meunier, C., & Rule, B. G. (1967). Anxiety, confidence, and conformity. *Journal of Personality, 35,* 498–504.

Michell, J. V., Jr. (1983). *Tests in print III: An index to tests, test reviews, and the literature on specific tests.* Lincoln, Neb.:

Buros Institute of Mental Measurements, University of Nebraska–Lincoln.

Miller, A. B. (1991). Is routine mammography screening appropriate for women 40–49 years of age? *American Journal of Preventive Medicine, 91*, 55–62.

Miller, J. O., & Phillips, J. (1966). *A preliminary evaluation of the Head Start and other metropolitan Nashville kindergartens.* Unpublished manuscript, George Peabody College for Teachers.

Millman, J. (1974). Criterion-referenced measurement. In W. J. Popham (ed.), *Evaluation and education.* Berkeley, Calif.: McCutchan.

Millman, J. (1979). Reliability and validity of criterion-referenced test scores. *New Directions in Testing and Measurement, 1*(4), 75–92.

Millon, T. (1969). *Modern psychopathology: A biosocial approach to maladaptive learning and functioning.* Philadelphia: Saunders.

Millon, T. (1983). *Millon Clinical Multiaxial Inventory Manual* (2nd ed.). Minneapolis, Minn.: National Computer Systems.

Millon, T. (1985). The MCMI provides a good assessment of DSM-III disorders: The MCMI-II will prove even better. *Journal of Personality Assessment, 49*, 379–391.

Millon T. (1987). *Millon Clinical Multiaxial Inventory-II (Manual).* Minneapolis, Minn.: National Computer Systems.

Minton, H. L., & Schneider, F. W. (1980). *Differential psychology.* Pacific Grove, Calif.: Brooks/Cole.

Mischel, W. (1968). *Personality and assessment.* New York: Wiley.

Mischel, W. (1984). Convergences and challenges in the search for consistency. *American Psychologist, 39*, 351–364.

Mitchell, J. V. (ed.) (1985). *The ninth mental measurements yearbook.* Highland Park, N.J.: Gryphon Press.

Mitchell, S. K. (1979). Interobserver agreement, reliability, and generalizability of data collected in observational studies. *Psychological Bulletin, 86*, 376–390.

Mitchell, W. G., Chavez, J. M., Lee, H., & Guzman, B. L. (1991). Academic underachievement in children with epilepsy. *Journal of Child Neurology, 6*, 65–72.

Monroe, S. M., & Simons, A. D. (1991). Diathesis-stress theories in the context of life stress research: Implications for the depressive disorders. *Psychological Bulletin, 110*, 406–425.

Moos, R. H. (1973). Conceptualizations of human environment. *American Psychologist, 28*, 652–665.

Moos, R. H. (1986a). *Work Environment Scale* (2nd ed.). Palo Alto, Calif.: Consulting Psychologist Press.

Moos, R. H. (1986b). *Group Environment Scale* (2nd ed.). Palo Alto, Calif.: Consulting Psychologist Press.

Moos, R. H. (1987a). *Ward Atmosphere Scale Manual* (2nd ed.). Palo Alto, Calif.: Consulting Psychologist Press.

Moos, R. H. (1987b). *Community-oriented Programs Environment Scale Manual* (2nd ed.). Palo Alto, Calif.: Consulting Psychologist Press.

Moos, R. H. (1987c). *Correctional Institutions Environment Scale Manual* (2nd ed.). Palo Alto, Calif.: Consulting Psychologist Press.

Moos, R. H. (1987d). *University Residents Environment Scale* (2nd ed.). Palo Alto, Calif.: Consulting Psychologist Press.

Moos, R. H., & Moos, B. (1986). *Family Environment Scale Manual* (2nd ed.). Palo Alto, Calif.: Consulting Psychologist Press.

Moos, R. H., & Truckett, E. (1986). *Classroom Environment Scale* (2nd ed.). Palo Alto, Calif.: Consulting Psychologist Press.

Moos, R. H., Finney, J. W., & Cronkite, R. C. (1990). *Alcoholism treatment: Context, process, and outcome.* New York: Oxford University Press.

Moreland, K. L. (1985). Validation of computer-based test interpretations: Problems and prospects. *Journal of Consulting and Clinical Psychology, 53*, 816–825.

Morgan, D. (1984). What do the SATs mean? SATs are getting in the way of education. *Current,* 9–13.

Mullins, C. J., Weeks, J. L., & Wilbourn, J. M. (1978). *Ipsative rankings as an indicator of job-worker match* (Tech. Rep. 78-70). U.S. Air Force Human Relations Laboratory.

Mungas, D. M., Trontel, E. H., & Winegardner, J. (1981). Multivariable-multimethod analysis of the dimensions of interpersonal behavior. *Journal of Research in Personality, 15*, 107–121.

Munsinger, H. (1975). The adopted child's I.Q.: A critical review. *Psychological Bulletin, 82*, 623–659.

Murray, H. A. (1938). *Explorations in personality.* New York: Oxford University Press.

Murray-Jobsis, J. (1991). An exploratory study of hypnotic capacity of schizophrenic and borderline patients in a clinical setting. *American Journal of Clinical Hypnosis, 33*, 150–160.

Murstein, B. I. (1963). *Theory and research in projective techniques.* New York: Wiley.

Museum of Modern Art (1955). *The family of man.* New York: Maco Magazine Corporation.

Myers, I. B. (1976). *Introduction to type.* Palo Alto, Calif.: Consulting Psychologists Press.

Myers, I. B. (1977). *The Myers-Briggs Type Indictor: Supplementary Manual.* Palo Alto, Calif.: Consulting Psychologists Press.

Myers, I. B., & Briggs, K. C. (1943/1962). *The Myers-Briggs Type Indicator.* Palo Alto, Calif.: Consulting Psychologists Press.

Naglieri, J. A. (1984). Concurrent and predictive validity of the Kaufman Assessment Battery for children with a Navajo sample. *Journal of School Psychology, 22*, 373–380.

Naglieri, J. A. (1985). Review of the Gesell Preschool Test. In

J. V. Mitchell (ed.), *The ninth mental measurements yearbook* (vol. 1). Highland Park, N.J.: Gryphon Press.

Naliboff, B. D., Benton, D., Solomon, G. F., Morley, J. E. (1991). Immunological changes in young and old adults during brief laboratory stress. *Psychosomatic Medicine, 53,* 121–132.

National Cancer Institute (1991). *Cancer Statistics Review.* 1973–1988, Bethesda, MD.

National Commission on Testing and Public Policy (1990). *From gatekeeper to gateway: Transforming testing in America.* Chestnut Hill, Mass.: National Computer Systems, Boston College.

Neisser, U. (1967). *Cognitive psychology.* New York: Appleton-Century-Crofts.

Neisser, U. A. (1991). A case of misplaced nostalgia. *American Psychologist, 46,* 34–36.

Nelson, E., Conger, B., Douglass, et al. (1983). Functional health status levels of primary care patients. *Journal of the American Medical Association, 249,* 3331–3338.

Nettelbeck, T. (1982). Inspection time: An index for intelligence? *Quarterly Journal of Experimental Psychology, 34A,* 299–312.

Nettelbeck, T., & Lally, M. (1976). Inspection time and measured intelligence. *British Journal of Psychology, 67,* 17–22.

Nolan, R. F., Watlington, D. K., & Willson, V. L. (1989). Gifted and nongifted race and gender effects on item functioning on the Kaufman Assessment Battery for Children. *Journal of Clinical Psychology, 45,* 645–650.

Norton, E. H. (1978). *The Bakke decision and the future of affirmative action.* Statement of the Chair, U.S. Equal Employment Opportunity Commission, at the National Association for the Advancement of Colored People convention, July.

Novick, M. R. (1981). Federal guidelines and professional standards. *American Psychologist, 36,* 1035–1046.

Nunnally, J. C. (1978). *Psychome-*

tric theory. New York: McGraw-Hill.

Nunnally, J. C. (1982). *Psychometric theory* (2nd ed.). New York: McGraw-Hill.

Nurius, P. S. (1990). A review of automated assessment. *Computers in human services, 6,* 265–281.

Nykodym, N., & Ruud, W. N. (1985). Intraview: Career development through business communication. *Journal of Employment Counseling, 22,* 161–165.

Nykodym, N., & Simonetti, J. L. (1981). *Communication: The key to business and organizational effectiveness.* Toledo, Ohio: Management Skills Books.

Oakland, T. (1979). Research on the ABIC and ELP: A revisit to an old topic. *School Psychology Digest 8,* 209–213.

Oakland, T., & Feigenbaum, D. (1979). Multiple sources of test bias on the WISC-R and the Bender-Gestalt test. *Journal of Consulting and Clinical Psychology, 47,* 968–974.

Oakland, T., & Parmelee, R. (1985). Mental measurement of minority-group children. In B. B. Wolman (ed.), *Handbook of intelligence: Theories, measurements, and applications.* New York: Wiley-Interscience.

Oei, T. P. S., Evans, L., & Crook, G. M. (1990). Utility and validity of the STAI with anxiety disorder patients. *British Journal of Clinical Psychology, 29,* 429–432.

Oei, T. P. S., Moylan, A., & Evans, L. (1991). Validity and clinical utility of the Fear Questionnaire for anxiety-disorder patients. *Psychological Assessment: A Journal of Consulting and Clinical Psychology, 3,* 391–397.

O'Leary, K. D., & Kent, R. N. (1973). Behavior modification for social action: Research tactics and problems. In L. A. Hamerlynck, P. O. Davidson, & L. E. Acker (eds.), *Critical issues in research and practice.* Champaign, Ill.: Research Press.

O'Leary, K. D., Kent, R. N., & Kanowitz, J. (1975). Shaping data collection congruent with experimental hypotheses. *Journal*

of Applied Behavior Analysis, 8, 43–51.

Olmedo, E. L. (1981). Testing linguistic minorities. *American Psychologist, 36,* 1078–1085.

Opton, E. (1977). From California, two views. *APA Monitor,* April, pp. 5–18.

Opton, E. (1979). A psychologist takes a closer look at the recent landmark *Larry P.* opinion. *APA Monitor,* December, pp. 1–4.

Osipow, S. H. (1983). *Theories of career development* (3rd ed.). Englewood Cliffs, N.J.: Prentice-Hall.

Osipow, S. H. (1987). Counselling psychology: Theory, research, and practice in career counselling. *Annual Review of Psychology, 38,* 257–278.

Owen, D. (1985). *None of the above: Behind the myth of scholastic aptitude.* Boston: Houghton Mifflin.

Palmer, F. H. (1970). Socioeconomic status and intellectual performance among Negro preschool boys. *Developmental Psychology, 3,* 1–9.

Parducci, A. (1968). The relativism of absolute judgments. *Scientific American, 219*(6), 84–90.

Parducci, A. (1982). Category ratings: Still more contextual effects! In B. Wegener (ed.), *Social attitudes in psychophysical measurements.* Hillsdale, N.J.: Erlbaum.

Parker, K. (1983). A meta-analysis of the reliability and validity of the Rorschach. *Journal of Personality Assessment, 42,* 227–231.

Parkinson, C. N. (1957). The short list, or principles of selection. In C. N. Parkinson (ed.), *Parkinson's law.* Boston: Houghton Mifflin.

Parsons, O. A. (1970). Clinical neuropsychology. In C. D. Spielberger (ed.), *Current topics in clinical and community psychology* (vol. 2). New York: Academic Press.

Pasamanick, B. A., & Knobloch, H. (1955). Early language behavior in Negro children and the testing of intelligence. *Journal of*

Abnormal and Social Psychology, 50, 401–402.

Patterson, C. H. (1974). *Relationship counseling and psychotherapy.* New York: Harper & Row.

Pattishall, E. (1992). Smoking and body weight. *Health Psychology,* in press.

Paul, G. L., & Eriksen, C. W. (1964). Effects of test anxiety on "real life" examinations. *Journal of Personality, 32,* 480–494.

Paul, S. M. (1985). The Advanced Raven's Progressive Matrices: Normative data for an American university population and an examination of the relationship with Spearman's "g." *Journal of Experimental Education, 54,* 95–100.

Payne, D. A., Goolsby, C. E., Evans, K. A., & Barton, R. M. (1990). Multivariate analyses of cognitive and cognitive style and cognitive style variables based on hemisphere specialization theory predictive of success in a college developmental studies program. *Perceptual and Motor Skills, 71,* 545–546.

Pearson, K. (1896). Mathematical contributions to the theory of evolution. III: Regression, heredity and panmixia. *Philosophical Transactions, A, 187,* 253–318.

Pedhauzer, E. (1982). *Multiple regression in behavioral research* (2nd ed.) New York: Holt, Rinehart & Winston.

Peoples, V. Y. (1975). Measuring the vocational interest of women. In S. H. Osipow (ed.), *Emerging women: Career analysis and outlooks.* Columbus, Ohio: Merrill.

Pettigrew, T. F. (1964). *A profile of the American Negro.* New York: Van Nostrand Reinhold.

Pfeifer, C., & Sedlacek, W. (1971). The validity of academic predictors for Black and White students at a predominantly White university. *Journal of Educational Measurement, 8,* 253–261.

Phelps, L. (1989). Comparison of scores for intellectually gifted students on the WISC-R and the Fourth Edition of the Stanford-Binet. *Psychology in Schools, 26,* 125–129.

Pierce, J. P., Burns, D., Gilpen, E., Rosenberg, B., Johnson, M., & Bal, D. (1992). *California baseline tobacco survey.* Unpublished report. San Diego: University of California.

Pinizzotto, A. J., & Finkel, N. J. (1990). Criminal personality profiling: An outcome and process study. *Law and Human Behavior, 14,* 215–234.

Piotrowski, C. (1984). The status of projective techniques: Or, "wishing won't make it go away." *Journal of Clinical Psychology, 40,* 1495–1499.

Piotrowski, C., Sherry, D., & Keller, J. W. (1985). Psychodiagnostic test usage: Survey of the Society for Personality Assessment. *Journal of Personality Assessment, 49,* 115–119.

Piotrowski, Z. (1947). Rorschach compendium. *Psychiatric Quarterly, 21,* 79–101.

Piotrowski, Z. (1964). Digital computer interpretation of inkblot test data. *Psychiatric Quarterly, 38,* 1–26.

Pirozzolo, F. J., Campanella, D. J., Christensen, K., & Lawson-Kerr, K. (1981). Effects of cerebral dysfunction on neurolinguistic performance in children. *Journal of Consulting and Clinical Psychology, 49,* 791–806.

Plaisted, J. R., Gustavson, J. L., Wilkening, G. N., & Golden, C. J. (1983). The Luria-Nebraska Neuropsychological Battery—Children's revision: Theory and current research findings. *Journal of Clinical Child Psychology, 12,* 13–21.

Polansky, N., Freeman, W., Horowitz, M., Irwin, L., Papanis, N., Rapaport, D., & Whaley, F. (1949). Problems of interpersonal relations in research on groups. *Human Relations, 2,* 281–291.

Polyson, J., Peterson, R., & Marshall, C. (1986). MMPI and Rorschach: Three decades of research. *Professional Psychology: Research and Practice, 17,* 476–478.

Pons, L. (1989). Effects of age and sex upon availability of responses on a word-association test. *Perceptual and Motor Skills, 68,* 85–86.

Price, K. H., & Garland, H. (1983). Compliance with a leader's suggestions as a function of perceived leader/member competence and potential reciprocity. *Journal of Applied Psychology, 66,* 329–336.

Prince, R. J., & Guastello, S. J. (1990). The Barnum effect in a computerized Rorschach interpresentation system. *The Journal of Psychology, 124,* 217–222.

Pugliese, M. D., Lifshitz, F., Grad, G., Fort, P., & Marks-Katz, M. (1983). Fear of obesity: A cause of short stature and delayed puberty. *New England Journal of Medicine, 309,* 513–518.

Quay, L. C. (1971). Language dialect, reinforcement, and the intelligence-test performance of Negro children. *Child Development, 42,* 5–15.

Radcliffe, J. A. (1965). Edwards Personal Preference Schedule. In O. K. Buros (ed.), *The sixth mental measurements yearbook.* Highland Park, N.J.: Gryphon Press.

Rahe, R. H. (1972). Subjects' recent life changes and their near-future illness reports. *Annals of Clinical Research, 4,* 250–265.

Raju, N. S., Normand, J., & Burke, M. J. (1990). A new approach for utility analysis. *Journal of Applied Psychology, 75,* 3–12.

Ralston, S. M. (1988). The effect of applicant race upon personnel selection decisions: A review with recommendations. *Employee Responsibilities and Rights Journal, 1,* 215–226.

Rapaport, D., Gill, M. M., & Schafer, R. (1945, 1946). *Diagnostic psychological testing* (2 vols.). Chicago: Yearbook Publishers.

Rapaport, D., Gill, M. M., & Schafer, R. (1968). *Diagnostic psychological testing* (rev. ed.)

(R. R. Holt, ed.). New York: International Universities Press.

Rappaport, N. B., & McAnulty, D. P. (1985). The effect of accented speech on the scoring of ambiguous WISC-R responses by prejudiced and nonprejudiced raters. *Journal of Psychoeducational Assessment, 3,* 275–283.

Rathus, S. A. (1973). A thirty-item schedule for assessing assertive behavior. *Behavior Therapy, 4,* 398–406.

Raven, J. (1986). *Manual for Raven's Progressive Matrices and Vocabulary Scales: Research Supplement No. 3.* London: H. K. Lewis & Co. Ltd.

Raven, J. (1990). *Raven Manual Research Supplement 3: American and International Norms.* London: Oxford Psychologist Press.

Rebok, G., Brandt, J., & Folstein, M. (1990). Longitudinal cognitive decline in patients with Alzheimer's disease. *Journal of Geriatric Psychiatry and Neurology, 3,* 91–97.

Recase, M. D. (1977). Procedures for computerized testing. *Behavior Research Methods and Instrumentation, 9,* 148–152.

Redfield, J., & Paul, G. L. (1976). Bias in behavioral observation as a function of observer familiarity with subjects and typically of behavior. *Journal of Consulting and Clinical Psychology, 44,* 156.

Reid, J. B. (1970). Reliability assessment of observation data: A possible methodological problem. *Child Development, 41,* 1143–1150.

Reid, J. B., & DeMaster, B. (1972). The efficacy of the spot-check procedure in maintaining the reliability of data collected by observers in quasinatural settings: Two pilot studies. *Oregon Research Institute Research Bulletin, 12.*

Reid, N. (1986). Testing the test: Wide Range Achievement Test: 1984 Revised Edition. *Journal of Counseling and Development, 64,* 538–540.

Reitan, R. M. (1967a). Neurological and physiological bases of psychopathology. *Annual Review of Psychology, 27,* 189–216.

Reitan, R. M. (1976b). Neuropsy-

chology: The vulgarization that Luria always wanted. *Contemporary Psychology, 21,* 737–738.

Reitan, R. M. (1986). Theoretical and methodological bases of the Halstead-Reitan Neuropsychological Test Battery. In I. Grant & K. N. Adams (eds.), *Neuropsychological assessment of neuropsychiatric disorders.* New York: Oxford University Press.

Reitan, R. M., & Wolfson, D. (1985). *The Halstead-Reitan Neuropsychological Battery: Theory and clinical interpretation.* Tucson, Ariz.: Tucson Neuropsychological Press.

Reschly, D. J. (1981). Psychological testing in educational classification and placement. *American Psychologist, 36,* 1094–1102.

Reschly, D. J., & Sabers, D. L. (1979). Analysis of test bias in four groups with the regression definition. *Journal of Educational Measurement, 16,* 1–9.

Reschly, D. J., Kicklighter, R., & McKee, P. (1988). Recent placement of litigation part III: Analysis of differences in Lary, P., Marshal and S-1, and implications for future practices. *School Psychology Review, 17,* 39–50.

Reschly, D. J., & Ward, S. M. (1991). Use of adaptive behavior measures and overrepresentation of black students in programs for students with mild mental retardation. *American Journal on Mental Retardation, 96,* 257–268.

Research and Education Association (1981). *Handbook of psychiatric rating scales.* New York: Research and Education Association.

Retzlaff, P., Sligner, N., & Gibertini, M. (1986). Predicting WAIS-R scores from the Shipley Institute of Living Scale in a homogeneous sample. *Journal of Clinical Psychology, 42,* 357–359.

Reynolds, C. R. (1980). An examination of bias in a pre-school battery across race and sex. *Journal of Educational Measurement, 17,* 137–146.

Reynolds, C. R. (1982). Determining statistically reliable strengths and weaknesses in the perfor-

mance of single individuals on the Luria-Nebraska Neuropsychological Battery. *Journal of Consulting and Clinical Psychology, 50,* 525–529.

Reynolds, C. R. (1986). Wide Range Achievement Test (WRAT-R), 1984 edition. *Journal of Counseling and Development, 64,* 540–541.

Reynolds, C. R., & Nigl, A. J. (1981). A regression analysis of differential validity: An intellectual assessment for Black and White inner-city children. *Journal of Clinical and Child Psychology, 10,* 176–179.

Rinn, W. E. (1988). Mental decline in normal aging: A review. *Journal of Geriatric Psychiatry and Neurology, 1,* 144–158.

Ritzler, B., & Alter, B. (1986). Rorschach teaching in APA-approved clinical graduate programs: Ten years later. *Journal of Personality Assessment, 50,* 44–49.

Ritzler, B. A., Sharkey, K. J., & Chudy, J. F. (1980). A comprehensive projective alternative to the TAT. *Journal of Personality Assessment, 44,* 358–362.

Robinson, J. P., Shaver, P. R., & Wrightsman, L. S. (1991). *Measures of personality and social psychological attitudes.* New York: Academic Press.

Roe, A., & Klos, D. (1969). Occupational classification. *The Counseling Psychologist, 1,* 84–92.

Roe, A., & Seigelman, M. (1964). *The origin of interests.* Washington, D.C.: American Personnel and Guidance Association.

Rogers, C. R. (1959a). A tentative scale for the measurement of process in psychotherapy. In E. A. Rubinstein & M. B. Parloff (eds.), *Research in psychotherapy.* Washington, D.C.: American Psychological Association.

Rogers, C. R. (1959b). A theory of therapy, personality, and interpersonal relationships, as developed in the client-centered framework. In S. Koch (ed.), *Psychology: A study of science* (vol. 3). New York: McGraw-Hill.

Rogers, C. R. (1961a). *On becom-*

ing a person. Boston: Houghton Mifflin.

Rogers, C. R. (1961b). A process conception of psychotherapy. In C. R. Rogers (ed.), *On becoming a person*. Boston: Houghton Mifflin.

Rogers, C. R. (1980). *A way of being*. Boston: Houghton Mifflin.

Rorschach, H. (1921). *Psychodiagnostik*. Bern: Bircher. (Hans Huber Verlag, trans., 1942.).

Rosenfeld, P. et al. (1989). Attitude assessment in organizations: Testing three microcomputer-based survey systems. *The Journal of General Psychology*, *116*, 145–154.

Rosenman, R. H., & Chesney, M. A. (1985). Type A behavior pattern: Its relationship to coronary heart disease and its modification by behavioral and pharmacological approaches. In M. R. Zales (ed.), *Stress in health and disease*. New York: Brunner/Mazel.

Rosenthal, R. (1966). *Experimenter effects in behavioral research*. New York: Appleton-Century-Crofts.

Rosenthal, R., & Fode, K. L. (1963). The effects of experimenter bias on the performance of the albino rat. *Behavioral Science*, *8*, 183–189.

Rosenthal, R., & Jacobson, L. (1968). *Pygmalion in the classroom*. New York: Holt, Rinehart & Winston.

Rosenthal, R., & Rosnow, R. L. (1991). *Essentials of behavioral research: Method and data analysis* (2nd ed.). New York: McGraw-Hill.

Rosenthal, R., Hall, J. A., DiMatteo, M. R., Rogers, P. L., & Archer, D. (1980). *Sensitivity to nonverbal communication: The PONS test*. Baltimore, Md.: Johns Hopkins University Press.

Rothlisberg, B. A., & Deran, R. S. (1989). Lateral preference and processing style. *International Journal of Neuroscience*, *48*, 243–245.

Rotter, J. B. (1966). Generalized expectancies for internal versus external control of reinforcement. *Psychological Monographs*, *80* (1, Whole No. 609).

Rotter, J. B. (1967). A new scale for the measurement of interpersonal trust. *Journal of Personality*, *35*, 651–665.

Rotter, J. B., & Rafferty, J. E. (1950). *Manual: The Rotter Incomplete Sentences Blank*. San Antonio, Tex.: Psychological Corporation.

Rourke, B. P., & Gates, R. D. (1981). Neuropsychological research in school psychology. In G. W. Hynd & J. E. Obrzut (eds.), *Neuropsychological assessment and the school-age child: Issues and procedures*. New York: Grune & Stratton.

Rourke, B. P., Young, G. C., Stang, J. D., & Russel, D. L. (1986). Adult outcomes of central processing deficiencies in children. In I. Grant & K. M. Adams (eds.), *Neuropsychological assessment of neuropsychiatric disorders*. New York: Oxford University Press.

Rowe, D. C. (1987). Resolving the person-situation debate: Invitation to an interdisciplinary dialogue. *American Psychologist*, *42*, 218–227.

Rubin, Z. (1970). Measurement of romantic love. *Journal of Personality and Social Psychology*, *16*, 265–273.

Rubin, Z. (1973). *Liking and loving: An invitation to social psychology*. New York: Holt, Rinehart & Winston.

Rubin, Z. (1979). Los Angeles says it with love on a scale. *Los Angeles Times*, February 21, 1979.

Rushton, J. P. (1991). Do r-K strategies underlie human race differences? *Canadian Psychology*, *32*, 29–42.

Russell, L. B. (1986). *Is prevention better than cure?* Washington, D.C.: Brookings Institution.

Rutter, M. (1978). Prevalence of types of dyslexia. In A. L. Benton & D. Pearl (eds.), *Dyslexia: An appraisal of current knowledge*. New York: Oxford University Press.

Ryan, J. J., & Rosenberg, S. J. (1983). Relationship between the WAIS-R and Wide-Range Achievement Test in a sample of mixed patients. *Perceptual and Motor Skills*, *56*, 623–626.

Saccuzzo, D. P (1975). Canonical correlation as a method of assessing the correlates of good and bad therapy hours. *Psychotherapy: Theory, Research and Practice*, *12*, 253–256.

Saccuzzo, D. P. (1976). *The practice of psychological testing in America: Issues and trends*. Paper presented at the meeting of the California Psychological Association, Los Angeles, April.

Saccuzzo, D. P. (1977). The practice of psychotherapy in America: Issues and trends. *Professional Psychology*, *8*, 297–306.

Saccuzzo, D. P. (1981). Input capability and speed of processing in mental retardation: A reply to Stanovich and Purcell. *Journal of Abnormal Psychology*, *90*, 172–174.

Saccuzzo, D. P. (1986). Information-processing theories of schizophrenia. In R. Ingram (ed.), *Information processing approaches to clinical psychology*. New York: Academic Press.

Saccuzzo, D. P., & Braff, D. L. (1981). Early information processing deficits in schizophrenia: New findings using schizophrenic subgroups and manic controls. *Archives of General Psychiatry*, *38*, 175–179.

Saccuzzo, D. P., & Braff, D. L. (1986). Information-processing abnormalities in schizophrenia and psychotic patients: Trait and state dependent components. *Schizophrenia Bulletin*, *12*, 447–458.

Saccuzzo, D. P., & Kaplan, R. M. (1984). *Clinical psychology*. Boston: Allyn and Bacon.

Saccuzzo, D. P., & Larson, G. E. (1987). Analysis of test-retest reliability for a battery of cognitive speed tests. *Technical Report*, 88-10. San Diego: Navy Personnel Research and Development Center, November.

Saccuzzo, D. P., Lewandowski, D. G. (1976). The WISC as a diagnostic tool. *Journal of Clinical Psychology*, *32*, 115–124.

Saccuzzo, D. P., & Marcus, A. (1983). *Speed of visual information-processing improves with practice in mental retardation*. Paper presented at the 91st

Annual Convention of the American Psychological Association, Anaheim, California.

Saccuzzo, D. P., & Michael, B. (1984). Speed of information-processing and structural limitations in retarded and dual diagnosis retarded-schizophrenic persons. *American Journal of Mental Deficiency, 89,* 187–194.

Saccuzzo, D. P., & Miller, S. (1977). Critical interstimulus interval in delusional schizophrenics and normals. *Journal of Abnormal Psychology, 86,* 261–266.

Saccuzzo, D. P., & Schubert, D. (1981). Backward masking as a measure of slow processing in the schizophrenia spectrum of disorders. *Journal of Abnormal Psychology, 90,* 305–312.

Saccuzzo, D. P., & Schulte, R. (1978). The value of a master's degree for the Ph.D. pursuing student in psychology. *American Psychologist, 33,* 862–864.

Saccuzzo, D. P., Braff, D. L., Shine, A., & Lewandowski, D. G. (1981). *A differential WISC pattern in the retarded as a function of sex and race.* Paper presented at the meeting of the Western Psychological Association, Los Angeles, April.

Saccuzzo, D. P., Hirt, M., & Spencer, T. J. (1974). Backward masking as a measure of attention in schizophrenia. *Journal of Abnormal Psychology, 83,* 512–522.

Saccuzzo, D. P., Kerr, M., Marcus, A., & Brown, R. (1979). Input capability and speed of information processing in mental retardation. *Journal of Abnormal Psychology, 88,* 312–317.

Saccuzzo, D. P., Larson, G. E., & Rimland, B. (1986). Visual, auditory and reaction time approaches to the measurement of speed of information-processing and individual differences in intelligence. *Personality and Individual Differences, 2,* 659–668.

Saigal, S., Szatmari, P., Rosenbaum, P., Campbell, D., & King, S. (1991). Cognitive abilities and school performance of extremely low birth weight children and matched term control children at age 8 years; a regional study. *Journal of Pediatrics, 118,* 751–760.

Sands, W. A., & Gade, P. (1983). An application of computerized adaptive testing in U.S. Army recruiting. *Journal of Computer-Based Instruction, 10,* 87–89.

Sands, W. L. (1972). Psychiatric history and mental status. In A. M. Freedman & I. I. Kaplan (eds.), *Diagnosing mental illness,* pp. 20–40. New York: Atheneum.

Sarason, I. G. (1958). Effects on verbal learning of anxiety, reassurance, and meaningfulness of material. *Journal of Experimental Psychology, 56,* 472–477.

Sarason, I. G. (1959). Intellectual and personality correlates of test anxiety. *Journal of Abnormal and Social Psychology, 59,* 272–275.

Sarason, I. G. (1961). The effects of anxiety and threat on solution of a difficult task. *Journal of Abnormal and Social Psychology, 62,* 165–168.

Sarason, I. G. (1975). Test anxiety, attention, and the general problem of anxiety. In C. D. Spielberger & I. G. Sarason (eds.), *Stress and anxiety* (vol. 1). New York: Halsted.

Sarason, I. G. (ed.) (1980). *Test anxiety: Theory, research, and applications.* Hillsdale, N.J.: Erlbaum.

Sarason, I. G., & Palola, E. G. (1960). The relationship of test and general anxiety, difficulty of task, and experimental instructions to performance. *Journal of Experimental Psychology, 59,* 185–191.

Sarason, I. G., & Sarason, B. R. (1980). *Abnormal psychology* (3rd ed.). Englewood Cliffs, N. J.: Prentice-Hall.

Sarason, I. G., & Sarason, B. R. (1985a). Life change, social support, coping, and health. In R. M. Kaplan & M. H. Criqui (eds.), *Behavioral epidemiology and disease prevention.* New York: Plenum.

Sarason, I. G., & Sarason, B. R. (1985b). *Social support: Theory, research, and applications.* Boston: Martinjus Nijhoff International.

Sarason, I. G., Johnson, J. H., & Siegel, J. M. (1978). Assessing the impact of life change: Development of the Life Experiences Survey. *Journal of Consulting and Clinical Psychology, 46,* 932–946.

Sarason, I. G., Levine, H. M., Bashhnan, R. B., & Sarason, B. R. (1983). Assessing social support: The social support questionnaire. *Journal of Personality and Social Psychology, 44,* 127–139.

Sarason, I. G., Sarason, B. R., & Pierce, G. R. (1990). *Social support: An interactional view.* New York: Wiley.

Sarason, I. G., Smith, R. E., & Diener, E. (1975). Personality research: Components of variance attributable to the person and the situation. *Journal of Personality and Social Psychology, 3,* 199–204.

Sattler, J. M. (1970). Racial "experimenter effects" in experimentation, testing, interviewing, and psychotherapy. *Psychological Bulletin, 73,* 137–160.

Sattler, J. M. (1973a). Examiners' scoring style, accuracy, ability, and personality scores. *Journal of Clinical Psychology, 29,* 38–39.

Sattler, J. M. (1973b). Intelligence testing of ethnic minority-group and culturally disadvantaged children. In L. Mann & D. Sabatino (eds.), *The first review of special education* (vol. 2). Philadelphia: JSE Press.

Sattler, J. M. (1973c). Racial experimenter effects. In K. S. Miller & R. M. Dreger (eds.), *Comparative studies of Blacks and Whites in the United States.* New York: Seminar Press.

Sattler, J. M. (1977). The effects of therapist-client racial similarity. In A. S. Gurman & A. M. Razin (eds.), *Effective psychotherapy: A handbook of research,* pp. 252–290. Elmsford, N.Y.: Pergamon Press.

Sattler, J. M. (1978). Review of McCarthy Scales of Children's

Abilities. In O.K. Buros (ed.), *The eighth mental measurements yearbook* (vol. 1). Highland Park, N.J.: Gryphon Press.

Sattler, J. M. (1979a). *Intelligence tests on trial: Larry P. et al. v. Wilson Riles et al.* Paper presented at the meeting of the Western Psychological Association, San Diego, April.

Sattler, J. M. (1979b). Standard intelligence tests are valid for measuring the intellectual potential of urban children: Comments on pitfalls in the measurement of intelligence. *Journal of Psychology, 102*, 107–112.

Sattler, J. M. (1980). Intelligence tests on trial: An interview with Judges Robert F. Peckham and John F. Grady. *APA Monitor*, November, 7–8.

Sattler, J. M. (1982). *Assessment of children's intelligence and special abilities.* Boston: Allyn and Bacon.

Sattler, J. M. (1988). *Assessment of children* (3rd ed.). San Diego, Calif.: Sattler.

Sattler, J. M. (in press). *Interviewing.* San Diego, Calif.: Sattler.

Sattler, J. M., & Gwynne, J. (1982). Ethnicity and Bender Visual Motor Test performance. *Journal of School Psychology, 20*, 69–71.

Sattler, J. M., & Theye, F. (1967). Procedural, situational, and interpersonal variables in individual intelligence testing. *Psychological Bulletin, 68*, 347–360.

Sattler, J. M., & Winget, B. M. (1970). Intelligence testing procedures as affected by expectancy and I.Q. *Journal of Clinical Psychology, 26*, 446–448.

Sattler, J. M., Hillix, W. A., & Neher, L. A. (1970). Halo effect in examiner scoring of intelligence test responses. *Journal of Consulting and Clinical Psychology, 34*, 172–176.

Satz, P., & Fletcher, J. M. (1981). Emergent trends in neuropsychology: An overview. *Journal of Consulting and Clinical Psychology, 49*, 851–865.

Saunders, B. T., & Vitro, F. T. (1971). Examiner expectancy and bias as a function of the referral process in cognitive assessment. *Psychology in the Schools, 8*, 168–171.

Sawyer, J. (1966). Measurement and prediction, clinical and statistical. *Psychological Bulletin, 66*, 178–200.

Sax, G. (1989). *Principles of educational and psychological measurement and evaluation* (3rd ed.). Belmont, Calif.: Wadsworth.

Scarr-Salapatek, S. (1971). Race, social class and I.Q. *Science, 174*, 1285–1295.

Scheuneman, J. D. (1981). New look at bars and aptitude tests. *New Directions in Testing and Measurement, 12*, 5–25.

Scheuneman, J. D. (1987). An experimental, exploratory study of causes of bias in test items. *Journal of Educational Measurement, 24*, 97–118.

Schmidt, F., & Hunter, J. E. (1983). Individual differences in productivity: An empirical test of estimates derived from studies of selection procedure utility. *Journal of Applied Psychology, 68*, 407–414.

Schmidt, F. L., Hunter, J. L., McKenzie, R. C., & Muldrow, T. W. (1979). Impact of valid selection procedures on workforce productivity. *Journal of Applied Psychology, 64*, 609–626.

Schmitt, N. (1976). Social and situational determinants of interview decisions: Implications for the employment interview. *Personnel Psychology, 29*, 79–101.

Schmitt, N., & Robertson, I. (1990). Personnel selection. *Annual Review of Psychology, 41*, 289–391.

Schneider, L. M., & Briel, J. B. (1990). *Validity of the GRE: 1988–89 Summary Report.* Princeton, N.J.: Educational Testing Service.

Schoggen, P. (1979). Roger G. Barker and behavioral settings: A commentary. *Journal of Personality and Social Psychology, 37*, 2158–2160.

Schroeder, H. E., & Kleinsaser, L. D. (1972). Examiner bias: A determinant of children's verbal behavior on the WISC. *Journal of Consulting and Clinical Psychology, 39*, 451–454.

Schuerger, J. M., Tait, E., & Tavernelli, M. (1982). Temporal stability of personality by questionnaire. *Journal of Personality and Social Psychology, 43*, 176–182.

Schultz, C. B., & Sherman, R. H. (1976). Social class, development, and differences in reinforcer effectiveness. *Review of Educational Research, 46*, 25–59.

Schwartz, R., & Gottman, J. (1976). Toward a task analysis of assertive behavior. *Journal of Consulting and Clinical Psychology, 44*, 910–920.

Science Agenda (1991). Department of Labor inundated with comments on GATB. *Assessing Assessments, 4*, 6–7.

Scott, L. H. (1981). Measuring intelligence with the Goodenough-Harris Drawing Test. *Psychological Bulletin, 89*, 483–505.

Scott, P., Burton, R. V., & Yarrow, M. (1967). Social reinforcement under natural conditions. *Child Development, 38*, 53–63.

Seguin, E. (1907). *Idiocy: Its treatment by the physiological method.* New York: Bureau of Publications, Teachers College, Columbia University. (Originally published in 1866.)

Self, P. A., & Horowitz, F. D. (1979). The behavioral assessment of the neonate: An overview. In J. D. Osofsky (ed.), *Handbook of infant development.* New York: Wiley.

Seligman, M. E. P. (1975). *Helplessness: On depression, development, and death.* San Francisco: Freeman.

Seligmann, J., Coppola, V., Howard, L., & Lee, E. D. (1979). A really final exam. *Newsweek*, May 28, pp. 97–98.

Sexton, M., Fox, N. L., & Hebel, J. R. (1990). Prenatal exposure to tobacco: II. Effects on cognitive functioning at age three. *International Journal of Epidemiology, 19*, 72–77.

Shaffer, L. (1953). Of whose reality I cannot doubt. *American Psychologist, 8*, 608–623.

Shakow, D., Hilgard, E. R., Kelly, E. L., Sanford, R. N., & Shaffer, L. F. (1947). Recommended graduate training in clinical psychology. *American Psychologist, 2,* 539–558.

Share, J. B., Webb, A., & Koch, R. (1964). The longitudinal development of infants and young children with Down's syndrome. *American Journal of Mental Deficiency, 68,* 689–692.

Sharkey, K. J., & Ritzler, B. A. (1985). Comparing diagnostic validity of the TAT and a new Picture Projective Test. *Journal of Personality Assessment, 49,* 406–412.

Shisslak, C. M., Pazda, S. L., & Crago, M. (1990). Body weight and bulimia as discriminators of psychological characteristics among anorexic, bulimic, and obese women. *Journal of Abnormal Psychology, 99,* 380–384.

Siegel, S. N., & Castellan, J. (1988). *Nonparametric statistics for the behavioral sciences* (2nd ed.). New York: McGraw-Hill.

Silver, N. C., & Dunlap, W. P. (1987). Averaging correlation coefficients: Should Fisher's Z transformation be used? *Journal of Applied Psychology, 72,* 146–148.

Silverstein, A. B. (1978). Review of McCarthy Scales of Children's Abilities. In O. K. Buros (ed.), *The eighth mental measurements yearbook* (vol. 1). Highland Park, N.J.: Gryphon Press.

Silverstein, A. B. (1982). Factor structure of the Wechsler Adult Intelligence Scale-Revised. *Journal of Counseling and Clinical Psychology, 50,* 661–664.

Simon, A. J., & Bass, L. G. (1956). Toward a validation of infant testing. *American Journal of Orthopsychiatry, 26,* 340–350.

Simon, W. E. (1969). Expectancy effects in the scoring of vocabulary items: A study of scorer bias. *Journal of Educational Measurement, 6,* 159–164.

Sines, J. O. (1970). Actuarial versus clinical prediction in psychopathology. *British Journal of Psychiatry, 116,* 129–144.

Singh, L. (1986). Standardization of n-power measuring instrument (T.A.T.). *Journal of Psychological Researches, 28,* 14–20.

Sinha, D. K. (1986). Relationships of graduation requirements and course offerings to Scholastic Aptitude Test performance of seniors in high schools. *The Journal of Educational Research, 80,* 5–9.

Sloman, J., Bellinger, D. C., & Krentzel, C. P. (1990). Infantile colic and transient developmental log in the first year of life. *Child Psychiatry and Human Development, 21,* 25–36.

Slosson, R. L (1963). *Slosson Intelligence Test (SIT) for children and adults.* New York: Slosson Educational Publications.

Smith, A. E., & Knight-Jones, E. B. (1990). The abilities of very low-birthweight children and their classroom controls. *Developmental Medicine and Child Neurology, 32,* 590–601.

Smith, B., & Sechrest, L. (1991). Treatment of aptitude X treatment interactions. *Journal of Consulting and Clinical Psychology, 59,* 233–244.

Smith, D. (1981). Unfinished business with informed consent procedures. *American Psychologist, 36,* 22–26.

Stanford-Binet: Fourth Edition with students with learning disabilities. *Journal of Learning Disabilities, 22,* 260–261.

Smith, G. A., & Stanley, G. (1983). Clocking "g": Relating intelligence and measures of timed performance. *Intelligence, 7,* 353–358.

Smith, J. E., Hillard, M. C., Walsh, R. A., Kubacki, S. R., & Morgan, C. D. (1991). Rorschach assessment of purging and nonpurging bulimics. *Journal of Personality Assessment, 56,* 277–288.

Smith, R. E., Ascough, J. C., Ettinger, R. F., & Nelson, D. A. (1971). Humor, anxiety, and task performance. *Journal of Personality and Social Psychology, 19,* 243–246.

Smith, S. H. (1977). *Refining cognitive behavior modification treatments for test anxiety.* Unpublished master's thesis, San Diego State University.

Smith, T. W., & Zurawski, R. M. (1983). Assessment of irrational beliefs: The question of discriminant validity. *Journal of Clinical Psychology, 39,* 976–979.

Snow, R. E. (1969). Review of *Pygmalion in the Classroom* by R. Rosenthal and L. Jacobson. *Contemporary Psychology, 14,* 197–199

Snow, R. E. (1991). Aptitude-treatment interaction as a framework for research on individual differences in psychotherapy. *Journal of Consulting and Clinical Psychology, 59,* 205–216.

Snyderman, M., & Rothman, S. (1987). Survey of expert opinion in intelligence and aptitude testing. *American Psychologist, 42,* 137–144.

Sostek, A. M. (1978). Review of the Brazelton Neonatal Assessment Scale. In O. K. Buros (ed.), *The eighth mental measurements yearbook* (vol. 1). Highland Park, N.J.: Gryphon Press.

Spearman, C. E. (1904a). General intelligence objectively determined and measured. *American Journal of Psychology, 15,* 201–293.

Spearman, C. E. (1904b). The proof and measurement of association between two things. *American Journal of Psychology, 15,* 72–101.

Spearman, C. E. (1923). *The nature of intelligence and the principles of cognition.* London: Macmillan.

Spearman, C. E. (1927). *The abilities of man.* New York: Macmillan.

Sperry, R. W. (1968). Hemisphere deconnection and unity in conscious awareness. *American Psychologist, 23,* 723–733.

Spielberger, C. D. (1972). Anxiety as an emotional state. In C. D. Spielberger (ed.), *Anxiety: Current trends in theory and research.* New York: Academic Press.

Spielberger, C. D., Anton, W. B., & Bedell, J. (1976). The nature and treatment of test anxiety. In M. Zuckerman & C. D.

Spielberger (eds.), *Emotions and anxiety: New concepts, methods and applications.* Hillsdale, N.J.: Erlbaum.

Spielberger, C. D., Auerbach, S. M., Wadsworth, A. P., Dun, T. M., & Taulbee, E. S. (1975). Emotional reactions to surgery. *Journal of Consulting and Clinical Psychology, 40,* 33–38.

Spielberger, C. D., Gorsuch, R. L., & Lushene, R. E. (1970). *Manual for the State-Trait Anxiety Inventory.* Palo Alto, Calif.: Consulting Psychologists Press.

Spiers, P. A. (1982). The Luria-Nebraska Neuropsychological Battery revisited: A theory in practice or just practicing? *Journal of Consulting and Clinical Psychology, 50,* 301–306.

Spiker, D. G., & Ehler, J. G. (1984). Structured psychiatric interviews for adults. In G. Goldstein & M. Hersen (eds.), *Handbook of psychological assessment,* pp. 291–304. New York: Pergamon Press.

Spilker, B. (1990). *Quality of life assessment in clinical trials.* New York: Raven Press.

Spitzer, R. L., Williams, J. B. W., Gibbon, M., & First, M. B. (1990a). *Structured clinical interview for DSM-III-R—patient edition* (SCID-P, 9/1/89 version). Washington D.C.: American Psychiatric Press.

Spitzer, R. L., Williams, J. B. W., Gibbon, M., & First, M. B. (1990b). *Structured clinical interview for DSM-III-R—personality disorders* (SCID-II, 9/1/89 version). Washington, D.C.: American Psychiatric Press.

SPSS (1990). *Statistical Package for the Social Sciences reference guide.* Chicago: SPSS Inc.

Squire, L. R., & Butters, N. (1984). *The neuropsychology of memory.* New York: Guilford Press.

Stallones, R. A. (1983). Ischemic heart disease and lipids in blood and diet. *Annual Review of Nutrition, 3,* 155–185.

Standage, K. (1989). Structured interviews and the diagnosis of personality disorders. *Canadian Journal of Psychiatry, 34,* 906–912.

Stanley, J. C. (1971). Reliability. In R. L. Thorndike (ed.), *Educational measurement.* Washington, D.C.: American Council on Education.

Stanley, J. C., & Hopkins, K. D. (1972). *Educational and psychological measurement and evaluation.* Englewood Cliffs, N.J.: Prentice-Hall.

Stanley, K. E. (1980). Prognostic factors for survival in patients with inoperable lung cancer. *Journal of the National Cancer Institute, 65,* 25–32.

Stephenson, W. (1953). *The study of behavior.* Chicago: University of Chicago Press.

Steptoe, A., & Johnston, D. (1991). Clinical applications of cardiovascular assessment. *Psychological Assessment: A Journal of Consulting and Clinical Psychology, 3,* 337–349.

Stern, W. (1912). [*The psychological methods of testing intelligence.*] *Die psychologische Methoden der Intelligenzprüfung.* Leipzig: Barth. (Baltimore: Warwick & York, 1914.)

Sternberg, R. J. (1981). Testing and cognitive psychology. *American Psychologist, 36,* 1181–1189.

Sternberg, R. J. (1984). The Kaufman Assessment Battery for Children: An information processing analysis and critique. *The Journal of Special Education, 18*(3), 269–279.

Sternberg, R. J. (1985). *Beyond IQ: A triarchic theory of human intelligence.* New York: Cambridge University Press.

Sternberg, R. J. (1986). *Intelligence applied: Understanding and increasing your intellectual skills.* San Diego: Harcourt Brace Jovanovich.

Sternberg, R. J. (1988). *The triarchic mind: A theory of human intelligence.* New York: Viking.

Sternberg, R. J. (1991). Death, taxes, and bad intelligence tests. *Intelligence, 15,* 257–269.

Sternberg, R. J., & Gardner, M. K. (1982). A componential interpretation of the general factor in human intelligence. In H. J. Eysenck (ed.), *A model for intelligence.* New York: Springer-Verlag.

Stevens, S. S. (1966). A metric for the social consensus. *Science, 151,* 530–541.

Stevenson, I. (1971). *The diagnostic interview.* New York: Harper & Row.

Stewart, A. L., & Ware, J. E. (eds.) (1992). *Measuring functioning and well-being: The medical outcomes study approach.* Durham, N.C.: Duke University Press.

Stewart, A. L., Ware, J. E., Brook, R. H., & Davies-Avery, A. (1978). *Conceptualization and measurement of health for adults (vol. 2), physical health in terms of functioning.* Santa Monica, Calif.: RAND Corporation.

Stokols, D. (1978). Environmental psychology. *Annual Review of Psychology, 29,* 253–295.

Strauss, M. E., & Brandt, J. (1990). Are there neuropsychologic manifestations of the gene for Huntington's disease in asymptomatic, at-risk individuals? *Archives of Neurology, 47,* 905–908.

Strauss, M. E., Gynther, M. D., & Wallhermfechtel, J. (1974). Differential misdiagnosis of Blacks and Whites by the MMPI. *Journal of Personality Assessment, 38,* 55–60.

Strauss, M., Lessen-Firestone, J., Starr, R., Jr., & Ostrea, E., Jr. (1975). Behavior of narcotics-addicted newborns. *Child Development, 46,* 887–893.

Streiner, D. L., & Miller, H. R. (1989). The MCMI-II: How much better than the MCMI? *Journal of Personality Assessment, 53,* 81–84.

Stricker, L. J. (1965). Edwards Personal Preference Schedule. In O. K. Buros (ed.), *The sixth mental measurements yearbook.* Highland Park, N.J.: Gryphon Press.

Strong, E. K., Jr., & Campbell, D. P. (1966). *Manual for Strong Vocational Interest Blank.* Stanford, Calif.: Stanford University Press.

Subkoviak, M. J. (1980). The

reliability of mastery classification decisions. In R. A. Burk (ed.), *Criterion-referenced measurement: The state of the art.* Baltimore, Md.: Johns Hopkins University Press.

Suinn, R. M. (1969a). The relationship between fears and anxiety: A further study. *Behaviour Research and Therapy, 7,* 317–318.

Suinn, R. M. (1969b). The STABS, a measure of test anxiety for behavior therapy: Normative data. *Behaviour Research and Therapy, 7,* 335–339.

Sundberg, N. D. (1961). The practice of psychological testing in clinical services in the United States. *American Psychologist, 16,* 79–83.

Super, D. E. (1953). A theory of vocational development. *American Psychologist, 8,* 185–190.

Super, D. E., & Hall, D. T. (1978). Career development: Exploitation and planning. *Annual Review of Psychology, 29,* 333–372.

Svanum, S., & Dallas, C. L (1981). Alcoholic MMPI types and their relationship to patient characteristics, polydrug abuse, and abstinence following treatment. *Journal of Personality Assessment, 45,* 278–287.

Sweet, R. C. (1969). *Variations in the intelligence test performance of lower-class children as a function of feedback or monetary reinforcement.* Doctoral dissertation, University of Wisconsin. (University Microfilms No. 70-37, 21)

Sweetland, R. C., & Keyser, D. J. (eds.) (1983). *Tests: A comprehensive reference for assessment in psychology, education and business.* Kansas City, Mo.: Test Corporation of America.

Sweetland, R. C., & Keyser, D. J. (1991). *Tests: A comprehensive reference for assessment in psychology, education, and business* (3rd ed.). Austin, Tex.: Pro-Ed Publishers.

Symonds, P. M. (1924). On the loss of reliability in ratings due to coarseness of the scale. *Journal of Experimental Psychology, 7,* 456–461.

Szasz, T. S. (1961). *The myth of mental illness.* New York: Harper & Row.

Tabachnick, B. G., & Fidell, L. S. (1989). *Using multivariate statistics* (2nd ed.). New York: Harper & Row.

Tannenbaum, A. J. (1968). Review of the IPAT Culture Fair Intelligence Test. In O. K. Buros (ed.), *The sixth mental measurements yearbook.* Highland Park, N.J.: Gryphon Press.

Taplin, P. S., & Reid, J. B. (1973). Effects of instructional set and experimenter influence on observer reliability. *Child Development, 44,* 547–554.

Tasto, D. L. (1977). Self-report schedules and inventories. In A. R. Ciminero, K. D. Calhoun, & H. E. Adams (eds.), *Handbook of behavioral assessment.* New York: Wiley-Interscience.

Taulbee, E. S., & Sisson, L. (1957). Configurational analysis of MMPI profiles of psychiatric groups. *Journal of Consulting Psychology, 21,* 413–417.

Taylor, C. W., Price, P. B., Richards, J. M., Jr., & Jacobsen, T. L. (1965). An investigation of the criterion problem for a group of medical general practitioners. *Journal of Applied Psychology, 49,* 399–406.

Taylor, H. C., & Russell, J. T. (1939). The relationship of validity coefficients to the practical effectiveness of tests in selection: Discussion and tables. *Journal of Applied Psychology, 23,* 565–578.

Taylor, J. A. (1951). The relationship of anxiety to the conditioned eyelid response. *Journal of Experimental Psychology, 41,* 81–92.

Taylor, J. A. (1953). A personality scale of manifest anxiety. *Journal of Abnormal Psychology, 48,* 285–290.

Taylor, R. L., Sternberg, L., & Partenio, I. (1986). Performance of urban and rural children on the SOMPA: Preliminary investigation. *Perceptual and Motor Skills, 63,* 1219–1223.

Temp, G. (1971). Test bias: Valid-ity of the SAT for blacks and whites in thirteen integrated institutions. *Journal of Educational Measurement, 8,* 245–251.

Templer, D. I., Schmitz, S. P., & Corgiat, M. D. (1985). Comparison of the Stanford-Binet with the Wechsler Adult Intelligence Scale—Revised: Preliminary report. *Psychological Reports, 57,* 335–336.

Teng, E. L., Wimer, C., Roberts, E., Damasio, A. R., Eslinger, P. J., Folstein, M. F., Tune, L. E., Whitehouse, P. J., Bardolph, E. L., & Chui, H. C. (1989). Alzheimer's dementia: Performance on parallel forms of the dementia assessment battery. *Journal of Clinical and Experimental Neuropsychology, 11,* 899–912.

Tenopyr, M. L. (1984, November). *So let it be with content validity.* Paper presented at the Content Validity III Conference, Bowling Green State University, Bowling Green, Ohio.

Teplin, L. A., & Schwartz, J. (1989). Screening for severe mental disorder in jails: The development of the Referral Decision Scale. *Law and Human Behavior, 13,* 1–18.

Terman, L. M. (1916). *The measurement of intelligence.* Boston: Houghton Mifflin.

Terman, L. M., & Merrill, M. A. (1937). *Measuring intelligence.* Boston: Houghton Mifflin.

Terman, L. M., & Merrill, M. A. (1953). Tests of intelligence. B. 1937 Stanford-Binet scales. In A. Weider (ed.), *Contributions toward medical psychology* (vol. 2). New York: Ronald Press.

Terman, L. M., & Merrill, M. A. (1960). *Stanford-Binet intelligence scale.* Boston: Houghton Mifflin.

Terrell, F., Taylor, J., & Terrell, S. L. (1978). Effects of type of social reinforcement on the intelligence test performance of lower-class Black children. *Journal of Consulting and Clinical Psychology, 46,* 1538–1539.

Thompson, D. E., & Thompson, T. A. (1982). Court standards for job analysis in test validation. *Personnel Psychology, 35,* 865–874.

Thorndike, E. L. (1904). *An introduction to the theory of mental and social measurements.* New York: Science Press.

Thorndike, E. L. (1920). A constant error in psychological rating. *Journal of Applied Psychology, 4,* 25–29.

Thorndike, E. L. (1921). Intelligence and its measurement: A symposium. *Journal of Educational Psychology, 12,* 123–147, 195–216.

Thorndike, R. L. (1968). Review of *Pygmalion in the Classroom* by R. Rosenthal and L. Jacobson. *American Educational Research Journal, 5,* 708–711.

Thorndike, R. L. (1971). Concepts of culture-fairness. *Journal of Educational Measurement, 8,* 63–70.

Thorndike, R. L. (1972). Review of the Torrance Tests of Creative Thinking. In O. K. Buros (ed.), *The seventh mental measurements yearbook* (vol. 1). Highland Park, N.J.: Gryphon Press.

Thorndike, R. L. (1973). *Stanford-Binet intelligence scale, Form L-M, 1972 norms tables.* Boston: Houghton Mifflin.

Thorndike, R. L., Hagen, E. P., & Sattler, J. M. (1986). *Technical manual: Stanford-Binet Intelligence Scale: Fourth Edition.* Chicago, Ill.: Riverside.

Thorndike, R. M. (1990a). Origins of intelligence and its measurement. *Journal of Psychoeducational Assessment, 8,* 223–230.

Thorndike, R. M. (1990b). Would the real factors of the Stanford-Binet Fourth Edition please come forward? *Journal of Psychoeducational Assessment, 8,* 412–435.

Thumin, F. J. (1969). MMPI scores as related to age, education and intelligence among male job applicants. *Journal of Applied Psychology, 53,* 404–407.

Thurstone, L. L. (1938). Primary mental abilities. *Psychometric Monographs, 1.*

Tiber, N., & Kennedy, W. A. (1964). The effects of incentives on the intelligence test perfor-

mance of different social groups. *Journal of Consulting Psychology, 28,* 187.

Tittle, C. K. (1983). Studies of the effects of career interest inventories: Expanding outcome criteria to include women's experience. *Journal of Vocational Behavior, 22,* 148–158.

Tomkins, S. S. (1947). *The Thematic Apperception Test: The theory and technique of interpretation.* New York: Grune & Stratton.

Topp, R. (1989). Effects of relaxation or exercise on undergraduate's test anxiety. *Perceptual and Motor Skills, 69,* 35–41.

Torgerson, W. S. (1958). *Theory and methods of scaling.* New York: Wiley.

Torrance, E. P. (1970). Broadening concepts of giftedness in the 70's. *Gifted Child Quarterly, 14,* 199–208.

Torrance, E. P. (1977). *Discovery and nurturance of giftedness in the culturally different.* Reston, Va.: Council for Exceptional Children.

Traub, R. E., & Lam, Y. R. (1985). Latent structure and item sampling models for testing. *Annual Review of Psychology, 36,* 19–48.

Tronick, E. Z. (1987). The neonatal behavioral assessment scale as a biomarker of the effects of environmental agents on the newborn. *Environmental Health Perspectives, 74,* 185–189.

Tronick, E., & Brazelton, T. B. (1975). Clinical uses of the Brazelton Neonatal Behavioral Assessment. In B. Friedlander, G. Sterritt, & G. Kirk (eds.), *Exceptional infant* (vol. 3). New York: Brunner/Mazel.

Trott, D. M., & Morf, M. E. (1972). A multimethod factor analysis of the Differential Personality Inventory, Personality Research Form, and Minnesota Multiphasic Personality Inventory. *Journal of Counseling Psychology, 19,* 94–103.

Truax, C. B., & Carkhuff, R. R. (1967). *Toward effective counseling and psychotherapy: Training*

and practice. Chicago: Aldine-Atherton.

Truax, C. B., & Mitchell, K. M. (1971). Research on certain therapist interpersonal skills in relation to process and outcome. In A. E. Bergin & S. L. Garfield (eds), *Handbook of psychotherapy and behavior change.* New York: Wiley.

Tryon, W. W. (1991). *Activity measurement in psychology and medicine.* New York: Plenum.

Tukey, J. W. (1977). *Exploratory data analysis.* Reading, Mass.: Addison-Wesley.

Turkheimer, E. (1991). Individual and group differences in adoption studies of IQ. *Psychological Bulletin, 110,* 392–405.

Turner, J. A., Herron, L., & Weiner, P. (1986). Utility of the MMPI Pain Assessment Index in predicting outcomes after lumbar surgery. *Journal of Clinical Psychology, 42,* 764–769.

Turner, J. H. (1970). Entrepreneurial environments and the emergence of achievement motivation in adolescent males. *Sociometry, 33,* 147–165.

Turner, R. J. (1981). Social support as a contingency in psychological well-being. *Journal of Health and Social Behavior, 22,* 357–367.

Turpin, G. (1991). The psychophysiological assessment of anxiety disorders: Three-systems measurement and beyond. *Psychological Assessment: A Journal of Consulting and Clinical Psychology, 3,* 366–375.

Tyler, L. E. (1969). *The work of the counselor* (3rd ed.). New York: Appleton-Century-Crofts.

Tyler, L. E., & Walsh, W. B. (1979). *Tests and measurements* (3rd ed.). Englewood Cliffs, N.J.: Prentice-Hall.

Uhl, N., & Eisenberg, T. (1970). Predicting shrinkage in the multiple correlation coefficient. *Educational and Psychological Measurement, 30,* 487–489.

Ulrich, L., & Trumbo, D. (1965). The selection interview since 1949. *Psychological Bulletin, 63,* 100–116.

Valencia, R. R. (1988). The Mc-

Carthy Scales and Hispanic children: A review of psychometric research. *Hispanic Journal of Behavioral Sciences, 10,* 81–104.

Valencia, R. R., & Lopez, R. (1992). Assessment of racial and ethnic minority students: Problems and prospects. In M. Zeidner & R. Most (eds.), *Psychological testing: An inside view.* Palo Alto, Calif.: Consulting Psychologist Press.

van Baar, A. (1990). Development of infants of drug dependent mothers. *Journal of Child Psychology and Psychiatry and Allied Disciplines, 31,* 911–920.

Vandenburg, S. G., & Vogler, G. P. (1985). Genetic determinants of intelligence. In B. B. Wolman (ed.), *Handbook of intelligence.* New York: Wiley.

Varble, D. L. (1971). Current status of the Thematic Apperception Test. In P. McReynolds (ed.), *Advances in psychological assessment* (vol. 2). Palo Alto, Calif.: Science and Behavior Books.

Vickers, D., Nettelbeck, T., & Willson, R. J. (1972). Perceptual indices of performance: The measurement of "inspection time" and "noise" in the visual system. *Perception, 1,* 263–295.

Wade, T. C., & Baker, T. B. (1977). Opinions and uses of psychological tests: A survey of clinical psychologists. *American Psychologist, 32,* 874–882.

Wagner, E. E., & Flamos, O. (1988). Optimized split-half reliability for the Bender Visual Motor Gestalt Test: Further evidence for the use of the maximization procedure. *Journal of Personality Assessment, 52,* 454–458.

Wagner, E. E., Alexander, R. A., Roos, G., & Adair, H. (1986). Optimum split-half reliabilities for the Rorschach: Projective techniques are more reliable than we think. *Journal of Personality Assessment, 50,* 107–112.

Wagner, R. (1949). The employment interview: A critical review. *Personnel Psychology, 2,* 17–46.

Wainer, H., & Braun, H. I. (eds.) (1988). *Test validation.* Hillsdale, N.J.: Erlbaum.

Walker, A. M., Rablen, R. A., & Rogers, C. R. (1960). Development of a scale to measure process changes in psychotherapy. *Journal of Clinical Psychology, 16,* 79–85.

Walker, S., & Rosser, R. (1992). *Quality of life assessment: Key issues for the 1990s.* Dordrect Netherlands: Kluwer Press.

Wallace, W. L. (1972). Review of the SAT. In O. K. Buros (ed.), *The seventh mental measurements yearbook* (vol. 1). Highland Park, N.J.: Gryphon Press.

Ward, T. J., et al. (1989). The effect of computerized tests on the performance and attitudes of college students. *Journal of Educational Computing Research, 5,* 327–333.

Ware, J. E., Jr. (1991). Conceptualizing and measuring generic health outcomes. *Cancer, 67,* 774–779.

Wasik, B. H., Ramey, C. T., Bryant, D. M., & Sparling, J. J. (1990). A longitudinal study of two early intervention strategies: Project CARE. *Child Development, 61,* 1682–1696.

Wasserman, A. L., Wilimas, J. A., Fairclough, D. L., Mulhern, R. K., & Wang, W. (1991). Subtle neuropsychological deficits in children with sickle cell disease. *American Journal of Pediatric Hematology/Oncology, 13,* 14–20.

Watson, C. W., & Klett, W. G. (1975). The Henmon-Nelson, Cardall-Miles, Slosson, and Quick Tests as predictors of NAIS IQ. *Journal of Clinical Psychology, 31,* 310–313.

Watson, D., & Friend, R. (1969). Measurement of social-evaluative anxiety. *Journal of Consulting and Clinical Psychology, 33,* 448–451.

Watson, R. I. (1951). *The clinical method in psychology.* New York: Harper & Row.

Webb, J. T. (1970). *The relation of MMPI two-point codes to age, sex, and education level in a representative nationwide sample of psychiatric outpatients.* Paper presented at the meeting of the Southeastern Psychological Association, Louisville, Ky., April.

Webster, E. C. (1964). *Decision making in the employment interview.* Montreal: Industrial Relations Center, McGill University.

Webster, J. S., & Dostrow, V. (1982). Efficacy of a decision-tree approach to the Luria-Nebraska Neuropsychological Battery. *Journal of Consulting and Clinical Psychology, 50,* 313–315.

Wechsler, D. (1939). *The measurement of adult intelligence.* Baltimore, Md.: Williams & Wilkins.

Wechsler, D. (1943). Non-intellective factors in general intelligence. *Journal of Abnormal and Social Psychology, 38,* 101–103.

Wechsler, D. (1955). *Manual, Wechsler Adult Intelligence Scale.* New York: Psychological Corporation.

Wechsler, D. (1958). *The measurement and appraisal of adult intelligence* (4th ed.). Baltimore, Md.: Williams & Wilkins.

Wechsler, D. (1981). *Wechsler Adult Intelligence Scale-Revised.* New York: Psychological Corporation.

Wechsler, D. (1991). *WISC-III manual.* San Antonio, Tex.: The Psychological Corporation.

Weekley, J. A., Frank, B., O'Connor, E. J., & Peters, L. H. (1985). A comparison of three methods of estimating the standard deviation of performance in dollars. *Journal of Applied Psychology, 70,* 122–126.

Weiner, B. (1991). Metaphors in motivation and attribution. *American Psychologist, 46,* 921–930.

Weiner, B., & Kukla, A. (1970). An attributional analysis of achievement motivation. *Journal of Personality and Social Psychology, 15,* 1–20.

Weiner, B., Graham, S., Peter, O., & Zmuidinas, M. (1991). Public confession and forgiveness. *Journal of Personality, 59,* 281–312.

Weiss, D. J. (1985). Adaptive testing by computer. *Journal of Consulting and Clinical Psychology, 53,* 774–789.

Weiss, D. J. (ed.) (1983). *New horizons in testing*. New York: Academic Press.

Weissman, A. N. (1979). The Dysfunctional Attitude Scale: A validation study. *Dissertation Abstracts International, 40* 1389A–1390B. (University Microfilms no. 79-19, 533)

Weissman, A. N., & Beck, A. T. (1978, November). *Development and validation of the Dysfunctional Attitude Scale: A preliminary investigation*. Paper presented at the meeting of the Association for the Advancement of Behavior Therapy, Chicago.

Weissman, M. M., Sholomskas, D., Pottenger, M., Prusoff, B. A., & Locke, B. Z. (1977). Assessing depressive symptoms in five psychiatric populations: A validation study. *American Journal of Epidemiology, 106*, 203–214.

Welsh, G. S. (1948). An extension of Hathaway's MMPI profile coding system. *Journal of Consulting Psychology, 12*, 343–344.

Welsh, G. S. (1956). Factor dimensions A and R. In G. S. Welsh & W. G. Dahlstrom (eds.), *Basic readings on the MMPI in psychology and medicine*. Minneapolis: University of Minnesota Press.

Welsh, K., Butters, N., Hughes, J., Mohs, R., & Hayman, A. (1991). Detection of abnormal memory decline in mild cases of Alzheimer's disease. CERAD Neuropsychological Measures. *Archives of Neurology, 48*, 278–281.

Wermiel, S., & Trost, C. (1986, June 20). Justices say hostile job environment due to sex harrassment violates rights. *Wall Street Journal*, p. 2.

Werner, H. (1937). Process and achievement: The basic problem of education and developmental psychology. *Harvard Educational Review, 7*, 353–368.

Wesman, A. G. (1971). Writing the test item. In R. L. Thorndike (ed.), *Educational measurement* (2nd ed.). Washington, D.C.: American Council on Education.

Westen, D. (1991). Clinical assessment of object relations using the TAT. *Journal of Personality Assessment, 56*, 56–74.

Wetzler, S. (1990). The Millon Clinical Multiaxial Inventory (MCMI): A review. *Journal of Personality Assessment, 55*, 445–464.

Wheeler, L., & Reitan, R. M. (1962). A presence and alaterality of brain damage predicted from response to a short aphasia screening test. *Perceptual and Motor Skills, 15*, 783–799.

Whipple, G. M. (1910). *Manual of mental and physical tests*. Baltimore, Md.: Warwick & York.

Wicker, A. W. (1979). Ecological psychology: Some recent and prospective developments. *American Psychologist, 34*, 755–765.

Wicker, A. W., & Kirmeyer, S. L. (1976). From church to laboratory to national park. In S. Wapner, S. B. Conen, & B. Kaplan (eds.), *Experiencing the environment*. New York: Plenum.

Wickham, T. (1978). *WISC patterns in acting-out delinquents, poor readers, and normal controls*. Unpublished doctoral dissertation, United States International University.

Wiederholt, J. L. (1978). Review of Illinois Test of Psycholinguistic Abilities. In O. K. Buros (ed.), *The eighth mental measurements yearbook* (vol. 1). Highland Park, N.J.: Gryphon Press.

Wiens, A. N. (1976). The assessment interview. In I. B. Weiner (ed.), *Clinical methods in psychology*. New York: Wiley.

Wiens, A. N., Matarazzo, J. D., & Saslow, G. (1965). The interaction recorder: An electronic punched paper tape unit for recording speech behavior during interviews. *Journal of Clinical Psychology, 21*, 142–145.

Wiesner, W. H., & Cronshaw, S. F. (1988). A meta-analytic investigation of the impact of interview format and degree of structure on the validity of the employment interview. *Journal of Occupational Psychology, 61*, 275–290.

Wiggins, J. S. (1973). *Personality and prediction: Principles of personality assessment*. Reading, Mass.: Addison-Wesley.

Wiggins, N. (1966). Individual viewpoints of social desirability. *Psychological Bulletin, 66*, 68–77.

Wiggins, N., & Kohen, E. S. (1971). Man versus model of man revisited: The forecasting of graduate school success. *Journal of Personality and Social Psychology, 19*, 100–106.

Wild, C. L., McPeek, W. M., Koffler, S. L., Braun, H. I., & Cowell, W. (1989). Concurrent validity of verbal item types for ethnic and gender subgroups. *GRE Publication Report 84-10p*. Princeton, N.J.: Educational Testing Service.

Wilder, J. (1950). The law of initial values. *Psychosomatic Medicine, 12*, 392–401.

Wilkinson, S. J., Downes, J., James, O., Davies, M. G., & Davies, A. D. M. (1986). Rating reliability for life events and difficulties in the elderly. *Psychological Medicine, 16*, 101–105.

Wilkinson, S. J., James, O., & Davies, A. D. M. (1985). Life stress and depression in the elderly: Experiences from a community survey. In A. Butler (ed.), *Aging: Recent advances and creative responses*. London: Croom Helm.

Williams, R. L. (1974). Scientific racism and I.Q.: The silent mugging of the Black community. *Psychology Today, 7*, 32–41.

Williamson, W. D., Wilson, G. S., Lifschitz, M. H., & Thurbers, S. A. (1990). Nonhandicapped very-low-birth-weight infants at one year of age developmental profile. *Pediatrics, 85*, 405–410.

Wine, J. D. (1980). Cognitive-attentional theory of test anxiety. In I. G. Sarason (ed.), *Test anxiety: Theory, research, and applications*. Hillsdale, N.J.: Erlbaum.

Wing, K. R. (1976). *The law and the public's health*. St. Louis, Mo.: Mosby.

Winter, D. G., & Stewart, A. J. (1977). Power motive reliability as a function of retest instructions. *Journal of Consulting and Clinical Psychology, 42*, 436–440.

Wishner, J. (1948). Rorschach intellectual indicators in neurotics. *American Journal of Orthopsychiatry, 18,* 265–279.

Wissler, C. (1901). The correlation of mental and physical tests. *Psychological Review, 3* (Monograph Supp. 16).

Witmer, J. M., Bornstein, A. V., & Dunham, R. M. (1971). The effects of verbal approval and disapproval upon the performance of third and fourth grade children of four subtests of the Wechsler Intelligence Scale for Children. *Journal of School Psychology, 9,* 347–356.

Witt, J. C. (1986). Review of the Wide Range Achievement Test-Revised. *Journal of Psychoeducational Assessment, 4,* 88–90.

Witt, J. C., & Gresham, F. M. (1985). Review of the Wechsler Intelligence Scale for Children-Revised. In J. V. Mitchell (ed.), *The ninth mental measurements yearbook* (vol. 1). Highland Park, N.J.: Gryphon Press.

Wolk, R. L., & Wolk, R. B. (1971). *Manual: Gerontological Apperception Test.* New York: Behavioral Publications.

Wolkind, S. (1974). Review of the Brazelton Neonatal Assessment Scale. *British Journal of Psychiatry, 125,* 216–217.

Wolpe, J. (1969). *The practice of behavior therapy.* New York: Pergamon Press.

Wolpe, J., & Lang, P. J. (1964). A fear survey schedule for use in behavior therapy. *Behaviour Research and Therapy, 2,* 27–30.

Wood, D. J. (1982). Talking to young children. *Developmental Medicine & Child Neurology, 24,* 856–859.

Wood, P. S., Smith, W. L., Altmaier, E. M., Tarico, V. S., & Franken, E. A. (1990). A prospective study of cognitive and non-cognitive selection criteria as predictors of resident performance. *Investigative Radiology, 25,* 855–859.

Woodcock, R. W. (1977). Wookcock-Johnson Psycho-Educational Battery: Technical report. Allen, Tex.: DLM Teaching Resources.

Woodworth, R. S. (1920). *Personal data sheet.* Chicago: Stoelting.

World Health Organization (1948). *Constitution of the World Health Organization.* Geneva: WHO Basic Documents.

Wright, O. R., Jr. (1969). Summary of research on the selection interview since 1964. *Personnel Psychology, 22,* 391–413.

Wright, T. L., & Tedeschi, R. G. (1975). Factor analysis of the interpersonal trust scale. *Journal of Consulting and Clinical Psychology, 43,* 470–477.

Yates, J. W., Chalmer, B., & McKegney, F. P. (1980). Evaluation of patients with advanced cancer using the Karnofsky Performance Status. *Cancer, 45,* 2220–2224.

Yerkes, R. M. (ed.) (1921). Psychological examining in the United States Army. *Memoirs of the National Academy of Sciences, 15*

Zales, M. R. (1985). *Stress in health and disease.* New York: Brunner/Mazel.

Zedeck, S., & Blood, M. R. (1974). *Foundations of behavioral science research in organizations.* Pacific Grove, Calif.: Brooks/Cole.

Zedeck, S., and Cascio, W. F. (1984). Psychological issues in personnel decisions. *Annual Review of Psychology, 35,* 461–518.

Zedeck, S., Tziner, A., & Middlestadt, S. E. (1983). Interviewer validity and reliability: An individual analysis approach. *Personnel Psychology, 36,* 355–370.

Zeidner, M. (1987). Test of the cultural bias hypothesis: Some Israeli findings. *Journal of Applied Psychology, 72,* 38–48.

Zeidner, M. (1990). Does test anxiety bias scholastic aptitude performance by gender and sociocultural group? *Journal of Personality Assessment, 55,* 145–160.

Zeidner, M., & Hammer, A. (1990). Life events and coping resources as predictors of stress symptoms in adolescents. *Per-sonality and Individual Differences, 11,* 693–703.

Zimet, G. D., Powell, S. S., Farley, G. K., Werkmen, S., & Berkoff, K. A. (1990). Psychometric characteristics of the multidimensional scale of perceived social support. *Journal of Personality Assessment, 55,* 610–617.

Zimmerman, I. L., Woo-Sam, J. M., & Glasser, A. J. (1973). *Clinical interpretation of the Wechsler Adult Intelligence Scale.* New York: Grune & Stratton.

Zimmerman, M., & Coryell, W. (1987). The inventory to diagnose depression (IDD): A self-report scale to diagnose major depressive disorders. *Journal of Consulting and Clinical Psychology, 55,* 55–59.

Zores, L. S., & Williams, P. B. (1980). A look at the content bias in IQ tests. *Journal of Educational Measurement, 17,* 313–322.

Zubin, J. (1972). Discussion of symposium on newer approaches to personality assessment. *Journal of Personality Assessment, 36,* 427–434.

Zuckerman, M. (1960). The development of an affect adjective check list measure of anxiety. *Journal of Consulting Psychology, 24,* 457–462.

Zuckerman, M. (1971). Physiological measures of sexual arousal in the human. *Psychological Bulletin, 75,* 297–329.

Zuckerman, M. (1990). Some dubious premises in research and theory on racial differences. *American Psychologist, 45,* 1297–1303.

Zytowski, D. G. (1976). Predictive validity of the Kuder Occupational Interest Survey: A 12–19 year follow-up. *Journal of Counseling Psychology, 23,* 221–233.

Zytowski, D. G. (1977). The effects of being interest inventoried. *Journal of Vocational Behavior, 11,* 153–158.

Zytowski, D. G. (1985). *Kuder Occupational Interest Survey Form DD manual supplement.* Chicago: Science Research Associates.

Name Index

Abrams, E. W., 462
Abramson, L. Y., 203
Abramson, T., 199
Ackerman, P. T., 349
Adair, H., 469
Adams, K. M., 530
Adamson, L., 320
Adkins, D. M., 364
Adler, A., 417
Ahern, S., 500
Aiken, L. R., 336
Akutagawa, D. A., 491
Albert, M. S., 530
Aldwin, C. M., 435
Alexander, R. A., 208, 469
Allard, A. M., 335
Allen, A., 191, 412
Allen, G. J., 519
Allen, J. J., 489
Allen, M. J., 107, 110, 164, 165, 169
Allison, J., 458
Alloy, L. B., 203
Allport, G. W., 439
Alpert, R., 514, 517
Als, H., 320
Alter, A., 456
Altmaier, E. M., 581
Amatruda, C. S., 322, 323
American College Testing Program, 370
American Educational Research Association, 123–124, 134, 179, 216, 624, 632, 637
American Psychological Association, 123–124, 134, 138, 179, 203, 216, 241, 484, 624, 627, 629, 630, 632, 637
Ames, L. B., 322, 326, 461, 463
Ammons, C. H., 341
Ammons, R. B., 341
Anastasi, A., 55, 134, 136, 151, 336, 376, 380, 411, 447, 619
Anderson, B. L., 625
Anderson, J. P., 150, 541, 549, 551
Anderson, N. B., 501
Anderson, N. H., 162
Ansorge, C. J., 365
Anthony, J. J., 570
Anton, W. B., 514, 517, 519
Anton, W. D., 519
Archer, D., 254
Archer, R. P., 638
Arkes, H. R., 201
Aronow, E., 469
Arthur, G., 296
Arvey, R. D., 247, 248, 251
Ash, R. A., 248, 252
Asher, J. J., 139
Atkins, C. J., 150
Atkinson, L., 326, 327
Atkinson, J. W., 106, 472, 476, 624
Auerbach, S. M., 511
Avolio, B. J., 382
Ax, A. F., 500
Azrin, N. H., 209, 499

Bacon, S. F., 505
Baehr, M., 248
Bagby, R. M., 511
Baglan, T., 229
Baird, L. L., 348
Baker, T. B., 220
Baltzley, D. R., 381
Balzer, 247
Bandura, A., 191, 192, 228, 626
Barbaree, H. E., 500
Barber, T. X., 200
Bardo, H. R., 364
Bardolph, E. L., 347
Bargh, J. A., 404
Barker, R. G., 406
Barlow, D. H., 492
Barnes-Farrell, J. L., 211
Baron, R. A., 248, 249
Barrett, G. V., 566, 574, 582
Barta, S., 496
Bartlett, C. J., 565
Bartley, J., 581
Barton, R. M., 368
Bashhnan, R. B., 525
Bass, L. G., 326
Baxter, D. J., 500
Bayles, K. A., 339
Bayley, N., 324, 325, 326
Beal, J. A., 320
Beamish, P., 437
Bearak, B., 613, 616, 617
Beatty, J., 500
Beck, A. T., 496
Beck, S., 21
Beck, S. J., 459
Bedell, J., 514, 517, 519
Beehr, T. A., 250
Bell, J. J., 345
Bell, T. K., 344
Bellack, A. S., 207, 208, 486
Bellak, L., 473, 477
Bellak, S. S., 477
Bellinger, D. C., 326
Belmont, L., 462
Bem, D. J., 191, 412, 413
Ben-Porath, Y. S., 22, 419, 432, 434, 435, 436
Bendell-Estroff, D., 327
Bentler, P. M., 100
Benton, A. L., 529
Benton, D., 521
Berenson, B. C., 237, 238
Bergan, A., 202
Bergan, J. R., 601
Berger, M., 272
Bergner, M., 541, 542, 543
Berka, C., 339
Berkoff, K. A., 525
Bernheimer, L. P., 322, 323
Berntson, G. G., 625
Berry, C. C., 149, 150, 546, 550
Bersoff, D. N., 12, 600, 601
Beyer, M., 313
Bhrolchian, M. N., 522
Bianchini, J. C., 559
Binet, A., 16, 257, 259, 265, 417, 458
Biondi, M., 521
Birk, J. M., 400

Birney, R. C., 472
Bitman, D., 436
Blake, D. D., 436
Blake, J., 504
Blanchard, E. B., 492
Blatt, S. J., 456, 458, 469, 470, 472
Block, J., 162, 434
Blood, M. R., 410
Bloom, A. S., 335
Bloom, B. S., 175
Bloom, E. T., 521
Blum, L. H., 337
Bobbitt, R. A., 541, 542, 543
Boll, T. J., 530
Bolton, L. S., 441
Bombardier, C., 151
Bonge, D., 497
Boor, M., 292
Borman, W. C., 154, 189, 577
Bornstein, A. V., 199
Bornstein, B. F., 523
Bortner, M., 378
Bowers, K. S., 412
Boyd, N. F., 546
Boyle, G. J., 280
Bracken, B. A., 281, 336
Bradbury, T. N., 404
Braff, D. L., 304, 502
Brand, C. R., 504
Brandt, J., 345, 347
Braun, H. I., 560
Braun, P. R., 494
Brayfield, A. H., 484, 630
Brazelton, T. B., 320, 321
Bredemeier, M., 609
Briel, J. B., 564
Briggs, K. C., 448
Brill, S., 595
Brill, W. J., 335
Brim, O. G., 258
Brittain, M., 272
Brogden, H. E., 189
Brook, R. H., 546
Brown, C. E., 340
Brown, D., 541
Brown, F. G., 571, 574
Brown, G., 496
Brown, G. W., 522
Brown, H. I., 136
Brown, J. S., 175
Brown, R., 502, 504
Bryant, D. M., 326
Bryson, S., 634
Buchwald, A., 177
Buck, J. N., 480
Bulpitt, C. J., 541
Buros, O. K., 193, 220, 221, 320, 321, 469
Burton, R. B., 175
Burton, R. V., 209
Burtt, H. E., 250
Bush, J. W., 149, 150, 541, 546, 550
Butcher, H. L., 369

Butcher, J. N., 22, 419, 432, 434, 435, 436, 505
Butler, L., 519
Butters, N., 530, 537, 540

Cacioppo, J. T., 625
Caine, E. D., 530
Callender, J. C., 247, 252
Cameron, R., 493
Campanella, D. J., 530
Campbell, C. B. G., 568
Campbell, D., 349
Campbell, D. P., 140, 388, 389, 395, 398, 400
Campbell, D. T., 147
Campbell, J. B., 94
Campion, J. E., 138, 247, 251
Canavan, A. G., 347
Cane, D. B., 496
Canfield, A. A., 55
Cannell, C. F., 203
Carkhuff, R. R., 237, 238, 239, 255
Carlin, J. B., 159
Carlson, R. E., 251
Carr, M. A., 536
Carroll, J. B., 8
Carter, W. B., 541, 542, 543
Carvajal, H., 280, 281
Cascio, W. F., 140, 171, 189, 594
Cash, H., 546, 547
Cash, T. F., 248
Castaneda, A., 578
Castenell, L. A., 558
Castenell, N. E., 558
Castner, B. M., 322
Cattell, J. M., 14
Cattell, R. B., 23, 274, 380, 439, 441, 510
Cautela, J. R., 492, 493
Cermak, L. S., 530, 537, 540
Chalmer, B., 546
Chambers, L., 547
Chambers, L. W., 541
Champney, H., 162
Chapman, S., 339
Chasnoff, I. J., 320
Chattin, S. H., 281
Chavez, J. M., 332
Cheiken, M., 208
Chelune, G. J., 530
Chesney, M. A., 521
Christensen, K., 530
Chudy, J. F., 477, 642
Chui, H. C., 347
Chun, 196
Chun, K., 94
Cialdini, R. B., 229
Cine, D. B., 138
Clarizio, H. F., 559, 571, 574, 598
Clark, C., 530
Clark, D. H., 558
Clark, K. E., 398
Clark, R. A., 472
Clarkson, Q. D., 566
Claussen, A. H., 327

Cleary, T. A., 144, 563, 565, 575, 577
Cliff, N., 90
Cobb, 196
Cohen, I., 202
Cohen, J., 121, 305
Cohen, S., 407, 523
Cole, N., 400
Cole, N. S., 558, 574, 576, 577
Coleman, J. C., 509
Coleman, M., 464
Coleman, W. W., 8
Coles, C. D., 320
Conger, B., 547
Conner, 327
Conner, R. E., 318, 322, 325
Connors, G. J., 490, 493
Conoley, J. L., 192, 194, 195
Conway, D. G., 339
Cook, M. L., 497
Cooper, D., 445
Cooper, W. H., 250
Coplan, J., 342
Copple, C. E., 559
Coppola, V., 612
Corah, N. L., 445
Corgiat, M. D., 280
Cornelius, E. T., 476
Coryell, W., 138, 139
Costa, P. T. Jr., 450
Costello, A. J., 241
Costello, J., 198
Cowell, W., 560
Cox, B. J., 511
Coyle, F. A., 430
Coyne, J. C., 523
Crago, M., 436
Cramer, P., 472
Crisco, J. J., 344
Crites, J. O., 402
Crockett, D., 530
Cronbach, L. J., 100, 110, 115, 118, 136, 147, 151, 152, 153, 189, 190, 205, 556, 570, 582, 620
Cronshaw, S. F., 247
Croog, S. H., 541
Crook, G. M., 511
Cundick, B. P., 479
Cureton, E. E., 8

Dahlstrom, W. G., 22, 425, 430, 432, 434, 435, 484, 630
Dakof, G., 523
Dallas, C. L., 421
Damarin, F., 325, 327
Damasio, A. R., 347
Dangel, H. L., 201
Daniels, M., 521
Danielson, K., 489
Dappelt, J. E., 294
Darlington, R. B., 574, 575, 576, 577
Darwin, C., 13
Das, J. P., 258, 311
Datta, L., 387
Dave, R., 320
Davidson, H. H., 459
Davidson, R. S., 435
Davies, A.D.M., 522
Davies-Avery, A., 546
Davis, J. D., 228
Davis, R. B., 175
Dearborn, G., 458
Dearborn, W. F., 362
Deffenbacher, J. L., 497
deGroot, A. M., 479
Delancy, M., 436
Delhees, K. H., 441
Delis, D. C., 530, 537, 538, 540

DeLongis, A., 523, 524
DeMaster, B., 208
DeMoivre, A., 100
Dent, H., 604
Depinet, R. L, 566, 574, 582
Deran, R. S., 334
DeRosa, A., 199
Diament, C., 209
Diamond, E. E., 387, 400
Dicken, C. F., 445
Dickie, J., 198
Diener, E., 413
Dietz, A., 209
Diller, L., 530
DiMatteo, M. R., 254
Dipboye, R. L., 248
Dittmann, A. T., 253
Dobbs, J. M., 344
Dobko, P., 561
Doctor, R., 341
Dodrill, C. B., 381
Donahue, D., 201
Donlon, T. F., 368
Doran, L. I., 190
Dorans, N. J., 144
Dostrow, V., 536
Dougherty, T. W., 247, 252
Douglass, 547
Dove, A., 568, 569
Downey, J., 345
Downs, H., 546, 547
Drake, L. E., 429
Draper, J. F., 561
Drasgow, F., 144, 561
Dreher, G. F., 248, 252
DuBois, P. H., 12, 582
Duker, J., 430
Dulcan, M. K., 241
Dun, T. M., 511
Dunham, R. M., 199
Dunlap, W. P., 108
Dunn, I. M., 338
Dunn, J. A., 380
Dunn, L. M., 338, 339
Dunnette, M. D., 139, 142, 154, 189, 577
Dupue, R. A., 524
Dush, D. M., 479
Dykman, R. A., 349

Eaton, N. K., 189
Ebel, R. L., 136, 163
Eber, H. W., 439, 441
Ebert, R. J., 247, 252
Edelbrock, C., 241
Educational Testing Service, 144, 351, 352, 353, 366, 371, 375, 597
Edwards, A. L., 163, 442
Edwards, G. A., 292
Edwards, P., 530
Egeland, B., 436
Egeland, B. R., 201, 337
Ehler, J. G., 240
Ehrhardt, A. A., 345
Eisenberg, T., 88
Eisenberger, R., 202, 203
Ekman, P. N., 210
Ekman, P., 253, 500
Ekren, V. W., 201
Elashoff, J., 200, 582
Elkin, E. J., 345
Elliot, R., 583
Ellis, A., 424, 453
Ellis, T. E., 497
Ellison, R. L., 580
Emory, E. K., 320
Endicott, J., 240
Endler, N. S., 411, 412, 511
Equal Employment Opportunity Commission, 593

Erdberg, S. P., 435
Eriksen, C. W., 516
Ernst, J., 162
Eslinger, P. J., 347
Esquivel, G. B., 348
Evans, K. A., 368
Evans, L., 494, 511
Evers, S. E., 493
Everson, H. T., 517
Ewart, C. K., 407
Exner, J. E., 457, 459, 461, 462, 464, 470, 476, 481, 642
Eyde, L. D., 637
Eysenck, H. J., 418, 456, 522, 556

Fagan, J. F., 321, 325, 327
Fairclough, D. L., 349
Falek, A., 320
Farley, G. K., 525
Farr, J. L., 142
Farrell, A. D., 501, 505, 638, 640
Fay, W. H., 566
Fechner, G. T., 15
Feifel, H., 523
Feigenbaum, D., 570
Feinstein, A. R., 546
Feldman, M. J., 445
Feldman, 199
Felsten, J. F., 561
Fidell, L. S., 90, 128
Fifer, G., 558
Filskov, F. E., 530
Fincham, F. D., 404
Finkel, N. J., 12
Finn, M. B., 519
Finn, S. E., 434
First, M. B., 241
Fisher, P., 531
Fisher, R. A., 651
Fiske, D. W., 147
Flaherty, V. L., 205
Flamos, O., 346
Flanagan, J. C., 175, 410
Flaugher, R. L., 559, 560, 574, 582, 583
Fleishman, E. A., 401, 411
Fleiss, J. L., 121
Fletcher, J. M., 530, 531, 532
Fletcher, J. N., 529
Flynn, P., 435
Fode, K. L., 200
Folkman, S., 523, 524
Follick, M. J., 541
Folstein, M. F., 345, 347
Foltz, D., 178
Forbes, E. J., 437
Ford, A. D., 545
Forrester, B. J., 582
Forsterling, F., 405
Fort, P., 59
Fowler, R. D., 173, 430, 505
Fowles, G. P., 304
Fox, N. L., 332
Francis-Williams, J., 531
Frank, B., 190
Frank, G. H., 298, 300, 418
Frank, L. K., 457
Franken, E. A., 581
Fraser, E. D., 272
Frederiksen, C., 578
Fredrikson, M., 499
Freeman, F. S., 257
Freeman, W., 490
Freeman, W. L., 349
French, J. L., 341
French, 196
Freud, S., 254
Friend, R., 492

Friesen, W. V., 253, 500
Fruchter, B., 55
Fuchs, D., 199
Fuchs, L. S., 199
Fuld, P. A., 531
Funder, D. C., 191, 413
Furby, L., 118
Furnham, A., 437

Gade, P., 382
Galton, F., 13, 14, 76, 261, 478
Gamble, K. R., 471
Garcia, J., 569
Gardner, E. F., 359
Gardner, H., 258, 305
Gardner, M. K., 311
Gardner, M. Y., 349
Garfield, S. L., 430
Garland, H., 248
Gates, R. D., 531
Gati, I., 400
Geer, J. H., 491, 494
Geiselman, R. E., 500
Georgoff, P. B., 462
Gerardi, R. J., 492
Gerritse, R., 430
Gersh, D., 435
Gessell, A., 321, 322, 323
Gessner, T., 347
Gianetti, R. Z., 205
Gibbon, M., 241
Gibby, R. G., 464
Gibertini, M., 304
Gilberstadt, H., 430
Gill, M. M., 288, 289, 292, 297, 459, 473, 478, 479, 484
Gillespie, R., 464
Gillingham, W. H., 201
Gilmore, D. C., 250
Gilson, B. S., 541, 542, 543
Glasser, A. J., 289, 292, 296, 297
Gleason, J. R., 342
Gleser, G. C., 100, 189, 190
Glutting, J. J., 280
Goddard, H. H., 265
Goetcheus, G., 468
Gohdes, D., 349
Goldberg, L. R., 192, 210, 419, 420, 628
Golden, C. J., 529, 534, 535, 536
Goldfried, M. R., 486
Goldiamond, I., 209
Goldman, B. A., 192, 195
Goldman, R. D., 578, 579, 580, 581
Goldstein, G., 530
Goldstein, L. H., 347
Goodman, J., 571, 574
Goolsby, C. E., 368
Gordon, E. W., 575
Gordon, W. A., 530
Gorsuch, R. L., 96, 510
Gotkin, T. D., 561
Gottfredson, G. D., 413
Gottfredson, L. S., 389
Gottlib, I. H., 138, 496
Gottman, J., 497
Gough, H. G., 162, 436, 449
Gould, S. J., 258, 584
Grad, G., 59
Graham, F. K., 347
Graham, J. R., 432
Graham, L. G., 497
Graham, S., 405
Grant, I., 530
Greaud, V. A., 505
Green, B. F., 505, 582
Green, B. I., 505

Green, D. F., 207
Green, D. R., 561
Greenfield, D. B., 327
Grenier, J. R., 210
Gresham, F. M., 311
Grieco, A., 546, 547
Groenweg, G., 339
Groth-Marmat, G., 205, 206
Grotz, R., 546, 547
Gruen, A., 524
Guastello, S. J., 640
Guertin, W. H., 298, 300
Guilford, J. P., 23, 55, 163, 438
Guion, R. M., 172, 210
Gulgoz, S., 313
Gunnison, J. A., 334
Gurie, 582
Gustavson, J. L., 535
Guttman, L., 173
Guyatt, G., 106
Guzman, B. L., 332
Gwynne, J., 198
Gynther, M. D., 419, 422, 435, 441, 442, 445, 446
Gynther, R. A., 419, 422, 441, 442, 445, 446
Gyurke, J. S., 313

Haber, R. H., 342
Haber, R. N., 514, 517
Haemmerlie, F. M., 437
Hagen, E. P., 256, 264, 272, 276, 280
Haith, M. M., 504
Hakel, M. D., 248, 411, 476
Hall, D. T., 386
Hall, E. M., 407
Hall, J. A., 254
Hall, J. C., 378
Hall, V. C., 566
Halstead, W., 533
Halverson, H. M., 322
Hambleton, R. K., 152
Hammer, A. L., 524
Hampson, E., 207
Hancock, P., 248, 252
Haney, W., 258, 556
Hanford, G. H., 368
Hansen, J. C., 388, 395, 400
Hardy, J. B., 558, 566
Hardy, K., 280, 281
Hargadon, F., 366
Harmon, H. H., 96
Harmon, K., 281
Harmon, L. W., 400
Harper, D. C., 436
Harris, D. B., 380
Harris, F. C., 208
Harris, M. M., 247, 251, 252
Harris, T., 522
Harrison, R., 476
Hart, B., 417
Hartig, L., 579, 580
Hartigan, J., 566
Hartlage, L. C., 566
Hartman, D. E., 206, 628
Hartmann, D. P., 121
Hartwell, S. H., 151
Harty, H., 364
Hase, H. P., 192
Hathaway, S. R., 426, 429, 430, 431, 435
Hatlelid, D., 223
Hattie, J., 348
Hayes, F. B., 339
Hayman, A., 530
Haynes, S. N., 486, 494, 499, 500, 637, 638
Hearst, E., 15
Heaton, R. K., 530
Hebb, D. O., 259

Hebel, J. R., 332
Heider, F., 404
Heilbrun, A. B., 444, 449
Heimberg, R. C., 248
Heitzmann, C. A., 525
Heller, K., 228
Henderson, M., 437
Henderson, N. B., 566
Henri, V., 417
Henri, Z., 458
Henrichs, T., 430
Henry, C. A., 634
Henry, P., 364, 634
Hensen, M., 208
Henson, R., 203
Herbart, J. F., 14
Herbert, W., 336
Herman, D. O., 305
Hernstein, R. J., 584
Herring, J. P., 265
Herrnstein, R. J., 265, 266
Herron, L., 436
Herron, E. W., 471
Herrzoff, N., 497
Hersen, M., 207
Hersen, M., 486, 494
Hersh, J. B., 201
Hertz, M. R., 459, 462, 463, 470
Herzoff, N., 436
Hewitt, B., 581
Hiester, D. S., 298, 300
Higgins, E. T., 404
Hilgard, E. R., 24, 192, 639
Hill, R. A., 497
Hillard, M. C., 464
Hindley, C. B., 326
Hirt, M., 502, 503
Hiscock, M., 497
Hodges, W., 292
Hodos, W., 568
Hofer, P. J., 505
Hoffmann, H., 435
Hogan, A. E., 327
Hogan, J., 620
Hogarty, P. S., 321
Holahan, C. J., 407, 408
Holland, J. L., 192, 389, 399, 413
Hollingworth, H. L., 250
Holmes, C. B., 281
Holmes, T. H., 521
Holmes, T. S., 519, 547
Holt, R. R., 25, 484, 628
Holtzman, W. H., 471
Holz, W., 209
Holzberg, J. D., 462
Hooper, 327
Hooper, S. R., 318, 322, 325
Hopkins, K. D., 163
Horn, J. L., 8, 274
Horowitz, F. D., 325, 326
Horowitz, M., 490
Horowitz, M. J., 524
Hosey, G. M., 349
Hotelling, H., 438
Houldin, A. D., 437
Howard, L., 612
Howell, K. W., 346
Hughes, J., 530
Humphreys, L. G., 565
Hunt, J. McV., 412
Hunt, E., 311
Hunt, T. V., 332, 503, 541
Hunter, J. E., 189, 191, 574, 575, 578
Hunter, J. L., 191
Hunter, R. F., 191
Huntley, R. M., 561
Huppertz, J. W., 566
Hurlburt, N., 321
Hutchinson, T. A., 546

Hyer, L., 436
Hynd, T. W., 530

Iacono, W. G., 489, 499, 500, 636
Ilg, F. L., 322
Ilgen, D., 589
Imada, A. S., 248
Imhof, E. A., 638
Ingram, R. E., 145
Ironson, G. H., 172, 561
Irwin, L., 490
Irwin, M., 521

Jackson, B. A., 545
Jackson, D. N., 445, 447, 631, 633
Jackson, E. W., 258
Jacobs, R., 142
Jacobsen, T. L., 580
Jacobson, L., 556, 582, 603
Jaffe, J., 254
Jaffe, M. W., 545
James, O., 522
Jenkins, C. D., 541
Jennings, J. R., 500
Jensen, A. R., 11, 336, 456, 503, 556, 563, 644
Jockusch, E., 175
Johanson, J. C., 399
Johansson, C. B., 398, 399
Johansson, G., 407
Johnson, 299
Johnson, J. G., 523
Johnson, J. H., 205, 522
Johnson, J. V., 407
Johnson, V., 500
Johnston, D., 499
Joint Committee on Testing Practices, 654, 658
Jones, E. E., 404, 405
Jones, M. B., 381
Jones, R. A., 497
Jung, C., 478
Jungeblut, A., 619

Kaemmer, B., 432, 435
Kagan, J., 558, 566
Kaiser, H., 55
Kalas, R., 241
Kallingal, A., 563
Kalonoff, H., 530
Kamhi, A. G., 337
Kamin, L. J., 556, 582, 584
Kammeier, M. L., 435
Kamphaus, R. W., 334
Kanfer, F. H., 485, 487, 494, 495, 506
Kanner, A. D., 523
Kanowitz, J., 208, 209
Kaplan, E., 538
Kaplan, R. M., 24, 59, 94, 106, 140, 142, 146, 149, 150, 151, 162, 203, 204, 206, 518, 519, 521, 525, 534, 535, 541, 546, 549, 550, 551
Karlsen, B., 359
Karnarack, T., 523
Karnes, F., 335
Karnes, I., 281
Karr, S. K., 281
Kaszniak, A. W., 339, 530
Katz, S. E., 424
Katz, S. T., 544, 545, 546, 547
Kaufman, A. S., 330, 334, 335, 338
Kaufman, N. L., 334, 335
Kaufman, R. W., 334
Kaufmann, S. H., 480

Kazdin, A. E., 207
Keane, T. M., 436
Kehoe, J. F., 561
Keir, G., 378
Keiser, R. E., 471, 475
Keller, J. W., 220, 456, 638
Keller, K. E., 248
Keller, L. S., 505
Kelley, D., 459
Kelley, E. L., 24
Kelley, T. L., 8, 18
Kelly, E. L., 447, 639
Kelly, H. H., 404
Kendall, B. S., 347
Kendall, P. C., 496, 497, 506
Kendrick, S. A., 565
Kennedy, R. S., 381
Kennedy, W. A., 202, 557
Kent, G. H., 478
Kent, R. N., 208, 209
Keogh, B. K., 322, 323
Kerner, J., 458
Kerr, M., 502, 504
Keyser, D. J., 192, 194, 195
Kicklighter, R., 610
Kiersh, E., 595
Kimura, D., 207
King, S., 349
Kirkpatrick, E. A., 458
Kirmeyer, S. L., 407
Klaric, S. H., 241
Klaus, R. A., 582
Kleinsaser, L. D., 201
Klerman, G. L., 541
Klett, W. G., 363
Kline, R. B., 280
Klinger, D. E., 205
Klinger, E., 496
Klopfer, B., 459
Klos, D., 403
Knapp, R. R., 403
Knight-Jones, E. B., 332
Knobloch, H., 322, 323, 582
Knotek, P. C., 339
Knox, H. A., 320
Knutson, J. F., 456
Koch, R., 272
Koffler, S. L., 560
Kohen, E. S., 628
Kohs, S. C., 296
Koksal, F., 512
Kolb, L. C., 492
Koller, P. S., 203
Komaroff, A. L., 521
Koppitz, E. M., 346
Korgeski, G. P., 496, 506
Kozin, F., 150, 551
Kraepelin, E., 16
Kraiger, K., 476
Kramer, J. H., 530, 537, 538, 540
Kramer, J. J., 192, 194, 195
Krentzel, L. P., 326
Krinsky, S. G., 339
Kubacki, S. R., 464
Kuder, G. F., 100, 112, 395
Kuhlmann, F., 265
Kuiper, N. A., 496
Kukla, A., 580
Kusysayn, I., 447
Kutner, B., 476

Ladd, C. E., 298, 300
Lahey, B. B., 208
Lakotas, L., 151
Lally, M., 504
Lam, Y. R., 171
Lambert, N., 604
Lamp, R. E., 566
Landis, C., 424
Landy, F. J., 136, 142, 151, 153, 211

Lang, P. J., 491, 494
Langlais, M. L., 339
Lanyon, B. P., 479
Lanyon, R. I., 479
Larrabee, L. L., 201
Larsen, G. E., 503, 504
Larsen, R. M., 220, 316, 456, 468
Larson, R., 422
Latham, V. M., 249
Lautenschlager, G. J., 205
Lauter, D., 613, 616, 617
Lawlis, G. F., 491
Lawshe, C. L., 136
Lawson-Kerr, K., 530
Lazarus, R. S., 523, 524
Lazovik, A. D., 494
Lee, E. D., 612
Lee, H., 332
Lee, J. A., 505
Lefever, D. W., 363
Leichsenring, F., 471
Lemke, S., 408, 409
Lerner, B., 621
Lessen-Firestone, J., 320
Lesser, G. S., 558
Lester, B. M., 320
Levenson, H., 436
Levenson, M. R., 435
Levenson, R. W., 500
Levi, A., 566
Levin, H. S., 529, 530, 531, 532
Levine, H. M., 525
Levine, S., 541
Levy, D., 21, 458
Levy, S., 595
Lewandowski, D. G., 24, 266, 300, 301, 302, 304, 464, 469, 484
Lewinsohn, P. N., 138
Lewis, J. F., 573
Lezak, M. D., 345, 401, 530, 537
Lichtenstein, E., 407
Liebert, R. M., 514, 517
Lifschitz, M. H., 321, 323
Lifshitz, F., 59
Likert, R., 159
Lillesand, D. B., 492
Lindemann, S. J., 566
Lindgren, S., 436
Lindzey, G., 457, 475, 481
Linn, R. L., 173, 175
Lipsitz, S., 198
Liss, P. H., 504
Little, K. B., 476, 628
Litz, B. T., 436
LoBello, S. G., 313
Locke, B. Z., 138
Loftus, E. F., 11
Lohman, D. F., 378
Lohr, J. M., 497
Long, C. J., 546, 547
Long, P. A., 570
Loper, R. G., 435
Lopez, E., 348
Lopez, R., 566
Lord, E., 459
Lord, F. M., 88, 120
Lorge, I., 337
Lotsoff, E., 462
Loughmiller, G. C., 580
Love, K. G., 250
Lowell, E. L., 472
Lowman, R. L., 448, 638
Loy, D. L., 430
Lubin, B., 220, 316, 380, 422, 430, 442, 456, 468, 492
Lumsden, J., 344
Lunemann, A., 566
Lunneborg, C., 503

Luria, A., 334
Luria, A. R., 533, 534
Lushene, R. E., 510
Lyman, B., 223
Lyon, 335

Machover, K., 480
Mackinnon, R. A., 227, 247
Mackintosh, N. J., 504
Macundy, C., 223
Magnusson, D., 412
Mahoney, M. J., 499
Mahoney, T., 496
Maisto, S. A., 490, 493
Majovski, L. V., 334
Maloney, M. D., 419, 420
Maloney, M. P., 239, 245
Mandes, E., 347
Mandler, G., 513, 514, 515, 516
Marcus, A., 502, 504
Marks-Katz, M., 59
Marlett, N. J., 516
Marshalek, B., 378
Marshall, C., 220, 422, 638
Marshall, H., 162
Marshall, W. L., 500
Martin, H. G., 438
Martin, 335
Martin, R. P., 339
Marting, M. S., 524
Maruish, M., 638
Marx, B., 436
Mask, N., 340
Massman, P. J., 530, 537, 540
Masters, B. N., 561
Masters, W., 500
Masuda, M., 521
Matarazzo, J., 220, 422
Matarazzo, J. D., 25, 206, 228, 254, 284, 294, 295, 305, 316, 456, 468, 638
Matarazzo, R. G., 254
Matias, R., 491, 494
Matthews, W. C., 150, 551
Mauer, D., 337
Maurer, T. J., 208
Mayfield, E. C., 247
Mayman, M., 476
McAnulty, D. P., 201
McCall, R., 30, 32
McCall, R. B., 321, 325, 326
McCall, W. A., 53
McCallum, R. S., 280, 281, 335
McCandless, B. B., 462
McClelland, D. C., 106, 472
McCordick, S., 518, 519
McCormick, E. J., 589
McCrae, R. R., 450
McDaniel, M. A., 188
McDonell, A., 411
McEwen, J., 541, 549
McFall, R. M., 411, 492
McGivern, R. F., 339
McGrath, R. E., 421
McGrew, 345
McGuinnes, S. G., 581
McKay, J. R., 490, 493
McKee, P., 610
McKegney, F. P., 546
McKenzie, R. C., 191
McKinley, J. C., 426, 429, 430, 435
McKnight, C., 175
McLarty, J. R., 561
McMahon, R. C., 435
McManis, D. L., 202
McMichael, A. J., 332
McNeilly, M., 501
McNemar, O. W., 424
McNemar, Q., 88, 268
McPeek, W. M., 560

Meehl, P. E., 147, 191, 430, 431, 628
Megargee, E. I., 437
Mehrens, W. A., 334
Meichenbaum, D., 498, 506, 518
Meikle, S., 430
Melchert, P. A., 202
Melei, J. P., 192
Mellits, E. D., 558, 566
Meloy, J. R., 456, 469
Mercer, J. R., 558, 565, 571, 572, 573, 574, 582, 598, 603
Mermelstein, R., 523
Merrill, M. A., 268, 270, 271
Merwin, J. C., 359
Messick, S., 136, 151, 619, 631, 633
Metalsy, G. I., 203
Metraux, R. W., 461, 463
Meunier, C., 516
Meyer-Bahlburg, H. F., 345
Michael, B., 504
Michels, R., 227
Middlestadt, S. E., 247, 252
Miller, A. B., 184
Miller, D. R., 464
Miller, H. R., 450
Miller, J. P., 198
Miller, S., 502
Millman, J., 120, 152
Millon, T., 450
Millsap, R. E., 517
Minor, J. S., 337
Minton, H. L., 400
Mischel, W., 404, 405, 486, 626
Mitchell, J. V., 192, 220, 221
Mitchell, K. J., 189
Mitchell, K. M., 235, 239
Mitchell, S. K., 489
Mitchell, W. G., 332
Mohs, R., 530
Monroe, S. M., 524, 526
Moos, R. H., 407, 408, 409
Moreland, K. L., 505, 628, 637
Moreno, K. E., 505
Morf, M. E., 447
Morgan, C., 22, 471
Morgan, C. D., 464
Morgan, D., 369
Morishima, A., 345
Morley, J. E., 521
Morris, L. W., 514, 517
Moskowitz, R. W., 545
Moss, H. A., 558
Most, R. B., 637
Moylan, A., 494
Muldrow, T. W., 191
Mulhern, R. K., 344, 349
Mullins, C. J., 444
Mungas, D. M., 447
Munro, E., 503
Munsinger, H., 556
Murphy, 247
Murray, H., 22
Murray, H. A., 442, 443, 445, 471, 472, 481
Murray–Jobsis, J., 447
Murstein, B. I., 474, 476
Museum of Modern Art, 477
Myers, I. B., 448
Myers, R. A., 228

Nader, R., 140
Naglieri, J. A., 323, 335
Nagy, V. T., 523
Naliboff, B. D., 521
Nanda, H., 100
National Assessment of Education Progress (NAEP), 351

National Commission on Testing and Public Policy, 484, 643
National Council on Measurement in Education, 123–124, 134, 179, 216, 632, 634, 637
Neher, L. A., 201
Neisser, U., 334, 502
Neisser, U. A., 11
Nelson, E., 547
Nettelbeck, T., 503, 504
Nichols, R. C., 192
Nigl, A. J., 564
Nisbett, R. E., 404, 405
Noble, C. A., 561
Nolan, R. F., 335
Norman, G., 106
Normand, J., 189
Novick, M. R., 216, 589
Nunnally, J. C., 30, 99, 107, 126
Nurius, P. S., 245, 254
Nykodym, N., 248

O'Connor, E. J., 190
O'Leary, B. S., 565
O'Leary, K. D., 208, 209
O'Malley, W. B., 421
O'Sullivan, M., 210
Oakland, T., 144, 570, 571, 574
Ober, B. A., 538
Obrzut, J. E., 530
Odbert, H. S., 439
Oehler-Stinnett, 335
Oei, T. P. S., 494, 511
Olinger, L. J., 496
Olkin, R., 436
Olmedo, E. L., 380, 584
Opton, E., 602, 604
Orenstein, D., 150, 551
Osbourne, W., 192, 195
Osipow, S., 401, 402
Ostrea, E., 320
Owen, D., 258, 559, 619

Paine, C., 220, 316, 380, 422, 442, 456, 468
Palmer, B. L., 281
Palmer, F. H., 566
Palola, E. G., 516
Pancheri, P., 521
Papanis, N., 490
Parducci, A., 160, 161
Parker, J. D. A., 511
Parker, K., 469
Parkinson, C. N., 13
Parmelee, R., 144, 571
Parra, E. B., 601
Parsons, O. A., 530
Partenio, I., 571
Pasamanick, B., 322, 323
Pasamanick, B. A., 582
Patalano, F., 199
Patterson, C. H., 239
Pattishall, E., 106
Paul, G. L., 209
Paul, S. M., 377, 516
Payne, D. A., 368
Pazda, S. L., 436
Pearson, K., 76, 100
Peca-Baker, T., 248
Pechacek, T. F., 497
Pedhauzer, E., 128
Pendleton, M. G., 530
Penk, W. E., 436
Peoples, V. Y., 400
Peter, O., 405
Peters, L. H., 190
Peterson, C., 497
Peterson, R., 220, 422, 638

Pettigrew, T. F., 558
Pfeifer, C., 563
Pfohl, W., 335
Phelps, L., 281
Phillips, J., 198
Pierce, G. R., 411
Pinizzotto, A. J., 12
Piotrowski, C., 220, 456, 470, 638
Piotrowski, Z., 459
Pirozzolo, F. J., 530
Plaisted, J. R., 535
Polansky, N., 490
Polkey, C. E., 347
Polyson, J., 220, 422, 638
Pons, L., 479
Pottenger, M., 138
Powell, J., 499
Powell, S. S., 525
Power, K. G., 512
Prather, E. N., 471, 475
Price, K. H., 248
Price, P. B., 580
Primoff, E. S., 637
Prince, R. J., 640
Prout, 339
Prusoff, B. A., 138
Pugliese, M. D., 59

Quaintance, M. K., 401, 411
Quay, L. C., 202, 559
Quigley, A. M., 620

Rabin, A. I., 298, 300
Rablen, R. A., 237
Radcliffe, J. A., 444
Rafferty, J. E., 479
Rahe, R. H., 519, 547
Rajaratnam, N., 100
Raju, N. S., 189
Ralston, S. M., 251
Ramey, C. T., 326
Ramirez, M., 578
Ramos, R. A., 189
Rapaport, D., 288, 289, 292, 297, 459, 473, 478, 479, 484, 490
Rappaport, N. B., 201
Rasmussen, 253
Rathus, S. A., 492
Rauchway, A., 469
Raven, J., 378
Rebok, G., 345
Recase, M. D., 205
Redfield, 209
Reid, J. B., 208
Reid, N., 349
Reitan, R. M., 533, 535
Reschly, D. J., 216, 564, 572, 610
Research and Education Association, 192, 196
Retzlaff, P., 304
Reynolds, C. R., 334, 349, 536, 561, 563, 564
Reynolds, D. N., 494
Reznikoff, M., 469
Richards, J. M., 580
Richardson, M. W., 100, 112
Richley, 610
Richman, L. C., 436
Rimland, B., 503, 504
Rinn, W. E., 294
Ritzler, B., 456
Ritzler, B. A., 477, 642
Roberts, E., 347
Robertson, G. J., 637
Robertson, I., 189
Robinson, J. P., 192, 195
Rodriguez, C. M., 517
Roe, A., 403

Rogers, C. R., 235, 237, 239, 449
Rogers, P. L., 254
Rohrbaugh, 247
Roos, G., 469
Rorschach, H., 21
Rosanoff, A. J., 478
Rosen, A., 430, 628
Rosenbaum, P., 349
Rosenberg, S. J., 305
Rosenfeld, P., 205
Rosenman, R. H., 521
Rosenthal, R., 200, 254, 556, 582, 603
Rosnow, R. L., 200
Ross, R. R., 581
Rosser, R., 542
Rossini, E., 536
Rothlisberg, B. A., 334
Rothman, S., 216, 221, 258, 578, 597, 634
Rothney, J. W. M., 362
Rotter, J. B., 94, 178, 476, 479
Rourke, B. P., 531
Rowe, D. C., 625, 626
Rubin, D. B., 159
Rubin, Z., 148–149, 178
Ruch, G. M., 18
Rudman, H. C., 359
Rule, B. G., 516
Rushton, J. P., 556, 584
Russel, D. L., 531
Russell, I. J., 151
Russell, J. T., 183, 184
Russell, 299
Russell, J. T., 183, 184
Russell, L. B., 550
Rutter, M., 530, 531
Ruud, W. N., 248
Ryan, J. J., 305

Sabers, D. L., 564
Saccuzzo, D. P., 24, 229, 255, 266, 299, 300, 301, 302, 304, 375, 378, 464, 469, 484, 502, 503, 504, 534, 535
Saigal, S., 349
Salmon, D. P., 530, 537, 540
Sands, W. A., 382
Sands, W. L., 247
Sanford, R. N., 24, 639
Sarason, B. R., 509, 522, 524, 525
Sarason, I. G., 411, 413, 509, 514, 515, 516, 522, 524, 525
Sarason, S. B., 513, 514, 515, 516
Saslow, G., 254, 485, 487, 494, 495, 506
Sattler, J. M., 144, 198, 199, 201, 202, 204, 208, 220, 241, 250, 251, 256, 264, 272, 276, 280, 297, 299, 305, 330, 340, 343, 566, 580, 582, 598, 603, 606, 609
Satz, P., 529, 530, 531, 532
Saunders, B. T., 201
Sawyer, J., 628
Sax, G., 163
Scarr-Salapatek, S., 558
Schafer, R., 288, 289, 292, 297, 459, 473, 478, 479, 484
Scheier, I. H., 510
Scheuneman, J. D., 559, 561
Schill, T., 292
Schmidt, F., 189
Schmidt, F. L., 191, 574, 575, 578
Schmitt, N., 189, 247, 252
Schmitz, S. P., 280

Schneider, F. W., 400
Schneider, L. M., 563
Schoggen, P., 406
Schrader, W. B., 560
Schuerger, J. M., 441
Schulte, R., 375
Schultz, C. B., 202
Schwartz, J., 241
Schwartz, R., 497
Sciarrino, J. A., 139
Science Research Associates, Inc., 397
Scott, L. H., 380
Scott, P., 209
Sebkovial, N. J., 561
Sechrest, L., 414
Sechrest, L. B., 210
Sedlacek, W., 563
Seever, M., 316
Seguin, E., 15, 319
Self, P. A., 325, 326
Seligman, M. E. P., 203
Seligmann, J., 612
Sellers, T. A., 281
Sexton, M., 332
Shaeffer, C., 523
Shaffer, L., 484
Shaffer, L. F., 24, 639
Shakow, D., 24, 639
Share, J. B., 272
Sharkey, K. J., 477
Shaver, P. R., 192, 195
Sheldon, 339
Sherman, R. H., 202
Sherry, D., 220, 456, 638
Sherwood, R. D., 364
Shimkunas, A. M., 435
Shine, A., 304
Shisslak, C. M., 436
Shisslak, C. S., 497
Shneidman, E. S., 476, 628
Sholomskas, D., 138
Shumaker, J., 205, 206
Siegel, I. E., 558
Siegel, J. M., 522
Siegelman, M., 403
Silver, M. J., 200
Silver, N. C., 108
Silverstein, A. B., 305, 332
Simon, A. J., 326
Simon, T., 16, 259, 265
Simon, W. E., 201
Simonetti, J. L., 248
Simons, A. D., 526
Sineps, J., 430
Sines, J. O., 628
Singer, J., 456, 469
Singer, R. D., 203
Singh, L., 476
Sinha, D. K., 369
Sisson, L., 430
Sligner, N., 304
Sloan, R. D., 497
Sloman, J., 326
Slosson, R. C., 341
Smith, A. E., 332
Smith, B., 414
Smith, G. A., 503
Smith, I. E., 320
Smith, J. E., 464
Smith, K. L., 280
Smith, R. E., 413, 518
Smith, S., 519
Smith, S. H., 519
Smith, T. L., 521
Smith, T. W., 497
Smith, W. L., 581
Smith, 335
Snow, R. E., 200, 378, 413, 582
Snyderman, M., 216, 221, 258, 578, 597, 634

Solomon, G. F., 521
Sostek, A. M., 320, 321
Sparling, J. J., 326
Spearman, C. E., 100, 257, 261, 417
Spencer, T. J., 502, 503
Sperry, R., 334
Spielberger, C., 292
Spielberger, C. D., 510, 511, 514, 517, 519
Spiers, P. A., 536
Spiker, D. G., 240
Spilker, B., 206, 542
Spitzer, R. L., 240, 241
Squire, L. R., 537
Stallones, R. A., 142
Stan, E. A., 339
Standage, K., 240
Stang, J. D., 531
Stanley, G., 503
Stanley, J. C., 163
Stanley, K. E., 547
Starr, R., 320
Steele, C. T., 566
Steele, J. W., 211
Steer, R. A., 496
Stehbens, J. A., 436
Stephenson, W., 162
Steptoe, A., 499
Stern, W., 266
Sternberg, L., 571
Sternberg, R. J., 258, 311, 336, 578, 642
Stevens, S. S., 161
Stevenson, I., 227
Stevenson, 339
Stewart, A. J., 476
Stewart, A. L., 546, 548, 549
Stokols, D., 406
Stone, B. J., 313
Strack, S., 523
Stracqualursi, F., 349
Strauss, M., 320
Strauss, M. E., 347
Streiner, D. L., 450
Stricker, L. J., 444, 445
Strong, E., 15
Strong, E. K., 387, 388
Subkoviak, M. J., 120
Succi, G. J., 559
Suinn, R. M., 494, 514
Sullivan, 199
Sundberg, N. D., 220
Super, D. E., 386, 402
Svanum, S., 421
Swartz, J. D., 471
Sweet, J. J., 536
Sweet, R. C., 202
Sweetland, R. C., 192, 194, 195
Swemer, W. A., 497
Symonds, P. M., 162
Sympson, J. B., 505
Szasz, T. S., 629
Szatmari, P., 349

Tabachnick, B. G., 90, 128
Tait, E., 441
Tannenbaum, A. J., 380, 381
Taplin, P. S., 208
Tarico, V. S., 581
Tasto, D. L., 490, 494
Tatsuoka, M. M., 439, 441
Taulbeee, E. S., 430, 511
Tavernelli, M., 441
Taylor, C. W., 580
Taylor, H. C., 183, 184
Taylor, J., 202
Taylor, J. A., 512, 513
Taylor, R. L., 571
Tedeschi, R. G., 94
Tellegem, A. M., 432, 435

Temp, G., 144, 564
Templer, D. I., 280
Teng, E. L., 347
Tenopyr, M. L., 136, 151
Teplin, L. A., 241
Teri, L., 138
Terman, L. M., 17, 18, 257, 259, 265, 266, 268, 270, 271, 417
Terpstra, D. E., 248
Terrell, F., 202
Terrell, M. D., 575
Terrell, S. C., 202
Testa, M. A., 541
Theye, F., 202
Thompson, D. E., 140
Thompson, H., 322
Thompson, T. A., 140
Thorndike, E. L., 100, 250, 418
Thorndike, R. L., 144, 200, 256, 264, 272, 276, 280, 348, 582
Thorndike, R. M., 261, 575, 576, 577
Thorpe, J. S., 471
Thumin, F. J., 435
Thurbers, S. A., 321, 323
Thurstone, L. L., 15, 272
Tiber, N., 202
Tikotzki, Y., 400
Timms, R. M., 150
Titchner, E. B., 15
Tittle, C. K., 400
Tomkins, S. S., 476
Topinka, C. W., 335
Topp, R., 519
Torgerson, W. S., 163
Torrance, E. P., 348
Toshima, M. T., 59
Traub, R. E., 171
Traxler, A. J., 566
Tronic, E. Z., 320
Tronick, E., 320, 321
Trontel, E. H., 447
Trost, C., 595
Trott, D. M., 447
Truax, C. B., 235, 237, 239, 255
Trumbo, D., 247, 251, 252
Tukey, J. W., 29
Tune, L. E., 347
Tunick, R. H., 304
Turk, D., 498
Turkheimer, E., 556, 584
Turnage, J. J., 381
Turner, J. A., 436
Turner, J. H., 472
Turner, R. J., 524
Turner, S. M., 491, 494
Turpin, G., 500
Twitchell, M., 518

Tyler, L. E., 229, 388, 389, 402
Tynan, W. D., 320
Tziner, A., 247, 252

Uhl, N., 88
Ulrich, L., 247, 251, 252
Ulrich, R., 209
Umansky, W., 318, 322, 325, 327
Upper, D., 492, 493

Valencia, R. R., 332, 566
van Baar, A., 325, 326
Van de Riet, V., 557
Vance, R. J., 211
Vandenburg, S. G., 544, 584
Varble, D. L., 476
Vickers, D., 504
Viglione, D., 464
Vitro, F. T., 201
Vogler, G. P., 544, 584

Wade, T. C., 220
Wadsworth, A. P., 511
Wagner, E. E., 346, 469
Wagner, R., 247, 251, 252
Wainer, H., 136
Waldman, D. A., 382
Walker, A. M., 237
Walker, E. L., 464
Walker, R. N., 461, 463
Walker, S., 542
Wallace, J. P., 151
Wallace, W. L., 294, 366, 368
Wallhermfechtel, J., 435
Wallis, H. R., 220, 316, 380, 422, 442, 456, 468
Walsh, R. A., 464
Walsh, S., 436
Walsh, W. B., 388, 389, 402
Walter, S., 106
Wang, W., 349
Ward, M. P., 239, 245, 419, 420
Ward, T. J., 205
Ward, 610
Ware, J., 151
Ware, J. E., 541, 546, 548, 549
Warner, M. H., 381
Wasik, B. H., 332
Wasserman, A. L., 349
Wasserman, G. S., 504
Watlington, D. K., 335
Watson, C. W., 363
Watson, D., 492, 516
Watson, R. I., 269
Weaver, K. A., 280
Webb, A., 272
Webb, J. T., 435

Webb, 418
Weber, E. H., 14
Webster, E. C., 247, 248, 252
Webster, J. S., 536
Webster, 313
Wechsler, D., 19, 271, 284, 285, 288, 289, 299, 300, 303, 304, 418
Weekley, J. A., 190
Weeks, J. L., 444
Weiner, B., 405, 580
Weiner, H., 521
Weiner, I. B., 461, 642
Weiner, P., 436
Weingardner, J., 447
Weiss, D. J., 172, 173, 639
Weissman, A. N., 496
Weissman, M. M., 138
Welcher, D. W., 558, 566
Welsh, G. S., 431, 434, 435
Welsh, K., 530
Wermiel, S., 595
Werner, H., 537
Wesman, A., 565
Wesman, A. G., 158, 163
Westen, D., 474, 475
Wetzler, S., 450
Weyand, K., 280
Whaley, F., 490
Wheeler, L., 533
Whipple, G. M., 15, 458
Whisman, M. A., 497
White, J. C., 557
Whitehouse, P. J., 347
Wicker, A. W., 406, 407
Wickham, T., 300, 301, 302
Wiederholt, J. L., 344
Wiens, A. N., 228, 230, 239, 249, 253, 254
Wiesner, A. N., 247
Wigdor, A., 566
Wiggins, J. S., 13, 419, 421, 447
Wiggins, N., 445, 628
Wilbourne, J. M., 444
Wild, C. L., 560
Wilder, J., 501
Wilimas, J. A., 349
Wilkening, G. N., 535
Wilkinson, S. J., 522
Williams, C. L., 434, 435
Williams, G. H., 541
Williams, J. B. W., 241
Williams, P. B., 560
Williams, R. C., 567, 569
Williams, S., 497
Williams, T. A., 205
Williamson, W. D., 321, 323
Willson, R. J., 504
Willson, V. L., 335
Wilmer, C., 347

Wilner, N., 524
Wilson, D. K., 151
Wilson, G. S., 321, 323
Wine, J. C., 509
Wing, H., 189, 207, 210
Wing, K. R., 586
Winget, B. M., 201
Winter, D. G., 476
Wishner, J., 462
Wissler, C., 259
Witmer, J. M., 199
Witt, J. C., 311, 349
Wolfson, D., 533
Wolk, R. B., 477
Wolk, R. L., 477
Wolkind, S., 320
Wolpe, J., 491, 518
Woo-Sam, J. M., 289, 292, 296, 297
Wood, D. J., 240
Wood, P. S., 581
Woodcock, R. W., 344
Woodward, J. A., 500
Woodworth, R. S., 423
World Health Organization, 547
Wright, O. R., 247
Wright, T. L., 94
Wrightsman, L. S., 192, 195
Wu, A. W., 150, 551
Wundt, W., 15
Wysong, E., 400

Yarro, M., 209
Yates, F., 651
Yates, J. W., 546
Yen, W. M., 107, 110, 164, 165, 169
Yerkes, R., 17
Yerkes, R. M., 265
Young, G. C., 531

Zales, M. R., 521
Zedeck, S., 140, 247, 252, 410
Zeidner, M., 517, 524, 565
Zelko, F. A., 335
Zimet, C. N., 458
Zimet, G. D., 525
Zimmerman, I. L., 289, 292, 296, 297
Zimmerman, M., 138, 139
Zimmerman, W. S., 438
Zmuidinas, M., 405
Zores, L. S., 560
Zubin, J., 424, 471
Zuckerman, M., 11, 500, 510, 556, 584
Zurawski, R. M., 497
Zytowski, D. G., 395, 400

Ability tests, 220–221
  defined, 7
  group tests, 351–384
  group v. individual, 353–356
  individual, 316–319
Absolute Zero, 31
Accounting Orientation Test, 382
Achievement Anxiety Test, 514, 517
Achievement tests
  v. aptitude tests, 358–359
  defined, 8
  group tests, 359–362
Actuarial prediction, 627–628
Adjective checklists, 162
Admission Test for Graduate Study in
  Business, 382
Adverse impact, 557, 589
Affect Adjective Checklist, 510
Affirmative action, 613, 618
Age deviation score (ADS), 337
Age differentiation, 260, 282
Age scale, 285
Albemarle Paper Company v. Moody, 614
Alpha coefficient, 110, 115, 130
  use in split-half reliability, 111
AMERICA 2000: An Educational Strategy,
  5
American College Test (ACT), 370–371
American Journal of Psychology, 100
American Psychological Association, 17,
  24, 210
*Ana Maria R. v. California Department of
  Education*, 604
Antimode, 174
Anxiety, 508–519
  defined, 509
  measures of, 510–518
  state v. trait anxiety, 510
  v. stress, 509–510
Aptitude tests
  v. achievement tests, 358–359
  coaching for, 619
Aptitude-treatment interaction, 413
Aquiescence, 435
Armed Services Vocational Aptitude
  Battery (ASVAB), 382, 640
Army Alpha, 17–18
Army Beta, 17
Assertive Behavior Survey Schedule
  (ABSS), 492
Assertiveness, 492
Assessment
  v. testing, 219
Association for Evaluation in Guidance,
  400
Attribution theory, 404–405

Barranquilla Rapid Survey Intelligence test
  (BRSI), 381
Basal age, 276
Base rate, 181, 196
Beck Depression Inventory, 138, 139
Beck, Sam, 21
Behavior analytic approach, 506
Behavior modification; *see* Behavioral
  assessment.
Behavioral assessment, 483–499
  cognitive-behavioral procedures, 495–
  499

Behavioral assessment (*continued*)
  computerization of, 505
  functional approach, 495
  v. medical model, 485–487
  operant conditioning and, 487–489
  procedures, 485–501
  self-report techniques, 489–494
Behavioral deficits, 487, 495
Behavioral excesses, 487, 495
Behavioral observation
  and drift, 208
  and expectancies, 208–209
  and reactivity, 207–208
  reliability of, 120–121, 130–131
Bell Adjustment Inventory, 423
Bender Visual Motor Gestalt Test
  (BVMGT), 346
Bennett Mechanical Comprehension Test,
  382
Benton Visual Retention Test (BVRT),
  345–346
Bernreuter Personality Inventory, 423
Best-fitting line, 69–70
Binet Intelligence scales, 16–17, 256–282
  deviation IQ, 271
  future of, 641
  historical development, 262–272
  modern (1986) Binet scale, 272–281
  reliability of, 278–279
  standard age score, 277
  theoretical basis, 259–262
  validity of, 279
  v. Wechsler scales, 285–288
  1905 Binet-Simon scale, 262–263
  1908 Binet-Simon scale, 263–265
  1916 Stanford-Binet scale, 265–266
  1937 Stanford-Binet scale, 268–269
  1960 Stanford-Binet scale, 270–272
  1986 Stanford-Binet scale, 272–281
Binet, Alfred, 16, 257, 259–265, 417
Binet-Simon scale, 16–17; *see also Binet
  Intelligence scales*.
Biserial correlation, 84
Bivariate distributions, 64
Black Intelligence Test of Cultural Homo-
  geneity (BITCH), 381, 569–570
Brazelton Neonatal Assessment Scale
  (BNAS), 320–321
British Journal of Psychology, 100
Brown v. Board of Education, 599
Burden of proof, 617

c scale, 55
California Occupational Preference Survey
  (COPS), 403–404
California Psychological Inventory (CPI),
  22, 23, 159, 416, 436–437
California Verbal Learning Test (CVLT),
  537–540
Career Assessment Inventory, 398–399
Career Maturity Inventory (CMI), 402
Career Testing, 385–415; *see also* Employment screening tests.
  aptitude v. interest, 400–401
  interest tests, 386–401
  personality tests for, 401–405
  social-ecology approach, 405–411
  template-matching technique, 413

Carnegie Interest Inventory, 15, 387
Carroll Depression Scale, 139
Case history interviews, 244–245
Category scales, 160–162
Cattell, James McKeen, 14
Cattell, R. B., 23, 439–441
Center for Epidemiologic Studies Depres-
  sion Scale (CES-D), 46–48, 138
Child Assessment Schedule (CAS), 241
Children's Apperception Test (CAT), 477
Children's Personality Questionnaire, 441
Chitling test, 568–569
Cholesterol Tests, 142
Civil service testing
  historical precedents, 12–13
Civil Rights Bill of 1991, 595
  and test score use, 617
Class interval, 36
Clinical Analysis Questionnaire (CAQ), 441
Clinical depression, 138, 139
Clinical neuropsychology, 529–530
Clinical prediction, 627–628
Code of Fair Testing Practices in Educa-
  tion, 654–658
Coefficient alpha, 115
Coefficient of alienation, 87, 97
Coefficient of determination, 87, 97
Cognitive Abilities Test (COGAT), 364–
  365
Cognitive-behavioral assessment, 495–499,
  506
Cognitive-functional analysis, 498
College Board Scholastic Aptitude Test; *see*
  Scholastic Aptitude Test.
College Entrance Tests, 366–371; *see also*
  Scholastic Aptitude Test.
Columbia Mental Maturity Scale (CMMS),
  337–338, 341
Commission on Sex Bias in Measurement,
  400
Common variance, defined, 441
Computer assisted instruction, 174–175
Computers
  behavioral assessment uses, 505
  computerized interviews, 245
  future uses in testing, 639–640
  psychophysical assessment and, 501
  signal detection procedures, 501
  test administration and, 172, 204–206,
  505, 639–640
Concurrent validity, 137–140
Conflict Resolution Inventory (CRI), 492
Connecticut v. Teal, 620
Construct, 147
Construct validity, 147–152
Content validity, 135–136
  and test bias, 558–561
Contrast effect, 208
Contrasted-group strategy, *see* Criterion
  group.
Convergent evidence, 147–151
Cooperative School and College Ability
  Tests (SCAT), 369–370
Coping Inventory, 524
Correction for attenuation, 129–130
Correlation coefficient, 66, 96
  statistical significance of, 78–79
Correlation, 66–67
  v. causation, 88–89

Correlation (*continued*)
  correlation coefficient, 66, 96
  related to regression, 76–78
Covariance, 77
  and test reliability, 113
Covert behavior, 7
Crawford et al. v. Honig et al., 605, 608–609
Creativity tests, 348
Criterion group strategy, 387, 420, 425, 431
Criterion keying, 387
Criterion referenced tests, 62
  and item analysis, 173–175
  reliability and, 120
  validity and, 152
Criterion validity, 80, 137–146
  concurrent validity, 137–140
  meaning of criterion and, 143
  predictive validity, 137
  test bias and, 562–566
Cross validation, 88–89, 421
Cultural bias; *see also* Test bias, Testing Legislation.
  alternative tests, 568–574
  Binet intelligence scores and, 281
  Cognitive Abilities test and, 364–365
  employment screening tests and, 132–133
  in interviews, 250–251
  ignorance v. stupidity, 567–568
  IPAT Culture Fair Intelligence Test, 380–381
  models of, 575–578
  race of tester, 198–199
  Raven Progressive Matrices test and, 378
  reinforcement effects, 202
  selection devices and, 575–579
  Wechsler Intelligence Scale for Children and, 311
Cutting score, 180

Darwin, Charles, 13
Debra P. v. Turlington, 610–612
Deciles, 54–55
Declining age standard, 294–295, 314
Degrees of freedom, 79
Dental Admission Testing Program, 382
Depression, 492
Descriptive statistics, 29
Detroit Edison Co. v. N.L.R.B., 620
Developing Cognitive Abilities Test (DCAT), 365
Developmental neuropsychology, 530–531
Developmental quotient (DQ), 322
Deviation IQ, 282
Diagnostic interview, 226
Diagnostic Interview Schedule for Children (DISC), 241
Diagnostic and Statistical Manual of Mental Disorders (DSM-III-R), 138, 240
Diana v. State Board of Education, 601–602
Dichotomous test format, 156–157
Difference scores, 116–118
Differential Aptitude Test (DAT), 382
Differential item functioning (DIF) analysis, 560–561
Differential prediction, 146
Differential process theory, 578–579
Differential validity, 558
Discriminability analysis, 128
Discriminant analysis, 92, 97
Discriminant evidence, 151
Distractors, 157–158
Divergent validation, *see* Discriminant evidence.
Domain sampling model, 107–116
Drift effect, 208, 211
Dysfunctional Attitude Scale, 496
Dyslexia, 530–531

Ecological psychology, *see* Social-Ecology.
Education for All Handicapped Children Act of 1975, 597–598
Educational Testing Service, 140–141, 145, 159, 560, 595–596
Educational tracking, 59, 61, 600–601
Edwards Personal Preference Schedule (EPPS), 442
Emotional impairment
  evaluation of, 16
Empirical validity, *see* Criterion validity.
Employment interviews, 226, 247–249
Employment screening tests, 137–140, 144, 381–383
  cost effectiveness of, 190–191
  decision analysis, 180–190
  legal issues, 614–620
  Wonderlic Personnel Test, 381
Endler Multidimensional Anxiety Scales (EMAS), 511
Environmental psychology, *see* Social-Ecology.
Equal Employment Opportunity Commission (EEOC), 557, 586
  testing guidelines, 588–595
Equal Intervals, 31
Error variance, 442
Essay exams, 159
Estimated learning potentials (ELPs), 572
Ethical issues, 631–636
Evaluation interview, 239–240
Examiner–test taker relationship, 199–200
Expectancy effects, 200–202
  in behavioral observation, 208–209
Experiential World Inventory, 177–178
Experimental psychology, 14–15
External-group strategy, *see* Criterion group.

Face validity, 135
Factor analysis, 23, 93–96, 116, 128, 261
  factor loadings, 96
  methods of rotation, 96
  principle components and, 93–94
Factor analytic strategy, 421, 437–442
Factorial validity, *see* Construct validity.
False negatives, 181, 182
False positives, 181, 183
Fear Survey Schedule (FSS), 490–491
  psychometric properties of, 494
Feedback, *see* Reinforcement.
Figure drawing tests, 480
Four Systems Anxiety Questionnaire (FSAQ), 512
Four-fifths rule, 589
Frequency distributions, 34–36
Frequency polygon, 35–36, 174

Galton, Sir Francis, 13–14, 76, 261
Gender bias, *see also* Test bias.
  sexual harrassment, 593, 594–595
  vocational testing and, 388, 400
General Aptitude Test Battery (GATB), 382
General cognitive index (GCI), 330, 331
General mental ability, 260–262
Generalizability, 145–146
Gerontological Apperception Test, 477
Gessell Developmental Schedules (GDS), 321–323
  developmental quotient, 322
Golden Rule Insurance Company et al. v. Washburn et al., 613–614
Goodenough-Harris Drawing Test (G-HDT), 379
Grade inflation, 374
Graduate Record Exam (GRE), 140–141, 143, 144, 371–376, 560, 563–564, 595
Graduate School Entrance Tests, 371–377; *see also* Graduate Record Examination.

Griggs v. Duke Power Company, 133, 614–616
Group ability tests, 7, 351–384
  achievement tests, 359–362
  v. individual, 353–356
  intelligence tests, 362–365
  nonverbal, 377
Guilford, J. P., 23, 438
Guilford–Zimmerman Temperment Survey, 438

Halo effect, 250, 255
Halstead-Reitan Neuropsychological Battery, 533, 534
Hamilton Rating Scale for Depression, 139
Handbook of Psychiatric Rating Scales, 192, 196
Health index, 150
Health status measurement, 540–541
Healy-Fernald Test, 319
Henmon–Nelson Test (H–NT), 363
Herbart, J. F., 14
Hereditary Genius, 13
Hit rate, 180
Hobson v. Hansen, 600–601
Holtzman Inkblot Test, 470–471, 481
House Subcommittee on Invasion of Privacy, 484, 630
Human ability, defined, 8
Human rights
  and testing, 629

Iconic storage, 502
Illinois Test of Psycholinguistic Abilities (ITPA), 342–344
Incremental validity, 190–192
Index of Activities of Daily Living (ADL), 544–546
Index of adjustment, 626
Individual ability tests, 316–319; *see also* Binet Intelligence scales, Wechsler Intelligence scales.
  special populations and, 316–319, 336–340
  v. group test, 353–356
Individual test, 7
Infant intelligence testing, 320–329
  Bayley Scales of Infant Development (BSID), 323–326
  Brazelton Neonatal Assessment Scale, 320–321
  Cattell Infant Intelligence Scale (CIIS), 326–327
  Gesell Developmental Schedules (GDS), 321–323
  memory, role of, 327–328
  recent developments in, 327–328
Inferences, 29
Inferential statistics, 29–30
Inherited validity, 271
Intelligence
  Binet's definition, 282
  defined, 8
  early definitions, 257–258
Intelligence quotient (IQ), 266–267, 282
  deviation IQ, 271
  full-scale IQ, 297
  performance IQ, 297, 299
  verbal IQ, 294–295, 299
Intelligence tests; *see also*, Binet Intelligence scales, Wechsler Intelligence scales.
  and bilingual children, 601
  group tests, 362
  historical development, 16–19, 258–259
  legal issues, 601–610
  socioeconomic bias, 258
  in young children, 328–336
Intelligence Test and Reviews, 193

Intercept, 69, 97
Internal consistency, 122
  tests of, 109–116
Internal-External Locus of Control Scale, 178
Interquartile range, 55
Interval scales, 33, 62
Interview techniques
  active listening, 236–239
  confrontation, 239
  evaluative statements, 230
  hostile response, 230
  levels of response, 236–239
  open-ended v. closed-ended questions, 231–232, 233, 255
  probing statements, 230
  reassuring response, 230
  stress interview, 229–230
  unstructured, 232–236
Interviews, 11, 223–255
  case history, 244–245
  computerized, 245
  cross-cultural bias, 250–251
  diagnostic, 226
  employment, 226, 247–249
  error sources in, 249–253, 255
  evaluation interview, 239–240
  halo effect, 250
  mental status examination, 246–247
  non-verbal communication in, 253–254
  reciprocal nature of, 228
  reliability of, 252–253
  standardized, 226
  structured clinical interview, 240–244
  tone, importance of, 228
  unstructured, 226, 232–236
  validity of, 250–252
Introduction to the Theory of Mental and Social Measurement, 100
Inventory to Diagnose Depression, 139
IPAT Anxiety Scale, 510
IPAT Culture Fair Intelligence Test, 380–381
Ipsative score, 444
Irrational Beliefs Test (IBT), 497
Isodensity curve, 563
Item
  defined, 6
Item analysis, 164–176
  criterion referenced tests and, 173–175
  extreme group method, 166
  internal criteria, 173
  item characteristic curve, 168–170
  limitations of, 175
  point biserial correlation, 167–168
Item characteristic curve, 168–170, 176
Item difficulty, 164–165, 176
Item discriminability, 166, 176
Item response theory, 171–173
Item sampling, 122

Jackson Personality Inventory (JPI), 445
Job analysis, 410–411
Job Testing; see Career Testing, Employment Screening Tests.
Jr. Sr. High School Personality Questionnaire, 441

Kappa statistic, 121
Karnofsky Performance Status, 546–547
Kaufman Assessment Battery for Children (K-ABC), 332–336
  correlation with Stanford–Binet scale, 280
  future role, 642
Kuder Occupational Interest Survey (KOIS), 395–398
Kuder Preference Survey, 387
Kuder-Richardson 20 (KR20), 112–115

Kuhlmann-Anderson Test (KAT), 362–363

Labelling, 629–630
Lack of Protection Scale (LP), 525
Larry P. v. Wilson Riles, 567, 585–587, 602–604, 606–609
Law School Admissions Test (LSAT), 181, 382, 560, 580, 595
Learning disabilities, 342–345
  (diagnostic tests)
Leiter International Performance Scale (LIPS), 340–341
Levy, David, 21
Lie detector tests, 210
Liebert-Morris Emotionality and Worry Scales, 514, 517
Life Experience Survey (LES), 522–523, 526
Likert format, 159
Logical content strategy, 419
  multidimensional scales, 423–424
  criticisms of, 424
Luria-Nebraska Neuropsychological Battery, 533–537

Magnitude, 30
Mammography screening, 184
Marshall v. Georgia, 609–610
McCall's T, 53–54
McCarthy Scales of Children's Abilities (MSCA), 328–332
McMaster Health Index Questionnaire, 541, 547–548
Mean, 41, 62
Measure and Appraisal of Adult Intelligence, 284
Measurement error, 100–103, 130
  reliability assessment and, 121–124
  sources of, 104
Measures of Personality and Social Psychological Attitudes, 192, 195
Measures for Psychological Assessment, 196
Medical College Admission Test, 382, 580–581
Medical Outcome Study Short Form-36 (SF-36), 548–549
Memory-for-Designs Test (MFD), 347–348
Mental age, 17, 260, 282
Mental Measurements Database, 193
Mental Measurements Yearbook, 192, 193, 220, 341, 342, 387, 422
Mental retardation,
  evaluation of, 15–16
Mental status examination, 246–247
Mental test, 14
Meta-analysis, 469
Metropolitan Achievement Test (MAT), 359–362
Miller Analogies Test, 376–377
Millon Clinical Multiaxial Inventory (MCMI), 449, 450
Minnesota Multiphasic Personality Inventory (MMPI), 22, 23, 159, 178, 221, 425–437, 533, 640
  demographic characteristics of subjects, 435
  future role, 642
  MMPI-2, 22, 432–434
  scales of, 426, 428, 429, 432
  validity of, 435
Minnesota Vocational Interest Inventory (MVII), 398
Mooney Problem Checklist, 423, 424
Multidimensional Scale of Perceived Social Support (MSPSS), 525
Multiple Affect Adjective Check List (MAACL), 525
Multiple choice exams, 158

Multiple regression, 91
Multivariate analysis, 90–96
Myers-Briggs Type Indicator, 448

Nader, Ralph, 140–141
National Education Association (NEA), 5, 18
NEO Personality Inventory, 449, 450–453
Neuropsychological assessment, 529–540
  of adults, 532–540
  clinical, 529–530
  developmental, 530–531
New York Truth in Testing Law, 595
Nominal scales, 32, 62
Nonverbal communication, 253–254
None of the Above: Behind the Myth of Scholastic Aptitude, 559
Nonproprietary test, 178
Norm referenced test, 61
Normal distribution, 35, 48–49
Normative sample, 219
Norms, 56–62
  age related, 57
  tracking and, 57–61
Nottingham Health Profile, 541, 549
Null hypothesis, 79

Observed score, 100–103
Observer differences, 122
Obsessive-Compulsive Disorder, 241–244
Operant conditioning, 487–489, 495
Ordinal scales, 32, 62
Origin of the Species, 13
Overt behavior, 6

Parallel forms reliability, 106
Parents in Action on Special Education v. Hannon, 604–605, 606–609
Partial correlation, 210
Pattern analysis, 299–302
Peabody Picture Vocabulary Test, revised (PPVT-R), 338–339
Pearson product moment correlation, 73, 106
Pearson, Karl, 76, 100
Percentile band, 362
Percentile rank, 36–40
Percentiles, 40–41
  and Z scores, 50–53, 645–647
Performance IQ, 19
Performance scale, 286, 313
Personality, defined, 417
Personality Research Form (PRF), 445
Personality tests, 221
  career testing and, 401–405
  defined, 9
  historical development, 19–23
  projective, 455–481
Personality Tests and Reviews, 193
Personality traits, 417, 625–626
Phi coefficient, 84–86, 121
Pictorial Test of Intelligence, 341
Piers-Harris Children's Self-Concept Scale, 449
Plessy v. Ferguson, 598–599
Point biserial correlation , 84–86, 167
Point scale, 285–286, 313
Polychotomous test format, 157–159
Porteus Maze Test (PMT), 341
Portfolio evaluation
  v. standardized testing, 18, 644
Positive manifold, 261
Predictive validity, 137
Principle of least squares, 70
Privacy rights, 630–631
Profile of Nonverbal Sensitivity (PONS), 254
Programmer Aptitude Test (PAT), 190–191

Projective personality test
  defined, 9
Projective personality tests, 21, 455–481,
  642
Projective hypothesis, 456–458, 480
Prophecy formula, 127
Proprietary test, 178
Psychological test
  defined, 6
Psychological testing
  current trends in, 636–640
  computerization of, 501–506
  defined, 10
  ethical isssues, 631
  future of, 640–644
  in health care settings, 528–551
  legal issues, 585–622
  moral issues, 629–631
  professional issues, 624–628
  social issues, 633–636
Psychometric g, 261
Psychophysiological assessment, 499–501
Psychophysical measurement, 14–16

Q-sort, 162–163
Qualified individualism, 575
Quality of Life assessment, 540–551
  decision theory approach, 541, 549–551
  health status and, 540–541
  measurement of, 542–551
  psychometric approach, 541
  quality-adjusted life-years, 549–550
Quality of Well-being Scale, 541
Quality-adjusted life-years (QALYs), 549–
  550
Quartiles, 54–55
Questioning techniques, *see* Interview
  techniques.
Quick Test, 341
Quotas, 575, 613
  and Civil Rights Act of 1991, 576

Randomly parallel tests, 108
Rathus Assertiveness Schedule (RAS), 492
Ratio scales, 33, 62
Raven Progressive Matrices (RPM), 377–
  379
Raw regression coefficients, 92
Reactivity, 207–208, 211
Reagan, Ronald, 613
Receptive vocabulary, 339
*Regents of the University of California v.
  Bakke*, 612–613
Regression
  related to correlation 76–78
  statistical, 67–84
Regression coefficient, 69, 97
Regression line, 67–69, 97
Regression plots, 80, 562–564
Reinforcement
  in attitudinal studies, 203
  effects of, 202
Reliability
  calculation by computer, 118–119
  defined, 10
  history of, 99–100
  methods of increasing, 126–130
  models of, 103–121
  professional standards for, 122–123
  relation to validity, 152–153
  and test use, 217
  theory of, 100–103
Reliability coefficient, 103
Representative sample, 16–17
Residual, 70, 86, 97
Revised Minnesota Paper Form Board
  Tests, 382
Rorschach, Herman, 21
Rorschach Inkblot Test, 9, 21–22, 23, 221,
  458–470, 480–481

Rorschach Inkblot Test *(continued)*
  administration of, 459–464
  determinant, 462
  future role of, 642
  historical development, 458–459
  interpretation of, 462–463, 466–467
  psychometric properties of, 468–470
  scoring, 464–465
Rosenthal effect, 200
Rubin, Zick, 148–149, 178
Rubin's love scale, 148–149

Scales of measurement, 30–33
  properties of, 30–31
  types of, 32–33
Scatter diagram, 65, 96
Schedule of Affective Disorders, 240
Scholastic Aptitude Test (SAT), 19, 26, 54,
  140–141, 143, 366–369, 560, 563–
  564
School testing
  future trends, 642–644
Scientific racism, 569
Scoring
  expectancy effect and, 201
  interpretation of, 177–192, 656
  theory of, 100–103
Seguin Form Board, 15
Seguin Form Board Test, 319
Selection ratio, 185
Self-concept, 417
Self-Directed Search (SDS), 399–400
Self-monitoring devices, 498–499
Self-report questionnaires, 418
Self-report techniques, 489–494, 495
  psychometric properties of, 20, 192,
  493–494
Senate Subcommittee on Constitutional
  Rights, 484, 630
Senior Apperception Test, 477
Sentence completion tests, 479
Sequential-simultaneous distinction, 334
Sexual harrassment, 593, 594–595
Shrinkage, 88
Sickness Impact Profile (SIP), 541, 542–
  544
Simon, T., 16
Sixteen Personality Factor Questionnaire
  (16PF), 23, 439
  primary source traits of, 440
Slope, 69, 97
Slosson Intelligence Test, 341
Social facilitation, 228
Social Support Questionnaire (SSQ), 5225
Social issues, 633–636
  access to service, 634–636
  dehumanization, 633
  usefulness of testing, 634
Social-Ecology, 405–411
Socioeconomic bias; *see* Test Bias.
Source traits, 439
Southern Mississippi Thematic Appercep-
  tion Test (SM-TAT), 477
Spearman, Charles, 100, 261
Spearman's rho, 84, 85
Spearman-Brown formula, 109–110
Special populations
  individual ability test for, 316–319, 336–
  340
  legal issues, 597–598
Split-half reliability, 109–111
  problems of, 112
Standard administration, 217
Standard conditions, 16
Standard deviation, 42–45, 62
  defined, 44
Standard error of estimate, 87
Standard error of measurement, 102, 124–
  125
Standard normal distribution, 48–49

Standardization samples, 16, 217
Standardized achievement tests
  future of, 642–644
  historical development, 16–19
*Standards for Educational and Psychological
  Testing*, 134, 143, 179, 203, 216, 624,
  655
Stanford Achievement Test, 360
Stanford Early School Achievement Tests
  (SESAT), 359
Stanford Test for Academic Skills (TASK),
  359
Stanford-Binet Intelligence Scale, 17, 18,
  19, 178, 220, 598; *see also* Binet
  Intelligence scales.
Stanine system, 55
State anxiety, 510
State-Trait Anxiety Inventory (STAI), 510–
  511
Statistical Package for the Social Sciences
  (SPSS), 118–119
Statistical symbols, 42, 44
Statistical validity; *see* Criterion validity.
Statistics, 28–62
  control of rating errors and, 210
  descriptive v. inferential, 29–30
Stell v. Savannah–Chatham County, 599–
  600
Sten scale, 55
Stress, 519–526
  v. anxiety, 509–510
  coping with, 523–524
  defined, 509
  illness and, 521–522
  measures of, 519–523
  social support, effect of, 524–525
Stress interview, 229
Strong Vocational Interest Blank, 15, 387–
  388
Strong-Campbell Interest Inventory, 387,
  388–395
  1985 Revision, 394–395
Structural Clinical Interview for the DSM–
  III-R (SCID), 241
Structured clinical interviews, 240–244
Structured personality test, 20–21
  defined, 9
  strategies of construction, 418–422
Subject population, 144
Subject variables, 206–207
Suinn Test Anxiety Behavior Scale, 514
Surface traits, 439
Survey of Recent Events (SRE), 519–522,
  526
Symmetrical binomial probability distribu-
  tion, 49
System of Multicultural Pluralistic Assess-
  ment (SOMPA), 571–574, 598

T-scores, 390
Taylor Manifest Anxiety Scale, 512–513
Taylor-Russell tables, 184–189, 196
Template-matching technique, 413
Tennessee Self-Concept Scale, 449
Test administration, 10, 197–211
  computer assisted, 172, 204–206, 383
  ethical codes for, 217
  expectancy effects, 200–202
  legal issues, 620
  race of tester, 198–199
  reinforcement effects, 202–203
  standard administration, 217
Test administrator, 7
Test anxiety, 206, 513–519
  and humor, 518
  measures of, 514–518
  treatment for, 518–519
Test Anxiety Inventory, 514, 517
Test Anxiety Questionnaire (TAQ), 514–
  515
Test Anxiety Scale (TAS), 514, 515–517
Test battery, 218–219

Test bias, 554–584, 657; *see also* Cultural bias, Gender bias.
  adverse impact, 557
  coaching and, 619
  content validity and, 558–561
  criterion validity , 562–566, 579–581
  differential item functioning, 560–561
  differential validity, 565
  EEOC guidelines, 557
  legal issues, 556–558
  regression plots and, 563–564
Test Critiques, 192, 194
Test manual, 178–179
Test takers
  rights of, 657–658
Test users
  responsibilities of, 632–633, 655–656
Test writing, 156–163
  dichotomous format, 156–157
  distractors, 157–158
  polychotomous format, 157–159
Test-retest reliability, 104
Test-retest method, 109, 130
Testing legislation, 585–622
  APA statement on, 597
  burden of proof, 617
  EEOC guidelines, 588–595
  federal regulations, 587–595
  four-fifths rule, 589
  judicial opinion, 586
  major lawsuits, 598–621
  truth-in-testing laws, 595–597
Tests; *see also* Psychological testing.
  defined, 6
  types of, 9
  history of, 12–27
  testing v. assessment, 219
  use and misuse of, 216–218
Tests: A Comprehensive Reference for Assessment in Psychology, Education and Business, 192, 194
Tests in Print III, 192, 193
Tetrachoric correlation, 85
Thematic Apperception Test (TAT), 22, 23, 227, 471–477, 481
  administration of, 472–473
  future role of, 642
  interpretation of, 474–475
  psychometric properties of, 476
Theoretical strategy, 420, 442–449
Third variable, 89, 96
Thorndike, Edward L., 100
Thought Sampling Questionnaire (TSQ), 496
Time sampling, 104, 122
  carry-over effect, 105
  practice effect, 105

Torrance Tests of Creative Thinking, 348
Tracking, 59–61, 600–601
Trait anxiety, 510
Trait validity, *see* Construct validity.
Traits, 7, 19
True score, 100–103
  estimation of, 107–108
True Response Inconsistency Scale (TRIN), 434
Truth in testing laws, 595–597

Uniform Guidelines on Employee Selection Procedures, 557
Unique variance, 442
United States v. City of Buffalo, 620
Unpublished Experimental Mental Measures, 192, 195
Unqualified individualism, 575

Validity, 132–154
  criterion v. predictor, 144
  defined, 10, 133
  differential prediction and, 146
  generalization of, 145
  relation to reliability, 152–153
  and sample size, 144
  and subject population, 144
  and test use, 217
Validity coefficient, 140–146, 186
  defined, 140
  factors in evaluating, 143
Variable Response Inconsistency Scale (VRIN), 434
Variance, 43, 62
Verbal scale, 313
Visiographic tests, 345–348
Vocational maturity, 402
Vocational Maturity Inventory (VMI), 402
Vocational Tests and Reviews, 193

Wards Cove Packing Company v. Antonio, 616–617
Washington v. Davis, 614
Watson v. Fort Worth Bank and Trust, 616
Ways of Coping Scale, 524
Weber, E. H., 14
Wechsler, David, 19
Wechsler Adult Intelligence Scale (WAIS), 289–305
  correlation with Stanford-Binet scale, 280
  declining age standard, 294–295, 314
  diagnostic significance, 300–302
  full-scale IQ, 297
  interprettive features of, 298–302

Wechsler Adult Intelligence Scale (WAIS) (*continued*)
  pattern analysis of scores, 299–302
  performance IQ, 297, 299
  performance subtests, 295–297, 313–314
  reliability of, 303–304, 314
  scaled scoring, 293, 314
  validity of, 304–305, 314
  verbal IQ, 294–295, 299
  verbal subtests, 289–292, 313
  weaknesses of, 305
Wechsler Intelligence scales, 19, 220, 283–314; *see also* Wechsler Adult Intelligence Scale, Wechsler Intelligence Scale for Children, Wechsler Preschool and Primary Scale of Intelligence.
  v. Binet scales, 285–288
  future role of, 641
  performance scale, 286, 313
  point scale concept, 285–286, 313
Wechsler Intelligence Scale for Children, third edition (WISC-III), 199, 306–311, 598
  correlation with Stanford-Binet scale, 279, 280
  cultural bias in, 311, 566
  reliability of, 310
  score interpretation, 309, 566
  validity of, 310
Wechsler Preschool and Primary Scale of Intelligence (WPPSI), 306, 312–313
  correlation with Stanford–Binet scale, 279, 280
Wechsler-Bellevue Intelligence Scale (W-B), 19
Wide Range Achievement Test, Revised (WRAT-R), 348–349
Wonderlic Personnel Test (WPT), 381
Woodcock-Johnson Psycho-Educational Battery, 344–345
Woodworth Personal Data Sheet, 20–21, 23, 422, 423, 494
Word association tests, 478–479
Wundt, Wilhelm, 15

Yale Tests of Child Development, *see* Gessell Developmental Schedules.
Yerkes, Robert, 17

Z scores, 45
  and percentiles, 50–53, 645–647
  Z score units, 49